WORLD RELIGIONS

AND

CULTS

Counterfeits *of* Christianity

VOLUME 1

General Editors

BODIE HODGE &
ROGER PATTERSON

First printing: August 2015
Fourth printing: September 2017

Master Books®, P.O. Box 726, Green Forest, AR 72638
Master Books® is a division of the New Leaf Publishing Group, Inc.

ISBN: 978-0-89051-903-5
ISBN: 978-1-61458-460-5 (digital)
Library of Congress Number: 2015910670

Cover by Left Coast Design, Portland, Oregon

Image credits:
Flickr: 224; Shutterstock: 8, 37, 46, 63, 96, 124, 130, 131, 154, 164, 167, 229, 290, 332; Wikimedia Commons: 12, 43, 71, 73, 76, 79, 81, 114, 121, 142, 181, 192, 193, 206, 216, 234, 235, 236, 257, 266, 284, 285, 291, 296, 299, 302, 304, 308, 338, 347, 353, 359, 368, 384, 392, 397; Wikipedia: 372

Please consider requesting a copy of this volume be purchased by your local library system.

Printed in the United States of America

Please visit our website for other great titles: www.masterbooks.com

For information regarding author interviews,
please contact the publicity department at (870) 438-5288.

Master
Books®
A Division of New Leaf Publishing Group
www.masterbooks.com

Acknowledgments

Our appreciation to the following for their contributions to this book: Dr. Terry Mortenson, Dr. Corey Abney, Steve Fazekas, Ken Ham, Roger Patterson, Bodie Hodge, Troy Lacey, Frost Smith, Pastor David Chakranarayan, Lori Jaworski, Linda Moore, Pastor Gary Vaterlaus, Dr. Georgia Purdom, David Wright, Pastor Brian Edwards, Dr. Tom Triggs, Brandie Lucas, Michael Houdman (and the Got Questions team), Dr. Royce Short, Steve Golden, and Mark Vowels (PhD candidate).

Contents

Preface

Bodie Hodge

Why is there a need for another book on world religions? The answer is simple. While there are many great resources that dive into various religions, I wanted to have a book series that did not shy away from origins accounts. Also, I had a desire to have a book series that offers a critique from a presuppositional apologetics perspective. Like other resources, we still wanted to explain the differences between various religions as to why they believe and practice certain things. I also wanted a book series that did not ignore the many secular religions, with their sects and cults, like secular humanism, atheism, and agnosticism. This book series is unique in those respects.

I hope this book series will be a welcome addition as a supplement for study when trying to understand world religions and why they fall short of God's standard. This book and those that will follow dive into various popular world religions, lesser-known religions, and also cults and philosophical systems.

"What is the difference?" you might ask. Sometimes it is quite nebulous. A cult is a religion, after all, and so is based in a philosophical system! They all subscribe to a worldview and govern how people live their lives, as well as attempting to explain the origins of life and what happens after death. They tend to have codes to live by, and many hold to a system of works to achieve some ultimate goal.

Typically, a *world religion* is a belief system that attempts to explain some aspect of reality and often how the physical and spiritual world operates; and yet it is independent of another world religion (though they often have different sects, cults, or denominations). But for all practical purposes, this is usually how a world religion is defined.

For example, Buddhism, secular humanism, and biblical Christianity are entirely different religions that do not share a common historical foundation. Each of these religions has variations within its constituents —

Buddhist statue in Japan

Buddhism has Mahayana and Theravada forms, biblical Christianity has Lutheran, Baptist, Presbyterian, etc., and secular humanism has atheism, agnosticism, and the like.

A *cult* is typically defined as a religious offshoot of a major world religion that no longer holds to the core tenets of that world religion. They would no longer be seen as orthodox by the majority of that religion's practitioners and are often seen as distant from them. For example, there are several cults of Christianity where there has been such a great deviation on core doctrines that they would no longer be considered orthodox. Usually this is due to one person's teachings that initially led people away from those core tenets.

Let's use Christianity as an example. There are cults like Mormonism and Jehovah's Witnesses (JWs), and some even include Islam as a cult of Christianity. Each affirms that the Bible is true, *to a certain degree*, but due to charismatic leaders like Joseph Smith (Mormons), Charles Taze Russell (JWs), or Muhammad (Islam/Muslims), their basic teachings have moved far away from the Bible's core doctrines. In each of these variations, the Bible has been demoted (or reinterpreted) in light of the new leader's views on the subject. These self-proclaimed prophets have produced "new revelations" such as *The Book of Mormon* (Mormonism), *Studies in the Scriptures* (JWs), and the Koran (Muslims).

The Book of Mormon

Instead of one God that is three persons (Father, Son, and Holy Spirit; making Christ God and Creator) as the Bible teaches, Mormonism says there are three gods (and many more, too) and you too can become a god within this universe. Jehovah's Witnesses and Muslims deny the three persons of the Godhead and say Jesus is a creature. So you can see how (on this one foundational point) their core tenets are radically different from biblical Christianity.

Many people overlook *philosophical systems* as religious, but they should be considered religions that frame the worldview of those who hold to the philosophy. This is why stoicism, Epicureanism, relativism, empiricism, hedonism, and naturalism are discussed in this series. These religious philosophical systems are all around us, but rarely do we treat them as such.

Naturally, we cannot examine every world religion, cult, sect, or system, so we have selected quite a few from different genres, which we will critique. At this stage, we are intending to cover over 50 religious views for this book series.

I hope that through these books, many will be equipped to not only understand the errors within these religious views, but also point the followers to the only hope of salvation — Jesus Christ. Jesus said,

> And I, if I am lifted up from the earth, will draw all peoples to Myself (John 12:32; NKJV).

> Most assuredly, I say to you, he who believes in Me has everlasting life (John 6:47; NKJV).

Introduction

God vs. Man — World Religions and Cults

Ken Ham and Bodie Hodge

Introduction to the Series

There are two religions in the world — God's and "not God's." Or another way of putting it: *God's Word* and *Man's Word*. Really, other than Christianity, there is only one other religion that comes in many forms — a religion built on man's fallible ideas. In fact, this battle between two religions began in Genesis 3 with the temptation. Really, Eve was tempted to doubt and not believe God's Word, and instead trust in her own word *(man's word)* when the tempter stated:

> "Indeed, has God said, 'You shall not eat from any tree of the garden'?" (Genesis 3:1).[1]

I hope you understand this basic concept, as it is very important. So important that it must be stated again to get us started: there are two religions in the world — God's and "not God's."

God only has one religion, and it is His true religion by virtue of it coming from a God who is the truth (John 14:6). All other religions do not come from God; so by default, where do they come from? They come from

---

1. Scripture in this chapter is from the New American Standard Bible.

Charles Darwin, circa 1874

man. All other forms of religion outside of God's religion are a religion of man (Psalm 118:8; Isaiah 2:22).

God created man (Genesis 1:27), yet in today's modern secularized culture, man is trying to elevate himself to be above God to say that man created God! Charles Darwin popularized this in modern form in his book *The Descent of Man* in the 1871. He said:

The same high mental faculties which first led man to believe in unseen spiritual agencies, then in fetishism, polytheism, and ultimately in monotheism, would infallibly lead him, as long as his reasoning powers remained poorly developed, to various strange superstitions and customs.[2]

But this is nothing new. Man's opinions have been used since the beginning when Adam and Eve elevated their own thoughts to be greater than God's Word and ate the forbidden fruit. This sin against a holy and perfect God demanded punishment, and the punishment for sin was death (Genesis 2:17). So man was thrust into a sin-cursed world where sin and death reigned and the need for a Savior was necessary to conquer sin and death (Genesis 3:15).

All false religions are based on man's opinions as they inadvertently, or sometimes intentionally, elevate man's autonomous[3] reason to be greater than God and the 66 books of His Word. It is true that Satan and demonic spirits could have their involvement, but either way a religion would still require the involvement of men and can rightly be called a *religion of man.*

---

2. Darwin, Charles, *The Descent of Man and Selection in Relation to Sex*, chapter III ("Mental Powers of Man and the Lower Animals"), 1871, as printed in the *Great Books of the Western World*, Vol. 49, Robert Hutchins, ed. (Chicago, IL: 1952), p. 303.

3. Autonomous reason is reason apart from God or "leaving God out of it" rather than taking every thought captive to the obedience of Christ.

Humanism, the religion of man in its broadest form, would encompass all religions that oppose God and His Word. When a religion elevates a book, books, or extra teachings to be Scripture, then they are taking man's opinions and elevating them to supersede or be equal to God's Word. When a religion deletes a book or books or otherwise subtracts teachings from Scripture, then they are taking man's opinions and elevating them to supersede or be equal to God's Word. Dr. Werner Gitt writes,

> We consider the phenomenon of the multitude of religions from the perspective of man's creative nature. Where man finds a gap, he invents something. He creates something. He fills the "hole" with either intellectual or material matter. Most people trust in inventions to solve problems. . . . But even religions are man-made inventions . . . born out of human creativity to fill gaps where knowledge of the Creator and His character are missing.[4]

In other words, some take man's ideas and use that to delete parts of God's Word, some completely reject all of God's Word as the truth, and others take man's ideas and elevate them to be equal or, in most cases, above God and His Word.

That is why it is so distressing to find (from research conducted by America's Research Group for Answers in Genesis in 2014) that of those aged 20–29 who currently attend church regularly, 20 percent believe there are other books (other than the Bible) that are inspired by God, and an additional 10 percent that don't know if there are.[5]

Man's religion, that is humanism in its broadest sense, is opposed to the truth of God's Word at its most fundamental level. Yet many religions that elevate man's ideas to that ultimate level often teach that they *are* in accord with God and His Word in one way or another; but we must be discerning and compare these beliefs to the 66 books of God's Word. Only by standing on the authority of God's Word, the 66 books of the Bible, will we be able to ascertain when man's ideas and religious philosophies are being elevated to be greater than God's revealed religion.

---

4. Werner Gitt, *What about the Other Religions?* translated by Royal Truman, (Bielefeld, Germany: Christliche Literatur-Verbreitung e.V., 1995), p. 12.
5. Britt Beemer, "Answers in Genesis Survey & Market Research Findings," Volume I & II (America's Research Group, Summerville, South Carolina), September 2014.

Forms of Man's Religion

There are a lot of forms of humanism (man's religions). But in a generic form, any time man's ideas are put on par with God's Word or elevated above God's Word, then that would encompass humanistic elements — the religion of man. Some religions honor man's ideas to such a degree that they completely reject God's Word. Some pay lip service to God's Word, but then change it to conform to their man-made religious system (by rewriting it, reinterpreting it, or otherwise attacking the Bible).

Some religions mimic God's Word but do not respect God's Word as coming from God. Only those who stand on God's Word as the absolute authority — inerrant, infallible, inspired, and sufficient in every way — will be in a position to see God's true religion from God's perspective. God will never be wrong in what He records in His Word, but man can and will be wrong as he seeks to stand in God's place.

Fallible mankind can never measure up to a perfect and infallible God and His Word. So all religions that have an element of man's ideas that have been elevated to be equal or to supersede God's Word are false. Sometimes these elements of human autonomy are deceptively clever, but one must discern if it comes from God or from man by comparing it to what God says in His Word. False religions may have elements of truth, but they have borrowed that truth from God and His Word, whether they realize it or not.

Even people who claim they are not religious are humanistic and base their religion on man's ideas — thus they are religious. Atheists claim they don't have a religion. However, they are religious, as they hold a worldview that is based on certain beliefs. Their religion is one of faith with the prominent tenet of naturalism — they believe the whole universe, including life, arose by natural processes. This belief is based on a faith — a blind faith, but a faith nonetheless. This is because they have already allowed their own human beliefs to sit in authority over God's Word and rejected it by suppression in their hearts (Romans 1:18–20). They are indeed religious, and do not let them deceive you into believing they are not.

When Bill Nye debated with Ken Ham in February 2014, he claimed the universe came into being by natural processes. He rejected that he has a religion (while inconsistently claiming to be agnostic and humanistic), but he cannot escape the fact he does have a religion — a faith that natural processes involving properties inherent in matter, produced the universe, including earth and all the life that inhabits it. Former radical Muslim turned Christian apologist Daniel Shayesteh confirms this when he writes,

> Willingly or unwillingly, every person in the world is affected by their beliefs. . . . Religious values are present everywhere we go; they are present in the lives of everybody with whom we have contact.[6]

There are two religions in the world — God's and "not God's." Man's religion ("not God's") is manifested in many ways that are being elevated to a position of being equal to or greater than God and His Word. But man's religions are purely based on man's arbitrary opinion that carries no weight when compared to the ultimate authority on the subject of religion — the triune God. Thus, they are refuted! Let God be true and every man a liar as we dive into the subject of world religions, cults, and philosophical systems, all of which are religious worldviews.

Preliminary Comments

Grouping of religions

There are several ways to group man's religions:

1. Polytheistic, monotheistic, pantheistic, and atheistic
2. Personal god(s), impersonal god(s), or no god(s)
3. Based on various alleged holy books
4. Spiritual, dualistic, or materialistic
5. Counterfeits of Christianity, mystical religions, and moralistic
6. Objective religion and subjective religion
7. Etc.

Although any of these classifications work, we've opted to select the breakdown that is similar to what philosopher and pastor Dr. Greg Bahnsen did when lumping religions into a philosophical framework. Our breakdown encompasses:

- Counterfeits of Christianity
- Mystical religions
- Moralistic religions
- Materialistic religions

---

6. Daniel Shayesteh, *Christ Above All* (Sydney, Australia: Talesh Books, 2010), p. 4.

We include a chapter that encompasses how religions can be broken down by the listing in #4 above (spiritual, dualistic, and materialistic) that will appear in a later volume but have opted to place materialistic religions as their own category within the framework of the listing in #5 (counterfeits of Christianity, mystical religions, moralistic; now including materialistic).

With this arrangement, and due to the nature of certain religious views, we sometimes had to make a judgment call on where to place them. In some cases, a religion has variations where some practitioners are materialistic where other forms are theistic (Satanism or Buddhism). In several cases, a religion could have been placed into more than one category, so we ask forgiveness if you feel a religion should have been placed under a different heading.

Due to the nature of our historical review of biblical Christianity (Protestantism or reformer-based Christianity brought on by the Reformation) and introductory material, we've opted to place Roman Catholicism and Orthodoxy prior to the counterfeits of Christianity section, even though some argue they could have been placed *under* this subheading (e.g., for those who hold to views like Mary being co-redemptrix [i.e., co-redeemer]). Again, it was a judgment call. But we do want people to read our thought-provoking and kind, yet bold, assessments of these deviations from biblical Christianity.

Refutations of Religions

There are several ways to refute false religions. The first and simplest is to point out where these religions are being *arbitrary* by appealing to fallible man as a being superior to God (arbitrariness). In many cases, their very foundation is simply arbitrary. Thus, they are refuted as logically untenable (proven false). Keep in mind that the opinion of man, whether Joseph Smith, Muhammad, Buddha, etc., regardless of who they are, carries no weight when an argument is arbitrary.

One might ask about the Bible's authors: are they arbitrary too? If an opinion came from Peter or Moses, it would carry no weight of its own accord. The fact that those books carry absolute weight in a debate is not due to their persons, but instead it is due to the weight of their co-author, the Holy Spirit, who is God, and not arbitrary in any way. Remember, all Scripture is "God breathed" (2 Timothy 3:16–17; 2 Peter 1:20–21).

Other forms of refutation can be done using *inconsistencies,* including logical fallacies. Pointing out where these religions are inconsistent with the truth of God's Word or inconsistent within their own religion can accomplish this type of refutation. For example, in an atheistic worldview, which is a materialistic religion by its very nature, immaterial things like logic, truth, reason, morality, and knowledge cannot exist. Hence, atheism is inconsistent within its own story when they try to use logic or say truth exists — they are refuted by their own self-contradictory inconsistencies.

Another way to refute a world religion or cult is to show where such has to borrow from God's Word to make sense of things like knowledge, clothing, reality, a week, and so on (this is called *preconditions of intelligibility* in philosophy). In other words, their own religion cannot make sense of their actions or beliefs, so we can point that out and show where they have actually borrowed from a biblical doctrine as a foundation for their own religion. It would be like asking what must be true for something to be possible. Allow us to explain this concept with a couple of examples.

First, let's say there is someone with a secular humanistic worldview. They believe that we are just evolved animals that came from the slime billions of years ago and that there is no God who sets what is right and wrong. And yet, these same people wear clothes. What must be true for people to believe it is right to wear clothes? Not the secular worldview, which should teach the opposite, as people are just animals. But instead, a biblical worldview where clothing came as a result of sin and shame in Genesis 3 gives a foundational reason for wearing clothing. The secularist is borrowing from the biblical worldview based on the Bible to make sense of clothing, and they don't even realize it.

Another example could be when an atheist says they hold to a particular "holiday." A holiday is a holy day and is predicated on God, who is holy, to make a day "holy." In the atheistic religion, there is no God and there is no holiness because there is no objective standard of right and wrong. So a holy day or holiday is actually meaningless in their religious worldview. But their actions betray their religion, demonstrating that they are actually borrowing from the Bible, whether the atheist realizes it or not.

So one way to refute a false religion is to show where their religion doesn't make sense of things and show where they must borrow from God and His Word to make sense of things. The presence for morality is another area where this lack of a foundation is evident and can be used to demonstrate how various worldviews borrow from the Bible while denying God is the standard of truth.

Another way to refute a false religion is to show where their religion leads (i.e., when it goes to *absurdity*). Many fail to realize that the religion they claim to adhere to when applied to other things becomes absurd. For example, in the atheistic religion there is no purpose, and many atheists are happy to promote this idea. But they fail to realize that by promoting the idea that there is no purpose, they are revealing that they *do* believe purpose exists!

Or when a follower of New Age mysticism says that whatever is true for you is true for you, but not for them, then they live in a way that presumes that everyone would agree that 2+2=4! When one points out where their religion leads, it shows the absurdity of their religious position and philosophy. They expect their banker to function in a way that is consistent with their understanding of truth, but then want truth to be relative in other areas — a fundamental absurdity.

To recap, some of the best ways to refute a false religion is by exposing:

- Arbitrariness
- Inconsistencies (with the Bible or within their own religion)
- Where they borrow ideas that are actually predicated on the Bible being true but not their own religion
- When their religion leads to absurdities

Because the Bible is true, we have a basis for using these tools to refute false worldviews. God is not arbitrary, being the ultimate authority (Isaiah 40:28; Romans 1:20). God cannot deny Himself, and His character is perfectly consistent (2 Timothy 2:13). This is why contradictions cannot exist within His Word or His nature, and why the law of noncontradiction does exist.

Building on this, we can use this law of logic to reveal people's inconsistencies and absurdities. God's Word is the basis for doctrine, and other religions often borrow from God and His Word (who is the source of all knowledge; e.g., Psalm 147:5; Colossians 2:3). In the character of the God who created this universe, the Christian has a logical foundation to stand on as he argues against false religious philosophies and claims, pointing others to repentance and faith in Jesus Christ as Creator and Savior.

Focus: Origins and Foundational Beliefs

There are many world religions books, articles, websites, courses, and so on. Why one more? The answer is our focus. We wanted a world religions series that viewed religions for what they are — either God's or man's. Furthermore, we wanted to emphasize the area of origins (cosmological and biological), which is an ideal place to spot man's arbitrary opinions and inconsistencies in a religion.

To get to the root of it, a false religion must borrow from God's Word for origins, or they must make up an arbitrary worldview to try to assemble a foundation for their religion. But a religion stands or falls on its foundation — its view of origins. So, unlike many other resources, many of which contain excellent information, we wanted to focus on origins and expose false thinking in their worldviews.

Diverse Authors — Yes, Indeed!

Authors for the respective chapters are from various theological walks. In fact, you will no doubt detect varied styles among the authors. We intend this to reduce monotony while reading. As you look through the author list, you might be wondering how this was possible. In fact, looking back on it, we too tried to figure out how we obtained such a diverse group of brilliant scholars, apologists, professors, pastors, Christian leaders, and a state congressman to work together on such a project! But it makes sense.

Yes, these authors would disagree with each other on a host of topics within their denominational or theological views like Calvinism vs. Arminianism, various eschatological positions, modes of baptism, covenant theology versus dispensational theology, and the like. These are indeed important issues, and we want to encourage everyone to know what they believe on these subjects and to do so *biblically*. Even though our authors try to avoid these denominational doctrine debates in a publication like this, there may be times where an author skirts along this line and may slightly cross into denominational issues unintentionally. For this, we ask forgiveness as well.

Denominational doctrines (secondary doctrines) are discussions that Christians have, by and large, while they are standing on the authority of the Bible. Though we save these doctrinal debates for other venues with each other to develop iron-sharpening-iron skills, we stand together when defending primary doctrines like the authority of the Bible against all other religions. Yes, there may be exceptions on particular arguments, however, when it comes to the issue of world religions and man's ideas being used to attack the authority of the Word of God, these Christians stand together to defend the authority of the Bible from the very first verse. And for this we praise the Lord and may He receive the glory.

Purpose of This Book Series: The Gospel of Jesus Christ and the Authority of His Word

The reason for this book series is first and foremost the promotion of the gospel of Jesus Christ. Jesus Christ and His Word, the 66 books of the Bible, have come under attack in this day and age. And with the multitude of religions that emanate from man, many get caught up in the popular notion that biblical Christianity is just one of many from which to choose.

However, biblical Christianity is not one of the many man-made religions to pick from a list like one would pick their favorite side dish from a menu. Instead, God's true religion revealed by Him in the Bible is the truth, and all other religions are deviants based on man's false ideas that have been elevated to challenge God's Word as the truth. So the second reason for this series is to challenge the false idea that there are many individual, compartmentalized religions.

There are only two — God's and man's — as we have already explained. When people realize that there are two religions, the true one and the false one (with many variations within these false religions), it becomes easier to see the so-called multitudes of religions for what they are. They are merely variants of the false ideas of man trying to take your attention away from the true religion — God's. Biblical Christianity that teaches the triune God is the Creator of all things and that Jesus Christ is the only Savior for all of humanity is the only true religion. There are not many paths that lead to God, but Jesus alone is the door (John 10:7–19, 14:6–7).

We pray this book series will open your eyes to the false aspects of man's religions and reveal where man's ideas have been used to supersede God's Word. In doing so, our hope is that you, the reader, will be able to see the truth of God's Word through the Holy Spirit by opening you up to see the gospel found only in the work of God through Jesus Christ our Lord and His work on the Cross for our sin. Let us share the good news that has brought us salvation with all those who are following man-made religions to the praise of the glory of God's grace.

And Jesus came up and spoke to them, saying, "All authority has been given to Me in heaven and on earth. Go therefore and make disciples of all the nations, baptizing them in the name of the Father and the Son and the Holy Spirit, teaching them to observe all that I have commanded you; and lo, I am with you always, even to the end of the age" (Matthew 28:18–20).

Chapter 1

Defending the Faith: Approaching World Religions

Dr. Kenneth Gentry

Biblical Christianity is a philosophy of life (worldview) surrounded by many opposing philosophies (worldviews). In this book we are promoting biblical Christianity over competing worldviews.

God calls upon Christians to "sanctify the Lord God in your hearts, and always be ready to give a defense [Gk., *apologia*] to everyone who asks you a reason for the hope that is in you, with meekness and fear" (1 Peter 3:15; NKJV). As we obey Him, we must defend the faith in such a way that it "sanctifies the Lord" in our hearts. This requires that we defend the faith from a position of faith. Simply put, the way that we argue for the faith must be compatible with the faith for which we argue.

In defending the faith we are engaging in what is called "apologetics." The English word "apologetics" is a compound of two Greek words *apo* ("from") and *logos* ("word"). Basically, an apologetic is a word from someone in his or her defense. It was originally a judicial term used in a court setting whereby someone defended himself from accusations.

The verb form of the word (*apologeomai*) occurs ten times in the New Testament (Luke 12:11, 21:14; Acts 19:33, 24:10, 25:8, 26:1, 26:2, 26:24; Romans 2:15; 2 Corinthians 12:19). The noun (*apologia*) appears eight times (Acts 22:1, 25:16; 1 Corinthians 9:3; 2 Corinthians 7:11; Philemon 1:7,

1:16; 2 Timothy 4:16; 1 Peter 3:15). Several of these appearances involve an actual court defense (e.g., Luke 12:11, 21:14; Acts 19:33, 24:10, 25:8, 25:16; etc.).

Gradually, apologetics evolved over time to become a branch of Christian theology that engages in a reasoned defense of the Christian faith. It sets forth the rational basis upon which the faith rests, and through that it challenges all forms of non-biblical truth claims. It challenges unbelieving thought with the confidence of "come, let us reason together" (Isaiah 1:18).

Unfortunately, too many defenses of the Christian faith today cede the method of approach to the unbeliever by arguing on his terms. This generally ends up "proving" at best only the *possibility* that *a god* exists — not the *certainty* that the *God of Scripture* exists. But we should argue from a "presuppositional" perspective that builds on the sure foundation of that which we believe. That is, we must believe that God's Word is the absolute authority in all areas of life and thought. This method of apologetics is called "presuppositionalism."

But what is presuppositionalism? And how does it effectively challenge all forms of unbelieving (non-biblical) thought? Answering these questions is the task of this chapter. To understand the presuppositional apologetic method, we must begin by considering the role of presuppositions in thought.

The Role of Presuppositions in Thought

As we begin to engage presuppositionalism, we must understand the following.

The Uniformity of Nature and Thought

We exist in what is known as a "*uni*verse." The word "universe" is composed of two Latin parts: "uni" (from *unus*, meaning "one," as in "unit") and "verse" (from *vertere*, meaning "turn"). It speaks of all created things as collective whole. This word indicates that we live in a *single* unified and orderly system that is composed of many diverse parts. These parts function coordinately together as a whole, singular, rational system.

We do not live in a "*multi*verse." A multiverse state of affairs would be a disunified, totally fragmented, and random assortment of disconnected and unconnectable facts. These unconnectable facts would be meaninglessly scattered about in chaotic disarray and ultimate disorder.

The concept of a *"uni*verse" is vitally important to science, for the very possibility of scientific investigation is totally dependent upon the fact of a *"uni*verse" — an orderly, rational coherent, unified system. If reality were haphazard and disorderly, there would be no basic scientific and mathematical laws that govern and control all the various physical phenomena of reality. And if this were so, there could be no unity at all in either reality itself, in experience, or in thought.

In such a multiverse, each and every single fact would necessarily stand alone, utterly disconnected from other facts, not forming a system as a whole. Consequently, nothing could be organized and related in the mind because no fact would be related to any other fact. Thus, science, logic, and experience are absolutely dependent upon uniformity as a principle of the natural world.

Uniformity and Faith

But now the question arises: how do we know assuredly that the universe is in fact uniform? Has man investigated every single aspect of the universe from each one of its smallest atomic particles to the farthest corners of its galaxies — and all that exists in between — so that he can speak authoritatively? Does man have totally exhaustive knowledge about every particle of matter, every movement in space, and every moment of time? How does man know uniformity governs the world and the universe?

Furthermore, how can we know that uniformity will continue tomorrow so that we can conjecture about future events? And since man claims to have an experience of external things, how do we know our experience is accurate and actually conforms to reality as it is? That is, how do we know that our senses are basically accurate and our memory is essentially reliable?

Such questions are not commonly asked, even though they are vitally important. The point of these questions is to demonstrate an important truth: we must realize that any and every attempt to prove uniformity in nature necessarily requires *circular reasoning*. To prove uniformity one must assume or presuppose uniformity.

If I set out to argue the uniformity of the universe because I can predict cause and effect, am I not presupposing the uniformity and validity of my experience? How can I be sure that my experience of cause and effect is an accurate reflection of what really happens? Furthermore, am I not presupposing the trustworthy, uniform coherence of my own rationality — a rationality that requires uniformity?

The issue boils down to this: since man cannot know everything he must *assume* or *presuppose* uniformity and then think and act on this very basic assumption. Consequently, the principle of uniformity is not a scientific law but an act of faith that undergirds scientific law. Thus, adherence to the principle of uniformity — though basic to science — is an intrinsically religious commitment.

Presuppositions in Thought

Scientists follow a basic pattern in discovering true scientific laws. First, they observe a particular phenomenon. Then on the basis of their observations they construct a working hypothesis. Next, they perform experiments implementing this hypothesis. This is followed in turn by attempting to verify the experiments performed. Then a verified hypothesis is accepted as a theory. Finally, a well-established theory is recognized as a scientific law that governs in a given set of circumstances.

Thus, the basic pattern of scientific activity is:

1. observation
2. hypothesis
3. experimentation
4. verification
5. theory
6. law

Christians agree wholeheartedly with the validity of this scientific methodology. We accept the notion of a uniform universe that allows for such, for "in the beginning God created the heavens and the earth" (Genesis. 1:1; NASB).

Physicist Thomas Kuhn, in his epochal 1962 work titled *The Structure of Scientific Revolutions,* notes that scientists *must* work from certain preconceived ideas, certain presupposed concepts about things in order to begin formulating their theories and performing their experiments.[1]

That presuppositions are always silently at work is evident in that when dealing with a particular problem, scientists select only a few basic facts to

1. Thomas Kuhn, *The Structure of Scientific Revolutions* (Chicago, IL: University of Chicago Press, 1962).

consider while rejecting or overlooking numerous others. They perform certain types of experiments while neglecting others. And *they do this in keeping* with *their presuppositions.* One of the most basic presuppositions held by scientists is the one we are considering: the universe is in fact one orderly, logical, coherent, predictable system. Were this not assumed, then science could not even get off the ground.

But, as a matter of fact, there are *numerous* presuppositions that *all* rational people hold that play a vital role in all human thought and behavior. The various presuppositions we hold govern the way we think and act, all the way down to how we select and employ specific facts from the countless number presented to us each moment. Basic presuppositions are the foundation blocks upon which we build our understanding of the world about us. Presuppositions are the very basis for what is known as our "world-and-life" view (or "worldview").

A worldview is the very framework through which we understand the world and our relation to it. Everyone has a particular way of looking at the world that serves to organize ideas about the world in his mind. This worldview must be founded on basic presupposed ideas that we hold to be truth. We begin with certain presuppositions and build from there in our learning, communicating, behaving, planning, and so forth. Because of this, we must recognize the impossibility of neutrality.

The Impossibility of Neutrality

Everyone holds to presuppositions. No one operates — or even *can* operate — in a vacuum. We simply do not think or behave "out of the blue." It is impossible to think and live as if we were aliens having just arrived to this world from a radically different universe, totally devoid of all knowledge of this world, absolutely objective and utterly impartial to ideas about truth. People behave in terms of a basic worldview that implements their conceptions regarding truth.

Consequently, neutrality in thought is impossible. Each person — the philosopher and scientist alike — has his own bias. This bias has predetermined the *facts* on the basis of his presuppositions. Yet almost invariably, scientists claim to be presenting neutral, unbiased, impartial, and objective facts in their research. But man is not and cannot be truly objective and impartial. *All thinking must begin somewhere!*

All thinking must have some fundamental, logically-primitive starting point or presupposition. At the very least, we must presuppose the reality of the external world, the rationality of mental activity, the compatibility between external reality and the mind, and the uniformity of nature, that is, the law of cause and effect. As noted previously, a certain *faith* is necessary in the selection and organization of the several facts chosen from the innumerable set of facts flowing toward us in every moment of experience.

Clearly, *presuppositions are necessarily self-authenticating or self-evidencing.* Facts are inseparable from their interpretation. Facts *cannot* stand alone. They must be understood in terms of some broad, unified whole or system. They must be organized in our rational minds in terms of their general relationships to other facts and principles.

This leads us then to our most basic questions: Which system of thought can give meaning to the facts of the universe? Which worldview can provide an adequate foundation for reality? Why is the world in which we live conducive to rational thought and behavior? What is the basis for an orderly universe?

Worldviews in Collision

When we contrast Christian thought with non-Christian thought we must realize that we are *not* contrasting two series of isolated facts. We are not comparing two systems of truth that share a basically similar outlook and that have only occasional differences between them at specific turns. *We are contrasting two whole, complete, and antithetical systems of thought.*

Each particular item of evidence presented in support of the one system will be evaluated by the other system in terms of the latter's own entire implicit *system* with all of its basic assumptions. Each fact or piece of data presented either to the Christian or the non-Christian will be weighed, categorized, organized, and judged as to its possibility and significance in terms of the all-pervasive worldview held.

Consequently, it is essential that we see the debate between the Christian and the non-Christian as between two complete worldviews — between two ultimate commitments and presuppositions that are contrary to one another. Two complete philosophies of reality are in collision. Appealing to various *scientific evidences* will be arbitrated *in terms of* the two mutually exclusive and diametrically opposed, presupposed truths held by the systems.

Thus, the debate between the Christian and the non-Christian *must eventually work its way down to the question of one's ultimate authority.* Every series of argument must end somewhere; one's conclusions could never be demonstrated if they were dependent upon an infinite series of arguments and justifications. So all debates must terminate at *some* point — at some premise held as unquestionable. This is one's foundational starting point, one's ultimate authority or *presupposition.*

The question that surfaces at this point is this: which system of truth provides the foundational preconditions essential for observation, reason, experience, and meaningful discourse? Thus, which *faith* system should be chosen: the Christian or the non-Christian?

The Christian System and Presuppositions

What is the Christian's starting point? What is his most basic presupposition upon which he builds his entire worldview? Where do we begin our argument?

Christian thought holds as its most basic, fundamental, all-pervasive, and necessary starting point or presupposition, the being of God who has revealed Himself in Scripture. Thus, our presupposition is God and His Word. The Scripture, being His own infallible Word (2 Timothy 3:16), reveals to us the nature of the God in whom we trust.

God is self-sufficient, needing absolutely nothing outside of Himself (Exodus 3:14; John 5:26). All else in the universe is utterly dependent upon Him (Colossians 1:17; Hebrews 1:3). God is the all-powerful Creator of the entire universe (Genesis 1:1; Exodus 20:11; Nehemiah 9:6). God is personal, thus giving meaning to the vast universe (Acts 17:28). And God has clearly and authoritatively revealed Himself in Scripture (2 Peter 1:20–21), so we may build upon His Word as truth (Psalm 119:160; John 17:17).

The entire Christian system of thought is founded solidly upon this God — the all-ordering God of Scripture (Psalm 33:9; Isaiah 46:10). We presuppose God for what He is. If God exists and demands our belief in Scripture, we cannot challenge or test Him in any area (Deuteronomy 6:16; Matthew 4:7). We recognize the independence of God and the utter dependence of man and the universe.

Because of this, we do not have to exhaustively know everything in order to be sure of anything. God knows all things and has revealed to us in

His Word the truth of uniformity (Genesis 8:22; Colossians 1:17; Hebrews 1:3) and all other truths we need in order to reason and to function in His world.

The Non-Christian System and Presuppositions

Against this presupposed system, what does the non-Christian presuppose as ultimate truth? What does the secularist have to offer as its ultimate authority?

The non-Christian must ultimately explain the universe *not* on the basis of the all-organizing, self-sufficient, all-wise, personal God as his starting point. In rejecting God and His Word, the default position for all other worldviews must be established on the ideas of man to one degree or another. Perhaps one of the most popular worldviews of man today is secularism, also known as humanism. It holds that reality is ultimately rooted in the nebulous, chaotic, and impersonal world. Due to its widespread and influential presence in our culture, this popular religious view will be compared and contrasted to the Christian worldview in the remainder of this chapter.

The secularist asserts that the universe was produced by a combination of impersonal chance plus an enormous span of time. Thus, in this worldview the ultimate starting point and the all-conditioning environment of the universe is time plus chance.

Because the unbeliever's worldview is based upon time plus chance, *rational* science is rooted in the *irrationality* of chance. The scientist cannot speak of design or purpose in the universe because there is no Designer or purpose. There can be no goal or purpose in a random system.

On this view, secular science *must* by the very nature of its non-Christian commitment assume facts to be bits of irrationalism strewn about awaiting rationalization by man. Thus, modern secular science is schizophrenic. On the one hand, everything has its source in random, ungoverned chance. On the other hand, evolution assumes all is not random, but uniform. It holds that all is ungoverned, yet, nevertheless, is moving in an upward direction from disorder to order, from simplicity to complexity.

In this regard, Christian apologist Dr. Cornelius Van Til has noted: "On his own assumption his own rationality is a product of chance. . . . The rationality and purpose that he may be searching for are still bound by products of chance."[2] To prove a rational universe by chance, man must believe the rational is the product of, and is dependent upon, the irrational.

Not only is all of reality founded on chance, but this leaves man to be the final criterion of truth. Man — sinful, fallible, finite man — becomes ultimate in the non-Christian system.

Presuppositions Make a Difference

Now let us consider four important areas of philosophy that govern our outlook.

Reality

When asked to give the basis and starting point for the orderly universe and all external reality, the Christian points to the self-contained, ever-present, all-powerful, all-wise, infinitely rational God of Scripture.

When the non-Christian secularist is asked to give the basis and starting point for the orderly universe and external reality, he points literally to . . . *nothing*. All has risen from nothing by the irrational mechanism of chance.

When asked if something can miraculously pop into being from nothing in an instant, the non-Christian vigorously responds in the negative. Instant miracles are out of the question. But when asked if something can come out of nothing *if given several billion years,* the non-Christian confidently responds in the affirmative. As Dr. Van Til has noted, the non-Christian overlooks the fact that if one zero equals zero, then a billion zeros can equal only zero.

Thus, the Christian has a *more than adequate reason* for the universe, whereas the non-Christian has *no reason whatsoever.*

Knowledge

The Christian establishes his theory of knowledge on the all-ordering, all-knowing God of Scripture. God has instantaneous, true, and exhaustive knowledge of everything, and He has revealed to man in the Bible comprehensive principles that are clear and give a sure foundation for knowledge. Such a foundation ensures that what man does know (although he cannot know all things), he can know truly. Knowledge does work because man's mind as created by God is receptive to external reality and is given validity by

---

2. Cornelius Van Til, *The Defense of the Faith* (Philipsburg, NJ: P & R Publishing, 1972), p. 102.

God Himself. We are, after all, made in the image of the logical, all-knowing God of truth (Genesis 1:26–27, 9:6)!

On the other hand, the non-Christian must establish his theory of knowledge on the same foundation upon which he establishes reality: nebulous chaos and irrational chance. If followed consistently, the non-Christian theory of knowledge would utterly destroy all knowledge, causing it to drown in the turbulent ocean of irrationalism. *There is no reason for reason in the non-Christian system.* The concepts of probability, possibility, order, rationality, and so forth, are impossible in a chance and purposeless system.

Thus, the Christian has a sure foundation for knowledge, whereas the non-Christian has none.

Morality

When we consider the issue of moral law, the standard for judging right and wrong, again the question must be settled in terms of one's foundational system.

For the Christian, morality is founded upon the all-good, all-knowing, everywhere present, all-powerful, personal, and eternal God of Scripture. His will, which is rooted in His being and nature, is man's standard of right. Since God is all good (Psalm 119:137; Mark 10:18) and all-knowing (Psalm 139; Proverbs 15:3), moral principles revealed in Scripture are always *relevant* to our situation. Since God is eternal (Psalm 90:2, 102:12), His moral commands are always *binding* upon men.

For the non-Christian there is no sure base for ethics. Since reality is founded on nothing and knowledge is rooted in irrationalism, morality can be nothing other than pure, impersonal irrelevance. In such a system as presupposed by non-Christian thought, there are no — *indeed, there can be no* — ultimate, abiding moral principles. Everything is caught up in the impersonal flux of a random universe. Random change is ultimate in such a system. And because of this, ethics is reduced to pure relativism. Non-Christian thought can offer no justification for any moral behavior whatsoever.

Purpose

To the question of whether or not there is *any* significance and meaning to the universe and to life, the Christian confidently responds in the affirmative. There is meaning in the world because it was purposely and purposefully created by and for the personal, loving, all-ordering, eternal God of Scripture (Nehemiah 9:6; Psalm 33:6–9).

In our system of thought, man came about as the direct and purposeful creation of the loving God who has revealed Himself in the Bible (Genesis 2:7). Furthermore, man was assigned a specific and far-reaching duty by God on the very day he was created (Genesis 1:26–29). Man and *his task* must be understood *in terms* of the eternal God and His plan, rather than in terms of himself and an environment of chance and change.

Non-Christian secularist thought destroys the meaning and significance of man by positing that he is nothing more than a chance fluke, an accidental collection of molecules arising out of the slime and primordial ooze. Man is a frail speck of dust caught up in a gigantic, impersonal, multi-billion-year-old universe. That, and nothing more.

The famous 20th-century atheist Bertrand Russell put it well when he wrote:

> The world is purposeless, void of meaning. Man is the outcome of accidental collocations of atoms; all the devotion, all the inspiration, all the noonday brightness of human genius are destined to extinction in the vast death of the solar system. Only on the firm foundation of unyielding despair can the soul's habitation be safely built. From evolution no ultimately optimistic philosophy can be validly inferred.[3]

Conclusion

To the question concerning which system is the most adequate for explaining external reality, the possibility of knowledge, a relevant and binding ethic, and the significance of man, the answer should be obvious: only the worldview presupposing the truth claims of the Bible is sufficient for the task.

Actually, the defense of Christianity is simple: we argue *the impossibility of the contrary.* Ironically, those who assault the Christian system must actually *assume* the Christian system to do so. That is, they must assume a rational world for which only Christianity can account. In fact, atheism assumes theism. If the God of Scripture did not exist, there would be no man in any real world to argue — there would be no possibility of rationality by which an argument could be forged, and there would be no purpose in debate!

---

3. Bertrand Russell, *Mysticism and Logic* (New York: Doubleday, 1917), p. 45–46.

Charles Darwin stated this problem in his personal letter to W. Graham on July 3, 1881:

> But then with me the horrid doubt always arises whether the convictions of man's mind, which has always been developed from the mind of the lower animals, are of any value or at all trustworthy. Would any one trust in the convictions of a monkey's mind, if there are any convictions in such a mind?[4]

Paul spoke powerfully when he declared in Romans 3:4, "Let God be true but every man a liar" (KJV).

The God of Scripture, the Father of our Lord Jesus Christ, is the ultimate and necessary foundation for a rational, coherent worldview. Every other system is built upon a lie — the fallible ideas of sinful and rebellious man. The Christian system begins with: "In the beginning God. . . ." And from that foundational reality, all the rest of a rational worldview falls into place.

---

4. Francis Darwin, ed., *The Life and Letters of Charles Darwin* (New York: Basic, 1959), 1:285.

Chapter 2

What Is Biblical Christianity, and Why Is It Different?

Dr. Joel R. Beeke and Pastor Paul M. Smalley

On April 18, 1521, Martin Luther stood before Charles V in Worms, Germany, a lowly monk before the emperor who ruled Spain, the Netherlands, Germany, and much of Italy. With the emperor stood powerful officials of the church and state who demanded that Luther renounce his teachings, saying they contradicted the traditions of men. Luther answered, "My conscience is captive to the Word of God. I cannot and I will not recant anything, for to go against conscience is neither right nor safe. God help me. Amen."[1] With those words, Luther provoked the wrath of the imperial court, which proceeded to condemn him as a heretic and a devil. Yet with these words Luther also fanned into flame a reformation and revival of biblical Christianity across Europe.

Christians have always been people of the Word. Jesus Christ said, "If ye continue in my word, then are ye my disciples indeed; and ye shall know the truth, and the truth shall make you free" (John 8:31–32).[2]

The term *Christian* means disciple of Christ (Acts 11:26). It refers to one who has submitted to Christ as Master, follows His teachings, and imitates His life no matter what the cost (Matthew 10:24–25, 16:24). The Word of

---

1. Roland H. Bainton, *Here I Stand: A Life of Martin Luther* (New York: Abingdon Press, 1950), p. 185.
2. All Scripture quotations in this chapter will use the King James Version of the Bible.

Christ is central to a Christian's life. By the Word, God gives faith (Romans 10:17), and by the Word, He makes His people holy (John 17:17). Today, that Word exists in the form of the ancient writings of the Bible, or Holy Scriptures, which were "given by inspiration of God" (2 Timothy 3:16).

Christianity is an ancient religion, as old as the promises of God. Its roots reach back thousands of years to the very first man and woman, whose faith grasped hold of God's first promise of salvation (Genesis 3:15, 3:20). Over the centuries, God revealed more of His Word to Noah, Abraham, Moses, David, Isaiah, and many others. Under God's direction, Moses began writing the Word of God down, and prophets who followed him added to these writings. These writings were preserved and brought together into what we call the Old Testament. The climax of God's plan was the arrival of God's Son, Jesus Christ, upon earth (Galatians 4:4). Through His Apostles and prophets, the Lord Jesus gave the final revelation of God and His will, with God testifying to the trustworthiness of His Word by signs and wonders (Ephesians 2:20, 3:5; Hebrews 1:1–2, 2:3–4). As a result, we have the New Testament, with four Gospels about Christ's life and teachings, and the Epistles, which were letters written to various churches and believers. The Apostles and their coworkers testified to Christ's death and Resurrection, and planted churches from Jerusalem westward to Rome and eastward to India.

The early Church in the pagan Roman Empire was often despised and at times suffered violent persecution. Yet the Church continued to expand into Europe, Africa, and Asia, bringing the message of the Bible to people who worshiped many gods and spirits and followed various philosophies. After the Emperor Constantine became favorable to Christians (A.D. 313), they experienced increasing freedom. At the same time, false teachings pressed believers to consider more carefully what the Bible says. They expressed their beliefs in the form of creeds. Over the first few centuries, basic Christian beliefs were summarized in the Apostles' Creed (though not written by the Apostles themselves). Also, Christian leaders met to work out statements of what they believed about God and Jesus Christ at the Council of Nicea (325), the Council of Constantinople (381), and the Council of Chalcedon (451).

Over the centuries, man-made traditions, rituals, and spurious forms of devotion crept into the Church. The bishop of the Church of Rome (the pope) gradually rose in authority and came to rule Christians of many nations as if he were a spiritual emperor. The Church increased in power, erecting massive cathedrals in Europe. Islam arose in the seventh century, and Muslims conquered the Middle East, North Africa, Spain, and Portugal, putting ever-increasing pressure on the Church. The Greek- and Aramaic-speaking Christians of the

The Cathedral at Cologne

eastern Mediterranean drifted away from Latin-speaking Christians· in the west, officially splitting with Rome in 1054. This resulted in a lasting divide between the Eastern Orthodox Churches and the Roman Catholic Church.

In the 16th century, the Reformation launched various churches in Europe and Britain, most notably the Lutherans, the Reformed, and the Anabaptists, as many people sought to return to the biblical Christianity of the early Church. They expressed their understanding of the Bible in confessional statements such as the Augsburg Confession (1530), the Heidelberg Catechism (1563), and the Westminster Confession of Faith (1646). Sadly, since the 19th century many Reformation churches have fallen prey to the influences of modern unbelief and no longer adhere to the teachings of their own creeds and confessions.

This is barely a sketch of Christianity. Rather than attempting to explore the subject of church history in more detail, this chapter will focus on what biblical Christianity teaches. While each church has its own confession and catechism, what follows is a summary of commonly held beliefs in the Reformation churches, organized in answer to seven key questions. In answering these questions, this chapter will cover more than 50 distinct points of doctrine. That may seem like a lot, but they are just a fraction of the truths taught in a typical Reformation confession of faith. Here, then, is a basic introduction to the teachings of biblical Christianity.

Question 1: Who Is God, and How Is He Active in the World?

The first words of the Apostles' Creed are, "I believe in God." Yet we can no more understand the depths of God than a three-year-old child can understand how a computer controls electronic ignition and fuel injection to make a car engine run. God is a Spirit (John 4:24); He does not have a body so we cannot see Him (Colossians 1:15). God is infinite; He is beyond any limitation, measurement, or understanding (Job 11:7). "His greatness is unsearchable" (Psalm 145:3). Martin Luther (1483–1546) said, "God hides himself" and yet wills to be "revealed" (see Isaiah 45:15, 45:19).[3]

We cannot completely understand God, but He has made it possible to know Him. We should not boast about being intelligent, powerful, or rich, for the only thing worth boasting about is knowing God (Jeremiah 9:23–24). God is beautiful (Psalm 27:4). Eternal life consists in knowing God (John 17:3). Therefore, we need to know God. Who then is God?

1. *God is one God and three persons.* Christians do not believe in three gods, nor do they believe in one person who acts in three different ways at different times. They believe in the Trinity: one God who has always existed in three distinct persons. We find the three persons at Christ's baptism (Matthew 3:16–17), and they are named in the baptism of Christians. As Matthew 28:19 commands, we baptize "in the name of the Father, and of the Son, and of the Holy Ghost." Each of the three persons possesses all the attributes of deity. In Deuteronomy 6:4, Israel was told, "Hear, O Israel: The LORD our God is one LORD." The Son is Lord and God (John 1:1, 20:28), one with the Father (John 10:30). The Spirit is Lord and God (Acts 5:3–4; 2 Corinthians 3:17). The Athanasian Creed (late fifth century) explains:

> Such as the Father is, such is the Son, and such is the Holy Spirit. . . . The Father eternal, the Son eternal, and the Holy Spirit eternal. And yet they are not three eternals, but one eternal. . . . The Father is almighty, the Son almighty, and the Holy Spirit almighty. And yet they are not three almighties, but one almighty. So the Father is God, the Son is God, and the Holy Spirit is God. And yet they are not three Gods, but one God.[4]

The Trinity is very mysterious and yet also beautiful. It includes three persons so close to each other that they share one essence, one wisdom, one power, and one love. That is the beauty of God.

---

3. Martin Luther, *The Bondage of the Will*, ed. and trans. Philip S. Watson, in *Luther's Works* (Philadelphia: Fortress Press, 1972) 33:139.

4. Athanasian Creed, in *Doctrinal Standards, Liturgy, and Church Order*, ed. Joel R. Beeke (Grand Rapids, MI: Reformation Heritage Books, 2003), p. 3.

2. *God is love and righteousness.* Though God is one, there are many ways of describing His beauty. If you hold a prism in the sunshine, one beam of light produces a lovely rainbow of many colors. Similarly, God is one, yet when He reveals Himself in His Word, we see His glory in many beautiful attributes. "God is love," says John 4:8. Exodus 34:6 says, "The LORD God, [is] merciful and gracious, longsuffering [patient], and abundant in goodness and truth." God is also righteous. As Deuteronomy 32:4 says, "He is the Rock, his work is perfect: for all his ways are judgment [justice]: a God of truth and without iniquity, just and right is he." God loves what is right and hates what is wrong (Psalm 11:5–7, 33:5). You can trust this God.

God is perfect in every way, and He alone deserves our worship. It is our highest duty to love Him with all that we are, for to know and worship such a great God is the deepest delight of man (Psalm 27:4, 63:3, 84:1–2, 84:10). Augustine (354–430), a pastor and theologian in North Africa, said, "Thou hast made us for Thyself, and our heart is restless until it rests in Thee."[5] Augustine knew this by experience, for prior to his conversion he spent many years seeking happiness in sex, in his work as a teacher, and by studying various human philosophies. When he turned from sin to trust in Jesus Christ, he prayed, "What things I feared to lose, now were a joy to cast away. . . . Thou didst cast them out and enter in to supplant them with a pleasure more sweet, brighter than light . . . more sublime than all honor."[6]

3. *God is Lord.* He is the great King. In His presence the angels cover their faces and cry, "Holy, holy, holy is the LORD of hosts" (Isaiah 6:3). He is very different from us. God has no beginning and no end (Psalm 90:2). He does not need us for anything (Acts 17:25). He is in every place at all times (Psalm 139:7–8; Jeremiah 23:24). He never changes in who He is or what He has planned (Numbers 23:19; Malachi 3:6). He knows everything (Psalm 33:13–15; John 16:30), even what we will do in the future, for He planned everything before we were born (Psalm 139:16; Isaiah 46:8–11). He is wise in all that He does (Psalm 104:24). He is all powerful (Daniel 2:20–21), doing whatever He desires to do (Psalm 115:3) and whatever He wills to do (Jeremiah 32:17).

---

5. Saint Augustine, *Confessions*, trans. and ed. Henry Chadwick (Oxford: Oxford University Press, 1991), 3 [1.1].

6. Augustine, *Confessions*, 155 [9.1]. We thank Ray Lanning for translations from Augustine's Latin in this paragraph.

4. *God created all things visible and invisible.* The first sentence of the Bible is, "In the beginning God created the heaven and the earth" (Genesis 1:1). In six days, the Lord made everything that exists (Genesis 1:1–31). Irenaeus said around A.D. 180 that the church received from the Apostles the belief that God is the "Maker of heaven, and earth, and the sea, and all things that are in them."[7] The universe has not always been here, nor was it shaped by accident. God is Lord not only of spiritual things but also of the physical world. Everything that we can see or that scientists can measure was made by God, so He is Lord of all (Acts 17:24). God also made what we cannot see, such as the invisible spirits of the angels (Colossians 1:16). God made everything very good, for He is good (Genesis 1:31). The things that He made show His glory (Psalm 19:1; Romans 1:20). Creation is the work of the Father, the Son, and the Holy Spirit, for these three are one God (Genesis 1:2; Job 33:4; John 1:1–3; Hebrews 1:2). We should thank Him every day, for every good gift is from Him (James 1:17).

5. *God provides for and controls all things.* God did not leave His world after creating it, but continues to uphold it by His power (Hebrews 1:3). He works through natural processes such as the falling of rain to keep plants, animals, and people alive (Psalm 104:10–15). God rules over all His creation (Psalm 103:19, 135:6). He gives life and takes life away. He makes one person rich and another person poor (1 Samuel 2:6–7). He controls the great kings of the world for His secret purposes (Proverbs 21:1; Isaiah 10:5, 10:15).

In His wisdom, God made a plan for His world. The Bible calls God's plan His "decree" (Psalm 2:7; Daniel 4:24), for it is the purpose and decision of the sovereign King. William Perkins (1558–1602) wrote of God's "eternal and unchangeable decree, whereby he has ordained all things either past, present, or to come, for his own glory."[8] That is a great comfort, for even bad things have a purpose in God's plan. Joseph's brothers sold him into slavery, so that he spent 13 years in bondage in a foreign country, but later he told the brothers that what they had intended for evil, God had planned for good (Genesis 50:20). If God had no plan, the world would be chaos. Imagine a construction site without a plan. The excavators do not know where to dig.

---

7. Irenaeus, *Against Heresies*, 10.1, in *Ante-Nicene Fathers* (New York: Charles Scribner's Sons, 1913), 1:330.
8. William Perkins, *An Exposition of the Symbole or Creed of the Apostles, According to the Tenour of the Scriptures, and the Consent of Orthodox Fathers of the Church* (London: John Legatt, 1595), p. 53.

The masons do not know where to construct walls. Everyone is arguing. You ask the supervisor to see the blueprints for the building. What if he says, "We don't have any plans. We are just putting the building together however it seems best, and we'll see what it turns out to be"? No self-respecting construction company would be so foolish! God is not like that either. When He created the world, He already had a definite plan for what He intended to do, and He is working all things according to His wise decree for His glory (Romans 11:33–36; Ephesians 1:4, 1:6, 1:11–12).

Question 2: Who Are We, and Where Do We Come From?

People have long marveled over God's purposes for mankind. Given how small we are compared to the vast reaches of outer space, we might expect God to pay no heed to us. David looked up at the stars and wondered, "What is man, that thou art mindful of him?" (Psalm 8:4). Abraham humbly considered himself to be only "dust and ashes" before the Lord (Genesis 18:27). However, David confessed, "thou . . . hast crowned him with glory and honour. Thou madest him to have dominion over the works of thy hands" (Psalm 8:5–6). What are we humans that we can be both dust and ashes and the crown of God's creation?

6. *God created the first man out of the earth.* God created man on the sixth day of creation (Genesis 1:26, 1:31). Genesis 2:7 says, "And the LORD God formed man of the dust of the ground, and breathed into his nostrils the breath of life; and man became a living soul." The first man did not evolve from a lower life form but was formed by God "of the earth" (1 Corinthians 15:47). God's creation of the first man from the dust is an important doctrine of the Christian faith. It is explicitly affirmed in the Belgic Confession (1561) and the Westminster Larger Catechism (1647).[9] The Lord took some flesh and bone from that man's side and made the first woman, who became his wife and the mother of all mankind (Genesis 2:21–24, 3:20). The Bible does not treat Adam and Eve as mythology but as real people (1 Chronicles 1:1; Luke 3:38), whom God made "from the beginning of the creation," as the Lord Jesus Christ said (Mark 10:6). Our humble origins from the dust remind us that we owe our life and breath — all that we are and all that we have — to God.

---

9. Belgic Confession, art. 14., in *Doctrinal Standards*, ed. Beeke, p. 11; Westminster Larger Catechism, Q. 17, in *Reformed Confessions of the Sixteenth and Seventeenth Centuries in English Translation, Volume 4, 1600–1695*, ed. James T. Dennison, Jr. (Grand Rapids, MI: Reformation Heritage Books, 2014), 4:302.

7. *God created man in His image for His glory.* God made man, male and female, "in the image of God" (Genesis 1:27). God designed man to visibly represent His glory, much as children are living images of their father (Genesis 5:3). Man was created to be a child of God (Luke 3:38; Acts 17:29). That means humans are far more valuable than animals (Genesis 9:3, 9:6), just as Christ taught us (Matthew 6:26, 10:31, 12:12). We are not just physical bodies but also souls (Matthew 10:28). When God created man, God commissioned him to rule over and care for all other creatures of the earth (Genesis 1:26, 1:28). The image of the Creator includes the ability to do such things as agriculture, architecture, the arts, and manufacturing (Genesis 4:17, 4:20–22). Yet man was to rule as God's obedient servant. God entered into a covenant of obedience with man so that if he continued to obey, he would continue in life; but if he disobeyed God's Law, he would surely die (Genesis 2:9, 2:15–17, 3:22). The essence of being created in God's image is to be endowed with spiritual knowledge, righteousness, and holiness (Colossians 3:10; Ephesians 4:24). The Westminster Shorter Catechism (1647) says that the chief end of man is "to glorify God, and to enjoy him forever."[10] It is a noble thing to be a human being, for each one of us has a high calling and a glorious privilege.

8. *Man fell into sin and misery.* Although God made mankind righteous, we have turned away from Him to our own ways (Ecclesiastes 7:29; Isaiah 53:6). When tempted by Satan, a fallen angel who had rebelled against God, the first man and woman broke God's Law (Genesis 3:1–6). Consequently, sin, death, and damnation afflicted the whole human race, for the first man was the representative of us all (Romans 5:12, 5:16–17). Sin turned us against God and against each other in hatred, fear, and shame (Genesis 3:7–12). Every thought of our hearts became evil; no one is righteous or seeks God (Genesis 6:5; Psalm 14:1–3). The entire human race became spiritually dead under the rule of Satan. By nature, we are driven by the lusts of our bodies and minds and thus deserve the righteous anger of God (Ephesians 2:1–3). We are no longer the children of God, but children of the devil, whom we follow in his lies and hatred (John 8:42–44; 1 John 3:10).

God made man as a beautiful temple in which He would dwell and reign as King. But that was defiled and became a ruin filled with filth and garbage,

---

10. Westminster Shorter Catechism (Q. 1), in Dennison, *Reformed Confessions of the Sixteenth and Seventeenth Centuries in English Translation, Volume 4, 1600–1695*, p. 353.

and haunted by demons. When you view the ruins of God's image in man, you still sense how beautiful he once was, but you also see how tragically broken and empty of God's glory mankind has become (Romans 3:23). We should be deeply humbled by knowing that God gave us so much, yet we have fallen so far from Him.

Question 3: What Is the Bible, and How Is It Different from Other Books?

Immediately after the Fall of man, God revealed His promise of salvation (Genesis 3:15). Just as God created the world by speaking a word of command, so He began a new creation in the fallen world by His Word of promise. Humanity's hope rests upon the Word of God.

9. *God has spoken, and the Bible is His Word.* One of the most common phrases of the Bible is, "Thus saith the Lord." God spoke to and through His prophets in various ways (Hebrews 1:1). The words of the prophets are the words of God (Jeremiah 1:9, 36:6, 3:10–11). The Bible does not merely contain the Word of God, or just provide a way to experience the Word of God. Christ said the Bible *is* the Word of God, and it cannot be broken (John 10:35; see Matthew 5:17–18). Calling this Word "the Holy Scriptures," which means "the sacred writings," the Apostle Paul said, "All scripture is given by inspiration of God, and is profitable for doctrine, for reproof, for correction, for instruction in righteousness" (2 Timothy 3:16). Literally, "given by inspiration of God" means *God-breathed,* meaning that the Bible came straight from God's mouth. The Holy Spirit moved men to write exactly what God wanted them to say (2 Peter 1:20–21). Thus, whenever we read or hear the Bible, we should respond with humble reverence to God, for He is speaking (Isaiah 66:2).

10. *The Bible consists of the 66 books of the Old and New Testaments.* The Lord has given His Word since the beginning of time. He directed His prophet Moses to write down God's words (Exodus 17:14, 24:4, 34:27; Deuteronomy 31:9). The first five books of the Bible were thus called the the *Torah,* meaning "Law" or "Instruction"

Papyrus P52 from the Gospel of John by papyrologist Bernard Grenfell, 1920, as preserved at the John Rylands Library

> **The Uniqueness of the Bible**
> *Here is the spring where waters flow,*
> *to quench our heat of sin:*
> *Here is the tree where truth does grow,*
> *to lead our lives therein:*
> *Here is the judge that stints the strife,*
> *when men's devices fail:*
> *Here is the bread that feeds the life,*
> *that death cannot assail.*
> *The tidings of salvation dear,*
> *come to our ears from hence:*
> *The fortress of our faith is here,*
> *and shield of our defense.*
> *Then be not like the hog that has*
> *a pearl at his desire,*
> *And takes more pleasure in the trough*
> *and wallowing in the mire.*
> *Read not this book in any case,*
> *but with a single eye:*
> *Read not but first desire God's grace,*
> *to understand thereby.*
> *Pray still in faith with this respect,*
> *to fructify [produce fruit] therein,*
> *That knowledge may bring this effect,*
> *to mortify [put to death] thy sin.*
> *Then happy thou in all thy life,*
> *what so to thee befalls,*
> *Yea, double happy shalt thou be,*
> *when God by death thee calls.*
> — Preface to the Geneva Bible (1599)

(Joshua 8:31; Mark 12:26; Luke 24:44). After Moses died, God continued to add to the Scriptures through the works of other writers. In time, the Hebrew Bible contained three parts: the Law, the Prophets, and the Writings (including the Psalms). Christ affirmed all of these as the Word of God (Luke 24:44), and they now comprise the 39 books of the Old Testament. Through Apostles and prophets sent by Christ, the 27 books of the New Testament were added to the Holy Scriptures (2 Peter 3:16; compare 1 Timothy 5:18 with Luke 10:7). Though men have tried to add other books to the Bible, the 66 books of the Old and New Testaments are the only divinely inspired books in the world. Other writings may be helpful, but they are only human and fallible at best, and false and misleading at worst.

11. *The Bible is true in all that it teaches.* God cannot lie (Titus 1:2; Hebrews 6:18), and His knowledge is unlimited (Psalm 147:5). All Scripture is "given by inspiration of God" (2 Timothy 3:16). Therefore, we can trust that everything the Bible says is true and without error, whether it is Genesis or a genealogy or Paul's Epistle to the Romans. God will not let one of His words fall to the ground (1 Samuel 3:19; 2 Kings 10:10). Proverbs 30:5–6 says, "Every word

of God is pure: he is a shield unto them that put their trust in him. Add thou not unto his words, lest he reprove thee, and thou be found a liar."

We should trust the Bible because it is God's Word. On one occasion, the horse of Napoleon, emperor of France, began to race off wildly in the midst of a parade. A low-ranking junior officer suddenly stepped forward, seized the animal's bridle, and forced it to stop so that Napoleon could mount his steed. Once on the horse, Napoleon said, "Well done, *captain*." The soldier did not question this unexpected promotion, but asked, "In what regiment, sire?" The commander-in-chief answered, "In my own."[11] The soldier's response showed that he believed he was promoted because he had the word of the emperor. We might have difficulty believing the promises of God's Word, especially when God promises so much grace to poor, believing sinners. But we honor Him by believing His Word, for it is the word of the greatest Emperor, even the King of kings.

12. *The Bible is our supreme authority.* We should receive the Scriptures not as the word of mere men, though God used men to write them, but as the Word of God (1 Thessalonians 2:13). We must submit to what God has said: "For the LORD giveth wisdom: out of his mouth cometh knowledge and understanding" (Proverbs 2:6). Sometimes the Bible seems to contradict the teachings of the wise men of this world regarding history, science, human nature, salvation, and church growth. It is possible that, at times, we are misunderstanding what the Bible says. But whenever God's Word contradicts man's ideas, God must be right.

13. *Scripture alone is the divine rule of faith and obedience.* Some people seek spiritual wisdom by mystical experiences and contact with spirits, but apart from the Bible we have no spiritual light (Isaiah 8:19–20). Other people would add to the Bible the traditions of men to decide how to worship and serve God, but Christ warned, "Howbeit in vain do they worship me, teaching for doctrines the commandments of men. For laying aside the commandment of God, ye hold the tradition of men" (Mark 7:7–8). The only foundation for what we are to believe about God is the Word of God (Proverbs 22:17–19; Romans 10:17). The Scriptures are sufficient to teach us God's will, to rebuke us for our sins, to correct us unto repentance, and to train us in doing what is right (2 Timothy 3:17). Man-made acts

---

11. William H. Ireland, *The Life of Napoleon Bonaparte,* 4 vols. (London: John Cumberland, 1828), 1:123.

of devotion are not what God desires; He seeks obedience to His Word (1 Samuel 15:22). We should read the Bible with the intent to do God's will, whatever it may be.

14. *The basic message of the Bible is clear.* The Bible itself declares that some parts of it are hard to understand, although this does not excuse people who twist the Bible into false teachings (2 Peter 3:15–16). However, the Bible as a whole is not an obscure book that only experts can understand. Psalm 119:105 says, "Thy word is a lamp unto my feet, and a light unto my path." The fundamental teachings of the Bible about salvation and righteous living are plain enough for anyone who studies it with an open mind to understand.

Earthenware oil lamp

15. *All of the Scriptures center upon Jesus Christ.* The Lord Jesus said that the Scriptures "testify of me" (John 5:39). The entire Old Testament points ahead to Christ, His sufferings, His Resurrection from the dead, and the preaching of the gospel of Christ to all nations (Luke 24:44–47). The Apostles preached Christ (1 Corinthians 2:2; 2 Corinthians 4:5), and the New Testament revolves around Jesus Christ, His work, and the implications for those who believe in Him. Thomas Adams (1583–1652) said Christ is the sum and center of the whole Bible, for He is the pattern of our joy, the fountain of life, and the foundation of all happiness.[12] The Holy Scriptures are precious because they are able to make us "wise unto salvation through faith which is in Christ Jesus," even if you are a child (2 Timothy 3:15). Therefore, we should read Scripture to know Jesus Christ, so that we might trust Him and have eternal life (John 20:31).

Question 4: Who Is Jesus Christ, and What Did He Accomplish?

The Bible teaches that God exists in three persons: the Father, the Son, and the Holy Spirit (2 Corinthians 13:14). The Son of God is Himself "the mighty God" (Isaiah 9:6), which means that He is the Lord and Jehovah (Isaiah 10:20–21). He already existed in the beginning of creation (John

---

12. Thomas Adams, *Meditations upon Some Part of the Creed*, in *The Works of Thomas Adams* (1861–1866 repr., Eureka, CA: Tanski Publications, 1998), 3:224.

1:1) and shares in all of the Father's works (John 5:19). The gospel reveals all three persons of the Trinity (Galatians 4:4–6), but it centers upon the person and work of the Son. John 3:16 says, "For God so loved the world, that he gave his only begotten Son, that whosoever believeth in him should not perish, but have everlasting life." God shows the greatness and glory of His love supremely in His Son (Romans 5:8; 1 John 4:9–10). Why is this so?

16. *Christ is the only Mediator of the covenant of grace between God and sinners.* The Apostle Paul wrote that there is "one mediator between God and men, the man Christ Jesus" (1 Timothy 2:5). A mediator is a middle-man, or broker, between two parties hostile to each other — someone who can put a hand on each and bring them back together (Job 9:33). Our sins have made us enemies of God, but "God was in Christ, reconciling the world unto himself," and "we were reconciled to God by the death of his Son" (2 Corinthians 5:19; Romans 5:10). Only Christ can bring sinners to God. Jesus said, "I am the way, the truth, and the life: no man cometh unto the Father, but by me" (John 14:6).

Christ is the mediator of the covenant of grace. Throughout the Bible, God made "covenants of promise" with nations and individuals (Ephesians 2:12). Robert Rollock (c. 1555–1598) observed that "God speaks nothing to man without the covenant."[13] The covenant of grace is God's solemn promise of faithful love to sinners, through faith in the gospel. Jesus as mediator brings sinners into a covenant relationship with God so that He is their God and they are His people (Hebrews 8:6, 8:10). In a sense, Christ *is* the covenant, for all its promises are fulfilled in Him (Isaiah 42:6; 2 Corinthians 1:18–20). The covenant can be compared to a spiritual marriage between the Lord and His people (Isaiah 54:5, 54:10; Hosea 2:18–23).

17. *Christ is the Savior of a people given to Him by God.* His very name means Savior, for the angel said, "thou shalt call his name JESUS: for he shall save his people from their sins" (Matthew 1:21). Jesus knew that God had given Him particular people to rescue from sin and to give them eternal life (John 6:37, 6:39, 10:29, 17:2, 17:6, 17:9). Christ called those people "my sheep" for He was their Shepherd and laid down His life for them, even before they had heard His Word and believed in Him (John 10:16, 10:27–29). The Bible calls this God's "election" (Romans 9:11, 11:5), for

---

13. Robert Rollock, *A Treatise of God's Effectual Calling, in The Works of Robert Rollock,* ed. William M. Gunn (repr., Grand Rapids, MI: Reformation Heritage Books, 2008), 1:33.

God made a selection before time began of whom He would save (Ephesians 1:4). The Holy Spirit works powerfully in God's chosen ones so that they believe in Christ and follow in His holy ways (1 Thessalonians 1:4–6; 2 Thessalonians 2:13–14). Election is the friend of sinners because unless God first chooses us, we would never choose Him. Election teaches us that the gospel is a love story in which the Father chose a bride for His Son — His Church — to whom His Son came in love. Various denominations may vary slightly on the detailed understanding of election, like many doctrines.

18. *Christ serves as the prophet, priest, and King of His people.* Though some people think that "Christ" is the last name of Jesus, it is actually a title. Literally meaning "anointed," the title tells us that the Lord Jesus is the person sent by God to be the mediator. As the Heidelberg Catechism (1563) explains, Jesus is called Christ "because He is ordained of God the Father, and anointed with the Holy Ghost" to be our chief prophet to teach us God's way of salvation (Deuteronomy 18:18; Acts 3:22), our only High Priest to atone for our sins (Psalm 110:4; Hebrews 7:21), and our eternal King to rule us and defend us (Psalm 2:6; Luke 1:33).[14] We need a prophet because of our ignorance and spiritual darkness, a priest because of our sins that deserve punishment under God's justice, and a King to defend us from the assaults of Satan and the world, and to preserve us in the enjoyment of salvation in the face of our continuing weakness through sin.

19. *The Old Testament points to Christ through promises, appearances, and types.* The first promise of the Bible looked ahead to Christ by referring to "the seed of the woman" who would suffer and yet conquer the devil (Genesis 3:15). The prophets also wrote about the coming Savior (for example, Numbers 24:17; Psalms 2, 22, 45, 110; Isaiah 9:6, 52:13–53:12; Ezekiel 34:23; Micah 5:2). The Son of God was at work throughout the Old Testament, sometimes appearing as the Angel of the Lord (Genesis 16:7–14, 22:11–19; Exodus 3:1–6). God designed particular persons such as Adam, events such as the Passover, and institutions such as the temple and its sacrifices as types that were imperfect yet true pictures of Christ and His work (John 2:19–21; Romans 5:14; 1 Corinthians 5:7). So even the Old Testament believers put their trust in Christ (John 8:56).

20. *God's Son became a man, born of a virgin.* When it was time for God to fulfill His plan, He sent His Son into the world as a human being, a baby

---

14. Heidelberg Catechism (LD 12, Q. 31), in *Doctrinal Standards*, ed. Beeke, p. 40.

Christ's Obedience and God's Law

Active Obedience	Passive Obedience
He voluntarily obeyed God's commands	He voluntarily suffered God's wrath
He satisfied the Law's precepts	He satisfied the Law's penalties
He merits glory and immortality	He saves from condemnation

born of a woman (Galatians 4:4). The eternal Son of God became flesh (John 1:14), taking upon Himself a truly human nature like ours in every way except sin (Hebrews 2:14, 2:17, 4:15). This is called the *Incarnation*. Mary of Nazareth, a young Jewish woman who had not had sexual relations with any man, conceived the child by the power of the Holy Spirit, so that her child was holy and the Son of God (Luke 1:31–35). Jesus grew tired and slept, and yet the stormy wind and sea obeyed His commands (Matthew 8:23–27). The Council of Chalcedon (451) concluded from Scripture that Jesus Christ is "truly God and truly man," having "two natures" with "the property of each nature being preserved," and yet "one Person," not "two persons, but one and the same Son."[15] Therefore, the Savior as God-man (Colossians 2:9) is uniquely equipped to bring sinful human beings to God. No other religion can offer such a mediator as Christianity.

21. *Jesus preached the Word to Israel and confirmed it with miracles.* After living and working as an ordinary carpenter for many years, Jesus began His public ministry in Galilee and Judea at about age 30 (Luke 3:21–23). He went out in the power of the Spirit, preaching the gospel, healing the sick, and casting out demons (Matthew 4:23–24; Luke 4:14–44). His miracles, or works of supernatural power, testified that God was with Him (Acts 2:22, 10:38). He called men to repent and believe the gospel, and to lead a life of self denial, cross-bearing, and obedience to His commands (Matthew 16:24).

22. *Christ lived a perfect life of obedience and died for sinners.* God's Son came as the Servant to do His Father's will (Psalm 40:7–8; Isaiah 42:1; John 6:38, 17:4; Galatians 1:4). The essence of His saving work is His voluntary obedience to God (John 10:18; Philippians 2:8; Hebrews 10:7). Though Christ is the Lord and lawgiver (Mark 2:28), He came as a man "under the

15. The Symbol of Chalcedon, in *The Creeds of Christendom*, ed. Philip Schaff, rev. David S. Schaff (1931; repr., Grand Rapids, MI: Baker, 1983), 2:62.

law" (Galatians 4:4). He lived and died as the surety who paid the debt of sinful men to God (Hebrews 7:22).

Christ's obedience consists of two aspects, answering to the two sides of the Law. His active obedience is His flawless keeping of the Law's commands. He could claim that "the Father hath not left me alone; for I do always those things that please him" (John 8:29). Thus, He represents His people as a man of perfect righteousness in God's sight (Isaiah 53:11; Hebrews 7:26; 1 John 2:1). His passive obedience is His voluntary suffering of the Law's penalties against lawbreakers, the curse of God (Galatians 3:10, 3:13). Thus, Jesus represents His people as the One who has completely satisfied God's justice for the sins of His people and propitiated or appeased God's wrath (Romans 3:25; 1 John 2:2).

Christ finished this work of bringing everlasting righteousness when He died on the Cross (John 19:30). As prophet, His death glorified God and commended God's love to us (John 13:31; Romans 5:8). As priest, He offered Himself once for all as the only sacrifice that atones for sin (Hebrews 10:12). As King, He conquered sin and Satan at the Cross (Colossians 2:15).

Many people think that they can atone for their own sins against God by feeling sorry and doing good works. To such people, Anselm of Canterbury (c. 1033–1109) said, "You have not yet considered what a heavy weight sin is."[16] It would be better for the universe to be destroyed than to commit the least sin, for sin is rebellion against the will of the Creator. If sinners could be saved by works of the Law, then Christ died for nothing (Galatians 2:21). The fact that God sent His Son to die for sinners shows that the price to atone for sin must be so great that we could never save ourselves.

23. *Christ rose from the dead as the living Savior.* Christ submitted to the powers of death for a time, but the decree and promises of God made it impossible for death to hold Him (Acts 3:24). On the third day, Christ rose bodily from the dead, leaving behind an empty tomb (Matthew 28:1–10). He appeared many times to individuals and to various groups of people, proving that He was not a ghost but the resurrected Son of man (Luke 24:36–43; Acts 1:3; 1 Corinthians 15:4–8). He will never die again, for He has conquered death for His people (Romans 6:9; Revelation 1:18). His resurrected life is the life of His people. He said, "Because I live, ye shall live also" (John 14:19).

---

16. Anselm of Canterbury, *Why God Became Man*, 1.21, in *A Scholastic Miscellany: Anselm to Ockham*, ed. and trans. Eugene R. Fairweather, Library of Christian Classics (Philadelphia, PA: Westminster, 1956), p. 138.

24. *The Lord Jesus ascended into heaven and sat down at God's right hand.* After visiting with His disciples for 40 days, the risen Lord was received up into the glory of heaven (Acts 1:3, 1:9–11). He sat down at the right hand of God in total triumph and absolute glory (Psalm 110:1; Ephesians 1:20–22; Hebrews 8:1). On the basis of the merit of His finished work, He intercedes as a living priest for His people so they will be saved to the end (Romans 8:33–35; Hebrews 7:25). He also continues to act as the living prophet and King of His people (John 10:16; Acts 11:20–21), working in them through the Word by the Holy Spirit (2 Corinthians 3:3, 13:3–4), whose ministry He obtains by His priestly intercession (John 14:16).

25. *Christ poured out the Holy Spirit on His Church at Pentecost.* Shortly after the Lord Jesus went up to heaven, He gave the Holy Spirit in great power to His gathered church in Jerusalem at the Feast of Pentecost, just as He had promised (Acts 1:4–5, 1:8, 2:1–4). The Spirit has been at work among God's people since the beginning (Psalm 143:10; Isaiah 63:10–11, 63:14; Haggai 2:5); however, Christ received the Holy Spirit as God's reward for faithful service, when He was lifted up to God's right hand and poured out His fullness on His Church (Acts 2:32–36). The Holy Spirit now does greater works than ever before to save sinners as the Spirit of the risen Lord Jesus Christ.

When we consider the love of the Father in sending His Son, and the love of the Son in coming to do His Father's will, we should be overwhelmed at the goodness of God. Jesus Christ is worthy of all our trust, all our love, all our obedience, and all our suffering. Samuel Rutherford (1600–1661) was banished from his church for faithfully preaching the Word of Christ. Yet as he prepared to leave his beloved home and congregation, he wrote, "My chains are gilded with gold." How could he say that? No matter what he lost, he had Christ. Rutherford wrote, "No pen, no words, no skill can express to you the loveliness of my only, only Lord Jesus."[17] Is Jesus Christ lovely to you? Is He like treasure hidden in a field that you are willing to let go of everything to gain? If the Holy Spirit opens your eyes to see the glory of Jesus Christ in the gospel, you will never be the same.

Question 5: What Is Christ Doing Now by the Holy Spirit?

The Gospels record what "Jesus began both to do and teach," but His activity did not cease when He went to heaven (Acts 1:1). As the mediator of the

---

17. Samuel Rutherford, Letter to Alexander Gordon of Earlston, Sept. 5, 1636, in *The Letters of Samuel Rutherford*, ed. Andrew Bonar (1891; repr., Edinburgh: Banner of Truth, 2006), p. 143. We have slightly modernized his words.

new covenant, Christ is working now to fulfill God's promises (Hebrews 8:6, 8:10–12). Christ did not leave His disciples alone but sent them "another Comforter," that is, "the Spirit of truth." With the coming down of the Holy Spirit from heaven to dwell in and among the disciples, Christ Himself has come to them and lives in them (John 14:16–23). What then is the Lord Jesus doing through the Spirit?

26. *The Spirit convicts sinners of their sin.* Christ said that He would send the Spirit to convict the world of sin (John 16:8). The fulfillment of this promise began when the Spirit filled the Apostles with power to preach the Word at Pentecost. Those who listened were pierced in their hearts as if by a spiritual arrow (Psalm 45:5) and cried out, "What shall we do?" (Acts 2:37). Ever since then, the Spirit has been convicting sinners so that they sense the weight of their sins against God and cry out, "What must I do to be saved?" (Acts 16:30).

27. *The Spirit causes sinners to be born again by grace alone.* Conviction of sin is not salvation from sin, for you can feel guilt and fear and yet put off turning to God (Acts 24:25). Sinners are dead in their sins; only God can make them alive by His grace (Ephesians 2:4–5). God does not do this in response to any good thing in us. Rather, as a gift of sheer mercy to foolish slaves of sin, He pours upon needy sinners the Holy Spirit through Jesus Christ. The Bible calls this work of the Spirit a "washing" because it takes away the guilt of our sins, a "regeneration" because it is a new creation or beginning of life, and a "renewing" because it gives a person a new heart and a new life (Titus 3:3–7; see Ezekiel 36:25–27; 1 Corinthians 6:9–11; 2 Corinthians 5:17; Ephesians 2:10). Believers are said to be "born again" as the Holy Spirit engenders a new life in the soul — a life of faith, repentance, love, and obedience (John 3:1–8; 1 John 2:29, 3:9, 4:7, 5:1, 5:4, 5:18).

28. *The Lord Jesus gives sinners faith and repentance.* The gospel of Christ calls all sinners to repentance and faith (Mark 1:15; Acts 17:30, 20:21). Through the Word, the Holy Spirit offers Christ, and promises "that whosoever believeth in him should not perish, but have everlasting life" (John 3:16). By nature, men resist the Holy Spirit (Acts 7:51). The Word is a light that exposes their evil deeds, and so they hate the light, love the darkness, and do not come to Christ in faith (John 3:19–20, 6:44). When God regenerates a sinner by the Spirit, Christ draws that sinner to Himself by the power of His saving death (John 12:32–33). Christ was lifted up to

God's right hand to give repentance to sinners (Acts 5:30–31). Faith and repentance are gifts of Christ. Thus we read in Acts 11:20–21, "And some of them were men of Cyprus and Cyrene, which, when they were come to Antioch, spake unto the Grecians, preaching the LORD Jesus. And the hand of the Lord was with them: and a great number believed, and turned unto the Lord." Only Jesus can open our hearts and our eyes (Acts 16:14, 26:18).

We need the Holy Spirit to show us our sins and also to show us the Savior. When Hector Macphail (1716–1774), a minister in the Scottish Highlands, was traveling to some church meetings, he stopped for the night at a household along the way. There he met a kitchen maid who knew little of the Christian faith. He told the girl that when he returned he would give her a scarf if she would pray this simple prayer every morning and evening, "Lord, show me myself." A couple of weeks later he came back, and discovered that she was in great distress over her sins. She told the minister, "He has shown me myself, and oh, what an awful sight it is!" The kind minister then explained the good news of Christ's saving work, and taught her another simple prayer, "Lord, show me Thyself." Many years later, he was delighted to meet her again, now a grown woman and mother of children. She told him that in the first prayer she came to feel her need of the Savior, and in the second she came to see the Savior that she needed.[18] Sometimes even pastors need to learn this lesson. Macphail was once a minister who preached mere morality and good behavior. However, the Lord used his wife's spiritual hunger to deeply convict him of his sins, and he became a godly believer and preacher of Christ for the rest of his life.[19] Whether adults or children, we all need the Spirit to open our eyes to our horrible sinfulness and to the beauties and perfection of the Savior.

29. *God unites people to Christ by the Spirit.* When God saves sinners, the Holy Spirit dwells in them as His temple and lives within him; as a result, they become one with Jesus Christ (1 Corinthians 6:17, 6:19). The same Spirit who lives in Christ also lives in Christians. God joins them to Christ in a living relationship, just as the members of the body are joined to the head (1 Corinthians 12:12; Ephesians 4:15–16). Jesus promised His disciples that the Holy Spirit would "abide with you forever" (John 14:16), and so Christ is always with them, too (Matthew 28:20).

---

18. "The Highland Servant-Girl," in *The Church* (July 1, 1866), 187.
19. F.R. Webber, *A History of Preaching in Britain and America* (Milwaukee, WI: Northwestern Publishing House, 1955), 2:226–28.

> Man, accordingly, has no works in which to glory before God; and hence, stripped of all help from works, he is justified by faith alone. But we define justification as follows: the sinner, received into communion [oneness and fellowship] with Christ, is reconciled to God by his grace, while, cleansed by Christ's blood, he obtains forgiveness of sins, and clothed with Christ's righteousness as if it were his own, he stands confident before the heavenly judgment seat.
>
> — John Calvin, *Institutes*, 3.17.8

30. *God justifies sinners by faith in Christ alone.* God is a righteous Judge, and He demands that mankind be righteous in His sight. Yet fallen mankind has no righteousness in itself (Romans 3:10). When God joins believers to Jesus Christ by faith, He becomes their righteousness (1 Corinthians 1:30). God credits them with "the righteousness of God" because they are in Christ, and Christ took upon Himself the penalty of their sins (2 Corinthians 5:21). God the Judge "justifies" or declares them righteous, not because of their own righteousness or works of obedience, but only because of their faith in Christ and because of His works of obedience (Galatians 2:16; Philippians 3:9). John Calvin (1509–1564), a French Reformer who served in Geneva, said that justification by faith alone is the hinge of true religion and the sum of godliness.[20] In justification, the sinner finds himself standing before the Lord as Satan accuses him of his sins. But by faith in Christ, the Lord takes away the filthy garments of our guilt and clothes us with the beauty of Christ's obedience (Zechariah 3:1–5). That is good news for sinners!

31. *The Holy Spirit makes people holy so that they do works of love.* Joined to the Lord Jesus, believers also find that Christ is their sanctification (1 Corinthians 1:30). The Spirit of Christ now dwells in them as the Spirit of life and freedom (Romans 8:2, 8:9). He changes their basic mindset to one of submission to God's Word, and leads them to increasingly put sin to death and live as obedient children of God (Romans 6:17, 8:5–9, 8:13–15). Their souls become a battleground where the Spirit moves them to fight against the sinful desires that once delighted them (Galatians 5:16–17). The Spirit produces love, joy, peace, patience, gentleness, goodness, faithfulness, meekness, and

---

20. John Calvin, *Institutes of the Christian Religion*, ed. John T. McNeill, trans. Ford Lewis Battles, The Library of Christian Classics, XX, XXI (Philadelphia: Westminster Press, 1960), 3.11.1; 3.15.7.

Double Grace in Christ

Justification	Sanctification
For all in Christ	For all in Christ
By faith Alone	Faith and works
Change in legal status	Change in nature and character
Immediate and complete at conversion	Beginning at conversion but growing through life
Invisible	Visible in fruits
Right to heaven	Fitness for heaven
Necessary	Necessary

self-control in believers so that by the power of Christ's Cross they increasingly obey God's Law (Galatians 5:22–24). While Christians never stop sinning in this life (1 John 1:8–9), they have begun a work of cooperation with the God who works in them to sanctify them (Philippians 2:12–13).

We must never separate justification and sanctification, though they are distinct blessings. As Calvin explained, God lovingly gives Christ to us to be grasped and received by faith, so that when we are united to Christ, we receive a *double grace*. First, by justification God does not condemn us as a Judge but accepts us as a Father. Second, by sanctification we change and grow in holiness and purity of life.[21] Anyone who is not being sanctified in daily life has not been justified, and those who have been justified will be made holy.

32. *The Spirit gives believers assurance by enabling them to trust fully in God's promises of salvation in Christ and by testifying that they are God's children.* The promise of God to all who receive Christ by faith is that they are the children of God (John 1:12; Galatians 3:26). Yet how can someone know if he has saving faith in Christ? God does not will that His children live in uncertainty and fear of punishment, but that they enjoy assurance of their salvation. John said, "These things have I written unto you that believe on the name of the Son of God; that ye may *know* that ye have eternal life, and that ye may believe on the name of the Son of God" (1 John 5:13, emphasis added). As John explains elsewhere in that letter, the signs of having eternal life are Christ's love in our hearts and Spirit-prompted obedience to God's

---

21. Calvin, *Institutes*, 3.11.1.

commandments (1 John 2:3, 4:12–13). By growing in the grace of God, we become sure that God has chosen and called us to Himself (2 Peter 1:5–10). The Holy Spirit witnesses to us that we are children of God by granting us to experience the marks and fruits of grace (such as the Beatitudes in Matthew 5:3–12 and the fruits of the Spirit in Galatians 5:22–23), and by moving us to live as children of God, even in hard times (Romans 8:13–17).

33. *The Spirit of Christ moves God's children to pray to their Father.* Prayer is as essential to the life of a Christian as breathing. The Holy Spirit works in God's children as "the Spirit of adoption," causing them to pray to God as their Father (Romans 8:15). Even when believers do not know what to pray, the Spirit intercedes for them, expressing the groaning of their hearts (Romans 8:26). Real spiritual prayer is far more difficult than many people think; the grace of God is necessary for even the least spark of prayer. John Bunyan (1628–1688) confessed that when he went to pray, he found his heart so reluctant to go to God that he must first ask God "that he would take my heart, and set it on himself in Christ, and when it is there, that he would keep it there," and help him to pray by the Spirit despite his weakness.[22]

The Spirit teaches us to pray by the Scriptures. While the entire Bible is a help in prayer, the Lord Jesus gave us special instructions on how to pray in Matthew 6:9–13. This prayer teaches us to come to God with faith in His love and majesty, to pray primarily for His honor and reign among people, to pray for all our needs, especially our need for justification and sanctification, and to praise Him for His glory.

34. *Christ empowers His people by the Spirit to serve Him to the glory of God alone.* Christ sends His people into the world to make disciples of

> **The Lord's Prayer**
> After this manner therefore pray ye:
> Our Father which art in heaven,
> Hallowed be thy name.
> Thy kingdom come,
> Thy will be done in earth,
> as it is in heaven.
> Give us this day our daily bread.
> And forgive us our debts,
> as we forgive our debtors.
> And lead us not into temptation,
> but deliver us from evil:
> For thine is the kingdom, and the power, and the glory, for ever.
> Amen (Matthew 6:9–13).

---

22. John Bunyan, *The Doctrine of the Law and Grace Unfolded and I Will Pray with the Spirit,* ed. Richard L. Greaves (Oxford: Clarendon Press, 1976), p. 256–57. See also *The Works of John Bunyan,* ed. George Offor (1854; repr., Edinburgh: Banner of Truth, 1991), 1:631.

all nations, and promises that He will always be with them as the Lord of all (Matthew 28:18–20). Christ imparts His gifts to each Christian so that every believer can help to fill the world with God's Kingdom (Ephesians 4:7–10). The Holy Spirit distributes these "spiritual gifts" to every member of Christ's Church to serve as God has willed (1 Corinthians 12:7, 12:11). God's grace comes in various ways to different people, some more gifted to speak and others to serve, but the purpose of all gifts and ministry is the same: ". . . that God in all things may be glorified through Jesus Christ, to whom be praise and dominion for ever and ever. Amen" (1 Peter 4:11). The Reformers used a Latin phrase to capture this idea: *soli Deo gloria* ("glory to God alone")! No one in the Church should be lifted up to receive glory for himself, for we are only servants who exist to glorify God.

Question 6: What Is the Church of Jesus Christ?

God's purposes revolve around the people of Jesus Christ (Ephesians 3:10–11). They are His true Church — not the building and not only the pastors and other leaders, but all the people of God. Through the Church, God will glorify Himself in Jesus Christ forever (Ephesians 3:21). Jesus Christ loves the Church (Ephesians 5:25). The gospel does not call us to follow Christ all alone but to stand in unity with the Church (Philippians 1:27). What then is the Church?

35. *The Church is the body of all who are united to Christ.* The word *Church* means an assembly called together "that belongs to the Lord." The Church is people who are called by the gospel into holy fellowship with God's Son, Jesus Christ, and with each other (1 Corinthians 1:2, 1:9). The same Greek word was used of the assembly of Israel in the old covenant (1 Chronicles 13:2; Acts 7:38) for "the congregation of the LORD" (Deuteronomy 23:1–3, 23:8; 1 Chronicles 28:8). The true Church consists of all those who are redeemed by Christ's death (Ephesians 5:25). It is the body of the Lord Jesus Christ (Ephesians 1:22, 5:23; Colossians 1:18, 1:24), joined to Him as closely as His own flesh and bones (Ephesians 5:29–30). The Church is Christ's creation and possession, for He said, "I will build my church" (Matthew 16:18). Joined with the One who sits at God's right hand, the Church is a heavenly people even while some of its members are still pilgrims on earth (Hebrews 12:22–24; see Ephesians 2:7; Philippians 3:20).

36. *The Church is one body with many diverse members.* The Apostle Paul wrote, "For as the body is one, and hath many members, and all the members

of that one body, being many, are one body: so also is Christ. For by one Spirit are we all baptized into one body, whether we be Jews or Gentiles, whether we be bond [slave] or free; and have been all made to drink into one Spirit" (1 Corinthians 12:12–13). Racial, cultural, and social differences cannot break the bond of oneness created by the Holy Spirit in Christ. Like the eye, hand, and foot of a human body, the members of Christ's Church have different strengths and weaknesses; every member is needed, needs the others, and should serve each other (1 Corinthians 12:14–26).

37. *The Church is organized into local congregations where Christians are members.* The vast majority of the uses of the word for *church* in the New Testament refer to particular churches gathered in specific locations (e.g., Acts 9:31, 15:41; Romans 16:1). Each Christian is a part of the life of the body (Ephesians 4:16; Colossians 2:19). Christians are not only members of Christ, but are also members of one another (Romans 12:4–5). Each church should have a clear sense of the value of membership as it receives new members (Acts 2:41, 2:47) and removes others when they refuse to walk in obedience to God despite repeated attempts by fellow Christians to lovingly call them to repent of sin (Matthew 18:15–17).

38. *Christ has given pastors to edify and equip His Church.* The risen and ascended Lord Jesus gives spiritual shepherds to build up His people (Acts 20:28; Ephesians 4:11–12). He calls them to devote themselves to prayer, the ministry of the Word, watching over the souls of their people, and living in holiness as an example to others (Acts 6:4; 1 Timothy 3:1–7, 3:14–15, 4:11–16; 2 Timothy 3:8–4:5; Titus 1:5–9). They are accountable to Christ to shepherd each member of the flock of God entrusted to them (Hebrews 13:17; 1 Peter 5:2). Each believer should be a member of a local church so that he is under the pastoral care of elders and overseers who can direct and comfort him (1 Corinthians 16:15–16; James 5:14).

39. *God commands His Church to keep His moral Law.* The moral Law of God obligates all mankind to obedience (Romans 3:19–20). God has placed His Law in the form of conscience in every man to commend right and condemn wrong (Romans 2:14–15). However, the Lord gave a special revelation of His Law to His people Israel after redeeming them from slavery in Egypt. He summarized its moral principles in the Ten Commandments, which the Lord spoke directly to Israel and wrote down on stone tablets, which were stored in the ark in the Most Holy Place (Deuteronomy

Summary of the Ten Commandments
(1) Thou shalt have no other gods before me.
(2) Thou shalt not make unto thee any graven image.
(3) Thou shalt not take the name of the LORD thy God in vain.
(4) Remember the sabbath day, to keep it holy.
(5) Honor thy father and thy mother.
(6) Thou shalt not kill [murder].
(7) Thou shalt not commit adultery.
(8) Thou shalt not steal.
(9) Thou shalt not bear false witness against thy neighbor.
(10) Thou shalt not covet . . . any thing that is thy neighbor's.

10:1–5). The Scriptures record these laws twice, which is also a sign of their great importance (Exodus 20:3–17; Deuteronomy 5:6–21). The commandments are stated in brief in the sidebar.

God does not give His Laws to keep people from real happiness, but for their good (Deuteronomy 10:13). If a three-year-old girl sees her father's blood-pressure medicine, she might think it is candy. Her father's command that she not eat the medicine is not an act of hatred but of great love. If she tries to eat it anyway and her father stops her, she might cry, pout, and think he is mean. However, she is being foolish and should trust her father. In the same way, we should trust that God's Laws are good for us, even if it seems at times that He is holding us back from enjoying something sweet and pleasant. Obedience to God enriches life.

Though Christ released His people from the ceremonies of the Old Testament, the Ten Commandments continue to direct their lives (1 Corinthians 7:19). Jesus Christ said that He did not come to abolish God's Laws, but to fulfill them. He taught that these commandments require not only outward action but obedience in the heart. Thus, the commandment against murder also prohibits sinful anger and hatred, and the commandment against adultery also prohibits sexual lust (Matthew 5:17–28). The Law shows us how much we all need a Savior, for even people with outwardly moral lives are full of sinful thoughts and desires. It also points us beyond mere good behavior to a life of obedience that springs from goodness in the heart.

40. *God summarizes His moral Law in love for God and man.* When asked what the greatest commandment is, Christ did not select any of the Ten

Commandments but instead summarized them all in two commandments: "Thou shalt love the Lord thy God with all thy heart, and with all thy soul, and with all thy mind. This is the first and great commandment. And the second is like unto it, Thou shalt love thy neighbour as thyself. On these two commandments hang all the law and the prophets" (Matthew 22:37–40). In the great commandment (Deuteronomy 6:5), Christ summarized the first four of the Ten Commandments, and in the greatest commandment the last six (Leviticus 19:18).

The Law and the gospel belong to each other. The Law shows us how sinful we are, so that we run to the gospel for salvation. The gospel shows us how loving God is so that we love Him in return and seek to obey His commandments. How can anyone not love God when his eyes are opened to see the love that sent God's Son to die for sinners? Bernard of Clairvaux (1090–1153) asked, "What is the result of contemplating such great mercy and mercy so undeserved, such generous and proven love, such unlooked-for condescension, such persistent gentleness, such astonishing sweetness?" He said that the result is that the church "runs eagerly" after God, "yet even when she has fallen wholly in love she thinks that she loves too little because she is loved so much. And she is right. What can repay so great a love and such a lover?"[23] Ultimately, Christians learn to love God for His own sake, "not because he meets your needs," as Bernard said, but rejoicing that you and all things exist *for Him*, and therefore finding no greater delight than to know His will is being done in your life.[24]

41. *God calls the Church to submit to civil authorities.* Though Christ is the only King of His people, His kingdom is not of this world. It is not a political kingdom but a spiritual kingdom created and preserved by the teaching of the truth (John 18:36–37). God has instituted human authorities ("magistrates") to rule in the political sphere, granting them the right to use force to punish evil-doers. God commands Christians to submit to the authorities as appointed by God, giving them appropriate honor and obedience (Romans 13:1–7; John 19:11). However, if the civil government or any human authority commands us to act against God's will, then we must say with the Apostles, "We ought to obey God rather than men" (Acts 5:29).

---

23. Bernard of Clairvaux, *On Loving God*, 4.13, in *Bernard of Clairvaux: Selected Works*, trans. G.R. Evans, The Classics of Western Spirituality (New York: Paulist Press, 1987), p. 184.
24. Ibid., p. 194–96.

42. *Christ blesses the Church with Christian freedom.* The Apostle Paul summarized the gospel in the word *liberty* because "Christ hath made us free" (Galatians 5:1) and "where the Spirit of the Lord is, there is liberty" (2 Corinthians 3:17). The essence of Christian liberty is "the glorious liberty of the children of God" (Romans 8:21). In the coming age, this will mean freedom from all sin and misery so that believers will behold the glory of Christ as God's beloved children (Romans 8:17–18; Revelation 21:3–7). In this present age, this means that Christ has released believers from the curse of God's Law, its rigorous demands for perfection in order to please God, the enslaving power of sin, the ceremonies of the old covenant, the tyranny of human expectations, and shame upon their consciences (John 8:31–36; Romans 6:17–18, 8:1–2; 1 Corinthians 7:22, 9:19, 10:25–31; 2 Corinthians 3:17–18; Galatians 5:1–2). It is not freedom to live however we please (2 Peter 2:19), but the liberty to serve God, for His commands are "the law of liberty" (Galatians 5:13; James 1:25; 1 Peter 2:16). In Christ, God overlooks the imperfection of our works and is genuinely pleased with our obedience (2 Corinthians 5:9, 5:19; Philippians 4:18), welcoming us to come freely into His presence (Ephesians 2:18, 3:12).

43. *God calls the Church to public worship.* Christ promises His special presence to the Church when it gathers in His name (Matthew 18:20, 28:18–20). Christians should also worship privately, for every Christian is a temple of the Holy Spirit (1 Corinthians 6:19). Believers should meditate on the Word and pray and sing privately and with their families every day (Psalm 1:2; James 5:13). They should talk with their children at home about the Word (Deuteronomy 6:6–7). However, the Bible's primary emphasis is on the temple of the Church (1 Corinthians 3:16; Ephesians 2:21–22). Christians worship God not as isolated individuals but as living stones fitted together into a holy temple in which His people declare His praises (1 Peter 2:5, 2:9). Christians who are filled with the Word and Spirit show this by building one another up through the teaching, preaching, and singing of the Church (Ephesians 5:18–20; Colossians 3:16). God has set aside one day a week for rest and worship, which since the time of Christ's Resurrection has been the first day of the week — the Lord's Day (Revelation 1:10). People who claim to be Christians but do not regularly participate in public worship, unless physically unable, are missing out on God's special presence, breaking the command of God, and discouraging His Church (Hebrews 10:22–25).

The Church is crucial to our spiritual growth, for we need each other. Wilhelmus à Brakel (1635–1711), a Dutch minister, wrote, "How refreshing it is for God's children, being hated by the world, to have communion with each other, to make their needs known to each other, and in love and familiarity may enjoy each other's fellowship!"[25] We isolate ourselves to our own harm.

A pastor once visited a Christian who had not attended his church's worship services for some weeks. The man sat down with his pastor by a fireplace, waiting to be rebuked for not coming to church. Instead, the pastor sat silent, looking into the fire. After a while, he took a pair of metal tongs from beside the fireplace and removed a coal from the center of the fire, placing it by itself on the stones of the hearth. The pastor and Christian watched as the glowing coal died out. Then the man looked at the pastor with pain in his eyes, and said, "I understand. I will be in church next Sunday."

44. *God marks the Church with baptism as a sign of its union with Christ.* God's people under the old covenant were required to keep a complex system of rituals for worship. Christ fulfilled the rigorous demands of the old covenant so that these ceremonies no longer bind believers (Colossians 2:16–17). Instead, Christ instituted a simple form of worship with only two visible signs. The first is baptism with water in the name of the Father, the Son, and the Holy Spirit (Matthew 28:19). Baptism does not save us, however. Paul wrote, "For Christ sent me not to baptize, but to preach the gospel," for "the preaching of the cross" is "the power of God" for salvation (1 Corinthians 1:17–18). Baptism is a sign of union with Christ (Galatians 3:27), especially in His death and Resurrection (Colossians 2:12). Reflecting upon one's baptism with faith in the gospel is a means of growth in grace, as the Apostle Paul shows when he appeals to the baptism of Christians to remind them that they have died and risen with Christ and therefore cannot live in sin (Romans 6:1–4).

45. *God provides the Church with the Lord's Supper as a sign of its communion with Christ.* The second sign is the sacred eating of the bread and drinking of the cup as instituted by Christ with His disciples on the night on which He was betrayed. Through the Lord's Supper, the Church remembers and proclaims Christ's death until He comes again (1 Corinthians 11:23–26). It is a sign of the new covenant between God and Christians, ratified by

---

25. Wilhelmus à Brakel, *The Christian's Reasonable Service*, trans. Bartel Elshout, ed. Joel R. Beeke (Grand Rapids, MI: Reformation Heritage Books, 1993), 2:100.

Christ's broken body and shed blood (Luke 22:20). Like baptism, the Lord's Supper is no guarantee of salvation (1 Corinthians 10:1–5), but it can be a means of fellowship with Christ (1 Corinthians 10:16). Eating a meal is a visible representation of receiving spiritual nourishment and love from the Savior by the exercise of faith in His Word (see John 6:35; Revelation 3:19–20).

Bread and cup for the Lord's Supper

46. *Christ commissioned the Church to preach the gospel to all nations.* After rising from the dead, the Lord Jesus explained to His disciples that the Scriptures foretold His death and Resurrection, and the preaching of repentance and forgiveness of sins in His name to all nations (Luke 24:44–46). The Lord entrusted this mission to the Church (John 20:21). He said to the Apostles, "All power is given unto me in heaven and in earth. Go ye therefore, and teach all nations, baptizing them in the name of the Father, and of the Son, and of the Holy Ghost [Spirit]: Teaching them to observe all things whatsoever I have commanded you: and, lo, I am with you always, even unto the end of the world. Amen" (Matthew 28:18–20). The mission of the Church continues today and will continue until the gospel is preached in every nation despite persecution, false teachers, and spiritual coldness (Matthew 24:9–14). The Lamb has purchased people of every nation, ethnic group, and language, and He will bring them into His kingdom (Revelation 5:9, 7:9, 7:14).

Trusting such promises, the Church should expect great things from God and attempt great things for God, as William Carey (1761–1834) said a year before leaving England to spend the rest of his life as a missionary in India.[26] The basic stance of biblical Christianity is optimism, not based on pride in mankind, but on confidence in the Lord who has promised to spread His Kingdom throughout the world by the gospel, and who will one day bring His Kingdom in open glory to the earth.

---

26. "Narrative of the First Establishment of This Society," *Periodical Accounts Relative to a Society Formed among the Particular Baptists for Propagating the Gospel among the Heathen,* no. 1, in *Periodical Accounts Relative to the Baptist Missionary Society, Volume 1* (Clipstone: J.W. Morris, 1800), p. 3, downloaded from "Expect Great Things; Attempt Great Things," http://www.wmcarey.edu/carey/expect/ (accessed Nov. 3, 2014).

Question 7: How Will Christ Bring His Kingdom to Earth in Glory?

The Christian life can be summarized in the words *faith, love,* and *hope* (1 Corinthians 13:13; 1 Thessalonians 1:3, 5:8). Faith looks back to the finished work of Christ and relies upon Him for salvation. Love responds to Christ's work by adoration of God and faithful service to other human beings. Hope looks forward to the future, when God's promises will come to full fruition (Romans 8:24–25). Biblical Christianity is a future-oriented religion that looks beyond this life to another world. It teaches that when the bodies of men die, the spirits of wicked men go to a place of conscious, fiery punishment, but the spirits of the righteous enter into Christ's presence in heavenly glory to rest from their labors (Luke 16:19–26, 23:43). However, the future hope of Christianity goes far beyond life after death; it looks primarily to everlasting communion with Christ, to the appearing of God's glory and Kingdom and the beginning of a new age.

47. *Jesus Christ will come again in visible glory.* The "blessed hope" of Christians is "the glorious appearing" of their God and Savior Jesus Christ in the Second Coming (Titus 2:13). Christ said, "For the Son of man shall come in the glory of his Father with his angels; and then he shall reward every man according to his works" (Matthew 16:27). He will come with a glory that is visible to all nations (Matthew 24:30, 26:64), returning bodily from the skies just as He ascended physically to heaven (Acts 1:9–11). Presently, believers on earth yearn to know their Bridegroom better. They long to see the One whom they love, but on the day of the Lord, their Bridegroom will return to their great joy (Matthew 9:15, 25:1–10; Revelation 19:7–9).

48. *Christ will raise from the dead everyone who has ever lived.* By the sheer power of His word of command, Christ will resurrect all deceased human beings, both the righteous and the wicked (John 5:28–29; Acts 24:15). The wicked will rise to experience everlasting shame, but Christ's people will shine with radiant beauty, sharing in the glory of their Lord (Daniel 12:2–3; Colossians 3:1–4). Christians who are still alive when Christ raises the dead will not die but be suddenly changed to share in His glory and immortality (1 Corinthians 15:51–53; 1 Thessalonians 4:13–18).

49. *The Son of God will judge everyone according to his works.* When Christ returns, He will come as the glorious King to sit in judgment on behalf of His Father, so that all men will honor the Son as they honor the

Father (Matthew 25:31; John 5:22–23). All living, intelligent beings will bow before Jesus Christ and acknowledge that He is Lord (Philippians 2:10–11). Using His divine knowledge of every heart and every act, Christ will judge everyone, great or small, rich or poor, according to his works (Romans 2:6–11, 2:16; Revelation 2:23). The Apostle Paul wrote, "For we must all appear before the judgment seat of Christ; that every one may receive the things done in his body, according to that he hath done, whether it be good or bad" (2 Corinthians 5:10).

50. *Christ will damn the wicked to forever suffer God's anger in hell.* The Lord Jesus will say to sinners, "Depart from me, ye cursed, into everlasting fire, prepared for the devil and his angels" (Matthew 25:41). Regardless of what outwardly religious acts or even miracles they may have done, their lifestyle of sin and failure to repent, put their faith in Christ, and obey God's commands will show that Christ never knew them in a saving relationship (Matthew 7:21–23). Condemned by the mouth of God incarnate, "these shall go away into everlasting punishment" (Matthew 25:46). This is hell, which Jesus repeatedly described as a place of "weeping and gnashing of teeth" (Matthew 8:12, 22:13, 24:51, 25:30; Luke 13:28). Christ once died as the Lamb (Revelation 5:6), but now the wicked will face the wrath of that Lamb (Revelation 6:17). Thomas Manton (1620–1677) said, "The majesty of Christ is the cause of their torments; and his look and face will be terror enough to sinners" (see 2 Thessalonians 1:9).[27] Their pain will never end (Revelation 14:10–11).

51. *Christ will bless the righteous with the enjoyment of God's love forever.* To the righteous, whose lives are characterized by love and compassion for other believers in their sufferings, Jesus Christ will say, "Come, ye blessed of my Father, inherit the kingdom prepared for you from the foundation of the world" (Matthew 25:34). Manton wrote, "To the wicked he saith, 'Depart,' but to the saints, 'Come.' . . . Come, draw near to me."[28] The essence of all that Christians have desired, and the glory of heaven, is to be near to the Lord forever (1 Thessalonians 4:17–18).

In the judgment of the righteous, their works will be assessed. They are not saved by their works, but their good works show that God has saved them and changed their nature through Jesus Christ (Matthew 12:33;

---

27. Thomas Manton, *Several Sermons upon the Twenty-Fifth Chapter of St. Matthew*, in *The Complete Works of Thomas Manton* (London: James Nisbet, 1872), 10:24.
28. Ibid., 10:49.

Ephesians 2:8–10). Though their acts of obedience deserve nothing (Luke 17:10), Christ will graciously reward even the smallest acts they have done for Him in obedience to His Word (Matthew 10:42). He will be like a master rewarding his servants for their work after a long absence, saying, "Well done, good and faithful servant; thou hast been faithful over a few things, I will make thee ruler over many things: enter thou into the joy of thy lord" (Matthew 25:23).

For all eternity, the triune God will glorify Himself by pouring out the riches of His grace and kindness upon His people through Jesus Christ (Ephesians 2:7). They will live with God in the new heavens and new earth where there is no sin or sadness (Revelation 21:1–3). They will look into the face of the Lord who died for them, and His glory will surround them and fill them (Revelation 22:4–5). The hope of believers is that "when he shall appear, we shall be like him; for we shall see him as he is" (1 John 3:2). Then Christians will truly know what it means to glorify God and enjoy Him forever.

The eternity of heaven shows us that God's love for His people is boundless. Someone might fear that he requires so much grace, love, and patience from God that it will all be used up and God will cast him away. But that will never be true of any who believe in Christ alone for salvation.

Charles Spurgeon (1834–1892) was coming home at the end of a weary day feeling depressed, when he remembered the promise, "My grace is sufficient for thee" (2 Corinthians 12:9). It struck him so forcefully that it made him laugh because it was absurd to think that God could run out of grace. He imagined a little fish being afraid that he might drink the River Thames dry, and the great river saying in response, "Drink away, little fish, my stream is sufficient for thee."[29] When Christ says, "If any man thirst, let him come unto me, and drink," He is not promising trickles of grace but "rivers of living water" (John 7:38).

Conclusion: The Simplicity and the Depth of Biblical Christianity

The study of biblical Christianity reveals a beautiful tapestry of many truths woven together. We have put our face close to the tapestry and traced over 50 threads of truth that run through it. However, when we step back from the tapestry, a single picture appears: *God gives eternal life to sinners through*

---

29. William Williams, *Personal Reminiscences of Charles Haddon Spurgeon* (London: Religious Tract Society, 1895), p. 19.

Jesus Christ. Thus, Christianity is both simple and deep. As Gregory the Great (540–604) said, "Scripture is like a river, broad and deep, shallow enough here for the lamb to go wading, but deep enough there for the elephant to swim."[30] Children, like little lambs, can understand enough of the Bible to trust Jesus Christ and follow Him as His disciples. Yet strong and mature Christians, who may be called elephants of the faith, still find truths in the Bible that are beyond their comprehension. Since God is God, we would expect to never completely understand Him. The great question is not whether you fully understand the Lord, but whether you know and trust Him.

This chapter has sought to summarize biblical Christianity by answering seven questions, which may be stated as the following.

1. Who is God, and how is He active in the world? God is one God existing eternally in the three persons of the Trinity. In His essence, God is the Lord, a being of infinite love and righteousness. He created all things visible and invisible. He provides for and controls all things.

2. Who are we, and where do we come from? God created the first man out of the earth. God made mankind, male and female, in His image for His glory, but we fell into sin and misery when the first man, Adam, disobeyed God's commandment. Yet God gave Adam and Eve a promise of grace, the first of many promises contained in the Bible.

3. What is the Bible, and how is it different from other books? The Bible, which consists of the 66 books of the Old and New Testament, is the written Word of God. Since God is God and cannot lie, the Bible is true in all that it teaches, and it functions as our supreme authority. It teaches all the essentials, what we must believe about God, and what God requires from us as His creatures. The basic message of the Bible is clear, and the central message that runs throughout the book is Jesus Christ.

4. Who is Jesus Christ, and what did He accomplish? Christ is the only mediator of the covenant of grace between God and the people given to Him by God. In particular, Christ serves as the prophet, priest, and King of His people. The Old Testament points to Christ through promises, appearances, and types. The New Testament tells us how God's Son was born of a virgin, grew to an adult man, preached to Israel, and worked miracles. He lived a perfect life of obedience and died for sinners to satisfy God's justice.

---

30. Gregory the Great, *Moralia or Commentary on the Book of Job*, Epistle, sec. 4, http://faculty.georgetown.edu/jod/texts/moralia1.html (accessed November 3, 2014).

Christ rose from the dead as the living Savior. He ascended into heaven, sat down at God's right hand, and poured out the Holy Spirit at Pentecost.

5. *What is Christ doing now by the Holy Spirit?* He convicts sinners of their sin, and causes people to be born again into a new life of faith and repentance. God unites people to Christ by the Spirit, and justifies sinners by faith in Christ alone. The Holy Spirit also makes people holy so that they do works of love. The Spirit gives believers the privileges of the children of God, including an assurance of God's fatherly acceptance, a heart to pray to the Father, and the power to serve Him so that He is glorified in the Church.

6. *What is the Church of Jesus Christ?* The Church is a people united to Christ. It is one body with many diverse members. It is organized into local churches in which Christians are members under the rule and care of Christ's appointed pastors. God commands His Church to keep His moral Law, which Christ summarized as love for God and man, and to submit to the authority and laws of civil government. However, in obeying God the Church is blessed by Christ with true spiritual freedom as children of their Father. God calls the Church to public worship, to baptism as a sign of union with Christ, and to partake of the Lord's Supper as a sign of oneness with Christ. Christ commissioned the Church to preach the gospel to all nations, calling sinners to come to Christ and become part of His Kingdom.

7. *How will Christ bring His Kingdom to earth in glory?* Jesus Christ will come again to earth in visible majesty and power. He will raise the dead, and judge all of us according to our works as signs of what we truly are. Christ will damn the wicked to suffer in hell forever, but He will bless the righteous to enjoy God's love forever.

There is, however, a final question that must be asked. *Are you a Christian?* Biblical Christianity is not just a set of ideas; it is an experience and a way of life. As William Ames (1576–1633) wrote, the major point of Christian teaching is "living to God." Christians do so "when they live in accord with the will of God, to the glory of God, and with God working in them."[31] Do you know the God of the Bible personally? Have you come to see, sense, and feel the evil of your sins against Him? Do you believe the Bible, submitting to it as the Word of God? Have you put your trust in

---

31. William Ames, *The Marrow of Theology*, trans. John D. Eusden (Grand Rapids, MI: Baker, 1968), 1.1.1, 6.

Christ alone to save you from God's wrath and your sins? Have you received Him as your prophet, priest, and King? Do you love and participate in the Church as a member of a local congregation that believes in the biblical faith? When Jesus Christ returns, will that be the happiest day of your life? Is Christ your Lord, your life, your righteousness, your love, and your hope? If this is not the case with you, then the Bible warns that you are in extreme danger. Today might be the day you meet your Maker, either through death or at Christ's return. Do not let it end without calling upon the name of the Lord Jesus Christ to save you.

If you would like to learn more about biblical Christianity, let me offer a few recommendations. First, read the Bible. There is no substitute for reading and thinking about the Word of God. Second, pray continually that God would show you both yourself and Himself, so that you would repent of sin and believe in Christ alone for salvation. Third, find a good church that believes, preaches, and practices the kind of biblical Christianity this chapter has described; be there every time it meets for worship and prayer, and make its members your best friends. Fourth, do not just read and hear the Word of God — *do* it. Put it into practice. Finally, read good books about Christian teachings, godliness, and the lives of exemplary Christians. God has blessed us with a rich heritage of good literature; we should make use of it. A disciple of Christ is always a learner.

Summary of Biblical Christianity Beliefs

Doctrine	*Biblical Christianity Teaching*
God	God is triune, existing in three persons of the God-head — Father, Son, and Holy Spirit; God is eternal and transcendent; the Son took on flesh to dwell on earth
Authority/ Revelation	God and His revelation of Himself in the 66 books of the Bible
Man	Man is created in the image of God; mankind is fallen as a result of Adam's sin; man is unable to do good and please God on his own
Sin	Any thought or action that is contrary to the will of God as revealed in the Bible

Salvation	Salvation is possible through the substitutionary atonement of Jesus on the Cross and His Resurrection; individuals receive salvation by repentance and faith in Jesus' work on their behalf; works have no merit for salvation; salvation is a free gift received by God's grace alone; eternal punishment in hell awaits those who die in their sins, while eternal joyful existence with God awaits those who receive salvation
Creation	The universe and all that is in it was created out of nothing in six, 24-hour days about 6,000 years ago; all living things were created according to their kinds in supernatural acts of God; mankind was specially created by God in supernatural acts

Chapter 3

A Brief Introduction of Christianity

Bodie Hodge

From the Apostolic Age to the Present

Christianity exploded in the first century and rightly so. Many were eyewitnesses of the risen Savior prior to His ascension into heaven to sit on the right hand of the throne of God. Massive numbers of Jews believed (3,000 in one day, no less) and became the saved remnant; then Gentiles (non-Jews) began repenting and pouring into ranks of the saved through the blood of Jesus Christ.

During these early years, it was not easy to be a Christian and follow Christ. Christians were undergoing persecution from the Jews, from people practicing local religions, and from those in the Roman government. Paul was beaten, flogged, left for dead, and arrested. The New Testament outlines much of this persecution.

Nero, the Roman emperor, was extremely cruel to Christians beginning about A.D. 64 until his suicide about three

Nero is one of the most well-known persecutors of the early Christian Church.

and half years later. It was under Nero that Church fathers recorded Paul's beheading and Peter's crucifixion upside-down (around A.D. 68). During Nero's reign, the Jews and Romans went to war, and by A.D. 73, Judea was utterly devastated. During the war, Jerusalem was destroyed and the Temple sacrifice had come to an end. Persecution from the Jews was significantly reduced, but others continued persecuting Christians. And in the mid-90s the Roman Emperor Domitian began attacking Christians.

For a couple of centuries, Christianity continued to explode, even in the face of persecution. Then the first Christian-influenced Roman emperor emerged. His name was Constantine. This obviously eased tensions and the harshness that Christians endured. By the power of the Holy Spirit, the gospel had moved slowly but surely from a few people near Jerusalem to the entire Roman Empire. Constantine moved the center of power from Rome to Constantinople. After his death, the Empire split into two: an eastern and western empire, and so the Roman Empire officially went into the pages of history. The western empire declined steadily with the sack of Rome in A.D. 410 and finally ceased about A.D. 476, according to most historians.

The eastern empire (Byzantine Empire) continued until the fourth Crusade in the 12th century. But even with some minor recoveries, the empire finally went into the pages of history in 1453 when the Ottoman Turks finally took Constantinople for good.

The Church had grown progressively, especially in Europe, the Middle East, and North Africa, but Muhammad began conquering much of Arabia and beyond in the early 600s. Muslims then controlled and stopped the growth of the Church by execution and compulsion by the sword for their new unitarian-based religion (i.e., the non-Trinitarian view of one God that they call Allah; Christ is not seen as God, but a prophet).

Christianity, though still growing in quiet circles in the Muslim world, has been forced into silence or persecution since those days. Even in our day, it is not uncommon to hear of Christians put to death in the name of Allah in Muslim lands on a regular basis.

The first major church split occurred in 5th century A.D. when the Oriental Orthodox churches (Coptic, Ethiopian, Eritrean, Syriac, Indian Orthodox, and Armenian Apostolic) split from the rest of the Church over and definitions at the Council of Chalcedon in A.D. 451. Another significant split in the Church called the Great Schism happened about A.D. 1054. It split the Church into the Eastern Churches led by Patriarch Michael Cerularius and the Western Church of Rome led by Pope Leo IX. There had been growing tension of numerous issues between the churches of the east and west as early as the 5th century. This culminated in the split.[1]

Fast forward, and we find that some within the Western Church were fed up with the direction that the Church was heading. It continued to move away from the Scriptures with indulgences (paying for dead loved ones to be freed from purgatory) and many other unbiblical doctrines and stances (e.g., image worship and praying to saints) that the popes of the Roman Catholic Church were imposing. These types of precursors finally led to the Reformation, generally acknowledged as beginning with Martin Luther, whose initial intention was to reform the Roman Church and get the leadership back to the authority of the Word of God. Luther's reform of the Roman Church failed, and Luther was commanded to recant of his "heresies."

Martin Luther
(Retouched restoration art by Lucas)

But Luther remained faithful to his testimony of standing on the Word of God as the supreme authority while standing before Roman Church authorities. This was the popular event that detonated the Protestant Reformation as people began going back to the Bible for their theology, ultimately leading to the Protestant denominations that we have today (from Anglican, Lutheran, Reformed, and Anabaptist to Presbyterian, Baptist, Mennonite, Methodist, Amish, Evangelical Free, Assemblies of God, Wesleyan, Christian and Missionary Alliance, Nazarenes, to independent churches, Christian churches, community churches, Calvary Chapels, and many more). While these denominations vary in particular doctrinal positions and styles of worship, all claim to look to the Bible rather than popes and tradition as the standard of truth.

---

1. The final nail in the coffin was over the *filioque* clause; for more on this see "What is the filioque clause/filioque controversy?" GotQuestions.org, http://www.gotquestions.org/filioque-clause-controversy.html.

Rome then reacted with the Counter-Reformation to reclaim those who left the grip of Rome. They formed the Jesuit order and began the Inquisition, among other tactics. Though not the main point of the meeting, the Council of Trent of the Roman Catholic church elevated the apocryphal books to a full canon status to support many of the doctrines disputed by the Protestant reformers (hence why Catholics and Protestants have two different listings of authoritative books in the Old Testament).[2]

Without going into the extensive distinctions of denominational doctrinal breakdowns, this is where we are today. The Church, by and large, is still evangelizing. It is reaching vast parts of the world and is still growing — as God wills until Christ returns.

The key to a healthy church, whether in its global or local expressions, is the authority of God and His Word in all areas — whether science, theology, history, logic, morality, education, and so on. Every deviation from the truth of God's Word has the mind and hand of man trying to supersede God's Word. The Church is not immune to these corrupting influences. We can and have all fallen short, and this brief review of Church history should simply remind us of this: we must humble ourselves to the truth of God's Word from the very first to the very last verse. God will never be wrong. We can be wrong, but God will never be wrong.

---

2. Protestants also enjoy the apocryphal books, but do not see them as inspired by God but valuable for history like Josephus (a Jewish historian in the first century) and other ancient books. Most Catholics such as Jerome (who translated the Bible from Greek and Hebrew into Latin about A.D. 400) up until the Council of Trent viewed the apocrypha as *second canon* or *deuterocanon* (useful but not Scripture).

Chapter 4

How Is Roman Catholicism Different?

Dr. Terry Mortenson

Since becoming a Christian in 1972, I have lived in four different countries and have shared the gospel and taught the Scriptures in 23 countries, many of them dominated by Roman Catholicism. While I have met numerous devout Roman Catholics who believe many of the things that I also believe, I have found that almost none of them had a good understanding of the gospel or a confident assurance of their salvation. From talking to many others, I learned that my interactions with Catholics are not unique, but commonplace. Why is that? That's what we want to explore in this chapter.

Today there are about 1.3 billion Roman Catholics in the world. The largest number of Catholics is in Brazil (128 million, which is 63 percent of Brazil), Mexico (98 million, 81 percent), the Philippines (81 million, 80 percent), the United States (76 million, 24 percent), and Italy (50 million, 81 percent). The top ten countries are these five followed by France, Congo, Columbia, Spain, and Poland, which together account for just under half of all Catholics.[1]

Compared to other major religions, as of 2013, Christianity has about 2.2 billion adherents (a little over half of them Roman Catholic), Islam about 1.8 billion, atheism/agnosticism about 1.1 billion, Hinduism about

---

1. http://en.wikipedia.org/wiki/Catholic_Church_by_country: statistics from 2010 put the number at 1.228 billion in the various independent countries of the world and about five million more people in several dependent territories.

Saint Peter's square from the St. Peter's Basilica's dome in Vatican City

1 billion, and Buddhism about 376 million (numbers tend to slightly vary depending on the source).

The Roman Catholic Church is the only religion that has its own political territory as an independent state (Vatican City, a walled enclave of 110 acres within the city of Rome) with its own coinage (though it uses euros), its own central bank, and diplomatic relations with other countries.[2]

The Roman Catholic Church claims to be the only church on earth that has Jesus Christ as its founder, and the pope is its earthly head. Within the church there are two dominant *rites* or *forms of liturgy*: the Western, Roman or Latin rite (practiced by the vast majority of Catholics) and the Eastern rite (found mainly in Romania, Ukraine, and India).[3] All other professing

---

2. http://en.wikipedia.org/wiki/Vatican_City.
3. Though the liturgies are different, there is complete unity on doctrine and submission to the pope.

Christians (Eastern Orthodox, liberal Protestants, evangelicals, etc.) are considered "separated brethren" whom the church wants to draw back into itself, where it claims the true gospel is preserved and taught.

Given the Roman Catholic Church's claims and its size, we need to carefully compare its doctrines and practices to what is taught in the Scriptures and the gospel revealed therein.

Structure of the Roman Catholic Church

The Roman Catholic Church is led by the pope, who is considered to be the supreme representative of Jesus Christ on earth. He serves for life or until he resigns. His headquarters are at the Vatican in Rome. Under the pope is the College of Cardinals, which is responsible to elect the pope and assists the pope in the governing of the church.

A cardinal is usually an ordained bishop or archbishop. Next down the chain of leadership are the archbishops, who are responsible for Catholic churches in a very large area, such as Boston, Chicago, or New York City. Under the archbishops are the bishops, who each head up a diocese and supervise all the church's teaching and activities in the various parishes of the diocese to ensure faithfulness to the doctrines of the church. Each parish is led by a priest, who gathers the faithful Catholics for worship, instruction, and service.

Besides these main positions of leadership, there are many other administrative positions serving along with these clerical leaders, as well as hundreds of religious orders of nuns, monks, and missionaries carrying out the work of the Roman Catholic Church. One of the most well-known and influential orders is the Society of Jesus, whose members are called Jesuits. They control most Catholic educational institutions of higher learning and were a dominant force in the bloody Counter-Reformation response to the early Protestants.

History of the Roman Catholic Church

Church history is a vast subject, and we have space only for the briefest sketch related to the development of the Roman Catholic Church.[4] The church claims that its history goes all the way back to the Apostle Peter. Catholics believe and teach that Jesus ordained Peter as the head of the

---

4. For an in-depth layman's treatment of church history, including the historical developments of Roman Catholicism, Eastern Orthodoxy, and Protestantism, see Earle E. Cairns, *Christianity Through the Centuries* (Grand Rapids, MI: Zondervan, 1996, 3rd ed.), and Bruce Shelley, *Church History in Plain Language* (Nashville, TN: Thomas Nelson, 2013, 4th ed.)

worldwide Church. Since they believe that Peter became the first bishop of the church in Rome, all his successors in that church (eventually called popes) also are the head of the true worldwide church. We will come back to these claims later.

The modern Roman Catholic Church is very different from the early Church in organization, doctrine, and practices. Changes took place gradually over many centuries. According to the New Testament, Jesus Christ is the cornerstone and the Apostles and prophets were the foundation (Ephesians 2:19–20). The Apostles taught that there were two offices in the Church: elders (also called bishops and pastors) and deacons.

The first three centuries of Christian history were a time of persecution, (sometimes extreme) throughout the entire Roman Empire. In addition to persecution, the Church had to deal with false teaching and heresy within. By the middle of the 2nd century, some church leaders were talking of the "catholic" (meaning universal) Church (but this did not mean Roman Catholic Church) and the role of bishop began to be distinct from and superior in authority to elders or pastors (also called priests). Soon bishops in key cities (Jerusalem, Antioch, Alexandria, and Rome, and in the fourth century, Constantinople) rose to preeminence. The Roman bishop was especially important because Rome was the capital of the empire, the city where the Apostles Paul and Peter were martyred, and the Church there was one of the largest and wealthiest. By A.D. 300, the doctrine of apostolic succession of bishops, each of whom had monarchial rule over a congregation, was a reality, and the bishop of Rome came to be seen at the "first among equals" of the bishops.

Also during this time a separation between clergy and laity developed, with the bishop being regarded as a dispenser of grace, and some began to view the Lord's Supper (communion) as a sacrifice to God. Whereas in the New Testament baptism was administered to a person after he believed, in the 2nd and 3rd centuries some bishops began to practice infant baptism as an initiation into the Christian faith.

Church and State Together

Things changed significantly in 313 when after almost three centuries of persecution against Christians the Roman emperor Constantine fully legalized Christianity. He restored confiscated property to the Church, made Sunday a day of worship and rest, and transformed Byzantium (modern-day Istanbul) by renaming it Constantinople and making it his eastern capital. He also ordered the building of the Church of the Holy Sepulchre near the supposed tomb of Jesus in Jerusalem, which soon became the holiest place in Christendom. Although Constantine was not baptized until 337 on his deathbed, and it is questionable if Constantine was ever truly saved, he called for and presided over the

The First Council of Nicea, wall painting at the church of Stavropoleos, Bucharest, Romania

Council of Nicaea (325) to solve the Arian doctrinal controversy about the deity and humanity of Christ. By 381, under Emperor Theodosius I, Christianity became the state religion of the empire. So began a long, increasingly spiritual and moral corruption of the church as first the state ruled the church and later the church, through the popes, controlled the state.

In the 4th through 6th centuries, monasticism[5] and asceticism[6] arose as people reacted against the growing worldliness of the institutional church. In addition to the Council of Nicaea, other emperors convened four other ecumenical (universal) councils of bishops to iron out doctrinal problems. These strengthened the office of the bishop and the power of the Roman bishop grew. Some historians consider Leo I as the first Roman Catholic pope because as he took the episcopal throne in Rome in 440, he began to assert his supremacy over all other bishops, a claim that was soon affirmed by the Roman emperor, but not by all the other bishops. Although he did not claim the title "pope,"[7] he certainly established the doctrinal basis of the papacy.

5. This is a system or way of life in which a person withdraws from society to live alone or in a residence (monastery) with other monks for religious reasons to try escape the corruption in the world.

6. An ascetic (monk or hermit) is someone who for religious reasons lives with rigorous self-denial and self-discipline without the usual pleasures and comforts of life.

7. The word "pope" comes from the Latin papa meaning father. "The term 'pope' itself is not crucial in the emergence of the doctrine of papal primacy. The title 'papa' originally expressed the fatherly care of any and every bishop of his flock. It only began to be reserved for the bishop of Rome in the sixth century, long after the claim of primacy." Shelley, *Church History in Plain Language*, p. 133.

During these centuries many pagans came into the church through mass conversions (i.e., a tribal prince or territorial leader "converts" and then forces everyone under his leadership to "convert"). To help such converts feel comfortable in the church, priests and bishops introduced the use of images into the liturgy and the veneration of angels, saints (martyrs from earlier centuries), relics, pictures, and statues.

More "holy days," including Christmas, were officially added to the church calendar. In addition to the sacraments of baptism (especially of infants) and the Lord's Supper (also called the Eucharist or Mass) the prominent theologian Augustine and other church leaders added new sacraments:[8] marriage, penance,[9] confirmation[10] and extreme unction.[11] Augustine also helped to develop the doctrine of purgatory (a spiritual state of final purification after death and before entering heaven). The veneration of Mary, the mother of Jesus, developed rapidly during this time. Belief in her perpetual virginity (introduced into churches in the middle of the second century) and in her sinlessness placed her at the head of the list of "saints,"[12] and festivals in her honor sprang up. People began to believe that she had intercessory powers to influence Jesus on behalf of believers. Veneration of other saints included the selling of relics from their bodies.

During the 7th through 8th centuries, the Eastern church dealt with the threat of Islam while the Western church sought to evangelize the Teutonic hordes of northern and western Europe. Gregory I ("the Great") became bishop of Rome in 590. He never accepted the title of "universal pope," but he exercised all the power and prerogatives of later popes, significantly

---

8. In the Catholic Church, a sacrament is a visible rite that imparts grace to the recipient who properly receives it. *Catechism of the Catholic Church* (Citta del Vaticano: Libreria Editrice Vaticana, 1997, second edition), #1131. Hereafter referred to as CCC, this document was approved and promulgated by Pope John Paul II. I will always cite the paragraph numbers (rather than page numbers) of the CCC, which is also available online.

9. Acts of fasting, prayer, and almsgiving are signs of a conversion of the heart toward God and serve as a means of forgiveness. CCC, #1431 and 1434.

10. Combined with baptism and the Eucharist, confirmation is part of Christian initiation more perfectly binding the person to the Catholic Church. CCC, #1285.

11. This is when the priest anoints with oil a person who is very sick or near death. CCC, #1499 and 1512.

12. While the Catholic Church uses the word "saint" to refer to all believers (as does the New Testament), in this instance and many others in Catholic literature (and through this chapter) the word refers to a special person whom the pope has canonized as a "saint" because of his or her "life of heroic virtue" or faithfulness to God through martyrdom (CCC, #828). But the New Testament never uses the word with this specialized meaning.

increased the wealth of the bishopric of Rome, and made the church a formidable power in politics. While he believed in the verbal inspiration of Scripture, he regarded church tradition as an equal authority, upheld the idea of purgatory, and considered each performance of the Eucharist to be a sacrifice of Christ's body and blood.

Pope Leo III crowns Charlemagne

In 800, Pope Leo III crowned the king of the Franks, Charlemagne, as emperor of the revived Roman Empire. The pope ruled the spiritual realm, and the emperor ruled the temporal realm, constituting together (so they thought) the kingdom of God on earth. But when Charlemagne died in 814 his Frankish empire quickly disintegrated, and for the next 250 years there was a power struggle between the popes and the Frankish rulers. Many of the more than 40 popes between 800 and 1054 were corrupt; in 1045, three popes claimed supreme authority at the same time!

Other developments at this time included the initial teaching that by divine miracle the bread and wine of the Eucharist was actually transformed into the body and blood of Christ (though without changing appearance). This further strengthened the power of the local priest and the pope and paved the way for the official doctrine of transubstantiation in 1215 and the final definition of it by the Council of Trent in 1545. In the 10th and 11th centuries reforms were made to deal with the wealth and corruption of the monasteries.

The Zenith of the Papacy

The Great Schism of 1054 occurred when the pope of Rome and the patriarch of Constantinople excommunicated each other because of disagreement about the use of unleavened bread in the Eucharist. This permanently divided the Roman Catholic Church (hereafter referred to simply as Catholic Church) from the Eastern Orthodox, and the mutual excommunications were not removed until 1965. After the schism and until 1305 the papacy attained its zenith of temporal and spiritual power over all of life in the Roman Empire.

In 1059, under Pope Nicholas II, the election of the pope was taken out of the hands of the Roman populace and given to the College of Cardinals, a group of priests and bishops in and near Rome that had begun in the 4th century.

From the beginning of his enthronement in 1073, Pope Gregory VII enforced the celibacy of the priesthood, and in his *Dictatus Papae* (1075) he declared the absolute supremacy of the papacy and that the Catholic Church has never erred and would never err.

According to church tradition, the rosary (a repetitious prayer with beads) became a part of the Catholic veneration of Mary after an "apparition of Mary" in 1214, and it has been promoted and modified by many popes from the 16th century to the present.[13]

Seven or eight major crusades and many minor ones occurred in the years between about 1095 and 1290. These were intended to resist the advance of Islam in Europe and retake control of the Holy Land. The popes offered crusading armies earthly riches and eternal blessings for killing Muslims, heretics, and anyone who rejected the supremacy of the pope.

Two important religious orders were formed in the 13th century. The pope approved the Franciscans in 1209 and the Dominicans in 1216. The Franciscans lived by alms and were committed missionaries for the church whereas the Dominicans produced scholars for the church.

The Catholic theologian Aquinas (1225–1274) presented arguments that cemented the doctrine of the perpetual virginity of Mary for her whole life, which added to the veneration she was already receiving as the "Mother of God."

The years 1305–1377 witnessed the "Babylonian Captivity" of the papacy, as French popes ruled not from Rome but Avignon, France. In 1378, the non-French objected, leading to the "Great Schism" of the papacy (not to be confused with the Great Schism of 1054), which lasted until 1415. For most of that time there were two popes, one ruling from Rome and the other from Avignon, each with his own College of Cardinals. The last six years the church suffered (as it had in 1045) under three simultaneous popes contesting the claims of each other! Finally, one resigned and the Council of Constance deposed the other two. After taking power from the College of Cardinals the Council elected a new pope.

---

13. http://en.wikipedia.org/wiki/Rosary, accessed February 27, 2015.

Attempts at Reformation

As we have noted, from time to time attempts were made to reform (return to the teachings of the Bible) the Catholic Church, though with limited success. John Wycliffe (1330–1384) made another attempt. An English priest, he translated the Bible into English so that the common man could know the truth and see the errors in the church. He died of disease but the Catholic authorities later exhumed his body and burned him as a heretic in 1428. The Czech priest Jan Hus adopted the ideas of Wycliffe and was burned at the stake in 1415 for his efforts at reform. But these men were preparing the ground for a German Augustinian monk named Martin Luther. In 1517, he nailed his Ninety-Five Theses on the door of the church in Wittenburg, Germany, exposing many doctrinal and practical errors in the Catholic Church.

One of those practices was the selling of indulgences — paying money to the church to obtain forgiveness for oneself and to free one from the temporal penalty of sin. Declared a dogma by Pope Clement VI in 1343, it was extended in 1476 by Pope Sixtus IV so that a person could pay to shorten a loved one's time in purgatory. Luther and others condemned this and other doctrines and practices that perverted the gospel and undermined the authority of Scripture. But the Catholic Church firmly rejected his efforts, triggering the Protestant Reformation, which led eventually to the development of Lutheran, Reformed, and Anglican state churches and various Anabaptist free churches mainly in northern and western Europe. Viewing Protestants as heretics, the Catholic Church fought this movement through the Counter-Reformation.

Throughout the 16th century its popes sought to make financial and spiritual reforms and new religious orders were founded which contributed to missionary expansion to Africa, Southeast Asia, Latin America, and Quebec led by the Jesuits, Franciscans, and Dominicans.

Pope Paul III authorized the Order of the Jesuits in 1540 to raise up well-educated preachers to convert the heathen and reconvert the Protestants. He also set up the Roman Inquisition in 1542, which, following practices of the Medieval Inquisition in the 1200s and the Spanish Inquisition in the 1400s, used confiscation of property and imprisonment as punishment for becoming Protestant.

The inquisitions were first instituted by Pope Innocent III (1198–1216), who used his crusading armies to torture and kill thousands of Albigensians and Waldensians (godly Christians that the church condemned as heretics) in southern France and northern Italy. Over the next 600 years, 75 popes ordered, devised, or approved some of the world's most brutal and horrific methods of torture and murder to try to force Jews, Muslims, and Bible-believing Christians to abandon their faith and trust in the "Holy Mother Church." Tens of millions of people (some historians estimate 50 million) suffered and died under these wicked and completely unbiblical inquisitions as the popes sought to establish their absolute rule over the church and society.[14]

In 1559, Pope Paul IV issued the Index of Prohibited Books, which forbid Catholics (on threat of damnation) from reading Protestant literature. The list was kept up to date until 1966 when Pope Paul VI abolished it.

A few years earlier, Pope Paul III had called the Council of Trent (1545–1563) to respond to the Protestant teaching. The Council affirmed that the Apocrypha[15] and church tradition are equal in authority with the Bible. It also affirmed the doctrine of transubstantiation as well as the doctrine of purgatory that the Council of Florence (1439–1445) had elevated to official dogma. It anathematized (condemned to hell) anyone who held to the biblical teaching of justification by faith alone, in Christ alone, through grace alone, as proclaimed by Protestant reformers. Still in force today,[16] those anathemas clearly condemn truly Bible-believing evangelicals.

After the Council of Trent, the structure and doctrines of the Catholic Church remained essentially as they are today. But a few new doctrines were officially added.

- In 1854, Pope Pius IX made the doctrine of the Immaculate Conception of Mary (that she was born without a sin nature and never sinned her whole life) an official dogma.

14. See the thoroughly documented research of David A. Plaisted, "Estimates of the Number Killed by the Papacy in the Middle Ages and Later," http://www.cs.unc.edu/~plaisted/estimates.html. This documentary film features, among others, a former Roman Catholic priest and a Roman Catholic layman who have done much research on the Inquisitions: https://www.youtube.com/watch?v=Rx8PdvOELvY&list=PLE1CB721E3CA65D76&index=94&feature=plpp_video. It describes and pictures a number of the torture techniques devised by the popes and also documents and quotes from Roman Catholic historians and official Catholic teaching.
15. Jewish writings between the last book of the Old Testament and the time of Jesus.
16. Except with respect to the Lutheran World Federation: http://www.vatican.va/roman_curia/pontifical_councils/chrstuni/documents/rc_pc_chrstuni_doc_31101999_cath-luth-joint-declaration_en.html. See point 2, paragraph 13, on "The Doctrine of Justification as Ecumenical Problem." However, theologically conservative Lutherans would not accept this Lutheran-Catholic joint declaration.

- Pope Pius IX also convened the First Vatican Council (1869–1870) and persuaded the gathered bishops to declare the doctrine of papal infallibility (i.e., the pope speaks without error when he speaks *ex cathedra* on faith and morals).

- Since Pope Pius IX, many popes have called Mary "Mediatrix," because, it is claimed, she intercedes for all believers and is the principal dispenser of grace. Pope Pius X (1903–1914) and other later popes have declared in papal documents that Mary is "Co-Redemptrix," referring to her indirect and unequal role with Christ in the redemption process.

- In 1950, Pope Pius XII declared the dogma of the Assumption of Mary (that she did not die and suffer decay but was miraculously taken body and soul to heaven).

The conflict between Roman Catholics and Protestants became very bloody during the Thirty Years' War (1618–48). Millions died from the conflicts, disease, and famine, and it took decades for devastated towns and villages to be rebuilt. But it did bring an end to religious persecution in Europe (except for the late 20th-century Catholic-Protestant conflicts in Northern Ireland), and the modern European system of states emerged from this conflict.

For the next 150 years, monarchs endeavored to limit papal power in their countries. From the end of the 18th century up to World War I, the Catholic Church lost many of its physical possessions and much of its political influence. Since then, the church has had increasing difficulties due to the spread of communism, liberal theology, and the havoc created by World War II. But it has pursued ecumenical relationships with the Eastern Orthodox and Protestants and has been significantly influenced by the charismatic movement.

The Second Vatican Council (1962–1965) created no new dogmas. But it was more open toward Protestants, calling them "separated brethren" rather than heretics and schismatics. It encouraged Bible reading (with interpretation directed by the Magisterium, the teaching authority of the bishops, cardinals, and popes) and partnerships with Protestants in Bible translation efforts and in social issues (such as abortion). It permitted the Mass to be conducted in the mother tongue of the worshipers (rather than only in Latin). It increased attempts for ecumenical unity with the Eastern Orthodox and Protestant churches, though without any compromise on official Catholic doctrine. It also opened the door to Roman Catholic dialogue with representatives of non-Christian religions.

It is clear from this survey of history that the doctrines, organization, and practices of the Catholic Church have been developing slowly since early in the post-apostolic age. The claim that the Roman Catholic Church goes back to the Apostles is simply not true. Some of its doctrines and practices do, but many others do not, and many of those are of very recent origin in the last few hundred years. As we shall see, they also seriously contradict the teaching of Scripture. It should also be noted that according to the teaching of the New Testament and the experience of the churches in the first few decades (as evidenced in the Book of Acts and the Epistles) it does not take centuries or even decades for false teaching and false practices to gain considerable influence among Christians.

But Roman Catholicism and Eastern Orthodoxy were not the only expressions of Christianity during the centuries leading up to the Protestant Reformation. There were local bodies of believers in North Africa, the Middle East, Europe, and elsewhere who sought to hold fast to the Word of God and sound doctrine and the true gospel of salvation through faith in Jesus Christ alone, and they opposed the growing corruption of the Catholic and Orthodox churches. Much of what we know about them, however, comes from the Catholics and Orthodox who condemned and persecuted them as "heretics." Therefore, they were not in a position to develop scholarship after the church became wedded to the state at the time of Constantine.[17]

One result of the efforts by the Catholic Church after Vatican II to seek ecumenical unity with non-Catholics was the "Evangelicals and Catholics Together" document signed or endorsed in 1994 by a number of prominent evangelical leaders and scholars and their Roman Catholic counterparts.[18] In sufficiently vague language to obtain agreement, this unofficial and non-binding document avoided serious doctrinal differences. Many evangelicals, including this author, believe that has contributed to a decline in doctrinal discernment among evangelicals. Before discussing some of the

---

17. Two excellent works, still available, that discuss these believers are Leonard Verduin, *The Reformers and Their Stepchildren* (Grand Rapids, MI: Eerdmans, 1964) and E.H. Broadbent, *The Pilgrim Church* (1931, republished by Resurrected Books in 2014).

18. Many evangelicals, including this author, were and are very concerned about this agreement between evangelicals and Catholics, for reasons discussed at http://www.gty.org/resources/Sermons/GTY54.

more important differences, we should note some of the important agreements between evangelicals and Catholics.

Roman Catholic Doctrines and Practices That Are Consistent with Scripture

There are many important doctrines and practices in the Catholic Church that are right in line with Scripture, and on these evangelicals can agree with Roman Catholics. These include:

1. Roman Catholicism is monotheistic: there is only one God who created the world. And the Church is Trinitarian. It teaches that God exists as three co-equal, co-eternal, and distinct persons: Father, Son (Jesus Christ), and Holy Spirit, each of which is fully God, and yet there is only one God.

2. The church affirms that the whole Bible is the inspired Word of God. The Bible teaches "without error that truth which God, for the sake of our salvation, wished to see confided to the Sacred Scriptures."[19] But the Roman Catholic Bible contains more books than the Bible used by Jews and Protestants, as explained later.

3. The church holds to the full deity and full humanity of Jesus Christ, His virgin birth and sinless life, and that He performed miracles, died for our sins, rose bodily from the dead, ascended to heaven, and will come again to judge the living and the dead.

4. It teaches that men and women are made in the image of God but are sinful and in need of salvation. Those who do not repent of their rebellion and respond to Christ's mercy and grace in this life will suffer eternally in hell, separated from God.

5. It teaches that marriage is sacred and instituted by God and is defined as one man united to one woman. It officially declares that homosexual acts are of "grave depravity" and "intrinsically disordered" and "under no circumstances can they be approved."[20] (However, Pope Francis seems to be warming up

---

19. CCC, #107.
20. Ibid., #2357.

to homosexuals as he gave VIP seats to members of an LGBT group from America at his October 15, 2014, speech at the Vatican.[21])

6. The Church has been strongly pro-life and therefore anti-abortion in both public declarations and actions, and historically this was so before many evangelicals began to express their concern about the holocaust of abortion.

Doctrines and Practices That Are Contrary to Scripture

While the Catholic Church holds to many beliefs and practices that are consistent with Scripture, it is critical to understand many other very important teachings and practices of the church that are incompatible with the Word of God. Here are just a few.

The Supreme Authority in the Church

The New Testament Apostles established only two offices in the local churches: elders and deacons. A comparison of the relevant passages[22] shows that the terms "elder" (or presbyter, from the Greek word *presbuteros*), "pastor" (or shepherd), and "overseer" (or bishop, from the Greek word *episkopos*) all refer to the same position of leadership. The Apostles gave no instructions for higher levels of leadership over multiple churches or over all churches in a large city or over the whole world. The New Testament indicates that the 1st-century local churches were to be independent congregations under the Lordship of Christ and the authority of the Word of God.

In contrast, as we have seen in the historical developments of the spread of Christianity in Western Europe, some bishops began to claim authority over more than one congregation, then over a city, and then over the world-wide church, and along the way cardinals, archbishops, and patriarchs were added to provide leadership under the absolute monarchy of the papacy.

The Catholic Church claims that the pope is infallible when he speaks *ex cathedra* ("from the chair of Peter"); when he speaks as the supreme teacher of the church he is incapable of teaching any false doctrine. Likewise, the bishops do not and cannot err when they teach religious and moral doctrines. This Magisterium (consisting of the pope and the bishops) is endowed

---

21. http://www.christianpost.com/news/vatican-gives-vip-seats-to-gay-positive-lgbt-catholic-group-at-pope-francis-speech-reportedly-first-gesture-of-its-kind-134384/.
22. 1 Timothy 3; Titus 1–2; 1 Peter 5; Acts 6 and 20:28–32.

"with the charism of infallibility in matters of faith and morals."[23] And, it is claimed, God has given this Magisterium the task of providing the correct interpretation of the Scriptures for the rest of the church.[24]

How does the Magisterium accomplish this task of interpreting Scripture without error? First, it includes in the Catholic version of the Scriptures the apocryphal books,[25] which are not accepted as the Word of God by either the Jews or Protestants.[26] But in those books, the popes and bishops find justification for some Roman Catholic doctrines, such as praying for the dead. Second, the Catholic Church equates unwritten "Tradition" with written Scripture. She "does not derive her certainty about all revealed truths from the holy Scriptures alone. Both Scripture and Tradition must be accepted and honored with equal sentiments of devotion and reverence."[27] This is because "Sacred Tradition and Sacred Scripture make up a single sacred deposit of the Word of God."[28] In Roman Catholic doctrine, "Tradition" (capital 'T') is the Church's "doctrine, life, and worship."[29] It is "a current of life and truth coming from God through Christ and through the Apostles to the last of the faithful who repeats his creed and learns his catechism."[30] And "Sacred Scripture is written principally in the Church's heart rather than in documents and records, for the Church carries in her Tradition the living memorial of God's Word."[31]

So the Catholic Church leadership relies heavily on man-made ideas and practices accumulated over the centuries as the basis for their interpretation of the Word of God.

The pope also claims his supreme authority by asserting that he inherited it from Peter who, according to official Catholic doctrine, was the bishop of Rome and the first pope over the worldwide church. "The Roman Pontiff, by reason of his office as Vicar [i.e., earthly representative] of Christ, and as

23. CCC, #890–891.
24. Ibid., #85.
25. Ibid., #120.
26. For reasons why the apocryphal books are rejected as Scripture, see https://answersin-genesis.org/OnlineBible/help/helpeng/source/html/apocryphainfo.htm and https://an-swersingenesis.org/bible-questions/is-the-bible-enough/.
27. CCC, #82.
28. Ibid., #97
29. Ibid., #78.
30. *The Catholic Encyclopedia*, quoted in James G. McCarthy, *The Gospel According to Rome: Comparing Catholic Tradition and the Word of God* (Eugene, OR: Harvest House, 1995), p. 291.
31. CCC, #113.

pastor of the entire Church has full, supreme, and universal power over the whole Church, a power which he can always exercise unhindered."[32]

But nowhere does the New Testament make either of those papal claims (infallibility and authority), nor does it teach the infallible authority of the bishops or describe any kind of magisterium. In fact, the Bible never says that Peter was in Rome (though we know from church history that he was martyred there), which is strange if he was the head of the church in Rome. And if he was the bishop of Rome, it is equally strange that when Paul wrote his letter to the church in Rome in about A.D. 57, he greeted many believers by name (Romans 16), but does not mention Peter. How could Paul overlook greeting the bishop, especially since his letter was giving very authoritative teaching to the Church there? Furthermore, Paul says that the Christian Church was built on the foundation of the Apostles (plural) and prophets, with Jesus Christ as the cornerstone (Ephesians 2:19–20).

It is also significant that in Peter's two letters written to all Christians in Asia Minor (modern-day Turkey) he describes himself as an Apostle and bondservant of Jesus Christ (1 Peter 1:1; 2 Peter 1:1), not as bishop of Rome. In Peter's first letter he humbly exhorts elders of the various churches as "a fellow elder," not as a supreme elder in authority over them and says they should not "lord over" the Christians that they shepherd in their flocks under the authority of the Chief Shepherd, Jesus Christ (1 Peter 5:1–4). In 2 Peter 3:2, he admonishes his readers to follow the commandments of Jesus and "your apostles" (plural), not his writings as uniquely authoritative.

It is true that Peter gave the "birthday sermon" of the Church to Jews in Jerusalem on the day of Pentecost (Acts 2). But it was the Apostles (plural: Acts 6) who led the Church there in the earlier years and there is no biblical evidence that Peter was the supreme leader of the Apostles then or any other time. Peter did lead the first Gentiles to faith in Christ in Caesarea (Acts 10), but when questioned about this by the Apostles a few days later in Jerusalem, Peter did not have supreme authority (Acts 11:1–18). When Philip led the first Samaritans to Christ, the Apostles in Jerusalem did not send Peter alone, but Peter and John together to confirm that the Samaritans were full members of the Church (Acts 8:5–17).

When Paul and Barnabas reported to the Church in Antioch about the many Gentiles coming to Christ, a dispute arose with other Jewish Christians

32. Ibid., #882.

who contended that Gentiles needed to be circumcised. The Church then sent Paul and Barnabas to the Apostles and elders (note: both are plural words, Acts 15:2, 15:4) in Jerusalem to resolve this matter. Peter was there and spoke, but so did Barnabas, Paul, and James. If anyone had supreme authority there, it was James, for it was after he spoke that "the apostles and elders with the whole church" decided to send Paul and Barnabas back to Antioch with instructions about Gentile believers (Acts 15:13–22). Peter had no unique authority in this situation.

Three years after Paul's conversion he went to Jerusalem and met Peter and James, the Lord's half-brother (Galatians 1:18–19). Then after 14 more years of ministry among the Gentiles, Paul went to Jerusalem again with Barnabas and Titus to explain to the Church there about their ministry among the Gentiles (Galatians 2:1–9). Paul says that God had committed him to take the gospel to the Gentiles, just as God had committed Peter to take the gospel to Jews, and Paul saw his apostolic authority as equal to Peter's. Paul names James, Peter, and John (in that order, again suggesting that James was the leader of the Church in Jerusalem) as ones who "seemed to be pillars" in the Church (Galatians 2:9). Those three together gave Paul and Barnabas the right hand of fellowship, signifying their equal authority in the churches, but with James, Peter, and John focusing on evangelism to the Jews and Paul and Barnabas going to the Gentiles.

But some time later Paul found Peter at the church in Antioch and had to confront and rebuke Peter in front of the other Christians for his hypocrisy, caving into peer pressure from Jewish Christians, and by his behavior undermining the truth of the gospel (Galatians 2:11–14). This is hardly consistent with the idea that Peter was the head of the whole Church. Peter obviously responded positively to this humbling rebuke, evidenced by his affirming statement that Paul's writings were Scripture (2 Peter 3:16).

There is no basis in Scripture for the papal claims of infallibility and supreme authority over the worldwide Church. The claims come from a long series of men grabbing more and more power, starting with Leo I in A.D. 440, and as we noted, it has led to a massive amount of political, moral, and theological corruption through the centuries.

Because the Catholic Church denies the supreme authority of Scripture, through its popes and bishops, it has been able to proclaim numerous doctrines that are contrary to Scripture. Clearly, this is a case of faith in man's word over faith in God's Word.

But the Apostles made it perfectly clear in the New Testament that the primacy belongs to Jesus Christ alone and is not shared with any man. "And he is the head of the body, the church: who is the beginning, the firstborn from the dead; that in all things he might have the preeminence" (Colossians 1:18).

The Bible is also clear that the "traditions" spoken of by the Apostles must be the same as the teaching in their New Testament writings, not contradictory to it or adding to or taking away from the doctrines in those books (2 Thessalonians 2:15, 3:6; 1 Corinthians 11:2). Because of the dangers of false prophets, false teachers, and false gospels (Matthew 24:4; Galatians 1:6–9; 2 Peter 2:1–3), Scripture repeatedly proclaims its supreme authority. Believers are not to turn to the right or the left from God's Word (Joshua 1:6–8) but walk in the ancient paths of the biblical prophets (Jeremiah 6:16–19; Isaiah 8:20). Jewish and Christian fathers were expected to know the Scriptures and teach them to their children (Deuteronomy 6:1–9; Ephesians 6:4).

Jesus taught His followers (not just church leaders) to treat the Word of God as their necessary daily food (Matthew 4:4), and that Scripture was the means by which God would produce holy maturity in their lives (John 17:17). His followers were to reject any man-made traditions that contradicted Scripture (Mark 7:6–13) and to test every truth claim against Scripture (Acts 17:11) because demonic spirits would seek to lead believers astray (1 John 4:1). Paul also warned that men would arise in the Church speaking perverse things to draw Christians away from the truth. So he urged people to follow the Word of God (Acts 20:28–32). This repeated insistence on the supreme authority of God's Word is a reflection of the fact that He has magnified His Word above His name (Psalm 138:2).

On the Question of Origins

Up until about 1800, the almost universal belief among those who identified themselves as Christians (whether Protestant, Catholic, or Eastern Orthodox) was that God created in six literal days about 6,000 years ago and destroyed the earth with a global Flood at the time of Noah. But with the development of the idea of millions of years by deistic and atheistic geologists and other scientists in the late 18th and early 19th centuries, most of the professing Christians abandoned that long-held belief. [33]

Today, most Roman Catholic clergy and laity would appear to be theistic evolutionists, although like most Protestants and Eastern Orthodox believers, Roman Catholics are very ignorant of the biblical and scientific evidence against microbe-to-microbiologist evolution and millions of years. This is not surprising given the Church's lack of commitment to the supreme authority of Scripture and its vague teaching on these matters in its official *Catechism of the Catholic Church* and in various pronouncements by popes and others.

Teilhard de Chardin (1881–1955), who was a Jesuit priest, philosopher, and paleontologist, took part in the discovery of the supposed ape-man "Peking Man" and likely was involved in the "Piltdown Man" hoax in 1912. He said,

> [Evolution] is a general postulate to which all theories, all hypotheses, all systems must henceforward bow and which they must satisfy in order to be thinkable and true. Evolution is a light which illuminates all facts, a trajectory which all lines of thought must follow.[34]

Many of de Chardin's writings were censored by the Catholic Church during his lifetime, primarily because of his views on original sin. "However, in July 2009, Vatican spokesman Fr. Federico Lombardi said, 'By now, no one would dream of saying that [de Chardin] is a heterodox author who shouldn't be studied.' "[35] Pope Benedict XVI has also praised him for his work.[36]

In a 1996 speech to the Pontifical Academy of Sciences, the Belgian Catholic priest and astronomer Georges Lamaître (1894–1966) was the first to propose the big-bang theory for the origin of the universe from a "cosmic egg."[37]

In 1996, in a speech to the Pontifical Academy of Sciences, Pope John Paul II commented about the 1950 encyclical by Pope Pius XII called

---

33. See chapters 1–3 in Terry Mortenson and Thane H. Ury, eds., *Coming to Grips with Genesis: Biblical Authority and the Age of the Earth* (Green Forest, AR: Master Books, 2008).

34. Cited in Francisco Ayala, "Nothing in Biology Makes Sense Except in the Light of Evolution: Theodosius Dobzhansky, 1900–1975," *Journal of Heredity*, (V. 68, No. 3, 1977), p. 3.

35. http://en.wikipedia.org/wiki/Pierre_Teilhard_de_Chardin, accessed February 27, 2015.

36. http://teilhard.com/2013/05/21/orthodoxy-of-teilhard-de-chardin-part-i/, accessed February 27, 2015.

37. http://en.wikipedia.org/wiki/Georges_Lemaître, accessed March 30, 2015.

Humani Generis:

> In his encyclical *Humani Generis* (1950), my predecessor Pius XII has already affirmed that there is no conflict between evolution and the doctrine of the faith regarding man and his vocation, provided that we do not lose sight of certain fixed points. . . . Today, more than a half-century after the appearance of that encyclical, some new findings lead us toward the recognition of evolution as more than a hypothesis.[38] In fact it is remarkable that this theory has had progressively greater influence on the spirit of researchers, following a series of discoveries in different scholarly disciplines. The convergence in the results of these independent studies — which was neither planned nor sought — constitutes in itself a significant argument in favor of the theory.[39]

But both of these documents indicate that these two popes and the Catholic Church are not necessarily opposed to evolution as long as Catholics still affirm that Adam and Eve were the first two humans and their souls were created and they fell in sin. The evolution of Adam's body from a pre-existing form of life is not categorically ruled out. Both of these popes' documents are filled with very vague language about the "fruitfulness of frank dialogue between the Church and science" and are completely devoid of reference to specific Scriptures relevant to the issue. Many observers have interpreted Pope John Paul II's statements to mean that he accepted biological evolution but only questioned the "mechanism of evolution." In other words, science has established that evolution is a fact, but scientists are not in agreement

---

38. The Roman Catholic "Eternal Word Television Network" had a footnote to John Paul's remark here stating, "The English edition at first translated the French original as: 'Today, more than a half-century after the appearance of that encyclical, some new findings lead us toward the recognition of more than one hypothesis within the theory of evolution.' The L'Osservatore Romano English Edition subsequently amended the text to that given in the body of the message above, citing the translation of the other language editions as its reason. It should be noted that a hypothesis is the preliminary stage of the scientific method and the pope's statement suggests nothing more than that science has progressed beyond that stage. This is certainly true with respect to cosmological evolution (the physical universe), whose science both Pius XII and John Paul II have praised, but not true in biology, about which the popes have generally issued cautions (as [in Pope John Paul's 1996 lecture] and *Humani Generis*)."

39. Pope John Paul II, "Message to the Pontifical Academy of Sciences: on Evolution," October 22, 1996, http://www.ewtn.com/library/papaldoc/jp961022.htm, accessed March 30, 2015.

about how it happened. So the popes have denied atheistic evolution but not theistic (God-guided) evolution.

More recently, Pope Francis has also affirmed theistic evolution with similar vague and pompous language. In his address to the Pontifical Academy of Sciences in 2014 for the dedication of a sculpture of Pope Benedict XVI, Francis said,

> When we read the account of Creation in Genesis we risk imagining that God was a magician, complete with an all powerful magic wand. But that was not so. He created beings and he let them develop according to the internal laws with which He endowed each one, that they might develop, and reach their fullness. . . . And thus Creation has been progressing for centuries and centuries, millennia and millennia, until becoming as we know it today, precisely because God is not a demiurge or a magician, but the Creator who gives life to all beings. . . . The Big Bang theory, which is proposed today as the origin of the world, does not contradict the intervention of a divine creator but depends on it. Evolution in nature does not conflict with the notion of Creation, because evolution presupposes the creation of beings who evolve. As for man, however, there is a change and a novelty. When, on the sixth day in the account of Genesis, comes the moment of the creation of man, God gives the human being another autonomy, an autonomy different from that of nature, which is freedom.[40]

Given the church's lack of commitment to the supreme authority of Scripture, the ambiguity of these papal pronouncements for over six decades, and the lack of any clear teaching in the official *Catechism* about evolution, the length of the creation days in Genesis 1, and the age of the creation,[41] it is no surprise that a great many Roman Catholics have a very shallow understanding of the issues and see no problem with accepting the evolution of the cosmos (from the big bang) and of living creatures, even possibly Adam's body, under the guiding hand of God.

---

40. Pope Francis, "Address of His Holiness Pope Francis on the Occasion of the Inauguration of the Bust in Honour of Pope Benedict XVI," October 27, 2014, https://w2.vatican.va/content/francesco/en/speeches/2014/october/documents/papa-francesco_20141027_plenaria-accademia-scienze.html, accessed March 30, 2015
41. See CCC, #282–289 and 337–342.

There are, however, some Roman Catholics who reject biological evolution and apparently hold to young-earth creation. The Kolbe Center for the Study of Creation, based in Virginia, was founded in 2000.[42] The Daylight Origins Society is a small Catholic group active in the UK.[43] But the influence of these groups in the Catholic Church appears to be very minimal.

The Catholic View of the Virgin Mary

Another area of very erroneous teaching in the Catholic Church relates to Mary, the earthly mother of Jesus.

Immaculate Conception

In 1954, Pope Pius IX first proclaimed as an official dogma the doctrine of the Immaculate Conception, which teaches that "The most Blessed Virgin Mary was, from the first moment of her conception, by a singular grace and privilege of almighty God and by virtue of the merits of Jesus Christ, Savior of the human race, preserved immune from all stain of original sin."[44] And so "by the grace of God Mary remained free of every personal sin her whole life long."[45]

This novel doctrine has no basis in Scripture. The Bible clearly teaches (through quoting her own words) that Mary was not sinless, but in need of the saving grace of Jesus Christ, just like all other humans. Mary said when she was pregnant with Jesus, "My soul exalts the Lord, and my spirit has rejoiced in God my Savior" (Luke 1:46–47; NASB).

Perpetual Virginity of Mary

The Catholic Church rightly teaches that Mary was a virgin when she conceived Jesus by the power of the Holy Spirit, but it goes on to claim that Mary remained a virgin all her life,

Statue of the Virgin Mary

42. http://kolbecenter.org/.
43. http://www.daylightorigins.com/.
44. CCC, #491.
45. Ibid, #493.

something that has no biblical support. In the church's liturgy they call her *Aeiparthenos*, the "ever virgin."[46] Furthermore, the Church affirms that,

> Jesus is Mary's only son, but her spiritual motherhood extends to all men whom indeed he came to save: "The Son whom she brought forth is he whom God placed as the first-born among many brethren, that is, the faithful in whose generation and formation she co-operates with a mother's love."[47]

Evangelicals and most other Protestants object to this doctrine because Scripture teaches that Joseph and Mary had four sons (James, Joses [Joseph], Judas [Jude], and Simon) and at least two daughters after Jesus was born (Matthew 13:55–56; Mark 6:3: cf. Mark 3:31–35; 1 Corinthians 9:5; Galatians 1:19). Aware of these verses, the Catholic Church responds,

> The Church has always understood these passages as not referring to other children of the Virgin Mary. In fact James and Joseph, "brothers of Jesus," are the sons of another Mary, a disciple of Christ, whom St. Matthew significantly calls "the other Mary."[48] They are close relations of Jesus, according to an Old Testament expression.[49]

But this reply fails for a number of reasons. First, while there are several women named Mary and more than one James and Simon named in the New Testament, the context in each case enables us to determine which individual is in view in each passage. Second, if the named brothers and sisters were cousins, why didn't Mark use the Greek word for cousin (*anepsios*), which Paul used in Colossians 4:10? Or for a more distant relative or kinsman Mark could have used *sungenis*, as Luke did to describe the relationship of Elizabeth to Mary (Luke 1:36). Instead, Mark used the normal Greek words for brother and sister. Third, the context of Mark 6:3 indicates that Jesus was in His hometown (Mark 6:1) and He refers to "his own relatives" in contrast to "his own household" (Mark 6:4). Fourth, in Mark 3:31–35, a crowd had gathered around Jesus and told Him, "Your mother and your brothers are outside looking for you." If "your brothers" were the sons of

---

46. Ibid, #499.
47. Ibid, #501.
48. Ibid., #500, footnote 158 says: "Matt. 13:55, 28:1; cf. Matt 27:56."
49. Ibid., #500.

some other Mary, then "your mother" would be referring to some other woman too, which is an impossible interpretation in this context. Fifth, Matthew 1:25 says that after the angel appeared to Joseph, he took Mary as his wife and kept her a virgin "until" she gave birth to Jesus, which strongly implies that they did have sexual relations after Jesus was born and thereby would have had children by her. Finally, Matthew 13:53–57 confirms this understanding because along with his mother, brothers, and sisters, the townspeople refer to Joseph, the supposed father of Jesus. It makes no sense for those people to mention his father and mother and then refer to more distant relatives.[50]

The Assumption of Mary

On November 1, 1950, Pope Pius XII proclaimed as official dogma that Mary did not die as all other humans have and will. Rather, God took both her body and soul to heaven supernaturally. The pope wrote,

> By the authority of our Lord Jesus Christ, of the Blessed Apostles Peter and Paul, and by our own authority, we pronounce, declare, and define it to be a divinely revealed dogma: that the Immaculate Mother of God, the ever Virgin Mary, having completed the course of her earthly life, was assumed body and soul into heavenly glory.[51]

The pope further dogmatically proclaimed,

> It is forbidden to any man to change this, our declaration, pronouncement, and definition or, by rash attempt, to oppose and counter it. If any man should presume to make such an attempt, let him know that he will incur the wrath of Almighty God and of the Blessed Apostles Peter and Paul.[52]

But there is no biblical support for this teaching, as the few New Testament verses that the pope footnoted demonstrate. Jesus never taught this and both Peter and Paul would certainly oppose this doctrine as false. Neither was this

50. For more on this topic, see Bodie Hodge, "Is the Perpetual Virginity of Mary a Biblical View?" in Ken Ham and Bodie Hodge, eds., *How do we know the Bible is True?* Volume 1 (Green Forest, AR: Master Books, 2011), p. 219–226.

51. Pope Pius XII, "Munificentissimus Deus," 1 Nov. 1950, point 44, https://www.ewtn.com/library/PAPALDOC/P12MUNIF.HTM, accessed March 30, 2015.

52. Ibid, point 47.

teaching in the "Apostles' Creed" or the Nicene Creed (which the Catholic Church highly regards), nor was it in the decisions of the 20 ecumenical councils recognized by the Catholic Church. So the only real authority for this is "our own," that is, the pope's and bishops' self-proclaimed authority.[53]

Titles and Roles of Mary

Given all the doctrines that have accumulated to the honor of Mary, it is not surprising that she has been given many titles. She is called the "Mother of the Church" who "by her charity joined in bringing about the birth of believers in the Church."[54] She is also called the "Queen over all things,"[55] "Mother of Mercy, the All-Holy One,"[56] and "the Mother of God." None of these titles have any basis in Scripture. Jesus Christ is the King (Luke 19:38; Revelation 19:11–16), but Mary is not His queen. The Bride of Christ is the Church (Ephesians 5:25–32), the assembly of individuals being gathered from every tribe, tongue, people, and nation — individuals who have personally repented of their sins and trusted in Christ alone for salvation (Revelation 5:6–9).

Mary is also said to be "a mother to us in the order of grace." She is the "Mother of God, to whose protection the faithful fly in all their dangers and needs."[57] The Catholic Church adds,

> Taken up to heaven she did not lay aside this saving office but by her manifold intercession continues to bring us the gifts of eternal salvation. . . . Therefore the Blessed Virgin is invoked in the Church under the titles of Advocate, Helper, Benefactress, and Mediatrix.[58]

But the Bible teaches that there is only one Mediator between God and people: the Lord Jesus Christ (1 Timothy 2:5). He alone is our advocate before our holy Judge, for He alone by His death was a propitiation for our sins, taking the wrath of God for us (1 John 2:2; Hebrews 2:17). There is no other name in all of heaven and earth by which we can and must be saved

---

53. For an enlightening discussion of how this doctrine was shoehorned into the category of infallible dogma, see James G. McCarthy, *The Gospel According to Rome* (Eugene, OR: Harvest House, 1995), p. 293–300.
54. CCC, #963.
55. Ibid., #966
56. Ibid., #2677.
57. Ibid., #971.
58. Ibid., #968–969.

(Acts 4:12). Jesus promised us another helper after He left the earth, but it was not Mary. It was the Holy Spirit (John 14:16–17, 16:7–15). Mary does not bring believers the gifts of eternal salvation. Jesus is the only source of eternal salvation (Hebrews 5:9). He is the only one to whom we should flee in our time of danger and temptation (Hebrews 2:18, 4:14–16). The Roman Catholic exaltation of Mary robs Jesus Christ of the honor and glory and trust and obedience that He alone deserves.

Veneration of Mary

The Roman Catholic *Catechism* says, "The Church's devotion to the Blessed Virgin is intrinsic to Christian Worship."[59] Catholics are instructed to venerate Mary above all people and angels. The church technically distinguishes between worship (reserved for God alone) and veneration (for Mary and "the saints"), but in practice it is hard to see the difference. The most common way that Catholics venerate Mary is by praying the rosary as they finger their way along a string of beads.[60] The church considers the rosary "the epitome of the whole Gospel."[61] The rosary involves the repetition of a prayer to Mary 50 times, punctuated after every ten with the Lord's Prayer. The repeated prayer to Mary is, "Hail Mary, full of grace, the Lord is with thee. Blessed are thou among women and blessed is the fruit of thy womb, Jesus. Holy Mary, Mother of God, pray for us sinners now and at the hour of our death. Amen."[62]

There is no biblical basis for venerating Mary or praying to her for help and intercession with her Son, Jesus. In fact, Mary is not even mentioned in the New Testament after Acts 1:14–15, where her name is in the middle of a list of some of the 120 disciples who after Jesus' ascension to heaven were waiting in Jerusalem for the coming of the Holy Spirit on the Day of Pentecost. Jesus once had a perfect opportunity

---

59. Ibid., #971.
60. With 1.3 billion Catholics in the world, the manufacture and sale of rosary beads in great variety is obviously big business: http://www.rosarymart.com/ is one of many places to buy one of the multitude of designs.
61. Ibid.
62. CCC, #2676–2677.

to teach His disciples to venerate and pray to Mary, but He did quite the opposite. Luke records,

> While Jesus was saying these things, one of the women in the crowd raised her voice and said to Him, "Blessed is the womb that bore You and the breasts at which You nursed." But He said, "On the contrary, blessed are those who hear the word of God and observe it." (Luke 11:27–28; NASB)

Christians are instructed to pray to the Father in Jesus' name (John 14:13–14, 15:16, 16:23–26). We are never told in Scripture to pray to Jesus in Mary's name or pray to Mary that she might intercede for us with Christ. The believer needs no mediator between himself and the Savior, and Jesus is the only mediator between the believer and God (1 Timothy 2:5–6). Jesus also taught that we should never use vain repetition as we pray (Matthew 6:7).

Apparitions of Mary

In addition to this Roman Catholic teaching, the many supposed appearances of Mary have increased devotion to Mary. The first appearance or apparition of Mary was to Pope John XXII (1316–1334). Another appeared in Guadalupe, Mexico, in 1531. But since 1830 there has been a growing worldwide movement of Roman Catholic devotion to Mary, fueled by the blessing and promotion of the popes. The apparitions have occurred in many countries, most notably in Europe. Some of the most well-known ones are Lourdes, France (1858), Fatima, Portugal (1917), and Medjugorje, Bosnia-Herzegovina (1981). In the latter case, the apparitions have been almost daily since 1981 and

> over 40 million people of all faiths, from all over the world, have visited Medjugorje and have left spiritually strengthened and renewed. Countless unbelievers and physically or mentally afflicted, have been converted and healed. You owe it to yourself and your loved ones, to investigate with an open mind and heart the events, which are occurring in Medjugorje. I invite you to explore the over 4000 pages of information contained on this Web Site, and decide for yourself whether you will answer Our Lady's call to prayer, and conversion.[63]

---

63. http://www.medjugorje.org, accessed February 27, 2015.

"People of all faiths" have been spiritually strengthened and renewed and unbelievers have been converted? A Muslim or Hindu or Buddhist or animist cannot be strengthened and renewed in his faith and also converted to Christ. Therefore the "conversion" referred to here must be a conversion to venerating Mary and mixing that veneration with the person's non-Christian religion. "Mary's" message on February 2, 2015, in Medjugorje was this:

> Dear children! I am here, I am among you. I am looking at you, am smiling at you and I love you in the way that only a mother can. Through the Holy Spirit who comes through my purity, I see your hearts and I offer them to my Son. Already for a long time I have been asking of you to be my apostles, to pray for those who have not come to know God's love. I am asking for prayer said out of love, prayer which carries out works and sacrifices. Do not waste time thinking about whether you are worthy to be my apostles. The Heavenly Father will judge everyone; and you, love Him and listen to Him. I know that all of this confuses you, even my very stay among you, but accept it with joy and pray that you may comprehend that you are worthy to work for Heaven. My love is upon you. Pray that my love may win in all hearts, because that is the love which forgives, gives and never stops. Thank you.[64]

These clearly are the words of a deceiving demon, not the words of Mary, the earthly mother of Jesus. According to the Bible, Mary, the mother of Jesus, was not pure. She herself admitted she was a sinner in need of a savior. The claim that the Holy Spirit comes through Mary and her purity is completely contrary to Scripture. Furthermore, Mary had no apostles. The apostles in the Bible were messengers of Jesus Christ sent into the world to glorify Him and proclaim His gospel (Mark 3:13–19; Acts 1:15–26; Ephesians 1:1; 2 Timothy 1:1; 1 Peter 1:1). Scripture never encourages Christians to mindlessly accept all messages that claim to come from God, but rather to test everything against Scripture (Acts 17:11; 1 John 4:1). Also, no Christian is worthy to work for heaven. Finally, it is not Mary's love that forgives, gives, and never stops. It is God's love through Jesus Christ alone that accomplishes those things.

---

64. Ibid.

We must conclude that these "apparitions of Mary" are not manifestations of her presence, but rather are demonic deceptions.[65] The Apostle Paul warned the 1st-century Christians about "false apostles, deceitful workers, disguising themselves as apostles of Christ. No wonder, for even Satan disguises himself as an angel of light" (2 Corinthians 11:13–14; NASB). He also warned about "deceitful spirits and doctrines of demons" (1 Timothy 4:1; NASB) who would bring people "another gospel" that is deceptively close to but significantly different from the gospel of Jesus Christ (Galatians 1:6–9). But that is exactly what these apparitions are doing as they reinforce devotion to "Mary," the Catholic doctrines about her and about salvation, and the authority of the pope, which keeps Catholics from the true faith in Jesus Christ for salvation revealed in Scripture.

Conclusion Regarding the Virgin Mary

Mary indeed was blessed to be the human mother of the incarnate Son of God. And for Christians, she certainly is a model of faith and submission to the will of God (when the angel announced that she would be the mother of our Lord, although later in the gospels she was not always an outstanding example of faith). But as James McCarthy succinctly states, "The Mary of Roman Catholicism is not the Mary of the Bible. Scripture says nothing of a woman conceived without sin, perfectly sinless, ever virgin, and assumed into heaven."[66] She is not the co-redeemer or the queen of heaven or the mother of the Church.

The Roman Catholic Mary never existed, but is the product of centuries of man-made traditions confirmed by demonic deception ("miracles" and "apparitions") that hinder millions of Roman Catholics and followers of other religions from coming to know the only one who can save them from sin and the holy judgment of God to come, that is, the Lord Jesus Christ. Mary plays no role in a person's salvation or sanctification. The gospel is all about Jesus.

The Catholic View of Salvation

Given the Catholic Church's erroneous views about Scripture and tradition, the authority of popes and bishops and the person and work of Mary,

---

65. Because of the claims of supernatural phenomena associated with the apparitions and the way they are attracting followers of other religions, it seems extremely unlikely to me that any of these apparitions are merely the result of humans deceiving themselves.

66. James G. McCarthy, *The Gospel According to Rome: Comparing Catholic Tradition and the Word of God* (Eugene, OR: Harvest House, 1995), p. 198.

it is no surprise that the Roman Catholic Church's teaching about salvation is a complicated mixture of truth and error that badly distorts the gospel and the process of sanctification in the life of a true follower of Jesus Christ.[67]

According to the Church, salvation from the coming judgment of God is a life-long process, not an event. It starts with baptism but then includes the repeated use of the sacraments and the person's cooperation with grace and then after death almost certainly some time in purgatory.

Baptism

The Catholic Church teaches, "Holy Baptism is the basis of the whole Christian life, the gateway to life in the Spirit, and the door which gives access to the other sacraments."[68] Except for adult converts to Roman Catholicism, Catholics are baptized as infants very shortly after birth. The Church teaches that baptism causes the new birth (making the person a child of God), frees the person from the power of darkness, and provides forgiveness of "all personal sins as well as all punishment for sin." It makes the person a temple of the Holy Spirit, a part of the priesthood of Christ, and incorporates him into the church. It gives the person the grace of initial "justification," enabling him to believe in God, giving him the power to live and enabling him to grow in moral virtues.[69]

In addition to baptism, the other six sacraments that also impart grace to the Catholic believer are the Eucharist, penance, confirmation (by a priest usually of a child at about age 12 after finishing a preparatory course on doctrine), the marriage ceremony, holy orders (ordination of men to the priesthood), and extreme unction (anointing of those who are seriously ill or nearing death).

Purgatory

Formulated by the Councils of Florence (1439) and Trent (1563), this doctrine says that when the Catholic faithful dies in an imperfect state, he must "undergo purification, so as to achieve the holiness necessary to enter the joy of heaven." To help those in purgatory, the Roman Catholic Church

---

67. For a fuller discussion than can be given here, readers are encouraged to get McCarthy's *The Gospel According to Rome*, which provides an excellent biblical refutation of Catholic teaching.
68. CCC, #1213.
69. Ibid., #1250, 1263–1270.

encourages prayer for the dead, almsgiving, indulgences, and penance on their behalf. But there is no actual biblical support for this doctrine.[70]

Penance and Indulgences

Penance is what the Catholic believer does "as means of obtaining forgiveness of sins." It begins with confession to a Catholic priest, but also is expressed primarily through fasting, prayer, and almsgiving. Additional means include efforts at reconciliation with one's neighbor, tears of repentance, prayers for the saints, acts of charity, reading Scripture, and praying parts of the liturgy.[71] But "taking up one's cross each day and following Jesus is the surest way of penance."[72]

Closely linked to the effects of penance is the doctrine and practice of indulgences.

> An indulgence is a remission before God of the temporal punishment due to sins whose guilt has already been forgiven, which the faithful Christian who is duly disposed gains under certain prescribed conditions through the action of the Church which, as the minister of redemption, dispenses and applies with authority the treasury of the satisfactions of Christ and the saints. An indulgence is partial or plenary according as it removes either part or all of the temporal punishment due to sin. The faithful can gain indulgences for themselves or apply them to the dead.[73]

By obtaining spiritual goods from the "Church's treasury," the repentant Catholic can "be more promptly and efficaciously purified of the punishments for sin." That treasury is "the infinite value which Christ's merits have before God." But it also "includes as well the prayers and good works of the Blessed Virgin Mary" which "are truly immense, unfathomable, and even pristine in their value before God," as well as the prayers and good works of

---

70. Ibid., #1030–1032. The only two Bible verses that the Catechism cites (besides one verse from the Apocrypha, which Protestants do not accept as Scripture) in support of this doctrine are taken out of context and twisted. First Corinthians 3:15 does not say that a person's sins will be burned away in purgatory so that they can enter heaven. Rather it teaches, in context, that the *quality* of the believer's works will be tested by fire on the day of judgment. First Peter 1:7 speaks of fiery trials in this life that test the believer's faith, not to a fiery purging of sins in the afterlife.
71. CCC, #1434–1437, 1456.
72. Ibid., #1435.
73. Ibid., #1471.

all the saints. This "treasury of the merits of Christ and the saints" obtains for the repentant Catholic the remission of the temporal punishments due for his sins.[74] But one can only wonder why the prayers and good works of Mary and the saints must or can be added to the "infinite value" of the merits of Christ.

But again, there is no basis in Scripture for indulgences or the merits of Mary or "saints" (those considered very holy Catholics, to whom the pope has assigned sainthood) that can remit temporal punishment for sin.

Eucharist (Mass, Holy Communion, Lord's Supper)

The night before His crucifixion Jesus instituted the "Lord's Supper" as an ordinance whereby Christians are to remember His saving work on the Cross and in the Resurrection on their behalf until He returns (Matthew 26:17–30; 1 Corinthians 11:17–34). The Catholic Church calls this the Eucharist or the Mass.

Whereas Protestants view it as a memorial, the Catholic Church says it a memorial *and* "the unbloody reenactment of the sacrifice of Calvary" which "perpetuates the sacrifice of the Cross by offering to God the same Victim that was immolated on Calvary . . . and applies the fruits of Christ's death upon the Cross to individual human souls."[75] When the priest consecrates the bread and the wine, the elements do not change in appearance but are transubstantiated into the literal body and blood of Jesus. As the Council of Trent says, the sacrifice of the Mass "is identical with the Sacrifice of the Cross" and is "propitiatory . . . atoning for our sins, and the sins of the living and of the dead in Christ."[76] The Church also teaches, "The sacrifice of the Mass is the most effective form of supplication which we humans can offer to the Eternal Father."[77] Catholics are told and believe that,

> When the priest bends low over the bread and wine and pronounces those tremendous words, the most momentous ever framed by human lips, "This is My body . . . this is My blood," the

---

74. Ibid., #1476–1477.
75. John A. O'Brien, *The Faith of Millions* (Huntington, IN: Our Sunday Visitor, 1974), p. 304. Written by a Catholic priest, this book has been endorsed by three prominent archbishops and translated into many languages to instruct Catholics and non-Catholics in the teachings of Roman Catholicism.
76. Ibid., p. 307.
77. Ibid., p. 308.

heaven of heavens opens, and the King and Ruler of the universe, Jesus Christ, comes down upon our altar, to be lifted up as a sacrificial Victim for the sins of the world.[78]

But Jesus Christ does not come down on thousands of earthly Catholic altars around the world every week at the beckoning of a priest. Scripture repeatedly teaches that ever since His ascension to heaven 40 days after His Resurrection, He has been seated at the right hand of God, constantly interceding before the Father for all true believers in Jesus Christ (Romans 8:34; Colossians 3:1; Hebrews 1:3–4, 8:1, 12: 1 Peter 3:22; 1 John 2:2).

In the consecration of the bread and the wine the priest prays,

> Receive, O holy Father, almighty, eternal God, this immaculate victim which I, Thy unworthy servant offer to Thee, my living and true God, for my innumerable sins, offenses and negligences, for all here present, and for all the faithful living and dead, that it may avail me and them to everlasting life.[79]

But the Bible teaches no such things regarding the meaning and results of the Lord's Supper or the consecration and prayer of the priest. On the contrary, referring to Jesus' death on the Cross, Hebrews 10:12–18 (NKJV) teaches,

> But this Man, after He had offered one sacrifice for sins forever, sat down at the right hand of God, from that time waiting till His enemies are made His footstool. For by one offering He has perfected forever those who are being sanctified. . . . Now where there is remission of these, *there is* no longer an offering for sin.

It is the death of Jesus on the Cross, not the memorial of that death, that provides the forgiveness of sins for the repentant, believing sinner. There is no bloodless sacrifice for sin (Hebrews 9:22).

The Catholic doctrine of transubstantiation is based on a literal interpretation of Jesus' words "This is my body" and "This is my blood" in the accounts of the Last Supper in Matthew 26; Mark 14; and Luke 22. But

78. Ibid., p. 317.
79. Ibid., p. 308.

these are not literal, just as Jesus' other statements are not: "I am the bread of life" (John 6:48), "I am the light of the world" (John 8:12), "I am the door" (John 10:9), and "I am the true vine" (John 15:1). These are all figurative statements to teach a spiritual truth. The bread and the wine in the Lord's Supper are simply symbolic or representative of the body and blood of Christ given for our salvation once for all on the Cross.[80]

Justification and Sanctification

According to the Catholic teaching, "Justification is not only the remission of sins, but also the sanctification and renewal of the interior man."[81] Volumes have been written on the difference between the Roman Catholic view of justification and the evangelical understanding of the biblical teaching.[82]

The Bible teaches four important truths about justification. First, justification is not gradual but *instantaneous*, at the moment a person trusts in Jesus Christ as Lord and Savior. Second, in justification the sinner is *declared righteous* in the sight of God, not actually made righteous in his experience. We are declared righteous by faith in the substitutionary atoning work of Christ on the Cross and in His Resurrection. Third, justification means that righteousness is *imputed* or reckoned into the spiritual account of the sinner, not infused into his person. And fourth, the sinner is justified *by faith alone in Christ's saving work alone*, not by faith in Christ plus the sinner's good works. We cannot add anything to His work. He took the wrath of God for our sins, so that in Christ we can be righteous in God's sight (2 Corinthians 5:21). We are saved by Christ's finished work at Calvary (John 19:30). According to the Word of God, we must individually repent of our sins and trust in Jesus Christ to be saved, born again, and justified (Ephesians 2:8–9; Romans 10:17; 1 Peter 1:23–24; John 1:12; Romans 3:20–28, 4:25). From that moment, we can be confident that we "have been justified" (Romans 5:1) and we can know (not hope) that we have eternal life (1 John 5:11–13).[83]

---

80. For a refutation of the Catholic view of the Mass, see McCarthy's *The Gospel According to Rome*, p. 133–144.
81. CCC, #1989.
82. Because of the vital importance of this doctrine, I encourage readers to consider James McCarthy's *The Gospel According to Rome* and John MacArthur's *Reckless Faith: When the Church Loses Its Will to Discern* (Westchester, IL: Crossway Books, 1994).
83. For biblical amplification of these points see, http://www.gty.org/resources/distinctives/DD09/roman-catholicism?Term=Catholic%20evangelical%20justification, which is a summary of the analysis in MacArthur's *Reckless Faith*.

That the Catholic Church denies this view of justification is clear from the response of the Council of Trent (1545–1563) to the Protestant Reformation. Its Canon 9 on justification (still in force) states:

> If any one saith, that by faith alone the impious is justified; in such wise as to mean, that nothing else is required to co-operate in order to the obtaining the grace of Justification, and that it is not in any way necessary, that he be prepared and disposed by the movement of his own will; let him be anathema.[84]

But once we are justified, born again, saved, redeemed, and reconciled to God, which happens the moment we repent of our sins and trust in Christ as Savior and Lord, we then begin the life-long process of sanctification. Biblically speaking, sanctification means becoming increasingly holy in our experience in the sight of men just as we already are in our judicial standing in the sight of God. Jesus said that believers are sanctified by the Word of God (John 17:17). As we trust and obey His Word (learned through personal study and fellowship in a Bible-teaching local church) and yield moment-by-moment to the Holy Spirit (who takes up residence in our hearts the moment we are saved), we grow in Christ-likeness in our thoughts, attitudes, and behavior (2 Peter 1:3–4; Galatians 5:16–23). We walk in the good works that God prepared for us to do (Ephesians 2:10).

The Bible clearly teaches that a repentant, believing sinner *has been saved* (justification), *is being saved* (sanctification), and *will be saved* completely and eternally in heaven (glorification). To confuse or equate these is to distort the gospel of Jesus Christ.

The Catholic Church terribly confuses these teachings of Scripture by mixing biblical truth with man-made dogmas accumulated over the centuries. It turns justification into a process that begins at baptism (*not* when a person repents and trusts in Christ) and doesn't end until the completion of purgatory. Through unbiblical doctrines and rituals it also introduces all kinds of error regarding the process of sanctification. The result is another gospel, a different gospel than the one revealed in Scripture, something Paul

---

84. Anathema means excommunication from the Catholic Church, which, it is claimed, is the only place where salvation is found. Therefore the anathema is a condemnation to hell, unless the person embraces the Catholic teaching on salvation and comes into (or back into) the Catholic Church.

sternly warned against (Galatians 1:6–9, 2:20–21). It is a gospel of faith plus works, which subtly subverts the totally sufficient, glorious, saving work of Jesus Christ and distorts the Word of God.

Conclusion

The Roman Catholic Church's horrendous persecution of true Christians, its brutal military crusades against the Muslim, Jews, and anyone else who would not submit to the pope, the unbiblical structure of its hierarchy and the political, moral, and spiritual corruptions of the papacy, the centuries of widespread homosexual and heterosexual immorality by the clergy (which is still occurring today),[85] its rejection of the supreme authority of Scripture by equating man-made tradition with Scripture, and its gospel-subverting doctrines about Mary, baptismal regeneration, the sacrifice of the mass, sainthood, justification, and sanctification lead us to only one conclusion. The Catholic Church is not the true church of Jesus Christ but is a false church that enslaves hundreds of millions of people in a false gospel that is a serious distortion of biblical Christianity.

I have no doubt that there are Roman Catholics who have a true saving faith in Jesus Christ. I have known some of them and prayed and studied the Scriptures with them. But in my experience of sharing my faith with many Catholics and serving as a missionary for almost 20 years in Eastern and Western European countries where Roman Catholicism is prominent or dominant, the true believers I have met who are still in the Catholic Church almost invariably were led to a proper understanding of the gospel either directly or indirectly by an evangelical Christian.

Sadly, most Roman Catholics are still lost in their sin, trusting in their baptism, good works, attendance at confession and Mass, and prayers to Mary and the saints. They need to hear a clear presentation of the biblical gospel and then be encouraged to trust in Jesus Christ alone for salvation, come out of the Catholic Church, and become involved in a Bible-teaching, gospel-preaching local church that gives all the honor and glory to Jesus Christ.

---

85. The sexual immorality of a staggering number of priests and bishops in recent decades and the concerted efforts by bishops, cardinals, and the popes to cover-up the scandals is documented in this 84-minute documentary: http://www.pbs.org/wgbh/pages/frontline/secrets-of-the-vatican/, accessed March 11, 2015.

Summary of Roman Catholic Beliefs

Doctrine	Roman Catholic Teaching
God	Trinitarian Godhead consistent with Bible. Jesus is an insufficient Savior.
Authority/ Revelation	The Bible is viewed as a revelation from God, but heavy emphasis is placed on tradition and teaching of the line of popes holding apostolic authority. Apocryphal books are considered part of the canon
Man	A sinful being who cooperates with God in the process of salvation.
Sin	Transgression of God's will consistent with the Bible, but divided into categories of mortal and venial. Must be confessed to a priest as a mediator between man and Jesus.
Salvation	A cooperation of man with God through sacraments. Sacraments are ministered through apostolic succession to members of the only true church. Jesus' atonement is insufficient to pay for sins. Purgatory following death is necessary for purification from sin. Merit of saints can be applied to others for payment for sin.
Creation	Originally believed in a literal, six-day creation, but influence of evolutionary views is now common. Several popes have made pronouncements that all forms of evolution are compatible with the Bible as long as Adam and Eve are preserved.

Chapter 5

How Is Eastern Orthodoxy Different?

Dr. D. Trent Hyatt

One sunny day in the late 1990s I was walking with friends near the center of Kiev, Ukraine, when I heard some chanting. I looked around and saw a small demonstration taking place. There were, perhaps, about 100 people marching in the street carrying a few placards. The man carrying the placard at the head of the marchers was dressed in the distinctive clothing of an Orthodox priest.[1] On his placard was the claim that the Orthodox Church was the "one, holy, catholic, and apostolic" church. Now, I was raised a Protestant and had personally placed my faith in Christ as a result of an evangelistic message given by a Protestant on the campus of the University of California at Berkeley while I was a student there. So, upon hearing the claim of the demonstrators, I immediately sensed a challenge in their claim. How could they claim something so exclusive?

Eastern Orthodoxy is indeed present in most parts of the world today, but is to a great many in the West little known and even less understood. In fact, the Orthodox Churches found in most countries of the West are immigrant churches, that is, churches started by immigrants from the countries of Eastern Europe (Greek, Russian, Armenian, Romanian, Ukrainian, Serbian, etc.). These churches may recruit new members through conversion of Protestants or Roman Catholics, but the majority of their flocks

---

1. When capitalized, "Orthodox" refers to the Eastern Orthodox Church in its various forms rather than an assent to orthodox biblical doctrine.

Eastern Orthodox Christians participate in a procession in Novosibirsk

are descended from these ethnic groups. Of course, marriage to a member of an Orthodox Church is one of the more common ways for people outside of the traditional ethnic communities to become Orthodox. This was humorously depicted in the wildly popular film *My Big Fat Greek Wedding*. However, since the 1980s a small but growing number of evangelicals have become Orthodox. Some of these have become part of the various national Orthodox churches, such as the Greek Orthodox or Russian Orthodox Churches, but most seem to have become part of the Evangelical Orthodox Church, which became associated with the Antiochian Orthodox Christian Archdiocese of North America. Some have also become part of the Orthodox Church in America, which began as a result of Russian Orthodox missionaries to Alaska in 1794.

How many people belong to the Orthodox Church in all its various expressions? The best estimates put the number between 200 and 300 million worldwide, depending on the way "members" is defined. In any case, the size of the Orthodox community would make it third behind the

Roman Catholics and the Protestants in the Christian tradition. Among those who are active members in Orthodox Churches there are many who are sincere and devout in their Christian faith. This essay, though written from the perspective of an evangelical Protestant, is not intended to simply discredit the faith of all Orthodox believers. Yet, in the spirit of 1 Thessalonians 5:21, I want to "examine everything carefully" and "hold fast to that which is good."[2]

Other than their exclusive claims to being the one true church, to which I will return later, what are the distinctive views of the Eastern Orthodox? I will attempt to survey their most important beliefs and practices by examining the following questions.

1. What is the highest authority in their tradition?

2. What is their view of creation?

3. What is their view of Christ?

4. What is their teaching on how one is saved, and what role do the "sacraments" play in their teaching on salvation?

5. How do they worship (including what an Orthodox Church service looks like)?

6. What is the justification for seeing orthodoxy as the one true church?

Authority

The Orthodox, like Protestants and Catholics, regard the Bible as the inspired Word of God. But like the Catholics, the Orthodox Bible contains a few books not found in the Hebrew Scriptures, that is, books called the Apocrypha (Maccabees, Judith, Tobit, etc.) and written between the close of the Old Testament and the writing of the New Testament.

The inclusion in the canon of Scripture of some books not regarded as canonical by Jesus and the Apostles (based on their lack of reference to them) is not an unimportant matter.[3] However, even more important and resulting in more serious consequences is the place of tradition in connection with the Scriptures.

---

2. All Scripture quotations in this chapter are from the New American Standard Bible.

3. Jesus also affirmed the three divisions of the Old Testament in Luke 24:44 being "the Law, the Prophets, and the writings (Psalms)," which excluded the apocryphal writings.

The Orthodox view of tradition is more complex than the Roman Catholic view. In the Catholic view, Scripture and tradition are both authorities. In other words, tradition exists alongside of Scripture as another authority. In the Orthodox view, the Scriptures are *a part* of tradition. According to their theologians, it is a mistake to pit Scripture *against* tradition. They are both part of one great tradition. They affirm that Scripture may be the highest tradition, but it is still tradition. But Scripture is not, in their view, the highest and final authority for faith and practice in the way Protestants since the Reformation have seen it and confessed it to be. Scripture, as part of the great tradition, must be interpreted *authoritatively*. Though the Orthodox do not have a *Magisterium*[4] comparable to the Roman Catholic Church, they do, practically speaking, have something functionally similar.

For the Orthodox, the church's tradition is the *authoritative interpretation* of the Scriptures. This means, practically, that no believer has the right to interpret Scripture on his or her own, so to speak. The proper way to read Scripture according to the Orthodox is with the writings of the church fathers[5] alongside the Bible, guiding us in our understanding of what the Bible says. Of course, in practice, there may be very few Orthodox who literally read their Bibles with the writings of the church fathers open beside them. But what they do seems (to this outside observer) to be: (1) they read the church fathers a good deal more than the Scriptures and then (2) when they do read Scripture, they come up with their understanding of what the Scriptures are supposed to mean from the church fathers and thus find in the Bible what they have already become convinced of by reading the church fathers. No doubt, this may facilitate a quicker and correct understanding of some parts of the Bible. However, the possibility that one or

---

4. The "magisterium" is defined as the official teaching authority of the church. This authority is "uniquely vested in the Pope and the bishops in communion with him. Further, the Scriptures and Tradition make up a single sacred deposit of the Word of God, which is entrusted to the Church," and the magisterium is not independent of this, since "all that it proposes for belief as being divinely revealed is derived from this single deposit of faith." Definitions found in the Catechism of the Catholic Church. This source can also be accessed on Wikipedia.

5. The "church fathers" refers to the theologians, bishops, or scholars from the first few centuries of the history of Christianity, whose writings played a significant role in shaping the church's doctrine and practice in the following centuries. These are also referred to as the patristics from the Latin form of "father." A few examples: Tertullian, Augustine, Basil the Great, John Chrysostom, Jerome, Ambrose, etc.

more of the church fathers has misunderstood or misinterpreted Scripture does not seem to come into play. When the church fathers and the church's tradition as a whole are used as a *means* of understanding Scripture, rather than using Scripture to correct and guide the church's beliefs and practices, the result is often seen in putting the church's tradition as an authority *over* or *above* the Scripture.

The implications of this approach to authority are clear. Paul's words to Timothy, his faithful disciple, in 2 Timothy 3:16–17 tell us that "All Scripture is inspired by God and is profitable for teaching, for reproof, for correction, for training in righteousness; so that the man of God may be adequate, equipped for every good work." This teaching, reproving, correcting, and training work of the Scripture in the lives of believers is at least partially shackled by the Orthodox approach to authority since the Scriptures can't do that *directly!* Any teaching or reproof that isn't grounded in the church's tradition must be set aside — disqualified.

A good example of how this works can be imagined, if this had been applied to the "discoveries" made by Martin Luther and the other Protestant reformers of the 16th century. Luther found peace for his tortured conscience when he discovered that he could be justified by faith alone (apart from works) and that God credited Christ's righteousness to him when he trusted in Christ and His work on the Cross for him. He *did not* find this understanding in the Roman Catholic Church's tradition. He found it in the Bible, particularly in Romans. If the Orthodox principle of reading the Bible only with the help of the church fathers and the church's tradition had been applied, Luther would have had no message. *Sola fides, sola gratia, sola scriptura, solus Christus, soli Deo gloria,*[6] the slogans of the Reformation, would have never corrected the practices and beliefs of the church. Though partial or basic understandings of these truths can be found here and there in some of the church fathers, no clear championing of them is to be found in the church's tradition.[7] Does that mean that the principles expressed in the slogans are wrong? According to the Orthodox understanding of authority, this would certainly be the case. But what about the fact that all of

6. The Latin phrases mean: by faith alone, by grace alone, by the Scripture alone, by Christ alone, and to God alone be the glory.
7. This is true of both Western (Roman) and Eastern traditions. Of course, the Reformation was an affair that took place only in the West. Eastern Orthodoxy has never had a Reformation-type movement and insists that it does not need one!

these principles that were of such life-changing significance for Luther and so many others in the Roman Catholic Church of the 16th century are found *explicitly* and *implicitly* in the Bible? If the Bible clearly teaches something, is it not valid, even if it is not found clearly in the church fathers? Luther, Zwingli, Calvin, and the other reformers insisted that the Bible's teaching was *over* the church's teaching, and when the church's teaching did not correspond to the Bible's, then it was the church's teaching that had to be changed, not the Bible's.

The Bible teaches its supreme authority repeatedly. For example, Moses taught the Israelites to trust and obey God's Word and teach it to their children (Deuteronomy 6:1–9). God told Joshua not to turn to the right or the left from following His Word (Joshua 1:6–9). Psalm 1 blessed the person who clings to God's Word, Psalm 19 says it is far superior to any truth we learn from nature, and Psalm 119 magnifies the importance of Scripture, making the believer wiser than his teachers (119:97–104). The prophets continually called the Jews back to the Word of God (e.g., Isaiah 8:20; Jeremiah 6:16–19; Hosea 4:6). Jesus condemned the Jewish religious leaders of His day for undermining the teaching of Scripture by their traditions (Mark 7:6–13). And the Berean Jews were commended for evaluating the truthfulness of Paul's teachings in the light of the Old Testament (Acts 17:11). Scripture is the only sure foundation and authority for the Christian.

Creation

Due to their high regard for tradition and belief that what the church fathers taught was permanently valid, the Orthodox Church has not been significantly involved in the debates of the last two centuries over creation and evolution. This is beginning to change as secular and rationalist thinking has come to dominate the sciences in the West. Andrew Louth is a theologian and professor emeritus from Durham University in England. He is at the same time a priest of the Russian Orthodox Church and serves the parish in Durham. Louth reveals the kind of approach likely to be taken with increasing frequency. He asks:

> Do Christians have to believe that Adam and Eve existed, and that they sinned, and that their sin has infected all subsequent human beings? Do we have to believe that there was an

original couple, that *Homo sapiens* emerged from some kind of *Homo erectus* as a single couple, in a particular place. . . . There are . . . Christians who believe this, and indeed not a few of them are Orthodox Christians. I do not, however, think we, as Orthodox, need to commit ourselves to such a position.[8]

Louth goes on to discuss the many characteristics that we humans share with animals. Thus a common origin is seen as quite reasonable. He does, of course, affirm that man possesses reason and is a higher being and in the image of God. Even so, this identity need not be tied to a historical Adam and Eve, according to Louth.

But what about the Fall? For Louth, the fallen state of humanity is an undeniable fact. Yet he is content to argue that man's condition is something that slowly evolved as humanity found "that the pull of more evident pleasure, or a sense of the self expressing itself in aggression towards the other, was too great to resist." What Louth is arguing is clearly a view of sin, but not just sin as we know it, but what he refers to as "ancestral sin" (the term he prefers to "original sin").

Ancestral sin, he thinks, is a consequence of man's ontology. In other words, man's nature is such that sin is a regrettable but unavoidable reality of his being. If, then, sin is more of an ontological problem than a moral or spiritual problem, a historical Adam and Eve and a historical Fall are not really necessary. These two perspectives, that is, our commonalities with the animal world and an obscure beginning for "ancestral sin" in the distant shadowy past, present no problem for Louth and those who agree with him in seeing an evolutionary beginning for life and a process of "millions" (his term) of years rather than a recently created historical pair who sinned by disobeying God's explicit command.

Father Serphim Rose (1934–1982), an American Orthodox monk and scholar, wrote a lengthy book surveying the teachings on Genesis 1–11 of Orthodox theologians and scholars down through the centuries. He documents with lengthy quotes from the "Holy Fathers" of Eastern Orthodoxy that up until the 19th century the Orthodox Church held to a literal six-day creation week about 6,000 years ago and a global catastrophic Flood at the time of Noah. But, he tells us, by the 20th century a very large percentage of

---

8. Andrew Louth, *Introducing Eastern Orthodox Theology* (Downers Grove, IL: InterVarsity Press, 2013), p. 74.

Eastern Orthodox believers had accepted the ideas of evolution and millions of years.[9]

Christ

Eastern Orthodoxy has historically maintained and defended a high view of the deity of Christ. The Orthodox make a great deal out of being "the Church of the seven councils," that is, the seven ecumenical councils of the early Church. The first five of these councils dealt with challenges to the full deity or full humanity of Christ. The first of these councils was held in Nicea and the fourth was held in Chalcedon. These two councils affirmed the biblical doctrine of Christ as being one person with two natures, thus fully divine and fully human. From the side of His divinity, He is the second person of the Trinity and is as fully God as are the Father and the Holy Spirit. From the side of His humanity, He is the virgin-born son of Mary and the heir of David. All these things the Orthodox Church faithfully teach and affirm. Thus, there is no debate between evangelical Protestants and the Orthodox on the deity of Christ or His incarnation. Difficulties emerge, however, when the meaning of the incarnation for redemption is considered. This is best considered in connection with the next question.

Salvation and the Sacraments

"What must I do to be saved?" This was the question the Philippian jailer asked Paul and Silas in Acts 16:30. It remains the critical question for all of mankind. Indeed, if we are given the wrong answers to this question, a catastrophic loss is the prospect we face. Strangely, in contrast to both Protestants and Catholics, the Orthodox do not seem to focus very much on this question. There are, of course, reasons for this.

Like Roman Catholicism, Eastern Orthodoxy places great emphasis on the "sacraments." Like Catholicism, Orthodoxy sees baptism as bringing about the regeneration of the person receiving the sacrament. The Orthodox

---

9. See Terry Mortenson's helpful review of Fr. Rose's book *Genesis, Creation and Early Man* on the Answers in Genesis website, December 1, 2002. For an in-depth biblical and historical defense of young-earth creation see Terry Mortenson and Thane H. Ury, eds., *Coming to Grips with Genesis* (Green Forest, AR: Master Books, 2008). For a layman's treatment see Ken Ham, *Six Days* (Green Forest, AR: Master Books, 2013). Jonathan Sarfati, in *Refuting Compromise* (Green Forest, AR: Master Books, 2011, second ed.) thoroughly, biblically, and scientifically refutes the progressive creationism of Hugh Ross. *The New Answers Book*, Volumes 1-4, edited by Ken Ham (Green Forest, AR: Master Books), answer the 130 most-asked biblical and scientific questions related to origins.

typically baptize infants but, of course, adult converts to Orthodoxy are baptized as well. In contrast to Roman Catholics, the Orthodox baptize by immersion. Immersion is carried out three times in succession, in the name of the Father and the Son and the Holy Spirit.

Unique to the Orthodox is a second sacrament applied immediately following baptism, called "chrismation." Chrismation is performed by the priest on the newly baptized individual by anointing him or her with oil and making the sign of the cross over the various parts of the body (the forehead, eyes, nose, mouth, ears, chest, hands, and feet) of the newly baptized and saying, "The seal of the gift of the Holy Spirit, Amen." According to Orthodox teaching, this sacrament brings about the indwelling of the Holy Spirit in the newly baptized individual. In the Orthodox view then, even if the individual being baptized is an infant, he or she is consequently a full member of the church from that point on. The oil used in the anointing

A gold vessel for chrism

of the person being baptized is called the "chrism." According to Orthodox belief, the chrism may be administered by a priest but the chrism must have first been blessed by a bishop.

The Orthodox do not believe that faith on the part of the person being baptized is necessary in order for these sacraments to be effective. Indeed, Orthodox theologians take great pains to clarify and emphasize that the effectiveness of the sacraments is entirely independent of any faith or particular desires for God or sanctity. To quote a prominent Orthodox theologian: "In no way is the efficacy of the sacrament contingent upon the faith or moral qualifications of either celebrant [i.e., priest or bishop] or recipient."[10] How is such a thing possible? The answer becomes clearer when we read Karmiris' explanation of what happens when the

---

10. John Karmiris, "Concerning the Sacraments," *Eastern Orthodox Theology: A Contemporary Reader*, ed. by Daniel B. Clendenin (Grand Rapids, MI: Baker Books, 1995), p. 22.

sacraments are dispensed: "Baptism and chrismation transmit justifying and regenerating grace."[11] Quite explicitly then, these two sacraments, according to Orthodox teaching, *automatically transmit* God's saving and regenerating grace.

How is it possible that a person can be baptized without any faith or spiritual hunger, by a priest of whom no moral qualifications are required, and yet that baptism be effective without fail? The answer to this question is that the sacrament itself, by virtue of being a genuine sacrament of the Orthodox Church, is certainly effective. In other words, all that is necessary is that the priest or bishop celebrating the sacraments must be a duly ordained minister of the Orthodox Church. The baptisms that take place in the Protestant Church or even the Roman Catholic Church are not regarded as valid baptisms. Why not? Karmiris explains this quite clearly:

> Furthermore, the Orthodox Catholic Church believes that divine grace is not dispensed outside of the true church, and thus the church does not recognize in their fullness sacramental acts which are performed outside of her, except in extraordinary cases.[12]

Thus, it is because of the belief of the Orthodox that the ancient maxim of Cyprian (3rd century) is true, that is, "outside of the church there is no salvation." Since only the Orthodox Church is the true church, then only the ministers of the Orthodox Church are genuinely in the apostolic succession.[13] Thus these ministers play the role of transmitting God's grace when they administer the sacraments.

It is ironic that the Orthodox regard the faith of the one being baptized as inconsequential while they at the same time believe that all baptisms administered by legitimate Orthodox ministers are effective. From the perspective of an outside observer, their faith is great but it is in the wrong thing. The Bible makes the faith of the believer the decisive thing. Notice Paul's response to the question of the Philippian jailor: "Believe in the Lord Jesus, and you will be saved" (Acts 16:31). As a *result* of his faith, the Philippian

---

11. Ibid., 22.
12. Ibid., 23.
13. The concept of apostolic succession is that the authority of the church has been passed on from the apostles in a direct line through the ministers of the church. Roman Catholics and Orthodox generally point to Matthew 16;13–20 as a justification of this belief.

jailor was *then* baptized (Acts 16:33). What a perfect situation for Paul to have clarified the effectiveness of baptism to bring salvation! All he would have had to say was, "Receive baptism from us and you will be saved!" But, of course, he did not say that. He placed the emphasis squarely on the faith of the individual sinner as the essential thing to receive salvation.

Two things must be said to clarify the picture further. It is quite true that Eastern Orthodoxy is a very sacramental tradition. The portal to enter the Orthodox Church is through the sacraments. Great emphasis is placed on these sacraments. There is a deeply rooted belief that the visible acts of the church's priests and bishops signify the invisible works of God. Because of the authority of the church to perform these acts and transmit the grace pertinent to the particular purpose, grace is transmitted to the recipient by virtue of the work of God through the church's ministers. Thus the members are taught that these sacraments are the means of salvation and becoming "deified." (More will be said about "deification" momentarily.) The point I want to make is this: the members of the Orthodox Church naturally assume that they can depend on the sacraments and that they will be effective. Consequently, the great majority of those within the Orthodox Church rely on the sacraments to "get them through," that is, to gain their salvation for them.

The second thing that needs to be said here is to clarify to people outside of the tradition that the salvation believed to have been imparted at one's baptism and chrismation is *not* viewed within Orthodoxy as a permanent possession. In fact, it is viewed merely as a beginning. Whether or not one will end up actually saved depends on a number of other things. Thus, it would be a misrepresentation of Orthodox teaching to leave people with the understanding that all that was needed was to be baptized and chrismated. Though it is true that the Orthodox believe that baptism and chrismation bring regeneration and justification, it is not true that they regard the new member of the church as having a "free pass to heaven," so to speak. The spiritual life in this newly baptized and chrismated individual must be nurtured. This is especially done through participation in "the Eucharist" (i.e., the Lord's Supper). But other matters are important as well. The main thing I wish to make clear at this point is that salvation in Orthodoxy is regarded as a process, indeed a life-long process. The sacraments play a very great role, but other things matter as well.

Salvation and Deification

One of the great points of confusion among outsiders trying to understand Orthodoxy is the concept of "deification" or "*theosis*." Translated, the thought is "becoming god." To most Westerners this concept is totally alien. Paul does, of course, speak of being "conformed to the image of Christ" (Romans 8:29). Is that all the Orthodox mean by *theosis*? No, it is not. In fact, the Orthodox have a major and complex theology built around the idea of deification.

An Orthodox icon depicting Athanasius

Most frequently quoted by the Orthodox is a statement by Athanasius: "God became man that we might become gods."[14] Athanasius was by no means the only church father to speak of deification in similar terms.[15] Outsiders might be tempted to think that the Orthodox have similar views to the Mormons, believing that humans can become divine, "gods" in an ontological sense. This would be quite mistaken. The Orthodox are quite clear in their Trinitarian belief that the divine essence resides only in the triune God. Man cannot by any means cross over the divide between the divine essence (the one true God) and human nature. But they do indeed mean more than what Protestants mean with their doctrine of sanctification. Where then does the Orthodox doctrine of *theosis* (deification) fit in their doctrine of salvation?

If, in fact, the Orthodox thought of deification only in terms of sanctification (i.e., the process of becoming more and more like Christ through faith and obedience and the work of the Holy Spirit), there wouldn't be a real problem with their doctrine other than the natural confusion that arises from the use of the term. But a careful survey of the writings of Orthodox

---

14. *Concerning the Incarnation of the Word*, De Inc 54.3; http://www.antiochian.org/content/theosis-partaking-divine-nature.

15. The concept is addressed by Basil the Great, Gregory Nazianzus, and Irenaeus among others!

theologians leads one to the conclusion that *theosis* is much more important than that. Indeed, it becomes clear that the Orthodox think of *theosis* as the process of salvation. In other words, one is *saved* by becoming "deified."

The basic perspective of the Orthodox on *theosis* is that it is a life-long process of becoming more and more holy, more and more like God, or as they often express it, more and more "a god." This transformation can also be spoken of as "union with God" or "sharing the divine nature."[16] The ultimate goal is not even reachable in this life. However, significant progress toward it can and must be made. How is progress toward *theosis* made? First of all, through active participation in the sacraments. According to one theologian,

> The road toward our theosis, our union with God, can be formulated in the following short statement: divine grace and human freedom . . . We *are* able to walk that road. We will be accompanied and strengthened by divine grace. The holy mysteries (sacraments) are what transmit this grace of the All-Holy Spirit. His sanctifying and deifying energy is actualized in the holy services of the church, especially in holy baptism, repentance, and the divine Eucharist.[17]

Two things emerge from this claim: *theosis* requires both divine grace and human action and the critical role played by the sacraments. The interaction of divine grace and human action is referred to often by Orthodox theologians and is called *synergy*. Of course, in the sacraments, according to the Orthodox view, grace is transmitted from God to man. However, in synergy, man must bring his part. Man's part is essential to the success of the venture.

The prominent and highly regarded Orthodox theologian Vladimir Lossky refers to what the Orthodox Church calls the "synergy of divine grace and human freedom." On this point Lossky quotes St. Macarius of Egypt as saying: *The will of man is an essential condition, for without it God does nothing*"[18] (my emphasis). This logically would mean that man is a participant in his own salvation. This is indeed what the Orthodox Church

---

16. Frequent reference is made to 2 Peter 1:4 where Peter uses the metaphor of "sharing in the divine nature" to refer to process of sanctification.

17. Christoforos Stavropoulos, "Partakers of Divine Nature" from Clendenin, *Eastern Orthodox Theology: A Contemporary Reader*, p.192.

18. Vladimir Lossky, *The Mystical Theology of the Eastern Church* (Crestwood, NY: St. Vladimir's Seminary Press, 1976), p. 199.

teaches. Lossky goes on to quote a 19th-century Russian ascetic writer to this effect: " 'the Holy Ghost, acting within us, accomplishes with us our salvation,' but he says at the same time that 'being assisted by grace, *man accomplishes the work of his salvation*' "[19] (my emphasis).

When one surveys the vast literature from Orthodox asceticism (as practiced by the countless monks in Orthodox monasteries), one finds this viewpoint that man participates in his own salvation in many places. *Theosis* is a synergistic process in which *the believer pursues the goal of union with God by means of* (my emphasis) denial of the flesh and pursuit of holiness. We are told that this involves struggle and striving: "Fastings, vigils, prayers, alms, and other good works which are done in the name of Christ are means which help us reach that goal which always remains the same: the reception of the Holy Spirit and the making him our own, that is theosis."[20]

Human effort, then, is an essential part of *theosis*; it is the *means* of pursuing union with God. Since *theosis* is accomplished by the synergy of God's grace and man's effort, then salvation depends not on God's grace alone — it is not a gift, but is a reward for man's effort. The seriousness of the Orthodox pursuit of holiness, at least on the part of many of the monks, is indeed impressive.

But is this explanation of how one is saved reconcilable with Ephesians 2:8–9? "For by grace you have been saved through faith, and that not of yourselves, it is the gift of God; not as a result of works, so that no one may boast." In fact, Paul's central thrust in the Book of Romans is to establish that "apart from the Law the righteousness of God has been manifested . . . even the righteousness of God through faith in Jesus Christ for all those who believe . . . being justified as a gift by His grace through the redemption which is in Christ Jesus" (Romans 3:21–24).

Romans and Galatians both speak eloquently of justification by faith and of the substitutionary atonement accomplished by Jesus Christ's completed work on the Cross. Strangely, these themes are scarcely, if ever, addressed by Orthodox theologians. When questioned about this deficit, the reply is that there are many metaphors for salvation in the Bible and that the Orthodox preference is to think in terms of union with God rather than in the legal terms so favored in the West. Is it not rather an error of perception to think

19. Ibid. p. 199.
20. Ibid. p. 190, Stavropoulos, "Partakers of Divine Nature."

in terms of preferences when discussing the great biblical theme of salvation? What does the Scripture itself emphasize? Is not the Book of Romans the longest and most systematic treatment of the doctrine of salvation in the New Testament? How can we ignore its clear teaching on grace, faith, the substitutionary atonement, and justification, and hope to have a truly biblical understanding of God's plan of salvation?

Salvation and the Atonement

A final point on the Orthodox teaching on salvation should be added before leaving this topic. There is comparatively little focus in Orthodoxy on the atonement or the Cross but a significantly greater focus on the doctrine of the Incarnation and the Resurrection. Protestants and Catholics are accustomed to thinking of the Incarnation as part of the process ending in the death of Christ on the Cross for our sins. Of course, the doctrine of Incarnation is a rich vein that bears many treasures for Christian theology, not the least of which is an affirmation by God of the inherent goodness of the material creation.[21] But in Scripture, the Incarnation of Jesus is seen first and foremost as a revelation of God to man of His goodness and character (Hebrews 1:1–3) to redeem man by means of the atonement. This is seen with great clarity in Jesus' own statement of the purpose of His coming: "to give His life a ransom for many" (e.g., Matthew 20:28; Mark 10:45). It comes as a surprise, then, to find the Orthodox perspective on the incarnation, which is captured well in this statement from Bulgakov:

> For God so loved the world that He spared not His Son to save and deify it. The Incarnation, first decreed to ransom fallen humanity and reconcile it with God, is understood by Orthodoxy as, above all, the deification of man, as the communication of the divine life to him. To fallen man the Incarnation became the supreme way for his reconciliation with God, the way of redemption. This produces the concept of salvation as deification.[22]

---

21. The creation is fallen and cursed because of sin (Genesis 3:14–19) and will be one day set free from its corruption (Romans 8:19–23; Revelation 21:3–5, 22:3), but it is not inherently evil. In fact, at the end of each day of creation, we are told that God saw what He had made and it was good, on the sixth day following the creation of man, "very good." Thus a doctrine of the goodness of the material world as created by God is explicitly present in the creation account in the Bible.

22. Sergius Bulgakov, *The Orthodox Church* (Crestwood, NY: St. Vladimir's Seminary Press, 1988), p. 108.

The incarnation is then said to be the effective "deification" of man. This deification is, according to Bulgakov, the Orthodox view of salvation. From a biblical point of view, it seems strange to gloss over the atonement and attribute to the Incarnation things never declared in Scripture and then end up calling it salvation.

Within the doctrine of redemption as set forth by Orthodoxy, there is also the surprising role attributed to the Resurrection. The Orthodox theologian and priest Andrew Louth makes the following assertions about the Resurrection and redemption:

> Orthodox theology . . . considers the question of Adam's sin and its consequences from the perspective of the resurrection of Christ. The icon, called 'The Resurrection' . . . is a depiction of Christ destroying the gates of hell and bringing out from hell . . . Adam and Eve, as the first of a crowd of people . . . who are being brought out of hell by Christ's victory over death in the resurrection. . . . Adam is commemorated as he is now: one whose penitence made it possible for him to be redeemed from hell by Christ at his resurrection.[23]

This is a remarkable presentation of the Fall and redemption! Though the reality of the Fall and the redemption are affirmed, notice that the Fall is the departure from the path of deification, and that redemption is accomplished *by the Resurrection*. And man's inclusion in the redemption is on the basis of his "*penitence*"! What is missing here? Absolutely no mention is made of the atonement or the Cross. No mention is made of the payment for sin or satisfying the wrath of God. For the Orthodox, Christ's victory over death and *not the Cross or atonement* is what saves from sin, death, and hell.

But Scripture is clear. Peter tells us, "He Himself bore our sins in His body on the cross, so that we might die to sin and live to righteousness; for by His wounds you were healed" (1 Peter 2:24). Luke 24:45–47 records Jesus' charge to His disciples before He ascended to Heaven:

> Then He opened their minds to understand the Scriptures, and He said to them, "Thus it is written, that the Christ would suffer and rise again from the dead the third day, and that

---

23. Louth, *Introducing Eastern Orthodox Theology*, p. 70.

repentance for forgiveness of sins would be proclaimed in His name to all the nations, beginning from Jerusalem."

In Romans 3:23–26, Paul instructs us:

> For all have sinned and fall short of the glory of God, being justified as a gift by His grace through the redemption which is in Christ Jesus; whom God displayed publicly as a propitiation in His blood through faith. This was to demonstrate His righteousness, because in the forbearance of God He passed over the sins previously committed; for the demonstration, I say, of His righteousness at the present time, so that He would be just and the justifier of the one who has faith in Jesus.

And in 1 Corinthians 15:3–4 he says, "For I delivered to you as of first importance what I also received, that Christ died for our sins according to the Scriptures, and that He was buried, and that He was raised on the third day according to the Scriptures." And in 2 Corinthians 5:21 we read, "He [God] made Him (Christ) who knew no sin to be sin on our behalf, so that we might become the righteousness of God in Him."

We cannot bypass the Cross. It is at the heart of the gospel, as Paul makes clear:

> I have been crucified with Christ; and it is no longer I who live, but Christ lives in me; and the life which I now live in the flesh I live by faith in the Son of God, who loved me and gave Himself up for me. I do not nullify the grace of God, for if righteousness comes through the Law, then Christ died needlessly (Galatians 2:20–21).

> But may it never be that I would boast, except in the cross of our Lord Jesus Christ, through which the world has been crucified to me, and I to the world (Galatians 6:14).

Worship

Christians from the West tend to be confused or even shocked when they first attend an Orthodox service. In Eastern Europe and Russia, Orthodox Churches generally do not have seating. (However, Greek Orthodox Churches in America do tend to have pews.) The inside of an Orthodox

Cathedral of Christ the Saviour in Moscow, Russia

Church is typically richly adorned with icons. The word "icon" is simply the Greek word for "image." At the front of the sanctuary is a wall of icons with a door (or doors) in it. This wall is called an "iconostasis" ("icon stand"). It plays an important part in Orthodox worship. The icons on the iconostasis only display the most important icons adorning a particular church. There are often many, many more icons distributed throughout the church. Westerners from the Catholic tradition, or who are familiar with Catholic Churches, are accustomed to religious art being featured prominently in the church. However, in an Orthodox Church, one is immediately struck with the number of pictures and the obvious importance they play in Orthodox worship. Why are icons so important to the Orthodox?

Worship and Icons in Orthodoxy

The place of icons in Orthodox worship is the result of a centuries-long development and some bloody battles. In the year 726, the Byzantine Emperor Leo III decreed that icons should *not* be used in Orthodox worship. This was immediately resisted, indeed violently resisted, and the famous "iconoclastic controversy" was underway. During the next 117 years, the Byzantine Orthodox Church and society were torn by this controversy. By and large, it was the state, the emperors, their families, the patriarchs, and the bishops who attempted to remove icons from the churches and to ban them from use during church services. The monks and many of the laity were vehemently opposed to the attempts of the iconoclasts to suppress the use of icons in the church.

Finally, in 753, Emperor Constantine V called a council of the church in Constantinople, which issued a condemnation of using icons in the church's

Ancient Orthodox icons

worship. This did not stop the controversy, however. There continued to be strong resistance to the prohibition against the use of icons in the church, and there was further persecution from the state against those who insisted on continuing to use icons in worship.

When the emperor died and his wife (Irene), a secret advocate for using icons, became empress, she called another council. This council, held in 787 in Constantinople, reversed all of the decisions of the 753 council and affirmed the correctness of the use of icons in worship. This second council to deal with the use of icons is recognized as the Seventh Ecumenical Council. Even this council did not end the conflict over icons. Not until 843 did the last iconoclastic emperor die. His wife had another synod called to confirm the decrees of the Seventh Council. This victory for the advocates of icon usage is celebrated every year as the Feast of Orthodoxy.

This bitter controversy and its final resolution in favor of those advocating the use of icons in worship has left a deep impression on Eastern

Orthodoxy. The love for and religious use of icons is a distinguishing mark of Orthodoxy. This raises the question: what justification is given for this practice? There is, after all, no mention of using icons in the New Testament. Not only that, there is the second commandment (Exodus 20:4) against making idols to worship and serve as well as the prohibition in Deuteronomy 4:23–27 against making any "graven images."

Those advocating the use of icons countered with the argument that the Apostles affirmed the use of icons even though they did not say anything about them in their surviving writings. We can, they claim, know this through oral tradition. This is, of course, a claim that can neither be proved nor disproved.

But the most important argument brought in support of the validity of icons was that the Incarnation made them acceptable. Since God chose to take on flesh when Christ was born, He made Himself visible. He took on a physical body, that is, made up of matter (Romans 8:3). Thus, the rejection of icons was arbitrarily said to be the denial of a genuine incarnation.[24] To believe that God became man meant that man could represent Him with material elements. The fact that God was able to incarnate Himself, to become man, is clearly a miracle of which only He is capable. It is a great leap to get from the historical Incarnation of God in Jesus to say that that means people are, therefore, competent to create holy images to be venerated in worship.

In fairness, it must also be said that the Seventh Council declared that it is wrong to *worship* icons but that it was acceptable to *venerate* (strong form of the word "to honor") them because they represented holy personages: Jesus, Mary,[25] and the saints. In venerating an icon of the Apostle Paul, for example, one is said to be recognizing and honoring his holiness, which he

---

24. This argument was set forth by the greatly admired (by the Eastern Church) church father from Syria, John of Damascus.

25. Orthodoxy has a very exalted view of Mary. "The Orthodox church venerates the Virgin Mary as 'more honorable than the cherubim and beyond compare more glorious than the seraphim,' as superior to all created beings. The church sees in her the Mother of God, who without being a substitute for the one Mediator, intercedes before her Son for all humanity. We ceaselessly pray to her to intercede for us. Love and veneration of the Virgin is the soul of Orthodox piety, its heart, that which warms and animates its entire body. A faith in Christ which does not include his virgin birth and the veneration of his mother is another faith, another Christianity from that of the Orthodox Church." Sergius Bulgakov, "The Virgin and the Saints in Orthodoxy" in *Eastern Orthodox Theology: A Contemporary Reader,* ed. by Daniel B. Clendenin (Grand Rapids, MI: Baker Books, 1995), p. 66.

achieved during his life. This is even said to result in making the venerator more holy. All of this became standard justification for the use of icons and remains so today.

Is it possible to use icons and not violate the second commandment? Is it possible to venerate icons and not slip over the line into worshiping them? Even the highly respected and prominent Orthodox theologian Alexander Schmemann admitted that the line dividing veneration and worship is a fine line that is easy to cross over. In his own words: the line "dividing the Chalcedoninan essence of icons from real idol-worship is [an] exceedingly fine line."[26] But, even if the worshipers are sufficiently schooled in theology and philosophy to stay on the right side of this fine line, is it an appropriate thing to do in a religious service of a faith that is "word-" and not image-based?

It is the *gospel* that is the power of God for salvation. Christ is said, in John 1, to be the *Word* which became flesh. All of this and much more in the rest of the New Testament emphasizes God's *speaking*. It seems at the least that the great emphasis on icons works counter to this biblical emphasis on the Word of God, what God says to us, and to which we must respond. Thus, with as much good will as we can muster, we still have to say that the particular form of icon veneration now practiced (bowing before, kissing) is rather far removed from speaking and hearing the Word of God, which is precisely what we all need much more than focusing on the image of a "saint."

The Importance of Icons in Orthodox Worship

Perhaps one of the most unfortunate consequences of the tragic iconoclastic controversy was that it actually ended up elevating icons in importance. Before it began, it was entirely possible to be an Orthodox believer and participate in Orthodox worship without venerating icons. Icon veneration, or worship in many cases, was widespread, but it was not a dogmatically defined practice and was not integrated into Orthodox liturgy.

After the Seventh Ecumenical Council of 787, veneration of icons was made an integral part of Orthodox worship and the meaning of icons was dogmatically defined by the council's decrees. This results in a role for icons within the Orthodox Church that is clearly far beyond anything that can be

---

26. Alexander Schmemann, *The Historical Road of Eastern Orthodoxy* (Crestwood, NY: St. Vladimir's Seminary Press, 1992), p. 203.

justified by Scripture. Though linking the making of icons with an affirmation of the Incarnation makes sense to many, just as many see the argument as far from compelling.

And, if that argument is not compelling and not based on any explicit Scripture, why should icon veneration have such an important place in the life of the church? Further, the prohibition against the making of "idols" or "graven images" from Exodus and Deuteronomy, though a part of the law, should still be taken as representing God's revealed will. We did have a supernatural intervention in Peter's life when the Lord wanted to make it clear that eating certain meats prohibited by the law was no longer prohibited (Mark 7:19; Acts 10:9–16). We have no such revelation regarding the making of graven images. It certainly does seem quite unjustified to claim that those of us who reject the use of icons in Christian worship deny the Incarnation.

When I was a very young child (two years old), my father was deployed to China at the end of World War II. I spent a whole year alone with my very young mother. She, of course, missed my dad terribly and wanted me not to forget him. She had a photograph of him by her bed, which I also shared with her that year. Every day she would hold the photo up to me and tell me to "give Daddy a kiss." I, of course, complied.

One day, however, he returned from China to his wife and son. I was initially a bit frightened of this man who had come in and taken my place in bed next to my mother. Wanting to help me get over my reservation about my dad, my mother told me to give my dad a kiss. I ran into the bedroom, got his picture and kissed it! I had become devoted to the image, but didn't know the person the image portrayed. Of course, I was quite limited in understanding images and representation, but until I was able to truly get to know my dad, could it be said that I loved *him*? Probably not. I may have loved the image because it made my mother happy, but I had to get to know him in order to grow in a relationship of love and trust.

It would, in my judgment, be an error to think that the great devotion to icons demonstrated by many Orthodox believers really betokens a great love for the one represented in the icon. And, even if it does indicate a great love for the one portrayed in the icon, is it fitting to develop such devotion to John Chrysostom or Basil the Great or even Mary? Should not our devotion be directed toward our Lord and Savior rather than His servants? That is the message the angel in Revelation gave to John when he prostrated himself at the angel's feet (Revelation 22:8–9). The angel's words make it abundantly clear that worship should *not* be given to fellow servants but only to God.

The Pattern of Orthodox Worship

A brief word about the conduct of Orthodox services should be added to this topic. The priest(s) perform the rituals of the Eucharistic service behind the iconostasis, out of sight of the worshipers. The liturgy is sung or chanted and is quite consistent. In other words, the worshipers who attend regularly know the liturgy and know how to enter into the process. The participation of the worshipers is seen in their responding at appropriate points in the liturgy and in much bowing, kneeling, and kissing of the icons. Some worshipers will stay through an entire service, but many will come in at some later point and many will leave before the service is over. In fact, there are at least two services that take place each Sunday, the first being "Matins," which lasts about an hour. The Eucharistic service lasts another hour and a half. Thus, many come and partake of whatever portion of the service they wish to be present for and participate in. As strange as it seems to Westerners, it is not considered inappropriate for people to come late or leave early during a service. There is a sense that entering into the liturgy when one arrives and praying and kissing the icons is enough. The liturgy is, after all, for God. Of course, participation in the Eucharist requires that one stay until the priest comes out from behind the iconostasis and distributes the bread and wine. This is the high point of the service. A sermon, generally called a "homily," is typically short and not many seem to wait to hear it. The important thing in the service is the liturgy and the Eucharist. Preaching does not tend to be valued very highly.

Curious to many, it is precisely this liturgy and the artwork (i.e., the icons) that have attracted many Westerners to Orthodoxy. There is, in the eyes of many, something worshipful about the solemn atmosphere and the ancient liturgy that gives a sense of connection with the past. However, the question that begs for attention is whether or not the exposition of the Scriptures should not play a central role in Christian worship. Paul's exhortation to Timothy in his last epistle before martyrdom was "Be diligent to present yourself approved to God as a workman who does not need to be ashamed, accurately handling the *word of truth*" (2 Timothy 2:15). Further, he tells him that it is *the Scriptures* that are "profitable for teaching, for reproof, for correction, for training in righteousness" (2 Timothy 3:16) and that he should "preach *the word*" (2 Timothy 4:2, emphasis added). Liturgy, per se, is certainly not a bad thing. The Greek word from which it comes simply means "service of worship." It was used of the pagan worship of the gods, but it is also used in the New Testament to refer to Christian worship. Thus, it is not the use of liturgy as such that I find questionable but rather the very limited place the exposition of the Scriptures have in Orthodox worship. Hearing Scripture read and expounded are clearly primary concerns of Paul in his pastoral letters. This should tell us something very important.

The Claim to Be the One True Church

As was pointed out at the beginning of this chapter, the Eastern Orthodox have a very exalted view of their church. Of course, the same could be said of Roman Catholics. In fact, from the fourth century until Vatican II (1962–1965), the claims made by Roman Catholics were just as great as those made by the Orthodox. However, with Vatican II it began to be possible for Catholics to see Protestants as "separated *brethren*" (my emphasis). This was a great advance over just seeing Protestants as heretics. From a Protestant perspective, it is possible to think in terms of different "denominations." Each denomination may be more or less close to what one sees as "fully biblical." The differences that Baptists have with Presbyterians need not lead to rejecting one another as "heretics." In fact, they may engage in various activities cooperatively to get the gospel out to an unbelieving world. From an Orthodox perspective, this notion of different *legitimate* denominations, different churches that have a valid justification for thinking of themselves as the people of the body of Christ, is not possible. In their view, there can only be one true church and they are quite confident that they are it! Why?

The reason is actually quite simple. The claim to be the one true church is connected to their claim to be "apostolic." By "apostolic," the Orthodox do not just mean that they believe and teach the message and doctrines of the Apostles. They do claim that — *and more*. What they are ultimately claiming is that their bishops and priests are the actual heirs of the Apostles, the "*successors*" of the Apostles. In other words, the claim is based on what theologians call "apostolic succession." The way this is claimed to have worked is simple. The Apostles appointed their successors before they died. These successors ordained priests and bishops in their years of ministry and, then, when they died, the ones they had appointed in turn appointed their successors. That means, they say, that there is an unbroken succession of appointees that goes right back to the Apostles, who started the succession. The implication for the Orthodox is also that anyone *not* in that succession is not regarded as a legitimate minister of the true Church, the one founded by Jesus and the Apostles. Even at this point in history, the Orthodox believe that all of their bishops stand in a direct line of succession, an unbroken chain, going all the way back to the Apostles and thus have been ordained to lead the true Church and to appoint (i.e., ordain) future ministers for that Church.

If we stop and reflect for a moment on the logic employed in this justification for the claim to be the one true Church, it should become obvious that there is a logical fallacy involved. Just for the sake of illustration, let us say John ordains Bill, who in turn ordains Jim, who ordains Carl. Now let's say that Jim begins to be influenced by a number of his friends and begins to add things to his teaching that did not come out of the Bible. Let's say further that in his teaching he also leaves out a few of the important points from the Bible. When Jim then appoints and ordains Carl to be his successor, he makes sure that Carl shares his values and viewpoints. As the process continues, we may find that by the time we get to Andy a few centuries later, he is teaching many things that the Apostles didn't teach and not teaching a number of things that they did teach. Is he in the "succession" beginning with the Apostles? Perhaps so, but this would be in a relational sense. But if he is not a *theological* successor in terms of holding to *the teaching of the Apostles*, how important is it that he has a formal link back to the Apostles? Can we doubt that the message, the teaching of the Apostles, is far more important, indeed decisively important, for the role of leading and serving the Church of Jesus Christ? We see exactly this kind of problem in the Gospels. Jesus pointed out that the scribes and Pharisees had seated themselves in the chair of Moses (being Jews, they had a relational link to him) but that their example should *not* be followed (Matthew 23:2ff) because their traditions undermined the truth of the Scriptures (Mark 7:6–13).

As the 16th-century reformers pointed out in their conflicts with the Roman Catholic Church of the time, where the gospel is truly proclaimed and the ordinances (baptism and the Lord's supper) are administered, there is the Church. Of course, they made it very clear that the Bible was the final authority for all things in the faith and practice of the Church, but they decisively rejected the notion of apostolic succession based on formal descent from the Apostles. It was the message and teaching of the Apostles, which is *found in the written Scriptures,* that give us the message and teaching that the Church must proclaim. Where Christ and His atoning death on the Cross and His Resurrection make up the central content of a community's faith, and the written Word of God *found in the Bible* is the final authority for faith and practice, the Church is present, whatever denomination or tradition it belongs to. This is a far more important measure of the true Church than the formal descent referred to as "apostolic succession."

A Concluding Question

One last question might trouble some. Is it possible for a born-again believer to be a practicing member of the Orthodox Church? Of course it is as long as they repent and believe on the Lord Jesus Christ and His death, burial, and Resurrection! As Jesus told Nicodemus, the Spirit blows where He wills (John 3:8). There are without doubt born-again believers in all kinds of places and churches. What is not possible is to claim that *all* in any particular church or denomination are saved just because they are members of that church or denomination. This certainly applies to the Orthodox Church, but it also applies to Protestant churches. Salvation and membership in the Body of Christ, the Church universal, is dependent on a personal relationship with the Christ of Scripture that comes about by personal repentance and faith in Him, not through belonging to any particular local church, denomination, or tradition. The Lord knows those who are His (2 Timothy 2:19)!

Many years of missionary work in Eastern Europe and Russia have led me to conclude that the gospel is not often proclaimed in the Orthodox Church. Church services are ritualistic exercises that focus on the icons and the sacraments. It is all too easy to trust in those sacraments to save one and on the icons to sanctify one rather than in the finished work of Christ on the Cross in our behalf. Though we cannot judge what is in the heart of another, we can certainly assume that most people in the Orthodox Church need to hear and respond to the good news of Jesus Christ and need to turn to Him for forgiveness of sins and to trust in *His* work on the Cross for their salvation. This is, indeed, the message that all people need to hear.

Summary of Eastern Orthodox Beliefs

Doctrine	Eastern Orthodox
God	Trinitarian Godhead consistent with Bible
Authority/ Revelation	The Bible is considered a part of tradition, thought the highest and most important tradition. The apocrypha is also considered part of Scripture, though on a lower level; tradition, particularly in the Church Fathers, gives the authoritative way to interpret Scripture.
Man	A fallen creature, yet not without the ability to cooperate with God in the process of deification (becoming "god," i.e., reaching salvation)
Sin	Transgression of God's will; sin is not seen as the powerful force controlling and enslaving people's will (cf. Romans 7; Ephesians 2:1–10).
Salvation	A cooperation of man with God; most important in this process is participation in the sacraments; the sacraments must be received from duly ordained ministers (priests and bishops) of the Orthodox Church who stand in the line of apostolic succession; beyond the sacraments, the individual believer must strive to become increasingly "holy"; the doctrine of the Atonement (the substitutionary death of Christ on the Cross for our sins) is not emphasized, but rather the Incarnation and Resurrection are the focus.
Creation	Originally believed in a literal, six-day creation, but influence of evolutionary views is increasing.

Chapter 6

Counterfeits of Christianity: The Overview

Bodie Hodge and Roger Patterson

In the grand scheme of religion in the world today, Christianity dominates and is currently the fastest-growing religion, particularly in conversions.[1] Recent numbers indicate 31.5 to 33 percent of the world's population are Christians and are evenly distributed around the world.[2] Most religions outside of Christianity dominate in *localized* regions of the world. The religion with the second most adherents is Islam (known as Muslims or Muhammadans) with about 23.2 percent.[3]

But note something profound: Over 50 percent of the world's religions are tied to the claim that the Bible is true. Obviously, the Bible claims its words are true many times, and this is consistent by virtue that it is from God who *is* the truth (John 14:6). But what many fail to realize is that Muhammad, founder of Islam, *also* affirmed that the Bible was true in the

---

1. Fastest Growing Religion, Fastestgrowingreligion.com, 2009, http://fastestgrowingreligion.com/numbers.html; see also: Brother Andrew, "The Myth about Islam Being the Fastest Growing Religion," Encyclopedia of Islamic Myths, Islam Review, http://www.islamreview.com/articles/mythaboutislam.shtml, accessed March 12, 2015.

2. Ibid.; Pew Research Center, "The Global Religious Landscape," Washington D.C., December 18, 2012, http://www.pewforum.org/2012/12/18/global-religious-landscape-exec/.

3. Ibid.

Koran (e.g., Surah, [chapter] 2:40–42, 126,136, 285; 3:3, 71, 93; 4:47, 136; 5:47–51, 69, 71–72; 6:91; 10:37, 94; 21:7; 29:45–46; 35:31; 46:11).

Take note that Jews affirm the Old Testament to be true (about 77 percent of the Bible); Mormons agree that the Bible is true (insofar as it is properly translated); Jehovah's Witnesses affirm the Bible is true (as they have translated it); and so it is the case with many variations and cults of Christianity. Of course, many groups say they see the Bible as the standard, but in practice they hold to authorities above the Bible. But in practice, only pure Christianity really views the Bible as being absolutely true.

Richard Dawkins at the 34th American Atheists Conference in Minneapolis, 2008

Furthermore, just because someone assumes the name Christian, does that mean they really believe in the Jesus Christ of the Bible and have repented of their sin and received Christ as Lord and Savior? Do they really believe the Bible is the sole authority in their lives? Or do they merely accept the name "Christian" without believing in Christ or His Word, as a "cultural Christian." A leading atheist, Dr. Richard Dawkins, will openly call himself a "cultural Christian."[4] Of course, he is an atheist and that is his religion, not Christianity by any means, but he sings carols at Christmas because he lives in a land (England) that was dominated by Christianity and Christian thought and a remnant of that still exists in cultural practices.

As we dive into this book series, we are not arguing for "a god" or merely a monotheistic view of God. Instead, we are arguing for the triune God of the Bible (Father, Son, and Holy Spirit) and no other. It is Christ above all others. So this includes arguing against those who may profess to be Christians but deny the Christ of the Bible, or, for that matter, claim to believe the Bible as the authority but then elevate other authorities higher than God's Word.

---

4. Dawkins, Richard on BBC's "Have Your Say," BBC News, December 10, 2007, http://news.bbc.co.uk/2/hi/uk_politics/7136682.stm.

This is a biblical authority issue where man's ideas have been elevated to be greater than what God has declared. It should be the other way around — our ideas need to be judged based on God's Word. The Bible is the standard that judges all other truth claims because it is the only written revelation from God to man. The arguments in this book will be made on the presupposition that the Christian God is the only God and that He has revealed Himself to us in the 66 books of the Bible.[5]

As biblical Christians, we are not arguing that we stand side by side with Jews, Muslims, Jehovah's Witnesses, Baha'i, or Mormons (and so on), saying that *together* we are arguing for theism in general. By no means! We argue for the God of the Bible alone, even against these religious views that *borrow* similarities from the God of the Bible, but deviate from the Bible. These are known as counterfeits of Christianity and we will focus on a few of these in this overview chapter from a big picture so you can better understand how counterfeits distort the truth about God. Each of the chapters in this volume will examine these counterfeits of Christianity in more detail.

Enter Man

As discussed in the introduction of this book, man's ideas often get elevated to be greater than God and His Word. Man's opinions begin to dilute or replace God's Word rather than serving as a sure foundation. And Christians are not immune! This disease or infection of thinking we are greater than God has even caused many Christians to adopt false beliefs by elevating man's ideas to be greater than God's Word.

This is clearly the case with religions like Islam, Judaism, Mormonism, Jehovah's Witnesses, and so on. Sadly, it is even the case within Christianity, and so it is a lesson for all of us. Furthermore, this is also the case with religions that have many similarities to Christianity but still deviate from the truth like Zoroastrianism, Deism, Gnosticism, and the like. This brings us to the issue of defining counterfeits of Christianity in more detail.

---

5. Since this volume focuses on the religious views that predominantly acknowledge the existence of God, our aim is to demonstrate that all other religions apart from biblical Christianity are false when compared to the Bible as God has revealed Himself to us. Discussions of the existence of God will be discussed elsewhere. For more information, see: "What Is the Best Argument for the Existence of God?" Jason Lisle, *New Answers Book 3*, Ken Ham, ed. (Green Forest, AR: Master Books, 2009), p. 263–270, https://answersin-genesis.org/is-god-real/what-is-the-best-argument-for-the-existence-of-god.

When it comes to paper money, a counterfeit is something pawned off or pretended to be the real thing, but isn't. It is not an authentic bill, but one that imitates the real bill, which has real value. Sometimes the bill is obviously faked but in other cases it can seem very convincing to deceive someone into believing that it is the real bill. There is a broad range of counterfeits! But what we know about a counterfeit bill is that it is ultimately without any value and fake.

In contrast to biblical Christianity (as defined by the 66 books of God's Word), a counterfeit of Christianity is any worldview that deviates from truths revealed in these 66 books by taking man's ideas to supersede God's Word by addition, deletion, unbiblical reinterpretation, syncretism with another religion, and so on; and yet, still has many elements of the Bible incorporated into its religious thinking and practices, whether they acknowledge it or not.

Now let's just put it right out there since this is what you are probably thinking: "But none of us get it exactly right except God, so how can *we* be expected to get it exactly right?" This is where the grace of God is extended, but each Christian is to strive to be as biblical as possible in all things (2 Timothy 2:15–16). It is a *process* whereby we are being made perfect, but that will not be brought to finality until we see the new heavens and new earth in consummate form where we will be in perfection with God for all eternity. But the greater point is that God gets it right, and the first step is realizing we can trust what He has revealed to us.

From a Christian worldview, we expect that there will be counterfeit religions very similar to a biblical worldview, and others that are heavily mutilated since this is exactly what Satan does. He cannot create but can only deceive by counterfeits (2 Corinthians 11:12–15). And so when we turn on our "radar," we can usually spot these variations. From a big picture, when cults and religions deviate from Christianity, they usually do it in a number of areas but none more often than the nature and work of Christ.

Arbitrariness: Looking at Counterfeits of Christianity

Let's start with two similar, but different, popular unitarian (God is not triune) counterfeits: Islam and Judaism. Both Muhammadism (Islam) and Judaism have much similarity to Christianity but have significant deviations. They both agree with Christians that there is only one God, and both have great respect for *much* of the Bible. But both of these groups deviate into a unitarian variant of God. Islam does so by adding to the Bible, making it subject to the alleged new revelation of Islam's Koran (Qur'an) and Hadith. Judaism does so by denying parts of God's Word as authoritative (the New Testament) while elevating man's traditions (Talmud) to the level of Scripture.

Note that in both cases, the 66 books of the Word of God were affected because man's ideas were elevated to be greater than God's Word. In the case of Islam, they held Muhammad's words to be higher than God's Word. With Judaism, Jews rejected Christ, elevating their own ideas to supersede the Word of God in the New Testament by denying its authority.

Jehovah's Witnesses, another unitarian counterfeit of Christianity, do something very similar. The founder of Jehovah's Witnesses, Charles Taze Russell, also claimed he was a prophet of God and introduced his writings as Scripture with his *Studies in the Scriptures* book series and set up what became the Watch Tower Bible and Tract Society whose publications (*Watchtower* and *Awake!* magazines) are seen as Scripture to the adherents of that cult. They produced a translation of the Bible in 1961 where many verses were changed to conform to their unitarian theology (New World Translation, NWT).

Now let us turn to the popular polytheistic (multiple-god) counterfeit of Mormonism (The Church of Jesus Christ of Latter-day Saints). They hold the Bible in high esteem, but, like Muslims and others, elevate a man's ideas to be greater than God's Word. Enter Joseph Smith Jr., who wrote several books that are seen by Mormons as being of greater authority than the Bible (*The Book of Mormon, Doctrine and Covenants*, and *The Pearl of Great Price*). Smith went so far as to rewrite the Bible, changing over 4,000 verses to conform to his new theology (Joseph Smith Translation, JST). The current Mormon organization still retains in its leadership people who claim to speak as prophets of God and thus sit in judgment over any previous revelation, including the Bible.

Note that in each case above, the ideas of man are used to overrule the Word of God. This makes their positions and their claims arbitrary, because man is not in a position to judge God and His revealed Word. God can speak for God, but man cannot without the help of God. In the case of the Bible, men were moved by God (the Holy Spirit) to write the inspired text (1 Timothy 3:16–17; 2 Peter 1:20–21). In the case of Muhammad, he claimed an angel informed him of this new "word of God" in trance-like revelations and ultimately found the word in his heart. Smith also encountered several angelic beings who he claims gave him special authority to receive revelations and do translations with special seer stones. Russell claimed of his own accord he was a prophet and spoke for God. The Jews, of their own accord, have merely set aside much of the Word of God and denied Jesus as the Messiah. Man cannot arbitrarily speak for God of His own authority and autonomy; only God can speak for God.

In most of these counterfeits, we find that a single person was the cause of deviation — whether Muhammad, Smith, Russell, Zarathustra (for Zoroastrianism), a pope, or another self-proclaimed leader. In some cases, when subsequent generations of followers came to power, such as the case with Jehovah's Witnesses and Mormons, the new leaders began to deviate from what was stated previously with further revelation! The arbitrary nature of these claims to new revelations from God became apparent as conflicting teachings surfaced within each group. If they had really been from God, they would not have contradicted one another.

But note that it is basically one person's views that are seen to supersede the Bible. In contrast, the Bible, which is unique in its authorship by having over 40 different authors with the same consistent message, is definitely a mark of the Holy Spirit's divine authorship.

Misconception: But Each Has Their Book and Their God(s) so It Is Like Preferring Chocolate over Vanilla?

So Muslims have the Koran, Mormons have *The Book of Mormon*, Jehovah's Witnesses have the *Awake!* magazine , the Jews have the Talmud, and the list continues. Christians have the Bible (Old and New Testament), so is the debate simply a matter of *preference*? Actually, this is a misconception.

These competing religious claims are not all equally valid. Not at all. It is not like a buffet, where you pick what you like, while someone else prefers to fill their plate with different foods. Truth is not a matter of opinion. If you pick what is truth based on your personal opinions, then truth is nonexistent since there would be no standard for truth! Thus, when we decide which "god" we feel like serving and what holy book is holy, it is merely arbitrary based on a human authority. Truth must be based on a standard. Only one God is the true God — all others are counterfeits.

When comparing the various religious views, there are some obvious conclusions we can draw. For instance, could it be true that Islam is a counterfeit of Mormonism? No. Mormonism was founded far later than Islam. Neither of their respective religious views hold the teachings of the other to be true — Muslims don't follow *The Book of Mormon*, and vice versa. Most of these counterfeits openly borrow or affirm the Bible, or at least parts of it, to be true whether Gnostics, Muslims, Mormons, Jehovah's Witnesses, Roman Catholic, Jews, Baha'i, and so on. Others borrow from biblical doctrines whether they realize it or not. (Zoroastrianism borrows a single God, creation, a need for salvation, final judgment, etc.) The Bible borrows teachings from none of these other religions, so it is obvious that they are counterfeits arising from the Bible. Biblical Christianity is the standard by which we can judge all other religious views.

Inconsistency

We are required to test these other religious worldviews against the truth of God's Word (1 Thessalonians 5:21; 1 John 4:1). In keeping with this, are they consistent? For example, let's look at two tests of consistency. First, it must be able to account for the existence of a rational universe in a consistent manner.[6] Second, it must contain no internal inconsistencies (e.g., false prophecies, truly contradictory revelations, competing omnipotent beings, etc.). The Bible, being the very standard at hand, obviously meets these two consistencies, so we judge all other truth claims by this same ultimate standard.

These different religions have gods that differ from the God of the Bible. Naturally, this is inconsistent when we consider that many popular cults tend to affirm the Bible is true! Further, their holy books do not agree with one another, so they can't all be from God (who cannot deny Himself). The God of the Bible is not arbitrary, is not inconsistent, and gives us a basis for knowledge. Other religions must borrow from the Bible to make sense of the world around us. In doing so, they inadvertently acknowledge the absolute truthfulness of the Bible.

Let's look at some examples. Mormons, Jehovah's Witnesses, and Muslims all affirm the Bible is true (to some degree), but then they deviate from that stated position. How?

---

6. Only the God of the Bible can consistently and logically account for the universe we live in; see Lisle, *New Answers Book 3*, p. 263–270.

	Bible true?	Are their subsequent Scriptures consistent with the Bible?	Their proposed solution?
Jehovah's Witnesses	Yes, but . . .	No	1. Rewrite the Bible to better fit their theology (NWT). 2. Say that when the Bible disagrees, then it must be corrected in light of their new revelations (*Awake!* or *Watch-tower*, etc.)
Muslims	Yes, but . . .	No	1. Christians and Jews changed the text of Scripture since Muhammad's day. 2. Later revelations like the Koran are to be used to correct the errors.
Mormons	Yes, but . . .	No	1. Rewrite the Bible to better fit with their theology (Joseph Smith Translation/JST). 2. Say that when the Bible disagrees, then it must be corrected in light of their new revelations (*The Book of Mormon*, etc.)

Of course, there are large problems with each of these tired responses. Where is the textual support for such changes to the Bible? It simply does not exist. The text of the Bible we have before and after Muhammad is essentially identical. No doctrinal conflicts exist. There are variants (updated words, variant spellings of a word, minor copyist mistakes), but due to the immense witness of the texts (thousands of manuscripts to analyze) we can demonstrate the authenticity of the historical work; the text of the Bible is easily seen.

So there is no basis to say Jews and Christians changed the text of the Bible — let alone teamed up to do it! Furthermore, both Christians and Jews would be irate if they found the other doing such a thing, as the text of the Old Testament is sacred in the eyes of both, while the New Testament is sacred in the eyes of Christians.

Thus too, any alleged translation like that of Jehovah's Witnesses or Mormons must ultimately be judged by the text of the Bible manuscripts, which have not changed. There is no reason for the blatant changes they have sought to put in their translations other than to force the Bible to match their man-made doctrines. For example, there is no textual witness for a prophecy of Joseph Smith in any ancient document at the end of Genesis as Joseph Smith's "translation" of the Bible conveniently adds (Genesis 50:30–36, JST).[7]

On the Koran's own claims, the Bible is true. This puts the Muhammadan scholars in a predicament, since the Koran clearly disagrees with the Bible on many points — the most important being the deity of Christ.

For example, in the Koran, Mary the mother of Jesus was mistaken for Miriam the sister of Moses (Surah 19:27–28 and 66:12).[8] Many sets of mental gymnastics have been offered to get around this conflict, but it is merely an error from the mind of Muhammad (or his scribe or subsequent successor) confusing Mary with Miriam in this oral-based culture at the time of this dictation. Jesus was not crucified according to the Koran, yet the New Testament makes it clear He was. Another intriguing glitch is that the Koran teaches that the Word of God cannot be changed (Surah 6:115), then the Muslim scholars proceed to argue that the Word of God in the Old and New Testaments (e.g., books of Moses, writings [Psalms], and the Gospels) have been changed, yet Muhammad, disagreeing with the later scholars, affirmed them to be true!

Another interesting situation arises when the Koran claims that the nature of Allah is so far beyond us in transcendence, that nothing in changing human experience can be used to describe him. This is the doctrine of *tanzih*. Dr. Greg Bahnsen writes:

> The two worldviews are dissimilar in pivotal ways when one reflects on Islam's unitarianism, fatalism, moral concepts, lack of redemption, etc. Islam can be internally critiqued on its own presuppositions. Take an obvious example. The *Koran* acknowledges the words of Moses, David, and Jesus to be the words of prophets sent by Allah — in which case the *Koran* may be, *on*

---

7. Genesis 50:30–36 from the Joseph Smith Translation, LDS.org, https://www.lds.org/scriptures/jst/jst-gen/50.

8. "Mary, Sister of Aaron & Daughter of Amram," Qur'an Contradictions, Answering Islam, accessed April 7, 2015, http://www.answering-islam.org/Quran/Contra/qbhc06.html.

its own terms, refuted because of its contradictions with earlier revelation (cf. Deuteronomy 13:1–5). Sophisticated theologies offered by Muslim scholars interpret the theology of the *Koran* (cf. 42:11) as teaching the transcendence (*tanzih*) of unchanging Allah in such an extreme fashion that no human language (derived from changing experience) can positively and appropriate describe Allah — in which case the *Koran* rules out what the *Koran* claims to be.[9] (Italics in original)

Also, the Koran says all of Noah's family survived the Flood, then says some of his sons drowned in the Flood (e.g., Surah 11:42–43 and 21:76). Hosts of contradictions with the Bible can be found within the Koran as well as internal contradictions.[10]

But is the Jewish God (from the Judean religion/Judaism) the same as the Christian God? It is also commonly claimed that the Muslims, Jews, and Christians believe in and worship the same God. If that were the case, then Jews and Muslims would pray to Jesus, right? They do not. So it is not the same God. There is a major difference. Jews hold to a unitarian God, whereas Christians hold to a triune God — one God that is three persons (the Father, the Son, and the Holy Spirit).

But like the Jews, Christians completely agree with the Old Testament. So why do they have different views of God? This occurred as Jews continued to deviate from what was clearly stated in the Old Testament Scripture and relied on the traditions of men to supersede what the Scriptures said, denying Jesus as the Messiah. The ideas of man became so elite that they were used to reinterpret the Old Testament into a unitarian God, despite so many clues to the opposite (see appendix 1).

From Genesis to Malachi, it speaks of Jesus, the second person of the Triune God — this is what the New Testament is primarily about. In types, shadows, and direct language, it is difficult to miss Jesus as the Christ (Messiah),[11] who is the Creator who humbled Himself and came to the Jews and

---

9. Greg Bahnsen, "Presuppositional Reasoning with False Faiths," *Penpoint* VII:2, Feb./Mar., 1996, http://www.cmfnow.com/articles/pa208.htm.

10. For more please see: "Contradictions in the Qur'an," http://www.answering-islam.org/Quran/Contra/qbhc06.html.

11. The New Testament writers refer to Jesus in various ways. He came as the Jewish Messiah, which is the Christ in its Greek form. Reference to Jesus, the Messiah, Christ, or various combinations are all referring to Jesus Christ, the Messiah.

took on flesh to become a man (Colossians 2:5–10). Christ is the seed of the woman in Genesis 3:15 (Galatians 3:16); Jesus is the Messiah (Daniel 9:25–26; John 1:41); Christ is the ultimate Passover lamb sacrificed once for all (1 Corinthians 5:7); Christ is the great *I Am* (John 8:58), and the fulfillment of *God with us*/Immanuel (Isaiah 7:14, Matthew 1:21–23); and Christ is the mediator of the new *everlasting* covenant spoken by Jeremiah (Jeremiah 32:40; Matthew 26:28; Hebrew 8:6–13, 13:20).

Even Old Testament language speaks of a non-unitarian God. Some examples are:[12]

	Lord speaking (emphasis added)	Reference
1	"Let Us make man in *Our* image . . ."	Genesis 1:26
2	Then the LORD God said, "Behold, the man has become like one of *Us,* to know good and evil."	Genesis 3:22
3	"Come, let *Us* go down and there confuse their language . . ."	Genesis 11:4
4	Also I heard the voice of the Lord, saying: "Whom shall I send, and who will go for *Us?*"	Isaiah 6:8

The point is that the Jewish religion has deviated to go against the teachings in the Old Testament in denying Jesus as Messiah and a person in the Godhead. As Christians, we want to call our Jewish friends to fully trust the Word of God in both the Old Testament and the New Testament. For our heart is that they too will be saved through Jesus Christ for all eternity.

Christianity — as described in the New Testament — fulfills and is judged by previous revelation — the Old Testament — and is not internally inconsistent (e.g., Deuteronomy 13:1–5; Acts 17:11; etc.). *The Book of Mormon, Watchtower*, Koran, and other religious writings try to go backward. Instead of allowing their books/writings to be judged by previous revelation from God, they claim the prior must be looked at in light of their new revelation, reinterpreting their predecessors or claiming the new supersedes the old. How convenient! But this is the mark of a false teaching — declaring your view as true and then saying all other things must be judged by your new view. Counterfeits simply do not stand up to scrutiny when judged by previous revelation from God.

---

12. All Scripture quotations in this chapter are from the New King James Version of the Bible.

Consider that what Islam tries to do with Christianity (add a later prophet's revelations to supersede what came before), Baha'i does to Islam! The Baha'i religion tries to supersede Muhammad with later prophets who reinterpreted the Koran and Bible and produced their own writings!

In Muhammadism (Islam), the only supposed guarantee of paradise is by dying in a holy war. So if there are no holy wars, then the certainty of salvation really diminishes, so this helps explain the bloody history of Islam. The rest of the non-militant Muslims then have hopes that good works will be enough to save them.

In fact, most counterfeits have this idea that good works will get them to heaven. But good works are expected from a good God who created man in His image. Good works should be a given, not a means of salvation! It is not good works that God looks at to decide if someone is worthy of heaven. Ever since Adam sinned, God looks at each person as sinful, and judgment will come for all sinners (Galatians 3:22). The punishment from an infinitely holy God is, by extension, an infinite punishment. So if 99.999 percent of all you do is good, then it still doesn't matter; that 0.001 percent will still be punished by an infinite God, which means you are not worthy to enter heaven. So what is the hope of heaven since all have sinned?

No created being could take that punishment — only the Lord Jesus Christ, who is God, could do it. The infinite Son of God became a man, lived a sinless life, and took the infinite punishment from the infinite Father, which is the only way the debt to sin can truly be covered. God was the only one in a position to take that punishment on our behalf. And this is what Jesus did on the Cross — He bore the wrath of God for sinners. To acknowledge His perfect sacrifice, the Father raised Him from the dead.

The only means of salvation is grace-based, not works-based, through Jesus Christ, by repenting of your sin and receiving by faith the Jesus Christ of Scripture as Lord of your life — not by dying in a holy war or trying to do "good works." The counterfeits of Christianity all demand righteousness earned by the individual — an impossibility — rather than trusting in the righteousness of Christ offered to all who trust in Him as Savior. When one receives Christ, the righteousness of Christ is transferred to you like a covering (imputed to you) so then you are seen as righteous in God's eyes and able to enter heaven.

Returning to an earlier idea, having later prophets (Joseph Smith, Charles Taze Russell, Muhammad, Ellen White, etc.) after the Bible was written has big problems. Most take a position that denies the Bible in saying sin hasn't been covered and that works are what is required to possibly achieve salvation.

Of course, none of these later prophets ever came back from the dead to prove they were right about the afterlife. Only the Lord Jesus Christ did. But consider other problems of having prophets after the Bible was written:

1. Apostles of Christ were given authority over prophets and, together with the prophets of the Old Testament, are the foundation with Christ as the chief cornerstone (e.g., 1 Corinthians 12:28–29; Ephesians 2:20; 2 Peter 3:2). The implication is that any alleged prophets after the Apostles of Christ are subject to the Apostles' teachings (i.e., the New Testament, which holds authority over any of them). This is consistent with previous revelation being used to judge any alleged new revelation.

2. In the New Testament, Jude 1:3 affirms that the faith was once for all delivered to the saints (Christians) now that Christ fulfilled the Old Testament (e.g., Matthew 5:17; Acts 3:18). So there is no reason for the faith to have to change; it was completed and salvation was made possible once and for all.

3. Some Christians hold to this third point as well: the Old Testament prophesied that prophecy (no more prophets) would cease upon the destruction of the Temple's sanctuary, when it would be burned with fire per Psalm 74:3–9. When the sanctuary is destroyed and the things in it with fire and broken down and all the meeting places (e.g., synagogues in Israel) are destroyed, there will no longer be any prophet in the land. This is confirmed by Daniel 9:24–27 when the vision and prophecy shall cease when the Holy City (that is Jerusalem, per Nehemiah 11:1; Isaiah 52:1) and sanctuary (that is, the Temple; e.g., 1 Kings 6:19) are destroyed, which occurred in the first century.[13] So vision and prophecy (i.e., new prophets)

---

13. Prophets like Jeremiah, Daniel, Ezekiel, and Obadiah still existed when the Babylonians came in and destroyed Solomon's Temple. Also, the items were largely taken out of the Temple by the Babylonians and were later returned and not destroyed (2 Chronicles 36:7; Ezra 5:14; etc.). This is why some Christians hold this Psalm/Daniel passages for what occurred in the first century. But as noted, not all Christians are in agreement here.

should no longer be possible after the New Testament was completed (i.e., in Muhammad's day about 500 years later, or Joseph Smith's day about 1,700 year later).

Borrowing from the Bible

Many religions borrow from the Bible, in particular those that have many similarities to Christianity. Many do this unknowingly while others are open about it.

Consider a big-picture simplistic point for a moment. God has all knowledge (cf. Psalm 147:5; Colossians 2:3). For anyone to have any knowledge whatsoever, it had to be borrowed from God. For example, for any religion to agree to the claim that there is one God, they had to borrow this concept from the one true God.

Have you ever considered that many other things are also borrowed from the God of the Bible? The concepts of good and evil are defined by the all-good God. So when people use terminology like "good" or "bad" or "better" or "worse" or "evil" or "proper" or "improper" and so on, then they are borrowing from the God of the Bible. Morality in and of itself is a Christian outworking from the God of the Bible who defines morality. Apart from a single, absolute standard, there can be no understanding of what is right or wrong, good or bad. The triune God of the Bible is that standard of goodness (Matthew 19:17).

Why do logic and reason and truth exist? They exist because God is the truth (John 14:6) and God is the standard of truth. Logic and reasoning are tools by which infinite truth can be better understood with our finite minds. But just because God makes logic, reason, and truth a possibility does not mean that man can reason. So why can man use logic to reason and know

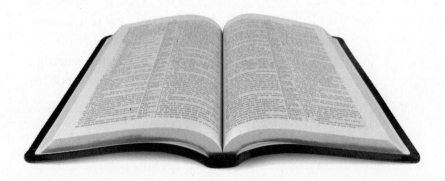

that truth exists? It is simple. The God of the Bible made man in His own image — the image of a logical, reasoning God who is the truth.

In what other religion is man made in the image of God? This idea comes from the Bible, though many borrow this openly. Islam and Mormonism both have creation stories that are similar to the account in the Bible. And when another religion doesn't borrow this openly, then they merely assume it (borrow it unknowingly) from the God of the Bible.

Consider other doctrines that are borrowed from the Bible with biblical references. Here are a few:

Clothing	Genesis 3
Marriage	Genesis 1
Marriage between a man and a woman	Genesis 1
Don't marry close relatives anymore	Leviticus 18
Logic exists and people can understand it	Genesis 1
Why people can often mess up logic	Genesis 3
Lying is wrong	Exodus 20,
Stealing is wrong	Exodus 20, Leviticus 19:11, etc.
Murder is wrong/preserving life	Genesis 4:8-14, Exodus 20, etc.
Knowledge exists	Genesis 2:9, Exodus 31:3, Colossians 2:3, etc.
Immaterial/spiritual exists	Genesis 1:1 (God is not part of creation), 1:2, 6:2, etc.
Why evil exists	Genesis 3

More Christian doctrines that the world must borrow from the Bible (still not exhaustive):

Trust exists

Honesty exists

Science possible (God upholds the universe in a particular uniform way)

Week

Weekend

Why death exists and is bad

Sadness exists

Joy exists

Love exists

Why hate exists

People have value

Safety due to things having value

Laws (why governing necessary)

Righteous judgments

Why disasters happen

Why a remnant of good in the world

Why the need for a Savior

Cleanliness

Why fight disease

Suffering is bad

Origins can be known

Gold/silver, etc., have value

Why eat vegetarian foods and meat

Why sin exists

Why things wear out (e.g., our bodies)

Why thorns and thistles exist

Agriculture/cultivation

Why people name things

Reproduction

Why classify things (class concept)

Work

Surgery possible

Sleep

Medicine

Timekeeping

Care for elderly, sick, orphans, etc.

Why sedimentary rock layers

Genealogies and their importance

Truth exists

Why hair should be kempt

Law of biogenesis

Astronomy, e.g., map and monitor heavens

Origin of languages

Communication possible

Why mutations exist

Miracles

Inheritance

Mercy exists

Grace is possible

Giving

Peace

Forgiveness is possible

Memorials

Mountains, valleys, landscapes

Music possible

Atonement

Existence of angels

Constellations

Animal husbandry

Language style and elements

Authority exists

Desire to do something

Education

Technology (e.g., to counter effects of the Curse)

Dominion

Preservation

Sympathy/Empathy

Honor exists

One race/all related

Holidays

Wearing shoes

History important

Mathematics

Sleep

Spirits/heavenly host exists

Soul

Animals have value

Anger exists

Moderation in certain things

Personal dignity

Morality; right and wrong (good and bad)

Other Smaller Cults with a Leading Human Authority

Cults existed in the first century. For example, Gnostics played off of a leader who led people down a different path. One variant form of Gnosticism in the early stages of the church was by Marcion. He tried to teach that only Paul's writings were Scriptures (neglecting much of the New Testament), but even then, he was selective about that!

Many modern cults usually have one leader (sometimes it can be more than one) who takes them down the wrong road and away from biblical teachings. Though there is no reason to be exhaustive, these examples should help you be able to spot what is occurring. This table outlines a few:

Who	Who was the authority seen to supersede the Bible?
Heaven's Gate	Marshall Applewhite and Bonnie Nettles
People's Temple	Jim Jones
Manson Family Cult	Charles Manson
Branch Davidians (Waco)	David Koresh
Children of God (The Family or Family of Love)	David Berg
Twelve Tribes	Elbert Eugene Spriggs
Christian Science	Mary Baker Eddy
Rastafari	Haile Selassie I

Note that in each case, man is used to supersede God's revealed authority. How sad that the creature would seek to usurp the Creator. Now there is a big point to be made here and it shouldn't go unrecognized. No one is immune from going down the path of a cult, even in what is seen as good biblical denominations. All it takes is one person to lead people down a path opposed to God's Word, claiming to have special revelations or authority that can lead to dangerous areas of compromise and destruction.

All teaching, regardless of its source, should be checked against the Word of God, the 66 books of the Bible. Paul commended the Bereans for doing just that with his teaching that Jesus was the Jewish Messiah (Acts 17:11) — and he was an Apostle of the Lord. So no teacher who really loves the Lord should be upset with having their work checked against Scripture (previous revelation).

With this said, there are some modern denominations moving in the wrong direction. Sometimes it is due to a person leading them there. In other cases, they are not checking certain teachings against the clear teaching in the Bible and gradually move in a false direction.

One great example of that is when people take the secular humanistic view of origins (a naturalistic view as opposed to the biblical view) and try to mix it with their Christianity. Usually, this is done by replacing biblical creation (in six days) with an evolutionary/big bang origins story that comes from the secular humanistic religion. This is not biblical and these types of teachings are leading people down the wrong path. These extra-biblical teachings lead to problems like the presence of death before sin that undermine the gospel of Jesus Christ.[14] We need to call many in various denominations back to God's Word, trusting what God revealed to us about creation as opposed to taking the human-concocted story about origins.

On the opposite end of the spectrum, we have groups that started out in the direction of a cult and have since moved to be more biblical in their outlook. One example comes with some Seventh Day Adventists (SDA). They departed from biblical truth by following Ellen White, who claimed to have visions, and many hailed her as a prophetess. Many within SDA hold to Ellen White's teaching as nearly infallible, so they could easily fit in the chart above. Many people within SDA have moved away from her teachings and tried to go back to the Bible in more modern times. Is this wise? Yes, and we want to encourage this, but the false doctrines must be abandoned for the truth of Scripture alone.

This is the lesson: no matter where you were raised or what circumstances you are in, you can always go back to God's Word to get the truth. The Bible is the Word of God inspired by the Holy Spirit and is the truth. *"All Scripture is given by inspiration of God, and is profitable for doctrine, for reproof, for correction, for instruction in righteousness"* (2 Timothy 3:16).

Conclusion: Christ above All

This first volume of World Religions and Cults dives into religions that seem like they have similarities to Christianity but deviate from the teachings in the Bible in various ways. Some can be considered "Christian" in a very

---

14. Bodie Hodge, "Biblically, Could Death Have Existed Before Sin?" Answers in Genesis, accessed March 2, 2010, https://answersingenesis.org/death-before-sin/biblically-could-death-have-existed-before-sin/.

broad and historical sense (as opposed to *biblical* Christianity), but we must be careful not to let that label become a stamp of truth in doctrine and a proper understanding of salvation.

In many of these cases, these religions openly affirm that the Bible is true, while others borrow from the Bible inadvertently. What is the common factor to the Bible's demotion from the position of absolute authority? It is man's fallible opinions that are elevated to be greater than what God has spoken in His Word. In each of these counterfeits, man's ideas are seen as greater than God's ideas. It is back to front.

One way or another, the Bible gets demoted or reinterpreted or completely ignored in light of man's ideas that are being used to throw the Bible's clear teaching out the window! To assume man sits in judgment above God and His Word is arbitrary and fallacious. So the key to not falling into this trap is biblical authority. To know the truth is to follow He who is the truth, and the only way to do that is by following the Bible that God, who is the truth, gave us.

Table of examples of some Bible-based religions that add or take away from the 66 Books of the Bible (included are faulty Christian views of origins where man's ideas have infiltrated) *Not exhaustive*

	Who?	Added to the 66 books of God's Word (man's opinions)?	Subtracted/ Changed from the 66 books of God's Word (man's opinions)
1	Roman Catholicism	Added OT Apocrypha Added papal authority	
2	Orthodox	Added Apocrypha Added authority of patriarchs	
3	Jehovah's Witnesses	Added Charles Taze Russell's writings (e.g., *Studies in the Scriptures*) and *Watchtower* and *Awake!* publications as supreme over the Bible Added Modern governing authorities of JW's	Changed the Bible to mean things other than what it plainly says (New World Translation)

4	Mormons (LDS)	Added Joseph Smith's writings (*The Book of Mormon, The Pearl of Great Price, Doctrines & Covenants*) Added modern prophets	Changed nearly 4,000 verses in the Bible to conform to their theology (Joseph Smith Translation, aka KJV 1833)
5	Islam (Muslims)	Added Muhammad's sayings (Koran and the Hadith) as superior to the Bible	Demoted the Bible as supreme, and Islamic scholars today say it was corrupted even though Muhammad said it was true and to be believed
6	Traditional Seventh Day Adventists*	Added Ellen White's teachings	
7	Theistic Evolution	Added astronomical, geological, and biological evolutionary ideas as supreme above the Bible, so the Bible (special revelation) needs to be reinterpreted in light of these general revelations as interpreted by secularists (i.e., mixing humanistic ideas with the Bible)	The Bible needs to be reinterpreted in light of the secular ideas
8	Progressive Creation	Added astronomical and geological evolutionary ideas as supreme above the Bible, so the Bible (special revelation) needs to be reinterpreted in light of these general revelations as interpreted by secularists (i.e., mixing humanistic ideas with the Bible)	The Bible needs to be reinterpreted in light of the secular ideas

9	Gap Theory	Added astronomical and geological evolutionary ideas as supreme above the Bible, so the Bible (special revelation) needs to be reinterpreted in light of these general revelations as interpreted by secularists (i.e., mixing humanistic ideas with the Bible)	The Bible needs to be reinterpreted in light of the secular ideas
10	Judaism	Adds traditions of the fathers (e.g., Rabbinic Literature like the Talmud, Midrash, etc.)	The 27 books of the New Testament are deleted from God's Word
11	Gnostics (or Marcionism)	Additions of spurious writings like the so-called Gnostic Gospels that some claim to be part of the New Testament or Marcion's claims	Deletion of New Testament texts except most Pauline epistles (they did not accept Paul's letters to Timothy and Titus) and an edited Gospel of Luke
12	Unitarian Universalism	Adds outside sources from other world religions	Demotes biblical teachings that Jesus and the Holy Spirit are the one true God along with the Father (Triune nature of God) Demotes the Bible in favor of false religions
13	Generic Cults	Elevates a leader's teachings to be supreme above the Bible	Because of a leader's authority, the Bible is usually seen as second rate and demoted

14	Deism	Human reason and nature are seen as absolute above God's Word	Demotes the character of God in the Bible Demotes Bible as a source of authority
15	Ba'hai	Added the teachings of Shoghi Effendi with the writings of Bahá'u'lláh, the Báb, and 'Abdu'l-Bahá	Denies the Bible is authoritative but recognizes the Bible as a holy text among others
16	Freemasons	Added Freemasonry teachings (Old Charges)	The Bible, though often revered by some within its ranks, is not the source of ultimate authority and many Masonic teachings contradict the Bible
17	Zoroastrianism	Add the book of Avesta, which includes the ideas of a man named Zarathustra and those following him	Deny the Bible's authority altogether

* Take note that many SDA today do not adhere to the teachings of Ellen White and hold that the Bible is the authority. We encourage this, by the way.

Chapter 7

Islam

Dr. Emir Caner

A Mosque for a Day: The Washington Cathedral Turns Its Prayers to Allah

In 1790, Congress declared Washington, D.C. to be the capital of the United States of America. The first president and namesake of the city, George Washington, diligently began construction plans for the newly formed city in order for it to be the seat of power of the young republic. President Washington appointed a three-person committee, including Frenchman Pierre L'Enfant, to develop the capital and its buildings. One such structure that Washington considered essential to the national welfare was a national cathedral. In 1791, L'Enfant planned a "church intended for national purposes, such as public prayer, thanksgiving, funeral orations, etc., and assigned to the special use of no particular Sect of denomination, but equally open to all."[1]

Unfortunately, due to a myriad of factors, the cathedral did not take shape until more than a century later. In 1907, President Theodore Roosevelt laid the cornerstone, which stated, "The Word became flesh and lived among us" (John 1:14).[2] The English Gothic cathedral, constructed in the shape of a cross and funded with private donations, was erected and given

---

1. Paul Kelsey Williams and Gregory J. Alexander, *Woodley Park* (Charleston, SC: Arcadia Publishing, 2003), p. 113.
2. All Scripture in this chapter is from the New King James Version of the Bible.

the official title "The Cathedral of Saints Peter and Paul."[3] Since its inception, the cathedral has hosted national events such as a national prayer service during the inauguration of Franklin D. Roosevelt and the state funerals of presidents Dwight Eisenhower and Ronald Reagan.

On November 14, 2014, another significant event occurred at the iconic cathedral — the first Muslim Friday prayer service ever held at the historic church. As Pamela Constable reported, "The Arabic call to prayer echoed among the vaulted stone arches and faded away."[4] Prayer rugs were laid out at the northern

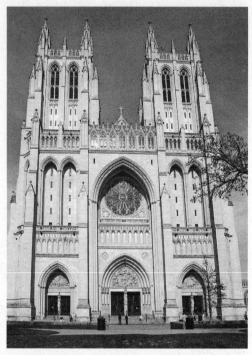

The National Cathedral in Washington, DC

precept of the cathedral, limited in its iconography, as rows of Muslim men and women prostrated themselves toward Mecca declaring, *Allahu Akbar* ("God is Great"). According to the National Cathedral website, organizers of the event believe "powerful things come out of praying together" and "demonstrates an appreciation of one another's prayer traditions and is a powerful symbolic gesture toward a deeper relationship between the two Abrahamic traditions."[5]

This historic precedent, though, illustrates theological infidelity far more than political correctness. The organizers of the event presuppose that Muslims and Christians worship the same god. How ironic that Muslim

3. Frederick Quinn, *A House of Prayer for All People: A History of the Washington National Cathedral* (Harrisburg, PA: Morehouse Publishing, 2014), p. vii-x.
4. Pamela Constable, "Washington Cathedral's First Muslim Prayer Service Interrupted by Heckler," *Washington Post*, 14 November 2014; at http://www.washingtonpost.com/local/2014/11/14/40c49d06-6c41-11e4-a31c-77759fc1eacc_story.html.
5. Stephanie Samuel, "National Cathedral Hosts Islamic Prayers; Lone Protester Interrupts Service," *Christian Post*, 14 November 2014; at http://www.christianpost.com/news/national-cathedral-hosts-islamic-prayers-lone-protester-interrupts-service-129726/.

rugs were laid out on the cathedral's foundation, which declares the deity of Christ — the Word (John 1:1) becoming flesh (John 1:14). Such a declaration of deity of anyone besides Allah is an unforgiveable sin (*shirk*) in Islam and considered the highest and most heinous sin (Qur'an 4:116).[6] Additionally, in a hope of a better relationship with Muslims, it seems Christian leadership in the cathedral were willing to sacrifice their relationship with the one true God (Isaiah 45:5). Like the nation of Israel under pagan leadership, who worshiped Baal along with Yahweh, so too have many American Christians added idols, including Allah, to their list of gods to worship. But like Elijah, we, too, must ask: "How long will you falter between two opinions? If the Lord is God, follow Him; but if Baal, follow him" (1 Kings 18:21). Any answer other than an exclusive allegiance to the Lord will lead to eternal damnation, not to mention the decline of a nation.

The Five Pillars of Islam: Struggling and Surrendering

Ye [Muslims] are the best of Peoples, evolved for mankind. Enjoining what is right, forbidding what is wrong, and believing in Allah. Qur'an 3:110

With a population surpassing 1.5 billion adherents, Islam[7] is the second largest religion in the world, only surpassed by Christianity. Birthed in the Arabian desert more than 1,400 years ago, Islam, an Arabic word that means "submission to Allah," prides itself as a simple religion that requires its followers to declare exclusive allegiance to Allah and to trust the messengers of Allah, in particular, the final messenger Muhammad (Qur'an 61:6). The creed (*shahada*) of Islam sums up the faith, stating, "There is no god but Allah. Muhammad is the messenger of Allah." All other beliefs are based on this one unchanging statement. In affirming there is only one god, Islam is a monotheistic religion.

This creed — or statement of faith — is required for anyone to convert to Islam. Once someone sincerely repeats this creed three times in Arabic, he or she is considered a Muslim, a follower of the Islamic faith. Such a person is then taught the "five pillars" of Islam, which are as follows:

---

6. The holy book of Islam is commonly spelled as Quran, Qur'an, and Koran. The divisions in the book are similar to the Bible's divisions of chapter and verse, but are called surahs (suras) and ayahs.

7. Islam is the name of the religion, and its practitioners are called Muslims.

1. The Creed (*Shahada*): Acknowledging Muhammad as the prophet of Allah, the believer now submits oneself to the teachings of Islam. The Qur'an, the holy book of Islam, becomes the guiding principle of life and eternity, and Muhammad is now the example by which a Muslim lives (Qur'an 33:21).

2. Prayer (*Salat*): The lifeline of Muslims, prayer is the central practice of Islam. Muslims are obligated to pray five times daily. The prayer ritual includes washing themselves beforehand (*wudu*) and reciting their prayers in Arabic while prostrating themselves before Allah. The Muslim is also required to pray with the Islamic community on Fridays (*jumu'ah*). If a Muslim does not pray regularly, he will forget about Allah and his greatness.

3. Almsgiving (*Zakat*): This pillar demands that Muslims reject individual greed and embrace generosity to others. Therefore, Muslims are commanded to give 2.5 percent of their incomes, excluding debts, to those less fortunate in the community.

4. Fasting (*Sawm*): According to the Qur'an, fasting is prescribed of the Islamic believer in order to learn "self-restraint" (Qur'an 2:183). For one month, from before sunrise to after sunset, the Muslim abstains from food, drink, strenuous activity, and even marital intimacy. In their place, the Muslim should devote himself to such things as reading the Qur'an.

5. Pilgrimage (*Hajj*): The climax of the Muslim experience, followers of Islam who are physically and financially able are required to visit the holiest city of Islam, Mecca (Saudi Arabia). The centerpiece of Mecca is a cube-shaped building called the *Ka'aba*. This structure, which Muslims believe was first established by the Old Testament prophet Abraham as the first house of worship on earth, had become corrupted with hundreds of idols by the time of Muhammad. But Muhammad destroyed all idols and restored the worship of Allah that Abraham had begun. Remember, Muslims face this building to perform their daily prayers from wherever they live in the world. And at least once during their lifetimes, Muslims are

Pilgrims pray at Kaaba, the Holy Mosque in Mecca

required to come, circle this cubed building, and pray. Additional duties include visiting Muhammad's last sermon site, throwing stones at the devil, and sacrificing an animal.

This brief description of the tenets of Islam gives the reader an understanding that Islam is not as simple as it first makes itself out to be. The Qur'an summarizes the pillars in one verse: "Those who believe, *and* do deeds of righteousness, *and* establish regular prayers, *and* give [almsgiving], will have their reward with the Lord" (Qur'an 2:277; italics mine). Notice the "ands" of the verse; that it is required for a Muslim to do all of these things in order to be rewarded, not merely some of the pillars all of the time or all of the pillars some of the time.

As one can easily see, Islam is not only a religion — it is a complete way of life. It engrosses all of life; from the way you dress to how you spend your money; from family life to the afterlife; from women to warfare; from purity to politics; from creation to end times. Muslims accept this lifelong struggle as a strength, not as a weakness of their faith. The faith is both theological and political, and for many Muslims these two cannot be separated. The law of Allah is, at minimum, the law for Muslims if not the accepted law of the land.

What was begun in the sands of modern-day Saudi Arabia has swept across much of the globe. The most populous Muslim nation is not found in the Middle East, near its geographical beginning, but in Indonesia, where more than 200 million Muslims reside. Three countries in South Asia — Pakistan, India, and Bangladesh — hold nearly half a billion Muslims. Indeed, Muslims are a majority in 49 nations of the world.[8] Islam is on the doorstep of the West, with millions of followers in the United States and tens of millions across Europe. The West, much of it known for its aversion to religion during the past century, must wake up from its religious illiteracy and once again begin studying the great religions of the world. If not, the world may just pass it by — or take it over.

The Rise of the Warrior-Prophet: Muhammad (A.D. 570–632)

> *We have truly sent you as a witness, as a bearer of Glad Tidings, and as a Warner: In order that you (O men) may believe in Allah and His Messenger, that you may assist and honour him, and celebrate His praises morning and evening.* Qur'an 48:8–9

In March of A.D. 632, an aged prophet rode on a camel one last time to the plain of Arafat, just outside the holy city of Mecca. A crowd, perhaps one hundred thousand strong, awaited his arrival and, with great expectation, listened intently to the last sermon of Muhammad, their prophet. It seemed he knew his life was fleeting and exclaimed, "O People, lend me an attentive ear, for I do not know whether, after this year, I shall ever be among you again." He then exhorted his followers to remain united in the faith and worship Allah alone for, one day, each person would answer for the deeds they have done.[9] The crowd cheered his farewell address, shouting, "You have fulfilled it, O Messenger of God."[10] Three months later, the prophet was dead. Muhammad had fulfilled his mission and handed the faith to his disciples. As one biographer noted, "Fired with the wild enthusiasm of the new faith,

---

8. Pew Research Center's Forum on Religion and Public Life, "Muslim," at http://www.pewforum.org/2012/12/18/global-religious-landscape-muslim.

9. For the full transcript of Muhammad's Farewell Sermon, see http://legacy.fordham.edu/halsall/source/muhm-sermon.asp.

10. John Glubb, *The Life and Times of Muhammad* (Chelsea, MI: Scarborough House, 1991), p. 21.

his followers poured out of their deserts, bent on conquering the world for God."[11]

Born in Mecca about A.D. 570, the early life of Muhammad was filled with tragedy. His father, Abdullah, died before his birth and his mother, Amina, passed away when Muhammad was just six years old. Muhammad's grandfather, Abd al-Muttalib, became the caregiver for a short while, but he died when Muhammad was only eight years old. Muhammad's uncle, Abu Talib, reared the young man into adulthood. By all accounts, Muhammad lived a normal Arab life; however, he refused to partake in the pagan rituals in his hometown of Mecca.[12]

In time, Muhammad met and married the first love of his life, Khadija, a wealthy merchant widow who had hired Muhammad to lead a caravan to Syria. Although she was 15 years his senior, Khadija bore six children, two boys and four girls. Both boys died in infancy, but the daughters followed the faith of their father, two of whom married future leaders of Islam.

Khadija also played a significant role in the formation of the Islamic faith. When Muhammad was 40 years old, he received his first revelation from Allah. While sitting in a cave in a mountain outside of Mecca, the archangel Gabriel supposedly appeared before the prophet and demanded that Muhammad recite the words of Allah. The encounter was so violent that he believed Gabriel was going to kill him. The prophet returned home, his "heart beating severely," and shared his experience with his wife. Muhammad wondered whether he was delusional or even possessed by an evil spirit. Khadija assured her husband that the revelation from Allah was authentic. Her consolation affirmed the first revelation, which birthed the sacred text of Islam, the Qur'an.[13]

Over the next 23 years in the life of Muhammad, two political events allowed Islam to rise to national prominence in the Arabian Peninsula. First, after Muhammad gained a small but zealous band of followers, the authorities in Muhammad's hometown of Mecca devised a plan to assassinate the emerging leader. Muhammad secretly eluded the assassins, journeyed about

---

11. Ibid., p. 21–22.
12. The earliest and most respected biography of Muhammad was written by Ibn Ishaq. The work, *The Life of Muhammad*, was translated by Alfred Guillaume and published by Oxford University Press (2002).
13. To read more about the encounter, see the collection of Hadith by Sahih al-Bukhari 1.3. The verses given to Muhammad, the very first verses revealed of the Qur'an, are surah 96:1–3.

200 miles to the town of Medina, and then quickly united the city under his political leadership. Muhammad had secured a home base for his religion where he could strategize the expansion and implementation of the Islamic faith.

Second, Muhammad rose as a military leader, a warrior-prophet, sanctioning raids on caravans in order to secure resources for their cause. Muhammad himself fought in dozens of battles over his lifetime and commanded others to do so as well, stating, "Fighting is prescribed upon you, and you dislike it. But it is possible that you dislike a thing which is good for you" (Qur'an 2:216). The prophet viewed war as a religious event, slaying those who "do not believe in Allah or the Last Day" (Qur'an 9:29). He eradicated Jews from Medina and ultimately conquered his hometown, Mecca, with very little resistance. There, Muhammad destroyed hundreds of pagan idols from the Ka'aba and established Islam as the official religion of the Arabian Peninsula. Mecca finally became the focal point of Islam, something it has sustained until this day.

A Trail of Blood: A Very Brief History of Fourteen Centuries of Conquest

And if you are slain or die in the way of Allah, forgiveness and mercy from Allah are far better than all they could amass. Qur'an 3:157

Immediately following Muhammad's death, Abu Bakr, an early convert to Islam, was named the leader (*caliph*) of the Islamic community. Yet some Muslims no longer desired to follow the religion after the prophet's passing and revolted against Islamic authorities. Abu Bakr quickly squelched the civil unrest and secured the entire Arabian Peninsula. The lesson: once a Muslim, you must always remain a Muslim.[14]

Over the next millennium, the world, in particular the Christian realm, witnessed the unprecedented growth of political Islam. As American missionary and scholar Samuel Zwemer explained, "To the follower of Christ, and especially to the student of Christian history, Islam possesses a melancholy interest peculiar to it among the religions of the world. It alone can claim to have met and vanquished Christianity."[15] The conquest of Christian lands by

14. Bukhari's Hadith declared, "If a Muslim changes his religion, kill him" (9.57).
15. Samuel M. Zwemer, *Islam: A Challenge to Faith* (New York: Student Volunteer Movement for Foreign Missions, 1907), p. 1.

Muslims was swift and stunning. British historian Bernard Lewis, who taught at Princeton, exclaimed, "For the first thousand years Islam was advancing, Christendom was in retreat and under threat. The new faith conquered the old Christian lands of the Levant and North Africa, and invaded Europe, ruling for a while in Sicily, Spain, Portugal, and even parts of France."[16] Consider the following Christian regions that were conquered by Islamic forces in the years given: Syria (634), Egypt (639), North Africa (700), Spain (711), and Morocco (722). In fact, although not overtaken, even Rome was sacked by Muslims (846). Muslims captured other territory including Persia (642), Afghanistan (670), Turkestan (715), and West Africa (late 900s).

Perhaps the greatest expansion of Islam occurred under the Ottomans, who conquered the city of Constantinople (1453), a city second only to Rome in Christian influence. The Turks would rule much of the civilized world over the next 450 years and challenge Christian supremacy in the very heart of Europe. By the mid-17th century, Turks controlled parts of Europe as far north as the Polish border and as far west as Hungary. In time, the Ottomans faded from political history, replaced by the very ones they attempted to conquer — Europeans.

Beginning in the 18th century, European colonialism halted the onslaught of Islamic expansion and drove back many of the advances made during the first one thousand years of Islamic history. Countries governed by Muslims for centuries, including Egypt, India, and parts of the Arabian Peninsula, were now controlled by British forces. The Dutch ruled Indonesia, the French controlled Morocco and Algeria, and the Italians ruled Libya. The Muslim world was in tatters, and the last Muslim power, the weakened Ottoman Empire, lost its final attempt at regaining any power after its defeat in World War I.

After the war, a new day dawned, a day of Muslim independence from European regimes. Brits and French made one final attempt at establishing rule over the Middle East, but emerging Islamic nationalism halted that effort. Over the course of the 20th century, Muslim-populated countries gained independence and began self-governance. At the same time Islam regained its political power, much of the religion was experiencing a cultural renaissance and theological reformation. Western values waned and Islamic

---

16. Bernard Lewis, "The Roots of Muslim Rage," *The Atlantic Monthly*, vol. 266, no. 3 (September 1990): 47–60.

law as described in the Qur'an and Hadith (*sharia*) came back in vogue. The more literally a Muslim read the Qur'an, the more political his faith became.

Today, many Muslim countries govern under the auspices of Islamic law and regard the holy texts of Islam as their constitution. Freedoms codified in law in the West, like freedom of speech and freedom of religion, are not accepted in Muslim countries. Many Muslim countries enforce criminal laws against proselytizing, and punish those who would criticize Islam in any way.[17] In the harshest of places, leaving the Islamic faith is punishable by death. Some blame the West and its oppression through colonialism for the backwardness and radicalization of these regimes. However, a fairer rendering of history, considering the life of Muhammad and the conquests throughout Islam's history, recognizes that an affirmation of Islamic law has little to do with colonial oppression and far more to do with Muhammad's words and actions. Political Islam, birthed in the seventh century by Muhammad himself, has seen a revival and, it seems, is here to stay for generations to come.

The Two Sources of Authority in Islam: Qur'an and the Example of Muhammad

> *We sent down the (Qur'an) in Truth, and in Truth has it descended: and We sent you but to give Glad Tidings and to warn (sinners). It is a Qur'an which we have divided (into parts from time to time), in order that you might recite it to men at intervals: We have revealed it by stages. Say: "Whether you believe it or not, it is true that those who were given knowledge beforehand, when it is recited to them, fall down on their faces in humble prostration.* Qur'an 17:105–107

The primary source of authority for Muslims is the "Glorious Qur'an" (Qur'an 85:22), the holy book of the faith. This book consists of 114 chapters, 6,616 verses, 77,943 words, and 338,606 letters — each and every part dictated by Allah. The story of the Qur'an comes through the prophet Muhammad, although the sacred text has little to say about him. Instead, the Qur'an affirms itself to be the irreproducible (Qur'an 2:23), incorruptible (Qur'an 15:9), and inspired (Qur'an 42:51) word of Allah recited in Arabic (Qur'an

---

17. For a good example, see Pakistan's blasphemy code (section 295c), which states, "Whoever by words, either spoken, or written, or by visible representation, or by any imputation, innuendo, or insinuation, directly or indirectly, defiles the sacred name of the Holy Prophet . . . shall be punished with death, or imprisonment, and shall also be liable to fine."

12:2). According to the Qur'an, it replaces the corrupted text of the Bible, "revealing to [Jews and Christians] much that you used to hide in the Book, and passing over much [that is now unnecessary]" (Qur'an 5:15). Like Mormonism, the words of Allah came on "a Tablet Preserved!" (Qur'an 85:22). This tablet, of course, does not exist and is only mentioned in this one verse of the Qur'an. As such, many Muslims regard the tablet as metaphorical, meaning Allah promises to preserve the Qur'an from distortion here on earth. Other Muslims believe this verse is literal and that there is a heavenly tablet secured for all of eternity as well.

A critical investigation of the Qur'an, though, contradicts the claims of a tablet preserved. Consider the following troublesome facts:

1. The Qur'an is said to be unchangeable (Qur'an 6:34, 10:64), but Allah removes verses as he pleases (Qur'an 13:39).

2. The Qur'an is regarded as preserved (Qur'an 85:22), yet Allah causes Muhammad to forget some passages (Qur'an 87:6–7).

3. The Qur'an states that it is dictated from Allah (Qur'an 39:1–2) and will be "guarded from corruption" (Qur'an 15:9), yet there were varying copies of the Qur'an during the earliest days of Islam. These differing manuscripts caused the third leader of Islam, Uthman, to choose one copy over another and burn all other irregular manuscripts. Additionally, a Qur'an discovered in Yemen in 1972, perhaps the oldest manuscript in existence, was found to have "small but intriguing aberrations from the standard Koranic text."[18] How can dictation by Allah have any irregularities, however small they may be?

4. Early leaders in Islam admitted they did not have the entire Qur'an. The second leader of Islam, Umar, stated, "Let none of you say, 'I have got the whole of the Qur'an.' How does he know what all of it is? Much of the Qur'an has gone. Let him say instead, 'I have got what has survived.' "[19]

The Qur'an is, as one professor describes it, "the charter of the community. . . . Islamic history has been the effort to pursue and work out the

---

18. Toby Lester, "What is the Koran," *The Atlantic Monthly*, 283:1 (January 1999): 43–56.
19. John Burton, *The Collection of the Qur'an* (Cambridge, MA: Cambridge University Press, 1977), p. 117.

commandments of the Koran in human life."[20] However, if the Qur'an is proven to be riddled with errors then "the whole Islamic struggle of fourteen centuries is effectively meaningless."[21]

But the Qur'an is not the sole and sufficient authority in Islam. The Qur'an itself notes, "Ye have indeed in the Messenger of Allah an excellent exemplar" (Qur'an 33:21). The sayings and practices of Muhammad provide Muslims a detailed example they are obligated to follow. More than two centuries after Muhammad's death, compilations of the prophet's sayings and conduct were collected in written form by Islamic scholars from oral narrations. These compilations, known as *Hadith* or Traditions, are only second to the Qur'an in importance and are regarded by Muslims as the rule of law and faith for the Muslim community. While there are six compilations of these Traditions, two are considered most authentic for Sunni Muslims: Sahih al-Bukhari and Sahih Muslim, named after the two men who collected them. The two editions combined hold more than 16,000 verses attempting to portray the virtuous life and teachings of Muhammad.

The question at hand is whether Muhammad is the noble prophet the Hadith declares him to be. Here is a warrior-prophet who built a faith upon military conquest and demanded allegiance to his cause. The Hadith itself records troublesome facts about the prophet including eradicating enemies who merely spoke against him (Bukhari 5.369), declaring capital punishment upon any Muslim who leaves the faith (Bukhari 9.57–58), and calling for the destruction of the Jewish people (Bukhari 4.177).

Muhammad's personal failures were also grave. Although Muslims are forbidden to marry more than four women (Qur'an 4:3), Muhammad received a special revelation that he could marry as many as he wished due to Allah's favor (Qur'an 33:37, 51). He took full advantage of this blessing. For example, Muhammad was infatuated with a woman named Zaynab. But there was one problem: Zaynab was married to Muhammad's adopted son, Zayd. Eventually the prophet convinced Zaynab to divorce her husband — Muhammad's son — and marry the prophet. Stunning as it sounds, Muhammad married his daughter-in-law. Yet that is not even the most controversial marriage of Muhammad by Christian standards. Such involved a young girl by the name of Aisha. Bukhari's Hadith states that Aisha was

20. Stephen Humphreys, in Lester, "What is the Koran?" n.p.
21. Ibid.

six years old when the couple was betrothed and she was nine years old when they sexually consummated the marriage (7.64). Recognizing that the Hadith is considered authentic and authoritative to Muslims, it is difficult to imagine any justification of this action by a biblical standard; much less a desire to consider Muhammad, as many do, as the "excellent exemplar" one should follow. But for the reader, this is why many Muslims marry children of such a young age.

Fundamentals of the Faith #1: Creation in the Qur'an

> *Your Lord is God, who in six days created the Heavens and the Earth, and then mounted the throne: He throws the veil of night over the day: it pursues it swiftly: and he created the sun and the moon and the stars, subjected to laws by His behest: Is not all creation and its empire His? Blessed be God the Lord of the Worlds!* Qur'an 7:54

The verse above seems to indicate that Muslims and Christians have remarkably similar accounts of creation. The Qur'an affirms the heavens and earth were created in six days (7:54, 50:38), that humans were given responsibility over creation (2:30), and that Eve was tempted by Satan in the Garden (2:36), and that the couple was removed from the Garden due to their transgressions (7:27).

But a more detailed comparison between the two monotheistic faiths illustrates a great chasm on this crucial issue. First, Christians must realize that the Qur'an does not have a detailed account of creation as is found in 80 verses of Genesis 1–3. The reader of the Qur'an, instead, must rely upon a simpler account given in the two main passages, 2:30–39 and 7:11–31, in order to garner an understanding of the Islamic view of creation. Second, while the Bible details clearly the order of creation in six days, thereby ruling out evolutionary models, the Muslim scholars give latitude to evolution due to both the lack of detail in explaining the six days of creation as well as maintaining an allegorical model when stating, "A day in the sight of the Lord is like a thousand years" (Qur'an 22:47). While the Bible has a similar verse to Qur'an 22:47, such an allegorical interpretation cannot be warranted due to the fact that the biblical passage is not dealing with creation but with the Second Coming of Christ (2 Peter 3:8). Finally, the stories of creation differ vastly in their accounts as can be seen in the following chart:

Bible	Qur'an
Precise detail on the six days of creation (Genesis 1)	Little detail on the six days of creation (7:54, 10:3, 11:7)
Jesus is the Creator (John 1:3; Hebrews 1:2)	Jesus is created (3:59)
Eve honored in creation (Genesis 2:18–25)	Eve never mentioned by name (20:117)
Mankind made in the image of God (Genesis 1:26)	Mankind is small part of creation (40:57)
Satan is seen as a cunning serpent (Genesis 3:1)	No mention of Satan as a serpent
Adam became a living being while the "last Adam" (Jesus Christ) gives life (1 Corinthians 15:45)	Adam was the first Muslim and the first prophet of Islam
Adam and Eve were tempted by Satan to eat from the Tree of Knowledge of Good and Evil (Genesis 2:17)*	Adam and Eve were tempted by Satan, who also tempts the rest of humanity (7:23–25)
Adam and Eve's sin recognized the need for a Savior (Genesis 3:15)	Adam and Eve's sin illustrated the need for guidance (30:30)

How important is one's view on creation? In Islam, creation and salvation (guidance) are directly linked. Since mankind is not fallen and death is natural, men and women need not a Savior to redeem them. They need a prophet to guide them. The path to heaven is paved by good works, not grace, by listening to the final prophet Muhammad, not God our Savior (1 Timothy 2:3). Thus, a burdensome struggle is the great virtue of the Muslim (Qur'an 35:18).

Fundamentals of the Faith #2: The Character of God and the Character of Christ

> *He begets not, nor is He begotten; and there is none like unto Him.* Quran 112:3–4

"We respect Jesus!" Such is the claim of Muslims who say they speak reverently of Jesus and His mission on earth. But no one can respect Jesus — Muslim or non-Muslim. Jesus declared Himself God (John 8:58) and the Son

---

* Directly for Eve, indirectly through Eve for Adam.

of God (Matthew 16:16–18) and, as such, each person only has two options regarding Christ: accept His free offer of salvation and bow to worship the King of kings, or reject His offer of salvation and refuse to bend the knee. But no one can state they respect Him; that is an insult to His character and work.

How the Qur'an speaks of Jesus is a complete contradiction to that of the Bible. In the Qur'an, Jesus is the created (3:47) "messenger to the Children of Israel" (3:49) who performed miracles (3:50) in order to declare "It is Allah who is my Lord and your Lord" (3:51). Jesus then rounded up "Allah's helpers" (3:52), the disciples, who bore witness that they were "Muslim" (3:52). In time, Jesus fulfilled His mission of calling Jews to worship Allah and was taken to heaven without experiencing death (3:55). According to the Qur'an, Jesus did not die on a cross but someone replaced Him (4:157–158). The Muslim rejects any notion that Jesus is God or the Son of God (19:88). Allah himself asked Jesus, "'O Jesus, the son of Mary! Did you say unto men, 'Take me and my mother for two gods beside Allah?' He will say: 'Glory to Thee! Never could I say what I had no right [to say]' " (5:116).

As the reader can see, the rejection of the deity of Christ goes hand-in-hand with the rejection of the triune nature of the Lord. Islam rejects the very nature and character of God as revealed in Scripture. Furthermore, any Christian should recognize that Mary is not seen as divine, but rather, it is the Holy Spirit who is God. Instead, the Qur'an reveals a god — Allah — who is transcendent, removed from mankind, and sovereign, arbitrarily choosing to work as he pleases (Qur'an 14:4). Here is a brief comparison between the Islamic god and the God of the Bible:

Yahweh — The God of the Bible	Allah — The god of the Qur'an
For God so loved the world that He gave his only begotten Son (John 3:16)	He begets not nor is he begotten (Qur'an 112:3)
God never changes (James 1:17)	Allah changes as he wills (2:106)
God is knowable (John 17:3)	Allah is ultimately unknowable (6:103)*

---

* Take note of the devastation of Islam here. If Allah is ultimately unknowable, then how can the Qur'an be what it claims to be: a revelation of an unknowable God? In other words, if the Qur'an is true that Allah is ultimately unknowable, then the nothing about Allah in the Qur'an can be trusted about Allah. That knowledge of Allah could not be accurate.

God is sovereign and intimate (John 14:8–9)	Allah is a dominant master and sovereign (4:78)
God became flesh (John 1:14)	Allah does not become flesh (5:72)
God is one essence (being) in three persons: Father, Son, and Spirit (Matthew 28:19–20)	Allah is one in mathematical terms (5:73)
God's love is unconditional (Romans 5:6–8)	Allah's love is conditional (2:190)
God's Word is truth (John 17:17; see also Titus 1:2 and Hebrews 6:18)	Allah is the greatest deceiver (3:54)
God's Son died on the Cross to atone for the sins of the world (1 John 4:10)*	Allah has no son (2:116)

Nonetheless, according to the Qur'an and Hadith, Jesus is coming back! (Qur'an 43:61). Jesus will one day descend onto a white minaret in the eastern side of Damascus (Muslim 41.7015). Fighting for the cause of Allah, a tradition tells the story of Jesus: "When you see him, recognize him: a man of medium height, reddish hair. . . . He will fight the people for the cause of Islam. He will break the cross, kill swine. . . . Allah will perish all religions except Islam. He will destroy the Antichrist and will live on the earth for forty years and then he will die. The Muslims will pray over him" (Dawud 37.4310). Simply put, Jesus will be the last Muslim warrior that ushers in the end times and witnesses Islamic world domination.

Fundamentals of the Faith #3: Salvation in Islam

And no burdened soul can bear another's burden, and if one heavy laden cries for (help with) his load, naught of it will be lifted. . . . He who grows (in goodness), grows only for himself. Surah 35:18

There is no such thing as redemption or vicarious atonement in Islam. According to the Qur'an, no one is lost (30:30) but all are born "weak" (4:28) and forgetful (20:115). Therefore, human beings are in need of guidance, wisdom that ultimately comes from the Qur'an, which states, "These are Verses of the Wise Book, a Guide and a Mercy to the Doers of Good"

* This chart was first published in Emir Caner, "Turning to the Triune God," *Decision* (December 2013): 19. I have modified it slightly.

(31:2–3). The equation for that salvation is three-fold: repentance + faith + works = possible salvation (Qur'an 25:70). Salvation begins with right belief as seen in the Creed, "There is no god but Allah. Muhammad is the messenger of Allah." There are six fundamentals to the faith that are also essential to his salvation: (1) belief in one God alone with no partners, (2) belief in angels, (3) belief in the revelations which came down, most notably, the Qur'an, (4) belief in Allah's prophets from Adam to Muhammad, (5) belief that Allah will judge all men and women, and (6) belief that all men and women will spend eternity in either Paradise or Hell.

But right belief is not enough. Right action must accompany right belief. Regular prayers, charitable giving, fasting, and the pilgrimage all must be done properly or there is little hope of heaven. One must act in accordance with the mandates of the Qur'an and the Hadith and, if not, "Allah loves not transgressors" (Qur'an 2:190). One day, when "the Trumpet is blown" (Qur'an 23:101), each person will give an account of his or her deeds. The Muslim hopes that his "balance (of good deeds) is heavy" (Qur'an 23:102) so that he can enjoy Paradise. For those whose sins are greater than their righteousness, "in Hell will they abide" (Qur'an 23:103).[22]

Salvation seems attainable at first glance. However, there is more to Islamic salvation than just the scale of justice between good and evil. Allah must first want you, for "Allah leads astray those who He pleases" (Qur'an 14:4). Furthermore, the ultimate cause for whatever action you undertake is Allah. The Qur'an states, "If some good befalls them they say, 'This is from Allah'; But if evil, they say, 'This is from you (O Prophet).' Say: All things are from Allah" (4:78). If that is truly the case, one wonders what to make of judgment. It seems the Cause (Allah) is judging the effect (the action). How could that be? Would not Allah be judging himself?[23]

---

22. Note the difference in the Bible. Even one sin is punishable by a Holy God for death (finally resulting in hell) for all eternity. For this is the nature of sin in regards to a perfectly infinite and holy God. Even one sin must be punished by death and that death is an eternal death, which would be infinite in nature due to the infinite nature of God. So no matter how many good deeds are done, the bad ones must still be punished by God according to the Bible. Since no one could take that ever-enduring punishment from God for our sin, only God Himself in the person of Jesus Christ could take that punishment on our behalf. Hence, salvation is by grace, through the work of Jesus Christ alone, not based on good deeds outweighing the bad.

23. Again, note the difference in the Bible. Where good and evil stem from Allah, the God of the Bible has only good stemming from Him. Evil is like a parasite that takes good things and corrupts them (i.e., from Satan who turned to sin or man who also turned to sin in Adam).

Additionally, the Hadith shed light on how many actions can lead to someone's eternal demise. Here is just a partial list:

1. Murdering another Muslim (Bukhari 1.30, 9.204)

   I have heard Allah's Apostle saying, "When two Muslims fight (meet) each other with their swords, both the murderer as well as the murdered will go to the Hell-fire." I said, "O Allah's Apostle! It is all right for the murderer but what about the murdered one?" Allah's Apostle replied, "He surely had the intention to kill his companion."

2. Unintentional Killing (Muslim 32.6338)

   Allah's Messenger (may peace be upon him) said: "None amongst you should point a weapon towards his brother, for he does not know that Satan might cause the weapon (to slip) from his hand and (he may injure anyone) and thus he may fall into Hell-fire."

3. Incorrect Ablution (Ritual Washings) (Bukhari 1.166)

   Perform ablution perfectly and thoroughly for Abul-Qasim (the Prophet) said, "Save your heels from the Hell-fire."

4. Arrogance and Stubbornness (Bukhari 6.440; see also Muslim 40.6835)

   I heard the Prophet saying . . . "And may I inform you of the people of the Hell-fire? They are all those violent, arrogant and stubborn people."

5. Careless Words (Bukhari 8.485)

   The Prophet; said: . . . "A slave (of Allah) may utter a word (carelessly) which displeases Allah without thinking of its gravity and because of that he will be thrown into the Hell-Fire."

6. Cruelty to Animals (Muslim 37.6638)

   Abu Huraira reported Allah's Messenger (may peace be upon him) as saying that a woman was thrown into Hell-fire because of a cat whom she had tied and did not provide it with food. Nor did she set it free to catch insects of the earth until it died inch by inch.

7. Giving in to Temptation (Muslim 40.6778)

   The Paradise is surrounded by hardships and the Hell-fire is surrounded by temptations.

A group of Muslims pray during Ramadan in Sana'a

How difficult is it to obtain Paradise according to Islam? Even infants are not guarded from Hell. In one Tradition, a woman, after her child dies, looks to Muhammad for comfort. She approaches the prophet with the hope that her baby is in Paradise. His response is chilling: "Don't you know that Allah created the Paradise and He created the Hell and He created the dwellers for this (Paradise) and the dwellers for this (Hell)" (Muslim 33.6435). Not even a child could be certain of Paradise.

Moreover, the differences between Heaven and Hell are literally night and day, as one can see below:

Paradise/Heaven	Hell
Gardens of Bliss (Qur'an 56:12)	Boiling springs (Qur'an 88:5)
Couches encrusted with gold and precious stones (Qur'an 56:15)	Tied with chains (Qur'an 14:49)
A feast with the best of food and drink (Qur'an 56:18–20)	Choke on liquid puss (Qur'an 14:16–17)
Sexual companions to meet every need (Qur'an 56:35)	Beaten with rods of iron (Qur'an 22:21)
No more grief; peace and security (Qur'an 43:68–73, 50:31–35)	Fire will consume and burn their faces; ice-cold darkness (Qur'an 14:49–50, 38:57)

In the end, there is absolutely no guarantee of Paradise with the sole exception of dying as a martyr for Allah's cause (Qur'an 9:111).[24] The Muslim must wait and wonder. Will the scales tilt in my favor? Does Allah desire my salvation? Does Allah love me and desire for me to be in Paradise? Is my fate the peace and security of a feast or the cold darkness of boiling springs? One thing is for sure — he cannot be sure.

An Eternal Conversation: Questioning the Claims of Islam and Sharing the Love of Christ

> *If you were in doubt as to what We have revealed to you, then ask those who have been reading the Book from before you: the Truth has indeed come to you from your Lord: So be in no wise of those in doubt.* Qur'an 10:94

Astounding as it may sound, the verse above asserts that Muslims who doubt can seek truth from those "before you," that is, Jews and Christians. Notice the Qur'an maintains the truth was given in the "Book," the sacred texts revealed by God. The Qur'an affirms three specific earlier books were sent from God: "And He sent down the Torah (of Moses) and the Gospel (of Jesus" (3:3), and "to David We gave The Psalms" (4:163). Muslims believe these books are now corrupt, as Jews and Christians "change[ed] the words from their (right) places and forget a good part of the Message that was sent them" (Qur'an 5:13). Regardless, the Qur'an, codified in the seventh century long after the Bible itself was accepted in its present form, contends that truth can be found through conversations with sincere Christian believers "who have been reading the Book." Furthermore, there is no textual support for the claim that the Bible has been corrupted.[25]

Therefore, the *message* of Scripture still stands as the sufficient means in defending the faith and winning a Muslim to Christ. And the *method* for reaching Muslims for the Lord is through conversational evangelism, defined as lovingly confronting an unbeliever with the gospel through sincere questions and honest dialogue. Such was the method of prophets in

---

24. This may be one reason for continual warfare within Islamic circles. If there is no war to die in, then there is no assurance of salvation. So Muslims need war, particularly holy war, not peace, for this possibility to exist.

25. There are variants in the biblical text, but these are not conflicts (such as variant spellings of words or copying mistakes, which are easily identified when looking at multiple texts, and these are expected when copying by hand). But none of these variants change theology or introduce conflicts.

the Old Testament like Elijah (1 Kings 18:21: "How long will you falter between two opinions?"), Jesus Himself in the Gospels (Matthew 16:15: "But who do you say that I am?"), and believers like Phillip in the New Testament (Acts 8:30: "Do you understand what you are reading?"). Having the privilege of speaking to someone on a deeply personal level not only requires the right answer; it demands the right questions.

Islam and Christianity present a clash of worldviews. Islam is a complete repudiation of Christianity, denying the very essentials of the faith including the death, burial, and Resurrection of Jesus our Lord. As such, Islam must be refuted in five key areas:

1. *The Prophet Muhammad.* There is an astonishing audacity for a prophet to come along nearly 600 years after Jesus and claim superiority to everything written beforehand without any historical evidence. Muhammad, an alleged prophet who never foretold future events or performed miracles, disregarded historical claims both inside and outside Scripture and arbitrarily denied the central claim of Christianity — the crucifixion and Resurrection of Christ. The Bible proves its own truthfulness — sources decades after Christ affirmed biblical accounts. Roman historian Tacitus (A.D. 56–117) spoke about the life and death of Christ, and Roman official Pliny the Younger wrote a letter (A.D. 112) detailing how Christians worshiped Christ.[26]

   It should be incumbent upon Islamic scholars not merely to deny Christian claims, but to find evidence from religious history supporting their own arguments. The typical Islamic scholar wishes to portray Muhammad as ignorant. I do not. He was a caravan trader that could have come into contact with many Trinitarian Christians in Damascus or other cities. He could have heard public readings of Scripture in Orthodox churches. One of his concubines was a Coptic Christian. He has more intimate knowledge of the Bible than many are willing to presume. For example, he nearly quotes Psalm 103:12 by heart during his prayers, that he would hope God would

---

26. Joseph M. Holden and Norman Geisler, *The Popular Handbook of Archaeology and the Bible* (Eugene, OR: Harvest House Publishers, 2013), p. 299–300.

remove his sin as far as the east is from the west. So many verses of the Qur'an are exact opposites of Scripture (surah 112:3 v. John 3:16; surah 35:18 v. Matthew 11:28). While there was obvious heresies within the Arabian peninsula, that does not excuse Muhammad's supposed ignorance.

Question to Ask a Muslim: What historical proof is there for the Islamic Jesus?

2. *The Qur'an.* As seen in this chapter, the Qur'an asserts that it is the fourth and final revelation of Allah, even though the Bible claims the faith was "once for all delivered to the saints" (Jude 1:3) through the Apostles of Jesus Christ. The earlier books included the Torah of Moses (Genesis–Deuteronomy), the Psalms of David, and the Gospels. Supposedly, these three sacred texts are corrupted and only the Qur'an can be trusted fully as "a Tablet preserved" (Qur'an 85:22). One can easily see the problem of such an argument. Why would Allah allow some of his texts to be corrupted yet preserve his final revelation? As Sovereign, isn't he able to preserve his words from the beginning? Wouldn't he want his word to be preserved from the beginning?

Questions to Ask a Muslim: Do you believe the Torah was inspired by God and then corrupted? Do you believe the Psalms of David were inspired by God and then corrupted? Do you believe the gospel was inspired by God and then corrupted? Why would I trust a god to preserve a word the fourth time when he didn't preserve it the first three times?

Another angle to take on the Qur'an is to ask: If the Qur'an is what it claims to be, that Allah is ultimately unknowable, then how can we trust the Qur'an to be accurate when it claims to reveal knowledge about Allah?

3. *The Trinity.* Questions regarding the Trinity often occur when speaking to a Muslim. In fact, in the author's own experience, Muslims will ask questions regarding the character of God more than any other question. Christians oftentimes mishandle the question and say something akin to the following: "I do not understand the Trinity but I worship the Lord anyway." Such a statement is dangerous as it may affirm to a

Muslim his own worldview — that Christians are ignorant of and in their faith. Instead, the question regarding the character of God comes down to two issues: sovereignty and purpose. God can do anything He pleases, which certainly means He can (and did!) become flesh. The incarnation of Christ demonstrates *why* He became flesh: "but [He] made Himself of no reputation, taking the form of a bondservant, and coming in the likeness of men. And being found in the appearance as a man, He humbled Himself and became obedient to the point of death, even the death of the cross" (Philippians 2:7–8). Jesus came to die for our sins, in our place, that we may obtain eternal life through His sacrifice.

Questions to Ask a Muslim: Can God do whatever He wishes? If so, is it not at least possible that He could become man? Why would He become man?

Also ask about the nature of Allah regarding sin as this relates to the triune nature of God. Ask: Is Allah infinite? If so, then why is his judgment upon sin not infinite? If Allah is infinite, then only Allah would be in a position to take the punishment for sin if he were perfectly holy. Where has Allah taken the punishment for man (which is death) upon himself? How then can Allah claim that salvation exists (to be able to attain paradise) if a means of escaping sin and death have not been dealt with at the ultimate level?

4. *The Crucifixion of Christ.* The Qur'an boldly declares that Jesus Christ never died upon a cross. It states, "But they killed him not, nor crucified him. Only a likeness of that was shown to them" (4:157). Note that Muslims argue that someone replaced Jesus and was a "likeness" of Him. It is key that you understand the biblical passages regarding the crucifixion. The eyewitnesses who watched the Savior's brutal death included Jesus's best friend, John the Beloved, and Jesus' own mother. It seems implausible that the two closest companions of Jesus would not recognize that He had been replaced.

Questions to Ask a Muslim: When was Jesus replaced before the crucifixion? Was it after He was scourged? Did not eyewitnesses see that the stripes were no longer on the back of the surrogate being crucified? How is it possible that Jesus' mother did not recognize Him? Have you read the Gospel accounts that Muhammad repeatedly affirmed were true yet to see what the Christ and His eyewitnesses claimed about the Resurrection, even after His Resurrection?[27]

5. *Salvation by Works.* Along with the affirmation that Allah has no partners, Islam requires the adherent to do works of righteousness in order to obtain Paradise (4:124). The Qur'an also states, "Things that are good remove those that are evil" (11:114). However, in a system of works-based salvation, God can be just or merciful, but He cannot be both. He can be just and punish all sin or He can be merciful (as seen in the verse above) and erase sin without punishment. But only in Jesus Christ, the God-man, can God be both just and merciful. The Lord is just, as He poured His wrath upon His Son to atone for the sins of the world (John 1:29), and He is merciful, as Jesus died in our place, for our sins. God is holy in His judgment yet loving in His mercy.

Questions to Ask a Muslim: If you perform more good works than evil works, can you earn Paradise? If so, what does Allah do with your sins? If he doesn't punish your sins, can he be just? Does Allah overlook sin and its consequences?

The issues above are theological in nature. But one must remember that a Christian's witness must also be personal and practical, speaking to a Muslim's heart as much as one speaks to his head. Here are some practical questions that may help begin a conversation with a Muslim:

1. Are you sure you will go to heaven? (Qur'an 46:9)

2. What has Allah personally said to you during your prayer times?

3. Is there anything in Christianity that if you found were true would cause you to become a follower of Christ?

4. Does Allah still love you when you do wrong? If you do wrong continually (Qur'an 2:190)?

5. Do you ever get tired of trying to earn heaven (Qur'an 35:18 v. Matthew 11:28)?

---

27. Editors, "The Bible as Seen by the Qur'an and the Muslim Traditions," *Answering Islam*, accessed December 29, 2014, http://answering-islam.org/Campbell/s2c1.html.

6. Have you ever read the Bible? Would you read it if I gave you a free copy in your native language?[28]

Muslims are not a different species in need of a unique way of sharing Christ with them. They are — as I once was — like all others, sinners in need of a Savior. Muslims are drawn to the Lord because of His promises — comforting words like, "I will never leave you nor forsake you" (Hebrews 13:5) and "Come to Me, all you who labor and are heavy laden, and I will give you rest" (Matthew 11:28). Like all others, Muslims are looking for an unconditionally loving God (John 3:16) who gives them the secure promise of eternal life (1 John 5:13), a relationship with the Lord that will never end. Our witness is simple: point them to the Lord and show them how Jesus still changes lives. Like two thousand years of Christian witness, believers must recognize that we overcome "by the blood of the Lamb and by the word of their testimony" (Revelation 12:11).

A Final Word: The Meaning of Total Surrender

A faith that's worth living for is a faith that's worth dying for (Romans 12:14–15). The heart of this New Testament message is not one of fame or comfort, but of faith and courage. The life of the disciples echoed this principle well as they gave their lives for their faith. In many parts of the Muslim world, surrendering one's life to Christ means just that — surrender. And, of all Muslim countries that persecute Christians, perhaps none is as unforgiving as Saudi Arabia, where becoming a Christian is punishable by death.[29]

Consider Ali, a young Saudi man who surrendered his life to Christ just a few years ago. Ali had not openly espoused his newfound faith, but the Saudi High Court, nonetheless, sentenced the young Christian to death for treason against Allah (Qur'an 5:33). Ali was to be beheaded. Within a few days of the verdict, Ali was escorted from his prison cell to the site of execution. Awaiting Ali were his wife and three-year-old daughter, forced to watch the execu-

---

28. These are but a few of the questions my students compiled during a graduate class I taught in Thailand. Students would use questions during their witnessing encounters and come back to class to discuss the effectiveness of these questions.

29. Let's just state this for what it is: a form of human sacrifice. This form of human sacrifice of non-Muslims for the cause of Allah has been common through Islamic history and is not restricted to Saudi Arabia but is also often found in Islamic Jihad (holy war). Such killings are seen in Iraq today (with groups like ISIS) and Africa where many Christians in particular are killed for Allah. Be praying for the gospel of Jesus Christ to permeate these lands and save the lost who are hopelessly kept in the darkness of Islam.

tion of their husband and father. The soldiers tied Ali's hands together and stretched Ali's neck out across a wooden block. His wife wept uncontrollably. The last words Ali spoke before the execution were these: "Father, into your hands I commit my spirit." Then he was gone, a martyr for Jesus.[30]

We are not called to be 21st-century Christians by following the culture of the day. We are called to be 1st-century Christians living in the 21st century, following Christ as our 1st-century brethren followed Christ. We are called to surrender. If the Muslim world is going to hear the gospel, it will be through Christians who are willing to sacrifice everything in order to share the beautiful gospel in a hostile world. May it be so. Truth is immortal.

Summary of Islamic Beliefs

Doctrine	Islamic Teaching
God	Deny the Trinity; believe Allah is the only god (monotheistic) and that Jesus is not the Son of God, but a prophet; Allah is transcendent and removed from mankind
Authority/ Revelation	The Bible is viewed as a revelation from God that has been corrupted, but the revelations of Muhammad in the Koran supersede the Bible; the Hadith are revered as traditions that tell of Muhammad's life and act as a sort of authorized commentary on the Koran
Man	Man is the highest creature made by Allah and is able to do good with his free will, though he needs guidance from Allah's prophets.
Sin	Transgression of Allah's will as revealed in the Koran and Hadith; no concept of original sin corrupting mankind; following the guidance of prophets will help you avoid sin and do good; the Five Pillars give a framework for obeying Allah
Salvation	Each person will be judged by Allah for his or her own actions; Allah will allow some into Paradise (Heaven) and send others to hellfire based on the balance of how many good and bad deeds they have done; there is no concept of a mediator or Savior and they deny that Jesus died on the Cross; martyrs receive entrance into Paradise

30. Emir Fethi Caner and H. Edward Pruitt, *The Costly Call, Book 2* (Grand Rapids, MI: Kregel Publications), p. 168–173.

| Creation | The Koran speaks of creation in six days, but many modern scholars allow for an allegorical interpretation and evolutionary views; conservative scholars would reject evolutionary ideas and hold a view very similar to the biblical timeline. |

Chapter 8

Jehovah's Witnesses

Got Questions Ministries

They're at your door again — Jehovah's Witnesses — with their smiles and their literature and their claims about Jesus and how He's been misunderstood all this time. So you open your door to talk to them. What do you say? What do Jehovah's Witnesses believe, and what makes them so dedicated to spreading their ideas about God?

Jehovah's Witnesses believe we are living in the last days, which gives impetus to their mission. They consider their time is short for spreading Jehovah's message. They also paint an appealing picture of eternal life. For example, they teach that virtually everyone who has died will be resurrected and given a second chance to be saved and inherit paradise — and who wouldn't like a second chance? They will cheerfully admit that they are not in the New Covenant, that Jesus is not their mediator, and what's more, there's no need to be born again in order to enter the kingdom (more on this in a moment).

Distribution and Basic Facts

The Watchtower Bible and Tract Society, commonly called the Jehovah's Witnesses, is an international religious organization based in Brooklyn, New York. Often labeled as a Christian denomination, the Watchtower Society is non-trinitarian and differs from orthodox Christianity in several other ways. It takes the name "Jehovah's Witnesses" from Isaiah 43:10, "'You are my

Watchtower Bible and Tract Society headquarters in Brooklyn, New York

witnesses,' declares Jehovah, 'Yes, my servant whom I have chosen' " (New World Translation).

In 2014, the Jehovah's Witnesses reported nearly 20 million members in over 113,000 congregations worldwide. Every month, the Jehovah's Witnesses conduct 9.2 million home Bible studies. Every day, hundreds of thousands of copies of their two magazines, *Watchtower* and *Awake!* are printed and distributed in nearly two hundred languages.

Overseeing the Watchtower Society is the Governing Body, a group of men known as "the faithful and discreet slave." This title comes from one of Jesus' parables: "Who really is the faithful and discreet slave whom his master appointed over his domestics, to give them their food at the proper time? Happy is that slave if his master on coming finds him doing so! Truly I say to you, he will appoint him over all his belongings" (Matthew 24: 45–47; NWT).

History

In the late 19th century, in Pittsburgh, Pennsylvania, 18-year-old Charles Taze Russell started a Bible class that he called "the Millennial Dawn Bible Study" in which he promulgated some aberrant doctrines that would later be part of the corpus of Jehovah's Witnesses' theology. Russell drew many of his ideas from Adventists and others who speculated about Bible prophecy, and he rejected many biblical doctrines that he found problematic. Intent on distributing his ideas as widely as possible, Russell published the first editions of the magazines *Watch Tower* and *Herald of Christ's Presence* in July 1879. In 1881, Russell formed Zion's Watch Tower Tract Society, incorporated in 1884 and renamed the Watch Tower Bible and Tract Society, and subsequently to Watchtower Bible and Tract Society.

Charles Taze Russell

Russell died in 1916, and the second president, Joseph Franklin Rutherford, began implementing some changes in the Society. By 1930, some 75 percent of the original Bible students had dropped out, citing conflicting doctrinal positions. It was during Rutherford's tenure that the name "Jehovah's Witnesses" was first applied to those who remained in the organization. Also under Rutherford's watch, several of the group's distinctive doctrines appeared, including the idea that Jehovah's Witnesses had replaced the Jewish people and the requirement that every Witness take part in literature distribution.

Joseph Franklin Rutherford

From humble origins, the Watch Tower Bible and Tract Society has grown into a worldwide organization. The Jehovah's Witnesses' expansion program is ambitious. To finance their worldwide outreach, each congregation is instructed to commit to regular monthly contributions, even though they themselves have no legal or financial control over the buildings they pay for or construct. The closer "the end of this wicked system of things"[1] draws, the more money pours into Society coffers. The "publishers" (door-to-door distributers of the literature) are admonished to work even harder in the interests of the kingdom because time is running out. The Governing Body stresses the imminence of the Tribulation and the need for Witnesses everywhere to do even more to prove their loyalty.

---

1. "But Jehovah's servants already belong to the only organization that will survive the end of this wicked system of things," *Watchtower*, Dec 15, 2007, p.14, http://jwfacts.com/watchtower/salvation-only-for-jehovahs-witnesses.php.

Means of Worship

Jehovah's Witnesses meet twice a week for worship and Bible study in Kingdom Halls. They do not call these buildings "churches," because that term is associated with Christianity, a false religion in their eyes. There are no stained glass windows, no images or statues, no candles, and absolutely no crosses, occupied or empty (Jehovah's Witnesses consider the Cross to be a pagan symbol). Kingdom Halls have no pews, no choir, and no organ. There is no baptistery, no altar or communion table, and no liturgical garb. The hall is plain and functional, with perhaps a lectern from which talks are delivered. The Jehovah's Witnesses do not sing hymns but have their own "Kingdom Song Book." Each meeting starts and ends with a prayer to Jehovah, asked in Jesus' name.

Distinctive Doctrines

- Their own translation of the Bible, the New World Translation (NWT), is the only version that can be trusted.

- Jesus was created by Jehovah as a spirit creature named Michael the Archangel.

- Jesus is not divine and has always been subordinate to His heavenly father, Jehovah.

- Jesus was a perfect man, but He could have sinned and failed in His mission.

- Jesus only became the "Son of God" at His baptism.

- Since He is not God, Jesus must not be worshiped or prayed to.

- Jesus died to atone only for the sin of Adam (inherited sin).

- Jesus was raised from the dead as a spirit creature — His body disappeared.

- Jesus started ruling God's Kingdom (invisibly, from heaven) in October 1914.

- Jesus chose the Jehovah's Witnesses to be Jehovah's earthly organization in 1919.

- The Jehovah's Witnesses have replaced Israel, and the 144,000 mentioned in Revelation 14:1 are "spiritual Jews."

- Only 144,000 persons since the time of Jesus can enter the New Covenant and go to heaven, there to rule with Jesus.

- Only 144,000 persons needed to be born again or anointed with Jehovah's impersonal "holy spirit."

- The Trinity is a pagan, polytheistic teaching.

- There is no such thing as an immortal soul — the dead know nothing (a doctrine related to soul sleep and annihilationism).

- Jehovah would never punish people for eternity — there is no such place as hell or the lake of fire.

- Jehovah exercises selective foreknowledge — He chose not to know that Adam and Eve would sin.

- Death acquits a person of his personal sin.

- After Armageddon, the dead will be physically resurrected to live on the earth.

- After their resurrection, the unsaved dead will get a second chance to be saved and live forever in a paradise on earth.

- Salvation depends upon works and being faithful and obedient to the end.

- There is no salvation apart from membership in the Jehovah's Witnesses' organization.

- There is no assurance of salvation, even for those with a "heavenly hope."

- Jehovah's revelation to His chosen representatives is progressive — the light keeps getting brighter. This accounts for changes made to previously held interpretations regarding the end times. Whenever those in the Governing Body modify a former belief, they attribute the change to "increased light."

Authority

Jehovah's Witnesses claim their authority comes from the Bible, the divinely inspired Word of God. However, the Bible can only be properly interpreted and applied "with the help of publications prepared by 'the faithful and discreet slave.' "[2] In fact, according to the Watchtower Society, a mature Christian "does not advocate or insist on personal opinions or harbor private ideas when it comes to Bible understanding. Rather, he has complete confidence in the truth as it is revealed by Jehovah God through His Son, Jesus Christ, *and* 'the faithful and discreet slave.' "[3] Thus, all of Scripture is filtered through the group's corporate leaders, and no other interpretation is given the least consideration, so they rely on the fallible ideas of men as their true authority.

Jehovah's Witnesses also claim their authority comes from Jehovah God through Jesus, because Jesus appointed them as His sole channel of communication to the world. The Society is Jehovah's one-and-only earthly organization, and it is only through a small group of men (the faithful and discreet slave) that spiritual food is dispensed from Jehovah to His people.

According to the April 15, 2013, *Watchtower*, "the earthly part of Jehovah's organization" is structured in this way:

1. The Governing Body

2. Branch Committees

3. Traveling Overseers

4. Bodies of Elders

5. Congregations

6. Individual Publishers (those who personally distribute the literature)

Such is the power and authority of the men who make up the Governing Body that no Witness dares challenge or question them. The Governing Body is perceived as Jehovah's representative on earth. A Jehovah's Witness cannot disagree with what he is told; he must accept the published literature and the word of the elders whose job it is to enforce loyalty. If he does disagree and

2. *Watchtower*, February 15, 2003, p. 31.
3. Ibid., August 1, 2001, p. 14.

makes his objection known, he will be disciplined. The ultimate punishment is to be disfellowshiped.

A disfellowshiped member is shunned by all Witness friends and family, sometimes resulting in decades of estrangement. Those still in the organization are advised not to have anything to do with shunned individuals: "Really, what your beloved family member needs to see is your resolute stance to put Jehovah above everything else — including the family bond. . . . Do not look for excuses to associate with a disfellowshipped family member."[4]

The Jehovah's Witnesses maintain a high level of control over what their congregations learn, and independent study is anathema: "All who want to understand the Bible should appreciate that the 'greatly diversified wisdom of God' can become known only through Jehovah's channel of communication, the faithful and discreet slave."[5] Submission to the Governing Body is seen as submission to Christ.

Foundations and Beliefs: Creation and Evolution

Jehovah's Witnesses claim to believe the creation account as recorded in the Book of Genesis. They have always rejected atheistic evolution, believing that Jehovah, through Christ Jesus, is the Creator of the universe. However, they are not young-earth creationists. While they reject Darwinian evolution, they accept astronomical and geological evolution (i.e., billions of years).[6] They do hold to a form of evolution, believing that God created the various "kinds" that were then allowed to diversify within their kind, though they mean, "remarkably different from one another."[7] Charles Taze Russell in *Studies in the Scripture,* VI, states:

> In the beginning we have merely the physical forces out of which the grand structure is made by a gradually unfolding, or if one prefers to say so, an 'evolutionary' process. . . . that there is a divine plan of evolution, appears on the face of the whole chapter.[8]

4. Watchtower Study Edition, January 15, 2013, p. 16.
5. Ibid., October 1, 1994, p. 8.
6. Watch Tower Bible and Tract Society of Pennsylvania, "Do Jehovah's Witnesses believe in Creationism?" 2015, http://www.jw.org/en/jehovahs-witnesses/faq/creationism-belief/.
7. Watch Tower Bible and Tract Society of Pennsylvania, "The Untold Story of Creation," *Awake!* March 2014, http://www.jw.org/en/publications/magazines/g201403/untold-story-of-creation/.
8. Charles Taze Russell, *Studies in the Scriptures*, Volume VI, In the Beginning, "Creation Was Gradual," 1904, p. 53.

198 — World Religions and Cults

This is denoted twice in a footnote on the same page that states: "As already indicated, it is only in respect to man's creation that the Evolution theory conflicts with the Bible — and only to attack this point does that theory exist or find advocates."

Jehovah's Witnesses believe that the six days in the creation account are actually "epochs" — each one a period of 7,000 years.[9] In addition, they believe the earth existed for an indefinite period of time before the creation of life began. This allows for the idea that the earth is millions of years old. The March 2014 *Awake!* states, "The Bible does not support fundamentalists and creationists who claim that the creative days were literal 24-hour days" ("The Untold Story of Creation").

A recent article in *Awake!* magazine takes the old-earth creationist position: "God created the universe, including the earth, in the indefinite past — 'in the beginning,' as Genesis 1:1 says. Modern science agrees that the universe had a beginning. A recent scientific model suggests it to be almost 14 billion years old."[10] The same article speaks of "the false ideas of creationists" that could lead one "to dismiss the Bible altogether" and never benefit from "its storehouse of 'practical wisdom.' "

The length of each creative day being 7,000 years long is so central to Jehovah's Witnesses' chronology that they have calculated that Adam was created in 4026 B.C. They reckon that the year 1975 marked 6,000 years since Adam was created, and from this they reckon that Jehovah's seventh day of rest must now have little more than 1,000 years left to go. This is hugely significant to Jehovah's Witnesses because they believe that the Millennial reign of Christ will take place during the final 1,000 years of Jehovah's 7,000-year-long "day of rest."

Jehovah's Witnesses claim to present "the real Bible story of creation," one that contains "a very logical and credible explanation of the beginning of the universe" that "harmonizes with scientific discovery."[11]

Foundations and Beliefs: The Character of God

Jehovah's Witnesses acknowledge that God is holy (Isaiah 6:3), loves justice (Psalm 37:28), and is all-powerful. And they make much of the fact that "God is love" (1 John 4:8). Jehovah is "merciful and compassionate, slow

9. *Watchtower*, February 15, 1970; Russell, *Studies in the Scriptures*, Volume VI, "In the Beginning, 'The Creative Week,' " 1904, p. 29–51.
10. *Awake!* "Creation," January 2014.
11. *Awake!* March 2014, "The Untold Story of Creation."

to anger and abundant in loyal love" (Exodus 34:6; NWT). Jehovah God created all things (Revelation 4:11). Jehovah alone is the Most High, the Almighty, righteous and true, and the King of eternity (Revelation 15:3). He alone has always existed. The view held by Jehovah's Witnesses denies the existence of a personal Holy Spirit and the truth of the pre-incarnate Christ as the eternal Word of God (John 1).

Apparently, Jehovah is so loving that He would never punish people for eternity. This belief makes the character of God *unjust,* which is in opposition to Witnesses' view that God loves justice. The idea of a place of eternal torment is abhorrent to Jehovah's Witnesses. They teach that the Bible does not provide any basis for a belief in hell fire — in spite of Jesus' warning in Luke 16:19–31 (and elsewhere). To support their view of a "loving" God, they teach that souls are not immortal and that the dead know nothing — the dead are in a state of "soul sleep." Thus, God does not punish sin justly.

Jehovah's Witnesses also refuse to acknowledge that God is omniscient or that He knows the end from the beginning. They think it would have been wrong for Jehovah to create Adam and Eve knowing they would sin and bring terrible consequences into the world. Their belief is that Jehovah exercised selective foreknowledge — He commanded Adam and Eve not to eat of the tree of the knowledge of good and evil, but He chose not to know how they would respond. When they disobeyed, God was surprised.

Jehovah's Witnesses try to constrain God, to make Him fit their view of how He should be. Whenever they come against a biblical teaching about God that they dislike, they reinterpret (or "retranslate") the Bible and assign to God the characteristics they want Him to have. In so doing, they have created a God in their own image.

Foundations and Beliefs: Life after Death

Jehovah's Witnesses base their belief that the soul is not immortal on Ezekiel 18:4: "Look! All the souls — to me they belong. . . . The soul who sins is the one who will die" (NWT). Jehovah's Witnesses say that someone who has died is simply a "dead soul" (Leviticus 21:11). Although the spirit, or "life-force," returns to Jehovah God, it does not actually travel to heaven; rather, "returning to Jehovah" means that any hope of future life rests with God. Only by God's power can the spirit return and a person be made to live again. At the resurrection, the dead will be given a new body, and Jehovah will bring it to life by putting the life-force into it. Jehovah's Witnesses use

Ecclesiastes 9:5–6, 10, and Psalm 146:4 to show that the dead know nothing at all and we mortals do not survive the death of the body. The dead simply cease to exist.

Jehovah's Witnesses also believe that death acquits a person from his own personal sin, so they reckon that billions of people will be brought back to life on earth with a new body into which Jehovah will place that person's personality. Some, however, will not be resurrected; Jehovah's Witnesses take Luke 12:5 to mean that some of the dead are currently in Gehenna, which they consider a symbol of everlasting destruction or non-existence.

Another aspect of Witness theology that does not align with biblical teaching is their view that those who are resurrected will be given a second chance to be saved. They suppose the "day of judgment" will last for 1,000 years, and during that time people who never knew about Jehovah will be physically resurrected and given time to learn how to serve Him. This teaching directly contradicts Hebrews 9:27, which says that man is destined to die once and after that to face judgment. The Bible does not teach a second chance after death.

In Jehovah's Witnesses' theology, there is no interim place of suffering or bliss and no place of eternal torment or joy — just soul sleep until the resurrection, and soul annihilation if you fail the final test. Many people find this an attractive proposition. They are comforted in thinking that no one will suffer after death and that virtually every person who has died will be resurrected (or re-created) and given a second chance to be saved.

Foundations and Beliefs: View of Christ

The person of Christ is the single most important issue in Christianity. Jesus is the cornerstone of our faith (Ephesians 2:20). Get the truth about Jesus Christ wrong, and the foundation of faith will collapse. Unfortunately, the Jehovah's Witnesses miss the truth about Jesus.

Jehovah's Witnesses believe that Jehovah created the pre-human Jesus as a spirit creature, Michael the Archangel (contradicting the whole of Hebrews 1). After the Virgin Mary was impregnated, the spirit of Michael the Archangel entered Jesus. They teach that Jesus lived a perfect life, although He could have sinned and failed in His mission. Jesus has always been subordinate to His Heavenly Father, and Jesus must not be worshiped or prayed to. Jesus died on a "torture stake" (not a cross) to atone for the sin of Adam. After Jesus died, His body disappeared, and what came out of the tomb was, again, a spirit creature. Although Jehovah's Witnesses say that Jesus is the Son of God, they deny He was fully man and fully God, and they deny His bodily Resurrection.

Foundations and Beliefs: Salvation — Grace, Faith, and Works

The Bible says that salvation is deliverance, by the grace of God, from eternal punishment for sin, granted to those who accept by faith God's conditions of repentance and faith in the Lord Jesus. Salvation is the result of faith in Jesus' substitutionary death and bodily Resurrection (Romans 5:10; Ephesians 1:7). Scripture is clear that salvation is the work of God, His gracious, undeserved gift (Ephesians 2:5, 2:8). Salvation is only available through faith in Jesus Christ (Acts 4:12). This faith involves repentance (Acts 3:19) and calling on the name of the Lord (Romans 10:9–10, 10:13).

Jehovah's Witnesses have a different view of salvation, one that relies on human works and careful obedience. For this reason, Witnesses promote high standards of morality and adhere to a strict set of rules. Some of their directives uphold the moral stance of the Bible; they forbid lying, sexual immorality, gambling (avoiding the love of money), etc. In those areas, the Witnesses are acting biblically. However, other rules, such as their prohibition against celebrating birthdays and holidays or their injunction against saluting flags, have no basis in Scripture.

Jehovah's Witnesses call Jesus the Son of God, and they believe in His atoning death — but with some twists. They clearly teach a works-based salvation and that only Jehovah's Witnesses will be saved. And they deny three foundational tenets of the Christian faith: that Jesus is God Incarnate, that Jesus died to cleanse us of our personal sins, and that Jesus rose bodily from the dead. The Bible says that "if Christ has not been raised, your faith is futile; you are still in your sins" (1 Corinthians 15:17; NIV). Thus, the Jehovah's Witnesses' denial of Jesus' actual Resurrection contradicts the very foundation of biblical faith.

Jehovah's Witnesses believe that Jesus was a perfect man who laid down His life as a ransom sacrifice to atone for Adam's sin. "Since a perfect human life [Adam's] was lost, no imperfect human life could ever buy it back. What was needed was a ransom equal in value to what was lost. . . . In a sense, Jesus stepped into Adam's place in order to save us. By sacrificing, or giving up,

His perfect life in flawless obedience to God, Jesus paid the price for Adam's sin. Jesus thus brought hope to Adam's offspring."[12] This sounds good at first, until one realizes the parameters they place on Jesus' atonement: *only* Adam's sin was atoned for. Our personal sin is still our responsibility. That's why the Witnesses say, "Those who in faith accept God's provision for atonement through Jesus Christ can gain salvation."[13] Note, according to this, faith does not *guarantee* salvation; it simply opens the *possibility* of salvation.

Jehovah's Witnesses believe that a person is acquitted of his sins when he *dies*, not when he believes in Christ. Romans 6:7 in the New World Translation says this: "He who has died has been acquitted from his sin." Of course, the whole chapter is talking about a *spiritual* death to sin, but Jehovah's Witnesses take verse 7 to mean that their personal debt of sin is paid when they die *physically*. They say that Jesus only died to take care of inherited sin, to give people *hope* of being saved. The Witness must still earn the right to be declared righteous, not by anything Jesus did, but by his own works.

Jehovah's Witnesses have to *prove* they have faith by doing everything the Governing Body tells them to do — attend the meetings, spend a minimum amount of time each month distributing literature and conducting home studies, and pledge to support the worldwide building program financially. And another stipulation: "We show that we appreciate the ransom by . . . attending the Lord's Evening Meal."[14] This meal is the annual memorial service of the death of Jesus, where only those of the "anointed remnant" partake of the bread and the wine. Everyone else is a mere spectator.

Not a single Jehovah's Witness has any assurance of salvation. They must all remain faithful and obedient until they die. Any Witness could stumble and fall and thereby lose the hope of living forever in the restored earthly paradise. Even the "anointed remnant" do not have any assurance of salvation because they, too, could fail to cross the finish line.

Sadly, this faith is placed entirely in man, a governing body that demands works, and not on the Lord God and His Word, the 66 books of the Bible. The Jehovah's Witnesses' view of salvation could be summed

---

12. Watchtower Editors, *What Does the Bible Really Teach?* (Brooklyn, NY: Watchtower Bible and Tract Society of New York, Inc., 2005, 2014), chapter 5. It is provided as part of a worldwide Bible educational work supported by voluntary donations.
13. Watchtower Editors, *Insight on the Scriptures*, Vol. 1 (Brooklyn, NY: Watchtower Bible and Tract Society of New York, International Bible Students Association, 1988), p. 212.
14. Watch Tower Bible and Tract Society of Pennsylvania, *What Does the Bible Really Teach?* p. 56.

up by this short statement: "Yes, to gain salvation it is not enough to have faith."[15]

Arbitrariness, Inconsistencies, and Refutations: Regarding Authority

For many years, Jehovah's Witnesses were taught that all "anointed" Christians were part of the faithful and discreet slave. However, the Governing Body has recently changed that. The *Watchtower*, July 15, 2013, article "Who Really Is the Faithful and Discreet Slave?" begins by sweeping aside the previous understanding that the slave was appointed in A.D. 33. The article then explains how Jesus' words only *began* to be fulfilled after 1914. The faithful and discreet slave is now identified specifically as "a small group of anointed brothers" that includes the Governing Body as a "composite slave." Thus, the Governing Body has more authority now than ever. It's strange that Jehovah's anointed channel of communication managed to get the interpretation of Jesus' Words so wrong for so long — unless their authority does not come from God but instead from the men who currently make up the Governing Body. However, this group still insists on total obedience:

> We need to obey the faithful and discreet slave to have Jehovah's approval.[16]

> All of us must be ready to obey any instructions we may receive [from Jehovah's organization], whether these appear sound from a strategic or human standpoint or not.[17]

There is no biblical basis for any of these claims of a right to rule over the people of God.

Arbitrariness, Inconsistencies, and Refutations: Regarding Salvation

According to the *Watchtower*,[18] there are four basic requirements for salvation that Jehovah's Witnesses must meet:

1. Take in knowledge of God and Jesus by studying the Bible.

2. Obey God's laws, especially with regard to being moral.

---

15. *Watchtower*, June 1, 2000, p. 12.
16. *Watchtower*, July 15, 2011, p. 24, Simplified English Edition.
17. *Watchtower*, November 15, 2013.
18. Ibid., February 15, 1983, p. 12–13.

3. Associate with God's channel, His organization (there is only one), and serve God as part of it.

4. Support God's government by loyally advocating God's Kingdom rule to others.

In regard to items 3 and 4, we rightly question whether these instructions come from God or men. Here is what the Jehovah's Witnesses say:

> Genuine Christians are now being gathered into a united brotherhood earth wide. Who are they? They are the Christian congregation of Jehovah's Witnesses.[19]

> We will be impelled to serve Jehovah loyally with his organization if we remember that there is nowhere else to go for life eternal.[20]

Nowhere in Scripture does it suggest that God is using Jehovah's Witnesses as His sole channel of communication or that the Society is His exclusive earthly organization or that you must belong to this organization to be saved. Such exclusivism is a mark of a cult. To the contrary, the Scripture says in 1 Timothy 2:5, "For there is one God and one mediator between God and mankind, the man Christ Jesus" (NKJV).

Arbitrariness, Inconsistencies, and Refutations: Regarding Core Teachings and Chronology

From its founding, the Watchtower Society has always proclaimed that the end is near. Yet their proclamations of just how near are constantly shifting. They have predicted the end of the world to happen in 1914, 1925, and 1975. Of course, they were wrong every time.

Here is a clearly false prophecy made in 1969: "If you are a young person . . . you will never grow old in this present system of things. Why not? Because all the evidence in fulfillment of Bible prophecy indicates that this corrupt system is due to end in a few years. . . . Therefore, as a young person, you will never fulfill any career that this system offers. If you are in high school and thinking about a college education, it means at least four, perhaps even six or eight more years to graduate into a specialized career. But

---

19. Ibid., July 1, 1994, p. 7.
20. Ibid., "Serve Jehovah Loyally," November 15, 1992, p. 21.

where will this system of things be by that time? It will be well on the way toward its finish, if not actually gone!"[21] The same line was still being touted in 2012: "No doubt, school counselors sincerely believe that it is in your best interests to pursue higher education and to plan for a secular career. Yet, their confidence lies in a social and financial system that has no lasting future."[22]

One of the Jehovah's Witnesses' core teachings is that Jesus took up His throne and started ruling (invisibly) from heaven in 1914. The outbreak of World War I "proved" that Satan had been ousted from heaven, which was supposed to be the first act of the new King. World War I was interpreted to be the Tribulation. However, since that time, the Society has been receiving huge quantities of "increased light."

Significantly, they admit they got a lot of things wrong about the Tribulation: "In the past, we thought that the great tribulation began in 1914 when World War I started. We thought that Jehovah 'cut short' those days in 1918 when the war ended so that the remaining anointed ones on earth could preach the good news to all nations. Then we realized that a part of Jesus' prophecy about the last days has two fulfillments. So we needed to change the way we understood some parts of the prophecy."[23] This revision is significant, given their claim that since 1919 they have been God's sole channel of communication. Why did Jehovah allow them to get the message wrong in the first place, and why did it take almost 100 years for them to realize they got it wrong?

Another core teaching that has been altered through the years concerns their view of "this generation" mentioned by Jesus in Matthew 24:34, Mark 13:30, and Luke 21:32. Originally, the Jehovah's Witnesses taught that this was the generation alive in 1914 — the World War I generation would live to see Armageddon. They openly taught that "Millions Now Living Will Never Die" (first proclaimed in 1920). Later, the Watchtower Society declared that 1975 marked 6,000 years since the creation of Adam, pointing to an imminent Armageddon. But the date of that final battle kept moving back. Such adjustments to previous teaching are explained away by saying, "The light gets brighter," and using Proverbs 4:18 as a proof text.

Other examples of Watchtower Society prophecies that were later modified include an assertion in 1989 that the Christian missionary work begun

---

21. *Awake!* May 22, 1969, p. 15.
22. *Watchtower*, June 15, 2012, p. 23.
23. Ibid., July 15, 2013.

in the first century would "be completed in our 20th century." However, when the *Watchtower* was republished in bound volumes, the phrase "in our 20th century" was replaced with the less specific "in our day." Another subtle change was made in Society literature in 1995. Up until October 22 of that year, the *Awake!* mag-azine declared its purpose was to proclaim "the Creator's promise of a peaceful and secure new world before the generation that saw the events of 1914 passes away." That was changed on November 8 to read, "The Creator's promise of a peaceful and secure new world that is about to replace the present wicked, lawless system of things."

1907 cover of *Watchtower* magazine

In the November 1, 1995, *Watchtower*, the previous under-standing of "this generation" (the generation alive in 1914) was modified to say, "In the final ful-fillment of Jesus' prophecy today, 'this generation' apparently refers to the peoples of earth who see the sign of Christ's presence but fail to mend their ways." All mention of 1914 was dropped. According to the current interpretation, Jesus' words refer to people born *after* 1914 who will comprise a "wicked generation" — "wicked" because they see the signs of Jesus' invisible presence but fail to become Jehovah's Witnesses.

Arbitrariness, Inconsistencies, and Refutations: Regarding Their Translation of the Bible

The New World Translation of the Holy Scriptures is the Jehovah's Wit-nesses' official Bible. The NWT is an anonymous work of a Watchtower Society committee. Jehovah's Witnesses claim that the anonymity ensures the credit for the work will go to God alone. Of course, it has the added benefits of shielding the translators from accountability for their errors and preventing independent scholars from checking their academic credentials.

The New World Translation is unique in that it is the first intentional, systematic effort to produce a complete version of the Bible edited and revised for the specific purpose of agreeing with one group's doctrine. The Watchtower Society realized that their beliefs contradicted the Bible. But rather than conform their beliefs to Scripture, they altered Scripture to agree with their beliefs.

For example, the New World Translation inconsistently translates the Greek for "Lord" or "God" as "Jehovah." In fact, the Watchtower adds the word *Jehovah* to the New Testament 237 times, even though it has no textual authority for doing so.

They also consistently add words to the Bible in order to make it fit their theological bias. One of the most glaring examples is John 1:1, which should read ". . . and the Word was God." The NWT adds the article *a*: ". . . and the Word was a god." There is absolutely no basis for adding this extra word. It is a blatant attempt to change the meaning of the verse and deny the deity of Christ.

Another egregious example of an added word meant to alter doctrine is found in the NWT translation of Colossians 1:16. In the NIV, this verse reads, "For in him all things were created. . . ." The NWT inserts the word *other* after *all,* despite its being completely absent from the original Greek text. The Jehovah's Witnesses make the verse say, "Because by means of him all other things were created . . ." (NWT). This wording gives the impression that Christ himself is also a created thing, which, of course, is exactly what the Jehovah's Witnesses teach. It is only the pre-conceived, heretical rejection of the deity of Christ that forces the Watchtower Society to translate the Greek text as they do, thus allowing their error to gain legitimacy in the minds of their followers.

Arbitrariness, Inconsistencies, and Refutations: Regarding Blood Transfusions

The Old Testament forbids consuming blood (Genesis 9:2–6) and says that the life of the flesh is in the blood (Leviticus 17:11). Jehovah's Witnesses use this truth to forbid their members from participating in blood transfusions. We know that blood transfusions aid in the preservation of life. When we use someone's blood to keep life going, we uphold the principle of the sanctity of life. However, Jehovah's Witnesses turn the *symbol* of life (blood) into something more important than what it symbolizes.

Furthering their error is the Jehovah's Witnesses' warped interpretation of Acts 15:20, which admonishes Gentiles in the early Church to "abstain . . . from blood." The passage is clearly speaking of eating meat with the blood still in it. But Jehovah's Witnesses apply this to blood transfusions as well. A blood transfusion is simply a transplant of blood; the blood is not absorbed, ingested, or taken as food in any way. It is transplanted just as a kidney would be. But the Jehovah's Witnesses see it differently. The Governing Body used to teach that organ transplants were a form of cannibalism; that vaccinations were useless, sinful, and caused demonism; and that blood transfusions and organ transplants would transmit the personality of the person it came from. Tragically, on the basis of these unscientific and uninformed opinions, many Jehovah's Witnesses have died. Here is a partial record of how the Jehovah's Witnesses have changed their view on this issue over the past 70 years:

1940 — Blood transfusions are acceptable

1945 — Blood transfusion are not acceptable

1956 — Blood serums should be treated as blood and are banned

1958 — Blood serums and fractions are acceptable

1959 — Storage of one's own blood is unacceptable

1961 — Blood fractions are not acceptable

1964 — Blood fractions are acceptable

1967 — Organ transplants are not acceptable

1974 — Blood serums are a personal choice

1975 — Hemophilia treatments (Factor VII and IX) are not acceptable

1978 — Hemophilia treatments (Factor VII and IX) are acceptable

1980 — Organ transplants are acceptable

1982 — Albumin is acceptable

1983 — Hemodilution is acceptable

1990 — Hemodilution is not acceptable

1995 — Hemodilution is acceptable

2000 — Blood fractions are acceptable

2004 — Hemoglobin is now acceptable

Again, we ask, if the Governing Body is the mouthpiece for God in this world, how is it that their decrees are so changeable?

In the past, any Witness accepting a blood transfusion faced disciplinary action at the hands of a judicial committee. Any unrepentant Witness was disfellowshiped and shunned by every other Witness, including members of his own family. Recently, the Society has withdrawn the overt threat of punishment for disobeying these rules. They now say it is a matter of conscience and sanctions will not be applied. Yet the prohibition against transfusions is still a *de facto* rule. There exist "hospital liaison committees" who intervene on behalf of Witnesses facing major surgery. These committees apply a great deal of pressure to the family of Witnesses who may face a life-or-death decision about blood transfusions. So the threat of being disfellowshiped is still implied, if not stated.

The Gospel for Jehovah's Witnesses

First, we should understand that Jehovah's Witnesses have been deceived. They have been taught a false gospel, and they do not know who Jesus really is. They have no assurance of salvation and must constantly strive to work harder to prove their loyalty and obedience to the organization. Make no mistake, they are sincere people who honestly believe they alone have "the truth," and they genuinely think Armageddon is imminent. They feel compelled to share their version of the gospel with anyone who will listen. They are sincere, but sincerely wrong.

Witnessing to the Witnesses must be done in Christian love and compassion. Let them know how much you care about their eternal salvation. Share your Christian testimony with them. It comes as a surprise to them to meet people who love the Lord, display the fruit of the Spirit, and use the Bible as the basis for their faith (Hebrews 4:12). Speak the truth in love (Ephesians 4:15). Lead your conversation to the person of Christ and the need to put total faith in what He has done. Focus on the gospel. Above all else, pray for them.

Here is the testimony of a former Jehovah's Witness:

> When nothing happened after 1975, I left the organization. So did thousands of other disillusioned Witnesses. The awful thing was I still believed Armageddon was just round the corner, and so I lived in fear that I would be destroyed. Also, I had nowhere else to turn because I had believed every other Christian denomination was part of a false religion, soon to be destroyed. For many years, I wandered in a spiritual wilderness. I still believed in God, in Jesus, and in the Bible, but I wanted

nothing to do with Jehovah's Witnesses in particular and with religion in general.

Years later I discovered my twin sister had also left the organization, and she had become a Christian. I had many questions for her, and she answered them in full. Unknown to me, she had been praying for me for many years because she knew the spiritual danger I was in. Praise God, her prayers were answered, and on March 30, 1996, the Lord broke down the last of my barriers and brought me to the foot of the Cross where I repented and was forgiven.

I finally understood what Jesus had endured to save a sinner such as I. It took several years before I came to understand that Jesus was not just a man and that He was not Michael the Archangel but the eternal Word of God who became flesh and dwelt with us — God incarnate. From that wonderful moment when I finally capitulated and gave myself to Him, my life was transformed. No longer do I fear Armageddon or feel the need to obey an organization. I now belong to Christ Jesus, who has given me rest. He is gentle and humble, his yoke is easy, and his burden is light (Matthew 11:29–30). He is the good shepherd, and I recognize His voice. It is God who draws people, and many Jehovah's Witnesses have come out of the dark into the light because Christians have prayed for them and gently shown them the true gospel, which is all about Christ.

People in a cult seldom realize they are in a cult until they try to leave. The price to be paid for walking out is sometimes so great that Witnesses will keep their fears and thoughts to themselves and go through the motions just to avoid being disfellowshiped and shunned. Christians can help such people by persistent prayer — and by being willing to be the answer to their own prayers. Rather than shut the door on Jehovah's Witnesses when they call, we should present the true gospel to them in love and gentleness. A key to helping Jehovah's Witnesses is to always point them to Christ Jesus because they do not understand who He really is. They must see the significance of Jesus' death and why they must be born again in order to have their sins forgiven.

The example of Christian love in action speaks volumes, and it is the work of the Holy Spirit to bring people to repentance and saving faith. For our part, we should be sensitive to the prompting of the Spirit and always be ready to be the Spirit's voice in presenting the gospel of salvation.

Summary of Jehovah's Witness Beliefs

Doctrine	Jehovah's Witness Teaching
God	Deny the trinity; Jehovah is the only god; Jesus was created as Michael the Archangel and became the Son at His baptism; the "holy spirit" is an impersonal force of Jehovah
Authority/ Revelation	The New World translation of the Bible; the Governing Body and its publications, which contain new revelations ("increasing light")
Man	A created being with a free will who must choose to obey Jehovah
Sin	Transgression of Jehovah's commands as well as other legalistic restrictions announced by the Governing Body; an individual's sins are removed at death
Salvation	Salvation comes from obeying laws and by doing good works; Jesus died to atone only for Adam's sin, not the sins of individuals; there is no concept of hell or eternal punishment; eternal paradise will be obtained by only a select few while others will have their souls annihilated
Creation	The Genesis account is acknowledged, but with a day-age understanding; the earth and universe are billions of years old; biological evolution to some extent is allowed, but man was specially created

Chapter 9

Judaism

David Abrahams

A Brief Historical Introduction

Have you ever wondered why there is so much strife between Jews and Muslims in the Middle East (and abroad)? The truth is, the Middle East has rarely been stable since the events that occurred at the Tower of Babel in Genesis 11.

There was the brotherly feud between Isaac (father of the Israelites and Edomites) and Ishmael (father of many Arabs), the two eldest of eight sons of Abraham whose progeny now dominates much of the Middle East (1 Chronicles 1:32). Abraham was also involved in a war where there were four kings against five in the Middle East (Genesis 14:7–16). Further conflicts arose due to strife between two more brothers, the sons of Isaac — Jacob (Israel) and Esau (father of the Edomites). And so it continues.

Needless to say, there have been problems brewing in the Middle East for ages. But why are the issues between Jews and Muslims so vicious today? They are clearly not on friendly terms. I suggest there was a culminating event that has triggered much of this aggression.

Two thousand years ago, the Jews, by and large, did not receive Jesus Christ as Messiah, the ultimate Passover Lamb, Savior, and deliverer who paid for sin once and for all. Because of this, they were still anticipating a messiah well after the time of Christ. In the days of Muhammad (late A.D.

500s and early A.D. 600s), some local Jews were familiar with the supposed prophet in Arabia, and some thought that he might be the long-awaited Messiah.[1]

Muhammad, favoring this idea, raised his hopes of being the Jewish Messiah and had many favorable things to say about the Jews (and Christians) in his dictated Koran. In time, however, the Jews realized that Muhammad did not fit the prophecies of the Messiah. When tested against the many messianic prophecies in Scripture, Muhammad wasn't even close (e.g., not born in Bethlehem [Micah 5:2], not a descendant of Judah [Genesis 28:14], etc.).

So, because of this (as well as for other reasons), Muhammad's attitude turned from one of kindness toward the Jews to hostility. From that time forward, there has been aggression toward the Jews (and Christians) from the Muslims because Muhammad labeled the Jews as "cursed" (Koran 4.46) and wanted his followers to "not take the Jews and the Christians for friends" (Koran 5.51). (Note that the Koran is not written in chronological order but from longest chapter to shortest chapter.)

Judaism in History

The words *Jew* and *Judaism* come from the name Judah, one of the 12 sons of Israel. Judah was one of the larger tribes that became dominant as its own country when the nation of Israel split into two kingdoms. The northern kingdom retained the name Israel (with 10 tribes), and the southern kingdom took the name Judah (with two tribes, one being Judah, naturally).

Although Judaism shares the same foundational history in the Old Testament with Christians — going back to God creating in six days and resting on the seventh — there is a stark contrast between what Judaism *has become* in comparison to what the Old Testament teaches. Judaism couldn't properly be named "Judaism" until after Judah came into being![2] Let me state this more succinctly: Judaism is an off-shoot, or deviation, from the Old Testament.

In Old Testament days, when Israelites followed the clear teachings of the Old Testament Scripture, they were following the true religion. Obviously, if

---

1. Mesbah Uddin, "Prophet Muhammad Was Revered as the Jewish Messiah in Medina," Media Monitors Network, March 3, 2008, http://usa.mediamonitors.net/Headlines/Prophet-Muhammad-was-Revered-as-the-Jewish-Messiah-in-Medina.
2. The name Jew/Jews was first used in the Book of 2 Kings 16:6 and 25:25, being men of Judah. If one tries to use this argument about Christianity not coming into being until Christ, then there is a flaw, as Christ is the Creator and preeminent to all things.

they were not following the Old Testament, they were not being godly and thus were not following the true religion!

In the first century, however, there was a division among those who followed the Old Testament: those of the Way (i.e., Christianity — e.g., Acts 19:23, 24:14) who followed Christ as the Jewish Messiah and all the implications thereof, and those who did not follow Jesus and were finally organized into the Jewish religion of Judaism, based on traditions as opposed to finding true freedom in the Messiah.

What Are the Holy Books in Judaism?

Where Christians follow the Old and New Testament Scriptures, those holding to Judaism follow the Old Testament and the Talmud (meaning the Babylonian Talmud).

The Talmud is defined by the World Book Encyclopedia as the following:

> A collection of legal and ethical writings, as well as Jewish history and folklore. It serves primarily as a guide to the civil and religious laws of Judaism. Orthodox Jews believe the laws in the Talmud were given to Moses by God and passed down orally from Generation to Generation. About A.D. 200, scholars wrote down these oral laws in a work called the *Mishnah*. Later scholars explained and interpreted the Mishnah. Their comments were recorded in the *Gemara*, which was written between 200 and 500. The Mishnah and Gemara together make up the Talmud.[3]

There is also a less authoritative Talmud that was compiled by about A.D. 400 called the Talmud of the Land of Israel (or the Jerusalem Talmud). It also contains two parts, a Mishnah and Gemara, but is shorter overall than the Babylonian Talmud.

The Talmud is made up of the traditions that were often spoken of in the New Testament (e.g., Matthew 15:3; Colossians 2:8; etc.). Of course, they were still in oral form at the time of Christ. There were times when Jews elevated these traditions above the Scriptures of the Old Testament (e.g., Matthew 15:4–9; Mark 7:3–13), hence they came to the wrong conclusions on certain issues such as, "Sabbath was made for man, and not man for the Sabbath"(Mark 2:27). This is why interpretation of Scripture is best done by

3. World Book Encyclopedia, Volume 11, Entry: Judaism, World Book, Inc., 1990, p. 178.

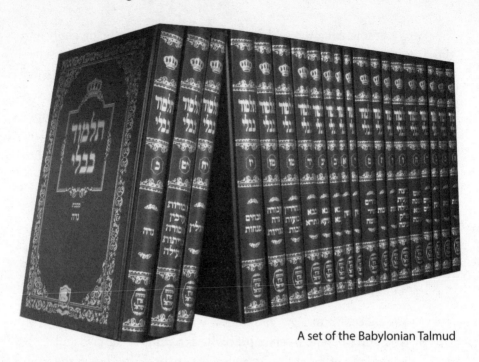

A set of the Babylonian Talmud

Scripture itself, as God is the best interpreter of His own Word, instead of relying strictly on the ideas of "scholars."

The infiltration of man's ideas has been a major issue in the history of the Israelite nation. How often does the Old Testament record deviations from the Word of God where Israelites began worshiping Baal or setting up high places to false gods? How many times did the Lord send prophets to call the Israelites back to His Word? Even the wise Solomon himself succumbed to the worship of false gods!

These types of seeds finally flourished into a version where man's interpretations of the Old Testament (in the form of the Talmud's Gemara) began to supersede the very Word of God. It becomes a major problem when man's ideas are elevated to be greater than the Word of God. Consider the words of Isaiah:

> Stop regarding man, whose breath of life is in his nostrils; for why should he be esteemed? (Isaiah 2:22; NASB).

What Are the Beliefs within Judaism?

Of course, it would require extensive time to develop all the beliefs within Judaism. So I will be concise in this section. But something must be stated up front: many who are Jews do not hold to Judaism. There are many who are secular (that is, the primary humanistic religion) and are of Jewish heritage. So just because someone says they are Jewish doesn't necessarily mean they hold to the tenets of Judaism. However, for the sake of simplicity, when I say "Jew" in this chapter on Judaism, I mean those who hold to the religion of Judaism, unless the context warrants otherwise.

Judaism is a set of informal beliefs about the world and how people should live their lives. Although Jewish beliefs vary, they can be summed up by medieval Jewish scholar Moshi ben Maimon's (Maimonides) 13 articles:

1. God alone exists and is Creator
2. God is one and unique
3. God is incorporeal and incomparable
4. God is eternal (both first and last)
5. We are to pray to God alone and to no other
6. The words of the prophets are true
7. Moses was the chief prophet, and Moses' prophecies are true
8. The Torah (first five books of the Bible) and oral Torah (Talmud) were given to Moses and divinely preserved
9. There will be no other Torah since it cannot be changed
10. God knows all things including the thoughts and deeds of men
11. God will reward the righteous and punish the wicked
12. The Messiah will come
13. The dead will be resurrected.[4]

Take note that Christians easily agree with most of these points. However, a Christian would disagree with the idea that the Talmud is of divine origin. Replacing the Talmud with the New Testament (along with the remaining Old Testament books) in point 8 would make this statement accurate. And in point 12, we would change "The Messiah will come" to "The Messiah has come, and He is Jesus of Nazareth."

In addition, although true, I would clarify point 11. All have sinned and fall short of God's glory (Psalm 116:11; Romans 3:23, 5:12), thus all

---

4. Tracey R. Rich, What do Jews Believe? Jewfaq.org, 1995–2011, http://www.jewfaq.org/beliefs.htm; John Parsons, Sheloshah-Asar Ikkarim, Hebrew for Christians website, Accessed April 15, 2015, http://www.hebrew4christians.com/Scripture/Shloshah-Asar-Ikkarim/shloshah-asar_ikkarim.html.

would be classed as sinful, hence wicked in God's eyes. The only way to be *made* righteous would be for God to assign the righteousness of His Son, the Messiah, to us so that we are seen as righteous and pure (clean) in the sight of God. More on this later.

Divisions in Judaism

There are several divisions within modern Judaism. The main divisions in religious outlook are Reform, Conservative, and Orthodox Judaism. This is not to be confused with cultures and traditions of various Jewish groups.

Allow me to explain the history of Jewish groups so that we can better understand the terms. Let's go back about 2,000 years to see the division that existed then. At the time of Christ, there were already divisions in Jewish thought.[5] These groups included Pharisees, Sadducees, Essenes, Scribes, and Zealots. Here are some of their views and differences.[6]

- Pharisees — those who held to strict adherence of the Law of Moses and the Old Testament, but *also* held to oral tradition as the truth. Interestingly, they set aside the divisions set up by God in the Law of Moses (i.e., Levites were required to do certain things for worship and priestly service, but the Pharisees proclaimed these things could be performed by any and all Jews). Positively, they held to the resurrection of the dead. This movement traces its roots back to the Maccabean revolt around 150 B.C. The Pharisaical view became the basis for modern Rabbinic Judaism after the fall of Jerusalem in A.D. 70.

- Sadducees — they trace their roots back to Zadok/Tzadok the priest (1 Kings 1:8) in David and Solomon's day. Their name actually is a variation of Zadok (think "s"adok or Sadoksees) and means "the righteous ones of Zadok." They held the priestly and ruling responsibilities at the Temple with prestigious positions. They did not believe in the resurrection of

---

5. One prior division before the first century that is worthy of note is the Samaritans. They, though not properly Jews, were a group of Israelites that had intermarried with pagans and had a form of primeval Judaism mixed with idolatry. They held to the Books of Moses and no other. They rejected the prophets and the oral traditions but often held to false gods.

6. For more on these groups please see: Daniel Sweet, *Who were the Pharisees, Sadducees, Scribes, Essenes, and Zealots?* God's Word First International Biblical Research & Teaching Ministry, 2010, http://www.gods-word-first.org/jesus-christ/pharisees-sadducees-scribes-zealots.html.

the dead (i.e., no afterlife, Matthew 22:23) and welcomed Roman rule.

- Essenes — they flourished for about 300 years ending prior to A.D. 100, likely due to the Romans. The Essenes may have been a division of the Sadducees and had become one of the three major divisions of the Jews around the first century. They lived in communes and abstained from worldly desires; they lived lives of poverty with very strict rules (think of something like monks and nuns within the Roman Catholic worldview). They were famous for the Dead Sea Scrolls, which were preserved in caves and not found for nearly 2,000 years.

- Scribes — these were highly trained scholars of their day who were often devoted to copying the Scriptures, but also had responsibilities as bankers, judges, governing authorities, and those sought for wisdom on some matters. There are still a few modern-day "Sofers," as they are called, who are scribes that still do work like those in the first century. The Masoretes who meticulously copied the Hebrew Old Testament until the tenth century were Scribes.

- Zealots — these people were often fanatic for the nation of Israel and wanted to try to do away with Roman rule. This group goes back to the Maccabean revolt against Rome that failed in about 150 B.C. They likely influenced many Jews to wage war against Rome, which led to the utter destruction of Jerusalem, the Temple and Sanctuary, and much of Judea (e.g., synagogues) by the Romans from A.D. 66 to 73.

Out of all these divisions, the Pharisaical system basically took over after the destruction of the Temple in A.D. 70 when the Jews were scattered or put into bondage. The added oral traditions, which were seen as Scripture, began to be put into written format about A.D. 200.

After the war with Rome that left millions dead in Judea, those Jews who survived were basically in two groups: those who fled from the grip of Rome and those who were taken captive by Rome. Of course, there were some who were left, but most in the region would fit into these two categories. Many of those taken captive by Rome became slaves that were sent to various parts of the Empire.

Sephardic Jews

Groups of captive Jews were taken by Rome to Spain, Portugal, North Africa, and the Middle East (while some fled "under the radar"). In subsequent years when tensions were reduced, they became their own people known as the Sephardic Jews. This group is divided into two groups. The first is the *Sephardim* in Iberia, or Spain and Portugal, and the *Mazrachim*, which include those in North Africa and the Middle East. Many Sephardic Jews in Spain were expelled in 1492 and made their way to communities among the Mazrachim.

Ashkenazi Jews

The *Ashkenazi* Jews are those who fled to the land of Germany. Ashkenaz was one of Noah's great-grandsons (Genesis 10:3), and it was his progeny that populated Germany.[7] Hence, many Jews refer to this land as "Ashkenaz," and the Ashkenazi Jews were those who lived in Ashkenaz, or Germany.

It makes good sense for Jews fleeing the grip of Rome to go to Germany, since Germany, which is relatively close to Rome, was never fully subdued by Rome. This was the ideal place to reach if you could make your way across the mountainous terrain to get to safety. Germany was also safer for Jews to stretch out to many other places in Europe as Rome's power diminished.

As a side note, this occurrence may be one reason for the tensions we still see today. Consider that these new German hosts were likely bitter about the massive numbers of new arrivals, and it might explain much of the tension between Jews and the Germans that has existed since that time. There were conflicts during the Crusades, and during the Reformation. And one cannot forget the utter devastation at the hands of the evil Nazis. Sadly, there are still tensions in Europe today between Europeans and Jews.

Messianic Jews

Another group called the *Messianic Jews* should really be mentioned at this point. Many Jews who *have* received Jesus Christ as Savior and Messiah in modern times take this name. In many ways, they are merely Christians with Jewish backgrounds or converted Gentiles, but in another respect, they

---

7. Bodie Hodge, *The Tower of Babel* (Green Forest, AR: Master Books, 2012), p. 151–157.

still retain certain aspects of Judaism (e.g., feasts, celebrations, and so on). They hold to the Old and New Testament as Scripture and Christ as the Son of God (one person of the one triune God; see appendix A).

Orthodox, Conservative, and Reform Judaism

As we have seen from our historical review, the modern groups within Judaism are primarily born out of Pharisaical teaching that held the Old Testament and the Talmud (traditions) as supreme authority. Even within this modern Judaism, there are divisions with three being the main groups:

- Orthodox Judaism — a movement holding traditional beliefs and practices such as kosher diets, Sabbath rest, and distinctive dress codes.

- Reform Judaism[8] — a modern movement begun in the 1800s that takes many liberal viewpoints and does away with conservative values and practices that are inherent to Orthodox Judaism.

- Conservative Judaism — a group that tries to balance between Orthodox Judaism and Reform Judaism.

There is one more group that is very prominent today that should be added to this section:

- Secular Judaism — those who still identify as Jews, most often by heritage, but are actually secular humanists (the popular religion of today). They have taken one more step beyond the Reform Judaist position to be purely secular in their religious outlook. They just retain the name for the sake of their ancestry.

Discussion

Now that we are familiar with the names, divisions, and some history of Judaism, let's proceed with the discussion. But before I go any further, let me speak my heart on this issue. I love the Jews, and I have a fondness for

---

8. In Christianity, the term "reformed" means that you go back to the Bible to reform your theology and beliefs to get it close to what God teaches (hence the name "Reform"). Reform Judaism is really the opposite. It seeks to take Judaism and reform it to modern, secular practices and beliefs.

them and have often defended them. But I still have the hope, as the Apostle Paul did (Romans 11:13–14), that they would repent of their sin and receive Jesus as Christ and Lord.

The Jews are loved on account of the patriarchs (Romans 11:28), and so I echo this same love. But like atheists, Muslims, and so many others, the Jews are enemies of the gospel of Jesus Christ, which is the good news that can set them free and guarantee eternal life (John 3:36, 10:28, 17:3; 1 Timothy 1:16; 1 John 5:11). Now that Gentiles have been offered the gospel, this puts Jews and Gentiles under the same need in equal fashion in the eyes of God (Romans 10:12). And with that, there is only one name under heaven that men must be saved (Acts 4:12) and only one way to peace with God for Jew or Gentile, and that is through Jesus Christ (Isaiah 9:6; John 14:6).

Even with many similarities, the differences between Judaism and Christianity are stark. And there is no reason we cannot be open about them.

Arbitrariness and Inconsistency

The Old Testament is the Word of God, and to say otherwise would be arbitrary opinions of man compared to the absolute of God's Word. Christians applaud those in Judaism who hold to the Old Testament as the truth. But at the same time, Judaists deny that the New Testament is the Word of God, based on their own arbitrary opinions.

Furthermore, adding oral traditions to the Word of God is also arbitrary. Naturally, these oral traditions are attributed to Moses by the Jews. But after 1,500 years of oral transmission in the hands of fallible and sinful men who were often in disobedience to the written Word, how can anyone know for sure that they are accurate? In the Old Testament, there were times when most Israelites knew precious little about the *written* Word due to so much false worship, let alone the *oral* traditions.

To prove this point, we could ask why is it that the Jerusalem Talmud and the Babylonian Talmud do not contain the same teachings when certain topics are discussed (e.g., agricultural laws or sacrificial rites and laws at the Temple)? Why do they disagree with each other (one being rather anti-Gentile [Babylonian] and one not so much [Jerusalem])? This shows they were not preserved as the Word of God.

In the two Talmuds, there are opinions of rabbis that disagree with each other concerning Bible passages — too many to cite! Such inconsistencies show that it is not the Word of God nor should it be elevated to a position of being greater than God's Word in the Bible. To cap the debate, Jesus Christ, who is God, affirmed that the traditions of men were not the Word of God and should not to be equated as such (Matthew 15:3–6; Mark 7:8–13).

To summarize, the Word of God was entrusted to the Jews. This is an honorable position — one that should not be taken lightly. All traditions should be judged by the written Word of God rather than allowing the written Word of God to be judged by oral traditions.

Borrowing from the Word of Christ

Obviously, those in Judaism have regarded much of the Bible as the truth, especially the Old Testament. Since Jesus, Immanuel, is God with us (Isaiah 7:14; Matthew 1:23), the Old Testament is His Word. Therefore, Judaists borrow from Jesus' Word for their religion. This helps clarify a misconception. Often, we hear that Christianity was born out of Judaism, but this is not the case. Judaism emerged as a response to Christianity.

The Old Testament is a Christian document that points to Jesus Christ who is the ultimate author of Scripture (Luke 24:27; John 5:46). Professor of Church History Dr. Phillip Schaff rightly states that the Old Testament Jewish religion "was the true religion before Christ but not perfect, or final."[9]

The New Testament, with Christ as the centerpiece, is like a blossomed flower with the Old Testament patriarchs, such as Abraham and Moses and the prophets as the stem, leaves, and roots. But where the New Testament perfected or finalized the Old Testament in God's perfect timing, the Pharisees deviated and held man's ideas in the oral traditions to be greater than God's Word. Judaism is just that: a deviation from the clear teachings of the Old Testament caused by elevating the traditions of men and rejecting the New Testament of God.

In other words, Judaism was born out of an improper understanding of Christ's religion (Old Testament) and a rejection of God's Word in the New Testament, particularly the rejection of the Messiah, Jesus. This happened because they misunderstood the promise, which led to a misunderstanding of its fulfillment.

But since Jews and Christians have the Old Testament in common, there will be some beliefs on which they agree. In fact, Christians and Jews share many similar doctrines because they draw many of them from the same pages of Scripture.

9. Philip Schaff, *Theological Propaedeutic* (New York: Charles Scribner's Sons, 1904), p. 55.

As a side note, Christians break the Old Testament books into 39 while the Jews have a listing that contains about 24. For example, where we split Kings, Chronicles, and Samuel into two books each, the Jews have one book for each of these. Ezra and

Orthodox Jewish men praying in Jerusalem

Nehemiah are put together into a single book, while all 12 of the minor prophets are combined as well. Nevertheless, it is the same content.

As Christians, we share the same foundation in Genesis as the Jews do, as well as draw from the patriarchal roots on up to the final prophets of the Old Testament. We both believe in one God (Genesis 1:1; Deuteronomy 6:4; Ephesians 4:6), hold to marriage as defined by God in the Garden of Eden (Genesis 1:27, 2:24), and have a basis for logic, knowledge, and the truth since we are made in the image of a logical, truthful God (Genesis 1:26–27). We both understand that we live in a sin-cursed and broken world (Genesis 3) and have a need for a Messiah (Deuteronomy 18:15; Daniel 9:25) and an everlasting covenant (Jeremiah 32:40).

There are many other doctrines in common, of course. But the differences begin where we start to see the outworking of the Old Testament as it flows into the New Testament (versus flowing into the Talmud). The Old Testament does not flow in two directions, so one direction must be wrong. The Old Testament naturally flows into the New Testament — its fulfillment. Because of this, there are many differences in doctrines, too many to discuss in one chapter, so we will focus on a few significant ones.

Obviously, diet is one well-known difference. In the New Testament, Jesus Christ (who is God) declared all foods clean in Mark 7:19. This initially shocked Peter, who was devout in his kosher diet (Acts 10:13–16)! The Judaists still maintain strict dietary restrictions (Colossians 2:16; 1 Timothy 4:3).

Christians recognize Jesus as the Messiah, or Christ — God who came in the flesh and dwelt among us (John 1:1, 1:14). But the Judaists still wait for a messiah and have a much lower view of who he will be. Their hope is that he will be a military leader to help free the Jews from some earthly crisis. Consider if the Jews had received Christ as Messiah the first time. Would they still have considered Muhammad to possibly be the Messiah? There would have been no reason to. Would there still be the conflicts with those of the Islamic faith? Only the Lord knows.

Of course, God's Messiah did so much more than the Judaists are looking for. He set us free for all eternity from sin and the cares of this world. The Messiah was put to death — the punishment that we all deserve for sin — to set us free forever. And those in the Messiah (Christ) have nothing to fear when the resurrection comes. Here are just 20 of the many Messianic prophecies in the Old Testament and where they were fulfilled in Jesus:

	Messianic Prophecy	**OT Reference**	**NT Reference**
1	Seed of the Woman	Genesis 3:15	Matthew 1:20; Galatians 4:4
2	Line of Abraham	Genesis 12:3, 22:18	Matthew 1:1–16; Luke 3:23–34
3	Line of Isaac	Genesis 17:19, 21:12	Matthew 1:1–16; Luke 3:23–34
4	Line of Israel	Numbers 24:17	Matthew 1:1–16; Luke 3:23–34
5	Line of Judah	Genesis 28:14	Matthew 1:1–16; Luke 3:23–34
6	Heir of David	2 Samuel 7:12–13; Isaiah 9:7	Matthew 1:1–16; Luke 3:23–34
7	Eternal throne and everlasting Kingdom	2 Samuel 8:13–16; Psalm 45:6–7; Daniel 2:44, 7:13–14	Luke 1:33; Hebrews 1:8–12; 1 Peter 5:11; Jude 1:25; Revelation 1:6
8	He will be a prophet	Deuteronomy 18:18	John 8:28–29
9	Savior of both Israel and Gentiles	Isaiah 49:6	Luke 2:29–32; John 8:12; Acts 13:46

10	Called the Son of God	2 Samuel 7:14; Psalm 2:7	Matthew 3:16–17
11	He will be King	Psalm 2:6; Zechariah 9:9	Matthew 27:37; Revelation 7:14, 19:16
12	He will resurrect	Psalm 16:10, 49:15	Matthew 28:2–7; Acts 2:22–32
13	Sits on the throne of God	Psalm 68:18, 110:1	Matthew 22:44; Mark 16:19
14	He would be a sacrifice for sin	Isaiah 53:5–12	Romans 5:6–8
15	He would be pierced in His side	Zechariah 12:10	John 19:34
16	As in a proper Passover sacrifice, His bones would not be broken	Exodus 12:46; Psalm 34:20	John 19:33–36
17	His hands and feet would be pierced	Psalm 22:16	John 20:25–27
18	Born in Bethlehem	Micah 5:2	Matthew 2:1; Luke 2:4–6
19	Born of a virgin*	Isaiah 7:14	Matthew 1:22–23
20	Called Immanuel (God with us)	Isaiah 7:14	Matthew 1:22–23

---

* The Judaist often professes that this doesn't mean "virgin" but merely "young woman." Refuting this, famed reformer John Calvin wrote in his commentary on Isaiah 7:14, "Although the word עלמה, (gnalmah,) a virgin, is derived *from* עלם, (gnalam,) which signifies to hide, because the shame and modesty of virgins does not allow them to appear in public; yet as the Jews dispute much about that word, and assert that it does not signify virgin, because Solomon used it to denote a young woman who was betrothed, it is unnecessary to contend about the word. Though we should admit what they say, *that* עלמה (gnalmah) sometimes denotes a young woman, and that the name refers, as they would have it, to the age (yet it is frequently used in Scripture when the subject relates to a virgin), the nature of the case sufficiently refutes all their slanders. For what wonderful thing did the Prophet say, if he spoke of a young woman who conceived through intercourse with a man? It would certainly have been absurd to hold out this as a sign or a miracle. Let us suppose that it denotes a young woman who should become pregnant in the ordinary course of nature; everybody sees that it would have been silly and contemptible for the Prophet, after having said that he was about to speak of something strange and uncommon, to add, A young woman shall conceive. It is, therefore, plain enough that he speaks of a virgin who should conceive, not by the ordinary course of nature, but by the gracious influence of the Holy *Spirit*."

Where Jews have looked to sacrifice and their good works for the possibility of salvation, Christians have looked to the ultimate sacrifice of Jesus in whom they believe and have faith and the assurance of salvation. Faith, or belief in God and what He has done, has always been the means of salvation. Those prior to Jesus looked forward to Him for their salvation in the same way Christians now look back to Christ for our salvation.

But salvation has always been of God alone. This is a major point of disagreement between Judaism and Christianity. The Judaist holds works to be essential, but the Christian holds faith in Christ through grace as the means of salvation. Christians do good works to please God, not to gain salvation. Leading modern Jews Dennis Prager and Joseph Telushkin write,

> Judaism stresses action more than faith.[10]

> The major difference between Judaism and Christianity lies in the importance each religion attaches to faith and actions. In Judaism, God considers people's action to be more important than their faith; acting in accordance with biblical and rabbinic law is the Jews' central obligation.[11]

This naturally has implication for theology. Consider what Prager and Telushkin continue to say:

> According to Judaism, one can be a good Jew while doubting God's existence, so long as one acts in accordance with Jewish law.[12]

> It is not, of course, our intention to deny the centrality of God in Judaism, but merely to emphasize that Judaism can be appreciated and practiced independently of one's present level of belief in God.[13]

Where Jews look to works for the *possibility* of salvation, the Bible teaches that works can't save a person. Sin still needs to be punished by an infinite and perfectly holy and just God. Josh McDowell pointed out the crux of the difference when he wrote:

---

10. Dennis Prager and Joseph Telushkin, *The Nine Questions People Ask About Judaism* (New York, NY: Simon & Schuster, 1975), p. 18.
11. Ibid., p. 78.
12. Ibid., p. 18.
13. Ibid., p. 19.

Judaism, while admitting the existence of sin, its abhorrence by God, and the necessity for atonement, has not developed a system of salvation teaching as found in Christianity. Atonement is accomplished by sacrifices, penitence, good deeds, and a little of God's grace. No concept of substitutionary atonement (as in Christianity in the person of Jesus Christ) exists.[14]

Yes, sin still needs to be dealt with properly — going back to the first sin in Genesis 3. Just as the coats of skins in Genesis 3:21, Abel's fat portions in Genesis 4:4, and Noah's sacrifices of clean animals after the Flood in Genesis 8:20, each pointed forward to the sacrificial laws given by Moses, so these sacrifices, as well as the Levitical sacrifices, ultimately pointed to Christ's final and eternal sacrifice once and for all (Hebrews 7:27, 9:12, 10:10). The sacrifices before the Law, and as a result of the Law, were still not sufficient to satisfy God's full wrath upon sin. They were mere shadows of what was to come in the blood of the ultimate Lamb of God, the Lord Jesus Christ.

The Bible makes it clear that the blood of bulls and goats are not sufficient to satisfy the wrath of God upon sin (Hebrews 10:4). An even better sacrifice, a sufficient sacrifice, was needed. And Christ, who is God, was that all-sufficient sacrifice (2 Corinthians 5:21). The Old Testament sacrifices pointed to the ultimate sacrifice of Jesus Christ on the Cross.

We (and the animals used in sacrifice) are only created beings — far less than the eternal God. No created being could take the punishment we deserve from an uncreated, infinite God. God Himself was the only one in a position to remedy His punishment upon sin. God, the infinite Son, Jesus, became a man fulfilling the promised seed of the woman (Genesis 3:15) and was the fulfilled seed of Abraham, Isaac, Jacob, Judah, and heir of David. The infinite Son, Jesus, took the infinite punishment from God, the infinite Father, when He was offered up as our ultimate Passover Lamb by the high priest of Israel nearly 2,000 years ago (Matthew 26:62–66; 1 Corinthians 5:7).

This is what makes salvation possible — not by our works, but by the necessary work of God so that He alone receives the glory. Salvation comes as a person repents of sin and receives Jesus Christ as Lord and Savior. And then Christ's righteousness is imputed to the sinner — whether Jew or Gentile. This is why sacrificial and ceremonial laws have been done away with

---

14. Josh McDowell, *A Ready Defense*, compiled by Bill Wilson (Nashville, TN: Thomas Nelson Publishers, 1993), p. 301.

— they are no longer necessary because they've been fulfilled in Christ. This is also why the Temple is no longer necessary. The body of the believer is now the new temple of the Holy Spirit (1 Corinthians 3:16, 6:19).

Where Judaists still hope for a new covenant (Jeremiah 31:31), Christians have recognized the coming of the new covenant (an eternal covenant) already in Christ's blood (Luke 22:20). He is our ultimate Passover Lamb (1 Corinthians 5:7). And we want those raised in Judaism to realize that they, too, need to receive Jesus the Messiah to be saved (Acts 4:12).

Although not a uniquely Jewish symbol before the 19th century, the Star of David, or Shield of David as it is known in Hebrew, has become a modern symbol of Judaism and the Jewish state of Israel.

Conclusion

Few realize that Christians have been among those who have supported the Jews for many years in their plight, not only because of their love for the ethnic Israelites, but for the sake of the biblical patriarchs. Even though many Israelites have been saved over the last 2,000 years, it seems that many Jews have been blind to the gospel for so long, yet the door seems so open for Gentiles. Why is that?

To answer this question, we first need to remember that God is the God of both the Jew *and* the Gentile (Romans 3:29)! What has happened is that Gentile believers have been grafted into the root of Israel in the same way that Ruth (a Moabite) and Rahab (a Canaanite) were grafted into Israel.

Sadly, by the rejection of God's Redeemer, Jesus the Christ, many Jews have been pruned from the tree of Israel. An Israelite Pharisee, Saul (Paul), who became a Christian nearly 2,000 years ago, writes about this mystery of why many Jews have been blinded to the truth (and only a remnant saved) and why the miracle of Gentiles being saved is so significant. He writes in the Book of Romans:

> So then faith comes by hearing, and hearing by the word of God. But I say, have they not heard? Yes indeed: "Their sound

has gone out to all the earth, and their words to the ends of the world." But I say, did Israel not know? First Moses says: "I will provoke you to jealousy by those who are not a nation, I will move you to anger by a foolish nation." But Isaiah is very bold and says: "I was found by those who did not seek Me; I was made manifest to those who did not ask for Me." But to Israel he says: "All day long I have stretched out My hands to a disobedient and contrary people."

I say then, has God cast away His people? Certainly not! For I also am an Israelite, of the seed of Abraham, of the tribe of Benjamin. God has not cast away His people whom He foreknew. Or do you not know what the Scripture says of Elijah, how he pleads with God against Israel, saying, "Lord, they have killed Your prophets and torn down Your altars, and I alone am left, and they seek my life"? But what does the divine response say to him? "I have reserved for Myself seven thousand men who have not bowed the knee to Baal." Even so then, at this present time there is a remnant according to the election of grace.

And if by grace, then it is no longer of works; otherwise grace is no longer grace. But if it is of works, it is no longer grace; otherwise work is no longer work. What then? Israel has not obtained what it seeks; but the elect have obtained it, and the rest were blinded. Just as it is written: "God has given them a spirit of stupor, eyes that they should not see and ears that they should not hear, to this very day." And David says: "Let their table become a snare and a trap, a stumbling block and a recompense to them. Let their eyes be darkened, so that they do not see, and bow down their back always."

I say then, have they stumbled that they should fall? Certainly not! But through their fall, to provoke them to jealousy, salvation has come to the Gentiles. Now if their fall is riches for the world, and their failure riches for the Gentiles, how much more their fullness! For I speak to you Gentiles; inasmuch as I am an apostle to the Gentiles, I magnify my ministry, if by any means I may provoke to jealousy those who are my flesh and save some of them. For if their being cast away is the reconciling of the world, what will their acceptance be but life from the dead?

For if the firstfruit is holy, the lump is also holy; and if the root is holy, so are the branches. And if some of the branches were broken off, and you, being a wild olive tree, were grafted in among them, and with them became a partaker of the root and fatness of the olive tree, do not boast against the branches. But if you do boast, remember that you do not support the root, but the root supports you. You will say then, "Branches were broken off that I might be grafted in." Well said. Because of unbelief they were broken off, and you stand by faith. Do not be haughty, but fear. For if God did not spare the natural branches, He may not spare you either.

Therefore consider the goodness and severity of God: on those who fell, severity; but toward you, goodness, if you continue in His goodness. Otherwise you also will be cut off. And they also, if they do not continue in unbelief, will be grafted in, for God is able to graft them in again. For if you were cut out of the olive tree which is wild by nature, and were grafted contrary to nature into a cultivated olive tree, how much more will these, who are natural branches, be grafted into their own olive tree? For I do not desire, brethren, that you should be ignorant of this mystery, lest you should be wise in your own opinion, that blindness in part has happened to Israel until the fullness of the Gentiles has come in. And so all Israel will be saved (Romans 10:17–11:26; NKJV).

As Christians, we need to remember that we, too, were enemies of God until the Holy Spirit saved us (1 Corinthians 12:3; Colossians 1:21). This is why our prayer is for those caught in Judaism to be set free by the promised Messiah, Christ Jesus our Lord. Our hope is for those in Judaism to receive the final Passover Lamb, Jesus, to have peace with God once and for all.

Just as God often left a remnant in the Old Testament, so a remnant of Israelites joined the firstfruits of the fulfillment of the Old Testament, such as Peter, Paul, John, Matthew, and many others. But the door is still open, as both Jews and Gentiles are called upon to receive Christ to be saved by the same measure (Acts 15:3–9; Romans 10:12). Gentiles, who were seen as unclean sinners by the Jews, are now made clean by the work of the Lord.

Is anything too hard for God (Jeremiah 32:27)? Is it too hard for God to take a pruned, natural branch and re-graft it in? Not at all! By receiving the Messiah, Jesus Christ, the natural branch will be made fruitful again.

Summary of Jewish Beliefs

Doctrine	Judaism's Teaching
God	Deny the Trinity; there is only one God; Jesus is not the Son of God or the Messiah; the Holy Spirit is not a person
Authority/ Revelation	39 books of the Old Testament; Talmud; various rabbis and traditions
Man	Man is created in the image of God; mankind is fallen as a result of Adam's sin; man is able to attain perfection
Sin	Disobeying the laws prescribed in the Old Testament
Salvation	Salvation is possible through the obedience of the individual to biblical and rabbinical laws; atonement is accomplished through personal acts of sacrifice and penitence; some see the future Messiah or the future restoration of the Temple sacrifices as a means of atonement
Creation	The universe and all that is in it was created out of nothing in six, 24-hour days about 6,000 years ago; all living things were created according to their kinds in supernatural acts of God; mankind was specially created by God in supernatural acts; many modern groups would accept certain forms of evolution

Chapter 10

Mormonism

Roger Patterson

As the story goes, a young man named Joe in upstate New York in 1820 was seeking after the right church to join. Seeing such strife and contention in the local churches — specifically the Methodists, Baptists, and Presbyterians — the 14-year-old was torn over the claims that each church was the true church. Longing to know the truth, Joe turned to the Bible where he read from the Epistle of James that those who ask God for wisdom would be given it.

Revival was breaking out in the area where Joe lived, but how could he know which church looked to the Bible to know the truth? Finding a secluded spot in the woods near his home, young Joe knelt down to ask God for wisdom about which church to join.

As Joe began to pray, an overwhelming force bound his body and tongue, and thick darkness enveloped him! Just as he thought he was about to die, a pillar of light descended from heaven delivering him from the power. Before him stood the Heavenly Father and His beloved Son engulfed in light. In answer to Joe's question, the Son told him that all of the creeds of these denominations were an abomination and their professors were all corrupt and that he should join none of them.

After three years of living a rebellious lifestyle, Joe sought another revelation. That night an angel named Moroni appeared to him and told young Joe that God had a great work for him and that he would receive a book written on plates of gold that contained the fullness of the everlasting gospel. Joe was to found a new church and restore the truth to the world — an answer to his prayer and the beginning of a legacy that continues almost 200 years later.[1]

History of the Church

You probably know the followers of young Joseph Smith Jr. as the Mormons. While officially called the Church of Jesus Christ of Latter-day Saints, or LDS, the common name comes from one of the books they consider to be "another testament of Jesus Christ," *The Book of Mormon.* The LDS Church claims to have over 15 million members spread across the globe and gathering in 29,000 local congregations (known as wards). They send missionaries to hundreds of countries and publish their literature in nearly 200 different languages. In 2014, there were a reported 84,000 Mormon missionaries actively

Portrait of Joseph Smith Jr., circa 1842

spreading the faith on six continents. There are nearly 150 temples used for religious rituals, with more being built each year. Additionally, the church runs three universities named after Brigham Young, an early prophet, in Utah, Idaho, and Hawaii.[2]

The Mormon Church was originally established in April of 1830 in Palmyra, New York, after Joseph had received golden plates from the angel Moroni and translated it to produce *The Book of Mormon.* As the message of the "restored gospel" spread, Joseph gained followers in New York, and soon there were followers and missionaries spreading the religion. It was necessary to restore the gospel because the true gospel laws and ordinances

---

1. For the full account of the First Vision in Joseph's own words, see "Joseph Smith — History," chapter 1, at https://www.lds.org/scriptures/pgp/js-h/1. It is also worth noting that the account of what happened during the First Vision changed over time, and there are discrepancies in the various accounts. The official version was recorded in 1839, almost 20 years after the original event.
2. "Facts and Statistics," accessed March 3, 2015, http://www.mormonnewsroom.org/facts-and-statistics.

had been lost shortly after the Apostles died — a time known as the great Apostasy.[3] Commanded to gather in Kirtland, Ohio, the LDS temple was built in 1836 as missionaries continued westward, establishing a community in Independence, Missouri, and proselytizing in Europe. A prophecy by Smith identified a valley near Independence as the original location of the Garden of Eden and the future site of the New Jerusalem, so the cornerstone of a temple was placed there but not completed.

Brigham Young

Eventually forced out of these areas by persecution, including the killing of many Mormons, Brigham Young led the growing congregation to establish the city of Nauvoo, Illinois, while Joseph Smith was imprisoned. Eventually escaping to Nauvoo, Joseph Smith took over as mayor and military leader, directing the building of the town and a large temple completed in 1846. However, the temple was completed only after Joseph Smith had been killed in a battle with a mob while he was under arrest in Carthage, Illinois, for treason. It was during this period in Missouri and Illinois that the doctrines most identified with the early Mormons, including baptisms for the dead and polygynous[4] marriage, were proclaimed by Joseph Smith (though plural marriages had been occurring since the time in Kirtland, Ohio).

After Smith's death, there was a dispute over the succession of leadership. This led to the eventual formation of several sects with various church leaders claiming authority. The largest surviving offshoot today is the Reorganized Church of Jesus Christ of Latter Day Saints (now known as The Community of Christ) under the eventual leadership of Smith's eldest son, Joseph Smith III, who was 11 at the time of his father's death. At the time of this succession crisis, other smaller sects led by prominent leaders formed and moved to different areas of the country, but the main denomination

---

3. "Apostasy," LDS.org, accessed April 8, 2015, https://www.lds.org/topics/apostasy.
4. While the practice is commonly referred to as polygamy, the Mormon doctrine only allowed men to marry multiple wives, so polygyny is a more accurate term. Within Mormonism, the euphemistic term "plural marriage" is generally used to avoid the stigma of polygamy.

that survives today was led by Brigham Young. After the Mormons had migrated to the Utah Territory in waves beginning in 1846, the main-line church was established. Since that establishment, various groups have split from the main branch over issues such as the doctrine of plural marriage. The groups identify themselves as Fundamentalist LDS groups (FLDS), believing that they are remaining faithful to the teachings of Joseph Smith that were abandoned by the leadership in Salt Lake City.

The Salt Lake Temple

Once they arrived in the Great Salt Lake valley, the pioneers began constructing a temple and the city that became Salt Lake City, Utah. The temple remains today, and the headquarters for the church are located just across the street. It is from here that the office of the president passed from Brigham Young through 13 other men to the current president, Thomas S. Monson. The president is the head of the church and is a modern prophet, seer, and revelator along with the two members of the First Presidency and the Quorum of the Twelve Apostles. Along with these 15 leaders, there are Quorums of Seventy, each with a president, to fulfill different functions of leadership and counsel over various church organizations. At the local level, stake presidents govern the various bishoprics, which serve the local groups called wards. The structure and function of these authorities are laid out in *Doctrine and Covenants* (*D&C*) section 107. These positions do not receive any direct compensation and are considered service positions.

Worship Practices

The typical Mormon attends a worship service and Sunday school classes on a Sunday. These meetings take place in the ward chapels, where several local wards make up a stake (similar to a presbytery or diocese). Meetings of the ward and the stake are held regularly. On a Sunday, the service and meetings would look very much like a typical evangelical church. There is a sacrament meeting of the whole ward where hymns are sung, communion of bread and water is offered, prayers are spoken, and speakers present teaching. Other classes are offered for separate ages and teach on topics from the Mormon scriptures. There are also meetings of the stake and biannual general conference meetings in Salt Lake City, which are broadcast around the world.

Additionally, Mormons have temples all over the world. As of 2015, there were 144 temples on six continents with more under construction. While the ward chapels are used for Sabbath worship by anyone, entrance into the temples is generally restricted to members of the church in good standing. Certain portions of the temples are restricted to those holding certain levels of the Mormon priesthood and those they are ministering to, and an identification card, called a temple recommend, is necessary for entrance. This is only granted to those who are living a faithful life as a Mormon as determined by the ward bishop.

The temples are used to practice the various ordinances that Joseph Smith received in his revelations and visions. One of the primary rituals is the endowment ceremony where doctrines are taught and certain ceremonies are performed. This ceremony typically happens just before young people go on their mission or before they are married. Converts can also receive this endowment. Marriages of Mormons are performed in the temple, and there are also special ceremonies where families are sealed to one another so that they can be together in eternity forever. The other main activities that happen in the temples are ordinances for the dead. Proxy baptisms are performed for dead family members and others (hence the emphasis on genealogical study among Mormons) so that they may participate in eternal life even if they were not baptized on earth. Sealing ordinances are also performed by proxy on behalf of other people so that their marriages and families may also continue in life after death.

Authority

When we talk about any worldview or religious system, it is important to understand where the authority in that system is drawn from. Mormonism is a relatively young religious system founded less than 200 years ago in 1830. In the vision that Joseph Smith claimed to see God the Father and

238 — World Religions and Cults

Jesus, he was told that there were no true churches on the earth. In light of that, Joseph claimed that he was told that he would be shown the truth so that the gospel could be restored to the earth. Mormons believe that it is under the direction of God the Father, typically referred to as Heavenly Father, through visions and revelations given to Joseph Smith that the fullness of the gospel has been revealed to mankind. Mormons claim that the God of the Bible is their ultimate authority, but because they believe in modern revelation through prophets and individual revelation through messengers from heaven, it is hard to justify that claim on a practical level.

The Mormons look to four written revelations as their scriptures (see section below), but they hold to the teaching that God has different plans in effect during different dispensations. Unfortunately, this becomes an arbitrary device by which any contradictions between their scriptures or the pronouncements of their prophets can be written off as God employing different rules at different times. For example, *The Book of Mormon* (*BoM*) condemns the polygamous relationships of David and Solomon (Jacob 2:23–29) and tells the readers not to participate in such abominations. In the early printings of the *Doctrine & Covenants* from 1835 to 1876, there was a strict condemnation of polygamy: "Inasmuch as this Church of Christ has been reproached with the crime of fornication, and polygamy: we declare that we believe, that one man should have one wife; and one woman but one husband, except in the case of death, when either is at liberty to marry again."[5] Later, under pressure of the U.S. Federal Government, polygamy was disavowed by Mormon President Wilford Woodruff after he claimed to have had a new revelation about the damage that would come to the church if polygamy continued.[6] Since that declaration in 1890, the LDS Church has officially forbidden polygamy, though there have been hidden instances within the church. The changing nature of these revelations, and other doctrinal changes, makes true authority an elusive and ever-moving target for the followers. Peering in from the outside, it is hard to see anything other than a system that constantly changes to fit new situations in the culture as new "revelations" are received.

5. This prohibition against polygamy was included in the original section 101:4 in printings up to 1876. At this point, the new revelation about the allowance for polygamy was included in sections 132:51–66, so the contradictory passage was removed. Jerald and Sandra Tanner, *The Changing World of Mormonism* (Chicago, IL: Moody Press, 1980), p. 205–207.
6. The declaration can be read in full at "Official Declaration 1," LDS Website, accessed March 16, 2015, https://www.lds.org/scriptures/dc-testament/od/1.

For the modern Mormon, the ultimate authority is vested in the current president of the church, since he is the "prophet, seer, and revelator" of the current dispensation. Elder Merrill C. Oaks, a member of the Council of the Seventy, presents the case for obedience to the modern prophet:

> Just over two years before his death, the Prophet Joseph Smith published the Articles of Faith. The ninth article of faith states, "We believe all that God has revealed, all that He does now reveal, and we believe that He will yet reveal many great and important things pertaining to the Kingdom of God." I will speak concerning the final sentence, "He will yet reveal many great and important things pertaining to the Kingdom of God." This principle of continuing revelation is an essential part of the kingdom of God. In the fourth and fifth verses of the Doctrine and Covenants section 21, the Lord declared to the Church their obligation to heed the guidance of His prophet: "Wherefore, meaning the church, thou shalt give heed unto all his words and commandments which he shall give unto you as he receiveth them, walking in all holiness before me; For his word ye shall receive, as if from mine own mouth, in all patience and faith."[7]

This continuing revelation denies the Christian doctrines of the inerrancy, sufficiency, and authority of the Bible as the source of authority for all areas of life. The Bible is not the ultimate authority for the LDS faithful, but instead it is the changing ideas of man as they receive ongoing revelations.

Mormon Beliefs

While the LDS Church would claim to be a part of the wider Christian tradition, the beliefs that they hold place them outside of traditional and biblical orthodoxy. Of late, the LDS church has made a significant effort to be included in the broad community of Christianity. This has not always been the case. Early prophets and teachers in the church sought to distinguish Mormons from Christians, teaching that all of the other expressions of Christianity had been corrupted beyond salvage. Modern media campaigns have sought to reverse this previous attempt at distinction, calling Christians to embrace Mormons as brothers and sisters in Christ. However, from their

7. Merrill C. Oaks, "The Living Prophet: Our Source of Pure Doctrine," *Liahona*, January, 1999, https://www.lds.org/liahona/1999/01/the-living-prophet-our-source-of-pure-doctrine.

understanding of who God is to their understanding of what awaits individuals in the afterlife, the majority of Mormon doctrines do not pass the test of being consistent with what is revealed in the Bible. Let's examine some of these key doctrines to expose the differences and make clear the chasm that separates Mormonism from biblical Christianity.

The Godhead

At a fundamental level, the Mormon view of the Godhead denies the biblical trinitarian explanation. In contrast to the biblical view of trinitarian monotheism, with God the Father, God the Son, and God the Holy Spirit as three persons in one God, Mormonism teaches that there are many gods. In its truest sense, Mormonism is a polytheistic religion since they believe that there are many gods occupying different sections of the universe. More accurately, Mormonism is henotheistic — they acknowledge many Gods but worship only the gods connected with this planet. The first Article of Faith sates: "We believe in God, the Eternal Father, and in His Son, Jesus Christ, and in the Holy Ghost." Notice the distinction of three beings rather than the trinitarian expression from confessions such as the Athanasian Creed. The online resources of the LDS church describe their view of God:

> These three beings make up the Godhead. They preside over this world and all other creations of our Father in Heaven. The Mormon view of the members of the Godhead corresponds in a number of ways with the views of others in the Christian world, but with significant differences. Latter-day Saints pray to God the Father in the name of Jesus Christ. They acknowledge the Father as the ultimate object of their worship, the Son as Lord and Redeemer, and the Holy Spirit as the messenger and revealer of the Father and the Son. But where Latter-day Saints differ from other Christian religions is in their belief that God and Jesus Christ are glorified, physical beings and that each member of the Godhead is a separate being.[8]

While Mormons deny that God is a Trinity, the gods they worship are described as being united in their purpose: "Although the members of the Godhead are distinct beings with distinct roles, they are one in purpose and

---

8. "Godhead," LDS.org, accessed March 19, 2015, https://www.lds.org/topics/godhead.

doctrine. They are perfectly united in bringing to pass Heavenly Father's divine plan of salvation."[9] The Mormon godhead is three divine persons united in purpose, not in being.

Heavenly Father

The Heavenly Father of Mormonism, called Elohim, was once a man who was created by another god (who was created by another god) and earned his status as a god by being glorified through obedience to his spiritual father. Unlike the biblical doctrine of the eternal nature of the triune God, the chief god of Mormonism is a created being who progressed through degrees of sanctification to eventually become exalted as a god. This is known as the law of eternal progression and applies to all spiritual beings in the universe. Humans can achieve godhood by being obedient to the "laws and ordinances of the gospel" defined by Heavenly Father. Additionally, Heavenly Father is a man of flesh and blood who has been exalted. He is not a spirit, but a man with a physical body. He is said to currently reside on a planet near the star Kolob (Abraham 3:1–4). In this doctrine, the LDS deny the biblical doctrine of omnipresence.

Joseph F. Smith, the sixth LDS president, wrote the following about Heavenly Father:

> I do not believe in the doctrine held by some that God is only a Spirit and that he is of such a nature that he fills the immensity of space, and is everywhere present in person, or without person, for I can not [sic] conceive it possible that God could be a person . . . . God the Eternal Father, whom we designate by the exalted name-title "Elohim," is the literal Parent of our Lord and Savior Jesus Christ, and of the spirits of the human race. Elohim is the Father in every sense in which Jesus Christ is so designated, and distinctively He is the Father of spirits.[10]

Even though the Mormon prophets constantly refer to the Father as an eternal being, there is no normal sense in which he can be eternal if he was once a man who was exalted to godhood. The teaching of god as an exalted man was an explicit teaching of Joseph Smith and has been perpetuated by all of

9. Ibid.
10. "Teachings of the Presidents of the Church: Joseph F. Smith," chapter 40, "The Father and the Son," https://www.lds.org/manual/teachings-joseph-f-smith/chapter-40

the LDS prophets. In a sermon delivered to the LDS gathered at a conference in 1844, Smith gave what is commonly called the King Follett sermon where he plainly described the character and origin of his god:

> God himself was once as we are now, and is an exalted man, and sits enthroned in yonder heavens! That is the great secret. If the veil were rent today, and the great God who holds this world in its orbit, and who upholds all worlds and all things by His power, was to make himself visible — I say, if you were to see him today, you would see him like a man in form — like yourselves in all the person, image, and very form as a man; for Adam was created in the very fashion, image and likeness of God, and received instruction from, and walked, talked and conversed with Him, as one man talks and communes with another. . . . for I am going to tell you how God came to be God. We have imagined and supposed that God was God from all eternity. I will refute that idea, and take away the veil, so that you may see. These ideas are incomprehensible to some, but they are simple. It is the first principle of the gospel to know for a certainty the character of God, and to know that we may converse with Him as one man converses with another, and that He was once a man like us; yea, that God himself, the Father of us all, dwelt on an earth, the same as Jesus Christ Himself did; and I will show it from the Bible.[11]

Lorenzo Snow, the fifth president, coined a well-known couplet to portray the law of eternal progression: "As man now is, God once was: As God now is, man may be."[12] While the Bible teaches that Christians are increasingly conformed into the image of Jesus Christ in godly character and will be ultimately glorified (Romans 8:28–30), to become a god with the same nature as God is far from orthodox biblical teaching.[13]

The natural extension of believing that Heavenly Father is a man of flesh and bones is to understand that he has at least one wife with whom

---

11. Joseph Smith, Jr., "The King Follett Sermon," *Ensign*, April 1971, https://www.lds.org/ensign/1971/04/the-king-follett-sermon.

12. "Becoming Like God," LDS.org, https://www.lds.org/topics/becoming-like-god.

13. The teaching of *theosis* or *divinization* has had various expressions in Christianity, but the idea that humans will become gods is not taught in the Bible. Humans are creatures that will never fully exhibit the divine nature of God.

he created the spirit children who would receive bodies to become humans. While the Mormon teaching on the Heavenly Mother is limited, she does not receive worship. Some in the LDS church, including President Brigham Young, have taught that there are multiple mothers, in line with polygamous earthly and celestial marriages, but this idea is not official doctrine of the church.

Table 1: A Comparison of the Mormon and Biblical Views of God the Father

Mormon God the Father	Biblical God the Father
A created being produced as a spirit child of another god and his wife	An eternal being of the same substance as the Son and the Spirit
Exalted to godhood by obedience to his father	Eternally God
Father of all spiritual beings, including Jesus	The Creator of all other beings outside the Trinity
One of three persons who are gods over earth	One of the three persons of the trinitarian Godhead
Seeks counsel from other gods to make his plans	Exercise absolute sovereign rule over the universe
A product of Joseph Smith described in contradictory ways in various revelations	Reveals Himself consistently in the Bible

Jesus

The Mormon view of Jesus diverges from the biblical Jesus in many of the same ways as God the Father. Jesus, also referred to as Jehovah, is believed to be the firstborn spirit child of Heavenly Father and Mother in a period and state known as the preexistence. Thus, the Mormon can affirm that Jesus is the firstborn over all creation (Colossians 1:15), but they must deny that He is the Creator of all things (Colossians 1:16), since He Himself is a created being and did not create other spiritual beings. But Jesus is not alone as a creature; there have been billions of spirit beings sired by the Heavenly Father who were all together in the preexistence, Jesus being the eldest spirit brother of all. The second-born was Lucifer, making the two spiritual brothers and siblings of all the other spirits. Jesus offered a plan of testing the worthiness of the spirit children that was favored by Elohim over Lucifer's plan. This led to a war in which Lucifer and those spirits who followed him were banished and doomed to exist as demonic spirits until they will be cast into outer darkness (the Mormon notion of hell).

While the Bible teaches that Jesus was born of Mary as a virgin and conceived of the Holy Spirit (Luke 1:26–38), LDS prophets and apostles have taught a different origin. Brigham Young was the first prophet to declare that the Heavenly Father directly sired Jesus with Mary in the flesh and not in a supernatural way: "When the time came that His first-born, the Saviour, should come into the world and take a tabernacle, the Father came Himself and favoured that spirit with a tabernacle instead of letting any other man do it."[14] President Orson Pratt later acknowledged the truth, teaching, "Each God must have one or more wives. God, the Father of our spirits, became the Father of our Lord Jesus Christ according to the flesh. . . . it was the personage of the Father who begat the body of Jesus. . . . The fleshly body of Jesus required a Mother as well as a Father. Therefore, the Father and Mother of Jesus, according to the flesh, must have been associated together in the capacity of Husband and Wife; hence the Virgin Mary must have been, for the time being, the lawful wife of God the Father."[15] In a more modern context, LDS apostle Bruce R. McConkie asserts, "Christ was begotten by an Immortal Father in the same way that mortal men are begotten by mortal fathers."[16] In this, the Mormon can affirm that Jesus is the only begotten Son of the father in the flesh, but not in the biblical sense of being the Son of God.

While many modern Mormons would reject the teaching as authoritative, the prophets and leaders of the church proclaim that Heavenly Father had normal sexual intercourse with Mary to conceive the earthly body of Jesus. This changes the biblical doctrine of the virgin birth into the idea of a virgin conception — the latter is no miracle, as virgins conceive children regularly through intercourse. With these things in mind, the Mormon view

---

14. "To Know God Is Eternal Life," Brigham Young, *Journal of Discourses*, vol. 4:42; available online at http://journalofdiscourses.com/4/42.

15. "Celestial Marriage," Orson Pratt, *The Seer*, (1853), 158. Facsimile available at http://mit.irr.org/files/imagecache/node-gallery-display/seerp158.gif.

16. Bruce R. McConkie, *Mormon Doctrine* (Salt Lake City, UT: Deseret Book, 1966), p. 388. Available in PDF at https://ia601505.us.archive.org/17/items/MormonDoctrine/mormon_doctrine.pdf.

of Jesus might be classified as some form of Arianism since Jesus is a created being that shares some of the nature of God.

Table 2: A Comparison of the Mormon and Biblical View of Jesus

Mormon Jesus the Son	Biblical Jesus
A created being produced as a spirit child of Heavenly Father and Mother	An eternal being of the same substance as the Father and the Spirit
Exalted to godhood by obedience to his father	Eternally God
Spiritual brother of Lucifer and all other beings	The Creator of all other beings outside the Trinity
One of three persons who are gods over earth	One of the three persons of the trinitarian Godhead
Provided a sacrifice that was not sufficient to pay for sins and offer full righteousness	Provided a sufficient sacrifice for sin once and for all to secure perfect righteousness
A spirit who entered a body formed by the sexual union of Elohim and Mary; conceived with a virgin	God who took on flesh; born to a virgin
Organizer of the earth from existing matter	Creator of the universe from nothing

The Holy Ghost

Following the language of the KJV, Mormons typically refer to the Holy Ghost, but also the Holy Spirit, as a third member of the Godhead. The concept of the Spirit is much more orthodox, though they still deny Him as a person of the Trinity. Rather than possessing a physical body, He is only a spirit who works in perfect unity with the Heavenly Father and Jesus to bring about their plans. Mormons believe that the Holy Spirit can influence people to do good and protect from spiritual and physical harm. After baptism, members of the Melchizedek priesthood can lay hands on an individual to impart the gift of the Holy Spirit to them (one of the ordinances of the gospel). This confirmation allows continual companionship of the Spirit if the person is obedient to the ordinances and commandments of the church, and allows them to experience various spiritual gifts.

Mankind

In Mormon thinking, all of humanity are children of the Heavenly Father and Mother(s). Believing that Heavenly Father is a man of flesh and bones, the natural extension is to understand that he has at least one wife with whom he created the spirit children who would receive bodies to become humans. It is the role of families on earth to provide bodies for the spirit children to inhabit and go through the probationary testing here on earth to determine their worthiness to return to live with Heavenly Father.

Because Heavenly Father is an exalted man, Mormons understand that mankind was created in the image of God in a most literal sense — having human form. There is great controversy within the LDS teachings about the nature of the creation of Adam and Eve, since some of the early prophets taught that Adam was Elohim — known as the Adam-God Doctrine. Most modern Mormons reject these inspired teachings of the early prophets as they were instructed to do by later prophets, particularly President Spencer W. Kimball in a 1976 address at the fall General Conference. (Here we find a prime example of the conflicting doctrines taught by the modern LDS prophets who both claim to be directed by their god.)

While the Bible teaches that all of mankind is fallen and damned in Adam (Romans 5:12–19; 1 Corinthians 15:20–28), Mormons acknowledge the consequence of physical death for all of Adam's descendants but not spiritual death. They believe that there is spiritual enmity against God, but that man has an autonomous will (called "free agency") that can strive after holiness and "yield to the enticings of the Holy Spirit."[17] "The Articles of Faith" 1:2 states: "We believe that men will be punished for their own sins, and not for Adam's transgression." Mormons deny any condemnation from original sin, focusing on individual disobedience as the source of any loss of rewards in the afterlife. Therefore, the Fall of man is a positive idea in Mormon theology, since without it the spirits could not be tested and learn and progress toward godhood (2 Nephi 2, *Book of Mormon*).

Salvation

While Jesus Christ appears in the church's name, the "restored gospel" of Joseph Smith is not a biblical expression of the gospel. From "The Articles of Faith," Mormons affirm: "We believe that the first principles and ordinances

---

17. Mosiah 3:19, *The Book of Mormon*.

of the Gospel are: first, Faith in the Lord Jesus Christ; second, Repentance; third, Baptism by immersion for the remission of sins; fourth, Laying on of hands for the gift of the Holy Ghost." And the article that comes just before this states: "We believe that through the Atonement of Christ, all mankind may be saved, by obedience to the laws and ordinances of the Gospel."

As these principal articles of faith are compared to Scripture, a glaring error becomes apparent. At its core, the Mormon view of salvation is one that is based on the works of man, not solely on the perfect life and substitutionary death of Jesus Christ. In 2 Nephi 25:23, the ancient Mormon prophet taught: "For we labor diligently to write, to persuade our children, and also our brethren, to believe in Christ, and to be reconciled to God; for we know that it is by grace that we are saved, after all we can do." The prophet Moroni related grace and works when he said, "Yea, come unto Christ, and be perfected in him, and deny yourselves of all ungodliness; and if ye shall deny yourselves of all ungodliness, and love God with all your might, mind and strength, then is his grace sufficient for you, that by his grace ye may be perfect in Christ; and if by the grace of God ye are perfect in Christ, ye can in nowise deny the power of God" (Moroni 10:32). In both of these citations, grace is only effective in addition to works of personal righteousness and not sufficient for the believer.

While Mormons are fond of talking about the peace they find in the atonement of Jesus, their concept of atonement is an unbiblical one. The Bible repeatedly affirms that the sacrifice of Jesus on the Cross was an act of substitutionary atonement that covered sins completely and requires no work on our part to complete (Ephesians 2:8–10; Titus 3:3–7; Hebrews 9:11–15). In this sense, *atonement* has a different meaning to a Mormon than it does to a Bible-believing Christian. Additionally, Mormons teach that the atoning sacrifice occurred during the suffering in the garden of Gethsemane only to be completed on the Cross.

Degrees of Glory in Heaven and Hell

To claim that Mormonism promotes a form of works-righteous salvation is clear from their teachings, but most Mormons would reject this claim. This is partly because they believe that almost all people will be saved from condemnation that leads to punishment in hell, known as outer darkness, and enter into one of the three levels of heaven (*D&C* 76:31–37, 76:40–45). However,

248 — World Religions and Cults

salvation is only possible if a person exercises faith, repents, receives baptism by immersion, and the laying on of hands by someone with the proper priesthood authority — only then are you born again. Their right standing before God is maintained by their obedience to the laws and ordinances of the gospel and making and keeping covenants in the temple. Only those who obey the Mormon teachings will achieve the ultimate salvation and exaltation to the highest level of heaven known as the Celestial kingdom where Heavenly Father will be (*D&C* 76:50–70, 76:92–96). The concept of three Kingdoms of Glory is drawn from 1 Corinthians 15:40–41, and ignores the biblical understanding of these three heavens referring to the atmosphere of the earth, space where the planets and stars reside, and the heavenly realm where God's presence exists. Based on this passage, the Celestial kingdom has the glory of the sun, the Terrestrial the glory of the moon, and the Telestial the glory of the stars. This is reflected in the architecture of some Mormon temples and the ornamentation on their exterior.

The spirits of those who have been obedient to the gospel rules and principles and have participated in rituals in the temple will proceed to Paradise in the Spirit World and be resurrected with a body of flesh and bone into the Celestial kingdom at the final judgment. Within the Celestial kingdom, there are three degrees of glory available based on obedience (*D&C* 131:1–4). It is generally taught that only those who have participated in temple marriage — sealed for time and all eternity — are eligible for the highest degree and can ultimately be exalted to godhood.

After death, the spirits of those who have not responded to the gospel or continued in the gospel rules and principles (being obedient Mormons) will enter into a place known as the Spirit Prison (*D&C* 138:32). There, the spirits in prison are "taught faith in God, repentance from sin, vicarious baptisms for the remission of sins, the gift of the Holy Ghost by the laying on of hands, and all other principles of the gospel that [are] necessary for them to know" (*D&C* 138:33–34). Those who respond with acceptance to this "second chance and have accept[ed] the principles of the gospel, repent of their sins, and accept ordinances performed in their behalf in temples, they will be welcomed into paradise."[18] At the judgment and resurrection, they will be conveyed into the Celestial kingdom at one of three levels.

---

18. "Death, Physical," LDS.org, accessed April 8, 2015, https://www.lds.org/topics/death-physical.

> People who have died without these essential gospel ordinances [baptism, laying on of hands (confirmation), temple marriage, and family sealing] may receive those ordinances through the work done in temples. Acting in behalf of ancestors and others who have died, Church members are baptized and confirmed, receive the endowment, and participate in the sealings of husband to wife and children to parents.[19]

The practice of baptisms for the dead is claimed to be one of the restored elements of the gospel that was lost in the Great Apostasy after the Apostles had died. Biblical justification for this practice is drawn from 1 Corinthians 15:29. Apart from baptism, no one will enter the Celestial kingdom, so this work is very important to Mormons as they seek to offer their spirit brothers and sisters the chance of the highest level of heaven.[20]

From the Spirit Prison, salvation to the lower kingdoms of glory, the Telestial being the lower and the Terrestrial being the middle, is possible for almost all people, even those who have never heard the gospel or responded to it on earth. Those who refuse the offer to repent after death and instead reject the fundamentals of the gospel, or have not received proxy baptism by someone on earth, will enter into the lower kingdoms after the judgment and resurrection. The Terrestrial is reserved for those who were moral (i.e., being good people) during the mortal probation, including unfaithful Mormons, and they will "receive of the presence of the Son, but not of the fullness of the Father. Wherefore, they are bodies terrestrial, and not bodies celestial, and differ in glory as the moon differs from the sun" (D&C 76:71–80). The Telestial is for those who were wicked on earth and continue to reject the gospel (D&C 76:81–90, 76:98–106). There will be no glory of any god in the Telestial kingdom, but even its glory "surpasses all understanding."[21]

What the Bible would call "hell" is typically referred to as outer darkness or perdition. This realm is reserved for Lucifer and those who fought with him in the battle in the preexistence (Satan and the demons). Along with these will

---

19. "Temples," LDS.org, accessed April 8, 2015, https://www.lds.org/topics/temples.

20. "Baptisms for the Dead," LDS.org, accessed April 8, 2015, https://www.lds.org/topics/baptisms-for-the-dead.

21. Some have claimed the Joseph Smith taught that the Telestial kingdom was so glorious that if one could get a glimpse of it they would commit suicide to get there. However, this is at best a third-hand idea in a journal of a man who heard President Wildrow Woodruff say it at a funeral 33 years after Smith's death. It is likely an apocryphal addition and is not found anywhere in Smith's own writings.

be those Mormons who have turned from the faith and denied the Mormon teaching, receiving resurrected bodies to rule in hell (*D&C* 76:30–49).

Eternal Progression

Those Mormon men who have been faithful in their probationary lives on earth and achieve the Celestial kingdom have the opportunity to progress toward godhood. Eventually, they use a special name to call their wife (or wives) whom they have been sealed to in the temple ceremony of celestial marriage to be goddesses with them. Smith taught:

> Here, then, is eternal life — to know the only wise and true God; and you have got to learn how to be gods yourselves, and to be kings and priests to God, the same as all gods have done before you, namely, by going from one small degree to another, and from a small capacity to a great one; from grace to grace, from exaltation to exaltation, until you attain to the resurrection of the dead, and are able to dwell in everlasting burnings, and to sit in glory, as do those who sit enthroned in everlasting power.[22]

By this law of eternal progression, a man may become a god, earning the privileges and powers of Elohim and being granted the ability to organize his own planet, where his wives will produce spirit children to continue the cycle of the four stages of existence — premortal existence, mortal life, spirit life, and resurrected life. The teaching that God was once a man and that men can become gods runs afoul of many biblical passages, but let's consider one in particular.

> "You are My witnesses," says the LORD, "and My servant whom I have chosen, that you may know and believe Me, and understand that I am He. Before Me there was no God formed, nor shall there be after Me. I, even I, am the LORD, and besides Me there is no savior (Isaiah 43:10–11).[23]

In concert with other passages (Deuteronomy 4:35; Isaiah 44:6–8), the Mormons must admit that their teaching on the nature of God and the exaltation of man is contrary to the Bible.

---

22. Joseph Smith, Jr., "The King Follett Sermon," *Ensign*, April 1971, https://www.lds.org/ensign/1971/04/the-king-follett-sermon.
23. Quoted Scripture in this chapter is from the New King James Version of the Bible.

Modern Prophets

Joseph Smith understood himself to be the first modern prophet who was to bring the restoration of the fullness of the gospel. As he gradually received revelations through various messengers, he identified these functions as prophet, seer, and revelator. These terms are used in various ways throughout his writings, but he taught the importance of a modern prophet to lead the church and speak on behalf of God.

Eventually, Smith was directed to reestablish the office of Apostle in the same form as the 12 Apostles who walked with Jesus. These modern apostles are said to have the keys of the kingdom of God and serve as modern prophets. Further, councils of 70 are called to serve the church in ways similar to the Jewish council of elders (Exodus 24:9; Numbers 11:16). Today, the Mormon leader, specifically the president, is designated a prophet, seer, and revelator.

Throughout the decades of the LDS church, the prophets have received revelations that have contradicted the Bible, *The Book of Mormon*, or one another.[24] These contradictions are prime examples of the arbitrary nature of a religious system that is based on the ongoing revelation given modern men. They depart from the authority of the Bible and cannot help but contradict the truth of Scripture and one another. One of these is the Adam-God doctrine taught by Brigham Young and early prophets, but rejected by the church's later prophets as false doctrine. If the first prophet was speaking authoritatively for God as a modern prophet, seer, and revelator, how could he have been in error? Which prophet is a true prophet who has the keys to the restored gospel?

> Brigham Young (2nd LDS President) — When our father Adam came into the garden of Eden, he came into it with a celestial body, and brought Eve, one of his wives, with him. He helped to make and organize this world. He is Michael, the Archangel, the Ancient of Days! about whom holy men have written and spoken — He is our Father and our God, and the only God with whom we have to do. . . . Jesus, our elder brother, was begotten in the flesh by the same character that was in the garden of Eden, and who is our Father in Heaven. Now, let all

---

24. For an extensive treatment of these contradictions and changes, see Jerald and Sandra Tanner, *The Changing World of Mormonism* (Chicago, IL: Moody Press, 1980). These references can also be found on various online resources that deal with apologetics to Mormons.

Mormon Worldview

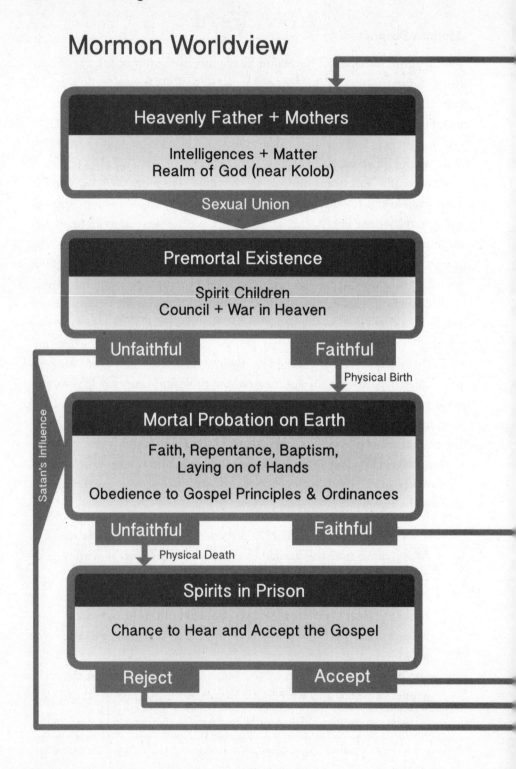

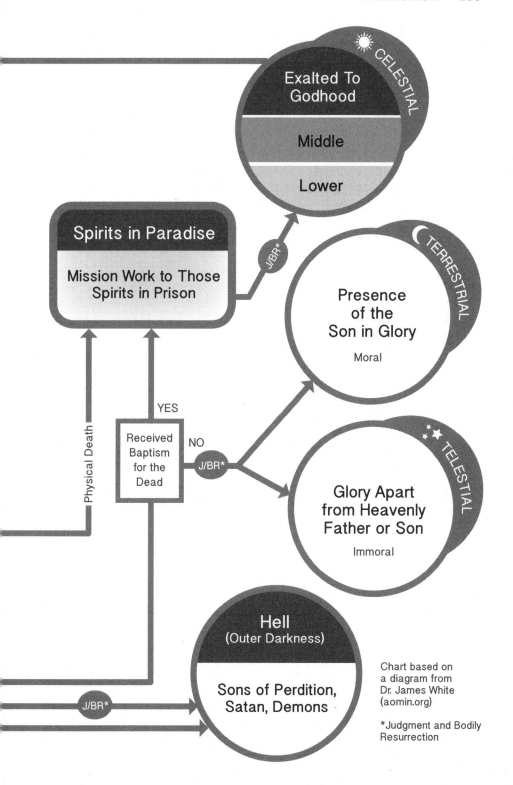

Exalted To Godhood

Middle

Lower

CELESTIAL

Spirits in Paradise

Mission Work to Those Spirits in Prison

J/BR*

Presence of the Son in Glory

Moral

TERRESTRIAL

YES

Received Baptism for the Dead

NO

J/BR*

Physical Death

Glory Apart from Heavenly Father or Son

Immoral

TELESTIAL

Hell (Outer Darkness)

Sons of Perdition, Satan, Demons

J/BR*

Chart based on a diagram from Dr. James White (aomin.org)

*Judgment and Bodily Resurrection

who may hear these doctrines, pause before they make light of them, or treat them with indifference, for they will prove their salvation or damnation. (Journal of Discourses, 1852)[25]

Spencer W. Kimball (12th LDS President) — We hope that you who teach in the various organizations, whether on the campuses or in our chapels, will always teach the orthodox truth. We warn you against the dissemination of doctrines which are not according to the scriptures and which are alleged to have been taught by some of the General Authorities of past generations. Such, for instance, is the Adam-God theory. We denounce that theory and hope that everyone will be cautioned against this and other kinds of false doctrine. (General Conference, October 1976)[26]

Additionally, there are failed prophecies of future events pronounced by Joseph Smith and other Mormon prophets. In one case, Smith announced that the building of a temple in Missouri would be completed within a generation of the revelation received in 1832:

Yea, the word of the Lord concerning his church, established in the last days for the restoration of his people, as he has spoken by the mouth of his prophets, and for the gathering of his saints to stand upon Mount Zion, which shall be the city of New Jerusalem. Which city shall be built, beginning at the temple lot, which is appointed by the finger of the Lord, in the western boundaries of the State of Missouri, and dedicated by the hand of Joseph Smith, Jun., and others with whom the Lord was well pleased. Verily this is the word of the Lord, that the city New Jerusalem shall be built by the gathering of the saints, beginning at this place, even the place of the temple, which temple shall be reared in this generation. For verily this generation shall not all pass away until an house shall be built unto the Lord, and a cloud shall rest upon it, which cloud shall be even the glory of the Lord, which shall fill the house. . . . For the sons of Moses

---

25. Brigham Young, "Self-Government — Mysteries — Recreation and Amusements, Not in Themselves Sinful — Tithing — Adam, Our Father and Our God," *Journal of Discourses*, vol. 1:8, http://journalofdiscourses.com/1/8.

26. Spencer W. Kimball, "Our Own Liahona," General Conference talk delivered October 1976, LDS.org, https://www.lds.org/general-conference/1976/10/our-own-liahona.

and also the sons of Aaron shall offer an acceptable offering and sacrifice in the house of the Lord, which house shall be built unto the Lord in this generation, upon the consecrated spot as I have appointed (*D&C* 84:2–5, 84:31).

While no temple has been built by the LDS church in Independence, Missouri (the designated spot), there has been a temple built by The Community of Christ (formerly the RLDS) and there is a visitor center run by the LDS church. While some Mormons would reinterpret "generation" to mean an indefinite period of time, a plain reading of Smith's prophecy shows that it failed to come to pass in the time he designated.

Applying the principle from Deuteronomy 18:20–22, Joseph Smith was a false prophet, and his teachings should not be followed nor his threats taken to heart. If the founder of the religious system was a false prophet, the foundation for the entire system crumbles and the church is exposed as fraudulent.

To make this point in a stronger way, Joseph Smith claimed that the gospel had been lost and that there was need for a restored gospel — a different gospel than the one preached by Paul and others as recorded in the Bible. Further, the messages were delivered to Smith by angels who appeared as beings surrounded by bright light. As we look at the Bible, we see that Paul warned the Galatian churches to reject any other gospel that came to them, whether from himself or an angel, describing those who would teach a different gospel as damned (accursed) by God (Galatians 1:6–9). The nature of the "restored gospel" given to Smith becomes apparent when we read in 2 Corinthians 11:13–15:

> For such are false apostles, deceitful workers, transforming themselves into apostles of Christ. And no wonder! For Satan himself transforms himself into an angel of light. Therefore it is no great thing if his ministers also transform themselves into ministers of righteousness, whose end will be according to their works.

Taken together, these verses help us understand the demonic origins of Mormonism and how Satan influences people to believe in counterfeit gospels that look like the genuine article on the surface, but are based on works rather than grace.

Modern Priesthood

Smith and his companions claim to have received visitations from various apostles and prophets who restored the laws and ordinances of the priesthood to the earth. In 1829, Smith and Oliver Cowdery claim that John the Baptist appeared to them and laid hands upon them to confer the Aaronic priesthood on them. This had been lost during the Great Apostasy that followed the death of the Apostles, but is now available to worthy Mormon men beginning at age 12. At some later point, Smith claims that Peter, James, and John appeared to him to confer on him and Cowdery the Melchizedek priesthood. Those who receive the Aaronic priesthood prepare to receive the greater Melchizedek priesthood by faithful service in the local wards. Then they can be considered for service as priests in the temples, service in higher offices, and they become eligible for exaltation. The particulars of these offices are described in *D&C* 107 and other writings.

Contrary to this Mormon teaching, only Jesus has the Melchizedek priesthood according to Hebrews 7, and He alone holds that priesthood forever, so this is a direct contradiction of biblical teaching. Further, the Aaronic (Levitical) priesthood was reserved by God only for those of the line of Levi, not Gentiles in New York in the 19th century.

Baptism and Laying on of Hands

Mormons are typically baptized at age 8 when they are believed to be able to make such a decision to follow the church's teachings willingly and of their own "free agency." Baptism must be performed by someone holding the proper priesthood authority and by absolute immersion. This act of baptism is one of the four key parts of the Mormon gospel (as described above). Additionally, they pursue baptisms on behalf of the dead. Apart from baptism, no one is eligible to enter into one of the levels of heaven. Therefore, Mormons see it as a duty to participate in these proxy baptisms (drawing on genealogical work) so that those who did not have that opportunity on earth might receive its benefits to be transferred from the Spirit Prison to Paradise by accepting this work done on their behalf.

After baptism, individually or by proxy, Mormons practice the laying on of hands for the receiving of the Holy Spirt as an essential part of the gospel ordinances.

Scriptures

For Mormons, the scriptures include the four "standard works" of the Bible, *The Book of Mormon* (*BoM*), *Doctrine & Covenants* (*D&C*), and *The Pearl of Great Price* (*PGP*). In *The Pearl of Great Price* we find a 13-point creed known as "The Articles of Faith." Regarding revelation, Articles 7–9 state:

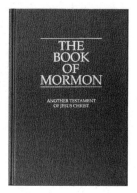

> 7) We believe in the gift of tongues, prophecy, revelation, visions, healing, interpretation of tongues, and so forth.

> 8) We believe the Bible to be the word of God as far as it is translated correctly; we also believe the Book of Mormon to be the word of God.

> 9) We believe all that God has revealed, all that He does now reveal, and we believe that He will yet reveal many great and important things pertaining to the Kingdom of God.

Bible

The Bible has a tenuous relationship to Mormon doctrine. While most Mormons in the West would use the KJV translation, as you will find posted on the LDS.org website and officially published by the church, the standard teaching is that the Bible has been corrupted to some degree over the ages. This is reflected in the phrase "as far as it is properly translated" in Article 8. With these errors in mind, Joseph Smith sought to "translate" the Bible correctly. His work was not a translation from the manuscripts, but simply a rewriting of the sections of text he believed were in error. In Mormon teaching, *translation* has a much broader meaning and includes receiving direct revelation audibly or in visions.[27] Smith's translation, referred to as the JST, was never completed, but includes what he believed to be corrections to texts and the removal of contradictions. However, these corrections added content to the Bible that sought to make sense of Mormon doctrines.

---

27. This broader view of *translation* and *translator* is discussed with respect to the Book of Abraham in the *PGP* in this article: "Translation and Historicity of the Book of Abraham," LDS.org, accessed March, 30, 2015, https://www.lds.org/topics/translation-and-historicity-of-the-book-of-abraham.

For example, Smith added to John 4:26 to remove the contradiction of Elohim having a body of flesh and bones when the Bible says "God is spirit": *For unto such hath God promised his* Spirit. And they *who* worship him, must worship in spirit and in truth (JST changes italicized). This alternate reading has no foundation in any Greek manuscript and is an entire fabrication of Smith to accommodate his peculiar teachings. The Mormon sect known today as The Community of Christ (formerly the RLDS) has published the most complete form of the JST, while most Mormons have only a portion of the JST in their scriptures and some of the changes in footnotes. Smith never finished the rewriting of the Bible, and it is a great curiosity as to why future prophets did not take up the work as the modern prophet, seer, and revelator of the church that claims to be the only true church on earth.

The Book of Mormon

For Mormons, *The Book of Mormon* is "the most correct of any book on earth, and the keystone of our religion, and a man would get nearer to God by abiding by its precepts, than by any other book."[28] The *BoM* is said to have been translated from a set of golden plates that Joseph Smith received after their location was revealed to him by the angel Moroni. After several years, Smith was allowed to take the plates. He also received a breastplate and spectacles, which are sometimes referred to as the Urim and Thummim. These spectacles allowed him to translate "by the gift and power of God." As Smith received the text, it was recorded by Oliver Cowdery who acted as principal scribe and one of 11 witnesses who testified to seeing the plates. Cowdery describes that Smith "translated his book, two transparent stones, resembling glass, set in silver bows. That by looking through these, he was able to read in English, the reformed Egyptian characters, which were engraven [*sic*] on the plates."[29] Other sections were recorded by Smith's wife Emma as he peered into a hat containing a seer stone. Interestingly, Smith did not look at the plates while he was "translating." David Whitmer describes the process:

> Joseph Smith would put the seer stone into a hat, and put his face in the hat, drawing it closely around his face to exclude

---

28. "What the Church Teaches about the Book of Mormon," LDS.org, accessed March 31, 2015, https://www.lds.org/topics/book-of-mormon/what-the-church-teaches-about-the-book-of-mormon.

29. "Book of Mormon Translation," LDS.org, accessed March 31, 2015, https://www.lds.org/topics/book-of-mormon-translation.

the light; and in the darkness the spiritual light would shine. A piece of something resembling parchment would appear, and on that appeared the writing. One character at a time would appear, and under it was the interpretation in English. Brother Joseph would read off the English to Oliver Cowdery, who was his principal scribe, and when it was written down and repeated to Brother Joseph to see if it was correct, then it would disappear, and another character with the interpretation would appear. Thus the Book of Mormon was translated by the gift and power of God, and not by any power of man.[30]

The confusion over the seer stone, the spectacles, the Urim and Thummim, and the breastplate in the various accounts of the translation process is further evidence of the spurious nature of the book that claims to be "Another Testament of Jesus Christ."

The *BoM* is supposed to be a collection of writings from two ancient groups recorded in Reformed Egyptian. The first group is said to have traveled to Central America in barges at the time of the dispersion at Babel and are called the Jaredites. A second group of writings in the *BoM* are supposed to be from a group of Jews who left Israel in 600 B.C. under the leadership of Lehi at the time of King Zedekiah. This line also comprised Native Americans of North America and ended with the prophet Moroni burying these plates of gold in upstate New York on the Hill Cumorah in A.D. 421. Significantly, 3 Nephi 11–28 describes Jesus appearing to the group of people known as the Nephites and teaching and performing miracles for them during the days He was believed to be buried in the tomb in Jerusalem before His Resurrection.

The archaeological and anthropological details of the *BoM* have had no external confirmation and have been contradicted on many levels, the most important of which are the contradictions with the Bible and tests that have confirmed that there is no genetic connection between the Jewish people and the Native Americans. All of the cities, temples, armies, and weapons described across Central and North America in the *BoM* are absent. On the other hand, there have been a multitude of archaeological and other historical confirmations of the things recorded in the Bible.

A portion of the plates were said to have been sealed and untranslated, with the anticipation of their translation at some future point. Conveniently,

30. David Whitmer, *An Address to All Believers in Christ* (Richmond, MO: n.p., 1887), p. 12.

the golden plates were returned to Moroni and are currently under his charge, not available for examination and verification as are the early manuscripts of the Bible. Some of the witnesses say that they are reserved in a cave in the Hill Cumorah awaiting a future time when they will be revealed. If the LDS church wanted to corroborate the 11 witnesses who claim to have seen the plates, all they need to do is conduct exploration and excavations on this small hill to produce the plates and verify their translation.

Doctrine and Covenants

In the introduction to this work we read, "The Doctrine and Covenants is a collection of divine revelations and inspired declarations given for the establishment and regulation of the kingdom of God on the earth in the last days."[31] *D&C* primarily includes revelations, noted in sections not chapters, given to Joseph Smith about specific points of doctrine as well as explanations of passages (section 74 explains 1 Corinthians 7:14). There are also a few revelations to other modern prophets near the end. Most of Mormon doctrine is found in this book as Smith formulated the various teachings over time. Earlier sections are contrary to later sections as Smith received new guidance for the dispensation of the church. For example, polygamy was condemned in early revelation (the original Section 101) and then commanded in later revelation (Section 132). Each of the sections includes headings that describe the time and setting of the revelations and brief explanatory notes.

The Pearl of Great Price

The Pearl of Great Price is the most interesting and eclectic book in the standard works. It was a collection of writings that was added to the LDS canon in 1880. The Book of Moses includes what Smith claimed to be a translation of writings of Moses, though what is written is not found in any form of the Hebrew Bible. The Book of Abraham is claimed to be a translation of a set of Egyptian papyri purchased by Smith in 1835. Smith "translated" these papyri and "discovered" they contained writings of Abraham. In these translations, Smith fabricated details of Abraham's life and revelations he received to validate doctrines such as the existence of Kolob (Abraham 3:3) and the spirits (intelligences) in the pre-existence (Abraham 3:22).

The papyri were lost for a time after being sold by Smith's family in 1856, but were discovered in a museum in New York in 1967 so the originals could

---

31. Introduction, *Doctrine and Covenants*, available online at https://www.lds.org/scriptures/dc-testament/introduction.

be examined to verify Smith's translation. Included in the papyri were diagrams that are printed as facsimiles in the *PGP*. As early as 1856, these printed facsimiles were recognized by a French Egyptologist as funerary scripts — a book of the dead for an Egyptian. Facsimile 1 supposedly shows the sacrifice of Isaac, but has actually been interpreted by Egyptologists as the burial rites of a man named Hor with the canopic jars where his organs would be placed.[32] Regardless of the clear fabrication of the translation, the Mormons accept these writings as coming from the prophet.[33] Ironically, the same textual criticism that has proven the Bible to be true is used to disprove the Book of Abraham and demonstrate it is a fabrication, not a translation. All the while, Mormons claim that the Bible has been corrupted and mistranslated, even when we have thousands of manuscripts that can affirm its modern accuracy.

The next two portions of the *PGP* contain a translation of a part of the Gospel of Matthew from Smith and an excerpt of the Joseph Smith History, which is the testimony and official history of Smith's life. The final section is the creed of Mormonism known as "The Articles of Faith." These 13 articles are typically memorized as a form of catechesis by young members and affirmed as true by all faithful Mormons.

Other Authoritative Writings and Teachings

Other works commended by the Mormons for study include: *Joseph Smith History*; *History of the Church*; *Journal of Discourses*; *Teachings of the Presidents of the Church*; *Mormon Doctrine* by Bruce R. McConkie; *Encyclopedia of Mormonism*; *Jesus the Christ* Teaching Manual; various teaching manuals and handbooks; messages from the apostles and prophets delivered biannually at General Conferences.

Official LDS magazines include *Ensign*, *New Era*, *Liahona*, and *Friend*.

At the LDS.org website you can find electronic versions of all of the Standard Works of Scripture as well as many other resources that describe Mormon teaching. You can also find many of the works referenced in this chapter in digital form for your own reference. I have attempted to use as many of the resources from the official LDS website as possible so that there

---

32. For a detailed analysis of the problems with the Book of Abraham translation, see: "The Book of Abraham," MormonThink.com, accessed April 6, 2015, http://mormonthink.com/book-of-abraham-issues.htm.
33. For the LDS response to these discoveries, see: "Translation and Historicity of the Book of Abraham," LDS.org, accessed April 6, 2015, https://www.lds.org/topics/translation-and-historicity-of-the-book-of-abraham.

may be no doubt about the source of the materials referenced to describe Mormon beliefs, as the reader can access them directly.

Various Doctrines of Mormonism

Creation and Evolution

As mentioned briefly above, the Mormon view of creation is not a creation out of nothing as the Bible teaches. Orthodox Christianity has understood the opening chapters of the Bible to describe the triune God creating the entirety of the universe out of nothing in a span of six days, resting on the seventh. In Mormonism, Elohim, with the cooperation of Jehovah and others, organizes the matter that we know as our solar system. This is described in detail, in a fashion similar to Genesis 1, in the Book of Abraham in chapters 3 and 4 (as well as in Moses 1–3). Working with a counsel of spirits in the premortal existence identified as Gods, Elohim sent Jehovah:

> And there stood one among them that was like unto God, and he [Jehovah/Jesus] said unto those who were with him: We will go down, for there is space there, and we will take of these materials, and we will make an earth whereon these may dwell; And we will prove them herewith, to see if they will do all things whatsoever the Lord their God shall command them. . . . And then the Lord said: Let us go down. And they went down at the beginning, and they, that is the Gods, organized and formed the heavens and the earth. And the earth, after it was formed, was empty and desolate, because they had not formed anything but the earth; and darkness reigned upon the face of the deep, and the Spirit of the Gods was brooding upon the face of the waters. And they (the Gods) said: Let there be light; and there was light (Abraham 3:24–25, 4:1–3).

As described, these gods took preexisting matter and organized it in a portion of the universe that was empty, forming earth. The verses that follow describe the rest of the creation over six days and rest on the seventh "time." Chapter 5 describes the creation of Adam and Eve and their placement in the garden in Eden.[34]

---

34. For a detailed explanation of Mormon views on the timing of creation, see: *Encyclopedia of Mormonism Online*, s.v. "Creation, Creation Accounts," accessed April 9, 2015, http://eom.byu.edu/index.php/Creation,_Creation_Accounts.

As mentioned above, there have been differing doctrinal positions on who Adam and Eve were. Brigham Young taught that Adam was Elohim and Eve was one of his wives, but the descriptions in the books of Moses and Abraham and declarations from other presidents contradict Young's teaching.

Most Mormons would reject the idea that biological evolution was involved in any sense in the formation of life on earth, but those views vary as they do in various religions. There is no official position from the leadership of the church on other forms of evolution, but the First Presidency has repeatedly affirmed the special creation of Adam and Eve. Under the heading "Evolution," the Mormon Encyclopedia, endorsed by the church, reads:

> The position of the Church on the origin of man was published by the First Presidency in 1909 and stated again by a different First Presidency in 1925:
>
> The Church of Jesus Christ of Latter-day Saints, basing its belief on divine revelation, ancient and modern, declares man to be the direct and lineal offspring of Deity. . . . Man is the child of God, formed in the divine image and endowed with divine attributes (see appendix, "Doctrinal Expositions of the First Presidency").
>
> The scriptures tell why man was created, but they do not tell how, though the Lord has promised that he will tell that when he comes again (D&C 101:32-33). In 1931, when there was intense discussion on the issue of organic evolution, the First Presidency of the Church, then consisting of Presidents Heber J. Grant, Anthony W. Ivins, and Charles W. Nibley, addressed all of the General Authorities of the Church on the matter, and concluded,
>
> Upon the fundamental doctrines of the Church we are all agreed. Our mission is to bear the message of the restored gospel to the world. Leave geology, biology, archaeology, and anthropology, no one of which has to do with the salvation of the soul of mankind, to scientific research, while we magnify our calling in the realm of the Church. . . .
>
> Upon one thing we should all be able to agree, namely, that Presidents Joseph F. Smith, John R. Winder, and Anthon H.

Lund were right when they said: "Adam is the primal parent of our race" [First Presidency Minutes, April 7, 1931].[35]

Missionary Work

You have probably seen the stereotypical Mormon missionary team riding their bikes or walking through a neighborhood. Their goal is to share their message of the Mormon gospel and make converts to Mormonism. These young people work in pairs, typically a first-year and a second-year missionary, and pay for their own expenses. While missionary work is not required in the church, it is considered an act of faithfulness and merits favor with God and the Mormon community as they seek exaltation. For males ages 18–25, they must be worthy to receive the Melchizedek Priesthood, receiving the title of elder, and be living lives of purity, chastity, and faithfulness to the teachings of Mormonism. Young women can begin mission service at 19 and are called Sisters while on their mission. These missionaries will ask to present a series of lessons about the teachings of the church as well as perform acts of service to those they contact.

Other mission work includes work within LDS organizations, at various visitor's centers and temples, and at food production facilities. People of all ages are involved in these missions, and the length of service varies.

Missionary work continues in the Spirit World when those faithful spirits in Paradise go to preach to those who are in the Spirit Prison. There, the spirits in prison who did not hear or did not respond to the gospel are offered the opportunity to accept the gospel and the proxy temple work done on their behalf.

Blacks and the Priesthood

Beginning with direction from Brigham Young in 1852 until 1978, men of black African descent (not just dark skin) were not allowed to hold the priesthood, though they could be baptized and considered members. Following Young's death, successive prophets also denied temple endowments and marriages to African blacks. There is no official church teaching as to why this was the case, but the most typical explanations involved the curse of Cain and the premortal existence. It was commonly taught in Christian circles that the curse of Cain in Genesis 4:10–15 involved black skin.

---

35. *Encyclopedia of Mormonism Online*, s.v. "Evolution," accessed April 9, 2015, http://eom.byu.edu/index.php/Evolution.

Additionally, the curse on Ham in Genesis 9:24–25 is suggested by some to include black skin (though the curse was actually on his son Canaan). From Mormon teaching, it was suggested that those who were less valiant during the premortal existence, and especially the war against Lucifer and his followers, were cursed with dark skin. This prohibition was removed in 1978 when President Spencer W. Kimball claimed to have received a new revelation. This is now included as Official Declaration 2 in *D&C*.[36] Most fundamentalist Mormon groups maintain the exclusion of black Africans from the priesthood and marriage to whites.

Native Americans

According to the various accounts in the *BoM*, there were two groups of people that traveled across the ocean to what we know as the Americas. The first group was called the Jaredites, and this group left from the Tower of Babel to a promised land in a group of barges. The book of Ether in the *BoM* gives their account, ending in their destruction after a civil war. Interestingly, no archaeological evidence has confirmed this group in Central America. The second group came at the time of King Zedekiah, leaving Jerusalem with a copy of the Torah and other writings under the direction of the prophet Lehi (1 Nephi 1–9). This initial group who traveled to North America is considered to include the ancestors of the current Native Americans. A group known as the Lamanites was cursed with dark skin (2 Nephi 5:20–25) for their disobedience, while the Nephites remained white. Those Lamanites who turned to follow God would have their curse removed, and their skin would become white and fair (3 Nephi 2:12–16).

About 200 years after Jesus is claimed to have visited them in North America, the Lamanites exterminated the Nephites and are considered the ancestors of Native Americans. Mormon prophets continued to teach that the conversion of the Native Americans would result in their skin changing color, leading to an adoption program of Native children into Mormon homes and claims of these becoming "white and delightsome" in supposed partial fulfillment of the prophecy of *D&C* 49:24.[37] Despite these claims, DNA analysis has shown that no Native American groups are descendants of

36. "Race and the Priesthood," LDS.org, accessed April 13, 2015, https://www.lds.org/topics/race-and-the-priesthood.
37. Bill McKeever and Eric Johnson, "White and Delightsome or Pure and Delightsome? A Look at 2 Nephi 30:6," Mormon Research Ministry, accessed April 13, 2015, http://www.mrm.org/white-and-delightsome.

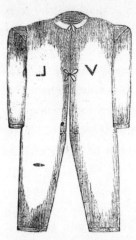

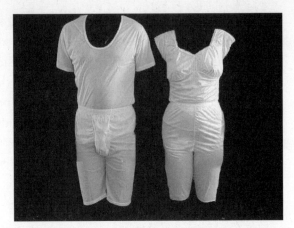

The Church of Jesus Christ of Latter-day Saints temple garments. Post-1979 two-piece temple garments end just above the knee for both sexes. Women's garments have cap sleeves with either a rounded or sweetheart neckline. Male tops are available in tee-shirt styles.

The early Mormon temple garments bore the square and compass symbol, demonstrating the link between Mormonism and Freemasonry.

Jewish ancestors, but rather of Asian descent as we would expect from migrations through Asia and across the Aleutian land bridge during the Ice Age.

Temple Garments

When a Mormon is deemed faithful and eligible to receive the temple endowments, they begin the practice of wearing special undergarments both day and night. The style has changed over time from one-piece to two-piece, and these are worn as symbols of purity and to promote modesty day and night. Symbols on the garments include a carpenter's square and compass (among other marks) that likely come from Smith's connection with Freemasonry. The garments are seen as a reminder to keep the covenants made in the temple, of God's protection, and to promote modesty. To mock these garments is very offensive to Mormons and is not a wise way to help LDS members to consider the true gospel.

Temple Work

Faithful Mormons are encouraged to participate in the various works and covenant ceremonies that take place in the temples. Beginning at age 12, young people begin participating in baptisms for the dead. Families can be involved in sealing ceremonies so that they will be "forever families" in the eternal realm. Likewise, Mormon marriages do not include the language "till death do us part," but rather "for time and all eternity," since they are sealed together in the temple to remain married in the afterlife. A man may be sealed to multiple wives in the case of the death of a wife or other circumstances. These and other ceremonies are considered sacred by the Mormons and are not shared publicly. When a temple is first constructed, non-Mormons can take a tour, but after the dedication non-members are only allowed in certain waiting areas. The exact nature of the covenants, vows, clothing, and ceremonies has changed over time, so many younger Mormons are not familiar with some of the older rituals. With that in mind, take care when discussing these issues with Mormons so that you do not accuse them of participating in something they have not done or do not believe.

Masonic Influence

Both Joseph Smith and Brigham Young were involved in the society of Freemasonry. The influence of the rituals and symbolism of Freemasonry in Mormon temple construction and rituals is evident. Some have made claims that the connection was much stronger than it is, but the connections cannot be denied. Joseph's father was a Master Freemason enrolled in a lodge in New York, and his older brother was also a Mason. While the relationship between the two groups has changed, the handshakes, oaths, and ritual dress of the LDS temple ceremonies are similar to those of the Masons and their progression from one level to the next in the society. Most notably, the square and compass markings on the temple garments are borrowed from the symbol of Freemasonry.

Occult Influence

Before finding the golden plates, the Smith family was involved in treasure seeking through occult practices known as "money digging." Part of this practice involved a seer stone which Smith would place in a hat to "see" the location of buried treasure. Smith was convicted of being a "glass looker" in a New York court on March 20, 1826. This occult practice continued even after Smith claimed to have received visits from the angel Moroni. Seeing the spirits that guarded the buried treasures was part of evading the evil spirits and claiming the treasure. Having opened himself to these occult influences, the deception of Satan in providing a different gospel was easy to accomplish. Remember that Smith did not claim to translate the golden plates directly, but he placed his seer stone into a hat where he saw the words appear. The same technique he used to "locate" buried treasure was used to "translate" *The Book of Mormon*.

Polygamy

As mentioned above, the teaching on polygamy changed over time and was practiced both openly and secretly at different times. Joseph Smith had approximately 40 wives, which were either married to him or sealed to him in temple ceremonies to be his wives in eternity if not on earth. At least 14 of these wives were married to other men at the time of their sealing or marriage to Smith.[38]

Tithing and Fasting

Mormons are directed to give 10 percent of their income, since the modern prophets have restored the ordinance of tithing for support of the work of the church (*D&C* 119). Failure to pay this tithe is seen as unfaithfulness to the ordinances of the church and a lack of trust in God to provide. Additionally, during fasting, Mormons are instructed to go without food or water for two consecutive meals during a 24-hour period, contributing the money that would have been spent to a special offering for those in need and devoting extra time to prayer and study. This is typically done during the first Sunday of each month and is accompanied by a testimony service in the local ward chapel.

Word of Wisdom

Mormons adhere to a dietary standard called the Word of Wisdom as a sign of honoring the bodies their god has given them. In general, the revelation instructs them to avoid alcohol, caffeine, various narcotic and hallucinogenic drugs, tobacco, and tea and coffee, and to eat meat sparingly and grains in abundance (*D&C* 89). Through obedience to these food laws, they are promised blessings of body, mind, and spirit. Biblically, these prohibitions run counter to Paul's instructions to the Galatian and Corinthian churches and brings to mind the warning to guard against those false teachers who

---

38. For the official LDS explanation of Smith's many wives, see: "Plural Marriage in Kirtland and Nauvoo," LDS.org, accessed April 15, 2015, https://www.lds.org/topics/plural-marriage-in-kirtland-and-nauvoo.

command people to abstain from certain foods which God gave to be received with thanksgiving (1 Timothy 4:3; Colossians 2:20–23).

Genealogical Work

In order to complete the work of proxy baptism and other temple ordinances, Mormons are devoted to studying genealogies. In order to do ordinances like sealing families "for time and all eternity," the names and relationships of families must be known.

Families

Large families are generally encouraged, as this allows physical bodies for those spirit children who are still waiting to enter their probation. Family unity is encouraged through various activities including family home evenings (often on Mondays) where there is teaching and time together as a family. Family prayer is also practiced. While the happy faces on many Mormons may make it seem that all is well, the high expectations of obedience and adherence to the church's teachings can create an environment of unrealistic expectations and standards. As with any legalistic religion, this can lead to depression, seeking to please others, and rebellion within the family. The claim of oppressive social and family structures within Mormonism are often dismissed as anecdotal, but various social surveys support these claims and they are consistent with my personal experience growing up as a Mormon and living in northern Utah and southern Idaho.[39]

Angels

Mormons believe in the continued communication with those who have died and entered into the Spirit World. To Mormons, angels are not spiritual beings created by God as distinct from humans, but spirit children along with all offspring of Heavenly Father. *D&C* 129:1–3 informs us that "There are two kinds of beings in heaven, namely: Angels, who are resurrected personages, having bodies of flesh and bones . . . [and] the spirits of just men made perfect, they who are not resurrected, but inherit the same glory." *D&C* 130:5 says that "there are no angels who minister to this earth but those who do belong or have belonged to it." These messengers were once

39. To be clear, an oppressive family life is not unique to Mormon families, but the doctrines of personal growth and the demands of obedience to such a high level of performance to achieve exaltation provide a justification for this high set of expectations. This type of dynamic can be experienced in any legalistic religious system.

people who lived on the earth and are now spirits. These messengers can communicate with those in the mortal existence. The angel Moroni was the prophet Moroni; the angel Gabriel was Noah; the angel Michael was Adam,[40] (*D&C* 107:54, "And the Lord appeared unto them, and they rose up and blessed Adam, and called him Michael, the prince, the archangel.") Other angels are said to have delivered the keys of the modern priesthood (as described above). Today, Mormons offer accounts of receiving messages in the form of visions from angels who offer them guidance.

Bearing Testimony / Burning in the Bosom

Knowing whether or not *The Book of Mormon* and the claims of Joseph Smith are true is not promoted through reasoned study and comparison to the Bible, but by an emotional response. Those who have interacted with Mormon missionaries on a doorstep or a Mormon friend have experienced the hearing of the person's testimony: "I bear you my testimony that this is the only true church, that Joseph Smith was a true prophet, that *The Book of Mormon* contains the restored gospel, and that there are modern prophets today to guide the church." They often invite you to read *The Book of Mormon* and then tell you to pray to God asking for a revelation of its truthfulness. If it is true, God will give you a "burning in the bosom" and a peace of mind that will make it clear. The absolutely subjective nature of this feeling leaves the individual open to personal and demonic influence.

This bearing of testimony is important for LDS members as only those who acknowledge Smith as a prophet of the only true church will be able to enter the Celestial kingdom. Brigham Young taught:

> . . . no man or woman in this dispensation will ever enter into the celestial kingdom of God without the consent of Joseph Smith. From the day that the Priesthood was taken from the earth to the winding-up scene of all things, every man and woman must have the certificate of Joseph Smith, junior, as a passport to their entrance into the mansion where God and Christ are — I with you and you with me. I cannot go there without his consent. He

---

40. If Adam was Elohim, as Young taught in the Adam-God doctrine, then Michael the archangel is also God and could not have been a spirit child. Again, the man-made doctrines of Mormon prophets contradict one another, demonstrating their falsehood and their satanic origin.

holds the keys of that kingdom for the last dispensation — the keys to rule in the spirit-world; and he rules there triumphantly, for he gained full power and a glorious victory over the power of Satan while he was yet in the flesh, and was a martyr to his religion and to the name of Christ, which gives him a most perfect victory in the spirit-world. He reigns there as supreme a being in his sphere, capacity, and calling, as God does in heaven. Many will exclaim — "Oh, that is very disagreeable! It is preposterous! We cannot bear the thought!" But it is true.[41]

Contrary to the Bible where Jesus Himself instructs us that all judgment has been given to Him by the Father (John 5:19–30), the Mormons rely on access to the highest degree of glory granted by a man named Joseph Smith. Again, Mormon doctrine shows itself contrary to the Word of God.

A Religion with a False Foundation

I trust that from the limited description above (entire volumes have been written on the details of Mormon doctrine and worldview) it is clear to the reader that Mormonism bears some resemblance to an orthodox view of Christianity based on the Bible, but it is not a Christian religion. Mormonism is focused on a god who used to be a man and has a physical body, a Jesus who is the spiritual brother of Lucifer and every other person, a Savior who does not provide a satisfactory atonement for sins once and for all to obtain eternal redemption (Hebrews 9:27–28). It is a religion based on human additions to the true Word of God that have been shown not only to contradict the Bible, but also one another.

The Mormon faith contains so many internal inconsistencies that it cannot provide a coherent framework for a worldview. If there are multiple gods who are all omniscient and omnipotent, how can we be sure that we should be worshiping one and not the other? How can we be sure that another god will not rise up to overthrow and disrupt Elohim's plans for the future? On top of this contradiction, the concept of eternal progression to godhood produces a great quandary — where did the first god come from, and why don't we worship him? Which of these gods determines what is true and establishes the laws of nature and morality? If Elohim was created by a

---

41. Brigham Young, "Intelligence, etc." *Journal of Discourses*, vol. 7:45; available online at http://journalofdiscourses.com/7/45.

god, who was created by a god, who was created by a god, we enter into an illogical condition called infinite regression. Just as the Hindu cannot answer what the lowest turtle which is holding up the world is standing on, neither can the Mormon answer who the first god was. From a biblical worldview with one triune God, He is the uncreated Creator who has created everything in the universe — the I AM who announced Himself to Moses.

Mormonism is built on a foundation that is arbitrary because it came from the mind of one man — and no man can speak authoritatively on his own. It is evident that Joseph Smith and the Mormon prophets who followed him were not speaking on behalf of God, but on their own arbitrary authority. That is why the doctrines and stories have changed so much over the years. Not only have the stories and doctrines changed, they are contrary to what God has revealed to us in the Bible and in the person of Jesus Christ. Mormonism offers a shifting and contradictory revelation and an insufficient Savior. The Bible offers us a perfect revelation telling us of a perfect Savior.

Keys to Reaching Mormons

As Christians seek to share the hope of a Savior who is able to save to the uttermost those who are perishing through the perfect sacrifice on the Cross and acknowledged in the Resurrection, we must do so prayerfully, boldly, and patiently. Having grown up in the Mormon Church, I have experienced the teaching, baptism, priesthood, and temple work up to age 14. After a period of rebellion and running far from God, He was pleased to draw me to Himself and has granted me salvation in Christ. I have experienced the burden of the yoke of seeking to be good enough to be accepted by those in my community and church and, ultimately, Heavenly Father. But that yoke is heavy. Having been conveyed out of that power of darkness and into the kingdom of God's beloved Son, I now know the freedom that comes from trusting in Jesus Christ alone for my right standing before the Father. I have traded the yoke of man-made legalism for the yoke of Jesus Christ — and it is light and easy because He is my righteousness, not my own works (Ephesians 2:1–10; Titus 3:4–7). As you talk with Mormons, begin to share with them about the rest offered by Christ (Matthew 11:25–30).[42]

---

42. Roger Patterson, "Every Mormon's Need for Rest," Answers in Genesis, https://answersin-genesis.org/world-religions/every-mormons-need-for-rest/.

While discussions over specific points of illogical or contradictory points of doctrine can expose contradictions, do not forget that it is by the convicting work of the Holy Spirit and the drawing of the Father that anyone will repent of their sins, and trust in Christ (John 6:44, 16:5–11). Those involved in Mormonism are involved in a culture that dominates their life. How would you respond if someone tried to persuade you to abandon Christianity and become a Mormon? Jesus taught that those who respond to the gospel message should count the cost (Luke 14:25–33). That cost can be very high for those involved in Mormonism as they will likely face being ostracized by friends and family. However, the benefits are eternal, and God's grace is available to them by the work of the Spirit, enabling them to take up their cross and follow Jesus as a perfect Savior. Be willing to invest time and love in this person who is perishing, knowing that God can use you as an instrument of His redemptive grace.

One of the most important things to consider when talking about Mormon doctrine is the use of terms. While Mormons will use the same language as Christians, their meanings are usually different. Mormons are fond of talking about the atonement, but the atonement they know is an incomplete atonement that only makes it possible for them to achieve ultimate exaltation if they work hard. Become skilled in asking good questions that draw out what they believe and why they do what they do:

- You talk a lot about the atonement. What does that mean to you?

- Have you ever been baptized for a dead person? Why do you do that? Where do you see that in the Bible?

- Can you explain to me why you think there are modern prophets? Why don't they always agree?

- I know some Mormon prophets have taught that Adam was Elohim (God). Do you believe that?

By asking questions rather than making rash accusations, you draw out the person's heart and help to expose the falsehoods and contradictions they are clinging to (Proverbs 20:5). Making accusations or telling them what they believe may put them on the defensive, especially if they don't believe those particular doctrines. For example, many Mormons may not have heard the teaching that Heavenly Father had sexual relations with Mary to prepare a body for Jesus. To announce, "Well, you guys believe God had sex with Mary, and that is weird" can be counterproductive, especially if they don't hold to that doctrine.

However, asking these types of questions can allow you to explain to them the contradictions in their worldview and point them to the truth that is found in the Bible (Proverbs 26:4–5). Help them to understand that if one prophet contradicts another, then they cannot both be speaking for God. Point them to the only omnipotent Creator and Savior who created and rules over the entire universe, not just this planet.

Another advantage to asking questions is that you don't have to remember every point of Mormon doctrine. You can ask them what they believe happens after someone dies, listen to their response, and then share what the Bible teaches on that topic. When they tell you there is a second chance to hear the gospel after death, point them to Hebrews 9:27 and ask them to explain why their teaching is different from the Bible. You should know your own doctrine and where to find those truths in the Scripture much better than you should understand any other worldview. You are not responsible to know every false teaching, just to be able to recognize them as false and point to the truth in Scripture. First Peter 3:14–17 instructs us to set apart Christ as Lord over our hearts as we seek to give a reasoned defense for the hope that we have in Christ, doing it with meekness and fear.

I leave you with the words of Paul to his disciple Timothy, and pray that God will use you to share the hope of Christ with truth, boldness, and love:

> But avoid foolish and ignorant disputes, knowing that they generate strife. And a servant of the Lord must not quarrel but be gentle to all, able to teach, patient, in humility correcting those who are in opposition, if God perhaps will grant them repentance, so that they may know the truth, and that they may come to their senses and escape the snare of the devil, having been taken captive by him to do his will (2 Timothy 2:23–26).

Table 3: This table describes the key events in the supposed restoration of the fullness of the gospel. Various angelic beings appeared to Smith and his associates to convey certain messages and ordinances. Revelations continued until Smith's death in 1844.

Date	Event	Agents	"Restoration"
1820	First Vision	Heavenly Father and Jesus	Message of the corruption of modern churches and the future restoration of the gospel
1823	Golden Plates	Moroni	Plates of gold that record "the fullness of the everlasting gospel"
1824–27	Joseph's mission	Moroni	Joseph visits the site where the plates are buried to receive further instruction until they are given to him on the fourth visit
1827–30	*The Book of Mormon* translated and published	Joseph Smith, Emma Smith, Martin Harris, and Oliver Cowdery using special seer stones	The testimony of Jews who lived on the American continents and their testimony of Jesus
1829	The first elders	John the Baptist	The Aaronic priesthood is given to Joseph Smith and Oliver Cowdery by John the Baptist, and they baptize one another, becoming the first elders of the restored church
1830 (?)		Peter, James, and John	The Melchizedek priesthood is given to Joseph Smith along with the authority to rule the church
1831	Bible translation	Joseph Smith	Work on retranslating the Bible begins to correct errors in the KJV

1833	New revelations	Joseph Smith	Joseph Smith receives 65 new revelations to direct the restored church, including the building of temples
1835–44	New revelations	Joseph Smith	A total of 138 revelations to direct the restored church are recorded as the *Doctrine and Covenants*
1836	Keys given	Jesus, Moses, Elijah, and Elias	At a temple service, the keys of the dispensation are given to Joseph Smith and Oliver Cowdery
1843	New revelation	The Lord	Baptism for the dead is instituted as a temple ceremony
1843	New revelation	The Lord	Eternal progression of man toward godhood is recorded

Summary of Mormon Beliefs

Doctrine	Teachings of Mormonism
God	Deny the Trinity One god (Elohim) rules this planet, but there are many gods (henotheistic) Elohim was once a man and has a body of flesh and bone Jesus (Jehovah) is a created being and our spirit brother The Holy Spirit is a god without a body The Godhead are three different gods who are united in purpose
Authority/ Revelation	Four standard works: Bible, *The Book of Mormon*, *Doctrine & Covenants*, *The Pearl of Great Price* *The Book of Mormon* is the most perfect book ever The Bible is correct only as far as it is translated correctly Modern prophets lead the church and determine doctrine
Man	All men are spirit children of Heavenly Father and his wives Man is sinful since the Fall of Adam Man has "free agency" to obey God Man can become a god by obedience to the gospel and other ordinances

Sin	Sin is disobedience to Heavenly Father's will Additional commandments not in the Bible (e.g., Word of Wisdom)
Salvation	The four ordinances of the gospel are faith, repentance, baptism by immersion, and the laying on of hands for the Holy Spirit Additional ordinances and covenants made in the temple are necessary for exaltation to godhood in the Celestial Kingdom All except Satan and the demons and a few "sons of perdition" will inherit one of three levels of glory in heaven
Creation	Jesus, with the assistance of others, organized matter in an empty part of the universe to form our solar system Generally reject biological evolution with varying views on cosmological (big bang) and geological evolution Believe the "days of creation" were phases

Chapter 11

The Baha'i Faith

Dr. Nagy Iskander

The Baha'i faith is arguably the youngest of the independent world religions. It was founded by Mirza Husayn Ali Nuri (1817–1892), who was given the title *Baha'u'llah*, which means "the manifestation of the glory of Allah" (the god of Islam). He is regarded by Baha'is as the most recent in the line of messengers from Allah.

Bahaullah claimed to be "he whom Allah will manifest" — not merely a teacher or prophet, but divine. Hence, his words were considered to be "of Allah" himself. He claimed to have knowledge no one else possesses or is even able to possess. And no one has the right to oppose him:

> The essence of being a Baha'i is boundless devotion to the person of the manifestation and a profound belief that he is divine and of different order from all other beings.[1]

It is estimated that there are about five million Baha'is worldwide. Baha'is believe that all previous religions lost their spirit; therefore, a new cycle must begin to enlighten the world. They believe that the great cycle that began in Adam had reached its culmination in Mirza Husayn Ali Nuri, known as "Baha'u'llah," the founder of their faith.

---

1. James Hastings, ed., *Encyclopedia of Religion and Ethics* (Edinburgh: T&T Clark Publishers, 1908–1927), ref "Bab."

The Historical Background of the Baha'i Faith

In order to understand the Baha'i faith, we need to understand its Islamic background. Although modern Baha'is would like to think of Baha'ism as a universal faith, this religion is considered to be an offshoot of Shi'ite Islam.

The Islamic faith was started by Muhammad, the prophet of Islam, in the year A.D. 570 and spread over the Arabian Peninsula. After the death of Muhammad, the Muslims chose Abu Bakr as *caliph*, or "successor." Abu Bakr ruled the state of Islam in Muhammad's place and was succeeded, in turn, by Umar, Uthman, and Ali. These four are known as the rightly guided caliphs who were all chosen by the majority of the known Muslim world.

Within the first century of Islam, a party developed whose members believed that the caliph, the successor of the prophet who rules the Islamic world, must be chosen by Allah rather than by the people. This sect is called *Shi'ite*, or "separatists." Though there were many divisions among the Shi'ites, they all held firmly to the belief that their leader, or the *imam*, must be a descendant of the prophet Muhammad and must be nominated explicitly by his predecessor.

The Shi'ites held that the first imam of the prophet Muhammad was Ali — the cousin and son-in-law of Muhammad. Thus the Muslim world was, from early times, divided between the Shi'ites and their opponents, the Sunnis (who differ on who should have succeeded Muhammad). This division has remained until the present day.

Though the Shi'ites have always been a minority in the Muslim world and were often divided among themselves as to who was the rightful imam of their time, they have often shown the most passionate devotion to their beliefs and to their leaders. The majority of the Shi'ites live in Iran where most Iranians believe in the doctrine of the divine right of kings, considering their rulers to be divine beings. Therefore they believe the imam has the divine right to rule over them in both civil and spiritual affairs.

The Shi'ites acknowledge 12 imams. The followers of this form of Islam affirm that Ali and ten of his descendants, who succeeded him one after another, suffered violent deaths at the hands of the Sunnis and are counted as holy martyrs. The fate of the 11 imams was bloody: Ali was assassinated with a dagger; Husain was killed after battle; and nine others were poisoned. The last one is believed to have mysteriously disappeared as a child in Iraq after the death of his father in the year A.D. 873.

However, the Shi'ites also believe that this 12th imam (also called *Imam Mahdi*) was given the titles "Lord of the Age" and the "Proof of Allah" and came from the family of Muhammad, the prophet of Islam; and it is believed that he is still alive and will appear again on earth.

For a period of 70 years after his disappearance, the 12th imam communicated his will to men through four leaders called *babs*, which means "gates" in Arabic. A bab is considered to be a channel of grace to mankind. When the fourth bab died, no one succeeded him, and so the Shi'ites thereafter were cut off from direct communication with the Lord of the Age.

Shi'ites earnestly look for the appearance of the hidden 12th imam. They believe that all of the former prophets and imams will return to earth to aid this Mahdi, or "Guided One." It is believed that the Mahdi (12th imam) will bring all oppression to an end and will fill the earth with justice. Only Shi'ites will then be found on the earth, and at last, the religion and government of all mankind will become one.

The Manifestation of the Bab

This brings us to the religious movement of Baha'i. Sayyid Ali Muhammad (1820–1850), known as the *Bab* (Bab means gate in Arabic), was born in Shiraz in the southern part of Iran on October 9, 1820. He was a descendant of the family of Muhammad, the prophet of Islam.

As he grew up, Sayyid was interested in religious matters, so he made a pilgrimage to the shrines of the Shi'ite imams near Bagdad in Iraq. Long meditation and much prayer brought him to the conviction that he himself had been chosen by Allah to bring a special message to mankind.

On May 23, 1844, at the age of 24, Sayyid made an historic declaration in his native city of Shiraz, marking the beginning of the Babi-Baha'i movement. He believed himself to be a major manifestation of deity — the "Gate of Allah" — greater than anyone who had preceded him.

Sayyid traveled through different parts of Iran, was opposed by the government, was imprisoned and then was executed on July 9, 1850, in the public square of the city of Tabriz. And some 20,000 of his followers perished in a series of massacres throughout Persia.

While the Bab, Sayyid Ali Muhammad, was imprisoned in Iran, his followers were busy traveling around the country calling upon the Shi'ites to accept him as their long-expected Mahdi.

Among the followers of the Bab was a young man named Husain Ali who was called *Mirza*, or "nobleman," from the village of Badasht in Iran. He was given the title of *Baha,* or "splendor" and later called himself *Bahaullah*, which means the "splendor, or the glory, of Allah." Those who followed him became known as *Baha'i.*

Baha'is believe that the Bab, Sayyid Ali Muhammad(1820–1850), was an independent messenger of Allah whose message was to start a new cycle in humanity's spiritual development and whose writings prepared the way for the mission of Bahaullah.

Who Is Bahaullah?

Bahaullah is an Arabic title meaning "the manifestation of the glory of Allah." He was born on November 12, 1817, in Tehran, Iran, and his given name was Husain Ali. He was the son of a wealthy government minister from the nobles of Persia. But instead of pursuing a life of power and leisure, Husain Ali chose to give all his energy to religious matters.

In 1844, when Sayyid Ali Muhammad declared himself to be the Bab and proclaimed the arrival of the "great day of Allah awaited by all religions," Husain Ali became one of the most active followers of the Bab.

In 1848 at the village of Badasht, Husain Ali hosted a gathering of the most eminent followers of the Bab known as the *Babis.* This led to Husain Ali's arrest. Most of the followers of the Bab who were arrested were put to death by the ruling Iranian authorities. But Husain Ali was spared the fate of his companions and was punished by being beaten with a rod on the soles of his feet.

The Babi movement swept Iran like a whirlwind and stirred intense persecution from the religious establishment. Its founder, the Bab, was executed in 1850.

Two years later, in 1852, Husain Ali was arrested and falsely charged with an attempt on the life of the shah of Iran. He was brought in chains and on foot to Tehran where influential members of the court and the clergy demanded a death sentence. Husain Ali, however, was protected by his personal reputation and his family's social position, as well as protests from Western embassies. So Husain Ali was cast into a dungeon known as the "black pit." The black pit had foul air, filth, and pitch darkness. Authorities hoped this would result in Husain's death.

Instead, the dungeon became the birthplace of a new religious revelation. Husain Ali spent four months in the black pit. During that time, he contemplated the full extent of his mission. Upon his release, Bahaullah, Husain Ali, was banished from his native land — the beginning of 40 years of exiled persecution. He was sent first to neighboring Baghdad. But after about a year, he left for the mountainous wilderness of Kurdistan where he spent two years. In 1856, Bahaullah returned to Baghdad where his reputation as a spiritual leader spread throughout the city.

Before leaving Baghdad, Bahaullah and his companions camped in a garden on the banks of the Tigris River. From April 21 to May 2, 1863, Bahaullah shared with the Babis in his company that he was the promised one foretold by the Bab and by all the world scriptures. The garden became known as the Garden of *Ridvan*, which indicates "paradise" in Arabic. The anniversary of the 12 days spent there is still celebrated by the Baha'is as the most joyous holiday, known as the Ridvan Festival.

On May 3, 1863, Bahaullah rode out of Baghdad on his way to the imperial capital, Constantinople, accompanied by his family and selected companions. After four months in Constantinople, Bahaullah was sent as a virtual state prisoner to Adrianople (modern Adrian), arriving in December of 1863. During the five years he spent there, Bahaullah's reputation continued to grow, attracting the intense interest of scholars, government officials, and diplomats.

Beginning in September 1867, Bahaullah wrote a series of letters to the world leaders of his time. In these letters, Bahaullah openly proclaimed his station as "the splendor of the glory of Allah."

Soon the continued agitation of opponents caused the Turkish government to send the exiles to Akka where Bahaullah and his family arrived in August of 1868. This was the final stage in his long exile. He spent the rest of his life — 24 more years — in Akka and its surrounding area.

Bahaullah's most important work was written in Akka, known more commonly among Baha'is by the Persian name *Katb-ul-Aqdas,* or "the most holy book." In it, Bahaullah outlined the essential rules and principles that are to be observed by his followers, laying the groundwork for the Baha'i administration.

In the late 1870s, Bahaullah was given the freedom to move outside Akka's city walls and his followers were able to meet with him in relative peace and freedom. Bahaullah passed away on May 29, 1892. His remains were laid to rest in a garden room next to his mansion known as *Bahji,* which means "joy." For Baha'is, this spot is the most holy place on earth.

Bahaullah's Son

Born Abbas Effendi (1844–1921), Abdul-Baha was Bahaullah's eldest son of his first wife. He was appointed by his father to be the successor — the one,

authorized interpreter of the Baha'i teachings and head of the faith after his father's passing. Abbas assumed the title of *Abdul-Baha*, or "the servant of Baha" being the "servant of Allah," and also called himself the "centre of the covenant."

From earliest childhood, Abdul-Baha shared his father's sufferings and his mission. He was imprisoned in Akka. But upon his release in 1908, he started traveling, reaching Europe and America in 1911 and 1913 to proclaim the message of the Baha'i faith to the West. Abdul-Baha wrote that he was the "interpreter of all the works and books of the blessed perfection," and therefore, no believer has any right to criticize. If someone does not understand the hidden secret of one

Abdul-Baha

of his commands or actions, they ought not to oppose it.

When Abdul-Baha died on November 29, 1921, thousands of people gathered on Mount Carmel to mourn his death. After his passing, the leadership of the Baha'i community entered a new phase evolving from that of a single individual to an administrative order.

The grandson of Abdul-Baha, Shogi Effendi, was designated "Guardian" of the Baha'i faith. His main task was to appoint the Universal House of Justice, which became the supreme authority over the Baha'i community. Although he did not have the authority to alter in any way what Bahaullah or Abdul-Baha had revealed, he performed the crucial tasks of clarifying points that may not have been clear before.

The Universal House of Justice

The Universal House of Justice, ordained by Bahaullah as the legislative authority of the Baha'i faith, finally came into existence in 1963. It has legislative, judicial, and administrative functions through a nine-member body elected at five-year intervals by the entire membership of the national government institutions of the Baha'i. It is believed that the House of Justice inherited both the position and the spirit of the "infallible guardian of the faith" and considers "divine agents" as representative of Allah.

The Baha'is International Centre

The Universal House of Justice at the Baha'i World Centre, Haifa, Israel

The Baha'i World Centre is established in the Haifa-Akka area of Israel, which is the location of Bahaullah's exile in 1868 and his death in 1892. Today the area is the site of the faith's most sacred shrines — the resting places of Bahaullah and his forerunner, the Bab — and is the seat of the international governing body.

Babi-Baha'i Scriptures and Customs

Sayyid Ali Muhammad, known as the Bab, wrote the book called the *Bayan*, which means "declaration" in Arabic. In it he explained the principles and customs of the Babi community, such as dividing the year into 19 months. Each month is 19 days (19 by 19 equals 361, almost being a year). The 19th month is the month of the fast. Immediately following the fast is the ancient Iranian festival of Nowruz, the Iranian New Year, which is to be observed with joy and gladness. The book also describes inheritance rules and many other aspects of social life for the Babis.

Bahaullah adopted what the Bab had prescribed in the Bayan, but he also wrote many other books and epistles in both Arabic and Persian, the most important being *Kitab-ul-Aqdas*, or the "most holy book." It was written at Akka in Palestine in the Arabic language. This is a book of laws — ceremonial, moral, civil, and criminal.

It's important to note that in Bahaullah's writings, he relegated the Bab to the background, putting the Bab into a position as a forerunner of himself. In fact, the fundamental assertion of Baha'ism is that Bahaullah is the manifestation of Allah. The Baha'is begin their writings with the phrase, "In the name of our lord El Baha," instead of "In the name of Allah."

In the development of the Baha'i faith, Abdul-Baha also added yet a third condition to the previous two conditions for being a true Baha'i. The first two conditions were the acceptance of Mirza Husayn Ali Nuri, known as Bahaullah, as the manifestation of Allah, and following him in complete obedience. The third condition that has been added since the death of Baha-ullah is the adherence to Abbas Effendi, known as Abdul-Baha, as supreme head — the center of the covenant. What's more, whoever rejects Abdul-Baha is cut off — no longer of the kingdom.

This is very similar to how most cults elevate their leaders, which is why the Baha'i religion is like a cult of both Islam and Christianity! The ethics of this religion permit polygamy (having multiple spouses). Their philosophy affirms the eternity of matter — which then begs the eternality of God in their view, unless matter is their God, which is self-refuting. The Baha'is have even aimed to create a new alphabet unlike the Arabic and Persian alphabets because their House of Justice must select one tongue out of the present languages — or a new language — to teach the children in the schools of the world.

Baha'ism Is Inconsistent with Christianity

If we were to ask a believer of the Baha'i faith what he thinks of God, he would most likely say that God is impersonal and "beyond the understanding of any mortal mind, though we may find expressions of His attributes in every created thing."[2] Though they believe God is unknowable, Baha'ism asserts:

> He has sent a succession of Divine Messengers, known as Manifestations of God, to educate and guide humanity, awaken-ing in whole populations capacities to contribute to the advance-ment of civilization to an extent never before possible.[3]

So, unlike the God of the Bible who reveals Himself to mankind through His Word and His Son, the god of Baha'i can only send messengers to guide us, and has no interest in a personal relationship with us.

Baha'ism asserts that the promises and prophecies given in the Holy Scriptures have been fulfilled by the appearance of the prince of the universe,

2. http://www.bahai.org/beliefs/god-his-creation/.
3. Ibid.

the great Bahaullah, and of Abdul-Baha. Of course, those familiar with biblical prophecies understand that these have precious little to do with Bahaullah! But the Bible warns of such persons:[4]

> For false christs and false prophets will rise and show signs and wonders to deceive, if possible, even the elect (Mark 13:22).

> But there were also false prophets among the people, even as there will be false teachers among you, who will secretly bring in destructive heresies, even denying the Lord who bought them, and bring on themselves swift destruction (2 Peter 2:1).

> Beloved, do not believe every spirit, but test the spirits, whether they are of God; because many false prophets have gone out into the world (1 John 4:1).

To accept Bahaullah and Abdul-Baha is to deny and forsake Christ. It is impossible for Christians to exchange the clear, consistent plan of salvation through the death and Resurrection of the Lord Jesus Christ for the mystical claims of Baha'ism simply because this man says so.

Baha'i is a religion that relies on the story of a man and the absolute adherence to that man without question. When Baha'i is judged by previous revelation, such as the Old and New Testaments in God's Word, we find contradictions on many fronts, including contradictions of itself, which shows that it is not from the God of the Bible. For example, compare the following two Baha'i quotes from their Messenger of God:

> God in His Essence and in His own Self hath ever been *unseen, inaccessible, and unknowable* (emphasis added).[5]

> Having created the world and all that liveth and moveth therein, He, through the direct operation of His unconstrained and sovereign Will, chose to *confer upon man* the unique distinction and capacity to *know Him* and to *love Him* (emphasis added).[6]

So the issue is simply whether to trust in God or trust in this man. The answer should be obvious: Christ came back from the grave to prove He

---

4. Quoted Scripture in this chapter is from the New King James Version of the Bible.
5. http://www.bahai.org/beliefs/god-his-creation/revelation/quotations; *Epistle to the Son of the Wolf.*
6. Ibid; *Gleanings from the Writings of Bahá'u'lláh,* XXVII.

was correct, whereas Bahaullah remains in his grave. This further shows that Bahaullah was not God incarnate but is himself subject to inescapable death, which is the punishment for sin since the Garden of Eden. Only Jesus Christ, being God, has power over life and death.

Finally, consider these stark differences between the words of the Messenger of Baha'i and Jesus Christ:

> The different religions have one truth underlying them; therefore, their reality is one.[7]

Now read what Jesus says about this claim:

> "Most assuredly, I say to you, I am the door of the sheep. All who ever came before Me are thieves and robbers, but the sheep did not hear them. I am the door. If anyone enters by Me, he will be saved" (John 10:7–9).

> Jesus said to him, "I am the way, the truth, and the life. No one comes to the Father except through Me" (John 14:6).

Jesus did not say there are many ways to God; there is only one way — and that is the truth of the gospel.

Summary of Baha'i Beliefs

Doctrine	Baha'i's Teaching
God	Allah; believe that all descriptions of gods from different religions reveal part of the truth about Allah
Authority/ Revelation	Writings of Bahaullah and his son; writings of other prophets sent by Allah; modern prophets and the House of Justice
Man	Man is generally good and is working to obtain his divine potential and harmony
Sin	Bringing injustice or disharmony to humanity
Salvation	Seeking enlightenment and connection with the divine; religions are all a part of achieving unity of the human race
Creation	Genesis gives a spiritual account of creation, but modern scientific theories provide details; accepting of all forms of evolution

7. Ibid.; *The Promulgation of Universal Peace.*

Chapter 12

Deism

Dan Fisher

Dust particles dance in the shaft of light penetrating the dirty window-pane as the soothing tick-tock of numerous clocks fills the small work-shop. Tiny springs, gears, and screws glisten in the morning sun as they lay scattered across the watchmaker's workbench, while the welcome heat from the crackling fire in the woodstove drives the chill from the morning air.

Softly whistling a favorite tune, the watchmaker carefully plies his trade, adding the finishing touches to his latest masterpiece. One by one, he meticulously assembles the individual pieces until he has crafted a beautiful work of mechanical timekeeping ingenuity. With a few tweaks here and a slight adjustment there, the job is finished. Polishing the crystal to a shiny luster, he holds the piece at arm's length and surveys his work. Nodding his approval, the great craftsman sets the hands, winds the spring, and then presses the piece to his ear to listen to the smooth sound of the steady ticking of the works. His job now complete, the watchmaker places the sparkling new pocket watch on the workbench, puts on his coat, and steps outside, locking the door behind him. The cold air forces a shiver from his body as he walks down the street, leaving the watch to run all alone.

Anyone who has studied anything about deism has no doubt heard the watchmaker story. Even though the simple story of a watchmaker who makes a watch only to leave it functioning on its own cannot fully explain what deists believe, it does, in a very general sense, state the core of their faith. At its basic level, deism teaches that God made the universe and its natural laws, and then left it running on its own, free from any divine interference or interaction.[1]

Deism often compares God to a watchmaker.

Admittedly, there is no uniform belief among deists on this point and their beliefs range from viewing the Creator as a distant, uninvolved deity to accepting the possibility that He can and does (although rarely) interact with His creation. As deist Brutus Tipton explains it:

> . . . the Creator, if he acts upon the manifest world at all, does so rarely and according to his own purpose . . . that is assuming he is "concerned" at all. That's not to say, of course, that some people and events are not possibly "acted" upon by the Creator.[2]

All Alone

Many struggle to understand why deists so eagerly embrace the concept of a distant and uninvolved Creator/God. Most people find the idea of being left all alone, for all practical purposes, in this vast universe incredibly unappealing. By nature, we humans crave social interaction, and the long history of human civilization certainly suggests that the interaction we most crave is that with our Creator. Civilizations from the earliest recorded periods of Mesopotamia, from the Greeks and Romans to modern times, all fashioned gods with whom they could interact. Distinct among those is Christianity, which teaches that the God of the Bible fulfilled the spiritual craving in the person of Jesus Christ, which is consistent, since we are made in the image of an interacting God in Genesis 1.

---

1. By affirming this position, the deist runs into a serious problem. If God upholds the universe's existence, then God is interfering and interacting. If God doesn't uphold the universe, then how can it remain in existence?
2. Brutus C. Tipton, "Deism: A New Beginning," World Union of Deists, http://www.deism.com/deismbeginning.htm.

On the opposite side of the religious spectrum is deism, which teaches that a personal, intimate relationship between man and his Creator is a practical impossibility, insisting instead, that all that can be known about God is revealed by the cold, impersonal laws of physics alone. Armed only with his sheer logic and reason, the deist hacks his way through the spiritual wilderness of life in his quest to understand a God who refuses to speak directly. Rejecting all divine revelation as spurious, deists rob themselves of any possibility of the deeply satisfying experience of actually "knowing" their Creator.

A Short History

Deism's relatively short story began when the term "deist" first surfaced in the middle 1500s in the writings of a Swiss theologian by the name of Pierre Viret. It appeared a few decades later in England in the early 1600s in Lord Herbert of Cherbury's work, *De Veritate*. Although not a deist in the truest sense (since deism would not become a distinct philosophy until years later), many consider Herbert the "father of deism" in the English world. In *De Veritate,* which means "concerning truth," Herbert postulated that man could use his human reason and other innate human faculties to discover truth, and by extrapolation, God. Extremely revolutionary for that time, his writings helped to ignite a firestorm of progressive thought that swept over Europe and led to the eventual development of deism as a distinct philosophy.

Swiss theologian Pierre Viret first used the term "deist."

Spurred on by unending wars in Europe, many of which were fought over religion, and the many advances in science, especially in astronomy, deism's star continued to rise into the late 17th and early 18th centuries. With the corruption that had taken hold in the "established" Christian Church of this time (which in many instances was far from the traditional, biblical Christian Church), many became disillusioned with traditional religion.

As the pendulum began to swing the other way, many of these disillusioned seekers turned to human reason (apart from the Scriptures or autonomous human reason) as an alternative to a faith that, in their view, had failed. Rejecting the idea of divine revelation altogether, deism became their default "religion." Finding a welcome home among these "seekers," deism spread to France, and with the efforts of men like Montesquieu, Voltaire, and Rousseau, it became a powerful engine of the age of enlightenment. Eventually jumping "the pond," this new "religion of reason" made its way to the shores of America. Once introduced to the American intelligentsia, numerous notables such as Thomas Jefferson[3] and Benjamin Franklin embraced deism, or at least were heavily influenced by it. Foremost among America's deists was Thomas Paine who, though not a Founding Father, did become deism's primary American evangelist and whose teachings continue to be heralded by deists to this very day.

A Working Definition

When studying any philosophy/religion, establishing a working definition is crucial. In his 1755 *A Dictionary of the English Language*, the English writer and literary giant Samuel Johnson defined deism as "the opinion of those that only acknowledge one God, without the reception of any revealed religion."[4] Seventy-three years later in his own dictionary, Noah Webster defined deism as:

> The doctrine or creed of a deist; the belief or system of religious opinions of those who acknowledge the existence of one God, but deny revelation: or deism is the belief in natural religion only, or those truths, in doctrine and practice, which man is to discover by the light of reason, independent and exclusive of any revelation from God. Hence deism implies infidelity or a disbelief in the divine origin of the scriptures.

---

3. There is still some debate over Jefferson's views to this day. In a letter to Charles Thomson on January 9, 1816, Jefferson openly proclaimed to be a Christian, which was clearly not the mark of a deist. Though he was likely influenced by deism to say the least and struggled in particular with the supernatural in the Bible, showing the influence of naturalism and deism. For all practical purposes, we will treat him as a deist in this chapter

4. Samuel Johnson, LL.D., *A Dictionary of the English Language* (London: 1755, 1785) Sixth Edition, accessed from http://publicdomainreview.org/collections/samuel-johnsons-dictionary-of-the-english-language-1785/.

Although numerous nuances have developed within deism since the time of Johnson and Webster, at its core, its basic tenets remain essentially the same. The World Union of Deists, a leading deist organization founded in 1993 by Robert Johnson, confirms this with their modern definition:

> . . . the recognition of a universal creative force greater than that demonstrated by mankind, supported by personal observation of laws and designs in nature and the universe, perpetuated and validated by the innate ability of human reason coupled with the rejection of claims made by individuals and organized religions of having received special divine revelation.[5]

So at the very heart of deism lies the emphatic declaration that, other than creation itself, there is no divine revelation of God. According to deists, not even the Holy Bible has a valid claim to divine inspiration. Thomas Paine, the "patron saint" of many deists, said:

> The creation is the Bible of the Deist. He there reads, in the handwriting of the Creator himself, the certainty of his existence and the immutability of his power, and all other Bibles and Testaments are to him forgeries.[6]

Adding insult to injury, The World Union of Deists harshly declares that the Bible ". . . paint[s] a very evil and insane picture of God."[7]

No Divine Revelation, No Divine Intervention

Rejecting all "spiritual truths" that cannot be substantiated by physical science, deists contend that any talk of sin, judgment, redemption, etc., is irrelevant, since creation teaches nothing of these concepts and can only be found in inspired writings like the Bible — a book they vehemently reject. Void of any divine revelation, the deist must resort to his imperfect reason/logic when attempting to understand God. Stating it succinctly, The World Union of Deists declares, "God gave us reason, not religion."[8]

In drastic contrast to Christianity, which teaches that the God of the Bible longs to have a meaningful and personal relationship with humans, deism

---

5. http://www.deism.com.
6. Thomas Paine, *The Age of Reason, In Two Parts* (New York: G.N. Devries, 1827), p. 173.
7. World Union of Deists, www.deism.com.
8. Ibid.

leaves man to make assumptions about a God who refuses to interact with His creation. Believing the Bible to be the divinely inspired Word of God, Christians base every belief concerning God's nature and His will on the clearly articulated doctrines laid down in Scripture. Relying on passages such as 2 Timothy 3:16–17, Christians believe the Bible to be the literal breath of God:[9]

> All Scripture *is* given by inspiration [*theopneustos* /Greek/ — God-breathed] of God, and *is* profitable for doctrine, for reproof, for correction, for instruction in righteousness, that the man of God may be complete, thoroughly equipped for every good work.

Unlike deists, Christians, do not speculate about God; they believe men can know with absolute certainty the things God has revealed about Himself in His Word.

At one level, Christians wholeheartedly agree with deists that creation does "scream" the existence of a God who *intelligently designed* and created a universe of space, time, and matter. Paul declared as much in Romans 1:20:

> For since the creation of the world His invisible attributes are clearly seen, being understood by the things that are made, even His eternal power and Godhead, so that they are without excuse.

Therefore, it is biblically correct to say that the creation is proof that there is a Creator/God. But this knowledge alone does not provide answers to such important questions as: "How did the universe come to be? How did mankind come to be? How should man relate to his Creator? What about the concepts of sin, righteousness, eternal life, and eternal judgment?" In short, a long list of questions essential to man's spiritual understanding and wellbeing cry out for answers that creation alone cannot provide.

For example, when Lord Herbert Cherbury articulated his early deistic postulations about truth, he summarized them with five "common notions":

1. There is a supreme deity.

2. This deity ought to be worshiped.

3. Virtue combined with piety is the chief part of religious practice.

---

9. Scripture in this chapter is from the New King James Version of the Bible.

4. Men are wicked and must repent of their sins.

5. There is reward and punishment from God, both in this life and after it.[10]

It is impossible to imagine how creation alone could have revealed all of that to Herbert. But let's take this one step further. From the creation alone, how can the deist know that logic and reason really exist? Reason has no mass and is conceptual (nonmaterial), so how can a *physical* creation reveal the *nonphysical* notion of reason? Even though this is devastating to the deist, let's grant that he can use reason and with that, it is easy enough to see how he might have conceived the first two notions from a "reasoned" study of the universe; but how could he possibly have understood the concepts of sin, repentance, and eternal punishment/reward without some additional source of divine revelation?

Formulating explanations to these deep spiritual issues without an authoritative, divine revelatory source is certainly a tall order indeed. Left to himself, the seeker of truth must either resort to his imagination for answers or he must simply ignore these critical issues altogether, hoping all eventually turns out well in the end; hence, this religion is purely arbitrary and left to the whims of each individual. What a terrible way to deal with such serious issues. Even more serious is the terrifying proposition of "guessing" incorrectly about these eternal questions or of completely ignoring them only to discover in the end that there actually was a divine revelation that provided answers to these critical queries. The eternal consequences will be catastrophic (Matthew 25:46).

Additionally, if man is left to develop his own explanations about spiritual essentials, what happens when these many explanations end up contradicting each other, as they no doubt will? Who decides which answers are correct? Can all positions be correct even if they contradict with each other? How can two opposing views of the same thing both be correct in the same sense at the same time? Wouldn't that contradict the law of non-contradiction?

This is the dilemma with which deists have grappled since the birth of their "religion" in the 1600s. Brutus C. Tipton, once an orthodox Christian and now leading deist, admits:

---

10. Accessed from christiandeistfellowship.com/truth.htm, cited 1/9/15.

As a Deist I must allow that there are very many things that are not currently known to us through scientific inquiry and perhaps there is much that will never be known. . . . As a Deist I am very much content to say that I just don't know when it comes to questions such as the existence (or lack thereof) of an afterlife. . . . Perhaps science will someday validate the belief in an afterlife (or at least some form of consciousness which continues after physical dewoath) and perhaps it may someday validate the power of prayer and other spiritual and religious practices. Nothing would please me more and although I personally stop short of faith I believe in keeping an open mind.[11]

Even the famed deist Thomas Paine was forced to admit his inability to possess any real certainty concerning his own afterlife:

I consider myself in the hands of my Creator, and that He will dispose of me after this life consistently with His justice and goodness. I leave all these matters to Him, as my Creator and friend, and I hold it to be presumption in man to make an article of faith as to what the Creator will do with us hereafter.[12]

Of course, if Paine was correct when he *reasoned* that the Bible is not God's divine revelation, then eternity may turn out well for him (this is what he hopes and placed his faith in). But, since he was wrong and the Bible is correct, then Paine is in for quite a rude awakening on Judgment Day. Interestingly, for those who believe and obey Scripture, right or wrong, eternity turns out well for them. This is a rehash of Pascal's Wager, but it leaves the truth of the God as a probability. Let's take this one step further for the readers: the God of the Bible does exist and we have certainty of that (e.g., 1 John 5:20).

Thomas Paine

11. Ibid., Brutus C. Tipton, "Deism: A New Beginning."
12. Thomas Paine, *The Theological Works of Thomas Paine* (London: R. Carlile, 1824), p. 261.

In spite of this eternal risk, deists remain adamant that their impersonal and disconnected God has provided no divine revelation of Himself short of creation. Since creation is subject to interpretation, then really the deist can't know anything for certain: not even their claim that creation is the only revelation, which is self-refuting. Sadly, the rank and file deist concludes that he is left with little or no hope of receiving any assistance or illumination from God. What a depressing and lonely existence this must be — especially in those moments of personal crisis when a personal, interactive God is what one needs most.

Deists and Revealed Religions

With their rejection of any valid source of divine revelation, it comes as no surprise that deists also reject all revealed religions as unreasonable, corrupt, and even insane. They argue that if these religions ever possessed any significant truth, centuries of human manipulation and myth have tainted and tarnished them beyond usefulness. And yet so often, deists fail to realize the human manipulation of their own religion! Even so, according to many deists, mankind would actually be much better off had he not been beguiled by the deceptive myths and superstitions of religion in the first place. The Union of World Deists implies as much when it declares:

> Much of the evil in the world could be overcome or removed if humanity had embraced our God-given reason from our earliest evolutionary stages.[13]

Deist Robert Johnson goes on to blame religion, especially Christianity, for much of the suffering in the world:

> I believe the Christian mind-set that is so eager to accept guilt and original sin, as well as the additional unnatural idea of redemption by proxy, is much to blame for the suffering of millions of people who allow themselves to be victims of negativity.[14]

Johnson even insinuates that had deism been the dominant religion centuries ago, life for mankind would be a virtual utopia by now:

> Every invention and discovery we have today could have been in effect 2,000 to 5,000 years ago. . . . We could be enjoying a

13. Ibid., World Union of Deists.
14. Robert Johnson, "The Beauty of Deism," http://www.deism.com/beautyofdeism.htm.

> virtually disease free, peaceful progressive society extending well
> beyond our planet Earth. . . . As we generate a peaceful world-
> wide religious revolution through Deism and the World Union
> of Deists we will bring about the emancipation of the individ-
> ual's mind and spirit. The soul of society will then be lifted to a
> new level, never before thought possible. A level of progress and
> international cooperation that will make warfare just an archaic
> oddity of the dark, superstitious past.[15]

Of course, Johnson and most other deists fail to mention the good that
religions, particularly Christianity, have brought to the human experience
(despite the fact that a true deist cannot state if something is really good or
bad as their god has not revealed what is good or bad!). They fail to mention
the massive humanitarian efforts performed throughout history mainly by
Christians. They fail to mention that most hospitals and medical missions
in America, and around the world for that matter, were originally founded
and operated by Christian organizations. They seem not to notice that in
every country where Christianity has become the dominant faith, those citizens experience the greatest amount of liberty, enjoy the most prosperous
economies, have the greatest opportunity for personal advancement, and
have, generally, enjoyed the best living conditions of all peoples. Like Johnson, Christians also wonder where mankind would be without these pesky
"revealed religions" — Christians simply draw a much different conclusion
than do Johnson and his like-minded deists.

Deism and America's Founding Fathers

(Editor's note to our international readers: this section dives into deism's
influence in the founding of the United States. Though you may not think
this is important, it could still be very valuable to understand what is occurring in the United States today and why certain debates occur in the United
States that are often seen on news sources around the world.)

"America was founded mostly by atheists and deists!" This is the incessant mantra that is peddled by the media/educational elites of our day. In
this post Christian era, rarely do these "authorities" mention our Founding
Fathers without insinuating or emphatically declaring that the majority of
them were either deists or atheists. Are they correct? Certainly not — but

---

15. Ibid.

most will not know this if they listen to the majority of today's commentators and educators. Those dining on a steady diet of their anti-Christian ranting are commonly quite surprised to learn that very few of our Founders even claimed to be deists. Accomplished historian Greg Frazer says that after some thirty years of research, he can only identify two Founders who were definitely deists.[16]

But does it even matter here in 21st-century America what religion our Founders embraced, if any? As it so happens, it matters a great deal — especially if we want to properly understand the philosophical roots of our form of government

George Washington
(Portrait by Gilbert Stuart Williamstown)

and if we are to properly interpret our founding documents. To our Founding Fathers, religion was essential to self-governance. Consider the sentiments of George Washington. Though it is unknown whether or not he was a "born-again" Christian (reasonable arguments concerning his faith can be made both ways), Washington considered "religion" vital to the survival of our Republic:

> Of all the dispositions and habits which lead to political prosperity, religion and morality are indispensable supports. In vain would that man claim the tribute of patriotism, who should labor to subvert these great pillars of human happiness. . . . And let us with caution indulge the supposition that morality can be maintained without religion.[17]

According to the "Father of Our Country," religion (most believe he was referring to Christianity) is the primary pillar that upholds our Republic;

---

16. Frazer/Mohler interview, "What Did America's Founders Really Believe? A Conversation with Historian Gregg Frazer," transcript, interview with Al Mohler on *Thinking in Public*, September 10, 2012, accessed from http://www.albertmohler.com/2012/09/10/what-did-americas-founders-really-believe-a-conversation-with-historian-gregg-frazer-transcript/, cited 1/7/15.

17. George Washington, Farewell Address, September 17, 1796, The George Washington Papers at the Library of Congress , 1741–1799.

therefore, any "ism" that would seek to strike at that pillar (as deism obviously does) would pose a real threat to our Republic's existence. Historian Greg Frazer observes:

> . . . for them [the Founders], the critical element in religion was morality. And this is where the left is wrong with their wall of separation notion and the idea that the founders wanted to keep religion out of public life. . . . they were creating a republic, a free society, without the iron fist of the government controlling people. And so the question they then had to deal with was, "How do you control such people? How do you get them to behave?" And their answer was that you get them to behave, you control them, through morality. And where do you get morality? You get it through religion. So they did not want to divorce or separate religion from public life; . . . they believed that morality was indispensible for a free society and that religion was the best source for morality. . . .[18]

This statement starkly contrasts to the common emphatic claim that our Founders intended to create a totally secular government completely free from religion and its influence (that is with the exception of the secular religions of course!).

It is important, though, to remember that these men were, among many things, also politicians. They were not attempting to lead a church or a denomination; they were attempting to create a new country with a form of governance (representative republic) that was a radical departure from the prevalent form of government for that time (monarchy). They understood that the success of self-governance would hinge on Christian morality — not necessarily Christian doctrine. For example, Benjamin Franklin said, "Only a virtuous people are capable of freedom."[19] In 1776, John Adams declared, ". . . it is religion and morality alone, which can establish the principles upon which freedom can securely stand. The only foundation of a free constitution is pure virtue."[20]

---

18. Frazer/Mohler interview.
19. Benjamin Franklin, *The Writings of Benjamin Franklin* (London: Macmillan & Co., 1906), Albert Henry Smyth, ed., Volume 9, Letter to Messrs. The Abbes Chalut and Arnaud, April 17, 1787, p. 569.
20. John Adams, letter to Zabdiel Adams, June 21, 1776, accessed from national archives, http://founders.archives.gov/documents/Adams/04-02-02-0011, cited 1/27/15.

Charles Carroll, signer of the Declaration of Independence, warned, "Without morals a republic cannot subsist any length of time . . . the solid foundation of morals, [is] the best security for the duration of free governments."[21] In 1798, John Adams, in commenting on the importance of morality to the effectiveness of our Constitution, said, "Our Constitution was made only for a moral and religious people. It is wholly inadequate for the government of any other."[22] Summing up this concept, Robert Winthrop, Speaker of the U.S. House of Representatives, declared in 1849, "Men, in a word, must necessarily be controlled, either by a power within them, or by a power without them; either by the word of God, or by the strong arm of man; either by the Bible, or by the bayonet."[23]

In defense of those who claim that deism greatly impacted our Founders, they are partially correct. By the middle of the 18th century, deism was definitely on the rise in America, due mainly to the influence of the French Enlightenment. Devout Christian and Founding Father Patrick Henry lamented the wave of deism sweeping over America:

> The view which the rising greatness of our country presents
> to my eyes is greatly tarnished by the general prevalence of deism,
> which, with me, is but another name for vice and depravity.[24]

Historian Greg Frazer argues that many of our Founders, who are today labeled as deists, actually embraced a "mixture of Christianity, natural religion (deism), and rationalism."[25] Coining the term "theistic rationalism" to describe their faith, Frazer says they "took elements of Christianity and elements of natural religion and then, using rationalism, kept what they considered reasonable and rational while rejecting everything else."[26] Unfortunately for some like Thomas

21. Bernard C. Steiner, *The Life and Correspondence of James McHenry* (Cleveland, OH: The Burrows Brothers, 1907), p. 475, letter from Charles Carroll to James McHenry, November 4, 1800.
22. Charles Francis Adams, *The Works of John Adams, Second President of the United States: with a Life of the Author, Notes and Illustrations* (Boston, MA: Little, Brown and Co., 1856), Vol. 9. Chapter: "To the Officers of the First Brigade of the Third Division of the Militia of Massachusetts, October 11, 1798."
23. Robert Winthrop, *Addresses and Speeches on Various Occasions* (Boston, MA: Little, Brown & Co., 1852), "An Address Delivered At The Annual Meeting Of The Massachusetts Bible Society In Boston, May 28, 1849," p. 172.
24. William Wirt, *Sketches of the Life and Character of Patrick Henry,* third ed. (Philadelphia, PA: James Webster, 1818), p. 836.
25. Mohler/Frazer interview.
26. Ibid.

The official presidential portrait of Thomas Jefferson. The debate continues over whether Thomas Jefferson was a deist.

Jefferson, that meant rejecting many of the supernatural parts of the Bible, especially in the New Testament. For example, Jefferson was willing to accept Jesus as a good moral teacher but refused to fully accept His claim to deity — denying that He had the power to work miracles defying the laws of physics.[27]

But even with deism's growing acceptance among America's ruling class, there remained a friendly coexistence between deists and Christians. Historian Gordon Wood claims that the major difference in the rivalry between deism and Christianity then and now is that "Enlightened rationalism and evangelical Calvinism were not at odds in 1776 . . ."[28] — certainly not to the extent they are today. Still, in the face of this rising tide of deism, Christianity remained by far the primary religious force in early America and was the religion of the masses and many of the Founders.

So how have the revisionist historians been able to convince a significant number of Americans that the Founders were mostly deists and atheists? Easy. They simply restrict their discussions to the views of the Founders who were mainly deistic — Thomas Jefferson and Benjamin Franklin. In a sound byte age when most people know little about our history, the results are predictable: these two Founders end up being the only ones most know anything about. From there, the next step is simple. Americans with a shallow view of their history are then easily led to believe that the spiritual views of Jefferson and Franklin were representative of most of the other Founders — when the exact opposite is actually true. Even conceding the point that Franklin was probably a deist and Jefferson a "theistic rationalist," it is worth

---

27. Miracles do not always defy natural law; some are by timing, and some may well be within the laws of nature, as we simply do not know all the laws of the physical creation. The fact that Christ did miraculous things was a testimony to His deity regardless; for more see Paul S. Taylor, "Did Miracles Really Happen?" Answers in Genesis, June 7, 2011, https://answersingenesis.org/apologetics/did-miracles-really-happen/.

28. Gordon Wood, *Creation of the American Republic 1776–1787*, "Republicanism," (Chapel Hill, NC: University of North Carolina Press, 1969), p. 60.

noting that they both retained a healthy respect for Scripture and certainly seemed to believe in an interactive God.

Consider Benjamin Franklin. Even though he was raised an Episcopalian by devout Christian parents and later attended a Presbyterian church for some time, in his own autobiography he called himself a "thorough deist" and said that, the "Arguments of the Deists . . . appeared to me much stronger [than the arguments of the Christians.]"[29] His deistic beliefs are clearly evident in a 1790 letter to Rev. Ezra Stiles, president of Yale:

> As to Jesus of Nazareth, my Opinion of whom you particularly desire, I think the System of Morals and his Religion, as he left them to us, the best the world ever saw or is likely to see; but I apprehend it has received various corrupt changes, and I have, with most of the present Dissenters in England, some Doubts as to his divinity; tho' it is a question I do not dogmatize upon, having never studied it, and I think it needless to busy myself with it now, when I expect soon an Opportunity of knowing the Truth with less Trouble. . . .[30]

Yet this same Benjamin Franklin, when the Constitutional Convention was gridlocked in Philadelphia during the summer of 1787, made the following appeal, which, sadly, was never officially adopted:

> In the beginning of the Contest with G. Britain, when we were sensible of danger we had daily prayer in this room for the divine protection. Our prayers, Sir, were heard, and they were graciously answered. . . . And have we now forgotten that powerful friend? I have lived, Sir, a long time, and the longer I live, the more convincing proofs I see of this truth — that God governs in the affairs of men. And if a sparrow cannot fall to the ground without his notice, is it probable that an empire can rise without his aid? We have been assured, Sir, in the sacred writings, that "except the Lord build the House they labor in vain that build it." I firmly believe this; and I also believe that without his concurring aid we shall succeed in this political building no better than the Builders of Babel: . . . I therefore beg leave to move,

---

29. Benjamin Franklin, *The Autobiography of Benjamin Franklin* (New Haven, CT: Yale University Press, 1964), p. 113–114.

30. Carl Van Doren, *Benjamin Franklin* (New York: The Viking Press, 1938), p. 777.

that henceforth prayers imploring the assistance of Heaven, and its blessings on our deliberations, be held in this Assembly every morning before we proceed to business, and that one or more of the Clergy of the City be requested to officiate in that service.[31]

These are hardly the words of a man who believed God was unconcerned and uninvolved in the activities of men. He was even quoting Scripture (e.g., Psalm 127:1, Matthew 10:29)!

Although not an orthodox Christian himself, Thomas Jefferson was certainly no enemy to Christianity. Con-

Benjamin Franklin, circa 1785
(Portrait by Joseph-Siffrein Duplessis)

sider the design for our national seal that he, John Adams, and Benjamin Franklin proposed to Congress. Although it unfortunately was not adopted, it was a circle with the words "Rebellion To Tyrants Is Obedience to God" written around its circumference with a drawing of Moses and the Children of Israel looking on as the Egyptians are drowning in the Red Sea, with God's presence depicted by a pillar of smoke and fire in its center, as described in the Bible. This is quite amazing considering the fact that these three supposedly rejected the Bible, all revealed religions, and an interactive God.

When serving as president, Jefferson exhibited no inclination to slight or diminish the importance of religion's role in America. For example, three times he signed into law extensions of a 1787 act that ordained special lands "for the sole use of Christian Indians" and reserved lands for the Moravian Brethren "for civilizing the Indians and promoting Christianity."[32] On April 10, 1806, he approved the rules and regulations for the Armies of the United

31. Library of Congress, "Religion and the Founding of the American Republic, Religion and the Federal Government, Part 1," http://www.loc.gov/exhibits/religion/rel06.html#obj145.

32. *The Laws of the United States of America, From the 4th of March, 1789, to the 4th of March, 1815, Including the Constitution of the United States, The Old Act of Confederation, Treaties, With Many Other Valuable Ordinances and Documents; With Copious Notes and References* (Philadelphia, PA: John Bioren and W. John Duane and Washington City: R.C. Weightman, 1815), Vol. 1, p. 569.

States, of which the second of the 101 articles began with the admonition, "It is earnestly recommended to all officers and soldiers diligently to attend divine service. . . ."

Clearly, even though Jefferson and Franklin were deistic in their thought, they harbored no hostility toward revealed religions and apparently embraced a God who was involved in the affairs of men. Though prominent among the Founders, their religious views were by no means predominant. Tragically, because of today's almost exclusive focus on the two, many Americans are led to the mistaken notion that the majority of our Founders were deists like Franklin and Jefferson.

In taking a closer look at the faith of our Founders, it is significant to note that most of them attended Christian churches that were orthodox in their teaching. Of course, this fact alone does not prove that they were true believers, but it does seem to strongly indicate that most of them were far from being deists. But there is an even greater source that reveals the authenticity of their faith — their official writings. Though imperfect and sometimes inconsistent, as all humans are, many of our Founding Fathers gave strong indications of the sincerity of their Christian faith. Consider:

- Charles Carroll, signer of the Declaration of Independence — "On the mercy of my Redeemer I rely for salvation and on His merits; not on the works I have done in obedience to His precepts."[33]

- Robert Treat Paine, signer of the Declaration of Independence — "I desire to bless and praise the name of God most high for appointing me my birth in a land of Gospel Light where the glorious tidings of a Savior and of pardon and salvation through Him have been continually sounding in mine ears. . . . in full belief of [H]is providential goodness and [H]is forgiving mercy revealed to the world through Jesus Christ,"[34]

33. The Last Will and Testament of Charles Carrollton, Life of Charles Carrollton, p. 226, accessed from https://play.google.com/books/reader?id=FkYSAAAAYAAJ&printsec=front-cover&output=reader&hl=en&pg=GBS.PA226, Kate Mason Rowland, *Life of Charles Carroll of Carrollton* (New York: G.P. Putnam's Sons, 1890), Vol. II, p. 373–374, will of Charles Carroll, Dec. 1, 1718 (later replaced by a subsequent will not containing this phrase, although he re-expressed this sentiment on several subsequent occasions, including repeatedly in the latter years of his life).

34. Robert Treat Paine, *The Papers of Robert Treat Paine*, Stephen Riley and Edward Hanson, editors (Boston: MA Historical Society, 1992), Vol. I, p. 98, March/April, 1749, https://books.google.com/books?id=-vcWuNWxNkwC&pg=PA98#v=onepage&q&f=false.

- Benjamin Rush, signer of the Declaration of Independence — "My only hope of salvation is in the infinite, transcendent love of God manifested to the world by the death of His Son upon the cross. Nothing but His blood will wash away my sins. I rely exclusively upon it."[35]

- Richard Stockton, signer of the Declaration of Independence — "I bequeath my Soul to the Lord that gave it me trusting in his mercies that he will Receive it again. . . ."[36]

- John Witherspoon, signer of the Declaration of Independence — "Believe it, there is no salvation in any other than in Christ. His atoning blood will reconcile you to God: His grace and love will captivate your souls; His holy and blessed Spirit will write His laws in your hearts. Believe in Him. . . ."[37]

- John Hart, signer of the Declaration of Independence — "Thanks be given unto Almighty God — therefore, and knowing that it is appointed for all men once to die and after that the Judgment. . . . first and principally I give and recommend my Soul into the Hands of Almighty God who gave it, and my Body to the Earth to be buried in a decent and Christian like manner . . . not doubting but to receive the same again at the General resurrection by the mighty power of God. . . ."[38]

- Roger Sherman (Signer of the Declaration of Independence & the U.S. Constitution) — "I believe that there is one only living and true God, existing in three persons, the Father, the Son, and the Holy Ghost. . . . that the Scriptures of the Old and

---

35. Benjamin Rush, *The Autobiography of Benjamin Rush*, George Corner, editor (Princeton, NJ: Princeton University Press for the American Philosophical Society, 1948), p. 166, accessed from http://books.google.com/books/about/The_Autobiography_of_Benjamin_Rush.html?id=g3IrAQAAMAAJ.

36. Richard Stockton's will, July 21st 1775, Albemarle County, Virginia, Will Book 2, page 324, accessed from http://www.genealogy.com/forum/surnames/topics/stockton/2235/, cited 4/2/15.

37. John Rogers, *The Works of John Witherspoon* (Philadelphia, PA: William W. Woodward, 1800), Vol. I, p. 256, accessed from http://books.google.com/books/about/The_works_of_the_Rev_John_Witherspoon_D.html?id=7kUVAAAAYAAJ, cited 4/2/15.

38. John Hart's last will and testament, attested April 16, 1779, which is in the custody of the State of New Jersey Library, Archives and History, Trenton, accessed from http://www.laurellynn.com/genealogy/hart/john_hart_marriage_children.htm, cited 4/3/15.

New Testaments are a revelation from God. . . . that God did send His own Son to become man, die in the room and stead of sinners, and thus to lay a foundation for the offer of pardon and salvation to all mankind so as all may be saved who are willing to accept the Gospel offer."[39]

- William Samuel Johnson, signer of the U.S. Constitutuion — "Remember, too, that you are the redeemed of the Lord, that you are bought with a price, even the inestimable price of the precious blood of the Son of God. . . . Acquaint yourselves with Him in His word and holy ordinances."[40]

- George Mason, member of the Constitutional Convention and called the "Father of the Bill of Rights" — "My soul I resign into the hands of my Almighty Creator, whose tender mercy's are all over his works, who hateth nothing that he hath made, and to the Justice and Wisdom of whose Dispensations I willingly and chearfully submit humbly hopeing from his unbounded mercy and benevolence, thro the Merits of my blessed Savior, a remission of my sins."[41]

- Patrick Henry, Governor of Virginia and leading patriot — "This is all the inheritance I can give to my dear family. The religion of Christ can give them one which will make them rich indeed."[42]

Though this is but a small sampling of our Founders' declarations of faith, it sufficiently reflects the beliefs of a good number of them and certainly refutes the notion that most of them were deists and atheists.

---

39. Lewis Henry Boutell, *The Life of Roger Sherman* (Chicago, IL: A.C. McClurg and Company, 1896), p. 272–273, accessed from http://books.google.com/books/about/The_life_of_Roger_Sherman.html?id=RVQCZ9VD0lIC, cited 4/2/15.

40. Beardsley Edwards, *Life and Times of William Samuel Johnson, LL.D.* (New York: Hurd and Houghton; Cambridge: The Riverside Press, 1876), William S. Johnson's address to the graduating class of Columbia Univ., 1789, p. 141–143, accessed from http://books.google.com/books/about/Life_and_times_of_William_Samuel_Johnson.html?id=rdm-fGCDg6YIC, cited 4/2/15.

41. George Mason, Last Will and Testament, March 20, 1773, accessed from http://www.virginia1774.org/GeorgeMasonWill.html; http://www.consource.org/document/george-masons-last-will-and-testament-1773-3-20/, cited 4/3/15.

42. Patrick Henry, Last Will and Testament, November 20, 1798, accessed from http://www.redhill.org/last_will.htm, cited 4/3/15.

What Really Motivates Deists?

Like all other religious/philosophical persuasions, there is a core conviction that drives deists to believe what they believe. In the final analysis, their rejection of divine revelation appears to be propelled by a deep desire to avoid any possibility of the unpleasant prospect of having their reason "shocked" by a faith-based religion. Essentially, deists adamantly refuse to embrace anything that offends human reason. Thomas Paine clearly articulated this when he wrote:

> There is a happiness in Deism, when rightly understood, that is not to be found in any other system of religion. All other systems have something in them that either shock our reason, or are repugnant to it, and man, if he thinks at all, must stifle his reason in order to force himself to believe them.[43]

In his search for God, the deist looks in two directions: outward at creation and inward to his own logic. His reliance on human reason alone to guide him to the truth makes him, in the words of Albert Einstein, a "religious nonbeliever":

Albert Einstein
(Photo by Oren Jack Turner)

> I cannot conceive of a personal God who would directly influence the actions of individuals, or would directly sit in judgment on creatures of his own creation. . . . My religiosity consists of a humble admiration of the infinitely superior spirit that reveals itself in the little that we can comprehend about the knowable world. That deeply emotional conviction of the presence of a superior reasoning power, which is revealed in the incomprehensible universe forms my idea of God. . . . I am a deeply religious nonbeliever. This is a somewhat new kind of religion.[44]

---

43. Thomas Paine, "Of the Religion of Deism Compared with the Christian Religion," *Age of Reason*, 1794-1796.
44. Walter Isaacson, *Einstein: His Life and Universe* (New York: Simon & Schuster, 2007), p. 387-388, 536.

Even though Einstein could not conceive of a god like the God of the Bible, billions of people across the centuries have (1 Corinthians 12:3). They have chosen to trust the most verified book in human history rather than "the little that we can comprehend about the knowable world."

Admittedly, the gospel is indeed "repugnant" to the natural man and its message definitely "shocks his reason." Paul taught this in 1 Corinthians 2:14 when he warned that human reason/logic cannot, on its own, comprehend the infinite God:

> But the natural man does not receive the things of the Spirit
> of God, for they are foolishness to him; nor can he know *them,*
> because they are spiritually discerned.

In Romans 9:33, Paul acknowledged to the Christians in Rome that God's message of redemption is indeed offensive to the unbeliever:

> Behold, I lay in Zion a stumbling stone and rock of offense,
> and whoever believes on Him will not be put to shame.

But before discounting Paul's teachings, one should seriously consider the strong words of Jesus to all who would ignore this "rock of offense." In Luke 20:18, Jesus warned: "Whoever falls on that stone will be broken; but on whomever it falls, it will grind him to powder."

No Faith, Just Reason

On the 1960s television series *Dragnet,* Sergeant Friday was famous for wanting only the facts. Similarly, deists also claim to be interested in only the "facts." In their search for the facts, they reject faith altogether, convinced that faith and fact are mutually exclusive. It is ironic that they have such faith in what they perceive as fact! The suggestion of a "factual faith" is anathema to them. They insist on seeing everything in life through the filter of human logic/reason (and human sense perception), thus eliminating any place for faith in their system of belief. Voltaire, the French philosopher and deist, put it this way:

> It is perfectly evident to my mind that there exists a necessary, eternal, supreme, and intelligent being. This is no matter of faith, but of reason.[45]

45. Voltaire, *Philosophical Dictionary,* "Faith," I, accessed from https://ebooks.adelaide.edu. au/v/voltaire/dictionary/chapter196.html.

Deists condemn faith as nothing more than the suspension of God-given reason for a subjective, experiential leap into a logical vacuum. Deist Stephen Van Eck put it like this: "When propagating a religion where proof is not available, one that contains logical absurdities, it is essential that the logical processes of the mind be short-circuited."[46] To them, faith masquerades as truth when it is actually nothing more than superstition/myth and is the bait spiritual hucksters in the church use to reel in the gullible to accept "such insane and unreasonable claims and ideas as original sin, walking on water, healing the sick without medical care, splitting the Red Sea, etc."[47] Deists naively believe that there is no objective proof to substantiate the "insane claims" of revealed religions. Of course, we can ask, what objective proof do they have of the contrary?

Although deists are certainly correct when they claim that most spiritual truths and absolutes cannot be proved using the laws of nature, this in no way means that the Bible's claims are completely without evidence or that faith and reason are mortal enemies.[48] After all, it was Jesus who said, "You shall love the LORD your God with all your heart, with all your soul, and with all your *mind*" (Matthew 22:37). Human reason, when illuminated by the Holy Spirit, can aid us in our search for truth. In spite of what deists claim, Christians are not required to "check their minds at the door" when they enter the faith.

Christians would argue that logic exists because God exists, and we are made in the image of this logical and reasoning God (Genesis 1:2–27). This is what makes logic possible for a person in the first place. In a deistic worldview, man is not made in the image of a logical God, so how can the deist really know that logic and reasoning really exist and that they are in a position to be able to do it and use it? Even so, are deists correct when they insist that there is no concrete proof to validate the claims of Scripture?

Consider the historical integrity of the Bible. It is no stretch to say that practically every time an archeologist sinks his spade into the sands of the Middle East, he unearths some new evidence that verifies the historical narrative of Scripture. Millar Burrows, biblical scholar and leading authority on

---

46. Stephen Van Eck, "Dissecting Christianity's Mind-Snaring System," accessed from http://www.deism.com/christianhype.htm.

47. World Union of Deists, www.deism.com.

48. Jason Lisle, "Faith versus Reason," *Answers* magazine, September 13, 2010, https://answersingenesis.org/apologetics/faith-vs-reason/.

the Dead Sea scrolls, put it quite simply: "More than one archaeologist has found his respect for the Bible increased by the experience of excavation in Palestine."[49]

Many are the historians who have eaten a huge piece of humble pie, admitting they were wrong in doubting the historicity of Scripture. As archeologist Dr. Joseph P. Free aptly said:

> Archaeology has confirmed countless passages which have been rejected by critics as unhistorical or contradictory to known facts. . . . Yet archaeological discoveries have shown that these critical charges . . . are wrong and that the Bible is trustworthy in the very statements which have been set aside as untrustworthy. . . . We do not know of any cases where the Bible has been proved wrong.[50]

Renowned archaeologist and Bible scholar William F. Albright said, "There can be no doubt that archaeology has confirmed the substantial historicity of the Old Testament tradition."[51] The famous Jewish Rabbi and archeologist Nelson Glueck echoed:

> It may be state[d] categorically that no archaeological discovery has ever controverted a biblical reference. Scores of archaeological findings have been made which confirm in clear outline or exact detail historical statements in the Bible.[52]

Given that Scripture has been repeatedly confirmed by the historicity test with flying colors (and every other apologetic test that can be employed to scrutinize its message), it is reasonable to say that the Bible and its message, though the most critiqued and attacked literary work in history, remains the most enduring account ever given to man. Compared to all other religions, Christianity, rather than being a "suspension of our God-given reason/ logic," is uniquely a faith accompanied and confirmed by logic and reason.

If deists would only embrace the claims of God's Word, they would discover that rather than taking a huge leap of faith into intellectual darkness,

---

49. Millar Burrows, *What Mean These Stones?* (New York: Meridian Books, 1956), p. 1.
50. Dr. Joseph P. Free, *Archaeology and Bible History* (Wheaton, IL: Scripture Press, 1969), p. 1.
51. William F. Albright, *Archaeology and Religion of Israel* (Baltimore, MD: Johns Hopkins Press, 1953) p. 176.
52. Nelson Glueck, *Rivers in the Desert* (New York: Farrar, Strous and Cudahy, 1959), p. 31.

they would, instead, be taking an illuminating step of faith into the wonderful light of God's truth. The renowned physicist/cosmologist Robert Jastrow put it this way:

> For the scientist who has lived by his faith in the power of reason, the story ends like a bad dream. He has scaled the mountain of ignorance; he is about to conquer the highest peak; as he pulls himself over the final rock, he is greeted by a band of theologians who have been sitting there for centuries.[53]

Summary of Deistic Beliefs

Doctrine	Deistic Teaching
God	A distant deity or force that has no intimate interaction with the world
Authority/ Revelation	Deny any special revelation from God; acknowledge natural law discerned by human reason and practice
Man	A rational being who directs his own destiny
Sin	Varies by individual; generally rejected as any absolute standard
Salvation	Varies by individual; some acknowledge an afterlife
Creation	Generally evolutionary explanations instigated by a deity

---

53. Robert Jastrow, *God and the Astronomers*, chapter 6, "The Religion of Science" (New York: Reader's Library, Inc., 1992), p. 107.

Chapter 13

Satanism

Bodie Hodge

The mere name of it rings out as a blasphemy against God. The conjuring of the name Satan, which literally means "adversary," often strikes fear in the hearts of many believers and unbelievers alike. Why does it strike the nerve of a Christian more than many other religions? I would suggest it is because, unlike other religions where supposed gods Zeus, Odin, and Vishnu are not really real, *Satan is real* and he is cleverly and viciously evil!

Many Christians are unfamiliar with what Satanism is. To a certain degree, this makes sense. For hundreds of years, many things have been labeled "satanic" or "Satanism," yet they are not the same thing. "Satanism" is a form of religion, whereas "satanic" is used to describe things that are characteristic of Satan, cruelty, or viciousness; however, that definition is changing in our modern day to include things that are merely atheistic.

The religion of Satanism has been difficult to document for one simple reason — Satanists were not out in the open but kept their secrets to themselves. Therefore, it has been tough to ascertain their specific doctrines and beliefs. With the dominance of Christianity in the Western world, few Satanists would have shouted from their rooftops, "I am a Satanist."

Collectively, it has been estimated that at the time of this writing, Satanism is a relatively small religion of less than 100,000 people in the world between all groups of those calling themselves Satanists. Precise numbers are hard to come by, due to the high number of unaffiliated Satanists. Regarding Satanism in recent years though, things have changed. Christianity's influence, though still quite strong in the Western world, has declined in politics and education, where the religion of secularism (with its many forms) has dominated. As a result of the culture becoming so relative (a product of secularism), anything seems to go, and this has been a springboard for Satanism to "come out of the closet."

The "coming out" of this religion has made it easier for Christians to refute it. Instead of relying on sketchy accounts of certain Satanists over the past few centuries, Christian apologists are now able to analyze Satanist publications to discover what Satanists believe. And that is what is being done here; taking a few moments to refute some of these Satanist religious forms (two in particular) collectively known as Satanism.

The Two Major Forms of Satanism

In the past, there have been various forms of Satanism, but today two forms have risen to dominance: Theistic (Traditional) Satanism and Modern or Symbolic Satanism (Church of Satan; or LaVeyan Satanism).

Theistic (Traditional) Satanism

In Theistic (Traditional) Satanism, Satan is real and is seen as a deity, in many cases to be worshiped. This is the group that has been known as "devil worshipers" or "Satan worshipers." Most hold to Satan by devotion, and some also partake of rituals. Some hold that magic really does exist (being channeled through Satan and his fallen angels).

There are various forms of traditional Satanism including: *Theistic Satanism* —Church of Azazel, Order of the Nine Angels, and Temple of the Black Light; *Theistic Luciferianism* with its unique differences and goals; and *Satanas* Ophite Cultus Satanas/Our Lady of Endor Coven founded in post-WWII era in Ohio. In a general sense, these variations each hold that Satan or Lucifer is a real being. Goals and specifics vary where some view Satan alone as *the* god, and some hold to pantheism, polytheism, or other popular pagan gods of the past.

Modern or Symbolic Satanism (Church of Satan; or LaVeyan Satanism)

LaVeyan or Modern Satanism was founded in the mid 1960s by Anton LaVey (1930–1997), hence, the name "LaVeyan Satanism." Its roots could be traced to occultist Aleister Crowley (1875–1947) who led a perverse life in opposition to Christian morality. Though Crowley was not seen as a Satanist, his influence set the stage for modern Satanism.[1]

LaVeyan Satanism (the Church of Satan) is a modern form that is massively different from Theistic Satanism. In fact, there is often strife between these two groups where Theistic Satanists often accuse the LaVeyan Satanists of being false Satanists or disguising themselves as Satanists but who are not true Satanists. Likewise, the LaVeyans lash out at Theistic Satanists saying "there is no such thing,"[2] since the LaVeyans hold to an atheistic position (more on this in a moment). LaVeyans are new to the scene of Satanism when compared to Theistic Satanists.

In a nutshell, Modern or LaVeyan Satanism is held in organization by the Church of Satan and adheres to Anton LaVey's teachings in his books *The Satanic Bible*, *The Satanic Rituals*, and *The Devil's Notebook* as well as other teachings imposed by the Church of Satan. Unlike Theistic Satanism, LaVeyan Satanism is an atheistic religion where people are seen as the absolute authority and their own desires are to be expressed and not inhibited, particularly in the area of lust. This means that even though the Law of God is written on their hearts (Romans 2:15), LaVeyan Satanists are fine with allowing their sin nature to rule supreme without an absolute moral code to rein them in from their sin. Anton LaVey writes in *The Devil's Notebook*, "Atheism wasn't tolerated when scriptural dictates were in fashion and accepted as the Word. Now, thanks to Satanic infiltration, it's safe to say, 'I don't believe in God.' "[3]

Even the Church of Satan website affirms, "Satanists are atheists. We see the universe as being indifferent to us, and so all morals and values are subjective human constructs. Our position is to be self-centered, with ourselves being the most important person (the "God") of our subjective universe, so we are sometimes said to worship ourselves."[4]

Furthermore, the LaVeyan form does not really believe in Satan, God, or any other alleged deities. "Satan" or the "Devil," to the LaVeyan, is likened metaphorically to the drives and desires within a person to do evil and unacceptable

---

1. George Mather and Larry Nichols, *Dictionary of Cults, Sects, Religions and the Occult* (Grand Rapids, MI: Zondervan Publishing House, 1993), p. 242–243.
2. Church of Satan Website, FAQ: Fundamental Beliefs, What is "Theistic Satanism"? Poughkeepsie, NY, 1999–2015, http://churchofsatan.com/faq-fundamental-beliefs.php.
3. Anton LaVey, *The Devil's Notebook*, (Port Townsend, WA: Feral House, 1992), p. 86.
4. Church of Satan Website, FAQ: Fundamental Beliefs, "Why do Satanists Worship the Devil?" Poughkeepsie, NY, 1999–2015, http://churchofsatan.com/faq-fundamental-beliefs.php.

things. For example, their ritual chant of "Hail Satan" doesn't reflect that they believe in Satan, but is merely a chant of rebellion to honor themselves.

Satanism Is Another Form of Man's Religion

In the grand scheme of religions, where there are two overarching religions — God's and not God's — obviously Satanism (in any form) is not God's, but man's. Both Theistic and LaVeyan forms of Satanism are "dedicated to the antithesis of the God of the Christian Bible."[5]

Some people might argue that this religion doesn't come from man, but comes from Satan. However, they need to realize that either way, it came through man and man's rebellious sinful nature to oppose God. For example, LaVeyan Satanism came from Anton LaVey, a man with roots back to another man, Aleister Crowley; hence, it is man's religion.

Theistic Satanism comes from men as well, each to their own individual forms. Sadly, these Theistic Satanists would rather "worship" Satan, a created and fallen entity, than the Creator. This warping of the mind is a result of what God reveals would happen in Romans 1, where people worship the creation rather than the Creator and are thus struck with a debased mind and given over to unnatural lusts, which is exactly what Satanism's fruit is. Consider Romans 1:20–28:[6]

> For since the creation of the world His invisible attributes are clearly seen, being understood by the things that are made, even His eternal power and Godhead, so that they are without excuse, because, although they knew God, they did not glorify Him as God, nor were thankful, but became futile in their thoughts, and their foolish hearts were darkened. Professing to be wise, they became fools, and changed the glory of the incorruptible God into an image made like corruptible man — and birds and four-footed animals and creeping things.
>
> Therefore God also gave them up to uncleanness, in the lusts of their hearts, to dishonor their bodies among themselves, who exchanged the truth of God for the lie, and worshiped and served the creature rather than the Creator, who is blessed forever. Amen.
>
> For this reason God gave them up to vile passions. For even their women exchanged the natural use for what is against

5. Mather and Nichols, *Dictionary of Cults, Sects, Religions and the Occult*, p. 241.
6. Scripture in this chapter is from the New King James Version of the Bible.

nature. Likewise also the men, leaving the natural use of the woman, burned in their lust for one another, men with men committing what is shameful, and receiving in themselves the penalty of their error which was due.

And even as they did not like to retain God in their knowledge, God gave them over to a debased mind, to do those things which are not fitting.

LaVeyan Satanism is exactly this — debased minds following after their own unnatural sexual lusts (it seems that anything goes, except godly marriage!). Theistic Satanism also illustrates Romans 1 where people worship the creation (i.e., Satan) instead of God, the Creator; they exchange God for a lie! Theistic Satanists have replaced Satan as the transcendent eternal being (i.e., God), and demoted the eternal Creator God as the created entity who is causing problems (Isaiah 5:20).

In either form, what these Satanists fail to realize is that when they do these sinful things, it proves they are under judgment by God and are merely waiting for death — the next judgment where an *eternal* punishment awaits them unless they repent and turn to God in the person of Jesus Christ and His death, burial, and Resurrection.

Satanism and Evolution

LaVeyan Satanism and Evolution

The Church of Satan and its atheistic stance is heavily influenced by the materialistic (atheistic/humanistic) view or origins, namely Darwinian evolution. Recall that Satanism is a form of atheism and atheism is a form of humanism. An early priest in the Church of Satan wrote in the introduction to *The Satanic Bible* in 1976:

> Satanism is a blatantly selfish, brutal philosophy. It is based on the belief that human beings are inherently selfish, violent creatures, that life is a Darwinian struggle for survival of the fittest, that only the strong survive and the earth will be ruled by those who fight to win the ceaseless competition that exists in all jungles — including those of urbanized society.[7]

---

7. Anton Szandor LaVey, *The Satanic Bible* (New York: Avon Publishing, 1976), introduction by Burton H. Wolfe, author and priest in the Church of Satan.

This echoes the exact sentiment of Anton LaVey, which is found in *The Satanic Bible*:

> Are we not all predatory animals by instinct? If humans ceased wholly from preying upon each other, could they continue to exist?[8]

> Satan represents man as just another animal, sometimes better, more often worse than those that walk on all-fours, who, because of his "divine spiritual and intellectual development," has become the most vicious animal of all![9]

Clearly, the Church of Satan or Modern Satanism is merely another form of a humanistic, atheistic religion. So any refutations of atheism and humanism can be applied to Modern Satanism. Specific refutations will be discussed later in this chapter.

Theistic Satanism and Evolution

Theistic Satanism is different. Where the Modern Satanists (LaVeyan) hold to atheism and its tenets of naturalism and materialism (prerequisites for evolution), Theistic Satanism is not so limited. Within the various forms of Theistic Satanism, some hold to much of the Bible being true, while others disavow much more. So you can have a broad range of origins accounts such as Satan being seen as "the creator."

Consider also that many Satanists of this vein hold to pagan forms of Satan or polytheism (e.g., Church of Azazel) so the range of origins options of this religion broadens. But based on the research that I've done, it seems evolution holds the most popular form of origins. For example, the Theistic Satanism website commented:

> Unlike the people in Bible times, scientists today do know quite a bit about the likely evolution of both the human species in particular and the Earth in general. Most likely, our species came into existence through natural evolution. Perhaps one or more gods had a hand in the evolution of humans now and then,

---

8. Ibid., p. 25.
9. Ibid., p. 33, reiterated: Church of Satan Website, The Nine Satanic Statements, http://churchofsatan.com/nine-satanic-statements.php.

too, at one or more times during the many millions of years that life has existed on this Earth.[10]

Evolution is a false philosophy that is often disguised as science. True science is based on repeatable observations. Evolution, big bang (cosmic evolution), and long ages (like millions and billions of years, which is geologic evolution) have neither been observed nor repeated. Clearly, evolution is not good science but rather an embarrassing view of origins. So having Theistic Satanists jump on board with the false view, and trying to tack Satan or other "gods" as the director of evolution is mere story-telling.

Satanism Is Not Particularly Special to Satan

One might think that Satanism is Satan's favorite religion as he receives "worship" by some, but I would suggest that it is merely one of many religions that Satan uses to distract people from the truth. You see, all false religions are religions that Satan uses to deceive people to miss the truth of biblical Christianity in Jesus Christ. Satan's goal is not necessarily for people to follow him; it is to keep them from following the Bible and particularly the Jesus Christ of Scripture. Keep in mind that Satan is fine if you follow Jesus, as long it is not the Jesus Christ of Scripture. Satan is fine with people following the Jesus of Islam (merely a prophet) or the Jesus of Mormonism (one of many people who became gods) or the Jesus of Jehovah's Witnesses (the created archangel Michael) and so on. So any religion that deviates from the Christ of Scripture and the 66 books of God's Word is a favorite of Satan.

Sadly, if Satan worshipers were aware that Satanism isn't necessarily that special to Satan, they might realize they are wasting their time, as their worship is really no different from someone worshiping a rock! Even Satan would be happy with that, as long they were not worshiping the Lord Jesus Christ.

For those who may entertain the idea of worshiping Satan so that they too may have a higher position in hell (favoritism), this is absurd. Satan has no power in hell, but will also be punished for all eternity in hell. Hell is likened to a fire in the Bible. One person in a fire is not ruling the other people in a fire. Sadly, I've heard people say, "I *want* to go to hell." Of course, their

10. Diane Vera, "The Here-and-Now Principle in Theology," Theistic Satan Website, 2004, http://theisticsatanism.com/CoAz/belief/here-now.html.

actions betray this. We don't observe these same people casting themselves into a fire to burn themselves up!

Refutations

How Do You Know about Satan and the Spiritual World?

One popular Theistic Satanism group, the Church of Azazel, states about knowledge (epistemology):

> What can we humans possibly know about the spirit world? Not much. And it is all too easy for us humans to deceive ourselves. We humans cannot really know the spirit world. At best, we can make educated guesses, based on our own and other people's spiritual and paranormal experiences, if any, and based on our knowledge of the history of religion and current religious trends.[11]

From their own viewpoint, they really can't know anything about the spirit world. But it is worse than that. They can't know *anything*. Theistic Satanists can't know that Satan exists; and yet as religious people, they are still devoted to a being that they can't know exists. It is purely arbitrary. Even knowledge itself breaks down at a fundamental level in this religion. They merely appeal to their own thoughts and whims (mere opinions). It is no different from a person arbitrarily saying, "I believe 3+7=8"! They obviously can't know it, but blindly believe it anyway.

Since people are not made in "Satan's image," and there is no inerrant personal revelation from an "all-knowing" Satan to mankind, people can't even be sure that their senses are reliable because nothing can be known about this Satan character. So Satanists can't even know that what we see, feel, smell, taste, and hear is actually real.

Consider also that the laws of nature might change tomorrow. Perhaps in the Satanic view, gravity might change tomorrow. After all, there is no revelation from an "all-knowing" Satan who knows the future that promised to uphold the world in the same fashion each day like the God of the Bible did (e.g., Genesis 8:22, etc.).

As for LaVeyan Satanists, how can they know anything either? They are atheists, which are *materialistic* by their very nature. In other words,

---

11. Diane Vera, "Epistemology: What Can We Know about the Spirit World, and on What Basis?" Theistic Satanism website, 2010, http://theisticsatanism.com/CoAz/belief/epistemology.html.

in atheism, only material things exist — nothing immaterial. But for that to be the case, then knowledge, which is not material, can't exist in their religion. So ultimately nothing can be known, which defeats the purpose of everything the LaVeyans have ever said.

Logic, reason, love, truth, or happiness are not material either. So why did LaVey write books or the Church of Satan run a website when their religion dictates that knowledge, logic, and reason can't exist? The only way they could do it is *by betraying the religion they claim to follow* because it cannot make sense of truth, logic, and knowledge. Neither should they involve themselves in anything that utilizes reason or logic or truth because such things are meaningless in their religion.

Refutations of False Nativities

During the Christmas season of 2014, The Satanic Temple (of the New York-based Church of Satan) did a public display in Florida to counter Christian nativity scenes. In it, Satan was falling from heaven into flames. On the display, it said, "Happy Holidays from The Satanic Temple" and quoted Isaiah where Satan (Lucifer, "Son of the Morning") fell from Heaven (Isaiah 14:12).

I found it quite interesting that they would say "happy," since their religion has nothing to do with happiness. Happiness is not material, so it is inconsistent for followers of a materialistic religion like this to discuss happiness. They say "holidays" (i.e., holy days), yet there is nothing holy in Satanism. Furthermore, apparently they felt they didn't have anything within their own religion to display so they had to borrow from the Bible. For those who claim to think independently, it is sad that they had to borrow from God's Word when they quoted Isaiah. Plus their Scripture quoting is very arbitrary, since they studiously avoid Revelation 20:10, which foretells Satan's final defeat.

Another false nativity was placed by Satanists (The Satanic Temple) in Detroit that had a snake with a book, a cross that had an inverted star in a circle (pentacle), and dead animal image affixed in the star. The display said, "The greatest gift is knowledge." As we learned in the previous section, Satanists have no basis for knowledge. These Satanists must give up their atheistic view and grab hold of the Christian worldview to even make sense of knowledge.

Furthermore, atheistic Satanists once again had to borrow from the Bible for the cross, snake (Genesis 3), and star (Numbers 24:17) used in their display. They had to borrow from Christianity in order to criticize Christianity!

Borrowing from the Bible: Marriage in Satanism

Believe it or not, even Anton LaVey got married at one point. But the origin of marriage comes from a literal Genesis where God created the first man (Adam) and first woman (Eve) in a perfect world. Today there are marital problems as well as sin and death in the world, thanks to Satan and the first couple's sin. But marriage comes out of a literal Genesis, and our Lord Jesus Christ defended this in Matthew 19 and Mark 10.

So in other religions, like Satanism, why get married? Getting married is a denial of one's own religion and openly affirms Genesis is true since it is a biblical doctrine. Each form of Satanism adheres, for the most part, to evolutionary origins, not a literal Genesis. So there is no need to get married. Mice don't wake up and say, "Let's get married." Marriage is strictly a Christian institution (instituted by Christ in the Garden of Eden), and yet religions all over the world have borrowed it. Satanism is no different.

In the Theistic Satanism perspective, they can't know anything about the spiritual world, so how can they know marriage exists? In the LaVeyan form, which is atheistic, immaterial institutions like marriage cannot exist. Again, they must give up their religion to make sense of marriage or love or happiness.

Inconsistency and Arbitrariness

Inconsistency

The Church of Satan makes it clear that they view people (i.e., themselves) as their own god and there is no other "god" in their view. "In Satanism each individual is his or her own god — there is no room for any other god and that includes Satan, Lucifer, Cthulhu, or whatever other name one might select or take from history or fiction."[12]

But then the Church of Satan goes on to give certain rules to its members such as: "Do not take that which does not belong to you."[13] "Do not

12. Church of Satan Website, FAQ: Fundamental Beliefs, "What is 'Theistic Satanism'?" Poughkeepsie, NY, 1999–2015, http://churchofsatan.com/faq-fundamental-beliefs.php.

13. Anton LaVey, "The Eleven Satanic Rules of the Earth," 1967, http://churchofsatan.com/eleven-rules-of-earth.php.

harm little children."[14] "Do not kill non-human animals unless you are attacked or for your food."[15] Naturally, this is inconsistent because if you are your own god and there is no other god, then why do they have rule-givers who have god-like status above you to make rules and impose them on you? If you are your own god, then you set your own rules. If you are your own god and there are no others, then other Satanists cannot be a "god" either and are not in any position to set authoritative rules over you.

Satan (yes, the biblical one who exists) is indeed clever. Do you realize that he has convinced these people they are their own "god"? The President of Puritan Reformed Theological Seminary Dr. Joel Beeke writes in the context of Satan's skill at matching his suggestions with our own corrupt reason, "Satan is a master at suggesting that we believe what we want to believe rather than believe the truth."[16]

In Satanism, people are seen as their own gods following their own evil desires. And yet, the atheistic Satanists still don't realize they have been deceived. This has been Satan's tactic since sin in Genesis 3 to convince people they can become their own "god" and thus neglect God's Word.

Interestingly, there is another inconsistency. In 1967, Anton LaVey wrote in *The Eleven Satanic Rules of the Earth*: "Do not give opinions or advice unless you are asked."[17] Yet LaVey was never asked for his opinion on Christianity by Christians. However, he openly gives it. So, by his own standard, he has refuted himself. No one asked for the Satanists' opinion at nativity scenes, and yet they gave it and betrayed their own inconsistent rules.

Another blatant inconsistency is when the Church of Satan states: "The Church of Satan does not condone illegal activities. If the use of certain drugs is illegal in your country of residence, they are just that: illegal."[18] Yet they openly advocated illegal activities such as homosexuality and adultery since 1966 which *was* illegal during much of that time. They openly admit this:

---

14. Ibid.
15. Ibid.
16. Joel Beeke, *Striving Against Satan* (Bryntirion, Bridgend, Wales, UK: Bryntirion Press, 2006), p. 72.
17. LaVey, "The Eleven Satanic Rules of the Earth."
18. The Church of Satan's Policy on Drug Abuse, Poughkeepsie, NY, 1999–2015, http://churchofsatan.com/policy-on-drug-abuse.php.

> We fully accept all forms of human sexual expression between consenting adults. The Church of Satan has always accepted gay, lesbian and bisexual members since its beginning in 1966.[19]

As previously seen, Theistic Satanism has no basis to know anything (epistemology), so for them to claim to know anything would be self-refuting due to its inconsistency. One popular independent Theistic Satanist, writing to Satanists who have left Christianity, advises:

> Learn the value of independent thinking, and introspection. Be inquisitive and don't accept everything at face value. These practices will help you to develop *independent thinking*, a method of living that I believe is necessary for experiencing life as a Satanist. You will wonder if what you have left behind, was the "real truth." In reality, there are no absolute truths in religion because there are so many beliefs and ideals that to accept one as an absolute truth is to be blind to the reality that ALL religions sanctimoniously claim to be the truth.[20]

There are a few glaring inconsistencies here. The first is that it is quite ironic for someone to be an independent thinker just because *someone else* says so. It defeats the purpose. The consistent independent thinker should reject someone telling him to be an independent thinker. Otherwise, it is a contradiction. Furthermore, when this Satanist writes, "Be inquisitive and don't accept everything at face value," then you shouldn't accept this Satanist's words either, for they are self-refuting.

Next are the claims of truth. Satanists are suppressing the truth in unrighteousness, as God said in Romans 1. There is really only one way to suppress the truth and that is to deny the truth and particularly its existence. This is precisely what this Satanist has done. She claims truth doesn't really exist when she blatantly states, ". . . there are no absolute truths in religion." This becomes a huge problem because she is stating as absolute truth that there are no absolute truths, which is a contradiction.

19. The Church of Satan Website, F.A.Q. Sexuality, Poughkeepsie, NY, 1999–2015, http://churchofsatan.com/faq-sexuality.php.
20. Venus Satanas (self-proclaimed name), Spiritual Satanist Website, "My Advice on Leaving Christianity," 2004, http://www.spiritualsatanist.com/articles/satan/exchristian.html.

Arbitrariness

Both Theistic Satanism and Modern Satanism (Church of Satan) hold to man's ideas about reality being the supreme authority. Hence, they are opinions, and thus, they are arbitrary. Arbitrariness is devastating for the *foundation* of a belief system. Mere human opinions show the bankruptcy of such a worldview at its very start.

Concluding Remarks

Satanism, in either form discussed here, is simply united in one purpose: to oppose God's religion as authoritative.[21] Satanists must borrow doctrines from the Bible to make sense of the world, all the while denying the God who owns them.

Yet so often Theistic Satanists and LaVeyan Satanists use terms like Satan, hell, devil, Lucifer, church, and temple, which ultimately have no meaning in their religion. But why? Did you ever stop to think why they spend so much time utilizing Christian terms and symbols (the upside-down cross of Peter,[22] a star, snake, and so on)? Because deep down they know the true religion is biblical Christianity. It is by their sin nature that they oppose Christianity, which is clearly their main target. Let's be frank here — Satanists don't run around chanting "Hail *Care Bears*" or have "The Temple of the Easter Bunny." They have chosen Satan to show their opposition to Jesus Christ.

In either Atheistic or Theistic Satanism, there is no absolute God, no ultimate right or wrong, and no salvation. Both religious forms lead nowhere. There is no hope and one is merely part of an illusionary evolutionary fairy tale that leads to utter meaninglessness. Any form that holds to Satan being real is purely arbitrary, unless they borrow that from the Bible.

21. The Church of Satan Website writes: "Anton Szandor LaVey never expected to be the founder of a new religion, but he saw a need for something publicly opposing the stagnation of Christianity, and knew that if he didn't do it, someone else, probably less qualified, would." Blanche Barton, Church of Satan website, Church of Satan History: Modern Prometheus, Poughkeepsie, NY, 2003, http://churchofsatan.com/cos-modern-prometheus.php. The Theistic Satanism Website also actively opposes Christianity as a requirement for members in Diane Vera, "Church of Azazel: Who We Are and How to Join," Theistic Satanism website, accessed January 8, 2015, http://theisticsatanism.com/CoAz/who.html.
22. Church fathers affirmed that Peter was crucified upside-down. This symbol has been part of the church for nearly 2,000 years.

Yes, There Is Hope . . . But Not in the Name of Satan

But there is hope. There have been many Christians saved out of Satanism. If you know people involved in Satanism, be praying that the Lord opens them up to salvation in Jesus Christ and further opens their hearts to the truth. Second Timothy 2:24–26 says:

> And a servant of the Lord must not quarrel but be gentle to all, able to teach, patient, in humility correcting those who are in opposition, if God perhaps will grant them repentance, so that they may know the truth, and that they may come to their senses and escape the snare of the devil, having been taken captive by him to do his will.

Although this chapter is designed for Christians, there may be some who have had satanic tendencies who are reading this. If you have been involved or dabbled in Satanism, it is time to stop running and realize that God does exist, and you know this in your heart of hearts (Romans 1). Logic, truth, reason, love, and knowledge also exist, which cannot in an atheistic and materialistic worldview (e.g., the Church of Satan). Knowledge, even about the spiritual and Satan, can be known (unlike Theistic Satanism or LaVeyan Satanism), because an all-knowing God made us in His Image and He has revealed what is sufficient to know Him and about spiritual things in His Inerrant Word.

I took note in this research that one of the main reasons Satanists deny God and Jesus Christ is that they see the world and the people in it as imperfect and broken, and they do not want to even consider that a God who may have made the world and people this way. Instead of finding out more about God and why the world and people are this way, they just reject Him outright and go for atheism (the popular religion of the day) or Satan (God's fallen adversary) or anything else they think can justify the world as it is.

But let's address this simple misconception. Originally, God made the world perfect (Deuteronomy 32:4) and very good (Genesis 1:31). There was no sin, bad things, suffering, anguish, brokenness, disasters, death, and so on. But Satan, who was also created perfect, sinned of his own accord with his pride to try to rise above God.[23] Hence, his fall into sin. He immediately went after mankind. He cleverly used a serpent (as a pawn) to

---

23. Bodie Hodge, *The Fall of Satan* (Green Forest, AR: Master Books, 2011), p. 27–28.

deceive mankind to sin, resulting in death, suffering, and pain entering the creation. This is the world in which we now live.

We are all fallen beings subject to a taste of punishment from God for sin. This world, full of sin and death, became a fallen domain, or as we say, "Satan's kingdom." A perfect God must punish sin. If not, He would not be perfectly just, since we are all sinners (Romans 3:23). We deserve eternal punishment. So, not only do we experience pain, death, and suffering on earth, we should be eternally punished after we die. But God made a way of escape because He loved us. Jesus Christ, who is God, came in the flesh to become one of us (also remaining 100 percent God). As a man, He lived a perfect life. (Romans 8:3). When Christ was offered up as a sacrifice by the Jews (Matthew 27:25; John 19:15; Acts 2:23, 3:13–15, 5:30, 7:52, 10:39), the Infinite Son of God (Jesus Christ, who is the second person of the one eternal triune God) took the infinite punishment that we deserve by the infinite Father (first person of the one triune God), which satisfied the wrath of God upon sin. The debt was paid entirely.

But Christ, our great God and Savior, did not remain in the grave but had the power to take up His life again to prove that salvation was possible unto eternal life (John 10:17; Acts 10:40; 1 Corinthians 15:11–24). So those who repent of their sin (Acts 17:30), no matter how many sins they have committed, and receive Christ (Colossians 2:6) and His Resurrection (Romans 10:9) will be saved for the new heavens and new earth when this sin-cursed world is finally done away with (Revelation 21–22).

And with salvation possible, the gospel (good news of Jesus Christ) is going forward. Pastor Warren Wiersbe wrote:

> Christ invaded Satan's kingdom when he came to this earth as a man. Satan, of course, knew that he was coming, and he did all in his power to prevent it. Satan even tried to kill Jesus after he was born. When he invaded Satan's kingdom, Christ also overcame Satan's power. "The strong man" came face-to-face with One who is stronger! In his life, death, and Resurrection, Jesus Christ has completely overcome Satan's power. Today he is claiming the spoils. He is rescuing sinners from Satan's dominion and then using those changed lives to defeat Satan's forces.[24]

---

24. Warren Wiersbe, *The Strategy of Satan* (Carol Stream, IL: Tyndale House Publishers, Inc., 1979), p. 149.

For those who may have been involved in Satanism, you and you alone must receive Christ to be saved; I cannot do it for you, and neither can anyone else. Please consider the claims of our Lord and Savior Jesus Christ who alone has all power and authority (Matthew 28:18):

Therefore submit to God. Resist the devil and he will flee from you (James 4:7).

Summary of Satanist Beliefs

Doctrine	Satanist Teaching
God	Views vary, but some are atheists and others view Satan as a god
Authority/ Revelation	The Bible is rejected as a revelation from God, but there is no formal revelation from Satan. Many would look to writings of various leaders like Anton LaVey as instructive.
Man	Atheistic Satanists view man as an animal with primal urges that should be followed; Theistic Satanists have varying views but generally deny the biblical view of man as a sinner in need of redemption.
Sin	Relativistic views of right and wrong based on the individual's beliefs
Salvation	There is no formal concept of an afterlife in most versions of Satanism, though some would believe in the continuation of life after death. Their unbiblical view of man does not require salvation from sin.
Creation	Most would believe in evolutionary views from the big bang to biological evolution, while some Theistic Satanists would assert that Satan or other gods were involved in the evolutionary process or see Satan as the creator.

Chapter 14

Freemasonry

Ryan McClay

The startled gathering raised their heads as the sharp rap of heels cut through the solemnness of the funeral home. Perfectly silent other than their walking, 16 men entered and marched to the front of the room. Each bearing a sprig of acacia and wearing white aprons over their black suits, they passed by and carefully placed the evergreen on the casket as they lined up along it. After all were in position, they performed a sharply executed salute, crossing both arms across their breast and in the process striking their shoulders. Then raising their hands above their heads with palms to the front, they let them fall down to the thighs.[1]

Such an experience is often the only exposure most people have to the religion of Freemasonry. Free Masons, Freemasons, or simply "the Masons" are a secretive organization that goes far beyond fraternal characteristics of social, professional, or honorary principles. Not to be confused with the building trade of a stone mason or a brick mason, Freemasonry is an elaborate, allegorical religion steeped in mystery. Given the secret nature of the religion and the infrequent, intriguing public displays, it is not surprising

---

1. Adapted from personal experiences and Grand Lodge of Iowa Handbook for Masonic Memorial Services, retrieved from http://grandlodgeofiowa.org/docs/ObituaryRites/MasonicMemorialHandbook.pdf.

that public perception of Freemasonry ranges widely from harmless benevolence to cautious suspicion to outright fear.

These perceptions have resulted in a voluminous amount of both "for" and "against" papers, books, articles, blogs, and websites. This chapter will not attempt to summarize or comment on these works, but for those interested in further study, be aware that these perceptions often color the material presented in a way that one must be cautious when evaluating various claims. The best way to evaluate any religion or claim is under the scrutiny of the lens of Scripture.

In order to better understand Freemasonry, a definition is in order, and what better source than Freemasonry itself. On page 26 of the Heirloom Masonic Bible — Master Reference Edition, "Freemasonry has been well defined as, 'A peculiar system of morality veiled in allegory and illustrated by symbols.' "[2] Since allegories by definition convey abstract or spiritual meanings through concrete or material forms, the exploration of Freemasonry must be handled with the knowledge that it has allegory as its basis.

Many religions use symbol and allegory, but the Freemasonry borrows from Christianity and specifically the Old Testament for much of its apologue. However, the fact that Freemasonry is a non-Christian religion becomes evident when carefully examined.

Status as Religion

Some may object that Freemasonry is not actually a religion, but is a harmless, benevolent fraternal organization. In order to evaluate that objection, consider the following definition of a religion:

> A set of beliefs concerning the cause, nature, and purpose of the universe, especially when considered as the creation of a super-human agency or agencies, usually involving devotional and ritual observances, and often containing a moral code governing the conduct of human affairs.[3]

We've already seen that Freemasonry defines itself as a system of morality and have seen evidence of its ritual nature in the funeral right, and more of the ritual will be explored later in this chapter. That, in and of itself, does not make Freemasonry a religion — after all, many non-religious social groups

---

2. http://www.emfj.org/dbr.htm.
3. http://dictionary.reference.com/browse/religion.

participate in funeral processes and have their own rituals and formality. However, Freemasonry goes much further. Consider the following statement one might hear in the liturgy that accompanies the ritual in the funeral:

> As Masons we put our trust in a Higher Power, a Supreme Being whom we call God, and we believe that He gives us each a task to do and looks down upon us, his children. We call ourselves builders because each one of us is trying to build his own spiritual temple of character, and because we believe that each one of us may have some little part in the building of that larger temple which is the sum of all human achievement, that great structure rising slowly through the ages according to the plans drawn by the Great Architect of the Universe on his Trestleboard, a temple whose foundations were laid in the beginning of time, and which will last through eternity — the great plan of the Supreme Builder of the Universe.[4]

One would hardly be able to read these statements without concluding that the Masonic funeral right fully expresses the nature of Freemasonry as a religion. It speaks of the natural ("human achievement") and supernatural ("a Supreme Being"), devotion ("a temple," "the Great Architect of the Universe"), and governance ("the building of that larger temple").

However, even with the components of a religion being present, some may argue that it still lacks some of the other characteristics of a religion. For instance, UCLA History Professor Margaret Jacob made this statement on CBS News:

> "Freemasonry is not a religion. Freemasonry has the look of a religion," said Jacob. "You think of religion as ritual, there's also this ritual element. But there are no priests, there are no ministers, there are no rabbis, there's no system of clergy of any sort. Everybody's their own thinker."[5]

The assertion by Professor Jacob is that somehow the presence of clergy is the defining nature of religion. Even if that were the case, Jacob's claim that Freemasonry does not have structure is simply not true. However, the key item

---

4. Grand Lodge Of Iowa A.F. & A.M. Masonic Memorial Handbook, p. 29.
5. http://www.cbsnews.com/news/9-things-you-didnt-know-about-freemasonry/.

in this statement is that "Everybody's their own thinker." This gives us a hint as to the true nature of Freemasonry and its relationship with another religion — that of humanism, which will be discussed in greater detail later in the book series.

One additional characteristic of a religion is its use of symbols. Freemasonry makes substantial use of symbols, and its members often have public display of these symbols either in the form of a ring, license plate, or other regalia. The square and the compass often combined with the letter G is the universal emblem of Freemasonry.

Freemason square and compass

The use of these symbols will be explored later in this chapter.

Despite all of this, many would still argue that Freemasonry is not a religion. Their rebuttal would be that structure, professed belief in a higher being, symbolism, and ritual do not make a religion and by that definition organizations such as the Boy Scouts of America are a religion. Furthermore, the argument points to other characteristics of a religion supposedly missing from Freemasonry: having a priesthood, teaching theology, ordaining clergy, defining sin and salvation (which Freemasonry does anyway), performing sacraments, publishing or specifying a holy book, or describing or defining the Deity. Of course, the religion of atheism doesn't have this either! But this type of rebuttal is a logical fallacy as it attempts to define religion in solely monotheistic characteristics common to a few religions such as Christianity or Islam and then attempts to show how Freemasonry does not fit that model. By comparing to such a specific example, the argument ignores addressing the actual practices of Freemasonry that are supposed to be secret and can't be talked about openly anyway.

In fact, if comparison is the metric for the definition of religion, Freemasonry has many similarities to the mystery religions associated with the Greco-Roman world. Those religions have the common characteristics of secrecy in their rituals and initiation of members. Freemasonry shares many similar characteristics with Rosicrucianism, another esoteric, secret society religion that arose out of the same school of thought as those ancient mystery religions.

Yes, Freemasonry is much more than a fraternal, social organization. In some of its own documents, it declares that it is not merely a social organization. The Masonic Declaration of Principles from the 1940s states, "It is a social organization *only so far as* it furnished additional inducement that men may forgather in numbers, thereby providing more material for its primary work of education, of worship, and of charity."[6] The education referred to is education in the religion. Worship would hardly be mentioned if Freemasonry wasn't religion, and charity doesn't make sense without the moral code ostensibly underlying the entire structure. Freemasonry is indeed a religion, but many of its own adherents may not realize that fact . . . after all, many Christians have even joined!

History, Structure, and Distribution

As with many religions, Freemasonry has a vague history along with its various sects and splinter groups. One undeniable fact is that it originated in Western Europe and was formalized in London in the early 18th century. Some histories of Freemasonry profess ties back to stonemason guilds of the Middle Ages, with one possible written reference in the late 14th century.[7] The closest thing to a "founding date" would be the year 1717 where the keeping of records became more formal with the formation of the first Grand Lodge in London, England,[8] although other public documents from the 1600s clearly reference (and often condemn) Freemasonry practices.

Freemasonry is organized in regional groups called "Lodges." A Masonic Lodge is analogous to a local Christian congregation and does not represent a physical building, but often has a physical building where adherents gather. Each Lodge has its own self-determined operating principles. Larger organizational structures called Grand Lodges represent amalgamations of the smaller Lodges and adapt standards by which all Lodges in the Grand Lodge operate albeit with local variations permitted.

Masonic Lodges in the Anglo-American tradition require a monotheistic belief in a "supreme being."[9] Despite the presence of the Bible in many Masonic Lodges, this does not necessarily mean that this "supreme being" is the God of the Bible. In fact, Masons in a given Lodge likely do not believe

---

6. Emphasis mine. Retrieved from http://masonicgenealogy.com/MediaWiki/index.php?title=GMMJohnson#DECLARATION_OF_PRINCIPLES.
7. The Regius Poem or Halliwell Manuscript c. 1390 seems to indicate the structure of Freemasonry. History prior to that is at best circumstantial.
8. http://www.masonicsourcebook.com/grand_lodge_of_england.htm.
9. This is not true of "Continental Freemasonry," the liberal split of the religion based in France with adherents largely in mainland Europe and Latin America.

in the same "supreme being." Freemasonry teaches that there is one God and men of all religions worship that one God using a variety of different names. In a Masonic Lodge, Masons join in corporate prayer to the Great (or Supreme) Architect of the Universe (GAOTU) to refer to the "supreme being." However, when a Mason prays, he is praying to his own view of that "supreme being" individually, but within the corporate prayer. This is consistent with a deist philosophy, but not a Christian one.

Within each Lodge, a type of clergy and governance does indeed exist. There are usually at least eight offices in each Lodge, with several others possible depending on the local jurisdiction.[10] Titles such as Deacon and Warden are progressive toward the highest office in a Lodge — the Worshipful Master. That role is analogous to the Chief Executive Officer (CEO) of a corporation rather than a spiritual leader, but the role does come with its own shepherding responsibilities. The leadership manages the affairs of a Lodge and is key in the instruction and advancement of its members through a series known as "degrees."

The degree of a Mason determines his rights and standing in a Lodge — also known as a Blue Lodge. There are three basic degrees through which an adherent progresses: Entered Apprentice, Fellowcraft, and Master Mason. Attainment of a degree marks advancement through the Masonic brotherhood. All Masonic Lodges have these three degrees in common. There are, however, degrees above Master Mason, but what those degrees are and represent will vary from region to region. These are often, but not always, referred to as "Rites" and have degrees that proceed from the fourth degree up to the 33rd degree and higher.[11] These degrees are often awarded by associated, but separate, Masonic bodies a Master Mason can join.

Another characteristic of this base level of Freemasonry or Blue Lodge Freemasonry is that it is limited to men only and is often referred to as a brotherhood.[12] There are several groups that are not Free Masons per se, but are appended or offshoot organizations. The Order of the Eastern Star and the Rainbow Girls are female-oriented groups affiliated with Freemasonry, for example. Another well-known all-male group is the Shriners, known for their children's hospitals, whose members must be a Free Mason.

---

10. http://en.wikipedia.org/wiki/Masonic_Lodge_Officers.

11. Higher degrees do not necessarily represent "rank" as they do in the 3 Blue Lodge degrees.

12. Some female-oriented lodges do exist in the Continental form of Freemasonry.

Although Freemasonry has its strongest presence in the British Isles and the United States, it is a global religion with over four million participants.[13] Given its London roots, it is not surprising that it is most prevalent in countries of the British Empire — most of North/South America, Western Europe, India, Australia, and sub-saharan Africa. It does not have a strong presence in Southeast Asia, with none in China.

Freemasonry arose in the early 1700s and spread rapidly across Europe. And although there is alignment with the language and terminology of Christianity, the Catholic Church and distrustful political leaders resisted its growth. *In eminenti apostolatus specula* was a papal bull issued by Pope Clement XII on April 28, 1738, banning Catholics from becoming Freemasons. As for Masonic involvement in the public square, a number of theories have emerged linking Freemasonry to major events such as the French Revolution. Whether or not these links are valid, they have occasionally led to restrictions on joining Freemasonry by other religious bodies or governments.

Fundamentally, there is no denying the philanthropic nature of Freemasonry and its associated organizations. Given its distributed nature, it is difficult to quantify the amount and nature of charitable support. The Shriner's Hospitals are a good example of public display of charity. There are two forms of Freemasonry charity: aid to non-Masons and mutual aid for fellow Masons. For example, one of the promoted benefits to new recruits is the care for a widow or orphans of a deceased Mason. These incentives, and the lack of government-sponsored social security in the 18th century, may have contributed to its rapid growth. These member benefits may extend into various societal benefits such as preference in hiring or promotion, lenience in legal issues, and similar things where a Freemason may be in a position of influence.

As Freemasonry has grown and spread, differences have developed. Although the three degrees of the Blue Lodge are common, several different Rites or advancement paths have developed. While difficult to quantify, there may have been over 100 Rites, and at least 1,500 Degrees or grades connected directly and indirectly with Freemasonry.[14] For example, The Ancient and Accepted Scottish Rite bends its efforts toward advancing individual freedoms and citizenship rights as well as responsibilities. On the other hand, York Rite Masonry, in its concluding Degrees or Orders of the Knights Templar, is said

13. http://www.msana.com/historyfm.asp.
14. http://www.masonicdictionary.com/rites.html.

to be a Christian organization.[15] Adding to these complexities, there are two key forms of Freemasonry — the Anglo-American Form that requires belief in a supreme being and the Continental Form that has no such requirement, and thus can include atheists. The Continental Form often takes a more liberal stand on social issues such as same-sex "marriages," but the Anglo-American Form is the most widely adopted and the primary subject of this chapter.

Authority

The diversity and complexity of Freemasonry is not surprising given that it is fundamentally a form of deistic humanism. While this may seem to be an oxymoron, it does capture the fundamental essence of Freemasonry. Freemason theology could be summed up as belief in a "supreme being" combined with layered allegories in which each adherent finds their own "truth." It is deistic in its belief in an agnostic supreme being, and humanistic in its belief that mankind is ultimately the source of truth. This is best captured in the following quote:

> In his private petitions a man may petition God or Jehovah, Allah or Buddha, Mohammed or Jesus; he may call upon the God of Israel or the First Great Cause. In the Masonic Lodge he hears petition to the Great Architect of the Universe, finding his own deity under that name. A hundred paths may wind upward around a mountain; at the top they meet.[16]

With such a wide possibility for interpretation of the practices and rituals in Freemasonry, it is not unusual that this diversity should exist and possibly extend to self-worship, demon or Satan worship, nature worship, or any other form of deity that one would like to ascribe.[17] This is not to say that all or even a majority of Free Masons seek their truth in one of these ways, but it is to point out that fundamentally the *primary* source of truth in Freemasonry is the individual and his interpretation of his religious experience.

15. http://srjarchives.tripod.com/1997-09/Duncan.htm.
16. Carl H. Claudy, *Introduction to Freemasonry* (Washington, DC: The Temple Publishers, c1931), p. 38.
17. One may attempt to argue that these are not "supreme beings," but if an individual accepts the tenets of Freemasonry as defining one's own truth, then why could these not be supreme beings?

The basis for much of the allegory and symbolism in Freemasonry comes from the Old Testament account of the building of Solomon's Temple. The central figure in Masonic allegory is Hiram Abiff, purported Grand Master at the temple project. Note, while there are several mentions of Hiram (or Huram) in the Old Testament, none precisely matches that of the allegorical Hiram Abiff (also Abif, Abi-ff, or Abiv among others). One such biblical reference is found in 2 Chronicles.[18]

> And now I have sent a skillful man, endowed with under-standing, Huram my master *craftsman* (the son of a woman of the daughters of Dan, and his father was a man of Tyre), skilled to work in gold and silver, bronze and iron, stone and wood, purple and blue, fine linen and crimson, and to make any engraving and to accomplish any plan which may be given to him, with your skillful men and with the skillful men of my lord David your father (2 Chronicles 2:13–14).

While there may be a historical basis for the builder of Solomon's Temple, all connection to actual history and biblical teaching ends there.

To summarize the basic allegory, Hiram Abiff went to visit the Temple. Entering the Temple from the West, Hiram — himself a Master Mason — was accosted by three Fellowcrafts. These Fellowcrafts wanted the secrets (or secret word) of a Master Mason. Hiram attempted to leave, each time attempting a different side of the Temple, going from South, back to West, and finally to the East and refused the Fellowcrafts who stopped him at each turn. The first two times he was wounded, but the third time he was killed by the assailant. The murderers fled after burying the body, but it was found after a search. In the end the assailants were found by searchers who overheard their lamentations coming in the form, "I wish that I had been killed in *such and such a manner*, rather than that I had been the cause of the death of our Master Hiram." The murderers were brought to Jerusalem and before Solomon, who sentenced them according to the punishments they had wished for themselves. The allegory concludes with Hiram interred in the Temple with great ceremony.[19]

---

18. Scriptures in this chapter are from the New King James Version of the Bible.
19. Many details and variations are omitted here for brevity. An interesting discussion of the variations is *The Evolution of the Hiramic Legend in England and France* by Joannes A.M. Snoek, himself a 32 degree mason (http://204.3.136.66/web/heredom-files/volume11/snoek.pdf).

In addition to the allegory above, the Blue Lodge draws allegorical symbolism from aspects of stonemasonry in their Lodge proceedings. Participants don aprons and participate in dialogue with references to the compass, square, gauge, plumb, and level to convey moral messages symbolically. The Entered Apprentice must go through a ceremony where he is led blindfolded around the Lodge ostensibly following the path of Hiram Abiff. During the Fellowcraft ceremony, initiates are taken into a room said to represent one of the chambers in Solomon's temple and the Master Mason's degree revolves around the Hiram Abiff allegory itself.

Advanced degrees may expand and expound on all of the above. For example, *Morals and Dogma* was published in 1872 by Alexander Pike of the Scottish Rite as an extensive commentary of the minutia of Masonic ritual. While an esoteric work, it does contain an emphasis on religious and cultural tolerance common to the thinking of his day. Philosophically, it expounded upon the idea that the root of all religion was the same. Concepts from ancient Egypt, Greece, and Phoenicia are linked with Buddhist, Hindu, Jewish, Islamic, and Christian doctrines to show the common traits in detail. Even though it was often given to a Master Mason upon attaining that degree, the work was not widely

Albert Pike

read (or understood) given its esoteric nature and immense size. *Morals and Dogma* nevertheless has had an influence on Masonic ritual as it has evolved through the past couple of centuries.

Although the source of authority in Masonic worship is ultimately oneself and the worshiper's own interpretation of the Hiram Abiff allegory, there is another major influence — that of the Lodge. Adherents to Freemasonry are required to make very serious oaths in order to advance in the three degrees of the Blue Lodge. These oaths are similar to the laments made by the three Fellowcrafts as they were discovered and summarily punished, and thus are the basis of the Lodge's authority over a Freemason.

Ostensibly a candidate has the opportunity to refuse these oaths because before he is given the obligation of the Entered Apprentice degree a candidate hears these words from the Worshipful Master:[20]

> Mr. _____, before you can proceed further in Freemasonry, it will be necessary for you to take an Obligation appertaining to this degree. It becomes my duty as well as pleasure to inform you that there is nothing contained in the Obligation that conflicts with the duties you owe to God, your country, your neighbor, your family, or yourself. With this assurance on my part, are you willing to take the Obligation? (Nevada ritual, circa 1984)

This same question is asked of the candidate before he proceeds with the obligation of the Fellow Craft degree, and likewise with the Master Mason degree.

Consider the penalties of the obligations (Nevada ritual, circa 1984):

> "To all of which I do solemnly and sincerely promise and swear, without any hesitation, mental reservation, or secret evasion of mind in me whatsoever; binding myself under no less a penalty than that of having . . .
>
> Entered Apprentice Degree: ". . . my throat cut across, my tongue torn out, and with my body buried in the sands of the sea at low-water mark, where the tide ebbs and flows twice in twenty-four hours, should I ever knowingly or willfully violate this, my solemn Obligation of an Entered Apprentice."
>
> Fellow Craft Degree: ". . . my left breast torn open, my heart and vitals taken thence, and with my body given as a prey to the vultures of the air, should I ever knowingly, or willfully, violate this, my solemn Obligation of a Fellow Craft.";
>
> Master Mason Degree: ". . . my body severed in twain, my bowels taken thence, and with my body burned to ashes, and the

---

20. Taken from http://www.emfj.org/oaths.htm

ashes thereof scattered to the four winds of Heaven, that there might remain neither track, trace nor remembrance among man or Masons of so vile and perjured a wretch as I should be, should I ever knowingly or willfully violate this, my solemn Obligation of a Master Mason."

And the ending for each of these obligations is:

"So help me, God, and make me steadfast to keep and perform the same."

These oaths represent a strong tie to the Lodge and the Freemason religion. Many Freemasons argue that the oaths themselves are allegorical, but regardless of whether they have any strength of validity or not, they clearly go against the teachings of Jesus in the Sermon on the Mount (Matthew 5:33–37):

Again you have heard that it was said to those of old, "You shall not swear falsely, but shall perform your oaths to the Lord." But I say to you, do not swear at all: neither by heaven, for it is God's throne; nor by the earth, for it is His footstool; nor by Jerusalem, for it is the city of the great King. Nor shall you swear by your head, because you cannot make one hair white or black. But let your "Yes" be "Yes," and your "No," "No." For whatever is more than these is from the evil one.

This warning should be a red flag against the religion of Freemasonry for anyone who professes faith in Jesus Christ.

Foundations and Beliefs

Fundamentally, the story of Hiram Abiff is the basis for most Masonic ritual, and many books have been devoted to sharing the story and associated rituals (despite the aforementioned oaths).

However, underlying the allegories is the true end of Masonic worship — pursuing Light. What is meant by the search for Light in the Masonic sense? It is not to be equated or confused with pursuing the Light of the World (Jesus), nor seeking absolute Truth, nor Christian salvation.[21] Recall

---

21. Many pro-masonic writings make the argument that it cannot be a religion because it does not offer a path to salvation — this is frankly untrue.

a portion of the funeral liturgy quoted earlier "We call ourselves builders because each one of us is trying to build his own spiritual temple of character. . . ." With that statement in mind, Freemasonry can be seen as fundamentally about the individual defining his own truth. After the vows, rituals of the Lodge, and the rules of Masonic body, there is a great amount of latitude to the adherent to interpret, visualize, and evaluate the allegories. At some point, the "truth" found in the allegories becomes a revelation and the Mason can be said to have gained more Light. No matter how confusing this may sound, all of Masonic teaching and ritual is a framework by which a Mason defines his own truth.

Given this premise and the growth of Freemasonry in the 17th and 18th centuries, it is reasonable to conclude that Freemasonry shares much of its religious basis with that of the intellectual movement from the same period known as the Enlightenment. The Enlightenment philosophy was characterized by "thinking for oneself" (as opposed to religious leaders for instance) and the employment and reliance on an individual's intellectual capacity in determining what to believe and how to act. These philosophies are very consistent with what is observed in Freemasonry. They are, however, contrary to biblical teachings of Christianity where the Word of God is the source of truth.

Use of Symbols

It is interesting to note the Freemasonry use of symbols in their allegorical exploration of truth. We've already seen the use of the square and the compass in the masonic emblem. These are used to express two of the three "Great Lights" in Freemasonry. A Wiccan Freemason, Robert Fisher, describes it like this:

> The Square means morality, honesty and fair dealing, whilst the Compasses are Freemasonry's most prominent symbol of truth and loyalty. The Compass, which is used to draw circles, can also be seen as representing the realm of the spiritual while the square, the symbol of earth and the realm of the material. Together, the compass and square represent the convergence of matter and spirit, and the convergence of earthly and spiritual responsibilities.[22]

---

22. Robert Fisher, http://pagantheologies.pbworks.com/w/page/13622064/Freemasonry.

Thus, Freemasonry symbols are used to illustrate the link between the material and the spiritual.

Before proceeding, one revealing quote by Mr. Fisher says:

> I can only say that as someone who was initiated as a Freemason first and as a Wiccan second I can honestly say that the Wiccan training and initiation opened my eyes to the magical potential that Freemasonry has and I think it so sad that in the main Freemasons are concerned with the externals of rite or organization rather than deeper content.[23]

There is also one other "Great Light" in Masonic ritual, the Volume of Sacred Law as it is referred to. In many cases, the Bible proper is used, but it does not necessarily need to be. In countries that are not predominantly Christian, the dominant religious text may be used. Whichever is used, it is displayed prominently with the other two "Lights" displayed upon it.

Rather than being an actual source of truth, like much in Freemasonry, the presence of the Volume of Sacred Law is symbolic.

> Like most other things in Freemasonry, the Holy Bible is itself a symbol of Divine Truth in every form. When viewed as a symbol, it represents that divine truth or knowledge from whatever source derived.[24]

Again, this appeal to truth from "whatever source" shows that the individual, not the true and living God and Creator, defines the truth. Also note in the quote the reference to "Divine Truth in every form." The emphasis is on many forms of truth, and ultimately centered upon the Mason's own interpretation.

Given the secret nature of Freemasonry, it is often tied to another secret society of the same era, the Illuminati. Illuminati symbolism and ties to revolutionary thought, conspiracy theory, and the relationship to Freemasonry are far beyond what can be described or addressed in this short chapter. For instance, it is widely believed that the pyramid on the U.S. dollar

---

23. Most Freemasons would argue that this is evidence of the individual truth that each one of them seeks. However, it illustrates the underlying influence of the allegories in leading men away from real truth.

24. http://www.themasonictrowel.com/Articles/degrees/degree_1st_files/the_great_light_of_fremasonry_gltx.htm.

bill, topped with the all-seeing eye is based on either Masonic or Illuminati symbolism or both. Regardless, there are undeniable ties to the Founding Fathers of the United States as James Madison, James Monroe, Benjamin Franklin, and George Washington were all Freemasons.

Theory of Origins

Since adherents to Freemasonry worship a "generic" god and reference a holy book symbolically, they do not necessarily have a consistent story of the origin of the universe. The Great Architect of the Universe is given credit for putting things in motion, and mankind is building upon that foundation (much like deism). The details of the origin of the universe are not important to developing Masonic allegory. However, an individual may draw upon their particular religious text or upon whatever individual experience one may have for the basis of their understanding of the origins of the universe.

This is an interesting consistency with Enlightenment principles of scientific thought growing rapidly during the same time that Freemasonry was building its philosophical underpinnings. In the Enlightenment, mankind — as the source of truth — rejected the revelations of Scripture, especially when it addressed the material world. Principles of geologic uniformitarianism (based on naturalism) arose during this same time. Observations surrounding the deposition of rock into layers over time led to an extrapolation and acceptance of millions or billions of years as to the age of the earth.[25] Secular "science" came in conflict with the authority of the Word of God. Theological and religious leaders at that time embraced the antiquity of the earth as a scientific fact. All of these factors combined to result in a rejection of the biblical account of origins. This type of thought aligns with the philosophical tenet of Freemasonry of a "supreme being," but denying that the Supreme Being is the ultimate source of truth.

Freemasonry has its influences in the growth and acceptance of evolutionary thought. Erasmus Darwin was a Mason as was Richard, Charles Darwin's father.[26] There is no formal record that Charles Darwin himself was a Mason, but there is no denying the influence of Enlightenment and Masonic thought on him. When Darwin observed the diversity in the

---

25. See Terry Mortenson, *The Great Turning Point* (Green Forest, AR: Master Books, 2012).
26. William R. Denslow, *10,000 Famous Freemasons* (Richmond, VA: Macoy Publishing & Masonic Supply Co., Inc., 1957). For mother lodge, cf. H.L. Haywood, *Supplement to Mackey Encyclopedia of Freemasonry* (1966), p. 1198, retrieved from http://freemasonry. bcy.ca/biography/darwin_e/darwin_e.html.

Galapagos, rather than interpret it in light of the revelation of God's Word, he chose to interpret it in the mind of his own truth and the anti-[Christian-based]-religious, anti-establishment nature of the Enlightenment.

Arbitrary Doctrines and Salvation

Some historical records of Freemasonry actually refer to the Trinity[27] and in particular "The Son," but as the religion has grown and evolved, that level of alignment with Christian teaching has been deemphasized or completely removed. This may explain why many Christians were part of it in the past, but today, there is no excuse for Christians to be part of this anti-Christian religion.

The religion of Freemasonry has changed and is continuing to change into something that is opposed to Christianity. Fraternal organizations, for example, are not necessarily a bad thing for a Christian, but when doctrines of such an organization change to oppose biblical doctrines, then should Christians be part of that organization . . . especially when they become a religion of themselves?

In fact, the recognized uniqueness of Christianity — Jesus Christ — is not mentioned in any Masonic teachings. Outside religion and politics as topics are forbidden in a Lodge, but this is quite odd given that Freemasonry is a religion itself. In reality, the prohibition is in reference to sectarianism and the fact that Masons worship the GAOTU generically and one member could not call out a particular deity or doctrine at the potential offense of another.

There are many, many sources, including ex-Masons, that claim that the underlying "god" of Freemasonry is demonic or satanic. It is true that making oneself the source of truth is absolutely consistent with satanic tactics (e.g., the Garden of Eden), but this may not be universally the case since each Freemason determines for himself who is his god. One biblical basis for why man was created was to worship God the Creator, not some generic Great Architect of the Universe. However, any religion that goes against this is in reality not worshiping Satan, but is advocating the worship of the individual. By denying the Creator, and more importantly the sacrifice by the Creator for the creation, one could be considered to be "worshiping Satan," but not as a deity per se. In this, I agree with Masons who say they do not worship demons or Satan or Lucifer. They simply agree with the tactics of the original liar.

---

27. http://www.rgle.org.uk/RGLE_Tenet.htm.

Let us consider the view of Freemasonry toward Scripture. The following excerpt details well the underlying basis of Freemasonry. Note the inconsistency in the insistence upon the existence of a Supreme Being, but denying that a common source of truth exists.

> Freemasonry invites men of all faiths to its teachings, requiring only a belief in a Supreme Being, knowing that we all pray to the God and Father of the Universe regardless of the actual name one uses to address Him. Thus, the Bible is often referred to as the Volume of Sacred Law, allowing men of differing faiths to use the Sacred Writings of their faith as the Volume of Sacred Law.
>
> What does this mean to the Freemason? The fact that the Holy Bible or some other Volume of Sacred Law rests open upon the Altar of Freemasonry means the Freemason must have some Divine Revelation. The Freemason must seek truth and wisdom from a source greater than that from human minds. Freemasonry makes no attempt at a detailed interpretation of the Bible. The Volume of Sacred Law lies upon the Altar open for all to read, open for all to study and interpret for himself. The tie that unites Freemasonry is strong, but it provides for the utmost liberty of faith and thought. It unites men not by creed or dogma, but upon the broad truth of a belief and faith in God, the Supreme Grand Architect of the Universe. Freemasonry is truly a Brotherhood of Man under the Fatherhood of God.[28]

Again, many Masons are strong in their statements that Freemasonry is not a religion and is not because it does not offer a plan of salvation or have specific doctrines. However, evaluate the concluding statements from the Master Mason Degree ritual:

> Then, finally my brethren, let us imitate our Grand Master, Hiram Abiff, in his virtuous conduct, his unfeigned piety to God, and his inflexible fidelity to his trust; that, like him, we may welcome the grim tyrant, Death, and receive him as a kind messenger sent by our Supreme Grand Master, to translate us from this

28. http://www.themasonictrowel.com/Articles/degrees/degree_1st_files/the_great_light_of_fremasonry_gltx.htm

imperfect to that all-perfect, glorious, and celestial Lodge above, where the Supreme Architect of the Universe presides.

Much of Masonic allegory does emphasize the sureness and inevitability of death. While it does not speak of the need for salvation per se, salvation is assumed by the acceptance of the Freemason by the "Supreme Grand Master . . . in the celestial Lodge above" through the process of death. In order to obtain that salvation, you are instructed to imitate Hiram Abiff so that you can get into heaven. The nature of the salvation message within Freemasonry is hard to deny given these statements.

So, how does one go about imitating Hiram Abiff? Think back to the allegory. Hiram traveled through the compass directions of West, South, and East. In much of Masonic allegory and ritual, the Light is "in the East," and adherents go through a sequence and eventually are "brought to the light" in the East which is where the Worshipful Master (CEO of the Lodge) sits.

Regardless of symbolism, there is an appeal that the Worshipful Master is the light or at least sits in the place of the light. The Worshipful Master holds the position that can bring the light to the adherent or at least get them on the path. The journey to the light embodies much of Masonic thought, and theoretically you cannot obtain all of the light that can be conferred in a lodge of Master Masons until you become the Worshipful Master yourself.[29] Of course, the Worshipful Master is the head of Blue Lodge Masonry and "additional light" can be gained through its many attached organizations. Unfortunately, this light is founded upon self-determination of truth and not the ultimate truth as revealed by the Holy Bible.

The problem is that this is a false gospel, one based on imitation of Hiram Abiff, rather than faith in Jesus Christ. Salvation is obtained through the efforts of imitating Hiram Abiff and becomes a works-based salvation. Also, in 1 Corinthians 15:26, "The last enemy that will be destroyed is death," but in Masonic teachings, death is a "kind messenger." These are just a few examples of the disparity between grace-based salvation through faith in Christ and the nature of salvation and death as described in Freemasonry.

Good News for Freemasons

A friend of mine asked me what I knew about the Masons, as he was considering joining. As a young Christian, he didn't see anything inherently

---

29. http://www.nj-freemasons.org/masoniclight.php.

wrong with joining a group that is known for its community service and its spirit of brother-hood. At the time, I didn't know a lot about the Masons and their beliefs, so rather than give unin-formed advice, I simply asked this question: "Why do you want to join? What is it about the Masons that is appealing to you?"

Stained glass window at St. John's Church, Chester, England, depicting Hiram Abiff

His response was typical in a world today where faith in the sustaining power of the Creator has been lost and the Church, by and large, has failed to serve its people. "I want to have assur-ance that if something happened to me, my widow would be taken care of and if I ended up in court, I could count on my fellow Mason's to take care of things for me." I was shocked at his response. Here was a young Christian looking to a secular group to serve his needs in an area that typically would fall to faith in Christ and the Body of Christ. My, how far the Church has fallen from influence, even among its own!

Even so, what would be the problem with a Christian also being a Free-mason? Let's examine this question further. A Christian (assuming that he was worshiping Jesus) walking into a Hindu temple to take part in the worship service and joining in corporate prayer to Vishnu is not unlike a Masonic ceremony where there is corporate prayer to GAOTU where you may have Christians, Muslims, Hindus, and Buddhists all together. Would Jesus Christ be willing to accept worship in this manner? The answer is found in Paul's first letter to the church at Corinth.[30] Paul wrote in 1 Cor-inthians 10:20–22:

---

30. http://www.emfj.org/mensclub.htm.

> I do not want you to have fellowship with demons. You cannot drink the cup of the Lord and the cup of demons; you cannot partake of the Lord's table and of the table of demons. Or do we provoke the Lord to jealousy? Are we stronger than He?

In this passage, Paul warns believers about mixing religions, especially those that are demonic in nature. As we have discussed, Freemasonry could be considered demonic in its approach to authority. This Scripture clearly warns against engaging in this kind of behavior.

Joining in a group prayer to a generic, self-determined God could be considered a heresy. And the acceptance of the Master Mason that he is to imitate Hiram Abiff for salvation is a false gospel. The penalty for teaching a false gospel is eternal in nature as Paul wrote in Galatians 1:8–10:

> But even if we, or an angel from heaven, preach any other gospel to you than what we have preached to you, let him be accursed. As we have said before, so now I say again, if anyone preaches any other gospel to you than what you have received, let him be accursed.
>
> For do I now persuade men, or God? Or do I seek to please men? For if I still pleased men, I would not be a bondservant of Christ.

Rather than imitate Hiram Abiff in order to gain salvation, Christians are to trust in the sacrifice of Jesus Christ and the truth of His Resurrection. As we see in 1 Corinthians 15:1–4:

> Moreover, brethren, I declare to you the gospel which I preached to you, which also you received and in which you stand, by which also you are saved, if you hold fast that word which I preached to you — unless you believed in vain.
>
> For I delivered to you first of all that which I also received: that Christ died for our sins according to the Scriptures, and that He was buried, and that He rose again the third day according to the Scriptures.

Paul repeatedly appeals to the authority of the Scriptures as his source of truth for the sacrifice of Jesus Christ. How much more should Christians do the same?

Additionally, the Scriptures document that Jesus, not Hiram Abiff, is the only way to salvation and reconciliation with God. In John 14:6, Jesus said:

> Jesus said to him, "I am the way, the truth, and the life. No one comes to the Father except through Me.

Even with the overwhelming weight of the words of Christ, some Masons may be concerned about their allegiance to the Lodge and the oaths that they took to join. Trust in Christ, and the oaths that you took are null and void. Leviticus 5:4–5 teaches that if something is hidden from a man and he takes an oath thoughtlessly, he is guilty of sin:

> Or if a person swears, speaking thoughtlessly with his lips to do evil or to do good, whatever it is that a man may pronounce by an oath, and he is unaware of it — when he realizes it, then he shall be guilty in any of these matters.
>
> And it shall be, when he is guilty in any of these matters, that he shall confess that he has sinned in that thing.

However, once he recognizes it and confesses it as sin, he can claim the promises of 1 John 1:8–9:

> If we say that we have no sin, we deceive ourselves, and the truth is not in us. If we confess our sins, He is faithful and just to forgive us our sins and to cleanse us from all unrighteousness.

If you are a Christian who has become ensnared in Freemasonry, I suggest that you confess your involvement in Freemasonry as sin, resign from your Lodge, and renounce your involvement. Scripture is clear that you are not to remain in such a state of dualistic allegiance. Second Corinthians 6:14–17 gives godly advice in this area:

> Do not be unequally yoked together with unbelievers. For what fellowship has righteousness with lawlessness? And what communion has light with darkness? And what accord has Christ with Belial? Or what part has a believer with an unbeliever? And what agreement has the temple of God with idols? For you are the temple of the living God. As God has said: "I will dwell in

them and walk among them. I will be their God, and they shall be My people." Therefore "Come out from among them and be separate," says the Lord. "Do not touch what is unclean, And I will receive you."

There are many resources to assist you in this process.[31] Forgiveness in Christ is available for those who repent and trust in Christ, but our repentance must be accompanied by works befitting that repentance (Acts 26:20).

Summary of Freemason Beliefs

Doctrine	Freemason Teaching
God	Whichever deity you choose to refer to as the Great Architect
Authority/ Revelation	There is a diverse tradition, but all based on man's ideas and personal religious interpretations; local Lodge leaders hold authority and teach the allegorical symbolism
Man	A being who has a duty to do good
Sin	Transgression of individual ethical codes
Salvation	Varies by individual; progressing through various degrees within the religious system
Creation	Varies by individual; generally a deistic view of origins that would accommodate evolutionary views

---

31. http://www.emfj.org/leave.htm.

Chapter 15

Zoroastrianism

Dr. Carl Broggi

Origins of Zoroastrianism

The founder of Zoroastrianism was a man named *Zarathushtra*, written in Greek as *Zoroaster*, from which comes the name *Zoroastrianism*. Most scholars say that Zoroaster lived around 650 years before Christ, though there is some debate as to precisely when and where he was born. One scholar in the field of world religions writes:

> The early history of Zoroastrianism is much in dispute. The religion was founded by Zoroaster, but it is not certain when he lived, where he lived or how much of later Zoroastrianism came from him. Tradition puts him in western Iran in the sixth century B.C., a little earlier than the Buddha in India, but it is now thought that he lived in northeastern Iran, in the area on the borders of modern Afghanistan and Turkmenistan. An alternate theory dates him much earlier, somewhere from 1700 to 1500 B.C., and places him in the plains of Central Asia, perhaps before the first groups of Aryans moved south from the plains into Iran and India.[1]

---

1. Richard Cavendish, *The Great Religions* (New York: Arco Publishing Company, 1980), p. 125.

Church historian Dr. Philip Schaff wrote about 100 years ago regarding Zoroastrianism:

> Zoroastrianism, or Fire-worship, is the ancient Persian religion, and traced to Zoroaster (Zarathustra), a priest in the temple of the Sun, who lived about B.C. 1300. It was the religion of Cyrus, Darius, Hystaspis, and Xerxes, and of the Wise Men from the East who came to worship the new-born Messiah at Bethlehem. . . . It is a system of dualism with a monad behind and, possibly a reconciliation in prospect. Ormazd is the good principle (the sun, the light), and Ahriman, the evil principle (darkness, winter), who corresponds to the Devil of the Scriptures; yet both were created by Zerana-Akerana. They are in constant antagonism, and hosts of good and bad angels under their banners. There is an incessant war going on in heaven as well as on earth. At last Ormazd sends his prophet (a kind of Messiah) to convert mankind; then follows a general resurrection, and separation of the just from sinners . . . the followers of this religion worship with the face turned towards the sun or the fire upon the altar; hence they are called fire-worshipers.[2]

This religion obviously has aspects similar to Christianity and may have been influenced by events from Genesis forward as they were passed down from generation to generation.

The Zoroastrian View of God

Regardless, Zoroastrianism is considered one of the world's oldest monotheistic religions — the doctrine or belief that there is only one God. However, while Zoroastrians say they believe there is one supreme God whom they call Ahura Mazda, they also recognize another immortal deity, known as Angra Mainyu, who represents the epitome of evil. So using the traditional definition of monotheism, many religious scholars would say it is more accurate to describe this religion as polytheistic. Polytheism is the belief or worship of more than one God, taken from the Greek word *poly*, meaning many and *theos*, meaning God. Polytheism is in contrast to the term "monotheism," derived from the Greek word *mono*, meaning one.

2. Philip Schaff, *Theological Propaedeutic* (New York: Charles Scribner's Sons Publisher, 1904), p. 49–50.

Nineteenth-century depiction of Zoroaster derived from a figure in a 4th-century sculpture, extracted from *Persia by a Persian* (Isaac Adams, 1906)

As Christians, it is important to understand that when God created us in His image, He wrote monotheism into our "spiritual DNA." In helping us to understand this reality, the Apostle Paul explains in the first two chapters of the Book of Romans that the existence of only one true God is evident to everyone in one of two ways. First, it is evident by the creation around us: "For since the creation of the world His invisible attributes are clearly seen, being understood by the things that are made, even His eternal power and Godhead, so that they are without excuse" (Romans 1:20).[3] The Bible reminds us that everything God has created in this world — every leaf, every flower, every drop of water — bears the stamp, "Made by God."

In addition to this outward revelation found in the visible creation, people also possess an inward knowledge of God known as the conscience. Romans 2 says that people of the world who have never even read a Bible instinctively understand certain moral parameters because God has "the law written in their hearts" (Romans 2:15). So when one reads in Zoroastrian literature of two deities who exist side by side, we immediately know that error has entered into this religion. Since people are born with a monotheistic view of God, it is only when they suppress the truth — seen outwardly in the creation and felt inwardly by the conscience — that they become polytheistic.

According to God's Word, people who believe in many gods are not displaying an earnest search for God, but are giving evidence of their rebellion against God (Romans 1:21–23). Having traveled to many countries of the world to share the good news, I understand that there are individuals

---

3. Scripture in this chapter is from the New King James Version of the Bible.

raised from birth in false religious systems like Zoroastrianism. Neverthe-less, I have also witnessed that many people caught up in a polytheistic religion know that it is not true. Therefore, it is our responsibility as Chris-tians to reason with them that there is only one God, who has revealed Himself in Jesus Christ.[4] People who practice Zoroastrianism are lost, and like everyone else in this world, they need to receive the forgiveness found in Jesus Christ.

The Zoroastrian View of Creation

Zoroastrians say that their supreme deity, Ahura Mazda, created the world. Their religions literature states:

> In the beginning, there was nothing in the world except Ahura Mazda, the Wise Lord, who lived in the Endless Light. And the Evil Spirit, Ahriman, who lived in the Absolute Dark-ness. Between them lay only emptiness.
>
> One day, Ahura Mazda decided to make different creations. First He shaped the sky made of metal, shinning and bright. Second, He made the pure water. Third, the Wise Lord created the Earth, flat and round with no mountains and valleys. Fourth, He made the plants, moist and sweet with no bark or thorn. Fifth, he created the animals, big and small. Then he created the First Man, Gayomard, bright, tall, and handsome. And lastly, he created Fire and distributed it within the whole creation. The Wise Lord ordered Fire to serve the mankind in preparing food and overcoming cold.[5]

Anyone who has read the opening chapters of Genesis can quickly see that there are major differences between the creation account in Genesis and the creation story in Zoroastrian literature; however, there are a few vague similarities. Because of these similarities, some liberal scholars have argued that Zoroastrianism predates the biblical record of Genesis and influenced the writings of Moses.

4. For some timeless lessons on how to reason with polytheistic people, study the Apostle Paul's interchange with the people of Athens on Mars Hill (Acts 17:16–34).
5. This creation account is taken from the *Book of Creation,* the *Bundahishn,* dating from the 6th century A.D. While this book draws on the Avesta, the official sacred text used by Zo-roastrians, because it reflects Zoroastrian scripture, today it is also considered authoritative by those in this cultish religion. Zorastriankids.com/creation.html.

Others argue that there was one common myth as to how the creation of the world took place and with time it gave birth to many different creation accounts. This view is very similar to those of liberal scholars who point out that there are over 200 different flood accounts found in ancient cultures. From these, it is contended that the different (but sometimes similar) accounts reflect commonly held ancient myths, but not historical fact. Commenting on this fallacious argument, Ken Ham writes:

> When I attended university in Australia (many years ago!), I remember one of my professors stating that there were Babylonian stories about a flood similar to the account in the Bible. Therefore he concluded, the Jews borrowed their "story" from the Babylonians! But I say it's really the other way round! There are flood legends in cultures all over the world because there really was an actual global Flood — Noah's Flood. As the account of the Flood was handed down (and particularly as people spread out around the world after the Tower of Babel), it was changed by many cultures. Yet many of these legends (including the Babylonian ones) have similar elements to the Bible's account. Because the Bible is God's inspired Word, it gives us the true account.[6]

This same line of reasoning could be used in helping to sort out the different, (but sometimes similar) creation accounts. On the one hand, even if one subscribes to the earlier and much highly debated date that places Zoroaster 1,700 years before Christ, this does not change the fact that in the early chapters of Genesis, Moses is writing of historical events that took place approximately 4,000 years before Christ.

On the other hand, if one ascribes to the founding of Zoroastrianism held by most scholars to be the 6th century B.C., the Bible still predates the writings of Zoroastrianism. Most historians and scholars, liberal and conservative alike, place the writing of the Torah (Genesis–Deuteronomy) between 1446 and 1406 B.C. when Moses and the children of Israel wandered in the desert for 40 years.

This would mean that the Old Testament pre-dates the oral traditions of Zoroaster, later recorded in the Avesta (the official religious text of

---

6. Ken Ham, Blog, January 27, 2014, answersingenesis.org/blogs/ken-ham/2014/01/27/was-noahs-ark-round/.

Zoroastrianism), by close to 900 years. Since the Bible predates the religious teachings of the false prophet Zoroaster, one should expect some similarities in Zoroastrianism and other ancient cultures concerning the creation of the world.

As with the Flood of Noah's day, the different creation accounts began with one authoritative account written by God through Moses and later disseminated through the peoples of the world after the Tower of Babel (Genesis 10–11).

The Zoroastrian Source of Revelation

The false prophet Zoroaster, purportedly at the age of 30, received a vision that he recorded in the Avesta. He was drawing water from the Daiti River and supposedly saw a "Shining Being," who called himself Vohu Manah. Most Zoroastrian scholars concur that this was an angel. According to Zoroaster, Vohu Manah led him into the presence of Ahura Mazda, the Zoroastrian god. This supposedly was the first in a series of visions in which Zoroaster asked questions and received answers from Ahura Mazda. The answers he received became the foundational tenets for the Zoroastrian faith. From these visions given uniquely to him, Zoroaster became the sole human author of the Zoroastrian religious literature.

Of course, as Christians, we know that Satan describes himself as "an angel of light" and that he uses fallen angels to communicate false doctrine (2 Corinthians 11:13–15; 1 Timothy 4:1). Typical in virtually every religious cult, there is some vision, some angelic messenger, or some revelation, usually given to a single person. I find it interesting that Zoroaster's method of enlightenment was very similar to Mohammed's enlightenment in Islam. Mohammed also supposedly received a vision from an angel, and this "revelation" became Islam's religious text, the Quran.

In both Zoroastrianism and Islam, the source of the religious revelation that is held to be authoritative is given to just one man, and in both instances it is given by an angel. By comparison, the revelation found and recorded in the Bible is so very different.

One of the amazing facts about the Bible is that although it was written by a wide diversity of authors (as many as 40), over a period of 1,600 years, from many different locations and under a wide variety of conditions, the Bible is uniquely one book, not merely a collection of 66 books.

The authors of the Bible lived in a variety of cultures, had different life experiences, and often were quite different in their personal make-up. They wrote their material from three continents (Africa, Asia, and Europe), in very diverse places — Moses in a desert, Solomon in a palace, Paul in a prison, John in exile, etc. — while employing three languages in their writings (Hebrew, Aramaic, and Greek). In addition, they represented a wide variety of backgrounds and professions. For instance, Moses was a political leader; Joshua a military leader; David a shepherd; Nehemiah a cupbearer; Solomon a king; Amos a herdsman; Daniel a prime minister; Matthew a tax collector; Luke a medical doctor; Paul a rabbi; and Peter a fisherman. And what is so amazing is that while most of the human authors never met each other and were unfamiliar with each other's writings, the Bible is still a unified whole, without a single contradiction! There is a perfect unity that runs from Genesis to Revelation. The only explanation is that the Bible is the Word of God. The only explanation is that behind the 40 human authors, there was one Divine Author, God the Holy Spirit.[7]

The Zoroastrian View of Good and Evil

Zoroastrianism teaches that there is a "cosmic dualism" that is unfolding in the universe. "Cosmic dualism" is a term used to summarize Zoroaster's belief that there is an ongoing battle, an ongoing tension, between good and evil. The "good power" is represented in their supreme being, Ahura Mazda, while the "evil power" is represented in Angra Mainyu. They believe that Ahura Mazda is responsible for the best in the world, while Angra Mainyu, existing alongside their supreme deity, infiltrates the universe with evil, making it impure. Therefore, Zoroastrians would attribute aging, sickness, famine, natural disasters, and death to this evil power. Zoroastrianism teaches that these two co-equal powers existed side by side from the beginning of time.[8] Furthermore, this "cosmic dualism" is reflected in man's "moral dualism" where he too makes both good and evil choices.

Of course, this teaching of moral dualism is contradictory to the revelation of God found in the Bible. When God created the world, "God saw

---

7. "Why Is the Bible Unique," Dr. Carl J. Broggi, p. 53, found in Ken Ham and Bodie Hodge, eds., *How Do We Know The Bible Is True*, Volume 2 (Green Forest, AR: Master Books, 2012).

8. For a helpful discussion on this topic with direct quotations from their religious writings, see *Early Zoroastrianism* by James Hope Moulton (London: Constable and Company, 1913), p. 344–349.

everything that He had made, and indeed it was very good" (Genesis 1:31). The Bible is clear that all of God's creation was very good, but sin entered into His creation through both the fall of Satan and the Fall of man.[9] The Bible does not present two cosmic powers dueling against each other from the beginning. There is one sovereign God who rules and reigns, who at a point in time made both angels and men with the capacity to choose. One-third of the angels (now called demons) rebelled, as did all of humanity since Adam (Revelation 12:4; Romans 5:12). The one true God of the Bible is very clear that it was not some cosmic evil force that brought aging, sickness, famine, natural disasters, and death into this world; it was man's sin (Romans 8:20–22). The Zoroastrian good god Ahura Mazda is co-eternal to the evil god Angra Mainyu. By contrast, the God of the Bible is sovereign over all. Furthermore, Satan is not the opposite of God; rather he is a created being and has limited power and by God's grace, limited time (Ezekiel 28:15; Job 1:12).

The Zoroastrian View of Salvation

Zoroastrianism teaches that man has a free will, and in the end he will be rewarded for his choices. Ahura Mazda, the "good power," is perfect and abides in heaven, as will all who live righteously. Alongside this "good power" is Angra Mainyu, the "evil power," who is wicked and dwells in the depths of hell, as will all who live wickedly. Zoroastrianism teaches that when a person dies he goes to heaven or hell depending on his deeds during his lifetime.[10] This religion is really no different from all the different "isms" found around the world: Confucianism, Mohammedism, Taoism, Sikhism, or Shintoism. All these religions teach that people are ultimately received by a Supreme Being or into some afterlife on the basis of what they have accomplished.

Why Should I Care about Zoroastrianism?

Why should you care about a subject that most of us can hardly pronounce? We should care because God has called us to reach the world for Christ, and tens of millions of people are trapped either directly or indirectly in this false religion of Zoroastrianism. Jesus Christ commissioned His followers to

---

9. To study the fall of Satan read Isaiah 14 and Ezekiel 28. To study the Fall of man read Genesis 3.
10. The above summary of these doctrines can be found in the following Zoroastrian scripture (Yasna 30:2, 4, 9-11; 31:8, 9; 43:12; 46:12; 51:6; 53:7-9). The Yasna is considered by Zoroastrians to be the most important portion of the Avesta.

"Go into all the world and preach the gospel to every creature" (Mark 16:15).

The U.S. Center for World Mission is an organization that, among other endeavors, catalogues all of the unreached people groups in the world. It continually stresses to Christians living in the West that most people who need to hear the gospel of Jesus Christ are located in the part of the world that missiologists refer to as the 10/40 window. The 10/40 window can be defined simply as, "the rectangular area of North Africa, the Middle East, and Asia, approximately between 10 degrees north and 40 degrees north latitude. This section of the world is often called 'The Resistant Belt' and includes the majority of the world's Muslims, Hindus, and Buddhists."[11]

The god Ahura Mazda on the rock relief of Shapour II at Taq-e Bustan The rock relief of Sasanian king Shapur II (309-379 CE) at Taq-e Bostan, also known as Taq-e Bustan I, shows a double scene of investiture and victory.

While this geographical region of the world comprises only about one-third of earth's total land area, nearly two-thirds of the world's people reside here. Included in this mass of humanity are the majority of those who practice Zoroastrianism. People groups found in India, Iran, Afghanistan, and Azerbaijan currently practice pure, undiluted Zoroastrianism. But there are also tens of millions who do not necessarily practice Zoroastrianism in its purest form, but who have adopted aspects of this cultish religion.

For instance, when describing the 650,000 Yazidi people of Iraq, many of whom have been attacked and slaughtered by ISIS,[12] Dan Scribner of the U.S. Center for World Mission writes: "The Yazidi people follow an

11. "What is the 10/40 Window?" by the Joshua Project, A ministry of the U.S. Center for World Mission.

12. The *Islamic State of Iraq and Syria* (ISIS), also translated as the *Islamic State of Iraq and the Levant* (ISIL), and known too by the self-proclaimed title of *Islamic State* (IS), is a Sunni, extremist, jihadist rebel group controlling territory in Iraq, Syria, eastern Libya, the Sinai Peninsula of Egypt, parts of Pakistan, and parts of India.

old religion which has remnants of Zoroastrianism, Hinduism, Judaism, and Christianity."[13] Those practicing the purest expression of Zoroastrianism number approximately 11,000 in the United States and approximately 300,000 worldwide. However, those practicing component parts of Zoroastrianism, mixed in with some other religion, number in the millions.

Americans might possibly meet someone living here who is practicing Zoroastrianism in its purest form.[14] God is bringing many different unreached peoples from around the world to our own land. Under current immigration law, the United States often grants refugee status to those who are persecuted for their religious beliefs.[15] This includes a people group known as the Parsis, who originate from the Bombay region of India and practice Zoroastrianism.[16] In addition, many of the Kurdish people of Turkey, Syria, Iraq, and Iran trace their religious roots to Zoroastrianism. Most Kurds in these nations are only nominally Muslims, of the Sunni branch.[17] "It has been said that Kurds hold their Islam lightly, due to several factors, one being that many Kurds still feel some connection with the ancient Zoroastrian faith. They feel it is an original Kurdish spirituality that far predates the seventh century A.D. arrival of Muhammad."[18] Overall, as more and more of the peoples from countries found in the 10/40 window come and take up residence in our own nation, we will meet an increasing number of individuals who embrace Zoroastrianism.

---

13. Dan Scribner, newsletter of the U.S. Center for World Mission, June 9, 2014.
14. According to the Federation of Zoroastrian Associations of North America, this number is small, estimated at approximately 11,000. For a demographic breakdown for North American, go to www.fezana.org.
15. For a helpful article explaining the *1951 United Nations Convention Relating to the Status of Refugees* which the United States bases its immigration policy on, see the University of Minnesota's Human Rights Library article on "Study Guide: The Rights of Refugees," Human Rights Education Associates 2003, http://www1.umn.edu/humanrts/edumat/studyguides/refugees.htm.
16. The Parsis, whose name means "Persians," are descended from Persian Zoroastrians, having immigrated to India in the last century to avoid religious persecution by the Muslims. They live chiefly in Bombay and in a few towns and villages mostly to the north of Bombay, but also in places like Karachi (Pakistan), Bangalore (Karnataka, India), and now in the United States.
17. Shiite Muslims are known for persecuting Sunni Muslims. The Sunni branch believes that the first four caliphs — Mohammed's successors — rightfully took his place as legitimate religious leaders of Muslims. Shiites, in contrast, believe that only the heirs of the fourth caliph, Ali, are the legitimate successors of Mohammed. See more at historynewsnetwork.org/article/934.
18. US Center for World Mission, article, "The Kurds" at www.http://joshuaproject.net/peoplegroups.

Increasingly, Christians in America who are faithful to share the gospel are discovering that religious beliefs once foreign to us have now moved into the American religious landscape. I recently baptized three individuals from India who have come to faith in Jesus Christ. Witnessing their conversions has heightened my awareness of other people from India who live in our community. India currently has a population of 1.3 billion people, and it is expected to pass China in population growth by 2025.[19] If Christ has not returned by that time, there will be more people from India alive on planet Earth than any other single people group. Being aware of this phenomena is important, because India is the primary nation where Zoroastrianism has been syncretized into Hinduism and the other religions found there.

According to *Operation World*, Hinduism is the principal religious faith of India, practiced by nearly 1 billion people living there.[20] So when you speak to Hindu people living here in America, you may be talking to people who knowingly or unknowingly embrace a number of the tenets of Zoroastrianism.

In addition, since Zoroastrianism has often been syncretized into many other world religions, and with the East moving West, being able to understand the beliefs of this false religion will better equip a Christian to win these people to Christ. All these factors combined should be enough motivation for any believer who takes the Great Commission seriously to want to reach a Zorastrian with the gospel.

Reaching a Zoroastrian with the Gospel

While there seems to be endless other issues in the Zoroastrianism cult that one could examine, like the manner in which they bury their dead, the so-called fire temples they worship in, or the allegiance they give to their seven archangels, to name just a few of dozens of topics we could have covered, we have nonetheless examined the principal components of Zoroastrianism. As

---

19. "India to Pass China in Population" by Sam Roberts, *The New York Times*, December 15, 2009.

20. *Operation World* is a wonderful resource to help Christians understand the religious climate of every nation in order to intelligently pray for the unevangelized. Their website (operationworld.org) indicates that the world's least-evangelized peoples are concentrated in India. Of 159 people groups of over 1 million people, 133 are unreached. Hundreds more groups of fewer than 1 million are unreached. Also, 953 ethnic groups have populations greater than 10,000; of these, 205 have no church and little to no outreach from Christians. About 700,000 of these people practice pure Zoroastrianism. However, nearly one billion people practice some form of Hinduism in which you will find components of Zoroastrianism. Only about 2.2 percent of the population is considered to be evangelical Christians.

in the study of any religious cult, what is critically important is not necessarily knowing every point of doctrine the religious cult ascribes to, but at least knowing the major points in order to be able to springboard into a discussion of the truth.

One should never be intimidated by the "strangeness" of so many new religions entering America. People are people, usually looking for meaning in life, and trying to find some way in which to relieve a guilty conscience. Never forget that no matter what people may tell you about their so-called god or even multiple gods, you can still appeal to what Christian theologians refer to as "general revelation."

General revelation is that truth that God has revealed about Himself to all people, wherever one may live in the world. People outwardly are able to understand that there is one Creator God who made the world we live in. God's fingerprints are all over His creation, and God wrote His moral dictates on each person's heart (Psalm 19:1–6; Acts 14:17; Romans 1:20, 2:14–15). God's laws are a reflection of God's character, which is why man innately knows what is right and wrong, and what is just and unjust. Certainly, people can sin against their conscience and develop a calloused conscience (1 Timothy 4:2; Titus 1:5; Hebrews 10:22), but they still know that they have sinned against a holy God (Romans 1:32). Our responsibility remains the same, and that is to make a defense for the truth found in the Bible. We are to share the forgiveness that is offered in Jesus Christ.

Remember, most other major religions in the world, including Zoroastrianism, claim that a person can achieve, on his own, some kind of afterlife by how he lives. However, the Bible alone teaches man cannot save himself, because the penalty for sin is death (Romans 6:23).

If You Have Been Influenced by Zoroastrianism

We have good news to share, how God in Christ took that death penalty for us, when He became a man and died on the Cross in our place (2 Corinthians 5:19). Jesus Christ then proved His sinless perfection, and therefore His ability to take our punishment as a sinless person, when He was raised from the dead (Romans 1:4, 4:25). The message of the Bible is that no one can possibly earn salvation, but each one must receive salvation by placing his or her faith in Jesus Christ alone (Ephesians 2:8–9).

God does not spell salvation "DO" — and God does not spell salvation "DON'T" — God spells salvation "DONE" (John 19:30). For this reason, with kindness and compassion, knowing that the Holy Spirit works with us as we share this message of forgiveness (John 16:8), we can boldly declare that Jesus Christ is the only way to heaven. We must never forget that Christ did not claim to be a good way to God. He did not even claim to be the best way to God. He claimed to be the only way to the Father (John 14:6).

Wherever you go in this country or this world, people need forgiveness. People need release from the wrong things they have done and the relief that only a clear conscience can bring. As Bible-believing Christians, we have the only message that both works and is true (Acts 4:12).

So look around the community you live in. You will probably find someone from Iran or Iraq or India or some place that either knowingly or unknowingly has embraced some tenet of Zoroastrianism. Share the good news of Christ with them.

Possibly before reading this chapter you were under the impression that your good deeds could save you, or at least they helped to save you. But maybe now you understand that it is only by the gospel, defined as the death, burial, and Resurrection of Christ, that you can be forgiven (1 Corinthians 15:1–3; Romans 1:16). It really does not matter what you may be guilty of in your past. God can forgive you, and He will forgive you, but He will only forgive you if you will call on His Son Jesus Christ to save you (Romans 10:13) I invite you to do that right now.

Summary of Zoroastrian Beliefs

Doctrine	Zoroastrian Teaching
God	Ahura Mazda is the supreme god who is worshiped, but there is also another immortal deity who represents evil, Angra Mainyu.
Authority/ Revelation	The Avesta is the scriptural record of the revelation announced by the prophet Zoroaster. Various sects hold to different sections as authoritative.
Man	The first man was created by Ahura Mazda but evil entered the universe and corrupted man; man must use his free will to choose to do good

Sin	Sin has physical and spiritual aspects and is not well-defined apart from doing good or evil.
Salvation	Those who do good deeds can earn their salvation; there is no concept of a mediator or Savior though all will ultimately be purged of sin to be in heaven.
Creation	Ahura Mazda is eternal and created the universe, including earth, plants, animals, and humans in a way that echoes Genesis.

Chapter 16

Worldwide Church of the Creator (The Creativity Movement)

Pastor Chuck Hickey

Dedicated towards developing the tremendous potential of nature's finest — the white race. May this book give our great race a religion of its own that will unite, organize, and propel it forward towards a whiter and brighter world. — Ben Klassen, P.M.E.

The White Man's Bible

On February 21, 1973, a book was published titled *Nature's Eternal Religion*. The author was Ben Klassen and the publisher was The Creativity Movement. This was the initial written work of a newly launched religious sect following a long line of Aryan cults that have dotted recent history. The above quote from *The White Man's Bible* (the second major publication of The Creativity Movement published in 1981)[1] encapsulates the essence of The Creativity Movement.

In the following pages, I will expose the teachings of The Creativity Movement, contrast those teachings with Christianity, and call those who have embraced the errors and heresies of The Creativity Movement to

---

1. The publication date of *The White Man's Bible* does not appear in the publication but does appear on The Creativity Movement website. The publication can be found at http://creativitymovement.net/Holy%20Books.html.

repentance. In endeavoring to accomplish these goals, a contrast between Christianity and Creativity will be undertaken under four philosophical headings: Epistemology (the study of how we know truth), Theology (the study of the transcendent being), Anthropology (the study of the nature and purpose of man), and Teleology (the study of the created order being directed toward an end or shaped by a purpose).

Throughout this writing, The Creativity Movement will be referred to as a cult. In Walter R. Martin's helpful book *The Kingdom of the Cults*,[2] Dr. Martin cites Dr. Charles Braden's definition of a cult: "A cult, as I define it, is any religious group which differs significantly in some one or more respects as to belief or practice, from those religious groups which are regarded as the normative expressions of religion in our culture."[3] As will become evident on the following pages, the beliefs of The Creativity Movement differ significantly from religious groups throughout North America, particularly Christianity. In fact, The Church of the Creator claims in its own documents (*The White Man's Bible*, *Nature's Eternal Religion*, and *Salubrious Living*)[4] that Creativity is a unique religion unlike all other religions. In many respects this is true, but in other respects, Creativity is as Solomon wrote in Ecclesiastes 1:9: "nothing new under the sun"[5]

The "sameness" of The Creativity Movement is found in its humanistic/evolutionary origins. These humanistic/evolutionary origins inculcate virtually every society throughout the world. When mankind is elevated to a position of the highest known creature and his origins are attributed to evolutionary processes, the uniqueness of The Creativity Movement is all but lost. In the case of The Creativity Movement, a third element is introduced that makes its humanistic/evolutionary beliefs a bit unique — the presumed superiority of the white race.[6]

---

2. Walter R. Martin, *The Kingdom of the Cults* (Minneapolis, MN: Bethany House Publishers, 1981).
3. Ibid., p. 1.
4. Each of these publications can be downloaded from The Creativity Movement website at http://creativitymovement.net.
5. In this chapter, Scripture quotations are from the New King James Version (NKJV) of the Bible.
6. "The whole objective and purpose of our religion, Creativity and the CHURCH OF THE CREATOR, is to advance the interests of the White Race, the finest creation in Nature's universe," Ben Klassen, *Nature's Eternal Religion* (New York: The Creativity Movement, 1973), Book II, paragraph 15. (This document is not paginated but appears on The Creativity Movement website www.creativitymovement.net in PDF format. The PDF document page is 274.)

Epistemology: Origins of the Creativity Cult

The beginnings of The Creativity Movement are somewhat muddled. It could be said that it began in 1973 as the Church of the Creator with the publication of Ben Klassen's first book, *Nature's Eternal Religion*. In Klassen's mind, the structure of religion is "eternal" and it is part of "nature." Thus, for Klassen, truth resides in nature alone. It is not revealed; it is merely observed. Klassen wrote, "When we reflect on the source of all our knowledge, we find that *the only real truths are in Nature and in Nature's laws. All that we know is rooted in the natural laws* that surround us. It is the White Man's uncanny ability to observe, to reason and to organize his knowledge of that small part of Nature's secrets from which he has lifted the veil"[7] (emphasis added).

It is interesting to note that although truth exists throughout nature for Creativity and its followers, it is only in the last 40-plus years that this "eternal" religion is distinguishable from all other religions. Furthermore, only "white" mankind is intelligent enough to discern this religion that is presumably eternal.

By way of contrast, Christianity asserts that truth is revealed to mankind by the eternal Creator/God who has codified His truth in the Bible. Therein we learn that God created all things in the space of six days, and all very good, by the power of His Word.[8] In John 17:17, Jesus Christ asserts without equivocation, when speaking of God the Father's revelation, "Your word is truth." This is really the heart of the issue — the arbitrary opinions of man versus the absolute truth of God.

Epistemology is the study of knowing truth. It endeavors to answer the question, "How do we know what we know?" Every religion or philosophy endeavors to answer this question. For The Creativity Movement, you must be of the white race to know and understand truth, and truth only exists in nature.[9] Truth has no other origin. For the Christian, truth is of two kinds, which are completely compatible with one another. Those two kinds of truth

---

7. Klassen, *Nature's Eternal Religion*, PDF p. 18.
8. "In the beginning was the Word, and the Word was with God, and the Word was God. He was in the beginning with God. All things were made through Him, and without Him nothing was made that was made. In Him was life, and the life was the light of men. And the light shines in the darkness, and the darkness did not comprehend it" (John 1:1–5).
9. "All truth and all knowledge originates from our observations of the laws of Nature." Klassen, *Nature's Eternal Religion*, PDF p. 140.

are "general" and "special" revelation. In the strict sense, God's revealed Word, the Bible, is His special revelation and is, in all its parts in the original autographs, the essence of truth. Additionally, Christian theologians have rightly asserted that God's revelation includes the "general" revelation of God's creation. From that "general" revelation, all mankind, including all peoples, regardless of skin shade, can observe things about God because He has created all that exists.[10]

Creation Movement logo

Thus, Creativity is at odds with the Christian understanding of the origins of "truth" and consequently "knowledge."

Theology: The Church of the Creator Rejects the Notion of a Creator God

All philosophies and religions deal with the concept of "God." Either they accept the concept of "God" and then endeavor to explain His person and character, or they reject the concept of a "God" and endeavor to explain why they reject any notion of "God." The Creativity Movement is no different. This movement rejects any notion of God while at the same time asserts that it is a "Church of the Creator."

In *Nature's Eternal Religion,* Klassen asserts the following:

1. The universe is governed by the laws of Nature.

2. The laws of Nature are fixed, rigid and eternal.

3. The laws of Nature apply to living creatures just as firmly and relentless as they do to inanimate objects.

4. The human race, too, is a creature of Nature.

5. Nature is interested only in survival of the species, and not the individual.

---

10. "For since the creation of the world His invisible attributes are clearly seen, being understood by the things that are made, even His eternal power and Godhead, so that they are without excuse" (Romans 1:20).

6. Only those species survive that can compete in the hostile face of all others and either hold their own or increase.

7. Nature continually tries to upgrade the species by the law of the "Survival of the Fittest." It ruthlessly culls out, generally before reproduction, all the misfits, the sickly and the weak.

8. In the struggle for the survival of the species Nature shows that she is completely devoid of any compassion, morality, or sense of fair play, as far as any other species is concerned. The only yard stick is survival.

9. Nature favors and promotes the inner segregation of each species and causes the sub-species to compete against each other.

10. Nature frowns upon mongrelization, cross-breeding or miscegenation. She has given not only each species, but each sub-species, the instinctive drive to mate only with its own kind.

11. Nature has evolved for each particular species a particular pattern in its life cycle which that species must follow. This is called instinct, a very important and vital part of its makeup. Any deviation, deadening or dulling of its instincts usually results in the extinction of that particular species. The White Race should note this well.

12. Not only has Nature usually assigned a particular lifecycle for each species, but usually also a certain type of environment that the species is limited to, such as fish can only live in water, polar bears in the Arctic regions, etc.

13. Nature is completely impartial as to which species survives, each being on its own, in the hostile faces of all others.

14. Each species is completely indifferent to the survival of any other species, and Nature tells each species to expand and multiply to the limit of its abilities. Love and tenderness are reserved exclusively to its own kind.

15. There are many species that realize the importance of territory and stake out limits of the territory that they need for the survival and raising of their families.

16. Many animals, birds, insects, and other categories have a well-developed social structure.

17. The leadership principle is instinctively ingrained and utilized by many species of animals, birds, and insects as well as the human race.

18. One species, for example a flock of gulls, will sometimes wage wholesale war against another species, such as a plague of locusts. A pack of wolves will attack a herd of musk oxen.

19. However, fratricidal wars among the species against its own kind are unknown in Nature, except for some misguided human species.

20. Nowhere in the realm of Nature does a stronger, superior species hold back its own advancement and expansion in deference to weaker, inferior species. There is no compassion between one species and another, only life and death competition.

21. Species themselves are continuously changing and evolving over the millenniums of time. This can even be greatly speeded up by means of deliberate selection, as in the breeding of dogs and horses. Some species die out. New species evolve. None remain static, but all, including the human species, are forever changing and evolving. Evolution is a continuous process.

22. Eternal struggle is the price of survival.

23. Nature has given each creature a strong natural instinct whose basic drive is the perpetuation of its own kind. Ingrained in this instinct is a complete blueprint for its whole life pattern that will propagate its own kind, generation after generation. A species must follow its ingrained instinctive pattern or perish.

24. Last, but not least, Nature clearly indicates that is her plan that each species continuously improve and up-grade itself, or be ruthlessly phased out of existence.[11]

From these assertions, it is evident that The Creativity Movement is devoid of any notion of a "creator." It is ironic, since the name of this cult is "The

---

11. Klassen, *Nature's Eternal Religion*, PDF p. 15–16.

Church of the Creator." (This inconsistency will be discussed later.) More importantly, these assertions are the presuppositions that color the entirety of this cult. From them, we can deduce these presuppositions as:

1. There is no creator; all that exists is a result of evolutionary process (see number 1 above).

2. Man is no different in his being from any other animal; man is merely a kind in the species of mammals, much like a bass in the species of fish, or fruit flies in the species of insects (see number 4 above).

3. Because mankind is merely a species, he is not a moral agent any more than a squirrel is a moral agent (see number 8 above).

4. Because species do not procreate with other species, neither should kinds procreate with other kinds (see numbers 10 and 11 above).

5. Species are continuously evolving and improving over time (see numbers 21–24 above).

Evolutionary processes, including the survival of the fittest, are at the core of the beliefs of this cult. Nowhere does this cult attribute the origins of creatures to the handiwork of a creator. In fact, *the very notion of a creator is, to this cult, utter nonsense.*[12]

Webster's Dictionary defines the word "creator" as: "one that creates usually by bringing something new or original into being; especially capitalized: god."[13] The very word "creator" presupposes a personage, whether a personal god or an individual who brings something new into being. Ironically, though this religion has the word *creator* in its name, the Church of the Creator attributes nothing of man's existence, the world or the cosmos to a "creator." The equivocation in the use of the word "creator" is undiscernible.

Though The Creativity Movement rejects any notion of a creator God, it does assert that those who are part of this movement are "creators." Ben Klassen

---

12. In speaking of the authors of the Old Testament, Ben Klassen states, "They are rambling about a God as unreal and imaginary as are Zeus, Mars, Jupiter and a thousand others concocted by the imaginary meanderings of the human fantasy," *Nature's Eternal Religion*, PDF p. 100.

13. http://www.merriam-webster.com/dictionary/creator.

wrote in *The White Man's Bible*, "Members of our religion are called CREATORS whether men, women or children, and the religion itself is known as CREATIVITY."[14]

Ben Klassen

Again, the Church of the Creator rejects any notion of a Creator God while the Christian faith believes in a transcendent God who is Trinitarian in His existence and the Maker/Creator of all things. In the early days of Christianity, assemblies of Christian leaders met in councils and made summary statements of the beliefs of the Christian Church. The summary statements are called creeds and were to be recited in the worship of the Church. At the Council of Nicea in A.D. 325, the Trinitarian God was described. The pertinent part is as follows:

> I believe in one God, the Father Almighty, Maker of heaven and earth, and of all things visible and invisible.
>
> And in one Lord Jesus Christ, the only-begotten Son of God, begotten of the Father before all worlds; God of God, Light of Light, very God of very God; begotten, not made, being of one substance with the Father, by whom all things were made.
>
> Who, for us men and for our salvation, came down from heaven, and was incarnate by the Holy Spirit of the virgin Mary, and was made man; and was crucified also for us under Pontius Pilate; He suffered and was buried; and the third day He rose again, according to the Scriptures; and ascended into heaven, and sits on the right hand of the Father; and He shall come again, with glory, to judge the quick and the dead; whose kingdom shall have no end.
>
> And I believe in the Holy Ghost, the Lord and Giver of Life; who proceeds from the Father and the Son; who with the Father and the Son together is worshiped and glorified; who spoke by the prophets.[15]

14. Klassen, *The White Man's Bible*, PDF p. 6.
15. http://reformed.org/documents/index.html.

These summary statements are based on statements found in the Bible that affirm the Trinitarian nature of the Maker/Creator God.[16]

In addition to the tripartite nature of the Christian Trinity, it is important to note that Christianity asserts that each of the persons of the Trinity have certain functions relating to creation. This understanding of differing functions by the persons of the Trinity is often referred to as the "economy" of the Trinity by Christian theologians.[17] These functions will be delineated shortly and will become more critical to understanding the difference between The Creativity Movement and Christianity in the section on anthropology.

The three persons of the Trinity — Father, Son, and Holy Spirit — share all things but are also distinct. The Westminster Confession of Faith (1647) gives a helpful description in chapter 2, paragraph 3, wherein we read:

> In the unity of the Godhead there be three Persons of one substance, power, and eternity: God the Father, God the Son, and God the Holy Ghost. The Father is of none, neither begotten nor proceeding; the Son is eternally begotten of the Father; the Holy Ghost eternally proceeding from the Father and the Son.[18]

What then are the differing functions of the three persons of the Trinity that make up the "economy" of the Trinity? First, God the Father, in complete cooperation with God the Son and God the Spirit, authors the decree of God.[19] Jesus, God the Son, in complete cooperation with God the Father and God the Spirit, executes God the Father's decree, particularly the portion that relates to salvation for men.[20] God the Spirit then "applies" the

---

16. Genesis 1:1–2; John 1:1–5; Matthew 28:19; Luke 3:21–22; see also, "God Is Triune," Bodie Hodge, Answers in Genesis, May 20, 2008, https://answersingenesis.org/who-is-god/the-trinity/god-is-triune/.
17. Not to be confused with modalism.
18. http://reformed.org/documents/wcf_with_proofs/index.html.
19. Isaiah 46:8–11 reads: "Remember this, and show yourselves men; recall to mind, O you transgressors. Remember the former things of old, for I am God, and there is no other; I am God, and there is none like Me, declaring the end from the beginning, and from ancient times things that are not yet done, saying, 'My counsel shall stand, and I will do all My pleasure,' calling a bird of prey from the east, the man who executes My counsel, from a far country. Indeed I have spoken it; I will also bring it to pass. I have purposed it; I will also do it."
20. Replete in the gospels of the New Testament is Jesus asserting that He came to do the will of the Father. See Matthew 7:21, 12:50; Luke 22:42; John 5:36, 17:4, 17:8.

salvation provided by Jesus, God the Son in accordance to the will of God the Father, to all who are called unto salvation that have been given to Jesus by God the Father.[21]

In summary, there is a stark difference between the Church of the Creator, which believes in no creator at all (only evolutionary processes in nature), and Christianity that believes in a Triune God who created all that exists, out of nothing, for His own glory.

Anthropology: The Nature of Man and His Purpose in The Creativity Movement

The study of mankind in philosophical and theological realms is known as "anthropology." Creativity has an extensive amount of writing relating to its understanding of anthropology. This is not surprising given the fact that Creativity is a humanistic cult that perceives man (specifically the white race of men) as the highest of all creatures. Ben Klassen wrote in *Nature's Eternal Religion*:

> If there is one thing in this wonderful world of ours that is worth preserving, defending, and promoting, it is the White Race. Nature looked fondly upon the White Race and lavished special loving care in its growth. Of all the millions of creatures who have inhabited the face of this planet over the eons of time, none has ever quite equaled that of the White Race. Nature endowed her Elite with a greater abundance of intelligence and creativity, of energy and productivity than she endowed unto any other creature, now or in the millenniums past. It has been the White Race who has been the world builder, the makers of cities and commerce and continents. It is the White Man who is the sole builder of civilizations. It was he who built the Egyptian civilization, the great unsurpassed Roman civilization, the Greek civilization of beauty and culture, and who, after having been dealt a serious blow by a new Semitic religion, wallowed through the Dark Ages, finally extricated himself, and then built the great European civilization.
>
> What other race can even come close to this remarkable record of creativity, achievement and productivity? The answer is

---

21. See John 6:39, 14:12–18, 15:26–27, 16:5–15, 17:24.

none. None whatsoever. None can even come close. In contrast, the black man of Africa never so much as even invented the wheel.

Yes, it is the White Man, with his inborn and inbred genius, that has given form to every government and a livelihood to every other people, and above all, great ideals to every century. Yes, we are the ones, racial comrades, who were especially endowed by Nature and chosen to be the ruling Elite of the world. Indeed, we were chosen by Nature to be masters of the world by building it ever better and better. We were destined to be fruitful and to multiply and to inhabit the entire hospitable face of this planet. This is our Manifest Destiny as ordained by Nature herself.[22]

In these short paragraphs, the essence of Creativity's anthropology is discerned. The white race is the highest form of all of nature's creatures. Apparently, the white race has evolved to that lofty position. It is unknown whether the "white race" could be supplanted by another race or other creatures (presumably it is possible given the concern expressed by Klassen in *The White Man's Bible* for the decline of the "white race":

But first, the White Race must, like all the other creatures, again learn to recognize its enemies, or it is certain that it will soon be as extinct as the dodo and the dinosaur. Let us again make this clear: our every position is and must be from the White Man's point of view. From the White Man's point of view the Jews, the niggers, and the mud races are his eternal natural enemies. This is as basic and unalterable as the conflict between the pioneering mother and the rattlesnake. . . .

At this crucial stage of world history, either the White Race will survive, or the Jews and their enslaved mud races. It will be one or the other, and this, too, is a grim unalterable fact of life, whether we like it or not. It is the supreme purpose of the CHURCH OF THE CREATOR to see to it that it will be the White Race that shall survive.[23]

In contrast to Creativity's view of anthropology, Christianity has a much different perspective. For the Christian, man is a created being of God, made

---

22. Klassen, *Nature's Eternal Religion*, PDF p. 17–18.
23. Klassen, *The White Man's Bible*, PDF p. 27.

in the image of God.[24] Man is not the product of an "evolutionary process"; he is a created being whose value and purpose are derived from his being created in the "image of God." Unlike all other creatures, mankind was endowed with moral agency, that is, the ability to discern right from wrong, good from evil. All other creatures have no such ability. Yes, creatures can perceive danger, feel emotions, and choose between alternatives (such as carnivores choosing one animal over another to eat), yet, they have no notion of right and wrong. Moral agency only exists in man because man is made in the image of God.[25] Furthermore, morality to the Christian is found in God's revealed Word, the Bible, which defines morality from the attributes of God. These are summarized in the Ten Commandments and the two great commandments of Jesus Christ.[26]

This notion of moral agency is not explained in Creativity. Words like morals, ethics, right, wrong, salvation, and redemption are all words that speak of morality. All of these words are used by the adherents of Creativity in their documents without any discussion of the origins of man's morality or an appeal to where one can find its origin. Only evolutionary processes in nature produce mankind's reality. Unfortunately for Creativity, men interpret their reality differently. Thus, what is morally right for adherents of Creativity is very likely wrong for other men. Even the white race (the highest of all living things in their view) cannot agree that it is the highest living thing. Many of the white race men believe that men are no better than the animals and therefore should never encroach on the habitats of animals. Some go so far as to argue that animals have "rights" that do not differ from the rights of men.

Another difficulty for The Creativity Movement, when considering problems of ethics from the perspective of nature, is that many creatures in nature exhibit behaviors that would presumably be reprehensible to the members of The Creativity Movement. For example, the black widow spider

---

24. Genesis 1:26–28: "Then God said, 'Let Us make man in Our image, according to Our likeness; let them have dominion over the fish of the sea, over the birds of the air, and over the cattle, over all the earth and over every creeping thing that creeps on the earth.' So God created man in His own image; in the image of God He created him; male and female He created them. Then God blessed them, and God said to them, 'Be fruitful and multiply; fill the earth and subdue it; have dominion over the fish of the sea, over the birds of the air, and over every living thing that moves on the earth.' "

25. Ibid.

26. See Exodus 20:1–17; Deuteronomy 5:6–21; Matthew 22:37–40; Mark 12:29–31; Luke 10:27.

kills and devours her mate after mating. Since morality is based on observations in nature, shouldn't "white women" consider such activity as normative? Many species of animals consume their young after birth either to avoid starvation or to allow only a few the opportunity to nurse at the mother. Again, since morality is based on observations in nature, shouldn't "white females" consider such actions for similar reasons?

In summary, Creativity believes mankind's origins are a result of evolutionary processes and that the "white race" of men is the highest of all creatures. This echoes early evolutionists like Charles Darwin and Earnst Haeckel (who popularized Darwinism in Germany and helped pave the way for Nazism). Both held firmly throughout their writings that what they defined as the Caucasian was superior and others were lesser evolved:

> At some future period, not very distant as measured by centuries, the civilized races of man will almost certainly exterminate and replace the savage races throughout the world. At the same time the anthropomorphous apes . . . will no doubt be exterminated. The break between man and his nearest allies will then be wider, for it will intervene between man in a more civilized state, as we may hope, even than the Caucasian, and some ape as low as a baboon, instead of as now between the negro or Australian [Aborigine] and the gorilla.[27]

> At the lowest stage of human mental development are the Australians, some tribes of the Polynesians, and the Bushmen, Hottentots, and some of the Negro tribes. Nothing, however, is perhaps more remarkable in this respect, than that some of the wildest tribes in southern Asia and eastern Africa have no trace whatever of the first foundations of all human civilization, of family life, and marriage. They live together in herds, like apes.[28]

Creativity cannot account for morality except as to what it believes can be observed from activities in nature. By contrast, Christianity believes that man was created by God and in God's image, which includes an understanding of morality. Morality to the Christian is a revelation of God's own attributes and is therefore normative.

---

27. Charles Darwin, *The Descent of Man* (New York: A.L. Burt, 1874, 2nd ed.), p. 178.
28. E. Haeckel, *The History of Creation*, 1876, p. 363–363.

Teleology: The Hope and Aspirations of The Creativity Movement

Every religion, philosophy, or cult has goals it wants to achieve. Creativity is no different. What is so very striking is the audacity with which they communicate those goals. This boldness may be part of their attractiveness to some. Following is a long quote from *The White Man's Bible* that is a summation of the hopes and aspirations of The Creativity Movement:

> Whether we like it or not (and we CREATORS accept it) a far reaching revolution is now in the making. Whether we like it or not, the impending upheaval is going to turn upside down the immediate affairs of mankind completely and irrevocably. The coming revolution is either going to totally degenerate mankind into a horde of miserable misfits, or could usher in the beautiful Golden Age of the Superman and a brilliant future beyond.
>
> We CREATORS are riding the wave of the future, and by foreseeing and planning that future we are determined to help mold it in such a way that we, our children and future generations can look forward to a Whiter and Brighter World of such magnificence as to stagger the imagination. The Future World we intend to build. Briefly, here are just a few of the broad outlines of the better world we are determined to build.

A Brighter World of Beautiful, Healthy People

> A world without cancer. A world without heart disease. A world in which there will be much more emphasis placed on building health rather than curing disease, and in which excellent health will be the norm rather than the exception. This we intend to accomplish by a program we call Salubrious Living.[29] We will have several chapters on this subject. We foresee a future world in which the intelligence of the average individual will be significantly raised in each ensuing generation. A world free of insane asylums, idiots, or morons. A clean world in which there will be very little pollution of the environment. A world

---

29. "Salubrious Living" for The Creativity Movement is primarily a form of "clean and healthy living" but is also the name of a book describing how clean and healthy living should take place. To this cult, "Salubrious Living" is indispensable to the movement. The book is found on their website at: http://creativitymovement.net.

virtually free of crime in which any man, woman or child can walk any time of day or night without fear of assault; a world of law and order; a world free of poverty; a world in which every person will be creatively and gainfully employed, in one way or another during their total lifetime, a lifetime that will be prolonged beyond that of the present world. However, let me quickly emphasize we are not nearly as much interested in prolonging life as increasing the individual's health and quality of life as long as it lasts. Longer life is only a secondary benefit as a result of superior well-being.

Racial Problems Solved

The future world as we envision it, will have no racial problems, no language barriers and no fratricidal wars. It will be well fed, but will have no problems of over-population or crowding. Nor will it have scarcities of food, energy supplies or resources. There will be abundance for all. A happy, affluent and well-rounded life will be within easy reach for everyone.

Superstitions Gone

We see a world in which superstition, fear of hell, and "spooks in the skies" will be buried with the superstitions of our barbarian ancestors. No longer will superstition be exploited for profit by con-artists to torment and dominate the minds of the gullible. We look forward to a world where a man and woman can join in raising a family of fine, beautiful, healthy, intelligent children in economic security. They will have the guaranteed prospects of a stable future world in which they can expect that their children, too, can look forward to having that same opportunity when they grow up.

Bringing Dreams to Reality

This is the future world of Creativity that we envision. A tall order, you say?

Fantastic? An impossible Utopia only contemplated by dreamers? Perhaps. But we not only envision it, we are determined to do our best to bring it into being. We are not merely dreamy visionaries, but on the contrary, we have the specific plans, realistic programs and a militant creed to bring it about. You are part of that program, my dear White Racial Comrade. With your help we not only can do it, we must do it and we will do it. It is our religion, our faith, *our reason for being*[30] (emphasis added).

From the above quotation, certain factual statements can be made of Creativity and its ultimate purpose. Creativity exists to promote and advance the "white race" to a utopian kind of civilization: to achieve this goal, a white person must live a salubrious life, exhibit religious devotion to Creativity, and embrace Creativity's "militant creed."[31] This is quite reminiscent of Hitler and the Nazis! Nothing short of this is acceptable to the Church of the Creator.

The teleological aspects of Christianity will be delineated in the following section.

Further Comparisons to Christianity

Creativity: A Religion That Is Not Creative

Throughout history, religious cults have sprung up and tried to mimic other religions. Christianity has been copied by so many artificial imitations that it is difficult to keep count. Some of those imitations endeavor to be subtle in their efforts to copy, while others (like Creativity) make no effort to disguise their efforts to copy Christianity. For example, Creativity has a "Bible" (*The White Man's Bible*),[32] a "Golden Rule,"[33] a form of the "Ten Commandments" (for Creativity, they have 16 Commandments),[34] titles (in the Christian Church, titles are used to delineate leadership in its various branches, e.g. elder, pastor, bishop, pope; in Creativity, the title of "Pontifex Maximus" is the highest leadership position),[35] and lastly, creeds (the Christian Church has creeds that summarize its beliefs, and Creativity has creeds

---

30. Klassen, *The White Man's Bible*, PDF p. 10–11.
31. Ibid.
32. Ibid.
33. Ibid., PDF p. 9. "What is good for the White Race is the highest virtue; what is the bad for the White Race is the ultimate sin."
34. Ibid., PDF p. 426–427.
35. Ibid., PDF p. 5. "From the traditions of Ancient Rome, not the Catholic Church, we have adopted the title of Pontifex Maximus as head of our church."

in the two books *Nature's Eternal Religion* and *The White Man's Bible*).[36] In short, for a religion that claims to be unique in all of history, it has borrowed so much structure from Christianity that it is a feeble, artificial imitation.

Creativity, like Christianity, speaks of "salvation" and "redemption," but in their documents, there is no defining of these terms and there is certainly no favorable reference to the Christian definitions of these concepts.

Salvation and Redemption in Christianity

Salvation and redemption have very important meanings in Christianity. "Salvation" means to be delivered from something and "redemption" means to be delivered unto or into something. Salvation is being delivered from the consequences of sin and death. Redemption is to be delivered unto eternal life and into the Kingdom of God.

To be saved from the consequences of sin and death means that there is a reckoning, or judging, for the actions of one's life. To the Christian, the one who exacts the reckoning or makes the judgment is the one who has created us, the God of the Bible. The Bible very clearly states, "For the wages of sin is death, but the gift of God is eternal life in Jesus Christ our Lord" (Romans 6:23). The Scriptures also state, "For by grace you have been saved through faith, and that not of yourselves; it is the gift of God, not of works, lest anyone should boast" (Ephesians 2:8–9). These verses speak of faith in something. That something is a person, the second person of the Triune God, Jesus Christ. In the Book of Ephesians we also read:

> In Him you also *trusted*, after you heard the word of truth, the gospel of your salvation; in whom also, having believed, you were sealed with the Holy Spirit of promise, who is the guarantee of our inheritance until the redemption of the *purchased possession*, to the praise of His glory (Ephesians 1:13–14, emphasis added).

These two verses are very profound as we consider the concepts of salvation and redemption. Both are mentioned in these verses and they both speak

---

36. Ibid., PDF p. 7. "One thing more. This book is not meant to be a scientific discourse, nor an historical review of the White Race. I make it very clear throughout: this book and NATURE'S ETERNAL RELIGION are conceived as a religious creed and program written for the masses, clearly and simply, so that anyone with an open mind and a modicum of common sense can understand it and grasp its import."

of a "purchased possession." What is the possession that was purchased? For the Christian, his salvation and redemption were purchased by the shed blood of Jesus Christ on the Cross.[37] Furthermore, God being the perfect judge of the universe then makes a declaration regarding our citizenship in the Kingdom of God. When Jesus rose from the dead, the Bible states that He did that for our "justification."[38] Justification is a legal term that means to be "declared just" or "right."

God stands ready to forgive any and all who confess their sins, turn from their sins, and declare Jesus Christ as Lord and Savior. He will declare "right" all who do so. He will also judge all for their sins that do not confess their sins, repent, and submit to the Lordship of Jesus.

This is reality — not a supposed master race of white men and women led by a self-proclaimed "Pontifex Maximus" who believes in a utopian society. I call on all who embrace The Creativity Movement to denounce the heresies of The Church of the Creator and bow their knees to the King of kings and Lord of lords, Jesus Christ.

Summary of Church of the Creator Beliefs

Doctrine	Church of the Creator Teaching
God	Nature is god and determines the laws of the universe
Authority/ Revelation	Truth originates from the laws of nature and can be understood only by those of the "white" race
Man	A creature of nature with no moral agency; the "white" race is superior
Sin	Whatever is bad for the "white" race is sin
Salvation	Largely undefined; a concept of a utopian society of "whites" only
Creation	Completely evolutionary in all aspects

---

37. Without the shedding of blood there is no remission of sin (Hebrews 9:22).

38. "It shall be imputed to us who believe in Him who raised up Jesus our Lord from the dead, who was delivered up because of our offenses, and was raised because of our justification" (Romans 4:24–25).

Chapter 17

Moonies / The Unification Church

Dr. Mark Bird

I stood there on the sidewalk, amazed at what I had just heard. The lady I was interviewing had told me that Rev. Sun Myung Moon married Jesus Christ to a woman from the Unification Church. "How could anyone believe that!" I thought. The pastor's wife explained that Jesus recently got married because that was the only way he (Jesus) could get out of Paradise and into Heaven. According to her church's theology, *anyone* who wants to go to heaven must be married with Rev. Moon's blessing.

The woman I interviewed was herself married to a man introduced to her by Sun Myung Moon, the founder of the Unification Church. She told me that on an appointed day she was waiting in a room with other women anticipating this "matching." Moon suddenly walked into the room with a gentleman, brought the two together, and left. Later, they wed in a ceremony that Moon conducted. Then, after a purification period of 40 days, they consummated their marriage and began having children. The now happily married lady claimed that because of this blessing and purification process, her children were born without sin. Noticing her kids playing nearby, I asked her, "So your children never do anything wrong?" She replied, "Oh, they're not perfect, just sinless!"

Many other members of the Unification Church can testify to a similar experience, since Rev. Moon matched thousands of couples during his lifetime. Why did he match couples, and why are their children said to be sinless? Because Moon was supposedly tasked by Jesus Himself to finish

Christ's mission to establish a pure new kingdom on this earth. Moon and his wife are the True Parents, whom Unification Church members call "Father" and "Mother." Moon started a new "race" of people, and a new movement to save the world.

According to the Unification Church, Jesus spoke to a 16-year-old Sun Myung Moon[1] in a vision while he was praying on a mountain in South Korea.[2] Moon learned that Jesus did not come to the earth to die, but to show people how to live, and to start a new physical kingdom on the earth. That first meeting with Jesus was the beginning of numerous encounters

Rev. Sun Myung Moon speaking in Las Vegas, Nevada, on April 4, 2010

Moon had with those from the spirit world, where he learned many truths that he shared with his followers.[3] A whole theology was developed, much of it contained in the "inspired" *Exposition of the Divine Principle*.[4] Most Unificationists would agree with the following presentation of these teachings.

1. He changed his name from Yong Myung (his birth name) to Sun Myung because Yong means dragon, which could be interpreted as serpent, or the devil.
2. From the introduction to a set of Moon's sermons: "On Easter morning in 1935, Sun Myung Moon was deep in prayer on a Korean Mountainside when Jesus Christ appeared to him and told him that he had an important mission to accomplish in the fulfillment of God's providence. He was then sixteen years old," (http://www.unification.net/nhtt/nhtt_prf.html). Koreans would have considered him to be 16, since in their traditional culture, someone is 1 year old when he is born. Moon was born in January, 1920.
3. Reverend Sun Myung Moon, *Exposition of the Divine Principle* (New York: The Holy Spirit Association for the Unification of World Christianity, 1996). Unificationists believe that some of those spiritual luminaries were Buddha, Mohammed, Confucius, and Moses. Moon would get all the information he needed to bring to light "all the secrets of heaven." "In the fullness of time, God has sent one person to this earth to resolve the fundamental problems of human life and the universe. His name is Sun Myung Moon," p. 12.
4. Ibid., preface, p. xxi. This book was put together by a disciple of Moon. It is based on many notes that Moon had written down. The most widely dispersed version of it (3rd version) was published in 1966 and the first English translation was made in 1973 by Dr. Won Pok Choi.

Unificationist Doctrine

God

God is dualistic — He has both a negative part and a positive part.[5] The positive or male part is God; the negative or female part is the Holy Spirit. This is reflected in the fact that every person is body (-) and soul (+), and the fact that male and female humans come together to become one flesh in marriage.

1st Adam (and Eve)

Adam and Eve were created as a reflection of the nature of God, and more than a reflection. Adam was the embodiment of God; Eve was the embodiment of the Holy Spirit. As such, they were to be the True Parents of Mankind.

The Trinity and the Fall

God intended for Adam and Eve to form a perfect trinity with him, and have perfect children.[6] But Eve was seduced by Satan and committed sexual sin with him. Feeling ashamed, Adam and Eve had sexual intimacy before they were perfected enough as a couple to receive the marriage blessing.[7] Through this sin of fornication, a new trinity (Adam, Eve, and Satan) was started.[8] God's purpose for Adam to physically procreate the kingdom of God on earth was thwarted.

From that time until Moon's own marriage, no marital intimacy was blessed by God. The consequences of the fall were devastating. Sin became commonplace in the human race. All humans were born with sin, and this evil nature spawned all kinds of problems and destruction.

Humankind needed to be redeemed. Prophets like Moses were sent to teach man God's ways, and Jewish obedience to the law brought us closer to God, but it was not enough. A new Adam was needed to reestablish God's kingdom.

---

5. Ibid., p. 16, "Everything in the created universe is a substantial manifestation of some quality of the Creator's invisible, divine nature. . . . Every entity possesses dual characteristics of yang (masculinity) and yin (femininity).

6. Ibid., p. 172, "If Adam and Eve had not fallen, but had formed this trinity with God and become the True Parents who could multiply good children, their descendants would have also become good husbands and wives with God as the center of their lives."

7. Ibid., p. 64, ". . . Eve, who in her immaturity had engaged in the illicit relationship with the Archangel, joined with Adam as husband and wife. Thus, Adam fell when he, too, was still immature. This untimely conjugal relationship in satanic love between Adam and Eve constituted the physical fall."

8. Ibid., p. 172, "When Adam and Eve fell . . . they formed a fallen trinity with Satan.

2nd Adam — Jesus

Fortunately, Zechariah (the priest who was the husband of Elizabeth and father of John the Baptist) impregnated the virgin Mary, and the Messiah was born.[9] With Zechariah of the priestly line, and Mary a descendent of David, they met the conditions for Jesus the Messiah to be born sinless.

Mary had been told, "You will conceive but not with your chosen husband." She cooperated with God's will, and had a child by the person who represented God on the earth. As the father of Jesus, Zechariah should have claimed Mary and protected her and Jesus, but he didn't. This led to problems later.

As the sinless Messiah (and second Adam), Jesus had a special mission to fulfill. He would redeem mankind both spiritually and physically. To redeem mankind physically, Jesus needed to find a perfect Eve, marry her, and start a perfect family. This would be the beginning of the restoration of the human race.

However, Jesus was killed before his time because the Jewish people, including John the Baptist, lost faith in him.[10] Jesus died before he could find his Eve — he should have married a half-sister (John the Baptist's sister) and started his perfect family, but his mother disallowed that.[11] However,

---

9. In Reverend Sun Myung Moon, *True Love and True Family* (New York: Family Federation for World Peace and Unification, 1997), Moon declares that, "Jesus was conceived in the house of Zechariah" (p. 12). Moon also said at a conference in 1995, "Who was the father of Jesus Christ? Zechariah. . . . The relationship between Elizabeth and Mary was just like that between Leah and Rachel. . . . The result of the relationship between Zechariah and Mary was the birth of Jesus Christ." (http://www.unification.net/1995/950207.html. Reverend Sun Myung Moon Speaks at the Leader's Conference, February 7, 1995, Washington, DC. Translator — Hideo Oyamada). Unificationists leave some room for doubt on this subject, but they also do not think there is a viable alternative to Zechariah being the father, since an actual virgin conception would contradict the natural laws that God has set up.

10. In this chapter, the pronouns for Jesus are not capitalized when referring to the Unification Church's false concept of Jesus.

11. According to Moon, "When Jesus Christ was seventeen years old, he told Mary whom he should marry. Jesus Christ spoke strongly about the necessity for this marriage, no matter what sacrifices might need to be made, but Mary could not accept it. . . . If Mary had confessed who her child's father was, there would have been a problem. Thus Jesus and John the Baptist's sister had the same father, but different mothers. They were half-brother/sister. . . . Under these circumstances, for Jesus to marry John the Baptist's younger sister was unacceptable. Although they had different mothers, they were both children of Zechariah. How could people accept such an incestuous relationship (Leviticus 18)?" (http://www.unification.net/1995/950207.html. Reverend Sun Myung Moon Speaks at the Leader's Conference, February 7, 1995, Washington, DC.).

Jesus did redeem mankind spiritually through his death on the cross, even though dying was not his original purpose for coming.[12]

Though Jesus was not God (any more than you and I are),[13] and even though he did not rise bodily from the dead (he rose spiritually instead), he was the only sinless man in history (before Moon), so he was able to redeem us spiritually.[14]

3rd Adam — Second Coming of Christ

Since Jesus left some of his mission unfulfilled, a third Adam was necessary. This third Adam would be the second coming of Christ, and was to be born in Korea soon after World War I.[15] This Messiah would not be Jesus, but someone else who would redeem mankind physically by finding a perfect Eve and starting a perfect family. Others who were blessed in marriage by him would become part of a restored human race, as their families too would be perfected. Children would be born sinless through marriages blessed by this Messiah.[16]

Who was this third Adam? After hinting at it for years, Moon publicly revealed himself to be the Messiah at a mass wedding in 1992.[17] He fit his own description of the Savior, since he was born in Korea in 1920, soon after the war. The pastor's wife I talked to was excited to tell me about this (our discussion took place later in 1992). She had suspected all along that the Messiah was Moon himself, but was thrilled to have had that recently

---

12. This is why in the year 2000 Moon held a campaign intended to get pastors to take crosses down from their churches. Moon thought that having a cross in a church was misleading. The crucifixion was not why Jesus came.

13. "While on earth, Jesus was a man no different than any of us except for the fact that he was without the original sin. . . . If Jesus were God, how could he intercede for us before Himself? . . . We can conclude with finality that Jesus was not God himself from the words he uttered on the cross, 'My God, my God, why hast thou forsaken me?' " (Moon, *Exposition of the Divine Principle*, p. 168).

14. According to Unificationists, the death of Jesus was not necessary. But since the people had lost faith in Jesus when he came the first time, the devil had a claim on them (it put them over on the devil's side), so Jesus gave himself in death for the people to bring them back over so that they could love again. In that sense, mankind is redeemed spiritually.

15. Moon, *Exposition of the Divine Principle,* p. 399, 382–383.

16. This chapter capitalizes Messiah even when referring to the Unification Church's false concept of the Christ, since the term Messiah is a title and the Unification Church capitalizes the term.

17. According to Moon, the Korean people happen to be the descendants of the lost tribes of Israel. They are the new Israel.

confirmed. The person who had matched her with her wonderful husband, and even had stayed in their home, was the Messiah!

Moon didn't keep the messianic honor to himself. At the wedding, he proclaimed that both he and his wife were Mankind's True Parents. He had married Hak Ja Han in 1960, and considered her his "Eve."[18] Moon and his wife eventually had a total of 14 children (one died as a baby), all of whom were considered perfect, since they were born to the True Parents of Mankind.

The 1992 public announcement was consistent with a declaration he had made a few years earlier. In a secret ceremony in 1985, Moon had crowned himself and his wife as Emperor and Empress of the Universe.[19]

In 2002, the *New York Times* reported on an ad that had been submitted by the Unification Church for publication. This full-page ad presented the text of a Christmas Day meeting in the spirit world attended by Jesus, Muhammad, Confucius, Buddha, and Martin Luther.

> According to the ad, which was presented to newspapers around the country this month, these men and hundreds of others in attendance proclaimed their allegiance to the Rev. Sun Myung Moon, the leader of the Unification Church. At the spirit meeting, the ad said, Jesus hailed Mr. Moon as the Messiah, proclaiming, "You are the Second Coming who inaugurated the Completed Testament Age." Muhammad then led everyone in three cheers of victory.
>
> God didn't attend, but sent a letter Dec. 28 seconding Jesus' remarks. Lenin and other leading communists also sent messages. Lenin said that he was in "unimaginable suffering and agony" for his earthly mistakes, and Stalin added, "We live in the bottom of Hell here."[20]

Two years later, Moon was photographed wearing a gold crown and regal robes. He had just declared in a ceremony before U.S. senators and

---

18. This was after a failed marriage to someone else years earlier, and after a child through that marriage.
19. Nansook Hong, *In the Shadow of the Moons: My Life in the Reverend Sun Myung Moon's Family* (Boston, MA: Little, Brown and Company, 1998), p. 148.
20. http://www.nytimes.com/2002/07/22/business/mediatalk-decisions-differ-on-religious-ad.html.

representatives that he was "none other than humanity's savior, messiah, returning lord and true parent."[21]

Moon also said that up until he started performing his marriage blessings, the only persons in history ever born sinless were Jesus and then Moon himself, as the third Adam.[22]

All these audacious claims came with a great benefit for Moon's loyal followers. It is through the True Parents (Rev. and Mrs. Moon) that God can now bless sexual relationships in marriage, and children can be born sinless. But there is a process by which that happens.

Unification Rituals and Salvation

Unification Church members are "born again" through a Holy Wine ceremony. In this event, original sin is forgiven, and now the believer can go to heaven after being blessed in marriage by the Moons. Children of these marriages have a special status. After the blessing and marriage, and a 40-day waiting period for purification, children will be born sinless — they won't need forgiveness.

Here is the process of salvation as described by a Unificationist Handbook:

> True Parents, standing on a historical foundation of victory, have the authority to engraft all humankind into the original lineage of God. The Blessing is the process through which we become God's original sons and daughters. It consists of these steps:
>
> ### A. Holy Wine Ceremony
>
> This ceremony restores the order of God's original love, cleansing us from the original sin. It is performed in precisely the reverse order of the process of the fall. True Parents give the wine to the woman first, who then shares it with her future husband.
>
> ### B. The Blessing Ceremony
>
> The Holy Blessing was traditionally officiated by Father and Mother Moon in their capacity as True Parents, or an officiating

---

21. http://www.washingtonpost.com/world/asia_pacific/sun-myung-moon-dies-at-92-washington-times-owner-led-the-unification-church/2012/09/02/001b747a-f531-11e1-aab7-f199a16396cf_story.html.
22. From interview of Unificationists Michael and Arlene Candelaresi, Feb. 5, 2015.

couple representing them. The officiators and their attendants cleanse the couples by sprinkling them with holy water, signifying their rebirth into God's lineage as a Blessed couple.

C. Chastening or Indemnity Ceremony

This simple ceremony provides an opportunity for each couple to indemnify[23] any personal sexual past and the historical abuse of each gender by the other. Each partner firmly strikes the other three times upon the buttocks, to repent for and resolve the history of sexual immorality and the misuse of our bodies. This ceremony is of course symbolic. Any abuse or violence between the couple whether emotional, verbal or physical, is a violation of the Blessing vows and not acceptable.

D. 40-day Separation Period

In this tradition, abstaining from sexual intimacy during the first 40 days of marriage is meant to separate the newly Blessed Couple from the history of selfishness between men and women. It can also help heal any painful personal sexual past.

E. Three-day Ceremony of Renewal

The couple first cleanses their bodies with the Holy Wine that now links them to God's lineage. Then with a prayer of offering, they invite the Heavenly Parent to enter their most intimate love relationship.[24]

The process of salvation, including everything that takes place after the renewal, takes time and a lot of effort. According to Unificationists, salvation is "95% up to God and 5% up to us, but it takes all we got to do the other 5%."[25] God does most of the work, but we contribute to our salvation through a complete adherence to the process. Unificationist Kwang-Yol

---

23. "What, then, is the meaning of restoration through indemnity? When someone has lost his original position or state, he must make some condition to be restored to it. The making of such conditions of restitution is called indemnity" (Moon, *Exposition of the Divine Principle*, p. 177).

24. Excerpts from an unpublished handbook made available to members online: DRAFT-Unificationist-Handbook_2013–12.

25. October 2014 interview with Michael Candelaresi, member of the Unification Church since 1974. Michael also happens to be a member of Mensa, having passed an intelligence test that only 2% of the general population can pass.

Yoo said that by following the Divine Principle, "man's perfection must be accomplished finally by his own effort without God's help."[26]

History of the Church

Origin and Nomenclature

The great promulgator of all this heretical theology, Sun Myung Moon, started the Unification Church in South Korea in 1954, calling it the Holy Spirit Association for the Unification of World Christianity.[27] Church members called themselves Moonies (and Moon himself used the term) until around 1990, when leaders in the church began to call "Moonies" a derogatory term. Since the Unification Church is a personality cult, "Moonie" still seems appropriate, but this chapter usually uses the term "Unificationists" to refer to the members.

Move to the United States

In the 1970s Moon came to the United States and preached to large stadium crowds. Thousands of young people were recruited in the '70s and '80s. Many parents during this time complained about the church's extreme indoctrination process and manipulation, since the children had been estranged from their families.[28]

In 1982 (the same year that he was convicted of tax evasion and sent to prison for 18 months), Moon founded *The Washington Times*, a conservative alternative to the *Washington Post*. This is probably the most successful enterprise he established, in terms of political influence, though the church has had to subsidize the paper with millions of dollars every year. The Unification Church also acquired the wire service United Press International, and it has had many other more successful business ventures.

Mass Weddings

Rev. Moon is most famous for the mass weddings he and his wife have conducted, beginning in the 1960s. Moon's followers have been told that through these weddings they would produce a new generation of sinless

---

26. Quoted in *Unification Church* by J. Isamu Yamanoto (Grand Rapids, MI: Zondervan, 1995), p. 82. Another Unification teacher (Young Oon Kim) taught, "We atone for our sins through specific acts of penance," Kim Young Oon, *Unification Theology* (New York: The Holy Spirit Association for the Unification of World Christianity, 1980), p. 230.
27. Its official name now is the Family Federation for World Peace and Unification.
28. http://www.4truth.net/fourtruthpbnew.aspx?pageid=8589952680.

Moon holds a mass "blessing ceremony"

children. Many of the participants in the latest mass weddings are these "sinless" children of the original followers.

The first wedding in 1961 had 36 couples; the next wedding doubled to 72, and the numbers kept increasing for more than 30 years. In 1992, the year Moon declared himself and his wife the True Parents, there were at least 30,000 couples married. In 1997, another 30,000 couples were married in Washington, D.C. In 1999, 21,000 couples exchanged vows in the Olympic Stadium in Seoul, South Korea.

These weddings have continued even after Rev. Moon's death in 2012. There were 3,500 couples married by Mrs. Moon in 2013. She blessed another 2,500 couples (from about 50 countries) in 2014.

These numbers do not include those who were part of the ceremonies via satellite. For example, in 2013, the church claims that 24,000 followers from other countries took part in that wedding through video link. For most of the Blessings, many couples had just met in person for the first time when the ceremonies took place, and in some cases, they spoke different languages.[29]

Beginning with the '90s, many of the participants were allowed to be non-Unification members, so that helped increase the numbers. The non-Unificationist participants only have to agree to be faithful to their spouse, to teach their kids abstinence before marriage, and to promote world peace. They don't have to accept Moon and his wife as the True Parents.[30]

---

29. http://www.dailymail.co.uk/news/article-2119753/Unification-Church-South-Korea-mass-wedding-2-500-marriages.html.
30. http://www.religionfacts.com/unification_church/.

Other changes over the years include having ministers of other faiths serve as co-officiators at the Blessing ceremonies. Also, since 2001, previously blessed couples have been able to help arrange marriages for their own children, without the Moons' direct guidance.[31]

Numbers/Growth of This Group

As of early 2015, the Unification Church claimed to have about 3 million members worldwide. Of these 3 million, 1 million are said to live in Japan[32] and another half a million are said to live in Korea. However, critics of the movement say that there are far fewer members than that; some say as few as 100,000 worldwide. Perhaps a better estimate would be about 1 million, with most of these living in Korea and Japan.[33] Unificationists believe that the church is growing across many of the approximately 100 countries in which it has a presence. Numbers are increasing in South America, Nepal, the South Pacific, and in Africa. Numbers have been shrinking in the United States since the death of Moon and a scandal involving his daughter In Jin, one-time leader of the American church.[34]

In the United States, there are now only around 10,000 Unification families.[35] In Ohio, for example, there are about 100 families, with 8–10 families in the Cincinnati area.

Besides the fragmentation that naturally resulted from Moon's death, another reason that there are fewer Unification members in the United States is that the intense recruiting efforts that took place in the '70s and '80s are no

---

31. http://www.dailymail.co.uk/news/article-2557521/Here-come-brides-2-500-Moonie-couples-met-just-days-wed-mass-stadium-ceremony-South-Korea.html#ixzz3Nz1Dx3rV.

32. http://familyfed.org/news-story/happy-anniversary-to-ffwpu-japan-6696/.

33. According to religionfacts.com, "Today, the church has a presence in more than 100 countries, though exact membership figures are difficult to estimate. The Unification Church says it has 3 million members, but other sources say it is far less, estimating membership at anywhere from 250,000 to just over 1 million." http://www.religionfacts.com/unification_church/#sthash.CA7t9o9k.dpuf.

34. This explanation of the declining numbers from long-time member Michael Candelesari. Interview Jan 29, 2015.

35. The source of these numbers is Michael Candelesari. There may be much fewer members in the U.S. than that. Here's data from an email correspondence in 2003 to adherents.com: "I have been a member since 1974 and it has always been hard to get a good estimate of the total number of members. One thing that did happen is that in February 2003, Rev. Moon asked one person from each church family in the USA to go to Korea for a two-week outreach program. A bit over 2,400 went, which was the goal. Not every family was able to send someone and a few families sent more. . . . So about 2,400 families, maybe 10,000 members in the USA." http://www.adherents.com/Na/Na_638.html.

longer generally practiced. Most Unificationists now live in their own homes, whereas many early Moonies lived in communal centers, attending many seminars, and working long hours to raise money and recruit new members.

Current Leadership

Since Rev. Sun Myung Moon's death in 2012, Mrs. Hak Ja Han Moon has taken charge of the church, as both the spiritual and physical leader. After she took over, she asked all of her children to give up their leadership positions of various branches of the church. In May 2014, Mrs. Moon appointed her fifth daughter, Sun Jin Moon, as the Director-General of Family Federation for World Peace and Unification International.[36]

Sinless Children?

As the True Parents of Mankind, Rev. and Mrs. Moon were to have their own set of pure children. However, the evidence suggests that their children are far from sinless. Their daughter In Jin, who at one time was the leader of the American church, had a child out of wedlock, after a three-year adulterous affair while in a leadership position.[37] Their eldest son Hyo Jin was deeply involved in drug abuse and sexual promiscuity. He physically abused his wife, Nansook Hong, who was afraid of him. She finally escaped the New York compound with their children and wrote a book in 1998 called *In the Shadow of the Moons*, a devastating exposé of what went on in the Moon family over many years.[38] Moon's daughter Un Jin, who also left an abusive relationship, confirmed Nansook's personal credibility and the accuracy of

36. On Feb 1, 2015, Sun Jin addressed the Interfaith Peace Festival in the Philippines. In the speech, she advocated the Unification Church concept of tribal messiahship. She said, "We are each called to fulfill the mission of a heavenly tribal messiah. That is, we should raise up other families to form our own heavenly tribe. Fulfilling our mission as heavenly tribal messiahs is the cornerstone for the complete establishment of *Cheonilguk,* God's eternal Kingdom. For this reason, last year True Mother was delighted to hear that two couples, one from Thailand and one from the Philippines, had each completed their tribal messiah mission by raising up 430 couples. Toward the end of October, she invited all those couples to come to Korea, and she held a great celebration for all of them. We celebrate each Blessing and spiritual rebirth with absolute joy! Thank you and congratulations to these tribes. May all 7 billion of Heavenly Parent's children soon be Blessed. We can then have the greatest celebration the world has ever known." http://familyfedihq.org/2015/02/sun-jin-nims-congratulatory-address-at-the-interfaith-peace-blessing-festival-in-the-philippines/.
37. http://www.newrepublic.com/article/115512/unification-church-profile-fall-house-moon.
38. http://www.washingtonpost.com/world/asia_pacific/sun-myung-moon-dies-at-92-washington-times-owner-led-the-unification-church/2012/09/02/001b747a-f531-11e1-aab7-f199a16396cf_story.html.

her book. (One thing Un Jin specifically confirmed in an interview was that Rev. Moon had an illegitimate son, named Sammy.) Another son in a troubled marriage committed suicide.

It is evident that being the Messiah's children did not keep them from the same vices and problems that plague the average human population. In some cases, the behavior has been more egregious. This contradicts a key element in Unification doctrine. Nansook said, "Rev. Moon has been proclaiming that he has established his ideal family, and fulfilled his mission, and when I pinpointed that his family is just as dysfunctional as any other family — or more than most — then I think his theology falls apart."[39] Though Unificationists explain that children born sinless still have the same choice that Adam and Eve had, and thus can still make bad decisions, it does seem ironic that the Messiah's own family has had that much trouble maintaining its purity. It not only contradicts Moon's theology but also fails to inspire confidence that other blessed couples will have children who remain true to their innate sinlessness.

Moon's Infidelity

The Reverend Moon didn't set a very good example for his children. In 1946, Moon abandoned his first wife and three-month-old son. He didn't return for six years. Sometime later came the divorce. His wife differed with him theologically, and unlike Moon, believed that when the Messiah came, He would literally return on the clouds.[40] But the problems were not just ideological; she also claimed that he was unfaithful to her. Other reports seem to confirm his straying tendencies. Nansook said:

> His wife's departure coincided with the first published reports of sexual abuse in the Unification Church. Rumors were rife that the Reverend Moon required female acolytes to have sex with him as a religious initiation rite. Some religious sects at the time did practice ritual nudity and reportedly forced members to have sexual intercourse with a messianic leader in a purification rite known as *p'i kareun*. The Reverend Moon has always denied these reports, claiming they were part of efforts by mainstream religious leaders to discredit the Unification Church. . . .

39. "Life with the Moons: A Conversation with Nansook Hong, Former Daughter-in-law of the Rev. Sun Myung Moon," *TIME Magazine*, October 13, 1998.
40. Hong, *In the Shadow of the Moons*, p. 25.

The record of those early days became all the more confused in 1993 when Chung Hwa Pak, the disciple whom the Reverend Moon is reputed to have carried on his back to South Korea in 1951, published a book entitled *The Tragedy of the Six Marias*. In it Pak states that the Reverend Moon did practice *p'i kareun* and contends that the Reverend Moon's first wife left him because of his sexual activities with other women. The Reverend Moon is said by Pak to have impregnated a university student, Myung Hee Kim, in 1953 while he was still married. . . .[41]

Moon apparently was also unfaithful to Hak Ja Han (True Mother). When Hyo Jin Moon told his wife Nansook that if his Father, Sun Myung Moon, could be unfaithful to his wife, then he could too, she took Hyo Jin's claim to Mrs. Moon. Nansook's mother-in-law became both furious and tearful:

> She had hoped that such pain would end with her, that it would not be passed on to the next generation, she told me. No one knows the pain of a straying husband like True Mother, she assured me. I was stunned. We had all heard rumors for years about Sun Myung Moon's affairs and the children he sired out of wedlock, but here was True Mother confirming the truth of those stories. . . .
>
> Mrs. Moon told Father what Hyo Jin was claiming and the Reverend Moon summoned me to his room. What happened in his past was "providential," Father reiterated. It has nothing to do with Hyo Jin. I was embarrassed to be hearing this admission from him directly. I was also confused. If Hak Ja Han Moon was the True Mother, if he had found the perfect partner on Earth, how could he justify his infidelity theologically?[42]

Moon's Dead Son Is Greater than Jesus

Besides calling himself the Messiah, what Moon said about one of his deceased sons may be his most bizarre claim. Just days after his 17-year-old son Heung Jin died from a car accident, Moon declared that Heung Jin

---

41. Ibid., p. 26–27. Moon later persuaded Pak to rejoin the church, and Pak disavowed his account of the early history of the church, but Nansook has always wondered what the price was of that retraction (p. 27). Support for the view that Moon practiced *p'i kareun* is found in the book *Change of Blood Lineage through Ritual Sex in the Unification Church*, by Kirsti Nevalainen (BookSurge Publishing, 2010).

42. Ibid., p. 196–197.

was already teaching the *Divine Principle* to those in the spirit world, and had actually displaced Jesus. Nansook said,

> Jesus was so impressed by Heung Jin that he had stepped down from his position and proclaimed the son of Sun Myung Moon the King of Heaven. Father explained that Heung Jin's status was that of a regent. He would sit on the throne of Heaven until the arrival of the Messiah, Sun Myung Moon.
>
> I was stunned by the instant deification of this teenage boy. I knew Heung Jin was a True Child, the son of the Lord of the Second Advent, so I was ready to believe that he had a special place in Heaven. But displacing Jesus? The boy I had helped search for a lost kitten in the attic of the mansion at East Garden, he was the King of Heaven? It was too much, even for a true believer like myself.[43]

Sun Myung Moon and his wife, Hak Ja Han

A few years later Moon also claimed that the spirit of Heung Jin had returned in the body of a Zimbabwean man who traveled the world giving messages and physically beating church members who misbehaved.[44] This abuse had Rev. Moon's support for a while.[45]

Instructions from the Spirit World

As the spiritual and physical leader of the Unification Church, Mrs. Hak Ja Han Moon claims to be getting instructions from her dead husband while in prayer. On the basis of these alleged messages from the spirit world, she has made quite a number of changes in the church, besides having her children

43. Ibid., p. 136–137.

44. Unificationists don't believe in reincarnation but believe we can come back to the world as spirits. They say that some who have died have misunderstood their purpose (they thought they should be reincarnated) and have come back to possess people. This has negatively impacted both the returning spirit and the person he "possessed."

45. http://www.nytimes.com/2012/09/03/world/asia/rev-sun-myung-moon-founder-of-unification-church-dies-at-92.html?pagewanted=all&_r=0.

step down from leadership. For instance, in 2013, Mrs. Moon declared that when church members pray, instead of saying "Heavenly Father" or "Heavenly Parent," the first words they must say are "Heavenly Parents" and then, "Loving True Parents of Heaven, Earth, and Humankind."[46]

Biblical Evaluation of Unification Church Theology

Could Rev. Moon Be the Returning Messiah?

Unificationists' belief that Moon is the second coming of Christ contradicts Jesus' own teaching on the end times. Whereas Christ said that he would return in the clouds (1 Thessalonians 4:17), Moon said just the opposite. He said in *Divine Principle*, "The idea that Christ will return on the clouds [literally] is totally unacceptable to the scientific mind of the modern age."[47] Moon uses a secular view of reality to support his anti-biblical position.

I asked one Unificationist if it bothered him that Jesus was supposed to return in the clouds. He replied, "No, that doesn't bother me; Rev. Moon did come in a cloud. Hebrews 12:1 speaks of a great cloud of witnesses. Korea has been a Christian nation, so it is a cloud (of witnesses).[48] Since Moon was born in Korea, then Christ came back in a cloud."[49] This Unificationist thought he had a way to interpret Scripture that would support Moon as the second coming of Christ.[50] But the angels said that Jesus would return like he left. How did he leave? He physically went up in literal clouds. Acts 1:9–11 says:

> Now when He had spoken these things, while they watched,
> He was taken up, and a cloud received Him out of their sight.
> And while they looked steadfastly toward heaven as He went

---

46. The change to praying to "Heavenly Parents" emphasizes that God is both male and female. It is not a reference to a literal, physical god and goddess (something taught or at least implied in Mormon teaching). It is a reference to the Yin/Yang qualities of God — that he has both positive and negative, or masculine and feminine characteristics as a spiritual being.
47. Moon, *Exposition of the Divine Principle*, p. 383.
48. Moon supports this idea in *Divine Principle*, p. 394. However, though South Korea is now about 29 percent Christian, when Moon was born, Korea was only about 5 percent Christian. Even now, it is not the majority. http://www.pewresearch.org/fact-tank/2014/08/12/6-facts-about-christianity-in-south-korea/.
49. "The great cloud of witnesses" is actually a reference to the believing OT saints mentioned in Hebrews 11.
50. My interaction with this Moonie on the return of Christ reminded me how important it is to take Scripture in a natural, plain way, according to how the original author intended it to be interpreted. Cultists are famous for spiritualizing Scripture and ignoring its original, plain reading. In doing so, they can make the Bible teach anything they want it to teach. But their twisted interpretations are still false.

up, behold, two men stood by them in white apparel, who also said, "Men of Galilee, why do you stand gazing up into heaven? This same Jesus, who was taken up from you into heaven, will so come in like manner as you saw Him go into heaven."[51]

There are corroborating passages that confirm his literal return in the clouds.[52] In claiming to be the Messiah, Moon also claims to be the third Adam. But the Bible says that Jesus, the second Adam, is the last Adam.[53] "And so it is written, 'The first man Adam became a living being.' The last Adam became a life-giving spirit" (1 Corinthians 15:45).

Salvation by Works?

The Unification Church teaches that members are "born again" through a Holy Wine ceremony, and can go to heaven after being blessed in marriage by the Moons. According to Unificationism, man's redemption is works oriented; it is not based on a full reliance on Christ's atoning work for the forgiveness of our sins. Salvation is "95% up to God and 5% up to us."[54] This viewpoint seems similar to what the Mormon scriptures say: "We are saved by grace, after all that we can do."[55] But salvation is not part grace and part works, even if just a little by works. The Unificationist view contradicts Ephesians 2:8–9, which says, "For by grace you have been saved through faith, and that not of yourselves, lest anyone should boast." Salvation is completely by grace. We are responsible to accept that grace (through faith), and cooperate with that grace (we must obey God), but we can't take credit for a portion of our salvation. Though we can reject what God has freely offered, salvation is 100 percent from God. Our works are the fruit of our salvation, not the means to become saved.

Who Is Jesus?

According to the Moonies, Jesus is not divine (any more than you and I are). He was not conceived by the Holy Spirit of the virgin Mary. He is not God incarnate. He did not need to die to redeem us, and he did not rise bodily

---

51. Scripture quotations in this chapter are from the New King James Version of the Bible.
52. For example, Rev. 1:7: "Behold, He is coming with clouds, and every eye will see Him." See also Luke 21:27; Daniel 7:13; Matthew 24:30, 26:24.
53. "Last" is translated from the Greek eschatos, which means "final." Eschatos never has the sense of "the latest" like the English "last" could have.
54. Quote from Michael Candelaresi.
55. II Nephi 25:23.

Comparison Chart on Key Doctrines

Doctrine	Unification Church	Biblical Christianity
Revelation	The Bible is revelation, but it is taken metaphorically when it conflicts with Unification theology. *Divine Principle* is a new revelation. Now that Mr. Moon is dead, Mrs. Moon claims to be getting messages/instructions from her husband in the spirit world while she is in prayer.	Only the Old and New Testaments are written revelation. This Scripture is inerrant, and must be interpreted the way the original authors intended it to be understood.
God	God is dualistic. He has a male and female part. God is Yin-Yang; positive, negative. God, in the act of creation, divided his nature into two, one representing God's masculinity, and the other representing God's femininity. There is no Trinity apart from creation. Jesus, as a separate and finite being formed a spiritual trinity with God and the Holy Spirit, but this is not the orthodox understanding of the eternal Trinity.	God is a Trinity. If there is only one God (Deuteronomy 6:4) and there are three distinct persons (Father, Son, and Holy Spirit) who are identified as this one God (Galatians 1:1; John 1:1, 1:14; Acts 5:3–4; and Mark 1:9–11), then the doctrine of the Trinity must be true — there must be one God who has revealed himself in three Persons, Father, Son, and Holy Spirit. See appendix A.

from the grave. Unificationists deny the essential facts of the gospel.[56] But our salvation rests in the fact that God the Son became flesh to be an adequate mediator between us and God.[57] It is only because Jesus is fully divine and fully human that a sufficient sacrifice could be made to atone for our sin against an infinite God.[58] Jesus not only had to die for our sins, but He also needed to conquer death through His bodily Resurrection.[59] It is only

56. I Corinthians 15:1–4.
57. Hebrews 2:14, 9:13–15.
58. Hebrews 9:14–15; John 1:1, 1:29.
59. Romans 6:9–10; Revelation 1:18.

Sin	Since literal serpents can't talk, this is symbolic. The symbol of the serpent represents Lucifer, a fallen angel. The first sin of Adam and Eve was sexual.	The first sin of Adam and Eve was disobedience to a simple command to not eat of the tree of the knowledge of Good and Evil. This was a literal disobedience of a literal command by literal people in a literal garden.
Christ	No virgin birth, no incarnation; Jesus is not the transcendent God. He is no more divine than we are. Though he died for our sins in some way, he did not rise physically from the dead.	Jesus is the transcendent second person of the Godhead who became a human. As the God-man, Jesus provided a full and sufficient sacrifice for the sins of the world, and then destroyed the power of sin and death through His Resurrection.
Salvation	We contribute to our salvation by our efforts. Members are "born again" through a Holy Wine ceremony, and can go to heaven after being blessed in marriage by the Moons. After the blessing and marriage, and a 40-day waiting period for purification, children will be born sinless — they won't need forgiveness.	Salvation is by grace alone through faith alone in Christ alone. Repentance is a necessary condition for faith to be real, but we cannot work our way toward God. Our works are the fruit of our salvation, not the means to become saved.
Last Things	There is an afterlife. Spirits come back to visit us, but there is no literal hell. Ultimately, everyone will be saved because God will keep giving chances until everyone accepts the truth.	Literal heaven; literal hell. Human spirits either go to heaven or hell when they die. They don't come back to visit us. Spirits that torment humans are actually evil spirits, who are fallen angels. There will be a general (physical) resurrection after which everyone will be judged and sent to their final destination, either an eternal lake of fire or an eternal heaven.

through the death and bodily Resurrection of the God-man that we can be saved.[60] Unificationists deny the essential doctrines regarding both the person and the work of Christ.

In response to my pointing out the importance of Christ's atonement for our sin against a holy God, one Unificationist said to me, "Jesus did not 'pay it all,' and he knew he didn't pay it all. That's why he came back [as Rev. Moon]. We did not really need atonement because ultimately God is a parent who disciplines, not a judge who punishes."[61] This response demonstrates an imbalanced view of the attributes and roles of God. It denies what God's Word says about the character of God.[62]

Why Jesus Came

Unificationists say that Jesus did not come to die, but to get married and set up a physical kingdom on the earth. But in Scripture, Jesus never talked about Himself getting married. He did not say that His purpose was to get a wife and have children. He said that His purpose for coming was to die, to lay down His life as a ransom for sinners.[63] Jesus also predicted His own Resurrection, and the Apostles claimed that this death and Resurrection were the fulfillment of Old Testament prophecy.[64] Peter said that Jesus of Nazareth was handed over to the Jews "by God's set purpose and foreknowledge; and you [the Jews] with the help of wicked men, put Him to death by nailing Him to the Cross."[65]

A False Christ

Rev. Moon is an example of the false christs that Jesus warned about in Matthew 24 and Mark 13:

---

60. John 14:6; 1 Corinthians 15:14–17.
61. Personal interview of Michael Candelesari, Jan 26, 2015.
62. God is a judge: Genesis 18:25; Psalm 82:8; Revelation 19:11. Jesus made a full payment for sin: Hebrews 9:15, 9:28.
63. Mark 10:45.
64. Matthew 16:21: From that time Jesus began to show to His disciples that He must go to Jerusalem, and suffer many things from the elders and chief priests and scribes, and be killed, and be raised the third day. Acts 13:32–34: And we declare to you glad tidings—that promise which was made to the fathers. 33 God has fulfilled this for us their children, in that He has raised up Jesus. As it is also written in the second Psalm: 'You are My Son; Today I have begotten You.' 34 And that He raised Him from the dead, no more to return to corruption, He has spoken thus: 'I will give you the sure mercies of David.'
65. Acts 2:23.

Now as He sat on the Mount of Olives, the disciples came to Him privately, saying, "Tell us, when will these things be? And what will be the sign of Your coming, and of the end of the age?" And Jesus answered and said to them: "Take heed that no one deceives you. For many will come in My name, saying, 'I am the Christ,' and will deceive many. . . . "Then if anyone says to you, 'Look, here is the Christ!' or 'There!' do not believe it. For false christs and false prophets will rise and show great signs and wonders to deceive, if possible, even the elect. See, I have told you beforehand. . . .

"Immediately after the tribulation of those days the sun will be darkened, and the moon will not give its light; the stars will fall from heaven, and the powers of the heavens will be shaken. Then the sign of the Son of Man will appear in heaven, and then all the tribes of the earth will mourn, and they will see the Son of Man coming on the clouds of heaven with power and great glory. And He will send His angels with a great sound of a trumpet, and they will gather together His elect from the four winds, from one end of heaven to the other."[66]

Rev. Moon claimed to be the Christ, but he did not appear in the clouds of heaven with power and great glory. There was no great sound of a trumpet and the gathering of the elect. Rev. Sun Myung Moon's claim to be the Messiah is false. He is not the second coming of Christ. He is not the Savior of mankind. He is a false christ, with many deceived followers. Unificationists, many of whom work hard to make a difference for good in our world, think they are on the right path to eternal life. But as the Bible says, "There is a way that seems right to a man, but its end is the way of death" (Proverbs 16:25). It matters what we believe, and the Unificationists have erroneous beliefs on issues that really matter. Moonies, such as the pastor's wife I interviewed, are putting their faith in someone who cannot save them from eternal death. Rev. Moon died, but did not come back to life. The true Savior of the world died and rose again, showing that He was who He claimed to be, and that He had power over sin and death. It is only through our trust in this Savior that we can be saved. Pray that followers of Rev. Moon turn from a false savior to the true Savior, who alone can eternally satisfy their longing for true love and purity.

---

66. Matthew 24:3–31.

Summary of Unification Church Beliefs

Doctrine	Unification Church Teaching
God	God is dualistic with a positive/male side and a negative/female side (Holy Spirit); Jesus is the sinless offspring of Zechariah and Mary; God is not sovereign; Sun Myung Moon was the new messiah (third Adam)
Authority/Revelation	Exposition of the Divine Principle; Reverend Sun Myung Moon's wife receives guidance through prayer to him
Man	Created as a reflection of God's dual nature to be parents of all mankind; Adam embodied God and Eve embodied the Holy Spirit; man must cooperate with God for salvation; children born in a blessed marriage are sinless while all others are sinful
Sin	Primarily focused on sexual sin and abusing others
Salvation	Largely accomplished by God but 5 percent involves man's adherence to the process of the Divine Principle; participation in the Marriage Blessing ritual is necessary; Jesus provided a spiritual atonement on the Cross; no eternal punishment
Creation	Deny naturalistic biological evolution

Appendix 1

The Triune God[1]

There are numerous passages that teach that God the Father, God the Son, and God the Holy Spirit are distinct persons and yet each hold the attributes of deity.

But the Bible also emphatically and unambiguously declares that there is only one God (Isaiah 44:8, 45:18; Deuteronomy 6:4; Malachi 2:10; James 2:19; Mark 12:29). Hence, taking all the Scriptures into account, orthodox Christian theology has always affirmed that the one true God is triune in nature — three co-equal and co-eternal persons in the Godhead.

This triune God (or Trinity) began to allude to this aspect of His nature right in Genesis 1:26–27. There we read that "God said, 'Let us make man in Our image' . . . God created man in His own image." Here God is a plural noun, *said* is in the third-person singular verb form, and we see both the plural pronoun *our* and the singular *His* referring to the same thing (God's image). This is not horribly confused grammar. Rather, we are being taught, in a limited way, that God is a plurality in unity. We can't say from this verse that He is a trinity, but God progressively reveals more about Himself in later Scriptures to bring us to that conclusion.

In Isaiah 48:12–16 we find the speaker in the passage describing himself as the Creator and yet saying that "the Lord God and His Spirit have sent Me." This is further hinting at the doctrine of the trinity, which becomes very clear in the New Testament. There are many other Old Testament Scriptures that hint at the same idea.

---

1. Used with permission from *Inside the Nye-Ham Debate,* by Ken Ham and Bodie Hodge, (Green Forest, AR: Master Books, 2014).

In Matthew 28:18–20 Jesus commanded His disciples to baptize His followers in the name (singular) of the Father, Son, and Holy Spirit. John's Gospel tells us that "the Word" is God who became man in Jesus Christ (John 1:1–3, 14). Jesus was fully man and fully God. Many other verses combine together to teach that God is triune.

The following chart is an accumulation of many of the passages that show the deity of the Father, the Son, and the Holy Spirit.

	God, the Father	God, the Son	God, the Holy Spirit
is the Creator	Genesis 1:1, 2:4, 14:19–22; Deuteronomy 32:6; Psalm 102:25; Isaiah 42:5, 45:18; Mark 13:19; 1 Corinthians 8:6; Ephesians 3:9; Hebrews 2:10; Revelation 4:11	John 1:1–3; Colossians 1:16–17; 1 Corinthians 8:6; Hebrews 1:2, 8–12	Genesis 1:2; Job 33:4; Psalm 104:30
is unchanging and eternal	Psalm 90:2, 102:25–27; Isaiah 43:10; Malachi 3:6	Micah 5:2; Colossians 1:17; Hebrews 1:8–12, 13:8; John 8:58	Hebrews 9:14
has a distinct will	Luke 22:42	Luke 22:42	Acts 13:2; 1 Corinthians 12:11
accepts worship	Too many to list	Matthew 14:33; Hebrews 1:6	—
accepts prayer	Too many to list	John 14:14; Romans 10:9–13; 2 Corinthians 12:8–9	—
is the only savior	Isaiah 43:11, 45:21; Hosea 13:4; 1 Timothy 1:1	John 4:42; Acts 4:12, 13:23; Philippians 3:20; 2 Timothy 1:10; Titus 1:4, 2:13, 3:6; 2 Peter 1:11, 2:20, 3:18; 1 John 4:14	John 3:5; 1 Corinthians 12:3
has the power to resurrect	1 Thessalonians 1:8–10	John 2:19, 10:17	Romans 8:11

is called God	John 1:18, 6:27; Philippians 1:2, 2:11; Ephesians 4:6; 2 Thessalonians 1:2	John 1:1–5, 1:14, 1:18, 20:28; Colossians 2:9; Hebrews 1:8; Titus 2:13	Acts 5:3–4; 2 Corinthians 3:15–17
is called Mighty God	Isaiah 10:21; Luke 22:69	Isaiah 9:6	—
is omnipresent/ everywhere	1 Kings 8:27; Isaiah 46:10	Matthew 28:18–20	Psalm 139:7–10
is omnipotent/ has power and authority	2 Chronicles 20:6, 25:8; Job 12:13; Romans 1:20; 1 Corinthians 6:14; Jude 1:25	John 3:31, 3:35, 14:6, 16:15; Philippians 2:9–11	1 Samuel 11:6; Luke 1:35
is all-knowing	Psalm 139:2; Isaiah 46:10; 1 John 3:20; Acts 15:8	John 16:3, 21:17	1 Corinthians 2:10–11
has the fullness of God in him (not just "a part of God")	N/A	Colossians 2:9	—
gives life	Genesis 1:21, 1:24, 2:7; Psalm 49:15; John 3:16, 5:21; 1 Timothy 6:13	John 5:21, 14:6, 20:31; Romans 5:21	2 Corinthians 3:6; Romans 8:11
loves	John 3:16; Romans 8:39; Ephesians 6:23; 1 John 4:6, 4:16	Mark 10:21; John 15:9; Ephesians 5:25, 6:23	Romans 15:30
has ownership of believers	Psalm 24:1; John 8:47	Romans 7:4, 8:9	—
is distinct	Matthew 3:16–17, 28:19; John 17:1	Matthew 3:16–17, 4:1, 28:19; John 17:1	1 Samuel 19:20; Matthew 3:16–17, 4:1, 28:19
is judge	Genesis 18:25; Psalm 7:11, 50:6, 94:1–2, 96:13, 98:9; John 8:50; Romans 2:16	John 5:21–27; Acts 17:31; 2 Corinthians 5:10; 2 Timothy 4:1	—
forgives sin	Micah 7:18	Luke 7:47–50	—

claimed divinity	Exodus 20:2	Matthew 26:63–64	—
is uncreated, the First and the Last, the Beginning and the End	Isaiah 44:6	Revelation 1:17–18, 22:13	—
lives in the believer	John 14:23; 2 Corinthians 6:16; 1 John 3:24	John 14:20–23; Galatians 2:20; Colossians 1:27	John 14:16–17; Romans 8:11; 1 Peter 1:11
has the godly title "I Am," pointing to the eternality of God	Exodus 3:14	John 8:58	—
is personal and has fellowship with other persons	1 John 1:3	1 Corinthians 1:9; 1 John 1:3	Acts 13:2; 2 Corinthians 13:14; Ephesians 4:30; Philippians 2:1
makes believers holy (sanctifies them)	1 Thessalonians 5:23	Colossians 1:22	1 Peter 1:2
knows the future	Isaiah 46:10; Jeremiah 29:11	Matthew 24:1–51, 26:64; John 16:32, 18:4	1 Samuel 10:10, 19:20; Luke 1:67; 2 Peter 1:21
is called "Lord of Lords"	Deuteronomy 10:17; Psalm 136:3	Revelation 17:14, 19:16	—

Appendix 2

Is Jesus the Creator God?
A Look at John 1:1–3

Bodie Hodge

Is this even an important question? Absolutely! If Jesus is not God, and therefore the Creator, then He is a created being. If Jesus is created, then how could He have been an adequate sacrifice to atone for sins committed against an infinite God? Jesus must have been God to adequately atone for our sins, which bring upon us unlimited guilt and cause us to deserve an eternal hell. Only the infinite God, Jesus Christ, can take the punishment from an infinite God to make salvation possible.

But does it really matter whether or not we believe that Jesus is God? Yes! If one places faith in a false Christ, one that is not described in Scripture (i.e., a created Jesus, Jesus as a sinner, Jesus as merely one of many gods, etc.), then can this false Christ save them? Not at all. Truly, the identity of Christ is of utmost importance. And yet, in today's culture there are people teaching that Jesus was a created being. They are leading people astray.

What sets biblical Christianity apart from cults and other world religions? It is the person of Jesus Christ — who He is. In Islam, Jesus was a messenger of God, but not the Son of God (i.e., a created being). In many cults, the deity of Jesus Christ is negated or changed,[1] and in many world religions and personal views, Jesus is just another wise teacher. But the Bible says that all things were created by Him and for Him:

> For by Him [Jesus] all things were created that are in heaven and that are on earth, visible and invisible, whether thrones or dominions or principalities or powers. All things were created through Him and for Him (Colossians 1:16).[2]

The biblical Book of Hebrews indicates that God calls Jesus, the Son, God:

> But to the Son He says: "Your throne, O God, is forever and ever; a scepter of righteousness is the scepter of Your Kingdom. You have loved righteousness and hated lawlessness; therefore God, Your God, has anointed You with the oil of gladness more than Your companions" (Hebrews 1:8–9).

We should expect Satan, the adversary of God and the Father of lies, to advance many variants of the person of Jesus Christ. Satan would want all the false views to succeed in some measure to lead people away from the true Jesus.

One may recall the temptations of Jesus by Satan in the wilderness (Mark 4:1–11). The great deceiver even (mis)quoted Scripture in his attempt to trick Jesus into sinning (Mark 4:6). The tactic of the serpent in the garden was to deceive the woman by distorting the plain meaning of the Word of God (Genesis 3:1–6).[3] Satan, through the serpent, quoted the words of God and abused their meaning. We must be aware of the devil's devices (1 Corinthians 2:11). Today, Satan misquotes Scripture through the cultist knocking on the doors in your neighborhood.

John 1:1–3 and the Deity of Christ

Jehovah's Witnesses teach that Jesus Christ is not the Creator God but a lesser created angel (Michael[4]) who was termed "a god" by John in the *New*

---

1. Mormonism, for example, changes the deity of Christ in the Bible to be something different. Jesus is merely one of many people who became gods in an infinite regression of gods in this universe/multiverse system.
2. All Scripture in this chapter is from the New King James Version of the Bible unless otherwise noted.
3. See Bodie Hodge, *The Fall of Satan* (Green Forest, AR: Master Books, 2006).
4. "The Truth about Angels," *The Watchtower*, November 1, 1995, Watch Tower Bible and Tract Society of Pennsylvania, http://www.watchtower.org/library/w/1995/11/1/article_02.htm, retrieved 9-18-2007.

World Translation (the Jehovah's Witnesses translation of the Bible). The NWT says:

> In [the] beginning the Word was, and the Word was with God, and the Word was a god. This one was in [the] beginning with God. All things came into existence through him, and apart from him not even one thing came into existence (John 1:1–3 NWT).

According to the Jehovah's Witnesses' theology (and other unitarian systems of belief), Jesus is something that came into existence. But even their own translation says that apart from Jesus not even one thing came into existence (John 1:3). So then, did Jesus create Himself? Of course that is a ridiculous proposition, but you see how Watchtower (Jehovah's Witness) theology contradicts the Bible, even their New World Translation.

Another contradiction surfaces in such a theology: Jehovah's Witnesses are firm that there is only one God.[5] But they also admit that there is at least one other god, though not as powerful as Jehovah. Jehovah's Witness literature states:

> Jesus is spoken of in the Scriptures as "a god," even as "Mighty God" (John 1:1; Isaiah 9:6). But nowhere is he spoken of as being Almighty, as Jehovah is.[6]

So even though Jehovah's Witnesses say they believe in one God, they really can't be called monotheists. If Jesus is not God Himself, then there is a plurality of gods, assuming Jesus is to be considered "a god" in their view.

Now let's compare the New World Translation of John 1:1–3 to more reputable translations:

> In the beginning was the Word, and the Word was with God, and the Word was God. He was in the beginning with God. All things were made through Him, and without Him nothing was made that was made (NKJV).

> In the beginning was the Word, and the Word was with God, and the Word was God. He was with God in the beginning.

---

5. *Reasoning from the Scriptures* (Brooklyn, NY: Watch Tower Bible and Tract Society of Pennsylvania, 1985), p. 150.

6. Ibid., p. 150.

Through him all things were made; without him nothing was made that has been made (NIV).

In the beginning was the Word, and the Word was with God, and the Word was God. The same was in the beginning with God. All things were made by him; and without him was not any thing made that was made (KJV).

In the beginning was the Word, and the Word was with God, and the Word was God. He was in the beginning with God. All things came into being through Him, and apart from Him nothing came into being that has come into being (NASB).

In the beginning was the Word, and the Word was with God, and the Word was God. He was in the beginning with God. All things were made through him, and without him was not any thing made that was made (ESV).

These translations show that the Word was God, not "a god." Why such blatantly different translations and, accordingly, different theologies? One starts with the Bible, the other starts from a false theology and takes that view to the Bible. The original passage was written in Koine Greek. Following is the Westcott and Hort Greek text (1881) for John 1:1–2:

1. εν αρχη ην ο λογος και ο λογος ην προς τον θεον και θεος ην ο λογος

2. ουτος ην εν αρχη προς τον θεον[7]

Elzevir's Textus Receptus (1624) is identical:

1. εν αρχη ην ο λογος και ο λογος ην προς τον θεον και θεος ην ο λογος

2. ουτος ην εν αρχη προς τον θεον[8]

Even non-Greek scholars can use lexicons and other tools to show without much difficulty that an exact English translation is:

7. *Westcott and Hort Greek New Testament (1881): With Morphology* (Bellingham, WA: Logos Research Systems, 2002), S. John 1:1–3.
8. Maurice Robinson, *Elzevir Textus Receptus (1624): With Morphology* (Bellingham, WA: Logos Research Systems, Inc., 2002), S. John 1:1–3.

1. In beginning was the Word and the Word was with God and God was the Word

2. He was in beginning with God

The Latin Vulgate of Jerome in the 5th century correctly translates John 1:1–2 into Latin:

1. *in principio erat Verbum et Verbum erat apud Deum et Deus erat Verbum*

2. *hoc erat in principio apud Deum*[9]

Word-for-word translation:

1. *in* (in) *principio* (beginning) *erat* (was) *Verbum* (Word) *et* (And) *Verbum* (Word) *erat* (was) *apud* (with) *Deum* (God) *et* (and) *Deus* (God) *erat* (was) *Verbum* (Word)

2. *hoc* (He) *erat* (was) *in* (in) *principio* (Beginning) *apud* (with) *Deum* (God)

If God was the Word, as John 1:1 is literally translated, then it is no problem for the uncreated Word to have created all things. As God, He created. How could the Word be with God and God be the Word at the same time? The doctrine of the Trinity (One God; three persons) is the solution here.[10] The Word was with God (the Father) and God (the Son) was the Word. This understanding, consistent with the rest of Scripture, eliminates any contradiction of multiple gods. There is only one God, revealed in a plurality of persons. The Jehovah's Witnesses do not have a solution to that alleged contradiction.

The primary reason Jehovah's Witnesses do not want John 1:1 translated accurately is due to influences *outside* the Bible. As the theological descendents of their founder Charles Russell, who began Jehovah's Witnesses in the late 1800s, they arrive at the Bible with the preconceived notion that Jesus the Christ is not God. Therefore, when a passage that clearly contradicts their theology comes up, there are two options: change their belief to coincide with what the Bible teaches or change God's Word to fit with their current theology. Sadly, they have opted to exalt their theology above

9. Jerome, *Latin Vulgata*, adapted from Online Bible, 2007.
10. See appendix 1, "The Triune God."

Jehovah's Word. So who is really the Jehovah's Witnesses' final authority? It is no longer a perfect God and His Word, but fallible, sinful men and their errant ideas about God.

Kingdom Interlinear and John 1:1

It is very interesting to see how the Jehovah's Witnesses Greek-English Interlinear translation compares with the NWT and with more accurate translations. One Jehovah's Witness said that their translation comes from an interlinear translation of the Westcott and Hort text and that the NWT is a good translation of it. But let's check into the two primary interlinear translations appealed to by Jehovah's Witnesses, the *Kingdom Interlinear* and the *Emphatic Diaglott*.

The Kingdom Interlinear[11] says:

KATA   IΩANHN

ACCORDING TO JOHN

1 Ἐν ἀρχῇ ἦν ὁ λόγος, καὶ ὁ λόγος
In beginning was the Word, and the Word
ἦν πρὸς τὸν θεόν, καὶ θεὸς ἦν ὁ λόγος.
was toward the God, and god was the Word.
2 Οὗτος ἦν ἐν ἀρχῇ πρὸς τὸν θεόν.
This (one) was in beginning toward the God.
3 πάντα δι' αὐτοῦ ἐγένετο, καὶ
All (things) through him came to be, and
χωρὶς αὐτοῦ ἐγένετο οὐδὲ ἕν.
apart from him came to be not-but one (thing).
ὃ γέγονεν 4 ἐν αὐτῷ ζωὴ ἦν, καὶ
Which has come to be in him life was, and
ἡ ζωὴ ἦν τὸ φῶς τῶν ἀνθρώπων· 5 καὶ
the life was the light of the men; and
τὸ φῶς ἐν τῇ σκοτίᾳ φαίνει, καὶ ἡ
the light in the darkness is shining, and the

1 In [the] beginning the Word was, and the Word was with God, and the Word was a god.* 2 This one was in [the] beginning with God. 3 All things came into existence through him, and apart from him not even one thing came into existence. What has come into existence 4 by means of him was life, and the life was the

Look carefully at John 1:1. The Interlinear doesn't translate *Theos* (θεος) as "a god," which is an unjustifiable change in the NWT (to the right of the interlinear above). Strangely, the interlinear does not capitalize "God" the second time it occurs, though it does the first.

One possible reason they tried distinguishing this particular word for God is due to the spellings of *Theos* (God) in this passage (θεον, θεος) is due to variant endings. Another variant ending is commonly "θεου." All three variants for God are in one passage and each translated as God:

11. *The Kingdom Interlinear Translation of the Greek Scriptures* (Bellingham, WA: Watch Tower Bible and Tract Society of Pennsylvania and International Bible Students Association, 1985), p. 401.

. . . who opposes and exalts himself above all that is called God (θεον) or that is worshiped, so that he sits as God (θεου) in the temple of God (θεον) , showing himself that he is God (θεος) (2 Thessalonians 2:4).

There is really no obvious reason for the change to "a god" or a lower case "god" by the NWT or *Kingdom Interlinear.*

Emphatic Diaglott and John 1:1–3

The next interlinear to be checked was the Diaglott. It translates John 1:1–3[12] as:

The interlinear this time incorrectly states that *theos* is "a god," but the side translation disagrees and says the *Logos* was God, instead of "a god." So again, there are mismatches that make no sense.

The Context of the Passage

Interestingly, in defending their translation of John 1:1, the Jehovah's Witnesses say:

Which translation of John 1:1, 2 agrees with the context? John 1:18 says: "No one has ever seen God." Verse 14 clearly says that "the Word became flesh and dwelt among us . . . we have beheld his glory." Also, verses 1, 2 say that in the beginning he

---

12. Benjamin Wilson, translator, *Emphatic Diaglott* (Brooklyn, NY: International Bible Students Association, Watchtower Bible and Tract Society, 1942).

was "with God." Can one be *with* someone and at the same time *be* that person?[13]

Trying to appeal to context, the Jehovah's Witnesses quote part of John 1:18 and John 1:14 while ignoring the teaching of verse 3 which shows Jesus made all things — no exceptions! John 1:3 makes it clear that everything was created by Christ (the Word). This puts Jehovah's Witnesses on the horns of dilemma. If Christ created all things, then Christ created Himself in their theology. But they say God created Christ, but this means that Christ didn't create all things that had been created and so their translation fails. Either way, they have a big theological problem. We have already shown how Jesus can be *with* God and *be* God — it is through the concept of the Trinity, which makes this passage perfectly readable as is.

Regardless, the context of the chapter should not be neglected. John 1:18 is referring to God the Father as the one no one has seen. We can interpret John 1:18 this way: *No one has seen God the Father at any time; the only-begotten God, Jesus — He has revealed the Father. Anytime anyone has ever seen God, he has seen the Logos, the Son, since the Son is the Word — the revealer.*

Expositor Dr John Gill explains the reference to God:

> That is, God the Father, whose voice was never heard, nor his shape seen by angels or men; for though Jacob, Moses, the elders of Israel, Manoah, and his wife, are said to see God, and Job expected to see him with his bodily eyes, and the saints will see him as he is, in which will lie their great happiness; yet all seems to be understood of the second person, who frequently appeared to the Old Testament saints, in an human form, and will be seen by the saints in heaven, in his real human nature; or of God in and by him: for the essence of God is invisible, and not to be seen with the eyes of the body; nor indeed with the eyes of the understanding, so as to comprehend it; nor immediately, but through, and by certain means: God is seen in the works of creation and providence, in the promises, and in his ordinances; but above all, in Christ the brightness of his glory, and the express image of his person: this may chiefly intend here,

---

13. *Reasoning from the Scriptures*, p. 416.

man's not knowing any thing of God in a spiritual and saving way, but in and by Christ.[14]

So we understand that Jesus reveals God and exists as God at the same time. There is not a contradiction between John 1:1 and John 1:18. In fact, they are amazingly consistent!

Islamic Appeal to the NWT

Muslims also deny the deity of Christ, so John 1:1–3 is also a problem to Islam if taken as written. Muslim apologists have appealed to the NWT in an effort to reduce the deity of Jesus Christ:

> "The Word" is only described as being "ton theos"(divine/a god) and not as being "ho theos" (*The* Divine/ *The* God). A more faithful and correct translation of this verse would thus read: *"In the beginning was the Word, and the Word was with God, and the Word was divine."* (If you read the New World Translation of the Bible you will find exactly this wording.)[15]

Christian apologists have responded:

> It should first be noted that all of known manuscripts and fragments of John's gospel contains this passage without any variation. It should also be noted that John 1:1 was quoted on several occasions by early Christian theologians and Church Fathers. . . . Clearly, there is no "ton theos," in this text as Al-Kadhi and Deedat claim. Both sentences have the phrase "ton theon." "Ton theon" is used because it is the accusative case (the nominative case is "ho theos" = "the God") In this [instance] we must use the accusative case, since the text uses the preposition "pros" which means "with" in this context.
>
> Al-Kadhi and Deedat should know that the article "ho" (nominative case) and "ton" (accusative case) both translate as "the.. Incidentally, the Greek word for "divine" is "theios, theia, theion," depending on the gender.[16]

---

14. Dr John Gill, Commentary notes on John 1:18, adapted from Online Bible, 2007.
15. Answering Christianity, Al-Kadhi, http://www.answering-christianity.com/john1_1.htm, retrieved 9-20-2007.
16. Answering Islam, http://www.answering-islam.org/Responses/Al-Kadhi/r01.2.2.06.html, retrieved 9-20-2007.

But this lets us know how influential the Jehovah's Witnesses and the NWT are. The NWT is being used in Islam to take people *away* from Jesus Christ. What is the typical Muslim response to the Bible? They claim that that the Bible was changed *after* Muhammad. Why after you might ask?

The reason is simple. Muhammad repeatedly stated the Bible to be true in the Koran (Qur'an). So the Bible, as Muslims agree, was indeed true in Muhammad's day. Muslims are even called to believe in in the Bible (the Books sent down aforetime).

> Surah 4:136: O ye who believe! Believe in God and His Apostle, and the Book which He hath sent down to His Apostle, and the Books which He hath sent down aforetime. Whoever believeth not on God and His Angels and His Books and His apostles, and in the Last Day, he verily hath erred with far-gone error.

The Qur'an declares the Bible to be a true revelation of God and demands faith in the Bible (e.g., Sura 2:40–42, 126, 136, 285; 3:3, 71, 93; 4:47, 136; 5:47–51, 69, 71–72; 6:91; 10:37, 94; 21:7; 29:45, 46; 35:31; 46:11). Furthermore, the Qur'an makes no distinction between God's revelations (Sura 2:136). Because Muhammad believed the Bible to be true, this puts Muslim scholars on the horns of a dilemma too, since the Koran (Qur'an) does not mesh with the previous 66 books of the Bible.

So their response is that the Bible must have been changed after Muhammad. Of course, there are two problems with this. First, the Koran (Qur'an) claims that *no one* can change the Word of God (e.g., Sura 6:34; 10:34). Second, there is no textual support for this at all. In other words, Bibles we have prior to Muhammad (around A.D. 600) and Bibles after Muhammad are virtually identical, both clearly teaching the deity of Jesus Christ.

Jehovah's Witnesses' Defense of the Word Being "a god"

Leading Jehovah's Witness apologist Rolf Furuli write extensively about John 1:1 and how *theos* should be translated in reference to the Word. He argues for the NWT's rendering of the Word being "a god" as opposed to "God." Several of his claims will be discussed here.

Mr. Furuli has a chart comparing the NWT with a couple of lesser-known translations, as well as the Greek text with *his* understanding of the word meanings. It is shown below:[17]

John 1:1 in Three Different Translations

NWT	"In [the] beginning the Word was, and the Word was with God, and the Word was a god."
NRSV	"In the beginning was the Word, and the Word was with God, and the Word was God."
Goodspeed	"In the beginning the Word existed. The Word was with God and the Word was divine."
Greek text	*ēn arkhē* ("in the beginning") *ēn* ("was") *ho logos* ("the word"), *kai* ("and") *ho logos* ("the word") *ēn* ("was") *pros* ("with") *ton theon* ("the god"), *kai* ("and") *theos* ("god" or "a god") *ēn* ("was") *ho logos* ("the word")

Let's evaluate Mr. Furuli's comments concerning the term *theos* (notice above how he defines *theos* as meaning either "god" or "a god"). He says:

> . . . in the Bible the word *theos* is also used for persons other than the creator, and therefore neither "creator" nor "YHWH" could be a part of its semantic meaning. . . . The word *theos* is a count noun, and John uses it in one of two ways: either in a generic sense or as a "singular noun." We might illustrate this point by use of the OT. Here we find that *elohim*, the Hebrew equivalent to *theos*, is used in the generic sense.[18]

Mr. Furuli takes about two pages to compare *theos* to the contextual uses of the Hebrew word *elohim*. But it would have been better to compare the uses of *theos* throughout the Greek New Testament and see how it was used in Greek context.[19]

17. Rolf Furuli, *The Role of Theology and Bias in Bible Translation With a Special Look at the New World Translation of Jehovah's Witnesses* (Huntington Beach, CA: Elihu Books, 1999), p. 200.
18. Ibid., p. 204–205.
19. Ibid., p. 211–213, again equating Theos with Elohim to argue against its Greek usage.

Perhaps the reason such was not done is that it would destroy the point Mr. Furuli was trying to make. A search of *theos* in the New Testament shows that *theos* is overwhelming translated as "God" (even when not preceded by an article) unless context warrants otherwise (only about six times). The NT context for John 1:1 overwhelming supports the idea that the Word is God the Creator, as John 1:3 indicates.

Mr. Furuli goes on to say:

> There are 322 examples of *theos* without the article. Because there is no inherent semantic contrast between the articular and the anarthrous *theos*, the question about the meaning of *theos* in some passages is pragmatic, and thus the context becomes essential.[20]

Mr. Furuli argues that John 1:1b can be translated: "And a god was the Word" since there is no article in front of *theos*, and thus the context must determine the meaning of *theos*. In response, we can first appreciate the concession that Furuli is making: the lack of the article in front of *theos* does not mean that the word *theos* is to be translated as an adjective (divine) or with an indefinite article (a god) rather than simply "God." (Even if it should be translated as an adjective, the verse would still teach the same thing — the Word is of the same essence as the Father.) It is obvious that there are many times that *theos* is translated as "God," referring to Jehovah, even when not preceded by an article. Furuli evidently concedes that.

So now it is a matter of context, says Furuli. We agree that context is crucial. But if context is so important, then why not look carefully at John 1:2–18? Furuli mentions only John 1:14, "with God" from John 1:2, and John 1:18. Why did he not refer to the other verses, including verse 3, which makes it clear that the Word made *all* things that have been made?

Furuli then attacked the eternality of the Word, Jesus Christ. In an attempt to downgrade that "in the beginning was the Word," Mr. Furuli tries to show that Jesus was not eternal, thus not God.

> Regarding the expression "in the beginning was the Word," all we can say with reasonable certainty is that at the particular

---

20. Ibid., p. 206.

point in time called "the beginning" the Word existed. This is a far cry from saying "the Word is eternal."[21]

But again, look at the context. If the Word made everything that was made (verse 3), then he must be eternal. If everything that was made (that is, had a beginning) had their beginning through Christ, then it must be the case that the Word never had a beginning; thus He is eternal. Christ, the Word, created time too, indicating His preeminent and eternal nature.

Ignatius (John's Disciple) and the Deity of Christ

Let's go one further step in this study. John, the author of the Gospel, did not simply write the account and disappear. On the contrary, he was the only disciple of Christ to live out his life and die of old age, even though he too endured tribulation for the Word of God (Revelation 1:9). He, like Christ, had disciples of his own, and the two most popular were Polycarp and Ignatius. It makes sense that John would teach his disciples the truth about Jesus Christ and who He was.

Polycarp wrote very little that has survived. Ignatius had quite a bit more. In Ignatius' letter to the Ephesians, it was clear that he viewed Jesus and the Father as the one true God. He said:

> . . . and elected through the true passion by the will of the Father, and Jesus Christ, our God. . . .[22]

> God existing in the flesh[23]

> Our Lord and God, Jesus Christ, the Son of the living God. . . .[24]

> For our God, Jesus Christ, was, according to the appointment of God. . . .[25]

---

21. Ignatius, Epistle of Ignatius to the Ephesians, in *The Writings of the Fathers Down to A.D. 325 Ante-Nicene Fathers*, Eds. A. Roberts and J. Donaldson (Peabody, MA: Hendrickson Publishers), 1:49 (Long version).

22. A. Roberts and J. Donaldson, eds., "Ignatius, Epistle of Ignatius to the Ephesians," in *Ante-Nicene Fathers: The Writings of the Fathers Down to a.d. 325* (Peabody, MA: Hendrickson Publishers), Volume 1, p. 49 (short version).

23. Ibid., p. 52 (short version).

24. Ibid., p. 56 (long version).

25. Ibid., p. 57 (short version).

> . . . God Himself being manifested in human form for the renewal of eternal life.[26]

> . . . God being manifested as man. . . .[27]

> We have also as a Physician the Lord our God, Jesus the Christ, the only-begotten Son and Word, before time began.[28]

After reading the words of a disciple of John who learned extensively from John, there should be no question what John was trying to say. So it is interesting that the founder of Jehovah's Witnesses, Charles Taze Russell, said with regard to John 1:1 and the Word being God:

> . . . except that where the word Theos is used twice in the same clause the Greek *Prepositive Article* is sometimes used, so as to give the effect of *the God* in contrast with *a God*. An illustration of this is found in John 1:1 — "the Word was with *the* God [*ho Theos*] and the Word was *a* God [*Theos*]." But the careful student (freed from Prejudice) will generally have no difficulty in determining the thought of the Apostle. Indeed, the language is so explicit that the wonder is that we were heedless of it so long."[29]

His interpretation of *Theos* as "*a god/a theos,*" he claims is so explicit that he wonders why it took so long for people to realize it. Pastor Russell wrote this in 1899 and yet John's own disciple Ignatius allegedly missed it? This makes little sense logically. The reason the early Church knew John was speaking of Jesus being God is not just from the Scriptures that confirm it, but they were taught this by John, who was their pastor for many years.

So really, what Mr. Russell was saying is that John's disciples, the early Church and the Church for about 1,800 years were wrong and that he [Pastor Russell] was right. This should be a red flag to anyone. Adam Clarke sums up the argument regarding John 1:1 with excellent comments:

> Should it be objected that Christ created *officially* or by *delegation*, I answer: This is impossible; for, as creation requires

---

26. Ibid., p. 57 (short version).
27. Ibid., p. 57 (long version).
28. Ibid., p. 52 (long version).
29. Charles Taze Russell, *Studies in the Scriptures*, Vol. 5, *The Atonement Between God and Man* (1899), reprinted in Bible Students Congregation of New Brunswick (Edison, NJ, 2000), p. 70.

absolute and unlimited power, or omnipotence, there can be but *one* Creator; because it is impossible that there can be *two* or *more* Omnipotents, Infinites, or Eternals. It is therefore evident that creation cannot be effected *officially*, or by *delegation*, for this would imply a *Being conferring the office*, and *delegating* such *power*; and that the Being *to* whom it was delegated was a *dependent Being*; consequently not *unoriginated* and *eternal*; but this the nature of creation proves to be absurd. 1. The thing being impossible in itself, because no limited being could produce a work that necessarily requires omnipotence. 2. It is impossible, because, if omnipotence be *delegated*, he to whom it is delegated *had it not before*, and he who delegates it *ceases to have it*, and consequently *ceases to be* GOD; and the other to whom it was delegated *becomes God*, because such attributes as those with which he is supposed to be invested are *essential* to the nature of God. On this supposition *God ceases to exist*, though infinite and eternal, and another not naturally *infinite* and *eternal* becomes such; and thus an *infinite* and *eternal Being* ceases to exist, and another infinite and eternal Being is produced in *time*, and has a *beginning*, which is absurd. Therefore, as *Christ* is the *Creator*, he did not create by *delegation*, or in any *official way*.

Again, if he had created by *delegation* or *officially*, it would have been *for* that *Being who gave him that office*, and delegated to him the requisite power; but the text says that *all things were made* BY *him and* FOR *him*, which is a demonstration that the Apostle understood Jesus Christ to be truly and essentially God.[30]

Conclusion

The reality is that John 1:1–3 clearly reveals the deity of Jesus Christ, the Word, being the Creator God (see also Colossians 1 and Hebrews 1). As such it confirms many other passages in Scripture that teach that Christ is God. Early Church fathers such as Ignatius, who was a disciple of John the Apostle, also recognized Jesus as God.

The significance of this is a matter of salvation. Without the true Jesus, can one really be saved? Only the infinite Son of God can satisfy the wrath of

---

30. Adam Clarke Commentary notes on Colossians 1:16, adapted from Online Bible, 2007.

an infinite God the Father upon sin to pay the debt in full. Any created Jesus could never have been able to endure the punishment that we all deserve for sin. Yes, having the right Christ is *crucial* to salvation being made possible.

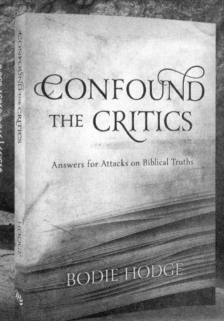

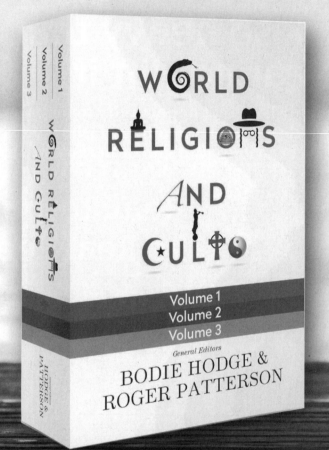

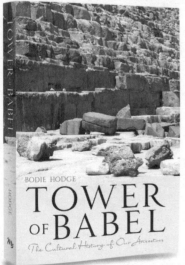

WORLD RELIGIONS

AND CULTS

Moralistic, Mythical
and Mysticism Religions

Volume 2

General Editors

BODIE HODGE &
ROGER PATTERSON

First printing: April 2016
Third printing: September 2017

Master Books®, P.O. Box 726, Green Forest, AR 72638
Master Books® is a division of the New Leaf Publishing Group, Inc.

ISBN: 978-0-89051-922-6
ISBN: 978-1-61458-504-6 (digital)
Library of Congress Number: 2015910670

Cover by Left Coast Design, Portland, Oregon

Scripture taken from the NEW AMERICAN STANDARD BIBLE® (NASB), copyright © 1960, 1962, 1963, 1968, 1971, 1972, 1973, 1975, 1977, 1995 by The Lockman Foundation. Used by permission.

Scripture taken from the New King James Version (NKJV), copyright © 1982 by Thomas Nelson, Inc. Used by permission. All rights reserved.

Scripture designated KJV is from the King James Version of the Bible.

Please consider requesting a copy of this volume be purchased by your local library system.

Printed in the United States of America

Please visit our website for other great titles: www.masterbooks.com

For information regarding author interviews,
please contact the publicity department at (870) 438-5288.

Master
Books®
A Division of New Leaf Publishing Group
www.masterbooks.com

Acknowledgments

Our appreciation to the following for their contributions and help to bring this book to fruition:

Troy Lacey, Ken Ham, Dr. Terry Mortenson, Dr. Corey Abney, David Wright, Dr. Royce Short, Dr. Dan Anderson, Pastor Don Landis and Ancient Man Team at Jackson Hole Bible College, Simon Turpin, Dr. Elizabeth Mitchell, Dr. Joseph Paturi, Dr. Thane Ury, Michiko Mizumuri, Tim McCabe, Joe Owen, Mark Vowels, Dr. James Johnson, Pastor Tom Chesko, Marcia Montenegro, Steve Fazekas, Dr. Mary Kraus, Dr. Ron Rhodes, Dan Zordel, and Shonda Snelbaker.

Contents

Introduction

Bodie Hodge

There are only two religions in the world. We reaffirm this in our second volume of *World Religions and Cults* as we continue to look at religious philosophies based on man's ideas and moralistic systems.

The two religions are God's and man's. God has only revealed one religion and it is the true religion because God is the truth and knows all things. So to have a proper understanding of truth and the one true religion would be to look at religion from the perspective of God (by looking at the 66 books of the Bible).

If a religion doesn't come from God, then it comes from man. This can occur in many ways; a group or individuals (e.g., ancient sages over time), a leading religious person (e.g., Confucius, Buddha), a king or ruler, or even through Satan and demons. But in any case, development of a religion requires the involvement of man. Sometimes the religion morphs into something different by later adherents, taking variant forms, or splintering into various sects.

All man-made religions are deviations from God's Word. They have used man's ideas to supersede God's Word. In other words and usually subtly, man is really seen as the supreme god sitting in authority over the true God. These religions of man are dubbed "humanistic" since they go back to the mind of man or a *human*. As Christians, we should not fear them.

> And do not fear those who kill the body but cannot kill the soul. But rather fear Him who is able to destroy both soul and body in hell (Matthew 10:28).[1]

There are a lot of variations of man's religion that can be broken in hosts of smaller religions. We have divided them by types similar to the way Christian philosopher and pastor Dr. Greg Bahnsen has done.

The religious divisions we are using for the book are:

- Counterfeits of Christianity — religions that look or act much like Christianity but deviate from the truth in some way, like Mormonism, Islam, Satanism, etc.

- Moralistic Religions — religions that teach a moral code that have no god, like Buddhism or Confucianism, or if they do have "gods" they are only slightly above humanity, like some forms of paganism and mythologies

- Mystical Religions — Eastern thought like Hinduism, Taoism, Sikhism, or New Age

- Materialistic/Atheistic Religions — secular humanism, atheism, agnosticism, hedonism, Epicureanism, etc.

Moralistic and Mysticism Religions

Volume 2 of *World Religions and Cults* focuses on moralistic and mysticism religions. This volume includes pagan religions like Greek mythology, witchcraft, and Druidism. Each is making a comeback in our Western world as people search for meaning in the world.

Some religions could have been included like Baal (Belus/Nimrod) worship, which was common in the days of the Old Testament. Baal worship was a blight that Israel often suffered when they rejected God's Word.

But this volume includes chapters of several other pagan systems that may be more relevant than Baal worship, like Egyptian mythology, Roman mythology, and Germanic/Norse mythology. These are having more of a comeback than Baal worship, though they have similar pagan styles. If you can refute one, then you can often refute others since they are based on the same false foundation.

---

1. All Scripture in this chapter is from the New King James Version (NKJV) of the Bible.

Other moralistic religions are Buddhism and Confucianism. These are probably the largest forms of organized moralistic religions. However, there are a lot of moralistic religions and many of these are unaffiliated.

One moralistic religion that could have been placed in this volume is secular humanism. It has a famous moral code (the various Humanist Manifestos) but no god. Since many secular humanists identify themselves as atheistic or agnostic, we opted to put it in the materialistic/atheistic section for volume 3.

As mentioned in the previous volume, some religions could rightly be lumped into more than one category. The chapter on Unitarianism that appears in this volume could have fit into volume 1 (Counterfeits of Christianity). There are some forms of Unitarianism (Oneness Pentecostalism, for example) that make it a counterfeit of Christianity. But the Unitarian churches have departed to the extent that they have become a moralistic religion.

Mystical religions include religious thought that often migrate from the East — Hinduism, New Age, Jainism, Taoism, Sikhism, and the like. They tend to deviate from reason, focusing on mystical experiences to understand the truth. These tend to be religions that have much similarity but they are packaged in different ways or have branched off from a common source.

Be sure to read the overview of moralistic and mystical religions at the beginning of each section to gain a better understanding of the types of religions they encompass. The overviews also show how their truth claims are refuted. But keep in mind the big picture as you read this volume: there are only two religions — the right one and the wrong one (that is manifest in many ways). In all of these, they are dependent upon a man or group of people who founded them, maintained them, and modified them. They are ultimately all humanistic religions — the religion of man.

Refutation Style

Refutations of these religions could be done in several ways. Any one refutation is sufficient to disprove a false worldview. Paul writes:

> All Scripture is given by inspiration of God, and is profitable for doctrine, for reproof, for correction, for instruction in righteousness: that the man of God may be complete, thoroughly equipped for every good work. I charge you therefore before God and the Lord Jesus Christ, who will judge the living and

the dead at His appearing and His kingdom: Preach the word! Be ready in season and out of season. Convince, rebuke, exhort, with all longsuffering and teaching. For the time will come when they will not endure sound doctrine, but according to their own desires, because they have itching ears, they will heap up for themselves teachers; and they will turn their ears away from the truth, and be turned aside to fables (2 Timothy 3:16–4:4).

All refutations of false worldviews must be predicated on the Word of God. It is God who does the refuting.

Arbitrariness

The authors have tried to show where each religion is arbitrary, which is not a good thing in debate or philosophical argument. Arbitrariness includes things like opinions or ideas based on the experience of one individual. If someone is of the opinion that the Constitution of the United States is actually an ice cream cone in the sky, then should that position be taken as truth? No. It is just an opinion.

Other forms of arbitrariness are conjecture, relativism, or unargued bias. Though I don't want to get too technical here, these are all forms of arbitrariness. A worldview or religion that is based on arbitrary ideas has no foundation or ultimate source of authority — it can't be shown to be superior to any other system. Arbitrariness is a fatal flaw in any worldview. Only biblical Christianity offers a non-arbitrary worldview with God as its ultimate source.

Inconsistency

If something is inconsistent, then it is a problem for a worldview. This is where logical fallacies come into play when refuting worldviews. If an argument has fallacies (formal or informal fallacies), then it is a bad argument.

Sometimes people are inconsistent by acting in a way that is contrary to what they say they believe. This is called a behavioral inconsistency. For example, if someone says they view all things in the universe as one but then they don't want a thief to steal their car, they are acting in an inconsistent way! After all, they and the thief would ultimately be the same since they are one with the universe, so why oppose the theft if you are just giving something to yourself?

Reduced to Absurdity

Another form of inconsistency could almost be placed in its own section. It is when you show where an argument leads if it were held in a consistent manner and applied to all aspects of reality. If the basic argument used in a worldview leads to absurdity, then it is inconsistent. Let's take the Taoists for example, who hold that all of the universe is one. They argue that Taoism is correct and Christianity is false. But within their own beliefs, all of reality is one, so Taoism and Christianity are one and the same, which is absurd.

Preconditions

Many religions do not realize that their worldview cannot account for the most fundamental aspects of reality. For example, people in many religions do not know why they wear clothes. Christians wear clothes because of the events of the Garden of Eden and the entrance of sin into God's perfect creation. Clothing covers the shame of nakedness introduced when Adam sinned, having his shame covered by the animals sacrificed to cover his sin (Genesis 3:21).

Many religions fail at explaining a host of these basic aspects of reality. A way to test a religion is to ask, within their professed story (worldview), how do we know that logic, truth, knowledge, or love exist? In the Hindu perception, all of reality is masked with illusion (maya). If this is true, all knowledge is illusion. So how can one even know that knowledge exists in the Hindu worldview?

In the materialistic worldview of many atheists, they claim all things are material (some expression of matter/energy). But the laws of logic have no mass or energy — they are immaterial — so logic is impossible to account for in their worldview even though they must use it to argue for their beliefs.

The Bible, with God as its ultimate author, accounts for all of these foundations of reality and gives a basis for such preconditions. Other worldviews fall short of these preconditions. They often *borrow* from God's Word but don't realize it. These refutations will be used from time to time throughout this volume to help you understand how to expose the false foundations.

Understanding the falsehoods can help you point people to the truth of the Bible and the hope that you have in Christ as Creator and Savior. The ultimate goal is not to simply dismantle someone's worldview, but to call them to build on the solid foundation of the triune God of the Bible.

Chapter 1

Eastern Mysticism Religions: The Overview

Bodie Hodge and Roger Patterson

Imagine seeing a person who has no clothes lying along the road, having been beaten, robbed of everything, and left for dead. Christians might recall the parable of the Good Samaritan (Luke 10:30–37) and honor God and their fellow man by helping the helpless. However, many people in mystical religions like Taoism or Hinduism may simply respond by "letting them be." Why?

In many forms of mystical thought, the person is getting what they deserve due to "karma" from a previous life. So it is not acceptable for someone to get involved and disrupt the karmic cycle by interfering with the consequences the person is experiencing. If the destitute person dies, they will be reincarnated for a type of "do over." By this reasoning, death isn't a big deal in the mind of the mystic. This is also the thinking reflected in those who would refuse to associate with or give aid to the "untouchable" caste within Eastern societies — bringing bad karma upon themselves for interfering.

Besides that, in the grand scheme of these mystical religions lies a concept that teaches nothing is real but is actually an *illusion*. It is called *maya* in Hinduism but has similar counterparts in other mystical religions. If we take this thinking to its natural conclusion, there really was no person who was injured, and you don't exist either, since all is an illusion and not the ultimate reality. This adds another level of confusion about the true nature of reality to Eastern mysticism.

Mystical Religions: Beliefs and Types

When people hear of Eastern religions they typically think of yoga, enlightenment, karma, oneness of being, reincarnation, and mystical contemplation and meditation. They may also think of the many gods in these religions. There are quite a few forms of Eastern mysticism, though Hinduism is surely the largest and most commonly seen in Western cultures.

There are also variants like Hare Krishna, which can be considered a "denomination" of Hinduism. In Hinduism, like some others, the gods are really just manifestations of one impersonal, universal force, Brahman (this is why Hinduism is often called Brahmanism in older literature).

Other forms of mysticism include Taoism (also known as Daoism) where their ultimate impersonal god is termed "Ultimate Reality." Another popular mysticism religion is the New Age movement. New Age is now progressing across the Western world much the way secular humanism (think atheism, agnosticism, evolutionism) has spread across Europe and North America.

Even Jainism is based in Eastern thought, having elements of Buddhism while retaining similarities with Hinduism. Any notion of a supreme god in these religions is *impersonal*.

There are similarities and differences among each of these variant mystical religions (as you can read in the chapters following). Mystical religions, unlike moralistic religions that will be discussed later in the book, go beyond human experience and rationality. So what does that mean? It means that they defy human experience and defy logic as fundamental aspects of reality.

Defying logic and experience might seem strange, but it is the norm in this way of thought. But this is apparent when we think of the notion of maya — that everything we experience is an illusion and not the ultimate reality. Even logic is an illusion, as are your experiences, in religions like Hinduism, Taoism, and Hare Krishna.

They teach that the problem with all of us is that we are blinded by this illusion to think there are distinctions, when in fact there is no distinction between anything. The logical person will obviously point out that there are distinctions based on their experiences (i.e., there is a distinction between a cat and a dog).

But the mystical mind would deny this. They would argue that both cat and dog are an illusion and we mistakenly think (based on our experiences) that there is a distinction. The mystic would say these are all just manifestations of the oneness that exists as the true reality (e.g., these are all emanations of Brahman in Hinduism).

This is why yoga and mystical meditation are required to move beyond experience and dive into the ideas that defy reason and experience. Thus, they argue that when you have entered deep enough into the mystical understanding that you can achieve the final state of bliss. The goal of life is to achieve nothingness, moksha, or nirvana[1] as you are spliced back into the oneness of being — "like a drop of water reentering the ocean of being."

If you have not achieved this perfect level at your death, then you are doomed to keep repeating life at a higher reincarnate level (come back as a human again) or lower level (e.g., come back as an animal or plant). This is done through stages of reincarnations, based on your good or bad karma, until you finally reach this state.

So the goal in many mystical religions is to stop drawing distinctions so that you can move up the reincarnation chain to finally get to nothingness. There are variations in the religions mentioned, but in the generalized sense, this is the basic goal of all mystical religions.

Arbitrariness

When we consider the validity of a religious worldview, the first question we need to ask is, "On whose authority do mystics know about their religion and its beliefs?" Did their impersonal god reveal the truth to mankind? No. The very notion of an impersonal god communicating to man is a logical contradiction — communication is an interpersonal act. They *do* have religious books, like the Vedas, Upanishads, Bhagavad Gita, etc. But these are not revelations from God to man as the Bible is.[2]

Instead, these religious books are merely the ideas or wisdom of ancients on the subject. Essentially, they are just the writings of man to recount old

---

1. These are just different names for essentially the same thing, depending on which Eastern religion is being discussed.
2. The Bible is not just written by men but *inspired by God* while using human authors to write the inspired text of Scripture.

philosophies. They often disagree with each other, but that is the flavor of writings of mere men.

These ideas all originate in the mind of man or are expressed through man (if they have a supernatural demonic origin). Thus, they are humanistic in their outlook.[3] The ideas of man are arbitrary next to the absolute standard of the Word of God, the Bible. The Bible comes with the authority of the *absolute authority*, God. The ideas promoted in the Vedas or Upanishads are just opinions of man. These opinions are arbitrary, having no ultimate source of authority.

In bold terms, *"so what"* if these ancients believed this mystical philosophy. Just because they believed it doesn't make it true any more than someone believing George Washington (the first president of the United States) was a green mushroom!

If one argues that these sages of old were exceptionally wise, then by what standard are they wise? The modern mystics? That again would be an arbitrary opinion. If someone came to me and said, "George Washington was a green mushroom," I would merely point out that their assertion is merely arbitrary and has no grounding in reality.

If they retort, "I heard this from someone who was exceptionally wise," does that really hold water? No. It is still arbitrary and thus a false premise upon which to base any argumentation.

If we consider any of the beliefs within these mystical systems, each is based on the opinion or idea of a mere man. For example, how does a Hindu or Taoist *know* he will be reincarnated? He doesn't. It is an arbitrary assumption that forms a belief.

Inconsistencies

There are also many inconsistencies with mysticism religions that allow us to see their false character. Consider just a few. Let's start with knowledge (in technical terms, this is "epistemology"). If all we experience is illusion, then knowledge is too. One can't consistently know anything in this religious system. To claim to know something based on experience would be to affirm that it is not illusory — a self-refuting position.

But it is just gets worse from here. No believer in Eastern mysticism can know anything about their religion if their religion is what it claims to be.

---

3. This reveals that there are indeed only two religions — God's and man's. All forms of mysticism are from the mind of man or part of the variations of man's religion.

Here is why. Their supreme god is *impersonal*. Since their god is impersonal, then it is impossible for that god to communicate to man, who is *personal*. This alleged supreme god couldn't use language, which is based on personal human experience. There can be no revelation *of any sort* to mankind to know anything about this alleged god. It would be inconsistent for any follower of Eastern mysticism to claim to know anything about their professed religion.

The mystic might argue that Brahman is impersonal but has an aspect where he[4] can be able to manifest as personal at certain times or as certain manifestations (as Brahma, Vishnu, or Shiva). But that would be a logical contradiction, as he would be both personal (relating to these other gods who have emanated from him) and impersonal at the same time and same instance as there is ultimately no distinction between Brahman and the personal manifestations. Besides, an impersonal Brahman cannot decide to manifest himself as personal, as decision making is personal in the first place.

The mystic might say that they can learn about their supreme god (Brahman, Ultimate Reality, etc.) based on utilizing the world in which we live. That also proves nothing since it is all supposed to be an illusion.

Another inconsistency is derived on their doctrine of *all being one* — that there is no distinction. Recall that our problem in mystical religions is that we draw distinctions. This is why we remain in the world of maya or illusion instead of entering into a nirvana, Moksha, or blissful state.

But here is the problem: in the Eastern mystical reality, there would be no distinction between the illusory and blissful states. So making the statement that they are distinct is self-refuting. Let's put it this way: if one argues that there is no distinction and that our problem is that we draw distinction, and they argue this by drawing distinctions, then that is illogical.

Just tell the mystical adherents that you are already in the state of bliss — what are they going to do — draw a distinction to say you aren't? Similarly, in Buddhism, and its variations, the goal is to rid one's self of all desires. So, you must desire to rid yourself of all desires to be released from being — a logical contradiction.

When one dies, who is the judge that determines if they had enough good or bad karma to know where and in what condition or form they will be reincarnated? Judging is a personal attribute, so their impersonal god cannot be the judge.

---

4. Brahman is viewed as a genderless force, but we will use a masculine pronoun here for ease of communication.

Another inconsistency is exhibited in the mystical believer's personal life. If *all is one* and *there is no distinction*, do they live in a manner consistent with that claim? No. If a Hindu says that *all is one* and *there is no distinction,* a good thing to ask for is . . . their wallet.

Would they give their money to you? No. But you could respond by staying, "I am you," since "all is one." You could go on and point out that the money is actually yours since the two of you are actually one as part of the principle of Brahman. If the mystic argues, just point out that they should stop drawing the distinction between you and them.

You need to understand that the mystical mind says one thing and lives their life another way. The believer of Hinduism or New Age or Taoism goes home and kisses their spouse as though they were real and distinct from other people's spouses. They handle their money as though it were real and distinct from someone else's money. Their lives are a walking inconsistency.

If a mystic resists the idea of converting to Christianity, ask them to consider this: if all is one and there is no distinction, then the mystic might as well become a Christian, since there is no distinction.

But remember, we pointed out that the Eastern mystical religions are not rational, i.e., they defy logic. As you talk with them, the mystic may respond by saying they are not bound to the laws of logic, so inconsistencies are acceptable in their religion since *all is one* — thus, logic and non-logic are one and the same.

If a mystic like a Hindu, New Ager, or Taoist says such a thing, just contradict them and point out that "they do believe in logic." What can they do? Would they appeal to logic (e.g., law of non-contradiction) to say that you contradicted what they just said (that they don't believe in logic)? That is inconsistent.

Borrowing from God's Word

The mystical mind cannot account for knowledge, logic, or even a single aspect of their professed religion because it is marred with inconsistences and arbitrariness. Even the lives of many mystics are plagued with inconsistencies within their professed religion.

Yet many held captive by these religions *do* believe in logic and that knowledge exists. They believe their wives or husbands are real and have distinction from any random person. They love their kids. But why?

The answer is because they are borrowing from a biblical worldview and don't realize it. Many of these doctrines were passed down from creation, through the Flood and Tower of Babel and are still retained today — even couched in many religions around the globe.

Man is made in the image of a personal God; this is why we are personal. We are made in the image of a logical God who knows all things. Thus, we are in a position to be logical and to know things. The Bible accounts for why things exist and have distinction — God created them.

The Hindu or Taoist understands that shame and love and dignity and honor exist. Yet these things should not exist, as they are merely illusions of experience in their worldview. But they are real concrete entities in the biblical worldview.

Consider memory. If all is illusion, then how can an Eastern mystic trust their memories? According to their worldview, they cannot. They cannot know that morality is a reality either.

Eastern religions cannot account for absolute morality, as there is no absolute lawgiver who communicated to mankind (thus, a personal God) that morality exists. For all the Hindu, Taoist, etc. knows, the correct path may have nothing to do with being *good enough or knowing enough,* as that can be an illusion, and being *bad and not knowing* may be how you move up a caste. In many respects, the adherents hold to some levels of morality. But why? It is because the law of God is written on their hearts. It is from the Christian viewpoint that morality makes sense.

When it comes down to it, the mystical worldviews cannot hold up to a Christian worldview that makes sense of knowledge, logic, truth, morality, memory, dignity, love, honor, and so forth. If the mystic wants to be logical and rational, they must give up mystical religions and move to the biblical position.

Conclusion

The mystical religions recognize there is a problem in the world and have devised all manner of works to seek to bring balance and harmony. We heartily agree. There *is* a problem in the world, but it doesn't have anything to do with drawing distinctions. It has to do with sin. When the mutual ancestors of us all, Adam and Eve, sinned in Genesis 3, the perfect world God had created became corrupt, and death and suffering came into the perfect creation as a result.

But Jesus Christ, who is the personal God (John 20:27–29), stepped into history to become a man (John 1:1–14; Philippians 2:8) to rescue us from sin and death where an eternal death, or second death, awaits (death is the punishment for our sin — Romans 6:23). Christ took the punishment we deserve on the Cross and died the death we deserved for sin (Colossians 2:13–14) and rose from the dead to demonstrate He had overcome death (Acts 10:40). God offers the free gift of salvation through the blood of Jesus Christ alone to attain heaven (Romans 5:15–18) where we will consciously be with God and His goodness and blessing for all eternity (1 Corinthians 2:9).

It is because we have been saved that we take the message of salvation to others. We want to help rescue unbelievers (those who don't believe in Jesus [yet]), even those trapped in mystical thought, in the same way that Christ rescued us.

We must remember that it was the power of the Holy Spirit (1 Corinthians 12:3) and the proclamation of the gospel that brought us (Romans 10:13–17), as Christians, from the kingdom of darkness and conveyed us into the Kingdom of Christ (Colossians 1:13). More than just showing those blinded by mystical ideas where their own thinking is flawed (2 Corinthians 10:4–5), we must point them to the only man who has ever perfectly understood all of life's mysteries — Jesus Christ.

So when Christians pass by those enslaved to mysticism, we should view them as a person who has no clothes lying along the road and has been robbed of everything and left for dead. They are in need of salvation through Jesus Christ and His death, burial, and Resurrection. The unbelievers need to repent (Acts 17:30) and receive Christ (John 1:12). This is why the Christian stops to help, applying the salve of the gospel to their wounds and calling on the Great Physician to bring them spiritual healing.

Chapter 2

The New Age Movement
(Pantheism and Monism)

Dr. Ron Rhodes

Cindy was exposed to the New Age movement through a human potential seminar sponsored by the company she worked for. The teacher of the seminar informed each attendee: "You are your own god," and "You can create your own reality." By embracing these ideas, he claimed, each employee could become much more successful at the workplace, ultimately leading to increased profits for the company.

Cindy was confused. If she was a god, wouldn't she already know it? Why does a god have to attend a seminar to *discover* that he or she is a god? She later found out that this seminar was part of the New Age movement. It didn't sit right with her. She decided to be very cautious in evaluating the New Age ideas she learned at the seminar.

The New Age movement first emerged in the West in the 1970s and then mushroomed in popularity in the 1980s. Even today the movement continues to influence people on the religious landscape around the world. Many no longer use the term "New Age" — they prefer the term "new spirituality," or something similar — but it is all part of the movement that emerged in the 1970s.

A major problem one encounters in discussing the New Age movement is defining it. Some have attempted to categorize it as a single unified cult.[1] It is probably wiser, however, to define it as a loosely structured network of individuals and organizations who share a common vision of a new age of enlightenment and harmony. Those who share this vision typically subscribe to a common set of core religious and philosophical beliefs — that is, they hold to a particular worldview. This worldview centers on *monism* (all is one), *pantheism* (all is God), and *mysticism* (the experience of oneness with the divine).

Despite these core beliefs, the collective body of New Agers around the world is organizationally diffuse. For this reason, we cannot properly categorize it as a unified cult. Cults are typically exclusivistic groups made up of individuals who subscribe to a uniform set of beliefs and operate according to a rigidly defined organizational structure. Movements, on the other hand, have an element of unity (core beliefs) but are also multifaceted — involving a variety of individuals and groups with different emphases. This is the case with the New Age movement. (More on this shortly.)

Factors which Gave Rise to the New Age Movement

There are a number of factors that contributed to the emergence of the New Age movement in the 1970s. First and foremost is 19th-century transcendentalism, a school of thought that was heavily dependent on Eastern scriptures, such as the Hindu Vedas. Transcendentalism emphasized intuition as a means of ascertaining truth. It also held that all religions contain divine truth, and affirmed that the goal of religion is to obtain conscious union with the divine. Such ideas helped set the stage for the eventual emergence of the New Age movement.

From the Vedas
(Shutterstock)

We can also point to the revival of occultism that took place in the late 19th century. This revival took form in the emergence of such groups as the Theosophical Society (1875), the Anthroposophical Society (1912), the Arcane School (1923), and the I AM movement (1930s). We need not investigate the unique teachings and features of each group. It is sufficient to recognize that spiritistic phenomena — that is,

---

1. An example is Walter Martin's book, *The New Age Cult* (Bloomington, MN: Bethany House, 1989).

contact with entities from the beyond, such as "ascended masters"[2] — was common in such groups. This helped set the stage for the emergence of modern New Age psychics and channelers.

Also contributing to the emergence of the New Age movement was a lesser movement called neo-gnosticism. As a backdrop, Gnosticism — from the Greek *gnosis*, "knowledge" — was a heresy that emerged in the second century A.D., purporting to offer knowledge of otherwise hidden "truth" as the indispensable key to human salvation.[3] Though gnosticism with its secret knowledge is long gone, a revival of certain gnostic ideas (called neo-gnosticism) occurred in the late 19th and early-to-mid-20th centuries. These ideas include, (1) Man has the spark of the divine within, (2) Man is ignorant of his divinity, and (3) Jesus came as a way-shower to bring enlightenment to humankind. These ideas eventually became prominent in the New Age movement.

Typical 1960s hippie look
(Shutterstock)

We might also point to the counterculture of the 1960s. Indeed, in the 1960s many people reacted against the West's traditional way of doing things. During the turbulent sixties, people were open to new ideas — religious and otherwise. The counterculture became saturated with fringe ideas. Common were antimaterialism, utopianism, communalism, interest in the occult, and a rejection of traditional morality. All this helped to lay the groundwork for the emergence of the New Age movement.

Also during the 1960s, the West experienced an Eastern tidal wave. The most pervasive interest was in transcendental meditation, reincarnation, chanting, visualization, and the idea that all of reality was divine and sacred. These ideas would soon become pervasive in the New Age movement.

Finally, we must recognize the failure of secular humanism. Cultural observers in the sixties and seventies recognized that human reason had not

---

2. "Ascended Masters" are believed to be formerly historical persons who have finished their earthly evolutions via reincarnation. Now, even as these Ascended Masters continue in their own evolution toward the godhead, they voluntarily help lesser-evolved humans on earth to reach the masters' present level. These masters allegedly give revelations to spiritually attuned human beings on earth.

3. Justo L. Gonzalez, *A History of Christian Thought,* Vol. 1 (Nashville, TN: Abingdon, 1970), p. 129.

been able to solve all of humankind's problems, as had been imagined by its proponents beginning in the Enlightenment. Moreover, with its relentless overemphasis on secularized reason, one's sense of the divine, the sacred, and the transcendent faded. In the New Age movement, people therefore sought a return to the divine and the sacred in all things. This is an example of the cultural "pendulum effect" — that is, there was a swing from the secular to the sacred, a swing from the merely rational to the transcendent and the mystical.

Maharishi Mahesh Yogi, developer of the Transcendental Meditation technique
(Jdontfight, Creativecommons)

These six factors, among others, collectively provided a rich and fertile soil for the emergence and worldwide growth of the New Age movement. The so-called Age of Aquarius blossomed and flourished.

Common Characteristics of the New Age Movement

We've already noted that core beliefs of New Agers include *monism* (all is one), *pantheism* (all is God), and *mysticism* (the experience of oneness with the divine). Along with these primary core beliefs are some secondary characteristics that are true of most New Agers. For example, most New Agers are highly eclectic. By this I mean that New Agers typically draw their religious and philosophical ideas from a variety of religious sources. They consult holy books like the Bible and the Hindu Vedas, but also feel free to consult psychics and channelers, whose "revelations" from spirit guides are considered just as authoritative as those found in holy books. They have no hesitation in consulting astrologers and others who practice the occultic arts of necromancy, palm readings, ball gazing, tarot cards, etc.

Tarot cards
(Shutterstock)

Not surprisingly, New Agers are also syncretistic. By this I mean that New Agers combine and synthesize religious and philosophical ideas from Jesus, the Buddha, Krishna, Zoroaster, alleged "space brothers" aboard UFOs, Ascended

Masters who live on planet Venus, and many others. New Agers believe there is truth in all religions and religious traditions. This willingness to pick and choose what they believe from various sources of enlightenment is a vivid demonstration of the arbitrary and inconsistent nature of the worldview.

Most New Agers are also transformational on two levels. First, New Agers believe that personal transformation takes place when a human being recognizes his or her oneness with all things in the universe. Second, planetary transformation takes place when a critical mass of human beings come into this same awareness. We are allegedly transforming — or *transitioning* — into a New Age with a new consciousness.

Not unexpectedly, New Agers are typically relativistic in their view of truth and ethics. One New Age curriculum that found its way into some school districts in the United States taught students how to discover *their own* values. The idea in this curriculum is that values are not to be imposed from without (such as from Scripture or from parents) but must be *discovered within*. The underlying assumption is that there are no absolute truths or values. New Agers are well known for their view that "you can have your truth and I can have my truth," and that "your truth should never infringe upon my truth." And yet, it is interesting that they are willing to impose (infringe) this alleged absolute truth upon everyone! This is a self-refuting position as it creates an illogical internal inconsistency within the worldview.

We might also observe that most New Agers are open to meditation. I am not referring to meditation on the Bible (e.g., Psalm 119:148). I am referring to an Eastern form of meditation in which one goes into a trance-like state and seeks to attain a sense of oneness with all things. The goal of meditation varies, but the common belief is that it allows one to connect to the divine or the force that permeates the entire universe. Emptying the mind and directing energies

Eastern meditation
(Shutterstock)

within the body allows the balancing of vital energies (present in meridians or chakras) which is used to promote spiritual and physical healing.[4]

---

4. Ron Rhodes, "Energies of Mind & Body," *SCP Journal,* Volume 21:3 Fall 1997; Ron Rhodes, *Miracles Around Us: How to Recognize God at Work Today,* Chapter 13: " 'Miracles' of New Age 'Energetic Medicine'" (Eugene, OR: Harvest House Publishers, 2000); Marcia Montengero, "The Religion of Life Force Energy," Christian Answers for the New Age, accessed October 30, 2015, http://christiananswersforthenewage.org/Links.html.

The use of crystals, essential oils, body positions (Yoga *asanas*), breathing practices, mantras, and other methods are used to connect to the divine force and release and balance divine energy within the person doing these practices.

Closely connected to meditation is the New Age view of visualization, which basically involves the idea of "mind over matter." One New Ager said, "Your thoughts are always creating your reality — it's up to you to take charge of your thoughts and consciously create a reality that is fulfilling."[5] Another said: "We literally create our reality through the beliefs we hold, so by changing those beliefs, we can change reality."[6] Today, this idea of manipulating reality through focus practices is called "mindfulness" and is commonly taught in arenas from public schools and children's programming to self-help seminars and corporate trainings.

The New Age View of Key Bible Doctrines

If New Agers are eclectic (open to many religious and philosophical sources) and syncretistic (combining and synthesizing religious and philosophical ideas from many different traditions), then one would naturally expect them to have deviant views on the key doctrines of the Bible. This has indeed turned out to be the case.

View of the Bible

The Bible is a good case in point, for New Agers believe it is merely one of many holy books communicating revelation from God, or the divine. New Agers believe it is incorrect to read the Bible in a straightforward way. Rather, they look for truth by seeking hidden, secret, or inner spiritual meanings of Bible verses, especially in the teachings of Jesus. For example, when Jesus said, "seek first the kingdom of God" (Matthew 6:33), He was allegedly teaching people to seek an awareness of their own inner divinity. Such Scripture twisting is common among New Agers.

Moreover, in place of the biblical Creator-God with whom we can have personal relationships is a pantheistic concept which says that God is all and all is God. In pantheism, all reality is viewed as being infused with divinity. The God of pantheism is an impersonal, amoral "it," and not a personal,

---

5. David Gershon and Gail Straub, *Empowerment: The Art of Creating Your Life as You Want It* (New York: Dell, 1989), p. 21.

6. Jennifer Donovan, "Seth Followers Spoon Up Fun in Their Goal to Enjoy Living," *Dallas Morning News,* July 1, 1986.

moral "He." The distinction between the Creator and the creation is completely obliterated in this view.

Views of Jesus

New Agers also have twisted views of Jesus Christ. Notice I said "views," for New Agers set forth many strange ideas about Jesus. Foundationally, New Agers distinguish between the human Jesus and the divine Christ. New Agers agree that Jesus became the Christ, but they have different interpretations as to how that happened. Some say that a divine cosmic Christ spirit descended upon the human Jesus at His baptism. Others say that Jesus underwent seven degrees of initiation — an occultic ceremony — in Egypt, the seventh degree being "the Christ." Still others claim Jesus traveled to India as a child and learned from Hindu gurus, and this eventually led to his Christhood. Regardless of how He became the Christ, New Agers agree that Jesus was an enlightened way-shower for humankind, demonstrating to humans how they, too, can become the Christ.

View of Man and Salvation

Since New Agers hold to monism (all is one) and pantheism (all is God), it is not surprising that they view human beings as divine. Because humans are divine, they are believed to have unlimited potential. Many Fortune 500 companies have sponsored human potential seminars.

The New Age view that humans are divine has powerful implications for the doctrines of sin and salvation. New Agers claim there is no sin, and hence there is no need for salvation. If human beings have any problem at all, it is allegedly an ignorance regarding their divinity. This being so, humankind's need is enlightenment, not salvation. All we need is "God-realization."

View of End Times

With their twisted views of the Bible, God, Jesus, humanity, sin, and salvation, it is no surprise that New Agers have also completely redefined the end times. New Agers offer different interpretations of the Second Coming. Some believe that prophecies of the Second Coming are fulfilled in the coming of a specific individual named Maitreya, who will allegedly take the primary role of leadership in the New Age. In this view, Maitreya has allegedly been living incognito among human beings since 1977 when his consciousness entered a specially created human-like body of manifestation, the Mayavirupa. In the near future, Maitreya will allegedly manifest himself to all humanity and usher in a new era of peace and happiness.

Other New Agers interpret the Second Coming in terms of the "cosmic Christ" (a divine spirit) falling upon all humanity so that human beings around the world come to recognize their divinity. This Second Coming is thus viewed as a "mass coming" involving not just one "Christ," but *all* humans coming to recognize their "Christhood."

Statistics of the New Age Movement

It is difficult to assess how many New Agers there are in the United States and around the world. After all, they are not a monolithic group that keeps membership roles like the Mormons and Jehovah's Witnesses. Moreover, as noted previously, not all who hold a New Age worldview actually call themselves New Agers today.

During the early nineties, it was estimated that around 12 million Americans were active participants in the movement, with another 30 million avidly interested in one or more different aspects of the movement. At present, the New Age tome titled *A Course in Miracles* has sold well over 1,000,000 copies and has spawned over 1,000 study groups in the United States alone. Such statistics point to a broad penetration of New Age ideas in Western culture. This broad penetration has been reflected in Hollywood movies (for example, *Ghost* and *The Sixth Sense*) and TV shows (for example, *Medium* and *Ghost Whisperer*).

Another way to gauge New Age influence is to consider statistics related to specific paranormal beliefs.[7] A Gallup poll reveals that 32 percent of Americans believe in some sort of paranormal activity. This statistic holds true for even graduating college seniors and college professors. Meanwhile, 28 percent of Americans believe we can communicate with the dead.

Among teenagers, some 73 percent have participated in psychic activities. Four out of five have had their horoscopes read by an astrologer. Seven million claim to have personally encountered a spirit entity, such as an angel or a supernatural entity. Two million claim to have psychic powers.

Even the United States government has been interested in the occult and the paranormal. According to government documents that were declassified

7. The word "paranormal" generally refers to that which goes beyond the normal — that is, beyond the five senses (sight, taste, touch, hearing, and smelling). In New Age circles, it often refers to attempts to gain secret or hidden knowledge or information outside the use of the natural senses — for example, by consulting a psychic or an astrologer.

in the 1990s, America — during the years of America's cold war with the Soviet Union — spent a whopping $20 million studying extrasensory perception and other psychic phenomena.

Such facts reveal that the New Age movement has indeed broadly penetrated American culture. For this reason, Christians ought to be equipped to answer the primary claims of New Agers.

Debunking New Age Claims

Someone said that the New Age movement is a target-rich environment when it comes to opportunities for critique. In what follows, I will provide a brief biblical response to some of the primary ideas set forth in the movement.

Relativism is not logically satisfying. One might interpret the statement "all truth is relative" to mean it is an *absolute* truth that all truth is relative. Such a statement is self-defeating. Or, one might understand the statement as saying it is *relative* truth that all truth is relative. But such a statement is ultimately meaningless. In contrast to such nonsense, absolute truth and morals are grounded in the absolutely true and moral God of the Bible (see 1 Kings 17:24; Psalm 25:5, 43:3, 100:5, 119:30; John 1:17, 8:44, 14:17, 17:17; 2 Corinthians 6:7; Ephesians 4:15, 6:14; 2 Timothy 2:15; 1 John 3:19; 3 John 4, 8).

All religions do not teach the same truths. One cannot rationally claim that the various world religions are teaching the same basic truths. This becomes evident by examining key doctrines in each religion. The doctrine of God is a good example. The Christian Bible reveals that there is one personal God who is triune in nature (Matthew 28:19; Mark 12:29; Romans 8:15). The Muslim Quran teaches there is only one God, but God cannot have a son, and there is no Trinity. The writings of Confucius affirm polytheism (there are many gods). Krishna taught a combination of polytheism and pantheism (all is god). Zoroaster set forth religious dualism (there is both a good god and a bad god). Buddha taught that the concept of God was essentially irrelevant. Clearly, the world's major religions hold completely contradictory views regarding the nature of God. The same is true in their view of Jesus and their view of salvation. This means that the New Age claim that all the religions teach the same basic truths is wishful thinking.

Pantheism — the view that "all is God" — is fraught with problems. In pantheism, all distinctions between the creation (which is finite) and the Creator (who is infinite) are destroyed. Biblically, God is eternally distinct from what He created (Hebrews 11:3; see also Genesis 1:1; Psalm 33:8–9). Moreover, pantheism contradicts common sense. If everything in the universe is truly God, then there is no difference between myself and anything else (or anyone else) in the world. Such an idea is nonsensical.

The truth is, the pantheistic God is an impersonal force, not a personal being with whom personal relationships can be established (see Mark 14:36; Galatians 4:6). The God of the Bible is infinitely more appealing and is the only source of the existence of everything in the universe (Colossians 1:15–18; Hebrews 1:3).

There are many problems with reincarnation. The concept of reincarnation finds its roots in Eastern religions and has no basis in any real experience. Even the most sophisticated views of ongoing cycles of birth and death are filled with logical inconsistencies and practical evils.

For example:

- Reincarnation is unfair, for one can be punished (via karma[8]) for things one cannot remember having done in previous lives.

- Reincarnation is ineffective. While it is claimed that karma progressively rids humanity of its selfish desires, the truth is that there has not been any improvement in human nature after millennia of reincarnations.

- Reincarnation yields social pacifism, for it urges that one should not interfere with someone else's bad karma (or bad circumstances). Thus, helping the poor and oppressed could yield bad karma for you since the lower classes are receiving what they have earned.

- Reincarnation is ultimately fatalistic, for the law of karma guarantees that one will inexorably reap in the next life what one has sown in the present life. There is no room for forgiveness and grace!

---

8. If one engages in good actions throughout one's life, one will allegedly build up good karma, which means one will be reincarnated in a desirable state in the next life. If, however, one engages in bad actions throughout one's life, one will allegedly build up bad karma, which means one will be reincarnated in a less desirable state in the next life. One might say this is a cosmic law of cause and effect.

- Reincarnation seems inconsistent with the New Age world-view, for if all is one and all is God, how can there be *individual souls* that reincarnate?

- Reincarnation is unbiblical, for every human lives once, dies once, and then faces the judgment (Hebrews 9:27).

Occultism is dangerous. Deuteronomy 18:9–12 warns that all forms of occultism are detestable to God. Exodus 22:18 even instructs that sorceresses were to be put to death — a penalty in Old Testament times that demonstrates how serious the sin of divination was. Leviticus 19:26 commands, "You shall not . . . practice divination or soothsaying." In Acts 19:19 we read that many who converted to Christ in Ephesus rightly destroyed all their paraphernalia formerly used for occultism and divination.

The New Age openness to channeling — consulting psychics in order to contact the dead, or to contact a guardian angel, or to contact "space brothers" aboard UFOs — is an especially heinous sin against God. Deuteronomy 18:10–11 is clear: "There shall not be found among you anyone who . . . [is] a medium, or a spiritist, or one who calls up the dead." Leviticus 19:31 instructs, "Give no regard to mediums and familiar spirits; do not seek after them, to be defiled by them: I am the LORD your God." In 1 Samuel 28:3 we read that "Saul had put the mediums and the spiritists out of the land." Later, we read that "Saul died for his unfaithfulness which he had committed against the Lord, because he did not keep the word of the Lord, and also because he consulted a medium for guidance" (1 Chronicles 10:13; see also Leviticus 20:27).

New Age meditation can be injurious. New Age (Eastern) meditation's stated goal of transforming one's state of mind into a monistic ("all is one"), if not an outright pantheistic ("all is God"), outlook lies in direct contradiction to the biblical view of the eternal distinction between God the Creator and His creatures (Isaiah 44:6–8; Hebrews 2:6–8). Moreover, Christian experts in occultism note that altered states of consciousness (which occurs in New Age meditation) can open one up to spiritual affliction and deception by the powers of darkness. Additionally, some New Agers may use drugs like LSD to enter these altered states, a practice Christians must avoid. Contrary to such Eastern meditation, Christians ought to practice biblical meditation. This involves objective contemplation and deep reflection on God's Word (Joshua 1:8) as well as God's person and faithfulness (Psalm 119, see also 19:14, 48:9, 77:12, 104:34, 143:5).

The New Age method of interpreting the Bible is faulty. The New Age method of seeking hidden, secret, or inner spiritual meanings of Bible verses violates the scriptural injunction to rightly handle the Word of God and not distort its meaning (2 Peter 3:16; 2 Corinthians 4:2). Among New Agers, the basic authority in interpretation ceases to be Scripture, but rather the mind of the interpreter (i.e., man is seen as the supreme authority over God and His Word). They rely on their own inner illumination as opposed to reliance upon the Holy Spirit (see 1 Corinthians 2:9–11; John 16:12–15). More often than not, New Agers superimpose mystical meanings on Bible verses instead of objectively seeking the biblical author's intended meaning.

Contrary to this New Age subjective approach to Scripture, it is better to interpret each verse in the Bible in its proper biblical context. Every word is part of a verse; every verse is part of a paragraph; every paragraph is part of a book; and every book is part of the whole of Scripture. It is wise to pay attention to both the immediate and broader contexts of Scripture. Moreover, one ought to consult history to get a better grasp on the historical milieu in which the biblical book was written. This objective approach will keep one on track in properly interpreting Scripture.

Jesus didn't train in the East as a child. Many New Agers suggest that the man Jesus studied under gurus in India as a child, returning to Israel as a master to perform miracles and spread the teachings He learned. There are many factors that argue against such an idea. First, Scripture explicitly states that Jesus was raised in Nazareth (Luke 4:16). As He grew up, He studied the Old Testament, as did other Jewish boys His age (see Luke 2:52).

Once an adult, those in His community seemed quite familiar with Him as a long-standing carpenter (Mark 6:3) and as a carpenter's son (Matthew 13:55). Had Jesus just returned from India, this likely would not have been the case (see Luke 4:22).

Some in His community were offended that Jesus was drawing such attention. They treated Him with a contempt born of familiarity (see

Matthew 13:54–57). Again, had Jesus just returned from India, this likely would not have been the case.

Consider also the Jewish leaders. They accused Jesus of many offenses throughout His three-year ministry, but never once did they accuse Him of teaching or practicing anything learned in the East. If they *could* have, they *would* have. This would have been excellent grounds for dismissing Jesus as the promised Jewish Messiah. The truth is, though, that Jesus didn't train in the East.

Jesus was the Christ; He didn't become the Christ. Jesus did not become the Christ as an adult, but rather was the one and only Christ (Messiah) from the very beginning. The angel said to the shepherds in the field, "There is born to you this day in the city of David a Savior, who is Christ the Lord" (Luke 2:11). Jesus' beloved disciple John wrote, "Who is a liar but he who denies that Jesus is the Christ? He is antichrist who denies the Father and the Son" (1 John 2:22).

It is noteworthy that the 100-plus prophecies of the coming Messiah in the Old Testament were fulfilled in a single person — Jesus Christ (for example, Isaiah 7:14, 53:3–5; Micah 5:2; Zechariah 12:10). Of course, the New Testament counterpart for "Messiah" is "Christ" (see John 1:41). Jesus was *uniquely* the Christ.

We might also observe that when Jesus was recognized as the Christ, He never said, "You too have the Christ within." Instead He warned that others would come falsely claiming to be the Christ (Matthew 24:5). Today, we see that fulfilled in the writings of teachers like Deepak Chopra, Eckhart Tolle, Edgar Cayce, and others who teach that each person can attain to Christ consciousness as promoted by spiritualists such as Oprah Winfrey and other popular media outlets.

Human beings are not divine. Contrary to the New Age claim that human beings are God, Scripture portrays them as creatures who are responsible to their Creator (Genesis 1–2; Psalm 100:3). Because human beings are creatures, they are intrinsically weak, helpless, and dependent upon God (you may wish to consult 2 Corinthians 3:5 and John 15:5). The recognition of creaturehood should lead human beings to humility and a worshipful attitude (Psalm 95:6–7). They have confused the fact that we are made in the image of the divine God (Genesis 1:26–27, 9:6) with falsely being equated to the divine God.

One cannot avoid asking: if human beings are God, then why do we have to buy and read New Age books to find out about it? Wouldn't we already know it? The fact that a person comes to realize he is God proves that he *is not* God. For if he truly were God, he would never have passed from a state of ignorance to a state of enlightenment as to his divine nature.

Still further, if it were true that human beings were divine, one would expect them to display qualities similar to those known to be true of God. This seems only logical. However, when one compares the attributes of humankind with those of God (as set forth in Scripture), we find more than ample testimony for the truth of Paul's statement in Romans 3:23 that human beings "fall short of the glory of God." Indeed, while God is all-knowing, all-powerful, and everywhere present (Matthew 11:21; Revelation 19:6; Psalm 139:7–12), man is none of these things (Job 38:4; Hebrews 4:15; John 1:50).

Human beings are fallen in sin and need to be saved. Contrary to the New Age claim that human beings are God and merely need enlightenment about this reality, the biblical truth is that human beings have a grave sin problem that is altogether beyond their means to solve. Human beings are sinners (Isaiah 64:6; Luke 15:10), are lost (Luke 19:10), are capable of great wickedness (Jeremiah 17:9; Mark 7:20–23; Luke 11:42–52), and are in need of repentance before a holy God (Mark 1:15; Luke 15:10). Because of sin, human beings are blind (Matthew 15:14, 23:16–26), enslaved in bondage (John 8:34), and live in darkness (John 3:19–21, 8:12, 12:35–46).

Jesus came into the world to offer a salvation based on grace. The word "grace" literally means "unmerited favor." "Unmerited" means this favor cannot be worked for. Grace refers to the undeserved, unearned favor of God. Romans 5:1–11 tells us that God gives His incredible grace to those who actually deserve the opposite — that is, condemnation. Eternal life cannot be earned. It is a free gift of grace that comes through faith in the Savior, Jesus Christ. As Jesus Himself put it, "Most assuredly, I say to you, he who believes in Me has everlasting life" (John 6:47; see also John 3:15, 5:24, 11:25, 12:46, 20:31).

Jesus is the only way. While the Jesus of the New Age is open to all religions, the Jesus of the Bible is God's exclusive means of salvation. Speaking of Jesus, a bold Peter proclaimed: "There is no other name under heaven given among men by which we must be saved" (Acts 4:12). The Apostle

Paul affirmed, "There is one God and one Mediator between God and men, the Man Christ Jesus" (1 Timothy 2:5). Jesus Himself said, "I am the way, the truth, and the life. No one comes to the Father except through Me" (John 14:6). Jesus also warned His followers about those who would try to set forth a different "Christ" (Matthew 24:4–5). Truly, Jesus is the only way of salvation, and only the Jesus who has revealed Himself in the pages of Scripture.

Jesus will come again at the Second Coming. Contrary to New Agers who claim either that the Second Coming has already taken place in the person of Maitreya, or through the cosmic Christ falling upon all humanity, Scripture reveals that the very same Jesus who ascended into heaven will come again at the Second Coming. Acts 1:11 tells us that angels appeared to Christ's disciples after He ascended into heaven and said to them: "Men of Galilee, why do you stand gazing up into heaven? This same Jesus, who was taken up from you into heaven, will so come in like manner as you saw Him go into heaven." This Second Coming will involve a visible, physical, bodily coming of the glorified Jesus, and every eye will see Him (Revelation 1:7). In Titus 2:13 Paul speaks of "looking for the blessed hope and glorious appearing of our great God and Savior Jesus Christ."

Suggestions for Dialoguing with New Agers

Following are some key considerations to keep in mind as you dialogue with your New Age acquaintances.

Befriend the New Ager. Befriending the New Ager means being *friendly* to the New Ager. As 2 Timothy 2:24–25 puts it, "a servant of the Lord must not quarrel but be gentle to all, able to teach, patient, in humility correcting those who are in opposition." The word *gentle* here carries the idea of being kind. When you witness, don't quarrel; instead, be kind.

Don't make false assumptions. Many New Agers use some of the same words Christians do — words like revelation, Jesus Christ, God, resurrection, and ascension. Do not make the false assumption that simply because they use such words, they mean the same thing you mean by these terms. You must be careful to define the terms you use.

Another false assumption to avoid is the idea that all New Agers believe exactly the same things. While they may be united in certain core beliefs, they also hold certain distinct beliefs. In view of this, it is important not to tell a New Ager what he or she likely believes. Ask questions about their views and then let the New Ager verbalize what he or she believes, and then you can accurately address what they've said (Proverbs 18:13).

Try to avoid unhelpful behaviors. For example, try to avoid arrogance and pride. Some Christians tend to carry a "spiritual chip on the shoulder." Acting like a spiritual know-it-all is a real turn-off. It is better to be humble, speaking with grace and truth.

It's also important to be patient. When witnessing, you will likely have to explain the same thing more than once. Expect this. Don't say, "I already told you this," or "Have you listened to anything I've said?" No matter how slow the New Ager may seem in grasping your points, be patient as you tell the truth about Jesus Christ.

Try to find common ground. As you interact with a New Ager, watch for common ground that you can use as a launch pad to dialogue about spiritual matters. (The Apostle Paul used this approach in Acts 17.) For example, if they speak about ecology, you might say that ecology is good, since God created the earth (Genesis 1:1–2) and the earth belongs to God (Deuteronomy 10:14). Or, if you want to talk about Jesus, you might mention how John 1:3 and Colossians 1:16 tell us that Jesus is the Creator of all things. If you watch for opportunities, it is easy to segue to spiritual matters based on something the New Ager said.

Address the inadequacy of mysticism. The truth is, so-called mystical revelations are too uncertain and insufficient as a ground upon which to build our knowledge of God (i.e., they are arbitrary and lead to an arbitrary understanding). Talk to any three mystics, and you will likely receive three different views on the same issue.

The Bible stresses the importance of objective, certain, historical revelation. For example, John 1:18 tells us: "No one has seen God at any time. The only begotten Son, who is in the bosom of the Father, He has declared Him." In the empirical world of ordinary sense perceptions, Jesus was *seen*

and *heard* by human beings on earth as God's ultimate revelation to humankind. This is why Jesus said, "If you had known Me, you would have known My Father also" (John 14:7).

The Apostle Paul also stressed the importance of objective, historical revelation. According to Acts 17:31, Paul warned religious people in Athens of the objective reality of a future judgment based on the objective evidence for Christ's Resurrection from the dead. Based on how people respond to this objective, historical revelation, they will spend eternity in a real heaven or a real hell.

There is another related matter worth noting. Those involved in New Age mysticism seem blind to the possibility of spiritual deception by the powers of darkness. Second Corinthians 11:14 warns that "Satan himself transforms himself into an angel of light." We are also told that Satan has the ability to blind the minds of unbelievers (2 Corinthians 4:4). Through mysticism, a New Ager might think he or she is having a positive spiritual experience, when in reality they are being deceived by the devil, who is the father of lies (John 8:44). Mysticism is a breeding ground for spiritual deception.

Point to pantheism's failure in accounting for the problem of evil. One great way to show the inadequacy of pantheism is to demonstrate its inconsistency with the problem of evil. If all is one and all is God, then God is evil as well as good, hatred as well as love, death as well as life. In such a view, life becomes an absurdity. How can it be said that Hitler's extermination of six millions Jews was a part of God (pantheism)? As hard as they might try, New Age pantheists cannot satisfactorily deal with the problem of evil.

Talk about the appeal of a personal God. An important component of your dialogue with a New Ager ought to be contrasting the personal God of Christianity with the impersonal "It" of the New Age movement. The idea of an impersonal God is utterly unsatisfying because one cannot have a personal relationship with a force. In this context, a good idea is to share your personal testimony, and speak openly about your own personal relationship with God.

Jesus was not a mere enlightened master. New Agers typically revere Jesus as an enlightened human being who came to help other humans attain enlightenment. Christians, by contrast, worship Jesus as the eternal God (John 1:1), who became a human (John 1:14), atoned for our sins at the Cross (2 Corinthians 5:21), rose from the dead (1 Corinthians 15:3–8), and ascended back to heaven (Acts 1:9–11), far above all other beings (Ephesians 4:10).

Let us be clear: Jesus was not a mere enlightened master. Rather He was and continues to be the Light of the world (John 8:12) who "gives light to every man coming into the world" (John 1:9). True "enlightenment" therefore involves believing in and following Him who is the Light of the world (see John 1:4–5). Note that the word "believe" occurs almost 100 times in John's Gospel. Salvation is found in believing in Jesus Christ, the Light of the world. It is He — as the Light of the World — who has delivered us from the kingdom of darkness (Colossians 1:13–14).

Closing Thoughts

At the top of this chapter, we learned that Cindy was exposed to the New Age movement through a human potential seminar sponsored by the company she worked for. The idea that she was a god who could create her own reality did not sit well with her. After all, why does a god have to attend a New Age seminar to discover that he or she is a god? This dilemma ended up motivating her to search for the truth.

Her search for truth led her to the following conclusions: there is such a thing as absolute truth; New Age mysticism can lead to deception; the idea that all is god is nonsensical; there is a personal and unique Creator-God; she herself is not a god but is rather a creature; her problems stem not from being unenlightened but rather from the sin that plagues all humanity; deliverance from this sin comes only in the person of Jesus Christ, the only true Savior.

Long story short — Cindy became a Christian, and now has a ministry that warns others about the New Age movement!

Summary of New Age Beliefs

Doctrine	Teachings of New Age
God	Most hold a pantheistic view of divinity, denying the Creator-God of the Bible. All of nature is connected to the divine or vital force. Divinity is within every person, though it is veiled in most. Jesus is not the Savior, but merely an enlightened master who can give guidance.

Authority/ Revelation	All spiritual views contain elements of truth, so various holy books (Hindu Vedas, Koran, Bible, etc.) are used to find hidden truths through mystical means. Revelation comes from spiritual guides who communicate those truths to humans through meditation, visualization, and channeling.
Man	All of humanity contains the divine spark within but needs to be awakened or the individual enlightened to the divine within. Some believe each person is bound by the deeds of former lives (karma), and their position in society or circumstances are based on those experiences (reincarnation).
Sin	The biblical idea of sin is denied. Most believe in the ideas of positive and negative forces/energies that need to be balanced for life to be connected to the divine.
Salvation	There is no need for salvation, in the biblical sense, since sin does not exist. The ultimate goal is to attain connection with the divine or vital force that connects all of humanity to the divine, vital force, or "Christ consciousness."
Creation	Various creation myths are seen as viable explanations for the creation of the universe. The common core is of the universe emanating from one source to which all in existence is connected.

Chapter 3

Taoism

Dr. Mary Kraus

Legend tells us that one day around 600 B.C. in the western province of Honan, China, an old man named Laozi (also spelled Lao-Tzu or Lao-Tze), meaning "the Old Boy" or "the Grand Old Master," climbed onto a water buffalo and rode toward Tibet. He had been keeping the imperial archives in his province and was so discouraged by the state of his society that he decided to abandon Honan and live as a recluse for the rest of his days. When he arrived at the Hankao Pass, the gatekeeper, knowing of Laozi's unusual wisdom, persuaded him not to leave before recording something that would help his countrymen. So Laozi turned around, went home, and three days later appeared with a slim little book of very short chapters that for 2,500 years has been a major influence on not only Chinese culture, but on all of Asia and is even now influencing many Westerners. Thus began Taoism (pronounced like Daoism[1]), one of the oldest Eastern philosophies, after Hinduism.

History and Authority

The *Daodejing*,[2] or *The Treatise on the Way and Its Power*, is traditionally regarded as the work of Laozi (604–531 B.C.), who was a contemporary of Confucius. Both lived during a time of social deterioration when their

---

1. For this chapter, we will use the spelling Taoism unless it is quoted from another source with an alternate spelling.
2. This book is also known as the *Tao Te Ching*, Lao Tsu, *Tao Te Ching*, trans, Gia`Fu Feng and Jane English (New York: Vintage Books, 1972).

society was fragmented into many warring factions. Both philosophers, worried about their societies, prescribed different but complementary solutions to social disintegration. Both men wanted people to be good, but while Confucius[3] taught that man can *learn* to be good by applying rational rules to his behavior, Laozi believed that following nature's way would make people good, solving man's troubles. One might regard these two as one regards rationalism and romanticism or reason and emotion — not as mutually exclusive, but as complementary, and still very inadequate solutions for man's unhappiness.

Taoism, along with Confucianism, has been a major underlying influence of Asian thought and now has become popular in the West as well. Zen Buddhism, for example, has adopted many Daoist principles. Many Eastern health practices that have been adopted by the West today have their origin in Taoism. The Mayo Clinic, for example, recommends *Tai chi chuan,* a slow kind of exercise that seems to bring many health benefits. Taoist *yoga* techniques are practiced by many Americans who seek better health or less stressful lives. The New Age Movement in America, which is really thousands of years old, has also adopted many Taoist ideas that will be discussed later in this chapter.

But the original text, *Daodejing,* which may actually be a reflection of many authors and editors, is the root of all the various beliefs and practices of *Taoism.* It consists of 81 short proverbial and paradoxical chapters that invite meditation on three different meanings of the Way or Dao:

1. *The Dao (Way) of Ultimate Reality* — the Source of all existence (no personal God)

2. *The Dao (Way) of the Universe* — the norm, rhythm, and driving power in all nature and the ordering principle behind all life

3. *The Dao (Way) of Human Life in Harmony with the Dao of the Universe* — the way people should live

Philosophical Foundations

1. The Way of Ultimate Reality

An excerpt from chapter 1 of the *Daodejing* begins by describing Ultimate Reality in negative terms:

---

3. See chapter 20 in this volume for a full description of Confucianism.

The Dao (Way) that can be told is not the eternal Dao.
The name that can be named is not the eternal name.
The nameless is the beginning of heaven and earth.[4]

These lines exemplify the first meaning, that there is an Ultimate Reality that lies beyond human ability to comprehend rationally or describe in language. This is an "eternal" reality without beginning or end. It is not irrational, but is beyond human reason to grasp. It is supra-rational. This Reality is the Source of all existence, but it is "nameless" because, unlike the biblical God, it is not personal and has not revealed itself to human reason. Nevertheless, human reason sees the self-evident principle that something cannot come from nothing, and so Laozi correctly concluded that the source of everything must be some kind of uncaused first cause. In practical terms today, Taoism is a panentheistic religion, teaching that the Dao is expressed in everything, but there are also polytheistic aspects to the religious practice of Taoism, which we will discuss later.

The radical difference between the *Daodejing*'s account of the Ultimate Reality and the biblical God is very clear. God's Word says, "In the beginning was the Word, and the Word was with God, and the Word was God. . . . All things were made through Him, and without Him nothing was made that was made. . . . And the Word became flesh and dwelt among us" (John 1:1–14).[5] Language, being a rational skill, is not able to describe the *Daodejing*'s Ultimate Reality adequately. But God revealed Himself in His Son and chose language, "The Word," to show Himself as a *person*, not an *it*. "For in Him [the Person of Jesus Christ] dwells all the fullness of the Godhead bodily" (Colossians 2:9).

In contrast to the "nameless" Ultimate Reality, the next line of the *Daodejing*, chapter 1 reads, "The named is the mother of ten thousand things," suggesting that the physical world which can be rationally investigated and experienced, is merely the manifestation of this Ultimate Reality that is its source, so that what people experience with their five senses, the visible world, points to an invisible reality as Romans 1:20 states: "For the invisible things of him from the creation of the world are clearly seen . . ." (KJV). However, in Taoism, there is no "Him," but only an It, the eternal source of everything.

---

4. Online site for *Daodejing*, http://www.taoism.net/ttc/complete.htm.
5. Unless otherwise noted, Scripture in this chapter is from the New King James Version (NKJV) of the Bible.

> The Dao begot one.
> One begot two.
> Two begot three.
> And three begot the ten thousand things.[6]

These lines indicate that the Dao began a kind of evolutionary process. There was no special creation in six days as the account in Genesis 1 describes: "In the beginning, God created the heavens and the earth." According to Taoism, the origin of the universe and everything in it is contrary to the account of special creation in God's Word.

2. The Way of the Universe

A second philosophical meaning of the *Dao* is the way the universe works, or the way of nature. This may be seen in the following lines from chapter 2 of the *Daodejing*:

> Under heaven all can see beauty as beauty only because there
> is ugliness.
> All can know good as good only because there is evil.
> Therefore having and not having arise together.
> Difficult and easy complement each other.
> Long and short contrast each other;
> High and low rest upon each other;
> Voice and sound harmonize each other;
> Front and back follow one another.

These lines accurately describe the dual nature of the universe. Everything is interconnected, interdependent, and closely related. Chapter 42 states, "The ten thousand things carry yin and embrace yang; They achieve harmony by combining these [opposite] forces."[7] *Yin* represents passivity while *yang* represents activity.

The yin yang symbol represents the principle of natural and complementary forces, patterns, and things that depend on one another and do not make sense on their own. These may be masculine and feminine, but they could be darkness and light (which is closer to the original meaning of the dark and light sides of a hill), wet and dry, or action and inaction.

---

6. *Daodejing*, chapter 42.
7. Ibid.

These are opposites that fit together seamlessly and work in perfect harmony. You can see this by looking at the yin yang symbol. Each element is pictured as a small circle within its opposite to show the interconnectedness of all things.

Yin yang symbol

The above lines from chapter 2 of the *Daodejing*, represented by the yin yang symbol, also suggest that to limited human intelligence without any outside or supernatural standard, all things are relative, even moral standards. This idea, called "the relativity of distinctions," was developed by the later Taoist philosopher, Zhuangzi (369–286 B.C.). He correctly explained that everyone is limited in his knowledge by his own limited perspectives, concepts, and experiences. No one can know absolute truth unless he identifies with some unlimited source of truth. Zhuangzi believed that true knowledge and happiness requires that one give up the ordinary way of rational understanding and identify with the infinity of the universe, the Way of Nature, which is the Dao or Ultimate Reality. "Forget the passage of time (life and death) and forget the distinction of right and wrong. Relax in the realm of the infinite and thus abide in the realm of the infinite."[8]

Here Zhuangzi correctly saw that human beings, because of their own limitations, needed something beyond themselves for guidance, "the realm of the infinite." But he had no knowledge of the infinite Creator/God or the catastrophe of the Fall, though he could surely see the evidence of it in his own society. However, the consequent damaging blow to all of nature, including human judgment and natural feelings, was somehow hidden from him, and he believed that man could, with his own power, return to the infinite Way of nature, the Dao or Ultimate Reality, and this return would solve man's trouble. All problems could be rectified by man himself.

But the infinite God tells us in His Word about what happened to nature when man first chose his own way over God's clear direction:

> Then to Adam He said, "Because you have heeded the voice of your wife, and have eaten from the tree of which I commanded you, saying, 'You shall not eat of it': Cursed is the ground for your sake; in toil you shall eat of it all the days of your life. Both thorns and thistles it shall bring forth for you, and you shall eat

8. Quoted in John M. Koller, *Asian Philosophies* (Boston, MA: Pearson Education, 2012), p. 232.

the herb of the field. In the sweat of your face you shall eat bread till you return to the ground, for out of it you were taken; for dust you are, and to dust you shall return" (Genesis 3:17–19).

So disobedience to the Creator's clear command plunged the entire human race into inescapable suffering and death. Laozi and Zhuangzi died. Attempting to identify with the Way of nature cannot cancel out God's wrath and the result of man's disobedience.

Another description of the way of nature is found in chapter 76 of the *Daodejing*:

> A man is born gentle and weak.
> At his death he is hard and stiff.
> Green plants are tender and filled with sap.
> At their death they are withered and dry.
> Therefore the stiff and unbending is the disciple of death.
> The gentle and yielding is the disciple of life.
> Thus an army without flexibility never wins a battle.
> A tree that is unbending is easily broken.
> The hard and strong will fall.
> The soft and weak will overcome.

These lines describe an important fact of the physical world, and conclude with a paradox that suggests something about the third meaning of *Dao* — humans should live gently and humbly.

3. The Way of Human Life When It Is in Harmony with the Dao of the Universe

Chapter 76 enjoins people to imitate nature by being flexible and gentle instead of rigid and forceful in their dealings with others and all of their surroundings. When on May 29, 1953, after many previous attempts, Edmund Hillary and Tenzing Norgay finally reached the summit of Mt. Everest, the tallest peak on earth, "the exploit was widely hailed as 'the conquest of Everest.' D.T. Suzuki, a Japanese remarked: 'We Orientals would have spoken of befriending Everest, rather than conquering it.' " This is very much in line with the Taoist principle of attuning and adapting oneself to nature. Much Taoist art reflects this principle very clearly. Note the prominence of trees, mountains, and mist in the picture following, while

Painting by Mossolainen Nikola (Shutterstock)

the boat and human dwellings blend into the scene so closely that one must look carefully to see them. This picture is seen as a visual lesson of the way people should live.

A Japanese team that scaled the Himalayan Mount Annapurna, the second highest peak in the Himalayas, climbed to within 50 feet of the summit and deliberately stopped. Why? Because "Taoism seeks attunement with nature and not dominance."[9]

This Taoist principle agrees in part with God's Word in regard to man's relationship with the natural world. People are to respect and care for it, rather than polluting and wasting it. After God had created Adam and planted the garden, "Then the LORD God took the man and put him in the garden of Eden to tend and keep it" Genesis 2:15). But rather than seeking to merely blend in with nature, God gave man dominion over nature, to use the earth and all its fullness for his benefit without exploiting its resources. In the *Daodejing* we read:

> Do not be concerned with loss or gain. . . .
> Surrender yourself humbly; then you can be trusted to care for all things.

9. Quoted by Huston Smith, *The World's Religions* (San Francisco, CA: Harper Collins, 1991), p. 212–213.

> Love the world as your own self; then you can truly care for
> all things.[10]

Some of the principles of Taoism are in beautiful agreement with Scripture principles because God created all men according to His master plan, and He intends them to see His invisible attributes, "His eternal power and Godhead" (Romans 1:20) by looking at the natural world. Nature has many lessons to teach those whom God intended to "tend and keep it."

Human Relationships

Humble leadership is one of these principles in which Taoism and Christian Scripture agree. In the *Daodejing*, Laozi asks,

> Why is the sea king of a hundred streams?
> Because it lies below them.
> Therefore it is the king of a hundred streams.
> If the sage would guide the people, he must serve with humility,
> If he would lead them, he must follow behind.
> In this way when the sage rules, the people will not feel oppressed:
> When he stands before them, they will not be harmed.
> The whole world will support him and will not tire of him.
> Because he does not compete,
> He does not meet competition.[11]

In God's Word, Jesus advises, "You know that those who are considered rulers over the Gentiles lord it over them, and their great ones exercise authority over them. Yet it shall not be so among you; but whoever desires to become great among you shall be your servant. And whoever of you desires to be first shall be slave of all" (Mark 10:42–44).

Again, regarding human relations, Laozi says,

> A good soldier is not violent
> A good fighter is not angry.
> A good winner is not vengeful.
> A good employer is humble.
> This is known as the Virtue of not striving.
> This is known as ability to deal with people.

---

10. *Daodejing*, chapter 13.
11. *Daodejing*, chapter 66.

This since ancient times has been known as the ultimate unity with heaven.[12]

In considering human relations and "ultimate unity with heaven," one cannot help noticing the much greater intensity and emphasis of the lawyer's answer to Jesus when asked, " 'What is written in the law? What is your reading of it?' So he answered and said, 'You shall love the LORD your God with all your heart, with all your soul, with all your strength, and with all your mind, and your neighbor as yourself.' And [Jesus] said to him, 'You have answered rightly. Do this and you will live' " (Luke 10:26–28). God, the Creator of the universe, is a person, not an impersonal Ultimate Reality, and so God's greatest command to human beings to love Him is not only reasonable, but wonderfully possible. It is actually man's whole reason for being.

The many similarities in biblical and Taoist thinking may come from a common source of truth transmitted through the ages from the dispersion at Babel or from drawing true principles from what we can observe of God's character in nature. Whichever is true, the Taoist ultimately has no true grounding in special revelation from God, but only in general revelation in nature. Because of this, it is ultimately an arbitrary standard. On what grounds is it best to co-exist with nature rather than exercise dominion and control over it? God's Word gives us a consistent foundation while Taoism is based on the opinions of men.

Vitality Cults

In addition to philosophical Taoism with its three meanings, another kind of Taoism arose and has now become popular in both East and West, the vitality cults. The aim of this kind of Taoism is to increase health and longevity. The feeling of vital energy that Taoists felt within themselves they named *chi* (also spelled *qi*). "The Taoists used it to refer to the power of the Tao . . . coursing through them — or not coursing because it was blocked — and their main object was to further its flow."[13] Today, Taoists use various methods in their attempt to increase this physical/spiritual vital force of chi that comes from the Dao. Many believe that chi can be increased nutritionally as it mixes with the innate chi that is generated in the kidney, and so hundreds of medicinal herbs are on the market. Here are just a few claims

---

12. *Daodejing*, chapter 68.
13. Smith, *The World's Religions*, p. 201.

of medicinal herbs (note that "energy" is used to refer to chi, not merely physical energy):

>**Ginkgo** (*Ginkgo biloba*) helps the brain better utilize oxygen, improves mental alertness, and improves peripheral circulation. Is an antioxidant, and kidney tonic.
>
>**Ginseng** (*Panax ginseng*) benefits exhaustion and helps the body deal with stress, adrenal exhaustion, fatigue, immune weakness, and postoperative recovery. Ginseng is an adaptogen, chi tonic, digestive tonic, immune stimulant, rejuvenative, restorative, stimulant, and tonic.
>
>**Hawthorn leaves, flowers, and berries** (*Crataegus species*) help break down fatty deposits in the blood and gently dilates the capillaries so that heart can function more efficiently. Hawthorn improves peripheral circulation and the body's ability to utilize oxygen.
>
>**Licorice root** (*Glychyrriza glabra*) is naturally sweet, helps normalize blood sugar levels and nourishes exhausted adrenal glands. Licorice is nutritive and rejuvenative.
>
>**Schizandra berries** (*Schisandra chinensis*) improve endurance and are an antioxidant. It improves fatigue and insomnia. Schizandra is considered to be an adaptogen, cerebral tonic, immune stimulant, kidney and liver tonic, rejuvenative and restorative.
>
>**Essential oils** can improve physical and psychological energy levels. Essential oils that benefit fatigue include basil, clary sage, geranium, lavender, lemon, orange, peppermint, and rosemary. Simply open a bottle of the pure essential oil and take no more than ten deep inhalations.[14]

The Internet is replete with various foods to boost chi, and various sources make claims about which forms of chi are promoted by various herbs and which organs benefit, with varying degrees of scientific validity. Obviously, foods have the nutrients that humans need to stay healthy, but chi, whose source is the *Dao,* is not at all the same thing as the life and vitality, both spiritual and physical, that the Creator God provides.

---

14. Various pages on the website of a Taoist herbalist and author, Brigitte Mars, brigittemars. com, accessed November 4, 2015.

Tai Chi Chuan

In addition to attempting to extract chi from food, Taoists engage in various kinds of bodily movements such as *tai chi chuan,* which is a kind of slow exercise that combines calisthenics, dance, meditation, yin/yang philosophy, and martial arts. Tai chi chuan is "designed to draw chi from the cosmos and dislodge blocks to its internal flow."[15] This exercise is practiced by many in the West and recommended by numerous health centers. It involves stretching and slow motion graceful dance movements that have a calming influence and help people's physical balance, particularly older people. It is believed that these movements allow the flow of chi through the meridians, invisible energy channels in the body. These benefits, however, are available with many kinds of exercises without depending on the flow of chi and belief in the Dao as its source. A Christian believer who loves God and wants to be loyal to

A group practicing tai chi chuan movements (Shutterstock)

Him will not go to the Dao or any other supernatural entity for spiritual or physical power *even if these activities are physically beneficial.*

The Creator's purpose for human beings is for them to give Him pleasure and glory. At the same time, God pours blessings on His children. But a believer's aim should not be merely to reap benefits from God, but to give Him love and glory. God's Word teaches that there really are "spiritual hosts of wickedness in the heavenly places" (Ephesians 6:12), and the enemy of souls would like nothing better than to entice God's people away from Him. God is a jealous lover and has repeatedly warned His people against idolatry of all kinds. "I am the Lord your God. . . . You shall have no other gods before Me" (Exodus 20:2–3).

Accupuncture

Another Taoist method of removing blockages to the flow of the body's chi is acupuncture. Taoism developed the view of an entire circulatory system

---

15. Smith, *The World's Religions,* p. 201.

of chi called meridians. Acupuncture meridians are called many names, including Chinese meridians, energy meridians, and chi meridians, to name a few. These meridians are believed to carry the life force that vitalizes all life forms and allows them to flourish and grow. Different cultures call this life force by different names like subtle energy, Spirit, Prana, and vital energy. Additionally, these meridians were developed for animals, and there is a modern resurgence of applying acupuncture to veterinary medicine.

This drawing from an ancient Chinese medical book represents the chi meridians described in ancient Chinese Taoist thinking.
(Shutterstock)

Believed to be similar to electricity, this energy is invisible to the human eye. However, the practitioners claim they can feel and trace these pathways of energy with their hands as they flow like streams through the body.

Western science has neither proven nor disproven the existence of chi meridians, and surely there are mysteries of the human body and mind that man has not discovered; but all that exists comes from the Person of the Creator God, who really is the personal Ultimate Reality. Christians would do well to steer clear of practices that were developed out of a philosophy that denies God as Creator and focuses on mystical healing.

Feng Shui

You may have heard the term on a popular home design show, but feng shui is also an outgrowth of Taoism's yin yang principle. The main idea is to develop environments where humans can interact with the normal flow of chi in the universe to nurture the chi of the individual. This idea comes from the connectedness of everything to the Ultimate Reality. Seeking balance of objects in a space and usage of light are believed to make an environment calming or energizing. There are various schools of thought about the criteria to be used in the design, showing that this concept is really just an arbitrary idea developed by people and reflecting their own opinions and preferences.

In Hong Kong, for example, with its beautiful architecture, buildings have been aligned and spaces created for the free flow of chi. This is again man's effort to exert some control over his life by appealing to what he believes is a natural power without acknowledging the true source of all nature, the Creator God, Yahweh.

Meditation

Meditation is another self-help method of imbibing more of the Dao's vital energy, or chi. "This practice involves shutting out distractions and emptying the mind to the point where the power of the Dao might bypass bodily filters and enter the self directly."[16] Trying to create a mental vacuum is not only dangerous, but is directly contrary to the instruction in God's Word to "be *filled* with the Spirit" (Ephesians 5:18, emphasis added). Taoist yoga is much like the psychosomatic exercise of raja yoga in Hinduism. The practitioner works through his body to reach the inner recesses of his mind, and eventually to lose all self-consciousness. He begins by trying to rid the body of physical cravings, then finds a posture that is neither too comfortable nor uncomfortable. The famous lotus position seems to be conducive to meditation for many. Then he works to control his breathing, "When, for example the yogi [practitioner] is doing a cycle of sixteen counts inhaling, sixty-four holding, and thirty-two exhaling, there is a stretch during which animation is reduced to the point that the mind seems disembodied."[17] This is his goal and allows connection with the Dao.

Divination

Another Daoist practice is using the *I Ching* or *The Book of Changes.* This is a divination manual that is composed of 64 hexagrams. Each one represents a particular tendency to change, and is accompanied with texts that help the user to interpret the hexagram. People use the *I Ching* to foretell the future and also to direct one in making decisions about personal or business relationships and other important matters.[18]

In general, Taoism doesn't make a rigid division between body and spirit, and regards physical activities, such as yoga, meditation, tai chi, and martial arts, as an important way to spiritual growth and a long life. This

16. Ibid., p. 202.
17. Ibid., p. 46.
18. Koller, *Asian Philosophies*, p. 170.

is exactly why believers in Jesus Christ are careful not to commit a kind of spiritual adultery by trusting in something supernatural that does not come from God. His Word repeatedly warns His people about seeking supernatural help from other gods or supernatural powers. "They provoked Him to jealousy with foreign gods; with abomination they provoked Him to anger. They sacrificed to demons, not to God. . . . Of the Rock who begot you, you are unmindful, and have forgotten the God Who fathered you" (Deuteronomy 32:16–18).

In addition to philosophical Taoism with its three meanings of the Dao or Way as Ultimate Reality, as the Way of the universe, and as the Way people should live, Taoism as a communal religion arose around the second century A.D. The Vitality Cults are a part of religious Taoism, but they are also an outgrowth of philosophical Taoism and have been discussed under the third meaning of the Dao, the Way people should live.

Religious Daoism

There is no unified Taoist answer to the question of what happens after this life. However, many Taoists believe that immortality is their main aim. "To attain it [immortality], people have to transform all their chi into the primordial [original] chi and refine it to subtler levels. The finer chi will eventually turn into pure spirit (*shen*), with which practitioners increasingly identify to become transcendent spirit people. The path that leads there involves intensive meditation and trance training as well as more radical forms of diet and other longevity practices. It results in a bypassing of death, so the death of the body has no impact on the continuation of the spirit person. In addition, practitioners attain super-sensory powers and eventually gain residence in otherworldly realms."[19] So immortality is earned by much earnest effort. Some Taoists believe that those who do not work for this goal will live in an eternal condition of suffering. Other Taoists believe that death is a perfectly natural part of the yin yang cycle, so when they die they simply go from the yang being to yin or nonbeing. In general, Taoists place most emphasis on living in tune with the natural way in the present.

This way of earned salvation is quite opposite of the Christian way in which trust in Jesus Christ alone is the single requirement. Jesus said, "I am the way, the truth, and the life. No one comes to the Father except through

19. Livia Kohn, *Health and Long Life the Chinese Way* (Dunedin, FL: Three Pines Press, 2005), p. 7–8.

Me" (John 14:6). All people, the Bible teaches, must live somewhere forever, either in heaven or in hell. But the fact of sin and the need for atonement is nowhere to be found in Taoism. Jesus Christ, the God-Man, is the bridge between sinful man and the righteous God. As the only innocent man, He took the world's sin upon Himself, and gives His divine righteousness in exchange to all those who trust in Him. "He [God] made Him [Jesus] who knew no sin to be sin for us, that we might become the righteousness of God in Him" (2 Corinthians 5:21). Taoists believe that one must work hard "to gain residence in wondrous other-worldly paradises," whereas Christians know that "by grace [unearned favor] you have been saved through faith, and that not of yourselves; it is the gift of God, not of works, lest anyone should boast" (Ephesians 2:8–9).

While the philosophical view of Taoism is panentheistic (teaching that everything is connected to the Dao in essence), Taoism is a polytheistic religion in practice. Unlike Christianity, there is not one single god to worship or honor. Taoist deities are part of the universe, as manifestations of the Dao, and are worshiped or venerated in Taoist temples. Religious adherents often choose one of many gods that is especially useful at a particular time. Taoist deities exist in a great pantheon [all the gods]. Within this pantheon is a structure, with various deities operating under the authority of other deities. The pantheon generally changes over time, and various Taoist sects have differing views of it. But all Taoist sects acknowledge the pantheon's existence. These deities are seen by some as a mixing of pure Taoism with Chinese folk religion and ancestor worship, but there is no formal structure or authority within the religion that would deny that this is an acceptable form of worship.

Some consider the Taoist pantheon as a heavenly bureaucracy that mimics the secular administrations of Imperial China. Since the Imperial administrations and the religious culture of the time were closely intertwined, it is also reasonable to think that the earthly structure was based on the heavenly organization, but there is no clear teaching on which view is true.

One of the sects, the Celestial masters, views Laozi as the chief god, with others organized below him:

> With the Way of the Celestial Masters, Laozi became a prin-
> ciple deity, and he continues to be the personification of Tao for
> many Taoists. He is usually regarded as one of the Three Pure

Ones, along with the Celestial Worthy of Primordial Beginning, the Celestial Worthy of Numinous Treasure. There are also the three Officials, the Emperor of the South Pole and Long Life, the Emperors of the Thirty-two Heavens, the Emperor of Purple Tenuity and the Northern Pole, and many, many more. All of these deities are divine emanations of celestial energy, pure cosmic qi, and have emerged from primordial chaos.[20]

The existence of this huge pantheon of many gods is an expression of man's instinctive need not only for supernatural aid, but also for *personal* supernatural aid. The impersonal "Ultimate Reality" will not do, and so the pantheon of personal deities arose to meet man's deep need. The very term "religion," which comes from the Latin *re ligare* and means literally "to bind again," indicates that people in all cultures recognize the fact that something that was once right has gone tragically wrong. So they have devised innumerable systems by which they attempt to bind themselves back to their origin and recapture their first condition of immortality, innocence, and bliss. There are 19 major religions in the world that are subdivided into a total of 270 large religious groups and countless smaller ones.[21] In fact, anthropologists have yet to discover a people anywhere who do not have some belief in the supernatural.

Taoism is like other religions — it relies on human effort to attempt to achieve immortality. Everyone wants to overcome death and live forever, as if they sense that man was not born to die. And they are right, for the Creator programmed all humans to know this truth. When the personal God first created the universe and placed man and woman in it, physical death was not part of the scene. He made the first humans with immortal souls like Himself, so they were His image-bearers with moral agency and the ability to love their Creator and one another. When they were tempted to go their own way instead of submitting to God, they gave in, and plunged their race into a condition of suffering and death, a condition that Taoism, along with all other religions, has been trying to change from its beginning until now. Death is the ultimate expression of a righteous God's wrath for the rebellion of His creation.

---

20. Julia Hardy, "Taoism: Ultimate Reality and Divine Beings," Patheos.com, accessed November 5, 2015, http://www.patheos.com/Library/Taoism/Beliefs/Ultimate-Reality-and-Divine-Beings.

21. http://www.religioustolerance.org/worldrel.htm, accessed November 5, 2015.

But this holy God is not only just and perfectly right, He is infinitely merciful and loving too. So He devised a way to bind man back to Himself. This would happen not by man's most heroic efforts at all, but by God's own action of saving His creatures who are unable to save themselves. The Triune God "so loved the world that He gave His only begotten Son, that whoever believes in Him should not perish but have everlasting life" (John 3:16). His Son is Jesus Christ, both God and man, who satisfied a holy God's justice by accepting death in place of all other sinful people, so that those who choose to trust Him may be with Him forever in heaven.

The Ultimate Reality of Daoism which cannot be named or known, the "unknown god," is actually the person "who made the world and everything in it. . . . He is not far from each one of us for in Him we live and move and have our being" (Acts 17:24–28).

Summary of Taoist Beliefs

Doctrine	Teachings of Taoism
God	Denies that God is a personal being, but refers to a nameless and impersonal Ultimate Reality or Source that has no beginning or end. There is a belief comparable to panentheism in philosophical Taoism, while many religious Taoists worship many gods (polytheism).
Authority/ Revelation	The writings of Laozi in the *Daodejing* are considered the founding principles of Taoism. Other important writings include the *Zhuangzi*, *I Ching*, and collections by various writers of the years. There is no direct revelation from the Ultimate Reality, but it is drawn from self-evident truths in nature and described by men.
Man	Man is a reflection of the universe and should seek harmony with the universe through pursuing the balance of yin yang.
Sin	The biblical concept of sin is denied, while the Taoist seeks to find balance of yin and yang.
Salvation	Since sin is denied, there is no need for personal salvation from judgment. The ultimate goal is to achieve unity with the Dao by purifying the spirit (shen).

| Creation | The universe is a continually existing force, chi, that is constantly recreating itself through physical emanations of yin and yang. The Dao is eternal, having no beginning or end. There is no clear teaching on when the earth came into existence. |

Chapter 4

Hinduism (with Hare Krishna)

Dr. Joseph Paturi with Roger Patterson

Hinduism (also known as Brahmanism in older writings and as a stage in the development of Hinduism) has ancient roots. It is unquestionably the oldest living major religious tradition not connected to the Bible. However, Hinduism has no known historical founder and has no firm date of its origin. The term *Hinduism* is derived from the word *Sindhu*. *Sindhu* is a Sanskrit word for the great Indus River in northwestern India.[1]

In Sanskrit, *sindhu* simply means a large mass of water. It was first applied to the people living on the Indus River who Alexander the Great, an early invader, called *Indu*, from which the words Hindu and India were derived. Further, the Muslims coming from Arab lands through the northwest side of India used the term *Hindu* to refer to the people who lived east of the Indus River. Hindus, whose history can be traced back for at least four thousand years, came to be known as Hindus on a wide scale only in the 18th century when the British and other Europeans who colonized India began to call them Hindus.

The actual term *Hindu* first occurs as a Persian geographical term for the people who lived beyond the Indus River. The term Hindu originated as

---

1. The reader should be aware that words translated from Sanskrit into English have various spellings in different resources. Some words may have an "aa" rather than a single "a" in their spelling (praana vs. prana), and include extra letters like "h" (astanga vs. ashtanga) that would be pronounced in certain dialects.

a geographical term and did not refer to a religion. Later, Hindu was taken by European languages from the Arabic term *al-Hind*, which referred to the people who lived across the Indus River. This Arabic term was itself taken from the Persian term *Hindū*, which refers to all Indians. By the 13th century, Hindustan emerged as a popular alternative name for India, meaning the "land of Hindus." The term *Hinduism* was introduced into the English language in the 19th century to denote the religious, philosophical, and cultural traditions native to India.

The term *Hinduism,* which was originally a geographic descriptor, presently stands for a singular religious identity of the Hindu tradition that incorporates multiple cultures and a variety of belief systems practiced by the Hindu people.

A Brief Biblical History of the Indian People

The region of India, beginning with the Indus valley, was populated early after the events at the Tower of Babel in Genesis 11. As peoples left Babel, some migrated by land to the subcontinent of India — others likely came by boat.

Some of Noah's descendants who can be traced to India include many of the sons of Joktan through the lineage of Shem. The sons of Joktan were Almodad, Sheleph, Hazarmaveth, Jerah, Hadoram, Uzal, Diklah, Obal, Abimael, Sheba, Ophir, Havilah, and Jobab. They originally settled in the Arabian Peninsula and then, as Arab records afford, 11 of these 13 sons' family groups continued to migrate over to India.[2]

The Coptic name for India is *Sofir* (think *Ophir* with an "*s*") — Ophir (named for one of Joktan's sons) was famous for its gold![3] A Jewish historian from about 2,000 years ago writes:

> Solomon gave this command: That they should go along with his own stewards to the land that was of old called Ophir, but now the *Aurea Chersonesus*, which belongs to India, to fetch him gold.[4]

---

2. Dr. John Gill, *John Gill's Exposition of the Entire Bible*, notes on Genesis 10:26, http://www.biblestudytools.com/commentaries/gills-exposition-of-the-bible/.
3. M.G. Easton, *Easton's Bible Dictionary*, s.v., "Ophir," http://eastonsbibledictionary.org/2796-Ophir.php.
4. Flavius Josephus, *Antiquities of the Jews*, translated by William Whiston, http://lexundria.com/j_aj/8.150-8.175/wst.

India is the source of the famed port of the famous gold of Ophir mentioned in the Bible (1 Kings 9:28, 10:11, 22:48; Job 22:24, 28:16; Isaiah 13:12). Considering that each of these sons (and others who settled here) brought an entire language family with them to India, it would make India a "melting pot" of languages. For those who know India, it is, even to this day!

Demographics

Hinduism has about 900 million adherents worldwide (15% of the world's population), which is just above atheism at 13%.[5] Along with Christianity (31.5%) and Islam (23.2%), Hinduism is one of the three major religions of the world by percentage of population. It is the third largest religion in the world, behind Christianity and Islam. The following are estimated adherents of these religions worldwide.

- Christianity: 2.1 billion
- Islam: 1.3 billion
- Hinduism: 900 million

A great majority of Hindus live on the Indian subcontinent, and India remains the heartland of Hinduism. However, there has been a global diaspora of south Asians that made Hinduism spread to over 150 countries today. About 2.25 million Hindus make North America their home, mostly immigrants.[6]

Defining Hinduism

It is difficult to define Hinduism in a comprehensive manner that would encompass all the facets of its practice. According to Klostermaier, "Hinduism is a state of mind rather an assembly of facts or chronological sequence of events."[7] Because of its relatively tolerant nature and ancient history, Hinduism has assimilated a variety of polytheistic beliefs, traditions, and practices.

Hinduism ranges from monotheism to polytheism, from monism to materialism and atheism to pantheism; from

---

5. Global Index of Religiosity and Atheism, Gallup International, 2012, http://www.wingia.com/web/files/news/14/file/14.pdf.
6. John L. Esposito, Darrell J. Fasching; Todd Lewis, *World Religions Today* (Oxford, UK: Oxford University Press, 2014).
7. Klaus K Klostermaier, *Hinduism: A Short History* (Oxford, UK: Oneworld, 2000), p. 4.

non-violence to moral system that see blood sacrifices to sustain the world; from supernatural other worldliness which both apotheosizes and marginalizes humans; defend social causes at any cost from critical, and scholastic philosophical discussion to the cultivation of sublime, mystical, and wordless inner experience.[8]

The most common term used by Hindus is *Sanatana Dharma*, meaning ancient or eternal religion, which is a descriptive word for Hinduism. As Christians, we would not believe that this is the eternal religion, holding the Creator God of the Bible, who is the Alpha and Omega (beginning and the end), as the ultimate authority on such matters. Based on God's Word, the Christian views Hinduism as a corruption due to sin since the events at the Tower of Babel as the arbitrary ideas of man are elevated to supersede God's Word, taking people down the wrong path.

Our hope is to bring the truth to those who have bought into Hinduism, giving them good news of great joy through Jesus Christ, the Creator God who has come to save them from sin.

General Beliefs

- Hindus believe in the divinity of their holy books, the *Vedas*, which are among the world's most ancient "scripture," and venerate the *Agamas* as equally revealed. These primordial hymns are assumed to be God's word and the bedrock of Sanatana Dharma, the eternal religion, which has neither beginning nor end.[9]

- Hindus believe in one all-pervasive Supreme Being (Brahman) who is both immanent and transcendent, both Creator and Unmanifest Reality.

- Hindus believe in the cyclical nature of time and that the universe undergoes endless cycles of creation, preservation, and dissolution.

8. Esposito, *World Religions Today.*
9. Being that the Hindu Brahman is impersonal, it is unclear how these *personal* books that utilize many *personal* things like human language are from the impersonal god, Brahman. If one argues, as some have, that Brahman is both personal and impersonal, then there is an internal inconsistency that makes his character illogical.

- Hindus believe in *karma*, the law of cause and effect by which each person creates his own destiny by his thoughts, words, and deeds.

- Hindus believe that the soul reincarnates, evolving through many births until all *karmas* have been resolved and *moksha*, spiritual knowledge and liberation from the cycle of rebirth, is attained. Not a single soul will be eternally deprived of this destiny.[10]

- Hindus believe that divine beings (*devas*) exist in unseen worlds and that temple worship, rituals, sacraments, and personal prayers create a communion with these *devas* and gods.

- Hindus believe that a spiritually awakened master, or *satguru*, is essential to know the Transcendent Absolute, as are personal discipline, good conduct, purification, pilgrimage, self-inquiry, and meditation.

- Many Hindus believe that all life is sacred, to be loved and revered, and therefore practice nonviolence and noninjury (*ahimsa*) to show universal compassion.

- Hindus believe that all revealed religions are essentially correct, and no particular religion teaches the only way to salvation above all others, but that all genuine religious paths are facets of God's Pure Love and Light, deserving tolerance and understanding.

These general beliefs are applicable to any Hindu person. However, Hindu beliefs and practices can deviate significantly. But let us pause for a moment and reflect. How can a Hindu know any of this for sure? In other words, how does the Hindu know these nine beliefs are *the truth*? Were they truly revealed from the Ultimate Reality?

How can an impersonal being reveal things in a personal fashion? It would be illogical. The obvious answer is that these beliefs are arbitrary. But what about the ancient wisdom books like the Vedas, Upanishads, Bhagavad Gita, etc.? Are these not like the revelation from God that Christians have?

---

10. If all people will eventually attain moksha, the practice of Hinduism is pointless.

Family performing an act of worship at a family shrine (Shutterstock)

Actually, no. The Bible is the revealed Word of God from a personal God to mankind created in the image of a personal God, which is what makes personal communication between the two possible. At best, these Hindu books like the Vedas are merely the suggested ideas of man about reality, being purely arbitrary compared to the Word of God (the Bible).

General Obligations

- Worship (*upasana*): Hindus are taught daily worship in the family shrine room from childhood — rituals, disciplines, chants, yogas, and religious study. They learn to be secure through devotion in home and temple, wearing traditional dress, bringing forth love of the Divine, and preparing the mind for serene meditation.

- Holy Days (*utsava*): Hindus are taught from childhood to participate in Hindu festivals and holy days in the home and temple. They learn to be happy through sweet communion with God at such auspicious celebrations. *Utsava* includes fasting and attending the temple on Monday or Friday and on other holy days.

- Virtuous Living (*dharma*): Hindus are taught from childhood to live a life of duty and good conduct. They learn to be selfless by thinking of others first; being respectful of parents, elders, and swamis; following divine law, especially ahimsa, which is mental, emotional, and physical noninjury to all beings. By doing so, they can resolve all karmas.

- Pilgrimage (*tirthayatra*): Hindus are taught from childhood the value of pilgrimage and are taken at least once a year for gazing at (*darsana*) holy persons or beings, temples, and places, near or far. They learn to be detached by setting aside worldly affairs and making god, gods, and gurus life's singular focus during these journeys.

- Rites of Passage (*samskara*): Hindus are taught from childhood to observe the many sacraments that mark and sanctify their passages through life. They learn to be traditional by celebrating the rites of birth, naming, head-shaving, first feeding, ear-piercing, first learning, coming of age, marriage, and death.

These general practices are applicable to any Hindu, though the expressions will vary to some degree.

Foundational Concepts

- Worldview: The worldview of a Hindu is based on the concept of karma, reincarnation, and caste. In fact, religion permeates every phase of existence.

- Ontology: The concept of three worlds is popular. It includes the world of the living, of the dead, and of the spirits (supernatural). There is no separation between sacred and secular. Hindus believe in the unity of all creation.

- Time: The concept of time is cyclical in nature. Everything is repeated age after age like seasons.

- Cosmology: The cosmological concept includes that nature is filled with spiritual beings and life forces that are all part of the universal force of Brahman (Gita, 4:35).

- Mankind: Man is brought into existence as *atman*, a spiritual emanation from Brahman. The atman is the essence of the individual, yet is part of the Divine. The self must experience the law of karma and come to realize that it is divine. In this sense, each person is divine and must recognize that the atman and Brahman are one.

- Maya: Reality as we know it is actually a form of illusion because we draw distinctions when there are no distinctions since all is one.

Major Divinities

Hinduism accommodates multifaceted concepts of god. The fundamental theological belief for a Hindu is in Brahman, the Impersonal Spirit, the Changeless and the Universal Force that comprises everything that exists. The Brahman is perceived in two different ways (with and without attributes). The Brahman, who is without attributes (*nirguna*), cannot be known by man. This naturally begs us to ask the question how it is possible for man to know that Brahman, the Impersonal Spirit, even exists!

The Brahman with attributes (*saguna*) demonstrates traits such as truth (*sat*), consciousness (*cit*), and blissfulness (*anand*), and can be known by man. The Brahman with these qualities is also known as *Isvara*, who is the creator of the world. Brahman, veiled with mysterious cosmic creative power known as *maya*, caused the material creation to come into existence. The whole of creation, which actually includes multiple universes, emanates from Brahman as the web that a spider weaves, and returns back into Brahman. Brahman exists in everything and everything exists in Brahman, making Hinduism a pantheistic worldview. Brahman alone is the Ultimate Reality. Maya and its created world is a created illusion and not eternal. Brahman creates this illusion for the purpose of joy or sport (*lila*).

In the functional aspect, Hindus believe in a triad of emanations made up of Brahma the creator, Vishnu the preserver, and Shiva the destroyer. So God is accepted as a person with personal attributes (saguna Brahman) such as being the creator, preserver, and destroyer of the universe. The three personal aspects of the Brahman can be referred to as a Hindu triad (*Trimurti*): Brahma the creator, Vishnu the preserver, and Shiva (Mahesha) the destroyer. In depictions of the triad, Brahma is shown as a multi-headed figure with Vishnu and Shiva.

There are many different incarnations (*avataras*) of Vishnu. *Avatara* is a Sanskrit word that refers to a divine incarnation that literally means "one who descends." Every Hindu believes in ten incarnations of the god Vishnu, of which nine avataras are already manifested and one more avatara is yet to come. The term *avatara* refers to a male or female person having divine powers. The term means an incarnation or appearance of a super-natural being or an illusion of that being. According to the *Bhagavad Gita*, whenever there is a decline of virtue and religious practice, Vishnu himself descends on earth to destroy evil and to uphold or re-establish righteousness. The most popular incarnations are *Rama* and *Krishna*. The final incarnation, *Kalki*, is yet to come into the world. All the avataras can be included in the second line of divinities.

Hindu Trimurti: gold statues of Brahma, Vishnu, and Shiva
(Shutterstock)

The ten avataras of Vishnu assume a prominent place in the Epics (the Hindu mythologies) and more so in the Puranas (a series of texts that describe specific gods).

The first three have a cosmic character and are foreshadowed in the hymns of the Vedas: *Matsya* (fish), *Kurma* (tortoise), and *Varaha* (boar).

The fourth incarnation belongs to a later age when the worship of Vishnu had become established: *Narsimha* (man-lion).

The fifth incarnation, *Vamana* (dwarf), whose three strides deprived the *asuras* of the domination of heaven and earth, follows the fourth avatara, and the three strides are attributed to Vishnu in the Vedic text as *Urukrama*.

The next three incarnations, *Parasurama, Ramchandra,* and *Krishna*, are mortal heroes whose exploits are celebrated in poems so fervently as to raise the heroes to the rank of gods.

The ninth avatara is the deification of any great teacher, known as *Buddha*. This is not a specific name, but a title. Most know this as the title taken by Siddhartha Gautama who achieved enlightenment and was known as Gautama Buddha. He is now a revered figure in Buddhism and various forms of Hinduism. According to the theory of the avataras, the Buddha himself was adopted as an avatara. In this way, Hinduism as the Vedic religion was able to enfold Buddhism under its large umbrella. Jainism also became, in essence, a doctrinal modification and adaptation of the Vedic religion.[11]

The final avatara is *Kalki*, who is yet to come and whose arrival will signal the end of the present age before the universe is annihilated and reborn. The idea resembles the manifestation of Jesus referred to in the Book of Revelation in the Bible. Jesus rides a white horse with a flaming sword (see Revelation 19:11–12) at the end of the world to usher in the new heavens and earth. It is possible that this is merely a corruption of early Christian teachings that have made their way into Hinduism since the Apostle Thomas and others (e.g., Luke 24:46–47; Acts 2:5; Romans 16:26) first brought the gospel into India nearly 2,000 years ago. What we supposedly know about Kalki is written primarily in the Puranas, which were written after the New Testament.

Popular Divinities

Many people have heard that there are millions of Hindu gods who are worshiped in various ways. This is due to the fact that there are so many popular deities and gurus who are worshiped and that individuals, families, and clans can create a deity to help with specific aspects of their lives.

Every Hindu family is supposed to have a family god or a personal deity to whom they show strong allegiance and worship by observing correct rituals, prayers, and festivals. The deities can be worshiped in public temples or shrines installed in homes. Certain sacred persons, living or dead, can be accepted as divine due to the miracles attributed to them before or after death. Popular Hindu deities include children of the major deities such as *Ganapati* (the elephant-headed god also known as *Ganesha*), who is a son of Shiva and Parvati. Ganapati is considered the god of knowledge and the obstacle remover. *Hanuman* or *Maruti* (the monkey-headed god), an associate of Rama, is believed to give health and strength.

Without the concept of female divinity, Hinduism would not be complete. A person, family, or a clan often worships female deities with great

---

11. See chapter 5 in this volume for a description of Jainism.

Hindu God Ganesha
(Shutterstock)

Illuminated statue of Hanuman
showing Rama and Sita in heart
(Shutterstock)

allegiance. Most female deities are mothers or consorts of major deities believed to have power (*shakti*) to protect a faithful devotee from evil powers. *Kali Mata* (Black Mother) of Calcutta is the most well-known female deity in India and is believed to have power to destroy evil and to protect and bless. She is believed to have seven sisters who are worshiped in different parts of India with different names such as *Durga Mata* or *Bhavani*.

Fertility cults are popular in rural India, and Shiva and *Parvati*, his consort, are associated with the male and female generative powers (similar to Priapus, the Roman god of generative power, who is worshiped in priapic or phallic symbolism). In addition to the above, there are 330 million gods traditionally accepted in Hinduism.

Spirits

Ancestral spirits are historical persons who are cultural, mythical, or religious heroes whom individuals may have experienced in dreams, visions, and miracles for benevolent results. These also include saints, gurus, and family heads. Recently deceased persons are remembered and honored through family rituals and family events. These are generally believed to be able to benefit the family.

A man killed in an accident or an unexpected mysterious death of a youth is often believed to exist as a bad spirit. Similarly, female malevolent spirits are created from unexpected deaths. However, ancestors can be both good and bad spirits and are ritually appeased by family members.

Demons and ghosts are believed to be living in abandoned houses, cemetery objects, trees, mountains, rivers, or strange places. Protection from these forces is sought from family gods, diviners, gurus, rituals, and magic.

Nature worship includes totem spirits of sacred trees, animals, birds, and imagined creatures. The cow is often considered the most sacred animal in the Hindu mythology. The Western expression "holy cow" comes from this bovine veneration. Since there is no meaningful distinction made between creator and the creation (or natural and supernatural), the whole cosmos is a sacred entity generally deserving reverence and worship.

The Living

Gurus (spiritual teachers or masters) have an important place in the Hindu tradition. A family or a person may have a guru according to their experience, sect, or background. A guru is also like a medium, a medicine man, an arbitrator, and a diviner who is believed to have power over human desires with supernatural abilities.

Saints or monks who live an ascetic life reside in the mountains, temples, or monasteries. Some are itinerant saints who travel from place to place and live on alms. This group of leaders generally stays away from social activities.

Magicians, though not very popular, are believed to have the ability to handle witchcraft, demons, and diseases in rural expressions of Hinduism.

Bhagats (self-taught priests) and priests born in a priestly family are the conductors of rituals, sacraments, and socio-religious events in temples or at homes. Magicians and Bhagats are very much a part of social life and participate in all community activities.

Concept of Karma

Karma simply means good or bad deeds considered as one of the paths to earn salvation. Whatever man receives or loses in life (including caste, spouse, children, family, and material things) and after life is believed to be the result of karma. It broadly describes the universal law of cause and effect. It is on a principle: "as you sow, so shall you reap." This means that what a man is now, is the result of what he has done in his past lives, and what he is doing now will determine what he shall be in the future life.

One of the arbitrary aspects of karma relates to determining what is good and what is bad. Since the individual experiences the world in an illusory form (maya), there is no ultimate standard of what is right or wrong. Additionally, there must be some form of accounting for good and bad deeds by a supreme being, but Brahman is supposed to be an impersonal force. This leaves the Hindu in a place of seeking to be judged by an impersonal force to determine his or her fate in a future incarnation — a logical inconsistency.

Scriptures

The Hindu scriptures can be categorized into two sections. The first category is *shruti* ("what is heard") and the second is *smruti* ("what is remembered"). *Veda* means "knowledge." The Vedas were oral traditions eventually written in ancient Sanskrit language and viewed as the most authoritative sacred texts. They are believed to have been developed from 1200 B.C. on.

The Vedas are considered shruti (heard) and have four parts: *Rig Veda, Sam Veda, Yajur Veda*, and *Atharva Veda*. All other scriptures are considered smruti (remembered).

The *Upanishadas* (dated from 600 B.C.), also called *Vedanta* ("final knowledge"), are philosophical discussions. These are written by gurus, and each of the vedas includes a section of Upanishadas at the end.

The most well-known epics are *Ramayana* and *Mahabharata* (fourth century B.C. to second century B.C.). The *Bhagavad-Gita* (200 B.C.) is a section from *Mahabharata* that has the story of *Krishna* and is considered the most popular book for Hindus to study and follow.

Many Christians reading this may immediately assume that the Hindu scriptures are like the Christian Scripture (the Bible). However, these are not in the same category. The Bible was inspired by God, who created man in His own image. God used chosen men to write His Word by the power of the Holy Spirit.

So when reading the Bible, we are reading what God has revealed to man. Thus, the Bible comes with the authority of God. The Hindu scriptures are not like this. They are merely the ancient writings of ancestors. Some are poems, prayers, and hymns; some contain history that reflects practices and beliefs; some have brilliant literary pieces, but not *inspired* or *inerrant* words by their god, Brahman.

So what is the source of authority of these Hindu scriptures? They are not authoritative like the Bible, but merely arbitrary writings of man (brimming with contradictions, no less). The Hindu may protest, "But this is the wisdom of the ancients," to which we might respond, "By what standard?" There is no greater standard than the true God.

The opinions of ancient people about various gods, Brahman, reality, and nature have no weight in an argument when compared to the Word of the personal Creator God in the Bible, who is the absolute authority on all issues. This is actually good news! The many peoples of India and elsewhere who have bought into Hinduism through the opinions of ancient peoples can be set free by the truth that only comes from the true Creator God.

Temples and Worship

India is famous for old Hindu temple architecture and its elaborate worship rituals. Temples, unlike churches or mosques, are not really meeting places but are the places of gods. The temple is built according to a sacred diagram that is described in the ancient sacred books. Much of a temple building is selected according to a divine sign and not according to human will.

A temple may be dedicated to a deity, and an icon of the presiding deity is placed in the sanctum. However, it is not surprising to see icons (many times formless objects) of many other gods and goddesses placed in different parts of a temple. Generally, a priest who presides over rituals may sit in the sanctum area. Icons in Hinduism are believed to have life or power of the divine. Devotees visit the temple for darsana (sacred gazing), to offer food or other items to the god, or to view and feel a sense of holiness.

A personal prayer or ritual in a temple may include facing a deity with folded hands; ringing a temple bell; offering water, fruits (especially coconut), food, or flowers; burning incense sticks; applying ash or red powder on the forehead; and circumambulation (*pradakshina*; walking around a shrine or temple). Congregational prayers could include group singing, dance, rituals, food in the temple hall, and preaching by learned gurus or monks during sacred days.

Pilgrimage in Hinduism is not mandatory, but the benefits are elaborately outlined in the Hindu texts: benefits such as healing, good karma, and personal purification. Kashi, also known as Banaras or Varanasi, is the most important center of pilgrimage for Hindus. It is believed that every religious act done in Kashi is multiplied good karma, impacting several lifetimes compared to the same act done elsewhere.

The largest human gathering on earth, called the *Kumbha Mela* ("pot festival"), happens every 12 years at Prayag ("the place of sacrifice") near modern Allahabad at the confluence of the Ganges, Yamuna, and the invisible Saraswati rivers. It also occurs at three other sites on a rotating basis. It is believed that immortal nectar (*amrita*) drips from a pot carried by Vishnu at each of these locations. About 30 million Hindu pilgrims gather to bathe ritually during Kumbha Mela time. This act of bathing in the river is believed to wash away the person's sins. There is also a procession of saints and blessings by various gurus and saints offered to the pilgrims. Here we can see a shadow of what the Bible teaches about baptism, but twisted in a way that denies the need for Christ's sacrifice to wash away sins.

Social Practices

While life for a Hindu is certainly colored by the particular culture they live in, there are certain aspects of Hindu life that cross borders of states and nations. Just as various Christian sects have different worship practices formed by their culture and the Bible, so Hindus vary in their personal expressions of worship.

Social Life

According to the scriptures, four divisions or castes (*varna*) regulate Hindu social life. Both Krishna (in the *Bhagavad Gita*) and a supernatural person's sacrifice in a creation myth in *Rig Veda* are considered the origin of the caste system.[12] A *Brahmin* caste has priestly duties, and *Kshatriya* is the warrior caste. *Vaysha* is the business caste, and *Shudra* is the lowest or servant caste. Those in the low castes are to serve the high caste and have been treated in the past as "untouchables." The detailed duties of the castes are mentioned in a controversial Hindu book called the *Laws of Manu*.[13] For centuries, the low caste community lived outside the Hindu socio-cultural circles. However, people are not allowed to observe the caste divisions in India today according to the constitution.

---

12. *Rig Veda*, tr. Wendy Doniger (New York: Penguin Classics, 1981).

13. James Fieser and John Powers, *Scriptures of the World's Religions* (New York: McGraw Hill, 2004).

Religious Life

Hindus believe in rebirth or innumerable births according to one's deeds. Every person is subject to the law of karma (cosmic law), and everything happens according to the law of karma. Salvation (moksha) is to liberate oneself.

While Hindus believe in a supreme force, most have individual or family gods and depend on them for daily needs. Observing strict rituals and customs related to deity is the mark of allegiance. Generally, a family consecrates a separate place for a deity that serves as a shrine in the house. An image of the presiding deity is placed in the center with multiple images of deities surrounding the centerpiece. The shrine orientation depends on the god of the household or family. Ritual or prayer times are common during daytime, sacred days, and special family or personal events.

Many perform daily *puja* (worship), especially the elderly. With folded hands, one stands or sits in front of a small family shrine. The shrine may contain the main family deity along with other preferred images, generally made of clay, wood, brass, copper, silver, or gold. The most popular deities in the central part of India are *Krishna, Rama, Ganapati, Durga,* and *Maruti.*

Other aspects of worship are the various *yogas* ("yoking") or *margas* ("paths") that an individual may perform. Various schools of thought will dictate an individual's practices, including acts of service, devotion, meditation, and seeking wisdom.

Festivals

Festivals are religious, cultural, and social events. Most are based on mythological stories of gods and goddesses such as *Ramanavami* that celebrates the birthday of the god Rama. The birth of the god Krishna is celebrated during *Gokulasthami,* and *Ganeshchuthrthi* celebrates the birth of the popular deity Ganesha.

The most popular Hindu festival is *Diwali* or the Festival of Lights. It is one of the most colorful and is a week-long community event. Families light earthen lamps throughout their homes, keeping them burning day and night. They put on new clothes and visit their extended families sharing sweets and gifts. Families pray to family deities at home or in temples and especially worship *Lakshmi,* the goddess of wealth, in hope of a prosperous year to come.

Family Life

Families usually live together under the authority of the family elders such as parents or grandparents. Marriages are typically arranged, though some of the cultural practices are changing in urban sections of India. Daily life is immersed with prayers, fasts, offerings, and rituals. Every Hindu — especially a person from the high caste group — needs to go through more than 70 *sanskaras* (sacraments).

Individual devotional elements and meditation are common in the Hindu community. A person who spends time in prayer, meditation, singing, and scripture chanting may be called the devotee of a deity. Devotional practices may include acts such as regular fasts, festivals, and observance of dietary laws and pilgrimages. Committed Hindus may practice meditation at home or in temples. These devotional and meditational aspects are perhaps the unique contribution made by India to the world religions, especially Buddhism and New Age.

Salvation as Liberation

Hindus believe in the concept of reincarnation (*punarjanma*), the idea that the soul is reborn in another body after death, and the quality of the future existence or next birth depends on one's current life lived or doing good deeds (karma).

When a Hindu dies, there is only one place he can go to, that is, back into Brahman. But since man and Brahman are so vastly separated, one must work his way up to Brahman through a *Samsara* (cycle of death and rebirth).

Striving to liberate (*moksha/mukti*) oneself from the Samsara cycle of death and rebirth called *karmabhadhan* (bound by the principle of karma) is the aim of a Hindu person. According to *Bhagavad Gita*, various paths to liberate oneself are: *karma marga* — the path of selfless action; *bhakti marga* — the path of devotion (personal worship); *astanga/raja marga* — the path of physical discipline and meditation; and *jnana marga* — the path of wisdom. As mentioned above, these paths to enlightenment are also called yogas. As a group, these can be seen as the religious salvific practices of Hindus, the ultimate goal being to escape all of the connection to the material world, achieving enlightenment and being united to Brahman, the universal reality.

Bahkti marga, total devotion to a god or avatara, is a popular path in India and depends on studying the religious texts and gurus. Many would agree that it is impossible to do only good deeds or live a perfect life, and thus assurance of liberation is impossible due to bad karma. *Jnana marg* (the path of wisdom) releases a person from the bondage of ignorance (*ajnana*) through inner enlightenment and finally unites the soul with Brahman forever. Various physical exercises, cleansings, and meditation allow one to realize the divinity of the soul revealed in the wisdom of the gurus by overcoming the distinctions produced through maya. Once the inner self realizes its divinity, laying aside all connections to the material world, the soul can escape the samsaras and be united with Brahman. As such, there is no notion of a heaven in Hinduism, but a form of annihilation of the soul as a distinct entity.

The Hindu caste system makes salvation harder for some. According to the *Laws of Manu,* a low caste person should attain high caste birth by serving the high caste community, and then the person may get the high caste birth and finally may get liberated if they are eventually able to live a good life and reach enlightenment.

Hare Krishna

Hinduism finds many different expressions and sects, but the development of specific systems is seen in Jainism, aspects of Buddhism, and Hare Krishna. You may know Hare Krishna practitioners as the saffron-robed men peddling flowers at an airport, but their religious views are Hindu at root. Officially known as the International Society of Krishna Consciousness (ISKCON), this group was formed in 1965 in America by a Hindu guru out of a devotion to Krishna, an avatar as the supreme god. This makes them a monotheistic expression of Hinduism (though they still hold pantheistic views). Hare Krishna followers see the stories of the warrior Arjuna's encounters with Vishnu in the Bhagavad Gita as the key texts to follow. Using Bhakti yoga practices of selfless devotion, meditation, physical postures, and song and dance, they believe they can achieve salvation through Krishna-consciousness, realizing their own divinity.

Krishna followers may lead normal lives as part of a society or be dedicated to living an ascetic lifestyle in a temple where they would abstain from various foods, alcohol, gambling, and illicit sexual activity. Vegetarianism is esteemed as the sanctified form of eating, and meat, fish, and eggs are avoided as to treat animals with reverence. The popularity of Hare Krishna increased when Beatles member George Harrison adopted the religion.

The main distinction of Hare Krishna comes from the mantra they believe to voice the supreme names of Krishna, Hare, and Rama. This chanting is believed to promote purification and connection with the true self, promoting peace and well-being. Using a string of 108 beads (*japa*; similar to a rosary), the chant is repeated 16 times each day for a total of 1,728 recitations. It is done in quiet meditation, aloud, or in groups with dancing. The chant states: Hare Krishna, Hare Krishna, Krishna Krishna, Hare Hare, Hare Rama, Hare Rama, Rama Rama, Hare Hare.

> The prayer or mantra that ISKCON devotees repeat is called the Maha Mantra, or the "great mantra for deliverance." It is made up of three words Hare, Krishna and Rama. Hare refers to God's energy. Krishna and Rama refer to God as the all-attractive and all-powerful one who is the source of all pleasure. Repetition of this mantra awakens the soul and brings strength, peace and happiness. It ultimately connects us with Lord Krishna and reveals our original spiritual life of eternal bliss and knowledge.[14]

In this we see the same goal of salvation through good deeds and realizing the divinity that lies within. While we can commend the Krishna followers for their care for creation and their desire to promote peace among all people, they are ultimately pursuing salvation through vain means — denying Jesus as the Savior and only source of salvation for fallen men.

Influence on the West

Hinduism's influence on the West can be seen in two major areas. The first is in the prominence of transcendental meditation. This practice was introduced to the West during the period of British imperialism. It gained traction among those who were looking for alternatives to traditional Western religious understanding of human consciousness. The modern view was popularized by Maharishi Mahesh Yogi in the mid-20th century. Meditation is prominent in Eastern religions, but the broad acceptance of this practice in various forms spread to the West as it was popularized by his disciples, especially the Beatles, Beach Boys, and many prominent entertainers.

14. http://www.iskcon.org/meditation/.

During the 1960s and '70s, many traveled to India to study under various gurus, yogis, and swamis, bringing those ideas back to the West, influencing cultural practices and beliefs. The New Age movement adopted many of these practices, seeking to empty the mind and connect with the inner divinity that was connected to the cosmos.[15]

Eastern meditation practices stand in stark contrast to biblical meditation. Biblical meditation focuses the mind on truths revealed by God with the goal of being conformed to His character. It is focusing on a truth that is outside of the self and revealed by a personal God. Eastern meditation attempts to clear the mind, using breathing techniques, repeated mantras or sounds, and looking within the self to recognize the inner divinity that is connected to Brahman.

The second major influence has been through what most Westerners would call yoga. Yoga means "to yoke" and is understood to be one of the paths to connect to the divine reality. The typical practice of yoga in the West involves various forms of Hatha or Ashtanga yoga — the physical exercises and meditative practices intended to be forms of Hindu worship and enlightenment. While there are many different schools of yoga, the postures and practices can be traced back thousands of years and are included in the Vedas and other writings.

Beginning in the mid 1800s, as Hindu philosophy was being introduced to the West, the practices of yoga were brought by Swami Vivekananda. He toured Europe and the United States, teaching yoga philosophy. Many other swamis and gurus have promoted their own versions since then. Rather than merely the postures and meditation, yoga encompasses an entire philosophy tied to the pantheistic view of Hinduism. Believing that each person is part of the Divine, having a divine spark within them, the popular schools of Hatha and Astanga yoga employ an eight-fold path to liberating the soul — the enlightenment of moksha that is the equivalent of salvation in Hinduism. These aspects of yoga include everything from purification, to controlling the body's vital force and senses, to meditation and absorption with the Divine force.

The various poses used in yoga, called *asanas*, are postures that are intended to bring relaxation. Many are based on various Hindu gods and aspects of nature, imitating them in a pose of worship. To strike the poses

---

15. See chapter 2 in this volume for a full description of New Age beliefs.

and meditate on them is to acknowledge the individual's connection with all of the cosmos and to remove thinking that makes distinctions. One common yoga progression is the sun salutation, a series intended to connect the inner self to the sun in an act of worship and meditation on how the sun expresses divinity. Additionally, these poses are intended to be practiced in concert with the other aspects. The breathing focus is intended to influence the vital force (*praana*) that flows through the body in channels called *nadi*. The use of focusing on objects, breath control, chanting mantras or sounds, and emptying the mind are all part of the practice. The postures facilitate this balancing of inner energy as well as moving inner focus through the various *chakras* in the body where the inner self can achieve enlightenment. This focus on the chakras progresses from the base of the spine up to the mind where the self recognizes its divinity. Many people report ecstatic experiences and spiritual connections during yoga.

Some refer to this as opening the third eye, by which the self is able to see past the illusions of the cosmos and approach moksha. The Tantric and Shaktic schools connect this flow of the force through the ascending chakras as the snake goddess, Kundalini, is awakened within and brings enlightenment. The Christian cannot miss the echoes of the promise of the serpent in the garden, promising Eve she could become like God. Several of these schools use various sexual expressions to achieve enlightenment, again showing a perversion of God's good gift and provision for new life through children.

The popularization of yoga practice in illustrated books and the philosophies that accompany it accelerated in the 1970s and continues today.

One modern proponent of yoga as a path to self-healing and self-realization writes:

> First and foremost, yoga is a systematic process of spiritual unfoldment. Yoga is a 5,000-year-old system of self-knowledge and God-realization, the aim of which is to unleash our full human potential — including our physical, ethical, emotional, mental, intellectual, and spiritual dimensions.
>
> The eight limbs are
> 1. Yama — Rules of Social Conduct
> 2. Niyama — Rules of Personal Behaviour
> 3. Aasana — Physical Postures
> 4. Praanaayaama — Control of Vital Force

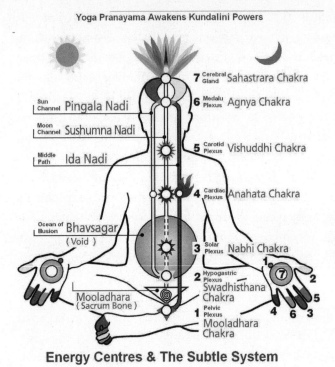

Yoga Pranayama Awakens Kundalini Powers

7 Cerebral Gland Sahastrara Chakra

6 Medalu Plexus Agnya Chakra

Sun Channel Pingala Nadi

Moon Channel Sushumna Nadi

Middle Path Ida Nadi

5 Carotid Plexus Vishuddhi Chakra

4 Cardiac Plexus Anahata Chakra

Ocean of Illusion Bhavsagar (Void)

3 Solar Plexus Nabhi Chakra

2 Hypogastric Plexus Swadhisthana Chakra

Mooladhara (Sacrum Bone)

1 Pelvic Plexus Mooladhara Chakra

Modern books, websites, and classes offer teaching on the utilizations of the eight aspects of yoga to achieve health benefits, supernatural powers, and salvation. (http://www.kentonbell.guru/what-is-kundalini/)

Energy Centres & The Subtle System

5. Pratyaahaara — Control of the Senses

6. Dhaarana — Right Attention or Concentration

7. Dhyaana — Meditation

8. Samaadhi — Absorption

The first five limbs (from Yama to Pratyaahaara) make up the outer aspect of Yoga and the last three (Dhaarana, Dhyaana, Samaadhi) are called Samyama or Integration. Yama and Niyama refer to the right attitudes, values, and lifestyle practices necessary for Yoga, its ethical foundation. Aasana, Praanaayaama, and Pratyaahaara are the means to control the outer aspects of our nature as body, breath, and senses. Attention or concentration naturally leads to Meditation, which in time results in Absorption or the Unification of the Perceiver, the Perceived and the process of Perception. We get the knowledge of our true Self.[16]

---

16. Sangeetha Rajah, "Ashtanga Yoga," accessed March 28, 2016, http://www.hindupedia.com/en/Ashtaanga_Yoga..

Both meditation and yoga practices have been embraced by the popular culture, integrated into government school systems, and used by individuals and corporations to promote inner peace and general well-being. While often cloaked in scientific and health-related terminology, these are both part of the Hindu paths to salvation and should not be practiced by Christians, despite their promotion by some churches. Doing so opens one to the influences of false teachings and even demonic activity and influence. Rather than looking inside the self (a self with a nature that is irreparably corrupted by sin) through yoga practices to find union with the Divine, looking to Jesus Christ in repentance and faith is the only way God has made available to be united with Him for eternity.

Hindu Attitudes

While it is difficult to describe the attitudes of such a large and diverse group of people, the Hindu religious beliefs color the thoughts and actions of the followers, just as any worldview does.

Theological

All paths lead to the same goal (Gita).[17] Hinduism is viewed as sufficient enough for salvation, and all people are free to take a suitable path, investing differently toward the afterlife.[18] Hindus generally claim that no one religion has the monopoly on the truth.[19]

Socio-political

Conversion to another religion is considered similar to denying one's own mother, and denial of one's religious heritage is denial of a great treasure. Conversion is a great form of violence against Hinduism. (This would seem to contradict the idea that "all are free to take a suitable path.")

Those who turn away from Hinduism can expect being disowned by the convert's family, friends, and society. Ridicule, persecution, and even death can be expected, especially by those who turn to Christianity. Though Hindus claim to be nonviolent, religious fervor often expresses itself in

---

17. Once again, this would render Hinduism as pointless.
18. By what standard? Impersonal Brahman has not revealed this, so it is arbitrary. But for the sake of argument, even if this statement were true, then it makes Hinduism meaningless.
19. In saying this, the Hindu is making an absolute religious truth statement to which he is imposing what he believes as an absolute truth, assuming his religion is the absolute truth; thus it is self-refuting.

violence against those who leave Hinduism or seek to convert others from Hinduism.

Doctrinal Differences between Hinduism and Christianity

Concept	Hindu Belief	Christian Belief
Brahman	Nirguna Brahman is impersonal, unknowable, relationless, and without personal attributes.	God is triune, personal, knowable, holy, loving, and man can enter into a personal relationship with Him.
Isvara	Saguna Brahman is personal, knowable, with attributes, though he never revealed himself in a written form.	God has revealed Himself as a personal being with personal attributes: the Father speaking to man as recorded through prophets; the Son coming in flesh, dwelling among us, and revealing words recorded in the Bible; the Holy Spirit inspiring the writings of the prophets and dwelling in believers.
Avatar	There are ten incarnations of Vishnu in various human and animal forms. The final incarnation will destroy the wicked and annihilate the universe.	There has been one incarnation of God, Jesus the Son, taking on flesh to bring redemption to the wicked and restore the universe to perfection.
Trimurti	Triad: Brahma as creator; Vishnu as preserver; Shiva as destroyer.	Trinity: Father, Son, and Holy Spirit — three persons but one God.
Maya	Maya veils Brahman from mankind, giving the illusion of distinction in the cosmos that is actually all united.	God creates a real, perfect world that is corrupted through man's sin.

History of the Creation	Cyclic: Everything is repeated in cycles of life and death, from individual lives to different universes.	Linear: Time moves forward from the point of creation, through corruption, and forward to a final consummation and restoration.
Atman	Man's spirit emanated from Brahman and is eternal.	God created man in His own image with an eternal spirit.
Ajnana	"Sin" is defined as ignorance and making false distinctions, but there is no revelation that describes this concept.	Sin is disobedience or unfaithfulness to God's revealed law.
Karma	An impersonal reckoning of "good" and "bad" deeds determines one's future state of reincarnation; dependent on one's own works; no possibility of forgiveness.	After death, individuals are judged based on their obedience to God's law; forgiveness is available through Christ's substitutionary atonement.
Samsara	Cyclical: Birth, death, and rebirth dictated by karma and the individual's deeds.	Linear: Born with a sin nature and born again by God's grace through faith in Christ's atonement apart from individual deeds.
Moksha	Release from samsara through enlightenment, recognizing self as deity, and eventually being absorbed into Brahman.	Redemption from sin as a gift of God through repentance and faith in Christ's atonement.

Arbitrariness and Inconsistency

The Hindu doctrine of maya presents a powerful point of discussion. The Ultimate Reality is supposed to be hidden behind the illusion of the physical reality while all is really united and emanates from Brahman. But do Hindus really live in a way that is consistent with the teaching of maya?

If they are honest with themselves, they do not. A Hindu can only live in the real world by acknowledging the distinctions between light and dark, love and hate, waking and sleeping. If the Hindu were truly consistent with the belief system, he would not be bothered if you took the money from his wallet — there is no difference between rich and poor, after all.

If clothes are not real but illusion, then why wear them? If there is no distinction and *all is one*, then why is there a caste system? If there is no distinction in Hinduism, then why should a Hindu follow Hinduism rather than follow Christ? If the Hindu were to respond and say, "But that is a different religion," then ask, "Why do you draw the distinction if all is one?"

If, as Hinduism teaches, our problem is that we continue to draw distinctions when we shouldn't, then we are all already in a state of moksha! To say otherwise is to draw distinction between the current state and the future potential state.

Notice the violations of logic inherent within the Hindu worldview. Some might argue that that is the point of Hinduism — to move *beyond* logic to the "transcendent" — so logic is not helpful when dealing with Hinduism. What can the defender of Hinduism say? Would they use a logical appeal to say that it was illogical to contradict their claim that logic isn't applicable? If so, they have used logic to argue that logic isn't useful in the Hindu worldview — this creates a self-refuting argument.

The point of this is to show that, when honestly and carefully considered, Hinduism is internally inconsistent. It is illogical. We've shown it to be arbitrary, being built on the opinions and writings of men rather than direct revelation from God. So having both internal inconsistency and arbitrariness logically reduces Hinduism to a false belief. Our hope though is to point Hindus to the truth of Jesus Christ.

Doctrinal Bridges to Reach Hindus

Common concepts shared between Christianity and Hinduism are the ideas of God, incarnation, sin, salvation, good deeds, and life beyond this present state. Hindus normally conclude by saying that Hinduism has the same basic teaching as Christianity or that things sound very similar. This should not close the doors but form bridges for sharing the gospel. We can reach out to the Hindu by asking them to carefully compare the differences between the doctrines — especially the person and work of Jesus Christ.

1. Brahman: As we have seen, Brahman, the ultimate reality, is the one behind many gods of Hinduism. This supreme Brahman is in the nature of spirit and remains unchanged. Likewise, in Christianity, God is One. He is Spirit and never changes.

2. Isvara: Isvara, the creator is similar to the Christian concept of Creator God. We can point to the Bible and explain how all three members of the Trinity were involved in creation (Genesis 1; Colossians 1; John 1).

3. Avatara: Since the Hindu accepts avatars, there is no problem accepting the fact of God taking on flesh in the person of Jesus Christ. In fact, some Hindus already accept Jesus as an avatar of Krishna or a yogi. It is always helpful to stay focused on the life and teaching of Christ when presenting the gospel to Hindus.

4. Trimurti: The triad of Hinduism paves the path to explain the Christian doctrine of the Trinity.

5. Cyclical History: In Hinduism, history is cyclical. Everything is presented age after age. History in Christianity is linear. The present world order is to be destroyed and a new one created which will continue forever. It is difficult for a Hindu to grasp the Christian affirmation that God is a God of history and entered into history as Jesus Christ. The centrality of historical facts of the Incarnation, the Cross, and the Resurrection of the Lord Jesus must be emphasized.

6. Atman: Both Hindus and Christians believe that the Atman (spirit) is eternal and comes under the bondage of sin. The Lord Jesus came to deliver people from the bondage of sin.

7. Karma: This doctrine of karma is similar to the biblical concept of "as you sow, so shall you reap." This can serve as a bridge to point Hindus to God's judgment of our sins. The Hindu has to be told how the Lord Jesus took upon Himself the

sins of the world on the Cross of Calvary as a substitute. The law of karma is the immutable law that a person pays for the evil he has done. There is no concept of forgiveness of sins for a Hindu. The Cross shows that God is not only a God of law (judging sin), but also a God of love. In the Cross of Christ, justice and love met and together granted forgiveness of sins. No amount of good works gives assurance of salvation. God alone has the power to save a person by grace through faith in Christ Jesus who paid the price for sins (Ephesians 2:8–9).

8. Samsara: The Hindu seeks to be free from the cycles of samsara. This keeps recurring until one finds liberation from samsara. The grace of the Lord Jesus Christ can deliver one from the clutches that bind one to the false wheel of samsara.

9. Moksha: Salvation is release from the wheel of karma-samsara. The Hindu longs for release from the cycle of births and deaths and from karma itself. When he is liberated, he wants to be united with Brahman. The Lord Jesus presents in Scripture how He can break the power of sin and satisfy the longing of those who search for liberation. Rather than being united to Brahman, we can be united to Christ and receive all of the benefits of being true children of God in this life and in eternity (Galatians 2:10–21).

As a gospel messenger, look for open doors and connecting bridges, prayerfully presenting the hope in Christ in a relevant and loving manner (Colossians 4:2–6). At the right time, communicate the difference between the two faiths and allow the Holy Spirit to work, trusting in the power of the gospel.

Practical Points for Communicating the Gospel to Hindus

Witness

Be the salt and the light that will help to earn the trust of Hindu friends and neighbors. As a follower of Christ, it is a lifelong commitment through word and action before, during, and after sharing Christ. Pray for specific families and rely on the Holy Spirit at every stage. Let your life and conduct reflect the change that Christ has worked in your life. As you speak, do so with grace and truth, not avoiding hard truths, but speaking in a winsome way.

Friendship

Hindu friends and neighbors are open to hear the gospel when facing critical situations such as sickness, failure, or death of loved ones. Most of the time they are open for prayer for healing because of fear, which can be a good opening to share Christ. Friendship allows them to see how Christians deal with trials and difficult situations.

Hospitality

Invite friends and neighbors for family events such as birthdays, anniversaries, or even Christian festivities like an Easter dinner. Try to avoid culturally offensive practices, foods, or expressions accordingly to make them feel at home. Some may be vegetarians or avoid certain foods. Don't be afraid to ask what things you should avoid serving in order to eliminate unnecessary offenses. This will show respect and keep the door open for future communication of the gospel.

Remove Hindrances

Most common objections against Christians in India are that church-going people discard Indian practices or become Westernized. This refers to dietary habits, dress, music, and language. Such hindering practices could be easily addressed by the believers for the sake of the gospel. In the West, Hindus may be more open to adopting various customs.

Christ Likeness

Christians can be sensitive to neighbors' lifestyles in order to keep the door open for the communication of the gospel. Some committed believers have sacrificed consumption of certain foods for the Kingdom cause. Most of all, neighbors will listen to the message through a Christ-like life lived by the believers and the message that accompanies it.

Conclusion

Jesus Christ is the true answer to the fervent prayer of Hindus as expressed in the Vedas:

> From untruth, lead me to the truth;
> From darkness, lead me to light;
> From death, lead me to immortality.

Finally, Jesus Christ is the fulfillment of the noble aspirations of Hinduism. He says to the Hindus (John 14:6):

> I am the Way — The Karma Marg
> I am the Truth — The Jnana Marg
> I am the Life — The Bhakti Marg

God loves the whole world, including Hindus, irrespective of any national, language, or cultural background: "For God so loved the world that He gave His only begotten Son, that whoever believes in Him should not perish but have everlasting life" (John 3:16; NKJV). Innumerable Hindus have come to the saving knowledge of Jesus Christ over the centuries; their lives were beautifully transformed by the power of the gospel and were used by God as mighty witnesses for Him in India and around the world. Even today the same continues to happen. Glory to God as the gospel message brings sinners to repentance and faith in Jesus Christ — even Hindus!

Summary of Hindu Beliefs

Doctrine	Teachings of Hinduism
God	Deny the existence of the biblical God. See Brahman as the supreme expression of the divine impersonal force that is in all of creation. There are many expressions of lesser gods known as avatars. The trimurti represents a triad of Brahma, Vishnu, and Shiva. Millions of popular and personal gods are worshiped for various protections and benefits. Some may view Jesus as a guru, but not as God.
Author-ity/Reve-lation	The Bible is rejected. The *Vedas*, *Upanishadas* (*Vedanta*), and the epics, *Ramayana* and *Mahabharata*, are seen as scrip-tures. The *Bhagavad-Gita* is often studied as a key text.
Man	All men are part of Brahman, individually as atman, which is bound to the laws of karma and samsara. The atman expe-riences the physical reality as false distinctions, maya, which must be overcome to realize that the atman is divine. Each person is divine, though flawed. The atman is reincarnated in various forms based on the law of karma and dharma. Bad karma results in reincarnation as lesser life forms or in a lower social caste.

Sin	Sin is vaguely identified as bad deeds. The law of karma relates good and bad deeds done during an individual's lifetime. There is no ultimate standard, though lists appear in the various scriptures as dharma.
Salvation	Escaping the cycles of samsara is the goal, achieving moksha as a state of oneness with Brahman. Moksha is achieved through yoga practices and creating good karma by doing good deeds and living a virtuous life.
Creation	There are many universes, each bound in a cycle, that emanate from Brahman. All of creation is an expression of Brahman (pantheism). There are many variations of creation myths in Hinduism, some of which would embrace evolutionary ideas as part of the process of the universal cycles.

Chapter 5

Jainism

Dr. Daniel Anderson

> There lived a family in a farm house. They were enjoying the fresh, cool breeze coming through the open doors and windows. The weather suddenly changed, and a terrible dust storm set in. Realizing it was a bad storm, they got up to close the doors and windows. By the time they could close all the doors and windows, much dust had entered the house. After closing all of the doors and windows, they started cleaning away the dust that had come into the house.[1]

This brief illustration has been used as an analogy to capture the essence of life as a follower of the religious system known as Jainism. What is the meaning of the recounting of this rather ordinary event? How does this analogy portray a spiritual concept or a religious system? To fully grasp how this "farmhouse" illustration summarizes spiritual ambition, it is necessary to explore the history, doctrine, and practices of Jainism.

Historical Background

Jainism (jī·nih·zəm), traditionally known as Jain Dharma, is a religious system originating in India during the sixth century B.C. as a reformation

---

1. Jainism Global Resource Center, "Introduction," accessed February 2, 2016, www.Jainworld.com/philosophy/fundamentals.asp.

movement within Hinduism.[2] The adherents of Jainism follow the religious teachings of Vardhamana Mahavira who, according to Jain tradition, was the last of a succession of 24 Tirthankaras (saints). In addition to liberating their own souls, these Tirthankaras spent their lives teaching others the path to *moksha* (salvation).

Mahavira was also known as the "Jina" (Victor), from which the term "Jainism" comes. The concept of victory describes the conquest of one's self over inner enemies such as pride or anger, as well as the conquering of any worldly passions through the practice of a rigid asceticism and a life of extreme self-denial. Motivating this life of denial is the hope that the cycle of rebirth can be broken by overcoming the consequences of the rule of karma.

Essential to the practice of Jainism is the emphasis upon observing a life of nonviolence (*ahimsa*) to purge the soul (*jiva*) of karma. This exercise of ahimsa is fanatically observed in the avoidance of killing any living creature to the point of refraining from activities such as wearing silk, picking flowers, swatting at bugs, or eating honey, as it is the food of bees. Thus, the followers of Jainism are characterized as being one of the strictest vegetarian communities of any religious sect. Observing these strict guidelines is seen as essential to achieving the spiritual enlightenment that leads to moksha.

The Founder of Jainism

Vardhamana Mahavira (ca. 599–527 B.C.) was born in Bihar, India.[3] According to tradition, he lived in the same general area as the Buddha during approximately the same time period. Some will even note comparisons between the two religions and the two persons.[4]

Mahavira was particularly revered because of his life of denial and self-imposed hardship. According to Jain tradition, Mahavira grew up in a life of comfort and ease, abandoning it all at the age of 30 to wander throughout India for 12 years in silence and nakedness, enduring deprivation and abuse. His dedication attracted a following of disciples.

---

2. See chapter 4 in this volume for a full description of Hinduism.
3. Western scholars differ from the traditional Jaina dates, suggesting Mahavira lived from 480 to 408 B.C. See Charles Taliaferro and Elsa J. Marty, eds. *A Dictionary of Philosophy of Religion* (New York: The Continuum International Publishing Group, 2010), p. 126.
4. Our earliest accounts of either person (Buddha and Mahavira) were written hundreds of years after they lived. Some have proposed that variations of these two developed in the oral accounts. Others argue that Buddha and Mahavira go back to the same person because they have many recorded similarities. Though interesting, it is still unlikely due to the recorded differences.

Claiming to have achieved the state of infinite knowledge (*kevala*), Mahavira began to promote his beliefs through an organized brotherhood of monks who took oaths of celibacy. Completely opposed to the idea of a supreme being, he even denied any gods existed to be worshiped. However, his disciples exalted him as a deity, with later Jain writings describing him as descending from heaven, free from sin and from all earthly desires. They present him as an ideal model for all to follow.

The Basic Structure and Tenets of Jainism

The followers of Jainism are part of a four-fold congregation of adherents composed of monks, nuns, laymen, and laywomen. The basic tenets of the corporate body are identified as the three jewels (*triratna*):

- right faith (*samyagdarshana*)
- right knowledge (*samyagjnana*)
- right conduct (*samyakcharitra*)

Observing these jewels is believed to lead one to a liberation from the bondage of karma. Both monastic and lay followers take solemn vows to comply with these basic beliefs. Jains believe that observing the strictest of ethical behavior restructures one's karma, expelling dark materiality (*pap*) and nurturing light (*punya*), thus advancing one's progress toward the release from the cycle of rebirth.

While the founder of Jainism was noted for his life of solitude, monks and nuns today typically live in a collected setting (*gana*) where they may benefit from the counsel and instruction of those deemed to be superiors among the brotherhood. A formal system of ordination is carried out for those joining the gana, which requires the departure from one's home, the abandonment of all property, and the shaving of one's head. The initiate then receives the "equipment" of a monk, which includes an alms bowl, a broom, a napkin, and loincloths.

Central to the practice of all Jains, whether lay or monastic, is the taking of vows. The Mahavratas (five great vows) of monastic Jains mandate abstaining from:

1. the killing of any living things, frequently referenced as non-violence (*ahimsa*)
2. false speech (*satya*)

3. taking what is not given (*asteya*)
4. sexual pleasure (*brahmacarya*)
5. worldly attachments (*aparigraha*)

The 12 Anuvrata (lesser vows) of a layperson are similar to the Great Vows but are less demanding and allow for a family life while still observing strict vegetarianism, diligent honesty, fidelity in marriage, and regular donations to religious persons and organizations. Additionally, both sets of vows forbid the taking of food or drink at night to minimize the risk of injury to insects, which might go unnoticed in the darkness.

Jain literature defines explicit guidelines for a monk's religious conduct on a daily basis involving such activities as begging, confession, and study. Compliance with the five great vows govern all of these activities. Beyond these five great vows, monks and nuns must comply with five rules of conduct known as *samiti*. Intended to increase awareness of the soul, both personally and in others, these five rules of conduct are:

- care in walking
- care in speaking
- care in accepting things from others
- care in picking up and putting down objects
- care in the performance of excretory functions[5]

In the first century A.D. a major division developed within Jainism leading to the formation of two distinct sects: the Digambaras and the Svetambaras. The primary issue was controversy over the practice of nudity as an evidence of ultimate deprivation and self-denial. Mahavira, the founder of Jainism, had practiced nakedness as a mark of rigid asceticism; loyal followers of Mahavira believed that they should do the same, determining that their nudity was in no way an act of moral impropriety. These Jains formed the Digambaras sect and were known as the "sky-clad" or "space-clothed."

The Svetambaras sect believed they should wear white robes and became known as the "white-clad." Because the basic tenets of Jainism had been well established by the time of this division, the Digambaras and Svetambaras adherents fundamentally agree in their primary beliefs.

---

5. John Cort, "Singing the Glory of Asceticism: Devotion to Asceticism in Jainism," *Journal of the American Academy of Religion,* vol. 70, no. 4 (December 2002): 83.

Ornate Jain temples exist around the world, including this one in Ranakpur, India.
(By Nagarjun Kandukuru, https://commons.wikimedia.org/w/index.php?curid=33434794)

The Growth and Spread of Jainism

Spread in India

Jainism originated in the northern state of Bihar, India. The ascetic life of Mahavira limited the extent of its influence during the early years of its existence. However, after Mahavira's time, the Jain community spread along the caravan routes from Bihar to the west and to the south where the teachings of Jainism were accepted by various princes and rulers. The Digambaras sect became particularly influential in the Deccan region with numerous variations of the sect being founded. The Svetambaras sect was especially successful in the Gujarat region with several of the kings of that area converting to Jainism. Adherents erected ornate worship centers such as that on Mount Abu, now in Rajasthan, during this period as well. Opposition resulting from Muslim invasions eventually led to the decline of Jainism in these locations.

Colette Caillat has noted that "although the Jain community never regained its former splendor, it did not disappear entirely; nowadays, the Digambaras are firmly established in Maharashtra and Karnataka and the

Svetambaras in Panjab, Rajasthan, and Gujarat. Jain businessmen are generally active in all the main cities of India, and many also outside India."[6] Currently, the Jains of India could be described as a small but influential and comparatively prosperous community engaged largely in commerce and finance. Many of India's prominent business leaders, financial leaders, and some political leaders are Jainists.[7]

Spread beyond India

Jainism has significantly spread outside India within the last 150 years. Prominent locations of Jains include the United Kingdom, the diamond business of Belgium, Singapore, Japan, Hong Kong, Kenya, Canada, and throughout the United States. In North America alone there are over 20 Jain Temples and 70 Jain Centers.[8]

Jainism first came to the United States in 1893 when Virchand Raghavji Gandhi delivered an address in Chicago at the World's Parliament of Religions (now identified as the Parliament of the World's Religions). In 1933, Champat Rai Jain gave a speech entitled "Ahimsa as the Key to World Peace" at the World Fellowship of Faiths. During the years following these initial occasions there was a small immigration of Jains. Turmoil in Kenya, Tanzania, and Uganda in the 1960s led to a significant increase in Jains fleeing those countries and eventually coming to the United States. They would often share worship areas with Hindus during these years. The Jain Center of New York was started in 1966, and the first designated Jain temple was opened in Boston in 1973. Additional temples and centers have been constructed in such prominent U.S. cities as Washington, DC, and Chicago. Every two years a major convention of Jainists sponsored by the Federation of Jain Associations in North America (JAINA) convenes. At the present time, JAINA estimates there are over 100,000 Jains living in North America.

Jainism has attracted significant attention in the United States in two ways related to their strong emphasis upon nonviolence (*ahimsa*). Because one of the prominent forms of charity practiced by Jainists is the provision of care facilities for diseased and disabled animals, such as the Jain Bird

---

6. Colette Caillat, "Jainism," *The Encyclopedia of Religion* (New York: Macmillan Publishing Co., 1987), p. 508.
7. *Columbia Electronic Encyclopedia*, s.v. "Jainism," 6th edition (2015): 1, accessed November 7, 2015.
8. According to JAINA: Federation of Jain Associations in North America in their JAINA/ Jain Vision 2020. www.jaina.org.

Hospital in Delhi, animal rights groups have become increasingly interested in and supportive of Jainism.

The second evidence of attraction is the inclusion of Jain ethics in thousands of yoga studios.[9] Yoga teachers are incorporating the ethics of Patanjali's Yoga Sutra, which is related to the five vows of Jainism. In fact, this blend of yoga and Jainism has even begun to include environmental concerns as illustrated by the following "Green Affirmations of the Yamas" adopted and promoted by prominent yoga instructor Clayton Burns Horton (shown here in a reduced form).[10]

- I observe the results of my actions so that I may discontinue my tendencies that are hurtful to myself, other human beings and all of creation.

- By eating a plant based diet, I am minimizing global warming and world hunger.

- As I recognize divinity in all of creation, I recognize the sacredness of fragile ecosystems, all beings and myself.

- I give thanks for the food I eat, the water that I drink and for the blessings that I receive from the material world.

- Acknowledging that I consume and receive so much from our Mother Earth, I try to give back something, however I can.

- I look inwards, study yogic texts and commune with nature so that someday the nature of reality will be revealed to me.

- I wake early to do my Yoga practice with the rising Sun so that I may connect with and be in harmony with the natural diurnal rhythms of the Earth and Sun.

Basic Doctrines of Jainism

Jainism is a religion of demanded legalism that requires extreme asceticism to achieve one's own salvation. This belief leads to a system of doctrine completely derived from human reasoning and dependent upon human endeavors.

9. Christopher Key Chapple, "Jainism, Ethics, and Ecology." *Bulletin for the Study of Religion* 39, no. 2 (April 2010): 5.
10. Clayton Horton, "Green Affirmations of the Yamas & Niyamas," accessed January 11, 2016, http://www.greenpathyoga.org/article_affirmations.html.

View of Scripture

Beginning shortly after the establishment of their religion, Jains were prolific writers, composing a wide variety of literary works intended to both serve the followers of Jainism as well as provide an apologetic for their beliefs. The oldest texts were written in the Prakrit language, reflecting their origin in northern India.

Later literary works made use of Sanskrit, which became the primary language used in scholarly discussion. "From the first to the fifteenth century [A.D.] an enormous mass of literature was produced, covering a wide range of topics: dialectics and logic, politics and religious law, grammar, scientific subjects, epico-lyric poems devoted to 'universal history,' narratives on the Jain law, short stories illustrating the doctrinal teachings, gnomic poetry and hymns."[11]

While these writings serve as a source of direction and influence for Jains, they are not seen as canonical in the way that Christians view the Bible. Jains believe there were 14 *Purvas* (ancient knowledge) taught by Mahavira which contained all the knowledge available in this universe. These texts were eventually lost, though Jains claim that parts of the material were incorporated into various treatises. The two sects differ on which parts of the Purvas were preserved and which books contain the information. However, Umasvati's writing from around A.D. 100, known as *Tattvarthasutra*, is accepted as the authoritative text on Jain philosophy and teaching by both sects.

View of God

Claiming that the world as we know it is made of living souls (*jiva*) and nonliving matter (*ajiva*), "Jainism believes that [the] universe and all its substances or entities are eternal. It has no beginning or end with respect to time. [The] universe runs [on] its own accord by its own cosmic laws. All the substances change or modify their forms continuously. Nothing can be destroyed or created in the universe. There is no need of some one [sic] to create or manage the affairs of the universe. Hence, Jainism does not believe in God as a creator, survivor [sustainer], and destroyer of the universe."[12] God, in the Jain theology, is ultimately the term used to describe the person

---

11. Caillat, *The Encyclopedia of Religion*, p. 508.
12. Pravin K. Shah, "Concept of God in Jainism"; *Jainism Literature Center*, Jain Study Center of North Carolina; The Pluralism Project at Harvard University (online compilation accessed January 14, 2016).

who has reached perfection by destroying all of his karmas, achieving liberation of the soul (moksha). Once the karmas are destroyed, the person is described as possessing infinite knowledge and power and ultimate bliss.

Because of this view, every living being has the potential to become a god. Therefore, it is accurate to say that Jains do not have one god. In fact, they believe the number of gods continuously increases[13] as more souls (*jivas*) attain moksha, receiving the status of *siddhas*.

View of Salvation

As has been repeatedly stated, Jainism is a religious system of self-imposed afflictions for the purpose of achieving release from the bondage of karma. Karma consists of miniscule karman particles floating throughout the universe which attach to souls (jivas). These particles can be either good (*punya*) or bad (*pap*). The amount of karma depends upon the nature of the activity as well as the depth of passion associated with the activity.

Passions are like glue which bind the karma to the soul; an unintentional action (whether physical, verbal, or mental) or an action without passion will be easily separated from the soul. The greater the vigor of activity and intensity of passion the longer the bondage of karma — up to thousands or millions of years. Once the accumulated karma matures (produces its results), the soul experiences either good things such as happiness and material comfort from the punya, or suffering and poverty from the pap. Karma can be dealt with passively by waiting for the results to conclude or actively by following austerities such as fasting, isolation, meditation, charity, atonement, or spiritual study. After death, the complete and final liberation of the soul from karma is called *moksha*. It is important to note that this process of eradicating karma is only possible as one places firm faith in the commands, primarily the five vows, of Mahavira, the founder of Jainism.

To stop the flow of karma particles, one must practice a synthesis of exercising care, restraint, sufferings, and contemplations. Care is demonstrated in such ways as avoiding injury to any living being as one walks, or avoiding any speech that may incite responses like violence, gossip, flattery, or condemnation. Care even encompasses the proper disposal of trash or bodily excretions so that no harm is done to any living being.

---

13. According to Jain tradition, the last person in this time cycle to reach moksha was Jambu, who was only two generations removed from Mahavira; he was a disciple of Mahavira's disciple Sudharman. Therefore, no souls have attained moksha for almost 2,500 years. Padmanabh S. Jaini, *The Jaina Path of Purification* (Berkeley, CA: University of California Press, 1979), p. 46.

Restraint describes the disciplining of the mind to restrict expressions of extreme emotions such as grief, anger, joy, or anxiety. Speech may be restrained to the point of taking a vow of silence. Sufferings include enduring hardship such as hunger, thirst, celibacy, cold, heat, or even ragged clothing while demonstrating a sense of serenity and contentment.

Contemplations refers to a process of meditating and reflecting upon 12 specific categories called *bhavanas*, where one must "contemplate" subjects to eliminate or discard in order to advance in the removal of karma. There are many types of karmas, but they have been broadly classified into eight categories:

1. Mohniya karma — it generates delusion in the soul in regard to its own true nature, and makes it identify itself with other external substances

2. Jnana-varaniya karma — it covers the soul's power of perfect knowledge

3. Darsana-varaniya karma — it covers the soul's power of perfect visions

4. Antaraya karma — it obstructs the natural quality or energy of the soul as charity and will power. This prevents the soul from attaining liberation. It also prevents a living being from doing something good and enjoyable.

5. Vedniya karma — it obscures the blissful nature of the soul, and thereby produces pleasure and pain

6. Nama karma — it obscures the non-corporeal existence of the soul, and produces the body with its limitations, qualities, and faculties

7. Gotra karma — it obscures the soul's characteristics of equanimity, and determines the caste, family, social standing, and personality

8. Ayu karma — it determines the span of life [at one's] birth, thus obscuring the soul's nature of eternal existence[14]

A Jain's ambition is to eradicate all eight karma categories before death. The destruction of the first four (called *ghati karmas*) results in achieving the

14. Shah, "Concept of God in Jainism."

status known as *arihant*, whereby the restoration of the original attributes of the soul (perfect knowledge, perfect vision, perfect power, and perfect bliss) are attained. While still a human being in this status, the arihant has achieved a level of perfection which will never be tarnished by an influx of karma.

Once a person has destroyed his ghati karmas, he will definitely destroy the remaining four karmas, called *aghati* karmas, before his death. The accomplishment of this stage of destroying karma provides complete liberation and results in a status called the siddha. Siddhas are totally free from the birth and death cycle. They do not possess a physical body but rather enjoy everlasting bliss at the top of the universe. They have achieved moksha.

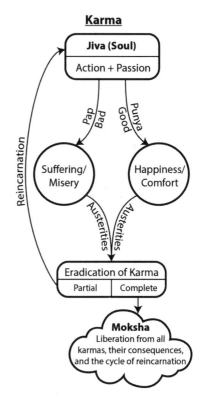

The removal of karma through various practices is believed to bring about liberation (moksha) of the soul.

Summary Illustration of Jain Doctrine

We began our discussion of Jainism by using an analogy that we can now interpret. The analogy stated the following:

> There lived a family in a farm house. They were enjoying the fresh, cool breeze coming through the open doors and windows. The weather suddenly changed, and a terrible dust storm set in. Realizing it was a bad storm, they got up to close the doors and windows. By the time they could close all the doors and windows, much dust had entered the house. After closing all of the doors and windows, they started cleaning away the dust that had come into the house.

The interpretation of this illustration incorporates some of the primary terms and beliefs of Jainism. That interpretation is as follows:

1. Jivas are represented by the people.

2. Ajiva is represented by the house.

3. Punya is represented by worldly enjoyment resulting from the nice, cool breeze.

4. Pap is represented by worldly discomfort resulting from the sand storm, which brought dust into the house.

5. Asrava is represented by the influx of dust through the doors and windows of the house, which is similar to the influx of karman particles to the soul.

6. Bandh is represented by the accumulation of dust in the house, which is similar to bondage of karman particles to the soul.

7. Samvar is represented by the closing of the doors and windows to stop the dust from coming into the house, which is similar to stoppage of influx of karman particles to the soul.

8. Nirjara is represented by the cleaning up of accumulated dust from the house, which is similar to shedding off accumulated karmic particles from the soul.

9. Moksha is represented by the clean house, which is similar to the shedding of all karmic particles from the soul.[15]

It obviously takes a great deal of understanding of Jainism to comprehend this analogy to its fullest degree. However, this succinct illustration, with its parallel meanings, quickly demonstrates the essence of the doctrine of Jainism which is dominated by a philosophy requiring a self-imposed abdication of fleshly gratification and devotion to the avoidance of harming others in order to achieve eternal "bliss." Tragically, one can never be certain of obtaining this bliss.

The Jain Symbol

Adopted by all sects of Jainism in 1975 in commemoration of the 2,500th anniversary of the death of Lord Mahavira, the official Jain emblem contains much symbolism.

---

15. Jainism Global Resource Center, "Introduction."

The hourglass outline symbolizes the shape of the universe as described in Jain literature.

The text below the hourglass reads, "All life is bound together by mutual support and interdependence."

The upraised hand includes the symbol for "ahimsa," the fundamental teaching of Jainism. This hand is intended as both a warning and a blessing — a warning to stop and consider one's actions so as not to perpetuate violence on another or on oneself, as well as a gesture of blessing for the soul who practices ahimsa. The circle further warns that the cycle of reincarnation awaits the soul who violates ahimsa.

The swastika's four arms (left figure above) represent the four primary types of souls: heavenly, human, animal, and hellish. During the cycle of reincarnation, faithfulness to ahimsa and diligence in austerities will determine into which of these four categories a soul may be reborn. In addition, the four arms represent the four classifications of Jain followers: monks (sadhus), nuns (sadhvis), and male and female laypersons (shravaks or shravikas).

Because of the swastika's association with Nazism, Jains in America have replaced that figure in the design with one that combines the word "Om" with the symbol for the Federation of Jain Associations in North America (JAINA) (figure on right above).

The three parallel dots at the top of the hourglass represent the "Three Jewels of Jainism" or what Jains consider to be the threefold path to moksha (liberation): Right Faith, Right Knowledge, and Right Conduct.

The crescent at the top of the hourglass stands for Siddhashila. In Jain cosmology, this upper part of the heavens is the final resting place for all liberated souls. The single dot above the arc represents a siddha (liberated soul).[16]

16. Information gathered from jainworld.com and pluralism.org; Illustrations: Official Jain Symbol clip art created by Mpanchratan as posted in Wikimedia Commons; Variant Jain Symbol clip art created by Etienekd as posted in Wikimedia Commons.

Primary Errors in Jainism

Jainism as a religious system has created its own terms and definitions. Part of the challenge of evaluating Jainism is understanding these terms so as to fairly assess their meaning and implications.

As has been noted, Jainism holds to a view of God that denies His very existence, instead defining "god" as humans who have destroyed all karma and have become gods. Jivas who have attained enlightenment are essentially seen as *god* in both existence and authority. There is no personal or separate person absolutely existing as God in Jainism.

Furthermore, there is no belief in a creation of the world by God. That denial of creation is further expressed as a rejection of any possibility of divine intervention in the history of the world, as seen in a Noahic universal Flood. Jainism claims that as humans we are the sole reason for suffering or happiness, both as an individual and on a corporate level.

A striking observation in all of the material about Jainism is their absence of any reference to Jesus Christ. They make no attempt to incorporate Him, even historically, into their religious system. Likewise, they make no inclusion of the Bible in their teachings.

Jainism will acknowledge the need for faith in order to reach the soul's intended destination of bliss. That faith, however, is placed in its founder, Mahavira, a mere man, and his teachings.

Concepts of heaven and hell are likewise erroneous in Jainism. Not only do souls exist on this earthly level, depending on the amount of good or bad karma accrued, a soul could also be punished in hell (infernal) until the bad karma is burned off and they are reincarnated into another body, or, for a time, a soul could enjoy a level of heaven (celestial) though not the complete liberation of moksha. The eradication of all karma and liberation from the reincarnation cycle would be equivalent to the classical definition of "heaven," but this destiny is never assured and certainly lacks any substantive hope. Hell as a place of punishment is not seen as an eternal reality; being trapped in the cycle of reincarnation because of the failure to destroy karma would be the equivalent to the classical view of "hell." Even at that, there is always the possibility in Jainism to eventually overcome the cycle of reincarnation and thus be freed from "hell."

The glaring error of Jainism in many ways is the utter hopelessness that exists in this religious system. There is no assured means of salvation, nor anyone to intercede for you. Any reference to salvation is usually identified with the word "liberated" and refers to the liberation from the reincarnation cycle. Without question, salvation to a Jainist is the performance of good works. One can never be certain that they have adequately achieved the necessary steps to eradicate karma and thus enter into eternal bliss. The depth of this hopelessness is powerfully illustrated in the description of what is called the "wise man's death," that is, the exalted fast-unto-death experience (*samlekhana*).[17]

Another question that arises is who judges the soul for good and bad? Judging is a specific action based on a standard of good and bad, and yet there is no true and absolute standard of good and bad or an absolute personal judge in the Jain view of the universe. If one is just to take someone's word for it (e.g., Mahavira or his early followers), then the definitions of good and bad are arbitrary, based on the opinions and writings of mere men.

Witnessing to Jains

While the religion of Jainism is relatively small in numbers, the followers of Jainism are widely scattered. This is somewhat due to the nature of occupations prevalent among Jainists that take them into cities all around the world. Therefore, it is important to be prepared to witness to these precious souls who need to trust Jesus Christ, since one never knows when an encounter with a Jain may occur.

As is true in any witnessing setting, it is imperative that a Christian prayerfully approach any opportunity to share the gospel with a sensitivity to the Holy Spirit's guidance. Likewise, a witness for the Lord must always rely upon the innate power of the Word of God, remembering that faith comes by hearing, and hearing by the Word of God (Romans 10:17).

One of the difficulties in reaching Jainists with the gospel is their tendency to restrict engagement with persons outside of their religious community. One of the primary reasons for that limitation is their strict vegetarian practices. That introduces one of the most important considerations in attempting to evangelize these people. Great caution must be exercised to avoid trespassing their vegetarian lifestyle. It is important to remember that the reason for their dietary practice is due to their dominant religious tenet of nonviolence (ahimsa). This tenet, more than any other, is central to their religious beliefs and is an intrinsic part of their culture.

---

17. Caillat, *The Encyclopedia of Religion*, p. 511.

This presents another important consideration when witnessing to a Jain. Because of their commitment to nonviolence, they are characteristically known for their gentle and contrite demeanor. Effective evangelization to Jains must be done with a spirit of gentleness and meekness. Simply stated, it is essential to demonstrate the fruits of the Spirit if one is to reach these souls with the gospel (Galatians 5:22–23).

At the same time, one must be careful not to amplify a Jain's tendency toward the promotion of wholesome, moral behavior. Moral conduct is a prominent component of their religion. Caution must be taken to avoid emphasizing the behavior of a Christian as though that is a part of becoming a Christian. Most dedicated Jainists are already well aware of and committed to a moral lifestyle. Care must be given instead to emphasizing the unique blessing of the grace of God as one shares that salvation is not by works of righteousness which we have done, but according to His mercy (Titus 3:5).

In seeking to witness to a Jain, one effective method to nurture a relationship is to regularly visit their shops. By engaging them in their area of business, it is possible to demonstrate the genuine love of the Lord to them in a way that is enviable to their desire to achieve moral goodness. There are ways to identify a business as owned by a Jain. First, many Jains take the name "Jain" as their last name. Second, the Jainists have a distinct symbol to identify their religion (as shown above). Observing either of these is a good indication that the individual is a Jain.

When seeking to introduce conversation about the gospel, it is valuable to identify Scriptures to relate to their concerns and interests. One passage which has proven effective when witnessing to Jains is the Sermon on the Mount, especially the Beatitudes, which emphasize the importance of moral behavior. Transitioning from interest in moral living to the One who gave these principles allows one to introduce Christ. Here one could also introduce them to the teaching of Jesus in Matthew 11:28–30, calling them to forsake their striving for perfection and accept that Jesus has accomplished our liberation on the Cross. Point them to the rest you have found in Christ.

Another effective avenue for witnessing is to discuss the meaning behind their word "Jaina," meaning "conqueror." Jains use that term to describe their founder who went to extreme measures attempting to conquer personal passions and sins. Presenting the message of the gospel and Christ's supreme example of sacrifice to assure us victory over sin can be used in an impacting way to a Jain.

Without a doubt, reaching Jains with the gospel can be a tedious and challenging task. May God give followers of Jesus Christ a dedication to living and giving the gospel that surpasses the dedication of those who have given themselves to the deception of Jainism. May each jiva come to know the true moksha as they realize that whoever calls upon the name of the Lord shall be saved (Romans 10:13).

Summary of Jain Beliefs

Doctrine	Teachings of Jainism
God	Deny the God of the Bible, including the possibility of a divine Savior. No mention of Jesus whatsoever. Each living soul (*jiva*) can progress to godhood by eradicating karma, thus achieving first enlightenment as a human (*arihant*) and then liberation after death (*moksha*) as a siddha. Jains consider both arihants and siddhas gods.
Authority/ Revelation	Fourteen original *Purvas* were recorded by Mahavira's disciples, but were largely lost. The later *Tattvarthasutra* writings are generally accepted as the authoritative text regarding Jain practices.
Man	All men are born carrying the karma from their previous life. There is no concept of an innate sin nature, but each individual must follow strict rules to avoid attracting additional karma.
Sin	Sin could loosely be defined as activities that attract bad karma. However, both good and bad karma are undesirable. The effects of karma can often be seen immediately in either suffering or enjoyment but may also carry over into the next life.
Salvation	Salvation is liberation from the effects of karma and the cycle of reincarnation. Karma is eradicated by austerities and keeping the 5 great vows or 12 lesser vows, the central tenets being nonviolence (*ahimsa*) and non-attachment. After death, liberated souls having achieved moksha ascend to the top of the universe (*siddhashila*).

Creation	The universe is eternal and uncreated, consisting of living souls (*jiva*) and nonliving matter (*ajiva*). There is no creator god. Evolutionary ideas are generally rejected, though some may accommodate them. Souls themselves may be seen as "evolving" as they progress through the karmic cycle, with the possibility that life may even exist within the most basic elements of nature.

Chapter 6

Sikhism

Steven Fazekas

Sikhism is a strange religion to people in many parts of the world. It has elements of Eastern religions like Hinduism and yet aspects of Middle Eastern thought like that of Islam. So what do we make of this?

The famous "duck test" is a humorous way of reasoning which asserts, "If it looks like a duck and swims like a duck and quacks like a duck, chances are it's a duck."

When it comes to the Eastern religions, there is a galaxy of gurus and a plethora of messiahs. Despite the things that differ, there is a consistent, almost monotonous sameness that, more times than not, gives the proverbial duck its "duckness," even though the respective beaks and webbed feet may appear a little bit different.

It is difficult to accept that the Sikh religion is a faith completely independent from Hinduism, Islam, or any other Eastern systems of belief. At some point, all of the foxes are joined at their tails.

In other words, Sikhism is a type of mixture between two religions — Hinduism and Islam. By the way, one might be tempted to argue, "Isn't this *sameness* found in the glut of Christian cults which are choking the Western mind as well?" Unfortunately, the answer is yes.

To the affirmative, there is a breathtaking surplus of mind-numbing views which have comfortably found a home in our Western culture where many groups borrow much of the Bible, then mix it with some other view to dilute to man's word.[1] Generally speaking, we might say that the heart of man worldwide is incurably religious.

What Is a Sikh?

Let's let the Sikh tell us what the Sikh is and does. The Rehat Maryada is the Sikh statement of beliefs and code of conduct. Article 1 states:

> Any human being who faithfully believes in: (1) One Immortal Being, (2) Ten Gurus, from Guru Nanak to Guru Gobind Singh, (3) The Guru Granth Sahib, (4) The utterances and teachings of the ten Gurus and (5) the baptism bequeathed by the tenth Guru, and who does not owe allegiance to any other religion, is a Sikh.[2]

The discerning mind, with a small amount of careful reading, will discover nothing unique in this definition. We have a call to belief in a supernatural Being, surrounded by a brotherhood of prophets who are devoted to a collection of prophetic writings, given to ritual, and devoted to no other worldview. We conclude, by way of definition, there is nothing unique that is not found in a hundred other religions.

Where Do I Find a Sikh?

The answer is "anywhere and everywhere." There are over 20 million followers of Sikhism, many of them having originated largely from the Punjab region of India, a highly cultural and religious area at a crossroads between areas dominated by Hinduism and Islam. In the day in which we live, Sikh communities are found in major population centers all over the world. Guru Nanak, who was born in 1469, was the founding apostle of Sikhism. We might say with a degree of accuracy that we are discussing a world religion that is comparatively young yet exceedingly well established.

The Sikh and the Nature of God

The Sikh view of God is distinctly different from the biblical view of God. They say:

---

1. These counterfeits of Christianity are explored in volume 1 of this work.
2. "Rehat Maryada," Sikhs.org, accessed November 19, 2015, http://www.sikhs.org/rehit.htm.

In Sikhism God is conceived in two forms i.e., in Nirguna form and in sarguna form. 'Ik' (meaning one) in Ikoankar defines Nirguna state of God. It is that state of God when He had not created the universe as yet. He was one and the only one at that time. He was in himself. There was no universe, no suns, no planets, no satellites, no living or non-living creatures, no good or bad deeds, no light, no days or nights. In fact there was total darkness at that time. God had not created in Himself His own powers, including the power of creation and the power of destruction. He was thus devoid of any characteristics or any qualities. He was one and only one. The ancient Hindu books describe this period of darkness, when God was one and only one, extending to 36 yugas (one yug is variously described as 1,000 years, 10,000 years or even more).

Once, Guru Nanak Dev Ji was asked by learned saints (Sidhas) to describe the "Nirguna" state of God. Guru Nanak Dev Ji replied that "Nirguna" state of God is a divine wonder. A man is too little a creature to even think of that state, let alone to describe that state. When God Himself had not acquired His power of creation, how can a created one, the human, think of that state of God? Everyone and everything is created by God. How can a created one think of the state of a creator when there was nothingness, no creation, only the creator. He, the creator, only knew about Himself of that state.[3]

Take note that God, in Sikhism, had to figure out how to create his own power and that man cannot comprehend this God.

Sikhs believe in one God who has gone by many names such as Ram, Rahim, Allah, Pritam, Yar, Mahakal, and Waheguru. To the Sikh, God is known by the inward eye of faith. Much like Islam, the Sikh God is omnipresent, timeless, universal, fearless, silent and self-existent, incomprehensible, genderless, and inaccessible with no form nor feature. Like Hinduism, communication between God and human beings can only take place through rigorous meditation, although you still can't really know God.

---

3. Sujan Singh, Guru Nanak Ki Bani website, "Concept of God in Sikhism," accessed 9/16/2015, http://www.gurunanakkibani.com/index.php/concept-of-god-in-sikhism.

These things being understood, many a devout Sikh has said, "We are all children of the same Universal Divine Love."

This concept of the Sikh God presents several internal problems. If this God is incomprehensible and inaccessible, then how can anyone know anything about the Sikh God? Since their God has not revealed truth, any human assertion about this God is unverifiable. This provides a logical refutation of the existence of the Sikh concept of God. For example, how can it be known that this God is loving if he is impersonal and incomprehensible?

Considerer that the Sikh God is not a *personal* God like the God of the Bible. This being the case, how then can anything in personal experience describe this God? There cannot be a personal revelation from an impersonal God; thus any alleged prophets claiming to speak for this impersonal Sikh God cannot be doing so.

The God of the Bible is a personal God who made us in His image (Genesis 1:26–28). Thus it is possible for personal revelation to exist through prophets and apostles by the power of the Holy Spirit revealing God to man.

The Word: Written and Living

The written authority for the faithful Sikh is their own version of the authoritative text called the *Guru Garanth Sahib*. It contains the writings of their designated holy men along with large portions of hymns and poetry claimed to have been passed down to them directly by God (see the explanation of this inconsistency above).

Guru Nanak (1469–1532), as the first guru and self-proclaimed prophet, was a prime contributor to this collection of writings; however, there were others who were highly esteemed in the Sikh community over the centuries whose works were added. The writing of the Sikh canon closed with the last guru (1709) making ten final prophetic voices, nine embodied as gurus in the flesh and one as written text. The *Guru Garanth Sahib* is considered the ultimate written source of spiritual encouragement for the devout Sikh.

Of course, we can ask, by what standard is this ultimate written source judged? By God's standard, revealed in the Bible, the alleged Sikh scriptures falls tragically short as the ultimate standard.

In contrast, the Christian holds the Bible as the only judge in all matters of faith and practice. For the Christian, the era of God revealing Scripture to men has ended. The Book of Jude teaches that the faith *was once for all delivered to the saints* (Jude 1:3). Thus, there was no need for further revelation after the New Testament was completed and no need for more prophets. Any alleged prophets after the New Testament must be considered false prophets.

The authority of the Old and New Testament is sufficient. The preface of the Chicago Statement on Biblical Inerrancy clearly states:

> The authority of Scripture is a key issue for the Christian Church in this and in every age. . . . To stray from Scripture in faith or in conduct is disloyalty to our Master. Recognition of the total truth and trustworthiness of the Holy Scripture is essential to a full grasp and adequate confession of its authority.[4]

In other words, this Christian truth claim also sets forth a revealed document (understood to be 66 unified books comprising the Old and New Testaments) that is inerrant, infallible, free from falsehood, duplicity, and deceit, and totally trustworthy in all that it asserts, as the dominant worldview. Unlike the Sikh God, the God of the Bible is personal and knowable, having made us in His image and revealed Himself to us because He loves us.

> Knowing this first, that no prophecy of Scripture is of any private interpretation, for prophecy never came by the will of man, but holy men of God spoke as they were moved by the Holy Spirit (2 Peter 1:20–21).[5]

Further, when examining other worldviews, the believing Christian is exhorted from the pages of the Bible to be clothed with a cautious discernment.

> Beloved, do not believe every spirit, but test the spirits, whether they are of God; because many false prophets have gone out into the world. By this you know the Spirit of God: Every spirit that confesses that Jesus Christ has come in the flesh is of God (1 John 4:1–2).

The caution in this text points to the "pseudo-prophet," the one who pretends to have special gifts from God and who invites the sincere seeker of the

---

4. http://storage.cloversites.com/gracechurch2/documents/CHICAGO%20STATEMENT. pdf.
5. Scripture in this chapter is from the New King James Version (NKJV) of the Bible.

truth to embrace a message which may sound enticing but will ultimately fail the test. Here are a few brief examples.

The Sikh teaches there are numerous pathways which lead to God.	The Christian embraces the words of Jesus: "No one comes to the Father except through Me" (John 14:6).
The Sikh denies being specially chosen by God.	The Christian claims an exclusive divine sonship rooted in faith: "To them He gave the right to become children of God, to those who believe in His name"(John 1:12).
The Sikh says that members of all religions share the same rights and privileges and liberties.	The Christian embraces the words of Scripture: "If we, or an angel from heaven, preach any other gospel to you than what we have preached to you, let him be accursed. As we have said before, so now I say again, if anyone preaches any other gospel to you than what you have received, let him be accursed" (Galatians 1:8–9).

The Christian faith teaches that God Himself has come to earth, clothed in flesh (which is purportedly to Eastern thought a bad thing), and having spoken to us through the prophets, has in these last days spoken to us through His Son, Jesus Christ (Hebrews 1:1–2). The difference, to all other claims, is found in the Son of God.

It is really against the truth claim of the Christian Scriptures as both the written and the living Word that we will attempt to address some of the components of the Sikh religion, its doctrine, philosophy, and spiritual claims.

Sikhism as Religion

The word "religion" itself is sometimes difficult to explain. Webster defines it as "beliefs embracing the cause, nature, and purpose of the universe and containing a moral code for the human race usually with a ritual observance of faith." This definition seems to work for our purposes, though a proper definition would involve much more than this.

There is disagreement among Sikh scholars with regard to its roots. However, Sikhism appears to be the product of a number of strong influences, such as the Sant tradition blended together with elements of Hinduism,

Jainism, and Islam. Sikhism appears to be a syncretism of Eastern religious ideas. Emerging from this milieu is the coming together of polytheism and monotheism, that is, one God manifesting himself in many different ways.[6]

The historic Christian confessions of faith, regardless of denomination, with one voice and without embarrassment proclaim the nature of God as three divine persons (Father, Son, and Holy Spirit) sharing one divine essence. Here is both unity and diversity blended together. Contrary to most Eastern religions is the Christian worldview that God is not a solitary unity but a composite unity. The words *Trinity, triune,* and *Trinitarian,* are not in the Bible, but they are necessary descriptive units indicative of both the mystery and reality of the God we love and serve and the things most surely believed among us who look to the Bible as the source of truth about God.

Sikhism as Philosophy

The underlying philosophic basis for most Eastern religions, including Sikhism, is what is known as "monism."

Monism can be illustrated in this way: Even as the river flows endlessly toward the ocean and becomes assimilated into that broad liquid expanse by finally "coming home," so the *self* enters its own journey, ever seeking, ever searching for home by way of a lifelong pilgrimage. Full liberation becomes "salvation" when the *finite* becomes one, merging with the *infinite.* This, to the Eastern mind, is redemption. It is the struggle of a good soul trapped inside an evil body of flesh wrestling to escape until full liberation takes place. In a sense, the human body to the Sikh is viewed as the prison house of the soul.

Monism is basically the idea that all is one, and our problem is that we don't realize that all is one! The human flaw is in continuing to draw distinctions that separate us from the "oneness of reality" rather than seeking unity of all things. Some claim that Christianity carries the same basic teaching since we are to "merge" with the Divine. The Christian "merging" may on the surface appear the same, but in fact is radically different. Hear the words of Jesus.

> . . . that they all may be one, as You, Father, are in Me, and I in You; that they also may be one in Us, that the world may believe that You sent Me (John 17:21).

---

6. Sean O'Callaghan, *The Compact Guide to World Religions,* "Sikhism" (Oxford, England: Lion Hudson, 2010), p. 129.

For the Christian, to be united with the Divine is permeated with sonship, as we are united to Christ as adopted sons and daughters and have the Spirit of God living within us.

The "Light" in All of Us

> Deep within the self is the Light of God. It radiates through-out the expanse of His creation. Through the Guru's Teachings, the darkness of spiritual ignorance is dispelled. The heart-lotus flower blossoms forth, and eternal peace is obtained, as one's light is merged into the Light.[7]

In 1974, a country and western song by Donna Fargo hit the charts:

> You can't be a beacon if your light don't shine.
> There's a little light in all of us by God's design.

It's a catchy little tune. However, the only problem with it is . . . it simply isn't true. The Sikh claim that men are all endowed with the same divine potential, that divinity permeates everyone and everything, is simply not true. It's a nice thought but totally opposite to the teaching of the Bible.

The Bible tells us that man's problem from the very beginning is the overwhelming desire to *be* the light of deity on earth.

> Then the serpent said to the woman, "You will not surely die. For God knows that in the day you eat of it your eyes will be opened, and you will be like God, knowing good and evil (Genesis 3:4–5).

As optimistic as this quest for inner light sounds, the Bible does not paint an overly optimistic picture of the heart of man. According to Jesus, who happens to be the One who exhaustively knows the human condition, we consider His words carefully.

> For out of the heart proceed evil thoughts, murders, adul-teries, fornications, thefts, false witness, blasphemies (Matthew 15:19–20).

The Bible also speaks of the heart in other passages:

---

7. Guru Amar Das, Majh, p. 126, http://www.sikhs.org/english/eg1.htm#p13.

> The heart is deceitful above all things, and desperately wicked; who can know it? (Jeremiah 17:9).

> And the LORD smelled a soothing aroma. Then the LORD said in His heart, "I will never again curse the ground for man's sake, although the imagination of man's heart is evil from his youth; nor will I again destroy every living thing as I have done" (Genesis 8:21).

Today's Western society practices self-deification of the individual (i.e., man is the ultimate authority, not God). The promotion of the "self" is also highly significant in the Sikh worldview. All men, to some degree, are practical Sikhs when it comes to their inner passions for deification and cosmic recognition. Frankly put, we all want to be the God of our life in one way or the other, which is contrary to the Bible.

Basic to Christian thought is the Fall of man and his rebellion toward his Maker. Whatever shines from man, it's hardly the "light of God" shining forth from the inner self.

> As it is written: "There is none righteous, no, not one; there is none who understands; there is none who seeks after God. . . . there is none who does good, no, not one. . . . destruction and misery are in their ways. . . . There is no fear of God before their eyes (Romans 3:10–18).

Sin has corrupted the human race, mind, will, and emotions. We have been affected, not only in our actions but also in our basic disposition toward sin. The Bible tells us we are slaves to sin (Romans 6:20) and our inner disposition is revealed with these words: Men love darkness rather than light because their deeds are evil (John 3:19).

The Six Badges of Sikh Identity

There are six insignias which the devout Sikh (Khalsa) wear as an outward sign of recognized piety.[8]

- KESH — uncut hair, kept in place by a turban (dastar), and a beard (for men) symbolizing dedication and a connection to other Khalsa

---

8. "The Khalsa," Sikhs.org, http://www.sikhs.org/khalsa.htm.

- DASTAR — a turban to signify dignity and self-esteem

- KANGHA — a comb worn in the hair symbolizing hygiene and discipline

- KIRPAN — a short sword indicating the desire to help the defenseless

- KARA — steel bracelet showing God's unity and as a reminder to show restraint

- KACHHAS — baggy shorts showing readiness to action and chastity

These six symbols are parts of the attire identifying Khalsa, "The Pure Ones," as a kind of righteous standard of initiation.

Under the Old Covenant, the Bible teaches the badge of Abraham's descendants as circumcision. This was a ritual ceremony of cutting the flesh performed on the male child usually around eight days of age.

It is made clear in the coming of Messiah that there is a New Covenant, and in Christ Jesus neither circumcision nor uncircumcision means anything,[9] but rather a new creation (Galatians 6:15). In other words, the significance of an external badge of distinction and identity is removed when Messiah comes and a new heart is given. Those with the "pure heart" are those with a spiritually circumcised heart. All the outer trinkets and symbols and gadgets and items of attire of Sikhism are insignificant when Jesus Christ grants a new heart, because along with it comes the power of a changed life.

There is an answer, and it is found in the absolute incomparable uniqueness of the Son of God Himself. The difference is in the Son!

The Things Surely Believed Among Us

To the Christian, every truth claim, including Sikhism, is held up against the incarnate Son of God in His life and death on behalf of a fallen race, and without exception, each claim is found woefully wanting.

The historic Westminster Confession of Faith sets forth one of the most marvelous statements on Jesus Christ in language worthy of committing to memory by every confessing believer in the gospel. Lofty language? Maybe.

9. Circumcision was a physical shadow of the *spiritual circumcision of the heart* for those who are descendants of Abraham who love the Lord their God with all their heart and all their soul (Deuteronomy 30:6; Luke 10:27–28; Romans 4:16, 9:6–8).

But we have here set forth to us a magnificent, majestic God who does not hide His glory, but has revealed Himself to the world in great humility and breathtaking condescension in the Person of the Son.

> The Son of God, the second person in the Trinity, being very and eternal God, of one substance and equal with the Father, did when the fullness of time was come take upon him man's nature, with all the essential properties, and common infirmities thereof, yet without sin; being conceived by the power of the Holy Ghost in the womb of the virgin Mary, of her substance. So that two whole, perfect, and distinct natures, the Godhead and the manhood, were inseparably joined together in one person, without conversion, composition, or confusion. Which person is very God, and very man, yet one Christ, the only Mediator between God and man.[10]

There is something radically life changing in the marketplace of world religions. There is something that has been elevated high above the "monotonous sameness" of world religions. It is God in Christ reconciling the world to Himself by the gospel.

Unlike Sikhism, in Christianity God became a man (the God-man) to suffer and die on our behalf to make salvation possible. Sikhism recognizes there is a problem of evil, but doesn't offer its origins or the way to escape it. According to God's Word, man (in Adam) sinned against God, bringing death, suffering, and evil as a punishment for sin (e.g., Genesis 2:17, 3:19; Romans 5:12).

Since we are all descendants of Adam, we are all sinners. God, being perfectly holy and just, must punish sin. The punishment for sin is death, and the power behind it is infinite in its force, being that God is infinite in His nature. This death would thus result in an eternal punishment for high treason against God.

Yet God did the unthinkable. God stepped into history in the person of His Son, Jesus the Christ, to become a man to take the punishment (on our behalf) from the infinite God in the person of the Father. The infinite Son took that infinite punishment. This then satisfied the wrath of God upon

10. Westminster Confession of Faith, "Of Christ the Mediator," chapter 8, par. 2, http://www.reformed.org/documents/wcf_with_proofs/index.html.

sin, and the Lord offers the unmerited free gift of salvation through the shed blood of Jesus Christ alone.

The Central Philosophy of Monism

Again, the overarching premise of most Eastern religions, including Sikhism, is what is known as *monism*.

Monism can be illustrated in a number of different ways. Even as a river flows endlessly toward the ocean and becomes absorbed and liberated into the wide expanse of waters, so the self enters a kind of lifelong pilgrimage whereby the individual becomes set free by merging with some impersonal God or ultimate source of reality.

This, of course, brings to mind a simple question: How can one know this? An impersonal God cannot communicate with man in a *personal* way to reveal this alleged truth. After all, language and communication is personal. A leading Sikh guru states:

> He who created the worlds, solar systems and galaxies —
> that God cannot be known.[11]

If the Sikh God cannot be known, then how can anyone know anything about him or even know that he cannot be known? When monism is mixed with monotheism it becomes inherently illogical.

Over time and through striving, the finite supposedly achieves unity with the absolute. Without some form of revelation, this idea becomes a mere arbitrary assertion.

Another way of explaining monism might be in a kind of migration of the soul as it goes through cycle after cycle of birth and death until it attains the form of humanity. A basic tenet of Eastern thinking is, "God is all, and all is God." Therefore, in some mystical metaphysical way, all of reality including man himself is, in a sense . . . deity. This is problematic logically. If all is already one, then there is no distinction, and if distinction really exists, then there cannot be an ultimate form that is pure unity.

Sikhism teaches that ultimate salvation is thus achieved by living an exemplary life, virtuous and truthful, frugal and honest until one may finally experience the merging of the Infinite with the finite.

---

11. SriGranth.org, "Sri Guru Granth Sahib," p. 907, http://www.srigranth.org/servlet/gurbani.gurbani?Action=Page&Param=907&english=t&id=38944#l38944.

The soul goes through cycles of births and deaths before it reaches the human form. The goal of our life is to lead an exemplary existence so that one may merge with God.[12]

But why? If there is really no distinction in the ultimate oneness that is monism, then lying and truth have no distinction. What real difference is there between an exemplary life and a miserable life?

Lamentably, there is an absence of grace in Sikh teaching. Here is where the Son makes the difference. How does the Sikh know for certain that he or she has lived a life that is commendable enough to gain assimilation into the One? How does the devout Sikh come to full knowledge that there are enough good works accrued to one's account to assure final peace with God? Assurance is virtually unknowable without the Son.

> For by grace you have been saved through faith, and that not of yourself, it is the gift of God; not of works, lest anyone should boast. For we are His workmanship, created in Christ Jesus for good works, which God prepared beforehand that we should walk in them (Ephesians 2:8–10).

The Sikh life of absorption into Oneness through good works is totally contrary to grace and the work of Christ on the Cross. While Christians pursue a virtuous life, it is not *for* salvation, but *because of God's grace in their life.* While the life of a Sikh and a Christian may appear similar on the outside, the motivation could not be more different.

Man in Creation

The Bible teaches the uniqueness of God's creation, especially His crowning achievement, man, whom He made in His own image.

> What is man that You are mindful of him, or the son of man that You take care of him? You have made him a little lower than the angels; You have crowned him with glory and honor, and set him over the works of Your hands. You have put all things in subjection under his feet (Hebrews 2:6–8).

---

12. "Introduction to Sikhism," Sikhs.org, accessed November 30, 2015, http://www.sikhs.org/summary.htm.

Sikhism has a low view of man and can never achieve the freedom found in Jesus Christ because it has a faulty, pessimistic view of humanity. To the Eastern mind, man is a good soul trapped in evil flesh trying to escape. The ultimate goal of man is the absorption of the human soul into the Great Divine Spirit. It might be called "the great escape."

This enslavement to the evil world (maya) is a product of the creation and is ultimately attributed to the divine, not man's actions in rebelling against the Creator. Man has been enslaved to evil since his creation rather than created perfect and experiencing a fall from that state.

Sikhs view the creation as having no ultimate beginning, but the physical aspects had a beginning and resulted from the will of the Creator. Describing the nature of creation, they say *the Lord is in his creation and the creation is in the Lord as all are in the One and the One is in all*. So the creation is the Creator, which is ultimately absurd. A Sikh apologetics website, Real Sikhism, states that the Sikh God created the entire universe and earth and life, though there is a twist. They write:

> Sikhism states that God created the entire Universe and the Universe including the Earth has been evolving since then. Earth while being in the Universe is a creation of God and all the life on the Earth is a creation of God. However, Sikhs respectfully disagree with Christians that the Earth was created 6000 years ago. Sikhism instructs that the Universe has been going on for billions of years. The Universe, including billion of stars, planets and the moons revolving the planets were created by God and it has been evolving since. In addition, this is not the first time God has created the Universe; He has done it many times.[13]

The Sikh God has allegedly made many universes over time! Universes include the *time dimension*. In light of this, their God must have created *time* more than once. Again we see how the arbitrary claims create internal contradictions. Sri Guru Granth Sahib Ji states:

> (Before the creation of the world) for endless eons, there was only utter darkness. There was no earth or sky; there was

---

13. Real Sikhism, "Sikh Views on Christianity: Do Sikhs believe in creation or evolution?" accessed November 30, 2015, http://realsikhism.com/index.php?subaction=show-full&id=1226710464&ucat=7.

only the infinite Command of His Hukam [will]. There was no day or night, no moon or sun; Vaheguru sat in primal, (like) in profound undisturbed meditation.[14]

If God existed in time, then time is superior to the Sikh God and he is bound by time. Os Guiness notes,

> Monism does not see man's dilemma as moral (in terms of what he has done) but as metaphysical (in terms of who he is). Monism thus leads to the notion that a man cannot be helped as an individual because it is his individuality which is the essential problem. He must be helped from his individuality; he must merge with the Absolute to reach salvation.[15]

Monism implies that human individuality must be lost or absorbed or assimilated into a larger whole in order to attain true freedom. In other words, to the Sikh it is a freedom *from* individuality. But how do they know this is really freedom? Did one rise from the dead to prove Sikhism was correct in the afterlife? No.

This idea of being absorbed into the Divine holds true in many Eastern religions. In contrast, the Bible sets forth the opposite. Man is amazingly complex, made in the image and likeness of God, and endowed with individuality, personality, mind, will, and emotions, all as an expression of the One who created him. The real problem is moral in its apostasy and expressed in rebellion toward a good and gracious Creator. The Sikh's problem is not finitude but sin.

Illusion of the Five Thieves

Chaucer had his Seven Deadly Sins. The Apostle Paul devastatingly cites what he calls the works of the flesh in Galatians 5:19–22. Sikhism has its "Five Thieves." All of these are simply variation on a theme and nothing new. "The Five Thieves," so called, are not just five bad acts, but rather they are the five bad acts from a bad heart. These acts come from the perception of reality and attachment to it, known as *maya*. To the Sikh, reality is a perceived illusion that must be escaped by avoiding the five forms of

---

14. Sikh Answers "How was the world created, according to Sikhi?" accessed November 30, 2015, http://www.sikhanswers.com/god-and-his-universe/creation-of-world/.
15. Os Guiness, *The Dust of Death*, "The East: No Exit," out of print; http://www.str.org/articles/reflections-on-hinduism#.VsysURh4yoI.

attachment. Whether these be *ego, anger, greed, worldly attachment, or lust,* "relentless devotion" cannot be the Sikh antidote to the things which so easily cause us to stumble. While the Christian can agree with the Sikh that these are vices, we know that they are sinful because they are contrary to the will of God and His character (revealed in the Bible). The cure is found in Paul's letter to the Romans 8:13–14.

> For if you live according to the flesh you will die; but if by
> the Spirit you put to death the deeds of the body, you will live.

The larger context of Romans chapter 8 will disclose the Trinitarian nature of the real antidote to these "Five Thieves," and many others that plague all of humanity. The "putting to death" of these five deadly sins are really the activities of the Father (Romans 8:15), the Son (Romans 8:3), and the Holy Spirit (Romans 8:9), and require so much more than mere "relentless devotion." The work of the Son on the Cross was not only relentless, but it was also thorough enough for Him to cry out, "It is finished."

There truly is no escape through any religion, Eastern or otherwise, which does not recognize the absolute uniqueness of the Son of God.

> O Christ our hope, our heart's desire, redemption's only spring,
> Creator of the world thou art, its Savior and its King.
> How vast the mercy and the love which laid our sins on Thee
> And led Thee to a cruel death to set Thy people free.
>
> O Christ be Thou our present joy, our future great reward,
> Our only glory may it be to glory in the Lord.
> All praise to Thee ascended Lord, all glory ever be,
> To Father, Son and Holy Ghost through all eternity.
> (Seventh to Eighth Century, Author Unknown)

Summary of Sikh Beliefs

Doctrine	Teachings of Sikhism
God	Deny the existence of the biblical God or a personal God, but are monotheistic. Deny that Jesus was God. View God as the Supreme Lord who created the universes and is described by many names. Their God is timeless, formless, fearless, universal, and self-existent.

Authority/ Revelation	The Guru Granth Sahib is a collection of sayings of the gurus and is viewed as the authoritative scripture of Sikhs.
Man	Men are conscious souls created by the Divine with attachment to the physical creation. All men are seeking to escape the cycle of births and deaths that attach them to the "unreality" of the physical world (maya).
Sin	Sin is viewed as five vices (ego, anger, greed, worldly attachment, and lust) that proceed from a bad heart and failure to realize that the world is not the ultimate goal.
Salvation	Salvation is equated with merging into the Divine of the universe. Salvation is achieved by following the guru's commands and meditating on the Divine Name. There is no concept of hell, but of returning to the cycle of births and deaths until achieving unity with the Divine.
Creation	The Creator created all of the universe and souls of living things with an attachment to the physical, evolving aspects of the creation. Life was created on many worlds. Many universes have been created.

Chapter 7

Moralistic and Mythological Religions: The Overview

Bodie Hodge and Roger Patterson

Does morality exist? If you don't want to get shot and killed, raped and tortured, stolen from and lied to, you are probably going to say yes! But why? *Why* does morality exist?

In the Christian worldview, morality exists because God is the *ultimate* lawgiver and the *supreme* basis for what is right and wrong. Thus, God's Word, the 66 books of the Bible, defines morality as a direct revelation of God's will for His creatures. Morality exists because God exists. Apart from God, there is no consistent grounding for determining what is true and holy.

But there are many people who believe in morality and yet do not hold the Bible as authoritative. Nor do they particularly hold to any God or gods in their worldview. Sometimes they hold to a vague notion of a universal force similar to a god or gods, but this god or force does not inform their morality. Morality comes strictly from man's experience and rationality in these systems. These are immanent moralistic religions, taking their cues of right and wrong based on what they immediately experience through nature or natural law.

Moralistic religions are *humanistic* by nature because they have elevated man's authority (human authority) to be greater than God and His Word on the issue of morality. In other words, people set their own morality or merely appeal to other people as those who define morality. Moralistic religions deny God's Word on morality and, by default, must appeal to their authority as absolute. Man is the ultimate standard of right and wrong in a moralistic religion.

Moralistic Religions

Moralistic religions encompass religious types that rarely have theistic elements but preach that there is some sort of code of behavior that needs to be adhered to. These sorts of religions basically believe there is some type of overarching code of morality that exists and should be followed but often do not include absolute morality.

Some of the more popular forms of this religion come from the East, such as Confucianism or Buddhism. In these, Buddha or Confucius (or other ancient sages) are seen as the ones who set the moral code to follow. Moralistic religions have appeared all over the world.

Even secular humanism could be classed as a form of this religion since there is a type of code of behavior, though it constantly changes and varies by individual. Although, we are placing secular humanism with the humanistic/atheistic religions in the third volume of this book series, it could rightly be in this volume. We have included Unitarian Universalism in this volume, though it aligns strongly with secular humanism. As mentioned elsewhere, with the classification system we are using, several of the religions could be placed in several categories.

Most of the adherents of moralistic religions might surprise you. They are individuals who often insist they have no religion or embrace multiple religious ideas! Of course, this is still a humanistic religious view that reflects one's morality and way of thinking about the world. This is why there are so many different forms of moralistic religions, since many are unaffiliated.

Moralism Invading the Church

This view has become a fixture of churches in the Christianized West. Sadly, it affects unsuspecting persons even in church pews. Often, many people consider themselves moral and believe this is good enough to be right with God. In other words, people walking on the street or attending churches may think that they are good enough for something better in the afterlife because they view themselves as "good people," often comparing themselves to some murderer or terrorist. Their moral code says, "As long as I am better than those wicked people, God will accept me." This is moralism and is a grave error — a damnable error.

Jesus dealt with a person who was a moralist. Consider Matthew 19:16–22:

> Now behold, one came and said to Him, "Good Teacher, what good thing shall I do that I may have eternal life?"
>
> So He said to him, "Why do you call Me good? No one is good but One, that is, God. But if you want to enter into life, keep the commandments."
>
> He said to Him, "Which ones?"
>
> Jesus said, " 'You shall not murder,' 'You shall not commit adultery,' 'You shall not steal,' 'You shall not bear false witness,' 'Honor your father and your mother,' and, 'You shall love your neighbor as yourself.' "
>
> The young man said to Him, "All these things I have kept from my youth. What do I still lack?"
>
> Jesus said to him, "If you want to be perfect, go, sell what you have and give to the poor, and you will have treasure in heaven; and come, follow Me."
>
> But when the young man heard that saying, he went away sorrowful, for he had great possessions.[1]

This person speaking to Jesus had the *basic* morality as he claimed to have kept the commandments, held to the concept of good coming from God, and wanted to do a good work to enter into heaven. But this man could not part with his possessions to follow Christ. He was focused on obeying a system and had deceived himself into thinking he had perfectly obeyed every command.

But he was missing something. He did not understand that the commandments pointed to Christ who fulfilled the law and is the epitome of good. Yet in his heart of hearts, this man chatting with Jesus realized he needed more. His hope was not in Christ, but in obeying a moral code to be good enough to be fit for heaven. What he did not realize is that the one who had already obeyed on his behalf was standing right in front of him. His own works, stained with his own sin and self-righteousness,

---

1. Scripture in this chapter is from the New King James Version (NKJV) of the Bible.

could never satisfy God's standard of perfect obedience. Only through Christ can we find the means to be good enough to inherit eternal life. This example shows how moralism invades even godly religion and makes it of no effect.

We find moralism influencing many unsuspecting people in church congregations. They often buy into this idea that if they are a "good person" or do some good works, then they will be saved in the end. But they are not good enough if they have committed even one sin. To go to heaven, you must be perfect — a standard none of us can achieve given our inherited sin nature and our individual choices to sin.

So is it impossible to go to heaven? One would think, but in steps, the Lord God helps us to do the impossible (Luke 18:27). Jesus, who is God, became a man and took our punishment upon Him through His shed blood. In doing so, Jesus was without sin and perfect. Those who receive Christ share in Christ's righteousness. His perfection is imputed (transferred) to us, so that we are seen as spotless and without blemish to enter heaven for eternity with God where we can share in His blessing and goodness (2 Corinthians 5:20–21).

Many within the Church mistake morality's role. They try to use morality to get to heaven or to find favor with God when the opposite is in order. It is because of our faith in Christ and the forgiveness we have received that we strive to be moral.

> Therefore gird up the loins of your mind, be sober, and rest your hope fully upon the grace that is to be brought to you at the revelation of Jesus Christ; as obedient children, not conforming yourselves to the former lusts, as in your ignorance; but as He who called you is holy, you also be holy in all your conduct, because it is written, "Be holy, for I am holy" (1 Peter 1:13–16).

Arbitrariness

Immanent moral religions like Buddhism, Confucianism, and any form of moralism, are *based on* human experience (man's ideas) unlike religions such as Hinduism, Taoism, Sikhism, etc., which go *beyond* human experience and rationality to establish a moral framework.

Any religion that comes from man (man's ideas) is arbitrary — man is simply not the absolute authority on any matter. Just because man says something is right or wrong doesn't mean it is. Many reading this may not realize how devastating this arbitrary nature is to an argument, but it shows it has no foundation beyond the changing opinions of men. Arbitrariness proves that something is without warrant (i.e., not a feasible defense).

It is as simple as that — moralistic religions are based on man's fallible opinions. When a moralistic religion states there is a moral code by which people should live, it is merely their *opinion*. How do they know that one person's opinion is absolute? They don't.

This is why moralistic religions have different rules and claims by which they make people (perhaps themselves) abide. Where one moral religion says not to murder or have multiple wives, another could say that murder and polygamy are acceptable within their allegedly moral religion. It is merely based on opinions and leads to the inconsistencies within a false worldview and between competing worldviews.

Some religions that are moralistic might claim that the sages of old (e.g., Confucius) or ancestors (mythological religions where ancestors became their gods like Oden, Zeus, Baal, etc.) have developed the code by which we are to live — but why trust their opinions? A potential response from those holding to moralistic religions might be, "But these ancients were exceptionally wise." To which we might respond, "By what standard? Your fallible *opinion*?"

Any way you slice the cake, moralistic religions are based on mere opinions. Furthermore, this is why there are so many of them — people's opinions vary. Having a lot of moralistic religions *is* a refutation of the underlying philosophy since they cannot all be right.

You need to understand that man's opinions are ultimately meaningless. If someone is of the opinion that 2+2=-3, who cares? Opinions have no merit in a debate or in determining truth from error. The only "opinion" that matters is the one that is grounded in ultimate reality. But in the moralistic religions, there is no absolute authority, creating a self-refuting position.

One might be tempted to say that this is a reversible argument to Christianity by *stating opinions* that Christians are also just offering arbitrary assertions for their theology, though they do not understand the Christian account.

In the Christian worldview, we have an absolute authority, God, who is not arbitrary by His very nature. That would be God's "opinion," which is the ultimate authority. He is not arbitrary but final and absolute. To object to this would be to appeal to a lesser, *arbitrary* authority and to claim to know more than God Himself.

God is the only one in a position to set true religious doctrine and moral standards. That perfect morality is demonstrated fully in Jesus Christ — and God said in Mark 9:7, "This is My beloved Son. Hear Him!" The point is that in the biblical worldview the reasoning is consistent and based in an ultimate authority and His revelations to us, but in the moralistic religious view we find inconsistency and arbitrary ideas, which produce a self-refuting worldview.

Inconsistency

The concept of inconsistency has to do with adhering to the law of non-contradiction — something cannot be both true and false at the same time in the same context. Why would moralistic religions hold to one person's opinions on matters of morality and not also take another person's opposing opinions on morality into account? When they allow these contradictions to exist, they become inconsistent, the second fatal flaw in these worldviews.

Inconsistencies within and between the Systems

Moralistic religions are inconsistent in two ways. First, there is no unity within the systems — they contradict themselves. Consider the words of Confucius:

> True wisdom is knowing what you don't know.[2]

Of course, if you are wise to know what you don't know, then you do know it. These are glaring inconsistencies that result from fallible men expressing ideas without full knowledge. Other moralistic religions also have inconsistencies. Consider when someone adheres to a moral code that says not to murder children and then turns around and supports abortion (the killing of children in the womb!).

The second inconsistency comes when we compare the systems to one another. While many of these systems will claim that other systems have a valid way of knowing truth, they wind up contradicting one another in significant ways. The boldest expression of this is the modern Unitarian Universalist Association, which allows its members to be atheists or polytheists and everything in between.

---

2. Confucius, Sayings of Confucius, http://www.goodreads.com/quotes/497572-true-wisdom-is-knowing-what-you-don-t-know.

The most important type of inconsistency is the failure to conform to the truth of the Bible. Any worldview that is not consistent with the revelation in the Bible is inherently false. If a worldview denies the Trinity or the fact that Jesus died to pay for the debt of sinners, they are false, contradicting the truth.

How Can One Be Perfected to Live Up to the "Code"?

We are told that we must live up to a particular code in moralistic religions like Confucianism or Buddhism. Of course, the problem is that no one lives up to that code. Thus, everyone is guilty of breaking that code and will continue to break that code. Therefore, everyone needs help to be able to live up to that code.

But this is not offered in these religions beyond looking inside yourself or seeking guidance from another imperfect person. What can make a person perfect and able to live up to the code? Nothing. And even if they could, that is not God's standard for redemption from our sinful nature and acts. We can never obey enough laws to be seen as righteous in God's eyes. There is truly no hope in these systems. These systems have no source of redemption, only a call to work harder and do more, even making up for wrongs done in past lives.

Hope for the Christian comes in the doctrine of redemption and union with Christ. Rather than trying to earn a righteous standing by following a moral law, Jesus Christ stepped into history as God in the flesh to take the punishment for our sin, rising on the third day for our justification. For those who repent and place their trust in Christ, God no longer sees them as failing to meet the standard, but as righteous through Christ (Isaiah 61:10). His blood and the work of the Holy Spirit are making us perfect (e.g., Galatians 3:3; Colossians 1:28, 4:12; Hebrews 12:23). The growth in holiness and the ability to do what is pleasing to God comes as a result of our redemption, not to gain it (Romans 8:1–8). This holiness arrives in its finality with a new heavens and new earth.

No Help for Past Wrongs

Another inconsistency is related to this. Even if one is able to live up to the code at some point, how have past wrong actions been dealt with? Let's use an extreme example here. Imagine that you murdered someone years ago. Now you try to live up to a code that says not to murder (and other positive actions).

How do you deal with the guilt for this past murder? How does justice work for the family of the murdered victim? What code of morality provides and satisfies for past wrongs? None. Moralistic religions just cannot consistently satisfy their own demands. Not doing wrong cannot make up for having done wrong.

Laws and Morality

Many try to follow the laws of a nation, believing they are "morally okay." But this is also inconsistent. There is a large difference between man-made laws and moral law as given by the absolute standard of God. Upon death, all will be judged by God's standard (Hebrews 9:27). They will not be judged based on the laws of the countries they lived in or the laws of the time they lived in. Christ will judge them based on His absolute Word and the standard of perfect righteousness.

Consider morality in Nazi Germany in the 1930s and 1940s. They had laws too, and what the leader Adolf Hitler did was *legal*, when he murdered millions and attacked nations in the hope of conquering the world. You see, the Nazis set the laws in their country and then they held these to be the standard of morality, murdering millions. They attacked all who held different sets of morality — particularly God's standard.

We observe similar things in our own Western countries today where certain government officials have passed laws to murder children (they call it abortion, but it simply means to end the life of a child) and impose the acceptance and promotion of homosexuality upon their respective realms. They even attack people who oppose such things as being immoral. The examples of governments promoting a false morality could be multiplied. Following man-made laws does not meet God's standard in the end. Apart from being found holy in Christ, the most obedient citizen of an earthly kingdom will not inhabit the heavenly kingdom.

Borrowing from God's Word (Openly or Inadvertently)

Moralistic religions have no valid basis for determining morality or offering hope for eternity. But we want people to realize something. Morality does exist, but it has nothing to do with moralistic religions and the wisdom of the sages. Morality exists because God exists and He determines morality. Any moralistic religion is therefore borrowing from God — whether they realize it or not.

Some might argue that Buddhists (or whomever) had no access to God's morality and yet they came up with some decent morals, so you can't say that they "borrowed it" from God. But this is false. In many cases, the moral codes agree with biblical morality. We would generally all agree that it is wrong to steal, murder, and rape. These things might in some cases encourage humanity to flourish for a short term in community, but if they are done for pragmatic reasons they are not pleasing to God (Romans 8:7–8). In other words, being good for goodness' sake is just arbitrary and does not please God. People have had access to God's Laws going back to early Genesis, and God made man in His own image with a knowledge of right and wrong (e.g., Genesis 1:26–27, 26:5).

Man has had knowledge of good and evil since the Garden of Eden (Genesis 3:22), being passed on from Noah after the Flood. Since God's Curse, man's fallible codes of behavior fail to perform properly, and men unrighteously suppress what they know to be true about God and His character (Romans 1:18–20). True morality is predicated on a true lawgiver, and that lawgiver is God alone.

Conclusion

If a religion is *moralistic*, they aren't hurting anyone so why oppose them? Actually, a moralistic religion is not moral, but immoral by God's standard. Redefined morality is not moral. As an example, consider marriage. Redefining marriage, which is a man and a woman by God's created standard, as anything else is endorsing what is immoral. But every man-made moral standard itself will be judged by God, and it will fall short of His perfect standard.

Many who have been entrenched in moralistic faiths (or one in particular) need to understand that they likely did it out of ignorance, as did their teachers before them. But the Lord has commanded those captured by a moralistic religion to repent and be converted that their sins may be blotted out. This is great news, as it can bring refreshment form the Lord and escape from the guilt of past sins, offering hope and redemption through the Lord Jesus Christ.

Chapter 8

Paganism

Pastor Tom Chesko

We Love Sin!

A young girl named Rachel decided to serve as a counselor at a Christian camp in the summer of 2014. She expected the usual mix of Christians who wanted to grow in their faith in an exciting environment, others undecided about what to believe who were there mainly for the fun, and some who were forced to go but didn't really want to be there at all.

What Rachel didn't expect was a few professing Wiccans (modern day pagan witches) who decided to make their beliefs known in a rather disturbing way. Acting in unison one night, they refused to obey the rules and began to shout, "We love sin." Campus security had to be called to quell the disturbance. The church group that brought the girls to camp was hoping to give them an exposure to the Christian way of life, not knowing what they truly believed.

This might be easy to write off as a few young girls seeking nothing more than attention, but their aberrant behavior was disturbing and frightening to other campers. Were they really part of the pagan community attracted to witchcraft? Probably not, because Wiccans do not believe in sin by Christian definition, but these young girls may have been familiar with Wicca to some extent and could very well adopt it as their personal expression of spirituality in the future.

Out of the Shadows

Paganism is a religion that has been experiencing growth in America since the 1960s, although the number of pagans is difficult to track. Many people don't openly admit to their belief in paganism, and pagans don't belong to denominations or structured religious groups. There are loose associations that cooperate, but paganism is an eclectic worldview that encompasses many specific views. You won't see a recognizable pagan meeting place like a church or synagogue, and pagans don't go door-to-door seeking converts like the Mormons and Jehovah's Witnesses.

Paganism is not as concerned about the growth and spread of their beliefs as much as the personal growth of the individual in what some simply refer to as "the craft." As a prelude, paganism can be expressed as ancient spiritism, Wicca, Druidism, witchcraft, polytheistic mythologies of the past, and a host of other variations.[1] In a practical sense, pagans value their own experience above all else. The majority of pagans are solitary and prefer to keep their religion to themselves. "Learning the craft" is being schooled in the beliefs and literature of the pagan way of life.

In a certain sense you don't become a pagan; you are a pagan. It is more of an inner discovery than a conversion. However, the Internet has helped pagans make their beliefs better known in a "try-before-you-buy" approach. It has moved paganism out of the closet — or should I say, the broom closet. Yes, brooms still have their place among the pagans, and not just at Halloween. They are used to symbolically sweep a place clean for certain rituals and in Wiccan handfast ceremonies.[2] In a handfast ceremony, two Wiccans make a binding commitment to each other for a certain period of time as a prelude to marriage, or the ceremony can be incorporated into an actual marriage ceremony. Sometimes the participants will jump over the broom at the end of the ceremony. When the bride and groom jump the broom at the end of the ceremony, they are sweeping the past away and jumping into their future together!

---

1. For specific information on groups referred to broadly as pagan, see the other chapters in this volume on Wicca, Norse and Germanic Mythology, Egyptian Mythology, and Greek and Roman Mythology.
2. The term may have come into English from the Old Norse word *handfesta*, which means "to strike a bargain."

Symbolism

Paganism employs many different symbols and symbolic actions like jumping the broom, but there is more to it than mere symbolism. Pagans will use various types of incense and candles on an altar to achieve certain objectives. Incense is believed to have therapeutic properties and is used in rites of purification. The same is true of essential oils, and various fragrant flowers and herbs are likewise employed to manipulate energies. An advertisement for a female human figure candle on the products page of a pagan online store called The Magickal Cat reads as follows:

> This reversible candle is made with black wax over red wax. Charged with reversing magic, it is intended to aid in returning negative energies and attentions to their source, leaving your enemies tasting what they have served. The female image in this candle can be particularly helpful if you are also calling upon the Goddess, using the candle to help protect a woman, or returning the negative energies in question to a woman.[3]

The Magickal Cat also sells a basic "Wiccan/Pagan altar set," scrying bowls, tarot cards, pendulums, spell-casting supplies, wands, gemstones, and your very own crystal ball, in addition to many other enchanting and exotic items to fill your pagan toolbox. It's kind of like an all-in-one, do-it-yourself pagan version of a home improvement store conveniently located on your computer. Pagans also use black cauldrons as pots to hold fire in which to brew potions. The witches' spell in Shakespeare's *Macbeth* contained the lines, "Double, double toil and trouble; Fire burn, and cauldron bubble."

Moving toward Paganism

The move out of the shadows by pagans can be seen by Christian apologists as a good thing in some ways, because it also reveals the darkness of paganism masquerading as light. The Bible gives repeated warnings about Satan's strategy to deceive in this manner (2 Corinthians 11:14). He is the "father

---

3. The Magickal Cat, accessed October 21, 2015, http://www.themagickalcat.com/Candle-Human-Figure-Female-Reversible-p/chrevf.htm.

of lies" (John 8:44). The world of false religion has many different shades of deception, and the lure of a powerful personal experience is a particularly attractive hue. Satan's first great lie to Eve in Genesis 3:5 included the promise of power and great enlightenment: "For God doth know that in the day ye eat thereof, then your eyes shall be opened, and ye shall be as gods, knowing good and evil."[4] This is what makes paganism so dangerous and attracts so many people to the New Age movement.

In addition, people are gullible by nature and tend toward sinful desires, especially those who are more open-minded to spiritual matters and personal growth apart from the wisdom and discernment that come from God's Word. Just witness the constant bombardment of products that the average person is subjected to every day. The advertisers know that if they can offer you something to enhance your life, it will probably sell. Highlight the benefits of a certain product and put it in an attractive package and people will buy it. It's a basic sales pitch, and Satan has a great marketing strategy to enlarge his kingdom of the cults and the occult.[5] Infomercials work because the claim is "Here is what I can do for you now." Paganism has the same message: "Here is what I can do for you now." The payoff is in this world, not a world to come.

People who have been disenchanted with organized religion constitute another class of potential pagans. They have tried other religious products, so to speak, and they did not work for them. These spiritual dropouts from the more traditional faiths may find the paganism packaging attractive, and when they buy it, they also find acceptance and encouragement to express their own beliefs rather than conform to a standard. They no longer feel like *outsiders*; they have become *insiders*. It's like belonging to a special club with all kinds of nice perks without the baggage of membership standards and dues.

Furthermore, the pagan man or woman can climb the ladder of paganism as high as they desire to go. There is no "top rung," and there is nothing like the clergy-laity separation they likely experienced in organized religion. Each person belongs to the priestly class in paganism, although advancement in the pagan covens (esbats) may take time. The prominent American pagan witch

---

4. All Scripture in this chapter is from the King James Version (KJV) of the Bible.
5. In general, the occult refers to gaining secret knowledge through spiritual practices. In paganism, this comes through channeling energies and spirits as well as entering altered states of consciousness. The occult is generally viewed by Christians as dealing with the supernatural realm of Satan and demons influencing humans through religious practices and rites.

Starhawk defined the coven as "a Witches support group, consciousness-raising group, psychic study center, College of mysteries, surrogate clan, and religious congregation all rolled into one."[6] On her personal web page under the listing "About Starhawk" we find the following:

- Starhawk is one of the most respected voices in modern earth-based spirituality. She is also well-known as a global justice activist and organizer, whose work and writings have inspired many to action.

- Starhawk is perhaps best known as an articulate pioneer in the revival of earth-based spirituality and Goddess religion. She is a cofounder of Reclaiming, an activist branch of modern Pagan religion, and continues to work closely with the Reclaiming community. Her archives are maintained at the Graduate Theological Union library in Berkeley, California.

- Starhawk is a veteran of progressive movements, from anti-war to anti-nukes, and is deeply committed to bringing the techniques and creative power of spirituality to political activism.

- Starhawk travels internationally teaching magic, the tools of ritual, and the skills of activism. She lives part-time in San Francisco, in a collective house with her partner and friends, and part-time in a little hut in the woods in western Sonoma County, California, where she practices permaculture in her extensive gardens, and writes.[7]

Like many traditional religions, paganism does not discriminate on the basis of age or gender, and women constitute the majority of pagans overall. This should not come as a surprise given the fact that in a masculine-dominated society, there are women seeking liberation and empowerment. Among the open-minded, the young spiritual explorers often dabble in some form of paganism often influenced by its prevalence and positive portrayals in popular media. Catherine Sanders notes, "The book *Teen Witch: Wicca for a New*

---

6. Helen A. Berger, "The Coven: Perfect Love, Perfect Trust," *A Community of Witches Contemporary Neo-paganism and Witchcraft in the United States* (Columbia, SC: University of South Carolina Press, 1999), p. 54.

7. "Starhawk," Transition United States, accessed October 21, 2015, http://transitionus.org/starhawk.

Generation has sold more copies for occult publisher Llewellyn than any other in its 95-year history."[8] Ruth La Ferla writes of two teenage witches:

> Ms. Trayer and Ms. Haddad-Friedman are members of a movement gaining an ardent following among teenagers, mostly girls, who are in part captivated by the glossy new image of witches portrayed on television shows and in the movies. No longer the hideous, wart-covered crone of folklore and fairy tale, witches in hit television shows like "Charmed," starring Shannen Doherty, and the 1996 movie "The Craft," a favorite with teenagers at video stores, are avatars of glamour, power and style. Other youthful adherents of Wicca, seeking an alternative path to spirituality, are attracted by the craft's lack of structure and dogma.[9]

Paganism and the Wiccan Connection

The term *pagan* comes from a Latin word for "country or village dweller" and was first used in the early Christian era in a broad sense to refer to the unconverted. In current usage, the word *pagan* is often associated with someone who behaves contrary to established norms. We often envision pagans as people with multiple body piercings, brightly colored hair, strange tattoos, and strange music. That stereotype does an injustice to the true nature of paganism; it's not about a certain outward appearance. You might find pagans fitting that mold, but you will also find them dressed in casual clothes or a business suit. They are typically middle class, educated, and come from all walks of life.

In the religious or spiritual sense, modern paganism, often referred to as neo-paganism, is more concentrated in Britain, North America, Australia, and New Zealand, according to author Barbara Jane Davy.[10] Although paganism is definitely not a mainstream religion like Protestantism, Catholicism, Buddhism, Islam, or Hinduism, pagans see it differently. They believe that paganism is the original religion from which all other religions eventually developed. This is not the case (as various forms of paganism are actually a

8. Catherine Sanders, "The Hidden Traps of Wicca," Focus on the Family, accessed October 21, 2015, http://www.focusonthefamily.com/parenting/teens/hidden-traps-of-wicca.

9. Ruth La Ferla, "Like Magic, Witchcraft Charms Teenagers," *New York Times*, February 13, 2000.

10. Barbara Jane Davy, *Introduction to Pagan Studies* (Lanham, MD: AltaMira Press, 2007), p. 3.

Cadet Chapel Falcon Circle, located on the hill top between the Academy Visitors Center and the Cadet Chapel, is dedicated May 6, 2011.
(Wikimedia Commons, U.S. Air Force/Photo by Mike Kaplan)

corruption of the truth as it was passed down since Noah), but there is an association of the word *pagan* with ancient religious traditions and heritage.

Some Wiccans refer to Wicca as the "Old Religion." Gerald Gardner, an Englishman, is considered the man who did the most to popularize modern Witchcraft and establish the Wiccan traditions beginning in the late 1930s. He said that the "Old Religion" had followers who preceded him, the religion having survived from the Middle Ages. However, Gardner's credibility is not without its doubters. In an essay titled, "History of Wicca in England: 1939 to the Present Day," author Julia Phillips, a Wiccan high priestess writes:

> Of course we can never really know the truth about the origins of the Wicca. Gardner may have been an utter fraud; he may have actually received a "Traditional" initiation; or, as a number of people have suggested, he may have created the Wicca as a result of a genuine religious experience, drawing upon his extensive literary and magical knowledge to create, or help create, the rites and philosophy. What I think we can be fairly certain about is that he was sincere in his belief. If there had been no more to the whole thing than an old man's fantasy, then the Wicca would not have grown to be the force that it is today.[11]

---

11. Adapted from a talk Phillips gave at the Australian Wiccan Conference in Canberra, 1991.

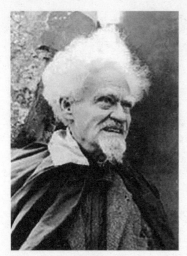

Gerald Gardner

Gardner's book, *Witchcraft Today*, published in 1954, was instrumental in the growth of American paganism, although he certainly leaned on others in his writing. He borrowed some of the rituals, which he incorporated into Wicca from a variety of sources including a Rosicrucian group, Kabbalah (a mystical offshoot of Judaism), the works of Aleister Crowley, and Free Masonry. For example, Gardner adopted the three-degree initiation rite of the Masonic order in his witchcraft.

Two of Gardner's followers, Rosemary and Raymond Buckland, established a coven in New York in 1964. In 1968, Buckland opened the Museum of Witchcraft and Magick on Long Island, New York. He has authored over 50 books, both fiction and nonfiction, the majority of them about witchcraft and magic. Wicca now had a foothold on American soil and would eventually spread westward. The first large gathering of pagans in the United States occurred in 1979 at the Pan-Pagan Festival in Indiana. These festivals provide a place and time for pagans to come together in a supportive environment to learn from one another and develop their individual skills in the craft.

Pagan Origins and Diversity

Wiccans comprise just a slice of the diverse pie of paganism that is composed of many different strands and elements of ancient and modern beliefs, some of which are identified in the Bible. When the Israelites entered the land of Canaan (the Promised Land), they saw an agriculturally prosperous region inhabited by people who worshiped nature gods and goddesses. The Canaanites attributed their agricultural success to these gods and goddesses who had power over the land.

Cuneiform tablets describing the Canaanite gods, including the chief god Baal ("lord" or "master"), were discovered in the Canaanite city of Ugarit (Ras Shamra), located in modern Syria.[12] Baal was a god who was believed to control the weather.

---

12. Excavations at Ras Shamra began in 1929.

The Ugaritic tablets credit Baal with sending the rains that make the land fruitful. He is called, "Prince, the Lord of the Earth," and "Baal, the Mighty One." In the texts Baal is also connected to the morning dew. 1 Aqht I, 42–46 says,

> Seven years shall Baal fail,
> eight the rider of the clouds.
> There shall be no dew, no rain;
> no surging of the two depths,
> neither the goodness of Baal's voice.[13]

Baal was sometimes pictured with a horned helmet that symbolized power and strength but is not to be equated with the image of a horned devil. If the Israelites could compromise their faith and worship these heathen deities, perhaps the ground would bring forth a plentiful harvest and they too would prosper economically as the Canaanites had. It was a strong temptation they could not resist.

The Book of Judges is a testimony to the apostasy of Israel during this early time in their history. During the lifetime of Joshua, the children of Israel followed the Lord, but things changed for the worse after his death:

> And Joshua the son of Nun, the servant of the LORD, died, being an hundred and ten years old. And they buried him in the border of his inheritance in Timnathheres, in the mount of Ephraim, on the north side of the hill Gaash. And also all that generation were gathered unto their fathers: and there arose another generation after them, which knew not the LORD, nor yet the works which he had done for Israel. And the children of Israel did evil in the sight of the LORD, and served Baalim: And they forsook the LORD God of their fathers, which brought them out of the land of Egypt, and followed other gods, of the gods of the people that were round about them, and bowed themselves unto them, and provoked the LORD to anger (Judges 2:8–12).

Elijah's dramatic confrontation with the false prophets of Baal was a divine rebuke and judgment of Baal worship; it was actually the God of Israel who brought rain to the land (2 Kings 18). Although many things have changed

---

13. Allen Ross, "The Miracles of Elijah and Elisha," Christian Leadership Center, accessed October 21, 2015, http://www.christianleadershipcenter.org/elijah.htm.

in the world since the Canaanites disappeared from history, paganism continued in the polytheism of the Greco-Roman gods/goddesses and their Celtic, Nordic, and Druid counterparts. The gods of Greece and Rome, which New Testament Christianity encountered, were all based on pagan mythology, rather than divine revelation. In the -isms of the world, animism, shamanism, Shintoism, and occultism all have their roots in religious beliefs going back a long time.

Other offshoots of the stream of paganism would include Native American religions, pantheism, and Totemism. Totemism is a system of belief in which humans are said to have kinship or a mystical relationship with a spirit being, such as an animal or plant.[14]

In an abstract on Canaanite Religion published in 2006, K.L. Noll from Brandon University states the following:

> Religion in an ancient Near Eastern context consisted of (1) acknowledgment of a supernatural reality usually defined as a god or gods, (2) reverence for objects, places, and times considered sacred, that is, separated from ordinary objects, places, and times, (3) regularly repeated ritual activities for a variety of purposes, including ritual magic, (4) conformance to stipulations alleged to have been revealed by the supernatural reality, (5) communication with the supernatural through prayer and other activity, (6) experience of feelings described by participants as awe, fear, mystery, etc., (7) integration of items 1–6 into a holistic, though not necessarily systematic, worldview, and (8) association with, and conformity of one's own life priorities to, a group of like-minded people.[15]

Noll's analysis, while true of many religions to some degree, fits well with neo-paganism as well. Sacred altars and shrines, places, days, ritual magic, meditation, divination, a sense of mystery, etc., all have a part in the lives of those who practice some expression of paganism. At the heart of it all is the attempt to make contact with the divine or essential world surrounding the practitioner. Immanence rather than transcendence is a key concept of paganism. The divine is seen as nature (pantheism) or in nature (panentheism) rather than a god/being that exists apart from nature. This idea of

14. For more information on these specific views, see chapter 12 in this volume.
15. K.L. Knoll, "Canaanite Religion," *Religion Compass* 1/1(2007):61–92.

immanence is the foundation for the experiential nature of pagan beliefs — connecting to nature is connecting to the divine.

Back to Nature

In paganism, nature is the temple of the sacred, so pagans, ancient and modern, attach deep reverence to the natural world, which leads many of them to be active in environmental causes today. In Greek mythology, Gaia (or Gaea) was the earth goddess who originated, or created herself, out of primordial chaos. According to some legends she gave birth to Pontus (the sea) and Uranus (the sky). Hesiod the poet wrote, "She [Gaia] bore also the fruitless deep with his raging swell, Pontus, without sweet union of love."[16] Earth Day, which has been celebrated in America since April of 1970, has become a pagan holiday of sorts.

> The spirit of Earth Day 1970 did not just happen; its roots could include the gradual stirring of environmental consciousness that accelerated in the 1960s, but that stirring itself had deeper roots in an American consciousness of a special relationship with the land, even if that relationship was often abusive. Still, if there was a year when Wicca (in the broad sense) became "nature religion," as opposed to the "mystery religion" or "metaphorical fertility religion," labels that it had brought from England, that year was 1970.[17]

Neo-pagan Gus di Zerega states:

> I think Earth Day is a particularly important moment for contemplation and commitment by us Pagans. Often American Christian critics accuse us of "pantheism," and in an important respect they are right. We do find the sacred, most of us, in the earth without reference to any transcendental spiritual force. In my mind there is a transcendental dimension as well, but it is not needed at all for us to honor the earth as sacred.[18]

---

16. "The Theogony of Hesiod," translated by Evelyn-White, accessed October 21, 2015, http://www.sacred-texts.com/cla/hesiod/theogony.htm.

17. Chas Clifton, *Her Hidden Children: The Rise of Wicca and Paganism in America* (Lanham, MD: AltaMira Press, 2006), p. 43.

18. Gus DiZerega, "Earth Day and the Sacredness of the Earth," *A Pagan's Blog,* Beliefnet, April 1, 2012, accessed October 21, 2015, http://www.beliefnet.com/columnists/apagansblog/2012/04/earth-day-and-the-sacredness-of-the-earth.html#more-1346.

Former Vice-President Al Gore is an environmental crusader and "prophet" of a global ecological crisis, who holds the view that earth does not belong to man, man belongs to the earth. This is the very opposite of what we find written in the first book of the Bible:

> And God said, Let us make man in our image, after our likeness: and let them have dominion over the fish of the sea, and over the fowl of the air, and over the cattle, and over all the earth, and over every creeping thing that creepeth upon the earth (Genesis 1:26).

Christians must be good stewards of God's creation, but the earth was made for man, not man for the earth. To be a good steward of the earth is to care for it as a gift and responsibility given to mankind from God. But Al Gore sees things a little differently. For him, there is a spiritual connection to the earth that was lost. He envisions a revival of interest in the belief that the earth is our Mother. In his *New York Times* best seller, *Earth in the Balance: Ecology and the Human Spirit*, Gore wrote:

> We feel increasingly distant from our roots in the earth. In one sense, civilization itself has been on a journey from its foundations in the world of nature to an ever more contrived, controlled, and manufactured world of our own imitative and sometimes arrogant design. . . . At some point during this journey we lost our feeling of connectedness to the rest of nature. We now dare now to wonder: Are we so unique and powerful as to be essentially separate from the Earth?[19]

Here Gore emphasizes the idea of regaining a "connection to nature." Our separation (distance) from the earth must be bridged. This is pagan thinking in a thinly veiled disguise.

It is similar to the New Age belief that "only the unity of all can bring about the well being of all."

In his speeches, Gore frequently reminds his audience of the need to seek the diversity and spiritual wealth that can be gleamed from the teachings and traditions of many different faiths. Paganism does not claim to be

---

19. Al Gore, *Earth in the Balance: Ecology and the Human Spirit* (New York: Houghton Mifflin, 1992), p. 1.

the one true way, just another way leading to some divine source. This is the syncretism of paganism, but their "openness" only goes so far. Pagans have no fondness for Christianity! Article X of The Principles of Wiccan Belief drawn up by the American Council of Witches in 1974 stated that Wiccans object to Christianity's claim to be the only way. But Jesus unapologetically made that very claim in the Gospel of John, and we find it essentially reiterated in Acts:

> I am the way, the truth, and the life: no man cometh unto the Father, but by me (John 14:6).

> Neither is there salvation in any other; for there is none other name under heaven given among men, whereby we must be saved (Acts 4:12).

Pagans would vigorously deny this assertion by and about Jesus Christ.

May the Force Be with You

Unlike systematized religions, paganism is primarily rooted in personal experience and power utilizing various forces of energy and nature to create beneficial changes in self, the life of fellow human beings, and the planet. Some shamans (spiritual mediators) identify this as a luminous energy field consisting of four layers: the spirit, the soul (psychic), the mental (emotional), and the physical (the body). As a form of paganism, the shaman works on the energy field to bring about a state of well-being. Anthropologist Michael Harner, a practicing shaman, describes his role in this fashion:

> The shaman moves between realities, a magical athlete of states of consciousness . . . a power-broker in the sense of manipulating spiritual power to help people, to put them in a state of equilibrium.[20]

To be a pagan is to be in charge of individual spiritual transformation through a variety of means at your disposal. There are chants, charms, spells, rituals, drumming, meditation, dance, and other such practices that all can be customized for the individual or group. These are the sacred rituals of

---

20. Michael Harner, *The Way of the Shaman* (New York, NY: Bantam New Age Books, 1982), p. 56.

paganism. They also have their holy days (sabbats) and seasons (of feasting and magic).

Pagans tend to believe that if things can be changed on an individual level, they can ultimately be changed on a universal level by "skilled practitioners" who collectively seek to improve mankind and the universe itself. It sounds far-fetched, and it is, but before you dismiss paganism as an insignificant system of beliefs (i.e., a religion), remember that just as the blind religion of evolution supposedly requires lots of time to bring about changes, the cosmic flow of positive energy takes time to redirect for the good of all. This is pagan thinking that borrows from a variety of sources from New Age to animism to Greek mythology.

The earth is supposed to have been around for a long time, so the pagan sees his religion more in the long term. He or she is just part of the circle of life occupying a sacred place on a planet in a vast universe for a certain amount of time and making the best of it. And for many, the pagan lifestyle is entertaining in the short term. It's like Halloween every day. They take their paganism seriously but have fun doing it. Just think of how many children and adults were spellbound by J.K. Rowling's *Harry Potter* books with sales totaling in the hundreds of millions. Fantasy yes, but some Potter fanatics delved deeper and deeper into the pagan, occult world of spiritual darkness.

According to a 2011 census, "Jedi" is now the most popular faith in the Other Religions category in England and Wales, taking seventh place among all the major world religions.[21] It is a church inspired by George Lucas' *Star Wars* films. The website of the Jedi Church states:

> The Jedi church believes that there is one powerful force [energy field] that binds all things in the universe together. The Jedi religion is something innate inside every one of us, the Jedi Church believes that our sense of morality is innate. So quiet your mind and listen to the force within you.[22]

---

21. Henry Taylor, " 'Jedi' religion most popular alternative faith," *The Telegraph,* December 11, 2012, http://www.telegraph.co.uk/news/religion/9737886/Jedi-religion-most-popular-alternative-faith.html.

22. Description on the Homepage at http://www.jedichurch.org, accessed October 21, 2015.

As the familiar saying goes, "buyer beware" — the Jedi religion is paganism pure and simple. The Jedi Church even warns its members to be cautious of the dark side of the force. It's territory that no Jedi should dare to enter. But how is someone to know when he crosses over from the light side of the force to the dark side by simply listening to the voice within? By what standard can good and bad be judged in this pagan belief? It would be arbitrary to assert some absolute good or evil in a religion where no absolutes, like the claims of Jesus Christ, are tolerated! In truth, there is no such thing as a light side of paganism. It's all darkness and it is a consuming darkness, like voodoo, which originated in sub-Saharan Africa that claims to be used to heal or to harm.

Pagan Polytheism

Paganism has some lofty spiritual goals, but it amounts to false worship based on teachings that are contrary to the Christian faith. It is both polytheistic (a belief in many gods) and pantheistic (all is god). It sprang from the seeds of polytheism sown in many different soils as people spread across the globe after the dispersion at Babel (Genesis 11). The pagan pantheon is composed of a variety of gods and goddesses, and the pagan may establish a close relationship with one or more of these gods. The spread of Hinduism in the West has also contributed much to the development of pagan thought and practice. An article on the history of modern paganism on the British Broadcasting Corporation website highlights this fact:

> The 1960s and 1970s were times of radical social change. Hinduism and Taoism helped shape contemporary Paganism as the hippy trail led people to become interested in Eastern religions and philosophies. North Americans rediscovered Native American traditions and the Afro-American traditions of Santeria, Candomble, and Vodoun. Paganism found an ally in the ecological and feminist movements of the 1960s. Pagan philosophies appealed to many eco-activists, who also saw Nature as sacred and recognized the Great Goddess as Mother Nature. The image of the witch was taken up by feminists as a role-model of the independent powerful woman, and the single Great Goddess as the archetype of women's inner strength and dignity.[23]

---

23. "History of Modern Paganism: Renaissance and Revival," BBC Religions, accessed October 21, 2015, http://www.bbc.co.uk/religion/religions/paganism/history/modern_1. shtml.

Thou Shalt Have No other Gods

The first commandment that God gave to Moses on Mount Sinai was: "I am the LORD thy God, which have brought thee out of the land of Egypt, out of the house of bondage. Thou shalt have no other gods before me" (Exodus 20:2–3). The Israelites were also warned about the diverse occult practices of the nations they would encounter:

> When thou art come into the land which the LORD thy God giveth thee, thou shalt not learn to do after the abominations of those nations. There shall not be found among you any one that maketh his son or his daughter to pass through the fire, or that useth divination, or an observer of times, or an enchanter, or a witch. Or a charmer, or a consulter with familiar spirits, or a wizard, or a necromancer. For all that do these things are an abomination unto the LORD: and because of these abominations the LORD thy God doth drive them out from before thee (Deuteronomy 18:9–12).

Rather than obey God, the Israelites failed to heed the Word of the Lord and fell into pagan idol worship and spiritism — the very thing God had warned them against in Deuteronomy 4:15–19. King Saul even went so far as to seek counsel from a medium called the witch of Endor (1 Samuel 28:1–8). In the New Testament, we read about Paul's trip to ancient Athens and the grief he experienced over what he saw: "Now while Paul waited for them at Athens, his spirit was stirred in him, when he saw the city wholly given to idolatry" (Acts 17:16). In Romans 1, we learn that when people fail to worship God as their Creator, they begin to worship the creation:

> For the invisible things of him from the creation of the world are clearly seen, being understood by the things that are made, even his eternal power and Godhead; so that they are without excuse: Because that, when they knew God, they glorified him not as God, neither were thankful; but became vain in their imaginations, and their foolish heart was darkened. Professing themselves to be wise, they became fools, and changed the glory of the uncorruptible God into an image made like to corruptible man, and to birds, and fourfooted beasts, and creeping things (Romans 1:20–23).

Christian author A.W. Tozer put it well: "Wrong ideas about God are only the fountain from which the polluted waters of idolatry flow; they are themselves idolatrous. The idolater simply imagines things about God and acts as if they were true."[24] The irrationalism of paganism is the belief in the multiplicity of gods, or no gods at all. Not all pagans believe the same about deity and divinity. Some make a distinction between the terms. Davy writes:

> "Deity" is a nonspecific word for divine beings, goddesses and gods, and The God and the Godess. Divinity is a more generic word for the sacred, not necessarily quantifiable as a distinct class of beings. Practitioners generally feel that belief in divinity is not a useful way of looking at Pagan religious practice, pointing to the strangeness of the idea one must "believe" in something to relate to it.[25]

Norm Geisler notes:

> Some neopagans debate about the ontological state of their "gods," assigning an idealistic or aesthetic role to them. But as one put it, "All these things are within the realm of possibility. It has been our nature to call these 'god.' "[26]

The confusion over the reality and nature of the gods in paganism is not a matter of confusion in the Scriptures. There is only one true God who created all things; all other gods and goddesses are false gods. They have no existence:

> For though there be that are called gods, whether in heaven or in earth, (as there be gods many, and lords many,) But to us there is but one God, the Father, of whom are all things, and we in him; and one Lord Jesus Christ, by whom are all things, and we by him. Howbeit there is not in every man that knowledge (1 Corinthians 8:5–7).

---

24. A.W. Tozer, Tozer Devotional, "The Essence of Idolatry," accessed October 21, 2015, https://www.cmalliance.org/devotions/tozer?id=1301.
25. Davy, *Introduction to Pagan Studies,* p. 14.
26. Norman Geisler, *Baker Encyclopedia of Christian Apologetics,* 1st ed., "Neopaganism" (Grand Rapids, MI: Baker Books, 1998), p. 523.

This is the pagan's real problem. They have no knowledge of the truth found in God's revelation of Holy Scripture and so they have opened themselves up to lying spirits posing as ancestral spirits, gods, goddesses, or other entities. "Now the Spirit speaketh expressly, that in the latter times some shall depart from the faith, giving heed to seducing spirits, and doctrines of devils" (1 Timothy 4:1). Christian researcher Dave Hunt sounds the warning:

> In all pagan/nature religions there is a presumed cause-and-effect relationship between the ritual or ceremony performed and the obtaining of the power or healing or other blessing sought. The whole idea of pagan ceremonies — the rites of the shaman or witch, the burning of candles, the making of potions, the use of fetishes, etc. — is that they will (if done correctly) elicit a response from the gods or spirits.[27]

The further one goes down the path of spiritual deception, the harder it is to escape because paganism is one of Satan's strongholds — it is a lie masquerading as enlightenment (2 Corinthians 11:4). The only hope for someone lost in its maze is the truth concerning Jesus Christ. He is the true light of the world who promised that those who follow him will not walk in darkness, but shall have the light of life (John 8:12).

The Pagan View of Jesus

One of the tests of a lying spirit is what it professes about Jesus:

> Who is a liar but he that denieth that Jesus is the Christ? He is antichrist, that denieth the Father and the Son. Whosoever denieth the Son, the same hath not the Father: he that acknowledgeth the Son hath the Father also (1 John 2:22–23).

Many pagans believe that Jesus did live at one time and was skilled in magical arts, which he passed on to his disciples, but that's as far as most pagans take it. Ultimately, the answer to the question "who is Jesus?" would invoke a variety of opinions depending on the pagan you talk to (i.e., each may have a different opinion). For the most part, Jesus hardly appears on the pagan radar screen. He is not part of their belief system. But I must ask, "How can He be so ignored by so many pagans?" The

27. Dave Hunt, "Native, Indigenous, and Nature Religion," *Occult Invasion* (Eugene, OR: Harvest House, 1998), p. 145.

American statesman Daniel Webster wrote: "All that is best in the civilization of today, is the fruit of Christ's appearance among men."[28] And Webster is not alone in recognizing the significance of Jesus Christ:

> I find the name of Jesus Christ written on the top of every page of modern history. (Historian George Bancroft)[29]

> I am an historian, I am not a believer, but I must confess as a historian that this penniless preacher from Nazareth is irrevocably the very center of history. Jesus Christ is easily the most dominant figure in all history. (Author H.G. Wells)[30]

> As the centuries pass by, the evidence is accumulating that measured by its effect on history, Jesus is the most influential life ever lived on this planet. (Historian Kenneth Scott Latourette)[31]

> All history is incomprehensible without Christ. (Historian Ernest Renan)[32]

> As a child I received instruction both in the Bible and in the Talmud. I am a Jew, but I am enthralled by the luminous figure of the Nazarene. . . . No one can read the Gospels without feeling the actual presence of Jesus. His personality pulsates in every word. No myth is filled with such life. (Albert Einstein)[33]

One thing that can be said for certain is that no pagan myth has the power to give life like Jesus did. In their defiance, pagans do not acknowledge Jesus as the Divine Son of God who came into the world to give them spiritual life. To possess spiritual life is what it means to be born again (John 3:5–7; 1 Peter 1:23; James 1:18).

---

28. Martin Manser, *The Westminster Collection of Christian Quotations,* 1st ed. (Louisville, KY: Westminster John Knox, 2001), p. 351.

29. J. Gilchrist Lawson, *Greatest Thoughts about Jesus Christ* (New York: George H. Doran, 1919), p. 122.

30. P.J. Clarke, *Lives That Made a Difference* (Cork: Publish on Demand Global LLC, 2012), p. 10.

31. Josh McDowell, *The New Evidence That Demands a Verdict* (Nashville, TN: Thomas Nelson, 1999), p. 321.

32. Britton H. Tabor, *Skepticism Assailed* (New York: S.S. Wood, 1895), p. 49–50.

33. George Viereck, "What Life Means to Einstein," *Saturday Evening Post,* October 26, 1929, p. 117.

Rejecting Christ, pagans stumble into their own destruction because Jesus said: "If ye believe not that I am he, ye shall die in your sins" (John 8:24). If you die in your sins, pagan or otherwise, you will spend eternity separated from the God in the lake of fire (Revelation 20:14).

Hell is not a state of mind; it's a place that was prepared by God for the devil and his angels (Matthew 25:41). Pagans may scoff at the idea of a literal hell and eternal punishment, but Jesus didn't. And if they refuse to repent (turn from their sin) and receive Jesus as Lord and Savior, they will ultimately learn of hell's awful reality. Most of what we know of hell in the New Testament comes from Christ's lips. In Revelation 1:18, Jesus said he had the controlling keys of death and hades (hell): "I am he that liveth, and was dead; and, behold, I am alive for evermore, Amen; and have the keys of hell and of death."

Notice that the one who holds the keys of hell and death is the one who conquered death. Jesus was not a wise sage, or spiritual teacher who came on the scene and died like all men. Though He died on a Roman Cross, He rose from the dead and presently sits in the position of all authority at the right hand of His Father in heaven on the throne of God (Ephesians 1:17–20). All authority is His (Matthew 28:18). Christ's Resurrection from the dead was proof that He is the eternal Son of God (Romans 1:4) and the foundation upon which the Christian faith rests. Without the Resurrection of Christ there would be no Christianity (1 Corinthians 15:13–19). One day the resurrected, historical Jesus is coming to judge the living and the dead.

The biblical case for the deity of Jesus is easy to make from Scripture (e.g., John 1; Colossians 1; Hebrews 1; etc.), but church history also affirms the fact. Quote after quote from Christian writers following the death of Apostles could be cited in this regard. Even some non-Christian sources testify to the Resurrection (e.g., the Jewish historian Josephus). I will not make the effort to do that here.

The belief in Jesus as divine was a fundamental doctrine of the early church and remains so today. Only those who were called heretics denied that Jesus was God manifest in the flesh. He suffered and died on the Cross as Savior of the world, rose again on the third day, ascended into heaven, and sits at the right hand of the father, waiting for the time He will come to judge the world in righteousness and establish His Kingdom. Contrary to some pagans' claims, the Council of Nicaea in A.D. 325 did not invent the doctrine of the deity of Christ. Rather, the Council affirmed the apostolic teaching of who Christ is, "The one true God and the Second Person of the Trinity." The proclamation states:

> We believe in one God, the Father Almighty, Maker of heaven and earth, and of all things visible and invisible.
>
> And in one Lord Jesus Christ, the only-begotten Son of God, begotten of the Father before all worlds; God of God, Light of Light, very God of very God; begotten, not made, being of one substance with the Father, by whom all things were made.
>
> Who, for us men for our salvation, came down from heaven, and was incarnate by the Holy Spirit of the virgin Mary, and was made man; and was crucified also for us under Pontius Pilate; He suffered and was buried; and the third day He rose again, according to the Scriptures; and ascended into heaven, and sits on the right hand of the Father; and He shall come again, with glory, to judge the quick and the dead; whose kingdom shall have no end.[34]

There Is No Salvation in Paganism

> God so loved the world, that he gave his only begotten Son, that whosoever believeth in him should not perish, but have everlasting life. For God sent not his Son into the world to condemn the world; but that the world through him might be saved (John 3:16–17).

Many people have seen John 3:16 on a placard at a sporting event, but, like the general population, have become so accustomed to the message that it is largely ignored. But it should not be ignored; it is a message about the grace of God to pardon sinners so they can become the heirs of salvation. However, since pagans do not recognize the biblical view of sin — an offense against a Holy God for which he or she is accountable — they believe there is no need for salvation. So where does that leave them? All dressed up in pagan garb and nowhere to go?

Do they depart this life for another state of consciousness? Will they face another life on earth as taught in reincarnation? Once again, pagans are free to decide for themselves what happens *when*, not *if*, they die, and some

---

34. Philip Schaff, *The Creeds of Christendom*, 6th ed., Vol. 1. (Grand Rapids, MI: Baker Book House, 1996), p. 27–28.

of them put the afterlife in the category of useless speculation that detracts from the joy of living. But how do they really know? Any answer they give is merely *arbitrary* and hence, logically fallacious. To the pagan, dying, after all, is just as natural as living; it is for the human what it is for a tree. It's part of sacred evolution; death as a return to the nature of one's elements. This is a pagan postulate. But what does the Scripture say?

> It is appointed unto men once to die, but after this the judgment (Hebrews 9:27).

Death is not an end to all existence as individuals, and there will be no second chances after death for those who die without Christ. Right now, pagans, as well as all people alive, are in a "grace period," if you will. We all deserve to suffer eternal separation from our Creator for the sins we have committed against His divine law. The good news is that Jesus bore the punishment for our sins on the Cross, and salvation is freely available to all who believe. This is why Christians are missionary minded: "Knowing therefore the terror of the Lord, we persuade men" (2 Corinthians 5:11). We want people, including pagans, to be saved!

The terror of the Lord is real, but for the Christian, death holds no uncertainty or apprehension: "We are confident, I say, and willing rather to be absent from the body, and to be present with the Lord" (2 Corinthians 5:8). Death has lost its power over those who belong to Jesus Christ (1 Corinthians 15:55–56). It will be a wonderful day of rejoicing when faith in Christ is turned into sight:

> But as it is written, Eye hath not seen, nor ear heard, neither have entered into the heart of man, the things which God hath prepared for them that love him. But God hath revealed them unto us by his Spirit: for the Spirit searcheth all things, yea, the deep things of God (1 Corinthians 2:9–10).

In paganism, since no single belief in the afterlife is normative, nobody knows for sure what will occur. This uncertainty comes from a lack of an authoritative revelation. Pagans think they have an ultimate spiritual destination in mind, whatever they may call it, but they have no reliable map to get them there. Christian philosopher Gordon Clark underscores the dilemma of pagan religion:

The beclouding effects of sin upon the mind as it tries to discover God and salvation in nature may best be seen in the divergent results obtained among the pagan religions. The ancient Babylonians, Egyptians, and Romans looked on the same nature that is seen by the modern Moslem, Hindu, and Buddhist. But the messages that they purport to receive are considerably different.[35]

Who Is in Charge?

Neo-paganism has no single authoritative book like the Bible. Therefore, they have no written creed, or standards acceptable to all pagans, which dictate what they do. This is an important distinction between paganism and Christianity. Unlike Christianity, paganism makes few absolute truth claims, but there are some basic beliefs that most pagans would generally hold to. One key view is the postmodern belief that truth is relative (it may change depending on the circumstances).

Pagans prefer situational ethics to moral absolutes. What might be right for one pagan could be wrong for another. An example of this would be in the diets pagans follow. Some are strict vegetarians while others are not. Some are heterosexual and others homosexual. Many are dedicated feminists; others are not. Paganism delights in personal choice and diversity. Oddly enough, pagans tend to think that the lack of written dogma unites them more than a universal statement of beliefs. It gives birth to self-expression, and pagans love to borrow techniques from one another. The more learned are still quick to teach the beginners the pagan way.

For many pagans, the lack of an ultimate authority is what made paganism attractive to them. Why become a disciple of some religious teacher when you can be your own spiritual master? Whatever it takes to be a good pagan and work for human enlightenment and progress is acceptable so long as it does no harm. Pagans are not interested in following a list of commandments like those found in Judaism or Christianity. Pagans do not like to feel guilty about anything. The closest thing one can find to a code of conduct would be the Wiccan Rede (counsel). There are long versions of the Rede and short versions that embody the idea of doing whatever you desire so long as you do not harm anyone. But in a relativistic religion (no absolute right and wrong), how do you determine what is harmful?

---

35. Carl Henry, ed., *Revelation and the Bible* (Grand Rapids, MI: Baker Book House, 1958), p. 27.

Some Wiccans also hold to a three-fold law that basically teaches that whatever you do will come back upon you magnified many times over. This is close to the Hindu concept of cause and effect stated in the law of karma.

> Even as I have seen, they that plow iniquity, and sow wickedness, reap the same (Job 4:8).

Instead of using a God-given conscience or revealed truth, the neo-pagan determines right and wrong for himself or herself, albeit with certain self-imposed restraints — do no harm. This is their golden rule, but it is a very subjective method of morality. What constitutes harm? Is abortion harmful to an unborn baby? Is it permissible to take recreational drugs without harming the body? Is lying with good intention permissible? The problem is that an undefined moral law is no moral law at all. It is why some witches' covens can perform certain rituals while they are naked. *Skyclad* is the term for ritual nudity. Starhawk believes that nudity establishes a bond among conveners. Gardner believed performing rituals in the nude was a sign of true freedom. It may be the freedom to do as one pleases, but it is condemned in the Bible as a sin of the flesh when it defies God's Word. When Adam and Eve sinned in the garden, they hid themselves from God and covered their shameful nakedness:

> And when the woman saw that the tree was good for food, and that it was pleasant to the eyes, and a tree to be desired to make one wise, she took of the fruit thereof, and did eat, and gave also unto her husband with her; and he did eat. And the eyes of them both were opened, and they knew that they were naked; and they sewed fig leaves together, and made themselves aprons. And they heard the voice of the LORD God walking in the garden in the cool of the day: and Adam and his wife hid themselves from the presence of the LORD God amongst the trees of the garden (Genesis 3:6–8).

For the Christian, the conscience is not a reliable guide. God has given man much more than a three-fold law. God has given his Word in the 66 books of the Bible. The Word of God tells the Christian what is right and what is wrong. "Thy word is a lamp unto my feet, and a light unto my path" (Psalm 119:105).

In Romans 3:20, Paul spoke of the law of God as that which brings the knowledge of sin. Psalm 119:11 reads: "Thy word have I hid in mine heart, that I might not sin against thee." Because paganism lacks spiritual insight from the source of all wisdom and knowledge, the Lord Jesus, it lacks moral judgment. Therefore, pagans feel free to live without a doctrine of sin to inhibit them.

Christians live by the Word of God, which gives the true perspective on sin because God's perspective is the only one that has *not* been tarnished by sin (e.g., Romans 1:28–32; 1 Timothy 4:1–3; 2 Timothy 2:24–26). But it also points us to the power to live a life pleasing to God through the Holy Spirit. The Christian has present joy and pleasures forevermore in the presence of God. "But as it is written, Eye hath not seen, nor ear heard, neither have entered into the heart of man, the things which God hath prepared for them that love him" (1 Corinthians 2:9). The pagan has myths and magic. Belief in magic among pagans is based on the idea that changing one thing can change other things because all things in the universe are connected. But no pagan magic can ever change the fate that awaits them if they continue in their present darkness. No magic spell or potion can make restitution for their sins or give them the hope of eternal life.

Final Analysis

In the end, paganism takes its place among the religions of the world, most of which lack inspired revelation, a clear path to God and His righteousness, and the certainty of final salvation. These things are found *only* in the inspired Word of God, the way of the Cross, and the promises of God:

> All scripture is given by inspiration of God, and is profitable for doctrine, for reproof, for correction, for instruction in righteousness: That the man of God may be perfect, thoroughly furnished unto all good works (2 Timothy 3:16–17).

> For the preaching of the cross is to them that perish foolishness; but unto us which are saved it is the power of God (1 Corinthians 1:18).

> For all the promises of God in him are yea, and in him Amen, unto the glory of God by us (2 Corinthians 1:20).

The true father of paganism is the prince of darkness who comes to steal, kill, and destroy. Jesus came to give life, and life more abundantly (John 10:10). Everyone must choose whom they will follow. It's one or the other.

I conclude this study on paganism with the exhortation of Joshua to the children of Israel as they were about to enter a land filled with pagan nations who practiced things God called abominations. They had a choice to make and so do each of us:

> And if it seem evil unto you to serve the LORD, choose you this day whom ye will serve; whether the gods which your fathers served that were on the other side of the flood, or the gods of the Amorites, in whose land ye dwell: but as for me and my house, we will serve the LORD (Joshua 24:15).

To God be the glory!

Summary of Pagan Beliefs

Doctrine	Teachings of Paganism
God	Pagans deny the existence of a supreme God. Various views are common, but worship or connection with various gods and goddesses (polytheism) are common, as well as worship of nature and the spirits of nature (pantheism or panentheism).
Authority/ Revelation	The Bible is rejected as authoritative. Individual experience is esteemed above any form of authority. Various forms of spiritual meditation and altered states of consciousness are used to gain secret spiritual knowledge.
Man	Man is seen as a self-defining and self-determining individual who is part of the whole of nature. Details about the nature of man vary widely among pagans.
Sin	The idea of absolute moral truths is denied, especially as related to the Bible. Each individual pagan determines morality by practicing the general guideline of "do no harm."

Salvation	There is no concept of salvation from a sinful nature. Various views on the nature of the afterlife are held by pagans.
Creation	The biblical account of creation is denied. Various views, including ancient pagan mythologies and various forms of evolution, are held by pagans.

Chapter 9

Voodooism

Dr. Corey Abney

Hollywood screenwriters and practitioners in New Orleans have shaped the modern perception of Voodooism, at least in Western culture. Movies depicting witch doctors, zombies, or voodoo dolls often shape the way people think about the religion. Major events like Mardi Gras draw attention to the city of New Orleans. There, voodooism has a significant presence and ongoing promotional opportunities, but partygoers often dismiss or overlook the number of people who practice voodoo.

The result of this Hollywood/Mardi Gras effect is that many people in our culture do not take voodooism seriously as a world religion, although millions of people around the world practice it, enslaved to its teaching. Voodooism powerfully influences many places around the world and can only be overcome by the gospel of Jesus Christ.

History

The modern term for voodooism comes from the African tribal word *vodu*, which means "god," "worship," or "fear of the gods." Voodooism originated in West Africa as a tribal religion,[1] and came to Haiti and eventually the United States as the result of the 16th-century slave trade that began in 1517. Many tribes in Sub-Saharan Africa claim exclusive rights to the origins of voodoo, but the specific origins of the religion cannot be verified.

---

1. See chapter 12 in this volume for more information on animistic religions.

The country of Benin (West Africa) is generally regarded as the birthplace and capital of voodooism, as voodoo remains the state religion of Benin to the present day.

The slave trade that launched in 1517 brought multitudes of Africans to the West Indies (Caribbean). When these African slaves settled in their new land, they possessed almost nothing beyond their deeply held religious convictions.

Their European masters, however, forced the Africans to embrace Roman Catholicism, which resulted in a mingled belief system that combined major tenants of Catholicism with traditional African rituals. Moreover, similarities existed between the two religions that allowed for faster integration. For example, Catholicism allows for the worship of saints, while voodooism promotes the worship of "lesser deities" and ancestors. Catholicism uses sacramental objects in worship, while voodooism uses charms. Many followers of voodooism added components of Catholicism to their religious practices, leading to a different brand of voodooism than was practiced in West Africa. Over time, Catholicism influenced voodooism in a profound way, especially in the New World.

Thus, modern voodooism has numerous variations and practices that reflect the geographical location of the practitioners. Additionally, modern voodoo practices continue to illustrate the influence of Roman Catholicism. For instance, many voodoo followers integrate Catholic rituals, prayers, and liturgies with old African animistic observances. Some voodoo places of worship have statues or pictures of Catholic saints and the virgin Mary. This modern version of voodooism is seen most profoundly in Haiti, a country that is said to have been dedicated to Satan over 200 years ago[2] and still has significant voodoo influences. Voodooism is also practiced in Trinidad, Jamaica, Cuba, and parts of North and South America, but its most significant following remains in West Africa and Haiti.

Beliefs

Voodooism is based on the idea that spirits in the spirit world interact with humans in a harmonious relationship. Humans provide various items to help the spirits make their way in the spirit world, while the spirits provide health, protection from evil, and good fortune to humans on earth. The

---

2. While this claim is popular, the details of the event are disputed. Regardless of its historicity, voodoo remains a strong influence in the country.

spirit beings are understood to be lesser gods, and the interaction between human beings and voodoo spirits is based largely on ritual ceremonies led by a voodoo witch doctor.

The core beliefs are difficult to nail down in a systematic way because of significant variations that exist around the world, with various tribes using different terminology to reference similar beliefs and concepts. Most voodoo followers share similar beliefs about god, authority, and salvation, however, which provide a starting point for understanding and engagement.

God

Voodoo practitioners believe in a supreme being who is responsible for creation and who possesses ultimate authority over the world. They do not believe that a person can know this god, however, because the "supreme being" is far removed from people (reminiscent of a deistic view of God).

Voodoo tribes use different names for the spirit world, but *loa* is the standard name for the spirits. These spirits take many different forms and fall ultimately under the control of the chief deity. Voodoo practitioners focus primarily on these spirits (loa) because they participate in the lives of individuals and are knowable. According to voodoo teaching, some loa are the souls of deceased ancestors who protect the family. Not all ancestors become loa, although every soul lives forever even if it does not become a lesser deity. Pre-existing spirits choose the spirits who become loa.

Some spirits have been present since the creation of the world and control all aspects of life. These spirits are typically associated with the magic aspects of voodooism. No detailed hierarchy of deities exists within voodooism, although

Voodoo charms, talismans, and idols are used in various ceremonies and in everyday life.
(Wikimedia Commons, by user: Doron, own work)

these "creation spirits" are considered to be the heart of the universe. Moreover, these spirits communicate their desires by possessing individuals and tormenting them, so voodoo worshipers appeal to loa in order to receive blessings and to avoid curses. One of the ways voodoo practitioners appeal to these deities is through the use of relics and charms.

Voodooism employs many rituals that are designed to invoke the help of loa. These rituals are held for securing help in times of difficulty, celebrating a holiday or significant event such as a marriage or the birth of a child, for healing, or to provide a smooth transition into the afterlife. During various ceremonies, loa take possession of individuals to act and speak through them.

A witch doctor presides over all ritual ceremonies as the priest of the community. The rituals include singing and dancing to the beat of drums in order to invoke the presence of the spirits. Offerings may be given and animals sacrificed. In some cases, worshipers may fall into a trance and manifest the spirit of loa by speaking, singing, or offering healing. These rituals are a necessary and important part of voodoo culture because of the impersonal nature of loa. Voodoo spirits participate in the lives of its practitioners without maintaining an ongoing, personal relationship. Additionally, various forms of divination are used to answer questions and give direction.

Authority

Voodooism does not possess a holy text that guides belief and practice. Key doctrines and practices are passed down orally from one generation to the next. This is the most significant reason that so much variation exists within voodooism. The lack of an authoritative text allows for wide variations of voodoo worship rituals and practices that vary greatly from one culture to another. For example, in many voodoo contexts, symbolic animals and plants represent certain elements of spirituality, with snakes (especially pythons) serving as a universal sign of voodoo power. In other contexts, people have a fear of ocean or river water because of the belief that evil spirits reside there.

Another example of variation within voodooism due to the absence of a holy text is the role of witch doctors. Witch doctors assume positions of great authority in many tribes of voodooism due to the absence of a holy text, especially in countries like Haiti. Many voodoo practitioners believe that witch doctors are chosen by loa, with selection often following family tradition as authority is passed down from generation to generation. Existing loa either confirm or deny an ancestor to take the mantle of a deceased witch doctor. In Haitian voodoo, male witch doctors are known as *houngan* and females as *mambos*. Additionally, *bokors* are involved in the practice of magic and sorcery.

Technically, anyone can be chosen to become a witch doctor by loa, even if an individual's family does not have a history of witch doctors, but the majority of witch doctors come from family units. They begin as apprentices who serve with more experienced witch doctors, start their own "practice," and achieve higher rank by gaining more knowledge of the spirit world. Witch doctors in contexts like Haiti place flags on top of their places of operation, with the most powerful witch doctors displaying more flags than their subordinates.

While Voodoo has no central authority, holy text, or governing body, witch doctors serve as authoritative voices and community leaders in many contexts. Haitian society, for instance, views witch doctors as men with the most understanding and wisdom. People seek them out for leadership, spiritual guidance, and even medical treatment. Witch doctors allegedly discern if people

Flags with various symbolism are used in voodoo rituals in the community.
(Wikimedia Commons, Voodoo banner by Valris, Sam Fentress, author)

suffer from physical maladies or something related to a spiritual cause. Their approach to attempted healing will differ based on whether or not "spirits" are involved. Typically, in cases that are determined to be physical in nature, witch doctors will use herbal remedies and organic "medicines" such as tea leaves and roots. In cases that are spiritual in nature, they turn to rituals and ceremonies that are designed to invoke direct action from loa. Ultimately, witch doctors are judged on their effectiveness to heal people and to lead their communities, and they can be replaced if the community determines that they are unable to heal and/or lead in a consistent manner.

Salvation

Voodooism does not articulate a doctrine of salvation where sin is forgiven or defeated. The focus of the religion is how to endure this life with as little trouble as possible. The Lao are called on to help voodoo followers navigate the present life and to move smoothly into the life to come. Fear is a motivating factor for voodoo practitioners and a reason that most followers demonstrate a high degree of morality. Many people are scared to do anything that may draw the ire of their Lao. In short, superstition rooted in fear trumps any notion of salvation rooted in love. In this way, voodooism is a religion that keeps its followers bound with fear and anxiety.

Engaging Followers

Engaging followers of voodoo begins with a description of the Creator God as the one, true, and living God of the Bible. Voodooism teaches that a supreme being created the world but is unknowable and removed from the world he made. Christians agree that a sovereign Creator made the world and that He is far greater than anyone or anything on the earth. Christians also believe, however, that God is personal and knowable. Therefore, the doctrines of transcendence and immanence are key starting points of Christian engagement with voodoo practitioners.

Transcendence

God's transcendence refers to His separation from all that He has made. He is infinitely exalted above all creation. God is set apart from everything else and in a class by Himself. God is not like man; rather, He is holy, sovereign, infinite, independent, all-knowing, ever-present, and perfect in all of His ways. Mankind is fully and completely dependent upon Him.

> Yours, O LORD, is the greatness, the power and the glory, the victory and the majesty; for all that is in heaven and in earth is Yours; Yours is the kingdom, O LORD, and You are exalted as head over all (1 Chronicles 29:11).[3]

> For You, LORD, are most high above all the earth; You are exalted far above all gods (Psalm 97:9).

> Who is like the LORD our God, who dwells on high, who humbles Himself to behold the things that are in the heavens and in the earth? (Psalm 113:5–6).

> "For My thoughts are not your thoughts, nor are your ways My ways," says the LORD. "For as the heavens are higher than the

---

3. Scripture in this chapter is from the New King James Version (NKJV) of the Bible.

earth, so are My ways higher than your ways, and My thoughts than your thoughts" (Isaiah 55:8–9).

God, who made the world and everything in it, since He is Lord of heaven and earth, does not dwell in temples made with hands (Acts 17:24).

The Scriptures present a clear picture of God's transcendence: He is greater than all that He created and separate from it. God is exalted above everything that exists in the universe and is not dependent upon anything or anyone.

Immanence

Thankfully, God is not only transcendent, He is also immanent. God is near to His people, present with them, active on earth, and involved in the world. He is present and involved in history and in the lives of individuals. He interacts with His people and assures them of His power and presence. He promised to never leave or forsake His own:

Be strong and of good courage, do not fear nor be afraid of them; for the LORD your God, He is the One who goes with you. He will not leave you nor forsake you (Deuteronomy 31:6).

Go therefore and make disciples of all the nations, baptizing them in the name of the Father and of the Son and of the Holy Spirit, teaching them to observe all things that I have commanded you; and lo, I am with you always, even to the end of the age (Matthew 28:19–20).

The ultimate demonstration of God's immanence and involvement in this world is the incarnation of Jesus Christ. The Son of God took on human flesh, was born of a woman, lived on the earth, interacted with others, and died among His people. God became what mankind is so that people can know Him and be like Him.

The Bible teaches that God's work of redemption is motivated by love for His people: "God demonstrates His own love toward us, in that while we were still sinners, Christ died for us" (Romans 5:8). Jesus came, died, and rose from the dead in order to reconcile men and women to Himself. God could have remained detached from His creation and left human beings without a way to know Him, but He initiated a relationship with them through His Word, His prophets and, most significantly, His Son.

Hebrews 1:1–2 says, "God, who at various times and in various ways spoke in time past to the fathers by the prophets, has in these last days spoken to us by His Son, whom He has appointed heir of all things, through whom also He made the worlds." The incarnation is the greatest manifestation of immanence and of God's desire to have a personal relationship with His people. John 1:14 notes that "the Word became flesh and dwelt among us, and we beheld His glory, the glory as of the only begotten of the Father, full of grace and truth." Literally, God "set up a tent" among His people so that He could have a personal relationship with them.

Balance

Scripture is clear that God is both transcendent (far from man) and immanent (near to man). Both truths must be affirmed and kept together in balance in order for a person to perceive God correctly. Only Christianity has a proper understanding and balance of God's immanence and transcendence.

> Therefore know this day, and consider it in your heart, that the LORD Himself is God in heaven above and on the earth beneath; there is no other (Deuteronomy 4:39).

> For thus says the High and Lofty One who inhabits eternity, whose name is Holy: "I dwell in the high and holy place, with him who has a contrite and humble spirit, to revive the spirit of the humble, and to revive the heart of the contrite ones" (Isaiah 57:15).

> "Am I a God near at hand," says the LORD, "and not a God afar off? Can anyone hide himself in secret places, so I shall not see him?" says the LORD; "Do I not fill heaven and earth?" says the LORD (Jeremiah 23:23–24).

Voodooism distorts God's transcendence and misunderstands God's immanence. Followers of voodoo maintain that the *supreme being* is unknowable, distant, and unconcerned about people on earth. If such were true, however, then how can they know anything about this god, even his existence? Moreover, they believe arbitrarily in lesser spirits that interact with human beings, mostly to possess them, harm them, or repay them for acts of wickedness.

Charms and relics are used, with blind hope, to appease the spirits and to persuade them to heal or bless voodoo practitioners. Voodoo practitioners participate with their gods without the comfort or confidence of a personal relationship. This stands in sharp contrast to the teaching of Christianity, which emphasizes that God is both the supreme Creator who is independent from man, but also the nearby Savior who stands ready to forgive anyone who calls on Him for salvation.

Philippians 2:5–8 says:

> Let this mind be in you which was also in Christ Jesus, who, being in the form of God, did not consider it robbery to be equal with God, but made Himself of no reputation, taking the form of a bondservant, and coming in the likeness of men. And being found in appearance as a man, He humbled Himself and became obedient to the point of death, even the death of the cross.

Jesus is both God and man. He came in both glory and humility. He is both the suffering servant and the sinless Savior.

The God of the Bible is both transcendent and immanent. Followers of voodooism need clarity concerning the nature of God that will bring together their view of a supreme being and the spirits who are present on earth (Deuteronomy 32:17; 1 Corinthians 10:20–21; Hebrews 1:14). Christians know the Creator God as the same God who is with us in a personal way. One God in three persons: Father, Son, and Holy Spirit.

The Ministry of Jesus Christ

Voodooism does not have a doctrine of salvation, so the need for a savior is glaringly absent. The presence of a mediator, however, is a significant part of voodooism, with witch doctors fulfilling the role of mediator within the religion. They invoke the presence of Lao, offer wise counsel to the people, and provide healing for spiritual and physical problems. Christians can engage voodoo followers with the concept of mediation, showing ultimately that Jesus Christ is the true mediator between God and man. Jesus is the only person who can reconcile mankind's relationship with God. He alone fulfills the roles of prophet, priest, and king that are so often fulfilled by the witch-doctors of voodoo culture.

Prophet

Followers of voodooism understand the concepts of good and evil, but they cannot know for sure that such concepts exist. Their distant god does not inform them of what is good or evil. Christians have the capacity to know good and evil, however, because of God's revelation, and one of the most significant ways God revealed Himself to His people was through His prophets. The Old Testament prophets communicated a clear standard of right and wrong to God's people and they spoke with a unique authority and clarity. Ultimately, this prophetic ministry was fulfilled by Jesus Christ, who came into the world as the divine Word of God.

As prophet, Jesus pronounced an end to all our sin. Prophets in the Old Testament served as God's mouthpiece to nations and individuals. Prophets spoke words of judgment when people sinned against God, and called them to repentance in order to be reconciled:

> Alas, sinful nation, a people laden with iniquity, a brood of evildoers, children who are corrupters! They have forsaken the Lord, they have provoked to anger the Holy One of Israel, they have turned away backward. . . . "Come now, and let us reason together," says the Lord, "Though your sins are like scarlet, they shall be as white as snow; though they are red like crimson, they shall be as wool" (Isaiah 1:4, 18).

Jesus is the greatest prophet who speaks God's Word because He is the very Word of God (John 1:1–4). Moreover, He fulfills the prophetic role by exposing sin and the need for repentance and saving faith. Jesus proclaimed pardon and forgiveness for all who believe. He speaks truth to all who will receive it and guides His people in wisdom and understanding. Unlike the witch doctors who are often wrong and unable to discern what is true, Jesus gives us a sure and perfect word.

Priest

Witch doctors presume their role as mediators and "priests" of their religion, yet their priests are not connected to their distant, unknowable god.

As priest, Jesus offered Himself as the ultimate sacrifice for the sins of His people. Priests in the Old Testament served as mediators between God and man. The high priest entered the Most Holy Place once a year on the Day of Atonement to offer a sacrifice to God on behalf of His people (Leviticus 16:34). The high priest sprinkled the blood of the sacrifice on the mercy seat "because of the uncleanness of the children of Israel, and because of their transgressions, for all their sins" (Leviticus 16:16).

Other sacrifices were made throughout the year as well, and these sacrifices were made on an annual basis. Jesus, however, is the true high priest who offered Himself as a sacrifice once and for all. Hebrews 9:12–14 states:

> Not with the blood of goats and calves, but with His own blood He entered the Most Holy Place once for all, having obtained eternal redemption. For if the blood of bulls and goats and the ashes of a heifer, sprinkling the unclean, sanctifies for the purifying of the flesh, how much more shall the blood of Christ, who through the eternal Spirit offered Himself without spot to God, cleanse your conscience from dead works to serve the living God?

Not only did Jesus offer Himself as the true, perfect sacrifice for His people, He continues to intercede on their behalf.

> Who is he who condemns? It is Christ who died, and furthermore is also risen, who is even at the right hand of God, who also makes intercession for us (Romans 8:34).

> But He, because He continues forever, has an unchangeable priesthood. Therefore He is also able to save to the uttermost those who come to God through Him, since He always lives to make intercession for them (Hebrews 7:24–25).

Jesus fulfills perfectly the priestly role described in the Old Testament, and He is the only one who can bring God and man together. His death, Resurrection, and ongoing intercession provide all that is required for mankind to draw near to God. Unlike the witch doctors who demand constant sacrifices and produce faltering results, Jesus' sacrifice was perfect and complete.

King

As King, Jesus conquers sin and death, securing an everlasting Kingdom of peace for His people. Monarchies in the Old Testament existed for the peace, prosperity, and welfare of nations. People looked to their kings for righteousness and justice. King David, for example, was a beloved king who ruled with equity and strength. Second Samuel 8:15 says, "So David reigned over all Israel; and David administered judgment and justice to all his people." David's reign served as a type of Christ, who rules with true righteousness, justice, equity, and power. Jesus came in the line of David to rule and reign over David's throne so that He is both David's son and David's Lord (Matthew 22:42–45). Jesus is "the ruler over the kings of the earth" and our "King of kings and Lord of lords" (Revelation 1:5, 19:16). His reign will never end and He will never be defeated. Followers of Christ can rest in His Kingdom of righteousness and peace.

Voodoo practitioners look to witch doctors, sacrifices, and rituals for what Jesus alone can provide. Jesus is infinitely wise, powerful, and loving. He offers salvation, healing, intercession, and comfort that bring peace, love, joy, and contentment. Followers of Jesus have no need for relics, charms, sacrifices, or spells, because the blood of Jesus grants access to God, and His ongoing intercession maintains the relationship. Ultimately, followers of voodooism don't need better education, an improved economy, or a more civilized religious system; rather, they need a mediator who can atone for their sin debt and satisfy the righteous demands of a holy God. They need a Savior who is present with them as prophet, priest, and King.

Those who are trapped in voodooism by the devil can know the true God and have a relationship with Him — particularly a God who destroys sin and evil. Furthermore, those who have been witch doctors and convert to Christ through repentance and faith can point people to the *true mediator* between God and man.

The Indwelling of the Holy Spirit

The Holy Spirit indwells every Christian from the moment of conversion (Acts 2:37–38). The nearness of God is so profound that God is not only *with* His people, He resides *in* them as well. The Apostle Paul writes, "But you are not in the flesh but in the Spirit, if indeed the Spirit of God dwells in you. Now if anyone does not have the Spirit of Christ, he is not His"

(Romans 8:9). The Holy Spirit stirs the conscience, enables understanding of the Scriptures, comforts God's people, guides into truth, cheers the soul, and convicts of sin. He interacts constantly with believers in such a way that God's Word is applied and Christ is glorified. Therefore, followers of Christ are commanded to walk in the Spirit and His many fruits. Galatians 5:16 states, "I say then: Walk in the Spirit, and you shall not fulfill the lust of the flesh."

Followers of voodoo long for their gods to be near them and act favorably toward them. Charms, relics, and sacrifices are offered to appease the gods and to provide some measure of assurance. Christians can engage voodoo practitioners with the hope of the one, true, and living God, who draws near to His people through Christ and indwells them with His Holy Spirit. God's Spirit will never withdraw from His own.

Furthermore, Christians do not live in fear and anxiety, striving to appease God constantly, because Jesus has already satisfied the righteous demands of the Father. The presence of the Holy Spirit in the life of a believer is a guarantee that he or she is loved by God and assured of everlasting life. People who are trapped within a culture of voodooism under the whims of a witch doctor and unseen dark spiritual forces need the confidence and assurance that can only come through the blood of Jesus and the indwelling of the Holy Spirit. As the Apostle Paul told the people of Athens, God "is not far from each one of us; for in Him we live and move and have our being" (Acts 17:27–28).

The Authority of the Bible

The nature and character of God as revealed in the Bible are the foundation of faith and morality for the Christian. The Scriptures provide a clear moral standard by which followers of Christ must live. Voodooism, however, does not possess a standard of doctrines, which leads to the loss of an ethical standard for voodoo followers and communities. Although a concept of law-breaking or wrongdoing exists in their culture, such "ethics" are sanctioned primarily by the specific community in which a follower of voodoo resides. No concept of sin is present within voodoo communities, nor is a clear moral standard taught throughout the religion. Evil magic can be applied to people or objects, and property can be destroyed for personal vengeance. The lack of an authoritative doctrinal foundation or moral standard is a source of tension within voodoo communities. Witch doctors assume authoritative roles with little accountability.

Christians should equip voodoo converts with the authority of the Bible, which provides a moral and doctrinal foundation for faith and practice. The Word of God is the foundation of faith, obedience, and Christian community. Followers of Christ have confidence knowing that in the Bible, God has spoken, revealed His nature and character, and provided clear principles of Christian conduct.

Converts from voodoo need the firm foundation of God's Word, which is always profitable to those who receive it:

> All Scripture is given by inspiration of God, and is profitable for doctrine, for reproof, for correction, for instruction in righteousness, that the man of God may be complete, thoroughly equipped for every good work (2 Timothy 3:16–17).

After all, God himself testifies that His Word "shall not return to Me void, but it shall accomplish what I please, and it shall prosper in the thing for which I sent it" (Isaiah 55:11).

Conclusion

Christian engagement with followers of voodooism should emulate the Apostle Paul's approach in Athens, where he stood at the Areopagus and made known the God who was previously unknown to the people. Paul speaks to the Athenians with appeals to the preeminence of God as Creator and the glory of God in general revelation. He finds a point of agreement in the Athenian belief in a supreme, unknown God. Paul then appeals to the authority of the one, true, and living God as Creator and Sustainer. Moreover, he points to the glory of God in general revelation and implies that people in Athens made an appropriate judgment based on general revelation about the presence of a Creator from whom man originates.

> Then Paul stood in the midst of the Areopagus and said, "Men of Athens, I perceive that in all things you are very religious; for as I was passing through and considering the objects of your worship, I even found an altar with this inscription: TO THE UNKNOWN GOD. Therefore, the One whom you worship without knowing, Him I proclaim to you: 'God, who made

the world and everything in it, since He is Lord of heaven and earth, does not dwell in temples made with hands. Nor is He worshiped with men's hands, as though He needed anything, since He gives to all life, breath, and all things. And He has made from one blood every nation of men to dwell on all the face of the earth, and has determined their preappointed times and the boundaries of their dwellings, so that they should seek the Lord, in the hope that they might grope for Him and find Him, though He is not far from each one of us; for in Him we live and move and have our being, as also some of your own poets have said, "For we are also His offspring." Therefore, since we are the offspring of God, we ought not to think that the Divine Nature is like gold or silver or stone, something shaped by art and man's devising. Truly, these times of ignorance God overlooked, but now commands all men everywhere to repent, because He has appointed a day on which He will judge the world in righteousness by the Man whom He has ordained. He has given assurance of this to all by raising Him from the dead' " (Acts 17:22–31).

Paul exposes the Athenians' mistake of crediting pagan gods with a power they do not possess. Thus, Paul appeals repeatedly to God's creative power and the subsequent implications manifested through general revelation as a point of agreement and as a launching pad for gospel proclamation.

Paul's method of evangelism in Athens is a helpful one for those who engage followers of voodooism. A point of agreement can be established with the belief in a Supreme Being who created the world. Mankind lives, moves, and has their being in the Lord of heaven and earth. But contrary to voodoo teaching, the true God is knowable and near to His people.

Moreover, He is not confined to temples made by human hands, nor is He shaped by art and man's devising. He is one God in three persons who extends grace and mercy to those who receive it. He commands that people repent of their sin because He has appointed a day on which He will judge the world in righteousness. This judgment will come at the hand of "the Man" whom God ordained and is the same Man who saves people from their sins. He is not a lesser deity or a voodoo priest; rather, He is the sinless Son of God who died for His people as an atoning sacrifice and rose from the dead as the victorious King of kings. Thus, the only hope for eternal life is found not in a witch doctor, but in a Savior, who is Jesus Christ the Lord.

Summary of Voodoo Beliefs

Doctrine	Teachings of Voodooism
God	Deny the God of the Bible, but believe in a creator god who is detached from his creation. Lesser gods (loa) and ancestral spirits are seen as ruling the affairs of man. Jesus is not acknowledged.
Authority/ Revelation	There are no standard writings. Oral traditions exist and vary by region. Syncretism with other religious views (e.g., Roman Catholicism) exist. Witch doctors are seen as the sages and priests in a community.
Man	All men are spiritual beings seeking to avoid trouble in this life and enter safely into the afterlife. There is no notion of a sin nature, though moral codes are to be followed.
Sin	Sin is based on local traditions and brings trouble in the present life. There is no notion of mediation or forgiveness of sins.
Salvation	There is no view of salvation apart from achieving a trouble-free life and entering the afterlife. All souls enter the afterlife, but some are able to become lesser gods (loa).
Creation	The creator god is responsible for creating, but not sustaining the creation. Evolutionary views vary, but are generally rejected.

Chapter 10

Wicca and Witchcraft

Marcia Montenegro

Author's Disclaimer: Since Wicca and Witchcraft are not centralized or monolithic, the disparities in beliefs and practices are widespread. Additionally, given the history of these beliefs, it can be challenging to sort fact from fiction. Therefore, some may dispute portions of the material given here due to these variations. For the sake of brevity, the words Wicca and Wiccan are used interchangeably with Witchcraft and Witch when possible, with the understanding that these terms are not always equated with each other by their followers. Since there are numerous and ever-evolving forms of Wicca and Witchcraft, this chapter gives a broad overview and cannot address all forms of Wicca and Witchcraft. To distinguish the generic use of the term "witch" and "witchcraft" from the modern religion of Witchcraft, "Witch" and Witchcraft" will be capitalized when referring to the contemporary religion.

You are in a circle. Protection from the Goddess and various spirits are invoked. The elements of earth, fire, air, and water are called in. You begin to dance slowly around the circle, then faster. There is chanting. The pace increases; the group is "raising energy." Or you are around a fire and each person, one by one, comes to the fire and throws something in while stating a personal truth or desire. In many such scenarios, a ritual will be performed, whether to call for protection, healing, a special favor, world peace, etc. The rituals vary from group to group, even person to person.[1]

Teen Witch, by Silver RavenWolf, a how-to manual for teens, came out in 1998 and sold so many copies that bookstore shelves were cleaned out, and several printings were required to fill the demand. Eventually, a small spell kit was sold alongside the book. It has become common to find books for children and teens featuring heroes who are Witches or cast spells and save the day by their magic arts (e.g., Harry Potter series, Disney's *Wizards of Waverly Place*). For adults, there are movies and television shows such as the popular series, *The Good Witch*, on the Hallmark channel or the classic *Bewitched*. These instances only indicate society's growing acceptance of Witchcraft and "good" Witches.

There are many myths and misunderstandings about Witchcraft, arising from sources as divergent as the entertainment industry, the early founders of the modern Witchcraft movement themselves, elaborate tales stemming from the European Inquisition, and dubious Internet data. Because of this, erroneous perceptions abound, and the result is a conflation of fact and fantasy. Christians, however, should make efforts to know the truth for the sake of those who need Christ, who is the way, the truth, and the life, so that our witness is both credible and compassionate.

History

The modern religion of Witchcraft, also known as Wicca, has drawn an increasing number of adherents for the last several decades in Europe and in the United States. The word "witchcraft" is a word of later origin than when the biblical canon was written; therefore, words in the Bible translated as "witchcraft" arise from Hebrew and Greek words that refer to sorcery, enchantment, or divination, and not to the modern concept of "Witchcraft"

---

1. These activities were open to outsiders; Wiccan rituals are normally closed and for adherents only. The author participated in these when she was an astrologer and New Ager.

as a religion. It is also useful to keep in mind the distinction between the generic term "witchcraft," which refers to occult practices and folk magic in many·cultures today, and the contemporary Western religious terms "Witchcraft" and "Wicca" that describe a modern religious practice.

Witchcraft and Wicca are a subset of neo-paganism, the alleged revival of ancient practices of worshiping and invoking gods (polytheism), belief in nature spirits, rituals to honor the cycles of nature, and occult practices such as divination[2] and spell casting. In the Old Testament, there are references to paganism that include the worship of false gods, rituals in the "sacred groves" or under trees with thick foliage, and ritual prostitution.[3]

Neo-paganism today exhibits itself as polytheism, seasonal rituals honoring nature and moon phases, worship of the Goddess (by some), and occult practices such as casting spells and the practice of divination. Neo-paganism is an umbrella term which covers Witchcraft, Wicca, modern Druidry, the worship of Norse and Germanic gods in Asatru and Odinism,[4] the worship of the ancient Greek and Roman gods, Italian witchcraft (*Stregheria* or *Strega*), and a number of other modern neo-pagan movements. Although neo-paganism includes modern Witchcraft or Wicca, they are not equivalent. Witches and Wiccans are pagans, but not all pagans are Witches or Wiccans. Wicca is also categorized by some as a subdivision of Witchcraft.

Wicca is a modern term for what is declared to be the religion of Witchcraft, particularly as it relates to Gerald Gardner (1884–1964), a native of England. Gardner, the main person responsible for initiating the modern Wicca movement, claimed he was reviving an ancient religion, a theory since discredited.[5] Gardner stated he was initiated into a Wiccan coven[6] by a

---

2. Divination in a pagan or an occult context is gaining information and advice through occult techniques and reading hidden meanings in esoteric symbols or omens. Divination is forbidden throughout the Bible (Leviticus 19:26; Jeremiah 14:14; Acts 16:16; Galatians 5:19–21; Revelation 21:8).

3. Deuteronomy 12:2, 16:20, 23:17; Judges 2:11–13, 3:5–7; 1 Kings 14:23; 2 Kings 16:4, 17:10; 2 Chronicles 28:4; Jeremiah 3:6, 13; Ezekiel 6:13, 20:28–29; Isaiah 1:29–30, 57:5; Hosea 4:13.

4. See chapter 14 for more information on Norse mythology.

5. The two most well-known works on this are Ronald Hutton, *The Triumph of the Moon: A History of Modern Pagan Witchcraft* (NY: Oxford University Press, Inc., 1999) and Margot Adler, *Drawing Down the Moon* (NY: Penguin Group, 1986); also Encyclopedia Britannica, http://www.britannica.com/EBchecked/topic/225915/Gerald-Brousseau-Gardner.

6. A coven is a small group of Wiccans or Witches that varies in number, usually anywhere from 3 to 20, although 13 is the usual limit. However, the number required will vary from coven to coven. The number 13 is thought by many to derive from anthropologist Margaret Murray's works; Murray's writings have since been largely discredited.

woman in the New Forest area of England, but there is only Gardner's word for the existence of this coven.

Gardner adapted many of the rituals and spells based on materials from occult sources and from the secret societies he joined and researched. Influences on Gardner include Margaret Murray (1863–1963), an Egyptologist, folklorist, archaeologist, and anthropologist, whose works on Witchcraft have been largely discredited;[7] the controversial 1899 work, *Ariada, or the Gospel of the Witches* by folklorist Charles Leland; James Frazer's *The Golden Bough,* published first in 1922; the 1948 book by Robert Graves (1895–1985), *The White Goddess*; and the writings of ceremonial magician and occultist Aleister Crowley (1875–1947).[8] Many enduring myths about a pre-Christian religion of Witchcraft and practices, as well as a supposed organized universal pagan religion, arose from these works and persist today.

In the 1960s, a Gardner initiate, Alex Sanders (1926–1988), started his own Witchcraft group in England, known as Alexandrian Wicca, a branch of Wicca still practiced today. The seed for Wicca was planted in the United States when Gardner follower Raymond Buckland (b. 1934) came to the United States and introduced Gardnerian Wicca in 1964. From that beginning, groups began to spread forms of Gardnerian and Alexandrian Wicca.

The late author and Wiccan priestess Margot Adler (1946–2014), in her landmark work on the modern neo-pagan movement, wrote, "The majority of Pagan scholars no longer accept Margaret Murray's theory of the witch cult, and they have come to accept that the persecution, torture, and killing of people accused of witchcraft in Europe involved a relatively small number of people accused of witchcraft."[9]

No matter what may be claimed, there is no historical evidence for an ancient religion of Witchcraft, or for the claim made by some present-day Goddess worshipers (some of whom who are Wiccans) that an ancient

---

7. Hutton, *The Triumph of the Moon*, p. 194–201; additionally, other portions of Hutton's book discuss the investigation of Murray's works on Witchcraft and resulting conclusions about its invalidity; Adler, *Drawing Down the Moon*, p. 45–46; "Margaret Murray's Unlikely History," http://wicca.cnbeyer.com/murray.shtml.

8. "Wicca and Neopaganism," Sacred Text Archives, http://www.sacred-texts.com/pag/.

9. Adler, *Drawing Down the Moon*, p. 235, also, Ellen Evert Hopman and Lawrence Bond, *People of the Earth: The New Pagans Speak Out* (Rochester, VT: Destiny Books, 2006), p. 349. The phrase used in Adler's title, *Drawing Down the Moon*, refers to a ritual during which the Wiccan priestess invokes the Goddess into herself so that while in a trance state the Goddess will speak through her.

matriarchal Goddess-worshiping culture existed.[10] There are Wiccans who admit that Wicca is a recent innovation but nevertheless choose to view the idea of an ancient religion as a useful metaphor, while others adamantly believe and claim it is humanity's oldest religion.

It is not that pagan practices did not exist in the ancient world, but rather that there is no evidence for a pre-Christian Witchcraft religion as practiced today, for ancient matriarchal societies that primarily venerated a Goddess distinct from the role as consort for a god, or for organized pagan religions such as described by Frazer, Murray, Gardner, and others. Interestingly, scholar Ronald Hutton writes in his highly respected work, *Triumph of the Moon*, that Frazer wrote *The Golden Bough* in part to discredit Christianity.[11]

Wiccans in ceremonial dress

Some Witches have divided modern Witchcraft into branches, such as Classical, Familial (passed down or inherited through a family line), Immigrant, Ethnic, and Feminist.[12] To this list can be added Natural, Eclectic, Dianic, Green, Neo-Shamanic, Hedge, and Faery (or Fari). Such divisions, and others, are still made by Wiccans and Witches.

Authority

There is no monolithic organization or central authority in Wicca with a stated creed or dogma (i.e., personal or self-authority). In fact, it is precisely this lack of structure that draws many to these groups. Each group or

---

10. Cynthia Eller, *The Myth of Matriarchal Prehistory* (Boston, MA: Beacon Press, 2000). This book is highly recommended as a scholarly work exploring the myth of ancient Goddess cultures and matriarchal societies.

11. Hutton, *The Triumph of the Moon*, p. 114. Frazer's work also influenced others, such as Margaret Murray and Gerald Gardner, and still holds sway today.

12. Adler, *Drawing Down the Moon*, p. 40. Adler attributes some of these classifications to Isaac Bonewits (1949–2010), an American Druid who wrote books on neo-paganism and magic, and founded a Druidic organization. Bonewits extensively researched the history of Witchcraft, concluding that there was no Witchcraft religion until the 20th century, and that the term "witchcraft" alluded to sorcery and other occult practices until the 14th century when baseless allegations of organized witches practicing a religion were made by those heading the Inquisition in Europe; Adler, *Drawing Down the Moon*, p. 65–67. This conclusion agrees with the research of others as well.

One of the *Book of Shadows* owned by Gerald Gardner
(Wikimedia Commons, Midnightblueowl)

person can form his own version of Wicca so that it can be a highly personal spiritual path; this is also an attraction.

For most who follow the Gardnerian teachings and British Traditional Witchcraft,[13] Gardner's *Book of Shadows*, first used in Gardner's coven in the 1950s, is the guide and instructions for rituals. Gardner's book included contributions from Gardnerian Wiccan, Doreen Valiente (1922–1999), who wrote many of the rituals, chants, and liturgies, including the well-known and well-used "Charge of the Goddess." The latter is an alleged discourse from the Goddess given through the high priestess after she invokes the Goddess in a ceremony known as "drawing down the moon." As is often true concerning Gardner, there is controversy about the sources Gardner used for this work. Valiente herself rewrote some of the material because she recognized that part of the content was from Crowley's writings, as well as that of others.[14] Although Valiente later broke with Gardner, she continued to accept some of Gardner's stories about his initiation into a coven despite the later exposés.

---

13. British Traditional Wicca also may refer to Alexandrian Wicca.
14. A detailed discussion of *The Book of Shadows* and the working relationship between Gardner and Valiente is found in Hutton, *The Triumph of the Moon,* p. 206–207, 226–236, 338–339, and Adler, *Drawing Down the Moon,* p. 79–81.

Others also criticized Gardner's claims about *The Book of Shadows,* noting that Gardner used modern writings as sources for the rituals.[15] Aidan Kelly, a neo-pagan who authored a book on the history of Witchcraft, explained that "the Gardnerian style deals with *The Book of Shadows* and the degree of adherence to it. At least the orthodox Gardnerians do it that way. The Liberal Gardnerians take the attitude that Gerald rewrote all the rituals, and if you truly want to follow Gerald, then *do what he did, rewrite the rituals.*"[16]

Indeed, there is no definitive *Book of Shadows* at present, since each Wiccan group or tradition have tailored their own to match their specific practices, and individuals may add material or write their own.[17]

Wiccans and Witches often follow a tradition from whatever teachers they learned from, and these teachings themselves may have been pieced together with others. Practices and beliefs can vary widely and do not have to be aligned with any specific teaching or doctrine. It is normal for followers to change groups or teachers. Solo practitioners, called Solitaires or Solitary Witches, practice alone and are not part of a particular group and may or may not adopt a particular lineage.

However, most Wicca and Witchcraft today incorporates aspects of the teachings of Gardner, Sanders, and Raymond Buckland, as well as influences from teachers and writers Stewart (d. 2000) and Janet Farrar (authors of the prominent work *A Witches Bible*); Wiccan teacher and writer Starhawk (b. 1951; real name, Miriam Simos); Margot Adler, Witchcraft teacher and popular author Scott Cunningham (1956–1993); and Wiccan High Priestess Selena Fox (b. 1949, founder of Circle Sanctuary in Wisconsin).[18]

Other notable voices include Z. (Zsuzsanna) Budapest (b. 1940), founder of the first documented women-only coven oriented to Goddess worship, called Dianic Wicca;[19] and Dion Fortune (1890–1946), who, although not a Witch, was an occultist and practitioner of ceremonial magic whose books influenced practices in Witchcraft.

---

15. Adler, *Drawing Down the Moon,* p. 61, 79, 115.
16. Hopman and Bond, *People of the Earth,* p. 272 (italics in original).
17. Rosemary Ellen Guiley, *The Encyclopedia of Witches, Witchcraft, and Wicca* (NY: Checkmark Books, 2008), p. 35.
18. According to the Circle Sanctuary website, Circle Sanctuary was founded in 1974 and is a "Wiccan church" that is "dedicated to networking, community celebrations, spiritual healing and education," https://www.circlesanctuary.org/. Fox is also a psychotherapist, https://www.circlesanctuary.org/index.php/organization/about-rev-selena-fox.
19. "Famous Witches: Zsuzsanna Budapest," Witchcraft and Witches, accessed October 15, 2015, http://www.witchcraftandwitches.com/witches_budapest.html.

Starhawk

Cunningham wrote a book on practicing as a Solitary, and this book was one of the top best-selling books on the topic, although many Wiccans thought he watered Wicca down.[20] Starhawk, whose book *The Spiral Dance* is considered a key source for modern Witchcraft practices and Goddess worship, has had a major impact on the Witchcraft and neo-pagan cultures. Starhawk has also authored other popular books on Witchcraft and neo-pagan practices.[21]

"Wicca" is allegedly an old English term for "witch" which originally meant to "bend," as in the use of magic[22] to alter reality, though there is dispute as to the word's true origins.[23] Many Wiccans refer to Wicca simply as "the Craft" or sometimes as "the Old Religion." Terms such as "Earth Religions" or "Earth Spirituality" are also used for neo-pagan, Witchcraft, and Wiccan beliefs, including by those outside of the religion.[24]

In fact, there is an organization of neo-pagans within the Unitarian-Universalist Church called The Covenant of Unitarian Universalist Pagans

20. Cunningham's book is *Wicca: A Guide for the Solitary Practitioner*. The criticism of some teachings being watered-down or being "fluffy Witchcraft" is not uncommon in the world of Wicca.

21. Some Witches may consider Starhawk, who is an activist in pagan, feminist, and ecological movements, too polemical. However, her influence on modern Witchcraft cannot be discounted.

22. "Magic" in this chapter refers to occult magic and not to stage magic, such as taking a rabbit out of a hat. Some spell it as "magick" to make the distinction between the two. Occult magic involves working with spirits, forces, or alleged gods using certain rituals and often various tools as symbols and aids in the ceremonies. There is disagreement among Christians as to whether there is any real power in this magic and if so, how demonic powers may be involved.

23. Adler, *Drawing Down the Moon*, p. 10; Starhawk, *The Spiral Dance* (NY: HarperCollins Publishers, 1999), p. 29. Some claim the word means "wise," referring to "wise women" who healed with herbs.

24. The following statement is from a Unitarian-Universalist website in reference to the UU churches: "Found in today's churches are humanism, agnosticism, atheism, theism, liberal Christianity, neo-paganism and earth spiritualism. These beliefs are not mutually exclusive — it's possible to hold more than one. While we are bound by a set of common principles, we leave it to the individual to decide what particular beliefs lead to those principles," http://www.uucnc.org/100q.html#q18. From the official UU website as part of a statement about the traditions from which they draw: "Spiritual teachings of earth-centered traditions which celebrate the sacred circle of life and instruct us to live in harmony with the rhythms of nature," http://www.uua.org/beliefs/principles/.

(CUUPS), which "is an organization dedicated to networking Pagan-identified Unitarian Universalists (UUs), educating people about Paganism, promoting interfaith dialogue, developing Pagan liturgies and theologies, and supporting Pagan-identified UU religious professionals."[25] The adoption of this group in the Unitarian-Universalist Church is arguably an indication of the mainstreaming of Witchcraft and other neo-pagan religions in the United States.

Wiccans may use the term Wiccan or Witch for themselves. Those who follow Wicca may reject the terms Witch or Witchcraft since they consider the term "Witchcraft" to be connected to black magic or casting evil spells, or worry that others view it that way.[26] Wiccans ordinarily perceive their religion to be white Witchcraft or white magic, which is deemed good. Some Wiccans, however, consider Wicca to be neutral in terms of good or bad. On the other hand, those who identify as a "Witch" may deny that Wicca is true Witchcraft, being only a recent innovation and not an ancient authentic religion such as the Witchcraft they follow. Their position may be that Wicca lacks depth or historic validity.

Many classify Wicca as Celtic Witchcraft and therefore different from non-Celtic forms. Then there are those who claim to practice paganism but may call themselves a Witch, and some Wiccans may also use that term. Many are apathetic about which label is used, and others disagree on the meanings, so it is wise to be cautious about applying such terms.

To summarize the view of authority among Wiccans, a person is their own absolute authority on matters of faith and practice within Wicca and Witchcraft, which is actually arbitrary.

Foundations and Beliefs

Doctrine is not primary for Wiccans or Witches.[27] They are more interested in experiences and practice, and they value their Wiccan community as well as the wider community of Wiccans and neo-pagans.

Wiccans "consider themselves priests and priestesses of an ancient European shamanistic nature religion that worships a Goddess who is related to

---

25. From the CUUPS website at http://www.cuups.org/.
26. Guiley, *The Encyclopedia of Witches, Witchcraft, and Wicca*, p. 371–372. This was also the author's experience with Wiccans as her astrological clients.
27. For the difficulty, if not impossibility, of defining Wicca and Witchcraft even among its practitioners, see Adler, *Drawing Down the Moon*, p. 95–103.

the ancient Mother Goddess," writes Adler.[28] Starhawk concurs, declaring that "Witchcraft is a shamanistic religion, and the spiritual value placed on ecstasy is a high one. It is the source of union, healing, creative inspiration, and communion with the divine — whether it is found in the center of a coven circle, in bed with one's beloved, or in the midst of the forest."[29]

"To be a witch," claims another, "means tapping into an ancient energy of wild nature. And also peaceful nature energy."[30] Because nature is sacred, rituals involve calling on spirits and hidden forces of the material creation. Nature spirits, "guardian beings that exist in all life forms in the plant, animal and mineral kingdoms," are called on in rituals for "cooperation and guidance."[31] It is worthwhile noting that using an inner force to cast spells or to summon gods or spirits is typically not seen as a supernatural activity, but as a natural one.

Eight seasonal rituals, called Sabbats, are celebrated throughout the year. Two are at the Summer and Winter Solstices, and two are at the Spring and Autumn Equinoxes. The others are midpoints between those four: February 2, May 1, August 1, and October 31.[32] The phases of the moon are also significant and normally merit a ceremony or ritual.

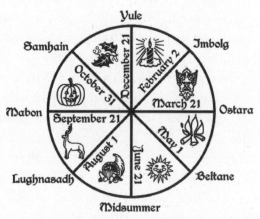

The Wheel of the Year

Divinity

Many Wiccans and Witches hold that Earth is the Goddess and consider Earth to be the source of life, calling the earth "Mother" of all life. Nature is the model and standard for life's principles. An example of this is found in the words of neo-pagan activist and Witch Starhawk: "The store-bought

28. Adler, *Drawing Down the Moon*, p. 10.
29. Starhawk, *The Spiral Dance*, p. 49.
30. Hopman and Bond, *People of the Earth*, p. 65.
31. Guiley, *The Encyclopedia of Witches, Witchcraft, and Wicca*, p. 244.
32. This is called the "Wheel of the Year." Normally Celtic names are given to these celebrations, although other terms can also be used, depending on the group and their tradition.

squash is an object, a dismembered part of the dead world, while the one in my garden is a whole process in which I have participated, from the composting of my garbage to the sense of wonder evoked when I find the vine still producing in November. . . . Our sense of self-worth is dependent on some direct contact with the broader cycles of birth, growth, death, decay, and renewal that do, in reality, sustain our lives."[33]

Male Wiccans and Witches use the same term as females. Although some men may identify as a "Warlock," it is normally used to refer to one who practices black magic, though some Wiccan men may be reclaiming the label.

The one core principle that most Wiccans agree on is what is called the Wiccan Rede: "An ye harm none, do what ye will."[34] Many believe Gardner adapted this from ceremonial magician Aleister Crowley's Law of Thelema, which states, "Do what thou wilt shall be the whole of the law."[35] The stand against doing harm leads Wiccans to think that they are practicing a good religion.

Basics of Wiccan belief about the divine typically include Pantheism or Panentheism, Duotheism, Polytheism, and regarding nature as sacred.

Pantheism is the view that all is God(dess), and that God(dess) is all and thus assumes divine forces within oneself and in nature.

Panentheism holds that all is in God(dess), and god(s), and God(dess) and god(s) are in all. This allows for the Goddess or gods to transcend creation.

Duotheism is the belief in two gods, commonly found in Wicca. In the case of Wicca, it is the Goddess and her consort, a male god. They are customarily referred to as the Lord and the Lady.

33. Starhawk, *Truth or Dare* (NY: HarperCollins Publishers, 1987, paperback edition, 1990), p. 200.
34. Adler, *Drawing Down the Moon*, p. 97; Guiley, *The Encyclopedia of Witches, Witchcraft, and Wicca*, p. 371–373.
35. Adler, *Drawing Down the Moon*, p. 97; Hutton, *The Triumph of the Moon*, p. 247–248. Aleister Crowley's Thelemic Law, "Do what thou will shall be the whole of the law" is routinely cited by modern-day Satanists as their creed, leading to the mistaken belief that Crowley was a Satanist. He was actually a ritual magician involved in many secret occult groups and activities, and notorious for debauched practices, though it is difficult to know what he actually did and did not do since he seemingly enjoyed his infamous reputation.

Polytheism is the belief there are many gods, or that many gods and goddesses are multiple separate manifestations of one god.

The Goddess is also known as the "Great Mother" or "Queen of Heaven." The focus on the Goddess comes in part from Robert Graves, poet Robert Bly, and others, positing that "matriarchy was not a historical state but a psychological reality with a great power that is alive and generally repressed in human beings today,"[36]

Wiccan Lady and Lord statues

This Goddess focus has created a feminist-oriented religion for many followers of Wicca.

The consort is usually referred to as the "horned god," who is the male principle of the creative force, sometimes identified with the mythical Greek god, Pan.[37] Starhawk writes that the horns of this god are the "waxing and waning crescents of the Goddess Moon, and the symbol of animal vitality."[38] Another asserts that the horns are antlers, standing for the animals killed by the hunter for the tribe.[39] This god is a hunter and a creature of earthy passions, representing the untamed woods and wildlife. The sun is one of his symbols, and the seasons symbolize his dying and rebirth.[40]

For some, the Goddess and/or gods are actual beings or forces of creation; for others, they represent the inner Goddess or god within each person. Still others may see the gods as psychological metaphors or illustrative of nature's powers. Additionally, there is belief in nature spirits and in forces or gods that inhabit and guide creation. A number of Wiccans and Witches

36. Adler, *Drawing Down the Moon*, p. 196.
37. Guiley, *The Encyclopedia of Witches, Witchcraft, and Wicca*, p. 169–170.
38. Starhawk, *The Spiral Dance*, p. 120. Starhawk often cites the discredited Margaret Murray or Robert Graves as sources.
39. Ashleen O'Gaea, *Family Wicca* (Franklin, NJ: The Career Press, 2006), p. 215.
40. Ibid. The "dying and rising" gods are ascribed to ancient pagan cults. Claims that Jesus is a "copycat Savior" based on these gods has been thoroughly refuted. Many online websites address this issue, such as Christian Think Tank at http://christianthinktank.com/copycat.html and Tektonics at http://www.tektonics.org/copycathub.html.

are non-theists or are even atheists, discounting belief in God or denying that God (or any god) exists.[41]

Many Wiccans revere what is known as the Triple Goddess.[42] She is maiden (or virgin), mother, and crone, the three aspects of the Goddess and the feminine nature, corresponding respectively to the new, full, and waning cycles of the moon. As maiden, she is youth, vitality, and pleasure. "Virgin" in this case is not sexual purity, but rather exemplifies that she is not possessed by anyone. The mother aspect is in her prime as nurturer and protector.

Image of Triple Goddess

This archetype is often related to the veneration of Earth as mother, nurturer, and healer. The last stage, crone, is considered the culmination of wisdom, representing independence and power. The stereotyped witch of an old woman with pointed chin and wart is, according to Witchcraft, a perverted version of the crone. Some Witches may even claim that the Trinity was a copy of the Triple Goddess.[43]

The Christian God is regularly stigmatized as patriarchal and oppressive to women, and the Bible is seen as the work of men who were toeing the line for those in charge of what is called "organized religion" (viewed as patriarchal, rules-based, and unjust to minorities).

---

41. The fact that there are agnostic and atheist Witches may be surprising. However, in Wicca and Witchcraft, the Goddess and gods are often metaphors or symbols and not always accepted as having substantive reality. Those who have this view may therefore decide that there is no actual Goddess or god.

42. Some believe the ideas of the Horned God and Triple Goddess came from Robert Graves' writings; Hutton, *The Triumph of the Moon*, p. 188, 194; or from Margaret Murray's works; Guiley, *The Encyclopedia of Witches, Witchcraft, and Wicca*, p. 238. Hutton touches on earlier (but later invalidated) prominent ancient goddesses or three-fold goddesses proposed by various scholars, p. 36–37.

43. In 1995, during a talk to a youth group at a church, the author was told by an eighth-grader that he was told by a Wiccan student at school that the Trinity was copied from the Triple Goddess, which predated it. He did not know how to respond to this. Although the author had known Wiccans and neo-pagans in her past as an astrologer and New Ager, this incident indicated that Wicca was in secondary schools in her area. This led the author to write her first article on Wicca, and to start speaking on it.

Jesus

There are differing assessments of Jesus Christ among Wiccans and Witches. Some reject Him as a symbol of Christian oppression of Witchcraft and/ or women while others regard Him as an enlightened spiritual teacher. Still others may consider Him another god and incorporate Him into their pantheon of pagan gods and goddesses. A few may deny Jesus existed. There is even a branch of Wicca called Christian Wicca that attempts to combine the ethical teachings of Jesus with Wiccan ethics (this is an example of syncretism, mixing two different religions together). Like many beliefs in Wicca and Witchcraft, there are spectrums with wide ranges. Most Wiccans I have encountered in my ministry experience are open to discussion about Jesus and generally are positive about Him.

Satan is rejected as real, and assessed to be an invention of the Christian church authorities in order to keep people subjugated. Although there can be individual crossovers from Witchcraft into Satanism, and though some Satanists might call themselves Witches, these two groups are separate (see chapter 13 on Satanism in volume 1). The line between the two groups becomes more blurred among those younger people who dabble in and mix several belief systems, but it is crucial to recognize that Witches and Wiccans are not Satanists, and, in fact, they do not generally like or get along with Satanists.[44]

Nature of Man

People are born basically good, but if hurt or damaged in life they may become out of balance within themselves and with nature. This can lead to the desire to do harm or to do wrong. Since there is no concept of a righteous God, there is no acceptance of the concept of sin, and thus there is no belief about being born with a desire to do harm or wrong. Wiccans and Witches will admit that they have flaws and make mistakes, and state this is why they need to adhere to the Wiccan Rede and strive to be better. The idea of being in balance is thought to bring harmony and to remedy potentials to commit harm.

Symbolism and Practices

Due to the experiential nature of Wicca, the use of symbols is important. The most well-known symbol is the pentacle or pentagram, a five-pointed

---

44. Nor do Satanists like Witches. Satanists regard Witchcraft and Wicca as a "white-light religion," whose followers attempt to hew to a moral code and do good, something for which Satanists have contempt.

star with the top point normally facing up, representing the four elements of earth, air, fire, and water, plus
Spirit.[45] Other symbols include the Ankh (an Egyptian
cross-like symbol associated with the worship of Isis
and topped by a noticeable loop, representing immortality and the union of male and female) and the crescent moon (symbol of the Goddess). Crystals, believed

Pentagram

to contain healing and spiritual properties, are frequently worn as jewelry,
on clothes, or even carried in small pouches.[46]

Meditation, visualization,[47] invocation,[48] calling on the four directions
of north, south, east, and west for rituals, chanting, burning candles, and
special rituals trigger a sense of the mystical, thus reinforcing the core belief
system. Practicing these techniques over a period of time can lead to ecstatic
or even what appear to be paranormal experiences because of the subjective
expectation, and there are demonic forces that will respond to those who
open themselves to such influence (1 Corinthians 10:19–22).[49]

Wiccans view magic and power as neutral, and it is in the intentions
of the Wiccan in use of such magic where good and evil lie. Most Wiccans
would agree with Aleister Crowley's definition of magic: "the science and art
of causing change to occur in conformity to the will."[50] Starhawk writes that
power is "the subtle force that shapes reality" and "is raised through chanting
and dancing and may be directed through a symbol or visualization."[51] This
is a common outlook of the use of magical power in Wicca.

Magic and rituals are inexorably linked in Wicca. Doing magic is done
in the context of rituals, and magic is invoking power from external gods or
forces through ritual and/or raising energy from within through ritual.[52] Magic
is perceived as a natural force, sometimes called a psychic force, resulting from

---

45. Typically, a pentagram with the two points up and the one point down is used by Satanists
    to represent the carnal (the two points) over spirit (the one point), although some Witch-
    craft groups use the pentagram with the two points up, according to a few Wiccan sources.
46. This is common also in the New Age.
47. Visualizing something for the purposes of bringing it into reality.
48. Summoning supernatural forces or gods/goddesses.
49. This is the personal belief of the author.
50. Guiley, *The Encyclopedia of Witches, Witchcraft, and Wicca*, p. 216.
51. Starhawk *The Spiral Dance*, p. 38.
52. For neo-pagan and Wiccan views of magic, see Adler, chapter 7, "Magic and Ritual," p.
    156; also see lengthy entry on magic in Guiley, *The Encyclopedia of Witches, Witchcraft, and
    Wicca*, p. 215–220.

the beliefs and the will of the practitioner done in concert with the ritual. As one Wiccan writes, "Magic at its most basic is energy collected from life's reservoir, shaped, and directed towards a goal. Wiccans work magic in particular ways, with certain words and gestures, because over generations, these forms have acquired power of our understanding-in-common."[53]

The state of mind achieved in this practice is considered to be an "altered state," that is, a state similar to a hypnotic or trance state. The person is still aware of one's surroundings but becomes receptive and open to another dimension of knowledge or understanding.[54] Starhawk writes extensively of "the trance state," and, while admitting it makes the mind more suggestible, extols it for opening the self to creativity, insight, growth of psychic powers, and revelation.[55]

Individual Wiccans may set up altars at home, consisting of representations of the Goddess and the god, items standing for the four elements, candles, a book in which to record spells, magical objects, and items with personal meaning. The altar serves as a base for ceremonies, rituals, and spells.

Wiccan altar

53. O'Gaea, *Family Wicca*, p. 99.
54. The author of this chapter is familiar with altered states, as she herself entered altered states during Eastern forms of meditation, past life regression exercises, and when reading astrological charts for clients during her years in the New Age. Seen as valid by those in the occult and New Age, this state is actually dangerous as it renders the mind more suggestible to outside influences, including from the demonic realm.
55. Starhawk, *The Spiral Dance*, p. 171; chapter 9 in this book, "Trance," is devoted entirely to this topic.

Wiccan and Witchcraft groups may combine their beliefs with or base their beliefs on cultural mystical traditions such as Celtic or Norse paganism, the Greek/Roman goddesses, ancient Egyptian spirituality, Eastern shamanism, or Native American spirituality. As an astrologer, I knew one group that was very involved in Native American rituals (or what they perceived to be) such as vision quests, sweat lodges, the wearing of a medicine pouch,[56] ritual dancing, having a totem animal, and other related practices. I had been on a retreat with them, and participated in what was called a "vision quest" to discover my "totem animal," a spirit animal that is a guide but also symbolizes the seeker's path in this life.

After a few years of knowing this group, the leader told me one day that what they thought were aliens were hovering over them and would not leave. I recall the leader showing real fear when relaying this. He said that he thought they were there to take over their bodies. At the time, I did not know how to process this information, especially since the whole group had experienced this. I knew the leader was sane and no one seemed unstable or deluded. Now, as a Christian, I believe that this was clearly the presence of demons who were drawn there due to the group's occult practices. Most in the group ended up leaving shortly after and went to another state.

Divination techniques[57] such as tarot cards, astrology, runes (stones with symbols connected to Norse pagan religions), the I Ching (from Chinese Taoism), clairvoyant or psychic readings, candle magic, and other occult practices are not only common but encouraged as well (though not practiced by all).

Many Witches and Wiccans are initiated via a ritual into covens, or they initiate themselves if they are solo practitioners. Opinions on initiation and when and how it is done vary widely. Traditionally, one is initiated after one year and one day of study, though this is not always followed.[58]

It is important to keep in mind that Wicca and Witchcraft are fluid systems, and can incorporate new ideas and discard old ones, although the

---

56. These pouches can contain bits of nature, such as stones or sticks, or anything representing something special or powerful to the wearer, sometimes something associated with the person's spirit animal, a guide from the spirit world in the shape of an animal. The pouch and its contents are considered an amulet, something which allegedly attracts protection.

57. Divination in a pagan or an occult context is gaining information and advice through occult techniques and esoteric symbols or omens. Divination is forbidden throughout the Bible.

58. Starhawk, *The Spiral Dance*, p. 188.

focus on earth, nature, and rituals remain. Also, many practitioners incorporate New Age beliefs.[59]

Although there are ritual magicians who cast spells, they follow another occult system and beliefs, and do not normally align themselves with Witchcraft.

Wicca has been around long enough now to have been passed down in families to younger generations; thus, there are more books and materials on Wiccan parenting and books for children in Wiccan families, such as *Family Wicca* by Ashleen O'Gaea (who also authored *Raising Witches: Teaching the Wiccan Faith to Children*, a book on how to organize religion classes for pagan children).[60]

Morality

Wiccans and Witches tend to disbelieve in absolutes, so there is no absolute good or evil, and no standard for it. Wiccans determine good and evil subjectively. Naturally this is a problem since they can't be *absolutely* sure that there is no absolute good or evil, which means this view is fallacious. Some adhere to the "Law of Three," which is the belief that what you do comes back to you threefold.

Many hold to a principle of opposites called Polarity. Polarity is based on a view of tension and balance between opposites. As one puts it, "The most crucial polarity is that between the life force and the death force, Eros and Thanatos if you will."[61] This latter notion has appeared to become more widespread since the initial days of the popular "white Witchcraft" standpoint.

Witches Janet and Stewart Farrar explain it this way: "The Theory of Polarity maintains that all activity, all manifestation, arises from (and is

---

59. The New Age, although some of it overlaps with neo-paganism, has a different worldview than that of neo-paganism. The New Age is more transcendent, future-oriented, God and Christ-oriented (though it is not the biblical God or Christ), and Gnostic in nature than neo-pagan beliefs like Wicca or Witchcraft; and the New Age regards mankind differently. The New Age is more apt to quote the Bible and use Christian terminology. Some Goddess-worshiping New Agers combine beliefs with neo-paganism; this could be considered a feminist-based Goddess religion existing apart from Wicca and the New Age, and is often called Goddess spirituality. But there are no objective, clear lines of demarcation apart from those drawn by the followers themselves or those who study these belief systems.
60. O'Gaea, *Family Wicca*, p. 79. O'Gaea admits to strong influences from Adler's *Drawing Down the Moon* and Starhawk's *The Spiral Dance*, p. 18.
61. "Why I Don't Like Scott Cunningham," Michael Kaufman, http://www.wildideas.net/temple/library/letters/cunningham1.html.

inconceivable without) the interaction of pairs and complementary opposites . . . and that this polarity is not a conflict between 'good' and 'evil,' but a creative tension like that between the positive and negative terminals of an electric battery. Good and evil only arise with the constructive or destructive application of the polarity's output."[62]

They further state that monotheists are trapped in the belief that good versus evil is a polarity and that "under the unchallenged rule of a non-polarized Creator, nothing can happen."[63] This is a misconception of the God of the Bible; I will discuss this in more detail in a moment. Furthermore, three essential ideas relevant to morality are stated here: (1) an all-good Creator is static, (2) the basis for polarity is not good versus evil, and (3) good cannot exist without evil.

Yin yang symbol

The Farrars use the Yin-Yang symbol to explain this concept. One side is black with a white dot in it, and the other side is white with a black dot in it. Most people think that this symbol represents opposites, but it actually represents the concept of polarity.[64] The dark and light sides are polarities that need to be balanced. Why does each side have a dot of the other color in it? It is because although they appear to be opposites, in actuality they are constantly changing and merging with each other, thus becoming each other. The dark becomes light and light becomes dark. There is no absolute dark or absolute light.[65]

Even the Goddess and gods are not viewed as absolutely good and are said to have a "dark side" to them. This stands in stark contrast to God who is good by His very nature (Psalm 100:5, 145:9). The natural result of this is that there is no final judgment on actions, certainly not from a divine source. In the book *Family Wicca*, while admitting that bad behavior should not be tolerated, the author writes that there is no "divine punishment for evildoing," only "the healing, only the learning."[66] Consider the

62. Janet and Stewart Farrar, *A Witches' Bible*, Part 2 (Custer, WA: Phoenix Publishing, Inc., 1996), p. 107.

63. Ibid., p. 111.

64. The Yin and Yang symbol arose from the ancient Chinese religion of Taoism (see chapter 3), and the idea expressed by the Farrars is very much like that in Taoism. In Taoist belief, the forces of Yin and Yang were produced by the morally neutral source of all, the Tao.

65. From a discussion of the New Age and occult stances on good and evil in the writer's website article, "The Dark Side: Beyond Good and Evil," http://christiananswersforthenewage. org/Articles_DarkSide1.html.

66. O'Gaea, *Family Wicca*, p. 129.

implications of this — without an absolute standard, an individual could justify any act by having good intentions. This is an example of the arbitrary nature of this worldview.

Although belief in evil entities or spirits is not uncommon among Wiccans, outside evil may be considered to be a psychological metaphor, representing a difficult or negative aspect within, which the Wiccan must confront and accept. In fact, Starhawk describes a ritual designed for this confrontation.[67]

Evolution, Death, and Salvation

Wiccans and Witches are very much oriented to the present, so issues about the origin of the universe or life on Earth, as well as ultimate destinies, are not of much concern. Individuals may have their own outlooks, but there are no prevailing beliefs on evolution or any scenario about the end of the world, although some hold to accounts from pagan mythologies as a creation story.[68] Some may regard the existence of Earth as part of a larger cycle that will end and then repeat, as is found in the natural world through the seasons.

Death is seen as part of life and is neutral, or is seen as the opposite polarity of life. "Death is not an end; it is a stage in the cycle that leads on to to rebirth," and "an immanent spirituality cannot deny death. Death is part of life. When we embrace life, we must also embrace the sorrow at its ending,"[69] writes Starhawk.

In email contact with a 13-year-old Wiccan over a period of several months, I once asked this young lady, who believed nature to be sacred, how she would understand it if she were in a forest and lightning hit a tree that fell on her, bringing death. She replied that death was natural, and had to be accepted. Death is not bad or evil.

Time may be seen as a series of cycles, and reincarnation is popular.[70] However, unlike in Hinduism, Wiccans see reincarnation as a "gift of the

---

67. Starhawk, *The Spiral Dance*, p. 166–167.
68. For example, see Starhawk, *The Spiral Dance*, p. 41–42.
69. Ibid., p. 51; Starhawk, *Truth or Dare*, p. 45.
70. Adler, *Drawing Down the Moon*, p. 109. Author's note: Reincarnation is a Hindu and New Age belief that one has many lives; that is, living, dying, and returning in a different body, and doing this repeatedly for thousands or tens of thousands of years. The person supposedly is learning lessons this way, ultimately leading to enlightenment and liberation from this cycle of reincarnation.

Goddess, who is manifest in the physical world. Life and the world are not separate from Godhead."[71]

Others believe in a place called Summerland where the dead are reunited with deceased loved ones in a beautiful place, an idea also found in Theosophy and Spiritualism.[72] One Wiccan states that in the Summerland, "we realize ourselves and our Self."[73] Those who accept reincarnation may see Summerland as the resting place between incarnations where one is "refreshed" and prepared for rebirth on Earth.[74]

Death is a "healing, a loving restoration rather than a punishing destruction" and mortality is sacred.[75] Writing further, the same Wiccan, who worships the Wiccan Goddess, declares that "Death's path to rebirth is the adventure for which all mythical and legendary quests are metaphors."[76]

Atheists and agnostic Wiccans generally hold that life ends at death, and their bodies go back to the Earth. The Goddess or gods are only symbolic for them. However, there are many Wiccans who think the Goddess and gods are merely symbolic but who, nevertheless, believe in life after death.

Since Wicca and Witchcraft reject the concept of sin, the teaching that death is a result of sin or is something to be eradicated is an alien concept, as is the idea of salvation. One must learn lessons to be a better person, but the need for salvation is foreign to Wicca.

The Christian Response

The worldview of Wicca and Witchcraft is remarkably different from the Christian one. It is best to be informed before speaking with those involved in these groups. Because there is such a wide array of beliefs, do not assume what someone claiming to be a Wiccan believes or attempt to refute ideas they may not hold. Asking questions is a good way to find out what the

71. Starhawk, *The Spiral Dance*, p. 51; Hinduism views the physical world as an illusion and an impersonal, transcendent force directs reincarnation.
72. Theosophy is an Eastern-based occult group started in the 1800s by Madame Blavatsky, who claimed to have learned secret teachings, mostly in India and Tibet. Theosophy was a major influence on the New Age Movement. Spiritualism is a religious practice and denomination based primarily on contacting the dead for guidance.
73. O'Gaea, *Family Wicca*, p. 129. O'Gaea refers to Irish paganism, and states that Summerland "encompasses the Underworld, Fairyland, and other realms, several astral planes, and a variety of states of mind and being," p. 221.
74. Ibid., p. 221; Starhawk, *The Spiral Dance*, p. 51.
75. O'Gaea, *Family Wicca*, p. 140–141.
76. Ibid., p. 142.

person believes and to direct the conversation in a way that deals individually with that person's views (Colossians 4:2–6).

Basic Wiccan Beliefs

- The natural world and experience are the basis for truth and ethics.

- There is a Goddess, a Goddess and god, many gods, or no gods.

- Power/magic is neutral.

- Good and evil are determined subjectively.

- Although there may be deceptive or even evil spirits, Satan does not exist as an actual, personal being.

- Nature is sacred and there should be a relationship with it.

- Death is not bad nor necessarily final.

Biblical Responses

In contrast, there is the truth as revealed by God, including responses to some assertions made in Wicca.

Absolute good and evil is taught in both the Old and New Testaments. God is absolutely good: "This is the message which we have heard from Him and declare to you, that God is light and in Him is no darkness at all" (1 John 1:5). God is described in 1 Timothy 6:16 as the one "who alone has immortality, dwelling in unapproachable light, whom no man has seen or can see, to whom be honor and everlasting power." Be fervently aware that non-Christians usually do not have the concept of what "righteous" means, much less the concept of a holy God who judges sin. Therefore, do not assume any understanding of these views. Be patient in explaining the nature of God and His righteousness without using theological words.

Satan is real, a fallen spiritual being, in total rebellion against a righteous God who created him, and is evil. Referring to Satan as a personal being, Jesus asserts, "When he speaks a lie, he speaks from his own resources, for he is a liar and the father of it" (John 8:44). Satan can disguise himself as something beautiful, as an angel of light, and in this guise, he is more deadly since he is not easily recognized (see 2 Corinthians 11:14–15).

The concept of polarity regarding good and evil is at odds with what God has revealed. Evil is not necessary for good, nor should we seek balance between light and darkness. Evil is the corruption or rejection of good. As Romans 12:21 puts it: "Do not be overcome by evil, but overcome evil with good." While current culture denies absolute good and evil, God's word is clear that there is a line between good and evil: "Woe to those who call evil good, and good evil; who put darkness for light and light for darkness; who put bitter for sweet and sweet for bitter!" (Isaiah 5:20).

Death, both physical and spiritual, is the result of sin due to man's disobedience, and is the "enemy," according to Scripture (see Romans 5:12–17; 1 Corinthians 15:26). Spiritual death after physical death is eternal separation from life in God's presence. Death will be thrown into the lake of fire at the time of God's final judgment that will be an eternal punishment with no rest (Revelation 20:14).

"Do no harm" is the Wiccan creed. However, since Wiccans deny absolute good or evil, they have no standard by which to decide what harm is or if this creed has any authority behind it anyway. Thus, their notions of what constitutes harm are totally subjective. Wiccans believe that dark and light need each other in order to exist and that dark and light will always balance each other out.

Witches may claim the Bible does not condemn Witchcraft, since they assert that the real interpretation of the Hebrew word for "witchcraft" should be understood as sorcery or divination. This is technically correct. However, the point is moot since the Bible strongly condemns the worship of gods or goddesses other than the biblical God, divination, and spell-casting, all of which are practiced or endorsed by most Wiccans (Deuteronomy 4:19, 12:1–4; Romans 1:22–23).

Wiccans may argue that sorcery is black magic used for evil, and that they practice white magic — magic for good. But the Bible makes no distinction between "good" or "bad" magic or magic versus sorcery. All occult magic has the same source and is abhorred by God.[77]

Witches and Wiccans may assert that the original religion was centered on the Goddess, and that Christianity, being a patriarchal religion,

---

77. Selected Scripture verses on divination, sorcery, and magic: Exodus 22:18; Leviticus 19:26, 31, 20:6, 27; Deuteronomy 18:10–12; 1 Samuel 15:23; 2 Kings 23:24; 1 Chronicles 10:13; Isaiah 2:6, 8:19–20, 47:13–14; Ezekiel 13:20–23; Daniel 2:27–28, 5:15–17; Acts 13:7–10, 16:16–18; Galatians 5:19–20; Revelation 22:15.

suppressed the Goddess religions like Witchcraft. As mentioned earlier, archaeological and historical research show that although many cultures worshiped Goddesses, the Goddesses were consorts or counterparts of male gods. Another point to make is that although God is Spirit, He makes it clear in His Word that He desires us to think of Him as Father when we come to Him through faith in Christ. Jesus called God His Father. Moreover, it is the Christian Scriptures that speak of women as equals to men as opposed to most other cultural and religious teachings or practices. In John chapter 4, Jesus talks to the Samaritan woman at the well, an astonishing thing for a Jewish man to do in that day and in that culture. Not only does Jesus talk to her, but He reveals Himself as the Messiah to her. Then she, an immoral woman of the village, is the one to take the news to the men. It was women who discovered and reported the empty tomb after the Resurrection of Jesus. Scriptural passages teach men to love their wives as their own body, and to love them as Christ loves the Church, which is pictured as His bride in Scripture (Ephesians 5: 25–33; Colossians 3:18–19). There is no biblical endorsement for male tyranny or abuse.

Witches may claim that theirs is an ancient religion which predates Christianity. However, Christ, being the Son of God and God the Son, is eternal, which means He has no beginning. It is Christ who predates all religions and God alone is worthy of worship from the beginning of time.[78]

Witches frequently do not know the true gospel; their opposition is to organized religion, which they arbitrarily see as an oppressive system of control and rules. It is true that religion is often just that. But biblical Christianity is a relationship with the living Christ, not a system of rules, rituals, or self-help.

Keep in mind that some Wiccans have had hurtful experiences in churches. All humanity falls short of the standard — which is a perfect, righteous God.[79] The standard is not man or other Christians. *God* is that ultimate standard. This is why Christ came, to live the perfect life and pay the penalty for our sins so that through faith, one is reconciled to God.[80]

Dialoguing with Wiccans

There is no formula for witnessing to someone in Wicca, especially since Wiccans are inclined to be individualistic. The Christian should first regard the

---

78. John 8:56–58; Colossians 1:15–17; 1 Peter 1:19–20; Revelation 1:17, 13:8.
79. Romans 3:23–24.
80. Romans 8:1–4; 2 Corinthians 5:18–20.

person as someone made in the image of God and not just a Wiccan, and pray for courage as well as love in sharing Christ. Always speak with grace: "Walk in wisdom toward those who are outside, redeeming the time. Let your speech always be with grace, seasoned with salt, that you may know how you ought to answer each one" (Colossians 4:5–6). Since occult views vary, begin by asking what his or her particular beliefs are; don't assume anything.

Ask the person what drew him or her into Wicca.

It is helpful as well to find out the person's spiritual background, and why they reject Christianity. Listen respectfully, and calmly correct any major wrong views about the gospel, which is of primary importance. Avoid rabbit trails and secondary issues.

Ask questions that will get the person to think specifically about their ideas. For example, if the person believes that good and evil are relative, ask for examples and how that works in real life. If the person regards God as an impersonal force, ask, "Why then do you think it is that we are all beings who seek personal relationships?"

Don't use terms the person may not understand such as *atonement, redemption, justification,* etc.; it's better to give examples of what these are and take care to explain them accurately.

Christians are to be prudent, vigilant, and discerning, but not afraid; therefore, have no fear in speaking to anyone involved in Witchcraft.[81]

Don't try to prove the Wiccan wrong at every point; instead, seek to discuss the nature of God and Jesus, especially Jesus' power over nature, demons, and illness, as narrated in the Gospels.

Don't hesitate to stand on the truths of Scripture, such as Jesus being the only way to God, but do this with gentleness and love.[82] Unbelievers tend to not respect people who waver on their beliefs.

Let the person see Jesus' love in you. The person may be suffering the scary or damaging effects of occult practice but most likely will not share this information in an initial conversation.

A mini-gospel that could be presented would be: "Jesus is the Son of God who came to earth as man to live a perfect life in complete obedience to God, because none of us can do that. We are born with a desire to do our will, not God's will, and we do things every day that are opposed to God.

---

81. 1 John 4:4; 2 Timothy 1:7.
82. 1 Peter 3:15.

This is called sin, and it leads eventually to dissatisfaction and despair. The ultimate penalty for sin is death, eternal separation from God. But since Jesus lived the perfect life, He was able to pay for the penalty of sins when He died on the Cross. He bodily rose the third day, conquering death, which is an enemy. By believing in who Jesus is and that there is nothing you can do to pay for your own opposition to the one true God, you are forgiven of all your sins and have eternal life."

An Encouraging Word

Jesus is the Light, and those who believe in Him become "sons of Light" and are to walk "as children of Light."[83] Treating Wiccans with kindness and respect is a way to show them this Light that indwells us through the Holy Spirit. Witnessing to someone in Wicca or Witchcraft not only reveals Christ's love and truth to that person, but permits the Christian to experience His amazing love and power as well.

Summary of Wiccan Beliefs

Doctrine	Teachings of Wicca
God	Deny the existence of a sovereign, supreme god. Beliefs vary, but many look to goddesses and spirits associated with aspects of nature; many worship the Earth as Mother Nature and goddesses that emanate from the Mother Goddess; some believe the Goddess has a consort, the Lady and the Lord; others are atheistic or view the "gods" as psychological aspects of the material world.
Authority/Revelation	There is no standard work of Wiccan beliefs and practices, but the *Book of Shadows* and other modern writings guide many. Various modern authors have developed specific sects that are often blended together, despite their contradictory elements. Experience is more valuable than absolute truth.
Man	Mankind is born basically good, but is subject to becoming out of balance with self or nature through harm or wrongs done to them.

---

83. John 12:36; Ephesians 5:8.

Sin	"Do no harm" is the Wiccan creed of ethics. Nature is the model and standard for life's principles. Good and evil are determined by intentions.
Salvation	One must learn lessons to be a better person, but the need for salvation is foreign to Wicca. The afterlife is often viewed as a peaceful place or a place of preparation for reincarnation.
Creation	Views vary, with some embracing general evolutionary views while others accept various pagan mythologies; the biblical account is generally rejected.

Chapter 11

Druidism

Bob Gillespie

"Druids Recognized as a Religion in the UK"

Druids have been worshipping the sun and earth for thousands of years in Europe, but now worshippers can say they're practicing an officially recognized religion.

The ancient pagan tradition, best known for gatherings at Stonehenge every summer solstice, has been formally classed as a religion under charity law for the first time in Britain. That means Druids can receive exemptions from taxes on donations, and now have the same status as such mainstream religions as the Church of England.

Phil Ryder, the chairman of the 350-member Druid Network, said "It will go a long way to make Druidry a lot more accessible."[1]

While Druidry may seem to be an obscure religion, there are up to 50,000 practicing Druids worldwide. Over a half a million people regard themselves as pagan, and many would consider themselves inspired by Druidism.

---

1. "Druids Recognized as Religion in the UK," CBS News, October 2, 2010, http://www.cbsnews.com/news/druids-recognized-as-religion-in-the-uk.

Druids participate in a ceremony at Stonehenge

Ancient Druids

History of Ancient Druids

Druidism was the ancient religious faith found in Gaul and later England and Ireland as the Romans pushed northward. The term "Druid" derives from an old Welsh term for oak, implying that they are the people who know the wisdom of the trees.

The Druid religion is most commonly associated with the Celts, a European cultural group first evident in the seventh or eighth century B.C. who eventually occupied much of northern Europe. The Celts arrived in Ireland by the second or third century B.C., and possibly earlier, displacing an earlier people who were already on the islands. The Gauls, Britons, and Irish were all Celtic people. The Romans never occupied Ireland, nor did the Anglo-Saxons who invaded Britain after the Romans withdrew in the fifth century, so Celtic culture survived more strongly in Ireland than elsewhere.

There is disagreement about whether or not the Druids actually built Stonehenge. It is not clear exactly when the Druids came to Britain, but it is likely that they arrived after Stonehenge was built.

Although the Celts had a written language, it was rarely used or what had been written was destroyed or lost. Their religious and philosophical beliefs were preserved in an oral tradition — and much of that has likely been altered, lost, or embellished. We have no writings from the Druids, and what we know about them is through secondary sources. Many modern authors have colored our understanding of the Druids with claims that have no legitimate historical basis. Little of their early history remains, and most of our legitimate information about the Druids comes from Greek and Roman writers.

According to Julius Caesar, who is the principal source of information about the Druids, the Druids took charge of public and private sacrifices, and many young men went to them for instruction. They judged all public and private quarrels and decreed penalties. If anyone disobeyed their decree, he was barred from sacrifice, which was considered the gravest of punishments. Once a year the Druids assembled at a sacred place in the territory of the Carnutes, believed to be the center of all Gaul. All legal disputes were submitted there to the judgment of the Druids.[2]

The early Christian missionary St. Patrick is credited for bringing Christianity to Ireland in the fourth century A.D. As the Christian religion spread into Northern Europe and the British Isles, the Druid influence began to fade and eventually all but disappeared.

Beliefs of Ancient Druids

Within ancient Druidism, there were three groups with different functions:

- The Bards were "the keepers of tradition, of the memory of the tribe — they were the custodians of the

---

2. Encyclopedia Britannica Online, s.v. "Druid," accessed February 9, 2016, http://www.britannica.com/topic/Druid.

sacredness of the Word." In Ireland, they trained for 12 years learning grammar, hundreds of stories, poems, philosophy, etc.

• The Ovates worked with the processes of death and regeneration. They were the native healers of the Celts. They specialized in divination, conversing with the ancestors, and prophesying the future.

• The Druids formed the professional class in Celtic society. They performed the functions of modern-day priests, teachers, ambassadors, astronomers, genealogists, philosophers, musicians, theologians, scientists, poets, and judges. They underwent lengthy training; some sources say as much as 20 years. Druids led public rituals, which were normally held within fenced groves of sacred trees. In their role as priests, "they acted not as mediators between God and man, but as directors of ritual, as shamans guiding and containing the rites."[3]

The Druids believed that the dead were transported to the Otherworld by the god Bile (also Bel, Belenus).[4] Life supposedly continued in the Otherworld much as it had before death. The ancient Druids believed that the soul was immortal. After the person died in the Otherworld, their soul reincarnated and lived again in another living entity — either in a plant or the body of a human or other animal. After a person had learned enough at this level, they moved on after death to a higher realm, which has its own Otherworld. This continued until the individual reached the highest realm, the "Source."[5]

St. Patrick's confrontation with Druidism of fifth century Ireland can give us much insight into that culture, and is especially instructional to Christians today who are dealing with modern Druidism or other neo-pagan religions. After having been enslaved by Irish Druids, Patrick escaped to return home to England. There he studied Christianity and eventually returned to Ireland as a missionary to the very tribes that had enslaved him.

---

3. "Celtic Druidism: Beliefs, Practices & Celebrations," Religious Tolerance, accessed February 9, 2016, http://www.religioustolerance.org/druid2.htm.

4. Bel or Belus has often been denoted as a variant name of biblical Nimrod by historians and ancient researchers.

5. "Celtic Druidism: Beliefs, Practices & Celebrations," Religious Tolerance, accessed February 10, 2016, http://www.religioustolerance.org/druid2.htm.

St. Patrick understood that to engage Celtic Druidic culture was indeed a spiritual battle. Missionaries in similar tribal cultures will attest to that spiritual warfare. Patrick is credited with using a song or chant as he went out to minister. This song acknowledged the spiritual battle he faced and pointed the Druids to trusting in Christ as their salvation rather than their man-made traditions.

Many people have attempted to connect some of the various aspects of modern celebrations like Halloween and various seasonal festivals to the Druids. However, no records of these celebrations exists and we are left with only third-hand accounts to substantiate such claims. One thing that we can be sure of is the co-opting of certain pagan festivals by the Roman Catholic Church. The pagan celebration of the dead that occurred at the end of October was absorbed into the Roman Catholic feast of All Saints' Day, preceded by All Hallows' Evening — from which the modern name "Halloween" is derived. How much of the specific traditions we currently associate with Halloween is rooted in Druid practice is speculative. Regardless of their origins, many of these practices are unbiblical and we should guard ourselves against engaging in them.[6]

Culture of Ancient Druids

Ancient Druids acted as shamans who, through various rituals, consulted their ancestors who dwelt in the spirit world. The modern-day equivalent to these ancient Druids would be the witch doctors found in tribal animism. Modern Druids freely admit that their beliefs are animistic in nature.

"Druidry is essentially an animistic tradition."[7]

"For many people, myself included, Druidry and Animism go hand in hand."[8]

Because of the similarity between the Druids of the past and current animism, much can be learned about the ancient Celtic culture by looking at the animistic tribes that exist today. Encyclopedia Britannica describes

---

6. Bodie Hodge, "Halloween History and the Bible," Answers in Genesis, October 29, 2013, https://answersingenesis.org/holidays/halloween-history-and-the-bible.
7. "Are All Druids Animistic?" Druid Network, accessed February 10, 2016, https://druid-network.org/what-is-druidry/beliefs-and-definitions/faq/druids-animistic.
8. "Druidry, Animism, and the Meaning of Life," Witches and Pagans, accessed February 10, 2016, http://www.witchesandpagans.com/sagewoman-blogs/druid-heart/druidry-animism-and-the-meaning-of-life.html.

animism as a "belief in innumerable spiritual beings concerned with human affairs and capable of helping or harming human interests."[9] Many secular historians assume that animism dominated the world in "pre-historic" times, and that all religions evolved from it.

These historians are coming from an evolutionary perspective. We know from the history found in Genesis that Noah and his family were monotheistic. They worshiped the One and true Creator. After the Flood, people began to reject the truth and disobey God again. We are not sure what false religions and beliefs arose before the dispersion at the Tower of Babel, but with the dispersion people took their false beliefs with them throughout the world.

The true accounts of creation, the Fall, and the Flood were passed down from Noah and his family; however, these accounts were distorted over time. This is why we find creation and flood legends all over the world. All have been changed and perverted over time, but most retain the seeds of truth as recorded for us in Scripture. One such example is the Druid obsession with

special knowledge. Ever since Eve desired special knowledge and ate of the tree of knowledge of good and evil, people have desired the same thing. The Druids even associated this knowledge with a tree; this may be why the sacred oak trees became important in their beliefs.

Satan often provides a counterfeit to the truth. One of these false beliefs involved the idea that ancestors in spirit form could influence daily life. Those who took the role of connecting with these spirits became powerful shaman figures of the Ovate or Druid class in their society. This ancestor worship spread throughout the world as people groups migrated. Today it is found in tribal cultures all over the world.

Symbols of trees are used as amulets, and sacred trees are often used in Druid rituals.

Modern Druids

History of Modern Druids

Modern interest in Druidism can be traced to John Aubrey (1676–1697), who delved into the classical texts about Druids and suggested that the

---

9. Encyclopedia Britannica, s.v. "Animism," http://www.britannica.com/topic/animism.

Druids had worshiped at the old stone monuments in Wiltshire. His work began the modern association between Druidism and Stonehenge. Modern Druidism emerged into public notice in the next century when, in 1717, deist writer John Toland (1670–1722) was elected the chief of the first modern Druid order.

Building on Aubrey's work, the physician William Stukeley (1687–1765) did extensive observations in Wiltshire and brought the monumental structures to public attention. He published a book about Stonehenge in 1740. There is dispute about how involved each of these men were in actual orders, but the Enlightenment attitudes and acceptance of "free-thinkers" freed many to explore these ancient religions. It was out of this social framework that the neo-pagan resurgence occurred and modern Druidry emerged.[10]

Interest in Druidism as the traditional pre-Christian religion of the British Isles led to the formation of several Druid organizations throughout the 18th century. The most important was the Ancient Order of Druids founded in London in 1781. In the 19th century, the Druid movement spread across Europe and through the British Empire, though these groups remained small. Druidism only began to grow on the coattails of the larger neo-pagan movement. One of the most important Druid groups to emerge in England was the Order of Bards, Ovates and Druids founded in 1964.

In America, a new and separate Druid tradition was initiated in 1963 by students at Carleton College in Northfield, Minnesota, as part of a protest of compulsory chapel attendance at the church-related school. In order to gain permission not to attend chapel, the students fashioned a separate religion based upon their reading of books on ancient religion. Once the rules on compulsory chapel attendance were dropped, the students discovered that they liked what they had created. Thus was born the Reformed Druids of North America that spread through the neo-pagan subculture. In Berkeley, California, the movement found a new leader in the person of Isaac Bonewits, who emerged as the most visible spokesperson of Druidism in North America. In 1983 he left the loosely organized Reformed Druid coalition to found the Ár nDraíocht Féin (ADF), the largest Druid group in North America. It has in turn given birth to additional groups. But just to clarify, beliefs of modern Druid groups are not the same as the beliefs of the ancient Druids.

---

10. Ronald Hutton, *Blood and Mistletoe: The History of the Druids in Britain* (New Haven, CT: Yale Univ. Press, 2009), p. 125–134.

Beliefs of Modern Druidism

Although modern Druids attempt to draw their beliefs and teaching from the ancient Celts, they also incorporate ideas from modern psychology and the Human Potential and New Age movements. Membership is open to followers of any religion.

The Order of Bards, Ovates and Druids express their beliefs as follows (condensed):

> One of the most striking characteristics of Druidism is the degree to which it is free of dogma and any fixed set of beliefs or practices. There is no "sacred text" or the equivalent of a bible in Druidism and there is no universally agreed set of beliefs amongst Druids. Despite this, there are a number of ideas and beliefs that most Druids hold in common, and that help to define the nature of Druidism today.
>
> Since Druidry is a spiritual path — a religion to some, a way of life to others — Druids share a belief in the fundamentally spiritual nature of life. Some will favor a particular way of understanding the source of this spiritual nature, and may feel themselves to be animists, pantheists, polytheists, or even monotheists. Others will avoid choosing any one conception of Deity, believing that by its very nature this is unknowable by the mind.
>
> Although Druids love Nature, and draw inspiration and spiritual nourishment from it, they also believe that the world we see is not the only one that exists. A cornerstone of Druid belief is in the existence of the Otherworld — a realm or realms which exist beyond the reach of the physical senses, but which are nevertheless real. This Otherworld is seen as the place we travel to when we die, but we can also visit it during our lifetime in dreams, in meditation, under hypnosis, or in "journeying," during a trance.
>
> Most Druids adopt the belief of their ancient forebears that the soul undergoes a process of successive reincarnations — which continues until the individual reaches the highest realm, the "*Source*." One Druid is quoted as saying, "All things are created from the Source, including the Gods. We are just sparks from its flame."

A clue as to the purpose behind the process of successive rebirths can be found if we look at the goals of the Druid. Druids seek above all the cultivation of wisdom, creativity and love. A number of lives on earth, rather than just one, gives us the opportunity to fully develop these qualities within us.

Woven into much of Druid thinking and all of its practice is the idea or belief that we are all connected in a universe that is essentially benign. Related to the idea that we are all connected in one great web of life is the belief held by most Druids that whatever we do in the world creates an effect which will ultimately also affect us.[11]

Within these claims, there are many arbitrary and self-contradictory claims. For example, the claim that they have no dogma and then go on to tell you what you believe if you are a part of Druidism is obviously self-refuting. The notion that there are many different ways to view Druidism shows the arbitrary nature of such a worldview. If there is no truth within the system, what value can it have and what hope can it offer? It can only offer self-fulfilling promise based on your own arbitrary opinions about the world.

Modern Druids in the Culture

In recent days, paganism, including Druidism, has seen a tremendous revival with a deliberate attempt to inject paganism into the mainstream culture. The founder of the ADF, Isaac Bonewits, has for his motto "paganize mainstream religion by mainstreaming paganism."[12]

This new paganism, sometimes called neo-paganism, traces its heritage back to native religious traditions of Europe and tribal traditions from North America. Many neo-pagan groups identify with Celtic (Druidic), Egyptian, Native American, Norse, or Roman traditions.

Ancestor spirits, a Mother Goddess, magic, witchcraft, sacred trees, and the like, are being incorporated into the mainstream through the media. The *Harry Potter* franchise is one such example. The *Lord of the Rings* movies brought magic, wizards, and a host of neo-pagan ideas. While these movies present a good over evil motif, one can see a not-so-subtle introduction of

---

11. "Druid Beliefs," Druidry.org, accessed February 10,2016, http://www.druidry.org/druid-way/druid-beliefs.

12. "Thirty Druid Groups," Reformed Druids of North America, accessed February 10, 2016, http://www.rdna.info/drulinks.html.

pagan practices into the mainstream culture. One is hard-pressed to find a Disney movie without pagan ideas mixed in. Children's cartoons are ripe with magic spells, ancestral spirit guides, and Mother Earth. There are countless video games that are full of pagan ideas. Children may even be exposed to paganism at school with the introduction of Eastern forms of meditation, talk of Mother Nature, and spirit guides. We can't leave out the influence of the *Star Wars* movies with the concept of the "Force," which is paganism dressed up in science fiction.

All of this has one intended goal, to mainstream paganism — starting with the children. As the older generation dies off, the younger generation will replace Christianity with a kinder, earth-friendly, and more "open-minded" belief. Of course, we must ask by what standard would they be kinder and on what basis would they hold such beliefs? After all, Christianity protects human life whereas the basis for pagan ideas like the Druids do not hold that life is special in any way, contrary to their assertions. They may promise the liberation from "outdated" Christian morality that holds us back, but it is all a cruel trick of Satan.

> While they promise them liberty, they themselves are the servants of corruption: for of whom a person is overcome, by him also he is brought into bondage (2 Peter 2:19; NKJV).

> There is a way which seemeth right unto a man, but the end thereof are the ways of death (Proverbs 14:12; KJV).

Satan's ultimate goal is to eliminate the truth from our culture and usher in the lies that will ultimately bring the very image bearers of God on earth into slavery. Without the truth found in the Bible and redemption in Christ, mankind is destined to the same fate as Satan himself, enslaved to outer darkness in eternal death.

Protecting Our Children from Neo-paganism

Children from Christian homes are prime targets of Satan and the influence of paganism. Neil Anderson and Steve Russo wrote a book on this topic called *The Seduction of Our Children*. They did a survey in Christian schools and found:

- 45% said they have experienced a "presence" seen or heard in their room that scared them

- 59% said they've harbored bad thoughts about God

- 69% reported hearing voices in their head

- 89% said they did not like themselves

As parents, we must help our children to bring "every thought captive to the obedience of Christ" (2 Corinthians 10:5) as we constantly point them to the salvation and renewal that comes only through repentance and faith in Jesus Christ.

Some of the first lies of Satan's influence on our children is that they are no good. They are just sinners so they might as well act that way. They don't know who they really are. All people are image bearers of our Creator.

While it is true that we are sinners, in Christ we become saints. The first step is to point your child to saving knowledge of Christ, and we must start while they are young. Second, we must immerse our children in the truth of who they are (or can be) in Christ. Pray as Paul did that your children's eyes may be opened, "that ye may know what is the hope of his calling, and what the riches of the glory of his inheritance in the saints, and what is the exceeding greatness of his power to us-ward who believe" (Ephesians 1:18–19; KJV).

While St Patrick was battling the Druids, his eyes were opened to the spiritual battle that he was in. We are in a spiritual battle as well, and we might want to pray the same type of spiritual affirmations over ourselves and our children that St Patrick did.

Satan is good at informing children how bad they are, so we must remind them of who they really are (or can be) in Christ.

- John 1:2 — I am God's child.

- Ephesians 1:1 — I am a saint.

- Ephesians 1:5 — I have been adopted as God's child.

- Ephesians 2:6 — I am seated with Christ in heavenly places.

- Ephesians 2:18 — I have access to God through the Spirit.

- Colossians 2:10 — I am complete in Christ.

- 1 Corinthians 3:16 — I am God's temple.

Reaching Neo-pagans for Christ

When engaging a Druid, or any neo-pagan for that matter, it is important to acknowledge, as did St. Patrick, that this is a spiritual battle with a demonic delusion and blindness to the truth. While they may pride themselves on claims of being tolerant and open-minded to all religions, being confronted with the truth from God's Word will often elicit an emotional response. The god of this world will not want them to hear the truth. A one-time confrontation with someone steeped in these beliefs will usually not bring about their conversion. Being a witness of the gospel is more of a conversation than a one-time presentation.

It is important to break out of our comfort zone and develop friendships with unbelievers — a relationship where the conversation can be picked up again at a later time, a relationship where one can feel safe and not threatened. Our actions will often say more than what we say in words. Our actions can go a long way in demonstrating the love that God has for them. Matthew 16:18 informs us that the gates of hell will not prevail again the rock of the gospel, so we can be confident in our witness (see also Daniel 2:35).

It can be beneficial to start with areas of agreement. Druids are correct in their assessment that there is more to life than this physical word. They also have a respect for life, love, and the improvement of self and all mankind. They also understand that our actions have consequences in the future.

Where does this commonality originate? Romans 1 tells us that all have an inborn sense of a Creator, and that the natural world screams of the Creator God. While Druids may be accepting of evolution, it is clear to them that there is some kind of spiritual, non-physical designer. Also inherent in the mind of all people is a sense of right and wrong and a desire to improve this world (Romans 2:15). From a purely materialistic, evolutionary perspective, there should be no need or compulsion for justice and improving the world if survival of the fittest is all there is, yet the neo-pagan are open about and embrace these ideas. Pointing out these similarities is a good non-confrontational way to start a conversation.

Some conversations could lead to pointing out why these ideas are predicated on Scripture to be true. Basic concepts like truth, love, right, and wrong are based on God and His Word, and the Druid has borrowed these concepts whether they realize it or not.

The difference between the Druid and the Christian is that the Druid has beliefs that are purely arbitrary. There is no source of authority that they can go back to; they claim that their beliefs are right purely because *they* say they are right. One might ask them how they can know for sure that they are right in what they believe.

If they are quick, they will probably return the question back to you, and your answer should be, "I am glad you asked." For here is the great difference — we have the truth directly from our Creator who revealed it to us. And since we are made in His image, we can know this. This truth is communicated to us in the context of the true history of the universe. The Word of God is what it says it is because the ultimate authority on all things (God) can only reveal Himself as the final authority. Thus, our beliefs are not arbitrary but are the only absolute truth directly from God.

But within the neo-pagan or Druid system of belief there is no absolute authority, that even the universe obeys. Who dictates what is right and wrong?

This is a great time to show the inconsistency of believing that all beliefs are true. The word "truth" itself implies that there is something called non-truth. Druids are accepting of any spiritual path, except the one that says Christ is the only way. So how can truth and not-truth both be acceptable? The fact is that they cannot. Thus, the neo-pagan belief is inconsistent right from the very start of their religious basis.

Here is also where logical arguments for the authority of Scripture come in. Starting with Genesis and just reading the truth is a powerful antidote to Satan's lies. At this point, they may be open to hearing good arguments against various forms of evolution, and how the Bible is consistent from beginning to end.

The main goal is to clearly explain the basic difference between Christianity and all other religions. All other religions seek a path to an alleged god, gods, or state of being, while Christianity is the only one where the Creator Himself has sought out a path to restore mankind back to Himself. Other religions often endeavor to do things to be united back with *"a creator"* (or the universe, etc.), while Christianity is just the opposite.

Our Creator has provided a way through Jesus Christ whereby we can receive grace. We can be brought back into fellowship with our Creator through nothing that we do but as a free gift. Finding oneness with our Creator is the heartfelt desire of all people, whether they know it or not.

Proclaimed from Genesis to Revelation, God's plan to restore man back to fellowship through Jesus Christ through repentance and faith is the key to reaching the neo-pagan for Christ. Jesus is God Himself, who took on human flesh, so He could die in our place and take our punishment. If we place out trust in Him, we are restored back to fellowship with our Creator.

Summary of Druid Beliefs

Doctrine	Teachings of Druidism
God	Deny the God of the Bible. Believe in a spirit world. Druids hold to a variety of beliefs about gods varying from a great "force" to various ancestor and nature spirits. Most would be polytheistic.
Authority/ Revelation	Reject the Bible as true. Do not look to any writing as divine or authoritative. Man is seen as the absolute authority. They pride themselves in accepting people and ideas of all beliefs.
Man	Various views exist. There is no concept of an innate sin nature. All men are born worthy of respect as part of the cosmos. Man is seen as a higher life form, but not entirely unique.
Sin	No absolute standard of sin exists. Sin is relative to the virtues of honor, loyalty, hospitality, honesty, justice, and courage to benefit all. Some hold a view similar to the law of karma.
Salvation	Various views exist. Through the process of reincarnation and acquiring special knowledge, individuals learn to be united with the ultimate "source" to live in an eternal state of unity or bliss.
Creation	Various views exist within modern Druidism. No known ancient creation myths exist. Many would acknowledge evolutionary ideas as consistent with their beliefs.

Chapter 12

Animism (Spiritism)

Mark Vowels

Do you have any superstitions? Have you heard that breaking a mirror causes bad luck or that walking under a ladder brings misfortune? What about the idea that seeing a black cat at night portends something bad might happen? Perhaps you know someone who says things like, "Knock on wood" or "Throw a penny over your shoulder." All of these ideas stem from the idea that somehow doing, or not doing, certain things affects the outcome of our future. When I was a child my schoolmates would say, "If you step on a crack it will break your mother's back!" As I walked to school each day I would carefully avoid stepping on cracks in the sidewalk for fear that the taunt might just be true.

In our culture, which places a high value on science and reason as a means of discovering what is true, most people grow out of their childhood fears and superstitions. We come to understand reasonable explanations for the mysterious happenings that we or others have experienced. We recognize that most superstitious beliefs come from incidents which took place at some point in time for which people had no explanation, therefore they assumed that something they had done, or not done, caused the problem and from that time took measures to avoid a similar experience in the future. Over time, those problem-avoiding measures, like not stepping on a crack or knocking on wood when wishing for something good to happen, become part of the culture and are continued out of habit. We see these concepts as mere fantasies or delusions.

What if you lived in a culture in which every aspect of life was governed by the thought that doing, or failing to do, prescribed behaviors would affect your future? Inevitably, you would develop a constant sense of fear that you might bring harm or misfortune upon yourself and your family. This is what it is like to live among people who are animists. Their entire lives are governed by fear. A typical Western view of superstitious practices holds that it is just bad luck or fate that produces negative consequences when the superstitions are violated. Animists, on the other hand, believe that spirit beings are directly responsible for everything that happens, both good and bad. So the only reasonable approach to this perceived reality is to do everything necessary to keep those spirit beings happy as much as possible.

All people everywhere have some sense that there is a spiritual dimension to life beyond the world they can see and touch. An innate sense of spiritual forces that in some way influence the destiny of one's life and fortunes is part of every person's perception. The world's various religions seek to provide some explanation for that basic sense that there is more to the world around us than simply what we can observe. Animism embraces the intuition that there are unseen spiritual forces at work around us that somehow affect what happens in life by attributing supernatural forces to all aspects of the natural world.

Definition of Animism

Animism takes its name from the concept that the physical world is inhabited, or *animated*, by spirits. Rocks, trees, rivers, lakes, mountains, valleys, and so forth, as well as animals, possess spirits that control all that takes place in a particular region. In order to procure favorable experiences in life, animists seek to interact with the spirits by either satisfying them or manipulating them. All religious practices in animism, which are often seen as primitive superstition by outsiders, are actually highly developed responses to the fear that animists have of offending the spirits, or rituals which are intended to in some way control the spirits.

Distribution of Animism

Animism is in many ways the default religion of the human soul. It has been described by some in the past as primal religion. Much of what the Old

Testament describes as paganism in ancient times was essentially animistic practice. Unlike most of the world's organized religious systems, animism has no sacred text or unified history, yet it is found literally throughout history and throughout the world. Any society or culture whose religious practice involves interaction with spirit beings is a manifestation of animism. This would include what is often referred to as indigenous religion, or the religions of indigenous peoples; that is to say, the religious practice of any people who are the original natives to a region. Most native African, North American, South American, Australian, Arctic, Asian, and even ancient European religion is either overtly animist or intertwined with animist beliefs and practices. In other words, the original religions of people in every part of the world are animistic.

The Bible's View of Animism

Why is this so? Are people simply incurably superstitious, or are there genuine spiritual beings who interact with human populations? The Bible clearly indicates that Satan and the demonic beings that assist him are at work in the world and seek to influence human activity. From the time when Adam and Eve were tempted by Satan in the Garden of Eden, actual spiritual beings have sought to manipulate human behavior. Likewise, from ancient times, humans have sought to manipulate the spirits. A prominent example from the Bible is the story of Elijah's interaction with the priests of Baal. In a contest to see whether Baal or Jehovah was the true God, Elijah challenged his opponents to call down fire from heaven. After all, Baal, it was supposed, was the god of lightning. According to 1 Kings 18:28, the servants of Baal "cried aloud and cut themselves after their custom with swords and lances, until the blood gushed out upon them" (ESV). Yet no fire fell on their altar. It is interesting that the Bible treats such examples of idolatry as worship of actual demonic beings rather than mere superstitious behavior.

Moses wrote about the idolatry of the Hebrews during their time in Egypt, saying, "They sacrificed unto demons, not to God; to gods whom they knew not, to new gods that came newly up, whom your fathers feared not" (Deuteronomy 32:17; KJV). Referring to the idolatrous practices of the people of Israel as they adopted the religious ways of the people of Canaan, the Psalmist wrote, "They served their idols: which were a snare unto them. Yea, they sacrificed their sons and their daughters unto devils, and shed innocent blood, even the blood of their sons and of their daughters, whom they sacrificed unto the idols of Canaan; and the land was polluted with blood" (Psalm 106:36–38; KJV).

Consider the attitude of the Syrians in 1 Kings 20:23, "And the servants of the king of Syria said unto him, Their gods are gods of the hills; therefore they were stronger than we; but let us fight against them in the plain, and surely we shall be stronger than they." As we will see further, this is a proto-typical animist response, assuming that various spirits control certain regions. They reasoned that Israel's God was no more powerful than their gods; He just happened to be powerful in the hills. In the New Testament, idol worship continued to be in practice among the Gentile people of the time.

The Apostle Paul gives his assessment of what took place in idol worship by saying in 1 Corinthians 10:20, "But I say, that the things which the Gentiles sacrifice, they sacrifice to devils, and not to God." In both Testaments, Scripture makes it clear that the earth is inhabited by deceptive evil spirits who in some way are organized for the purpose of opposing God's plan for humanity.[1] So the Bible's perspective on animistic practices is that they represent interaction between real demonic forces and people who are ignorant of God's way of salvation.

Beliefs and Practices of Animism

Because the actual practice of animism is closely tied to the specific experiences of the people among whom it is found, variations in animistic expressions abound. While there are similarities between the forms of worship of different animists, each expression of the religion will in some ways be unique. As already mentioned, there is no binding sacred text, no universalizing creed, no single creation myth, nor any unifying method of worship. The two things that all animists have in common is fear of the unseen spirits in their region and their attempt to coexist successfully with these spirit beings.

One of the questions that must inevitably be answered in animist societies is where did the spirits originate? Many believe that they are created beings that have varying degrees of power based on some kind of hierarchical relationship. In fact, this is similar to what the Bible teaches about evil spirits. Others believe that they are part of the earth itself and are manifestations of their view that nature is a living entity. The great majority of animists believe that at least some of the spirits are their deceased ancestors.

---

1. See Daniel 10:13 and Ephesians 6:12.

Good and Evil

Animists believe that there are both good and bad spirits, and that both types can be beneficial if properly engaged. Good spirits bring good things to the individual or to the community, such as good harvest, good health, fertility, or wealth. In order to encourage good spirits to serve their desires, animists make offerings of food or animals, or in some cases even of human beings. Each spirit is also believed to have a retinue of actions that either please or displease it, so believers are careful to say the right words, wear the right clothes, and perform the right rituals. These activities are sometimes referred to as *taboos*, meaning actions that must be properly performed (or not performed) in order to placate the spirits. This may include *talismans* or *amulets,* articles made to be worn or carried on one's body, which have some spiritual significance, in order to please good spirits or repel bad spirits.

Bad spirits can be either mischievous or outright sinister. They can play dirty tricks to entertain themselves or they can bring disease or disaster or even kill people. Part of the worldview of all animists is that *everything* that happens is the result of interplay with the spirits. Nothing occurs without a spiritual cause. The key to successful living is to prevent the spirits from doing harm and cajole them to do good. If someone becomes ill, it is not because a virus has infected his body; it is because a spirit has afflicted him. If someone has a good crop, it is not because he planted well and carefully nurtured his plants; it is because he has found favor with the appropriate spirit. Therefore, it is essential that an animist knows what the spirits like or do not like so that he or she can effectively satisfy them.

Interacting with the Spirits

Since there is no sacred text in animism to reveal what pleases the spirits, some sort of religious specialist must develop the ability to communicate with the spirits and discover their preferences. In all examples of animist religion it is thought that there are certain practitioners who can mediate between people and the spirits. These spirit mediums are called by different names in different cultures. Some are called *shamans* or *medicine men.* Others are called *witches* or *witch doctors.* Some are called *sorcerers* or *wizards.* In many situations, there will be different types of spirit mediums with different roles and powers. Some only interact with the evil spirits and some only with the good. Some use *magic* or *sorcery* to help, and some use it to damage.

If, for example, a wife wanted to ensure that her husband would love her and remain faithful to her, she might go to a witch who could provide some potion that would make the wife more attractive to her husband or make her husband become more devoted to her. The formulations of such concoctions are secrets known to the practitioner that may have been passed down for many generations or revealed by some spirit. In either case, the origin of such knowledge is supposed to have been derived from the spirit world. If a child dies, it is assumed that someone has either broken taboo or that a curse had been placed on the child. A shaman or sorcerer would determine which was the actual cause. Perhaps someone would need to be ritually punished for breaking taboo and may be disfigured or exiled from the community. If the shaman determines that the ill fortune was a result of someone placing a curse on the unfortunate sufferer, then he will practice some form of *divination* (using some ritual to discern a spiritual reality) in order to figure out who is responsible. Forms of divination may include reading the entrails of a slaughtered animal, seeing patterns in shells or sticks cast on the ground, using special cards (like tarot cards) in random sequence, or any other technique intended to reveal hidden spiritual realities. He may then, in return for some fee, place a curse back on the culprit. All of this sounds like fantasy to our Western minds, but this is just a small glimpse into the everyday life of those in an animist culture.

Variations of Animism

Today, animism is most directly associated with tribal people who live in relative isolation from modern society. For this reason it was once often supposed that if a group of animists was exposed to modern technology and scientific understanding, they would naturally abandon their religious practices as mere superstitions. This expectation, however, fails to take into account the fact that people who practice animism are not merely superstitious. They really do interact with spiritual beings (demons) and remain fearful, in spite of modern scientific advances, of offending them. That is not to say that all of their fears are valid and that none of their practices are simply superstitious. It is, rather, a recognition that at the root of their belief system are genuine experiences of supernatural interaction with the spirit world for good or for ill. This underlying characteristic of animism makes it a pervasive religious influence even where other religions have ostensibly superseded it.

For example, throughout most of the Muslim world, people adopt the external customs and doctrines of Islam while continuing to actively practice animism. Likewise, most Buddhists in the world do not practice pure Buddhism; instead, they mix Buddhist teaching with animistic practices. Even Christianity can be ostensibly practiced on the surface while people continue to use the rituals and taboos of animism to interact with the spirit world. These blended religious forms are known as "folk" religions, such as Folk Islam, Folk Buddhism, Folk Judaism, or Folk Christianity. As a general rule, adherents of folk religions look to the doctrinally pure form of the religion (Islam, Buddhism, Judaism, or Christianity) for existential reality, or big-picture thinking. These religions address the major issues of what is real and why we exist. They offer explanations about what happens after death. For the problems of everyday living involving relationships and wellness and personal success, folk religionists look to the spirits and shamans while continuing the practices of animism. When we take into account the number of people in other religions who also practice animism on some level, we see that, in actuality, billions of people around the world are animists.

Authority of Animism

There is no central founder of animism. Its roots go back to earliest times, making it the world's most ancient false religion. There are no universal writings or sacred texts that are common to animist peoples. In fact, because animism is most often associated with tribal peoples, many of whom have no written language, what is thought to be true is passed down orally.[2] For this reason, animism is sometimes labeled "oral religion." What then is the basis for authority among any group of animists? It is their tradition passed down from generation to generation. The multitude of taboos and customs, rituals and observances necessary to maintain balance with nature and the spirits inhabiting it are taught through stories and legends which become the core of that people's *worldview* or understanding of what is real.

Certain locations or landmarks are held to be sacred or, conversely, taboo. There may be a sacred tree or stone where important religious events are celebrated. Certain places may be avoided in order to not break taboo and consequently bring misfortune. How are these things known? They were found to be so through experiences that took place at some point in the people's

---

2. Some animists are literate and may have their own locally written materials. These usually take the form of magic books of secret formulas or spells. See Acts 19:19.

history and have ever since been marked as special. These beliefs guide the life cycle of animist peoples. All animists have some types of ceremonies to ensure proper interaction with the spirit world during important life events such as birth and death, puberty and marriage, planting and harvest, and so forth, but animism is non-institutional. Authority for daily spiritual direction rests with whatever person is most in tune with the spirit world, such as a shaman or witch. This person is able to enter the spirit world through a trance or by means of being inhabited by a spirit and can therefore know hidden mysteries which guide the decisions of an individual or the entire group.

Understandably, the leader (shaman, witch doctor, medicine man, etc.) frequently abuses this authority for personal gain in terms of wealth or power. While claiming to manipulate the spirits, the shaman may in fact be manipulating the tribe. This is certainly a common characteristic of sinful humans in any religion or society, but it is a mistake to assume that this is all that is taking place within the practice of animism. Though much of what is seen as supernatural in animism is surely attributable to the trickery of devious leaders, the practice of animism has continued through all these centuries, in spite of modernity, because there is real interplay between humans and the spirit world.[3]

Creation Beliefs of Animism

Interestingly, most animist systems hold to a belief in one supreme deity who is the creator of all that is. Variations exist about how or why this great being made the world and man to inhabit it, but some commonality exists regarding the character of the high god. Animism's view of God could generally be described as *deistic*. That is, God is indeed all-powerful, but He is also uninterested. At some time in the past He made the world and set things in order, but then something happened to offend Him and cause Him to depart. Though He still exists, He no longer interacts directly with humans, but allows lesser deities, or spirits, to do so. Animists generally perceive the high god to be angry and unreachable by humanity. There are a host of explanations for why the creator is angry, but most are simply fabulous tales of him being mistreated in some way.

---

3. A good example of this in the Bible is found in Acts 19:13–16. Apparently, the sons of Sceva were fraudulently taking advantage of the Ephesian people's fear of spirits. Yet in an attempt to use the name of Jesus as some sort of magic word, they discovered to their regret that a real evil spirit was at work.

For example, one African myth relates that God came to visit a family while the wife was preparing dinner. Because she was late in her preparations, she was working rapidly to pound her corn. In her haste she poked God in the eye and He became angry and left, never to return to interact with humans again.[4] The universal presence of such legends among animists allows for their universal denial of personal responsibility for being alienated from the Creator. In all animist creation myths, the creator left man and not vice versa. Therefore, man is not guilty of rebellion against God but still suffers the consequences.

The spirits that remain active in the world generally fit into several categories in animist thought. There are good spirits, which are lesser gods and perhaps related to the high god in some way. There are evil spirits, which are the enemies of both the high god and his associated lesser gods (good spirits) as well as humans. Finally, there are ancestral spirits, which can be either good or bad, depending on how they are treated.

While animists generally do not introduce evolutionary ideas into their creation accounts, they misunderstand the nature of God. The idea that He is offended with humanity is in fact correct, but it is not because He is capricious. Rather, He rejects man's sinful rebellion against Him. He has not abandoned man but has, in fact, sent His only Son in order to repair the relationship with man by atoning for our sin and accounting us as righteous. He has not, as animists suppose, relegated human affairs to lesser spirits, but is directly responsible for the good things that are evident in nature.[5] The Apostle Paul explained this to the animist thinkers at Lystra when he reasoned in Acts 14:17, "He did good, and gave us rain from heaven, and fruitful seasons, filling our hearts with food and gladness" (KJV). Part of Paul's message to these people was that God the Creator was actively involved in their daily lives whether they realized it or not.

Theological Concepts of Animists
Sin

Because animists generally dwell in corporate or tribal social environments, that is to say that they are more concerned with the group than

---

4. Philip M. Steyne, *Gods of Power: A Study in the Beliefs and Practices of Animists* (Columbia, SC: Impact International Foundation, 2011), p. 74.
5. The Bible clearly indicates that God often uses angelic beings to accomplish His work among people, such as the angels who rescued Lot, closed the lions' mouths to save Daniel, and freed Peter from prison.

the individual, concepts of evil are based upon what is deleterious to the group as a whole. Animists do not feel guilty because they have transgressed against God, but will sense shame if their actions are seen as harmful to the group. Acting in ways that bring the wrath of the spirits, such as breaking taboo or failing to perform prescribed rituals, is considered evil, and the group may move to punish the offender. Shame and fear are employed

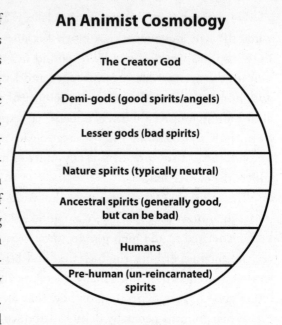

An Animist Cosmology

The Creator God

Demi-gods (good spirits/angels)

Lesser gods (bad spirits)

Nature spirits (typically neutral)

Ancestral spirits (generally good, but can be bad)

Humans

Pre-human (un-reincarnated) spirits

to motivate individuals to comply with social expectations. For the animist, iniquity is not a violation against God, but against one's social group. Right and wrong are not issues of personal morality, but of their practical effect on the group as a whole.

Death

For the animist, death is part of the continuous cycle of nature. Everyone dies, but no one dies without some spiritual cause. Life can be shortened by living out of harmony with nature, by offending a spirit, or because an enemy has placed a curse. Animists believe that upon death, a person continues to live on in a different plane as a spirit. Eventually the spirit of the deceased will be forgotten from the living memory of the tribe and will then be reincarnated as a new baby among the same people. Animist society consists of the spirits of the yet unborn, the living, and the dead. They view each group as equally alive, and believe that they should continually interact with one another.

Salvation

Animists believe that death is simply the continuation of life, but in a different sphere, and that individuals continue as ancestral spirits until they are forgotten, and are eventually reborn as new persons. Therefore, there is little thought for salvation in the sense of eternal rescue. For the animist, the principal goal in life is to interact with the spirit world successfully so as to provide for tranquility and prosperity in the here and now. There is no single savior for the animist. He may look to a powerful spirit to vanquish other spirits, but the idea that God provides some ultimate means of conquering the power of the spirits and eliminating the need to manipulate them is unknown in animist thinking.

Communicating the Gospel to Animists

It is important to communicate with animists using concepts that are familiar to them and that speak to their central religious concerns (Colossians 4:2–6). Here is a sample of how one might present the truth of God's salvation through Christ to an animist:

> The Creator God made the original human parents and placed them in a perfect garden where all of their wants were satisfied. He forbade them to eat a fruit which would cause them to think and act independently of His loving kindness to them. An evil spirit, who was once one of the Creator's special and most powerful servants, but who had rebelled against Him, spoke lies to the first parents and deceived them into believing that God was not kind. They ate the forbidden fruit and immediately realized that they had acted in rebellion against God. Clearly, God was rightly offended by their hostile act. He had not abandoned them, but His cherished children had made themselves His enemies. This caused them to experience fear and shame for the first time. But the Creator God in perfect kindness came to search for them, even though they tried to hide themselves.
>
> He made a way for their rebellion to be forgiven and instituted a plan in which the sacrifice of an innocent animal could temporarily cover the stain of their shame and rebellion against Him. He gave them instructions for how they should live in compliance with His will for them. Most importantly, He promised that someday a man would be born who would be His own Son, one who would be both God and man, and this One would provide salvation once and for all for all people who believed on Him. He would give His life as the ultimate sacrifice for humanity's rebellion against the Creator God and completely remove all of

CONCEPTS ASSOCIATED WITH ANIMISM

Synonyms for Animism
Spirit Religion — so called because all animism by nature involves interaction with the spirit world
Oral Religion — so called because many animistic societies are pre-literate
Natural Religion — so called because animistic practice is highly holistic in its understanding of the relationship between humanity and nature
Primitive or Primal Religion — so called because many animistic peoples are pre-modern in their use of science and technology
Tribal Religion — so called because the majority of the world's animistic peoples live in tribal societies
Folk Religion — so called because animism is not a formal religion (no sacred writings or universal practices). Most formal religions have localized folk varieties (Folk Buddhism, Folk Islam, Folk Judaism, or Folk Christianity) which are highly dependent on interaction with spirit powers.

Elements of Power
Mana — a neutral force which is thought by some animists (mostly throughout Polynesia) to exist in nature, which can be harvested for use by humans
Witchcraft — the use of rituals, ceremonies, potions, or incantations to effect some result, usually harmful, which is beyond natural occurrence
Magic — any form of interaction with non-human powers. White magic involves using powers to bring benefit, while black magic involves using powers to bring harm. Specific types of magic include contagious magic, which uses something from a person's body (hair, nails, tooth, feces) to bring them harm or blessing, and imitative magic which uses a representation of a person to bring harm upon them (as in a voodoo doll).
Spirit Manipulation –—direct interaction with a spirit being for the sake of garnering its favor for doing good or evil. This may involve sacrifice, offerings, deprivation, taking an oath, or allowing the spirit to use one's body for some purpose.
Taboo — a prohibition against saying certain words, going to certain places, performing certain acts, looking at certain things, etc. for the sake of not offending a spirit and thereby bringing misfortune upon oneself or one's community
Power Words — special words which are thought to have power in themselves to invoke either good or ill. These can include incantations, curses, or blessings pronounced to repel evil spirits.

Objects Associated with Power
Charms — any item, naturally occurring or specially created, which is thought to have power to ward off evil or draw good fortune
Talismans — a type of charm which has been prepared specifically for the purpose of providing good luck or protection from harm
Amulets — any form of wearable charm

Fetishes — an object specially prepared by a religious specialist (shaman, medicine man, etc.) that is thought to create a special relationship between the possessor and a particular spirit

Totems — physical representations of spirit beings, often associated with certain animals.

Sacred Objects or Places — items or places where a specific spirit or spirits is thought to abide and therefore to exercise special power. Examples could include things like sacred trees, rocks, streams, or hills.

Kinds of Non-Physical Beings

Creator God — animists have some concept of a single supreme being, but he is thought to be distant and unknowable.

Gods — powerful spirits which control the lives of animist peoples. Various explanations occur for the origin of these gods.

Ancestors — the spirits of the dead who are still remembered and are believed to continue to be dwelling among and interacting with the living. Ancestral spirits are generally considered helpful as long as they are respected.

Ghosts — the spirits of the dead who are no longer remembered and are therefore disconnected with the life of the animist society. They are angry as a result and are thought to be generally malicious.

Nature Spirits — less powerful spirits which inhabit all of nature. These are generally considered good and helpful.

Totemic Spirits — many animist peoples believe that they have a special relationship with the spirits of certain animals and therefore must interact with those animals in prescribed ways. These spirits are often represented through totems.

Religious Specialists*

Priest — any person who generally instructs animists in the proper functions of the religion

Medicine Man — name given in some animist societies to the person who attempts to use magic and spirit manipulation to bring healing and other benefits

Shaman — a general term for someone who has special spiritual knowledge through dreams or visions or by means of some connection with the spirit world

Witch — a person who has naturally occurring supernatural power, often inherited from a parent or grandparent. Witches can be male or female and are characterized by using their powers to bring harm.

Sorcerer — a person who has acquired supernatural power through ritual or study and uses that power to do harm for profit

Medium — a general term for anyone who has regular contact with the spirit world. Often a medium has a special connection with one particular spirit and experiences times of possession by that spirit.

---

* Note that while most organized animist societies feature each of these types of religious specialists, different expressions of animism use these terms interchangeably or not at all.

Means of Divination
Reading Signs — any method of discerning the otherwise unknowable by detecting random patterns understood only by the diviner. Examples include studying animal entrails, casting cowry shells, reading tarot cards, reading palms, reading tea leaves, etc.
Astrology — attempting to understand the future based on the movements of the stars
Interpreting Omens — recognizing certain occurrences (e.g., comets, eclipses, earthquakes) as portending the arrival of either good or bad fortune upon an individual or group
Ordeal — a test by which truth is revealed. Such tests usually involve afflicting a person physically or chemically and determining his or her guilt or innocence, suitability, or worthiness based on the reaction to the affliction.
Dreams/Visions — information revealed through the separation of the spirit from the body. Animists believe that the spirit is able to leave the body and return. Sometimes information that would otherwise be unknowable is discovered during this state of separation.
Spirit Possession — all forms of animism involve some kind of activity whereby the spirits take control over and communicate through particular human beings, generally spiritual practitioners such as the shamans.

the consequences of our rebellion, including our fear and shame. Salvation could be received by believing in this great promise.

Sadly, the great deceiving spirit, the enemy of God, continued to work to cause people everywhere to live in rebellion against their Creator. The deceiving spirit, Satan, has many other spirits who were also created by God to serve Him but who also chose to rebel and follow the deceiver. They inhabit the whole world and present themselves as friendly and helpful spirits, but they are not. Throughout the entire history of humanity they have made promises of power and success if people would serve and worship them. They have presented themselves as spirits of animals or of rivers or trees or mountains. When people serve them they sometimes give people power. But they continue to lie and say that the Creator God is unkind and unfair, just as Satan lied to our first parents. Worst of all, they say that there is no judgment for man's rebellion against the Creator. According to the deceiving spirits, people simply live and die and return again.

Fortunately, God, because He is actually so kind and good, has never stopped caring for humanity. He has always provided good by sending rain and harvests and by giving health and prosperity to many. He has also communicated to us through a special book, revealed to men who obeyed Him over many years. In His book, He explains that the One who was promised from the beginning, the One who would be both God and man, has come and did give His life as a sacrifice for our rebellion. He suffered a cruel death involving great pain by which He paid the cost of every evil deed and rebellious act ever committed. Then, He arose from the dead to prove that He had gained victory over all rebellion and death itself! When we stop believing the deceiving spirits and believe in the One who died to remove our shame and restore our honor with the Creator, God considers us as one of His own special children. Rather than being far removed and acting as one offended by us, He becomes our spiritual Father and we begin to know Him personally. When we die, He does not leave us here to wander about as an ancestral spirit, but takes us directly to live with Him in His home beyond the stars.

Only those who choose to believe these promises and turn away from serving any other spirits can experience the joy of becoming one of God's spiritual children. The spirits you have served will lie to you and tell you that they are more powerful than the One who was both God and man. But the truth, stated to us in God's book, is that when Jesus (the name of the God-man) paid for our rebellion and conquered death, He also conquered God's enemy, Satan, and all those spirits who followed him. In fact, by His victorious life, death, and Resurrection, Jesus gained all of the power of the universe. He alone can give us true harmony with the world we live in and with the Creator God to whom we are responsible. Those who follow Jesus are not victims of fate or of the spirit world; the lives of those who believe God's promises are controlled by God Himself and by the power of Jesus they live in victory over all of the spirits, even Satan.[6] If you will choose to follow the Creator God and His unique Son, the

---

6. It is important to communicate to animists the victory and power of Jesus over demon spirits. The New Testament often refers to this reality and the promise of genuine spiritual power to all believers. See, for example, John 12:31; Romans 8:31; Colossians 1:13; Hebrews 2:14; 1 John 3:8, 4:4.

God-man, you will join His side against all the other spirits in world who, in reality, are the enemies of God and all people.

Conclusion

We typically think of animism as something associated with pre-modern peoples — images of tribalists with scant clothing, led by shamans or witch doctors. Wild dances or animal sacrifices come to mind at the mention of the term animism. In reality, however, any form of interaction with the spirit world is a manifestation of animism. Witchcraft, the occult, fortune telling, communicating with the dead, and praying to those who are no longer living are all manifestations of animism on some level. In each case there is an attempt to obtain knowledge or manipulate circumstances through contact with the spirit world. Attempts to receive spiritual guidance from any source other than God and His Word are strictly forbidden for those who know Him.[7]

Animism is not an organized religion like many other religions. There are no sacred writings or historic founders featuring ordered systems and hierarchical structures, yet more than half of the people on planet earth practice some form of animism on a regular basis. Jesus conquered Satan and all of the fallen spirits who serve him by defeating sin and death at the Cross and through His physical Resurrection from the tomb. As followers of Christ, we must never fall for the lies of demonic spirits who would replace hope and grace with fear and promises of spiritual manipulation.

Satan wants us to believe that God only loves us when we are good or when we do things that please Him, but God loves us because He is good, not because of what we can do to gain His favor. He saves us, not because of what we have done, but because His Son paid the ultimate sacrifice for our rebellion against Him (Titus 2:11–14). We can never make God love or accept us more than He already does through Christ our Savior. That great deceiver, Satan, still tries to introduce animist concepts even into our relationship with our Creator. He wants us to believe that we can negotiate with God in order to receive good, or that we must do penance for our sin in order to restore God's favor. We must resist the devil's lies and wholly believe in God's love and forgiveness that was so fully demonstrated through Christ Jesus.

---

7. Deuteronomy 18:10–12; Isaiah 8:19–20.

Summary of Animistic Beliefs

Doctrine	Teachings of Animism
God	Acknowledge a supreme god, but generally have a deistic view. God is seen as distant and disconnected rather than personal. There are various views of lesser gods or spirits who interact with humans and nature.
Authority/ Revelation	There are no authoritative texts, but each group has its own oral traditions that are passed down. Shamans or other leaders are seen as the authorities that can interact with the spirits.
Man	Man is a spirit that is part of nature and is reborn in cycles.
Sin	Sin is generally viewed as bringing harm to the tribe rather than an individual affront to a holy God. There is no concept of original sin.
Salvation	There are various views, but generally no view of a judgment in the afterlife.
Creation	Generally, a Creator God made the world but has abandoned it (deism). Generally deny evolutionary concepts or have no connection to them.

Chapter 13

Egypt's Ancient Religion

Dr. Elizabeth Mitchell and Troy Lacey

The ancient Egyptians were a very religious people. Hundreds of years after Homer sang epics about gods meddling in the Greek war with Troy, the Greek historian Herodotus of Halicarnassus (c. 484-425 B.C.) wrote of his visit to Egypt, then under Persian rule.

Herodotus recorded his observations and interviews for posterity. Though he himself came from a polytheistic people to whom the Apostle Paul later said, "Men of Athens, I perceive that in all things you are very religious" (Acts 17:22),[1] Herodotus wrote that Egyptians "are religious to excess, far beyond any other race of men."[2]

The pervasive influence of Egyptian religion on every facet of ancient life is evident in the artwork and inscriptions on its many monuments and artifacts and in papyrus documents that survived for millennia in the dry heat of northern Africa. Not only do the tombs of royalty and temples reveal the importance of religion, but the existence of many local village shrines and household shrines from the Middle Kingdom period onward affirm that religious interest was not reserved for the ruling classes.

Though then eclipsed by foreign powers, for much of its history Egypt had been a key power in the Mediterranean world. Herodotus deduced that

---

1. All Scripture in this chapter is from the New King James Version (NKJV) of the Bible.
2. Herodotus, *The History of Herodotus*, trans. George Rawlinson, vol. 2, section 37, Encyclopaedia Britannica, 1952.

ancient Egypt was the source of much in the classical Greek pantheon. He wrote, "Almost all the names of the gods came into Greece from Egypt."[3] Through its trade, might, and inherent appeal, ancient Egypt's religion influenced cultures near and far.

Egypt's pyramids and mummies are familiar testimonials to a culture seemingly devoted to death. Religious beliefs and practices reflect how people deal with the uncertainties of both death and life. For instance, the ancient Egyptians believed that proper preparation of a dead body, be it the body of a beloved family member or a revered ruler, was essential for the individual's eternal well-being.

Egypt's dry climate has preserved much evidence to help us piece together what ancient Egyptians generally believed about their origins and their eternal destinies. Their religion dictated how kings, priests, and people should interact with their gods in order to hold back chaos, ensuring a good life, a stable nation, and a secure future.

Unity of Religion and the State

Religious symbolism appears in Egypt's most ancient artifacts. Egypt's religion likely developed among those who settled it after the dispersion from Babel and therefore existed before its unification as a nation. Egypt's religion and government eventually became inseparable. Its king was seen as an incarnation of the god Horus, son of Osiris, and its economy, art, and architecture were devoted to the satisfaction and sustenance of the gods in order to preserve the natural order and protect the dead. A look at Cleopatra's Needle, now gracing the bank of the Thames in London, is a reminder of this theocratic union.

The obelisk was not commissioned by the famous Cleopatra VII but was named because it was moved to an Alexandrian temple that Cleopatra built to honor her Roman lover. The 68-foot obelisk had been constructed centuries earlier at the order of Pharaoh Thutmose III to mark sunset at Atum-Ra's temple in Heliopolis. As the supposed offspring of the sun god Ra and the vital link between Egypt and the gods, it was the pharaoh's duty to facilitate the daily life-giving cycle of the sun god, and he commissioned two obelisks for this purpose.

The companion to the obelisk on the Thames, taken from the eastern gate of the same temple, was built to mark Ra's daily rebirth or resurrection.

---

3. Ibid., vol. 2, section 50.

It now stands in New York City's Central Park. These obelisks, like the pyramids, also symbolized an element common to all Egyptian creation myths — the primeval mound from which the creator god Atum emerged to conquer chaos.

Battle with the God of Moses

Egypt's religious beliefs accumulated over time and were never codified in a holy book. They were, however, recorded in every facet of its culture. Certainly by the time of Moses and the Hebrews' Exodus, Egypt's system of gods was a force over which the Creator God, as the only true God, chose to show Himself powerful for the benefit of the Hebrews and the watching world.

When God announced the tenth plague to Moses, He explained, "against all the gods of Egypt I will execute judgment: I am the LORD" (Exodus 12:12). The Hebrews had long lived in Egypt exposed to Egypt's religion and, as God forged them into the nation through which He would reveal His Word (Romans 3:2) and eventually send the Savior into the world, they needed to be shown the power of the only true God. The Egyptian people themselves needed that lesson, and God told Moses:

> But Pharaoh will not heed you, so that I may lay My hand on Egypt and bring My armies and My people, the children of Israel, out of the land of Egypt by great judgments. And the Egyptians shall know that I am the LORD, when I stretch out My hand on Egypt and bring the children of Israel from among them (Exodus 7:4–5).

People of other pagan nations (such as Jericho, according to Rahab; see Joshua 2:8–10) also needed to see the proof of God's power over the false gods of this mighty nation. Pharaoh was considered the incarnation of the god Horus and the son of the sun god, Ra. If not divine during his time on earth (a status that varied over the centuries), he anticipated unification with the god Osiris after his death. Pharaoh represented Egypt to the gods. He therefore was not just a stubborn obstacle to Hebrew freedom but the point man for Egypt's "gods" in the battle that played out before Israel's departure.

Egypt's creation stories held that the gods emerged to create order out of chaos, and they themselves were part of that order. Keeping chaos at bay was one of the chief goals of Egypt's religion in general and therefore of pharaoh in particular. According to inscriptions recounting religious rituals, the pharaoh was pictured as Egypt's representative even as the priests ministered to the mythological beings they believed to be the authors and sustainers of all that was not chaos.

The office of pharaoh was identified with the god Horus. At death, if all rites were observed, the pharaoh was thought to become one with Horus' father, Osiris, the god of the underworld. Thus, the ten plagues preceding the Exodus under Moses dealt a series of blows to the status of many elements of nature that were personified as gods as well as to the quasi-divine pharaoh, son of the sun god, who was Egypt's intermediary with its pantheon.

It is difficult to be dogmatic about which plagues dealt blows to Egyptian perceptions of which specific gods. After all, Egypt honored around 1,500 gods, many manifested in nature. Two of the more obvious are the plague of frogs, in which the frog-headed fertility goddess Heket certainly lost face among her worshipers, and the plague on livestock, which took a shot at the sacred Apis bull and the bovine goddess Hathor.

Life and prosperity in ancient Egypt depended on certain cycles. For ancient Egyptians, the sun's daily renewal and the Nile River's annual flood were particularly important. Egyptians believed that properly cared for gods and goddesses would maintain these cycles on which their lives depended. Thus, the plague of darkness was a direct assault on the normally dependable sun god, Ra.

The Nile River also had divine status, and Hapy was the god of the all-important annual flood that imparted life-sustaining fertility to Egypt's soil. The first plague, turning water into blood, struck at the heart of Egypt's agricultural prosperity, the water that kept the dry desert's chaos from claiming Egypt's fertile lands. Ultimately, the ten plagues culminated in the death of the firstborn of Egypt, including the firstborn of Egypt's quasi-divine pharaoh.

Foreign Threat

As evident from Herodotus' testimony during his visit to a Persian-ruled Egypt, Egypt's religion weathered foreign rule, but not unscathed. Persia conquered Egypt in 532 B.C. and promptly slew the Apis bull and destroyed the statues of many gods. Cambyses, the Persian conqueror, even had the mummy of Pharaoh Ahmose II, who died in 526 B.C., taken from its tomb and cremated — thus destroying the essential nightly home on which the pharaoh's *ka* and *ba* depended for their eternal existence (see section below for an explanation of this concept).

Persian efforts to replace Egypt's religion with their own form of sun worship left a mark, even on some monuments. For instance, the sun's rays seem to have been added to some religious carvings, yet Egypt's ancient religion survived. Later, under the Ptolemaic rule that followed Alexander's Greek conquest of Egypt, Egypt's ancient religion, though mixed with elements of other religions and mysticism, continued to accord divine status to the Egyptian king.

Egypt's theocracy finally crumbled under the rule of Christianized Rome in the fourth century A.D. With the Renaissance, the modern world took an increased interest in all things ancient, especially things Egyptian. Egyptian symbolism and the enticing mysteries of the as-yet-then-indecipherable hieroglyphics intrigued many, including philosophers of the Enlightenment, theologians, mystics, secret societies, and revolutionaries.

Modern Interest in Egyptology

Things Egyptian became much more accessible to Europeans after Napoleon's conquest of Egypt and his subsequent defeat by the British at the 1801 Battle of Alexandria. Antiquities were popular and available. The cornerstone of Egyptology in the 19th century and beyond was the inscription on the Rosetta stone unearthed during Napoleon's brief rule. Its simple message recorded in three languages contained the key to deciphering Egyptian hieroglyphics. As Egyptology blossomed with the abundance of artifacts and the excitement of linguistic breakthroughs, some scholars hoped to discover the mysterious wisdom of a superior ancient philosophy, while others expected to find corroborating evidence for many historical accounts in the Bible's Old Testament.

Finding the footprints of a highly civilized, complex ancient culture in the monuments, artifacts, inscriptions, and documents they unearthed in Egypt, 19th-century scholars were puzzled to discover that evidently advanced people had worshiped gods represented as animals and animal-human hybrids. Mummified people was understandable to modern Western cultures with their own elaborate funeral rites, but what should the modern mind make of the many mummified crocodiles, cats, and bulls?

How could a highly civilized nation have arisen harnessed to a religion that seemed barbaric or even silly? And so began the quest to piece together the truth about what ancient Egyptians, from farmer to pharaoh, really believed about their origins, how they worshiped their gods, and what they thought would happen to them after they died.

Polytheism in an Advanced Civilization

Though ancient Egypt's religion is documented in surviving papyrus documents and artwork covering monuments, temples, and coffins, Egypt never developed a Bible-like book containing an official, authoritative version of their beliefs. Much of Egyptian mythology seems contradictory, but given the fragmentary nature of the evidence from which it has been recovered this isn't surprising.

Moreover, Egyptian gods and goddesses were believed to have co-existing multiple manifestations and characteristics. Thus, the sun god has more than one name, but the name changed according to the time of day. The rising sun was generally the scarab-headed Khepri, the midday sun Ra (or Re), and the setting sun Atum. And Aten was the name eventually applied to the radiant disk of the sun in the time of the Pharaoh Ahkenaten. Furthermore, every being also had a secret name reflecting his or her essence, and the goddess Isis once gained power over the sun god by tricking him into revealing his secret name to her. Thus, differing names were not seen as contradictory.

From the abundant yet fragmentary evidence, scholars have pieced together a reasonable understanding of the roughly 1,500 named gods the Egyptians revered and how they worshiped them. About some there is little more known than a name, but for many there is a great deal of information. Well-known are the mythological stories of Seth's murder of his brother Osiris — by tricking him into climbing into a box in which he was subsequently drowned — and of Osiris' ultimate resurrection as god of the underworld with the help of his wife, Isis, the posthumous conception and birth of their son Horus, and Horus' eventual revenge upon Seth.

In some ways, Egyptian myths resembled familiar Greco-Roman myths, though early Egyptologists had to wrestle with the philosophical nature of polytheism in addition to linguistic challenges and the cryptic preponderance of apparent animal worship in such an advanced culture.

Over the past couple of centuries there has been much debate about the nature of Egypt's religion. Some, perhaps spurred by the idea that only intellectually backward people would worship a pantheon of animal-like deities, theorized that Egypt's polytheism was a sublimated form of monotheism with multiple divine manifestations. (This view was even showcased in G.A. Henty's 19th-century historical novel *The Cat of Bubastes*.)

Some Egyptologists have suggested Egypt's ancient religion moved in a trajectory toward a "more civilized" monotheistic religion or recognition of some sort of omnipotent divinity. Each of these positions finds some support in various texts, but we should be cautious in trying to stretch those concepts to interpret the totality of Egypt's theology. In fact, during the New Kingdom, the pharaoh Akhenaten promoted a nearly monotheistic worship of Aten, often depicted as the radiant solar disk, to the exclusion of the rest of Egypt's menu of deities. After his death, Akhenaten's efforts were regarded as heretical and Egyptian worship returned to its firmly polytheistic form.

Animal Gods

Some of Egypt's gods, such as Nut, the goddess of the sky, were accorded human form. But of course, many were depicted as animals, animal hybrids, or animal-human hybrids. Though Egyptians took care to avoid offending sacred animals and revered zoologic manifestations of their deities, most scholars now believe that Egyptians did not think their gods necessarily looked like the animals in their divine menagerie. Rather, they believed their gods could manifest themselves as certain animals, often more than one.

Some gods were depicted alternately as a complete animal or an animal-human hybrid. For instance, Thoth, the god of writing and knowledge, who in one mythological story had healed the eye of Horus, could appear as a baboon, an ibis, or an ibis-headed man. Ra could be depicted by a falcon or by a human body with a falcon's head. The primary creator god Atum was depicted in fully human form wearing the crowns of Upper and Lower Egypt, as a man with the head of a ram, or in animal form as a serpent, a scarab beetle, a lion, a bull, a lizard, an ape, or a mongoose.[4]

The animal manifestation of a god sometimes provided a visual metaphor for some aspect of the god's character or behavior. The cat-headed goddess Bastet was generally a protector. In one depiction she is seen beheading

---

4. Richard H. Wilkinson, *The Complete Gods and Goddesses of Ancient Egypt* (London: Thames and Hudson, 2003), p. 100–101.

the serpent Apophis, promoter of chaos and enemy of Ra. She was seen as a protector of the dead and as a patroness of mothers, protecting women during pregnancy.

Litters of kittens were suitable gifts to commemorate the new year, perhaps in celebration of Bastet's protective role during the "demon days" that marked the end of each year. Sekhmet, Egypt's most prominent divine lioness, had a more mercurial nature. While Sekhmet could be a goddess of healing, she was also a goddess of plagues or war. Functioning as the all-seeing eye of Ra early in human history, Sekhmet is said to have wreaked havoc on mankind, nearly destroying the human race. Many mummified cats are preserved in cemeteries at Saqqara and Thebes. The cats appear to have died with broken necks at uniform ages, suggesting their mummies were not just remains of beloved pets, and reflecting the importance of feline manifestations in the Egyptian pantheon.[5]

In time, scholars came to understand that neither polytheism nor the worship of gods depicted as animals meant the ancient Egyptians were intellectually inferior. The unusual animal representations of deities in their various combinations carried symbolic meaning. For instance, Sobek was the crocodile god and lord of the Nile. But in a statue found in the temple of

Wall of relief of the Crocodile God Sobek in Egypt
(Shutterstock)

Luxor in 1967 at a pit in which the sacred animals were likely kept, Sobek-Ra is depicted as a crocodile god with a solar disk on its head and the body of a man. Sobek-Ra's statue, because it has a man's body, is able to embrace a stylized statue of Amenhotep III, and Sobek-Ra is giving him an ankh. The *ankh*, a cross with a loop on the top, was a symbol for life. Scholars believe this statue indicates the sun god, the creator and sustainer of life, manifested himself merged with the crocodile god Sobek, which in turn passed the symbol of life

Ankh

5. John H. Taylor, *Death and the Afterlife in Ancient Egypt* (Chicago, IL: University of Chicago Press, 2001), p. 256.

to the pharaoh.[6] In other myths, Sobek shared his crocodile form with other gods, including Seth — the jealous, sneaky, power-hungry murderer of Osiris and enemy of Horus.[7]

Sophistication, Paganism, and the Gospel

Thus, Egyptologists today, having pieced together bits and pieces of information and studied the Egyptian religion though art, artifacts, inscriptions, and other written material, can now be confident that Egypt's polytheism, complete with all its animal forms, was highly abstract and sophisticated. It was, nevertheless, an utterly pagan substitute for the worship of the true God. As Romans 1 tells us of all such religions that reject the true Creator God, regardless of their level of sophistication or whether they are monotheistic or polytheistic:

> For the wrath of God is revealed from heaven against all ungodliness and unrighteousness of men, who suppress the truth in unrighteousness, because what may be known of God is manifest in them, for God has shown it to them. For since the creation of the world His invisible attributes are clearly seen, being understood by the things that are made, even His eternal power and Godhead, so that they are without excuse, because, although they knew God, they did not glorify Him as God, nor were thankful, but became futile in their thoughts, and their foolish hearts were darkened. Professing to be wise, they became fools, and changed the glory of the incorruptible God into an image made like corruptible man — and birds and four-footed animals and creeping things (Romans 1:18–23).

In his book *Eternity in Their Hearts,* missionary Don Richardson, also the author of *Peace Child,* notes that many pagan cultures with ancient roots harbor deep-rooted cultural beliefs that make it easy for them to understand biblical Christianity once it is presented to them. So it was with Egypt. For centuries, Egyptians believed their priest-like pharaoh was a son of their sun god, Ra, their intermediary with the gods, and a divine or semi-divine being identified with the god Horus. They believed that upon his death he would

---

6. Geraldine Pinch, *Egyptian Mythology: A Very Short Introduction* (Oxford: Oxford University Press, 2004), p. 53–54.

7. Ibid., p. 64.

become one with Osiris, his father and god of the underworld. As such, this "son of a god" and mediator would continue to influence the fate of those who died.

For anyone familiar with the biblical gospel of Jesus Christ, the parallels are impossible to miss. When Christianity was introduced in Egypt, many aspects of the true gospel had a familiar ring. Unfortunately the popularity of the Isis-Horus mother-child myth concerning Isis' care of her son Horus, miraculously conceived after the brutal murder of his father, Osiris, lent itself to counterfeits in the form of cultic associations. These mystery religions rivaled Christianity for centuries.

Nevertheless, the past had prepared the hearts of many to be forever changed by the knowledge and worship of the true Son of God, which came to Egypt early in Christianity's history. The hour had come when, like the Samaritans of whom Jesus said "you worship what you do not know" (John 4:22), many Egyptians would turn to "worship the Father in spirit and truth" (John 4:23), having learned that "there is one God and one Mediator between God and men, the Man Christ Jesus, who gave Himself a ransom for all, to be testified in due time" (1 Timothy 2:5–6).

By the end of the second century, Christianity had put down deep roots in the Nile Valley.[8] This long preceded its official acceptance as the religion of the Roman Empire. Yet in A.D. 452, after a century of Christianized Rome's domination and almost two centuries before seventh century Muslim forces overran Egypt, there is record of a group of Egyptians taking an Egyptian goddess (idol) south to visit "her" relatives in Nubia. The powerful and persistent influence of Egyptian religion on surrounding cultures is evident in the "mystery religions" that rivaled Christianity in the Greco-Roman world.

An Egyptian temple actively devoted to the worship of Isis and Osiris on the Nile island of Philae, built under Egypt's Ptolemaic rulers, co-existed with Christian worship until closed by order of the Byzantine emperor Justinian in the sixth century A.D. A cult based on the worship of Isis and Osiris acquired a widespread international following and long outlived the popularity of the Egyptian gods in Egypt itself.

Worldview, Mythology, and Eternal Concerns

There is great value in understanding the worldview of others past and present, though today you will not likely encounter worshipers of Ra and Isis

---

8. Wilkinson, *The Complete Gods and Goddesses of Ancient Egypt*, p. 242.

Temple of Isis from Philae at Agilikia Island
(Wikimedia, Ivan Marcialis)

in your evangelistic efforts to win your neighbors to Jesus Christ. Egyptian mythology reveals what these intelligent people valued and how they thought. For instance, their concern with the preservation of the body and elaborate provisions for the future of the dead reveals their concern about the afterlife. And their beliefs about judgment to be faced after death shows not only their concern with justice but also their appreciation that not just the letter of the law but also truth and the condition of the heart are important indicators of character and even eternal destiny.

The myths the Egyptians developed represent their attempt to explain their origins, understand their place in the world, justify their cultural norms and institutions, lend stability to their government, make sense of their sorrows, and to face death and the uncertainties of the afterlife. In short, Egypt's ancient religion dealt with the same questions that all humans face. In examining ancient Egypt's worldview, we see how, having rejected whatever knowledge of the true God the people retained from their Babel-based ancestors and from others like Abraham who crossed their path, they attempted to answer these timeless, universal human questions through the wisdom of men.

Egyptian mythology, with its rich imagery, despite its pagan roots, has, like classical Greco-Roman mythology, made a rich contribution to literature, even showing up in the writings of John Milton's *Paradise Lost* and in Mozart's opera *The Magic Flute*. Egyptian mythology lives on today in vivid fantasies built around the colorful and imaginative figures that populate Egyptian mythology — especially those in animal form.

The actual worship of these characters now being long past, such stories intrigue Christians and non-Christians alike. But we must remember that real people — people who built a complex, powerful, and influential civilization under the shadow of this pantheon — believed these gods and goddesses held the keys to their past, their present, the afterlife, and their national well-being. Therefore, they devoted their lives and their treasure to worshiping these gods in all their manifestations.

Given that God saw fit to have Moses record in Exodus His battle with the demonic forces personified as Egyptian gods, it is worthwhile for us to learn more about the beliefs of this mighty nation that so greatly influenced its neighbors. Some claim that the Genesis account of creation was influenced by Egyptian creation myths — though we would claim that any similarities to the corrupted versions in Egypt's mythos stem from a cultural awareness of the true history handed down by the descendants of Noah's family who eventually moved from Babel to Egypt.

Satan has been in the business of prompting people to create counterfeit religions that twist the truth of God into a lie and worship the creature instead of the Creator (Romans 1:25) for a very long time. In ancient Egyptian rituals for dealing with death and preparing for the afterlife, we see the earmarks of the same satanic lies that still abound in works-based religions that deny the grace of God available in Christ.

Egyptian Views of Creation

Nearly a dozen Egyptian creation stories distilled from archaeological evidence can be boiled down to three basic forms, based largely on documents and artifacts from three of ancient Egypt's religious centers. While on the surface they seem contradictory, it is best to consider them as complementary stories revealing various perspectives on origins, for there is no evidence that these stories competed with one another. (In a similar way, many people today erroneously think that the biblical accounts of creation recorded in Genesis chapters 1 and 2 are in conflict, when in reality they only focus on different aspects of the same event.)

Egyptians would have viewed these creation accounts — like many seemingly contradictory "versions" of the relationships between and actions of their gods — as simultaneously true, equally valid layers of the same reality. Furthermore, the creation stories all contain several common elements.

The primeval mound was one such common element. Ancient Egypt's religion at times seems like a personified metaphor based on the natural world in which many key elements are deified. Thus, it is quite possible that the primeval mound was a larger-than-life version of the mounds of land that appeared in the Nile River, the river without which life in Egypt could not exist.

These mounds of sand, silt, and clay called *geziras* are particularly prominent in the Nile Delta. Rising above the cultivated land, they were used in ancient times for settlements. In one story, when the mound rises up from the surrounding chaos, a bird lands on it and cackles so loudly that the silence is broken and life begins. In most Egyptian creation myths, a father of other gods somehow emerges from the mound and begins the work of creation, starting with the creation of many other gods.

From the "City of the Sun," Heliopolis, the original home of Cleopatra's Needle on the western gate of the Temple of Ra, comes one of the three creation myths. Heliopolis was a religious center devoted to the worship of the creator god Atum. Atum is often identified with the sun god Ra, though in some scenarios Atum is seen as the dying sunset that travels the underworld at night, and Ra is revered as the rising reborn sun.

In the Heliopolis mythos, in the beginning there was only the chaos of primeval water. Out of this water arose a mound from which the god Atum emerged. Standing on the mound, Atum sneezed out the air god, Shu, and spat out the moisture goddess, Tefnut. The offspring of these two were the sky goddess, Nut, and the earth god, Geb. The offspring of Nut and Geb were Osiris, Isis, Seth, and Nephthys, key players in Egypt's most memorable stories. These nine gods and goddesses, a group called the *Ennead*, were then responsible for different creative acts or attributes that built the world in which Egyptians played out their lives.

When a pharaoh — the offspring of Ra — died, he hoped to become one not only with Osiris but also with Atum, traveling the underworld each night to bring new life each morning (Pyramid Texts 147). Not just creator and one with the sun, Atum was also seen as the one who would someday un-create everything, returning the world to chaos and settling down to reign over it all as a serpent.[9]

From the fifth dynasty city of Hermopolis come texts describing a primeval egg in the waters of chaos. In this egg Atum, or Ra, the sun god, existed until he brought himself forth, initially as a lotus blossom, and stood on his mound. From there the sun god created four male-female pairs of gods — Nun and Naunet representing water, Heh and Hauhet representing infinity, Kek and Kaukey representing darkness, and Amun and Amaunet representing hiddenness. These eight divine elements then, of course, produced all the other gods and goddesses and the physical world they represent. Thus once again, to the life-sustaining sun, earth's nearest star, is ascribed the original creative power to produce all that makes our world habitable.

From the city of Memphis comes one of the best-preserved Egyptian creation myths. Recorded on the 25th dynasty Shabbat stone housed in the British Museum, the Memphite view of origins contains the oldest extrabiblical record of creation *ex nihilo* through the power of the spoken word. In the Memphis mythos, the god Ptah was the primeval water who formed himself into dry land — the primeval mound — and, embodying the male-female divine elements within himself, spoke into existence the familiar Egyptian pantheon, to whom he delegated further creative acts.

In all these Egyptian creation myths, the creation of the world was paramount. Although many of the Egyptian gods are depicted in animal forms, creation of man and the animals is something of an afterthought. In some versions, the creator god Ra sent his eye to search for his missing offspring, Shu and Tefnut. Returning, the eye — having become the lion goddess Sekhmet — is distressed that Ra has grown another eye and weeps. Those tears became humanity.[10]

For the most part, however, Egyptian mythology leaves the creation of each man to a lesser god, Khnum, who fashions people out of clay from the Nile River. By contrast, the Bible, God's eyewitness account of creation, in Genesis 1 and 2 explains that God spoke the physical world and all kinds of

---

9. In *Book of the Dead* 175, the god Atum makes this apocalyptic pronouncement to Osiris: "You shall be for millions of millions, a lifetime of millions. Then I shall destroy all that I have made. This land will return in to the Abyss, into the flood as in its former state. It is I who shall remain together with Osiris, having made my transformations into other snakes which mankind will not know, nor gods see."

10. Geraldine Pinch, *Egyptian Mythology: A Very Short Introduction* (Oxford: Oxford University Press, 2004), p. 60.

living things into existence in an orderly fashion. Then, having prepared the world, God created Adam and Eve and presented the world to them, placing it under man's dominion (Genesis 1:26, 28), giving Adam the responsibility of tending and keeping the Garden of Eden (Genesis 2:15).

Thus, in Egyptian mythology we see man as an afterthought at best and a product of divine distress at worst. By contrast, from the Bible we infer that man is the culmination of God's creative work (being the only creature made to bear God's image) and the designated recipient and steward of the created world. Furthermore, upon man's rebellion against God, humanity became the focus of the saving grace that God planned from the foundation of the world (1 Peter 1:20).

The late Dr. Henry M. Morris suggested that Satan believes that he was not created, but that "all of the angels as well as God Himself had just arisen from the primeval chaos . . . and that it was only an accident of the priority of time that placed him, with all of his wisdom and beauty, beneath God in the angelic hierarchy."[11] If that were the case, it would be natural for fallen man to carry forward mythologies in which a god came forth from nothingness. Satan desires to be worshiped as God, and we know that idols and false gods really are surrogates for demonic worship (Deuteronomy 32:17; 1 Corinthians 10:20). Sadly, many fall into this sort of trap — worshiping the creature, rather than the Creator.

These three creation myths share some common elements — a primeval watery chaos, a primeval mound of dry land, and the deification of many elements of nature. Because Egyptian mythology deifies only certain aspects of nature and not nature itself, it differs from truly pantheist religions. Nevertheless, ancient Egyptian religion is a vivid example of what the Apostle Paul describes as worship of "the creature rather than the Creator" (Romans 1:25).

In one of these ancient Egyptian myths we find the first mention, outside the Bible, of the idea that creation was accomplished through the power of the spoken word. Recall that Genesis prefaces each of God's creative acts with "And God said . . ." and in the New Testament John 1:1–3 identifies Jesus Christ as the *Logos,* the Word through whom creation was accomplished long before He came into the world as a man to die for and redeem mankind. The Apostle John, under God's inspiration, penned the New Testament verses describing the creative power of God's words long after the heyday of Egyptian

11. Henry M. Morris, *The Genesis Record* (Grand Rapids, MI: Baker Book House, 1976), p. 107–108.

religion, and Moses recorded the creation account preserved in Genesis at a time when Egyptian religion was already highly developed.

While we cannot be dogmatic about the path of ideas over the millennia, we know that the Egyptian people, like all people in the world, descended from Noah's family dispersed from the Tower of Babel. We can reasonably hypothesize that those people who came down to Egypt knew the true history of creation through this family heritage. Perhaps this creation-by-spoken-word — unusual in ancient mythology — is an element of the true origins history that survived in corrupted form to become part of the Memphite creation story.

The same may be said of many other elements in Egypt's creation myths, such as the raising up of dry land from an initial watery chaos, that bear some resemblance to the actual conditions prevailing at the time of creation as recorded in Genesis 1:9–10 under the inspiration of history's reliable eye-witness, the Creator God.

Egyptologists and other scholars have noted that the chaotic conditions prevailing early in the biblical creation week described in Genesis 1 are mir-rored in Egypt's creation stories. This naturally has prompted some liberal theologians to speculate that Egypt's creation myths were source material for the Mosaic account. After all, Moses was educated in Egypt in pharaoh's household and would have known all about them.

Furthermore, the Hebrew people Moses led out of Egypt had been living under the influence of Egypt's gods for several generations at the time of the Exodus. Yet, according to the God-inspired Scripture, Jesus Christ clearly accepted Mosaic authorship of the Pentateuch under divine inspiration. Did Egyptian mythology influence the sacred text God inspired Moses to write? If so, God's true version of origins would have shown the ancient Hebrews what little truth was embodied in the corrupted Egyptian accounts. Strip-ping away Egyptian corruptions would have revealed, by contrast, "In the beginning God created the heavens and the earth."

God's truth about origins — then as now — refutes man's imaginative but baseless stories about the creation and the character of the Creator.

The creation account preserved in Genesis 1 and 2 and the history of man's rebellion against our holy omnipotent Creator in Genesis 3 is God's own eyewitness version of our history. In Egyptian creation stories, the first god (at best) exists in a primordial egg that emerges from chaos with the first dry land and proceeds to create other gods to help him out. Here we see an illogical construction, since the god who created the world must have been created by another god before that.

By contrast, the Bible reveals that the real Creator is one all-powerful, uncreated, eternally existent God. And while the Egyptian creator is part of the created order even as he commands it and fashions it from chaos, the biblical Creator transcends nature. The biblical Creator is above and outside His creation, though He is intimately involved with both the world and the people He created. In fact, God is so intimately involved that the Son took on flesh and became part of mankind to offer salvation through His life, death, and Resurrection.

While in some Egyptian myths the creator god creates by the power of the spoken word, even then the ancient Egyptian concept of a creator never separates the god from his creation. Like the modern "god" of evolution, the Egyptian god appears from chaos through natural processes and then puts the world in order. And though endowed with mythological divinity, the elements of nature — like those in evolutionary scenarios — create the rest of nature and eventually life itself from the natural elements.

Egypt's Gods and the One True God

Moses wrote in Deuteronomy 6:4, "Hear, O Israel: The LORD our God, the LORD is one!" The people to whom this was originally addressed had lived for four generations among the pantheon of Egypt. They were surely accustomed to hearing about a multiplicity of gods, regardless of what they believed. Children had grown up perhaps hearing the truth from their parents but nevertheless exposed to Egyptian mythology, not as fanciful stories but as the truth that ruled the government and day-to-day Egyptian life. In that context and for that audience, the boldness and the importance of this statement — *There is only one God!* — is apparent.

From Scripture we learn that God exists in three persons but He is one God. Furthermore, the biblical God does not create other gods or lesser gods as in the Egyptian myths. God created angels, but they are not gods. Hebrews 1:5–6 makes this clear:

> For to which of the angels did He ever say: "You are My Son, today I have begotten You"? And again: "I will be to Him a Father, and He shall be to Me a Son"?

But when He again brings the firstborn into the world, He says: "Let all the angels of God worship Him."

Unlike angels, Jesus Christ, the only begotten Son of God, though He entered our history and was born of a virgin in the flesh, actually co-existed with the Father from eternity past — He was not created. John 1:1–3 reveals for instance "In the beginning was the Word, and the Word was with God, and the Word was God. He was in the beginning with God. All things were made through Him, and without Him nothing was made that was made." Indeed, the Bible is clear that Jesus Christ is not only the author of our salvation but also the author of all creation. Colossians 1:15–17 informs us that Jesus "is the image of the invisible God, the firstborn over all creation. For by Him all things were created that are in heaven and that are on earth, visible and invisible, whether thrones or dominions or principalities or powers. All things were created through Him and for Him. And He is before all things, and in Him all things consist."

Egypt's Unholy Pantheon and the Holy God of the Bible

The Bible — starting in Genesis — reveals not only information about the origin of all things — the physical universe, life, man, male and female, marriage, sin, suffering, and death — but also reveals much about the character of God. We learn in the Bible that God is holy, just, merciful, gracious, loving, all-powerful, eternally pre-existent, all-knowing, and transcendent above His creation even as He interacts with it and with the people He created.

In contrast, in Egyptian mythology we meet multiple gods that are themselves created, flawed, capricious, and finite. They do not transcend creation but instead form parts of it. Though they spring into existence at the behest of the first god — himself a part of the creation to emerge from chaos — Egypt's gods require assistance from each other to create the elements of the physical world.

Far from holy, Egypt's gods engage in all manner of immorality, deceit, and cruelty to gain their ends. Sekhmet the lion goddess, and originally the eye of the creator Ra, for instance, went on a rampage to destroy humanity. Ra finally tricked the bloodthirsty goddess — actually a manifestation of the more benign Hathor — by getting her inebriated on blood mixed with beer in order to spare the rest.[12]

---

12. Pinch, *Egyptian Mythology: A Very Short Introduction*, p. 61.

Lust, promiscuity, murder, and complicated paternity issues are rampant among the members of the Egyptian pantheon. For instance, jealous of Isis, faithless Seth tricks and murders Isis' companion, his brother Osiris, dismembering Osiris's body parts in an attempt to ensure they cannot be reunited and reanimated. And just who exactly is Horus's father? Perhaps not even the gods know for sure — but after being posthumously conceived and raised by his mother Isis, Horus makes war to avenge his putative father's murder. As an aside, some skeptics try to say that the virgin birth is actually mimicking the story of Horus and Isis, but the details are often stretched or fabricated to make the two seem more similar than they are.

The goddess Isis poisons Ra, king of gods, and then tricks him into yielding up much of his power in exchange for a cure. Ra subsequently retires to the sky for a daily transit, his nightly underworld journey, and a glorious morning of rebirth. Interesting stories, to be sure. But the Egyptians created their larger-than-life gods in their own image — in humanity's sinful image. As such, their gods and the myths surrounding them reflect the capricious and cruel character of human beings, not the holy character of the biblical God.

Satan and Seth

Does Egypt's religion have an evil character corresponding to Satan? Some suggest Seth (Set) was essentially a Satan counterpart, but this is a poor analogy. Seth, one of the more disagreeable Egyptian gods, is one of the original group of gods in the Ennead. Following death, the person who fails his test with the feather of truth (see explanation below) would consider Seth his fearsome enemy, for the Seth animal would devour him. And while Seth is a god of violence and anger, a jealous murderer who killed his brother and went to war with his nephew, he also has constructive activity attributed to him. For instance, Seth rides the back of the sun god during his daily journey across the sky to combat the serpent of chaos, Apophis. And a winged Seth slays the serpent Apophis in artwork in the temple of Hibis.[13] Apophis, in contrast to Seth, is a uniformly reprehensible serpent deity that was not revered or worshiped.

While Egyptian mythology contained numerous serpent deities, most were not malevolent; Apophis was. In contrast, Amun and Osiris will supposedly one day be transformed into everlasting serpents to reign forever over an apocalyptic return of chaos. However, Egypt's pantheon provided

13. Wilkinson, *The Complete Gods and Goddesses of Ancient Egypt*, p. 199.

enough malevolent characters to go around, and trying to assign one to the role of Satan is an oversimplification. In any case, the numerous capricious actors in the Egyptian hit parade of gods provided ample explanation for the evil and suffering in the world.

A Most Religious People

Ordinary people would have had no access to the temple services and ceremonies by which the pharaoh and priests served the gods so that they would keep chaos far from Egyptian sands. Priests, even though they might hold ordinary jobs too, underwent rites of purification to even enter the inner regions where they bathed, dressed, and fed the statues representing Egypt's gods.

Nevertheless, evidence suggests that religion did not touch the personal lives of ordinary people. For one thing, ordinary people could make offerings of flowers, food, or votive statues in the outer courts of the temples. And during processions on festive occasions they could watch as priests carried the statues of the gods in sacred boats through the streets and put on mystery plays for the public.

Ancient Egyptians could seek advice from the gods through priestly oracles at the temples. They could even try to influence the gods by leaving offerings at "hearing ear" shrines built into the outside walls of many temples. Some picture a worshiper kneeling in prayer before a series of large ears.

Additionally, many local shrines were available where supplicants could leave offerings, beg healing, and touch sacred objects. People could leave statues of themselves there to beg for healing, interceding with the gods for them while they went about the business of living. Excavations have shown that the homes of ordinary people had places for household gods along with the images of dead family members.

This stela depicts a person in prayer appealing to the hearing ears of the gods. Artifacts like these are associated with the later centuries of ancient Egypt's history, during the New Kingdom.

Artifacts from the New Kingdom, later in ancient Egypt's history, reveal that some people were concerned with the problem of sin. "Penitential texts" recovered from excavations at Deir el-Medina include both brief and elaborate prayers. One of the best examples found there on the Stela of Nebre may be translated:

> Though the servant was disposed to do evil,
> The Lord is disposed to forgive.
> The Lord of Thebes spends not a whole day in anger,
> His wrath passes in a moment, none remains.
> His breath comes back to us in mercy,
> Amun returns upon his breeze. . . .[14]

Eventually, a personal relationship with the goddess Isis and the availability of salvation through her became a part of Egyptian religion accessible to those without royal blood or riches. The awareness of sin and concern about death reminds us that ancient Egyptians had the same concerns as modern people, even though they had rejected the God who could answer their needs.

Man and the Afterlife

Egyptian temples were devoted to the care and worship of the gods on whom the Egyptians depended to keep back the forces of chaos until the end of time. But with death, a person's fate became a more immediate concern. Unlike atheistic evolutionists, Egyptians did not assume that man was only an animal and that life ended forever at the grave.

What is man? Understanding the ancient Egyptian view of the afterlife requires knowledge of their answer to this question. While not much concerned with the origin of man, Egyptians were concerned with the essential elements of a person — his body, his name, and his shadow, his *ka* and his *ba*. Though scholars suspect that in early days the ancients believed only the pharaoh possessed all these elements, by later times the nobility and likely even common people were dignified by a nature worth preserving and protecting through ritual.

The Egyptians believed the physical body was inhabited by an invisible ka and ba that departed at death but were able to return to a properly preserved body. While the ka was more associated with attaining sustenance,

---

14. Wilkinson, *The Complete Gods and Goddesses of Ancient Egypt*, p. 51.

the invisible ba was more like a ghostly manifestation of the person, able to go to the world beyond and interact with the cosmos inhabited by the gods. Ongoing existence beyond the grave demanded a preserved body, one processed by rituals that often included various types of mummification. The body was not thought to physically move about or eat, but rather to provide a home to which the ka and ba would return from their excursions. Surrounding this preserved body would be instructions and amulets to assist the dead in facing judgment and in navigating the afterlife.

Like other ancient cultures that have left tombs filled with grave goods and evidence of companions to serve the departed in the life beyond, the ancient Egyptians' careful treatment of the dead and particular concern with the preservation of the body attest to their belief in an afterlife and some preoccupation with doing what they could to make the passage into death a safe one and the ongoing existence happy. Unlike some other ancient cultures, Egyptians were not in the habit of routinely slaughtering large numbers of people to serve the royal dead in the afterlife, at least not after the earliest years. From the Middle Kingdom onward the dead were instead supplied with statues called *shabti* — figurines of servants to take care of their needs in the beyond.

These shabti, housed at the British Museum, were once placed in ancient Egyptian tombs with the expectation that they would answer their master's call, not only serving his or her needs, but performing by proxy whatever labor might be required of the dead in an agricultural afterlife.

Monumental tombs of various sorts were built to house royals and nobles, so naturally there remains more evidence to reveal their expectations after death. The grave goods that accompanied such wealthy people included food, jewelry, furniture, and even boats. Artwork in the grave was supposed to have power to maintain the normalcy of life. Moreover, inscriptions containing spells, poems, and instructions for the dead person were carved on the walls of many tombs and on coffins. The oldest of these discovered thus far are the Pyramid Texts, about 800 inscriptions carved on the walls in nine Old Kingdom pyramids, some in language associated with pre-dynastic Egypt.

During the Old Kingdom, Egyptians may have believed that only pharaoh could have an afterlife, and these texts explain that he would undertake a journey fraught with peril, but if successful continue his existence as either the sun god or Osiris. Yet the discovery of ancient Egyptian bodies buried beneath desert sand, desiccated by natural processes and accompanied by grave goods, suggests that even common people had some expectation of life beyond the grave, regardless of whether that belief was reinforced by the official religion.

Later, Egyptians came to officially believe that the afterlife was also available to non-royal nobility. How far down the social scale this extended remains a matter of speculation. Men, and even women, could hope to become one with Osiris. Even later in Egypt's history, many people were therefore buried with little corn mummies made of grain, clay, and sand wrapped in bandages and decorated with pictures of Sokar, the falcon god of craftsmanship.

On the other hand, women — and even men — could hope to join with Hathor, the nurturing protective goddess of women and motherhood often depicted as a cow. This bovine deity — believed to give birth to the sun god each day and to travel with him — was naturally associated with rebirth and resurrection. It seemed only natural that Hathor might greet the dead as well as each day's dying sun with water to purify and refresh.[15]

The availability of the afterlife to the populace is attested to by over 1,000 "Coffin Texts," inscriptions and spells carved on coffins to provide instruction and protection to the deceased. By the time of the New Kingdom, many of these were collected as the *Book of the Dead*, also called "The Beginning of the Spells for Going Forth by Day," after the opening title.

15. Ibid., p. 143.

Though lengthy passages continued to be carved in tombs and on grave goods, personalized papyrus copies of the *Book of the Dead* inscribed with the name, genealogy, and occupation of the deceased were often buried with people. Amulets were also blessed with or even inscribed with spells from the *Book of the Dead* and buried with the body.

Importance of Preserving the Body

An Egyptian's afterlife was doomed to be disastrous if the body was not preserved. The elaborate ritualized process of mummification removed and preserved the vital organs in jars and essentially pickled, wrapped, and preserved the body itself, perhaps with a covering of sweet spices and a beautiful mask, in hope that the sleep of death would give way to a happy future existence. Egyptians would be particularly upset if the body of a loved one were not recovered. Thus, being devoured by a hungry crocodile or other beast was particularly distressing, even more than just the gruesome nature of such a death itself would warrant. And cremation was unheard of.

Many additional rites ensured the best chance for a safe trip into the afterlife. For instance, in the ceremony of the Opening of the Mouth, a priest would recite spells intended to revitalize the dead in the afterlife and enable a statue or image of the departed to act as the surrogate of the dead person.

Why would the dead need a body? Assuming the dead person passed through judgment successfully, the ba and ka could sail into eternal bliss on Ra's boat and then rise each day forever. The ba could look after the family left behind. Accordingly, Egyptians would write letters to a dead relative they believed had become a powerful *akh*. The ka could enjoy a variety of pleasant places and activities and commune with gods like Osiris, Hathor, Ra, or Thoth.

But the body needed a nametag of sorts, lest the ba and ka land in the wrong place. This was the purpose of the cartouche attached to each coffin. If the body was destroyed or the name obliterated, the ba and ka could not find their way back and would disappear forever. Though families were expected to pay mortuary cults to keep the dead supplied with food, just in case the generations eventually failed in their commitment, the images in the tombs were symbolically thought to assume the necessary roles.

So what did the ancient Egyptian — at least one wealthy enough to have a fully decked out tomb — expect after death? The cow goddess Hathor might welcome him or her to the underworld with water. Many Coffin Texts found on tombs throughout Egypt reveal the dangers people feared after death — hunger, thirst, aggressive serpents, fire, darkness, dismemberment by demons, wading upside-down through sewage, or having an uncooperative shabti.[16]

Coffin Texts empowered the deceased with the secret names of gods and demons, provided them with maps of the underworld so they could follow Ra's boat during its nightly transit toward the morning of resurrection, reminded the dead person to declare his heart to be pure, told him how to take on the role of a god and escape danger by reenacting his mighty acts, and gave him the words to spur a lazy shabti to obediently go work in the fields for his master.

After Death, Judgment

Worst in the gauntlet of dangers in death was judgment. Failure had dire and irrevocable consequences: to be devoured by Ammut, a ferocious goddess with the head of a crocodile, the front legs of a lion, and the back parts of a hippopotamus. The Egyptian concept of truth, justice, righteousness, and order was personified in the goddess Maat. Immoral and unrighteous behavior was considered a threat to order, so to enjoy the richness of the afterlife a person needed to be guiltless.

The jackal-headed god Anubis — who, myth held, had transformed Osiris into the first mummy — would escort the deceased to face a panel of 42 gods, presided over by Osiris.[17] The deceased greeted each and declared himself innocent of specific sins ranging from lying and theft to blasphemy and murder of a sacred bull.

Declaring innocence was only the first step in judgment. The heart had to be weighed on a balance against Maat's feather of truth. The heart, considered the seat of intelligence and preserved in place in the body, contained the record of a person's life and thus a memory of all guilt. Just as the Bible informs us that all are sinners (Romans 3:23), the Egyptians must have realized that they were not guiltless.

They feared their hearts would reveal the truth when weighed on Maat's scale. The *Book of the Dead,* a collection of spells to assist the deceased in his or her journey, was often buried with people and included a spell, activated

---

16. Pinch, *Egyptian Mythology: A Very Short Introduction,* p. 245.
17. Ibid., p. 206.

during the ceremony of Opening of the Mouth at the time of burial, commanding the heart to not reveal its owner's guilt.

Among the most important amulets placed with or even in a person's corpse was the heart scarab. The scarab beetle was associated with several gods, but none more important than Khepri, the scarab-headed man that represented the rising sun, reborn each morning after successfully negotiating the nightly journey through the underworld to bring "his" life-sustaining rays to the day.[18] Thus, the scarab was associated with resurrection. The heart scarab, an oval or heart-shaped scarab made of stone and inscribed with spells from chapter 30 of the *Book of the Dead*, was supposed to keep the dead person's heart from testifying against him or her when

This heart scarab, housed at the Brooklyn Museum, is inscribed with chapter 30 from the *Book of the Dead*. (Wikimedia)

facing judgment. Thus, while the judgment faced by the dead was concerned with weighing the works done in life to achieve justice, the condition of the heart was also relevant to the outcome of the scales of justice.

Osiris ruled the underworld and was generally the chief judge of the dead and much to be feared. He earned his place there after being murdered and dismembered by his brother Seth. Because Seth separated the pieces of the body in hopes they would not be recovered, the supremely heinous nature of the murder is apparent. In later times, Osiris' son, a hawk-headed Horus, is depicted as the judge holding two scepters, and possibly offering greater mercy than could be expected from Osiris.

Perhaps recognizing that no one is completely good, the Egyptian concept of innocence before judgment was, like that of so many people today, a relative thing — a matter of having done more good things than bad. Declaring himself or herself innocent before the 42 gods sitting in judgment, the dead person's heart was weighed by Anubis against the feather of Maat, the goddess of truth. Though other organs were ordinarily removed from the body and preserved in canopic jars, the heart was buried inside the body so that it would be available for this auspicious ceremony.

---

18. Wilkinson, *The Complete Gods and Goddesses of Ancient Egypt*, p. 231.

This illustration from a papyrus copy of the *Book of the Dead* depicts the jackal-headed Anubis weighing the heart of the deceased on the scale of Maat.
(Wikimedia)

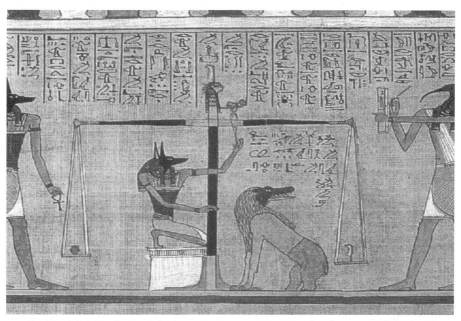

During this "Weighing of the Heart" ceremony, Ammut the devourer of the dead waits expectantly in case the deceased's heart is found wanting. Meanwhile, the ibis-headed scribe Thoth records the results.
(Wikimedia)

If the heart was heavy with evil outweighing the good, the person was declared a liar and the crocodile-headed demonic beast Ammut devoured his heart. With the neck, mane, torso, and forelegs of a lion or leopard, and the rear of a hippopotamus, Ammut was a composite of the most dangerous animals in Egypt. Pictured in the *Book of the Dead* chapter 125, waiting by the fateful scale, Ammut loomed as a fearsome danger that various spells — such as those inscribed on a heart scarab buried inside the chest — were expected to circumvent.

Egyptians properly equipped to face the dangers of death feared their own version of purgatory, but seemed to generally expect a good outcome, not so much through their own purity but through the spells that stacked the deck in their favor. If Ammut devoured a person's heart, he ceased to exist. Otherwise he could go on to various possible happy fates — joining with Osiris like the pharaoh, working on the crew of Ra's all-important ship as it sailed the underworld each night, traveling with Hathor in Ra's retinue, living in a mansion with Thoth the god of wisdom, or enjoying the rich fruits of his shabti's labors in the Field of Reeds. Some saw the eternal state of the justified as one of blissful sleep enlightened nightly by the passage of the sun god through the underworld.

Works, Grace, and the Good News

Sadly, without knowledge of God's grace available through faith in the God of the Bible, the ancient Egyptian's hope of escaping judgment and entering into a paradise was in vain. The Bible explains in the Book of Romans that even people who do not know the law of God from the Bible have knowledge of right and wrong. The Egyptian concept of the afterlife confirms this.

Like many people today, ancient Egyptians thought that if the good they did outweighed the bad, they would emerge unscathed from judgment and enjoy paradise. Yet God is holy and He is the true standard by which everyone in His creation is judged. God's Word makes clear that all people are sinners with a sinful nature, justly deserving condemnation.

No amount of good works can obliterate and nullify the evil a person does. Justice cannot be satisfied and sin paid for by burying it beneath an overwhelming number of good deeds. James 2:10 indicates that even one sin in a person's life is too much: "For whoever shall keep the whole law, and yet stumble in one point, he is guilty of all." Justice requires the price for sin be paid, and from the time Adam sinned, God began unveiling His plan to provide the payment for sin Himself. Salvation is therefore a matter of grace through faith in God's provision.

The ancient Egyptians also realized that true justice would consider not only the deeds a person had plainly done but also the hidden motives and secret sins. The Egyptians suspected that a divine being would be able to see the secrets of the heart. They thought that if the heart didn't condemn them, if the conscience were truly clear, the goddess that weighed the heart against a feather would pass them on toward paradise.

Yet God's Word indicates that — except for Jesus Christ, God's Son — every person born since Adam sinned has a sinful nature. We cannot through our own efforts purify ourselves, but the sinless Son of God offered Himself as a sacrifice for us so that we could be reconciled to God — so that we could truly become "the pure in heart" who "shall see God" (Matthew 5:8).

The ancient Egyptians were correct to expect judgment for their sins after death. Hebrews 9:27 says "it is appointed for men to die once, but after this the judgment." But they had unfortunately abandoned faith in the true Creator God known to their forebears descended from Noah's family. They put no trust in the God of Abraham, who had walked among them. Abraham was saved by faith; he believed God and His promises (Romans 4:2–5). Instead, the Egyptians put their trust in the false gods they invented and in their own abilities to meet the standards for good works that they themselves contrived. And like people who die today trusting in their own good works to save them, they stand condemned. Instead of fearing a false god like Ammut, they should have feared the true God of the Bible. It is a fearful thing to fall into the hands of the living God (Hebrews 10:31).

Summary of Ancient Egyptian Religious Beliefs

Doctrine	Teachings of Egyptian Mythology
God	Deny the biblical God. Various myths describe a supreme god and a pantheon of gods created by him or arising from the earth. Polytheistic in its reverence of many gods.
Authority/ Revelation	Various eras held to different sources of authority, but the *Book of the Dead* is a popular source describing the views of the afterlife.

Man	Various myths describe man as being created by different gods from tears, clay, and other sources. Man is not seen as particularly important within the world.
Sin	Sin is not clearly defined, but extends beyond actions to the intents of the heart.
Salvation	Upon death, the heart is weighed against the feather of truth in the presence of the gods. The dead use spells to conceal their guilt from the gods. If the heart weighs less than the feather, the person can pass to various places in the underworld. If not, it is devoured by a demonic beast. Simply, salvation is achieved if the good of your life outweighs the bad.
Creation	Various myths describe a supreme god creating the world and other gods from nothing, or the earth forming into various gods and man and creatures.

Chapter 14

Norse and Germanic Mythology

Dr. James J.S. Johnson

The Lord Jesus Christ endorsed Genesis truth while He walked the earth, including the origin of creation and the history of the worldwide Flood.[1] Inexcusably, however, the biblical account of creation is recklessly spurned by modern fans of Darwin's evolutionary model — sometimes even to the extreme of comparing ancient Norse mythology (i.e., the worship of Thor and Odin) to the Genesis record that the Lord Jesus endorsed.

For example, in one federal lawsuit (involving biblical creation–informed science education), the trial judge glibly said — in open court — that he could give justice to the case because he had already adjudicated controversies involving Thor worship and a marijuana cult, so adjudicating a case about biblical creation should be easy enough.[2]

Some might excuse the irreverence as attempted humor, but the result was not funny. How can such disrespect for God's truth be so outrageous?

Yet, evolutionary mythology is ubiquitous — it is "everywhere" — it is promoted by television, movies, cereal boxes, military leaders, closed-Bible

---

1. Ken Ham, "Did Jesus Say He Created in Six Literal Days?" chapter 20, *The New Answers Book*, 12-20-2007), posted at https://answersingenesis.org/days-of-creation/did-jesus-say-he-created-in-six-literal-days/ , citing John 5:45–47; Mark 10:6, 13:19; Luke 11:50–51, 13:14; etc.

2. *Institute for Creation for Research Graduate School v. Texas Higher Education Coordinating Board*, 2010 WL 2522529 (W.D. Tex.—Austin 2010) (erroneous naming of plaintiff in the original). Revealingly, the legal phrase "academic freedom" was never used anywhere within the federal judge's 39-page ruling.

pastors, and even in recipe books![3] Ironically, however (and perhaps not surprisingly), the underlying mythological beliefs and practices of ancient Norse and Germanic pagans are "reincarnated" in the evolutionary pantheism ("everything is god") of today's pagans.[4]

Where did the Norse and Germanic pagans go wrong?

There was never any legitimate excuse for these pagan mythologies. So why did they ever exist? Why were Norse and Germanic myths so popular in many lands for several centuries of time?

To really understand *why* ancient Scandinavians and Saxons held to these false religions, we must understand why false religion is so universally attractive to human sinners. *Why is false religion so popular, so attractive, anyway?*

How Do We Make Sense of Norse and Germanic Mythologies?

The introductory questions above presume that the pantheism of many modern-day evolutionists is comparable to the ancient polytheism of ancient Norse and Germanic pagans — but is it, really?[5]

If so, how does the comparison of those ancient and modern mythologies fit the modern world of evolution-dominated false religions?

---

3. James J.S. Johnson, "Hidden in Plain View: Evolution's Counterfeit History is 'Everywhere,'" *Acts & Facts*, 41(2):8–9 (February 2012), posted at http://www.icr.org/article/hidden-plain-view-evolutions-counterfeit/.

4. Edd Starr, "Can an Evolutionist Celebrate Earth Day?" Answers in Genesis, https://answersingenesis.org/theory-of-evolution/can-an-evolutionist-celebrate-earth-day/, saying: "Many of the people in this category would not consider themselves 'pantheists'; rather, they would simply consider themselves agnostics. However, individuals in this category believe that, regardless of evolution and the lack of a distinct god, nature is to be seen as inherently good, to be worshipped or honored, etc. Many common phrases associated with this type of environmentalism have a pagan origin — for example, 'Mother Earth' or 'Mother Nature,' the 'circle (or web) of life.'"

5. This study could have more precisely used the phrase "Scandinavian and Saxon mythologies" but the terms "Norse" and "Germanic" are more popularly understood as terms that fit this current chapter. Some writers prefer to combine those demographic categories under the term "Teutonic," so that term is sometimes used here, to avoid always saying "Norse and Germanic." Technically speaking, the term "Norse," when used as a linguistic label, refers to the Old Norse language that survives (to a large degree) today as the Icelandic language. But when used as an ethnic or cultural term, the word "Norse" often refers only to Western Scandinavians, at the expense of the Swedes and Swedish Finns. Here "Norse and Germanic" will refer to all of the Nordic peoples who spoke Old Norse, plus all of the continental European peoples who spoke a variant of German ("Saxon") during the Dark Ages, especially during the centuries known collectively as Europe's "Great Migration Period" (AKA the Völkerwanderung, the era when barbarian invaders broke up the Roman Empire, from just before A.D. 400 to 800) and the slightly overlapping "Viking Age" (from the late 700s to the century before or including the 1200s).

All of these questions require that we learn — at an overview level, at least — what the ancient Norse and Germanic mythologies were all about. Those false religions involved much more than comic-book stories about imaginary gods whose names appear on our calendars (e.g., Thursday from Thor's Day; Wednesday from Wodin's Day). The Norse and Germanic mythologies (sometimes labeled in combination as Teutonic mythologies) painted a confusing and magic-dominated hodgepodge of humans, gods, goddesses, giants, elves, and others, some of whom changed from one form into another.

> The old Norse religion . . . may be classified as an ethnic religion, meaning that it belongs to a specific people or group of people, in contrast to, for example, a religion like Christianity, which has become a universal or multi-ethnic religion. Traditional Scandinavian religion was polytheistic and comprised a large numbers of gods and goddesses, called *aesir* and *Vanir*, as well as many other groups: mythic giants . . . dwarves . . . female *norns* who sat in the center of the world and held power over the fate and fortune of individuals . . . valkyries . . . elves [who appeared to be] departed ancestors.[6]

To analyze the heartbeat of these false religions we need to review some relevant Scriptures, because *God's Word is always our starting point when we try to understand anything.*

Biblical insight #1: pagans prefer falsehoods over truth

> And this is the condemnation, that the light has come into the world, and men loved darkness rather than light, because their deeds were evil (John 3:19).[7]

These mythologies were accepted and promoted because unredeemed sinners prefer darkness over light, falsehoods over truth, and immoral priorities

---

6. Anne-Sofie Gräslund, "Religion, Art, and Runes," in *Vikings, The North Atlantic Saga* (Washington, DC: Smithsonian Books, 2000; edited by William W. Fitzhugh & Elisabeth I. Ward), p. 55. The Nordic mythology is perhaps best represented by the contents of Old Norse poetry fragments and the *Prose Edda*, which in aggregate describe "mythology, gods, and other supernatural beings," compiled by Snorri Surluson, the pre-eminent Icelandic/Nordic scholar of the A.D. 1200s, when the Viking Age closed near the end of the Dark Ages. (The Dark Ages finally broke with the "morning star" of the Protestant Reformation, John Wycliffe.)

7. All Scripture in this chapter is from the New King James Version (NKJV) of the Bible.

over moral values. People shy away from accepting the idea of God being holy and omniscient, knowing all of our faults, and disapproving all of our sins. People also like having "excuses" for their sinful thoughts and sinful actions — something a less-than-perfect deity can provide.

If a (mythical) god is selfish, it appears to excuse human selfishness. So, in order to deal with God's holiness, people imagine unholy substitutes for God, such as imaginary gods and goddesses who are selfish themselves.

Accordingly, if the gods practice fornication, that behavior appears to excuse the same sin when it is committed by humans. Likewise, if the goddesses tell lies in order to manipulate their personal agendas, that usage of deceit appears to excuse similar deceit by selfish humans.

Furthermore, if people dislike the Bible's report about our origins (which include the Bible's report on how our sin originated in Eden, how death originated, why husbands have primary responsibility for a marriage honoring God, etc.), people invent fables of their own liking, to explain the origins of things.

The root problem, here, is a refusal to accept truths about God Himself, compounded by a refusal to accept truths about how (and why) He made creation, and how He has been ruling it ever since.

In sum, the ancient pagans — such as those living during the Dark Ages, in lands speaking Germanic and Scandinavian languages — failed to accept God for who He really is, and His deeds, so they tried to imagine substitutes for God and His actions.

This can be analyzed as a series of three failures:

1. failure to give God due credit for *being the kind of divine Being He always is*

2. failure to give God due credit for *His past work of creating creation as He did*

3. failure to give God due credit for *His present work of ruling creation as He does*

The writings of the New Testament — especially Acts 17 and Romans 1 — help us to understand how these three errors ruined their worldview, leading them to adopt idolatrous mythologies. The overall result of these forms of paganism was a culturally accepted system of disgracefully wrong beliefs and tragically wrong behaviors.

Consider how plainly God has communicated Himself to His human creatures — God employs His creation to teach us how powerful He is, how knowledgeable He is, and how caringly and carefully He has designed and constructed and balanced His creation. Creation's components, both living and nonliving, prove to us that we are incapable of making the kind of creation we live in.

The real maker of all creation must be *more* powerful than we are, *more* knowledgeable than we are, *more* caring than we are, *more* careful than we are — He is immeasurably superior to us in all of these characteristics.

Obviously, therefore, we have no excuse for thinking that God is like us self-centered and finite-minded humans. If He were, which He is not, He could not have successfully made the creation we see all around us.

But what do unredeemed humans all too often do, when thinking about who deserves credit for creation?

Biblical insight #2: pagans replace God, in myths, by corrupt substitutes for God

For since the creation of the world His invisible attributes are clearly seen, being understood by the things that are made, even His eternal power and Godhead, so that they are without excuse, because, although they knew God, they did not glorify Him as God, nor were thankful, but became futile in their thoughts, and their foolish hearts were darkened. *Professing to be wise, they became fools, and changed the glory of the incorruptible God into an image made like corruptible man — and birds and four-footed animals and creeping things.* Therefore God also gave them up to uncleanness, in the lusts of their hearts, to dishonor their bodies among themselves, who exchanged the truth of God for the lie, and worshiped and served the creature rather than the Creator, who is blessed forever. Amen (Romans 1:20–25, emphasis added).

Notice that the Apostle Paul taught that humans who reject the evidence of God's creatorship "become fools" — they forfeited their earlier opportunities (with proper judgment) about issues of true versus false, right versus wrong, good versus bad, and worthy versus unworthy. Those who reject creation's witness of God's truth routinely receive a severe penalty, during this earthly lifetime: *ruined thinking*. The biblical name for this ruined thinking is a "reprobate mind" (Romans 1:28).

Only a truth-shunning (i.e., reprobate) mind can invent the kind of mythologies that the Norse and Germanic pagans invented — with beliefs in a pandemonium of imagined gods and goddesses (and other mythical beings), that *substitute for the real God* who created the heavens and the earth. Many of these imagined gods and goddesses are imagined as existing in images *made like corruptible man* (Romans 1:23) and behaving like sinful humanity (cheating, lying, stealing, coveting, etc.).

Sometimes reprobate thinking descends below attributing the traits of human sinners to deity — the notion of animals and nonliving substances are imagined as explanations for the existence of a god or goddess. This is the essence of a pantheistic religion with natural elements having god-like characteristics.

In the ancient Norse myths, the origin of some gods was deemed traceable to nonliving material components of creation, such as snow, or frost! In the best known collection of Nordic myths, the *Prose Edda*, Gangleri inquires about the origins of the world and of humanity. The reply is a fairy tale every bit as magical and pantheistic as the Mayas' *Popol Vuh* and Darwin's evolutionary story: storm waves hardened into a strange ice and the ice exuded icy rime that thawed and magically formed a giant:

> It [the thick ice and rime] thawed and dripped at the point where the icy rime and the warm winds met. There was a quickening in these flowing drops [of ice-melt water] and life sprang up [magically], taking its force from the power that sent the heat. The likeness of a [gigantic] man appeared and he was named Ymir. The frost giants called him Aurgelmir, and from him come the clans of the frost giants. . . . It is said that as he slept he took to sweating. Then, from under his left arm grew a male and female, while one of his legs got a son with the other. From here came the clans that are called the frost giants. The old frost giant, him we call Ymir.[8]

This pantheistic myth, therefore, begins its evolutionary tale with an inanimate physical substance, ice, somehow converting ("transforming") into a

---

8. Jesse L. Byock, *The Prose Edda: Norse Mythology* (London: Penguin Books, 2005), translating Snorri Sturluson's *Prose Edda* (12th–13th centuries), p. 13–15.

non-human life form, a frost-giant named Ymir. More rime-ice melted and dripped, magically forming a cow (named Audhumla) who produced four rivers from her udder.[9] From this cow's milk, Ymir is nourished. This magical cow, the *Prose Edda* creation myth continues, then proceeded to produce the gods that were imagined as the collective powers who produced and ruled the world thereafter.

How did this occur, according to Norse mythology?

The giant cow licked a salty ice-block, and out came a "whole man," Buri, who fathered Bor, who fathered Odin and others. Eventually, Odin and his brothers kill the frost-giant/ice-monster, Ymir, and transform his various body parts (flesh, bloody sweat, hair, eyelashes, and brains) into the earth, the sea, the air, the clouds, and the heavens.[10] Soon afterward, Odin and his brothers made a human man and woman from two tree logs they found on the seashore, magically providing the first "regular" humans with breath, life, intelligence, movement, shape, speech, hearing, and sight.[11]

Sound ridiculous and absurd? Of course it is.

Biblical insight #3: pagans worship inanimate stuff, rather than worship God

Yet the fairy tale described above is *no more nonsensical* than today's evolutionary big-bang-to-stardust-to-pondscum-to-humanity explanation of the origin of the universe and the life in it. All such nonsensical and insulting depictions of deity misrepresent God's dignity and glory, an obvious fact that Paul once proclaimed to ignorant-yet-arrogant Athenians:

> Then Paul stood in the midst of the Areopagus and said, "Men of Athens, I perceive that in all things you are very religious; for as I was passing through and considering the objects of your worship, I even found an altar with this inscription:
> TO THE UNKNOWN GOD.
> Therefore, the One whom you worship without knowing, Him I proclaim to you: God, who made the world and everything in it, since He is Lord of heaven and earth, does not dwell in temples made with hands. Nor is He worshiped with men's hands, as though He needed anything, since He gives to

9. Ibid., p. 15.
10. Ibid., p. 15–17.
11. Ibid., p. 18.

> all life, breath, and all things. And He has made from one blood every nation of men to dwell on all the face of the earth, and has determined their preappointed times and the boundaries of their dwellings, so that they should seek the Lord, in the hope that they might grope for Him and find Him, though He is not far from each one of us; for in Him we live and move and have our being, as also some of your own poets have said, 'For we are also His offspring.' Therefore, since we are the offspring of God, we ought not to think that the Divine Nature is like gold or silver or stone, something shaped by art and man's devising" (Acts 17:22–29).

Yet we read of the Norse gods being represented by physical images — idols — inside temples made by human hands, and we later read of Christian Vikings, such as Olaf Tryggvason, who destroyed such physical idols.

A. Idolatrous belief in various gods and "goddesses" as substitute for the real God

In the ancient Norse/Germanic mythology's "pantheon(s)" there were various major and minor gods and "goddesses," a few of whom are listed below:[12]

1. *Odin/Wodin* (Old Norse: Óðinn; Old Saxon: Wôdan; Old High German: Wôtan) The presiding god of the heroic Aesir tribe of gods, the idolized ancients who migrated from Asia to a special place called Asgard (which Snorri identifies as Troy), a royal estate that included Valhalla, a hall of honored warriors killed in battle. Odin's name connotes "fury" or "frenzy"; he was imagined as the divine creator of other gods and of humans, as well as expert in wisdom, magic, poetry, illusion, deception, and prophecy, acquiring half of the warriors who die in battle. Wednesday is derived from ancient words meaning "Wodin's Day."

2. *Thor/Donar* (Old Norse: Þórr; Old High German: þonar; Saxon runic: ᚦᛟᚾᚨᚱ) The god of thunder and lightning, physical strength, and strong things like oak trees; Thor's name means

12. As in other ancient cultures, these gods could have been ancestors who lived unusually long lifespans after the Flood and viewed as demigods by their descendants whose lifespans were rapidly declining. Odin is present in several royal lineages in northern Europe.

"thunder"; Thursday is derived from ancient words meaning "Thor's day" (in German it is spelled "Donnerstag," i.e., "Donar's Day").

3. *Tyr/Teiws* (Old Norse: Týr; Gothic: Teiws; Old High German: Ziu; Old English: Tīw) The god of war, heroic glory, authority, law, and justice; Tuesday is derived from ancient words meaning "Teiws' Day" (Alemannic German "Zischtig," i.e., "Zîes' Day").

4. *Frey* (Old Norse: Freyr; Old English: Frea) The god of male fertility, sunshine, and fair weather, fruitfulness/agricultural fertility, and worldly prosperity; Frey's name means "lord" or "noble."

5. *Freya* (Old Norse: Freyja) The goddess of female fertility, female beauty, "love," sexuality, sorcery, and gold, and was imagined to select half of the warriors killed in battle, as well as women who died noble deaths. Freya's name means "lady" or "noblewoman." Friday is derived from ancient words meaning "Freya's Day."

6. *Loki* (also Loptr and Hveðrungr) A devilish god of evil, hatred, and deception, who is sometimes portrayed as a jötunn (frost-giant) and a bisexual shape-shifter. Loki's devilish nature is portrayed by his role in parenting Jörmungandr (the world-snake monster), Hel (queen of the dead doomed to an inglorious afterlife), Fenrir (a wetland-dwelling wolf-monster), and Sleipnir (an eight-legged horse).

7. *Balder/Baldur* (Old Norse: Baldr; Old High German: Baldere; Old Saxon: Baldag) The god of daylight, brightness, and purity, as well as light-like shining brilliance, bravery, and boldness. Balder was imagined as a son of Odin and a brother of Thor.

8. *Hel* (Gothic: Halja) The goddess of deadly plagues, graves, and ignoble deaths, was imagined as owning and operating the misty underworld "hall" of the dead who died of diseases

or old age, as opposed to dying noble deaths (such as in battle, in order to belong to Odin or Freyja). Hel's name is the root for the Anglo-Saxon word "Hell" (a short form of Helheim, meaning "Hel's home") as a label for the abode of those who die ignobly. Ancient pagans believed that Helheim was a huge underground hole beneath one of the three roots of Yggdrasil (the world tree).

In addition, the Norse myths imagined the existence and activities of other supernatural beings (i.e., non-humans with magical powers), such as frost-giants, fire-giants, trolls, valkyries, fates, etc.

Notice also that the reprobate-minded unbelievers — in their rebellious imaginations — insultingly transform the proper recipient of worship (God) into a collection of objects of worship that do not deserve our worship, such as animals and humans and other components of creation (Romans 1:23). By doing this, God was replaced in the minds of such idolaters by God-substitutes.

There are two idolatries here, where God is cheated out of glory and the credit due Him, namely (1) falsely attributing credit to someone or something other than God, for *creating* various components of creation; and (2) falsely attributing glory and credit to someone or something other than God, for *ruling* various components of creation. A few representative examples follow.

B. Idolatrous attribution of God's powers to someone/something other than God

In the Teutonic pantheon, various gods and goddesses are given credit for both *creating* and for *ruling* various components of creation. This is idolatry because it steals credit from God who alone *created* and *rules* all of creation.

> As in other polytheistic religions, the Viking gods [supposedly] ruled over different aspects of human life. The most important were Odin, Thor, and Frey.[13]

Also, various giants or gods were accredited, by the Norse and Germanic pagans, as creating and forming the world and all of its life forms. One

---

13. John Haywood, "Pagan Religion and Burial Customs," in *The Penguin Historical Atlas of the Vikings* (London: Penguin Books, 1995), p. 26. See also Gwyn Jones, *A History of the Vikings*, revised edition (Oxford: Oxford University Press, 1984), p. 73–74, 333–345.

example of such polytheistic idolatry is the Norse worship of Odin, known as Wodin by the Saxons:

> Odin was a rather sinister deity who, with his brothers, had created the human race and gave man the knowledge of poetry and of writing in runes [alphabetic letters]. Odin was the god of wisdom, power, war, and poetry: he was a sorcerer and could deprive men of their wits and exercise his power of life and death in wildly unpredictable ways. Odin's attributes made him the god of kings, chieftains, warriors and poets: both the Danish royal family and the Earls of Hlaðir claimed descent from him.[14]

Notice that Odin worship gave Odin credit for wisdom and knowledge, as well as its divine impartation to humans.[15] This blasphemously steals credit due the true and living God. Likewise, only the real God has power over life and death.[16] But, as the New Testament teaches us, only God has the power to deprive men of their reason by giving them over to a "repro-bate mind"[17] and a "strong delusion"[18] as punishments for blasphemous imaginations.

Another example of such idolatry is the worship given to Thor, known as Donar by the Saxons:

> The most popular god among the peasantry was Thor, the god of physical strength, thunder and lightning, wind, rain, good weather and crops. Using his mighty hammer Mjöllnir, Thor defended the world against the destructive power of the giants [such as the ice-giants and the fire-giants]. Unlike Odin, Thor was straightforward, reliable god [*sic*], but he was none too bright and the myths concerning his deeds often highlight in a humorous way the limitations of brute strength. Pendants fashioned in the sign of the hammer were often worn by Thor's devotees.[19]

---

14. Haywood, *The Penguin Historical Atlas of the Vikings*, p. 26.
15. See James 1:5–6, 3:17; see also 1 Corinthians 1:19–31, especially verses 20–21.
16. See Psalm 68:20, 102:18, 139:13–16; Matthew 10:29–31.
17. See Romans 1:28.
18. See 2 Thessalonians 2:11–12.
19. Haywood, *The Penguin Historical Atlas of the Vikings*, p. 26.

Yet only God controls the weather. All of the world's winds,[20] rain,[21] hail,[22] thunder,[23] and lightning bolts[24] are His, and His only, to command. Thor is an imaginary counterfeit and a miserably unholy one. But the ancient pagans preferred an unholy counterfeit because unholy gods do not condemn unholy sinners for unholy behaviors.

A third example of such idolatry is the worship given to Frey (Freyr), which overlapped with the idolatrous worship of his sister Freya (Freyja):

> Freyr was the god of [material] wealth, health and fertility: he was portrayed [in a vulgar anatomical depiction]. Offerings were made to Freyr at weddings. The Swedish Yngling dynasty traced its ancestry to a union between Freyr and Gerd, a giant woman [i.e., a monstrous ogress]. Freyr had a sister [Freyja], who gave luck in love [as pagans defined "love"] and represented sensuality. Freyja was the leader of the *disir*, a race of female demi-gods who presided over fertility in nature and in humans.[25]

But what accounts for fertility in crops or in livestock or in human families? The pagans in Scandinavia and in Saxland (the ancient name applied to all European lands where the ancient German language dominated) gave credit to the vulgar Frey and Freyja, but that was profane idolatry. The Scriptures teach that God alone enabled His creatures to "be fruitful, and multiply" so that His earth could be filled with humans, plants, and animals.[26]

The Scandinavian polytheism did not attempt to portray gods who were inherently holy. Rather, like other heathen polytheists (such as the ancient Babylonians, Egyptians, Greeks, and Romans), they were as corrupt as sinful humans, and Loki even more so — Loki was somewhat like (though not completely like) the Satan of Scripture.

---

20. See Genesis 8:1; Psalm 107:25, 135:7, 147:18, 148:8; Jonah 4:8; Matthew 8:26–27; Mark 4:37–41; Luke 8:23–25.
21. See Genesis 2:5–6, 7:4, 7:12, 8:2; Deuteronomy 11:14; Isaiah 55:10; Jeremiah 10:13, 14:22, 51:16; Amos 4:7; Matthew 5:45; Acts 14:17; James 5:17.
22. See Exodus 9:18–29; Joshua 10:11; 2 Samuel 22:15; Job 38:22; Psalm 78:47–48, 148:8; Isaiah 30:30; Haggai 2:17; Revelation 8:7, 11:19, 16:21.
23. See Exodus 9:23–34; 1 Samuel 2:10, 7:10, 12:17–18; 2 Samuel 22:14; Job 28:26, 38:25, 37:4–5; Psalm 18:13, 29:3, 77:18, 104:7; Revelation 4:5.
24. See Job 37:3, 38:35; Psalm 18:14, 77:18, 97:4, 135:7, 144:6; Jeremiah 10:13, 51:16.
25. Quoting John Haywood, *The Penguin Historical Atlas of the Vikings*, p. 26. See also Jones, *A History of the Vikings*, p. 330.
26. See Genesis 1:20–22, 1:28, 8:16–17, 9:7; Psalm 102:18, 127:3–5, 128:3.

The god Loki was a cunning, witty mischief-maker [i.e., worker of wickedness], whose schemes were always getting the gods and himself into trouble. Though he was not an unambiguously evil figure like Satan, Loki was capable of great wickedness and treachery, and the Vikings believed that this scheming would lead in the end to [the doom of] Ragnarök.[27]

In the ancient Teutonic mythologies pantheism blurred with polytheism. Inanimate glaciers were imagined as ice-monsters, jötunn (also known as rime-giants and frost-giants). The fire from a volcano was imagined as a fire-monster (e.g., Surtr).

In other words, inanimate components of nature — such as volcanoes and glaciers and huge granite rocks — were believed to have spirits associated with their physical substance, and sometimes were believed to have shape-changing ("transformative") powers to resemble humanoid giants (i.e., ogres or trolls). Rocks and glaciers were deemed to have powers to think and to act, so all of the physical creation was imagined to have selective powers.

Theologically speaking, this generalized animism is *pantheism blurred with and into polytheism*, an inane idolatry that worships elements of creation rather than the Creator.

Ironically, the pagan Norsemen and Saxons were ancestors to many who would evangelize the world, by boat, in partial fulfillment of Noah's blessing to their common ancestor, Japheth.[28] This providential pivot in world history is illustrated in the Viking-to-Christianity conversions that led to Nordic and Anglo-Saxon nations sending Christian missionaries all over the world, following the Apostle Paul's Macedonian call.

From the westernmost shore of Asia [e.g., including Jerusalem and Antioch], Christianity had turned at once to the opposite one in Europe [beginning with Paul's missionary journeys to Macedonia and other parts of Europe]. The wide soil of the

---

27. Haywood, *The Penguin Historical Atlas of the Vikings*, p. 26.
28. See Genesis 9:27 with 10:2–5. Linguistically speaking, it appears that the Scandinavians and Saxons are two closely related offshoots of one subset of Japheth's descendants, the people descended from Ashkenaz. Since the original dispersion of people groups was caused by linguistic division (Genesis 11:1–9), that makes demographic sense. Notice how the consonants in the ethnic terms "Scandians" and "Saxons" resemble those in the ethnic term "Ashkenaz."

continent which had given it birth could not supply it long with nourishment; neither did it strike deep root in the north of Africa [despite Philip's evangelism of the Ethiopian eunuch]. Europe became, and remained, its proper dwelling-place and home. It is worthy of notice, that the direction in which the new faith worked its way, from South [Europe] to North [Europe], is contrary to the current of migration which was then driving the nations from the East and North to the West and South. As spiritual light penetrated from one quarter, life itself was to be reinvigorated from the other. . . . Slowly, step by step, Heathendom gave way to Christendom. Five hundred years after Christ, but few nations of Europe believed in him; after a thousand years the majority did. . . .[29]

As experienced mariners,[30] many of Japheth's descendants connected lands and peoples by seagoing travel and transactions. Even the distant shores of Iceland would receive the Christian religion.

> The summer Christianity was made law in Iceland, one thousand years had passed from the Incarnation of our Lord Jesus Christ. That summer, King Olafr disappeared from the Long Serpent [longboat] by Svoldr in the south [Baltic Sea] on the fourth [day] before the ides [i.e., 15th day] of September. He [i.e., King Olaf] had been king in Norway for five years.[31]

In time, even distant Iceland would embrace the Lutheran Reformation. (The details of that history exceed our current study.)

How Were Norse/Germanic Mythology Religions Practiced?

Unlike the Holy Bible, the Scandinavian/Saxon pagans had no authoritative book of theology, much less any sacred book that provided a logically

---

29. Jacob Grimm, *Deutsche Mythologie*, volume 1, translated from the 4th edition, as *Teutonic Mythology* by James Steven Stallybrass (Mineola, NY: Dover Publications, 2004), p. 1.

30. Notice that the Scandinavian Vikings (who sailed oceans and the Baltic Sea habitually), as well as the coastal Saxons, easily fit the coastal mariner lifestyle indicated by Genesis 10:5. In Old Norse a saltwater inlet was called a "vik" (e.g., Reykjavik = "smoky bay"), so even the word "Viking" indicates a people who were famous for their coastal activities.

31. Siân Grønlie, *The Book of the Icelanders: The Story of the Conversion* (London: University College London & Viking Society for Northern Research, 2006), translating Ari Þorgilsson's Íslendingabók Kristni Saga (early 12th century A.D.), p. 50.

consistent systematic theology of big-picture truth.[32] Rather, the beliefs of the Teutonic pagans are recognized in bits and pieces, as they are illustrated in the surviving poems, sagas, and other writings that show what the ancient pagans thought and taught.

> Unlike Christianity, Scandinavian paganism [and the same was true for Germanic paganism] did not have a systematic theology and lacked absolute concepts of good and evil or of the afterlife. Religion was a matter of correct performance and observance of sacrifices, rituals and festivals, rather than personal spirituality. There was no full-time priesthood [or full-time clergy]; it was usually the king or local chieftains who had the responsibility for ensuring that festivals were observed.
>
> A cycle of cosmogonical myths told of the creation of the world and of its ultimate destruction at Ragnarök]. Vikings believed that all things were subject to fate, including the gods who would perish at Ragnarök, the final cataclysm that would destroy the world.[33]

However, just because the Teutonic myths were not organized in written forms for many centuries, does not detract from the fact that these heathen beliefs steered the behaviors of those who held those beliefs.

Biblical insight #4: believing pagan myths routinely produced pagan behaviors.

> For as he thinks in his heart, so is he (Proverbs 23:7).

In the Norse and Germanic myths, the gods and goddesses were imagined as killing and stealing whenever doing so was deemed a prudent deed, similar to modern "situational ethics" immorality.

Unsurprisingly, the Vikings copied the immorality of their gods and goddesses, and practiced a "might-makes-right" approach to social behavior. Slaves and peasants were offered as human sacrifices because the lives of humans were not valued as precious people made in God's own image.[34] Kidnapping the weak was deemed a valiant display of manly power,

---

32. Jones, *A History of the Vikings*, p. 73–74, 330, 333–345.
33. John Haywood, *The Penguin Historical Atlas of the Vikings*, p. 26.
34. Genesis 1:26–28.

so Vikings and Saxon warriors routinely killed, raped, plundered, and enslaved victims — anywhere in Europe where they raided or conquered. Ancestors were worshiped, as were imaginary gods (often depicted by physical idols "dwelling" in temples), and even the forces of nature (such as thunderstorms) were venerated as if divine manifestations of the pagan pantheons.

Because the inherited sin from Adam was not believed, and many sins were even praised as meritorious accomplishments of selfish "winners," there was no concept of redemptive salvation in the Norse and Germanic mythologies. Living a "noble" life should qualify one for an afterlife of fighting and drunkenness in Valhalla (or in Freyja's many-seated hall), but those who died "weakly" — such as by disease or accidental injury — were "doomed" to a dark and humble afterlife in Helheim (Hel's underworld).

Ironically, the Norse belief in giants appears to be a corruption of pre-Flood memories — an oral tradition that recalled how super-powerful giants (*nephelim*) raged violently against ordinary humans.[35] In fact, the ancient Anglo-Saxon epic Beowulf appears to include some memories of the world-wide Flood as a divine punishment of such giants.[36]

Should We Reach Out to Norse and Germanic Pagans Today?

This may seem like an obsolete question, because the ethnic Scandinavians and Germanic tribes no longer adhere to the mythologies they endorsed during the Dark Ages. But is that really the case?

There has been a resurgence of various forms of pagan mythology in the 19th and 20th centuries, including the worship of Thor, Odin, and other gods, known as Asatru, Germanic neo-paganism, or Heathenry. While there are a relatively small number of followers of various sects primarily in Europe, North America, and Australia, you may find yourself talking to one of these practitioners on a plane or park bench. Their religious convictions are often blended with other practices, but they will commonly perform rites at certain times of the year while wearing traditional dress and guided by priests and priestesses. During a blót, sacrifices of various forms are offered along with feasting and alcoholic drink. Some adherents will

---

35. It is also reasonable to think that these references could refer to the post-Flood giants mentioned in the Bible, including the descendants of Anak (Deuteronomy 9:2).

36. Bill Cooper, *After the Flood* (Chichester, West Sussex, England: New Wine Press, 1995), p. 146–147.

place idols around shrines in homes and wear various pendants — often of Thor's hammer, Mjölnir. Some holidays include Yule (winter solstice) and Merry Moon (May Day).[37]

These groups have no authoritative sources upon which to base their religious practices or their moral code. As such, many of their practices are blended with traditions from various pagan beliefs. Their moral code often focuses on loyalty, hard work, courage, and integrity. While these are noble ideas, they have no source of truth to look to and no honorable models of these behaviors in their gods and goddesses.

While sacrifices to the various gods and spirits are seen to gain their favor, there is ultimately no solid notion of sin or salvation within this religious view. This makes sense when we consider the character of their gods and heroes. As Christians, we need to help these people see the futility in worshiping gods that were invented in the minds of men — an invented god is no god at all. We must help them to see that there can only be one true God who is the Creator and ruler over all who would claim to be gods (Isaiah 41:23–24). We need to point them to the perfect life, sacrificial death on the Cross, and death-defeating Resurrection of Jesus Christ, which called them to repent of their fundamental sin of rejecting the true Creator-God — by trusting in His amazing solution for sin, the Lord Jesus Christ — thereby rejecting the idolatrous worship of the pantheon including Odin and Thor.

And there is another similar group to consider. Although the myth-makers in northern Europe (and in other lands dominated by what we call Western Civilization) rarely speak of Ymir, Audhumla, Odin, Thor, Freyr, Freyja, Hel, valkyries, and frost-giants, that doesn't mean that another group of modern pagans has escaped similar myths that blend pantheism with polytheistic animisms. Anyone who says that natural elements like fire and ice and rain and stone can create and "select" and "favor" some animals over others, or some humans over others, is not that far from the magical myths of the ancient Teutons.

How were Teutonic myths defeated in the hearts and minds of medieval pagans such as Leif Eiriksson and Olaf Tryggvason? By the gospel of Christ, of course, and one soul at a time. It's the same with today's educationally

---

37. "Asatru: Norse Heathenism," Religious Tolerance, accessed September 30, 2015, http://www.religioustolerance.org/asatru.htm.

evolutionized pagans, who nowadays embrace the "Big Bang-to-stardust-to-pondscum-to-humanity" cosmogony as an explanation for the origin of the universe and the life in it.

Are we ashamed of the Lord's gospel? Shame on us if we are. For God has chosen to empower the message of the gospel for reaching the souls of men and women, boys and girls, regardless of the false system of beliefs they embrace. And the proper foundation for the gospel message summarized in John 3:16 is the book of beginnings — Genesis.

Summary of Germanic and Norse Mythology Beliefs

Doctrine	Norse Mythology
God	A pantheistic and polytheistic collection of various beings and gods who have no absolute power or authority and are in conflict with one another. The gods include Odin, Thor, Frey, Freyr, and others.
Authority/Revelation	There are no authoritative sources apart from the collection of myths and sagas in the *Prose Edda*.
Man	Odin and his brothers made a human man and woman from two tree logs they found on the seashore.
Sin	There is no clear idea of sin apart from loose moral codes based on honor and integrity.
Salvation	There is no consistent view on the afterlife, but many believe that one will enter other realms after death based on the worth of one's life and the manner of death. Some also believe in reincarnation or the continuation of various aspects of the soul.
Creation	The world was formed by the gods from the remains of an ice-giant they killed. This ice-giant and a cow had been formed from thawing ice in a gap between the fire and ice realms. Many different realms where different beings exist are connected to different parts of the world tree, Yggdrasil.

Chapter 15

Syncretism in Latin American Religions

Joe Owen

B efore I was a Christian, I remember how I was convinced that part of critical thinking was to disassociate myself from what I heard as a child with respects to a biblical understanding of the world. I learned to watch documentaries on other cultures and see their beliefs from a relativistic point of view. At least that is what the narrator of these clips pushed on the viewer.

Although we see the depths of human depravity in these cultures as a result of the effects of Genesis 3, we are told by *our* depraved culture that what we observe is only natural, and any objection to cultural differences is a result of closed-mindedness.

Latin American Culture and Background

Being that North America is a neighbor to the Latin American countries, many of us have been conditioned to look at the paganism there as a cute aspect of our vacation destination. We are expected to celebrate the cultural diversity without acknowledging the utter hopelessness experienced in paganism.

The first book in Spanish that I read was *Las Leyendas Mexicanas (Mexican Legends)* when I was in my second year of Spanish in high school. I was enamored by the legends like the creation of the "new sun and moon" by a meeting of the gods in Teotihuacán (about 25 miles north of modern-day Mexico City) and the history of the pyramids.

What I did not even care to understand then is what many admirers of such legends fail to understand — where such a worldview came from and how it is still prevalent today. Although the legends are considered by most to be just that — legends — the underlying worldview has *not* suffered the same fate. These beliefs remain active throughout Latin America today. There are many ways in which this belief system, which is a direct contradiction to Scripture, manifests itself, but we will extract the three most basic tenets and the three ways that they affect people's worldviews in Latin America today.

Pre-colonial Latin America consisted of three major people groups (Aztecs, Mayas, and Incas) and many minor offshoots. These groups were polytheistic, animistic, and involved in ancestor worship, although the practice of each differed throughout the regions.[1] There was a dualistic system of dark and light similar to Manichaeism (an old Persian mixture of religions), including a constant need to appease their pantheon of gods.

On some of the ziggurats (step pyramids) used in their religious practice they conducted countless human sacrifices to satisfy their gods. There are many interesting documentaries that you can watch to learn about this fascinating, yet disturbing, history. Nonetheless, you will have a difficult time finding much written on how this worldview has not only survived colonization, but has flourished under diverse religious garb.

The three major ways that these beliefs have survived (in order of least to most subtle) are outright witchcraft, syncretism with Roman Catholicism, and syncretism with Evangelicalism. Syncretism, "the combination of different forms of belief or practice,"[2] is often not as obvious as one might think and can get a little complicated. There are different degrees of syncretism and they will be discussed below.

Syncretism in the Latter Apostolic and New Testament Age

The error of syncretism is not a new challenge to the proclamation of the pure gospel message. The Apostle John was already dealing with what seems like the inception of what would later be known as the heresy of Gnosticism. According to Gnosticism (from the Greek *gnosis* — knowledge), the

---

1. For example, the Mayans left artifacts that "reveal gods and goddesses, creators of rain and winds . . .": John Lynch, *New Worlds, A Religious History of Latin America* (New Haven, CT: Yale University Press, 2012), p. 7.
2. Merriam Webster Online, s.v. "Syncretism," accessed January 4, 2016, http://www.merriam-webster.com/dictionary/syncretism.

universe is a dualistic system where all matter or flesh is inherently evil and the spiritual is inherently good.

In this worldview, a person can move up the deification ladder by gaining secret knowledge. Gnosticism not only served as a denial of the biblical deity of Christ, but also found itself in a crucial quandary: if all flesh is inherently evil, then how could Jesus have been born as a human and not be evil?

This is where someone has to pay the bill. You can't have both contradictory doctrines — either the dualistic system was wrong or Jesus couldn't have come in flesh, but only in an illusory body. And that is why these groups denied the physical body of Jesus, in order to not have to discard their foundational belief of dualism.

What is most interesting, though, is the Apostle John's response. His intolerance of this religious system would be considered quite closed-minded in our days. Here, though, we can come to an understanding that truth is exclusive in nature and that unity or social peace does not take precedence over biblical conviction. In other words, truth is not up for a vote.

> And every spirit that does not confess that Jesus Christ has come in the flesh is not of God. And this is the spirit of the Antichrist, which you have heard was coming, and is now already in the world (1 John 4:3).[3]

> For many deceivers have gone out into the world who do not confess Jesus Christ as coming in the flesh. This is a deceiver and an antichrist (2 John 1:7).

The Apostle John had already made it clear with this assertion:

> And the Word became flesh and dwelt among us, and we beheld His glory, the glory as of the only begotten of the Father, full of grace and truth (John 1:14).

With this in mind, we deal with false religions with a grace-filled proclamation of the truth without compromising on either of the two — just as Jesus is full of grace and truth.

Witchcraft — Brujería

Latin America has many *curanderos* (healers) who will perform ritual healings for the right price, as well as *brujos* (witches) who practice either "white

3. Scripture in this chapter is from the New King James Version (NKJV) of the Bible.

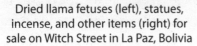

Dried llama fetuses (left), statues, incense, and other items (right) for sale on Witch Street in La Paz, Bolivia

magic" or "black magic." In places such as Bolivia, the Aymara people sell sacrifice kits and llama fetuses used to appease gods for various reasons. I personally witnessed an Aymara woman burning a sacrifice kit on a curb in La Paz, Bolivia, hoping to bring protection to drivers experiencing a high accident rate in that area. One of my most interesting travel experiences has been a trip to see where these kits sell for a bargain price on *La Calle de las Brujas* (the Witch Street).

Where in the world would somebody come up with a basis for this idea? Although there are some written sacred texts in these regions, like the *Book of Chilam Balam*, most people will never see a copy in their lifetime. This worldview is passed from generation to generation, and the belief that "the world of the spirit and the flesh were closely merged."[4] In an animistic belief, humans have the power to direct much of the spirit world, and certain humans have more power than others.[5]

Animism remains the belief that all things material have a spirit. Special ceremonies were the way in which humans could move or even control the interaction between the spiritual and physical. The sobering fact about such a mythical mindset is that it continues as a prevalent belief throughout Latin America. Of course, this view is purely arbitrary and based solely in man's explanation of the world around him without revelation from God.

4. Lynch, *New Worlds, A Religious History of Latin America*, p. 7.
5. See chapter 12 in this volume for a full description of Animism.

Additionally, the refutations given in the witchcraft chapter in this volume also apply here as well.[6]

What Does the Bible Say?

These people groups mentioned are not the only ones dabbling in witchcraft. We know from Scripture that God took the Hebrews from slavery in Egypt to settle in Canaan, and that He took them the long way.

> Every commandment which I command you today you must be careful to observe, that you may live and multiply, and go in and possess the land of which the LORD swore to your fathers. And you shall remember that the LORD your God led you all the way these forty years in the wilderness, to humble you and test you, to know what was in your heart, whether you would keep His commandments or not. So He humbled you, allowed you to hunger, and fed you with manna which you did not know nor did your fathers know, that He might make you know that man shall not live by bread alone; but man lives by every word that proceeds from the mouth of the LORD (Deuteronomy 8:1–3).

Although provoked by the people's disobedience, one of the reasons why God made a 40-year journey out of a 250-mile stretch was to set apart a nation for Himself that would depend wholly on God and submit to His Word for direction. This preparation would be crucial, as they were to settle in a land surrounded by many different pagan religions and practices, in which sorcery and witchcraft were included. God gave this nation a stern warning:

> When you come into the land which the LORD your God is giving you, you shall not learn to follow the abominations of those nations. There shall not be found among you anyone who makes his son or his daughter pass through the fire, or one who practices witchcraft, or a soothsayer, or one who interprets omens, or a sorcerer, or one who conjures spells, or a medium, or a spiritist, or one who calls up the dead. For all who do these things are an abomination to the LORD, and because of these

---

6. See chapter 10 in this volume for a full description of Witchcraft.

abominations the LORD your God drives them out from before you (Deuteronomy 18:9–12).

The question of why it is an abomination for mankind to seek out the spirit world and communicate to help manage how daily circumstances are played out in the physical realm is important. The answer can be found back in the created order. In Genesis 1 and 2, we see that God created mankind and walked with them in the garden. We see a relationship in creation that mankind enjoyed that had no extra-human involvement as man was created in God's image and likeness, apart from all other life. This relationship was severed by man's disobedience in Genesis 3, but God's eternal plan to provide and appeasement to satisfy His own just wrath against sin was given in Genesis 3:15:

> And I will put enmity between you and the woman, and between your seed and her Seed; He shall bruise your head, and you shall bruise His heel.

A non-mortal blow (to the heel) would be given to the Seed of the woman, as He would deal a mortal blow (to the head) to the serpent. God would provide a way to reconcile Himself to mankind in the Seed, Jesus Christ. There is, though, an entire spiritual realm. The Bible is clear that man was originally given dominion over the earth (Genesis 1:26–28) but had essentially forfeited that dominion to Satan, the serpent, along with one-third of heaven's angels, which were cast down along with Satan in the great rebellion.[7]

The Bible also reveals that there is much interaction between the spiritual realm and the physical realm. For instance, Satan fought the archangel Michael over the physical body of Moses (Jude 1:9), and followers of Christ are in battle against "principalities, against powers, against the rulers of the darkness of this age, against spiritual hosts of wickedness in the heavenly places" (Ephesians 6:12).

This is all to say that although it is an abomination for humans to communicate and make use of spirits, it doesn't mean the extreme opposite in denying their existence. Naturalism is not the answer to this evil, but would simply be an "out of sight, out of mind" way of ignoring such a great reality. The answer is the gospel of Jesus Christ and a total repentance of any interaction with spiritual mediums. You need to understand that we have

7. Isaiah 14:12; Luke 10:18; Revelation 9:1, 12:3–9; Hebrews 12:22.

a perfect mediator, Jesus Christ, the great High Priest. He is the promised Seed who reconciles repentant believers to God by grace through faith in His all-sufficient substitutionary sacrifice on the Cross and His subsequent Resurrection from the dead on the third day.[8]

Syncretism: Roman Catholicism, Witchcraft, and Ancestral Worship

When Hernán Cortés reached Mexico, he brought with him a Roman Catholic tradition and power structure. Major Aztec temples (such as the Templo Mayor in Tenochtitlan, or today's Mexico City) were destroyed or covered and a physical cathedral erected in their place. Many idolatrous customs of the indigenous people groups were banned by force, replaced with a Roman Catholic tradition.

The Templo Mayor, the historic center of Mexico City, where many pre-colonial human sacrifices took place.
(Shutterstock, Javarman)

This conquest may look like the vanquishing of a pagan, murderous religious society, but the truth is that there is one irreplaceable word that is missing: gospel. To better understand how this happened, we need to skip back about a thousand years before

Metropolitan Cathedral, Mexico City, next to the Templo Mayor
(Shutterstock, Nfoto)

Roman Catholicism reached the New World. By the fifth century A.D., the bishop of Rome, Leo I, had gained much political power due to the fact that the other major bishops (in Jerusalem, Antioch, Alexandria, etc.) were part

8. 1 Timothy 2:5; Hebrews 4:14–16, 9:11–12, 10:10–14; 2 Corinthians 5:18; 1 Corinthians 15:3–4.

of the Eastern church. The Roman Emperor was in Constantinople in the east, and there was a consolidation of church and state that resulted in the Holy Roman Empire. The bishop of Rome took on the title "Pope."[9] By the 15th century, the Roman Catholic "church" had dominated Europe with its political power. So when the Catholic Spaniards reached the shores of the New World, a focus on individual regeneration through the gospel had long since been lost, having been replaced by an imperial attitude.

Instead of hearing of the "new creation" experience of a hopeless sinner being reborn into the Last Adam, Jesus Christ, wherein he learns to have a renewed mind, a large society was forced into submission under the standards of the Roman Catholic empire. The natural consequence was a syncretism that is found throughout Latin America to this day.

The best way to understand how this syncretic system works is to give practical examples of how it is carried out in day-to-day life.

Witchcraft

In Mexico, many believe in what is called *el ojo* (the eye). In instances when a baby cries or gets a fever, it is believed that an adult stared too long at the baby and passed on a bad energy or spirit to the baby. The remedy is to use an egg, a special branch, oil, etc., and chant. Added to this spell is the recitation of the Lord's Prayer, Ave Maria, a Rosary, etc. As spell casting is concerned, there is a false belief in a white, good magic and a black, bad magic. If someone would like to cast a spell for good luck, fortune, or love, that spell can be considered white magic and in accordance with a good, Catholic lifestyle by the majority of the Latin American society. Also, on Witch Street in La Paz, Bolivia, Roman Catholic saints stand among the pagan sorcery items and trinkets for sale.

Seen in this picture from a storefront on Witch Street, La Paz, Bolivia, is Saint Expeditus, a Christian martyr from the late second century. The writing on this incense package states, "For redemption, hope and to attract money." The fact that this saint is used in a superstitious way to "expedite" things does not come

from Inca syncretism, though. These superstitions are found throughout Roman Catholicism, making it clear that syncretism started many centuries before reaching the shores of the New World and added to the folk religions.[10] And as far as witchcraft goes, these are only a small sampling of its saturation and how it plays a major role in Latin American societies.

Ancestor Worship

The indigenous ancestral worship found a compromise with the Roman Catholic Church (RCC) in exchanging ancestral "worship" for the "veneration" of RCC saints. For even the moderately observant tourist, the fact that Mexico has a peculiar endearment for their saints becomes obvious very quickly. The roadways have temples in curves and mountainsides with different saints for protection. Markets are full of trinkets for different saints in promise of different favors or relief. Streets are closed for processions as flowers are laid down for the carrying of large statues of saints for various festivals. But, again, it is worth mentioning that this "veneration" of dead saints past is practiced around the world. This unbiblical practice was brought to Latin America and simply incorporated into the folk religions — praying to ancestors was replaced with praying to saints.

Another example of an instance where compromise appears via syncretism is in All Saints Day. *Día de los Muertos* (Day of the Dead) is celebrated on All Saints Day every November 1.[11] This is mostly a Mexican celebration involving a parade to the cemetery to visit dead ancestors. This ceremonial celebration predates the colonization period, but has really only changed dates to comply with the RCC's tradition.[12] In Mexico

Typical Day of the Dead cemetery vigil

---

10. Example: http://catholicherald.com/stories/A-patron-saint-for-procrastinators,18693, accessed January 4, 2016.

11. Bodie Hodge, Halloween History and the Bible, Answers in Genesis, October 29, 2013, https://answersingenesis.org/holidays/halloween-history-and-the-bible/.

12. Some sources state that the Día de Muertos was originally celebrated in the beginning of the summer before the Spanish rule.

City, the deceased children are visited on November 1 and the deceased adults on November 2. The families cook the loved one's favorite dish, taking it to the cemetery in hopes that their spirit will visit to dine once again. In some villages, the bones of the deceased are dug up and washed.

This unhealthy interest in death has brought on a new "saint" for Latin America — *La Santísima Muerte* (Saint Death). This brand of "venerating" or worshiping a personification of death comes out of a great admiration and respect for death's power. Saint Death is found on trinkets, shirts, hats, and even full statues of what many in the Western world would consider to be the Grim Reaper as seen in the picture. According to a leading popular webpage that gives specific prayers to Saint Death, this is the beginning and end of the structure of a prayer:

> Lord, before Your Divine Presence God Almighty,
> Father, Son and Holy Spirit,
> I ask for your permission to invoke the Holy Death.
> My White daughter.

And then it ends with:

> (Pray three "Our Fathers")[13]

What does the Bible say?

Interestingly, the Bible doesn't allow for communication with any spiritual being except God, whether saint or death itself. The Bible speaks of death as an enemy that was brought into the world through sin and will one day be defeated forever. Jesus Christ defeated death through His work on the Cross (1 Corinthians 15:24–28; Colossians 2:13–15; Revelation 20:11–15). To offer prayers to the enemy of Christ while invoking His name is a strange fire to offer at the altars to Saint Death.

The prophet Habakkuk, after his inquiry on why God allows evil, and after God's response, continues to exhort, then, those who speak to idols:

> What profit is the image, that its maker should carve it,
> The molded image, a teacher of lies,
> That the maker of its mold should trust in it,
> To make mute idols?

13. "Very Powerful" Prayer of Protection, La Santa Muerte, http://www.santamuerte.org/oraciones/3745-plegaria-de-proteccion.html, accessed January 4, 2016.

Statues including the Grim Reaper

An altar of *Santísima Muerte*, Saint Death

> Woe to him who says to wood, "Awake!"
> To silent stone, "Arise! It shall teach!"
> Behold, it is overlaid with gold and silver,
> Yet in it there is no breath at all.
> But the Lord is in His holy temple.
> Let all the earth keep silence before Him (Habakkuk 2:18–20).

In the case of any idol, whether saint or death, just because one recites a prayer asking God to give permission to speak with this person doesn't mean that God grants the permission. On the contrary, the Bible teaches the opposite. When King Saul wanted to beg the dead prophet Samuel for help, he didn't go to God asking for permission because he knew it was against God's will. He foolishly went to a medium (witch) to get an audience with the dead. In doing that he broke God's law. The only mediator (not medium) that we have to communicate to a Spirit is Jesus Christ — granting us an audience with the Father (1 Timothy 2:5).

Animism

As previously mentioned, the foundation of these mystical, superstitious, and pagan beliefs in Latin America, as well as in some other parts of the world, is animism. Instead of a sovereign God who directs the affairs in the material and spiritual realms, animism is taking a stab at achieving human sovereignty. If a human can pronounce a spell or mix just the right elements in a potion of eggs and oil he can manipulate the spiritual world, which in itself coordinates the affairs of the physical world.

In this system there is recognition of a world where things are not as they should be, but there is no hope. There is no great systematic storyline of a holy, just, and loving God who is working out His will to usher in the

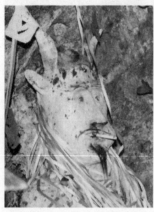

consummation of His plans for an eternity of a pure, perfect, and reconciled relationship with humans. There is no notion of being redeemed through Christ as He redeems everything that is in heaven and earth (Colossians 1). There is just each man on his own, working things out to the best of his abilities for his own personal benefit. In this sad system, you can beseech the spirit of the wind for tranquility, sacrifice and chant to *Pachamama* (Mother Earth) for a good harvest, and bring offerings to *El Tío* (the Uncle, god of the underworld) for safety in the mines, but there is no guarantee for any of it.

El Tío, the Uncle, in the mines of Potosí, Bolivia

Animistic attitudes, with only a small degree of discernment, can be seen in their most common manifestation — superstition. In superstition, fate is considered easily controlled by certain words or actions. For example, in Latin America (at least in most parts, especially with the least amount of European immigration), sarcasm is not taken well. A sarcastic statement is thought to be dangerous. By declaring something sarcastic, the spirit world is not privy to your real intentions but will react according to what was said.

That said, the manner in which animism has found itself into a syncretic system is more disturbing and, in a more subtle way and unbeknownst to multitudes, has invaded what many might consider evangelicalism. This most subtle syncretism is probably the largest problem facing the Latin American church at this time.

There has been a type of spin-off of Montanism (an early Christian heresy)[14] from the second century that has resurfaced in churches throughout

---

14. New Prophecy heresy from the middle of the second century wherein much attention was given to an imminent Second Advent that would take place in Phrygia, in that certain people receive new prophecy that was very sporadic and nonsensical, even speaking in the first person, "I am neither angel nor ambassador, but I God and Father, who am come." Epiphanius, *Heresies*, 48.11; Stevenson, 107. http://earlychurch.org.uk/article_montanism.html, accessed January 4, 2016.

the globe. The exceptional challenge that this brings to Latin America is that it closes the gap by reconciling an experiential religious anomaly and animism, and therefore has exploded in the last few decades.

This is known to most as Prosperity Theology or Prosperity Gospel and has taken over whole communities throughout Latin America. Every Sunday, many "templos" are filled to the brim with thousands upon thousands of devoted followers. Thankfully, a growing number of Christians are concerned about this syncretism

Cash Luna, Guatemalan prosperity leader, one of Latin America's most well-known prosperity animists

and are working to usher in a biblical gospel message alongside the barrage of confusing messages.

> The evangelical movement in Bolivia began over a hundred years ago in rural areas. But the country actually banned evangelical churches from cities until 1945 due to its bad reputation for mysticism and animism (influenced by Andean culture). Decades later, the church remains weak, characterized by captivating faith and prosperity teachings that replace reliance on God's word with a confidence in leaders referred to as apostles and prophets.[15]

There are a number of movements that have "Apostles" as the directors who speak as if from the Lord, or at least convince many to believe so. They will make such statements as, "Don't get lost among so much knowledge of the Word: Believe! That is what is important!"[16] And, "What are the 7 things that you desire in 2016? I declare 21 days of miracles over your life as you begin this New Year in prayer, fasting and offerings!"[17]

15. Patti Richter, "Bolstering Biblical Ministry in Bolivia," The Gospel Coalition, http://www.thegospelcoalition.org/article/bolstering-biblical-ministry-in-bolivia, accessed January 4, 2016.

16. Cash Luna, http://restablecidos.com/wp-content/uploads/2015/03/cash-luna-no-te-sumerjas-tanto-conocimiento-palabra-solo-cree.png, accessed January 4, 2016.

17. https://www.facebook.com/apostolgmaldonado/?fref=ts, accessed January 4, 2016.

What these false teachers figured out was how to play off of an animistic culture's superstition and "declare" how they can thus move the spirit world and circumstances of their life. Playing off of the misunderstanding about the relationship between laypeople and clergy, the average person is not "spiritual" enough to make much of a demand, so mediums are put in place and the syncretism is made clear by the title of "Apostle."

A sad truth is that in many cases these "Apostles" cannot be confronted in even the most biblical of ways without an all-out excommunication of the soul who dared to make such a challenge. According to many of their followers, they have the authority to make certain declarations that, in all practicality, carry the weight of Scripture within the community they control.

They are modern-day mediums for fortune and good luck and sadly claim the title *Evangelical*. In many of these cases, somewhere down the line many people adopted the title "evangelical" but never believed that Jesus is sufficient. This group has fallen into dualism again, and a demoted Jesus merely ends up being a superhero in the background on our side with our local Apostle fighting against the powers of darkness in the universe to take back what has been stolen — our health, wealth, and happiness.

What Does the Bible Say?

No matter what the culture or people group, we all spread out over the face of the earth from Babel until now with our own versions of man-made religions that all stem back to what was trying to be accomplished there — man making his own way to his idea of a god, deciding his own purpose and what was most important in life. This is humanism in its broadest sense.

Most people recognize the fact that we are spiritual beings, and not just material (except for the staunch naturalists and materialists). Most try to reach out for contact with the spiritual world they are certain exists. This venture, unassisted by the Word of God and carried out by an unregenerate person, is already doomed to failure. It is easy to say that the gospel is the answer, but as we have noted in this chapter, many people try to add a false version of the gospel to their animistic worldview, and thus miss out on the true, saving message of salvation in Jesus Christ alone.

The answer to this false religion is a biblically based message of hope through Jesus without the leeches of syncretistic falsehood that suck the lifeblood from the gospel, keeping so many from hearing the unadulterated Word of the living God.

> But we have renounced the hidden things of shame, not walking in craftiness nor handling the word of God deceitfully, but by manifestation of the truth commending ourselves to every man's conscience in the sight of God. But even if our gospel is veiled, it is veiled to those who are perishing, whose minds the god of this age has blinded, who do not believe, lest the light of the gospel of the glory of Christ, who is the image of God, should shine on them (2 Corinthians 4:2–4).

So if they who are lost die in their disbelief, let it only be due to their blindness, not accompanied by our deceit.

> If anyone teaches otherwise and does not consent to wholesome words, even the words of our Lord Jesus Christ, and to the doctrine which accords with godliness, he is proud, knowing nothing, but is obsessed with disputes and arguments over words, from which come envy, strife, reviling, evil suspicions, useless wranglings of men of corrupt minds and destitute of the truth, who suppose that godliness is a means of gain. From such withdraw yourself (1 Timothy 6:3–5).

Because the true gospel is:

> For I delivered to you first of all that which I also received: that Christ died for our sins according to the Scriptures, and that He was buried, and that He rose again the third day according to the Scriptures (1 Corinthians 15:3–4).

Chapter 16

Greek Mythology

Don Landis and the Ancient Man Team at Jackson Hole Bible College

Come hither, tell of Zeus your father and chant his praise. Through him mortal men are famed or un-famed, sung or unsung alike, as great Zeus wills. For easily he makes strong, and easily he brings the strong man low; easily he humbles the proud and raises the obscure, and easily he straightens the crooked and blasts the proud — Zeus who thunders aloft and has his dwelling most high.[1]

What we now refer to as "Greek mythology" began as unreliable, convoluted oral tradition passed down from generation to generation. In fact, there is no single document or text that outlines and describes the complete Greek system of beliefs. Instead, there are various pieces of written literature, poems, and stories that describe and elaborate on the origins, purposes, and characteristics of these alleged gods and man's purpose.

According to the myths, it appears that the ancient Greeks had a religious system similar to the majority of the pagan religions of their day (950–250 B.C.). Various deities governed the natural forces of the world. The gods and goddesses of Greek mythology controlled everything from the sky and

---

1. Hesiod, *Works and Days*, translated by Hugh G. Evelyn-White, http://www.sacred-texts.com/cla/hesiod/works.htm, accessed February 20, 2015.

sea to vegetation, earthquakes, and marriage. They were powerful but quarrelsome and seemed to lack self-control and wisdom.

Like all pagan religions, the beliefs of the ancient Greek culture stood in direct contrast to the truth of God's Word. The Greeks resolutely dismissed the existence of the one true God and history as outlined in Scripture. Their religion was sourced in their own authority. Remember that long before the Greeks started making up stories about gods like Zeus, Prometheus, and Aphrodite, mankind had decided to reject the truth and forge their own way.

The origin of all post-Flood pagan religions was the Tower of Babel, when mankind came together in an effort to usurp God's authority and proclaim their own. Even after being scattered across the planet, their defiance against God didn't die but rather blossomed into paganism of various forms — all sourced in the original rebellion.[2]

Greek mythology is perhaps one of the most famous and well-known ancient mythological religions. It had a profound impact on the ancient world because it was spread so widely by the conquest of Alexander the Great, and later broadly adopted by the Romans (they merely changed the names of the gods). By studying Greek beliefs about origins, God, man, morality, and the afterlife, we will gain insight into the minds of the ancient people and even learn about our own pagan tendencies.

Although not in written form for years, it is clear that the average Greek had a general knowledge and understanding of the gods and goddesses. When early authors like Homer (whom scholars date around the eighth or ninth century B.C.) wrote literature about the gods, they did not describe much about their character or origins. This knowledge was assumed to be already well-known. It wasn't until around 700 B.C. when the poet Hesiod wrote *Theogony* that the origins and nature of the Greek pantheon (all the gods and goddesses of their religion) were officially described. Other authors, playwrights, and poets elaborated on the myths, expanding the narratives individually. In the first century B.C. the Roman historian Gaius Julius Hyginus compiled all this mythological literature into a structure.

The Origin of All Things

The first Greek creation story was written around 700 B.C. by Hesiod (quite late in comparison to other origin myths). According to Hesiod, though

---

2. Don Landis, ed., *The Secrets of Ancient Man: Revelations from the Ruins*. 1st ed. (Green Forest, AR: Master Books, 2015).

there are variations of the story among other writers, the universe started out as Chaos (the primeval void) and out of Chaos came Erebus (darkness) and Nyx (night). It wasn't until the coming of Eros (love) that Erebus and Nyx bore light (Aether) and Hemera (day). After the coming of light, the great domains, Gaia (earth), Ouranos (sky), Pontos (sea), Tartarus (underworld), and other primordial beings personifying everything from sleep to fate, were born from the union of these beings. The Titans, Olympians, monsters, and minor gods were born from these primordial beings. In ,Theogeny, Hesiod focused on the emergence and lineage of the gods and monsters, all connected in a large convoluted family tree. He also described many fantastic tales about the wars and struggles between the gods, Titans, and monsters.

Primordial Gods	Titans	Olympians	Heroes	Monsters
The first deities who created the universe and produced the next generation of gods, the Titans	Sometimes known as the elder gods, the children of Earth (Gaia) and Sky (Ouranos)	Twelve gods who ruled from Mount Olympus after the overthrow of the Titans	Individuals who achieved semi-divinity or were specifically recognized for their greatness	Monsters and other mythical creatures feature prominently in many Greek tales
Gaia Ouranos Eros Tartarus Chaos Pontos Ourea Aether Hemera Nyx	Rhea Cronos Helios Phoebe Theia Hyperion Perses Prometheus Epimetheus Atlas Mnemosyne Tethys Themis Oceanus Coeus	Zeus Poseidon Hera Artemis Athena Dionysius Demeter Ares Apollo Hermes Hephaestus Aphrodite Sometimes included: Hestia Hades	Heracles Achilles Callisto Theban Helen Theseus Odysseus Perseus Orpheus	Pegasus (winged horse) Centaurs (part man part horse) Sphinx (part woman and part lion) Cyclops (one-eyed giant) Unicorns Gorgons Minotaurs Satyrs Dragons

Because the ancient Greek religion does not have any one specific and comprehensive text to reference, charts like the one above are likely to differ from one another depending on the sources used to obtain the information. The chart above is simply a helpful reference for common classification of some of the mythical Greek characters.

Atlas was a Titan who was supposedly punished by Zeus and forced to hold up the earth.
(Wikimedia Commons, Biatch)

Prometheus delivers fire to mankind, previously in darkness.
(Wikimedia Commons, Heinrich Füger)

The Origin of Mankind

According to the Greek myths, there was a long time in history when only the immortal gods existed. It was not until after the war between the Olympians and the Titans (in which the younger Olympian gods defeated the elder Titans) that humans and animals appeared on the earth. Zeus, the new Olympian king of the gods, rewarded two of the Titans who had joined their side (Epimetheus and Prometheus) with the creation of animals and humans. Epimetheus made all of the different animals, giving them gifts of speed, strength, wings, fur, and other strong attributes. This left Prometheus without any gifts, so he made man out of clay and then Athena (goddess of wisdom) breathed life into his clay forms. Prometheus created them in the image of the gods, standing upright with the same countenance. He also stole some skills from Hephaestus (god of craftsmanship) and Athena to bless his new favorites. In an effort to help them, he gave them control over fire. The first humans were all male and lived in harmony with the gods.[3]

---

3. *The Prometheus of Aeschylus* (Cambridge, MA: Harvard University Press, 1888), p. 343, https://books.google.com/books?id=YkygMobybKUC.

However, Zeus (god of storms) was angry that man had been given fire, forming a rift between men and the gods. According to the myths, in his anger he punished them with the gift of womankind.[4]

The first woman was called Pandora. Zeus had Hephaestus create her, and she was given gifts of beauty and guile. In Hesiod's tale *Works and Days,* the gods created her and gifted her out of spite to cause suffering to mankind. The gods created her with "cruel longing and cares that weary the limbs" and a "shameless mind and deceitful nature." She was "bedecked with all manners of finery" and yet filled with "lies and crafty words." She was given as "a plague to men."[5]

Hesiod claims that before women appeared, men lived "free from ills and hard toil and heavy sickness." But Pandora

Artist's impression of Pandora attempting to close the box she opened out of curiosity as the evils she has released taunt her while they escape.
(Wikimedia commons, F.S. Church)

brought a jar with her (commonly referred to as Pandora's Box). Though warned never to open it, she could not resist the temptation. Upon opening the jar she released every kind of evil upon mankind including toil and death. And yet the one thing that didn't escape was Hope. It remained in the jar, closed under the lid.[6]

Judgment

Because of the evil unleashed and the resulting chaos as man was given over to corruption, Zeus and the other gods punished them by sending a flood to wipe out all mankind. Only a noble man named Deucalion and his wife Pyrrha (daughter of Pandora) were spared because Prometheus warned them of the coming disaster. They built a boat and floated for nine days before landing on Mt. Parnassus. Upon landing they were told to throw stones behind them; each stone thrown by Deucalion turned into a man, and each stone thrown by Pyrrha turned into a woman. They then sired their own

---

4. Stephanie Lynn Budin, *The Ancient Greeks: An Introduction* (New York: Oxford University Press, 2009), p. 244.
5. Hesiod, *Works and Days.*
6. Ibid.

children from whom all Greeks are descended. (The stones populated the other areas of the world.)[7]

Drawing Comparisons

Without delving any further into the convoluted details of Greek mythology, the basics of this pagan religion are already clear and lie far outside of biblical truths.

Gods and Goddesses

As seen in the tale of the origin of the universe and the creation of mankind, the Greek gods are nothing in comparison to the one true God. Though some of the gods, Zeus in particular, seem to mirror many of the characteristics of the God of the Bible, they were certainly not all-powerful or all-knowing, and they often got tricked by others, even mortal men. They show themselves to be petty, quarrelsome, unjust, and cruel. They were violent, jealous, prone to anger and deceit, and often shown to be limited in their abilities and strength. The Greeks replaced the incomparable, omniscient, omnipotent God, in whose image they were made, with a myriad of weak, unreliable gods and goddesses created in their own image.

The ancient Greeks considered the gods morally perfect. (Hesiod claimed that "true judgment is of Zeus and is perfect.")[8] However, even cursory readings of Greek mythology prove that idea to be completely untrue from a biblical perspective.

Yet to the Greeks, the most defining attribute of a god was not goodness or omniscience or perfection, but *power.* And usually that power defined a god as a specific kind of force or action (Aphrodite was the force of love, Zeus was the god of the storm, etc.).[9] Perhaps this explains why the gods were often attacking each other and seemingly capricious. They were defined and directed by their power, they did not command or control it.

The Nature of Man

According to the origins story, mankind was originally and internally good; it was not until Pandora released evil into the world that mankind started to

---

7. John H. Haaren and Addison B. Poland, *Famous Men of Greece* (New York: American Book Company, 1904), p. 20–24, https://books.google.com/books?id=OLsBAAAAYAAJ.

8. Hesiod, *Works and Days.*

9. *God and Men in Greek Religion*, http://faculty.gvsu.edu/websterm/gods&men.htm., accessed February 19, 2015.

do wrong. Even then, the evil of mankind is attributed to the evil spirits that had been released around them, not to man's internal evil nature.

In fact, according to Hesiod's *Works and Days*, women in general are the source of evil and trials. In contrast to God's Word, women were apparently sent as a punishment to mankind, not created as a helpmate and fellow image-bearer. Pandora is called a "beautiful evil" in *Theogony*, a "deadly race and tribe of women who live amongst mortal men to their great trouble, no helpmeets in hateful poverty, but only in wealth." They were "an evil to mortal man, with a nature to do evil."[10]

In this perversion of biblical truth we can see traces of Adam and Eve's history and the effects of the curse visible between the lines. This mythology reflects Satan's lies as a distortion of what really happened.

Morality

From their literature it is clear that the Greeks believed in some sort of moral code and that it was somewhat governed by the gods. Hesiod teaches that Zeus gave man "right," in contrast to the animals who knew nothing of right and wrong. According to *Works and Days*, doing right would lead to prosperity. But those men who lied and "hurt Justice" and sinned "beyond repair" would be left to obscurity.[11] Moreover, "badness can be got easily and in shoals: the road to her is smooth, and she lives very near us. But between us and Goodness the gods have placed the sweat of our brows: long and steep is the path that leads to her, and it is rough at the first; but when a man has reached the top, then is she easy to reach, though before that she was hard."[12]

This passage from *Works and Days* describes how Zeus continued to create many generations of men that always fell into evil. The author bemoans his life among the evil of his generation, and his description of those evils is intriguingly similar to biblical passages:

> Thereafter, would that I were not among the men of the fifth generation, but either had died before or been born afterwards. For now truly is a race of iron, and men never rest from labour and sorrow by day, and from perishing by night; and the gods shall lay sore trouble upon them. . . . The father will not agree

---

10. Hesiod, *The Theogony of Hesiod.*
11. Hesiod, *Works and Days.*
12. Ibid.

with his children, nor the children with their father, nor guest with his host, nor comrade with comrade; nor will brother be dear to brother as aforetime. Men will dishonour their parents as they grow quickly old, and will carp at them, chiding them with bitter words, hard-hearted they, not knowing the fear of the gods. They will not repay their aged parents the cost their nurture, for might shall be their right: and one man will sack another's city. There will be no favour for the man who keeps his oath or for the just or for the good; but rather men will praise the evil-doer and his violent dealing. Strength will be right and reverence will cease to be; and the wicked will hurt the worthy man, speaking false words against him, and will swear an oath upon them. Envy, foul-mouthed, delighting in evil, with scowling face, will go along with wretched men one and all.[13]

Many of these are biblically based ideals (similar to verses such as those found in Proverbs and Ecclesiastes). How is it that the Greeks seemingly borrowed from the Bible in their pagan mythology? They definitely had no intention of aligning themselves to the teachings of God, and yet the author ached for justice and righteousness, for honesty, love, and kindness. Is it any surprise that these good attributes were missing from their society when the gods and goddesses they worshiped were constantly manifesting evil tendencies?

As the Psalmist rightly notes, "those who make [idols] are like them; so is everyone who trusts in them" (Psalm 135:18; KJV).

Life after Death

The ancient Greeks believed that death occurred when the breath left the body. They believed in a soul-like, ghost-like entity called a *psyche* that left the body upon death to enter an afterlife. They believed that the next life would be spent in the underworld, which was ruled by the god Hades. It appears from the literature that the afterlife was a depressing reality to the Greeks — a weary and tedious place (as described by Achilles in Homer's *Odyssey*).

And yet an alternate condition is also described in later Greek literature with three areas of the underworld offering a more hopeful, positive outlook.

---

13. Ibid.

The first area was Tartarus (also known as the pit), which was split into two different sections. The first and lowest section was the prison of the gods; monsters and other powerful beings were placed in this area.[14]

The second section of Tartarus was imagined by fifth-century Greek poets like Homer and Hesiod who repurposed the pit to include the most despised sinners. It was the lowest area where humans could be sent and was the place where the worst of the worst went to endure eternal torment.[15]

The middle area, the Fields of Asphodel, was where the vast majority of people went. These had done nothing particularly evil so as to deserve the punishment of the lower realm but had also

Hades was the god over the underworld, pictured here with the three-headed dog, Cerberus.
(Wikimedia Commons)

not done anything particularly good in order to deserve Elysium. Here they would experience neither joy nor torment; instead it was listless, dull, and forgetful.

The highest area was Elysium, the goal of all people. In Elysium there was endless celebration. It was reserved for those who did good works to earn their way in. Only the greatest heroes and most honorable humans would achieve Elysium.

Even later, another shift occurred in the Greek ideology about death as many came to believe in a form of reincarnation. If a person died and went to the Fields of Asphodel, they could choose to live again for a chance to receive the reward of Elysium. They would not remember who they were; they would be different people (though they started out as animals, Herodotus made the statement that it took three thousand years to return to human form), allowing them a chance to receive the greater reward. Clearly influenced by Eastern and/or Egyptian ideas, the Greeks believed if you

14. These aspects are described in various sections of Homer's *Iliad* and other writings.
15. Sarah A. Scull, *Greek Mythology Systematized* (Philadelphia, PA: Porter & Coates, 1880), p. 99–104, https://books.google.com/books?id=Lm0ZAAAAYAAJ.

lived enough good lives, you would eventually end up in Elysium.[16] These ever-changing ideas about the afterlife are evidence of the truly arbitrary nature of their beliefs, having no grounding in a legitimate authority.

The Purpose of Life

For the Greeks, the purpose of life was twofold — to worship and please the gods and to achieve honor and glory for themselves to gain entrance to Elysium. Since pleasing the gods was the primary way to reach Elysium, these purposes were closely tied together.

Man was created to be subject to the gods and to please them with sacrifices and other forms of worship. However, the true reason a Greek would strive to live a life of honor, and the reason they wanted to perform great deeds and to become well known, was simply because they desired Elysium. Therefore, just like every other man-made religion in the world, the Greeks relied on their own works to be saved from punishment.

They were constantly working to appease the fickle gods, both for blessings in this life and in order to achieve happiness after death. It was a tedious way of living, involving various sacrifices, rituals, and careful maneuvering in order to avoid upsetting the deities.

While Elysium was the goal of most men (one only achieved by great heroes such as Achilles, Odysseus, Helen, Menelaus, Perseus, Theseus, etc.), the very greatest of heroes were granted an even greater reward — godhood. This was the ultimate gift granted to a select few, including the great heroes such as Heracles and Dionysus (the only one to become an Olympian). Most men could not hope to achieve such standing, but it is interesting to see how they still believed it was possible.[17]

Once again we see the ancient goal of Babel reflected in Greek religion — mankind desiring the domain and authority of God, trying to make a "name" for himself.

Judeo-Christian Beliefs in Greek Mythology

To be clear, it should be noted that Greek mythology did not *intentionally* borrow anything from God's revealed religion (that would eventually reach its fullest expression in Christianity). Like all man-made religions, Greek

---

16. Budin, *The Ancient Greeks: An Introduction*, p. 301.
17. The explanations of deifications, known as apotheosis, are found in later writers like Cicero and Pausanias.

mythology has its origins at the Tower of Babel. At Babel, Satan influenced mankind to start a one-world religion and government that was anti-God. However, it is important to remember that Satan cannot create, he can only pervert. Therefore, he set up a *counterfeit kingdom* and a *counterfeit religion*. Aspects of this counterfeiting can be seen in all of the false religions in the world. They all take a portion of truth and then twist it so it is almost unrecognizable. These truths were known by the people at Babel and carried with them as they traveled around the globe, being distorted in various ways over time.

Creation

The creation story of Hesiod's *Theogony* is a clear distortion of biblical truth. Now this may seem like a strange claim as the mythology of the Greeks seems to be far different than the truth of God's Word. However, look at the first two things that came into being from the Chaos — darkness and light. While it may seem inconsequential, it is something taken directly from true history as recorded in the Bible. Also the claim that at the beginning of creation Chaos was simply a great void is another distortion of the creation account in the Book of Genesis (Genesis 1:2). Other aspects of their creation story, such as the forming of man from the clay, even the creation of animals and man around the same time and man being created before woman has a kernel of biblical truth.

Sacrificial System

Another aspect the Greeks borrowed from the Judeo-Christian worldview is the sacrificial system. This religious practice was borrowed by every single ancient culture — they all had some form of a sacrificial system created to appease whatever gods they served. In the Bible, this system was initiated right after the Fall of Adam and Eve when God killed two animals and made clothes out of them. This first sacrifice was developed further in the account of Cain and Abel. Throughout the Old Testament, sacrifice as a covering for sin is practiced by Job, Abraham, and others. It is codified for the Israelites under Moses, but finds its perfect fulfillment in Jesus Christ and His death on the Cross. Because of His amazing sacrifice to take away the sins of those who believe in Him, there is no longer any need to maintain the old sacrificial system described in the Old Testament. The Greeks sacrificed to appease their gods as well, yet they had no promise or assurance of salvation from a coming Messiah. In reality, their sacrifices were piteously ineffective, proving the disastrous results of perverting God's system.

The Appearance of Evil

The next similarity is the entrance of evil (sin) into the world. According to the Greeks, the first woman, Pandora, was given a jar that she was not allowed to open. Her curiosity of what might be in the jar proved to be too strong and she opened it, releasing evil into the world. This story is a twisted version of the account of the Fall of Adam and Eve in Genesis chapter three. Eve, the first woman, was tempted by Satan to eat from the one tree that was forbidden by God. Satan tempted Eve by appealing to her curiosity and pride.

The Flood

Another piece of the biblical account taken by Greek mythology is the story of Deucalion and the flood. Just as in the biblical account, a flood is sent by the gods to punish the wickedness of mankind. Again, the Greeks skew the history — only Deucalion and his wife are spared and the flood only lasts for nine days. However, the concept was clearly taken from the true account of Noah and the Flood sent by God as described in the Bible. There are many religions from ancient times that twist the account of the Flood; they are merely distorted versions of the actual event that remains in their cultural memory from Babel.

The Afterlife

The last primary element that seems to have similarities to the Judeo-Christian worldview, is the organization of the underworld. In the Old Testament, the temporary holding place of those who died is set up in a fairly similar way. Recall that Tartarus in Greek mythology was a prison for supernatural beings including the gods. In the Bible, Peter uses the same word to name the holding place for the angels who sinned (2 Peter 2:4). Furthermore, when studying the Old Testament and the Jewish understanding of Sheol, it appears as if the Jews believed in a multi-level place with an area of rest and waiting (Psalm 86:13) but also a lower part of fire and torment (Deuteronomy 32:22). In Psalm 16:10 and 45:15 David indicated that he would not stay in Sheol, but somehow be redeemed.

The Foolishness of Greek Mythology

The inconsistencies and arbitrariness of Greek mythology make it a truly sad religion to follow, especially in light of the similarities to biblical truths. The basic lack of any clarity and definitive teaching make it seem hopeless and unfulfilling. Imagine trying to serve and please the dozens of gods and immortal creatures of the ancient Greeks. All of them were so different — by pleasing one you might upset another. The gods were constantly turning on each other, so how would you know who was currently more powerful and who to side with?

Moreover, there was no authority to rest upon — it seems like any deep thinker or writer could simply use their imagination and expand on the existing myths with details that suited their own purposes. The Greek religion was an ever-changing story that, though fascinating and exciting to read about, seems to leave the follower/believer in a state of confusion and anxiety. There is no security and, like the story of Pandora's jar, no real hope of redemption.

It seems like much of their literature was written to critique, analyze, and make sense of the world around them. Yet the literary works were inconsistent and constantly evolving because their authors lacked the authority and knowledge to correctly explain reality. The angst, bitterness, struggle, and conflict outlined in the epics and poems portrays the state of the human souls living according to this system of flawed paganism, always striving but never finding rest.

As Romans 1:21–23 proclaims:

> Because, although they knew God, they did not glorify Him as God, nor were thankful, but became futile in their thoughts, and their foolish hearts were darkened. Professing to be wise, they became fools, and changed the glory of the incorruptible God into an image made like corruptible man — and birds and four-footed animals and creeping things.

There is no better way to describe the elaborate and confusing tangle of Greek mythology than "futile thinking." They rejected God and were forced to worship a mere distortion based on their own fallible, sinful imagination.

Salvation from the Snare of Greek Paganism

You may wonder why this chapter has found its way into a book on world cults and religions when it is obviously a dead mythology that no one believes anymore. Or so you may think.

Many today worship the god of reason with the proclamation of "I think, therefore I am."
("The Thinker" by Rodin, Wikimedia)

In reality, our culture is not so different from that of the ancient Greeks — and neither are our beliefs. People may not sacrifice to Zeus or Poseidon or erect temples to Athena or Artemis anymore, but we have made gods of the same powers and forces around us. Remember that it was the force or power that defined the Greek gods and goddesses. Those powers and forces still govern our lives today and demand our worship — if we let them.

Who can say that Dionysus, the god of wine, is not alive and well today, worshiped and sacrificed to by millions?

What about Athena, the goddess of reason? Have many not bowed down to her, denying the God of the supernatural and worshiping science, logic, and human intellect?

Aphrodite was the goddess of love, desire, and beauty. Who can deny that humanity still worships sex, is overpowered by lust, and constantly seeks to worship beauty?

What about Ares, the god of war, or Apollo, the god of youth and healing? How many put their hope in these false gods?

It is evident that many people in our culture still worship the same powers that the Greeks revered. In truth, we all struggle with them in some sense.

> For we do not wrestle against flesh and blood, but against
> principalities, against powers, against the rulers of the darkness
> of this age, against spiritual hosts of wickedness in the heavenly
> places (Ephesians 6:12; NKJV).

But there is good news! Unlike the Greek's false religion, there is true hope! Christians know the one true God who conquered all powers and all authorities. He alone is the truth, undistorted and pure. He is not arbitrary or capricious. He remains the same forever, and He loves us! He created us male and female in His own image with a purpose — to glorify, love, and enjoy Him forever. This is only possible by His mercy and grace, shown by the ultimate act of love: sending His Son to die on the Cross in our place. And He has given us assurance of this by sealing us with His Holy Spirit.

This good and gracious God commands us to love Him first and to have no other gods or idols before Him (Exodus 20:3–6). His Son, Jesus Christ, deserves all glory and praise.

Is He the one and only pursuit in your life? Or have you bought into the ways of this world, the ways of the ancient Greeks, the ways of Babel? Heed the Apostle Paul's warnings and flee from idolatry (1 Corinthians 10:14)!

> And we know that the Son of God has come and has given us an understanding, that we may know Him who is true; and we are in Him who is true, in His Son Jesus Christ. This is the true God and eternal life. Little children, keep yourselves from idols. Amen (1 John 5:20–21).

Summary of Greek Mythological Beliefs

Doctrine	Teachings of Greek Mythology
God	Deny the God of the Bible. Hold to a pantheon of gods beginning with the primordial gods and proceeding to many lesser gods including the Titans, Olympians, and others. The various gods personify different aspects of the universe.
Authority/ Revelation	Oral traditions that were eventually recorded in various epics and poems that changed over time
Man	Men were created by the gods from clay as morally good beings that were influenced to evil and corruption through the influence of evil spirits and gods. Women were created later.
Sin	Sin is poorly defined and often associated with offending various gods.
Salvation	The pursuit of a moral life and achieving greatness through pleasing the gods could earn one a spot in various levels of the afterlife. A few were able to achieve godhood through extreme valor and pleasing the gods.
Creation	The primordial god Chaos gave rise to the physical creation and other aspects of the universe. Gaia is the goddess that represents the earth, with other equal and lesser gods creating the various aspects of reality.

Chapter 17

Stoicism (with Notes on Epicureanism)

Dr. Greg Hall with Troy Lacey

> Beware lest anyone cheat you through philosophy and empty deceit, according to the tradition of men, according to the basic principles of the world, and not according to Christ (Colossians 2:8).[1]

I (Dr. Hall) work where ideas are highly valued. Higher education is a marketplace of ideas. Ideas operating in this marketplace have changed the world. The great advances in technology, scientific discovery, or medicine that have come from institutions of higher education have blessed the human race in unimaginable ways. God has blessed mankind, and we see an important aspect of the Imago Dei (being created in God's image) when we consider the great power and results of human reason applied to solving problems we face.

But I have found when it comes to engaging the deepest and most profound issues of human existence and purpose such as why we are here, how we got here, where we are all going, why the world is in such a mess and the potential solution, that not all ideas are equally valid. It is not that mankind has not thought about these questions or postulated answers. It is, however, that when their answers are not based upon Scripture they become futile

---

1. Scripture in this chapter is from the New King James Version (NKJV) of the Bible.

speculation that darkens the mind, and the result is a captivity of the mind that ends in deceit. It is the mind full of the ideas of men instead of the mind devoted to Christ.

The Bible is a book devoted to presenting the truth of the Creator, God. God is the source of this book and it's tantamount to reading the "Owners Manual." It teaches us the truth about origins, about purpose in life while living in this world, and about the coming consummation of all things. The Bible gives answers to the questions our Creator knew would perplex the human mind. God created mankind with an insatiable appetite for understanding. We have a deep-seated need to contemplate the profound questions of life. Our problem is that we are looking for comprehension, understanding, and knowledge in all the wrong places. I say again, not all ideas are equally valid.

Paul and the Stoics

In chapter 17 of the Book of Acts, the apologist and Apostle Paul was sent to confront the prevailing philosophers of the day with the truth of God's Word. He knew God's Word alone gives understanding to the inquiring mind. God's Word is what Francis Schaeffer called, "true truth." It is here in Acts 17 at the Areopagus that Paul faced off with the Stoic and Epicurean philosophers, giving us not just an understanding of the humanistic philosophical mind, but the exact way to confront it and offer the truth of God as the remedy for false ideology. This is the great legacy of Acts 17.

The Areopagus was located in Athens, Greece, and it seems to have looked a lot like the universities of our culture. The "intelligentsia" of the day spent their time doing nothing more than hearing and promoting the latest "ideas." The Areopagus has traditionally been understood to be a place near the Acropolis, but it may actually be a reference to an advisory council in Athens that dealt with ethical, cultural, and religious matters, and the supervision of education.[2]

Paul was apparently quite familiar with both the Stoics and the Epicureans, and this assisted him in framing his conversation with them. When you consider Paul's message in Acts 17, how he formulated his argument, and what he wanted these philosophers to know about truth, it becomes apparent he was quite well versed in Greek philosophy. In fact, as we shall

2. Robert L. Thomas, *New American Standard Updated Edition Exhaustive Concordance of the Bible* (La Habra, CA: The Lockman Foundation, 1994) p. 4770.

see later, Paul utilized the same divide and conquer strategy between the Stoics and Epicureans as he had when getting the Pharisees to side with him over the Sadducees (Acts 23:6–9).

Founding Beliefs

According to John Drane in *Introducing the New Testament,* Stoicism was based on philosophical speculation about the nature of the world and its people. The philosophy was founded by Zeno in Greece during third century B.C. and developed by later thinkers including Marcus Aurelius, Seneca, and Epictetus. At its heart, matter was considered the ultimate reality. To the Stoic, God was an abstract of human thinking sometimes referred to as Fate. But God is also the source of humanity's soul through the primordial essence of fire (logos), which was given to the primordial couple and passed on to their offspring through procreation. The Stoic's god was ill-defined, generally based in pantheism with God as the Creator and essence of everything in the universe.

Morality was determined by human reasoning and generally consisted of avoiding passions and aligning one's actions with the natural course of things. Wisdom, justice, temperance, and courage were the four principle virtues viewed as honorable. For Stoics, "salvation" was found in self-sufficiency and alignment with the cause and course of the cosmos. They sought self-mastery over themselves so as to be "one with nature." Stoics had no future hope or expectation of rewards or judgment beyond the grave.[3] It is a philosophy of hopelessness. Based in the pure arbitrary opinions of each individual, there is no ultimate source of truth or determining what is right or wrong. We can see these same ideas present in various forms of Humanism today.

Shared Beliefs

Paul also recognized a few commonalities and used them as a wedge to gain a foothold for the gospel, and to openly denigrate the Epicurean position. For example, Stoics did believe in some form of divine creation, which the Epicureans denied. The Stoics also believed that there was something beyond the strictly material. The Stoics also believed that animals and mankind were not just created, but that this creation involved a purpose and design in

---

3. "Stoicism," Internet Encyclopedia of Philosophy, http://www.iep.utm.edu/stoicism.

body parts and functions.[4] The Epicureans were truly the complete evolutionists, believing that everything came about through random chance and was purposeless, but only mimicked design because of the massive amounts of variation in nature.[5]

In fact, early in Paul's gospel defense on Mars Hill, he quickly uses the creative works of God to gain a foothold with the Stoics in the crowd. "God, who made the world and everything in it, since He is Lord of heaven and earth . . ." (Acts 17:24). The Stoics would have immediately thought to themselves that this foreigner aligned more with their philosophy than with the Epicureans. Paul further gains the attention of the Stoics toward the end of his speech with his declaration of man's moral responsibilities toward God and also the partial quotation from two Greek poets (Acts 17:27–30). The poets Paul quotes are Aratus and Cleanthes; the first was revered among the Stoics, and the second was the Stoic "patriarch" who studied under Stoicism's founder, Zeno.

However, Paul was also aware of the many differences between Stoicism and Christianity. His closing words were intended to show that both Stoics and Epicureans needed to turn from their sin and embrace the risen Savior, Jesus Christ. His rather pointed phrasing about living in ignorance and needing to repent in order to avoid judgment (Acts 17:30–31) would have been regarded as shocking or offensive to many in the audience. Paul would have known that the more learned Stoics thought that they were self-sufficient and morally righteous, and the Cross of Christ would have indeed been regarded as "foolishness" to them. Dr. David Naugle in his paper "Stoic and Christian Conceptions of Happiness" attributes this predisposition to intellectual elitism on the part of Stoic sages:

> Stoicism aggrandizes the individual who through practice and self-discipline is able to make the whole life harmonious by bestowing upon him the title of "Sage." The Stoic sage is completely self-sufficient and happy because of his virtue. For the "virtuoso," the conduct of life presents no problem. His life consists in a regular and effortless flow in harmony with human rational and ultimate metaphysical nature all of which constitutes

---

4. David Sedley, *Creationism and Its Critics in Antiquity* (Oakland, CA: University of California Press, 2009), p. 206–208, 214–216.
5. Ibid., p. 150–155.

genuine virtue. The Stoic sage has advanced to a point where a life of courage and wisdom, justice and temperance comes easily and naturally, without struggle and without repining.[6]

So, how amazing it is that as Paul confronted the vain, deceitful philosophy of the Stoics he first began his presentation of the truth by proclaiming the God who is Creator of everything that exists, something the Stoics would have mentally assented to, at least in principle. It is Paul employing the use of creation evangelism.[7] Paul did what we should do — any apologetic approach to philosophers of any pagan ideology must begin with establishing the truth on origins. Paul begins by getting the attention of the philosophers.

> Then Paul stood in the midst of the Areopagus and said, "Men of Athens, I perceive that in all things you are very religious; for as I was passing through and considering the objects of your worship, I even found an altar with this inscription: TO THE UNKNOWN GOD. Therefore, the One whom you worship without knowing, Him I proclaim to you" (Acts 17:22–23).

Once he has captured their attention, he launches his defense of Scripture and the God of the Bible with these inspired words:

> God, who made the world and everything in it, since He is Lord of heaven and earth, does not dwell in temples made with hands. Nor is He worshiped with men's hands, as though He needed anything, since He gives to all life, breath, and all things (Acts 17:24–25).

To clearly proclaim the truth of God beginning with the claims of Genesis 1:1 is the way to contend with any pagan philosophy. The late Francis Schaeffer said if he had an hour to talk to someone about the gospel, he would spend the first 55 minutes establishing the truth of creation and the last 5 minutes explaining the gospel of Christ. The reason is, he knew what the Apostle Paul knew — you cannot understand the gospel and our need for a Savior without first establishing faith in the true account of the God

---

6. http://www3.dbu.edu/naugle/pdf/stoic_christian_views.pdf, extended quote taken from p. 15.
7. For more on creation evangelism please see Ken Ham, *Why Won't They Listen?* (Green Forest, AR: Master Books, 2002).

who created *ex nihilo* (out of nothing) and to whom we will give an account of our lives.

A Modern Echo

The late Dr. Henry Morris, a scientist and well-known refuter of evolutionary philosophies, in his book *The Genesis Record*, put it like this:

> It is quite impossible, therefore, for one to reject the historicity and divine authority of the Book of Genesis without undermining, and in effect, repudiating, the authority of the entire Bible. If the first Adam is only an allegory, then by all logic, so is the second Adam. If man did not really fall into sin from his state of created innocency, there is no reason for him to need a Savior. If all things can be accounted for by natural processes of evolution, there is no reason to look forward to a future supernatural consummation of all things. If Genesis is not true, then neither is the testimonies of those prophets and apostles who believed it was true. Jesus Christ Himself becomes a false witness, either a deceiver or one who was deceived, and His testimony concerning His own omniscience and omnipotence becomes blasphemy. Faith in the gospel of Christ for one's eternal salvation is an empty mockery.[8]

All worldly philosophies have the same goal: produce ideas that will give mankind so-called "answers" to the great metaphysical questions of all time. Where did we come from? What is our purpose? Where are we going? Is there any meaning to life? Is there life beyond the grave? But the worldly philosophies do not generally allow for God to enter the equation, and if the concept of God is allowed in the conversation, it is an anemic, powerless deity, the exact opposite of the God of Scripture. It is an "unknown god" as Paul described in Acts 17:23.

Again, quoting from Dr. Henry Morris:

> Actually all such false philosophies are merely different ways of expressing the same unbelief. Each one proposes that there is no personal, transcendent God; that ultimate reality is to be found in the eternal cosmos itself; and that the development

---

8. Henry M. Morris, *The Genesis Record* (Grand Rapids, MI: Baker Book House, 1976), p. 22.

of the universe into its present form is contingent solely on the innate properties of its own components. In essence, each of the above philosophies embraces all the others. Dualism, for example, is a summary form of polytheism, which is the popular expression of pantheism, which presupposes materialism, which functions in terms of evolutionism, which finds its consummation in humanism which culminates in atheism.

The entire system could well be called the system of atheistic evolutionary humanism. Other philosophical ideas could also be incorporated into the same monstrous structure: naturalism, uniformitarianism, deism, agnosticism, monism, determinism, pragmatism, and others. All are arrayed in opposition to the great truth — marvelously simple, and understandable to a child, yet inexhaustibly profound — that "in the beginning, God created the heaven and the earth."

It is remarkable that, when there have been so many antitheistic philosophies (ancient and modern) affecting untold millions of people, the book of God makes no attempt to prove that God exists. The opening verse of Genesis simply takes this fact for granted, as though it were so obvious that only a fool could say "there is no God" (Psalm 14:1).[9]

So Paul, under the direction of the Holy Spirit, confronts the pagan ideology and worldly philosophy of the Stoics with a clear and simple, yet profound, proclamation of the Creator, God. He reminds them of "the God who made the world, and everything in it." He knew that the philosophy promoted by these ancient philosophers and their forebears all end in the same direction: the supposed explanation of the origin of life without reference to the Creator God of the Bible. While the Stoics believed in a creator and rejected random chance as the originator of the universe, they had in mind a notion of a vague and impersonal intelligent designer.

The Role of Chance

By contrast, the Epicureans totally embraced "chance" as the agent responsible for all matter. This is the very fabric of the philosophical naturalism being presented to a generation of students today, and naturalism is not

---

9. Ibid., p. 38.

based on scientific inquiry — it qualifies only as a false religion. You must have great faith in fallible man's ideas about the origin and nature of the world and universe around us to buy into naturalism. Naturalism is religion, and evolution is its dogma.

Students who have been told evolution is scientific fact may find it hard to comprehend that it is more a philosophical position than a scientific one. Even evolutionary scientists will admit evolution is a fundamental tenet of the ideology of humanism, a secular religion — a full-fledged alternative to Christianity. This was true of evolution in the beginning, and it is true of it still today.[10]

This is why Dr. Henry Morris says that today's secular scientist must believe in evolution in spite of all the evidence, not because of it. And speaking of deception, note the following remarkable statement that Dr. Morris comments on:

> We take the side of science in spite of the patent absurdity of some of its construct. . . . in spite of the tolerance of the scientific community for unsubstantiated commitment to materialism. . . . we are forced by our a priori adherence to material causes to create an apparatus of investigation and set of concepts that produce material explanations, no matter how counterintuitive, no matter how mystifying to the uninitiated. Moreover, that materialism is absolute, for we cannot allow a Divine Foot in the door.[11]

[Morris] The author of this frank statement is Richard Lewontin of Harvard. Since evolution is not a laboratory science, there is no way to test its validity, so all sorts of just so stories are contrived to adorn the textbooks. But that doesn't make them true! An evolutionist reviewing a recent book by another (but more critical) evolutionist, says:

> We cannot identify ancestors or "missing links," and we cannot devise testable theories to explain how particular episodes of evolution came about. Gee is

10. Michael Ruse, "Saving Darwinsim from the Darwinians," *National Post* (May 13, 2000), p. B3.
11. Richard Lewontin, review of *The Demon-Haunted World*, by Carl Sagan, New York Review of Books, January 9, 1997.

adamant that all the popular stories about how the first amphibians conquered the dry land, how the birds developed wings and feathers for flying, how the dinosaurs went extinct, and how humans evolved from apes are just products of our imagination, driven by prejudices and preconceptions.[12]

[Morris] A fascinatingly honest admission by a physicist indicates the passionate commitment of establishment scientists to naturalism. Speaking of the trust students naturally place in their highly educated college professors, he says:

> And I use that trust to effectively brainwash them. . . . Our teaching methods are primarily those of propaganda. We appeal — without demonstration — to evidence that supports our position. We only introduce arguments and evidence that supports the currently accepted theories and omit or gloss over any evidence to the contrary.[13]

[Morris] Creationist students in scientific courses taught by evolutionist professors can testify to the frustrating reality of that statement. Evolution is, indeed, the pseudoscientific basis of religious atheism, as Ruse pointed out. Will Provine at Cornell University is another scientist who frankly acknowledges this.

> As the creationists claim, belief in modern evolution makes atheists of people. One can have a religious view that is compatible with evolution only if the religious view is indistinguishable from atheism.[14]

[Morris] Once again, we emphasize that evolution is not science, evolutionists' tirades notwithstanding. It is a philosophical worldview, nothing more.[15]

---

12. Peter J. Bowler, review of *In Search of Deep Time* by Henry Gee (New York: Free Press, 1999), *American Scientist*, vol. 88, March/April 2000, p. 169
13. Mark Singham, "Teaching and Propaganda," *Physics Today*, vol. 53, June 2000, p. 54.
14. Will Provine, "No Free Will," in *Catching Up With the Vision*, ed. By Margaret W. Rossiter (Chicago, IL: University of Chicago Press, 1999), p. S123.
15　Henry M. Morris, The Scientific Case Against Evolution, www.icr.org/resources.

Together, the humanistic philosophy and the evolutionary science, so far, seem to have won the day in the classroom, having declared evolutionary storytelling to be true, in spite of the growing evidence against it. The reason the interaction of the Apostle Paul with the Stoic philosophers in Acts 17 at the Areopagus is so significant in our times is it shows how philosophy and ideology drive the marketplace of ideas and how worldly philosophy mitigates against the Word of God. In a very real sense the issue of our day, the origins debate, is ultimately driven by the philosophers masquerading as scientists.

Answers in Genesis has shown for a long time, and in highly academic fashion, that the science behind evolutionary claims is very suspect to say the least and, in reality, based on falsehood. Many world-class scientists believe today that the evolutionary model is massively implausible, if not entirely false. So how does it persist? The answer can be seen in this Acts 17 passage, and it is why understanding the prevailing philosophies of the day is so important. We need to understand the Stoics and every philosophical system since and argue against them just like Paul did at Mars Hill (Areopagus).

In the origins debate today, philosophy rules, not science. This may surprise you. Naturalism is the religion of the age, and evolution is its dogma. It is the philosophy of naturalism most at stake in the battle, not the science that is used to promote evolution or creationism. The science of creationism clearly wins the day. Evolution persists because naturalism demands it persist! Naturalism demands the origin of everything must be explained without reference to a Creator.

And so, under the anointing of the Holy Spirit, the Apostle begins his apologetic masterpiece in Acts 17:22–23.

> Then Paul stood in the midst of the Areopagus and said, "Men of Athens, I perceive that in all things you are very religious; for as I was passing through and considering the objects of your worship, I even found an altar with this inscription: TO THE UNKNOWN GOD. Therefore, the One whom you worship without knowing, Him I proclaim to you.

This is where evangelism should begin today and why apologetics is such an important discipline: we begin with the Creator and His creation. This fact must be presented in all its clarity and power before the gospel will ever be understood. It should be obvious that the foundation of the gospel must be present so that he gospel will make sense. The gospel is only understood in terms of God being both Creator and Redeemer.

> In the beginning, God created the heavens and the earth (Genesis 1:1).

It was the starting point in ministry to the Stoics at Mars Hill and to every philosopher since. It is so crucial to see the apologetic argument unfold as Paul confronts the pagan philosophy of the Stoics and Epicureans because it is the divinely inspired thought that still reaches the pagan philosophies and philosophers of our day. They may no longer be called Stoics, but their "offspring" has as its purpose to replace the truth of the Creator and His creation with the false explanation of moral self-sufficiency, naturalism, or any number of other vain philosophies.

Paul teaches them of "the God who made the world and everything in it" (Acts 17:24).

He made from one man (Adam) every nation of mankind to live on all the face of the earth (yes, Adam and Eve *are* the sole progenitors of the human race). He further determined periods and boundaries, with the intent of mankind seeking God (verse 27). God is close to us, Paul teaches, "In Him we live and move and have our being" (verse 28). Paul quotes one of the Stoic poets, Aratus, from his poem, "Phainomena," when he says, " 'For we are also His offspring.' Therefore, since we are the offspring of God, we ought not to think that the Divine Nature is like gold or silver or stone, something shaped by art and man's devising. Truly, these times of ignorance God overlooked, but now commands all men everywhere to repent, because He has appointed a day on which He will judge the world in righteousness by the Man whom He has ordained. He has given assurance of this to all by raising Him from the dead" (verses 28–31).

So there it is — the perfect, God-given argument for pagan philosophy of any kind. God is Creator, ruler, judge, and redeemer. This is an argument with no further debate. It is settled by the God with sovereign power to create everything out of nothing (*ex nihilo*) by His spoken Word, alone!

The Response to Paul

The result of this apologetic presentation is what can be expected in our evil, sinful, and broken world: "And when they heard of the resurrection of the dead, some mocked, while others said, 'We will hear you again on this matter.' So Paul departed from among them. However, some men joined him and believed . . ." (verses 32–34).

To the Stoics who professed to shun creature comforts in favor of what they termed virtuous acts (but was really self-righteousness), the only "good" they could conceive of was devotion to Stoic principles. So when confronted with Christ's death, burial, and Resurrection for their sins, they were confounded.

For example, Christians think of Christ's sacrifice in terms of John 15:13 — "Greater love has no one than this, than to lay down one's life for his friends." This was antithetical to Stoic thinking, as Charles Taylor notes that "the Stoic sage is willing to give up some 'preferred' thing, e.g., health, freedom, or life, because he sees it genuinely as without value since only the whole order of events which, as it happens, includes its negation or loss, is of value. . . . The [John 15:13] sentence would lose its point in reference to someone who renounced life from a sense of detachment; it presupposes he is giving up something."[16] Therefore, the Stoics couldn't reconcile Christ's death as meaningful to them.

Personally, I find that students coming to the university from state schools have obviously been fully inculcated with the beliefs of evolution as a worldview. I have also found there is great confusion about the very term "evolution," especially in its biological sense. Many students do not understand the meaning of evolution in the scientific sense, and especially in its implication in the areas of cosmology, geology, and biology. Some students believe evolution simply means "change." Creationists believe in change, and by this simplistic definition could be called evolutionists! So clearly this simplistic view is unacceptable.

Some believe the term *evolution* is equivalent to the concept of "natural selection," or "survival of the fittest," but they have merely confused evolution with these ideas that are part of the supposed evolutionary process. I find many students surprised that evolution in the naturalistic scientific community ultimately means that at a time in the primeval past, inanimate (nonliving) material through the mechanism of random chance and natural laws become animate (living) matter (chemical evolution). This

---

16. David Naugle, "Stoic and Christian Conceptions of Hapiness," http://www3.dbu.edu/naugle/pdf/stoic_christian_views.pdf, extended quote taken from p. 29.

living matter somehow obtained the ability to reproduce itself through the passing of information (whether RNA or DNA), and a single cell became the common ancestor of all living things (biological evolution). This unobservable and unrepeatable belief requires great faith to believe — it is far from the scientific method and actually a dogma of the philosophy of naturalism.

Many students also attribute the concept of evolution to Charles Darwin's writings in *On the Origin of Species*. They are sometimes surprised to learn evolutionary ideas, as a proposed alternative to biblical creationism, precedes Darwin by many generations — including the Epicureans that Paul also confronted in Acts 17.

This is why the presentation of Paul at the Areopagus is so significant. The concept of evolution as a proposed explanation of origins goes back into antiquity, even prior to the Stoic and Epicurean philosophers addressed by the Apostle. True philosophy is always Christ-centered (Colossians 2:8–10). Vain or worldly philosophy is always an attempt to explain origins, or any other of the profound issues of life, without reference or commitment to God — particularly the God of Genesis, the God of Scripture.

The Stoics and Epicureans of Acts 17 represent a long line of philosophers before them, and a longer line since, who offer humankind an alternative to biblical creation and instead try to explain origins in terms of impersonal design or "chance" evolution. In truth, of the science behind evolution and the philosophy behind the science, neither one are compatible with the biblical truth.

For a full treatment of the history of the idea of evolution, see Dr. Henry Morris' book *The Long War Against God*. Of special note is the chapter entitled "The Conflict of the Ages." You will see that evolution is an idea as old as man himself. It certainly did not originate with Charles Darwin. Dr. Morris writes:

> All these ancient atheistic philosophers, as well as the ancient pantheistic philosophers (Pythagoras, Plato, Aristotle, etc.) were highly intelligent men and made many great contributions to science, mathematics and general learning. Nevertheless, all rejected the true God of creation and promoted one or another evolutionist system of cosmogony and primeval life history. The evolutionary philosophy that completely dominates the modern

Western world has now been traced back all the way to ancient Greek philosophy, beginning about 2,500 years ago.[17]

I think, too, that beyond the ancient Greek or pre-Socratic philosophers, evolutionary concepts can be traced back to early descendants of Noah listed in Genesis 10 and 11. That argument, however, is beyond the scope of this chapter. The point again is clear — evolution is a very ancient idea possibly going back to early people after the Flood.

At this, it is crucial students see the point. Evolution, to quote one author, "is a theory in crisis."[18] It is based on extrapolation of certain changes and taught as a "fact" of science to unsuspecting multitudes of students. Though scientific evidence is used to support the evolutionary interpretation of our origins, this view is at the very least "massively implausible." It persists among those who adhere to the philosophy of naturalism because of a prior commitment to the philosophy and with a clear goal — to get God out of the picture.

This is why today the creation/evolution debate is predominantly a philosophical debate, not a scientific one. This is a point worthy of repeating.

To make this abundantly clear, consider this quote from the book, *Total Truth*:

> A few more examples drive the point home. During the Ohio controversy, one of the drafters of the controversial state guidelines wrote a letter to *Physics Today*, insisting that, in order to be considered at all, "the first criterion is that any scientific theory *must be naturalistic*."[19] In other words, unless a theory is naturalistic, it will be ruled out before any consideration of its merits. The editor in chief of *Scientific American* then entered the fray, stating that "a central tenet of modern science is methodological

---

17. Henry Morris, *The Long War Against God* (Green Forest, AR: New Leaf Publishing, 2000), p. 218.

18. Michael Denton even titled his book *Evolution: A Theory in Crisis* in 1985 as a result of his research on evolution.

19. Mano Singham, a physicist at Case Western Reserve University, writing in *Physics Today*, June 2002, emphasis added. To buttress his argument, he quoted paleontologist George Gaylord Simpson, who wrote, "The progress of knowledge rigidly requires that no non-physical postulate ever be admitted in connection with the study of physical phenomena . . . the researcher who is seeking explanations must seek physical explanations only" in *Tempo and Mode in Evolution* (New York: Columbia University Press, 1944), p. 76.

naturalism — it seeks to explain the universe purely in terms of observed or testable natural mechanisms."[20] But who says we have to accept naturalism as a "central tenet" of science? As one professor I know retorted, "Who made up that rule? I don't remember voting on it."

In other words, why should we acquiesce in letting philosophical naturalists prescribe the definition of science itself? The only reason for restricting science to methodological naturalism is if we assume from the outset that philosophical naturalism is true — that nature is a closed system of cause and effect. But if it is not true, then restricting science to naturalistic theories is not a good strategy for getting at the truth.[21]

Today, a naturalistic definition of science is taught as unquestioned dogma throughout the public [state-run] education system, even to young students who lack the background to challenge it. Read this quotation from a typical high school textbook: "Many people believe that a supernatural force or deity created life. That explanation is not within the scope of science."[22] Notice that the book does not say creation has been proven false or discredited by facts, but only that it falls outside a certain definition of science. It has been ruled out by definition.

Another high school textbook says, "By attributing the diversity of life to natural causes rather than to supernatural creation, Darwin gave biology a sound scientific basis."[23] Note how the text equates "sound" science with philosophical naturalism.

Clearly, philosophy has gained primacy over the facts.[24]

---

20. John Rennie, "15 Answers to Creationist Nonsense," *Scientific American*, June 17, 2002.
21. See Del Ratzsch, *The Battle of Beginnings: Why Neither Side Is Winning the Creation-Evolution Debate* (Downers Grove, IL: InterVarsity Press, 1996), p. 167. For a more recent and more academic, discussion of philosophical issues, see Del Ratzsch, *Nature, Design, and Science: The Status of Design in Natural Science* (New York: SUNY Press, 2001).
22. *BSCS Biology: A Molecular Approach*, 8th ed., Jon Greenberg, revision editor (Everyday Learning Corporation, 2001), p. 446.
23. Neil A. Campbell, Jane B. Reece, and Lawrence G. Mitchell, *Biology*, 5th ed. (Reading, MA: Addison Wesley, 1999), p. 426. A helpful analysis of textbooks can be found in Norris Anderson's "Education or Indoctrination 2001," at http://www.alabamaeagle.org/education_or_indoctrination_2001.htm.
24. Nancy Pearcey, *Total Truth* (Wheaton, IL: Crossway Books, 2005) p. 169.

Responding in a Modern Marketplace of Ideas

In this current environment, students are asked to discriminate among the various ideas of the marketplace, distinguishing between truth and falsehood. It is possible for us, with careful study, using the minds with which we were created and especially under the instruction of the Holy Spirit, to determine what is true. In fact, Scripture promises the Holy Spirit will "guide [us] into all truth" (John 16:13).

But we must see, it is all about the "starting point," and what we believe is foundational to our epistemological approach. Epistemology is the study of knowledge, the study of how we know what we say we know.

Consider this: in the creation/evolution debate, all scientists are looking at the same information and data — everyone has the same evidence. How is it that they reach such different conclusions? The answer is in the philosophy that undergirds their investigation. As we have seen, if that philosophy is naturalism you will reach naturalistic conclusions and exclude any supernatural explanations. If that foundation is the Word of God you will view all the data through that lens. We need to be honest and acknowledge that our starting points will influence our conclusions.

Paul knew the debate of origins or any other concept of significance was going to have a "starting point" issue for the philosophers at the Areopagus. So he stood firmly upon the Word of God. And if you are a believer you should too. There is absolutely no reason to deviate from the message of Scripture. It is God's revelation to us. And I, for one, will stand on God's revelation any day rather than the ideas of human philosophy.

I have heard scientists say, "Well, science has proven the Bible is false." That is manifestly not true. Scientists have not proven anything about Scripture untrue, nor could they, since God's Word is always true. I've heard others say, "Well, the Bible is not a textbook on science." That may be true, but as the Word of God, it has given us the truth on every subject it speaks of, including scientific topics. But I would go further — because the Bible is true, science is possible. The truths about God and nature in the Bible provide the necessary framework for observable and repeatable science to be possible.[25] This foundational element was missing from the philosophy of the Stoics and Epicureans, and it is missing from the naturalists of the modern era.

---

25. Jason Lisle, *The Ultimate Proof of Creation* (Green Forest, AR: Master Books, 2009).

The issue at stake in the creation/evolution debate and in the interaction with Paul and the Stoics is this: to whom will you look as the source of truth, God or man? The matter of truth seeking must be of paramount importance to the source of truth, God himself. In Romans 1:18 we read:

> For the wrath of God is revealed from heaven against all ungodliness and unrighteousness of men, who suppress the truth in unrighteousness.

To suppress truth is obviously egregious to God. To pursue truth, the student finds a clear plain path in the Word of God. The very character and nature of His invisible attributes, His eternal power, and divine nature are clearly perceived, *since the creation of the world,* in the things that have been made. We are without excuse if we suppress the truth that is evident in nature and even more clearly expressed in the Bible. God's Word is clear and understandable, though admittedly deep and mysterious in areas. But He has made the main thing the plain thing (Romans 1:18–20).

We can know Him, honor Him, and turn from futile thinking, like the hopeless ideas of the Stoics, on these eternal matters. Our foolish hearts need no longer be darkened.

Summary of Stoic Beliefs

Doctrine	Teachings of Stoicism
God	Deny the Creator God of the Bible, but have a vague deistic view of a god as Nature or Fate. As the entire universe is considered all that exists and expresses itself in living things, Stoicism can be seen as a form of pantheism.
Author-ity/Reve-lation	Through reasoning in accord with Nature, man can determine what is true and virtuous apart from any direct revelation from Fate. Deny religious writings as authoritative, but recognize they may contain truths in accord with Fate.
Man	The souls of men and animals are emanations of the active Fate (Logos) of the universe. The goal of man is to avoid suffering by living in accord with Reason and Nature.
Sin	Sin is equivalent to acting contrary to nature and reason (vice), bringing misfortune and unhappiness on an individual. Wisdom, justice, temperance, and courage are the four principle virtues. If these are present in the soul, the soul is good.

Salvation	The soul may return to its union with the universal Fate, as it is not a distinct entity. There is no concept of punishment or rewards in an afterlife.
Creation	The universe is eternal and composed of passive matter generated by active Fate. The Fate (a fiery ether) directs the passive matter as it wills.

Chapter 18

Shinto

Michiko Mizumura

An article in *Asahi Shinbun* in December 2014 reveals this intriguing news: "A Tokyo project will avoid building over 'cursed' grave associated with samurai's head." The large 1.43-billion-dollar project involves construction of two skyscrapers which house offices, a hotel, and multipurpose concert halls in central Tokyo. Yet they avoid removing the small grave of a 10th century samurai because they fear a curse. We live in the 21st century, and this antiquated, superstitious thinking may cause many of us to wonder! But many Japanese still feel uneasy about upsetting spirits of the dead that had become gods. This reflects the Shinto way of thinking.

Another modern news topic concerns Japanese politicians making visits to Yasukuni shrine, which was built to commemorate the war dead. Because the shrine is Shinto, the war dead (even war criminals) become gods, and about 2,460,000 gods are enshrined there. Many cabinet members, including the prime minister, visit Yasukuni to pay their respects to the spirits of the dead as gods. This has led to a controversial issue in foreign diplomacy — most likely concern over enshrining war criminals and violating the principle of separation of church and state. Yet most Japanese are lenient about it because of Shinto culture.

The Japanese people of today are still deeply affected by Shinto, both in their culture and thinking. This is one of the reasons it's difficult for them to accept monotheistic religions such as Christianity. Looking closely at Shinto can give us a better understanding of the underlying fundamental beliefs that shape the thinking of the Japanese people. In this chapter we'll examine what Shinto is.

What Is Shinto? Brief Overview

Shinto is an indigenous religion originating with the Japanese. It is only practiced within Japanese communities, and it provides the backbone of Japanese culture and national identity.

The annual statistics of the religious population, taken by the Japanese Agency for Cultural Affairs in 2011, show that there are over 100 million Japanese people adhering to Shinto (51.2%), 85 million to Buddhism (43.0%), 1.9 million to Christianity (1.0%), and 9.5 million in other religions (4.8%).

It is important to note that the total number of the religious population exceeds the actual population of Japan, which is about 130 million. Some people identify with multiple groups, and the history of Japanese religions is responsible for this phenomenon. This will be further explained later.

Shinto Definition of "God"

Shinto is written in two Kanji (Chinese characters), 神道, namely, 神 which is "god(s)" and 道 which is "way." So it can literally mean "god's way" or "gods' way" (in Japanese, there are no explicit singular or plural forms, so it is determined by context).

In Shinto, a god is not like the God of the Bible who is the omnipotent Creator of the world. Shinto gods are basically spirits that are everywhere in nature and also in men — hence the assumption of many gods. Exactly how many? One may wonder. The phrase *Yaoyorozu* (meaning 8,000,000) is used to express the innumerable gods in Japan.

Shinto originally began as a form of animism. The early Japanese feared the natural forces and believed those forces came from the power of the spirits living in various natural entities, such as forests, rocks, oceans, etc. The habitats of the spirits, considered sacred, were called *Yorishiro*, but Yorishiro themselves were not the subjects of worship. In Shinto, therefore, the subjects of worship are not creatures or visible idols but spirits that are believed to have supernatural power. Both benevolent and malevolent spirits are called *kami* in singular or *kami gami* in plural, meaning "gods."

As Shinto developed, not only spirits living in nature but also ancestors' spirits were enshrined as gods. After death, ancestors' spirits were believed to become guardian gods, watching over and protecting their living descendants. Furthermore, some distinguished persons became enshrined for various reasons. Michizane Sugawara, a famous scholar and aristocrat of the ninth century who is now viewed as a god of academics, was originally thought to have become an *onryo*, a cursing spirit, because he was falsely charged with treason and died a regrettable death. Tenman Shrine was originally built to placate his spirit to avoid his *tatari* (curse). Another famous enshrined person is Ieyasu Tokugawa, the primary shogun who established the Tokugawa administration. He was enshrined in Nikko Toshogu Shrine to authenticate and authorize the supremacy of the Tokugawa family to rule over the nation during the Edo period.

Shinto Beliefs

Shinto does not have scriptures such as the Torah of Judaism or the Bible of Christianity. Instead, its adherents rely on the folklore and ancient histories that are kept in *Kojiki* (meaning "old matters") and *Nihon Shoki* (Japan chronicles), which give some background accounts to Shinto beliefs. In those books are written the accounts of how the gods created various physical entities including the islands of Japan. They also explain how gods and men once lived, even marrying each other. Those gods are now viewed as guardian angels, thus they are respected. *Kojiki* and *Nihon Shoki* also record that Japan's emperors are the direct descendants of the famous Amaterasu, the goddess of the sun — with special care being taken to explain how emperors are fully sanctioned to rule over Japan. This leads to worshiping the emperor as a living god — seen recently in the days of World War II.

Because Shinto gods are related to the nation's folklore and legends, some people view Shinto merely as tradition and culture — not as a religion. Shinto deals mostly with this life, and issues such as personal salvation or life after death are not discussed.

Shinto Practices

There are over 80,000 Shinto shrines in Japan. Some distinguished shrines, such as Yasukuni, Ise Jingu, and Izumo Taisha gather many visitors from all over Japan, but most shrines are visited locally, as they enshrine gods of the area or *Uji-gami* (guardian gods of clans living in the area).

Shinto does not require one to affiliate with it by denying other religions, so it welcomes anyone who visits Shinto shrines to pay respects to gods whenever the individual wishes. This explains why many Japanese can identify with Shinto and other religions at the same time. When visiting shrines, the following is the common protocol:

1. Bow at the *Tori-i* gate before entering the shrine precinct.

2. Wash hands and mouth (there is usually a water fountain at the entrance of the shrine precinct).

3. Move forward to *Haiden*, the hall of worship building, located in front of *Honden*, the main sanctuary building where gods reside.

4. Make offerings at the offertory box.

5. Ring the large bell by pulling the attached rope to call the gods' attention.

6. Make a specific worshiping action, such as "bow twice, handclap twice, and bow once." Usually prayers are made after the handclapping.

Quintessentially, the Japanese people visit shrines on New Year's Day to pray for safety, good health, and prosperity in the coming year. This tradition is called *Hatsumoude* (meaning the first visit of the year). People also visit shrines for traditional festivals or seasonal events, as each shrine holds annual *Matsuri* (meaning festival or ritual ceremony).

At different life stages, typical Japanese follow specific Shinto traditions. When a baby is born and reaches the age of one month, parents usually take the infant to a local shrine to give thanks and pray for good health for their little

Main Gate at Ise Grand Shrine in Ise, Mie, Japan
(Kanchi1979, Creative Commons)

one. The same is done for children turning three, five, and seven years old. When students take entrance exams for schools, they go to the shrine of gods of academics to ask for success and to buy good luck charms. Some young couples choose to get married at a shrine, as there are gods of good marriage, and they also go to a shrine devoted to the gods of childbearing when they wish to conceive, praying also for a safe delivery. As life advances, some families opt for funerals in Shinto style, though most of them are done according to Buddhist rites because of traditions added to the culture during the Edo period.

Shinto and Politics

Shinto has always been present on the political scene of Japan. In ancient times, a shaman or shamaness was the leader who enshrined and performed rituals to please gods. He or she also practiced divination to discern the will of the gods so that people knew such things as when to sow seeds. In the early days of Japan, shamans held high positions not only in rituals but also in politics. Later, the imperial family, viewed as the descendants of gods of Japan, became responsible for performing rituals and governing the country. Japanese political structure emerged from the integration of Shinto rituals and government (similar to a theocracy), and this was kept until the end of World War II. The remnants of such customs can be seen even today.

History of Japan and Shinto

In this section, let us examine more closely how Shinto was shaped throughout Japanese history.

Early Form of Shinto

Where did the first people of Japan originate? It is believed that during the Ice Age[1] Japan was connected to the Asian continent by land, enabling various people to migrate across the Asian continent to the far eastern end of it after spreading out from Babel. This area later became the islands of Japan as the sea level rose. But even after the islands were disjoined from the continent, people were able to make the trek by sea, as recorded in ancient texts. Nothing definite can be said as to exactly which ethnic tribes reached

---

1. Mike Oard, "Where Does the Ice Age fit?" *New Answers Book 1*, ed. Ken Ham (Green Forest, AR: Master Books, 2006), p. 207–220.

Japan. In all likelihood, it was not a single tribe but multiple tribes bringing different cultures.[2]

With distinct seasons and with abundant natural resources such as the ocean, rivers, and forests, the Japanese islands provided a perfect environment for fostering in its residents a sense of awe toward nature. Climate and topography were both instrumental in nurturing animistic beliefs and provided a background for developing folklore, especially the mythological stories of spirit gods living with and interacting with men.

When rice cropping was brought to Japan in the third century B.C., people started to settle down into villages, forming units in an agricultural society. It is most likely that at that time the prototype of Shinto was formed. People tried to placate perceived spirits by worshiping them as gods and making sacrificial offerings to them — even going so far as to offer up the lives of women and children (according to lore). This was done in order to secure the villagers' lives and crops from natural disasters. Festivals were held according to the farming calendar, and shamans exercised paramount roles in practicing divinations and instructing people in the will of the gods. This early form of Shinto, therefore, consisted of animism and shamanism.

Rise of Yamato Dynasty (the Imperial Family)

Several ancient Chinese records (*Records of Three Kingdoms* and *Book of the Later Han*) explain that there was a countrywide war in Japan in the second century A.D., a conflict lasting over 70 years. The war finally ended when they placed Himiko as their common ruler. Himiko was a female shaman and the queen of Yamataikoku; she lived from late second century to mid-third century A.D.

Himiko was also mentioned in another record as having sent her delegates to China, where she was recognized as ruler of Wa, the name given to Japan at that time. Himiko was given a special golden seal by the Chinese emperor around 238 A.D., confirming that she had great power in Japan in her day. It is not exactly known where Himiko's kingdom Yamataikoku was, but it is said that Yamataikoku ("Yamatai kingdom") could be related to the Yamato dynasty — the only dynasty that ever existed in Japan, becoming the imperial family that includes the present emperor of the nation.

By the fourth century, Yamato kings reigned as the rulers of Japan. Both governing and performing rituals were important duties of the ruler.

---

2. For more on some of the possible tribes please see Bodie Hodge, *Tower of Babel* (Green Forest, AR: Master Books, 2013), p. 166–167.

They made sure to perform ceremonies for Amatsukami, gods who live in the heavens and created the land of Japan, and Kunitsukami, gods who reside on the earth and protect the land of Japan. The Yamato dynasty also enshrined Amaterasu, the goddess of the sun who is viewed as their ancestor, in Ise Jingu Shrine, the most prestigious Shinto shrine in Japan.

Emperor Tenmu ordered the compilation of national chronicles in the late seventh century. The writing of *Kojiki* was completed in 712 and *Nihon Shoki* in 720. These two texts are the foundational sources upon which Shinto beliefs are based. Both of these texts cover stories of the creation of Japan as well as the genealogies of Yamato kings. Folklores about stories of the gods are much like Greek mythologies, since gods of Japan are very much like humans, emotional and imperfect, getting married, and having children. The genealogies inform us that Yamato kings were descendants of Ninigi, the grandson of Amaterasu. It is important to note that one of the reasons these two texts were written was to authenticate the Yamato kings as the authorized rulers of Japan by tracing back their bloodline to the gods of Japan, especially to Amaterasu.

By the beginning of the eighth century the Yamato dynasty achieved centralized power and established a new governmental structure called the *Ritsuryo* system, similar to the one in China. In this new structure, a specific religious bureau was installed wherein the government could carry out Shinto rituals. The rituals, *Matsuri*, defined under Ritsuryo system, are listed in Table 1. The religious bureau became superintendent of all the shrines in the country. The shrines were ranked, and 22 shrines related to the imperial family or to the dominant clans were chosen to be operated at public expense. An interesting fact is that this system evaluated and put rankings on gods, just as it did on human officers. In Shinto, gods became ranked according to their abilities and titles.

Ritsuryo system was in operation for about three centuries. By the end of the tenth century, it became difficult for the government to keep centralization of power, and a new system was installed. For religious matters, the spread of Buddhism changed the position of Shinto in the culture.

Introduction of Buddhism

The introduction of Buddhism had an enormous impact on Shinto.

In the mid-sixth century, Buddhism was officially brought into Japan from Baekje (one of three kingdoms of Korea at that time). Seong, the king

Table 1: List of Matsuri under the Ritsuryo system

Time	Name of the Rituals (Matsuri)	Religious Practice
February	Pray for the Year Matsuri 祈年祭（としごいのまつり）	To pray to Amatsukami and Kunitsukami for abundant harvest year
March	Flower Appeasing Matsuri 鎮花祭（はなしずめのまつり）	To pray for plague or diseases to depart from the country, at Oomiwa Shrine and Sai Shrine
April & September	God Clothing Matsuri 神衣祭（かんみそのまつり）	To offer clothes to Amaterasu at Ise Jingu Shrine
April	Three Branch Matsuri 三枝祭（さいぐさのまつり）	To decorate Sake (rice wine) barrel with lilies at Isagawa Shrine
April & July	Large Sacred Matsuri 大忌祭（おおいみのまつり）	To pray for good rain and harvest for rice crops at Hirose Shrine
April & July	Wind God Matsuri 風神祭（かぜのかみのまつり）	To pray for rice fields to be protected from bad storms or floods at Tatsuta Shrine.
June & December	Monthly Matsuri 月次祭（つきなみのまつり）	To pray for the welfare of the imperial family at Ise Jingu Shrine (it used to be done every month)
June & December	Feasting God Matsuri 道饗祭（みちあえのまつり）	Make a feast for evil spirits so that they don't come into the town

June & December	Fire Appeasing Matsuri 鎮火祭（ひしずめのまつり）	To pray for safe fire
September	God's Meal Matsuri 神嘗祭（かんにえのまつり）	To offer the first fruit of the year to Amaterasu at Ise Jingu Shrine
November	Partaking God's Meal Matsuri 相嘗祭（あいにえのまつり）	To offer the first fruit to gods and partake of it together
November	New Meal Matsuri 新嘗祭（にいなめのまつり） 大嘗祭（おおにえのまつり）	To celebrate the harvest, the emperor offers the new meal to gods, and he partakes too
November	Soul Appeasing Matsuri 鎮魂祭（たましずめのまつり）	To pray for peace of the emperor's soul
June & December	Purification Ceremony 大祓（おおはらえ）	To remove the impurity accumulated over the 6 months, done on the last day of June and December.
As needed	Special New Meal Matsuri 践祚大嘗祭	The first New Meal Matsuri since the emperor's enthronement

of Baekje, presented Buddha statues and scriptures to Kinmei, the emperor of Japan. Unsure of what to do, Kinmei consulted his court advisors. Some said to accept Buddhism, as it was already accepted in countries such as

China and Korea, while others said to refuse it, for Japan had its own gods, and accepting a new god like Buddha might upset the nation's original gods. Therefore, from the onset, Buddhism was not accepted well in Japan. To make a definitive contrast with Buddhism, Japan's indigenous religion began to be called Shinto.

But it was not long before Buddhism began to be accepted in Japan. The famous Prince Shotoku, who was regent to Queen Suiko in late sixth century, adopted and promoted Buddhism. Buddhist temples and statues began to be crafted at public expense. But Prince Shotoku was wise enough not to deny Shinto worship, issuing a law ordering people to continue worshiping Amatsukami and Kunitsukami. He was politically savvy enough to respect both the new and the old to avoid religious conflicts.

The Buddhism brought into Japan was Mahayana Buddhism with influences from other religions such as Confucianism, Taoism, and even Christianity.[3] Compared to this Buddhist admixture, Shinto is a simple ritualistic religion with few doctrines. Shinto deals with present happiness and not with personal salvation or afterlife. Folklore and traditions, on which Shinto is established, do not offer ethics or discipline to improve one's character. On the other hand, Buddhism has doctrines of enlightenment and commandments to follow. Sacred texts of Buddha can be studied by erudite scholars, and mysterious disciplines can be performed by practitioners. Buddhism offered what Shinto could not. Consequently, Buddhism attained the higher position in Japanese religious circles.

Syncretization of Shinto and Buddhism

As Buddhism became widely accepted in Japan, there followed a phenomenon called *Shin Butsu Shugo*, which means syncretization of Shinto with Buddhism.

This syncretization can be seen in the following phenomena:

- Shinto gods were accepted as the guardian gods of Buddhist temples, and Shinto shrines were built on the grounds of Buddhist temples.

- Temples were also built on the grounds of Shinto shrines to help Shinto gods to become Buddha, since Shinto gods were

---

3. See chapter 19 in this volume for a full description of Buddhism, chapter 20 for Confucianism, and chapter 3 for Taoism.

acknowledged as lower than Buddha and therefore needed to attain nirvana in the manner of humans.

- Certain Shinto priests became Buddhist monks hoping to attain their own personal "salvation" or enlightenment.

Further advancing the amalgamation of Shinto and Buddhism, the concept of *Honji Suijyaku* was developed. Shinto gods who supposedly created Japan and had been protecting the nation came to be viewed as the Buddha's personification. In this, worshiping Shinto gods was understood to be worshiping Buddha. In some cases, Buddhist monks even performed Shinto rituals. This strange mixture of Shinto and Buddhism was present in Japan for a long time, from the 10th century until the end of the Edo period in the mid-19th century when a new government ordered the separation of Shinto and Buddhism.

Uji-gami Beliefs at Local Shrines

Buddhism also affected Shinto's Uji-gami beliefs that were seen among common people at local shrines.

In Shinto the places of worship were at Yorishiro, the sacred dwelling places of gods such as woods, rocks, mountains, and other monumental natural objects. In the early days there were simple altars at Yorishiro, but later, larger buildings were constructed on premises as shrines.

In these local shrines each clan (Uji) or village enshrined its own guardian gods of their ancestor (Uji-gami) or of their village (Ubusuna-gami). Seasonal festivals were held at shrines to please these gods, and participation in various events at the local shrine was mandated in order to be part of the village community. This simple, traditional Shinto belief among common people was called Uji-gami belief, and it dealt with the interest of the entire village, not with personal interests or wishes.

When Buddhism, which deals with personal faith and "salvation," came along and began to spread among the common people, it profoundly affected and modified Shinto practices. It became acceptable to pray about personal matters at shrines.

Also, the efficacy of each god was defined so that people would visit shrines whose gods seemed to answer their specific prayers. Shrines began to recruit gods with certain efficacies from other shrines. By a process called *bunshi*, a god's spirit could be split to live in a new shrine as well as in the original shrine. In this way, popular gods were invited into many shrines and shared by more people. By way of example, the Inari god, originally living in Fushimi Inari Shrine, had the purported power to bring agricultural harvest and business success. This was a popular god, and his spirit was split into as many as 32,000 bunshi shrines that still exist today. This is an example of the arbitrary way Shinto gods are viewed.

Corruption of Buddhism and Re-evaluation of Shinto

During the 16th century Samurai wars, Catholic missionaries such as Francisco Xavier arrived and evangelized Japan. Amazingly, many Japanese received the good news of salvation through Christ, and as many as 1,000,000 people, including samurai lords and common people, converted to Christianity. But by the end of the century, Christianity was banned by Hideyoshi Toyotomi, the top Samurai who had become the ruler of the country. Severe persecution against Christians started. Shogun Ieyasu Tokugawa overturned Toyotomi and ended the long age of Samurai wars by establishing the Tokugawa Administration as the unified governing power in the Edo period (1603–1868). But the Tokugawa Administration also enforced anti-Christian policy.

As part of its thrust against Christianity, the Tokugawa Administration utilized the Buddhist temples as monitoring offices to ensure that people did not practice Christianity. They initiated a system called "Temple Binding" (*Tera-uke*), which mandated that every person had to belong to a Buddhist temple. Without a registration document from the temple, a person could not do any business, could not travel to other towns, and could not get married or conduct funeral services. This system led to corruption and secularization of many Buddhist temples and monks because they all too easily procured for themselves much capital and labor from the indigenous populace bound for the temple. The oppressed people were unhappy, but they had no choice.

Over the span of 250 years in the Edo period, peace was maintained within Japan enabling art and literature to flourish. Scholars again studied *Kojiki* and *Nihon Shoki* and were reawakened to the significance of these Japanese classics. They established a new field of study called *Kokugaku*, meaning "national studies." *Kojiki* and *Nihon Shoki* provided not merely information on the early history of the nation but also the reminder that the original Shinto was the vital religion and true identity of Japan. The inevitable conclusion was that the Japanese people should go back to original Shinto. This brought about the rejection of Buddhism-influenced Shinto as secular and the removal of Buddhist influences to restore the nation's original religion.

This movement to restore Shinto by the Kokugaku scholars provided the philosophical base for the revolutionists who overturned the Tokugawa Administration, ending the Edo period. The new Meiji government elevated the emperor, believed to be the true descendant of Japan's gods, as the ruler of the country, established a policy of "Separation of Shinto and Buddhism," and tried to restart the Shinto rituals at the national level as in the Ritsuryo system of the eighth century. Thus began the National Shinto system, under which all Japanese citizens were viewed as servants or children of the emperor, a living god.

Emperor Meiji ordered construction of the predecessor of the Yasukuni Shrine in Tokyo to enshrine the war dead from the civil battles that occurred during the transition from Edo to Meiji. Since then, Yasukuni enshrines all Japanese who die in any war for the country.

View of Divine Nation and "Kamikaze" in War Times

In Shinto, there is always the concept of Japan being the gods' country or "divine nation," protected by its guardian gods. This concept emerges whenever Japan engages in battle with foreign countries.

The mention of a "divine nation" first appears in *Nihon Shoki* with respect to an incident as early as the third century. When Empress Jingu sent troops to rule over three kingdoms of Korea, one of the kings surrendered without a fight, saying, "They are divine troops from a divine nation, sent by a holy king of the East; therefore we are better off not to resist." This quote of a Korean king may not be authentic, as it was probably written to glorify the emperors of Japan, yet it verifies that there was already the concept of Japan as a divine nation from the early days.

Another incident worth mentioning is that of a Mongolian invasion in the late 13th century. The Mongol Empire, which extended its power over China and Korea, tried to approach Japan twice. However, with the help of strong *Kamikaze*, which translated means "divine wind," Japan was able to chase off the outnumbering Mongolian troops from the coastline both times. At this point in history, the myth developed that Japan could not be invaded because the guardian gods of Shinto protected its islands.

When the samurai age ended and the modern nation started in the mid-19th century, the National Shinto provided the image of the new Japan as being the divine nation since antiquity. Eager to catch up with technologies and military powers of Western countries, the Meiji government utilized Shinto to unite Japanese citizens by ordering them to pay respects to the guardian gods of Japan and their descendants, namely the emperor and the imperial family.

After winning the wars with China in 1895 and with Russia in 1905, Japan was recognized internationally and became confident enough to enlarge its territories over Asian countries to create "Greater East Asia Co-Prosperity Sphere." The Shinto view enabled Japanese military officers to rationalize it as Japan, the divine nation, being given the authority to free and protect Asian countries from control by Western nations.

In 1910, Japan annexed Korea. In 1932, Japan assisted in establishing the independent Manchukuo nation from China. Believing that America was trying to stunt Japan's advancement, Japan eventually entered the war with America by attacking Pearl Harbor in 1941. When the war situation worsened, the Japanese government put enormous emphasis upon the idea of the divine nation under the emperor, the living god, to prevent any resistance from its citizens. This emphasis also served to motivate soldiers that it was an honor to die for the living god. Thus were born the famous Kamikaze (divine wind) pilots, who gave their lives in suicide attacks on American war ships. Even ordinary citizens were commanded not to surrender but to die for the nation and the emperor. Tragic suicidal death took its greatest toll in victims among the citizens of the Okinawa Islands, with many women and children included.

Post WWII Shinto

When World War II drew to a close, the Allied Powers sent General Douglas MacArthur and his team to occupy and restructure Japan. They spared the lives of the emperor and the imperial family since they were merely used by the government and the military, but they made the emperor declare himself to be an ordinary man and not a god. Today the emperor of Japan is a figurehead and cannot be engaged in political issues. However, he still performs the Shinto rituals as the head of the country, according to traditions of the imperial courts. Even the head of the Cabinet (i.e., the prime minister), the head of the Congress, and the head of the Supreme Court attend some of the major rituals performed by the emperor. It is not discussed openly in public, but there still exists the problem of separation of religion (Shinto) and government in Japan.

The National Shinto was disassembled right after the war, and all Shinto shrines became private religious corporations according to the new constitutional policy of the separation of religion and government. Yasukuni Shrine also became a private corporation, though it still embodies the notion of a national reposing monument. As mentioned in the story at the beginning of this article, the problem of politicians visiting Yasukuni exists because now it is a private Shinto shrine.

For most Japanese people, the long history of religious syncretization deeply affects their religious positions. Shinto and Buddhism — both cultivated in Japan for many centuries — are regarded as a tradition and culture. Affiliations with Shinto shrines or Buddhist temples are just the remains of the Uji-gami community or Temple Binding system from the previous eras. A person can be counted in both Shinto and Buddhist populations, but it does not mean that the person has an active personal faith in these religions. Therefore, when asked about his or her faith, many Japanese would find that question difficult to answer.

Comparison between Shinto and Christianity

It is easily recognized that Shinto is quite different from Christianity. The following summarizes the views of Shinto and Christianity with respect to some fundamental doctrines.

Table 2: Comparison of Shinto and Christianity

	Shinto	Christianity
View on God	Polytheism (Innumerable gods)	Monotheism (Triune God)
Character of God	Not omnipotent Gods can die Good and bad	Omnipotent God lives forever Good all the time

Sacred Text	None *Kojiki* and *Nihon Shoki* are used as the source for Shinto mythology	The Bible
Target	Japanese only	All mankind
Human nature at birth	Neither good nor bad	All men inherit the original sin committed by Adam
Sin	Can be cleansed by a ritual called *Misogi*, washing with water	Cleansed by animal sacrifice in Old Testament pointing to Jesus' final atoning blood in the New Testament
Salvation	Not discussed	Through faith in Jesus Christ
Life after death	Existence of the underworld where all the dead go is mentioned.	The saved go to heaven, and the unsaved go to hell.
Judgment	Not discussed	All mankind must face God in judgment
Moral Value	Not explicitly stated General respect toward nature and life is suggested	Laws and commandments in Old and New Testaments
Believer's priority	Man-centered worship of gods in order to receive safety, success, health, and prosperity	God-centered worship because of love toward God

Unlike Christianity, Shinto does not claim to be the only truth nor the only way to heaven. Therefore, arbitrariness and inconsistencies inherent in Shinto are not considered to be of great significance.

- Shinto mythology is not to be taken literally; even Shinto priests would say it's a folk tale.

- Shinto gods act like humans — imperfect and quite emotional. They demand being enshrined and respected by making people fear a curse.

- Many Shinto practices are merely customs and traditions for the Japanese, but most Japanese don't know how such practices originated and why they do what they do.

- Shinto is superficial. Sin and uncleanness are easily relieved by performing some outward rituals, without any inward repentance. Success and prosperity are ensured by purchasing *ofuda* (paper with a god's name on it) or *omamori* (good luck charms) at shrines.

For people accustomed to monotheism, Shinto probably appears to be naïve or unsophisticated, yet this religion is what has been fostered in Japan for nearly two millennia. Most Japanese would not care how illogical or inconsistent Shinto is; they respect it out of a deeply ingrained sense of tradition and ethnic identity.

Further Discussion

Early Christian Influences on Shinto

From the basic facts (as shown in the chart above) and histories, Shinto looks quite different from Christianity. Interestingly, though, influences from Christianity are still evident. This is due to the unofficial but probable historical accounts detailing how early Christians from the school of Assyrian Churches of the East had come to Japan between the second and seventh centuries with teachings from the Bible, which then became syncretized with Shinto mythology and practices.

According to "official" history, Christianity was first brought to Japan in 1549 by a Jesuit missionary, Francisco Xavier, from Europe. Although many believers came to faith during this time, under the fierce persecution in the Edo Period from the 17th to mid-19th century, only a few survived. In 1873, the Meiji government once again permitted the practice of Christianity, making way for the arrival of Protestant missionaries from the United States and Europe. In both cases, these missionaries had come from the Western countries. Thus, in the minds of many Japanese today, Christianity is still viewed as Western religion, and this view continues to serve as a chief alienating factor.

In studying the "unofficial" historical accounts (preceding 1549), researchers have found that missionaries could have arrived from Eastern countries as early as the second to third centuries with the emigration of a group of Christians of the clan of Hata (秦) from the ancient country of Yutsuki in central Asia. There is little information on Yutsuki, but the country is believed to be a small Christian nation evangelized by missionaries from Assyrian Churches of the East.

Shinsen Shoujiroku, compiled in A.D. 816, records that the prince of Yutsuki and his people arrived in Japan and became naturalized either in the 8th year of Emperor Chuai (A.D. 199) or in the 14th year of Emperor Oujin (A.D. 283). The clan of Hata had a reputation for excelling in the production of silk. If the clan of Hata brought not only the advanced technologies and skills available in Assyria and Persia but also the biblical cultures and teachings that had spread to those nations, then some traces should be seen mixed in and syncretized with the original culture of Japan. Vestiges of Christianity should be detected in the account of mankind's origins and in various objects and rituals of Shinto.

First, let us look at the origins account in Shinto and see if there are some influences of the Bible present.

Origins Account in Shinto

As mentioned previously, Shinto's mythology is recorded in two ancient texts, *Kojiki* and *Nihon Shoki*, compiled in the early 8th century. The following is a summary of the relevant origins stories of Shinto.

- The beginning of the heaven and the earth
    - *Kojiki* describes that in the beginning, when the heaven and the earth were separated, there were three gods, Amenominakanushi (天之御中主神, the central master in heaven), Takamimusuhi (高御産巣日神, high creator god), and Kamumusuhi (神産巣日神, divine creator god) in *Takamanohara*, the heaven.
    - When the earth was without a form, "like oil in water and floated like jellyfish," two gods sprang up like reeds.
    - Then the names of two gods and five pairs of gods are listed and are known as seven generations of gods, *Kamiyonanayo*. The last pair on the list are Izanagi (man deity) and Izanami (woman deity), who would create the islands of Japan.

• Creation of islands of Japan by Izanagi and Izanami

  * Other heavenly gods ordered Izanagi and Izanami to make something firm out of the formless earth. The two gods stood on the bridge between heaven and earth, and pierced a halberd-like long spike into the earth and stirred it. When they took the spike out, salty water dripped and crystalized into a small island. The two gods went down to the island, mated, and produced the islands that compose Japan.

• Izanagi and Izanami bearing various gods, death of Izanami

  * After bearing the Japanese islands, Izanagi and Izanami bore the many gods who reside in nature (ocean, river, mountains, etc.), in housing, and in many other objects. Finally Izanami bore a god of fire, but she was burnt by the fire and died. When she died, she went to the underworld, a place like hades.

  * Saddened at losing his wife, Izanagi visited Izanami in the underworld, but her body was already decomposing. Izanagi grew terrified and ran away. Upset by his escape, Izanami cursed the living world to kill 1,000 people a day. But Izanagi blessed the world by bringing 1,500 births a day to counteract it.

• Purification bathing of Izanagi and the birth of three noble gods

  * Coming back from the underworld, Izanagi performed purification bathing, called *misogi*, in the ocean. Out of his clothing, gods were born, and through his bathing, more gods were born. Finally, as Izanagi washed his eyes and nose, three noble gods were born: Amaterasu (goddess of the sun, in charge of the heavens), Tsukuyomi (god of the moon, in charge of the night), and Susano-o (god of the storm, in charge of oceans).

• Amaterasu's hideaway in a cave

  * Susano-o was a rough god, causing much harm in both the heavens and on the earth. This disturbed Amaterasu greatly, and she decided to hide away in a cave and shut the door. Darkness filled heaven and earth, and evil prevailed. The gods in heaven conferred with one another and decided to throw a

big noisy party in front of the cave to interest her. Eventually she got curious and opened the door slightly. A powerful god pulled her out of the cave, thus returning light to the world.

- Ninigi as the ruler of Japan

  * Ookuninushi, the descendant of Susano-o, rose up as the first ruler of Japan since its creation. Watching it from above, Amaterasu decided her son should be the ruler instead. So she sent several messengers to Ookuninushi, and eventually he agreed to hand over the position without much ado. Ninigi, the grandson of Amaterasu, descended from heaven along with some attendant gods and three sacred treasures to assume the throne. Ninigi became the first heavenly approved ruler of Japan.

  * The great-grandson of Ninigi, Iwarebiko, known as Emperor Jinmu, was the first emperor of Japan. Thus, the present imperial family is viewed as the direct descendant of Ninigi and Amaterasu.

It is logical to acknowledge these accounts as nothing but myth, yet mythological stories may contain traces or evidences of real incidents or of borrowed stories from other folklore or religions. Some researchers say that the concept of "the beginning of the heaven and the earth" is not originally in Shinto mythology and is most likely included because of early Christians introducing the Genesis account. It is also possible that a clan of people brought this history to Japan with them after the scattering at the Tower of Babel. It merely became corrupted and mythologized as history proceeded. Consider that the first three gods that were present from the beginning of creation seem also to have their origins in the triune God of the Bible.

Early Eastern missionaries could easily account for other corruptions or even information emanating from Solomon's day where people came from around the world to hear Solomon's wisdom. For example, the story of Amaterasu's hideaway in a cave could be related to Joshua's long day in Joshua, chapter 10, in the Bible. If the sun stood still in the middle of the sky for a day in Israel, allowing Joshua's troops to overtake the Amorites, a night would have fallen for the same amount of time in Japan, which is on the other side of the globe. It must have been frightening in Japan not to see the sun rise for a whole day, and this may have led to the folklore that the sun goddess had hidden away in a cave.

Similarities in Objects and Rituals

There are some objects and rituals that bear resemblance to Christianity. This resemblance cannot be used as conclusive proof of the Bible's influence on Japan's indigenous religion, but the observations are fascinating and might encourage one to do further research.

Mikoshi vs. the Ark of Covenant

Mikoshi is a temporal housing for gods, used during ceremonies or festivals to move gods from one place to another. It is a gold-covered wooden box supported by two wooden carrying bars. An ornate golden phoenix stands on top of the housing.

Mikoshi
(By 663highland, Wikipedia Creative Commons)

The general appearance of Mikoshi resembles the ark of the covenant in the Bible. The golden phoenix, a fictional bird with its wings spread out on top of the box, reminds us of cherubim with their outspread wings on top of the ark. Both are carried on poles by men in a similar way.

Shrine Structure vs. Tabernacle/Temple Structure

In early Shinto there was no shrine structure. Yorishiro alone or simple altars in front of it were the places of worship. However, by the fourth century, shrine buildings were constructed. The layout of a shrine precinct is similar to that of the biblical tabernacle or temple with the holy of holies.

Tori-i vs. Passover Gate

At the entrance to the shrine area, or precinct, there is a gate called Tori-i, which is composed of two columns and a beam across the top. The purpose of the gate is to separate the secular world and the sacred place. Today unpainted Tori-i are quite common, but many are painted red, bringing to mind the doors of the Israelites' homes on the day of Passover, where the blood of the lamb was applied to the top and sides of the doorframes.

A tori-i at the entrance of Yasaka Shrine in Kyoto
(I, KENPEI, Wikimedia Commons)

Purification Rituals: Misogi and Harae

Shinto holds to the concept of ritual uncleanness, brought upon one's person when touching dead bodies, etc. Shinto values purification before facing gods; therefore, there are cleansing rituals known as *misogi* and *harae*.

Misogi is ritual bathing. A person goes into water to wash off the ritual uncleanness and sins — similar to Jewish customs.

Harae is a ritual whereby a Shinto priest shakes *onusa*, a wooden staff with a bundle of zigzag-shaped white papers, over an unclean person or thing. The uncleanness is taken away from the person or thing and gets attached to the onusa or a doll used for the purpose. This could be related to the custom of Azazel, the scapegoat of Israel, upon which the nation's sins were placed, as well as the ritual cleansings performed by Israelite priests.

Assyrian Churches of the East and Keikyo, the Luminous Religion

It is worth mentioning that Christianity is not just a Western religion but should also be considered an Eastern religion. Acknowledging the work of the churches of the East is imperative because Japanese people would note the geographical proximity and would be more open to Christianity if its history in the East would be emphasized to a greater degree.

Assyrian Churches of the East, which had headquarters in Edessa (Urfa in modern Turkey), exerted great influence in the evangelization of Asian countries such as Persia, India, and China. Thomas, one of the 12 disciples of Jesus, was known to have gone to Assyria to build churches before going farther eastward to Persia and India. Also, there were Assyrian witnesses at Pentecost in Acts 2, who in all likelihood went home with the good news of salvation through Christ and probably helped establish churches with Thomas.

The Assyrian Church is also known as the Nestorian Church. It was rejected as heretical by the Roman Catholic Church in 431 because Nestorius denied Catholicism's veneration of Mary as the "Mother of God." From the biblical point of view, of course, Nestorius' teaching was not heresy. But the unfortunate labeling of the Nestorian Church as heretical resulted in Western Christian schools' lack of appreciation for the great work and history of Assyrian Churches.

Assyrian missionaries officially visited the Chinese emperor in A.D. 635. They were called the "Luminous Religion" (*Keikyo*, 景教 in Japanese) and were allowed to publicly teach the Bible. They built Keikyo temples in Chang'an, the capital of China at that time.

When the famous Japanese monks Kuukai and Saicho visited Chang'an to study Buddhism in the seventh century, they probably encountered Keikyo missionaries and learned some biblical concepts. They probably did not distinguish between Buddhist and Christian ideas, thus bringing back to Japan a conglomeration of Buddhism, Keikyo, and other religions and philosophies. This is probably why Buddhism in Japan is somewhat different from the Buddhism in other countries. And of course this mixture also affects Shinto.

Assyrian missionaries probably reached Japan well before the 16th-century time frame of Francisco Xavier, though this is not recorded officially. It's possible that the history was rewritten to hide Christian influences, or the teachings were simply taken as a style of Buddhism and all got syncretized. It would be interesting and eye opening if researchers studied this matter further.

Analysis of the Japanese Mindset

It is important to know that Shinto still exerts a profound effect on the unique worldview that runs deep within the hearts and minds of the Japanese populace. To sum up, there are three main characteristics found in the typical Japanese mindset influenced by Shinto:

- *Superstitious:* Today's Japanese people are fond of horoscopes and other fortune telling means in their daily lives. They buy good luck charms (*omamori*) from shrines. Some even like to visit "power spots" where they hope to get healings and energies from spirits or gods. Japanese people like to "feel" rather than "think logically" in spiritual matters.

- *Tolerant:* Throughout the ages, Shinto was able to accept Buddhism and other ideas, and it allowed syncretization to maintain the co-existence of various religions within the nation. Therefore, the Japanese are good at tolerating and respecting assorted religions and views. It is difficult for the Japanese to sympathize with religious conflicts that involve violence, such as that which occurs in the Middle East.

- *Very little interest in an afterlife:* Shinto deals with this life. People go to shrines to pray for safety and prosperity in the here and now. The general picture of life after death is that every dead person becomes a spirit and then watches over the living in the air or from the sky (heaven). There is no concept of judgment, so no ultimate motivation for living a moral life pleasing to God.

To ponder the mindset of the 21st-century Japanese is truly a fascinating, compelling study in contrasts. As mentioned in the opening paragraph of this chapter, builders of a 1.4 billion dollar skyscraper project in modern Tokyo avoid moving one small samurai grave because they are afraid a curse may fall on their new buildings. This kind of news and stories are not uncommon in today's modern Japanese societies, as it has deep roots in a centuries-old thinking process that has been fostered through Shinto, Japan's indigenous religion. Therefore, it is especially meaningful and helpful for Christians who are evangelizing the Japanese to know and understand this background.

Good News for the Japanese

The Japanese people are, in a sense, quite devout — seen in the fact that they are capable of respecting not only Shinto gods and Buddha but also other gods that are highly valued. Sadly, the one eternal God is not known by most Japanese. This eternal One is the only absolute and omnipotent God, the Creator of the world.

Because this Creator God is completely different in power and authority from other gods, the word "God" with upper case "G" is used to distinguish

Him, in English, from the many other so-called "gods" with lower case "g" who are not absolute and omnipotent.

> In the beginning God created the heavens and the earth (Genesis 1:1).[4]

The Bible testifies that this God alone created the physical universe. Therefore, He is more powerful than the universe itself. God created the earth as the perfect environment for mankind and for all His creatures as well — the birds of the air, the fish in the sea, and the animals on the ground. When mankind sinned against God, God's Curse fell upon the earth. This God who created our earth with such intricacy and beauty is without a doubt the Almighty One of incomparable intellect, possessing the highest, ultimate artistic sense.

Today, however, we are taught the religious ideas of evolution (which is now being syncretized into Japanese culture as well). Especially in Japan, school textbooks and television proclaim that everything came into existence through the natural process of evolution and that it is proven by "science." Most Japanese think "science" is the way to the truth and would be surprised that there are people who "still" believe in the biblical creation view. They consider the Bible's description of there being one God who created everything an old-fashioned religious myth. Also, the biblical creation idea is seen as coming from Western cultures, thus the Japanese do not generally respect it or feel responsible to study it.

Most Japanese are not exposed to learning that evolution is not supported by "observable science" and is merely an idea that actually contradicts many observations and laws of nature. They have no opportunity to learn that "observable science" better supports the biblical creation view. When properly confronted with scientific facts supporting creation by the Intelligent Designer, people can start to see how illogical and unreasonable it is for evolution to bring this intricate world into existence.[5] If evolution is not the truth, then considering the Creator God and the biblical account should be taken more seriously by everyone — including the Japanese.

According to the Bible, God created the entire universe. He created the earth and filled it with plants and animals and then, finally, created the

---

4. Scripture in this chapter is from the New American Standard Bible (NASB).
5. The entire discussion of creation and evolution can be studied through the website and publications of Answers in Genesis (answersingenesis.org), so it is not discussed here.

first man and woman with special care. All men and women, regardless of their ethnic or religious identities, are the descendants of the first man and woman God created — Japanese included.

Not only is there one true Creator of all races, but the Creator is also the Savior of the world. Shinto does not explain the afterlife or what happens to a person after death, but that does not spare a person from the ultimate judgment. The Creator God, who loves His creatures deeply, made a sacrifice and prepared a way for any person to be saved, if he or she repents and places faith in Him.

The Bible tells us mankind was created in God's image; thus, they have a moral will. But the first man and woman freely chose not to obey God but to do their own thing. This sin unleashed upon mankind unspeakable suffering and death — death not only of the body but also of spiritual separation from the Creator Himself. This sinful state also includes the certainty of facing God in the final judgment and eternal punishment in the afterlife.

> For the wages of sin is death, but the free gift of God is eternal life in Christ Jesus our Lord (Romans 6:23).

The Bible proclaims that Jesus Christ is the Creator God: "For by Him all things were created. . . . He is before all things, and in Him all things hold together" (Colossians 1:16–17). As the King of the universe, He has infinite power and authority. Yet, in His infinite love, He humbled Himself and became a man to provide a way to save people from eternal suffering. Jesus took the sins of mankind upon Himself, endured suffering and death on the Cross, and endured from the wrath of God the Father on behalf of His people. His death paid the penalty for their sin. Jesus was resurrected from the dead with a glorified body on the third day and now sits enthroned in heaven. The good news is that anyone who turns from their sin and trusts Jesus as his personal Savior can have his own sins forgiven as a free gift from God. Along with this forgiveness comes wonderful, beautiful eternal life.

I sincerely wish for these Japanese to come to know their true identity and accept their true Creator and Savior. They would be free from fearing curses of Shinto gods or spirits. They would truly be "children of God" and be a member of the true divine nation, the eternal kingdom of God, mentioned in the Bible. How much better to live for the true God than for whimsical Shinto gods!

As maintained throughout this chapter, Shinto is mythology deeply entwined with Japanese national history and ethnic identity. For those who wish to share the gospel with the Japanese, it is important to understand how their mindset is influenced by these Shinto roots and approach them carefully. Logic would demand that the sincere Japanese seeker of truth would serve himself best by turning to the One who knows him best, his omnipotent Creator and Savior, Jesus Christ. May the Japanese people open up their hearts to know the One who said, "I am the way, and the truth, and the life" (John 14:6).

Summary of Shinto Beliefs

Doctrine	Teachings of Shinto
God	Deny the God of the Bible, but worship many local gods and ancestors
Authority/ Revelation	*Kojiki* and *Nihon Shoki* are used as the source for Shinto mythology
Man	Men are neither good nor bad
Sin	Sin can be cleansed by a ritual called *Misogi*, a washing with water
Salvation	Existence of the underworld where all the dead go is mentioned, but there is no concept of judgment
Creation	Several gods were involved in the creation of the earth and the land

Dedication

This chapter is dedicated to my daughter, Rieko. May she find the Savior Lord in her life even while she grows up in the Shinto culture of Japan.

Acknowledgments

My beloved husband, Souta, who always stands beside me, encourages me, and honors the Lord. Mrs. Pat Kovacs, my dear sister and mentor in the Lord, who took much time to read and check my English thoroughly.

Chapter 19

Buddhism

Dr. Thane Hutcherson Ury

Some say if you compare the Sermon on the Mount, Buddha's *Dhammapada*, Lao-tzu's Tao-te-ching, Confucius' *Analects*, the Bhagavad *Gita*, the Proverbs of Solomon, and the *Dialogues* of Plato, you will find it: a real, profound, and strong agreement. Yes, but this is ethics, not religion. . . . Ethics may be the first step in religion but it is not the last. As C.S. Lewis says, "The road to the Promised Land runs past Mount Sinai." — Peter Kreeft[1]

About six centuries before Jesus walked the earth, a young Hindu prince is said to have escaped the trappings of materialism and found the path to enlightenment. Now known as the Buddha — *the enlightened one* — he left behind a formula to help others trace the same nirvanic path. These teachings have been distilled in the belief system known as Buddhism, a humanistic and essentially monistic religion.[2] As one of history's oldest surviving global religions,[3] it is one of today's fastest growing faiths, and currently boasts almost

---

1. Peter Kreeft, "The Uniqueness of Christianity," http://www.peterkreeft.com/topics-more/ christianity-uniqueness.htm.
2. Some Buddhistic strains have animistic, deistic, and/or polytheistic elements.
3. Unlike other religions, Buddhism has no deity, resembling more of an ethical school. But in the centuries following Gautama Buddha's death, various devotees have revered him as a godlike figure.

half a billion adherents worldwide. This makes it one of the largest blocks of people groups unreached with the gospel.

In countries like Thailand, Tibet, Bhutan, Cambodia, Laos, Myanmar, and Sri Lanka, over 60 percent of the populace could be described as "folk Buddhists." Thailand is 95 percent Buddhist, with Myanmar and Cambodia about 90 percent. But Buddhism is not just for the Far East anymore, as the United States has become a prime mission field for Buddhism, gradually achieving mainstream acceptance. "Probably the most attractive of all the non-Christian religions to the Western mind,"[4] notes J.N.D. Anderson, America now has two million homegrown Buddhists. Though it took millennia for Buddhism to be established in Asia, it has taken deep root in Western countries in a fraction of that time — perhaps due to compatibility with the naturalistic evolutionary worldview that now permeates the Western World.

Historical Overview

If Gautama Buddha or his earliest disciples ever wrote down his teachings, such has perished, meaning no one has been able to claim with high confidence exactly what he taught. In fact, written records about Siddhartha don't appear until at least four hundred years after his death. Before this we have only scattered Sanskrit accounts and oral tradition. Thus a pale of historical uncertainty has resulted, with Buddhist scholars even conceding that falsehoods have leached into most biographical accounts about the Buddha, not to mention outlandish embellishments. For example, one account says that within seconds of birth, he stood, walked, and scanned in all directions before nobly claiming that he was the foremost being in the world, and that this would be his last rebirth. During his quest for enlightenment he is said to have survived on one grain of rice daily for a few years. The last two years before his "awakening," he completely abstained from food or water.[5]

---

4. J.N.D. Anderson, *Christianity & Comparative Religion* (Downers Grove, IL: InterVarsity Press, 1970), p. 46.

5. When it comes to the *Bibliographical Test*, the Buddhist "Pali Canon" fails miserably. Since we do not have the original manuscripts of any ancient religion, how confident can we be that what we read today is the same as the original writing? Thankfully, scholars have developed ways to assess this very issue. The gold standard in this regard has been to combine the *External Test, Internal Test,* and *Bibliographical Test*. Since copyist errors, copyists' redactions, or embellishments have crept into the copying process over so many centuries, the Bibliographical Test centers on assessing the transmissional fidelity of extant copies. The test focuses particularly on two factors: the number of manuscripts we now have, and the estimated time gap between when the originals were first written and the date when the oldest existing copy was penned. The layperson is generally unaware that (1) these tests

Roughly 2,500 years ago in Kapilavastu at the foothills of the Himala-yas, a young aristocrat named Siddhartha Gautama was born in the lap of luxury. His father carefully insulated his heir from the real world beyond the palace walls, and allegedly gave him three palaces and 40,000 dancing girls.[6] However, Siddhartha inadvertently caught glimpses here and there beyond the royal walls. The following sights in particular gripped Gautama's heart: 1) a crippled man, 2) a leper, 3) a rotting corpse, and 4) a pious ascetic. These later came to be known as the *Four Passing Sights*, which so moved him that he renounced his life of comfort and luxury to pursue enlightenment. This *Great Renunciation*, as Buddhists call it, included Gautama abandoning his wife and child, for "distractions"[7] such as these would impede his quest to untie the Gordian knot of pain, sickness, old age, and death. The driving motivation of Buddhism's founder was to pinpoint the origin of pain and suffering and to propose a solution.[8]

As with many Hindus (the culture and worldview he was born into), Gautama found the standard Indian theodicy[9] for pain and death to be dreadful and deeply unsatisfying. Legend has it that six or seven years after his *Great Renunciation*, his long search paid off. Tranquilly seated in the lotus position under a fig tree (later commemorated as the Bodhi tree[10]), Gautama meditated for a long time.[11] Freed from distractions, he persevered, he was

---

are in the background of everything they read and take for granted in ancient history, and (2) based on these tests alone, the Christian Scriptures' credibility is empirically demon-strated to be eons ahead of all the scriptures of the world. The comparison is really not even remotely close.

6. Some embellish the opulence of Gautama's life so as to magnify the gravamen of his re-nunciation.

7. Siddhartha's son was named *Rahula*, meaning "hindrance" or "chain." In the Dhammapa-da, part of the Buddhist canon, we find this teaching: "Those who love nothing and hate nothing, have no fetters."

8. Sadly, he never encountered the theodicy of Genesis 3, which answers the question of the origin of death and suffering, and points to the need for a Savior who conquers both.

9. Theodicy describes the general understanding of how a good god — usually the biblical God who is all-loving and all-powerful — and evil can exist at the same time. Hinduism denies the actual reality of evil; it is illusion (*maya*). Karmic debt must be paid for our injustices performed in previous lives. Any Buddhist or Mother Theresa–like compassion disrupts the karmic cycle and brings bad karma. Hinduism and Buddhism both agree that we are in a cycle of misery, but disagree on the "entrance and exit ramps" of life's carousel of suffering.

10. Note the similarity of the words *bodhi* and *Buddha*. The first means enlightenment (or wisdom), and the second means enlightened or awakened one.

11. Some sources add that at this time Māra, the demon of sensual desire, threw all his minions and tactics at Gautama. Buddha was tempted to enter nirvana immediately, so the story goes, so he couldn't tell others the way to enlightenment. But Brahma, the Hindu creator god, came and told him to continue on (become a bodhisattva) for the sake of others.

able to recall his previous lives and learn the cycles of birth, death, and rebirth. The rubrics of Buddhist dharma were then revealed to him, and he attained ultimate bliss,[12] becoming the enlightened one — hereafter simply *the* Buddha.

In the wake of attaining *nirvana*, the Buddha began traveling itinerantly with five companions, sharing with them the insights learned under the tree of wisdom. His first teaching was the *Sermon at Benares*, which included *The Four Noble Truths* and *The Eightfold Path*. These two groups of dharma, if followed while navigating *The Middle Way*, will guide imperfect aspirants to escape from the cycle of reincarnation and attain enlightenment.[13] The Buddha did retain some of his former Hinduism, but added nuance to reincarnation and a few other precepts. In fact, he simply hoped to be a force of reform within Hinduism.

An Answer to Suffering: Buddha's Main Quest

Ever since the *Four Passing Sights*, Gautama's *Great Renunciation* was fueled by a hunger to find an answer for the pain and suffering in life. When it came to solving the problem of evil, the Buddha took a very different path from Hinduism. The latter saw evil as *maya* (illusion), while the Buddha taught evil is not only real, but that it can be overcome by methodically removing desire — the source of all suffering.[14] Eliminate this craving and you eliminate suffering. Such gives birth to the stereotypical view Westerners have of monks seated yoga-like and seeking complete detachment from the world. Through discipline and patient determination all passions can be "blown out."

For the last 45 years of his life, the Buddha pointed encumbered seekers toward the way of liberation from the cycle of birth and death. The timing

---

12. As legend has it, at the exact moment of bliss, the moon lit up the heavens, the earth shook, and lotus blossoms rained down from the heavens.

13. Before discovering *The Middle Way* of meditation that paved the path to enlightenment, the Buddha had experienced the extreme opposites of princely abundance and extreme self-mortification, both of which hinder spiritual growth. Thus, striving for a middle ground between too much worldliness (self-indulgence) or too much of asceticism has become a non-negotiable commitment for bona fide Buddhists ever since.

14. The Scriptures tell us that the evil desires and sin nature that permeates us all can be attributed to the Edenic fall. James 1:13–15 clearly teaches that our desire brings forth sin, and sin brings about death, which is the punishment for sin. This explains why Jesus had to suffer and die in our place to make salvation possible. He substituted Himself for us. The Buddhist recognizes that suffering and death is real, but they have no basis for why it exists and how it has been conquered by God. The only way to remove this sin-nature desire is through Christ, not meditation.

In a monastery in NW China, one monk among many trying to follow the precepts of the Buddha.
(Photo: Thane Ury)

could not have been better, as his method came in a period when there was a huge discontent with the drudgery and vagaries of Hinduism. The Buddha's teachings seemed logical, elegant, and appealing — especially with the suffering class — and so his views progressively gained traction. For the next few centuries Buddhism spread widely in East Asia, across China, and over to Japan and Korea. The desire for some viable, but god-free, answer to the problem of pain and suffering, partially explains why many moderns adopt the Buddhist path.

For all the superficial similarities some may propose between classical expressions of both Buddhism and Christianity, when it comes to theodicy any notion of a concord implodes immediately. For most of the time prior to the advent of Charles Lyell's uniformitarianism, traditional Christianity applied a normative reading to the opening chapters of Genesis; i.e., tending toward accepting the creation and Flood narratives at face value. This meant that Christianity's dominant theodicy for its first 18 centuries was that it was the original disobedience of a historical Adam and Eve that ushered in both moral and natural evils. When our *imago dei*, was fractured, perfect communion with God was lost, and all sufferings and relational dysfunctionalities flowed from this breach. E.L. Mascall succinctly explains:

> It was until recent years almost universally held that all the evils, both moral and physical, which afflict this earth are in some way or another derived from the first act by which a bodily creature endowed with reason deliberately set itself against what it knew to be the will of God.[15]

---

15. E.L. Mascall, *Christian Theology and Natural Science: Some Questions and Their Relations* (New York: Ronald Press Company, 1956), p. 32. See also Thane Ury, "Luther, Calvin, and Wesley on the Genesis of Natural Evil: Recovering Lost Rubrics for Defending a Very Good Creation," in *Coming to Grips with Genesis: Biblical Authority and the Age of the Earth,* Terry Mortenson and Thane Ury, eds. (Green Forest, AR: Master Books, 2008), p. 399–423.

It is perhaps not surprising that evolutionary thinking finds greater unity with Buddhism in particular and Eastern thought in general, but exploring this is beyond the scope of this present chapter.

Present-day Buddhism

> Entering Zen is like stepping through Alice's looking glass. One finds oneself in a topsy-turvy wonderland where everything seems quite mad — charmingly mad for the most part, but mad all the same. It is a world of bewildering dialogues, obscure conundrums, stunning paradoxes, flagrant contradictions, and abrupt non sequiturs, all carried off in the most urbane, cheerful, and innocent style imaginable. — Huston Smith[16]

Through two and a half shaky millennia, Buddha's philosophy has not only survived but it has flourished.[17] And although it is the majority or state religion in a dozen countries, it has remained anything but monochromatic in the 21st century. Variant forms and sects abound, with at least 238 distinct ethnolinguistic Buddhist people groups.[18] Theravada (or Hinayana) and Mahayana are the two major sects of Buddhism and are actually quite different from one another.

Theravada Buddhism

Theravada (The Teaching of the Elders), about 38 percent of all Buddhists, has remained the school truest to original Buddhism, and is more conservative. It tends to be more dominant in China, Japan, Korea, Mongolia, Taiwan, and Tibet. It is also called Southern Buddhism and holds that only monks can reach nirvana. This school is deeply monastic, seeing meditation as the main key to "salvation" and quite inwardly focused.

Mahayana Buddhism

Mahayana (The Greater Vehicle) is more popular at 56 percent, and more liberal than Theravada, and dominates in Cambodia, Laos, Myanmar, Sri Lanka, Singapore, and Thailand. It is also called Northern Buddhism, and contends that even the laity can reach enlightenment. Meditation is vital

---

16. Huston Smith, *The Religions of Man* (New York: Harper & Row, 1958), p. 140.
17. Buddhism has survived episodic setbacks, including a resurgence of Hinduism in India, rivalries with Confucianism and Taoism, a backlash in the Tang Dynasty, plus Hun and Islamic invasions.
18. Paul Hattaway, *Peoples of the Buddhist World* (Carlisle, UK: Piquant, 2004), p. xx.

for this school, but puts more emphasis on selflessness and altruism (i.e., helping others in order to help yourself) to attain salvation (in their belief system); and thus is more outwardly focused than Theravada Buddhism. Additionally, about 700 years after Buddha died, this school had a tendency to see him as a divine. They also have many tantric and occult-like practices.

Other Buddhist Sects

The *Vajrayana* school (The Diamond Vehicle, aka Lamaism or Tantra) is a third, much smaller group at 6 percent, and prevalent in Tibet. It would hardly bear mention were it not for its most famous representative, the exiled Dalai Lama. But all factions of Buddhism can be traced back to this triad of the Mahayana, Theravada, and Vajrayana schools. While each has distinctive dogma, all embrace what we will call "mere Buddhism."

Other variants bear brief mention. *Zen Buddhism* is a spinoff of Mahayana Buddhism, concentrated in Japan. Generally, Zen is a non-doctrinaire road to transcendence, is extremely esoteric, and believes enlightenment is attained by chanting rote phrases, names, or texts. It is not preoccupied with logic and is the most philosophical school. Zen is characterized by an emphasis on detachment from one's desires, seeking to attain extinction (*parinirvana*), with the distinct nuance of experiencing *satori* (the sudden awareness of one's absolute Buddha nature, accompanied by inner joy and harmony).

Pure Land Buddhism (aka Amidism) splintered off of the Mahayana school as well. Pure Landers regard the personality Amitabha Buddha as a savior through whose merits one can achieve nirvana. Pure Land targets the layperson. Engaging in something as simple as a mechanistic chanting of "Praise to Amitabha Buddha" (the *nembutsu*) can clear the way to be reborn in the paradise called Pure Land. This is a mythical place "created" by Amitabha where pursuing enlightenment takes less effort.

Last, *Nichiren Buddhists* are very mystical and stress that they represent true Buddhism. This school is enticing because of its emphasis on materialism, basically being an Eastern expression of prosperity theology — a view thoroughly at odds with the Buddha. Devotees follow scriptures like *The Lotus Sutra* and teach that by chanting before the *Gohonzon* (a scroll or box with the names of key religious figures in the *Lotus Sutra*), one can bring his life into balance, achieving health and wealth. This sect is also unique in that it seeks to refute other schools and proselytize.

The above distinctions in the Buddhist family tree are crucial for apologists hoping to penetrate hearts from each offshoot. But with so many schisms — and the blurring within each — classification will remain exceedingly difficult.[19] Try to imagine, for example, being invited to chart the common Christian ground of a Pentecostal in the Appalachians, with those of a Filipino Roman Catholic, or a Nigerian Seventh-day Adventist. Since an equally wide swath exists with Gautama's heritors today, we must join leading missiologists and think more in terms of *Buddhisms* on a vast spectrum. Our evangelistic tack with a saffron-robed Buddhist in Qinghai will be quite different than with the Buddhist in the pew in Ulaanbaatar. Zen Buddhism in Japan and Vajrayana Buddhism in Tibet "feel" similar, but look very different. And a Nepali villager may never have been taught Buddha's *Four Noble Truths*, but if you showed them to her she'd likely say she shares such convictions.

East Is East, and West Is West, and Never the Twain Shall Meet?

Contra Kipling's poem, through Buddhism the twain have met indeed. And in America it is the list of high-profile converts that has given it some major street cred.[20] Sports personalities like Tiger Woods, David Beckham, and Phil Jackson (former NBA coach) have turned their hearts East, as have Jerry Brown (governor of California) and luminaries like the late Steve Jobs and Rosa Parks. While not a convert, Bill Clinton has adopted a vegan diet and hired a Buddhist monk to tutor him on proper meditation technique. And the Dalai Lama, the figurehead of an oppressed people group, is treated like a rock star in America, having been invited to the White House, the UN, and wining and dining with the cultural elite.

Los Angeles has been called the most diverse Buddhist city in the world. Complementing this is a list of Hollywood elites who have embraced Buddhist principles, including Richard Gere,[21] Keanu Reeves,

19. See Christmas Humphreys, *Buddhism: An Introduction and Guide* (London: Penguin Books, 1951), p. 71–73, for a proposed platform of 14 tenets that every Buddhist can embrace.
20. Buddhism first established a beachhead in America via Chinese railroad laborers. By the end of the 19th century, hundreds of "joss houses" had sprung up on the West coast.
21. On the heels of 9/11, Gere was booed off stage at a memorial. Why? For asking for a moment of silence . . . for the terrorists! He was also interviewed by ABC Radio, where he counseled Americans to respond with "the medicine of love and compassion." While it's natural for Americans to identify all those murdered and the massive suffering in the wake of the attacks, Gere asked us to also have compassion for "the terrorists who are creating such horrible future lives for themselves because of the negativity of this karma," http://

Tina Turner, and Harrison Ford.[22] Iconic director George Lucas was very transparent that his agenda for the Star Wars series was to introduce Buddhism to the West.[23] The *Force* symbolizes the impersonal energy of Eastern mysticism.[24]

Authors like Thomas Merton, D.Z. Suzuki, Alan Watts, and popular movies like *Seven Years in Tibet, The Little Buddha*, and *What's Love Got to Do with It?* have all contributed to the romanticizing, allure, and mainstreaming of Buddhist-type thinking. Even TV, movies, and music have

been adopting subtle Buddhist elements, like the TV series *Lost* (think Dharma initiative), *Point Break* (with Bodhi — a lead character) and the band Nirvana.

Buddhism's Allure

A full assessment of the Buddhistic worldview's popularity is beyond the scope of this chapter, but a few suggestions for its appeal can be posited. Becoming disillusioned with one's own religious background, Western culture in general, or the rat race of American society have all contributed to hearts turning East.

In all of God's image bearers is a longing soul, like this woman searching for truth at a Buddhist temple. (Photo: Thane Ury)

abcnews.go.com/Entertainment/story?id=101959&page=1. We address karma below, but consider the worldview between Gere's ears. Those in the Twin Towers were not victims, but somehow deserving of their fate, and any suffering in the aftermath of 9/11 was a rebalance for past offenses. Further, the efforts of the Red Cross and Salvation Army, and any relief effort is to be frowned upon, for such bucks against the law of karma. And the sword cuts both ways, for those who escaped the tragedy must somehow be morally upright.

22. Others in Hollywood tied to Buddhism include Orlando Bloom, Oliver Stone, Angelina Jolie, Brad Pitt, Jennifer Lopez, and Leonardo DiCaprio. Raised a Buddhist, Uma (meaning *Great Middle Way*) Thurman holds herself more Buddhist than not. Her father was the first Westerner ever to be an ordained Tibetan Buddhist monk.

23. Buddhist scholar Alexander Berzin notes that prior to making *Star Wars*, Lucas visited a Tibetan monk named Tsenzhab Serkong Rinpoche, who in fact became the basis for the diminutive Grand Jedi Master known as Yoda. In a 2002 interview with *Time*, Lucas was asked if he held a religion, and responded: "I was raised Methodist. Now let's say I'm spiritual. It's Marin County. We're all Buddhists up here." See, John Baxter, *George Lucas: A Biography* (London: Harper Collins, 1999), p. 165, passim. It is known that Joseph Campbell and Carlos Castaneda also deeply influenced Lucas' thinking.

24. Others claim the series also contains subtle hues of Hinduism, Taoism, and/or Zoroastrianism. In an interview with Bill Moyers, Lucas noted that he included mythical elements from multiple cultures and religions, but it is clear that Buddhism is the core philosophy in the universe of *Star Wars*.

Buddhism's rubrics of tolerance, wisdom, compassion, lovingkindness, nonviolence, and personal transformation have also no doubt enticed spiritually awakened and hungry souls. With so many varieties to choose from, Buddhism has enough flavors to accommodate the palates of any individual, even the raging atheist. Consider further that in our sensate world of chaos, materialism, and the erotic, Buddhism's combo of inner tranquility, enlightenment, and easy-believism are an irresistible escape hatch. Our society has also accepted meditation and yoga as great stress relievers, with little regard that these have become gateway disciplines to a deeper exploration of Gautama's path.[25]

Others are no doubt uncritically enamored by the idea of reincarnation, conditioned perhaps by countless wholesome portrayals in modern films.[26] At a superficial level, some may think reincarnations gives them endless chances to get things right. Hollywood, academia, the media, and the social elites all too often give Buddhism a free pass from critical assessment simply because they love its non-judgmental, non-theistic, and non-violent emphases. In addition to appearing hyper-tolerant, Buddhism offers a guilt-free ethical framework with no external god to whom we are accountable. Such is not too far from the flaccid convictions of liberal Christianity — a view paying lip service to a wrath-free deity, whose ecumenical arc has no room for sin, a Christ on a Cross, the exclusive truth claims of a risen Savior, or any suggestion of a final and lasting judgment.[27]

Does Buddhism Have Its Own Scripture?

Islam has the Qur'an, Christianity has the Bible, but Buddhism has no absolute canonical authority binding on all its splinter groups. That being stated, a key textual authority providing some uniformity for most Buddhists is found in the *Pali Canon* — a collection of writings 11 times larger than the Christian Scriptures! The *Pali Canon* is divided into three parts — each called *pitaka* or "basket" — and thus has come to be known as the Tripitaka.

---

25. Esther Baker, an ex-Buddhist nun, provides a fuller list as to why Buddhism may be so attractive to Westerners in her *Buddhism in the Light of Christ* (Eugene, OR: Resource Publications, 2014), p. 3–4.
26. Films like *Avalon High, Brother Bear, Fluke, Cloud Atlas*, and *Birth* contain reincarnation themes.
27. H. Richard Niebuhr famously conveyed such sentiment in his work *The Kingdom of God in America* (New York: Harper & Row, 1937) p. 193.

Tripitaka, or Pali Canon		
Vinaya Pitaka:	Sutra Pitaka:	Abhidhamma Pitaka:
(Basket of Order)	(Basket of Discourses)	(Basket of Higher Teachings)
Code of monastic discipline for the community of monks	Conventional teachings believed to have come straight from Gautama Buddha or his closest followers	Texts in which the Sutta teachings are arranged to help in the study of the nature of mind and matter

Opinions vary within Buddhism regarding the authority of these writings.

Some claim the whole Pali Canon is binding. Others contend that no "basket" can relay rationally warranted beliefs, so the Buddhist canon carries no binding authority. Additional thinkers hold that the enlightened Gautama provided reliable knowledge through his lectures, but no Buddhist texts are authoritative.[28]

While there is no god in Buddhism, the thoughts and teachings of the Buddha (written centuries after his death) are generally taken as an underlying authority to guide Buddhists. But really, at base, a traditional Buddhist takes *himself* as an authority, as he must work out his own salvation. The Buddhist *ordo salutis* is very self-oriented.[29] Regardless, the authorities listed here are *man*. Man is ultimately seen as the absolute authority on Buddhist teachings. This is actually arbitrary, creating a system that allows all things to be true while nothing is true — a state that cannot logically sustain its own weight.

Last, while Buddha's image is often worshiped by some of his followers around the globe, he never considered himself a god or even a revelation from a god. He never even intended to start a new religion, but originally hoped to be a force for reform within Hinduism.

Two major misconceptions linger in the West. The first is that Buddha is the name of a god. But Buddha is just a title that means "enlightened/ awakened one" or "teacher." Anyone who has grasped the nature of ultimate

---

28. Other writings looked to as authoritative in the Buddhist world include the *Abhidaharma* (philosophical discourse of Buddhist teaching), the *Vinaya* (monastic regulations), and the *Mahavastu, Milindapanha, Saddharma Pundarika*, and *Prajnaparamita Sutras*.
29. In a famous excerpt from the Tripitaka, the Buddha tells a young monk, Ananda, that monks are to be their own lamps and take refuge in nothing outside of themselves.

Many in the West wrongly associate the portly statues of Budai (left) with the founder of Buddhism (right).
(Photo on left: Creative Commons; photo on right: Umanee Thonrat, Shutterstock)

reality or has been enlightened is a Buddha, and thus, in Buddhism, there are many Buddhas. The second erroneous view is thinking that the corpulent, laughing figurine popular in many Chinese restaurants is the Gautama Buddha of history. But this is actually Budai, a tenth-century quirky Chinese Zen monk, who carried a stick with a bag on it. The Buddha fasted regularly and walked thousands of miles, so a chubby Buddha statue is about as plausible as a chubby Jesus.

Foundations and Beliefs

There are several common beliefs that all Buddhists embrace. Front and center are the "Three Jewels" in which all Buddhists find refuge, reassurance, and dignity. They are the *Buddha* (the yellow jewel), the *teachings* (the blue jewel, or *dharma*), and the monastic order (the red jewel, or *sangha*). One can hear these three gems in the following popular mantra that Buddhist monks chant through the day:

> *Buddham Saranam Gachchami* [I take shelter in Buddha]
> *Dhammam Saranam Gachchami* [I take shelter in dharma]
> *Samgham Saranam Gachchami* [I take shelter in community with monks]

Then we have The Four Noble Truths, which essentially retraces Gautama Buddha's own road toward enlightenment. They are as follows:

1) *Dukkha*, or suffering, is inescapable plight of existence
2) *Samudaya* (or craving) causes dukkha, and grates against all reality
3) *Nirodha* (cease) is the key to overcoming dukkha
4) *Marga*, cessation of suffering comes by following The Eightfold Path

This *Eightfold Path* is key to the cessation of suffering and is congruent with one's move toward enlightenment. The eight steps are:

Training in Wisdom (*Prajan*)	**Right views** — believe The Four Noble Truths, rejecting all false views
	Right intention — improper thoughts must be purged
Training in Morality (*Shila*)	**Right speech** — truthful, clear, non-harmful communication
	Right action — live non-exploitatively and properly toward others
	Right livelihood — live simply
Training in Concentration (*Samadhi*)	**Right effort** — work toward detachment from the world
	Right mind — understand the nature of oneself and reality
	Right meditation — dispel all distractions, total focus on enlightenment

One cannot help but ask who defines "right." If it is just a man, like a monk, Buddha, or anyone else, why presume that they have all knowledge to know the true nature of reality? To know absolute right, one must have absolute knowledge, which no man has. The only one in a position of knowing absolute right (and absolute wrong) is an all-knowing God, not a man. Yet Buddhism has no all-knowing God nor a revelation to man. When men merely have the opinion that something is right or wrong, then it is merely an opinion, a form of arbitrariness.

Several Buddhist tenets are familiar, at least in name, to non-Buddhists in the West. These include karma, reincarnation, the transmigration of the soul, nirvana, and dependent organization.

- Good or bad *karma* dictates everything. Depending on the virtue or depravity of one's actions in prior lives, such determines how one will be manifested in the next life. You literally will sow what you reap. What we are now is a direct effect of actions from a previous incarnation, which in turn are based on the previous lives *ad infinitum*. While Hindus held that one can't break free from this cycle, Buddha iconoclastically claimed not only that one could break free, but also that this escape was available to all castes.

- In the Buddhist view, *reincarnation* normally refers to the endless cycle of birth, life, death, rebirth, and redeath that all must experience on their journey toward enlightenment. The Buddha denied that individual souls come back in other forms, so Buddhism typically rejects the theory of a transmigrating permanent soul.[30]

- *Transmigration of the soul* refers to the passage of the soul from one body to the next in successive incarnations. In Buddhism one doesn't die, but just keeps coming back again and again until enlightenment is achieved. The Mahayana sect embraces the concept of an individual soul, so rebirth is also seen as transmigration. In contrast, however, the Theravada school rejects the idea of the transmigration of the soul (i.e., self, person, or enduring mind) from a prior life.[31]

- *Nirvana* has different nuances among Buddhists, but there is agreement that at nirvana the fires of greed, hatred, ignorance, delusion, and attachment are snuffed out. For some, nirvana denotes a state of absolute bliss, while for others it is the ultimate

30. Recalling how many varying schools of Buddhism there are, we can expect that there will not be uniformity in how terms are understood across "denominational lines." Some sidestep the issue, by claiming differences between reincarnation and transmigration are mere semantics, and thus the terms can be used interchangeably. While that practice is generally acceptable, we must try here to capture some of the subtle differences. Metempsychosis and palingenesis are other terms used with varying nuances in discussing different schools of thought on "rebirth."

31. A few other suggested differences between reincarnation and transmigration deserve mention. Some see reincarnation as rebirth in human form, whereas transmigration refers to a rebirth into a non-human form. Many reincarnationalists (mostly in the West) resist the idea that a human soul can be "rehoused" in anything other than a human being; but transmigrationalists (so we're told) believe that a human can be re-embodied as a wombat, fruit bat, or meerkat. Some say that reincarnation refers to each instance of being reborn, whereas transmigration refers to the whole process. As we can see, there's no boilerplate for either of these categories in today's Buddhism.

liberation where the soul — like a candle's flame — is completely extinguished.[32]

- *Dependent Organization* is the Buddhist metaphysical idea that all things arise together as an interdependent whole. Given our ever-changing, impermanent, essenceless cosmos, this arbitrary "law" accounts for the order and consistency we "observe."[33]

View on Origins

As noted above under the umbrella of Buddhism, while the Theravada, Mahayana, and Vajrayana strands share common ground, they also have doctrinal convictions that totally clash with each other. This holds true for a Buddhist perspective on origins, which is anything but lock step. Yet even allowing for variations, a few precepts remain uniform across their spectrum. Since Buddhism holds that there is no god, no schools can accommodate a supreme creator.

Given Gautama Buddha's opposition to key features of India's Brahmanism, its not surprising that he never was even remotely concerned with accounting for the order in our world[34] or any notion of a first cause. For us to be concerned with the origins of the cosmos (or other "unconjecturables") is a distraction, as Buddha attempted to demonstrate in his famous parable of the poisoned arrow. Picture a man, he asks, shot with a poison arrow. He could alleviate his suffering by simply removing the arrow. But would it not be odd if the wounded refused to have the arrow removed until a number of queries were answered first, questions like the archer's identity, details of the bowperson's family tree, and plotting the arrow's trajectory, aerodynamic integrity, color, weight, composite material, and whether this was volitional or accidental (a hunter's arrow intended for small game?), etc. Buddha's point was that just as suffering would not be alleviated in the least by such conjectures, neither will cosmological contemplations do anything to address our current sufferings. Since the Buddha's main goal was

---

32. The root meaning of the word *nirvana* literally means "to blow out," as in a candle being extinguished.
33. We clearly hear echoes of Heraclitus here, the pre-Socratic who — about the same time as the Buddha — invoked the *ad hoc* doctrine of *logos* as an "ordering principle" for a reality that he also claimed was impermanent and in continual flux.
34. In the *Pali Aggañña Sutta*, Buddha parodies Brahmin views, instead of offering a model of origins.

the elimination of suffering (pulling out the poison arrow), speculations on the origins of the cosmos are relegated to the dustbin of uselessness.[35]

> Some people prefer to call Buddhism a way of life and thought. In Asia, "Buddhism" is often [seen] as an alien term, because to them it merely refers to reality. Because the Buddha wouldn't deal with certain questions basic to metaphysics, there are reasons why his path isn't considered a philosophy. Likewise, because he never resolved questions about God or gods or an afterlife, his teachings aren't precisely a religion. And since it teaches that self is an illusory construct, it can be tricky to categorize it exactly as a psychology. — Gary Gach[36]

Since the Buddha is not known to have ever speculated on human origins, it is warranted to infer that he didn't see such as basic to proper spirituality. This is not surprising because his opinion was that most theological issues were unedifying and unworthy of reflection. Paradoxically enough, for one whose majority platform was built on illusion, it is ironic that the idea of discussing origins involved too much metaphysical speculation for the Buddha.

Thus, on the Buddhist view there is no other option except to believe the universe arose through random and impersonal natural laws. Further, the Buddhist quest to raise cosmic consciousness has even been called *spiritual evolution*, a mantle the New Age movement has been all too happy to pick up.

We generally find crude evolution-like (Chain of Being) underpinnings in all major Asian worldviews. This is true of Confucianism, Taoism, and

---

35. This is clearly a gratuitous and false analogy, for in the real world if a homicidal archer shot arrows one's way, only an irrational person would behave in the manner implied by the parable; i.e., focus on the arrow only. In the real world, one would instinctively and quickly try to determine from whom and which direction the arrow came, to immediately seek cover, and avoid further piercing. Every sane person would agree that tending to the wound is paramount. In failing to consider that a Hindu just might be able to limp and chew gum at the same time, Buddha commits the either–or fallacy (false dichotomy) by omitting a third option: namely, one could, in triage fashion, address the arrow while *also* deducing as much evidence as possible to avoid being a target for follow-up woundings. In the real world, Buddha ultimately succumbed to the arrow's wound — an effect of sin — and regrettably never learned the true genesis of the arrow of suffering and death.

36. Gary Gach, *The Complete Idiot's Guide to Understanding Buddhism* (New York: Penguin Group, 2002), p. 16.

Hinduism. But the Buddhistic cosmogony is unlike other major non-Christian religions in that it has no creation myth.[37] Wayne House distills the Buddhist creational view as follows.

> Buddhism does not refer to the creation of the universe. Instead it refers to everything in the universe as "reality," with all phenomena of the world originating interdependently. Reality is characterized by impermanence,[38] insofar as everything eventually perishes. Reality is understood in terms of processes and relations rather than entities or substances. Human experience is analyzed in five aggregates (*skandhas*). Form (*rupa*) denotes material existence. The other four refer to psychological processes: sensations (*vedana*) perceptions (*samjna*), mental constructs (*samskara*), and consciousness (*vijnana*). The causal conditions for such human experience are found in a 12-membered chain of dependent organization (*pratitya-samatpada*). The links in the chain are ignorance, karmic predisposition, consciousness, name-form, the senses, contact, craving, grasping, becoming, birth, old age, and death.[39]

A Buddhist believes the cosmos is fragmentary and impermanent, and that in a sense, *he* continually creates and recreates his world through karma. We can clearly see that the Buddhist idea of origins is multi-layered, not prone to falsification, and thus has precious little to bring to the empirical table in the contemporary discussion on origins.

View of the Afterlife

All Buddhists believe if they follow the *Eightfold Path* they can achieve liberation from the hamster-wheel of birth, death, and reincarnation. The great yearning is release from this world of maya (illusion), detachment from craving, and that perfect state bliss (nirvana), where pain and suffering are no more (cf. Revelation 21:4). Nirvana is the final state of nothingness for Buddhists. They don't hold to any type or heaven or believe in any type of eternity whatsoever. In other words, their goal is a form of final death with vain hopes that there is nothing beyond this death.

---

37. Some Buddhists allude vaguely to a "creative cloud" with waters initiating a "water cycle."
38. Buddhism's dogma of impermanence is so pervasive that nothing has a permanent essence.
39. Wayne House, *Charts of World Religions* (Grand Rapids, MI: Zondervan, 2006), chart 67.

The idea of hell is also foreign for most of Buddhism, but is allowed for in certain strains of their worldview. I grew up in Asia, and vividly remember as a boy seeing murals on the wall of a Buddhist temple — grotesque frescos of the horrors that awaited some Buddhists.[40] Like Dante's *Inferno*, the images stuck to the canvas of my mind for years, and I've seen similar gruesome vignettes in my nearly 40 trips to China. Those depictions capture the fate for truly

Beijing hell mural
(Photo: Thane Ury)

wicked souls. The silver lining for these Buddhists is that there's a purgatory-like limit to this purging, meaning one will eventually be "freed" to return to the cycle of birth, death, and reincarnation on the path toward nirvana.

Consider the psychological effect of such fatalistic indoctrination. If one's whole existence is determined and the benefits of our current actions are not realized until some successive stage, hopelessness seems assured. Something of this despair can perhaps be seen empirically. Buddhist-dominant countries tend to have very high suicide rates. In fact, J. Warner Wallace has noted that the "the top twenty most suicidal countries are almost all countries with strong Buddhist or Communist (atheist) histories."[41] In Buddhist countries,

---

40. Buddhism's view on the afterlife is multifaceted, with differing models of hell arising in splinter groups. One view arose in the T'ang dynasty, suggesting hell had 18 levels, each one lasting twice as long as the previous, and each being 20 times more excruciating. Another suggestion arose that there are 12,800 hells beneath us, and 84,000 miscellaneous hells on the cosmic periphery. Assorted Buddhist writings describe these abysses in gruesome detail. Punishments in some hells include being perpetually skewered, dismembered, disemboweled, fried in cauldrons of boiling oil, mauled and ripped to shreds by predatory animals, boiling liquids forced down one's throat, and perpetually forced through a meat grinder with dogs waiting on the receiving end to consume sinners. These ghastly punishments never bring death, and are repeated until one is returned to the reincarnation cycle. These barbaric stations are theoretically tailored to match a person's deeds. Thus, those in occupations as butchers, fishermen, or exterminators would be treated likewise, and so it's not surprising that seeing such graphic murals was enough to terrify many into changing their profession.

41. J. Warner Wallace, "22 Important Questions for the Buddhitic Worldview," Cold-Case Christianity, September 11, 2014, http://coldcasechristianity.com/2014/22-important-questions-for-the-buddhistic-worldview.

the suicide rate is about 18 in 100,000 annually. In Thailand there is a suicide every two hours, and in China there is a suicide every two minutes.

> How many people have provoked this question — not "Who are you?" . . . but "What are you?" . . . Only two: Jesus and Buddha. — Huston Smith and Philip Nova[42]

Buddhist Perspectives on Christ

While every biblically grounded Christian holds to the divinity of Jesus, Buddhists of any variety deny that Jesus was divine. They do not deny, however, that he is a pivotal person in history. Interestingly, since Buddhists believe the Buddha had a miraculous birth, they have few quibbles with Jesus' miraculous birth. They deeply admire his social teachings and particularly his selfless work on behalf on others, but a deity he was not. Instead, he is to be revered as a *bodhisattva*, who allegedly postponed nirvana for the sake of others.[43] Terry Muck even points out that high-level Buddhists show far greater respect for the historical Jesus than liberal exegetes of the Jesus Seminar."[44] But even if the honor these Buddhist leaders accord Jesus as a great teacher seems genuine, fans of C.S. Lewis will wonder how these doyens might respond to the *trilemma*. Lewis wrote:

> I am trying here to prevent anyone saying the really foolish thing that people often say about Him: I'm ready to accept Jesus as a great moral teacher, but I don't accept his claim to be God. That is the one thing we must not say. A man who was merely a man and said the sort of things Jesus said would not be a great moral teacher. He would either be a lunatic — on the level with the man who says he is a poached egg — or else he would be the Devil of Hell. You must make your choice. Either this man was, and is, the Son of God, or else a madman or something worse. You can shut him up for a fool, you can spit at him and kill him

42. Huston Smith and Philip Novak, *Buddhism: A Concise Introduction* (New York: Harper-One, 2003) p. 21.

43. In Buddhism, a *bodhisattva* is one who postpones enlightenment to help others attain nirvana. While Buddhism is atheistic, some schools express devotion to various "deities," which often are merely bodhisattvas — somewhat reminiscent of the canonization of saints seen in Roman Catholicism. Besides Gautama, Buddhism recognizes at least 27 other bodhisattvas.

44. Terry C. Muck, "Jesus Through Buddhist Eyes," Books and Culture, accessed February 2, 2016, http://www.booksandculture.com/articles/1999/marapr/9b2046.html.

as a demon or you can fall at his feet and call him Lord and God, but let us not come with any patronizing nonsense about his being a great human teacher. He has not left that open to us. He did not intend to.[45]

Similarities between Buddhism and Christianity

When it comes to dovetailing Christian theism and Buddhism, there has been no shortage of thinkers like Thomas Merton (Trappist monk) and Thich Nhat Hanh (Buddhist monk)[46] — who are among many who have become apologists for such syncretism. And at first glance, superficial parallels between Buddhism and Christianity are abundant. For example, Buddha taught that "self" is the most deceitful of delusions, and Christianity seems to find agreement in Paul's writings,[47] but such agreement is superficial, for *self* is referred to in very different ways. Buddhists have no concept of the sin nature to which Paul is pointing.

Another obvious similarity is the prospect of ultimate peace promised by both religions. But again, the Buddhist brand of peace is unlike Christianity because it is "works-based," where one attains peace through mere meditation. Christianity, on the contrary, contends that real peace only comes through being made new creations in accepting Jesus, the Prince of Peace, as Savior.

Many suggest that Jesus and the Buddha wore comparable halos, and few would disagree that the similarity between their lives is indeed interesting. Consider that each was a monastic leader who . . .

- didn't seek personal power
- taught through parables
- didn't leave any personal writings behind[48]
- established an all-encompassing way of life
- condemned prevailing religious and social norms of the day

---

45. C.S. Lewis, *Mere Christianity* (London: Collins, 1952), p. 54–56.
46. Thich Nhat Hanh, *Living Buddha, Living Christ* (New York: G.P. Putnam's, 1995). Hanh asserts, "When you are a truly happy Christian, you are also a Buddhist. And vice versa."; *Jesus and Buddha: The Parallel Sayings*, ed. Marcus Borg (Berkley, CA: Ulysses Press, 1997); and Paul F. Knitter, *Without Buddha I Could Not Be a Christian* (Croydon, UK: Oneworld Publications, 2013).
47. Cf. Romans 6:11; 2 Corinthians 5:17; Galatians 2:20, 5:24. See also Luke 9:23–24 and John 12:24.
48. Although we have no words written by His own hand, we must acknowledge His words recorded in the Bible, which is Jesus' Word.

- experienced huge opposition from local authorities
- stressed living simple, righteous, and compassionate lives
- condoned strong moral conduct (e.g., prohibitions against killing, stealing, sexual misconduct,[49] lying, and a litany of abuses)
- taught that materialism interferes with spiritual growth
- urged adherents to strive toward perfection
- encouraged community and altruism in his followers
- emphasized a love and respect for all people

Yet, as interesting as these parallels are, the fundamental and irreconcilable contrasts between the two faith systems are quite stark, as highlighted in the following table.

No additional antidote is needed to vanquish futile attempts by creative inclusivists who propose a compatibility between the Buddhist and Christian traditions. The core teachings are hopelessly irreconcilable, and yet the "politically correct tractor beam" of modern pluralism and "forced neutrality" is relentless. Many in the Christian church have gone along for fear of being labeled Buddhaphobic, or similar epithets.

In fact, the motivation behind the production of the volume you are now holding will be judged by many as bigoted and intolerant. It is not because of material presented here (which is written in an honest fashion), but because of intolerant and bigoted positions of those projecting their intolerant and bigoted position toward Christianity. But such is the risk of lovingly and thoroughly assessing the truth claims and congruity of Christianity's contemporary rivals to which we are called (2 Corinthians 10:4–5; 1 Peter 3:15, etc.). The perspicuity of John 14:6 does not cease to exist just because it is ignored — Jesus is *the* way, *the* truth, and *the* life. Ecumenical bartering to dissolve the sharp distinctions listed above can only be done at the high price of abandoning true truth. Additionally, to trivialize the vast chasm between the teachings of the Buddha and those of Jesus is to do a great injustice to the intent of both men. Any promise of a pluralistic potluck reveals a substantial ignorance of both systems as classically understood and of the milieus in which they were birthed.

For most of Asia the rhythm has hardened into a recurrence.

---

49. Almost every country with a Buddhist tradition has made pornography illegal.

Some Incongruities between Buddhism and Christianity	
Buddhism	**Christianity**
No personal God exists (atheistic)	A personal God exists (theistic)
No creational model	God is the creator of all that is
There may be a moral law, but not absolute	There is absolute moral law because God is the absolute law-giver
The fundamental problem is suffering	The fundamental problem is sin, which is responsible for suffering and finally death
"Sin" is ignorance of reality's true nature	Sin is rebellion against God
"Redemption" comes from within	Redemption only comes through Christ
Key moment happened *under* a tree	Key moment happened *on* a tree
Buddhist teachings do not depend on Buddha	There is no Christianity without Christ
Buddha died and was cremated	Jesus died and rose incorruptible
Personhood hinders liberation	Personhood is central*
The ultimate goal is nirvana	The ultimate goal is a personal relationship and reconciliation with God
Completely subjective	Grounded in objective reality
An inward focus prevented development of science	A love and study of creation gave rise to science
Followers should resist critical analysis	Followers are instructed to test all things (1 Thessalonians 5:21–22)
Piety is inwardly focused	True piety looks beyond self
We die perhaps tens of thousands of times	We die just once (Hebrews 9:27)
Merit accrues over thousands of lives	Salvation by faith through God's grace alone
Ultimate reality is *sunyata* (emptiness)	Ultimate reality is fullness in Christ

Cyclical view of life and history	Linear (telic) view of life and history
Followers must empty themselves of desire	Followers can overcome unholy desires; Jesus fulfills our desire
Buddha: "Be ye lamps unto yourselves"	Jesus: "I am the light of the world"
The soul does not exist	The soul does exist
There is no afterlife	There is an afterlife

* So much could be added here. For example, Buddhism sees enduring personhood as an illusion, with nirvana annihilating personhood. But for Christians, we are image bearers of a three-person God, so personhood is essential to Trinitarian thought, and our person endures beyond the grave — being made in the image of an eternal God. The individual (person) is often underemphasized or completely ignored in most Asian traditions. When personhood is ignored, a preoccupation with caste, family, or society rushes to fill the vacuum.

It is no longer merely a rather topsy-turvy sort of world; it is a wheel. . . . [Asia has] been caught up in a sort of cosmic rotation, of which the hollow hub is really nothing. In that sense the worst part of existence is that it may just as well go on like that forever.
— G.K. Chesterton[50]

Arbitrariness and Inconsistencies within Buddhism

Buddhism resembles more of a mystical construct than a tightly formed philosophy with a healthy respect for logic and empirical data. Gautama Buddha himself saw theological reflection as mere speculation, unedifying, and not conducive to attaining spiritual liberation. It is nothing short of painful irony that his view itself would be hard to exceed in its metaphysically conjectural scope.

Christianity of course is also a faith. But it is a faith that is said to rest on historical events. In fact, given the centrality of the Christ's Resurrection, it can truly be said that the Christian faith stands or falls on a single historical

---

50. G.K. Chesterton, *The Everlasting Man* (New York: Dodd, Mead & Co., 1925), http://www.areading.net/The_Everlasting_Man/40.html.

event that is claimed to have taken place in space and time (1 Corinthians 15:12–19). In strong contrast, traditional Buddhists place little to no emphasis on objective data. Ultimate reality is indescribable, indefinable, unknowable, deep things that can only be met with "noble silence."

> "If one cannot empirically know the minds of other people, then pursuing knowledge of other minds is inconsistent with the Buddha's doctrine regarding the kind of knowledge necessary to end suffering. . . . Is not compassion then inconsistent with the kind of knowing that leads one to be able to end one's suffering?" A head monk answered, "If someone truly understands the Buddha's teaching, they will see that compassion is meaningless." Collender comments, "If metaphysical claims are that which we cannot possibly verify, then the Buddha cannot verify . . . that there are any individuals beyond himself. This makes the Buddha's epistemology an enemy of compassion." — Michael Collender[51]

Those who give credence to things like the law of non-contradiction may find encounters with Buddhists quite frustrating. Reasoned arguments and logic will not typically fall on fertile soil, as *Tripitaka* faithful Buddhists seem relegated to mere subjectivism and experientialism at every turn.

But picture a monk looking both ways before crossing a busy Bangkok street to beg for alms; the incongruity of how his meta-rational convictions fits with (1) avoiding being run over, and (2) dependence on others, is perhaps not even realized much less explained. To the average Westerner such irreconcilable contradictions seem pervasive throughout Buddhist dharma. Non-Buddhists, for example, might note the following conundrums:

- Since souls are impermanent — i.e., there is no real self — how can Buddhism refer to nirvana as *achieved* or *experienced*?

- When Buddhism teaches reincarnation, but also denies that souls exist, what then is reincarnated? With no self to be reborn, how can cycles of rebirth occur?

- If all things are impermanent, does not that very conviction implode?[52]

---

51. Michael Collender, sharing his experience during a visit to Wat Thai, a Theravada monastery in the Los Angeles area. *To End All Suffering* (Eugene, OR: Wipf & Stock Publishers, 2014), p. 190.
52. This is an example of *self-referential incoherence*, or a self-defeating assertion. Famous ex-

- Karma entails that past acts and future incidents are inseparably linked together (i.e., we truly reap in this life what we've sown in a previous one). But how can this be if nothing is permanent?

- The Buddhist's whole worldview is predicated on overcoming suffering, but how can this be if (some of the same) Buddhists deny that suffering is real?

- Buddhism infers one has no personal significance. But then why do some Buddhists seem to live as if they *do* have some modicum of significance?

- How can Buddhism claim that suffering comes from the pursuit of private fulfillment, and then pursue (desire) a private fulfillment like nirvana?

- As part of our world of sensory illusion, how are ethical notions (like *good* and *evil* or cruelty and non-cruelty) even sustainable?[53] Specifically, what objective moral basis can Buddhism provide to distinguish between them?

- It is commendable that Buddhists live ethically. But by holding that ultimate reality is impersonal — with distinctions between good and evil being illusory — isn't such an ethic wholly arbitrary with no objective underpinning?[54]

- With no personal God, who/what decides whether an act deserves "good" or "bad" karma?

- How is it even known that the search for enlightenment is worthy?

---

amples are, "All things are relative!" and "There are no absolutes!" Each collapses under its own logic.

53. Buddhism's pessimistic view that life is suffering is logically inconsistent. L.T. Jeyachandran frames it this way: "Philosophically, one cannot define a negative entity such as suffering or evil except as the absence of corresponding, positive entities, namely pleasure and good. If everything were suffering, we would not know it to be suffering!"; L.T. Jeyachandran, *Beyond Opinion: Living the Faith We Defend*, ed. Ravi Zacharias (Nashville, TN: Thomas Nelson, 2007), p. 92–93.

54. Buddhists and New Agers, like secular humanists, all hold to moral values of course. But what ties them together is that neither can provide an objective, ontological rationale for such convictions; forced instead to subjectively embrace a moral framework by sheer fideistic fiat. If no personal God exists, a concept like *The Four Noble Truths* becomes problematic, for on what objective basis are we to determine what is *noble* and what is *truth*? The same applies to the eight *rights* in *The Eightfold Path*. Right by whose standard?

- If self-effort is imperative to curry good karma, how does this mesh with the aid of a bodhisattva?

The list could go on, but one last glaring fallacy bears mention. Buddhism advocates selflessness and liberation from craving. And yet the whole goal of *attaining nirvana* ironically appears to be the ultimate form of selfishness, since it is a completely self-centered experience. Johnson summarizes the contradiction clearly.

> The moral contradiction is precisely this: A person should want to get saved from desire or selfishness. But wanting to save oneself is just as selfish as any other act for selfish ends. If a person wants enlightenment, he still *wants*. And *wanting, desiring*, is the very fault which [sic] prevents enlightenment.[55]

Illogical thinking, of course, is not the exclusive domain of Buddhists, as such manifests itself at some level with all views opposing biblical truth. Nor is it implied that those who pride themselves in logic are automatically superior or logical, much less correct. But with Buddhism (and Taoism also) contradiction actually seems essential to the system, and thus is not only tolerable but even somewhat of a badge of honor. All this comes as no surprise; being the logical outcome of a worldview that teaches that reality is just an illusion. Since any "rules of reasoning," whatever they may be for each individual, are part of a reality that is illusory, then such rigid laws cannot exist, much less be codified in an ethereal worldview.

> Even among the Zen masters themselves there is a great deal of discrepancy, which is quite disconcerting. What one asserts another flatly denies or makes a sarcastic remark about it, so that the uninitiated are at a loss what to make out of all these everlasting and hopeless entanglements. — D.T. Suzuki[56]

Intra-faith dialogues with diehard Buddhists will have no shared appreciation of the logical and linear reasoning that Westerners take for granted. In fact, it will be extremely difficult to fathom why Buddhists themselves fail to see logical contradictions within their framework, their holy books,[57]

---

55. David Johnson, *A Reasoned Look at Asian Religions* (Minneapolis, MN: Bethany House, 1985), p. 130.
56. D.T. Suzuki, "The Koan," in Nancy Wilson Ross, *The World of Zen, an East-West Anthology* (New York: Vintage Books, 1964), p. 54.
57. See https://www.jashow.org/articles/apologetics-2/contradictory-teachings-in-zen-buddhism/.

their practice, or why the law of non-contradiction is not taken as a universal truism. Greg Bahnsen suggests that if someone denies the law of non-contradiction, you could just respond, "Oh, so you don't deny it." When they counter with, "No, I do deny it," then you can simply respond, "Yes, but if you deny it, then you also don't deny it." Since they have given up the law of non-contradiction, then they can't appeal to that law when you contradict their position. The force of Bahnsen's words is hard to escape.

Tips for Sharing the Gospel with Buddhists

Having been introduced to *mere Buddhism*, you can see that this religion is every bit as diverse as Christianity (this happens when a religion has been around for a long time), and as such, just about every assertion and assessment in this chapter could be endlessly qualified. The same holds true for strategies in sharing Christ with Buddhists. There is no cookie-cutter approach. What may have been fruitful for the T'ang dynasty Nestorians will prove sterile 1,300 years later in Marin County.

We all know how daunting it can be to share Christ with family and friends, but getting to Calvary with Buddhists can be even more overwhelming, especially when tacking on cultural and language barriers. Yet be encouraged, as God has helped many just like you to handle these hurdles. A powerful and proven mix involves three things: a little preparation, courageously stepping out in faith, and knowing that God is with you! You will learn, grow, and gain confidence with each encounter. Additionally, previous evangelism by others has plowed the way for you, just as you may be tilling the ground for others or watering what they planted (1 Corinthians 3:5–8). Centuries of prayer cover precedes you too.

Some have long ministered in the Buddhist world. When they share methods that have proved fruitful, and others that have flopped, we should listen. The following common sense suggestions can be adapted according to context.

- This is spiritual warfare, so start with prayer! The Holy Spirit has long tilled the soil in Buddhist hearts, and will continue to do so.

- The demonic is often in play. Do not tread flippantly onto the battlefield.

- Be pre-emptive (1 Peter 3:15). Research Buddhism. Truly understanding a Buddhist's faith is key and shows respect. Familiarity with things like *The Four Noble Truths*, *The Eightfold Path*, and *The Middle Way* is imperative. If you get pressed into a discussion, do not be afraid to ask questions about what the Buddhist believes so that you can properly discuss the issues.

- Similarly, have you delved into a personal study of theodicy (the existence of suffering, especially in the creation of an omnipotent and holy God)? Indications that you've reflected deeply on pain and suffering will send a positive signal. We must be as serious about our beliefs as Buddhists are about theirs.

- You must learn to distinguish original Buddhism from modern variants, in addition to determining which school of Buddhism your friend embraces. When in a discussion, do not be afraid to ask respectful probing questions.

- Buckle in for the long haul. There really are no shortcuts to the time it takes to earn trust and the right to speak truth to the Buddhist.

- Building relational bridges is essential. Do whatever it takes to understand their personal world, listen, and answer questions.

- Dialogical approach is best — listen very well. Residual aggressiveness or condescension must give way to gentleness and reverence (1 Peter 3:15). Being overly confrontational is a killer in general, but more so in an Asian context. Become familiar with and avoid tactics that cause one to "lose face."

- Speaking the truth *in love* is essential in witnessing to Buddhists, respectfully and patiently highlighting essential differences.

- Timing is crucial. Ask God when it's right to advance — and when it's best to pull back. Premature attempts to draw the net can be counter-effective if proper foundations aren't in place.

- Christians committed to their own spiritual disciplines have better rapport with Buddhists. But casual Christians who don't know their sources, or who don't pray, fast, etc., don't foster the same sense of credibility with Buddhists.

- Drawn-out diatribes of comparative religion have rarely worked. Aside from Christ, don't focus on the Buddha or other personalities. Concentrate on issues.

- Share Christ winsomely and patiently. Buddhists usually know little about Jesus, so while an overview of His uniqueness may take time, it is non-negotiable.

- Make no assumptions and patiently clarify key terms. Buddhists are rarely conversant with biblical concepts and terms Christians take for granted. Don't assume Buddhists understand sin, judgment, vicarious atonement, heaven, hell, or resurrection. This is doubly important because some, like the Dalai Lama, substitute terms like *compassion, peace*, and *harmony* with Tibetan words that have very different meanings.

- The concept of a relational God offering forgiveness to His image-bearers has deep appeal for Buddhists.

- The thinking Buddhist wants escape from the cycle of karma, suffering, and incessant striving for self-perfection. Sharing your personal narrative of how Christ freed you from similar bondage and what it's like to have a personal relationship with a living God will be quite powerful.

- Be prepared to explain the differences between *heaven* and *nirvana*.

- Engaging in too much comparative religion (i.e., highlighting common ground) can be a diversion. Focus on Jesus, Jesus, Jesus.

- As you would expect, nomenclature like "born again" or "regeneration" and the like can be problematic, being heard very differently by Buddhist ears. Such terms can't be avoided, of course, but exercise extreme wisdom in explaining the differences between regeneration and reincarnation. One source wisely suggests substitute terminology like "endless freedom from suffering, guilt, and sin," "new power for living a holy life," "promise of eternal good life without suffering," or the "gift of unlimited merit."[58]

- Make sure to give Buddhist friends a Bible, stating your willingness to answer questions. Suggest the Gospel of Mark as a starting point.

- As you began with prayer, likewise end with prayer. In the wake of each encounter, ask God to continue to work on the heart of each

58. North American Mission Board, http://www.4truth.net.

future ex-Buddhist.

Summary of Buddhist Beliefs

Doctrine	Teachings of Buddhism
God	Deny the existence of the biblical God. In its pure form, Buddhism is atheistic; however, some sects revere the Buddha as a godlike figure. Other sects are polytheistic, honoring various lesser gods. All deny Jesus was divine, but many would acknowledge His miraculous birth and see Him as an enlightened teacher.
Authority/Revelation	The authority of the *Tripitaka*, or *Pali Canon*, while variously revered among the sects, is at least acknowledged as a source of Buddhist teachings. Other assorted writings are used by rival sects. Ultimately, each individual is his own authority.
Man	All life forms and men are part of a cycle of life and death whose self is seeking to achieve nirvana. Individuals are born subject to the law of karma, not with a sinful nature, based on their performance in the previous life.
Sin	Sin is loosely defined as doing wrong and having desires that attach one to the world. All suffering is the result of wrong desires and holding wrong thoughts and intentions. Sin is seen as the ignorance of true reality.
Salvation	The individual is intent upon removing all desires and attachments to the world to remove any form of suffering. Following the Eightfold Path, each person can achieve the state of nirvana, having their existence extinguished and removed from the cycle of reincarnation and suffering.
Creation	Deny the existence of a supreme creator. Consider questions about origins a distraction from achieving enlightenment. May embrace evolutionary ideas as a part of the chain of being.

Chapter 20

Confucianism: A Humanistic Wisdom Tradition

Dr. Thane Hutcherson Ury

"Confucianism buried the Chinese . . . it became the curse on China!"[1]

Confucius (551–479 B.C.) has been referred to as China's first teacher; even as the Socrates of the East,[2] and an "unsceptred king, ruling over the Chinese intellectual world for over two thousand years."[3] Far from being a mere punch line or patron sage of fortune cookie wisdom, he is one of the most influential figures in world history. His moral school evolved to become the State-cult in imperial China. Confucius saw the need for ethical scaffolding at every societal tier, and felt precise moral education and the practice of virtues and rites could accomplish that.

---

1. Church leader to author, Sichuan province 8/11/2015.
2. Western philosophy has often been facilely likened as mere footnotes to Socrates, but in the East it is much less hyperbolic to say that all post-Confucian philosophy is a series of footnotes to his ideas.
3. Chen Jingpan, *Confucius as a Teacher: Philosophy of Confucius with Special Reference to Its Educational Implications* (Beijing: Foreign Languages Press, 1990), p. 11.

Historical Overview

Five hundred years before Christ, the "wild union" of a 60-something general and a teen concubine, led to the birth of Kong Qiu,[4] born into a feudal state near present-day Qufu, Shandong province. While data on Confucius' early life is either skimpy or unreliable, there is a consensus that he was born into a good family, the youngest of 11 children. After the death of his father,

Confucius

the family fell on hard economic times, but he was still able to get a good education.[5] His early years were challenging. At age 19 he married, had a few children, and later divorced. As time went on, he found employment as a granary bookkeeper, clerk, cowherd, and "Minister of Crime,"[6] before he found his calling as a teacher.

Confucius was self-taught, never had a job of any clout, didn't seek fame, and never imagined he'd become a cultural hero. He did not pretend to be a prophet, promised no riches, power, or fame to his pupils, and none of his disciples ever became a famous leader. Still, he dedicated his life to the battle for the mind and soul of China, and ultimately changed the course of history with a philosophical influence that's lasted two and a half millennia. His ethics continue to impact the lives of well over 1.6 billion people.

Confucius' teachings were initially rejected,* but finally and posthumously percolated through every echelon of Chinese society, and took center stage during China's gilded age. While the taxonomy of Confucianism is

---

4. The honorific title, K'ung Fu-tzu (Grand Master Kong) came later. In the 16th century, Jesuit missionaries Latinized this to "Confucius." Outside of China, the terms "Confucianism" and "Confucian" are common but are virtually unheard of referents in Mainland China.

5. Early data on Confucius's life has been notoriously spotty, most turning to Han dynasty historian Sima Qian, but recent scholarship has often found Qian unreliable, and thus we can be justifiably dismissive at times of what appear to be romanticized embellishments by a Confucian apologist. The process of demythologizing the apocryphal Confucius from the Confucius of history is ongoing.

6. For a sampling of the outrageous apocryphal hagiography that was glommed on Confucius's birth, see Lee Dian Rainey, *Confucius and Confucianism: The Essentials* (Malden, MA: Wiley-Blackwell, 2010), p. 12. Spoiler alert: it involves unicorns, dragons, celestial music, and vomiting out jade books.

resistant to easy classification, we here submit that it is that school founded on the premise that people can achieve moral perfection by self effort, frequent introspection, following rules of good conduct, and having a committed sense of duty toward family and society, which all lead to harmony. While there was some fine-tuning or minor straying in subsequent generations, Confucius' basic precepts wavered little, and his legacy and continued influence on the intellectual and social history of South East Asia are incalculable.

He eventually started a school to train leaders, and his reputation as a wise teacher grew. He was a true polymath,[7] and became known as a "one-man university." With an "at-home feel" and Socratic teaching style, he taught history, government, philosophy, and ethics. He also placed a high premium on music, poetry, and the arts in general. And while he shied away from what we would call "theological reflection," he did delve into divination.

Confucius lived during the Zhou dynasty, which had ruled in relative harmony for half a millennia. For a maze of reasons, this calm gave way to storm with a growing disregard for time-honored values. Destabilization rushed into the moral vacuum, and surrounding states became red in tooth and claw. Huston Smith offers the following graphic snapshot.

> Instead of nobly holding their prisoners for ransom, conquerors put them to death in mass executions. Soldiers were paid upon presenting the severed heads of their enemies. Whole populations unlucky enough to be captured were beheaded, including women, children, and the aged. We read of mass slaughters of 60,000, 80,000, 82,000, and even 400,000. There are accounts of the conquered being thrown into boiling caldrons and their relatives forced to drink the human soup.[8]

We could also add oppressive slave labor, crushing taxation, etc. to the mix to highlight the state of moral mayhem confronting Confucius. The collective Chinese mind had an excessively romanticized view of earlier dynasties; a supposed *Golden Age* characterized by harmony and order. But now that societal standards and respected traditions were hemorrhaging badly, a new social philosophy was needed. Confucius was not looking for his 15 minutes

7. A person with a wide-range of knowledge.
8. Huston Smith, *The Religions of Man* (New York: Harper and Row, 1965), p. 166.

of fame, but it was looking for him. And he became the architect of a plan that would eventually restore China back to more pastoral days.

Various dueling ideologies in the background added to the drama. The triumvirate of Buddhism, Confucianism, and Taoism — which would later collectively shape the majority worldview of the Chinese — were all gaining traction at this time in history.[9] Yet, in the immediate context, it was the legalist/realist view that was most resistant to Confucian reforms. According to this school, the lives of the citizenry had to be tightly regulated. And while mere overregulation would also be a hallmark of mature Confucianism, the legalists saw the best manner to secure domestic stability was via the "rule of law" — with laws, intimidation, and harsh punishment.

Confucius' sociopolitical model, in contrast, began with individual hearts. The idea was that if the relational mortar of benevolence, trust, and fidelity were refined at the family level, such would result in societal cohesion. The legalist/realist model has been accurately described as an attempt to legislate morality from the top down, whereas Confucius was attempting to reform culture by cultivating goodness from the bottom up.

> In the last 4,000 years, China has produced only one great thinker: Confucius. In the two-and-one-half millennia since his death, China's literati did little more than add footnotes to the theories propounded by Confucius and his disciples, rarely contributing any independent opinions, simply because the traditional culture did not permit it." — Guo Yidong, aka "Bo Yang"[10]

It sounds odd, but there are two reasons that Confucius was not technically the founder of Confucianism as we know it.[11] First, he said, "I have transmitted what was taught to me without making up anything of my own." He was merely a conduit of the paleo-orthodoxy from China's golden past; reviving for China and his disciples the "seminal expressions"[12] of Chinese civilization.

9. Few are aware that many philosophies arose concurrently during this pivotal era. At about the last known sighting of the ark of the covenant (586 B.C.), we have the advent of the pre-Socratics, the Upanishads being written, and the arrival of Zoroaster, Buddha, Lao Tzu, and Confucius.

10. https://www.thechinastory.org/yearbooks/yearbook-2013/forum-counting-and-corruption/the-ugly-chinaman/.

11. What we label Confucianism today was originally just called the "School of the Learned"; *ru*, referring to the word scholars. In the annals of Chinese history, the school was also called "the way of the gentleman" and "the forest of the learned."

12. Raymond Dawson, trans., *Confucius: the Analects* (Oxford: Oxford University Press, 1993).

Second, as will be shown below, most of Confucius' ideas and sayings were recollected and recorded by his followers long after his passing. So ripened Confucianism, then, has derivative and collaborative qualities — drawn from material *before* Confucius and basically reconstructed from second-hand accounts *after* Confucius. Having said this, the Confucian repository of materials written, edited, and compiled by Confucius and his followers were quite distinct.

Religion or Philosophy

According to Cantwell-Smith, the question "Is Confucianism a religion?" is one that the West has never been able to answer, and China never able to ask.[13] That may be true, yet the perennial question remains: Is Confucianism[14] a religion or merely a philosophy? Quick answer: Yes, as it seems to be a wisdom tradition with religious qualities. But the question's hidden value is that it forces us to more fully engage the subject. Namely, it forces us to parse and grasp the meanings of *religion* and *philosophy* — which are intricately interconnected. While Confucianism has been labeled a "moral code" or, more creatively, as a "wisdom tradition" — something akin to a cultural foundation[15] — we must look at why the wrangling over "religion or philosophy?" has taken place, and why the issue will probably never be settled.

Some Reasons Confucianism Is Considered a Philosophy

Those who deny that Confucianism is a religion, highlight the obvious demarcation that it has no deity. As such, this wisdom tradition downplays the supernatural, stressing ethical conduct instead. Yes, there are statues of Confucius all over Asia and countless Confucian temples, but these were not originally intended for worship but only as a display of deep reverence directed toward mortals.

---

13. Wilfred Cantwell Smith, *The Meaning and End of Religion* (Minneapolis, MN: Fortress Press, 1991), p. 69.
14. Here we will attempt to engage the root; i.e., *original* Confucianism. Further, with Confucianism sprouting in China — along with most Confucians, past and present, residing there — this chapter will tend toward assessing matters mostly through a Chinese filter. This will be somewhat artificial for scholars and followers of Confucius, but until the topics at hand can be fleshed out in a book-length treatment, such delimitations are needed.
15. The present government in China officially recognizes only five religions: Buddhism, Catholicism, Taoism, Protestantism, and Islam. While it is interesting that Chinese authorities perceive Catholicism and Protestantism as two different religions, the salient point here is that they do *not* categorize Confucianism as a religion, despite it being freely and widely practiced across China.

Confucius never claimed to be a prophet, or claimed divinity, though long after his passing he was venerated. Neither has a claim of divine inspiration ever been made for Confucian texts. There is no organized membership, and instead of a priesthood, we find only an official scholar class.

Classic Confucianism frowned on asceticism,[16] monasticism,[17] and ritual, practices *allowed* within but not *generated* by Confucian principles. Last, Confucianism is decidedly mute on origins or a theory of the afterlife. Additionally, there is no conversion process, no renunciation of another faith to become Confucian, and no moment of transformation, much less marking such with baptism or other ritual.

Another suggested point, often overlooked, is Confucianism's ability to be grafted into other religions, even allegedly exclusive ones. If Confucianism were a religion, this couldn't be done, or so the thinking goes. Those making this point contend in this way: just as Thomism pairs well with Christian convictions, or as some fancy themselves Christian Platonists, so too Christianity can embrace much of Confucianism.

In fact, Dr. Gregg Ten Elshof, philosophy professor and director of Biola University's Center for Christian Thought, sees no reason why there can't be "Confucian Christians."[18] Similar impulses can be found as far back as Matteo Ricci in the 16th century and in any number of more recent luminaries who suggest that Christianity need not replace other faith traditions,[19] but are ripe for a healthy comingling.

Clear-thinking Christians can recognize that there is much moral good in Confucianism, and assuming one is firmly grounded in Christian theology, there is nothing spiritually unhealthy about observing interesting parallels between Confucian convictions and Christian dogma. But what we are not obligated to do is let down our guard every time syncretists drag

---

16. Avoiding indulgence and self-discipline.
17. Renouncing worldly pursuits to follow spiritual pursuits.
18. Jonathan Merritt, "Confucius for Christians? Evangelical College Professor Learns from Unlikely Source," September 8, 2015, http://jonathanmerritt.religionnews.com/2015/09/08/confucius-for-christians-evangelical-college-professor-learns-from-unlikely-source. Reticent souls will want to hear from Ten Elshof how he decides which Confucian rubrics are compatible with Christianity, and which ones are not. Consider Confucius's assertion that "Absorption in the study of the supernatural is most harmful." Lionel Giles, *The Sayings of Confucius* (London: John Murray, 1917), p. 94.
19. William Hocking, Paul Tillich, et al. Even the magisterial sinologist, James Legge, felt that Confucianism is not antagonistic to Christianity in the way that Buddhism and Islam are.

their "electromagnetic crane" over Taoism, Buddhism, and Islam. Something always sticks.[20]

In exploring the Christian-friendly aspects that radiate from Confucianism, perhaps Ten Elshof is only highlighting such as indicators of the natural law that the Lord has lodged in the human conscience, or something equally nonthreatening (see below). If that's all, then we can live with that. But if left unchecked, let's envisage "Elshof 2.0" in the future; some colleague willing to push the envelope just a hair further. What might we brace ourselves for in this future scion?

- Perhaps 2.0 would agree that a *dual belonging of faith* is unacceptable for Christians, instead only affirming that dual citizenship of culture is unavoidable. Perhaps not.

- Perhaps 2.0 will preach the dangers of "Jesus *plus*" thinking. Perhaps not.

- Perhaps 2.0 knows that the suggestion that Christians can accommodate adjectives like "Confucian" will find little support in Scripture,[21] Church history, or the premier Christian apologists of our day. Perhaps not.

- Perhaps 2.0 could point us to references where Paul, Augustine, Luther, Calvin, Wesley, or similar icons would buy into exhortations that there should be "Confucian Christians." Perhaps not.

- Perhaps 2.0 would draw the line if his students began worshiping or offering sacrifices to ancestors in a local Confucian temple, or worked the *I Ching* into their devotions. Perhaps not.

- Perhaps 2.0 will specify how Christianity benefits from even the appearance of a philosophical liaison with a worldview that so many Chinese Christians consider a curse on China. Perhaps not.

---

20. Similarity in moral systems does not make them equal. Other systems that have truth are merely confirming Romans 2, which indicates that in each image-bearer is a God-given conscience (natural law) that reigns in our conduct.

21. See Paul's thoughts on this in 1 Corinthians 1:12–13, 10:18–22.

- Perhaps it will just appear that 2.0 is suggesting that Christianity is internally lacking in something that can only be supplemented (for some) by wrestling with the *Analects*. Perhaps not.

- Perhaps 2.0 will be even more open than his predecessor to "the rich tradition stretching back" to Buddha or Muhammad becoming "God's chosen instrument for affecting change for the better?" If not, perhaps he'll spell out why not.

When considering the supposed merits or pressures of hyphenating our faith, we would do well to remember the Chinese proverb, "A small hole not repaired, in time will become more difficult to mend."

While spirited in-house debates on inclusivism will continue in the West, an inclusive spirit comes "pre-installed" in most Asian religions. For example, Confucian temples often double as Buddhist and Taoist temples.[22] Ralph Covell also notes this interpenetration of Confucianism with adjacent religions, a comingling so pronounced that Chinese could worship in a Confucian facility one day and not think twice about burning joss sticks in a Buddhist temple the next. And as if that's not enough, priests in those very temples often can "not explain to visitors whether the temple was Daoist, Buddhist, or Confucianist."[23]

Two popular Chinese sayings are "Every Chinese wears a Confucian cap, a Taoist robe, and Buddhist sandals" and "Chinese are Confucians at work, Taoists at leisure, and Buddhists at death."

Some Reasons Confucianism Is Considered a Religion

On the other hand, some say that Confucianism bears some of the classic earmarks of religion, siding with Robert Bellah who labels it a "civil religion."[24] It has been variously referred to as a "diffused religion" and

22. Such pluralism, largely a hallmark of Asian culture, can be seen in the Hanging Temple of Hengshan. Hailed as one of the world's architectural wonders, this temple is dedicated to Confucianism, Taoism, and Buddhism. Any concern to keep clinically precise lines between the triumvirate may be a predictable, if not artificial, Western construct. Stated very broadly, Western ideas of religion are usually tethered to recognized canons, formal authority structure, distinct dogma, faiths named after founders, and membership rolls, etc. But in Eastern thought we find a much more nuanced allowance for the comingling of disparate beliefs. See Jordan Paper, *The Spirits are Drunk* (New York: SUNY Press, 1995), p. 7–8.
23. Ralph Covell, *Confucius, the Buddha, and Christ: A History of the Gospel in Chinese* (Eugene, OR: Wipf & Stock Publishers, 2004), p. 9.
24. Robert Bellah, *The Broken Covenant: American Civil Religion in a Time of Trial* (New York: Seabury Press, 1975).

"religious humanism." Michel Masson, a Jesuit scholar, has convincingly demonstrated that faith permeates the Confucianism paradigm.[25]

What are we to make of the claim that Confucius himself followed no deity and downplayed otherworldly matters? We could suggest that this was merely pragmatic or utilitarian, namely, to get folks focused on this world. Even if we grant some truth here, compelling arguments must be built on something more than interesting conjecture.

The same applies to those on the other side who point out that Confucius *did* favor practices which objective observers would immediately recognize as religious. The nuances in this debate cannot be teased out here, and the debate will never be settled, but we can at least highlight why some believe the label of *religion* is warranted.

For example, like its neighboring non-theistic constructs, Buddhism and Taoism, Confucianism also impacts every significant area in one's life. Moreover, Confucianism has seldom been mute about spiritual things, making a generous place at the table for what we might call *soft supernaturalism*. A prime example is the deified principle of *Tian* that brings order to the cosmos. In honoring the teachings from China's past, Confucius not only allowed for "the way to Tian," but in many ways his goals depended on such. Thus, we shouldn't be surprised when some detect, correctly or incorrectly, the faintest brushstrokes of the supernatural in mature Confucianism.

Confucius also saw rituals as essentially non-negotiable to the inner stability of the individual at the micro level — which in turn fortified families and society at the macro level. The man in the street was given wide berth in animistic rites. The thought was that they had a duty to honor spirits of departed ancestors. This intense reverence involved prayers and sacrifices. And of all the issues that early missionaries to China wrestled with, "ancestor worship" proved one of the most delicate and heated.

It is of no minor consequence that Confucius condoned the presenting of sacrifices to *Tian*,[26] that faceless force which governs our life from the

25. See Michel C. Masson's Philosophy and Tradition: The Interpretation of China's Philosophical Past: Fung Yu-lan, 1939–1949 (Taipei: Ricci Institute, 1985).

26. For Peter Berger this alone determines the answer of the "religion or philosophy debate," http://blogs.the-american-interest.com/2012/02/15/is-confucianism-a-religion/. Lit-Sen Chang, a former Confucian, concludes that Confucianism is not a religion. See his Asia's Religions: Christianity's Momentous Encounter with Paganism (Phillipsburg, NJ: P&R Publishing, 1999). It could also be the case that those who energetically push the "religion card," at least in China, do so because they feel an inferiority that their country does not have its own homegrown religion.

cosmos, and kept rulers accountable to the "mandate." He warned that "He who offends against Tian has no one to whom he can pray."[27] While not personally believing in a god(s), Confucius had the reformational zeal of a Martin Luther.

His ardent disciples also exhibited what is indistinguishable from what in any other context would be labeled "religious character." These followers attempted to wed the sacred and the profane, minus the God hypothesis. Confucians, in the wake of their founder, were decidedly worldly, allowing no spiritual distractions. Instead of focusing on the afterlife, they saw it better to focus on healing wounds on this side of eternity. Stephen Prothero summarizes the Confucian's concerns as "ethical rather than eschatological, practical rather than metaphysical."[28] And in forfeiting any possibility of a transcendent relationship, Confucians had to settle for a form of religiosity in its most sterile form — they wanted morality and a moral culture, without bothering to clarify how such could be done without reference to an absolute, transcendent, objective source of moral authority like a personal God.

We've seen that the question of whether Confucianism is a religion or a philosophy is thorny. The better part of valor might be to recognize this as a false dilemma. If so, when asked if Confucianism is a religion or a philosophy, we would be wise to don our Confucian caps and answer, "Yes!"

Does Confucianism Have Its Own Scriptures?

A few years before his death, Confucius undertook the task of collecting, editing, and adding commentary to key historical writings. The result was an anthology of the most pivotal works in Chinese history. Most people are unaware that the Shandong sage was determined to be unoriginal, that most of the key Confucian texts long predate him, or that he did not actually pen much of the teachings attributed to him.

It was only after Confucius' death that followers collated and redacted his thoughts, so we cannot be certain about any of the precise words attributed to him. And it must be noted that no scholar of any merit has ever suggested that the transmissional fidelity of key Confucian texts can hold a candle in comparison to the painstaking copyists' methods

---

27. Analects III: 13. Some translations have "sin" instead of "offends."
28. Stephen Prothero, *God is Not One: The Eight Rival Religions that Run the World and Why Their Differences Matter* (Victoria, Australia: Black Inc, 2010), p. 113.

and trustworthiness boasted by the Old and New Testament documents.[29] Still, it is generally, albeit arbitrarily, accepted by critical scholars that even though we may not have Confucius' exact words in most cases, we can be confident that we have the basic contours of his thoughts.

The following nine works constitute the Confucian canon and became the embodiment of moral law for the collective Chinese conscience. The works are the Five Classics and the Four Books —though some also refer to the Thirteen Classics.[30]

The Five Classics of Confucianism[31]

These works form the core of Confucianism teachings, represent the zenith of Chinese culture, and were developed *before* Confucius. Their centrality became clear when considering that for more than a thousand years anyone considering a career in civil service had to memorize all five works!

1. *I Ching (Book of Changes)*: A work on yin/yang,[32] cosmology, divination, magic, etc. It attempts to chronicle the readings from *plastromancy* and *scapulimancy* (reading the cracks from heated tortoise shells and ox scapula). The book was considered so vital to Chinese tradition that Emperor Qin spared it from flames during his infamous purge. Confucius placed this work above the other eight, and toward the end of his life said he'd need 50 more years to grasp the *I Ching's* wisdom.

2. *The Classic of Poetry*: A compilation of 305 poems used widely by Confucius, dealing with customs concerning courtship, marriage, war, feasts, sacrifices, agriculture, etc.

3. *The Classic of History*: Includes history, ancient documents, and speeches. Importantly, Emperor Shun from the first recorded

---

29. See F.F. Bruce's timeless *The New Testament Documents: Are They Reliable?* (Downers Grove, IL: IVP, 1943), and Walter Kaiser's *The Old Testament Documents: Are They Reliable and Relevant?* (Downers Grove, IL: IVP, 2001).
30. The Thirteen Classics are the Five Classics and *The Analects* and *The Book of Mencius*. In addition, these texts include three commentaries on the *Spring and Autumn Annals* and five other texts, including the *Classic of Filial Piety*, and the work *Near to Correctness*.
31. A sixth work, *The Book of Music*, has not survived antiquity.
32. The yin and yang symbol is sometimes used to represent the balance found in Confucian ideals. China is philosophically dualistic in many ways, due in large part to the influence of the *I Ching*.

dynasty is said to have sacrificed to *Shang Di*.[33] It also contains reference to *The Mandate of Heaven*, by which every ruler (the *Son of Heaven*) was expected to abide.[34]

4. *The Book of Rites*: Book of ceremonial rituals and etiquette.[35]

5. *Spring and Autumn Annals*: A history of the Dukes of Lu, Confucius' native province.

The Four Books of Confucianism

1. *The Analects*[36] (or "edited conversations") of Confucius: A compilation of nearly 500 of Confucius' thoughts that reached its final form around the second century B.C.[37] The content is mostly on ethics and government. Elias Canetti sees *The Analects* as "the oldest complete intellectual and spiritual portrait of a man. It strikes one as a modern book."[38]

2. *The Great Learning*: Author unknown. A philosophy of the self-made man and the ideal leader.

3. *Doctrine of the Mean*: Written by Confucius' grandson, with the idea that the harmonious development of human nature, decorum, sincerity, and other virtuous conduct comes from following the middle way.

33. *Shang Ti* is a common variant spelling.
34. NB: In all of Confucius's known teachings, he personally refers to *Shang Di* only once.
35. As with most of the Confucian canon, this work in its present format is considered to have come after Confucius. Former Confucian, Lit-Sen Chang, notes that in his role as compiler of elements in the *Book of Rites*, Confucius "winnowed away some materials of high spiritual value" and could thus be likened to liberal or modernist theologians: Lit-Sen Chang, *Asia's Religions: Christianity's Momentous Encounter with Paganism* (Phillipsburg, NJ: P&R, 2000), p. 42.
36. Though surviving manuscripts of the *Analects* have variant readings and uncertainties that textual criticism may never solve, it remains the best source for understanding Confucius's thinking. Scholars like E. Bruce and A. Taeko Brooks in *The Original Analects* (New York: Columbia University Press, 2001) argue that only 16 of the *Analects* are actually from Confucius, and that the Confucius of history is much different than the sage presented in past and contemporary literature. See also Lionel M. Jensen, *Manufacturing Confucianism* (Durham, NC: Duke University Press, 1998).
37. Here is one of the most famous aphorisms: "Tzu-kung asked, 'Is there a single word which can be a guide to conduct throughout one's life?' The master said, 'It is perhaps [reciprocity]. Do not impose on others what you yourself do not desire.' "
38. Elias Canetti, *The Conscience of Words*, trans. Joachim Neugroschel (New York: Farrar, Straus & Giroux, 1984), p. 173.

4. *The Book of Mencius*: Written by Mencius, who helped to make Confucius' teachings a national philosophy in China, it includes treatises on good government and the essential goodness of humans.

Emperor Wu, of the Han dynasty, made mastery of the Confucian canon essential for those going into civil service. Such cushy positions used to be the birthright only of the noble class, but the long reach of Confucius shifted things more toward a meritocracy. The penetration continued such that eventually a cult of Confucius developed, where it became compulsory for all those in government to make sacrifices to Confucius. The Classics were later engraved on huge tablets, now preserved in Xi'an, Shaanxi province.[39]

Confucianism 101: Ten Fundamentals

With all the social and ideological unrest in the air in Confucius' day, a blueprint was needed to defuse the chaos and restore social harmony. His solution was as ingenious as it was foolhardy: simply cobble together a mosaic of the best of all possible moral rubrics from China's past: educate everyone about the duty and benefits of the new paradigm, and push the restart button. Space constraints allow us to list only ten of a whole cluster of fundamentals that Confucius pulled together, and/or which post-Confucius adherents deem derivative from his teachings.

Fundamental 1: Benevolence

Ren (also *jen*), for Confucius, was the keynote virtue of the "superior man." Ren is variously translated as righteousness, love, benevolence, empathy, and very often human-heartedness. Attributes like strength, guileless, and reserve come close. But ren was understood in Confucian circles as the loftiest trait — one of always thinking of others — a quality that the present writer calls "othercentricity." This spirit of altruism (*shu*) essentially says, "Judge others as you wish to judged." Confucius affirmed, "The good man is one who, wishing to establish his character, self-deprecatingly establishes the character of others, and, wishing to develop himself, develops others. To be able to use one's own needs as an example for the treatment of others is

---

39. If the reader is ever in Xi'an, it must be a priority to visit the Beilin Museum (Forest of Steles), housed in a former Confucian Temple. Here you will see key Confucian works etched in huge slabs of stone, and nearby the famous Nestorian tablet.

the way to practice ren." When a disciple asked Confucius how to practice ren, the simple answer was "Love people."

Classic Trinitarians, who appreciate the richness of what it means to be image-bearers of a triune God, will appreciate this facet of Confucianism. We were made as social beings, to live a life of ren with others if you will, in pure selfless love. So when Confucians practice this, it is merely an expression of having been stamped deeply with the divine image. We can appreciate the similarity, but must note a least one huge difference: Christians see sin as relationally destructive to the "five bonds," whereas for Confucianism education is the key to eradicate disharmony.

The idea of reciprocal faithfulness is another parallel between Confucianism and Christianity. This is seen clearly in Confucius' negative version of the golden rule. In the *Analects*, he asserts "What you do not want yourself, do not do to others," an idea later echoed in Matthew 7:12.

Confucius urged a return to a golden age when wise rulers were men of ren. Those times were golden because of ren, not vice versa. He insisted that everyone on the social spectrum — from emperor to rice farmer — was obligated to perform certain righteous duties (*yi*). If ren is the inner essence of goodness for the gentleman, yi serves as the external praxis by which the gentleman's character may be authenticated.

Fundamental 2: Etiquette

The concept of *li* (variously translated as etiquette, custom, propriety, or ritual action) is key to developing ren. Li is very complex and laced with nuances. Confucius felt a civilized life would be characterized by ritualizing an entire way of life. The cultural ground and grammar of a harmonious society is made up of individuals "within a framework of fixed convention" who intentionally own up to their ethical role. They must do this almost as performing a sacred rite. Our conduct should reflect goodwill in an appropriate, honorable, and virtuous way in *every* sphere and action.

These social norms are to be expressed in the relationships between (a) ruler and subject, (b) father and son, (c) husband and wife, (d) elder brother and younger brother, and (e) elder friend and younger friend.[40] A dual assumption is at play in these "five bonds." First, these five relations are

---

40. With the hindsight of history, the first "three bonds" have long been assessed as contributing to (not causing) despotism, patriarchalism, and chauvinism. See brief mention below of the stark contrast between early Confucian and early Christian attitudes toward women.

infused with something like the honor a son gives his father (filial piety). Second, with varying degrees, there are reciprocal obligations between both parties. Friendships outside the family are "ritually constrained."

Confucius stated, "Do not look in a way which is not li, do not listen in a way that is not li, do not speak in a way that is not li, do not move in a way that is not li" (*Analects* XII: 1). Li has to do with respecting all rites, social mores, ethical norms, conventions, and political protocol — from the minutia of social etiquette in marketplace greetings, to the elaborate ceremonies of the emperor and ancestor worship, all is tightly prescribed.[41] Morally binding social customs filter down to everything from what to wear, who bows first, to honoring the departing. Nothing is improvised. Ames and Rosemont capture the span of li, as having to do with:

> meaning-invested roles, relationships, and institutions which facilitate communication, and which foster a sense of community. The compass is broad: all formal conduct, from table manners to patterns of greeting and leave-taking, to graduations, weddings and funerals, from gestures of deference to ancestral sacrifices — all of these, and more, are *li*. They are a social grammar that provides each member with a defined place and status within the family, community, and polity.[42]

Essentially, as we have inherited *li*, so too are we to pass on this hermeneutical repository of social grammar to the next generation. To cultivate these is to cultivate harmony. But for Christians, constraining outward human action says nothing about reining in a carnal heart. For those who claim that Confucianism is only a philosophy, they must admit this pervasive ritualizing of all of life does emit the persona of a religion.

---

41. For an example of the meticulous scripting in Confucianism, consider the manner of grief and mourning that a filial son must follow in the wake of his father's passing: "When mourning, a filial son weeps without wailing; he performs funeral rites without attention to personal adornment; he speaks without rhetorical flourish; he feels uncomfortable in fine clothing; he feels no joy on hearing music; he does not relish good food. . . . After three days he breaks his fast. . . . The period of mourning is not allowed to exceed three years. . . . The body shrouded, is lowered into the encased coffin. . . . Beating the breast and jumping up and down, the mourners bid the last sad farewell. The body is laid to rest in the burial place selected by divination." Quoted in Kenneth Kramer, *The Sacred Art of Dying: How the World Religions Understand Death* (Mahwah, NJ: Paulist Press, 1988), p. 88–89.

42. Roger T. Ames and Henry Rosemont, Jr., trans., *The Analects of Confucius: A Philosophical Translation* (New York: Ballantine Books, 1998), p. 51.

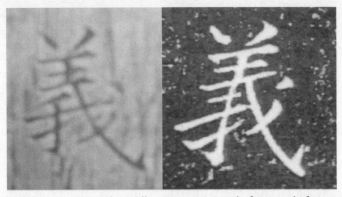

Early Chinese characters were basically pictograms, and often made from combining radicals/words to form a new word. In its traditional form, the character yì offers a staggering example of this. Yì is a composite of two words/characters; the upper portion 羊 [lamb] and the lower portion 我 [me] are fused together into a single word, yì, which means "righteous." Non-theists have yet to offer a convincing explanation for this character's origin. In other words, at least six centuries before Christ, what would have been the basis for ancient Chinese to pictify righteousness as "a lamb over me"? Biblically, righteousness comes when we put ourselves under the blood of the Lamb, so it is fascinating to find this character embedded in the content of the I Ching! The author took these photos in Xi'an, at the Forest of Steles. Yi can be seen carved in stone, on both the I-Ching (left) and on a rice paper rubbing of the Nestorian Stele (right).

Fundamental 3: Ideal Man

Junzi means the "ideal man." While Confucius had faith in humanity's innate goodness, he also believed it was best for us to follow an example. Thus, our great need is for a superlative model for society to emulate — what Confucians call a junzi (contrasted with *xiao ren*, meaning "small man" or "commoner"). The word *junzi* is ideally rendered as "superior man" or "gentleman," but previously meant "son of a ruler."

The junzi exhibits the qualities of yi, ren (see below), and *de* (moral force) in all they do. The junzi combines not just the qualities of a gentleman, but also a saint and scholar. The junzi is calm and at ease, while the small man is nervous and uncomfortable. The junzi is a moral guide for the rest of society. He is the model partner in any relationship, the perfect gentleman, who displays honesty, confidence, generosity, humility, and openness. In Confucianism, everyone should strive to be a junzi.

Fundamental 4: Moral Righteousness

Yi, most often rendered as righteousness, is central to Confucianism. The idea is that of "moral sense" and refers to that ethical penchant to do what is right according to one's virtue. This also has to do with discerning what is right according to the situation. Yi is probably second only to jen of all the Confucian virtues. They are companion virtues logically, for how could we radiate "humaneness" toward others without yi? Yi is also closely tied to ritualism, which gives outsiders the distinct impression that Confucianism is a religion. Before Confucius, yi was focused more on things like ritualized ancestor worship. But Confucius widened and applied yi to every area of life.

Fundamental 5: Middle Way

The *Doctrine of the Mean* is to Confucians what the *Tao Te Ching* is to Taoists, and the *Diamond Sutra* is to Buddhists. Aristotle and the Buddha also had their versions of the middle way. Many essential teachings for Confucians are elaborated here, and with an entire book in their canon dedicated to the *mean*, it should be clear just how essential this idea is. Consider the range of translations given for the title: *The Doctrine of the Mean* has been variously translated by some scholars as *Constant Mean*, *Middle Way*, *Unwobbling Pivot*, and even *Focusing the Familiar*.

The common denominator is to pursue proper conduct between the ways of two extremes. The essence of the mean is to never act excessively, and as such, the mean is so all-encompassing that it represents every venue in life, particularly equilibrium, honesty, moderation, objectivity, rectitude, sincerity, propriety, truthfulness, and dispensing with prejudice. The objective of the mean is to pursue, reach, and preserve a state of perfect balance in all of life.

Fundamental 6: Right Names

The *Rectification of Names* is a key idea in Confucianism. If chosen to govern a state, Confucius said he would first rectify the names. This meant calling things what they truly are, with the other side of the coin being that things should actually correspond to what they are called. For Confucius, subjects must behave in a manner fitting to their social position as subjects. Sons must behave like sons, fathers like fathers, rulers like rulers, ministers like ministers, and so on. Society must know (1) what each term means, (2) the social roles denoted by these, and (3) act consistent with one's role. Failing to do so is sure to initiate the ripples of disharmony throughout every stratum of society. Harmony comes when a person's behavior corresponds to his name. To reduce the rectification of names to mere observance, manners, and ritual — as so many do — is to trivialize Confucian thought.

Fundamental 7: Knowing Ming

> If my principles are to prevail in the world, it is *Ming*. If they are to fall to the ground, is also *Ming*.[43]

> He who does not know *Ming* cannot be a superior man.[44]

Knowing *Ming*. Ming has been translated as fate, destiny, decree, mandate, forces of the heavens, or Will of Heaven. According to Yu-lan Feng, for Confucius, knowing Ming referred to "the Decree of Heaven or Will of Heaven" which "was conceived of as a purposeful force."[45] For some, this means that while there are other things we can affect, most things in our lives are beyond our control. We are to do all we can, of course, but beyond that we must calmly accept most outcomes as inevitable. This is what most Confucians mean when teaching of "knowing Ming."

Others flesh this out differently, asserting that "knowing Ming" allows one to act virtuously with complete disregard for personal gain. One should do what one ought to do simply because it is the right thing to do. So a Ming-knowing ruler will behave virtuously no matter what the potential fallout might be for himself. And since acting morally always benefits the selfless altruist, at least in Confucius' mind, our moral choices should never be deterred by possible negative consequences. The ideal Confucian, then, acts nobly with no thought of self, and accepting the results as his Ming (fate).

Fundamental 8: Tian

Every key component in Confucianism is disputed to some degree but few more vigorously than the idea of *Tian*, and the debate won't be settled here. Some see Tian as the Zeus in the pantheon of Chinese mythology. Others reduce Tian to something akin to the pre-Socratic notion of *logos*, an impersonal dynamism which is the ordering principle of all reality, and not too unlike Buddhism's *Dependent Organization*.

Show the character Tian (天) to contemporary Chinese and the first thing they'll think of is sky. But in ante-Confucian times Tian signified the Heavenly Emperor who ruled over everything. The idea was far from monochromatic, and could accommodate notions of fate, impersonal nature, and deity.

---

43. Confucius, *Analects* XIV: 38.
44. *Analects* XX: 2.
45. Yu-lan Fung, edited by Derk Bodde, *A Short History of Chinese Philosophy* (New York, NY: Free Press, 1948), p. 45.

A.C. Graham notes that Confucius himself seems conflicted about Tian. Sometimes he seems "convinced that he enjoys the personal protection and sanction of Tian," while at other times "he seems caught in the throes of existential despair, wondering if he has lost his divine backer at last."[46]

Deeply embedded in China's past are six tacit ideas of Tian: (1) Tian is anthropomorphic, (2) Tian's "will" is unpredictable, (3) Tian is absolutely sovereign, (4) Tian is in some degree dependent on mere mortals, (5) Tian is always associated with moral goodness, which, (6) gives moral authority to the emperor, who was seen as the "Son of Heaven" with a mandate derived from *Tian*.[47] In all of these we can hear echoes of the truth about God, likely maintained in the culture from the time of Babel.

Nothing from Confucius suggests that he would challenge these assumptions. He said, "He who offends against Heaven (Tian) has no one to whom he can pray." To be sure, his use of Tian is not to be taken as a pure synonym for God (*Shang Di*[48]), which can be somewhat confusing since the two terms were widely interchangeable at times. Could it be that earlier Chinese were more concerned with plumbing Tian's relationship with man than with philosophical abstractions? If Tian were personal, then of course prayer, worship, and obedience would be approached very differently.

But if Tian is merely an impersonal, ordering force, one is relegated to religion without relationship. It cannot be pursued here, but it is widely held that long before Confucius, China embraced a clear monotheistic view, but this conviction degraded over time.[49] Aside from all the yet-to-be-settled points above, there is no scholarly disagreement regarding the centrality that Tian

46. A.C. Graham, *Disputers of the Tao: Philosophical Argument in Ancient China* (La Salle, IL: Open Court, 1989). The author's thoughts in this section are considerably indebted to Graham's insights.

47. The *Mandate* was conditional. Emperors were to "rule by virtue," but if it were determined they ruled non-virtuously (evidenced by disharmony or natural disaster, etc.), the mandate was nullified.

48. In the early-Shang dynasty, *Shang Di* literally meant 'Heavenly ruler' or Supreme Being. With the Zhou era, the term Tian gradually displaced the term Shang Di, though there was an element of interchangeability between the two. *Shang Di* was more personal, while Tian captured more of a flavor of abstraction for the Almighty. See G. Wright Doyle's insightful assessment of this very point at http://www.globalchinacenter.org/analysis/articles/names-for-god-shang-di.php.

49. On China's alleged primordial monotheism, see John Ross, *The Original Religion of China* (Edinburgh: Oliphant, Anderson & Ferrier, 1909), p. 18–25; James Legge, "A Letter to Professor Max Müller," *The Chinese Recorder and Missionary Journal*, XII (1881): 35–53; Matteo Ricci, *The True Meaning of the Lord of Heaven*, trans. Douglas Lancashire and Peter Hu Kuo-chen, ed. Edward Malatesta (St. Louis, MO: Institute of Jesuit Sources, 1985).

played in Confucianism — not to mention other Chinese -isms like Taoism and Moism. For all of these, Tian was the source of moral law in the cosmos.

Fundamental 9: Filial Piety

Far prior to Confucius, filial piety was deeply rooted in feudal China as the bedrock of ethical conduct, social harmony, and sociopolitical stability. Confucius elevated filial piety as the moral gold standard, which in turn was the foundation for ren. So filial piety undergirds Confucian ethics. It can be summarized as follows: the respect, devotion, loyalty, duty, and/or obedience owed by younger members of a family toward elders and ancestors — and more particularly, the loyalty of a son toward his father. For Confucius, reverence for parents was the linchpin virtue for all other social relations. Without filial piety, no other virtues are possible.

> Few of those who are filial sons and respectful brothers will show disrespect to superiors, and there has never been a man who is respectful to superiors and yet creates disorder. A superior man is devoted to the fundamental. When the root is firmly established, the moral law will grow. Filial piety and brotherly respect are the root of humanity.[50]

Fundamental 10: Wen

Wen, in essence, is an appreciation of art and a direct antithesis to "brutishness." Far beyond mere appreciation, though, disciples of the Confucian way are to be conversant in each skill. The arts are not just inspiring but become a cultural vehicle for moral education. Confucius spread his views using arts, ritual, drama, and song. He and his disciples sang and played instruments together, and learning the "Odes" was mandatory. Confucius personally mastered archery, calligraphy, charioteering, and mathematics, and listed calligraphy, poetry, painting, and music as the prime arts. Tian is peppered with creativity, order, and patterns, and mankind is to reciprocate; not just in the visual arts, but even in ritual patterns.

View of Origins

As with Buddhism and Taoism, Confucius and his followers barely thought of origins. Some of this is due to Confucianism being "long on practice and short on the theory . . . [with] an almost pathological horror

---

50. *Analects* I: 2.

of abstractions."[51] But truth be told, it is rare to find *any* early Asian thinker deeply reflecting on ultimate origins, and Confucius is no exception. In Confucianism, since the universe was seen as self-generated, self-contained, and self-maintained, there is no need for a creator. There was a consensus with the scholar class that family, marriage, and government — the key rubrics of social order — were but echoes of the structure of the cosmos. And most notably, the office of emperor was deeply ingrained in the celestial order.

Zhu Xi, an important 12h century Neo-Confucian, and subsequent thinkers, made primitive stabs at cosmological reflection, but given the era, they can't be faulted for only going so far. China was forced to borrow ideas from Indian and Islamic astronomies until the telescope was finally introduced in the 17th century. With longtime disregard for ultimate origins, the dye was cast whereby Confucians never let a Creator's foot in the door. The situation hasn't changed with current "naturalism, materialism, or agnosticism," whereby the living and Almighty God is expelled and has "no relation with the lives of the Chinese people, though they are not aware of this serious fact!"[52]

View of the Afterlife

Though Confucius was very meticulous on how ancestors were to be venerated after their passing, he did not delve into the hereafter. This, as cited above, is one of the main reasons Confucianism is received more as a philosophy than of a religion.

His focus was on the here and now and has nothing to offer on the soteriological (salvation) or eschatological (final and afterlife events) plateaus which are so important in Christianity. Confucianism offers no hope beyond the grave. When asked about death, Confucius famously replied by saying, "If we don't know about life, how can we know about death?" But such answers only serve to underscore the stereotype that Confucian apologists often sound profoundly sagacious, when in fact they regularly only traffic in non-answers or mere platitudes.

Two Key Proponents of Confucianism

Such a melee of intellectual activity arose between 551 and 233 B.C. that the era became known as the *Period of the One Hundred Schools*. Tucked in the

---

51. Diane Morgan, *The Best Guide to Eastern Philosophy & Religion* (New York: Renaissance Books, 2001), p. 178.

52. Lit-Sen Chang, *Asia's Religions: Christianity's Momentous Encounter with Paganism* (Phillipsburg, NJ: P&R Publishing, 1999), p. 51.

middle we have the Warring States Period (401–256 B.C.), that bloodstained era when the Zhou Dynasty was split between eight states. In this epoch, two thinkers arose who expanded Confucius' scope — Mencius (372–289 B.C.) and Xunzi (310–220 B.C.).

These two remain the most well-known early interpreters of Confucian thought. Mencius became known at the "Second Sage," being the most influential Confucian after the "Supreme Sage," Confucius. Areas of concord between them are not hard to find, but we must highlight perhaps the most significant point of disagreement. Many centuries before Pelagianism[53] hit the West, Mencius in the East was already stressing the inherent goodness of human nature, and that we are corrupted only by external factors. This was a key plan in Confucian thought. For nearly two thousand years, the first sentence a Chinese child was taught to read was the Confucian maxim, "Human beings are by nature good."[54] Of course, such could not be more contrary to Scripture (Genesis 8:21; Jeremiah 17:9).

Xunzi, however, did later contend that we are born with an evil nature. On the surface, this reminds us of Pauline dogma (Romans 3:10)., but the similarity is only superficial in that, in Xunzi's view, the evil nature is nothing like the sin-cankered state man is in due to Eden's curse. Xunzi's "cure" for innate evil nature was education; quite different from biblical regeneration which comes only through Christ's atoning work on the Cross. Xunzi offers a Band-Aid, while Paul knows a heart transplant is needed.

Negative Reception

Confucianism's road to becoming *the* orthodox school of thought in China — supported by the majority of emperors for two thousand years — was anything but smooth. To "teach a new dog old tricks" of this magnitude — i.e., to salvage and reanimate the dead, antiquated ritualism of China's past — would require more than one lifetime, and Confucius never lived to see the Chinese utopia of his dreams.

While pursuing reform, Confucius survived near-starvation, endured banishment, and dealt with much rejection. Three rulers were so threatened by Confucius that they tried to have him assassinated. Toward the end of his

---

53. Pelagianism is a 5th century A.D. heresy denying that man inherited a sinful nature. Human nature being unmarred by original sin, thus can freely choose to be good without divine aid.

54. Huston Smith, *The Religions of Man* (New York: Harper and Row, 1965), p. 166.

life, Confucius considered himself a failure, and others agreed. Little could he or they have known the profound influence his ideology would eventually have on billions of Asians through time.

Subsequently, emperors — even up to the modern era — have tried to mold Confucius in their own image, and Confucianism has been bent to symbolize either the good or bad in Chinese history. Emperors and ministers in the Han Dynasty (206 B.C.–A.D. 220) co-opted Confucianism to legitimate their reign, shore up the kingdom, and of course control the populace. But any illusion of uniform respect is dispelled when considering the likes of Han Fei Tzu, a post-Confucian philosopher and apologist for the Legalist philosophy, who ridiculed Confucianism as a parasite. And Liu Bang — first emperor of the Han Dynasty — so despised Confucians that whenever he ran into them, he'd snatch their pointy caps and urinate in them. Under the reign of Emperor Qin, Confucian scholars were severely persecuted. Qin decreed a book burning, consigning many ancient texts to oblivion. Hundreds of Confucian scholars who resisted the edict were buried alive or slaughtered.

After falling out of favor for a season, Confucianism once again became the state ideology from 1392 to 1911. Both the Nationalists under Chiang Kai-shek and Mao's Communist Party (holding to humanistic and materialistic religions) rejected Confucianism. Mao depicted Confucianism as a relic of the imperial past, an ideology of reaction and repression. He vilified Confucius during the Cultural Revolution and compared him to an enemy general who had tried usurping Mao's rule. In an anti-feudalistic rage, Confucian temples and ancient writings were torched.

In contrast, Deng Xiaoping, the communist leader of China after Mao, saw Confucianism as a means for establishing national order and stability. China's current president, Xi Jinping, references the "brilliant insights" of Confucius quite often to back up his own views. He recently touted the Chinese Communist Party as a defender of ancient virtues epitomized by Confucius and his collected teachings, *The Analects*.

The Chinese government spends a great deal of money on the restoration of ancient Confucian temples, and places statues of Confucius in tourist areas. Across the board in Asia, a resurgence of Confucianism and Taoism is taking place. Clearly, Confucius' worry that he made little impact has proven to be inaccurate.

A Snapshot of Present-day Confucianism

While it would be a reckless generalization to say that all of East Asia is Confucian, it would not be an overstatement to claim that Confucian ripples are felt everywhere. Current data estimates there are a mere 6 million Confucians worldwide — a comparatively minor worldview. This number becomes even more modest when considering that 99.4 percent reside in Asia, and the numbers dip further if we count only those who strongly embrace the *entire* Confucian worldview.

However, the important thing here is that more than one-fifth of the world has been seriously conditioned (culturally if not subliminally) by Confucian precepts, and could be labeled "cultural Confucians." Add to this that the Chinese government has funded the establishment of nearly 500 Confucius Institutes worldwide,[55] and Christians have a worldview that needs to be reckoned with.

We cannot lump all Confucians together; like Buddhism, there are many different branches. In this chapter we are focusing for convenience on what we will coin as "mere Confucianism," fully aware any designation will fall short somewhere. The Confucian family tree has many branches, including:

- Neo-Confucianism
- Korean Confucianism
- Japanese Confucianism
- Singapore Confucianism
- Contemporary Neo-Confucianism
- Cultural-Nationalist Confucianism
- North American New Confucians

Confucianism's Allure Today

Quietly gazing over every Supreme Court decision in Washington, DC, Confucius joins an elite group of moralists like Hammurabi, Moses, and Solomon in a marble frieze at the U.S. Supreme Court. While Jews and

---

55. Over the last decade, Beijing has sponsored at least 70 Confucius Institutes in the United States. The Confucius Institute is a Chinese state-run venture which partners (mostly) with American schools to promote Mandarin language and foster cross-cultural collaborative initiatives. However, concerns about lack of transparency and curbing of academic freedom have led the University of Chicago, Penn State, and Stockholm University to shut down these institutes on their campuses. A spirited debate continues as to whether these institutes serve as a Trojan horse for political propaganda.

Christians might quibble over the merits of including some of the 18 lawgivers immortalized there (Muhammad?), there's no question that Confucius can be respected. Thomas Paine, one of the founding fathers of the United States, respected Confucius and Jesus as the two most influential moral teachers in history.

For a variety of reasons, Confucianism strikes a positive note with many. Whether this is due to its non-sectarian bent or the precise opposite, each heart has its reasons. Confucianism might also be seen by some as a "preservative" of Asian culture. We should also recall that Confucianism arose in response to chaotic times. It is not a huge news flash, therefore, that given the moral mayhem of our day we find some hoping for a revival of Confucianism,

Confucius immortalized in marble at the U.S. Supreme Court, Washington, DC

even recommending that it be added as a sixth official religion in China.

But what are we to do when mere respect gives way to something more? Consider the aforementioned Biola professor who sees no incongruity in the idea of "Confucian Christians." Is it such a stretch to envisage an impressionable student, perhaps disillusioned with institutional religion, finding some implied imprimatur (if not invitation) from Prof. Ten Elshof? The student — let's call him Blake — a missionary kid who grew up in Japan might quietly ponder and put in an email:

> Dr. Elshof . . . what a godsend. So cool!! How could he know when he spoke in class today that it's been ages since I've felt any meaningful depth in my spiritual walk? Interesting that his book talks about "a life in pursuit of Confucian Christian ideals." Maybe exploring the merits of being a Confucian Christian — to "find my way into flourishing" as he mentioned — could be the ticket. I'm curious to know if reflecting on the *Analects* could also increase and expand my humanity — my humanness on the way. Sounded kind of odd to hear him put it that way, but he's not just a believer — and not just a PhD — but in fact an administrator no less, at my parents' alma mater, right? And yet, as one with 14 years in Japan, I can't help but think how

my Asian pastor would process Prof. Ten Elshof's invitation to "integrate Confucian categories and emphases with Christian commitment."[56] Prof's optimism seems so radically at odds from most of the Asian voices I've heard in my experience. But Prof said reflecting on the *Analects* has aided his pursuit of the Way of Jesus . . . well, why not me too.

The main issue is not whether this has happened or not, but only if Ten Elshof would be concerned over such a scenario. To read his book, one would have to conclude that he would say, "Mission accomplished."

We already have a group made up largely of university professors currently in North America, who have long been proselytizing on behalf of a Confucian ethos. These are called the *New Confucians*. So Confucianism has already being wooing the Blakes of this generation. It's not surprising that such an enticement might not come from beyond the pale, but we must beware that Confucianism might be covertly (or even unintentionally) promoted by ambassadors within the church.[57] For decades, Blake's Japanese pastor has been helping recovering Confucians to place their faith in Christ alone. His concern regarding Blake's email, prompted the following responses:

1. The *I Ching* is a work on divination, which Confucius placed above all other texts, even adding ten appendices (called the

---

56. Gregg A. Ten Elshof, *Confucius for Christians: What an Ancient Chinese Worldview Can Teach Us about Life in Christ* (Grand Rapids, MI: Eerdmans, 2015). Ten Elshof's motives seem noble, and his work is short and lucid. But if it ever gets translated, it will be interesting to hear the response of Chinese House Church leaders to the premise that Christians should learn at the feet of Confucius.

57. Ten Elshof is not promoting "double belonging," but his thesis would seem to open the door in that direction. A choir of apologists for "double belonging" can be found in Catherine Cornille, ed., *Many Mansions? Multiple Religious Belonging and Christian Identity* (Eugene, OR: Wipf and Stock, 2010). In the introduction, Cornille muses: "In a world of seemingly unlimited choice in matters of religious identity and affiliation, the idea of belonging exclusively to one religious tradition or of drawing from only one set of spiritual, symbolic, or ritual resources is no longer self evident. Why restrict oneself to . . . one religious tradition amid the rich diversity of symbols and rituals presenting themselves to the religious imagination? . . . A heightened and widespread awareness of religious pluralism has presently left the religious person with the choice not only of *which* religion, but also love how many religions she or he might belong to." For attempts to defend "dual-citizenship," see, John H. Berthrong, *All Under Heaven: Transforming Paradigms in Confucian-Christian Dial* (Albany, NY: SUNY Press, 1994), p. 165–186; and Gavin D'Costa and Ross Thompson, *Buddhist-Christian Dual Belonging: Affirmations, Objections, Explorations* (Surrey, UK: Ashgate Publishing, 2015). Compare Han Küng and Julia Ching, *Christianity & Chinese Religions* (New York: Double Day, 1989), p. 273–283.

"Ten Wings"). Is your professor OK with students chewing on these ten wings? Why or why not?

2. When counseling your classmates to plumb Confucius for wisdom, there's so much that goes against Scripture. What standard does your teacher use to disentangle which Confucian tenets to revere and which ones to avoid? Confucius says, "Heaven does no speaking!" How are we helped on *the way* with that?

3. Additionally, does he give clear examples of necessary insights that we can learn from this wisdom tradition that couldn't be garnered from sources in our faith? Is he suggesting that if Confucius had never been born that Christians would in some manner be spiritually or philosophically impoverished?

4. Perhaps he's only intimating that Confucius can be used of the Lord to help unearth our deep-seated cultural or theological biases? Can't that be done without proselytizing for Confucian Christianity?

5. Since key thinkers like Calvin, Luther, and Wesley didn't extol the benefits of sipping at the fount of Southeast Asian thought. Please ask your professor to spell out why it is that his wisdom exceeds theirs.

6. I agree with your professor's counsel to be wary of our cultural blinders. Very wise! But this must cut both ways. Confucius was humanistic and rationalistic to the core — two very serious blinders. You said Ten Elshof has yet to highlight any of the serious weakness in Confucianism. As a former Confucian priest myself, this huge omission is very telling to me.

7. A major focus of your parents' mission here has been to teach that we're all in desperate need of a Savior. Confucius, however, suggested that human nature is basically good, and that we must focus on self-effort, not preoccupied with otherworldly distractions. You're grounded enough to see what's going on here.

8. So many in our congregation here have repented of Confucianism, due to some of its underlying false teachings. They'd be quite concerned to hear that your parents' alma mater is comfortable with the idea that Christians can meditate on

the *Analects*; fashioning these as somehow a handmaiden to theology and Christian devotion.

9. Does your professor arbitrarily stop with Confucius? Why not plunder any humanist for devotional insight? Why not become a Taoist or Buscaglian Christian, or even move to Christian Confucianism with a Whiteheadian emphasis? Where would the quest stop and why?

10. Confucius' words, so often very wise, carry little more authority or inspiration than the obituaries in your local newspaper. Remember, Confucius was just a man. "Thinking Christianly" is our mandate from heaven; thinking otherwise can be dangerous business indeed.

11. Please check your library for the most recent works by Lit-Sen Chang (even Paulos Huang and Abraham Poon) to get another perspective from an Asian sharing something of his own emancipation from Confucianism.

From all I've heard, your favorite prof is a great guy. Please let me know how he responds to the concerns above.

Cordially,
Pastor Taoshiro

Common Ground between Confucianism and Christianity

Common emphases abound between Confucianism and Christianity. One of the more obvious parallels is that both traditions see "ego is a weapon of mass destruction." With this comes an "other centeredness" that both traditions hold as praiseworthy, stemming into other similarities: respect, love, strong morality, centrality of family and tradition, filial piety, justice, leading by example (vs. coercion), and the cultivation of self-discipline, virtue, and wisdom, etc. Such matters and many others have no doubt captured Prof. Elshof's imagination.

Consider also that Confucius' master plan was to train up a small band of young men in virtuous education, sending them out to take leadership positions in and become agents of transformation in their world. Sound familiar?

Moreover, Confucianism has always put a high premium on the importance of education. As with Christianity, understanding accompanies thoughtful study. Taoism's accent toward passivity in educational (and political) processes, on the other hand, is one of many strong contrasts with Confucianism. Confucius' pedagogy and passion attracted many, and he welcomed students from any social background. His greatest student was a commoner, and he was widely known for taking students who could repay him with nothing more than dried meat and gratitude.

The history of the Church boasts similar impulses: that there should be no class distinctions in education; that those of humble means can improve their plight through education and hard work; that meritocracy outweighs entitlement; etc. Confucius deserves accolades for these kinds of things. But man's deepest need is not information or even virtuous modeling, but true heart transformation found in Christ alone. Mere education can't provide that. Education without reformation is vacuous; reformation without transformation is — well — Confucianism. Our greatest need is a redeemed heart that praises, walks, and communes with our Creator.

Last, Christianity strongly concurs with Confucianism that only in community are we fully human. We are not built for isolation; we are built for relation. We can admire Confucius' "five bonds" as the glue for a stable cultural environment. But we lament that he missed the most important relationship a person can have — a personal relationship with God. This "sixth bond" gives a whole different motivation to how the other five relationships are ordered. It is perhaps this single factor that best accounts for the skyrocketing growth of Christianity in China today.

Differences between Confucianism and Christianity

Many more likenesses could be given. But it behooves Christians to discern truth form error. In fact, the similarities above are incidental if not superficial, given that they emanate from radically different origins, and operate with starkly contrasting motives. Some of this can be seen in the following chart showing representative contrasts between Confucianism and Christianity.

Arbitrariness, Inconsistencies, and Weaknesses in Confucianism

Given our investigation so far, the reader can understand why Johnson insists that "Confucian theory is difficult to criticize."[58] Given its broad scope, ambitious humanistic soteriology, "soft supernaturalism," numerous abstractions, toggling between inclusivism and exclusivism, we see why. It

---

58. David Johnson, *A Reasoned Look at Asian Religions* (Minneapolis, MN: Bethany House, 1985), p. 41.

Some Differences between Confucianism and Christianity	
Confucianism	Christianity
Main Goal: To have a structured society.	Main Goal: Love God and follow His will
Humans are inherently good	Humans are inherently fallen and sinful
"Sin" is breach of the rule of piety toward a superior, parents, family, or homeland	All have inherited a sin nature. Sins are willful violations of known laws of God
Claims the Way (Dao) has been lost	Jesus said, "I am the way"
One foot in present, the other in the past	One foot in present, the other in the future
Founder wrestled with moral weakness	Founder was sinless
"Earthly salvation" achieved through education behavior modification	Eternal salvation comes in acknowledging Jesus' atoning sacrifice and receiving Him as Savior
An inclusive wisdom tradition	An exclusive worldview
No teaching about redemption for sin	Gospel message: there is redemption for sin
Right doing leads to right being	Right being leads to right doing
Anthropocentric	Theocentric/Christocentric
Silver rule: "Do not do unto others . . ."	Golden rule: "Do unto others . . ."

is difficult to criticize in part because it is hard to grasp. Still, for Christians who find much common ground with Confucianism and Christianity, they should be aware of some of its shortcomings. There are many, but we will mention only eight here.

The Biggie

The early Confucian consensus was that man is good by nature and can be perfected by education. In Confucian terms, each person must "rectify himself," which means he must regulate his own conduct. But as lofty and admirable as this sounds, it only bubbles forth from human thinking, making it entirely arbitrary. Thus, outside of being justified by the Holy One of Israel, there is no eternal hope for those placing any salvific weight in these man-crafted guidelines.[59] Again, the many merits of Confucianism mustn't be allowed to camouflage that it is in large part a failed experiment. The Confucian quest for a perfect utopia never materialized — and never will — simply because it was and remains a human construct.

Human beings cannot make themselves good through sheer act of the will, and "human nature being what it is, the lack of *external* checks and balances on power led to the gradual corruption of dynasties all through history."[60] The notion that man is basically good denies the doctrine of original sin and has made evangelism in Asia very difficult. This biggest weakness latent in Confucianism gives birth to the following remaining shortcomings below.

The Elitist Criticism

Johnson highlights a defect of Confucianism missed by most, one found compelling by those on the right (who embrace democratic principles of social order) and those on the left (like Marxists and Maoists). It relates to Confucianism's "anti-democratic and aristocratic cultivation of a cultural elite."

Recalling our prior mention of the junzi, we noted the strong emphasis Confucianism puts on the development of the "ideal" gentleman — but Johnson highlights the obvious, that not everyone can become a gentleman. Those who "make it" tend to enjoy a privileged and refined life. As he rises up the privileged social ladder, he lacks less and less, finding opportunity to accept or reject things according to his (subjective) inner sense of appropriate behavior.

But doesn't this "refinement and taste" come at the expense of everyone else who cannot attain such position? And this is exactly what happened, as the canyon between an elite (and often corrupt) class and the underprivileged was vast. The former enjoyed a palatial and splendid world, while such blessings never trickled down to those in greatest need. Most people influenced by democratic ideas about equality and the rights of the common man saw something wrong with this Confucian elitism, where a few people are raised "to a level where they are considered to be somehow *better* than others." It's

---

59. A few references suggesting exclusivism are John 14:6; Acts 4:12; 1 Timothy 2:5; 1 Corinthians 15:21–22; Hebrews 9:12.

60. Rob Gifford, *China Road: A Journey into the Future of a Rising Power* (New York: Random House, 2007), p. 104.

no shock that Communists castigated "the scholar gentleman" as representative of all that was "repressive, oppressive, and exploitative about the old system."[61]

The Not-so-Golden Rule

A disciple of Confucius, Zi Gong, asked, "Is there any one word that could guide a person throughout life?" The master replied, "How about [reciprocity]? Do not do unto others what you would not want others to do unto you." This is so similar to Jesus' Golden Rule (Mark 12:31) that some have even suggested Jesus plagiarized Confucius! But this charge lacks punch when noting one key difference. While Confucius (and many religions) frames the rule as a negative, Jesus' states the rule as a positive. Jesus exhorted his disciples to "Do unto others as you would have them do unto you." This is a call to a *higher* degree of service than merely refraining from doing bad things to others.

The Christian rule implicitly challenges us to seek opportunities to do good for others. Yamamoto goes so far as to say that in Confucius' version of the Golden Rule, he was instructing his disciples to focus on *themselves*, and references C. George Fry who contends that the first saving virtue for Confucius was "self love."[62]

Inferiority of Women

In the vast majority of Confucianism's earliest chapters, women are accorded very low status and always ranked below men. He spelled out how to become the "ideal man," but nothing of the ideal woman. He shook the social structure by saying that any *man* could become a junzi and scholar, but females factor in very little in the *Analects*. Confucian teaching, as a whole, did nothing to upend the consensus view that girls were to be subordinate, and essentially servant girls in the making.

Additionally, at temple altars, only the names of male ancestors could be listed. And in the *Book of History*, women seem to only be mentioned when it is to blame them for bad happenings. All this stands in stark contrast to Jesus, whose attitude and compassion toward women was breathtakingly inclusive. You might recall that it was women who were the first bear witnesses to His Resurrection.

---

61. Johnson, *A Reasoned Look at Asian Religions*, p. 41–42.
62. J. Isamu Yamamoto, *Buddhism, Taoism, & Other Far Eastern Religions* (Grand Rapids, MI: Zondervan Publishing House, 1998), p. 59.

We can extend Confucius a modicum of slack, as he certainly didn't create China's patriarchal persona. All of Chinese society was male-centered, and he was a product of his time and culture. Having said that, we are saying that long before the practice of foot binding,[63] Confucian ideology did nothing to loose the psychological fetters women had in being valued less than men.

Consider also the lines from a very famous poem (Book IV, *Odes*, vi)

> Sons shall be born to him:
> They will be put to sleep on couches;
> They will be clothed in robes;
> They will have scepters to play with;
> Daughters shall be born to him:
> They will be put to sleep on the ground;
> They will be clothed with wrappers;
> They will have tiles to play with.

The clear and sad message is that girls are inferior to boys in this religious philosophy.

Note also the yin and yang motif — that famous concept in Asian philosophy where everything in the universe is divided into opposite but complementary elements that interact harmoniously. The male-biased principle of yang is portrayed with positive traits like luminous, fast, moving, and aggressive. The female principle of yin is associated with negative qualities like cold, darkness, graves, death, passivity, ghosts, submission, emptiness, and fear.

The harmony of all things in nature and the mutual relationship between good and evil are often represented with the yin-yang symbol.

Imagine the psychological straitjacketing to millions of women over the centuries, having their gender undeservedly linked with negative things (as was portrayed with the main character in the Disney film *Mulan*). Imagine how this conditioned not just young girls, but also the equal damage of millions of men over the centuries having their gender undeservedly linked with the positive. The long arc of justice is slow but sure, however. With 83 documented generations in Confucius' ancestry, in 2009 women were finally officially recognized in Confucius' family tree.

---

63. This was the constricting of young women's feet to prevent growth, done so as a symbol of beauty and status. The barbaric practice was finally ended in the early 20th century.

God's Word vs. Man's Opinion

Another point bears mention — even though it will only carry force with those who accept the truth claims of Christianity — namely that the claims of Confucius and the Confucianism canon have no grounding in divine revelation. The Confucian classics reveal the vanity of relying on human doctrine without the aid of divine revelation. As such, they carry no more authority than any other man-made proclamations.

Confucius' wisdom is nothing but the opinion of one man. Many moral rubrics espoused in Confucianism can be appreciated and even in part practiced by a Christian, and that may be all that Elshof is suggesting. But it must be constantly borne in mind that the Confucian system is humanistic to the core, and thus large parts of it must be courteously, if not firmly, rejected. Christianity, when properly understood, is not weighed and found in want of something that Confucianism offers. But Confucianism, when properly understood, is weighed and found in great need of what Christianity offers.

Sez Who?

We must make a "typically Western" inquiry here. Confucius' exhorted his followers to make truth a priority in their lives. In the *Analects* VII: 24, he highlighted the priority of "culture, conduct, loyalty, and truthfulness." Consider also some of his famous aphorisms:

> The object of the superior man is truth.

> They who know the truth are not equal to those who love it, and they who love it are not equal to those who delight in it.

> Speak the truth, do not yield to anger; give, if thou art asked for little; by these three steps thou wilt go near the gods.

No one denies that Confucius sincerely promoted virtue, wisdom, morality, and the pursuit of truth. But herein lies a dilemma, according to John Ankerberg. The unstated premise is that all of these lofty standards presuppose an absolute standard; these ideals must be "true for everyone — everywhere and always. Yet, what if these qualities are merely relative concepts, untethered from objective truth? If truth is reduced to mere personal whim — for example by an Emperor Qin type in a power grab — then all the

Confucian ideals are gutted of objective meaning, and thus have no authentic or lasting value.

Presupposing that words have meaning, Ankerberg asks us to consider how Confucius might counsel the *superior man* (i.e., the genuinely virtuous) "to learn truth prudently, with humility and attention to detail."[64] Saying this is one thing, but how exactly do we follow his sagacious advice; how do we learn absolute truth? How do we transcend the wisdom to be found in the routine and practical matters of this earthly life? How do we learn the truth where it matters the most, discovering real answers to the great questions of life that everyone is unavoidably curious about? What about finding the true purpose of life, or how to secure enduring peace and happiness, or knowing what happens when we die, or the nature of ultimate reality? This is where, if we honor Confucius admonition to place truth first in our lives, we discover a dilemma.

But Ankerberg is merely exploiting a philosophical weakness which Arthur Leff calls "The Grand Sez Who?" Why do the rights of the ruler (be he the emperor or Mao) outweigh those of the rice farmer or even the whole country? Leff says that without an objective source of moral authority handing down laws from above, what reason do we have to designate any action or school of thought as "virtuous" as opposed to another?[65]

If a Christian suggests we act more generously to the needy, someone might ask "Sez who?" When she quotes Luke 3:11, it's implicit that she's saying, "Jesus — the Creator and Sustainer and absolute authority in all things! That's who!" Cultured despisers of our faith aren't swayed by this, but that's not the point. We are just saying that this is the *basis* on which we should build our convictions and from which we act.

But think about any exhortation that Confucius ever uttered, or pick any of his pithy proverbs, and immediately ask, "Sez who?" We are not denying that many elements in Confucianism are good, moral, and edifying. We are simply trying to get at the meta-ethical bedrock of what makes the good things *good* that Confucius advocates? For a Christian, the answers come easier than most. Namely, it is the absolute objective moral authority undergirding Christianity — the Almighty God — that permits the Christian to judge elements in Confucianism as good or bad. But anyone should wonder if Confucian precepts should be accepted on

---

64. https://www.jashow.org/articles/general/the-religions-of-china-and-the-power-of-jesus/.
65. http://www.firstthings.com/article/1993/03/002-nihilism-and-the-end-of-law.

their own ground. Aside from begging the question, we can hear Dr. Leff chime in, "Sez who?"

With Friends Like These

Given China's cyclic anarchy, cruelty, wars, crime, societal discord, government corruption, innumerable manifestations of inhumanity, and collapse of the family in Confucius' day, it is difficult to fathom how Confucius (and Mencius later) could embrace the premise that "mankind is innately good." Mencius agreed. Xun Zi, in the third century B.C., on the other hand, examined the empirical data of life, claiming that man naturally tended toward evil.

Confucians of every stripe, however, were collectively mistaken in thinking that all foibles could be purged through mere education and *self*-cultivation. It was *self*-cultivation, in a sense, that caused all problems in the first place. Mankind has been crippled since that scene played out in the Garden.

The River Elegy

A church leader in central China recently told the author that, "Confucianism buried the Chinese . . . it became the curse on China!" Confucius' philosophy carved out deep ruts that the Chinese slavishly followed for 2,000 years. This observation was from a prominent believer, but it's also a fairly common sentiment on the street that Confucianism has generally held China back.

This exact point was loudly and surprisingly made when CCTV (Chinese state TV) aired a documentary series in 1988 called *River Elegy*, partly blaming Confucianism for China's isolationism and backwardness. It suggested that blindly following traditions had hindered China's modernization. The series brought on a maelstrom, and its proximity to the deadly Tiananmen confrontation a year later should not be missed.

But what of the series title? It refers to the Yellow River, which has come to represent the cradle of Chinese culture and civilization. The earliest written records verify that she was known as the mother river of the nation, and most Mainland Chinese see themselves as offspring of the Yellow River. It has long been called "China's Sorrow" because of its propensity for devastating floods. But now we have reference to an elegy, or "a lament for the dead." Rob Gifford explains why the series title was chosen.

There is an old Chinese saying that "a dipperful of Yellow River water is seven-tenths mud," and *River Elegy* took the silt and sediment of the river as a symbol for the weight of Confucian tradition, clogging up the Chinese mind. The elegy of the title was an aspirational one, a hope that the traditional cultural of China, which has held the country back for so long, might die and be replaced by a more progressive, Western-style way of thinking.[66]

So the suffocating sediments of the Yellow River (in part) symbolized the mud that has suffocated Chinese minds for ages. The creators of *River Elegy* were trying to raise awareness that China's cultural stagnation had many culprits, and Confucianism was a key player.[67] Christians, of course, see a much deeper need here, as this presents an opportunity for the gospel to penetrate Asia's rocky soil. Such, in fact, has already been firmly established in Korea, and missiologists estimate that at present, 22,000 souls turn to Christ every day in China. From river elegy to river of life?

Tips for Redemptive Outreach with Confucians[68]

God-fearing Christians can and do disagree on their approaches to reaching the Confucian soul. Where can we accommodate, and where must we hold firm? Those long-immersed in the Asian world have found some approaches more fruitful than others when sharing Christ with those who are deeply imprinted with Confucian convictions. The author's own parents modeled for him several decades of love for the Asian harvest, and he watched countless souls befriended in his living rooms, seeing questions addressed with biblical truth, barriers come down, and — over time — these souls loved into the Kingdom. The following common sense suggestions can be ignored or adapted according to context, and will often apply just as well when witnessing Buddhists, Taoists, or anyone from a traditional Asian background.

---

66. Gifford, *China Road*, p. 166.
67. Other weaknesses in Confucianism are too numerous to list here. See also, J.N.D. Anderson, ed., *The World's Religions*, 3rd edition (Grand Rapids, MI: Eerdmans, 1955), p. 178–179; and Stuart C. Hackett, *Oriental Philosophy: A Westerner's Guide to Eastern Thought* (Madison, WI: University of Wisconsin Press 1979), p. 140–152.
68. See also "Christian Witness to the Chinese People" at https://www.lausanne.org/content/lop/lop-6, and https://www.lausanne.org/content/lga/2014-11/the-path-to-confuciuss-ideal. Cf. Paulos Huang, "Basic Problems in the Confucian-Christian dialogue," in *Confronting Confucian Understandings of the Christian Doctrine of Salvation* (Leiden, The Netherlands: E.J. Bill, 2009), p. 245–265.

- Spiritual warfare is serious. Begin with prayer! The Holy Spirit has long tilled the soil in Confucian hearts, and will help you.

- To fully comprehend the Chinese psyche it is imperative, as one thinker put it, to "reckon with the long shadow of Confucius." Familiarization with the *Analects* is essential if you are preparing for missions work anywhere with high concentrations of Confucians.

- Huang gives five positives which have increased Confucian receptivity to the gospel: (1) the enthusiasm of Chinese Christian believers; (2) the attractive personalities of many Western missionaries; (3) the respect for, and use of, Confucian classics by many missionaries in their presentation of the Gospel; (4) the dialogical approach that has replaced a more confrontational stance of earlier years; and (5) the employment of natural reasoning by missionaries and Chinese converts, which appeals to the rationalistic bent of Confucianism (i.e., we need the solid grounding in apologetics).[69] This still holds.

- Ancestor worship is not likely to come up in early encounters, but could arise later. Be prepared! How to express deep veneration without worship is not a topic for armchair missionaries. Areas of contextualization at this depth must sometimes be wrestled with for years, to discern which elements Scripture is asking us to adopt, adapt, or abolish.

- Honest seekers have wondered for ages whether they are called to reject their culture when becoming Christian. It's unfortunate and embarrassing that missionaries have botched this so often. Add to this the anti-imperialism mantra of the May Fourth Movement (1919), "One more Christian, one less Chinese," and we get a feel for the psychological warfare that still constricts the Chinese heart. So many Asians continue

---

69. I am indebted to G. Wright Doyle for this tidy summation, as well as drawing my attention to Huang's work, http://www.reachingchineseworldwide.org/blog/reviews/confronting-confucian-understandings-of-the-christian-doctrine-of-salvation. Huang's study should be indispensible reading for anyone serious about the present Confucian-Christian dialogue, and learning how Confucians from the Ricci era to the present have adopted, adapted, or abated the Christian message.

to labor under the illusion that coming to Calvary means betraying family and cultural identity. Be prepared to show how Chinese can be followers of Christ without having to jettison their ethnic identity. Also, anticipate some version of the question as to whether one can be Confucian and Christian.

- Discussing the Father relationship is often helpful as such an exploration can help Confucians form a more accurate concept of our personal God.

- Two Confucian ideals are personified by Jesus — namely the virtues of being (1) junzi, the ideal man, and (2) a son of perfect filiality. Tracing these trajectories for a sensitive seeker is an effective way to find common ground and point to Christ as the perfect image of God.

- Consider adapting this parallel: "China's history is replete with emperors who have utterly failed in their *Mandate* to govern wisely and maintain harmony, But *Shang Di*, the Father, sent His Son of Heaven who sacrificed himself to fulfill his Father's will and usher in reconciliation." To frame things like this is to preemptively address the charge of the gospel being a foreign answer to an indigenous problem, and (again) highlight the Confucian ideal of filial piety.[70]

- Wherever biblically warranted, emphasizing parallels between Christianity and Confucianism in order to evangelize Confucians can be fruitful. But doing so in a way to suggest that becoming a "Confucian Christian" is okay, or that condones "double belonging," is extremely problematic.

- The realization that the Christian message is the missing piece to Confucius' puzzle of the Noble Man could be extremely significant for a cultural Asian considering the claims of Jesus.

- Don't get mired in cherry picking inconsistencies of Confucianism. Such does not fly in Asia. Paint an irresistible narrative of how Christ fulfills the longings of the Confucian heart. Use words as necessary.

70. Adapted from http://rzim.org/just-thinking/jesus-the-path-to-human-flourishing.

- Again, spiritual warfare is serious! The enemy will not easily re-linquish territory he's fought millennia to conquer. Pray, pray, pray!

Summary of Confucian Beliefs

Doctrine	Teachings of Confucianism
God	Confucians pursue social ethics, and all traditional Asian cultures see the spiritual realm as carrying the potential for impacting society and all relationships. Deny the God of the Bible, but allowance is made for an impersonal Tian that resembles an ultimate force or ordering principle. Elements of ancestor worship are common.
Authority/ Revelation	Confucius is seen as the pre-eminent leader. The Five Classics, the Four Books form the core Confucian canon. Among these the *Analects* is most revered, and for Confucius himself it was the *I Ching*.
Man	All men are innately good. Only in relation to others can one establish virtuous character. Education, virtuous living, and ritual can create the ideal man. External influences cause moral corruption.
Sin	In early days there was a moral obligation to follow the Mandate of Heaven. To not do so was "sin," but sin was also the result of external corrupting influences or failing to follow *li* or *yi*. Creating disharmony and defying social structures and rites are seen as corruptions of the created order.
Salvation	Man can achieve moral perfection, social harmony and benevolent governing through human effort and proper ritual, including veneration of ancestors. There is no defined concept of an afterlife, or a "reward and punishment" dialectic.
Creation	View the universe as self-existent, so there is no notion of a Creator. Modern adherents may accept various ideas regarding evolution.

Chapter 21

Unitarianism

Roger Patterson

As a writer, I often interact with people on social media platforms who are commenting on my articles or articles from Answers in Genesis. One of the most alarming ideas I encounter from professing Christians is the unitarian view of God.

In articles that talk about the trinitarian God of the Bible, commenters quickly turn to castigating the authors and other commenters for believing in the Trinity. They insist that God has revealed Himself as the "one, true, and living God." "If God is one, how can you say there are three gods?" "The Trinity was invented by Constantine/Council of Nicaea/Roman Catholics." "If you are worshiping the Trinity, you are worshiping false gods."

While these are common responses, they do not reflect the biblical presentation of God. While we must admit that the word "Trinity" does not appear in the Bible, we dare not deny that the concept is presented.[1] This is such an important issue because it is a dividing line between those who know the Father and those who do not. The Apostle John warns the first-century Christians that denying Jesus as God in the flesh is to deny the Father, as well.

> Who is a liar but he who denies that Jesus is the Christ? He
> is antichrist who denies the Father and the Son. Whoever denies

---

1. See Appendix 1, "The Triune God," in volume one of this series for a scriptural validation of the Trinity.

the Son does not have the Father either; he who acknowledges the Son has the Father also (1 John 2:22–23).[2]

The early church had to deal with this question on many occasions. The outcome of every challenge to the doctrine of the Trinity was to denounce the unitarian views of God as heresy — a doctrine that leads to damnation to all who deny the triune God. The fullest summary expression of these trinitarian ideas is contained in the Athanasian Creed. Earlier creeds, like the Nicene and Apostles' Creed, do not have an expressly trinitarian formula that continues to allow non-trinitarian groups to claim allegiance to Christianity through these less-precise creeds.

While these false views are damning, the modern expressions of Unitarianism has moved further away from its historic Christian roots to the point that Dr. Walter Martin has called it "the cult of the intellect."[3] Blending ideas of New Age thinking with rationalism and moral relativism, biblical morality has been abandoned for a truly man-centered view of truth and morality. Within Unitarian Universalism, *man* is truly the measure of all things.

Defining Unitarianism

The term "unitarian" has both a general sense and a more precise theological sense. The focus of this chapter is the religious movement known as Unitarianism and its later expression of Unitarian Universalism, but we will also look at how the term can be applied in a general sense. At its root, a unitarian view of God insists that God is one person and one being. This is practically synonymous with monotheism, believing in one God, but is distinguished from a trinitarian monotheism that believes in one God existing in three persons. The trinitarian distinguishes between the being and the persons of the Godhead while the unitarian denies the distinction in various ways.[4]

In its specific sense, Unitarianism is a system of religious thought that developed in Europe in the mid-16th century. It is characterized by the acknowledgment of one God, denying that Jesus and the Holy Spirit are persons of the Godhead. Jesus is seen as the "son" of God in some sense, and the Holy Spirit is seen as a force or an aspect of God's will in the world.

---

2. Scripture in this chapter is from the New King James Version (NKJV) of the Bible.
3. https://www.youtube.com/watch?v=RVwGaXt4pOk.
4. When referring to the religious movement, Unitarian will be capitalized; when used as an adjective describing the generic view of the nature of God it will be lowercase. The same format will be followed for the use of trinitarian.

Variations on a Theme

Today, we can find many expressions of the unitarian view of God within the broad scope of Christianity. Christadelphians, Jehovah's Witnesses, and others teach a monotheistic unitarian view of God. Additionally, several unitarian groups developed out of trinitarian churches in the US. United Pentecostalism and Oneness Pentecostalism are non-trinitarian groups that teach God is one being manifested in three different modes. This unitarian belief is often referred to as *modalism* and bears strong resemblance to *Sabellianism*, a unitarian view promoted by Sabellius in the third century. Other denominations, some bearing "Church of God" or "Apostolic" in their names, also hold a unitarian view of God while claiming the Bible as an important aspect of their religious views. Judaism and Islam can also be considered unitarian in this general sense, each acknowledging that there is only one God.

There is also a rise in unitarian teaching among groups associated with the modern "Hebrew Roots" movement. Aligning strongly with Judaism, these groups view Jesus as the human Messiah, but deny the Trinity. Similarly, a rise in Biblical Unitarianism in the West has been championed by teachers like Anthony Buzzard, but seeking to distinguish themselves from rational Unitarianism, especially Universal Unitarianism. Biblical Unitarians consider themselves within orthodox Christianity and appeal to the Bible as an authoritative source.

These forms of unitarian religious systems fit within the category of counterfeits of Christianity, the subject of volume one of this series. They are briefly covered here because of the potentially confusing terminology, allowing a clear distinction between unitarian beliefs and the Unitarian movement. At their origin, the Unitarian churches were overtly biblical. In their modern expressions, Unitarianism and Unitarian Universalism can be seen as moralistic religions that draw ideas from many different sources. Both are ultimately grounded in human reasoning and natural law rather than God and His revelation to us in the Bible.

Unitarian History

Unitarian thinking was present in various groups from the beginning of Christianity. As with much of our modern understanding of Christianity, Unitarianism rose out of the Protestant Reformation. You may be familiar with the name Michael Servetus — probably associated with John Calvin — but you may not know why his teaching was being challenged as heresy by both the Roman Catholics and the Protestants. Servetus' views were rejected for good reason — he was openly promoting a unitarian view of God and other false ideas. This ire came to a head in 1531 with the publication of his *Trinitarian Misconceptions*.

Additionally, the Protestants saw him as a dangerous false

Unitarians, including Michael Servetus and Thomas Jefferson, have compared the doctrine of the Trinity to turning the one true God into the three-headed beast, Cerberus.
(Campana Collection, 1861, Louvre Museum, by Eagle Painter, Wikipedia)

teacher because he rejected the biblical teaching of justification by faith alone.[5] He was arrested by Roman Catholics but he escaped. Later, he was arrested in Geneva by Protestants. During his trial in Geneva in 1553, he was questioned on his views of the Trinity, having compared the doctrine of the Trinity to the mythical three-headed Greek beast, Cerberus. Holding a unitarian view of God, he saw the doctrine of the Trinity as unbiblical and denied that Jesus was the eternal Son of God. Unfortunately, Servetus was charged as a heretic and burned at the stake for his heresies by the civil authorities, and much controversy surrounds this event.[6]

Various scholars in Europe continued to study the writings of Servetus, especially in light of his refusal to recant at his martyrdom. While he had not founded a movement, he surely paved the way for a young Italian to do so. Following in the footsteps of his soft-spoken uncle Lelio, Fausto Sozzini would carry Servetus' ideas to the founding of the first unitarian church. While various spellings of his name are found, we often see it presented in its Latin form as Faustus Socinus. It is from this spelling that the anti-Trinitarian view of Socinianism is named.

5. Frederick B. Mott, *A Short History of Unitarianism since the Reformation*, 2nd ed. (Boston, MA: Unitarian Sunday-School Society, 1893), p. 15–24, accessed digitally at https://books.google.com/books?id=jHcRAAAAYAAJ.
6. Standford Rives, *Did Calvin Murder Servetus?* (Charleston, SC: BookSurge Publishers, 2008), p. 288–289, accessed digitally at https://books.google.com/books?id=MlPrYQ5srKEC.

Faustus Socinus continued to promote the anti-Trinitarian views of Servetus and began to develop a more robust system of thinking — the system that would ultimately be known as Unitarianism. Beyond teaching against the Trinity, he also promoted an unbiblical view of Christ's sacrifice. Socinus denied that Jesus was a vicarious (substitutionary) sacrifice for sins, but that obedience to God was still necessary.[7]

Rather than Jesus reconciling God to men, the consensus of a majority of the Reformers, Socinus taught that men were reconciled to God through piety, demonstrations of love, and obedience to God — through works. Jesus is seen more as an example for us to follow than a substitute who died in our place having taken upon Himself the penalty for our sins. He also denied the idea of original sin, the pre-existence of Jesus as the Word before His birth, and that God's knowledge of the future is limited to necessary truths.

The Transylvanian and Polish Churches

Socinus was called to Transylvania (in modern-day Romania) to help settle a dispute within the Unitarian Church of Transylvania. Simultaneously in Poland, a Unitarian church was gaining popularity. The Minor Reformed Church, a group who had split from the majority, formed in 1565. Commonly known as the Polish Brethren, this group was banned from Poland in 1656. Many of its members moved to Transylvania, Netherlands, and England, where there had already been considerable Unitarian influence.

Through the writings of Socinus, formal doctrines of Unitarian thought were formulated. Published after his death, the Racovian Catechism provided the platform of Unitarian teaching. Though there were factions that denied miracles and other aspects, these teachings relied heavily on the Bible for their foundation. Though Socinus promoted the use of human reason to validate what the Bible taught (i.e., *man* sitting in judgment over God), it was in England that the secular rationalism of the Scientific Revolution and Enlightenment era would add color to Unitarian thinking.

Spread to England

In 1609, a Latin version of the unitarian Racovian Catechism was produced and eventually banned by the English Parliament, which ordered all of the copies to be burned. Not long after, a version emerged from Amsterdam in

---

7. Mott, *A Short History of Unitarianism since the Reformation*, p. 25–26.

English. Some credit this translation to John Biddle.[8] Biddle had used his own reasoning from the Bible to come to the conclusion that the Trinity was a doctrine foreign to Scripture.

Upon encountering the works of Socinus, Biddle found a kindred spirit and began promoting his ideas in writing and speaking. This promotion of anti-Trinitarian ideas brought the ire of the government who had outlawed anti-Trinitarian teaching as blasphemy, landing him in jail on multiple occasions. Biddle's views also brought condemnation in John Owen's *A Brief Declaration and Vindication of the Doctrine of the Trinity*. Owen specifically targeted the false views of the Trinity and the atonement presented by Biddle and other Socinians.[9] Jonathan Edwards would later argue in a similar manner against John Locke's rationalistic view of Scripture and Socinian views.[10]

Along with the increasing secular humanistic influence of the period before the Enlightenment, Biddle saw human reason as the only appropriate way to interpret Scripture. This influence led Biddle and others to reason that Jesus was not divine, nor was the Holy Spirit a part of the Godhead. The Trinity was deemed irrational by fallible human standards, and they found Bible passages that they twisted to support their ideas. In this, their error is exposed — they used man's fallible reasoning to judge the truth of God's infallible Word. Through the distribution of tracts and preaching in various venues, the application of rationalism to the interpretation of the Scriptures flourished.

This influence is later seen in the writings of John Locke, Isaac Newton, and John Milton. All of these men, though often propped up for their Christian beliefs, denied or questioned the Trinity and the deity of Christ while subjecting the Scriptures to their own rational standards. While acknowledging God's role in the world and even His revelation through Scripture, they used Scripture to support their ideas where it was helpful and set it aside where it was not useful. This rationalistic approach to Scripture would become a hallmark of Unitarianism as it grew in England and spread to America.

---

8. Ibid., p. 28. Also spelled Bidle.
9. John Owen, *A Brief Declaration and Vindication of the Doctrine of the Trinity*, 8th ed., (Glasgow, Scotland: Napier and Khull, 1798), p. viii–xii, accessed digitally at https://books.google.com/books?id=NwM3AAAAMAAJ.
10. J.D. Bowers, *Joseph Priestley and English Unitarianism in America* (University Park, PA: Pennsylvania State University Press, 2007), p. 20.

Because of the strong connection between church and state in 16th- and 17th-century Europe, Unitarians were pushed out of government involvement and generally persecuted for their beliefs by both the Roman Catholic and Protestant regimes. It was not until 1774 that the first Unitarian congregation was established by Theophilus Lindsey. Lindsey was a vicar in the Anglican Church, and you may know him as an early champion of Sunday school. But his rejection of Trinitarian doctrines and subscription to all of the Thirty-Nine Articles of the Anglican Church led him to join a petition to parliament in 1771 to allow the Unitarians and others to remain in the church without holding to the Anglican doctrines in total. After the petition failed, he resigned his vicarage and began teaching at Essex Street Chapel in London. At the dedication of the chapel in April of 1774, Benjamin Franklin made an appearance. Within four years they had purchased more property on Essex Street and a "proper chapel" was built.[11] The headquarters of the British Unitarians remains there to this day.

Lindsey was also a friend of one of the greatest British scientific minds, Joseph Priestley. Priestley took his great analytical mind and applied it to theology. The rational spirit of the age was turning many theists toward deism, though atheism was still socially unacceptable. Mott notes that "Priestley's great help to the growth of Unitarian principles was in the use of shears and pruning-knife. He relentlessly trimmed away conventionalities, the poetry of tradition, and the mystery of accepted faith, and left only the sturdy stock of rational theology, a strong plant for others to cultivate."[12] Priestley's influence stretched beyond his scientific endeavors to philosophy and religious thought.

Other notable Unitarians in England include Josiah Wedgewood, Emma Darwin, John Locke, John Milton, Charles Dickens, and Neville Chamberlain.

Spread to America

Priestley was basically forced out of England for his political and social views. He chose to find a new home in America. Landing there in 1794, he was not the first to bring rationalism and Unitarianism across the Atlantic. As many different groups moved to the English colonies, Unitarian thinkers and teachers were among them, but Priestley unified the movement with his

---

11. Bowers, *Joseph Priestley and English Unitarianism in America*, p. 15.
12. Mott, *A Short History of Unitarianism since the Reformation*, p. 42.

leadership.[13] While the colonies were strongly influenced by biblical Christianity, the rationalism of the Enlightenment blended with the moralism that found its primary basis in the Bible. While many dismissed the miraculous elements of the Bible, it was still an influential book. But as with Biddle and others, reason sat as judge over revelation. Natural law was the standard, and the Bible was used where it was helpful in affirming proverbial wisdom.

Unitarianism as a formal American denomination took root in Boston with the founding of King's Chapel in 1784. Colonial New England was heavily influenced by Calvinist theology, so Socinian ideas denying the divinity of Jesus and substitutionary atonement raised the hackles of the orthodox Christians. However, James Freeman found a sympathetic audience when he arrived at King's Chapel. The congregation was so amenable to his ideas that he reformed the Episcopal liturgy to align with Unitarian doctrines. Being refused ordination as an Episcopal minister, the congregation ordained him as their minister.[14] With the assistance of William Hazlitt and the writings of Priestley and his students, tracts and other writings promoting Unitarian beliefs were distributed, and Unitarianism spread in the fledgling nation.[15]

Unitarian Ideas among the Founding Fathers

If the defining doctrines of Unitarianism are placing reason above Scripture, denying the divinity of Jesus, and rejecting man's sinfulness and need for Christ's atoning blood, its doctrines were broadly accepted even before a church was established. Reading the 18th-century American political discussions, the influence of John Locke cannot be denied. His use of principles from Scripture, acknowledgment of the Divine, and emphasis on reason ring through his work and those who followed his thinking.

While the Bible was revered by many as book of good moral value, even ministers like John Witherspoon taught that reason sat in judgment over revelation. It was his influence that took Princeton from a school training ministers of the gospel to one training rationalists who would greatly influence America's founding period. Dr. Gregg Frazer has dubbed this view "theistic rationalism," documenting how key men involved in writing

---

13. Bowers, *Joseph Priestley and English Unitarianism in America*, p. 2–3.
14. Mott, *A Short History of Unitarianism since the Reformation*, p. 44–46.
15. George Willis Cooke, *Unitarianism in America: A History of Its Origin and Development*, vol. 4 (Boston, Massachusetts: American Unitarian Association, 1902), p. 76–80; Bowers, *Joseph Priestley and English Unitarianism in America*, p. 53.

America's founding documents used biblical principles in the spirit of John Locke's rationalism. While acknowledging God is involved in the affairs of man (acknowledging providence and denying Deism), they looked to their own reason to judge what was useful and true in Scripture.[16]

The influence of Servetus, Priestley, Lindsey, and others seems clear in the writings of Thomas Jefferson who likewise compared the doctrine of the Trinity to Cerberus and promoted Unitarianism as the only rational view of God, though expressing that in public was politically problematic. His view that Trinitarian teaching had corrupted true Christianity and the prominent role of reason are clearly presented in a letter to James Smith from 1822:

> I have to thank you for your pamphlets on the subject of Unitarianism, and to express my gratification with your efforts for the revival of primitive Christianity in your quarter. No historical fact is better established than that the doctrine of one god, pure and uncompounded was that of the early ages of Christianity; and was among the efficacious doctrines which gave it triumph over the polytheism of the ancients, sickened with the absurdities of their own theology. Nor was the unity of the supreme being ousted from the Christian creed by the force of reason, but by the sword of civil government wielded at the will of the fanatic Athanasius. The hocus-pocus phantasm of a god, like another Cerberus, with one body and three heads had its birth and growth in the blood of thousands and thousands of martyrs. And a strong proof of the solidity of the primitive faith is its restoration as soon as a nation arises which vindicates to itself the freedom of religious opinion, and its eternal divorce from the civil authority. The pure and simple unity of the creator of the universe is now all but ascendant in the Eastern states; it is dawning in the West, and advancing towards the South; and I confidently expect that the present generation will see Unitarianism become the general religion of the United States. The Eastern presses are giving us many excellent pieces on the subject, and Priestly's learned writings on it are, or should be in every hand. In fact the Athanasian paradox that one is three, and

16. Gregg. Frazer, *The Religious Beliefs of America's Founders: Reason, Revelation, Revolution* (Lawrence, Kansas: University Press of Kansas, 2012).

three but one is so incomprehensible to the human mind that no candid man can say he has any idea of it, and how can he believe what presents no idea. He who thinks he does only, deceives himself. He proves also that man, once surrendering his reason, has no remaining guard against absurdities the most monstrous, and like a ship without rudder is the sport of every wind. With such persons gullibility which they call faith takes the helm from the hand of reason and the mind becomes a wreck.

I write with freedom, because, while I claim a right to believe in one god, if so my reason tells me, I yield as freely to others that of believing in three. both religions I find make honest men, & that is the only point society has any authority to look to — altho' this mutual freedom should produce mutual indulgence, yet I wish not to be brought in question before the public on this or any other subject, and I pray you to consider me as writing under that trust. I take no part in controversies religious or political. at [sic] the age of 80, tranquility is the greatest good of life, and the strongest of our desires that of dying in the good will of all mankind. and [sic] with the assurances of all my good will to Unitarian & Trinitarian, to Whig & Tory accept for yourself that of my entire respect.[17]

Having traveled to England, Benjamin Franklin had been acquainted with Priestley, even offering letters of introduction to his friends in Philadelphia for one of Priestley's students who traveled to America to promote Priestley's writings.[18] While Franklin and Jefferson seem to have gone closer to Deism than Priestley was comfortable doing, the influence and shared ideas are obvious.

In a letter to Jefferson, John Adams wrote of his study of Priestley's writings, the superiority of reason over Scripture, and his denial of the Trinity:

Dear Sir, I owe you a thousand thanks for your favor of August 22d and its enclosures, and for Dr. Priestley's doctrines

---

17. "From Thomas Jefferson to James Smith, 8 December 1822," Founders Online, National Archives, http://founders.archives.gov/documents/Jefferson/98-01-02-3202. Digital copy available through the Library of Congress at https://www.loc.gov/resource/mtj1.053_0578_0579.

18. Bowers, *Joseph Priestley and English Unitarianism in America*, p. 52.

of Heathen Philosophy compared with those of Revelation. . . .
The human understanding is a revelation from its Maker which
can never be disputed or doubted. There can be no skepticism,
Pyrrhonism, or incredulity, or infidelity, here. No prophecies,
no miracles are necessary to prove the celestial communication.

This revelation has made it certain that two and one make
three, and that one is not three nor can three be one. We can
never be so certain of any prophecy, or the fulfillment of any
prophecy, or of any miracle, or the design of any miracle, as we
are form the revelation of nature, I.E., Nature's God, that two
and two are equal to four. Miracles or prophecies might frighten
us out of our wits; might scare us to death; might induce us to
lie, to say that we believe that two and two make five. But we
should not believe it. We should know the contrary.

Had you and I been forty days on Mount Sinai, and been
admitted to behold the divine Shekinah, and there told that one
was three and three one, we might not have had courage to deny
it, but we could not have believed it.[19]

As Adams speaks of revelation, he elevates natural revelation above the
Scriptures, even saying he would deny the Trinity on that basis if God spoke
to him. In the letter, Adams goes on to deny the biblical concept of hell
based on his own reasoning from nature. While these men may not have
been official members of any Unitarian church, the thoughts they express
on religion betray their allegiance to Unitarian doctrines and not orthodox
Christianity. Adams payed homage to Priestley throughout his later writings
and consistently elevated reason above Scripture, even though he acknowledged the Bible's usefulness:

Philosophy, which is the result of reason, is the first, the
original revelation from the Creator to his creature, man. When
this revelation is clear and certain, by intuition or necessary
induction, no subsequent revelation, supported by prophecies
or miracles, can supersede it. Philosophy is not only the love of
wisdom, but the science of the universe and its cause. . . . Phi-

19. "Letter to Thomas Jefferson, September 14, 1813," *The Writings of Thomas Jefferson*, vol.
6 (Washington, DC: Taylor and Maury, 1854), p. 204–207, accessed digitally at https://
books.google.com/books?id=LmMSAAAAYAAJ.

losophy looks with an impartial eye on the terrestrial religions. I have examined all, as well as my narrow sphere, my straitened means, and my busy life would allow me; and the result is, that the Bible is the best book in the world. It contains more of my little philosophy than all the libraries I have seen; and such parts of it as I cannot reconcile to my little philosophy, I postpone for future investigations.[20]

You will note that Adams mentions the Bible as a great book, but only so far as it fits his "little philosophy." Adams has not subjected his thoughts to God's Word, but the reverse. From there, he goes on to extol the virtues of the morality of Zoroaster, Confucius, and the Hindu writings, noting their "sublime" and "transcendent" qualities, offering that there could not "be found theology more orthodox, or philosophy more profound, than in the introduction to the Shasta."[21] As long as a religious writer or philosopher agreed with Adams' perception of the world through his own reasoning, he was obliged to say it was true. Those parts that did not accord with his view of the world were to be set aside for "future investigation." This line of thinking would develop as the fundamental core of Unitarianism, culminating in the eventual emergence of the Unitarian Universal Church of today.

Other notable American Unitarians include John Quincy Adams, Paul Revere, Ralph Waldo Emerson, Susan B. Anthony, Mary Shelley, Alexander Graham Bell, Louis Agassiz, Linus Pauling, and Frank Lloyd Wright.

From Biblical to Universal

Early American Unitarianism, like its English mother, was rooted in the Bible. To varying degrees, the Bible was seen as the source of religious thought and morality. As with Socinus and Servetus, the denial of the divinity of Jesus and the unorthodox view of His death were argued from Scripture mingled with human reason. We should view early (1790–1840) American Unitarianism as a spectrum. Ministers like William Ellery Channing still denied the Trinity but thought of Jesus as more than just a man, as the more liberal Unitarians like Andrews Norton who went beyond Channing in denying the Virgin Birth and

---

20. "Letter to Thomas Jefferson, December 25, 1813," *The Works of John Adams*, vol. 10 (Boston, MA: Little, Brown, and Company, 1856), p. 82–86, accessed digitally at https://books.google.com/books?id=jRXOAwAAQBAJ.
21. Ibid., p. 85.

most of the miracles in the Bible.[22] All shared the elevation of human reasoning above biblical inspiration, but some denied the Trinity and deity of Christ in the form of Arius while others followed Socinus' reasoning.

In 1825, under the initial leadership of Channing, and later Aaron Bancroft, Unitarian congregations in the East joined together to form the American Unitarian Association (AUA). This was the formal denominational structure of Unitarianism in America, holding conferences and publishing various journals and literature. Later, Western Unitarians (e.g., Illinois, Ohio, and Kentucky) joined the association.[23] It was during this period that Unitarianism took hold within Harvard Divinity School and spread to the pulpits supplied with its graduates.[24]

A Transcendental Shift

In the 1830s, a large shift began within the Unitarian movement. Based in the German transcendental philosophy, this shift took Unitarians away from external sources of truth and sought a natural religion that was affirmed by the inner witness of the soul. Much to the consternation of Channing and others, Ralph Waldo Emerson and other young Unitarians continued to move away from Scripture as a foundation, looking to the inner self to define the divine.

Ralph Waldo Emerson and other transcendentalist writers had a strong influence on the liberalization of Unitarianism in America. (Wikipedia)

Having studied at Harvard and served as a pastor, Emerson eventually came to espouse the transcendental philosophy after travels in Europe. This influence took a strong hold in Unitarian circles, setting personal intuition and inner divinity as the next liberalizing tide. This tide led to the acknowledgment of other religions as valid ways to connect with God, bringing waves of pluralism and syncretism to erode the biblical underpinnings of Unitarianism. As loose as this footing was, it provided little resistance. Unitarianism had become a broadly inclusive religion by the end of the 19th century.[25]

22. Cooke, *Unitarianism in America*, p. 92–107.
23. Ibid., p. 127–138.
24. Ibid., p. 108–110.
25. Ibid., p. 412–435.

Influenced by Frederic Hedge and other writers and preachers, Emerson, Henry W. Longfellow, Oliver Wendell Holmes, Louisa May Alcott, and many other poets and writers spread the new form of Unitarianism far and wide. This new era of pluralism was accompanied by the notion of universal salvation on the grounds that every individual was already connected with the Divine — Emerson's Over-Soul — as a part of nature. This had the positive effects of promoting an end to American slavery, supporting various cultural causes, and the enfranchisement of women, but a detrimental effect on the spiritual health of the nation's population. Additionally, an increasing acceptance of materialistic science colored the teaching of the AUA as humanism was advancing within its ranks.

A Humanist Manifesto

Moving forward to the early 20th century,[26] there was a controversy within the association between those who wanted to promote humanism and those who wanted to maintain a theistic view. In 1921, this controversy came up at a national conference as John Dietrich gave a speech that swayed the core of AUA principles from "faith in God, into faith in the Commonwealth of Man." It was from this point that the full "rejection of divine revelation and the affirmation of reason and the scientific method" was solidified in the AUA.[27]

Desiring to have a summary of the beliefs of the Humanist Fellowship, Roy Wood Sellars was asked to draft such a document. With the help of Edwin Wilson, Raymond Bragg, and Curtis Reese, all Unitarian ministers, the document was prepared for publication in 1933. It was widely distributed after being signed by 34 prominent men, creating another wave of controversy with the AUA theists.[28] The first Humanist Manifesto, often called Humanist 1 since there have been more recent versions, promoted the idea that outdated religions should be replaced with a view that is based on "man's larger understanding of the universe."

The document denies God as Creator, appeals to evolution, and generally points to man as the hope for the betterment of society and mankind.[29]

---

26. For a brief overview of the history of Unitarianism, see Walter Martin, *The Kingdom of the Cults*, ed. Ravi Zacharias (Minneapolis, MN: Bethany House, 2003), p. 339–342.
27. William R. Murry, *Reason and Reverence: Religious Humanism for the 21st Century* (Boston, MA: Skinner House Books, 2007) p. 40–43, accessed digitally at https://books.google.com/books?id=pTnDx1HvEj0C.
28. Ibid., p. 43.
29. "Humanist Manifesto I," American Humanist Association, accessed February 17, 2016, http://americanhumanist.org/humanism/humanist_manifesto_i.

The later, and much expanded, Humanist Manifesto II was signed by several Unitarian ministers, as was the current third version. These manifestos have been signed by influential people like John Dewey, Isaac Asimov, Francis Crick, Alan Guttmacher, B.F. Skinner, and Richard Dawkins.

A Parallel Universalism

At the same time Unitarian thought was developing in America, there was also a universalist form of Christianity. The first Universalist church was started by John Murray in Gloucester, Massachusetts, in 1774, though he was preceded by preaching and writing from people like James Relly (Welsh) and Adams Streeter.[30] In 1866, the Universal General Convention formed as a denominational entity teaching the universal salvation of all of mankind through Jesus. While there have been universalist teachings since soon after Christ's death, this American expression was born out of the rationalistic views popular in 19th-century theology.

Seal of the Universal General Convention (Wikipedia)

Using ideas from the Bible and combining them with natural arguments against eternal punishment for men who were considered generally moral, these churches taught that all men will ultimately receive salvation because of what Christ had accomplished. These churches changed their organizational name to the Universalist Church of America in 1942. Beginning in the late 1940s, there was a move toward a very pluralistic religious ideal. The definition of universalism changed from one of salvation to one of universal religion.[31]

The shift from merely a universal view of salvation in Jesus to one of pluralism makes perfect sense. If you begin from the point that Jesus' death satisfied the debt of all of mankind's sin, it is not long on your journey before you step off of the bus at the base of the mountain where all paths lead to God. This was true of both the Unitarians and the Universalists.

---

30. Richard Eddy, *Universalism in America: A History*, vol. 1 (Boston, MA: Universalist Publishing House, 1884), p. 107–142, accessed digitally at https://books.google.com/books?id=_X4AAAAAYAAJ.

31. Martin, *Kingdom of the Cults*, p. 341.

Unitarian Universalism

Two streams that both began with the Bible as their reservoir had been flowing in channels created by denying biblical truths and adding man's own ideas to the supply. These two streams found a common pit to fill in 1961 when the Unitarian Universalist Association (UU) was formed from the union of the AAU and UCA. Picking and choosing which parts of Scripture to believe combined with setting man's own natural reasoning above God's written revelation turned these streams into a stagnant and lifeless pool rather than a vibrant spring of refreshing, life-giving water.

The UUA symbol of a burning chalice encircled by two rings is generally believed to represent holy oil burning on an altar. A chalice is often lit during UU worship services.

These groups both neglected to consider the corrupted nature of mankind. Although man was created upright, Adam's sin has brought corruption to not only our actions but also our faculties of reasoning. Assuming that man can use his God-given reason to examine the world and determine what is true is a fatal flaw found in both groups. Adding to that the corrupted state of the natural world itself, the ideas of humanism and naturalism have no hope of discerning the true state of reality. Because they have forsaken God's Word, Universalist Unitarians (UUs) have sought the wisdom of the world and pursed a pluralism that is almost unimaginable.

UU Beliefs

UUs claim that they follow no creed and have no dogma. Rather, they hold to seven principles and six sources as affirmations:

> Unitarian Universalist congregations affirm and promote seven Principles, which we hold as strong values and moral guides. We live out these Principles within a "living tradition" of wisdom and spirituality, drawn from sources as diverse as science, poetry, scripture, and personal experience.[32]

---

32. "Our Unitarian Universalist Principles," Unitarian Universalist Association, accessed February 18, 2016, http://www.uua.org/beliefs/what-we-believe/principles.

The seven principles are:

1. The inherent worth and dignity of every person

2. Justice, equity, and compassion in human relations

3. Acceptance of one another and encouragement to spiritual growth in our congregations

4. A free and responsible search for truth and meaning

5. The right of conscience and the use of the democratic process within our congregations and in society at large

6. The goal of world community with peace, liberty, and justice for all

7. Respect for the interdependent web of all existence of which we are a part[33]

From these principles, the pluralistic nature of this religious system should be quite obvious. While a Christian can generally agree with these ideas, their true expression can only be met while resting on the authority of the Bible and the person regenerated in Christ. Apart from a standard, these principles ae merely the arbitrary views of the collective wisdom of UUs — each of whom are creatures with a sinful, fallen nature.

> Our faith is not interested in saving your soul — we're here to help you unfold the awesome soul you already have.[34]

Of each of these principles, we can ask, "By what standard?" From the Bible, we know that each individual has inherent worth because they are made in the image of God. In denying God as the Creator (a dogma that cannot be affirmed), UUs may pick from any source to affirm their ideas but have no consensus on the reason. Sadly, the persons in the womb are not seen as having inherent dignity. Under the ironic banner of "Reproductive Justice," UUs work to support the murder of the unborn. Among advice given to UU members is celebrating the history of *Roe v. Wade* and the following points:

---

33. Ibid.
34. Andrea Lerner, in Peter Morales, ed., *The Unitarian Universalist Pocket Guide*, 5th edition (Boston, MA: Skinner House Books, 2012), p, 7.

- Volunteer with and/or provide financial support to organizations that provide reproductive health services at little or no cost, abortion clinics, women's shelters, and child and family community support centers.

- Support reproductive health/abortion clinics that are experiencing intimidation and spiritual or physical violence.

- Accompany anyone wanting support (e.g., while seeking government assistance, in making decisions for their families about pregnancy and adoption, during abortions, and during childbirth).

- Advocate for comprehensive reproductive health services, including contraception, prenatal care, abortion, and infertility treatment.[35]

Under the banner of "Standing on the Side of Love,"[36] UU members actively advocate for legal abortion, showing their lack of love for the unborn. While claiming to welcome all views, the acceptance is true "only to a point." As an example, when a pro-life group interrupted a UU worship service to share the view that abortion is murder, they were asked to leave with the sentiment "You are welcome to your beliefs and behaviors. Now please take them outside the threshold of our church."[37]

I will leave you to consider the arbitrary nature and inconsistencies that follow from each of the affirmations, but principle five can serve as an example. If each person is to determine what is right based on their conscience, there can be no determination of right and wrong in an absolute sense. This creates a system of thought in which true contradictions can exist — showing the illogical nature of the worldview. When each person does what is right in their own eyes, sin reigns over all.

A Big Umbrella

To guide UUs in their understanding of the world and the seven principles, they look to six sources:

35. "Reproductive Justice," Unitarian Universalist Association, accessed February 18, 2016, http://www.uua.org/statements/reproductive-justice.
36. "Homepage," Standing on the Side of Love, accessed February 18, 2016, http://www.standingonthesideoflove.org.
37. Darcy Baxter, "All Are Welcome, to a Point," UU World, September 15, 2014, http://www.uuworld.org/articles/all-are-welcome.

Standing on the Side of Love" is a public advocacy program of the UUA which promotes abortion, immigration, racial issues, and other social justice issues from a liberal and anti-biblical perspective. They aim to "harness love's power to stop oppression," but do not call sinners to repentance and trust in Christ — the truly loving act.

1. Direct experience of that transcending mystery and wonder, affirmed in all cultures, which moves us to a renewal of the spirit and an openness to the forces which create and uphold life

2. Words and deeds of prophetic women and men which challenge us to confront powers and structures of evil with justice, compassion, and the transforming power of love

3. Wisdom from the world's religions which inspires us in our ethical and spiritual life

4. Jewish and Christian teachings which call us to respond to God's love by loving our neighbors as ourselves

5. Humanist teachings which counsel us to heed the guidance of reason and the results of science, and warn us against idolatries of the mind and spirit

6. Spiritual teachings of earth-centered traditions which celebrate the sacred circle of life and instruct us to live in harmony with the rhythms of nature

Again, the pluralism in these sources of wisdom indicates how far from Servetus and Socinus Unitarianism has come. Though these men devalued certain parts of Scripture, they still saw the Bible as a revelation from God and submitted to its authority to some degree.

The UU will affirm that truth is not found in any single source, but spread among all of the religious ideas from around the globe. This mentality is the ultimate expression of the religious buffet where each person fills his spiritual plate with whatever catches their eye and delights their tongue. In this list of sources you can find everything from personal visions and insights to interpretations of the Bible or Hindu Vedas to the oral traditions of the Cherokee Indians. Within UU spirituality, studies in particle physics and evolutionary relationships are just as valid for understanding reality as are mystical Eastern practices of meditation and yoga. In this sense, UU is simply a moralistic religion that allows each individual to determine what is moral — right and wrong are a matter of preference.

The most obvious problem with this view is that it cannot be internally consistent. The UU will respond to this concern by suggesting that life is so complex that truth can't be limited to one culture or one religious tradition. But how can they be absolutely sure this claim is true?

Here we see an allusion to the broad path that Jesus warned leads only to eternal destruction. Those on the broad path look around and see everyone far to their right and far to their left. They consider all of those around them, reasoning in their hearts that there are so many on this path headed in the same direction that it couldn't possibly be taking them in the wrong direction. But this reasoning is folly. It abandons the call of Jesus Christ to follow Him through the narrow gate — He is the way, the truth, and the life who leads to the Father.

> There is a way that seems right to a man, but its end is the way of death (Proverbs 14:12).

Unitarian Universalists can be agnostics, atheists, theists, deists, animists, pagans — there is no firm concept of God within the association. God can be seen as anything from something that resembles the biblical Creator, to oneself, to a "unifying force," to the spirit of humanity that binds us together.

Similarly, Jesus is not viewed as God, though many would consider Him a good teacher or example to follow. However, others may arbitrarily consider

Him immoral for calling people to repent of their sin or for His judgmental words. How are these people to come to any agreement? Without an authority higher than each individual's view, there can only be a false unity based on shifting opinions as each person "journeys" to find the truth. "That may be true for you, but it's not true for me" is an ideology that can only lead to destruction for all as it denies the Creator of truth.

Under the UU umbrella you can find the UU Humanist Association, UUs for Polyamory Awareness, UUs for Jewish Awareness, UU Buddhist Fellowship, UU Christian Fellowship, Unitarian Baha'i Fellowship, BDSM Awareness, Covenant for UU Pagans, and others, each promoting their views within the broader UU fellowship and its local expressions. Religious services are typically held on Sundays, and would look much like a Protestant worship service with hymns, prayers, a sermon, and other related activities. All of these activities would use inclusive language and could invoke Buddhist meditation, pagan circle dances, or chanting Jewish prayers.

While UUs speak openly about promoting tolerance, they don't tolerate those who hold to exclusive views and dogmatic statements (e.g., Jesus is the only way of salvation). The rhetoric becomes, "You are accepted in our group as long as you affirm every view. If you do not affirm all views, we will not affirm your views." I trust you can see the absurdity of such an idea. This demonstrates that the UU worldview is not able to live up to its own standard of accepting all views as valid and is self-refuting.

From a biblical perspective, God has prescribed what is good, beautiful, and true. It is by *His standard* that we can make judgments, not on our own authority. We can know what it means to reflect the image of God because Jesus Christ has demonstrated that for us. We should not look inside of ourselves to recognize the divine within us,[38] but to Christ to save us from Adam within us.

What Is Man?

While there are variations, UU teaching generally acknowledges the evolutionary progression in the formation of the universe and life on earth. This teaching begins with children's materials and continues to adults. One curriculum promoted on the UUA website, "Riddle and Mystery," promotes

---

38. When people look to worship the inner divine of humanity, they are worshiping the fact that they are made in the image of God instead of worshiping the God who created us in His image.

evolutionary ideas to grade 6 students as a better way to understand the world than religious "myths." Of course, they fail to teach that evolution can be considered a religious myth, following the religion of scientism. Falsely pitting *myth against science*, students are led along a path from the big bang to human consciousness, with the teacher repeating "riddle and mystery" where there are chasms cutting across the evolutionary path.[39] In the Unitarian tradition, modern UUs value personal reason above God's revelation. In light of this humanistic philosophy, evolutionary processes, from theistic to atheistic, are seen as the best explanation available and advocated within the association.

UUs view humanity as basically good, each soul a part of the journey of truth. Many would adopt John Locke's *tabula rasa* concept — each person is born as a blank slate and is influenced by parents, culture, education, and all of life's experiences. Each person is influenced for good or bad (whatever those terms might mean) by their surroundings and influences.

Contrary to the biblical teaching, they would deny the dogmatic idea that sin has corrupted every human being. It is hard to find any notion or definition of sin within their writings since there is such a broad base of beliefs. With the explicit endorsement of all forms of sexual expression and the refusal to be dogmatic about what actually constitutes immoral behavior, UUs have no foundation for defining right and wrong. A probing question that exposes the inconsistency in this view would ask the UU how the first people who did evil learned how to do evil if they were the first to do so. Additionally, how can they ever call any act good or bad, right or wrong, without a standard? The Bible offers us the only true explanation for the corrupted condition of mankind — our inherited sin nature and personal choice to act on that nature — and the only true standard of right and wrong. The truths in the Bible reflect the perfect character of God. Because of this absolute standard, we can discern truth from error and good from evil.

In the *Unitarian Universalist Pocket Guide*, published by the UUA, one member summarizes his journey. Having been disillusioned with the Christianity of his youth, he was reading a book on Protestant denominations. When he read the UU chapter, the ideals resonated within him.

---

39. Richard S. Kimball, "Riddle and Mystery; Session 5: Out of Nothing," Unitarian Universalist Association, accessed February 18, 2016, http://www.uua.org/re/tapestry/children/riddle/session5.

I realized that I was a Unitarian Universalist and had been for a long time. The words came to me like manna from heaven and I ate every one. Newton's lyrics arose in my mind: "Amazing grace how sweet the sound that saved a wretch like me." Soon after that experience, I found a Unitarian Universalist church that was exactly what I expected — warm, friendly, and open. I was home. Here I wasn't weird. Here I was fully human, fully accepted, and fully loved. I found a place that gave credence to who I was at my core. . . . Being found means, in the words of Unitarian Walt Whitman, that "you shall listen to all sides and filter them from yourself." Being found is not a destination but a journey.[40]

While Christians should affirm that all are welcome and consider what all sides say, we must not determine truth from within ourselves. This is nothing more than a validation of the self (Proverbs 16:2, 26:12; Isaiah 2:22). From the Christian worldview, this is a foolish practice that leads to the denial of sin and its consequences. It is only by the work of the Holy Spirit that one can recognize his own sinfulness and recognize that, at our core, we are sinners in need of salvation from God's wrath (Romans 8:7–8; John 16:8–11). If all we seek is others to affirm our unregenerate nature, then the destination of our journey will be hell and God's just punishment. Jesus calls us to repent and believe the gospel, not to look for affirmation of the self.

Is There an Afterlife?

While there are no affirmative ideas about the afterlife, the one thing that all UUs would reject is the idea of any judgment or punishment after death. Here the metaphor of all of the various religious paths leading up a mountain to the place of God's residence is fitting (whatever "god" might mean). Because of the broad influence of Eastern thought, biblical ideas, pagan myths, and atheism, opinions will vary from a heaven-like state to no existence after death (Daniel 12:1–3; Matthew 25).

Many UUs may be quite unsure of what they believe. For this reason, discussions of final judgment after death are likely to elicit strong reactions from the typical UU. Wisdom and prayerful consideration of how to address

---

40. Morales, *The Unitarian Universalist Pocket Guide*, p. 13–15

the issue is warranted. Asking questions about what they believe happens after someone dies can open up the opportunity to share the truth that all men are appointed to die and face God's just and holy judgment.

Sharing Hope with Unitarians

When you encounter someone who professes to be a unitarian, the first thing you must establish is what they mean by that identification. Simply asking, "What do you mean by 'unitarian'?" is a great place to start. It opens a line of communication and establishes that you are interested in what they believe. If you hear someone claim to be unitarian and begin persuading them that the Bible is true and the miracles in it are real, thinking they are UU, they will know you do not understand what they believe.

While you should never shy away from speaking the truth, you must first understand what their disagreements with Christianity are and proceed from there. Regardless of their concerns, they need to hear of their sinful condition before God and the remedy that Christ provides, calling them to repent and put their trust in Him alone.

Regardless of which unitarian position they hold, they need to acknowledge the truths contained in the God-breathed revelation of the Bible. Rather than sitting in judgment over the Word of God, picking and choosing what they believe, they need to submit to its truths as authoritative. This is where you must pray for each individual, asking God to open blinded eyes and unstop deaf ears — that more would come to know Him and worship around His throne forever.

Summary of Unitarian Universalist Beliefs

Doctrine	Teachings of Universal Unitarianism
God	Reject the biblical teaching on God, especially Trinitarianism. Have no official beliefs on the existence of specific deities. Views range from atheistic to pantheistic to pagan.
Authority/ Revelation	There are no authoritative texts or revelations, but each individual draws from all of human learning and myth to determine their own version of reality.
Man	Man is born as a blank slate. Man is likely the product of evolutionary processes.

Sin	Sin is generally viewed as bringing harm to self and others rather than an individual affront to a holy God. There is no concept of original sin. Biblical morality is denied, with diverse sexuality promoted as normal.
Salvation	There are various views, but generally no view of a judgment in the afterlife. Many believe existence ends at death.
Creation	Various views from atheistic evolution to incorporating various mythical or biblical ideas with evolutionary processes.

Chapter 22

The Gospel and World Religions

Simon Turpin

The world is flooded with a mixture of religions, but where do they come from and how does the Bible view them?[1] These are important questions for Christians to consider in our desire to share the gospel with those from other religions.

Where Does Religion Come From?

If we want to know the meaning of anything we have to understand its origin. The origin of religion began in the Garden of Eden when God clearly revealed himself to Adam. However, Adam and Eve rejected that revelation and chose to believe a falsehood about Him.[2] Their sin was that they wanted to be gods themselves (Genesis 3:4–5). In this act of disobedience, Adam chose to follow Satan's worldview over God's worldview.

Adam's disobedience had consequences for the rest of his descendants, as it affected how they viewed God and creation.[3] This can be seen at the event

---

1. By the term *religion*, I mean a system of belief that is a person's ultimate standard for reality — their worldview.
2. The falsehood was that they chose to disbelieve what God had said and instead chose to accept Satan's lie.
3. The New Testament uses various words to describe the ruin of humanity's intellect: futile (Romans 1:21); debased (Romans 1:28); deluded (Colossians 2:4); darkened (Ephesians 4:18).

of the Tower of Babel, which was the beginning of religious diversity.[4] At the Tower of Babel, monotheism devolved into polytheism, pantheism, and the worship of anything other than the one true living God. When the people were dispersed at Babel, they would have taken with them a hybrid of the truth of the true and living God mixed with the twisting and distorting of the truth of that revelation about Him (Romans 1:18–32). Religion then is first of all a response to God's revelation — it is either in faith or rebellion.

How Does the Bible View other Religions?

This is an important question since how we answer it will determine how we engage people of other religions with the gospel.

From Paul's teaching in Romans 1:18–20 we can understand that religious consciousness is a product of two things: 1) God's revelation, and 2) suppression of that revelation. Because God has clearly revealed himself in creation, there is no one who is "without excuse" for not believing in His existence. However, because of mankind's fallen nature, the truth of God's revelation of His eternal power and divine nature is held down and suppressed. The suppression of that revelation ultimately expresses itself in idolatry. In an attempt to capture the essence of human fallenness, John Calvin wrote that man is a maker of idols:

> Hence we may infer, that the human mind is, so to speak, a perpetual forge of idols. . . . The human mind, stuffed as it is with presumptuous rashness, dares to imagine a God suited to its own capacity.[5]

Idolatry is exchanging the glory of God for the image of the creature, which is ultimately "the de-godding of God."[6] In this exchange, idolatry is a subjective response to objective divine revelation, which only has negative consequences: sin → suppression of the truth → exchange for idolatry → darkness → guilt = God's wrath (Romans 1:18–32).

---

4. The Bible links false religion with Babylon (Revelation 17:5). For an exposition of the Tower of Babel as the origin of religious diversity, see James Montgomery Boice, *Genesis Volume 1; Creation and Fall* (Genesis 1–11) (Grand Rapids, MI: Baker Books, 1998), p. 420–426.
5. John Calvin, *Institutes of the Christian Religion*, trans. H. Beveridge, 2nd ed. (Peabody, MA: Hendrickson Publishers, 2009), p. 55.
6. D.A. Carson, *Christianity and Culture Revisited* (Grand Rapids, MI: W.B. Eerdmans, 2008), p. 46.

Since the "gods" of the nations are idols (Jeremiah 10:1–11), it is only God's special revelation through the gospel that turns people from their idolatry to trust in the living and true God (1 Thessalonians 1:5, 9).

The Gospel and World Religious

Once we realize that misdirected religion is an idolatrous response to God's revelation, it will help us think about communicating the gospel to those of other religions.

Paul's speech to the Greeks of the Areopagus in Acts 17:16–34 is the classic text for guiding us in sharing the gospel with those from different religious backgrounds. At his arrival in Athens, Paul was so "provoked"[7] at seeing the idolatry in the city that he was moved to preach the gospel in the marketplace.[8] It was because Paul was preaching Jesus and the Resurrection (Acts 17:18–19) that some Epicurean (those who were indifferent to the gods) and Stoic (those who were pantheistic) philosophers invited Paul to the Areopagus (on Mars Hill) in order to know more of what he was teaching. These two philosophies had a different worldview from Paul's. For example, the Epicureans were indifferent to the gods, as they believed them to be too removed to be objects of concern. The Epicureans were basically like today's agnostic secularists.[9] The Stoics, on the other hand, were pantheists who argued for the unity of humanity and relationship with the divine.[10] Both the Epicureans and Stoics were essentially materialists who, unlike Paul, did not believe in one God who created the world and was sovereign over it (Acts 17:24–26; cf. 14:16).

Since Paul understood the people he was preaching to and their religious background, he knew the topics he needed to speak on. For instance, in seeing the idol to an "Unknown God," Paul uses it as a springboard for explaining who God is. Paul began by explaining that God is the Creator of the heavens and earth and that He created mankind from one man.[11] This idea contradicted the Athenians, who believed that they originated from the

---

7. New Testament scholar Darrell Bock states: "The verb παροξύνω (*paroxuno*) means "provoke" (Deut. 31:20 LXX; Ps. 73:10 LXX [74:10 Eng.]). It is used of God's anger at idolatry." Darrell L. Bock, *Acts: BECNT* (Grand Rapids, MI: Baker Academic, 2007), p. 560.
8. Paul would have understood the idolatry in Athens as evidence of the suppression of truth (Romans 1:18–20).
9. Bock, *Acts*, p. 561.
10. Ibid.
11. The "one man" Paul has in mind is clearly a reference to Adam (Romans 5:12–19; 1 Corinthians 15:21–22, 45).

soil of the ground.[12] His mention of the Resurrection and future judgment is also important since in the Athenian view, death was seen as immaterial, as the "body is not restored in any form."[13]

Paul started with who God is because he knew that the idols present in Athens were not there by virtue of their ignorance but by virtue of the suppression of the truth in unrighteousness.[14]

Paul then connected the truth of who the Creator God is with the truth that God had already given to them by way of natural revelation. He did this by quoting Greek poets to these Athenian philosophers.[15] Paul used these Greek poets as a part of his defense and persuasion of the gospel. By taking what they already knew and bringing it in to his defense, Paul then used God's revelation in nature to persuade them of what they already knew to be true. He connected that inner knowledge to who God is, adding explicitly Christian content to it.

In this way, the gospel can be seen as subversively fulfilling world religions. The gospel is subversive as it stands as the contradiction and confrontation to all manifestations of world religions. It makes a call of repentance from idolatry to the true and living God (Acts 17:30). But it also is the fulfilment of what these false religions seek. Since idols are counterfeits of the one true God, the metaphysical and epistemological questions that other religions ask (but ultimately cannot answer) are answered by the triune God.[16]

This connection with the knowledge of God that the Athenians already had led to a bridge for Paul to share the gospel.

Paul tells the Athenians that God has overlooked the ignorance of the nations[17] who find themselves in need of repentance and reconciliation to God through Christ. However, unlike the Stoics, who had a cyclical view of the world, Paul concludes that there will be a definitive judgment on the

---

12. Ben Witherington III, *The Acts of the Apostles: A Socio-Rhetorical Commentary* (Grand Rapids, MI: W.B. Eerdmans, 1998), p. 526.
13. Bock, *Acts*, p. 571. This is why by the cultural standard of wisdom the Cross was foolishness to the Greeks (1 Corinthians 1:23).
14. In Acts 17:24–25 there is an allusion to Isaiah 42:5, which is in the context of an anti-idol polemic.
15. The quotation "In him we live and move and have our being" is probably from Epimenides of Crete. The quote "For we are indeed his offspring" is from Aratus' poem "Phainomena."
16. See Daniel Strange, *For Their Rock Is Not As Our Rock: An Evangelical Theology of Religions* (Nottingham: Apollos, 2014), p. 237–273.
17. God in his mercy has not judged the idolatry of the nations as severely as he might have (see Romans 3:25).

world by Christ so it is incumbent of all men to repent of their sin and turn to Him in faith.

Conclusion

World religions are a rebellious, idolatrous response to God's revelation of Himself in creation. Because God has made himself known to every person, we need to communicate the fullness of the truth of the gospel in such a way that it connects with the truth that God has already communicated by way of natural revelation. The good news is that God is now redeeming people from false religions throughout the earth and uniting them into one people of God through the gospel of Jesus Christ.

Appendix 1

Tools for Engaging People from Other Religions

Roger Patterson

If you are a Christian reading this book series, you are probably doing so with a desire to be a more effective ambassador of Jesus Christ. Knowing the basic foundations and doctrines of different religious views is wise. If you are meeting for lunch with a Muslim coworker and you order a ham sandwich or invite a Mormon to a coffee house, you could be placing an unnecessary stumbling block in the path of sharing the gospel. While we must trust God's sovereignty in salvation, we are also responsible to represent Jesus Christ and share the gospel in a way that is filled with grace and truth (Colossians 4:2–6).

Don't Divorce Evangelism, Apologetics, and Discipleship

The classic verses used to inform us about evangelistic and apologetic encounters are often disconnected from one another, but we should think about evangelism and apologetics as two sides of the same coin. And then, we must not forget about the connection to discipleship. When we consider 1 Peter 3:15, the classic apologetics passage, we often forget the context of verses 13–17. When we give a defense or reason for the hope that is in us, we have to remember that our hope is in the person and work of Jesus Christ, not tearing down human evolution or telling people how dinosaurs and humans were created on the same day. While we may use those topics as we discuss the truthfulness of Christianity, we must remember that Christ and the hope of salvation He offers is the focal point of Christianity.

Likewise, in Matthew 28:18–20 we often focus on the "go and make disciples" aspect — evangelism — and forget the "teaching them to observe all things that I have commanded you" aspect — discipleship. Once someone has confessed Christ as Lord and Savior, we now have the opportunity and privilege of helping them grow to be more like Christ as disciples who are being sanctified (Romans 8:28–30) — remembering that we are always growing in our discipleship too.

Our evangelistic encounters should naturally flow into a discipleship relationship.[1] Whether we do this personally in our own local church or help the person connect to a local church body that teaches the Bible, we would be negligent to divorce evangelism and discipleship.[2] In summary, evangelism, apologetics, and discipleship should all be in view as we share the gospel message with those who are not yet children of God (John 1:9–13).

Know Your Own Beliefs Better Than the Counterfeits

In understanding the various religious philosophies, there is a danger to be aware of. Spending too much time studying false views may lead to spiritual dangers. It is not advisable or necessary for every Christian to know every doctrine of every religion and its various cults and sects. First, you will not likely encounter people from all of those views, making your time studying the details a "waste."

Second, if you spend too much time studying the false you will have less time for studying the truth of the Bible. Third, there are other Christians in your own local church or in other areas who have studied the details and are serving the Body of Christ with those gifts and knowledge. This book, and other resources, can give you a summary of the views and a starting point for discussions without being immersed in the falsehoods. Christians who have come out of false religions can be a great source of information and wisdom

---

1. Since this book series focuses primarily on making converts of those who are from other religions, we will not discuss the role of discipleship of young children in a home with Christian parents (or other similar situations).
2. However, in the instance of using tracts, books, or audio/visual forms of communicating the gospel, we can trust that the Holy Spirit's work in the person's heart will direct them to finding a local church. Including contact information on these types of gospel tools is always advisable.

and encouragement. Also, if there is a dominant religious group in the area you live (e.g., Mormonism in the states around Utah), you may want to spend more time understanding those views than a specific cult view you are unlikely to encounter. It's not every day you bump into a Wiccan.

Rather than exhaustively studying all of the counterfeits, you would do much better to know the truth God has revealed to us in the 66 books of the Bible. Knowing the truth in a deep and intimate way will be much more profitable than studying all of the false views. While understanding some basic differences can be very helpful, the strategy of asking wise questions can help you learn about a person's beliefs even if you don't know much about their religion.

Additionally, there are many sects and denominations within religious systems. It is not wise to accuse the person you are speaking to of holding a doctrinal view that they may not hold. If a Muslim told you that they could never believe like you do and pray to Mary, you would dismiss them as ignorant since you don't pray to Mary as most Roman Catholics do. Likewise, if in speaking to a Mormon you ask them why they believe the Heavenly Father had sexual relations with Mary, they might tell you they don't believe that (as some Mormons have never been taught that particular point of doctrine or don't accept it).

Ask Good Questions

Rather than telling others what they believe — or what you assume they believe because of the religion they identify with — ask questions. "Counsel in the heart of man is like deep water, but a man of understanding will draw it out" (Proverbs 20:5; NKJV). Learning how to ask questions about what others believe is an invaluable strategy for learning what a person thinks about the meaning of life and the future after death.

For example, if you encounter a man on a plane coddling his Buddhist prayer beads, open a conversation by asking him what the beads mean to him and why he uses them. Ask him what he thinks happens when people die. Ask him how he knows what is right and wrong. Ask him if it is hard to work and strive for his own future state. Ask him . . . okay, you get the point.

As you are asking and showing genuine interest in the person, be listening for ways his worldview is different from the Bible, and then be prepared to tell him what the Bible teaches. But to do that you need to know more about the Bible, who God is, and what Jesus has done for us than you know about the Buddhist Eightfold Path to enlightenment. Being filled with the truths of the Bible allows those truths to flow from your heart to your lips and to offer the good news of salvation in Christ. Being filled with love and thankfulness for your own salvation and all Christ has done for you will flow out of your heart into words and actions that will demonstrate your hope in Christ (1 Peter 3:13–17).

Point Them to Rest in Christ

It may be a bit cliché, but it has been noted that all the other religions in the world are based on what a person must *do* to achieve the ultimate state (nirvana, exaltation, paradise, oneness of being, etc.) while Christianity is a religion that is based on what has been *done* for us in Jesus Christ. *Do* vs. *Done*. In pursuing their own righteousness or concept of perfection, people will become weary and discouraged — and rightly so! But there has only been one person who has lived a life of perfection — Jesus Christ.

Jesus knew the weariness of perfectly obeying God. He saw those He walked with striving to please God but falling short (Romans 3:23). Rather than encouraging people to try harder, Jesus called them to find rest in Him, to take His easy yoke rather than striving to do more (Matthew 11:25–30). As we point people to resting in Christ, we can remind them of their own sinfulness, their accumulating debt of sin (Romans 2:5–11), and the fact that Christ bore the wrath of God for sin in His body upon the Cross (1 Peter 2:23–25). We can ask them to trust that their sin is placed on Christ and they can receive His righteousness — the great exchange that makes peace with God and resting in Christ possible (Isaiah 61:10; Titus 3:3–7).

Take Out Your Sword and Use It

As you interact with others in your evangelistic and apologetic discussions, never be afraid to open the Bible and use it — draw your sword! Even if the person claims not to believe in the Bible, it is still the only source of absolute truth God has revealed to us. Just as a soldier would be foolish to set aside his sword in a battle if his enemy said he didn't believe in swords, a Christian is foolish to set aside the most powerful weapon God has given us (Hebrews 4:11–13; Ephesians 6:14–20).

Rather than providing your own opinion, appeal to the authority of the God of the universe who created all things and rules over all things. Declare the true history of the universe and the nature of mankind and explain how the triune God who has revealed Himself in the Bible is the only source of existence, truth, and hope.

Following the analogy, we must know how to wield the sword as an effective weapon. A basic familiarity with what the Bible teaches and the ability to accurately report that truth requires some training and attention to the Holy Spirit at work in you. If they disagree, it is not with your opinion, but with what God has proclaimed. As you faithfully proclaim the truth from God's Word, it will accomplish the purpose He has sent it for (Isaiah 55:10–13). The Word of God is your powerful weapon that the Holy Spirit will use to bring conviction, not the wisdom of men in persuasive words (1 Corinthians 1:17–2:16).

Don't Be Like the Fool

In Proverbs 26:4–5, we are given a basic strategy for dealing with those who are foolishly denying God's existence or pursuing false gods to serve and worship. Rather than following along with the fool and arguing from his beliefs, we should show him how his views lead to foolishness (absurdity), as they are not founded in the truth of God and His Word. We can then present the biblical worldview and the message of the gospel, calling them to submit to God and acknowledge Jesus as Lord and Savior.[3]

As we listen to what people believe and try to understand them, we should not spend an inordinate amount of time arguing fine points of doctrine and debating evidences back and forth. It can take time and patience to continue to witness to people in our lives who deny the gospel, but we need to move beyond secondary issues to deal with the root of their false worldview. As an analogy, we should not spend time trying to pluck nails and boards from their house hoping that it will fall, but take a jackhammer to the foundation and expose the fact that their house is standing on nothing.

As they recognize their need for a true foundation, invite them into the household of God to be adopted as His child. Apart from God and a submission to the truth of the Bible, there is no consistent foundation upon which we can build a worldview (Matthew 7:24–27). Apart from Christ, there is no Creator and Savior. Jesus Christ is the foundation upon which we *must* build our worldview (Ephesians 2:19–22; 1 Peter 2:1–10).

---

3. For a fuller explanation of this presuppositional apologetics view, see Jason Lisle, *The Ultimate Proof of Creation* (Green Forest, AR: Master Books, 2009); for a condensed explanation, see Jason Lisle "Fool-Proof Apologetics," *Answers*, January–March, 2009, p. 66–69, available online at https://answersingenesis.org/apologetics/fool-proof-apologetics.

While exposing the faulty foundation of someone's worldview is no guarantee that they will drop to their knees, repent, and turn to Christ for salvation, it may give them pause and a means by which the Spirit can work in their hearts to bring conviction of sin. While we do our part to be faithful ambassadors, planting seeds and watering those that have been planted, it is God who brings the growth resulting in a harvest of righteousness. The fear of the Lord is the beginning of wisdom (Proverbs 9:10). All the treasures of wisdom and knowledge are found in Jesus Christ (Colossians 2:1–10). Let us embrace the truth and proclaim it boldly to the glory of God.

Questions to Use in Evangelistic Encounters

Doctrinal Questions

- Why do you wear that pendant/head covering/emblem/tattoo?
- Where and how do you worship?
- What is the ultimate goal in your religion?
- How do you achieve the ultimate state?
- How do you know when you have done enough?
- How are you doing in your progress to that goal?
- How did you decide which sect/denomination to follow?
- Who is the leader or main authority that informs your religious views?
- How do you understand the beginning of the universe/world/mankind?
- Is mankind basically good or bad in its nature? Why?
- What writings do you study to help you grow in your faith?
- What is the source/object of your faith?
- How do you view God? How do you know what He is like?
- What do you think happens when someone dies? What will happen to you?

Ultimate Questions

- How do you know what is right and wrong or good and evil?
- How does your worldview account for truth/reality?

- Is it possible that you are wrong about the way you see the world?

- How do you know what the purpose of mankind/your life is?

- If God judged you by your own actions/sins, would you deserve to spend eternity in heaven?

- If you stood before God and He asked you why you should be allowed to spend eternity with Him, what would you say?

- Why do you deny that Jesus Christ is the only Savior of the world?

- The Bible says that everyone knows that God exists based on His attributes displayed in creation, so why do you suppress what you know to be true?

- If there is more than one god, how do you know which god is the right one to obey?

- If the universe/being is an impersonal force, how does it interact with the material world?

- If you believe that matter and energy are all that exist, how do you account for transcendent immaterial entities (logic, numbers, morality, laws of nature)? Do you have a soul?

- How does your worldview account for morality, uniform laws of nature, reasoning, logic?

- Is it possible that you are wrong about everything you believe?

- What would the consequences be if you were wrong?

- How do you know that is true?

- Since your worldview contradicts the Bible's teaching, how do you know you are right and the Bible is wrong?

- Jesus said He was the way, the truth, and the life, and that no one would get to heaven apart from Him. Why do you deny His claims?

- Who do you say Jesus is?

Appendix 2

The Irrationality of Atheism, Polytheism, Deism, and Unitarianism

Timothy McCabe

Abstract

Ultimately, all possibility of rational thought is grounded in the Trinitarian Christian God. This appendix will offer an internal analysis of atheistic, polytheistic, deistic, and unitarian systems. It will find that each of these four systems, by its own nature and according to its own claims, denies mankind all possible grounds for justified conclusions, thereby eliminating all possibility of human rationality. By comparison, it will also offer an internal analysis of Trinitarian Christianity and will find that the problems inherent in the other four systems are refreshingly absent.

Definitions

Throughout this appendix, *atheism* will refer to any claim or set of claims rejecting the existence of a sovereign, rational author of the universe; *polytheism* will refer to any claim or set of claims that there are many sovereign, rational authors of the universe who are equally ultimate; *deism* will refer to any claim in which a sovereign, rational author of the universe exists but has no ongoing involvement with what is created apart from the initial act of creation itself; and *unitarianism* will refer to any claim in which a sovereign author of the universe exists, continues to be involved with the created realm, and whose divinity is not shared in any sense.

These views will each be contrasted with *Trinitarian Christianity*, or *Trinitarianism*, in which one sovereign and rational author of the universe exists, is involved with what is created today, and yet whose divinity is effectively shared between *God the Father* and the *Image of God, the Son*.[1]

Starting Points

From the moment we begin to draw conclusions as individual human beings, we already know how to learn. Knowledge of the basic and fundamental process of learning is already well established in our minds before we begin using it to draw conclusions. Before we learn anything at all, we assume (or presuppose) a method of learning. This initial knowledge of how to learn is not itself learned, rather, acceptance of the method is a precondition of our usage of it. Accepting a method for judging truth claims is common to humanity as one of our starting points. We begin life under the assumption or presupposition that the ways we learn things will actually produce accurate conclusions about the world around us.

When we begin drawing conclusions, when we first start learning things, we do so with certain presupposed assumptions or "first principles." For example:

> Nothing can both be and not be at the same time and in the same way.

This is known as the law of non-contradiction. Before we can learn anything at all, we must first presuppose this rule of thought. Evidence, assertions, conclusions, and thinking itself would all be completely meaningless to us if we did not initially grant that all of reality is non-contradictory.

That we have this initial assumption is true for all humans from the time we begin to think. The infant knows that milk is milk. Milk is not non-milk. If the infant allowed the possibility that milk were non-milk, he would have

---

1. It is not my intent to suggest that these definitions are the only correct definitions of these terms. For example, *Trinitarian Christianity* was often designated as *atheism* by the ancient Romans because Christians rejected the entire pantheon of Roman gods and refused to worship the emperor. I will not be defining atheism as the rejection of Roman gods, but rather, as a rejection of a sovereign, rational author of the universe. As a second example, a hypothetical view may assert that the universe was never created at all but has existed forever, and many gods exist: a god of the sea, a god of the sun, a god of the moon, a god of fire, etc. Typically, such a view would be as *polytheistic*. However, in the course of this appendix, it will be referred to as *atheistic*, since it denies a sovereign rational author of the universe. My intent is not to be militant about "proper" definitions for these terms, but rather to be internally consistent throughout this appendix in my usage of them in the hopes that the discussion itself will be easier to understand.

no reason to believe that he had received what he had been crying for, even as it fills his mouth. The infant simply grants or assumes — the infant *knows* — that the law of non-contradiction is universal and invariant.

It is not my claim that the infant can *articulate* the law of non-contradiction, or *teach* it, or *defend* it, but rather that he inherently *believes* and operates in accordance with the law even if he has never consciously pondered it.

And so do you.

Further, every single correct conclusion the infant ever comes to, and every single correct conclusion the adult ever comes to, is based upon this assumption that the law of non-contradiction is universally valid, both now and forever. We not only start off *believing* it without ever actually *learning* it, but everything we ever conclude is founded on or grounded in that initial assumption.

But what if we're wrong? Is that initial assumption *justified*? Is there a good reason for us to hold to it? Is it a blind invention of random chance? Is the author of our initial assumptions rational? Is this universal truth claim merely an unfounded, dogmatic assertion made by someone without authority over the entire universe such that the universe is not bound to fulfill his dogmatic claims? Could the law of non-contradiction fail to work in some parts of the universe? And what connects our own thoughts with our environment? Why should there be any similarity at all between our own internally presupposed rules of thought and the way that our external environment behaves?

If genuine contradictions could actually exist, it would be impossible for anyone to know anything at all. If contradictions were viable, then even if a conclusion were accurate, it may not be accurate. Assertions would not necessarily be any different than their exact negations. Even if it were true that you are reading this, it may not be true that you are reading this.

That last sentence is completely meaningless and impossible to understand because it asserts a *contradictory proposition*. If it were possible for reality itself to be contradictory, like that sentence, reality itself would be equally impossible to understand. It would not be possible to know anything at all. But this is not the case. We all automatically believe that reality is not contradictory.

Rational Thought Requires Rational Justification

In order for an idea to be *rational*, holding the belief must be *rationally justified*. Even if a belief happened be accurate or factual, this alone is not enough to make that belief *rational*. The process by which the person came to hold that belief is actually more important than the belief's truth value in terms of whether or not the belief is *rationally* held. A belief may be true, yet still be irrational.

For example, any wishful thinker may assert without grounds that there are exactly 501,043 pink flying unicorns on a planet in the next galaxy. For that individual to believe such a thing would be irrational, because they themselves have asserted it groundlessly or without reason. Even if this bizarre, groundless assertion happened to be true, its factuality would not make belief in the assertion any more *rational*, since it was asserted *groundlessly* — without justification or reason.

On the other hand, a belief may be false while being perfectly rational. For example, consider the man who believes that pushing the brake pedal in his car will slow the car and eventually bring it to a complete stop. He believes this because he has been told this is true by his parents and friends, and he tested their claims on thousands of occasions. One hundred percent of the time, the car behaved exactly as he expected. But then one day it didn't, and the man died.

He was wrong to believe his car would stop when he pushed the brakes on that day, but nonetheless, based on all of the evidence, he held to this false belief *rationally*. He had testimony from multiple witnesses, observations, and lots of experience upon which he grounded his belief. It was *rationally justified* in spite of being incorrect.

Now, is our belief that all reality is non-contradictory *rationally justified*? Or are we irrationally, without reason, holding to an idea that is only asserted groundlessly?

Rationally Justifying Rational Justification

While it is true that some beliefs may be rationally justified while being completely false, the same cannot be said of every belief. Consider, for example, the following assertion:

> *Rational justification is possible.*

In addition to the law of non-contradiction, the assertion above is another one of our initial starting points, our "first principles." As humans, we begin the learning process *already believing* that this assertion is true, that *rational justification is possible*. But note that this statement can only be rationally justified if it is also true; if it is false, nothing can be rationally justified, including the statement itself.

The idea that "*rational justification is possible*" must itself be true in order for it to be rationally justified. For any worldview to allow for rational human thought, it must not only allow for our initial assumptions about the non-contradictory nature of the universe to be true, but it must also allow for *the possibility of rational justification itself*. It *must* allow for a mechanism whereby *rational justification is possible.*

Atheism

Atheism *prohibits every imaginable mechanism* whereby rational justification is possible. Truth claims from atheists demand that there is no sovereign rational author of the universe. No one exists who has authority over the universe. No one exists who is justified in claiming that the entire universe is, and always will be, non-contradictory. No person can guarantee these things. Therefore, by whatever random mechanism the bizarre and ground-less notion of a non-contradictory universe got into our heads to begin with, that initial assumption of ours is necessarily irrational. All of our conclusions are based upon this rationally unjustified starting point, making all of our conclusions rationally unjustified, or irrational.

If our initial assumptions about reality don't find their origin in a rational sovereign author of the universe, they are rationally unjustified. In other words, if there is no sovereign rational author of the universe, if the claims of atheism are accurate, then all human conclusions are irrational or without reason.[2]

"But what about observable evidence?" one may ask. In the example of the man hitting the brake pedal, he couldn't absolutely guarantee that it would work, yet he was rationally justified in believing it would. Here, no one can guarantee that the universe is non-contradictory, but can't we still be rationally justified in believing that it is, just like the man with the brake pedal?

Surely, even if we initially believe in the complete universality of the law of non-contradiction without having any rational justification for our initial

---

2. While the argument above deals with all worldviews that deny a rational, sovereign Creator, an additional argument against the possibility of rational thought can be offered against materialistic naturalism, a popular atheistic religion that denies that immaterial things exist. Reason, truth, knowledge, logic, and so forth cannot be adequately explained within this atheistic format since they are not material. By the very foundational beliefs of materialistic naturalism, logic and reason are an impossibility.

belief (a claim no atheist could rationally dispute), our present-day usage of that belief can be justified after-the-fact by observing the world around us and recognizing the non-contradictory nature of things, can't it? The more we observe non-contradictory behavior, surely the more justification we have for asserting the universality of the rule.

This inductive argument could be described as follows:

1. We would expect that in a non-contradictory universe we would never find any true contradiction.

2. Thus far, we have never found any true contradiction.

3. Therefore, we rationally conclude that *the universe is most probably non-contradictory.*

But note that points (1) and (2) can only be meaningfully accepted if we first presuppose that the universe is invariantly non-contradictory, making the argument wholly circular in all its points. While circular arguments can be perfectly valid, this one is still founded upon an indisputably irrational starting point, the unjustified initial assumption of non-contradiction. The admitted irrationality of the foundation upon which the circular argument is built negates all possibility of rationality in the conclusion.

The man with the faulty brake pedal believed what he believed *as a result of* meaningful experience, and was therefore justified. On the other hand, we consider our experiences meaningful *as a result of* our belief in the law of non-contradiction, not the other way around. It is the *exact reverse* of the brake pedal example.

The atheist has put the cart before the horse. To see what I mean, let's assume for a moment that the universe is *not* bound by the law of non-contradiction. Let's assume that contradictions are perfectly acceptable statements of truth. There would then be no reason to reject the following argument:

1. We would expect that in a non-contradictory universe we would never find any true contradiction.

2. Thus far, we have never found any true contradiction.

3. Therefore, we rationally conclude that *the universe is full of contradictions.*

"Wait, that doesn't make any sense!" you shout. *The conclusion contradicts the premises — it can't be right!*

Remember, when we formulated the above argument we assumed contradictions could be acceptable statements of truth. The only way the conclusion above could possibly be meaningfully rejected is if we presuppose that the universe is non-contradictory before we even attempt the argument, and since, under atheistic premises, we have absolutely no rational justification for making that initial assumption about the universe before observing it, the entire process, and indeed inductive inference itself, is reduced to meaningless irrationality.

There is, under atheism, no greater reason to prefer the coherent conclusion than to prefer the incoherent one. They are equally unjustified. In short, the absence of any universal and invariant rational authority under atheistic premises demands a lack of rational justification for any kind of universal or invariant claim.

If God doesn't exist, we simply cannot think.

This nonsense can be described via the following deductive syllogism:

1. Conclusions are irrational if they are built upon unjustified premises.

2. Under atheism, all of our conclusions are built upon unjustified initial premises.

3. Under atheism, all of our conclusions are irrational.

This, of course, does not mean that everything an atheist says is wrong or false; rather, it means that his worldview cannot justify *rationality*. When we say that atheism renders everything meaningless, we are not simply referring to some kind of greater purpose in life that appears to be lacking under atheism, or some kind of eternal value that we hope and wish humans had that seems absent without some kind of God. No, indeed, atheism renders every sentence meaningless. Every word. Every thought. Absolutely every concept.

Polytheism

Polytheism, likewise, *prohibits every imaginable mechanism* whereby rational justification is possible. Polytheistic claims, as I am defining them, mandate that there are many sovereign, rational authors of the universe who are equally ultimate.

As these multiple sovereign authors of the universe create our reality, try to imagine what our reality would be like if they disagreed. One god decides certain trees will have abundant green leaves on its branches, but the other god decides these same trees will not have any leaves at all under any circumstances whatsoever. The question we as humans are then faced with is *do these trees have abundant green leaves, or do they not?*

The answer, of course, is that both options are completely and wholly true and both are also completely and wholly false. The trees have leaves and it is not the case that the trees have leaves. At the same time. And in the same way. Not only does this make our reality incoherent and incomprehensible; not only does this make our presupposed universality and invariance of the law of non-contradiction invalid (though if it is invalid it may also be valid at the same time and in the same way); but this also points out an interesting fact about exactly what the gods themselves, the ultimate authorities over our reality, each individually hold to be correct.

Our first god who is sovereignly authoring the universe determines that these certain trees have abundant leaves. Therefore, he knows that those trees do in fact have abundant leaves. However, even though he is right, *he is also wrong.* Even if this sovereign god directly informed us that the universe he created was non-contradictory, his personal opinion on the matter would not be trustworthy given the presence of the other equally authoritative god. Indeed, this first god cannot authoritatively guarantee *anything at all* for his created humans, so he cannot be trusted to present us with an accurate view of his very own creation.

To misappropriate an old saying, if everyone is sovereign, no one is.

If the law of non-contradiction is an untrustworthy test of truth, as it would necessarily be with multiple sovereign gods who are equally ultimate, then, just as under atheism, it is not possible to guarantee any kind of meaning for anything at all. Things may mean what they don't mean. Arguments may prove what they disprove. Assertions and their negations may be equivalent. No one, not even the gods, could be justifiably certain of anything at all. Rational thought, dependent upon the universality and invariance of the law of non-contradiction, would be nonexistent.

Under such a scenario, the very concept of rational justification (which here may entail what it doesn't entail) becomes meaningless. Since there is then no such thing as rational justification, it is therefore impossible to rationally justify anything at all, and thus, every belief is irrational, or without reason.

In short, the equally ultimate sovereignty of polytheistic gods leads to a lack of rational justification for any and every claim.[3]

This nonsense can likewise be described via the same deductive syllogism as was used to describe atheistic epistemology:

1. Conclusions are irrational if they are built upon unjustified premises.

2. Under polytheism, all of our conclusions are built upon unjustified initial premises.

3. Under polytheism, all of our conclusions are irrational.

Deism

Deism, too, *prohibits every imaginable mechanism* whereby rational justification is possible. Deistic claims demand that a sovereign author of the universe exists but has no ongoing involvement with what is created apart from the initial act of creation itself. Such a god cannot justifiably guarantee anything about any moment beyond creation.

The unfolding of time is independent of the deistic god. Future moments are not created by him. Somehow, both future moments and therefore time itself exist autonomously, independently, and apart from his sovereignty. If this were not the case, every moment would depend upon him for its existence, in which case he would by definition continue to be intimately involved with his creation, even today.

If anything is independent of the deistic god, he cannot authoritatively guarantee that it will behave according to his expectations or deterministic decrees. This means that his expectations or truth claims may not be valid. Indeed, if time is independent of god, even if we tried to believe that god himself were perfectly rational, time could hypothetically behave in a completely irrational manner. Logical contradictions could become perfectly viable — or perhaps they always have been.

The deistic god cannot guarantee anything about those things he has no control over. Even if he has caused humans to reproduce in such a fashion that each successive generation assumes that the law of non-contradiction is always valid, without variation — even if our initial beliefs somehow had his

---

3. According to Plato's *Four Dialogues*, Socrates made this same case against the conflicting sovereignty of the Greek pantheon of gods in *Euthyphro*, but restricted his argument in his particular discourse to moral facts. Here, I have merely expanded Socrates' argument to all facts.

486 — World Religions and Cults • Volume 2

own mark of authority on them and were not randomly produced — then, since our assumptions were determined by one who had *no authority to make such claims*, we are not rationally justified in accepting our own assumptions. With absolutely all of our conclusions being based solely upon his ultimate authority, authority that is lacking, we are then never rationally justified in holding to any of them.

"But couldn't the deistic god observe time for a while and see how it behaved?" you ask. "And then, based upon this observable evidence, cause humans to believe that it is non-contradictory? Even if he were wrong, wouldn't we still be rationally justified in trusting our initial assumptions based on god's careful consideration of the evidence?" Actually, no.

As demonstrated when we discussed atheism, the use of probability and evidentiary claims is meaningless without the establishment first of the universality and invariance of the law of non-contradiction, which the deistic god simply cannot establish. Evidential inference is subject to the law of non-contradiction, not the other way around. The deist, just like the atheist, has put the same cart before the same horse.

Yet again, just as in atheism and polytheism, our initial assumptions about reality are arbitrary and unjustified in a deistic framework. They have come from a being that cannot guarantee their accuracy, since time is an influence on both us and on our universe and time is not under his control.

Deism, like atheism and polytheism, prohibits us from being justified in believing that the law of non-contradiction is valid, thereby denying the possibility of rational justification. In short, the deistic god's lack of authority over time (and over time's functionality) dictates a lack of sufficient justification for trusting our starting assumptions today.

If our initial premises are unjustified, it is irrational for us to believe any conclusions based upon them. We see that the same syllogism properly applies to deism:

1. Conclusions are irrational if they are built upon unjustified premises.

2. Under deism, all of our conclusions are built upon unjustified initial premises.

3. Under deism, all of our conclusions are irrational.

Unitarianism

Finally, unitarianism (e.g., the god of the Jehovah's Witnesses, Unitarian Universalism's concept of god, or the Islamic god) also *prohibits every imaginable mechanism* whereby rational justification is possible.[4]

Unitarian claims demand that a sovereign author of the universe exists and continues to be involved with the created realm. Further, the unitarian holds that his god's divinity is not shared in any sense. A unitarian god's beliefs, conclusions, actions, decisions, purposes, intentions, preferences, and decrees, etc., would then be both unjustified and unjustifiable, making every such god irrational.

Yes that was a bold claim, but let me explain. Under our definition of unitarianism, and from within a unitarian perspective, the one creator god himself is, in the ultimate sense, the only reason for anything at all. He alone is the originator of all things other than himself. According to unitarianism, he is the reason they exist. He is the reason things are the way they are. Otherwise, things would not be under his control, and he would have no justification for making universal claims about them, as we have already seen above with three other worldviews. As a supposedly rational being, he would necessarily reflect upon his reason for his beliefs, his reason for his conclusions, his reason for his actions, his reason for his decisions, his reason for his decrees, and so forth. And, of course, in reflecting upon his reason, he is reflecting upon himself, because ultimately, he is his own reason. As he reflects upon himself, however, he himself is reflected.

To grant unitarianism the benefit of the doubt, the unitarian god must know himself perfectly, or else he would not be able to guarantee what he himself will do, and we would then have no rational justification for trusting his assertions about the non-contradictory nature of anything under his control. Because the unitarian god knows himself perfectly, when he reflects upon himself, his reflection, the image that he holds of himself, has all of the same attributes that he knows himself to have, with the exception, of course, of those attributes that necessarily differentiate anything from its reflection.[5]

---

4. For definition sake, monotheism is not necessarily unitarian. While all unitarians are monotheists, biblical Christianity is monotheistic trinitarianism, which holds to one God existing in three co-equal and co-eternal persons — the Father, the Son, and the Holy Spirit.

5. As Jonathan Edwards writes in *An Unpublished Essay on the Trinity*, "The knowledge or view which God has of Himself must necessarily be conceived to be something distinct from His mere direct existence. There must be something that answers to our own reflection. The reflection as we reflect on our own minds carries something of imperfection in it.

As the unitarian god himself is eternal, so his image of himself, that is, his reason, is likewise eternal. As he himself is consistent, so his image of himself is consistent. His conception of himself must eternally be the exact representation of himself, sharing divine sovereignty, since this conception is the reason for everything that occurs.[6] This presents the problem in unitarianism, which denies that divine sovereignty is shared in any manner, though we have seen that it must be for the sovereign creator to be rational.

Since any rational author of reality could have no reason other than Himself, and as the *unitarian god does not have a divine conception of himself, the unitarian god, if he is the author of reality, cannot be said to be rational.* Whatever his ultimate reason is, it is either nonexistent, since he alone is the self-existent one, or it is an attribute of himself rather than himself. Therefore, it is not ultimate in the fullest sense.

The unitarian god's rationality is thus insufficient to provide us with universal and invariant guarantees about reality. Understanding this, we now see that unitarianism could actually fall under our definition of atheism, since under atheism there is no sovereign *rational* author of the universe, and while the unitarian god (under unitarianism) is the sovereign author of the universe, he is certainly not rational. Remember, if our initial assumptions about reality don't find their origin in a rational sovereign author of the universe, they are rationally unjustified — completely without reason.

In short, the faulty thinking of the unitarian god dictates a lack of sufficient justification for trusting any and all of his claims. Under unitarianism, then, every human's initial assumption, given to us by the god who created us, that the universe is invariantly non-contradictory, is therefore unjustified. Yet again, we see the same syllogism applied to unitarianism.

However, if God beholds Himself so as thence to have delight and joy in Himself He must become his own object. There is God and the idea (the λόγος) of God. Therefore as God with perfect clearness, fullness and strength, understands Himself, views His own essence, that idea which God hath of Himself is absolutely Himself. This representation of the Divine nature and essence is the Divine nature and essence again: so that by God's thinking of the Deity must certainly be generated. Hereby there is another person begotten, there is another Infinite Eternal Almighty and most holy and the same God, the very same Divine nature. And this Person is the second person in the Trinity, the Only Begotten and dearly Beloved Son of God; He is the eternal, necessary, perfect, substantial and personal idea which God hath of Himself; and that it is so seems to me to be abundantly confirmed by the Word of God." http://www.ccel.org/ccel/edwards/trinity/files/trinity.html.

6. As the Nicene Creed states in its modern wording, "We believe in one Lord, Jesus Christ, the only son of God, eternally begotten of the Father, God from God, Light from Light, true God from true God, begotten, not made, of one being with the Father."

1. Conclusions are irrational if they are built upon unjustified premises.

2. Under unitarianism, all of our conclusions are built upon unjustified initial premises.

3. Under unitarianism, all of our conclusions are irrational.

Woe Is Me

Thus far, every worldview we've examined has collapsed in upon itself. Each of these four religious concepts (atheism, polytheism, deism, and unitarianism) have exhibited a lack of a rational and permanent authority behind the universe, making it impossible for human beings to rationally justify anything at all. Our prospects of ever actually being rational, of ever having good reasons for what we think and what we do, are looking dimmer by the minute. Must we now conclude that there is no reason to hold to any idea at all? That every assertion is just as rational as its negation? That truth, if it exists at all, is completely unknowable?

Before we give up on thinking entirely, we do have one more worldview to consider.

Trinitarian Christianity

Unlike atheism, which has no one in authority to guarantee the universality and invariance of the law of non-contradiction, Trinitarian Christianity holds that there is a sovereign author of the universe.

> In the beginning God created the heavens and the earth (Genesis 1:1).[7]

> All things were made through Him, and without Him nothing was made that was made (John 1:3).

> For by Him all things were created that are in heaven and that are on earth, visible and invisible, whether thrones or dominions or principalities or powers. All things were created through Him and for Him (Colossians 1:16).

> You are worthy, O Lord, to receive glory and honor and power; for You created all things, and by Your will they exist and were created (Revelation 4:11).

---

7. In this chapter, all Scripture is from the New King James Version (NKJV) of the Bible.

> By faith we understand that the worlds were framed by the word of God, so that the things which are seen were not made of things which are visible (Hebrews 11:3).

Unlike the gods of polytheism, the monotheistic God of the Bible exists as one God, yet three persons — Father, Son, and Holy Spirit. The persons of the trinitarian God, since they are the same God, are guaranteed to always agree with one another, obey one another, and to be perfectly consistent with one another, never denying Himself as one God. God even claims that His existence directly corresponds to His existence rather than ever being contrary to it.

> If we are faithless, He [God] remains faithful; He cannot deny Himself (2 Timothy 2:13).

> Father, if it is Your will, take this cup away from Me [Jesus]; nevertheless not My will, but Yours [the Father], be done (Luke 22:42).

> And being found in appearance as a man, He [Jesus] humbled Himself and became obedient to the point of death, even the death of the cross (Philippians 2:8).

> Then Jesus answered and said to them, "Most assuredly, I say to you, the Son can do nothing of Himself, but what He sees the Father do; for whatever He does, the Son also does in like manner" (John 5:19).

> And God said to Moses, "I AM WHO I AM." And He said, "Thus you shall say to the children of Israel, 'I AM has sent me to you' " (Exodus 3:14).

Unlike deism, the Trinitarian God is the author of time, sustaining His creation every moment, Himself being both eternal and omnitemporal.

> And He is before all things, and in Him all things consist (Colossians 1:17).

> Declaring the end from the beginning, and from ancient times things that are not yet done, saying, "My counsel shall stand, and I will do all My pleasure" (Isaiah 46:10).

Now to the King eternal, immortal, invisible, to God who alone is wise, be honor and glory forever and ever. Amen (1 Timothy 1:17).

I am the Alpha and the Omega, the Beginning and the End, the First and the Last (Revelation 22:13).

For a thousand years in Your sight are like yesterday when it is past, and like a watch in the night (Psalm 90:4).

And finally, unlike unitarianism, the Trinitarian God is wise enough to genuinely understand what the only possible rational justification, or reason, for all things is — namely, Himself.

For My own sake, for My own sake, I will do it; For how should My name be profaned? And I will not give My glory to another (Isaiah 48:11).

This people I have formed for Myself; they shall declare My praise (Isaiah 43:21).

Jesus said to him, "I am the way, the truth, and the life. No one comes to the Father except through Me. If you had known Me, you would have known My Father also; and from now on you know Him and have seen Him." Philip said to Him, "Lord, show us the Father, and it is sufficient for us." Jesus said to him, "Have I been with you so long, and yet you have not known Me, Philip? He who has seen Me has seen the Father; so how can you say, 'Show us the Father'?" (John 14:6–9).

He is the image of the invisible God, the firstborn over all creation (Colossians 1:15).

God . . . has in these last days spoken to us by His Son . . . who being the brightness of His glory and the express image of His person . . . sat down at the right hand of the Majesty on high, having become so much better than the angels, as He has by inheritance obtained a more excellent name than they (Hebrews 1:1–4).

But even if our gospel is veiled, it is veiled to those who are perishing, whose minds the god of this age has blinded, who do not believe, lest the light of the gospel of the glory of Christ, who is the image of God, should shine on them (2 Corinthians 4:3–4).

Let this mind be in you which was also in Christ Jesus, who, being in the form of God, did not consider it robbery to be equal with God, but made Himself of no reputation, taking the form of a bondservant, and coming in the likeness of men (Philippians 2:5–7).

But of Him you are in Christ Jesus, who became for us wisdom from God — and righteousness and sanctification and redemption — that, as it is written, "He who glories, let him glory in the LORD" (1 Corinthians 1:30–31).

For Jews request a sign, and Greeks seek after wisdom; but we preach Christ crucified, to the Jews a stumbling block and to the Greeks foolishness, but to those who are called, both Jews and Greeks, Christ the power of God and the wisdom of God (1 Corinthians 1:22–24).

In the beginning was the Word, and the Word was with God, and the Word was God. . . . And the Word became flesh and dwelt among us, and we beheld His glory, the glory as of the only begotten of the Father, full of grace and truth (John 1:1–14).

Conclusion

By standing on the Bible and the God it professes as the absolute authority, it is perfectly rational for the Trinitarian Christian to assert the premises of rationality, like the permanent universality of the law of non-contradiction, to proclaim these premises and uphold them. He may also use them as an unfailing standard for judging and discerning truth claims. The same cannot be said for the unitarian, the deist, the polytheist, or the atheist. For these groups, it is inconsistent to assert the premises of rationality as an unfailing standard for judging truth claims since, according to their own worldviews, rationality is not within the domain of human capability.

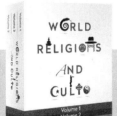

WORLD RELIGIONS

AND CULTS

Atheistic *and* Humanistic Religions

Volume 3

General Editors

BODIE HODGE & ROGER PATTERSON

First printing: November 2016
Third printing: July 2018

ISBN: 978-0-89051-970-7
ISBN: 978-1-61458-039-3 (digital)
Library of Congress Number: 2016917109

Cover by Left Coast Design, Portland, Oregon

Please consider requesting a copy of this volume be purchased by your local library system.

Printed in the United States of America

Please visit our website for other great titles: www.masterbooks.com

For information regarding author interviews, please contact the publicity department at (870) 438-5288.

Master
Books®
A Division of New Leaf Publishing Group
www.masterbooks.com

Acknowledgments

Our appreciation to the following for their contributions and help to bring this book to fruition:

Roger Patterson, Bodie Hodge, Troy Lacey, Ken Ham,
Dr. Terry Mortenson, Dr. Elizabeth Mitchell, Frost Smith,
Dr. Georgia Purdom, Avery Foley, Dan Zordel,
Shonda Snelbaker, Walt Stumper, Dan Lietha, Steve Ham,
Todd Friel, Pastor David Chakranaryan, Dr. Nathan Merrill,
Dr. Jerry Bergman, Dr. Carl Broggi, Bryan Osborne,
Eric Hovind, Dr. Stuart Burgess, and Jeremy Ham.

Contents

Introduction

Bodie Hodge

There are only two religions in the world. If there is only one thing to be remembered from reading this three-volume set (dealing with world religions, cults, and philosophical systems), it is that all religions outside of God's true religion are religions of man. They are simply variations of humanism (in its broadest sense).

It is the case of God's Word vs. man's word. In one fashion or another, man's ideas have been elevated to take people away from the truth of God's Word and deposit them in one version or another of a man-made religion. God vs. man is still the consistent theme with the final book in this series. This final volume focuses on religions that tend to oppose God by claiming He doesn't exist or reduces God to a strange concoction of illusion and irrelevancy.

These variations of humanistic/secular religions now dominate the state school systems, museums, media, universities, and so forth in our Western world. It has been causing a culture change from Christian to secular. Beginning about 200 years ago, there was a slow and gradual takeover — simply because few Christians have opposed this religion for so long.[1]

Interestingly, most of the secular religions in this volume usually have no problem calling themselves "humanistic." In fact, they are often proud of it. For example, they revel in the religion of man so much that secularists even have a "humanist of the year" award since 1953. Over the years, it

---

1. This is in part because many Christians began incorporating elements from secular religions into their doctrine. For example the most common way was to accept the secular origins account over the Bible's origins account. See chapter 11 on Christian syncretism in this volume for more on this subject.

included the likes of Sir Julian Huxley (agnostic), Dr. Carl Sagan (atheist), Dr. Richard Dawkins (atheist), and TV personality Bill Nye (agnostic)!

Notice how humanism can incorporate varied secular beliefs like agnosticism or atheism and so forth (materialists, naturalists, etc.). We see this clearly with the secular emblems frequently placed on cars that say "COEXIST." It is cleverly written out using each letter as a symbol of various religions like Islam's crescent moon and star for the "C" and the Yin Yang symbol of Taoism for the "S." And of course, they end with the "T" being the Christian cross symbol.

It is not unlike the cover of this book series where we have utilized certain letters from various world religions to be letters that are used in the title, *World Religions and Cults*. For example, the "A" in our *World Religions and Cults* title is the atheist "A," and the "C" in cults is the Muslim symbol of the crescent moon and star.

However, COEXIST has a much different purpose than this world religions book series. COEXIST is meant to impose or promote a religious belief (that all religions are acceptable except those that say they are the only way, like Christianity). In other words, the COEXIST worldview is that people, like Christians, should be tolerant and stop saying there is only way — through Jesus Christ. Make no mistake, COEXIST is a means to try to silence Christianity and any religion that would claim an exclusive answer to mankind's problems.

COEXIST is essentially a subtle statement that Christianity is false and those promoting COEXIST are right. Would those holding to a COEXIST philosophy, be tolerant of the Christian belief that Christ is the only way? Not at all. They cry for tolerance but are intolerant themselves. Notice how it is a self-refuting attack on Christianity.

Yet COEXIST appears on the bumpers of those holding to religions like atheism, agnosticism, and secular humanism. Interestingly, secularists like this are usually more than happy to allow for multiple lines of belief (this is *syncretism*, where more than one religion is mixed with another), as long as it is not biblical Christianity.

On several occasions, I have personally spoken to a number of humanists who have pushed for atheism, then switch to agnosticism, and then switch to argue positively for something else like angelology or Eastern religions. It sounds like religious schizophrenia — and it is! But this is more common than you might realize.

For example, the Darwinfish.com website (clearly secular) will sell you the COEXIST symbol, alien symbol, Yin Yang symbol of Taoism, satanic pentagram symbol and a Devil fish plaque, Egyptian mythology of Isis symbol, Namaste (Hindu greeting), evolutionary religious symbols, Buddha emblem, Jewish Gefilte fish, and an angelology emblem.

At the same time, Darwinfish.com has some items that mock Christianity like a no-preaching emblem, an evolution symbol raping a Christian Ichthus fish, a dinosaur eating the popular Christian fish emblem, and an emblem that mocks Jesus with "Jeebus."[2] Do you see how they are inconsistent with their profession of tolerance?

One might object and say that COEXIST simply means that we coexist alongside one another in a pluralistic society. But that would be like a bumper sticker that states the obvious like "Air Exists." It essentially becomes meaningless. Even if this were the case, we already coexist in a sin-cursed world *for now*.

The point is that in heaven only those who have repented and received Jesus Christ and His death, burial, and Resurrection will be saved. In hell, those who have not repented and did not believe will be punished for their sins for all eternity from an eternal and all-powerful God. There will be no rest from the wrath of God upon their sin.

This brings us to the final point of this introduction. As Christians, we want to see people repent and find salvation through Christ, who is the only way. But from a secular perspective, why actively promote a secular belief? There is no god commanding someone to proselytize a secular faith in that viewpoint. So pushing atheism, agnosticism, materialism, naturalism, and the like is a self-refuting position right from the word "go"!

It shows that in the heart of hearts of the unbeliever, they know God exists and they have no excuse so they actively try to suppress that knowledge of God. Romans 1:20–32 reveals this state of the heart and mind of those in willful rebellion. It explains why secularists entertain great acts of sinfulness and actively oppose the Christian God with their words and lifestyle. Their minds have become futile, debased, and are under judgment already. Romans 1 says:

> For since the creation of the world His invisible attributes are clearly seen, being understood by the things that are made, even His eternal power and Godhead, so that they are without excuse, because, although they knew God, they did not glorify Him as

2. www.darwinfish.com, accessed Monday July 11, 2016.

God, nor were thankful, but became futile in their thoughts, and their foolish hearts were darkened. Professing to be wise, they became fools, and changed the glory of the incorruptible God into an image made like corruptible man — and birds and four-footed animals and creeping things.

Therefore God also gave them up to uncleanness, in the lusts of their hearts, to dishonor their bodies among themselves, who exchanged the truth of God for the lie, and worshiped and served the creature rather than the Creator, who is blessed forever. Amen.

For this reason God gave them up to vile passions. For even their women exchanged the natural use for what is against nature. Likewise also the men, leaving the natural use of the woman, burned in their lust for one another, men with men committing what is shameful, and receiving in themselves the penalty of their error which was due.

And even as they did not like to retain God in their knowledge, God gave them over to a debased mind, to do those things which are not fitting; being filled with all unrighteousness, sexual immorality, wickedness, covetousness, maliciousness; full of envy, murder, strife, deceit, evil-mindedness; they are whisperers, backbiters, haters of God, violent, proud, boasters, inventors of evil things, disobedient to parents, undiscerning, untrustworthy, unloving, unforgiving, unmerciful; who, knowing the righteous judgment of God, that those who practice such things are deserving of death, not only do the same but also approve of those who practice them.

Even so, the souls of unbelievers are still not far from being rescued by the Holy Spirit unto salvation. We see secularists come to know the Lord all the time in sincere repentance. Just as Paul outlined the offenses of those who reject God in Romans 1, he also stated to the Corinthian church that they had formerly been in such a state (1 Corinthians 6:9–10), but now it could be said of them: But you were washed, but you were sanctified, but you were justified in the name of the Lord Jesus and by the Spirit of our God (1 Corinthians 6:11).

Our hope with this final volume is to help open the eyes of Christians and non-Christians to the futility and illogical positions of secular religions. Our prayer is for the Holy Spirit to use this for His Glory unto salvation of many through the gospel of Jesus Christ.

Chapter 1

Secular and Atheistic Religions: Overview

Bodie Hodge and Roger Patterson

Secular religions (e.g., atheism, agnosticism, secular humanism, naturalism, etc.) possess a unique status in our Western world. Having a past that has typically been uneventful, the 1800s saw an explosion of these religious variants.

Fueled by the likes of Charles Lyell in the 1830s (geological evolution or "millions of years") and Charles Darwin beginning in 1859 (biological evolution from a common ancestor), the secular takeover of the West continued. We still see the fruit of these religious views in our day and age.

Secular religions now dominate areas like the media, education, law, museums, sexual expression, and, sadly, the minds of the next generation, according to recent statistics.[1] This makes sense since secular religious views flow freely in the education system due to secular laws imposed upon state schools. Young minds are molded into secular form, and few realize it until it is too late.

In the Western world (United States, United Kingdom, Germany, etc.), these secular religions are the biggest stumbling block for the next generation of Christians and Christian missionaries seeking to proclaim the gospel.

---

1. See Ken Ham, Britt Beemer with Todd Hillard, *Already Gone* (Green Forest, AR: Master Books, 2009); Ken Ham with Jeff Kinsley, *Ready to Return* (Green Forest, AR: Master Books, 2015).

The once great West, whose churches sent missionaries out to the whole world, is now crumbling at a foundational level due in part to the influence of secularism. Secular religious doctrines are even infiltrating the Church!

Essentially, the West needs missionaries to rise up and "rebuild the wall," so to speak, of the Church in the West. But to do so, we need to deal decisively with the religion of the day — the secularism that stands like Goliath in our culture. So how do we, as a Church, deal with it?

Immunizing the New Missionaries

Consider this hypothetical situation with which missionaries have to deal. Missionaries are sent to minister with the gospel to a place that has deadly diseases. The missionaries contract a disease and the missionaries die. You send more missionaries; they contract the same disease and die.

Now, if you were a sending church, what would you do? Do you simply send more missionaries to their potential doom? Or do you take the time to prepare your missionaries with the proper protection for what they are about to encounter — medicine or inoculation from the disease? Obviously, you want to protect your missionaries and give them what they need to be effective for the gospel work for which they are sent.

Now consider this same problem, but from a spiritual angle in our Western world. The United States and the United Kingdom were once nations greatly influenced by Christians, and churches could be found in abundance, particularly in cities. But now, churches have closed their doors *en masse* in many places in England. The same trend is happening to the United States, albeit at a delayed pace.

Today, cities have precious few churches, and those that are there are typically shallow with little doctrine (there are exceptions) and compromise the authority of God's Word. In other words, they are struggling and dying themselves. Many Christians recognize that there is a need for churches in cities. The cities like Cincinnati, New York, Salt Lake City, Los Angeles, Chicago, London, and Bristol are ripe for church plants.

Interestingly, few of these church plants are as effective as hoped. Some church plants grow slowly, others plateau, some merely take people from other churches, and others struggle and die. A lot of excuses are given — wrong church model, not enough funding, wrong music, too traditional, etc. But the main problem is that they were not dealing with the false religion that has entwined the people of the mission field.

When a missionary goes to Africa or the Amazon or Papua New Guinea, they train themselves to know what religions are in the area (e.g., Animism, Islam, Spiritism, etc.), and they learn how to refute those false beliefs so they can be an effective witness in presenting the truth of the Bible and the gospel. They don't go with the intent of just telling people to be moral and to add Jesus to what they believe.

How many church planters in cities in the UK and the USA have trained their missionaries to refute secular humanism, Darwinism, atheism, etc.? How many pastors in church plants in New York are trained to refute secular attacks on Christianity like radiometric dating, alleged missing links, big bang, and so on? The even bigger problem is that many of the church planters may have *agreed* with the secularists and believe the big bang is true, embrace millions of years, or even prefer evolution over the Bible's origins account. Imagine if we sent a missionary to Muslims who had bought into many tenets of Islam!

While we must certainly affirm that the message of the gospel is the power of God to salvation, apologetics is an important aspect of evangelism. While we proclaim the truth of Jesus as Lord and Savior, we must also help others see how their own religious views are insufficient to deal with their sin. We might also need to answer questions that explain the foundational elements of how sin entered the world and why they need a Savior.

If a missionary is not refuting the false religion prevalent in their mission field (i.e., secularism in much of the Western world), then why would we expect that missionary to be effective? Dealing with secularism and refuting it is a key to mission work in the "new" Western world. But refuting it is only part of the step. Secular refutations should not be divorced from the preaching of the gospel and teaching disciples to obey all Jesus commanded, embracing the authority of the Bible in all areas — starting in Genesis.

What Are Secular Religions?

There are a lot of forms of secularism. They are religions that are humanistic (i.e., man is the supreme authority). Here is a list of some of the forms or aspects of secular/humanistic religions:

- Atheism and New Atheism
- Agnosticism
- Existentialism

- Extraterrestrial Humanism
- "Nonreligious" Religious Humanism
- Naturalism
- Stoicism
- Materialism
- Relativism
- Nazism
- Hedonism (including perverted sexual expression)
- Communism
- Nature Worship
- Idealism/Dualism
- Satanism (Church of Satan)
- Epicureanism (Evolutionism)
- Modernism
- Scientism
- Post-modernism
- Secular Humanism

As you can see, there is a wide variety of secular/humanistic religious views. Those who profess a humanistic religion often blend these aspects in various ways. For example, a person might identify generally as an atheist and hold to a materialistic view of the universe and a relativistic understanding of morality. Professor Richard Dawkins is a new atheist but also believes in aliens/extraterrestrial life as a possible explanation for the origin of life on earth. Bill Nye professes to be an agnostic (he can't know for certain if God exists), but then proceeds to argue from an atheistic perspective (no God exists, cf., Psalm 14:1).

Sometimes these religions have great variations while sharing many commonalities. For example, Hedonism promotes sexual perversions like homosexuality (e.g., LGBT) and Nazism absolutely opposes them. Yet both share the same view that man is the supreme authority, and both share an evolutionary view of origins, opposing the Bible, looking to bring human prosperity, etc.

Some of these are philosophical aspects that are utilized by each variant — like naturalism, materialism, and relativism. Even *within* the various flavors of humanistic religions you can have variations. For example, within hedonism (cf., Ecclesiastes 9:7–10) there are two very different forms:

Quantitative Hedonism (get as much as you can for your enjoyment before you die)

Qualitative Hedonism (enjoy the highest quality of things in life before you die)

There are even variations within atheism. One view presents itself from *classical atheism* — says there is no God(s) but refrains from caring what others believe, also known as soft atheism. Then there is *new atheism,* which doesn't believe God(s) exists but tries to force this view on others, also known as hard atheism.

You may also notice that some of these religious flavors sometimes cross over with the moralistic religions described in *World Religions and Cults Volume 2.* Why such great variation and yet such similar commonalities based on the authority of man?

Consider what the Bible says:

In those days there was no king in Israel; everyone did what was right in his own eyes (Judges 17:6).

That we should no longer be children, tossed to and fro and carried about with every wind of doctrine, by the trickery of men, in the cunning craftiness of deceitful plotting (Ephesians 4:14).

It should not surprise us that a religious view that sets man as the authority has as many variations as there are people — since each person considers themselves the captain of their own soul. Man can invent all sorts of evil (Romans 1:30) and diversity of evil and deceptive doctrine (2 Timothy 3:12–13). These things should be tested against the absolute standard of God's Word (1 Thessalonians 5:21).

How Secular Religions Took Over the West — and the Failure of the Church to Properly Respond

About 200 years ago, the United States and England were strongly influenced by Christianity. England, at least in a legal sense, is a Protestant nation headed by a Protestant monarch. The queen or king is the supreme governor of the Anglican Church. They cannot take the throne without being of the Protestant faith — there is a long history to this establishment.

This influence extended to the British colonies and the nations that developed from those colonies.

But when we see the culture today, the USA, UK, and many other Western nations are highly secular. The ubiquity and brazen display of lies, immorality, murder, greed, hatred of Christians, child sacrifice, idolatry, the love of money, and many other evils are a daily reminder that our culture has changed. So how did it get this way?

One part of the answer is the failure of the Church to seriously engage these issues. And, *Deo volente* (God willing), they will be in a better position to address the trend. But the Church has failed in two areas:

1. Instead of combatting the slow secularization that began to unfold in the West in the early 1800s, many in the Church and their leaders embraced various aspects of secularization.
2. The Church gave most teaching of children over to a third party (that became secular), so subsequent generations within the Church were not equipped and fell to the secular onslaught.

In America in the 1800s, for example, Christians began giving their children over to state schools to educate them. At the time, it seemed like a good idea, as state schools used the Bible in the classroom. They used it to teach history, logic, philosophy, literature, science, and so forth.

So the Church, by and large, didn't have to focus on those subjects. Instead, they began concentrating on teaching the gospel, theology, and morality. As man's ideas about long ages, millions of years, astronomical evolution, and biological evolution began taking over school systems, most Christians either didn't notice or fell victim themselves.

By 1925, geological evolution (millions of years) and animal evolution were being taught in schools with full backing by the state. As human evolution began to be taught, the battle lines finally erupted with the famous Scopes Trial.

Even so, as the humanistic religion began to permeate the state schools under the influence of men like John Dewey, the Bible was removed, creation was taken out, prayer was silenced, the Ten Commandments banished, and so on. Now entire generations of kids have been raised up being taught the religion of secular humanism.

But what did the Church do to specifically counter this false religious teaching? By and large — nothing! Many churches still teach morality, the gospel, and theology (not that these are bad things), but then most parents (90 percent by the latest stats)[2] still send their children to state schools to be taught a different religion. So for about 40 hours a week, kids from Christian homes are taught the religious tenets of secular humanism, and the Church (who scarcely teaches the kids 2–3 hours per week) wonders why the kids are walking away from the faith and following after humanistic religions. Those that remain in the Church have often brought secular baggage with them. They often hold to evolution and millions of years, secular morality, secular views of sexuality, marriage, race, and so on.

What does this do to a local church? It causes it to be stagnant, impotent, or die as members are actually mixing secular religions with their Christianity. It is no different from the former godly Israelites in the Old Testament mixing true worship of God with worship of Baal. The mere difference is with *which religion* the modern Christians mix their Christianity — secularism rather than Baal.

With this in mind, we as Christians have to "pull the plank out of our own eye" in the Church before we "reach for the speck of sawdust" in the culture's eye. The Church needs to get back on the right track first. Thus, the Church has a big job to re-educate their congregations in the truth of the Bible in all areas like history, science, logic, and so forth.

"But We Don't Have a Religion!"

The secularists are the first to cry, "We are not part of a religion!" Why is this the case? There are a couple of reasons.

First, they don't want to be kicked out of the place of influence in the government school classrooms. Second, the secularist can more easily deceive kids into thinking that it is okay to believe what they teach and that it should have no conflicts with their respective religious beliefs.

Secular and humanistic religions like evolution, atheism, and agnosticism are part and parcel of the same pie. They have free reign under tax-supported dollars in the UK, USA, Australia, Germany, and so many other places. It is strange that Christianity was kicked out of the classroom and yet another religion is taught in its place.

---

2. Ken Ham, "Yes, We Are Losing the Millennials," Answers in Genesis, May 13, 2015, https://answersingenesis.org/christianity/church/yes-we-are-losing-millennials.

Tax dollars are spent on the secular religions through schools, state-funded museums, science journals, and so on. All the while, there is a false claim that "secularists aren't religious."

There is a simple way to test this claim. If something isn't religious, then it cannot oppose religious claims. Does the secular origins view (big bang, millions of years, and evolution) oppose the religious claim of special creation by God in six days and subsequently a young earth? Yes. Thus, secular views are religious. Anyone who claims that they are not religious and then makes judgments about religious topics (e.g., the deity of Christ, the existence of God, the morality of adultery, the truthfulness of the Bible, etc.) has made a religious statement. Though they may claim to be irreligious, they show that they are religious when they try to refute another religious view.

Does atheism, which says there is no God, oppose the religious claim that God exists (as found in the pages of the Bible)? Again, yes. Thus, atheism is religious. It is easy to prove that humanistic religions are religious.

Even many secularists openly admit to their faith. One instance is John Dunphy while writing for a secular magazine:

> I am convinced that the battle for humankind's future must be waged and won in the public school classroom by teachers who correctly perceive their role as the proselytizers of a new faith: a religion of humanity that recognizes and respects the spark of what theologians call divinity in every human being. These teachers must embody the same selfless dedication as the most rabid fundamentalist preachers, for they will be ministers of another sort, utilizing a classroom instead of a pulpit to convey humanist values in whatever subject they teach, regardless of the educational level — preschool day care or large state university. The classroom must and will become an arena of conflict between the old and the new — the rotting corpse of Christianity, together with all its adjacent evils and misery, and the new faith of humanism.[3]

The U.S. Supreme Court, in *Torcaso v. Watkins*, 81 S.Ct. 1681 (1961), stated the following: "Among religions in this country which do not teach what would generally be considered a belief in the existence of God, are

---

3. J. Dunphy, "A Religion for a New Age," *The Humanist*, Jan.–Feb. 1983, p. 23.

Buddhism, Taoism, Ethical Culture, Secular Humanism, and others." Additionally, these groups are eligible for the same tax benefits as other religious groups, and secular and atheist chaplains even function within the military. You can't have your cake and eat it too. Humanists are religious and they act in religious ways.

Is Science Secular?

Many people today insist that science can only be done by people who have a secular worldview — or at least by those who are willing to leave their religious views at the door as they enter the science lab. Several popular atheists and evolutionists have contended that people who reject the big bang and the evolution of living things are so backward that they cannot even be involved in developing new technologies.[4]

But is this really the case? Or are these opponents of a biblical worldview simply making assertions that cannot be supported with facts and substantial arguments, having an incorrect understanding of true science?

A friend of Answers in Genesis was challenged by the comment that science can only be done through a purely secular, evolutionary framework. Such statements are blatantly absurd and are a type of arbitrary fallacy called an "ignorant conjecture." In other words, these people simply do not know the past, nor are they familiar with what science really is.

Examples of Scientists Operating from a Christian Worldview

If science is a strictly secular endeavor without any need for a biblical worldview, then why were most fields of science developed by Bible-believing Christians? For example, consider Isaac Newton, Gregor Mendel, Louis Pasteur, Johannes Kepler, Galileo Galilei, Robert Boyle, Blaise Pascal, Michael Faraday, James Joule, Joseph Lister, and James Clerk Maxwell. Were these "greats" of science not doing science? Francis Bacon developed the scientific method, and he was a young-earth creationist and devout Christian.

Even in modern times, the inventor of the MRI scanning machine, Dr. Raymond Damadian, is a Christian working with Christian principles. The founder of catastrophic plate tectonics, Dr. John Baumgardner, is also a devout Christian. And those who recently founded the scientific field of

---

4. As an example of this dismissive attitude, Eugenie Scott (formerly) of the National Center for Science Education (NCSE), a leading religious humanist, says, "Like other pseudo-sciences, 'creation science' seeks support and adherents by claiming the mantle of science." http://ncse.com/rncse/23/1/my-favorite-pseudoscience.

baraminology are also Christians. Also, I (Bodie Hodge) developed a new method for production of submicron titanium diboride for the materials science and ceramics industry. Professor Stuart Burgess developed a new mechanism for the two-billion-dollar European (ESA) satellite *Envisat*. Dr. John Sanford developed the gene gun. And let's not forget Werner von Braun, the young-earth Christian who was the founder of rocket science and led the United States to the moon. These are but a few examples of people who held to a biblical worldview and were quite capable as scientists and inventors of new technologies.

The Foundation for Science Is Biblical Christianity

Furthermore, science comes out of a *Christian* worldview. Only the God described in the Bible can account for a logical and orderly universe. God upholds the universe in a particular way, such that we can study it by observational and repeatable experimentation (see Genesis 8:22). Because God upholds the universe in a consistent manner, we have a valid reason to expect that we can study the world we live in and describe the laws that God uses to sustain the universe (Colossians 1:17).

In the secular view, where all matter originated by chance from nothing, there is no ultimate cause or reason for anything that happens, and explanations are constantly changing, so there is no *basis* for science. Though many non-Christians do science, like inventing new technologies or improving medical science, they are doing it in a manner that is inconsistent with their professed worldview. On what basis should we expect a universe that came from nothing and for no reason to act in a predictable and consistent manner? When non-Christians do real science by observable and repeatable experimentation, they are actually assuming a biblical worldview, even if they do not realize it.

It makes sense why "science" in the United States is losing out to other nations since our science education system now limits science in the classroom exclusively to the religion of secular humanism (and its subtle variations).

It Is Not "Science vs. Religion"

So the debate is not "science versus religion." It is really "religion versus religion." Sadly, science is caught up in the middle.

The battle is between the religion of *secular humanism* (with its variant forms like agnosticism, atheism, and the like), which is usually called *secularism* or *humanism* for short, and *Christianity.* They both have religious documents (e.g., the Humanist Manifestos I, II, and III for humanists, and the Bible for Christians); both are recognized religions by the Supreme Court;[5] and both receive the same 501(c)(3) tax-exempt status. Both have different views of origins.

Humanism has astronomical evolution (big bang), geological evolution (millions of years of slow gradual changes), chemical evolution (life came from non-life), and biological evolution (original, single-celled life evolved into all life forms we have today over billions of years) in its view of origins. In other words, evolution (as a whole) is a tenet of the dogma of the religion of humanism in the same way as biblical creation (as a whole, with six-day creation, the Fall, global Flood, and the Tower of Babel) is a tenet of the dogma of Christianity. It is a battle between two different religions.

In recent times, the state and federal governments kicked Christianity out of the classroom, thinking they kicked religion out; but instead, they just replaced Christianity with a godless religion of humanism. This was done as an attack designed by humanists.

An Evolutionary Worldview Equals Science?

There is a misconception that this evolutionary subset of humanism *is* science. Science means knowledge and scientific methodology that is based on the scientific method (observable and repeatable experimentation). However, evolution (whether chemical, biological, astronomical, or geological) is far from scientific. Consider the following facts:

1. No one has been able to observe or repeat the making of life from non-life (matter giving rise to life or chemical evolution).

2. No one has been able to observe or repeat the changing of a single-celled life-form like an amoeba into a cow or goat over billions of years (biological evolution).

3. No one has been able to observe or repeat the big bang (astronomical evolution).

4. No one has observed millions of years of time progressing in geological layers (geological evolution).

---

5. U.S. Supreme Court, *Torcaso v. Watkins.*

The reason some people are confused about the religion of humanism — and specifically its subset of evolution — as being science is a bait-and-switch fallacy. Let me explain. One of the key components of humanism is naturalism. Basically, it assumes *a priori* there is nothing supernatural and no God. In other words, nature (i.e., matter) is all that exists in their religion (only the physical world).

As a clarifying note, Christians also believe in the natural realm; but unlike the naturalist or humanist, we believe in the supernatural realm, too (i.e., the spiritual, abstract, conceptual, and immaterial realm). Logic, truth, integrity, concepts, thought, God, etc., are not *material* and have no mass. So those holding to naturalism as a worldview *must* reject logic, truth, and all immaterial concepts if they wish to be consistent, since these are *not* material or physical parts of nature.

This is very important because naturalism or natural science has been added as one of the dictionary definitions of science. For example, it was not found in the 1828 Webster's dictionary, but it was added in one form in the 1913 edition. And, interestingly, they removed the definition that "the science of God must be perfect" in the 1913 edition.

So, although many appeal to observable and repeatable science through methodology to understand how the universe operates, another definition has been added to muddle this.[6] Science is now defined as "knowledge or a system of knowledge covering general truths or the operation of general laws especially as obtained and tested through scientific method."[7]

For example, evolutionists have continued to popularize Darwin's scientific observation of the changes in beaks of Galapagos finches as proof for the evolution of one animal kind into another. This is a great example of the bait-and-switch fallacy where scientists present real scientific evidence (the difference in finch beaks) but stretch the truth to say it gives validity to the mythology of microbes-to-man evolution (the "switch" part of the fallacy). This trick leads many to believe that evolution is real science. The only real science in this example is the observation of the difference in finch beaks.

People are baited with this good methodology of observational science (again developed by a Christian named Francis Bacon), and then they are

---

6. There is also the issue of operational science versus historical science. For more, see: http://www.answersingenesis.org/articles/ee/what-is-science.

7. Merriam-Webster Online, s.v. "science," accessed March 8, 2013, http://www.merriam-webster.com/dictionary/science.

told that evolution is science while subtly appealing to another added definition: that of "natural science" or "naturalism." This is like saying another definition of science is "Nazism." Then Nazis could say they are "scientists" and get into a classroom! This is what has happened with humanism. The religion of humanism (with its founding principle of naturalism) has been disguised as *science* by adding another definition to the word *science*. But it is not the good science we think of that makes computers, space shuttles, and cars. It is a religion. To call evolution science is a bait-and-switch tactic.

So, Is Science Strictly Secular?

No. In summary, science can never be strictly secular for these reasons:

1. Real science is observable and repeatable experimentation that only makes sense in a biblical worldview where God's power keeps the laws of nature consistent. In other words, science proceeds from a biblical worldview.
2. Secular humanism, with its subset of evolution, is in reality a religion and not science.
3. Many of the greatest scientists were Bible-believing Christians whose biblical worldview motivated their scientific studies, showing that a strictly secular view is not necessary for performing science.

Where Humanism Leads

Christians will continue to conduct scientific inquiry and invent things, processes, and science fields as we always have. If the United States and other places neglect our accomplishments and inventions and continue to push the religion of humanism on unsuspecting kids in the classroom (usually unbeknownst to most) by limiting its definition of science to the humanistic worldview, then my humble suggestion is that they will continue down the same road humanism leads. That is, people who are consistent in their naturalistic worldview shouldn't care about true science or the world, since nothing ultimately matters in that worldview.

Refutations

Secular worldviews like atheism (and the like) have serious problems. When refuting false worldviews, there are three ways that are typically used to prove them false. They are:

1. Arbitrariness
2. Inconsistency
3. Borrowing from the Bible (preconditions of intelligibility)

Arbitrariness includes things like mere opinions, relativism, conjectures (prejudicial), and unargued biases.

Inconsistencies include logical fallacies, "actions speak louder than words" in behavior and attitudes, presupposition issues that are irrational, and views that are *reduced to absurdity*, based on where the argument is heading.

Borrowing from the Bible is couched in philosophical terminology like preconditions of intelligibility. In brief, it is when a worldview cannot account for something that is foundational. For example, in a materialistic worldview, why would love exist? Love is not material. You don't drink some love to increase your daily dose of love.

So when a secular materialist claims they love something or someone, then it is highlighting a problem with their preconditions. In other words, the materialist in this case believes love exists, but his religious convictions say otherwise. Some of the problems with secular viewpoints will be analyzed using these criteria (arbitrariness, inconsistencies, etc.) without being exhaustive, of course.

Arbitrariness

In the case of God and His Word, they are not arbitrary. This is because there is no greater authority than God (cf. Hebrews 6:13). There is no greater authority that can be appealed to than God — and by extension His Word.

However, all secular views fail to appeal to God as their final authority, instead appealing to man. Man is a lesser authority and not absolute. Thus, any authority of man is a mere opinion to the absolute and supreme authority of God and His Word. All secular religions are based on the ideas of fallible man and thus arbitrary next to God.

The fact that many secular religions deviate from one another in their belief systems shows how relative they are regarding man's opinions. Thus, relativism reigns supreme among them. But relativism is fallacious, being arbitrary. So from two fronts, secular religions fail to pass the test.

In response, some secularists have touted that there is variation among Christians and the outworkings of the Bible, thus the Bible is arbitrary, too.

However, this misses the point — it is not about what Christians believe, but about what God says. Christian outworkings (e.g., denominations, church splits, doctrinal misinterpretations) are based on man's (less than perfect) understanding of the Scripture. But this has nothing to do with God being the absolute authority. Just because an authority is misinterpreted or misunderstood does not undermine its authority.

Inconsistent

Have you noticed that many secularists want to be good and want to do the moral thing? Herein lies the problem. If there is no God who sets what is right and wrong or defines good and bad, then why be moral and how can "good" be defined? It is utterly inconsistent to try to do good or be moral when your religion, *at its very base*, says there is no need or compulsion to do so.

We've seen atheists, agnostics, hedonists, and others get upset with brutality, people lying and deceiving, and terrorist activities, and yet they hold to positions that encourage abortion (murdering babies in the womb). Note the inconsistency.

Christians are commonly attacked for believing God's authority regarding the truth of the Bible, but they turn around and hold to a position based on trusting man's authority! Think of it like this:

> Secular claim: You Christians blindly take the Bible as an authority because the Bible tells you to.

> Christian response: By what authority do you reject God's Word?

> Secular response: I read a book (or heard someone) that told me to believe the Bible is wrong, and I trust them.

Again, note the inconsistency. The difference is that man's authority is meaningless when compared to the absolute authority that is God's Word. If God *is* God, then what authority would supersede God's? There is none. God must reveal Himself as the final and superior authority.

Another secular claim, particularly from empiricists, is that "seeing is believing." They argue that truth claims can only be known through the senses. But there is an inconsistency here. How does the secularist know that alleged truth claim is true? Their senses are not involved in that alleged truth claim (that all truth claims can only be known through the senses).

To further elaborate, they claim that all truth claims are known by senses, but how do they know that? Did they see or sense that truth? Sadly, they usually hold such a position because someone told them to — like a book or teacher.

Secular religions are largely materialistic and naturalistic. Matter (including energy and space-time) is all that exists — nature is all that exists . . . thus, the term *naturalism*. This stands in direct opposition to the Christian worldview based on the Bible where the supernatural also exists. God is God of both the natural and supernatural (i.e., spiritual realm). This is why Christians are not as limited as secularists on many issues.

But a materialistic/naturalistic worldview causes undeniable problems for secular views. If matter is all that exists, then nonmaterial (immaterial) things cannot exist. There are many things that cannot exist if materialism is correct. They include:

- Logic
- Truth
- Abstractions
- Propositions
- Concepts
- Rights
- Shame
- Reason
- Knowledge
- Dignity
- Honor
- Love
- Sadness

It would be inconsistent (i.e., a behavioral inconsistency) for a secularist to appeal to logic, reason, truth, etc., to argue for a secular worldview that says immaterial things cannot exist!

Another absurd inconsistency reveals itself during discussions of God's Word being the authority. Some secularists go so far as to proclaim that they don't believe the Bible, as though that settles the debate. But it doesn't. When a secularist (or anyone else) professes that they disagree with the Bible, then they are claiming to be God. To disagree with God is to view oneself as God. This is fallacious reasoning.

Allow me to explain this further. When one claims to disagree with God, then they are elevating their own thoughts to be greater than an omniscient, omnipotent, and omnipresent God. Therefore, one is (usually inadvertently) elevating themself to *be that* God! This is clearly absurd.

Borrow from Bible

Many secularists live their lives borrowing from God's Word, though they fail to realize it. If people are merely evolved animals and there is no God who sets right and wrong, then why wear clothes? Why get married? Why get an education? Squirrels don't set up universities to discuss philosophical methodology.

Why celebrate the popular Christian holidays called weekends, which is based on the Sabbath Day and the Lord's Day? Why have holidays anyway? A holiday is a holy day, yet there exists nothing holy in a secular worldview.

Why heal sick people (medicine) when survival of the fittest should take its course as it has in the past without our interference? Why have laws? God may set laws, but if we are our own authority, then law is meaningless.

Why waste time on science? In fact, how can the secularist know the laws of nature won't change tomorrow? (From a Christian perspective, God has promised to uphold nature as it is in the future.) From a secular viewpoint, they can't know the future will be uniform. If they argue that it has always been like that, then it begs the very question at hand! Thus it is a fallacious circular argument. Yes, even the possibility of observable and repeatable science is based on God's Word being true.

Conclusion

When it comes down to it, secular views fail on a number of aspects. Even more discussion and refutation is found in the various chapters in this volume. Sadly, many have been deceived into believing that secular worldviews are the truth, when in fact truth cannot exist if secular worldviews are correct (as truth is not material).

Our hope is that those caught up in secular religions, whether they knew it or not, will repent. Our hope is to see them realize the truth of the Scripture by the power of the Holy Spirit. Secular religions ultimately say things came from nothing, are going to nothing, and nothing matters. But with Christianity, there is the power of hope based on a truthful God who made a way to save us for all eternity. See chapter 15 in this volume for more on this precious subject.

Chapter 2

Atheism

Ken Ham and Bodie Hodge

The fool has said in his heart, "There is no God." They are corrupt, and have done abominable iniquity; there is none who does good (Psalm 53:1).

The religion of atheism is nothing new. The godly have dealt with it since sin took a foothold in a fallen world (after Genesis 3).[1] King David dealt with it in the Old Testament; the Apostle Paul dealt with it in the New Testament when he argued against the atheistic Epicureans in Acts 17.

In our day and age, the atheistic religion is alive and thriving in the wake of declining Christianity in the Western world. Atheists make up about 3.1% of the U.S. population according to the Pew Research Center in 2014.[2] The UK has about 13% who profess the religion of atheism.[3]

These increases come as no surprise as the government schools in the West teach the religious tenets of atheism without restriction in many classes. One

---

1. Consider the very thoughts of the Pre-Flood world. Genesis 6:5 says, "Then the LORD saw that the wickedness of man was great in the earth, and that every intent of the thoughts of his heart was only evil continually."
2. "America's Changing Religious Landscape," Pew Research Center: Religion & Public Life, May 12, 2015, http://www.pewforum.org/2015/05/12/americas-changing-religious-landscape.
3. "Brits among the least religious in the world: UK comes 59th in poll of 65 countries after only 30% of population say they have a faith," DailyMail.com, April 12, 2015, http://www.dailymail.co.uk/news/article-3036133/Brits-religious-world-UK-comes-59th-poll-65-countries-30-population-say-faith.html.

of the founders of modern, atheistic evolutionary views, Charles Darwin, argued that man invented the idea of God.[4] Being from England, his views have been imposed on generations of people in the UK and beyond.

What Is Atheism?

Atheism is the king of the secular humanistic religious variations. It is the pinnacle of secular beliefs, taking the position to its extreme.

Atheism is the religious belief system that professes there is no God or gods. While agnostics claim it is not possible to know whether a god exists, atheists are absolute in their insistence that there are no gods. Many people who claim to be atheists will actually acknowledge they are agnostics when pressed.

Inherent to atheism is materialism — the concept that only material things exist. The atheist claims there is no immaterial realm (i.e., no spiritual realm), otherwise God could exist in that nonmaterial realm and thus atheism would be refuted. So there is an absolute commitment to the idea that every phenomenon can be explained as the result of matter interacting.

The term *theism* is based in belief in God (*theos* is "god" in Greek). Atheism means *without God* (*a-* without, *theos-* god). The term has been in use since the 1600s. Atheism is a fancy way of saying that they try to maintain a belief system without any notion of God. Some prefer the moniker *non-theist*. In reality, these are just different names of the same basic philosophy with slight variations in their outlook.

As with any religious worldview, there are variations in atheism:

- Classical Atheism (atheism without any flair)
- New Atheism (evangelistic and aggressive to impose the religion of atheism on people through schools, media, etc.)
- Non-theism (opposed to God but usually disinterested in discussions; also called soft atheism)

---

4. Charles Darwin, *The Descent of Man and Selection in Relation to Sex*, reprinted from the 2nd ed. (New York: A.L. Burt, 1919), p. 105–109. Some may object and suggest that Darwin was a theist because the name God does appear a few times in *On the Origin of Species*, the 6th and final edition. However, Darwin's fist edition had no mention of God. Due to his views being attacked for years by those who believed in God, Darwin's later editions added "God" as a possibility, though Darwin only ever described himself as an agnostic at best in his correspondence. His final book *Descent of Man* showed where his view of God truly was — that man invented the idea of God. For more, see Randall Hedtke, *Secrets of the Sixth Edition* (Green Forest, AR: Master Books, 2010).

- Anti-theist (opposes religions other than itself — outspoken and confrontational; also called hard atheism)
- Church of Satan (LaVeyan Satanism)
- Epicureanism (among the first atheistic evolutionists, a form of Greek philosophy)
- Ritual atheists (e.g., Atheist Church which models rituals after Christian elements but without God)

There are several religions that are atheistic in their outlook or act like atheism in practice. Without being exhaustive, two examples are agnosticism and Buddhism. Buddhism has elements of a "transcendental heavens" that lies outside the natural realm, but in practice it is atheistic in denying a being acknowledged as a god.

Though distinct from atheism but still a variation of Secular Humanism, agnosticism receives an honorable mention because many of its adherents act more like practical atheists. Agnostics (a- without; gnosis- knowledge) claim that it is not possible to know if a god or gods exist since they are not part of the natural realm. In his debate with Ken Ham, Bill Nye, a professing agnostic, used and argued for atheistic positions while not claiming to know with certainty whether God exists.

As a reminder, this book series is not arguing for a mere theistic position, but instead for *Christian* theism. We are unashamed about proclaiming and arguing for the God of the Bible.

Atheists — Seeing through the Facade

Professor Richard Dawkins, a well-known atheist and former professor at Oxford University in England, openly argues against gods — especially the Christian God — and claims that he doesn't believe in the God of the Bible. Nor does he believe in the Easter Bunny, Dionysus (an alleged Greek god), or the Tooth Fairy![5]

Interestingly enough, Dr. Dawkins doesn't spend his energy and effort arguing against the Easter Bunny, Dionysus, or the Tooth Fairy. Instead, he has spent much of his life writing books and articles and offering interviews and commentary arguing against the God of the Bible. Why the inconsistency?

Have you ever stopped to think about why Dr. Dawkins and other professing atheists spend so much of their waking hours arguing against God's

---

5. Although, Dawkins gets nervous about being critical of the Allah of the Koran.

existence? It is because in his heart of hearts (innermost part of his mind) Dr. Dawkins knows God exists and he is trying to suppress that knowledge and justify his denial of the obvious. It is an easy task to let go of the alleged existence of the Easter Bunny, Tooth Fairy, and so on. But the God of the Bible is not so easily cast aside. And there are good reasons.

Romans 1:18–25 says:

> For the wrath of God is revealed from heaven against all ungodliness and unrighteousness of men, who suppress the truth in unrighteousness, because what may be known of God is manifest in them, for God has shown it to them. For since the creation of the world His invisible attributes are clearly seen, being understood by the things that are made, even His eternal power and Godhead, so that they are without excuse, because, although they knew God, they did not glorify Him as God, nor were thankful, but became futile in their thoughts, and their foolish hearts were darkened. Professing to be wise, they became fools, and changed the glory of the incorruptible God into an image made like corruptible man — and birds and four-footed animals and creeping things. Therefore God also gave them up to uncleanness, in the lusts of their hearts, to dishonor their bodies among themselves, who exchanged the truth of God for the lie, and worshiped and served the creature rather than the Creator, who is blessed forever. Amen.

The Bible gives a consistent witness to the fact that God's existence as the eternal and divine Creator is obvious from the creation He has made, including man himself.

> He has made everything beautiful in its time. Also He has put eternity in their hearts, except that no one can find out the work that God does from beginning to end (Ecclesiastes 3:11).

> Who show the work of the law written in their hearts, their conscience also bearing witness, and between themselves their thoughts accusing or else excusing them (Romans 2:15).

> The heavens declare the glory of God; and the firmament shows His handiwork. Day unto day utters speech, and night

unto night reveals knowledge. There is no speech nor language where their voice is not heard. Their line has gone out through all the earth, and their words to the end of the world (Psalm 19:1–4).

Dr. Dawkins and others are trying to suppress their knowledge of God, which God has made evident to them. However, they cannot escape it, so they do what they can to hide from it, seeking to justify that God doesn't exist — with bold, yet bad, arguments no less. But there is no escaping that fact that God exists.

Why Is This Significant?

It means that atheism, though professed, doesn't really exist. In other words, there are no true atheists, just those who *claim* to be. If we agree with God we must disagree with atheists. An all-knowing and all-powerful God informs us that all people do have the knowledge of God's existence. Therefore, atheism is impossible. What you have are 3% of Americans who are openly suppressing that knowledge of God and lying, whether consciously or not, to say they are atheists.[6]

Here is an illustration to help understand the point. Imagine if someone professes that logic doesn't exist. Then they proceed to use logic to try to prove that logic doesn't work. Do you really believe them when they claim they don't believe in logic? No, they demonstrated that their claim was false the moment they used logic to disprove logic.

Furthermore, when atheists spend immense time trying to disprove God, it proves where the battle in their heart is. It is against the God they are trying to suppress.

Atheistic Origins: Big Bang, Millions of Years, and Evolution

Since materialism is one of the core tenets of atheism, naturalistic, evolutionary processes provide the foundation of the belief of origins. So the atheist must try to figure out where the universe came from naturalistically, *without* appealing to a Creator.

Big Bang

In the past, some atheists posited an eternal universe (which most now reject). The second law of thermodynamics destroys this position. If the

---

6. It is also possible that many of these professing atheists simply don't know what atheism is.

universe was eternal in the past, there should be no usable energy left whatsoever. So the fact that stars shine disproves this position.

Others have observed that the universe is expanding (which the Bible suggests was the case, e.g., Isaiah 40:22, 44:24; Zechariah 12:1; etc.). But those opposing God proposed that if the expansion of the heavens could be wound backward (in a general sense), there was a "creation point" or singularity (an almost infinitely hot and dense particle). Then this singularity blew apart (expanded outward in all directions rapidly) and this is where the space, matter, and energy came from to form the universe. But they say there was no God involved — pure naturalism.

This singularity could not have been eternal, as the second law of thermodynamics destroys that idea as well. It should have run down to a point where there is no more usable energy as eternity progressed. So the atheistic position is that there was nothing — no time, no space, no matter — and then this singularity just popped into existence from nothing and then expanded. This is essentially what the big-bang model promotes.

Based on modern observations of the expansion of the universe and measurements of distance between galaxies, scientists postulated that the expansion could be viewed in reverse. At some point, the universe must have been smaller, so the calculations attempted to determine when the universe began. This assumes that God had not created the universe in the recent past or with any initial size.

As time went on, the model was adjusted in light of new findings. But to rescue the model in the face of contrary evidence, ideas like cosmic inflation were added to make the numbers "fit" the model. There have been many changes to the initial concept and so many layers added that it barely resembles the original "cosmic egg" idea. Today, many scientists appeal to the unobserved idea of a multiverse to explain how something came from nothing — the origins fairy tale for the atheist.

The biblical creationist explains these modern observations as well, so the observations are not exclusive to the big-bang idea. Take note that this whole model is built on pure speculation! The big bang is not repeatable or observable at its very root, which means is it not observational or repeatable science. It is just fairy tale stories to fit with their preconceived religion of atheism and naturalism. As a loud and clear point, no God or gods are required in any big-bang model. It was always meant to explain the origin of the universe from a totally naturalistic, materialistic viewpoint. So for Christians who might consider the option that God could have *used* the big bang, then they are essentially adding God to a view that was formulated to explain the universe without God!

Millions of Years

Millions of years (in fact, billions of years) are a prerequisite for an atheistic worldview. We've never heard of a young earth atheistic evolutionist. For the earth to form as we know it through naturalistic processes, there must have been billions of years for its evolution, beginning with the big bang.

To the atheist, one must have *millions of years* for stars to form after the big bang, then *millions of years* for stars to supposedly make heavier elements, then *millions of years* for stars to explode, then *millions of years* for the heavier elements to coalesce into planets and asteroids and so forth. All of these naturalistic evolutionary processes are referred to as cosmological evolution.

Then the atheist needs *millions of years* for the molten planets to cool. Then one needs *millions of years* of naturalistic processes to finally arrive at sufficient water and a protective atmosphere for life to form. Then the atheist needs *millions of years* for the right planet to be at just the right size and just the right distance from a stable star. Then they need *millions of years* of chemical processes to occur so that maybe one of them accidentally produces the first life. As the earth continued to form, geological evolution supposedly produced the rock layers, seas, and landforms that we see today.

Keep in mind, we're just hitting the highlights. But see this for what it is: blind faith. This is just one arbitrary story layered upon another with no observable verification or witness.

Chemical and Biological Evolution

Chemical evolution or "abiogenesis" is how matter supposedly gave rise to life from non-living elements. The problem is that this has never been observed. Furthermore, one of the few laws in biology is the law of biogenesis that says life only comes from life. So to blindly believe in abiogenesis is not scientific, as it violates this verified law of science. Despite the evidence against it, atheists must believe it happened at least once in the past to be consistent in their materialistic worldview.

At any rate, once life supposedly formed, what did it eat? How did it excrete its waste? How did it protect itself from harsh chemicals all around it? How did it know to reproduce? Where did the coded information in its DNA come from? This complex initial life form apparently just happened by accident in the atheistic worldview — at least that is how the story goes.

Assuming life happened, this single-celled organism must evolve over billions of years, adding complex information to its genome like a circulatory system, a brain, a nerve system, ears, eyes, hair, immune system, and so forth. Of course, we do not observe these kinds of changes happening in nature today, nor have we been able to repeat this via naturalistic experiments. It is a story based on blind arbitrary assertions and opinions based on what we actually observe today.

From a big-picture perspective, atheism, based on its origins teaches that man (and the universe) is just an accidental mixture of chemicals doing what chemicals do. There is no purpose, no right, and no wrong — everything is ultimately meaningless.

Bahnsen-Stein Debate: When the World's Leading Atheist Met His Match

Along with Dr. Richard Dawkins, Dr. Gordon Stein (d. 1996) was another well-known champion of atheism. Dr. Stein was a brilliant man. He was an atheist and proud of it.[7]

Dr. Stein was well versed in the classical arguments for the existence of God (first cause, grand design, etc.) espoused by persons like Thomas Aquinas and Rene Descartes. Each of these arguments began with human reason and tried to derive a position that *a god* probably exists.

Starting from a possible god, the Christian would then argue that *that god* might be the God of the Bible. Each classical argument for the existence of God is *probabilistic*. In other words, the best you can argue is that a god probably exists and it might be the biblical God.

Dr. Stein knew this. He also figured out how to annihilate Christians in debate because of these faults, even writing a book on the subject. This should come as no surprise, since the arguments are flawed from the onset. These arguments rest on the premise that one should leave God out of the argument and stick strictly with human reason as the sole authority.

---

7. In the famous debate with Greg Bahnsen, Gordon Stein had a strange definition of atheism that was more akin to the definition of agnosticism (i.e., that an atheist just doesn't know if God exists). Perhaps this was a debate ploy, because atheism is rather easy to debunk.

Why would a Christian, who believes God is the absolute authority, argue on the basis that God *isn't* the absolute authority to develop a position based on the premise that man *is* the absolute authority? The moment that a Christian leaves God's absolute authority out of the debate, he has already lost the debate over God being the absolute authority!

Dr. Stein, with his string of victories, was set to debate philosopher and pastor Dr. Greg Bahnsen. Dr. Bahnsen didn't use the flawed classical arguments for the existence of God. Instead, he started with God and His Word as the absolute authority and didn't waiver.

Dr. Bahnsen argued that all other positions, including atheism, must borrow from God and His Word to make sense of anything — knowledge, logic, truth, morality, and so forth. This is called the Transcendental Argument for the Existence of God (TAG for short), although, it really isn't an argument as the name seems to imply, but rather a starting point for God being the absolute authority *in all arguments*.

In other words, Dr. Bahnsen stood on the authority of God's Word, which is what makes argumentation possible — even Dr. Stein was borrowing from God's authority and didn't realize it. This was devastating to Dr. Stein's case. Dr. Bahnsen pulled the rug out from underneath the atheistic position of Dr. Stein.

Dr. Bahnsen used the subject of logic (as well as absolute morality, and uniformity of nature) to destroy Dr. Stein's atheistic position. How did he do this? Dr. Stein was a professing atheist who had a materialistic worldview. Thus, when Dr. Stein argued that immaterial entities, like God, don't exist (based on his professed worldview), Dr. Bahnsen caught him in a trap.

Dr. Bahnsen kindly pointed out that logic, which is not material either, could not exist in Dr. Stein's atheistic view. Logic is not material. It is abstract, invariant, and universal. Truth, knowledge, information, absolute morality, etc. are not material either. Thus, Dr. Stein couldn't even make a logical case without presuming his professed religion of atheism was wrong in its materialistic foundations. Dr. Bahnsen pointed out that Dr. Stein must borrow from God's Word just to argue against it.

Dr. Stein kept trying to figure out how to answer and words came out of his mouth, but he left the debate in utter defeat. He and Dr. Bahnsen wrote letters back and forth until they died in 1995 and 1996. To his dying day,

Dr. Stein could not answer the devastating case made against his atheism. In subsequent debates, Dr. Bahnsen ultimately earned the name "The Man Most Feared by Atheists." Let's look more closely at specific refutations of the religion of atheism.

Arbitrariness

> Stop regarding man in whose nostrils is breath, for of what account is he? (Isaiah 2:22; ESV).

Would you believe something just because someone tells you to believe it? We should hope not! Next to God, the ideas of man are but a breath. God's ways are much higher than man's (Isaiah 55:9). This is logical, as God is all-knowing (Psalm 147:5) and man isn't.

When the opinions of man sit as the absolute authority on a subject, then they are arbitrary. Each person sits in the supposed position of authority, so no one is the authority. This is the case for atheism. There is no God or ultimate authority to appeal to in an atheistic mindset. In the absence of God, man is viewed as the final authority on all matters.

Appealing to man's opinions as the truth is a faulty appeal to authority. Thus, it is illogical. The entire philosophy of atheism is based on man being the ultimate authority on all matters — an arbitrary position that can never provide a source of truth.

Inconsistency and Borrowing from the Bible

Absolute Morality

If everything came from nothing and all things that happen are merely chemical reactions doing what chemicals do, then there is no such thing as right and wrong. In other words, if someone decides to kill all the atheists in the world, from an atheistic position that is okay since they cannot argue that killing atheists is wrong *within* their own worldview. If people are merely a sack of chemicals interacting, then there is no consistent reason to forbid killing others.

Don't get me wrong, many atheists want some sort of moral code (i.e., they don't want to get murdered or be lied to), but that doesn't come from *their* religion. Instead, it comes from God who has written the law on their hearts, and their consciences know it. Really, atheists must borrow morality from God's Word, whether they realize it or not.

Atheists might argue that they could borrow morality from other religions, but that fails too. First, all those other religions are also borrowing morality from the God of the Bible (they all have the law of God written on their hearts too). So the atheist is still ultimately borrowing it from God.

Second, if the atheist opts to borrow morality from other religions that have deviated from the Bible in their morality (like Islam or Eastern religions), it doesn't help them. Islam is generally fine with the extermination of the atheists (infidels).

Eastern thought says all things are illusions (doctrine of *maya*) — including people like atheists. If someone kills them it is no big deal since they don't really exist anyway. It merely changes their karma for the next life.

Absolute morality comes from God, as God is the ultimate and final lawgiver (Hebrews 6:13). Only God explains why morality exists in the universe that He created.

Laws of Logic

The atheist holds that all things consist of matter and energy (nature and matter only). They argue with the loudest voice that there is no immaterial, spiritual, or ideal realm. Their position relies on strict materialism.

If an atheist professes that he believes there are immaterial things that exist, then he is not an atheist. He would be a dualist. That is an entirely different religious framework.[8]

Atheists argue against the existence of an immaterial realm. If they left open the idea that the immaterial exists, then God, who is not material, could exist and atheism would be wrong. If this were the case, the atheist would be forced to move to a different religious system like dualism or agnosticism, conceding that atheism would be impossible.

This is why aspects like materialism and naturalism (everything can be explained by natural processes) must be held to unwaveringly in an atheistic religion. As a result, this also makes atheism one of the easiest religions to refute.

Consider things that are immaterial or abstract: truth, logic, knowledge, concepts, dignity, respect, love, care, conclusions, information, and so forth. The logically consistent position is that the atheist cannot believe these exist either. They are not material; they must not exist. To get around this issue they claim that love is an aspect of matter interacting, but they have no way

---

8. See chapter 10 in this volume on dualism.

to verify such a claim. They go on using the immaterial laws of logic while adhering to a materialistic worldview.

For example, what is the mass of logic or by what means would we measure it? It is an illogical question to ask what the mass is of something that has no mass because it is an abstract, immaterial concept. Yet logic, which is invariant and universal, exists, as the universe even obeys the laws of logic. For example, you cannot have the moon and not the moon at the same time in the same relationship (law of non-contradiction).

Many atheists appeal to reason and logic, but their worldview cannot account for either. So they must step out from under their atheism and borrow the Christian worldview that does make sense of logic. God created all things and He upholds things in a logical fashion. Logic is a tool we use to think God's thoughts after Him.

Consider truth, information, love, etc. These things cannot exist in a purely materialistic worldview. Even argumentations, reasons, conclusions, and so forth cannot exist in an atheistic worldview. The atheist cannot, based on his own professed worldview, make an argument for atheism without first giving up his atheism.

Uniformity of Nature

Doing scientific inquiry is predicated on the Bible being true. God upholds the world in a consistent fashion and has promised to do so (Genesis 8:22). So the Christian can do observable and repeatable science, knowing that the result will be the same day to day.

God, who knows all things past, present, and future, has promised the future will be like the past — not in the conditions of course, but in the way God upholds things. To clarify, the wind may not blow at the same speed each day, but the laws that govern the wind will be the same each day, allowing predictions about the future.

In an atheistic worldview, laws of nature changed in the past (i.e., the big bang defies the laws of physics; there were no laws, now there are laws). In the future they may change again. Since no one really knows the future in the atheistic framework, the laws of nature could change as early as tomorrow. Why do science if the laws of science might change tomorrow?

The atheist might argue that we know the future will be like the past, because in the past the future was like the past. But this is circular reasoning. It begs the very question we are asking.

Unless God reveals to us that the future will be like the past, science is impossible. It makes sense that leading scientists held a Christian worldview (Francis Bacon, Isaac Newton, Galileo Galilei, Johannes Kepler, Gregor Mendel, Michael Faraday, Robert Boyle, Raymond Damadian, etc.). Secular scientists are still resting on the shoulders of great Christians and their scientific works.

A Path to Absurdity

Let's assume for a moment the atheistic position could make sense of logic. To say there is no God would logically require someone to look everywhere in the entire universe at the exact same time *and* for all time, past and future, and find no God.

Furthermore, the atheist would have to be powerful enough to look in the immaterial, spiritual realm for all time too. They would also have to be powerful enough to supersede God to make sure God was not cloaking Himself from their search. In other words, for an atheist to say "there is no God" would require the atheist to be omnipresent and omnipotent. The atheist would essentially have to be all-knowing to say God doesn't exist (omniscience).

Thus, for an atheist to claim there is no God would require them to be God! Thus, it is an absurd and self-refuting worldview.

Regarding the Atheist

Do atheists get tired of all the evil associated with the philosophy of atheism — Stalin, Hitler, Pol Pot, and so on?[9] After all, most murderers, tyrants, and rapists are not biblical Christians, and most have rejected the God of the Bible. Even if they claim to believe in the God of the Bible, they are not really living like a true Christ follower (who strives to follow God's Word), are they?

Does an atheist feel conflicted about the fact that atheism has no basis in morality (i.e., no absolute right and wrong; no good, no bad)? If someone stabs an atheist in the back, treats them like nothing, steals from them, or lies to them, it doesn't ultimately matter in an atheistic worldview where everything and everyone are just chemical reactions doing what chemicals do. And further, knowing that a person is essentially no different from a

9. Bodie Hodge, "The Results of Evolution," Answers in Genesis, July 13, 2009, http://www.answersingenesis.org/articles/2009/07/13/results-evolution-bloodiest-religion-ever.

cockroach in an atheistic worldview (since people are just animals) must be disheartening.

Do atheists struggle with the fact that atheism has no basis for logic and reasoning?[10] Wouldn't it be tough to get up every day thinking that truth, which is immaterial, really doesn't exist? Would the atheist be bothered by the fact that atheism cannot account for uniformity in nature[11] (the basis by which we can do real science)? Why would everything expand from nothing and, by pure chance, form beautiful laws like $E=MC^2$ or $F=MA$?[12]

Perhaps the atheist would like a weekend to recoup and think about these things. Interestingly, the concept of a weekend is really meaningless in an atheistic worldview since animals, like bees, don't take a day of rest or have weekends. Why do atheists borrow a workweek and weekend that comes from the pages of Scriptures, which are despised by atheists? A consistent atheist should just work every day until they die.

Weeks and weekends come from God creating in six literal days and resting for a literal day; then the Lord Jesus resurrected on the first day of the week (Sunday). And why look forward to time off for a holiday (i.e., holy day), when nothing is holy in an atheistic worldview?

Does the atheist feel conflicted about proselytizing the faith of atheism, considering that if atheism were true then who cares about proselytizing? Let's face it, life seems tough enough as an atheist without having to deal with other minor concerns like not having a basis to wear clothes, or no basis for marriage, no consistent reason to be clean (snails don't wake up in the morning and clean themselves or follow other cleanliness guidelines based on Levitical laws), and no objective reason to believe in love.

In fact, why would an atheist care to live one moment longer in a broken universe where one is merely rearranged pond scum and all you have to look forward to is . . . death, which can be around any corner? And in 467 trillion years, no one will care one iota about what an atheist did or who they were or how and when they died — because death is the ultimate "hero" in an atheistic, evolutionary worldview.

10. Jason Lisle, "Atheism: An Irrational Worldview," Answers in Genesis, October 10, 2007, http://www.answersingenesis.org/articles/aid/v2/n1/atheism-irrational.
11. Jason Lisle, "Evolution: The Anti-science," Answers in Genesis, February 13, 2008, http://www.answersingenesis.org/articles/aid/v3/n1/evolution-anti-science.
12. Jason Lisle, "Don't Creationists Deny the Laws of Nature?" in Ken Ham, Gen. Ed., *The New Answers Book 1* (Green Forest AR: Master Books, 2006), p. 39–46, http://www.answersingenesis.org/articles/nab/creationists-deny-laws-of-nature.

The religion of atheism is a lie (Romans 1:25). As Christians, we understand that truth exists because God who is the Truth exists (John 14:6), and we are made in His image.[13] Unlike an atheist, whose worldview doesn't allow him to believe in truth or lies, the Bible-believer has a foundation that enables him to speak about truth and lies. This is because believers in God and His Word have an authority, the ultimate authority on the subject, to base their beliefs upon.

Atheists have no consistent reason to proselytize their faith, but Christians do have a reason — Jesus Christ, who is the Truth, commands us to (Matthew 28:19). We want to see people repent of their evil deeds and be saved from death to worship the God who created them (Acts 8:22, 17:30).

Where atheists have no basis for logic and reason (or even for truth, since truth is immaterial), Bible believers can understand that mankind is made in the image of a logical and reasoning God who is the truth. Hence, Christians can make sense of things because in Christ are "hidden all the treasures of wisdom and knowledge"(Colossians 2:3). Christians also have a basis to explain why people sometimes don't think logically due to the Fall of mankind in Genesis 3. The most logical response is to give up atheism and receive Jesus Christ as Lord and Savior to rescue you from sin and death (Romans 10:13). Instead of death, God promises believers eternal life (1 John 2:25; John 10:28) and in 467 trillion years, you will still have value in contrast to the secular view of nothingness.

Christians do have a basis to wear clothes (to cover shame due to sin; see Genesis 2:25, 3:7), a reason to uphold marriage (God made a man and a woman; see Genesis 1:27; Matthew 19:4–6), a reason to be clean (Leviticus contains many provisions to counter diseases in a sin-cursed world), and a source of real love (since God made us in His loving image; see 1 John 4:8). As Christians, we have a solid foundation for saying that things like back-stabbing, theft, and lies are wrong (see the Ten Commandments in Exodus 20).

The day is coming when we all will give an account before God for our actions and thoughts (Romans 14:12). For those who are atheistic and reading this, I invite you personally to become an ex-atheist, join the ranks of the saved through Jesus Christ, and become a new creation (2 Corinthians 5:17) as we continue to advance with the gospel in peace that only God can provide (Romans 5:1)

---

13. Keep in mind that Christians do fall short due to sin and the Curse, but God never fails.

Chapter 3

Agnosticism

Steve Ham, M.Div.

There is an old joke that has been going around for many years. Did you hear about the agnostic, dyslexic insomniac? He stayed awake all night wondering if there really is a *dog*. As silly (and funny) as that joke is, it actually captures the skeptical nature of an agnostic.

In this chapter, we will define agnosticism and look at its history. We will also answer the main concern for every agnostic. Agnostics are concerned with the concept of *knowing*. While agnostics swim in the sea of skepticism, Christians can confidently stand knowing that the God of the Bible exists and has powerfully revealed Himself. We don't just know *about* Him, but we also know Him.

Understanding the Dilemma

The Apostle Paul stood right in the midst of the Greek philosophers as they deliberated over the religious and civil life of Athens. One can only imagine Paul's spectacular view from the Areopagus (Mars Hill) as he looked over the city with its paths and buildings and statues to the various Greek gods. For Paul, the statues of these gods had not gone unnoticed. The inscription on one in particular had caught Paul's eye and gave him the theme for his famous Acts 17 sermon. Who is the *Agnosto Theo* — the "Unknown God"?

Most Greeks believed in many gods and, just in case they missed one, they built a statue to cover themselves. The Greeks wondered if these gods were all that there are. Are there more? Is there a god of the gods? Who is he, she, it? The questions are countless and lead people to the one huge question — *Is it possible to know if there really is a god at all?*

Derived from the same term as the inscription on the statue at Athens, agnosticism is basically about "not knowing." *Gnosis* means "knowledge" in Greek and *a-gnosis* would be "without knowledge." The fact that agnosticism has now been termed as an "-ism" means that for some people it has turned into a whole belief system.

There are varying degrees of agnosticism. When somebody uses this identifier, Christians should dig a little deeper to find out with what sort of agnostic they are conversing. There are agnostics who say that they *don't know* whether there is a god, and there are agnostics who say that *nobody can know* if there is a god. There are also different versions of these two positions.

Popular author and New Testament critic Bart Ehrman calls himself an Agnostic Atheist.[1] By this, he means that he believes that one cannot know if there is a god and therefore cannot believe that there is a god. The "not knowing" part makes him an agnostic, and the "not believing" part he claims makes him an atheist.[2]

On the other end of the agnostic scale are those who are much more pragmatic than Bart Ehrman. They are willing to say that they do not know whether a god exists, and may not even care since they believe that there is no real consequence either way. So the range of agnosticism is somewhere from "We cannot know and we cannot believe" to "I don't know and I don't care."

The Christian must, however, see the common denominator in all agnostic positions. Whether they lean in an atheistic or pragmatic position, the agnostic is always resting on his or her own autonomous judgment. This is an arbitrary position.

The agnostic has made a judgment, not just about "a god," but also about the God of the Bible who has specially revealed Himself to us in the

---

1. Bart D. Ehrman, "Am I an Atheist or an Agnostic," *The Bart Erhman Blog*, June 2, 2012, https://ehrmanblog.org/am-i-an-agnostic-or-an-atheist/.

2. Ehrman's argument is a leap in logic in which the conclusion does not follow. If one cannot know if God exists, then the conclusion that he doesn't is arbitrary and illogical. One can rightly profess the opposite by the same logic. Imagine if someone says one cannot know if God exists, therefore God exists. Besides, atheism is not about *believing* whether God might exist or not, but about the absolute denial of His existence, and atheists profess to "know" this. Ehrman's position is foolish (Psalm 14:1).

person of Jesus Christ and in His Word. Furthermore, as the Creator of all, He has positioned all mankind without excuse, having clearly revealed His power in creation (Psalm 19:1–4; Ecclesiastes 3:1; Romans 1:18–32).

In stark contrast to the agnostic position, the Christian can and does know God through the powerful gospel. Paul encouraged the Thessalonian church with this message when he told them, "knowing, beloved brethren, your election by God. For our gospel did not come to you in word only, but also in power, and in the Holy Spirit and in much assurance" (1 Thessalonians 1:4–5). The Thessalonians truly knew God in the one true saving sense, and this came through the proclamation of the gospel and the power of the Holy Spirit. First John 5:11–13 also reveals that Christians can *know* they are saved by God.

A Foundation for Agnosticism

In reality, a discussion of the history of agnosticism would require a survey of skepticism concerning the existence of deity well beyond the limits of this chapter. One can, however, trace a distinct line from some of the philosophies of the Enlightenment to the man who first used the term "agnostic" in a self-descriptive way. The period known as "the Enlightenment" ranges from the mid-17th century through to the 19th century. It is peppered with some of the names of the world's great philosophers such as Descartes, Spinoza, Locke, Hume, and Kant.

If there is one common word to describe this period, it is "rationalism." These philosophers placed confidence in the ability of unaided human reason to discover the truth in all areas of reality.

This is a significant factor for the Christian understanding of the basis of the agnostic worldview. The men of the Enlightenment, some of them theists, paved the way for a large-scale rejection of God's revelation as the authoritative basis for reason. It is important to have a short glimpse of how this happened and the wide-ranging effects of the impact.

Descartes (1596–1650) is best known for his statement, *"Cogito Ergo Sum," I think therefore, I am.* This statement is an example of what is known as deductive rationalism. Also evident in the works of the Greek philosopher Plato, deductive rationalism has its source of knowledge in human intuition, or innate ideas. In other words, man is seen as the absolute authority on the subject of reason, and God has been demoted or removed and subjected to man's judgment.

Descartes commenced with a journey of skepticism, doubting his very existence. He came to the conclusion that he could not doubt his existence unless there was a doubter, thus, "I think, therefore I am."[3] This statement triggered a generation of voices that says man is the authority over God. Unlike Descartes, God professes, I Am Who I Am (Exodus 3:14; John 8:58). God is the "I Am," and the existence of man and reason itself is predicated on God, not man. With Descartes, *God* was traded for *man* and this led many down a path of "man is the measure of all things" instead of God being the ultimate standard. Far too many were deceived in this movement, and we still feel the effects of it in today's culture.

In 1690, John Locke published his *Essay on Human Understanding* in which he denied the concept of innate ideas and posited that all ideas come from sense experience or reflection. His disagreement with Descartes' skeptical application of innate ideas was not subtle.

> If any one pretends to be so skeptical as to deny his own existence, (for really to doubt of it is manifestly impossible,) let him for me enjoy his beloved happiness of being nothing, until hunger of some other pain convince him of the contrary. This, then, I think I may take for a truth, which every one's certain knowledge assures him of, beyond the liberty of doubting, viz. that he is something that actually exists.[4]

Contrary to deductive rationalism, Locke opened the enlightenment period to *inductive* rationalism, also described as *Empiricism*.[5] More in line with the Greek philosopher Aristotle, empiricism only claims knowledge that comes through the senses — something must be observed through sense perception or testing to be known to be true. For Locke, if anyone were to claim intuitive knowledge, they were claiming something that was simply "self-evident," (an orange is not an apple).

Locke discussed different types of knowledge that could all be explained in terms of sense experience and reflection. He believed that demonstrative

3. Rene Descartes, *Discourse on the Method of Rightly Conducting the Reason and Seeking for Truth in the Sciences*, in Vol. 31 of *Great Books of the Western World*, edited by Robert Maynard Hutchins, et al. (Chicago, IL: Encyclopedia Britannica, Inc., 1952), p. 51.
4. John Locke, *Concerning Human Understanding*, in Vol. 35 of *Great Books of the Western World*, edited by Robert Maynard Hutchins et al. (Chicago, IL: Encyclopedia Britannica, 1952), p. 349.
5. See chapter 14 in this book for a full description of Empiricism.

knowledge derives from reason, sensitive knowledge from the senses, and, when considered together, one can make judgments based on probabilities.[6] In reasoning methodology, most modern agnostics would be examples of the school of inductive rationalism.

Neither Locke nor Descartes were agnostics. Both men believed in God, and Descartes was Roman Catholic. While Descartes reasoned that God must have placed innate ideas in the mind of man (the famous mind-body separation model),[7] Locke reasoned that beings cannot produce themselves and, therefore, something must have existed from eternity. Locke reasoned that God was the eternal, all-powerful, all-knowing being.[8]

Neither did Locke completely reject the idea of revelation. Revelation was acceptable only under the magisterial authority of reason (i.e., man determines which parts of revelation to accept).[9] In his discussion of revelation and reason, he states:

> In any truth that gets not possession of our minds by the irresistible light of self-evidence, or by the force of demonstration, the arguments that gain it assent are the vouchers and gage of its probability to us; and we can receive it for not other than such as they deliver it to our understandings. Whatsoever credit or authority we give to any proposition more than it receives from the principles and proofs it supports itself upon, is owing to our inclinations that way, and is so far a derogation from the love of truth as such: which, as it can receive no evidence from our passions or interests, so it should receive no tincture [tinge or infusion] from them.[10]

Five years after his *Essay on Human Understanding*, Locke published *The Reasonableness of Christianity*. While not accepting all the tenets of the Christian faith, Locke did note that Christianity was the most reasonable of all religions (by *his* fallible standard, no less). Church historian Justo L. Gonzalez summarizes his analysis of this work, stating that, "In the final

---

6. Locke, *Concerning Human Understanding*.
7. Justin Skirry, "René Descartes: The Mind-Body Distinction," Internet Encyclopedia of Philosophy, accessed 10/5/2016, http://www.iep.utm.edu/descmind/.
8. Locke, *Concerning Human Understanding*, p. 349–354.
9. Note Locke's fallacy here. He believed God was all-knowing, eternal, and all-powerful except when it comes to man's fallible and imperfect reason which must be elevated above God to make such a claim. This is self-contradictory.
10. Ibid., 384, definition added.

analysis, Christianity was little more than a very clear expression of truths and laws that others could have known by their natural faculties."[11]

Locke could be described as having a rational theism wherein the only revelation that was acceptable is that which could be naturally reasoned by the mind of man. This thinking had a wide and lasting effect. Locke's system of rationalism founded the philosophical basis for democracy, motivated some of the thinking behind the French Revolution, and even influenced the framing of key documents such as the United States Declaration of Independence.[12]

After Locke's work on rationalistic theism, deism became a popular alternative to Christian orthodoxy. Deism is a belief system that rejects any idea of particular revelation. In this way, deists took the demotion of revelation a step further than had Locke.

Deists believe that religion is universal and available through the natural instincts of all human beings. Basing his work on the foundation provided by John Locke, John Tolland, a British deist (1670–1722), wrote *Christianity Not Mysterious, A Treatise Showing That There Is Nothing in the Gospel Contrary to Reason nor Above It, and That No Christian Doctrine Can Be Properly Called a Mystery.*[13] This work (and others like it) was written in order to show that any real quality claimed in orthodoxy could be derived through natural reason apart from direct revelation.

It was also on the basis of Locke's work that philosopher David Hume brought a new type of skepticism, moving from Locke's ideas concerning rationality and revelation. David Hume's new empiricism was a great diving board from which to jump into agnosticism. Hume (1711–1776) held that logic was a mere habit of the mind and not demonstrable truth.

Like Locke, Hume did agree that all knowledge comes from the senses. He further argued, however, that no one has ever seen or experienced the principle of *cause and effect.* Cause and effect is not a result of experience but a result of our mental habits linking the phenomena we have experienced through our senses. Therefore, concepts such as cause and effect have no basis in Hume's empirical observation.

---

11. Justo L. Gonzalez, *The Story of Christianity, Vol. 2: The Reformation to the Present Day,* 2nd ed. (New York: HarperOne, 2010), p. 241.

12. Gregg L. Frazer, *The Religious Beliefs of America's Founders: Reason, Revelation, and Revolution* (Lawrence, KS: University Press of Kansas, 2014), p. 216–217.

13. John Toland, *Christianity Not Mysterious: Or, a Treatise Shewing, That There Is Nothing in the Gospel Contrary to Reason, nor Above It, and that No Christian Doctrine Can Be Properly Called a Mystery* (Gale ECCO, Print Editions, 2010).

Furthermore, supernatural phenomena such as miracles must also be denied unless individually experienced. Specifically, one cannot believe in a resurrection unless they themselves have risen from the dead. Declaring his inability to experience any part of it, Hume also rejected any consideration of a universal cause.

> It is confessed, that the utmost effort of human reason is to reduce the principles, productive of natural phenomena, to a greater simplicity, and to resolve the many particular effects into a few general causes, by means of reasonings from analogy, experience, and observation. But as to the causes of these general causes, we should in vain attempt their discovery; nor shall we ever be able to satisfy ourselves, by any particular explication of them. These ultimate springs and principles are totally shut up from human curiosity and enquiry.[14]

One would be hard pressed to find any more complete definition of agnosticism than this statement from Hume. Reading words such as this, we can understand why many have attempted to class Hume as an agnostic or even an atheist. And so it is, with the stage set and the curtain drawn, that we introduce the man as the first to name himself an agnostic, Thomas Huxley.

The Agnostic and the Anglican

It is reported that the term *agnostic* was first heard in public in 1869 at a party when spoken by the famous anatomist, Thomas Huxley (1825–1895). Huxley, today often referred to as Darwin's Bulldog, was negative toward organized religion. His term, *agnosticism*, gained immediate traction and was soon being debated, not only by Christian rivals, but also among those who shared Huxley's empiricism.

A strong opponent of agnosticism was a senior Anglican priest from St. Paul's Cathedral in London by the name of Henry Wace (1836–1924). Wace and Huxley, with others, commenced a series of papers and arguments against each other's positions.

The precise definition of agnosticism has remained debatable through to present times. Even so, the sole reliance upon human reason and/or empiricism for knowing truth, especially concerning deity, has remained a

---

14. David Hume, *Concerning Human Understanding*, p. 460.

common element. In 1888, Wace quoted the Oxford dictionary as already having a basic definition for the term.

> An agnostic is one who holds that the existence of anything beyond and behind natural phenomena is unknown, and (so far as can be judged) unknowable, and especially that a First Cause and an unseen world are subjects of which we know nothing.[15]

Apparently, Huxley, who did not want to be known as an atheist, coined the term referencing Paul's discussion of the *Agnosto Theo*, the "Unknown God," in Acts 17. Paul, of course, was not in any way advocating agnosticism by using the inscription on the statue in Athens. On the contrary, Paul referred to the "unknown God" to proclaim to the Greeks that the Creator had become the Savior and specially revealed Himself in the Lord Jesus Christ. Paul was seeking the Greeks to believe on the basis of this magnificent revelation. Wace, in a similar manner as Paul to the Greeks, was taking the position of revelation against Huxley's unknowable deity.

> But if this be so, for a man to urge as an escape from this article of belief that he has no means of a scientific knowledge of the unseen world, or of the future, is irrelevant. His difference from Christians lies not in the fact that he has no knowledge of these things, but that he does not believe the authority on which they are stated. He may prefer to call himself an agnostic; but his real name is an older one — he is an infidel; that is to say, an unbeliever.[16]

In a later argument, Wace also states in similar vein that,

> Prof. Huxley's learning is justified in being ignorant that it is not upon such knowledge, but upon supernatural revelation, that Christian belief rests. However, as he goes on to say, my view of "the real state of the case is that the agnostic does not believe the authority on which these things are stated, which authority is Jesus Christ."[17]

15. Henry Wace, "On Agnosticism," in *Christianity and Agnosticism: A Controversy*, 1889 (repr. London, England: Forgotten Books, 2013), p. 5.
16. Ibid, p. 8–9.
17. Henry Wace, "Agnosticism: A Reply to Professor Huxley," in *Christianity and Agnosticism: A Controversy*, 1889 (repr. London, England: Forgotten Books, 2013), p. 59.

Huxley's arguments for his agnosticism were many, but none of them were surprising. He denied miracles, Jesus' knowledge of the unseen world, and the basic biblical history of creation, the Fall, and the Flood. Since he saw these as the historical basis for Paul's theology, he rejected Paul's teachings.[18] Influenced by the textual critics of the Bible of his time, Huxley also denied the authenticity of the New Testament text itself. He questioned the credibility of the Gospels, particularly noting as a supposed contradiction the differing accounts of the same event in the Gospels.

Wace's argument was simple and profound. He did not agree with the textual critics who denied the credibility of the inspired text and the authorship of the Gospels; but he also noted that those same critics did believe that the Sermon on the Mount was the authentic sermon of Christ. In this sermon, however, Christ displays His authority, speaks of coming judgment and the Kingdom of heaven, and speaks often of God. The Lord's Prayer alone confirms all of these things. To say that no human has the ability to know that God exists, or to know anything about the unseen world, is to make a statement about the revelation of Jesus Christ. Wace writes:

> The position of an agnostic involves the conclusion that Jesus Christ was under an "illusion" in respect to the deepest beliefs of his life and teaching. The words of my paper are, "An agnosticism which knows nothing of the relation of man to God must not only refuse belief to our Lord's most undoubted teaching, but must deny the reality of the spiritual convictions in which he lived and died." The point is this that there can, at least, be no reasonable doubt that Jesus Christ lived, and taught, and died, in the belief of certain great principles respecting the existence of God, our relation to God, and his own relation to us, which an agnostic says are beyond the possibilities of human knowledge; and of course an agnostic regards Jesus Christ as a man. If so, he must necessarily regard Jesus Christ as mistaken, since the notion of his being untruthful is a supposition which I could not conceive being suggested. The question I have put is not, as Prof. Huxley represents, what is the most unpleasant alternative to belief in the primary truths of the Christian religion, but what

---

18. Thomas H. Huxley, "Agnosticism," in *Christianity and Agnosticism: A Controversy*, 1889 (repr. London, England: Forgotten Books, 2013), p. 22.

is the least unpleasant; and all I have maintained is that the least unpleasant alternative necessarily involved is, that Jesus Christ was under an illusion in his most vital convictions.[19]

Today we have heard this same argument put in a similar way by such people as C.S. Lewis and Josh McDowell. To deny the Lordship of Jesus Christ one must call Him either a lunatic or a liar. For Wace, as it should be for all Christians, we stand before agnostics concerned not so much for the limitations of their empiricist position, but for their denial of the authority of the revelation of Jesus Christ as Lord and Savior. They have made a choice about magisterial authority when it comes to human reason. They have chosen to submit to the fallibility of human autonomy rather than to the infallibility of the Word of God to inform reason.

It is no coincidence that the same man who coined the phrase "agnostic" and rejected biblical revelation also became the greatest cheerleader for Charles Darwin. Darwin, as a naturalist, also ignored revelation. He observed variation within animal kinds resultant from natural selection. This actual observation is something that perfectly corroborates the Genesis account of the reproduction of animals after their own kinds. Darwin's speculation about an evolutionary progression of kinds was in essence a rejection of God's Word. Huxley believed in this unobservable, untestable, non-repeatable idea of evolution, and became Darwin's bulldog.

Let's pause for a moment and reflect on the overall historical position of agnosticism. The position has been to reject God (no God allowed) but slyly take God's gift of reasoning and then falsely accredit it to autonomous man (who then messes it up due to sin). From there, agnostics (and their brothers) have used fallible man's reason as the absolute standard to reject God's revelation piece by piece.

Agnostics continued to judge God's revelation and demote it one piece at a time based on man's fallible and arbitrary opinions. And now they come to the idea of Jesus Christ and conclude, "He is false." Thus, no God is allowed.

What few realize is that the agnostic assumed the very thing for which he argues in the first place. He started with the premise, "no God allowed" and arrived at the conclusion "no God allowed." This is the fallacy of begging the question.

---

19. Henry Wace, "Agnosticism: A Reply to Professor Huxley," p. 60.

Modern Agnosticism

It would seem that Huxley's ideas of agnosticism are present, largely unchanged, in today's culture. Unbelief remains as unbelief. While there are some like Bart Ehrman who are prepared to call themselves agnostic atheists, others such as Ron Rosenbaum are careful to differentiate the terms in light of the "New Atheism" movement.

The new atheists, led in the vitriol of Richard Dawkins, the late Christopher Hitchens, and Sam Harris, are no longer content to simply not believe in God. They are zealous recruiters engaged in an anti-theistic battle as preachers of nothingness. The confidence of the new atheists has caused agnostics such as Ron Rosenbaum to call others to embrace an agnostic identity in a brotherhood of solidarity who have the "humility" to say they "just don't know." In an article for *Slate*, Rosenbaum wrote:

> Why has agnosticism fallen out of favor? New Atheism offers the glamour of fraudulent rebelliousness, while agnosticism has only the less eye-catching attractions of humility. The willingness to say "I don't know" is less attention-getting than "I know, I know. I know it all."[20]

"I Just Don't Know" is the T-shirt slogan Rosenbaum suggests. Perhaps a better slogan might be, "We're here, but it's just not clear!"

As much as some agnostics may wish to distance themselves from atheist terminology, there is a common ground when it comes to the practicality of living.[21] Both staunchly confident atheists and staunchly unconfident agnostics (oxymoronic statement intended) live without any accountability to the God that they don't, won't, or can't believe in. At the end of the day, they are both living under the autonomy of self-rule.

Australian agnostic blogger John Wilkins describes yet another group of agnostics that are not staunchly unconfident but only provisionally unconfident. For provisional agnostics, "a question is not *yet* — capable

---

20. Ron Rosenbaum, "An Agnostic Manifesto," *Slate*, June 28, 2010, http://www.slate.com/articles/life/the_spectator/2010/06/an_agnostic_manifesto.html.
21. Bill Nye, for example, claims to be an agnostic, but in the debate with Ken Ham he argued for the atheistic position repeatedly; see Ken Ham and Bodie Hodge, *Inside the Nye Ham Debate* (Green Forest AR: Master Books, AR, 2014).

of being answered, not that the evidence is equivocal or evenly balanced."[22] This still means that they are under self-rule until something better turns up. Either way, there is a practicality that brings all atheists and agnostics together.

Ron Rosenbaum uses the term "humility" to describe the agnostic position. One must also ask what sort of humility rejects any consideration of a special revelation of the world's history from the one revealing Himself as the Eternal Creator. Wouldn't humility require a serious consideration of looking at the world through these glasses before placing one's trust in human autonomy to seek knowledge? It is unlikely that any self-described agnostic can be found expending their energy in an attempt to find God rather than defending his or her own skeptical position. In Romans 3 (quoting Psalm 14)[23] there is a verse that points directly to the human condition in general, but also aptly describes the specific agnostic attitude: "None is righteous, no not one; no one understands; no one seeks for God" (Romans 3:10–11; ESV).

The Agnostic Problem

There are three basic problems that should be apparent from our introduction to agnosticism. There is a logic problem, a definition problem, and, most importantly, a spiritual problem.

A Matter of Logic

In a logical argument there are a series of premises (at least two) that lead to a conclusion. The validity and/or soundness of a conclusion will depend on the validity of both the premises and conclusion. As an example, a valid and sound logical argument might flow as follows:

A. All mammals have kidneys

B. All dogs are mammals

C. Therefore, all dogs have kidneys

---

22. John Wilkins, "On the Suspension of Belief and Disbelief," *Evolving Thoughts*, accessed February 23, 2015, http://evolvingthoughts.net/2011/11/on-the-suspension-of-belief-and-disbelief/.

23. Psalm 14:1–3: The fool has said in his heart, "There is no God." They are corrupt, they have done abominable works, there is none who does good. The LORD looks down from heaven upon the children of men, to see if there are any who understand, who seek God. They have all turned aside; they have together become corrupt; there is none who does good, no, not one.

This argument is valid because it does not violate the laws of logic and the conclusion necessarily follows from the premises. It is sound because its premises are verifiably true.

The basic argument used by agnostics to support their position is often presented in the following way:

A. If we want to know that God exists, then we must be able to test His existence empirically
B. We cannot empirically test God's existence
C. Therefore, we cannot know if God exists

If you follow the reasoning of the premises leading to the conclusion, this argument is reasonable and logically valid. The conclusion follows necessarily from the premises. This is the valid logical form of *modus tollens*.[24]

The problem with this argument, however, is that it is not sound because there are other forms of testing that can be employed, so the premise is not verifiable. It makes a truth claim that is circular in nature — I believe things must be empirically testable to be true because all true things are empirically testable. This is the fallacy of begging the question — arguing in a vicious circle. Based on the faulty premise, the conclusion has become unsound. This objection holds true even if the argument is presented in a logically valid form.

The premise states that something must be empirically testable to know that it is true, but this assumes that empirically testing something is the only way to know truth. This premise in itself is not empirically testable, so how can anyone know that it is true? The basic empiricist argument, therefore, is unsound at its most foundational level — it is a self-refuting argument. Further, it is an arbitrary assertion that is not based on any ultimate authority. Why should empiricism be considered true? The agnostic can offer no ultimate reason.

A Matter of Definition

As one wades through the history of empiricism, a common word consistently mentioned is "science." The term "science" is most often recognized as the observable, testable, repeatable method of proving or falsifying hypotheses and forming theories. This is called *observational science*. It is this type of science where scientists who believe in God can work side by side with agnostic

---

24. Jason Lisle, *Discerning Truth* (Green Forest, AR: Master Books, 2010), p. 68.

or atheistic scientists doing the same experiments and coming up with the same conclusions. From this type of science we describe natural laws, cure diseases, and discover new technologies.

There is another form of science, however, that should be differentiated from observational science. *Historical science* is the discipline of assessing "evidence from past events based on a presupposed philosophical point of view."[25] Because the past is not observable or repeatable, we cannot test the past. We have evidence in the present that was left from past events that needs to be interpreted, and this is only possible within the worldview of the interpreter. In other words, our ideas about the past will determine the way we interpret the evidence in the present.

An agnostic and a Christian have very different assumptions about the past. The agnostic believes there must only be a natural explanation for past events (naturalism alone), whereas the Christian accepts God's revelation through biblical history that accounts for the major events in the history of the created world.[26]

Christians will often hear statements from both atheists and agnostics that they believe only in what can be determined through scientific study. This type of statement often suggests that Christians — and specifically biblical creationists — are religious while atheists and agnostics are scientific. This, too, is a logical fallacy called *equivocation*. Christians, atheists, and agnostics have the same observational science, but the definition of science used in conjunction with ideas such as evolution is a different type of science called historical science. The agnostic changes the definition of *science* to suit his argument. Once correct definitions are adopted, the Christian and the agnostic can discuss the interpretive worldview assumptions that each of them adopt before coming to the evidence.

A Matter of Spiritual Corruption

The most important problem that agnostics face is the same problem that every single human being faces from fertilization (formerly known as conception). There are many Scriptures that describe the corrupt nature of human beings as a result of our inherited sin nature from our original parents, Adam

25. Roger Patterson, "What Is Science?" Answers in Genesis, accessed February 23, 2015, https://answersingenesis.org/what-is-science/what-is-science.
26. The Christian is not limited to natural explanations alone, as the agnostic has imposed upon himself. Instead, the Christian holds to both supernatural and natural events in the past.

and Eve. Ever since humanity rebelled against our Creator in the Garden of Eden, we have been spiritually separated from God and from the knowledge of His divine glory. Through the biblical authors, God has described this position to us as "blindness" and "death."

> And you He made alive, who were dead in trespasses and sins, in which you once walked according to the course of this world, according to the prince of the power of the air, the spirit who now works in the sons of disobedience, among whom also we all once conducted ourselves in the lusts of our flesh, fulfilling the desires of the flesh and of the mind, and were by nature children of wrath, just as the others (Ephesians 2:1–3).

> But the natural man does not receive the things of the Spirit of God, for they are foolishness to him; nor can he know them, because they are spiritually discerned. (1 Corinthians 2:14).

> But even if our gospel is veiled, it is veiled to those who are perishing, whose minds the god of this age has blinded, who do not believe, lest the light of the gospel of the glory of Christ, who is the image of God, should shine on them (2 Corinthians 4:3–4).

> But He answered and said, "Every plant which My heavenly Father has not planted will be uprooted. Let them alone. They are blind leaders of the blind. And if the blind leads the blind, both will fall into a ditch" (Matthew 15:13–14).

The agnostic problem is not their problem alone. It is the same problem that every human being faces. Romans 3:23 places all humanity in the same position: "For all have sinned and fall short of the glory of God." All of humanity is conceived with the same sin problem and deserving of the same just, eternal condemnation. The good news is that this common problem that all humanity shares with agnostics has the same solution.

Can We Know God?

Modern agnostics, founded on the thinking of Locke, Hume, and Huxley, are primarily concerned with what they can know through sense experience. Christians, while not dismissing any degree of sense experience, understand that coming to the knowledge of God is not an autonomous exercise. "But as it is written: 'Eye has not seen, nor ear heard, nor have entered into the heart of man the things which God has prepared for those who love Him.' But God has revealed them to us through His Spirit. For the Spirit searches all things, yes, the deep things of God" (1 Corinthians 2:9–10).

Paul was referring to something that Christians know as illumination. Illumination happens through the work of the Holy Spirit drawing us through the power of his revealed Word, and specifically, the gospel of Jesus Christ. In short, we know God through the Spirit and the Word, and the two are never separated. Discussing this same passage, professor of apologetics John Frame, states, "The Spirit testifies to *words* that He has given to the apostles. The same is the case in 1 Thessalonians 1:5 and 2:13. Indeed I know of no passage in which the Spirit's witness has any object other than the Word."[27]

A wonderful explanation of this is seen in Ephesians 1. Paul talks of how the Ephesians have heard "the word of truth," the gospel of their salvation, and that they believed in Jesus Christ and were sealed with the promised Holy Spirit (verses 13–14). He has great joy that he has heard of their faith in Jesus Christ and their love for each other (verses 15–16) and further prays for this continued revelation and wisdom in them, "that the God of our Lord Jesus Christ, the Father of glory, may give to you the spirit of wisdom and revelation in the knowledge of Him, the *eyes of your understanding being enlightened; that you may know* what is the hope of His calling, what are the riches of the glory of His inheritance in the saints, and what is the exceeding greatness of His power toward us who believe . . ." (verses 17–19, emphasis added).

There is both an objective and subjective element working in coming to a true knowledge of God. The objective element is the objective propositional truth conveyed in God's revealed Word. Jude describes this as the faith "once for all delivered to the saints" (Jude 3).

God's Word is authoritative, infallible, and, therefore, trustworthy in totality. But how is the sin-corrupted human to open his or her eyes to this truth? Scripture makes it clear that their own thinking is futile and darkened and their hearts are blind due to the effects of original sin (Ephesians

---

27. John M. Frame, "a Presuppositionalist's Response," in *Five Views on Apologetics*, edited by Steven B. Cowan (Grand Rapids, MI: Zondervan Publishing Company, 2000), p. 74–75.

4:17–19). Further, the god of this world, Satan, has blinded their eyes to the truth of the gospel and they do not see the "glory of God in the face of Jesus Christ" (2 Corinthians 4:3–6). This requires the subjective enablement of the Holy Spirit (1 Corinthians 12:3).

Only in the union of these two factors — proclamation of the Word of God and the working of the Holy Spirit — is this illumination possible. This is why the Christian can have such confidence in the proclamation of the gospel. Christians are those who have heard the gospel proclamation and, in the power of the Spirit, come to repentance and faith in Jesus Christ, illuminated to the truth. The Apostle John writes, "But you have an anointing from the Holy One, and you know all things. I have not written to you because you do not know the truth, but because you know it, and that no lie is of the truth" (1 John 2:20–21).

When Saul was converted on the road to Damascus, it was through the revelation of Jesus Christ and the power of the Spirit (Acts 9:17–18). Perhaps this is why Paul later describes the gospel as the power of God unto Salvation (Romans 1:16).

Christians never need to fear discussions with agnostics, atheists, or anyone. Yes, we should attempt to answer the skeptical questions, and correct the logical fallacies. We should understand the definitions of observational and historical science, and do all we can to sanctify our hearts in the Word of God in preparation to give an answer for the hope we have within us (1 Peter 3:14–17).

Above all, however, we should use all these things to guide conversations toward the most powerful message that God uses to illumine the minds of His sheep and bring them into the knowledge of His truth, the gospel of Jesus Christ. Only by means of this message can the scales on the eyes of unknowing skeptics fall away, allowing the eyes of their hearts to be enlightened and causing them to find life in the Creator and Savior.

So, as prime importance, let us prioritize this one message to all we speak to. "For I delivered to you first of all that which I also received: that Christ died for our sins according to the Scriptures, and that He was buried, and that He rose again the third day according to the Scriptures" (1 Corinthians 15:3–4).

And let us seek all mankind everywhere, calling them to repent and believe the gospel.

In Conclusion

Agnostics are not just people who don't know. They are people who don't know what they don't know. They don't know the gospel of Jesus Christ, at least not in a saving way. Through this magnificent revelation of God, people can come to knowledge of God and they can come to actually know God.

We do not come to this knowledge through skeptical empiricism but through the Spirit and the Word. This truth should cause the Christian to rejoice in God's grace, and to gain a heart to reach out to agnostics everywhere with the message that is "the power of God unto Salvation."

Summary of Agnostic Beliefs

Doctrine	Teachings of Agnosticism
God	Deny the certainty of the existence of God, but in various forms. They would generally reject the idea of Divinity, the Trinity, and Jesus as the Son of God or Savior.
Authority/ Revelation	Mostly reliant on materialistic, empirical thinking with human reasoning coupled with sense perception being the ultimate standard of truth. Reject any form of supernatural revelation, including the Bible.
Man	Generally accept an evolutionary view of man. No concept of a sinful nature. Man is a mortal being and part of the animal kingdom, with no particularly special role in the universe.
Sin	Sin is not generally a part of agnostic thinking, though some would adopt certain cultural taboos. There is no view to judgment of sin since they reject knowledge of deity.
Salvation	There is no concept of salvation apart from some cultural ideas. Reject the need of Jesus as Savior.
Creation	Generally hold an evolutionary worldview, embracing cosmological, geological, and biological evolution. Reject the biblical creation and young-earth creation ideas.

Chapter 4

Secular Humanism

Todd Friel

Here are three recent headlines that will make your Christian head spin.

- 100,000 Atheists Are "Unbaptized"[1]
- California School Bans All Christian Books[2]
- InterVarsity "Derecognized" at California State University[3]

What is the cause of this contemporary outbreak of insanity? Two words: Secular Humanism.

Unfortunately, you will have more success naming the waves on the ocean than labeling secular humanists; atheists, agnostics, rationalists, empiricists, skeptics, and deists all fall under the banner of "Secular Humanism." What brings such a broad range of people together? God. Or more specifically, a lack of God's existence or involvement in the affairs of men.

Because secular humanism is arguably the fastest growing worldview in the Western world, Christians would do well to be acquainted with this very anti-Christ philosophy.

---

1. Jim Denison, "100,000 Atheists are 'Unbaptized,'" http://www.christianheadlines.com/columnists/denison-forum/100-000-atheists-are-unbaptized.html, accessed 5/20/2016.
2. Carey Lodge, "California School Bans All Christian Books," *Christianity Today*, http://www.christiantoday.com/article/california.school.bans.all.christian.books/41072.htm, accessed 5/20/2016.
3. Ed Stetzer, "InterVarsity 'Derecognized' at California State University's 23 Campuses: Some Analysis and Reflections," http://www.christianitytoday.com/edstetzer/2014/september/intervarsity-now-derecognized-in-california-state-universit.html, accessed 5/20/2016.

Identifying Secular Humanism

Humanism is a broad religious view that encompasses all religions that use human ideas rather than God and His Word as the foundation of truth. All religions outside of God's one and true religion are influenced by humanistic beliefs.

Secular Humanism is an umbrella that covers a vast number of subgroups, all claiming to be free of religious dogmas.[4] These groups could be likened to different denominations within Secular Humanism. While they share some similarities, their distinctions are worth noting:

Rationalism — a belief that all human opinions and actions should be based on reason and knowledge as opposed to religious belief or emotional response.

Empiricism — the philosophical theory that all ideas are derived from some form of experience, be it internal or external. This theory posits that this is the sole foundation of true knowledge. It developed in the 17th and 18th centuries, expounded in particular by John Locke, Francis Bacon, and especially David Hume.[5]

Agnosticism — the view that the truth-values of metaphysical claims, such as the existence of a god, are either unknown or, in fact, unknowable.

Atheism — the view that rejects or disbelieves the existence of God or gods.

Nihilism — the rejection of all religious and moral principles.[6]

The History of Secular Humanism

In the broadest sense, anyone who denies the existence of God is a secular humanist. Anyone who believes that there may be a god who created the universe, but is not involved in the daily oversight of the universe (deism), is also influenced by secular humanistic thought. That means secular humanism's principles are as old as the rebellion of Adam and Eve in the Garden of Eden.

Throughout history, men have denied the existence of a supreme being. The Old Testament informs us that atheism was alive and well when the

---

4. While Secular Humanists claim to be irreligious, all worldviews are religious in that they seek to explain being and meaning and to act in accord with those beliefs. Secular Humanism is acknowledged as a nonprofit group for receiving tax benefits in the United States.
5. Walter A. Elwell, *Evangelical Dictionary of Theology*, 2nd ed. (Grand Rapids, MI: Baker Academics, 1984), p. 375–376.
6. The religion of nihilism is self-refuting. If they were consistent in rejecting all religious principles, then they should reject nihilism as well.

Psalmist wrote, "The fool has said in his heart, 'There is no God' " (Psalm 14:1). In ancient Greece, Socrates was executed, in part because of a charge that he was an atheist who rejected the Greek pantheon of deities.

History is replete with individuals who have either outright denied the existence of any god or lived in a way that demonstrated that conviction. However, the rise of secular humanism as a prominent worldview began to simmer in the 17th century, in part due to the Protestant Reformation. It came to a full boil in the 1700s and would change the course of history in the West.

A Foundation for Skepticism

During the 1500s, Luther, Calvin, Zwingli, Knox, and many others risked their necks to wage theological war against the Roman Catholic Church based on their deviations from biblical doctrine. While the Protestant Reformation was an overwhelming success in reclaiming the doctrine of justification (grace alone, through faith alone, in Jesus Christ alone), Protestant challenges to the predominant Christian authority (the Roman Catholic Church) unwittingly gave everyone permission to challenge the authority of the Church and Scripture. While it was certainly not the intention of the great Reformers to launch a secular humanist revolution, that was certainly a result of their godly efforts.

Seventeenth Century

The Enlightenment Era Philosophers of the 17th century took advantage of the "question authority" zeitgeist and began to argue against the Roman Catholic Church and even the very existence of God. Prominent names include:

> **Baruch Spinoza** (1632–1677) — "My opinion concerning *God* differs widely from that which is ordinarily defended by modern Christians. For I hold that God is of all things the cause immanent, as the phrase is, not transient."[7]

> **John Locke** (1632–1704) — "The end of a religious society, as I have already said, is the public worship of God, and from that the acquisition of eternal life."[8]

---

7. Baruch Spinoza, Benedict de Spinoza, *The Chief Works of Benedict de Spinoza, vol. 2, On Improvement of the Understanding, Ethics, Select Letters, Letter 21 (73) to Henry Oldenburg,* 1662; http://oll.libertyfund.org/titles/1711/144137, accessed 1/26/2015.

8. John Locke, *A Letter Concerning Toleration* (Ontario: Broadview Press, 1950), p. 54.

Voltaire (1694–1778) — "Every sensible man, every honorable man, must hold the Christian sect in horror."

David Hume (1711–1776) — "Survey most nations and most ages. Examine the religious principles, which have, in fact, prevailed in the world. You will scarcely be persuaded, that they are any thing but sick men's dreams: Or perhaps will regard them more as the playsome whimsies of monkeys in human shape, than the serious, positive, dogmatical asseverations of a being, who dignifies himself with the name of rational."[9]

Immanuel Kant (1724–1804) — "The wish to talk to God is absurd. We cannot talk to one we cannot comprehend — and we cannot comprehend God; we can only believe in Him. The uses of prayer are thus only subjective."[10]

Some scholars, such as Rene Descartes and Marin Marsenne, actually endeavored to prove the existence of God. Unfortunately, the way they attempted to do this was on the basis of pure reason (man's opinions alone). They sought to show that the existence of God could be demonstrated without the use of inspired Scripture. This proved to be a huge blunder.

In some regard, these men were geniuses; Descartes reinvented geometry, for instance. Yet their proofs for the existence of God were lacking. Not only did others begin dismantling many of their arguments, the Christian philosophers battled to promote their own pet views at the expense of other views. This ended up causing a framework of doubt on two fronts.

1. If the Bible is the inspired word of God, then why would the Christian set it aside to attempt to prove the existence of God?
2. Why are the Christian's arguments so inconsistent that they themselves cannot even come to an agreement on virtually any point?

---

9. David Hume, *Four Dissertations: I. The Natural History of Religion, II. Of the Passions, III. Of Tragedy, IV. Of the Standard of Taste* (London: Printed for A. Millar, 1757), p. 115.
10. H.L. Mencken, *A New Dictionary of Quotations on Historical Principles from Ancient and Modern Sources* (New York: AA Knopf, 1946), p. 955.

Godless Enlightenment philosophers saw these disagreements as proof that Christianity was demonstrably false. They concluded that the use of man's pure reason was the only way that humanity could reach its full potential.

Eighteenth Century

The 18th century successfully watered the secular humanist seeds planted in the previous century. However, it was one event that ultimately launched secular humanism into prominence — the French Revolution of 1789 and the subsequent advance of the Age of Enlightenment.

In 1788, there was a severe food crisis in France. In desperation, the king called a meeting of the estates to come up with a plan to deal with the problem on May 4, 1789. This council was made up of three estates: the aristocracy, the clergy, and the bourgeoisie (middle class). During the assembly, little attention was paid to the middle class, so the bourgeoisie broke away from the estate and formed a document called the "Declaration of the Rights of Man and of the Citizen." This declaration was aimed at bringing equality to all men under the law.

Article four in the document reads, "No corporate body, no individual may exercise any authority that does not expressly emanate from it. Liberty consists in being able to do anything that does not harm others: thus, the exercise of the natural rights of every man has no bounds other than those that ensure to the other members of society the enjoyment of these same rights. These bounds may be determined only by Law."

Notice that human rights actually come from other *humans*. Contrast that to the American Declaration of Independence, which acknowledges that our rights come from God: "We hold these truths to be self-evident, that all men are created equal, that they are endowed by their Creator with certain unalienable Rights, that among these are Life, Liberty and the pursuit of Happiness."

The French Declaration was a humanist manifesto that proved to be wildly popular and led to a massive uprising and ultimately the overthrow of the government. It also led the culture to a deep mistrust of not only the oppressive Catholic Church, but of religion in general.

While the French Revolution seemed to be the dawning of the age of the dominance of a secular humanist worldview, it was a short-lived victory. First came a time known as the Reign of Terror (1793–1794). Tens of thousands of people suspected of anti-revolutionary sentiment were sent to the guillotine. In 1799, Napoleon conquered France, and Catholicism was swiftly reinstated. Still, this period developed many ideas that would be expanded on more by future secular humanists. While this was a brief period, it left its mark on history as perhaps the first, and most certainly the largest, culture that operated free from God in Western history.

Nineteenth Century

One of the men who would further develop the godless worldview was none other than Karl Marx of Russia (1843–1881). Marx believed that the world consisted only of matter. He wrote that religion was an opiate; it was a way for the oppressed to deal with their plight. If oppression would end, then people's need for the opiate of religion would end, putting an end to religion itself.[11] These ideas would be used as the basis of communism,[12] and some of the most brutal governments in history would sprout from these seeds.

Enter Charles Darwin

Out of all the secular humanists that have ever lived, perhaps the most influential is Charles Darwin. Darwin doesn't easily fit into a category when it comes to his religious beliefs. Historian Frank Burch Brown, states it this way:

> His beliefs concerning the possible existence of some sort of God never entirely ceased to ebb and flow, nor did his evaluation of the merits of such beliefs.
>
> At low tide, so to speak, he was essentially an undogmatic atheist; at high tide he was a tentative theist; the rest of the time he was basically agnostic — in sympathy with theism but unable or unwilling to commit himself on such imponderable questions."[13]

Overall, his thought regarding theological matters could best be described as what he himself called a "muddle." In a letter he wrote to a theistic evolutionist, Asa Gray, he wrote that he couldn't completely affirm the idea of the world being designed, but it did not appear to have come into being purely by chance.

---

11. The primary religion in mind was Christianity, not Marx's religious humanism.
12. See chapter 7 on Communism in this volume.
13. Frank B. Brown, *The Evolution of Darwin's Religious Views* (Macon, GA: Mercer University Press, 1986), p. 27.

One thing is clear — Darwin was not a Christian. In his book *The Descent of Man*, Darwin went so far as to say man created the idea of God.[14] He loathed the idea of eternal punishment, referring to it as a "damnable doctrine."[15] It is impossible to understand Darwin rightly without being aware of this backdrop since his worldview colored his explanation of the past.

While on his journey aboard the *Beagle*, Darwin meticulously examined the flora and fauna of South America and its accompanying islands, as well as the geological features. Famously, he noted that the length and shape of finch beaks on the various Galapagos Islands differed. He assumed these variations happened according to the needs of the bird in obtaining food. Darwin posited that all the finches had a common ancestor from which they descended. Based on this and other observations, he concluded that small change was occurring within populations. Simply stated, the parents with the most advantageous characteristics would survive and pass those traits on to their progeny, who would then thrive and produce more of these organisms with the advantageous trait.

While this hypothesis is detectable and valid (even Christians like Ed Blyth described this process before Darwin), Darwin extrapolated it far beyond what is observable. He stated that these small changes could accumulate over millions of years to account for all life. He stated that all life on earth could be traced back to a single ancestor, and, over time, different advantageous mutations occurred and were passed on, while the organisms that lacked these advantages died off. This errant understanding of variation within a species gave a plausible hypothesis to those eager to explain life without God. Richard Dawkins famously stated, "Darwin made it possible to be an intellectually satisfied atheist."[16]

In line with the philosophy of modernism that was prevalent in the West, Darwin clearly saw man as just another animal: "My object in this chapter is to show that there is no fundamental difference between man

---

14. Charles Darwin, *The Descent of Man and Selection in Relation to Sex*, reprinted from the 2nd ed. (New York: A.L. Burt, 1919), p. 105–109.

15. For a person who opposed hell, which is what damning is, Darwin was not afraid to use the terminology. But notice that Darwin, whether he realized it or not, was holding religious convictions of humanism to take his own thoughts on a subject and then judge God and His Word based on his own fallible mind.

16. Richard Dawkins, *The Blind Watchmaker* (New York: Norton, 1986), p. 6.

and the higher mammals in their mental faculties."[17] Since man was just an animal, Darwin suggested that mankind would be better off if only the fit had children.

> With savages, the weak in body or mind are soon elimi-
> nated; and those that survive commonly exhibit a vigorous state
> of health. We civilised men, on the other hand, do our utmost
> to check the process of elimination; we build asylums for the
> imbecile, the maimed, and the sick; we institute poor-laws; and
> our medical men exert their utmost skill to save the life of every
> one to the last moment. There is reason to believe that vacci-
> nation has preserved thousands, who from a weak constitution
> would formerly have succumbed to small-pox. Thus the weak
> members of civilized societies propagate their kind. No one who
> has attended to the breeding of domestic animals will doubt that
> this must be highly injurious to the race of man. It is surprising
> how soon a want of care, or care wrongly directed, leads to the
> degeneration of a domestic race; but excepting in the case of
> man himself, hardly any one is so ignorant as to allow his worst
> animals to breed.[18]

Not only did Darwinian evolution become the skeptic's mechanism and cudgel for denying God's existence, social Darwinism justified much of the 20th century's eugenics atrocities. Unbelievers from Adolf Hitler to Margaret Sanger cited Charles Darwin as their source for justifying the murder of "inferior races" or unwanted children. The results of secular humanism have invariably led to licentiousness and death.

> Margaret Sanger — "As an advocate of birth control I wish
> . . . to point out that the unbalance between the birth rate of
> the 'unfit' and the 'fit,' admittedly the greatest present menace
> to civilization, can never be rectified by the inauguration of a
> cradle competition between these two classes. In this matter, the
> example of the inferior classes, the fertility of the feeble-minded,
> the mentally defective, the poverty-stricken classes, should not

---

17. Darwin, *The Descent of Man*, p. 74.
18. Ibid., p. 151–152.

be held up for emulation. . . . On the contrary, the most urgent problem today is how to limit and discourage the over-fertility of the mentally and physically defective."[19]

Adolf Hitler — "The law of selection justifies this incessant struggle, by allowing the survival of the fittest. Christianity is a rebellion against natural law, a protest against nature. Taken to its logical extreme, Christianity would mean the systematic cultivation of the human failure."[20]

Darwinian evolution gained entrance into American schools following the so-called "Scopes Monkey Trial" of 1925. The defendant in this case was John Scopes, a biology teacher accused of teaching human evolution. His defense attorney, Clarence Darrow, used many evolutionists to promote the scientific merits of evolutionary biology. Darrow put the prosecutor, William Jennings Bryan, on the stand to show he had little to no knowledge of what evolution was and to show his willingness to compromise the literal truth of the Bible. While Bryan won the battle and Scopes was fined $100, the war was lost; evolution had gained a level of popular acceptance and began moving into schools, replacing the creationist curriculums that were the norm. Secular humanism was on a roll.

Twentieth Century

The 20th century gave us Dr. Sigmund Freud, the father of modern-day psychoanalysis, who further expanded secular humanist ideas stating that God is merely an illusion: "Religion is an illusion and it derives its strength from the fact that it falls in with our instinctual desires."[21] He taught that the belief in God comes from a variety of different psychoses, such as the need for a father. To Freud, God was the imaginary figment of a delusional mind; a fictional father that some people needed in order to cope with reality, "At bottom God is nothing other than an exalted father."[22]

---

19. Margaret Sanger, *The Eugenic Value of Birth Control Propaganda* (1921), p. 5; http://www.nyu.edu/projects/sanger/webedition/app/documents/show.php?sangerDoc=238946.xml.
20. Adolf Hitler, *Hitler's Table Talk: 1941–1944*, trans. Norman Cameron and R.H. Stevens (New York: Enigma Books, 2000), p. 51.
21. Sigmund Freud, *New Introductory Lectures on Psycho-analysis*, trans. James Strachey (New York: W.W. Norton, 1965), p. 216.
22. Sigmund Freud, *Totem and Taboo; Some Points of Agreement between the Mental Lives of Savages and Neurotics*, trans. James Strachey (New York: W.W. Norton, 1950). p. 147.

In the meantime, a Christian movement attempted to combat liberalism in the early 20th century: Fundamentalism. This orthodox movement holds to a group of non-negotiable fundamentals of the Christian faith, such as the inerrancy of the Bible, the literal (plain/straightforward) nature of the Bible, the virgin birth of Christ, the bodily Resurrection and physical return of Christ, and the substitutionary atonement of Christ. These fundamentals came largely from 12 volumes of articles published in Chicago between 1910 and 1915.[23]

The articles were written polemically against liberalism and apologetically in defense of the sufficiency of the Bible. Unfortunately, this movement was soon overshadowed by the rising tide of liberalism, and fundamentalists were eventually on the outside looking in on many of the key areas of culture such as arts, entertainment, and academia.

The fundamentalist outlook fell out of favor with the "scientific community," and they were largely shunned.

> In science they [fundamentalists] were steadfastly committed to the principles of the seventeenth-century philosopher Francis Bacon: careful observation and classification of facts. These principles were wedded to a "common sense" philosophy that affirmed the ability to apprehend the facts clearly, whether the facts of nature or the more certain facts of scripture.[24]

The scientific landscape shifted, however, and the fundamentalists were now the outsiders. "These largely unspoken assumptions, as well as their faith in the Bible, separated the fundamentalists so entirely from the most of the rest of the twentieth century thought that their ideas appear simply anomalous. Thus in the fifty years following the 1870s, the philosophical outlook that had graced America's finest academic institutions came to be regarded as merely bizarre."[25]

Twentieth Century Postmodernism

The fall of the Berlin Wall in 1989 brought a crashing end to classic secular humanism and modernist thinking. Prior to the reuniting of East and West

23. Walter A. Elwell, *Evangelical Dictionary of Theology*, 2nd ed. (Grand Rapids, MI: Baker Academics, 1984), p. 475.
24. George M. Marsden, *Fundamentalism and American Culture* (Oxford: Oxford University Press, 1980), p. 7–8.
25. Ibid., p. 8.

Berlins, secular humanist modernists believed that human reason was superior and sufficient for determining morality. World Wars I and II undermined that notion. The bloodiest century in human history led philosophers and culture to conclude that man does not have the ability to make the world a better place.[26]

Unfortunately, the death of modernism gave birth to an even uglier stepchild — postmodernism.[27] It was clear to philosophers that neither God nor man had the solution for evil, so who does? Interestingly, the answer was "nobody and everybody."

Secular philosophers concluded that God doesn't exist and humans had made a mess of things, therefore, no single authority has the right or ability to declare universal truths for all men. Postmodernism insisted that truth could not be objectively known, therefore, each individual must determine what is true for himself. This philosophy is called moral relativism. Christians battle this form of relativistic humanism (postmodernism) today.

History Is Like a Baseball Game

Prior to the French Revolution, Western culture largely submitted to the Word of God — truth was determined by our Creator. Secular humanists insisted that God does not exist and only man has the answers to the problems that plague us. Unfortunately, the bloodiest wars in human history (World Wars I and II) left man with the sense that we don't know the answers.

Think of the history of the Western world like a baseball game where the umpire is determining the accuracy of the pitches, calling them as balls or strikes.

> **Premodern era:** Time of Christ until c. 1789. An umpire of a premodern baseball game would "call them as they are."
> **Modern era:** 1789 until c. 1989 (the fall of the Berlin Wall). An umpire of a modern baseball game would "call them as he sees them."
> **Postmodern era:** 1989 until today. An umpire of a postmodern game would "call them, and that is what they are."

---

26. Bodie Hodge, *The Results of Evolution*, Answers in Genesis, July 13, 2009, https://answersingenesis.org/sanctity-of-life/the-results-of-evolution.
27. See chapter 8 on Postmodernism in this volume.

Presently, we are living in a postmodern world where "all truth is valid truth" — at least that is what we are told. Nobody is wrong about anything. According to postmodernism, one man's truth is as valid as any other man's truth; even if the two "truths" are diametrically opposed to one another. Postmodernism's ultimate battle cry is, "All truth is valid truth."[28]

Twentieth-century French philosophers Jacques Derrida and Michael Foucault led the charge against modernism claiming that truth is not external but internal.

> Jacques Derrida — "I speak only one language, and it is not my own."[29]

> Michael Foucault — "Knowledge is not for knowing: knowl-edge is for cutting."[30]

What does postmodernism sound like today? "If being a Christian works for you, then it's true for you. But I don't believe Jesus Christ is God, and that is true for me. Which one of us is correct? Both of us." Logic is thrown out the window, which proves their postmodernism view is false.

While that sounds bonkers to your biblically trained mind, it makes perfect sense to godless secular humanists who exalt man to the position that only God should inhabit. The implications of this are considerable. Not only must a Christian wage war against an unbeliever's worldview, the Christian must battle against an entirely different way of thinking and perception. The Christian does not have the same starting point as the postmodern secular humanist. It is the Christian task to understand this if we are going to be effective witnesses for Jesus Christ.

Unfortunately, far too many Christians are adopting a postmodern mindset that allows for other religions to be equally as valid as Christianity. There are two deviant forms of Christianity that have embraced aspects of postmodernism:

1. Universalist Christians: while this term is an oxymoron (John 14:6), liberal denominations like the Unitarian Universalist[31]

---

28. Naturally, this position is illogical and self-refuting. The opposite claim, "all truth is not valid truth" would also be seen as true and valid to the postmodernist.
29. Jacques, Derrida, *Monolingualism of the Other: or, The Prosthesis of Origin* (Stanford, CA: Stanford University Press, 1998).
30. Michael Foucault, *The Foucault Reader* (New York: Pantheon, 1984).
31. See the chapter on Unitarianism in volume 2 of this book series.

sect believe that ultimately everyone will go to heaven, regardless of their religious beliefs.

2. Anonymous Christian view: liberal theologians like Tony Campolo and even the Roman Catholic Church since Vatican II believe that people who do not possess any knowledge of Jesus can still be saved by Jesus if they are striving to know God and be good.

Both of these views are grossly heretical. If people do not need to know Jesus to receive salvation, then the Bible is very wrong:

- Go therefore and make disciples of all the nations, baptizing them in the name of the Father, and of the Son, and of the Holy Spirit, teaching them to observe all things that I have commanded you; and lo, I am with you always, even to the end of the age (Matthew 28:19–20).

- How then shall they call on Him in whom they have not believed? And how shall they believe in Him of whom they have not heard? And how shall they hear without a preacher? (Romans 10:14).

- So then faith comes from hearing, and hearing by the Word of God [Christ] (Romans 10:17).

Twenty-first Century: The New Atheists

In the early 21st century, a group of secular humanists emerged who became popularly labeled as the "new atheists." The group sought to obliterate the Christian religion (and a few others) by attacking it verbally and in written form in an extremely abrasive manner. Some of the most notable members of this group are the "Four Horsemen of the Non-Apocalypse": Sam Harris, the late Christopher Hitchens, Daniel Dennet, and Professor Richard Dawkins.

While the New Atheists were excellent at making headlines, their scholarship was far less impressive. Their lack of philosophical prowess was exposed quickly in debates with Christians like Frank Turek, Dinesh D'Souza, William Lane Craig, and even Christopher Hitchens's brother (and professing believer) Peter Hitchens. Nevertheless, books by the New Atheists sold millions of copies to non-discerning secularists who continue to parrot their flimsy arguments.

Thanks to their efforts, a 2012 Pew Forum on Religion and Public Life study concluded, "The number of Americans who do not identify with any religion continues to grow at a rapid pace. One-fifth of the U.S. public — and a third of adults under 30 — are religiously unaffiliated today, the highest percentages ever in Pew Research Center polling."[32]

Here is the bad news: America's non-religious, or "Nones," is growing at a faster rate than any other time in U.S. history. But just because they claim to have no formal religious affiliations does not mean that they are not religious. These individuals have a worldview that informs how they act and think about the world around them. Their religion is merely a secular religion that leads them to worship man as the supreme being, and they do so outside of the walls of a traditional church building.

Here is the good news — Secular Humanism is perhaps the easiest of all worldviews to undermine.

The Foundations of Secular Humanism

In order to engage with secular humanists, it is important that we rightly understand the foundations of their worldview. Since secular humanists claim that there is no higher power that has communicated his will, they are forced to base their worldview on one of two shaky foundations.

The first foundation is nature. According to some secular humanists, we are merely animals formed by evolutionary processes. Therefore, the most logical way to live and form our society is in a like manner. The problem with this? It is utterly impossible.

Animals live in a way that no secular humanist, if they were honest, would want to live. Animals are the epitome of selfishness; they kill each other so they can survive. Sometimes they care for their young, but some species frequently eat their young or their mates for nourishment or to promote the spread of their own genes. Certainly, no animal cares about the environment. Locusts don't worry about the damage they do to the planet when they eat everything they can in a swarm. The animal mentality is simple: Want. Take.

Ironically, evolution supports the "dog-eat-dog" lifestyle of animals, and yet no evolutionist would like to actually live in his own worldview. In other words, secular humanists believe one thing but live another (often borrowing from Christian morality).

---

32. " 'Nones' on the Rise," Pew Research Center, October 9, 2012, http://www.pewforum.org/2012/10/09/nones-on-the-rise, accessed May 24, 2016.

Furthermore, and despite Darwin's assertion, it is self-evident that man is different than every other creature. Observation reveals that we are superior in thinking, morality, creativity, wisdom, memory, emotions, and behavior. No matter how much the secular humanist may claim that he is just like every other animal, he betrays his own worldview by living in a house with heat, air conditioning, and running water.

The second secular humanist foundation is "common values." Secular humanists shun God's laws but find themselves in a conundrum that ultimately exposes the arbitrary nature and implausibility of their own worldview. Secular humanists recognize the need for morality in order to live in a safe and orderly society, so they must "create" values. Unfortunately, their worldview collides with their desire.

The secular humanist recognizes a need for laws, but their postmodern worldview demands there are no objective laws. So how does the secular humanist create laws?

1. By claiming that whatever doesn't cause someone harm is permissible.
2. By claiming that whatever promotes the greatest common good is best.
3. By getting amnesia. The secular humanist constantly creates laws that come from their God-informed conscience.

Unfortunately for the secular humanist, the argument for "common values" overlooks two glaring problems:

1. A secular humanist cannot explain where the concepts of right and wrong come from.
2. Common values cannot objectively condemn behavior. By pointing out that cannibalism is accepted in a few societies, the secular humanist is forced to admit that "common values" morality is not objectively wrong, only our temporary societal preferences.

Over the years, Secular Humanists have attempted to codify their beliefs while shunning any type of dogmatic formulations. In 1933, prominent humanists penned *A Humanist Manifesto* to lay out their beliefs. Among these are the self-existence of the universe, evolutionary processes, the rejection of supernaturally revealed morality, looking to human reason and natural cause to understand the world, and a rejection of old attitudes of worship and prayer.[33]

The second iteration came in 1973 with the addition of promoting the right to birth control, divorce, and abortion as well as speaking out against weapons of mass destruction and any notion of judgment or need for salvation. Among the most notable lines is the denial of any supernatural being:

> But we can discover no divine purpose or providence for the human species. While there is much that we do not know, humans are responsible for what we are or will become. No deity will save us; we must save ourselves.[34]

In 2003, a third and shorter version was created, still upholding the same godless, evolutionary views that make man the measure of all things, using seven guiding principles. If anyone doubts that Secular Humanism is a religion, you can direct them to this statement of faith to bolster your argument.

Today, the International Humanist and Ethical Union is the umbrella group under which the secular humanist groups around the world sit. The American Humanist Association represents American humanism and publishes *The Humanist* magazine as well as maintains several websites and promoting humanism as a 501 (c)(3) charitable organization. The brights, freethinkers, skeptics, secularists,

GOOD WITHOUT A GOD

The official logo of the American Humanist Association depicts the "happy human" who can be good without a god. Used with permission. (Source: Wikipedia)

humanists, and other varieties all look to man as the standard of truth rather than God and His Word. They revere naturalistic science, rationalism, and human autonomy as their platform of beliefs. A reading of these humanist manifestos will help you see what the typical humanist affirms and allow you to have an informed conversation about why they believe what they believe.[35]

---

33. "Humanist Manifesto I," American Humanist Association, accessed May 24, 2016, http://americanhumanist.org/humanism/humanist_manifesto_i.

34. "Humanist Manifesto II," American Humanist Association, accessed May 24, 2016, http://americanhumanist.org/humanism/humanist_manifesto_ii.

35. Youi can read the entire manifesto here: "Humanist Manifesto III," American Humanist Association, http://americanhumanist.org/humanism/humanist_manifesto_iii.

Dismantling Secular Humanism

The Secular Humanist worldview is one of the easiest worldviews to demolish. It is as simple as a country road.

If a governing authority determines and announces that the speed limit on a country road is 35 mph, then you will receive a ticket if you exceed 35. If there are no signs posted by someone in authority demanding that your speed not surpass 35 miles per hour, then you are free to drive like the Dukes of Hazzard.

If the law does not determine which speed is right and which speed is wrong, then no speed is wrong and every speed is right. If the law does not determine what is lawful and what is not, then there are only speed preferences but no speeding laws. Without a posted sign, an old farmer on his porch can only yell at a speeding teenager, "I prefer you don't drive that fast."

That is the undoing of secular humanism. Without an objective standard of morality, the secular humanist is left in a world of preferences, but no absolute rights and wrongs. Without an objective, absolute lawgiver, the secular humanist cannot definitively claim, "That is evil."

- A secular humanist cannot state that murder is wrong, he can only claim that murder is not his preference, as it does not promote "human welfare."
- A secular humanist cannot find incest immoral, only not preferable.
- A secular humanist cannot call a rapist evil, he can only inform the rapist he does not prefer his raping behavior.
- A secular humanist cannot even claim with any certainty that Christianity is wrong because nothing can actually be wrong to a secular humanist.

If you would like to demonstrate the absurdity of the secular humanist worldview, simply grab the wallet or purse of a secular humanist and run away shouting, "You may not prefer this, but this is right for me! It promotes my happiness and helps me enjoy a good life."

If that is too bold for you, then ask the secular humanist who doesn't believe in moral absolutes if he can pay whatever he wants for a Quarter Pounder. The secular humanist adamantly denies the existence of God, yet he speaks and lives like a Christian. The secular humanist denies the existence of a moral lawgiver, but he lives and talks like a deist (at the least). Every time a secular humanist makes a moral judgment, he is admitting that God exists.

The plight and irrationality of secular humanism gets worse. The secular humanist should never do a laboratory experiment or try to solve a math equation. Without "laws of nature," lab work and math are a total waste of time, as no consistent outcome can be expected without "laws of nature." If we are accidents of time and chance, there is no rational grounding for physical laws of nature, and science and math should not exist.[36]

While it is quite easy to expose the incoherence of secular humanism, leaving a person with his crumbled worldview around his feet does not change his eternity.

How Not to Witness to a Secular Humanist

Many argue that the best way to reach this group is to dismantle their worldview by reasoning with them and exposing the inconsistency of their worldview apart from any use of the Bible. This approach cannot work because 1 Corinthians 1–3 informs us that an unregenerate man cannot and will not rightly reason his way to God (cf., 1 Corinthians 1:18–31, 2:14, 3:18–23).

> But the natural man does not receive the things of the Spirit
> of God, for they are foolishness to him; nor can he know them,
> because they are spiritually discerned (1 Corinthians 2:14).

To reason with someone who has no ability to reason about spiritual things is to try to teach algebra to a dog. An unregenerate man cannot see the folly of his worldview through reason and logic alone because he is entirely unreasonable and illogical when it comes to discerning spiritual matters. This is not to say that there is no value in showing someone the inconsistencies within their own worldview, but that cannot bring about conversion of the soul — a job only the gospel can accomplish.

Other approaches suggest we provide them with the overwhelming evidence for the Christian religion. When faced with this, they should be able to come to the conclusion that Christianity is true and bow the knee in repentance and faith. This approach attempts to bridge the vast differences between humanism and Christianity through man's intellect alone.

36. Jason Lisle, "Evolution: The Anti-science," Answers in Genesis, accessed May 24, 2016, https://answersingenesis.org/theory-of-evolution/evolution-the-anti-science.

This is what Rene Descartes did, and his method resulted in a colossal failure. This method is destined to fail every time it is used because it assumes some unbiblical points. It assumes that the natural man is simply ignorant of the existence of God and just needs to be shown that He exists. The natural man will meet the Christian on common ground, and if he is shown sufficient proof he will come around to a belief in God. This is simply not true.

Romans 1:18–32 instructs us that every person already knows God exists through the created world. Secular humanists *suppress* this truth, they refuse to give thanks to the real God, and they turn their praise back onto things created by God — namely nature or themselves. They aren't standing on common ground with an open mind. They stand on God's planet, knowing God created it, and shake their fist at Him.

> For the wrath of God is revealed from heaven against all ungodliness and unrighteousness of men, who suppress the truth in unrighteousness, because what may be known of God is manifest in them, for God has shown it to them. For since the creation of the world His invisible attributes are clearly seen, being understood by the things that are made, even His eternal power and Godhead, so that they are without excuse, because, although they knew God, they did not glorify Him as God, nor were thankful, but became futile in their thoughts, and their foolish hearts were darkened (Romans 1:18–21).

How to Witness to a Secular Humanist

If man's intellect, logic, or reason is not the connecting point, what is? To find this answer we need to consult our ultimate authority, the Bible. Genesis 1:27 tells us that God created man in His own image, meaning, unlike all the other creatures on earth, man has a moral aspect, absent from all other animals. Romans 2:14–15 states:

> For when Gentiles, who do not have the law, by nature do the things in the law, these, although not having the law, are a law to themselves, who show the work of the law written in their hearts, their conscience also bearing witness, and between themselves their thoughts accusing or else excusing them.

You have an ally in the conscience. A universal courtroom is hardwired into the brain of every human. Attack the conscience rather than merely the intellect (2 Corinthians 4:1–5). Use the laws of God to bring about the knowledge of sin (Romans 7:7). Let the law act as a schoolmaster to bring the secular humanist to the Cross (Galatians 3:24).

Every man bears the image of God and has the moral law of God written on his heart (Romans 2:15). This is "common ground" that acknowledges the sinfulness of each human being. The secular humanist needs to see their need for a Savior, not to be barraged with evidences and proofs. They need to see that they have broken the law that God has given them. They have sinned over and over by lying, stealing, blaspheming, and denying Jesus as Lord. They need to be confronted with the fact that they are criminals, and if they die in that state they will pay the eternal penalty for their rebellion against a perfectly holy God in a place called hell.

Then, once the humanist trembles before a just and holy law, give them the greatest news they can ever hear — "Jesus died for sinners!" (cf., Romans 5:6–8; 1 Corinthians 15:3). Jesus rose from the grave and defeated death so that secular humanists can be forgiven and reconciled to the Creator they know exists. Through the proclamation of the truth of God's Word, God the Holy Spirit will bring conviction of sin and open blinded eye and unstop deaf ears to the glorious gospel of Jesus Christ.

This is not to suggest that apologetics do not play an important role in evangelism. They do. Apologetics support the truth of the gospel, but apologetics can never save — only the proclamation of God's Word saves. "Faith comes from hearing and hearing from the word of God [Christ]" (Romans 10:17).

When, if ever, do we introduce apologetics? When the stony heart of the secular humanist heart is softened by the law and the gospel that utterly refutes their worldview, then you can reason with an unbeliever. Think of it like this:

You and a friend/spouse/sibling get into an argument and exchange angry words. After a period of separation, one of you makes a move toward reconciliation. There are two approaches one of you can make:

1. "So, are you still going to be an idiot or what?"
2. "I hate it when we fight; can we please sit down and work through our differences so we can get along?"

Which approach works and which approach leads to more fighting? The answer is obvious. If you are witnessing to an argumentative, belligerent, aggressive secular humanist, apologetics without the law will not silence their mouth. Only the law can do that:

> Now we know that whatever the law says, it says to those who are under the law, that every mouth may be stopped, and all the world may become guilty before God. Therefore by the deeds of the law no flesh will be justified in His sight, for by the law is the knowledge of sin (Romans 3:19–20).

If a secular humanist sincerely seeks to understand the answers to the questions that have plagued him, then answer him apologetically. Should the humble humanist ask questions of genuine concern (the age of the earth, why evil exists, supposed contradictions in the Bible, etc.), then bring out your apologetics to wipe away their confusion, never neglecting to share the hope of the gospel.

Be Encouraged

Witnessing to a secular humanist is not hard — you have every advantage. You have the power of a "two-edged sword" (Hebrews 4:12). Take it out and use it. You are engaging in a spiritual battle (Ephesians 6); use the spiritual weapon that God has provided you. Use the Word.

Sadly, all you have to do is leave your home to find a secular humanist. Unfortunately, they are everywhere. But fortunately, God loves secular humanists so much that He died to save them.

So find a secular humanist, and share the law and the gospel, trusting that God will work through you to bring many to worship Him around His throne.

Summary of Secular Humanist Beliefs

Doctrine	Teachings of Secular Humanism
God	Deny the existence of God or any divine being; or they acknowledge a god may exist, but he is not involved in the affairs of man. Believe nature is self-existing. Reject Jesus as Savior or God.
Authority/ Revelation	Man is the measure of all things. Naturalism, materialism, and rationalism are key concepts in determining truth. Scientific inquiry is the highest pursuit of truth.
Man	All men are the result of "unguided evolutionary change" and have no existence beyond this earthly life. The goal of man is to maximize his own pleasure without harming others. Man is a social animal.
Sin	Sin is denied as any type of moral absolute. "Ethical values" are based in "human welfare" and change with new experience and knowledge.
Salvation	There is no belief in an afterlife and no need to consider salvation since death is the end.
Creation	The universe is self-existent and its physical structure originated at the big bang. Naturalistic evolutionary processes explain all of existence.

Chapter 5

Nazism: A Variant of Secular Humanism

Jerry Bergman, PhD

The main religious influence on the Nazi movement can best be described as Secular Humanism, the belief that human reason, not Christianity or any theistic religion, is the solution to human social and psychological problems. Especially important to the Nazi variation of Secular Humanism is secular science and the use of the scientific method, both tools that the Nazis applied with abandon. Claims that they relied on the occult or some other religious influence were found to be without foundation. Their religion was totally secular and materialistic.

The Occult Claim

Determining the occult aspects of Nazism is fraught with misinformation, especially as to the putative influence of the occult on its major leaders. As indicated by the number of books, films, and articles about the topic, much fascination with the occult exists in both America and Europe, both in the early 20th century and today.

One reason for the popularity of the occult explanation is that in attempting to explain the horrific atrocities committed by Nazi leaders, some writers have made various claims about the alleged involvement of Hitler and his close associates in various occult movements and practices. This involvement, the supporters of this view claim, is important in understanding Nazi behavior. Most of these claims, though, have proven to have little solid substantiation. It is well documented that Hitler and most of the leading Nazis had disdain for the occult in all its forms, but rather relied on the science of eugenics for their conclusions.[1] Some writers have focused on the occult in an effort to divert attention from the major influence of Darwinism and eugenics on the Nazi atrocities.

The two highest-ranking Nazi officials who had occult interests were Heinrich Himmler and Rudolf Hess. Many others, including Hitler, Goebbels, and Heydrich, were openly opposed to involvement in the occult. Hitler's opposition is illustrated by an incident when Hess flew on his own to Scotland to, he claimed, obtain a peace agreement to end the war. Hitler blamed the escapade on Hess's occult interests and ordered a roundup of astrologers, fortune-tellers, and other occult prognosticators. Goebbels recorded in his diary that none of the occult prognosticators foresaw their arrests coming, which occurred in May of 1941, sarcastically remarking that this was "not a good professional sign" of their ability to predict the future. Himmler's own police forces and the SS were responsible for these arrests. However, Himmler rescued Wilhelm Wulff, one of the astrologers, from the concentration camp to work as his personal astrologer.[2]

The use of astrology was a desperate attempt toward the end of the war to respond to the critical problem that the German military position had progressively worsened, forcing Himmler to rely more and more on Wulff's astrological predictions, which obviously failed. Wulff himself concluded that the Nazis had little regard for astrology except as a propaganda tool. Likewise, the British also exploited astrology for its propaganda value by publishing phony astrological forecasts to boost British morale and dire astrological predictions for the Third Reich that were smuggled into Germany in an effort to undermine German morale.

Rejection of Christianity

One thing can be said with certainty — most of the leading Nazis rejected Christianity, and many leading Nazis sometimes aggressively opposed Christianity.[3] Another truism is that the 12 years of Nazi dictatorship occurred in the heart of Europe in one of the most educated, civilized, and industrially

---

1. Ken Anderson, *Hitler and the Occult* (Amherst, NY: Prometheus Books, 1995).
2. Wilhelm Wulff, *Zodiac and Swastika: How Astrology Guided Hitler's Germany* (New York: Coward, McCann & Geoghegan, 1973).
3. Richard Weikart, *Hitler's Ethic: The Nazi Pursuit of Evolutionary Progress* (NY: Palgrave MacMillan, 2009).

advanced countries in the world. This movement was in vivid contrast to the moral and religious values that existed in the Christian world at that time. How could this have happened?

One factor that helps to explain the Nazi movement is the fact that the main religious influence on the Nazi leaders was a form of Secular Humanism, the belief that mankind can create a better society by applying reason and science to society apart from any theological influence or revelation. A major conclusion of the first part of the 20th century was Darwinism, especially eugenics. The Nazis garnered strong support from most secularists, especially those in academia, mostly the biologists and the medical establishment.[4] The involvement of academia was so strong that a separate trial was held for them at the end of the war called the doctors' trial.

"Inferior Races"

The Nazis claimed that it is difficult to snuff out the lives of many millions of persons, but the Nazi genocide program would, in the end, produce both a superior race and society. An example is that Hitler and some of his leading Nazis compared their genocide goals to a surgeon that removes a cancer, causing much suffering to the patient, but in the end saving the patient's life. So too, what they had to do was difficult now, but would be a boon to humanity. To produce a superior society requires a superior race that must not be allowed to be polluted by breeding with "inferior races," namely Jews, Gypsies, and Slavic peoples, especially Poles and Russians.

To create this perfect people and perfect society, or at least a society as close to this ideal as possible, the "Aryan race" (mostly Germans and Scandinavians) must reproduce faster and the non-Aryans must reproduce slower, or, ideally, not at all. And the Nazis believed that Aryans breeding with the inferior races always brings down the superior race, causing race degeneration.[5] Thus, only two years after the Nazis' takeover of Germany, Nazi Germany passed laws forbidding marriage and sexual intercourse with Jews and other inferior races. These racist laws were called the Nuremberg Laws because they were formally introduced to the faithful Nazis at the annual Nazi Party Nuremberg Rally of 1936.

4. Heather Pringle, "Confronting Anatomy's Nazi Past," *Science* 329:274–275. July 16, 2010; Dieter Kuntz. *Deadly Medicine: Creating the Master Race* (Washington, DC: United States Holocaust Memorial Museum, 2004).
5. Regardless of the Nazi's beliefs, there is only one race, the human race, descended from Adam and Eve.

The Nuremberg Laws classified people with four Germanic grandparents as German or "kindred blood"; those persons that descended from three or four Jewish grandparents were classified as pure Jews. A person with one or two Jewish grandparents was a *Mischling*, a crossbreed or a person of "mixed blood." These laws were later extended to people described as "Gypsies, Negroes or their bastard offspring." These laws deprived Jews and other non-Aryans of German citizenship and prohibited mixed sexual relations and marriages between Germans and other non-Aryans.[6] These rules proved difficult to implement for several reasons and were consequently modified or even ignored at times, especially in cases where an esteemed German general or other Nazi military man was classified as Jewish according to these rules.[7] In these cases, certain Nazi leaders are claimed to have famously proclaimed, "I will determine who is a Jew."

Hitler realized that his end-goal of a world populated only by Aryans would take a long time to implement, and he worked slowly at first toward this goal. As time went on, he accelerated this goal, even using troops and trains to murder non-Aryans instead of using these resources to support the war effort in the Eastern front. This clearly showed his priorities — elimination of putative "inferior races" was more important than winning the war.[8]

Hitler's Main Opposition Was Christianity

Hitler and his leading Nazis realized very early that the main opposition to their eugenic goals was Christianity.[9] The Nazi Darwinists deduced that under Christianity the natural struggle for existence, which in the long run allows only the strongest and healthiest to survive, would be replaced by the mistaken Christian anti-evolutionary desire to aid the weakest and sickest. Naturally, this would interfere with the Nazi goal of the stronger race eventually replacing the weaker. Hitler reasoned the result of what he regarded as this misguided approach would be that the progeny of the strong who breed

6. Eric Ehrenreich, *The Nazi Ancestral Proof: Genealogy, Racial Science, and the Final Solution* (Bloomington, IN: Indiana University Press, 2007), p. 9–10.

7. Bryan Mark Rigg, *Hitler's Jewish Soldiers: The Untold Story of Nazi Racial Laws and Men of Jewish Descent in the German Military* (Lawrence, KS: University Press of Kansas, 2002), p. 82.

8. Ron Rosenbaum, *Explaining Hitler: The Search for the Origins of His Evil*, 2nd edition (Boston, MA: Da Capo Press, 2014), p. 398–399.

9. Joseph Keysor, *Hitler, The Holocaust, and the Bible* (Greenwood, WI: Athanatos Publishers, 2010).

with the weak would be inferior to the strong, resulting in the degeneration of the race.

It was for this reason that the Darwinian drive for survival would decimate what Hitler described as germs, bacilli, and weak "so-called humaneness of individuals." In other words, the inferior "races" must be destroyed to make room for the superior "races." What Hitler believed was that misplaced Christian humaneness would only interfere with this goal.[10]

Hitler also knew that the vast majority of the German population was at least nominally Christian; thus, he realized he must move slowly against the churches. One illustration of this is the belt buckles and cigarette lighters issued to Nazi soldiers with Christian phrases, such as *Gott Mit Uns* (God with Us). The first step was to endeavor to get the churches' cooperation, a goal in which Hitler was largely successful.[11] Then smaller steps

Propaganda tools like Christian slogans on belt buckles have led to confusion about the religious beliefs of the Nazi regime.
(Source: Daderot, own work, Creativecommons)

were implemented, such as the Nazi Bible (Third Reich Bible or Hitler's Bible) — a rewriting of the Bible to promote Nazi views instead of pure Christianity. Even the 10 Commandments were rewritten into Hitler's 12 commandments. Then finally, after the war was supposed to have been won by Germany, his plan was to work toward Christianity's total eradication. Like the Secular Humanists in the modern West, so too the Nazi Secular Humanists were at war against Christianity.[12]

An example is Martin Bormann, Hitler's right-hand man and the second most powerful man in the Third Reich. Although the Nazis were forced to tolerate Christianity until after the war, Bormann let his colleagues know that a clear conflict existed between Nazism and Christianity, stating that

---

10. Jerry Bergman, *Hitler and the Nazis Darwinian Worldview: How the Nazis Eugenic Crusade for a Superior Race Caused the Greatest Holocaust in World History* (Kitchener, Ontario, Canada: Joshua Press, 2012).
11. Erwin Lutzer, *Hitler's Cross* (Chicago, IL: Moody Press, 1995).
12. Bruce Walker, *The Swastika against the Cross* (Denver, CO: Outskirts Press, 2008).

"National Socialism and Christianity are irreconcilable."[13] Hitler supported this view openly by proclaiming that "one day we want to be in a position where only complete idiots stand in the pulpit and preach to old women."[14] To replace the old religion, the Nazis offered the German people a new religion openly based on Secular Humanism and secularized science. The fact is "the Nazis were no different here to earlier revolutionaries who tried to offer the people a brave new secular world. It was no surprise that racial supremacy played a large part in the new 'religion.' "[15]

Bormann made his absolute disdain for Christians and his open hostility and support of breaking them absolutely clear as rapidly as possible.[16] He was one of many high-level Nazis who "intended eventually to destroy Christianity" for the reason that "National Socialism and Christianity are irreconcilable," because in his mind, Nazism was based on science, and science had superseded the Christian church, which he regarded as anti-science.[17] He added that "National Socialism and Christian concepts are incompatible" because the Christian Churches were all built on

> the ignorance of men and strive to keep large portions of the people in ignorance because only in this way can the Christian Churches maintain their power. On the other hand, National Socialism is based on scientific foundations. Christianity's immutable principles, which were laid down almost two thousand years ago, have increasingly stiffened into life-alien dogmas. National Socialism, however, if it wants to fulfill its task further, must always guide itself according to the newest data of scientific researchers.[18]

Bormann added that the "Christian Churches have long been aware that exact scientific knowledge poses a threat to their existence" and instead have relied on pseudo-science such as theology. Furthermore, Bormann concluded the church takes "great pains to suppress or falsify scientific research.

---

13. Ibid.
14. Ibid.
15. Matthew Hughes and Chris Mann, *Inside Hitler's Germany: Life Under the Third Reich* (New York: MJF Books, 2000), p. 80.
16. Keysor, *Hitler, the Holocaust, and the Bible*, p. 180–181.
17. William Shirer, *The Rise and Fall of the Third Reich* (New York: Simon and Schuster, 1960), p. 240.
18. Bormann, 1942, reprinted in George L. Mosse, *Nazi Culture; Intellectual, Cultural, and Social Life in the Third Reich* (New York: Schocken Books, 1966) , p. 244.

Our National Socialist worldview stands on a much higher level than the concepts of Christianity." This rhetoric is very similar to that offered by Western Secular Humanists today.[19]

Support of the Scientific and Academic Establishment

As is true of Secular Humanism today, a major source of supporters of Hitler was the German scientific establishment. During the 20th century, Germany was more scientifically advanced than any other nation in the world at the time. Cambridge University historian John Cornwell wrote that during the first three decades of the last century Germany held the premier position for scientific achievement compared to all other nations of the world. German scientists were then among the most accomplished and honored in most fields, as demonstrated by the fact that they were then awarded the lion's share of Nobel prizes.[20]

One professional group that did not become active supporters of Hitler, at least after the persecution against them began, were Jewish professors. Professor Kater concluded that by expelling Jews "Germany may have lost as many as 40 percent of its medical faculty to racist fanaticism; the harm to science and education [in Germany] was unfathomable."[21]

The well-documented fact is that the leading German "scientists played a significant role in the formulation of Nazi racial ideology."[22] German academics provided the scholarship, the putative scientific support, and the "techniques that led to and justified . . . unparalleled slaughter" of Jews, Catholic Poles, and other groups that the Nazis deemed biologically inferior, a conclusion well supported by numerous scholars such as Weinreich.[23]

Both "Nazi medicine and science . . . were integral" to the Holocaust and "the monstrous crimes committed in occupied Europe out of hatred for . . . so-called inferior races and groups."[24] The fact is, "biomedical scientists played an active, even leading role in the initiation, administration, and execution

19. Michael D. LeMay, *The Suicide of American Christianity: Drinking the "Cool"-Aid of Secular Humanism* (Bloomington, IN: WestBowPress, 2012).
20. John Cornwell, *Hitler's Scientists: Science, War and the Devil's Pact* (New York: Viking, 2003).
21. Michael Kater, *Doctors Under Hitler* (Chapel Hill, NC: The University of North Carolina Press, 1989), p. 142.
22. Aaron Gillette, *Racial Theories in Fascist Italy* (New York: Routledge, 2002), p. 185.
23. Max Weinreich, *Hitler's Professors* (New Haven, CT: Yale University Press, 1999), p. 6.
24. Elie Wiesel, "Without Conscience" foreword to Vivien Spitz 2005, *Doctors from Hell.* (Boulder, CO: Sentient Publications, 2005).

of Nazi racial programs . . . scientists actively designed and administered central aspects of National Socialist [Nazi] racial policy."[25] Professor Caplan opines that a major reason for the "innocuous rise of eugenics in Weimar Germany" was because the Germans saw eugenics as

> an adjunct to efforts at public health reform. Germans eager for a rebirth after the disaster of the First World War eagerly seized on the hope extended by physicians, geneticists, psychiatrists, and anthropologists that using social Darwinism to guide public health was the vehicle for German regeneration.[26]

The level of support by doctors in Nazi Germany was so strong that "there were so many doctors and scientists involved in the Nazi crimes that to weed them all out would have left post-war Germany with hardly any at all, an intolerable situation in a nation reeling from starvation and decimation."[27] Medawar and Pyke documented the major loss of scientists that ended Germany's 50-year record of world supremacy in science.[28] The many scientists deemed to be members of an inferior race who managed to escape from Germany, mostly Jewish, turned out to be Hitler's gift to America.

Recognizing their central role in the Holocaust, "professors Astel, de Crinis, Hirt, Kranz and Dr. Gross committed suicide, and so, later, did Professors Clauberg, Heyde and Schneider, when charges [of genocide] were brought against them" by the victorious Allies.[29]

The importance of Darwin and his disciples' writings in causing the Holocaust was illustrated by Viktor Frankl, a Jewish physician who survived the horrors of Auschwitz. Dr. Frankl astutely evaluated the influence of modern scientists and academics in helping to prepare the way for the Nazi atrocities by concluding:

> The gas chambers of Auschwitz were the ultimate consequence of the theory that man is nothing but the product of

25. Robert Proctor, *Racial Hygiene: Medicine Under the Nazis* (London: Harvard University Press, 1998), p. 6.
26. Arthur Caplan, "Deadly Medicine: Creating the Master Race," *The Lancet*, 363:1741–1742, May 22, 2004, p. 1742.
27. Ibid.
28. Jean Medawar and David Pyke, *Hitler's Gift: The True Story of the Scientists Expelled by the Nazi Regime* (New York: Arcade Publishing, 2001).
29. Benno Müller-Hill, *Murderous Science: Elimination by Scientific Selection of Jews, Gypsies, and Others in Germany, 1933–1945* (New York: Oxford University Press, 1988).

heredity and environment — or — as the Nazis liked to say, of "Blood and Soil." I am absolutely convinced that the gas chambers of Auschwitz, Treblinka, and Maidanek were ultimately prepared not in some Ministry . . . in Berlin, but rather at the desks and in the lecture halls of nihilistic scientists and philosophers.[30]

Dr. Frankl accurately summarized the case for academia and the scientists in Germany causing, or at least making a major contribution to, the Holocaust and the horrors of World War II and the loss of 55 million lives.[31]

Dr. Josef Mengele: Darwin's Angel of Death

Dr. Josef Mengele best personifies the Secular Humanists of Nazi Germany. Today, he symbolizes the worst of the Nazi Germany criminals for his grossly barbaric and often lethal medical experiments on prisoners. He is a prime example of where the logical implications of Darwinism can lead. Mengele was awarded a PhD for a thesis completed in 1935 "proving" that a person's "race" could be determined by examining their jawbone. Mengele's chosen fields of anthropology and genetics were especially influenced by the racist theories of Nazi dogma. His strong

> interest in genetics and evolution happened to coincide with the developing concept that some human beings afflicted by disorders were unfit to reproduce, even to live. Perhaps the real catalyst in this lethal brew was that Mengele, first at Munich and later at Frankfurt, studied under the leading exponents of this "unworthy life" theory. His consummate ambition was to succeed in this fashionable new field of evolutionary research.[32]

Unfortunately, he succeeded all too well, but in ways that the world now regards as one of the worst tragedies in human history. The evolutionary ideas that Mengele so enthusiastically absorbed at his university "were precisely the ones that would propel him down the road to Auschwitz. His apprenticeship as a mass murderer formally began not on the selection

30. Victor Frankl, *The Doctor and the Soul: From Psychotherapy to Logotherapy*, third ed. (New York: Vintage Books, 1986), p. xxxii.
31. Richard Weikart, *Socialist Darwinism: Evolution in German Socialist Thought from Marx to Bernstein* (Lantham, MD: International Publications, 1998).
32. Gerald L Posner. and John Ware, *Mengele: The Complete Story* (McGraw-Hill Books Company, 1986), p. 9.

lines of the concentration camp but in the classrooms of the University of Munich."[33]

Jewish historian Robert Lifton, in his extensive study of Nazi doctors, wrote that he (Lifton) "began and ended" his study of Nazi crimes with Mengele.[34] Indeed, few men are as closely associated with the horrors of the Holocaust in the public's mind as Professor Josef Mengele, MD, PhD.

Conclusions

The dominant religion in the Nazi German hierarchy and government policy was that which is today called Secular Humanism. Nazism would properly be considered a variant or subset of Secular Humanism. Although differences exist and most Secular Humanists today rightly condemn some aspects of Nazi Germany, numerous major parallels exist. Some of these include both Nazism and Secular Humanism's endorsement of anti-Christian policies, and the long-term goal of both groups is to replace Christianity with a highly secular society. Another parallel is that both the Nazis and the modern Secular Humanists strongly support secular science (e.g., geological evolution, "millions of years," and astronomical evolution) and especially Darwinism (biological evolution).

Both movements are totalitarian and use the government to suppress Christianity, first in state-supported entities, such as government institutions and government-controlled schools and colleges, then later in the private sphere, such as requiring denominational schools to teach evolution or risk loss of state funds and accreditation, as occurred in Nazi Germany[35] and is now beginning to occur in the West and particularly in America.[36]

33. Lucette M. Lagnado and Sheila Cohn Dekel, *Children of the Flames: Dr. Josef and the Untold Story of the Twins of Auschwitz* (New York: William Morrow, 1991), p. 42.
34. Robert Jay Lifton, *The Nazi Doctors: Medical Killing and the Psychology of Genocide* (New York: Basic Books, 1986).
35. Anonymous, *The Persecution of the Catholic Church in the Third Reich Translated from the German* (Fort Collins, CO: McCaffrey Publishing, 2007). Originally published in 1941.
36. Jerry Bergman, *Slaughter of the Dissidents: The Shocking Truth About Killing the Careers of Darwin Doubters* (Southworth, WA: Leafcutter Press, 2012); and Jerry Bergman, *Silencing the Darwin Dissidents* (Southworth, WA: Leafcutter Press, 2016).

Chapter 6

Scientology (Thetanism/Church of Scientology/Hubbardism)

Pastor David Chakranarayan

The Church of Scientology spent millions of dollars to air a Super Bowl XLIX ad in light of ongoing controversy over a documentary centered on the religion.[1] The ad features a voiceover accompanied by quick clips of footage including a person hiking, a DNA strand, and a close-up of an eye. The announcer in the ad says:

> We live in an age of searching: to find solutions, to find ourselves, to find the truth. Now imagine an age in which the predictability of science and the wisdom of religion combined. Welcome to the age of answers.

The commercial is filled with real-life experiences and the latest innovations in science meant to portray a union capable of giving human beings the answers to life. This is not the first time the church has paid to air an ad during the pricey platform. Scientology ads aired during the Super Bowl in 2013 and 2014 as well, promoting their message to the largest audience in the United States during the most popular sporting event.

The ad followed the 2015 release of the documentary *Going Clear: Scientology and the Prison of Belief* debuting at the Sundance Film Festival. The

---

1. "Scientology Super Bowl Commercial 2015, 'Age of Answers,'" YouTube video, 0:32, Scientology, February 1, 2015, https://www.youtube.com/watch?v=jXf3pWVJOkA.

church launched a Twitter account to discredit the film, which focuses on Hollywood's connection to the faith.

The Church of Scientology has many famous followers such as actors Tom Cruise and John Travolta, actress Kirstie Allie (who claims the church helped her overcome cocaine addiction), singer Beck Hansen, TV personality Greta Van Susteren (who says she is a "strong advocate of their ethics"), and EarthLink founder Sky Dayton. Dayton notes on his website that "communication is the solvent for all things" — the words of none other than L. Ron Hubbard, the founder of the Church of Scientology.[2]

The Origin of Scientology

It is no secret that the religion was inaugurated by Hubbard in the 1950s. Hubbard was a science fiction author who struggled financially. His book *Dianetics: The Modern Science of Mental Health* eventually became a bestseller and was the foundation for his emerging religious philosophy. Dianetics began as Hubbard's explanation of the connection between the mind and the body and the urge to survive. While he promoted Dianetics as a scientific idea, its rejection by the scientific community led him to adapt his thinking into a self-help religious philosophy. He had this idea that religion, particularly a cult, is where the money was. Hubbard said:

> You don't get rich writing science fiction. If you want to get rich, you start a religion.[3]

> I'd like to start a religion. That's where the money is![4]

So start one he did — the Church of Scientology, or what might rightly be called Hubbardism (as it is purely the invention of Hubbard). It was an interesting mixture between modern secular humanism, self-help psychology, and Eastern thought with a little science fiction thrown in. And the money came in for him. Was Hubbard worried about his venture? Not at all. He openly wrote, "The only way you can control people is to lie to them.

2. Aly Weisman, Kirsten Acuna, and Ashley Lutz, "21 Famous Church of Scientology Members," *Business Insider*, November 26, 2014, http://www.businessinsider.com/famous-scientology-church-members-2014-11.

3. Sam Moskowitz, Affidavit, regarding the Eastern Science Fiction Association meeting of November 11, 1948, that Hubbard made this statement, April 14, 1993.

4. L. Ron Hubbard to Lloyd Eshbach, in 1949; quoted by Eshbach in *Over my Shoulder: Reflections on a Science Fiction Era* (Hampton Falls, NH: Donald M. Grant Publisher, 1983).

You can write that down in your book in great big letters. The only way you can control anybody is to lie to them."[5]

The religion was meant as a money maker, and it succeeded with its ups and downs throughout Scientology's early years. This chapter is a Christian response to Scientology, as Christians have seen it as a challenge to Christianity and want to have a response. Hubbard taught "that all men have inalienable rights to their own religious practices and their performance."[6]

Christians are commanded to demolish arguments and every pretension that goes against the knowledge of God (2 Corinthians 10:4–5). According to Hubbard, we have the inalienable right to practice our religion, which means responding to Hubbard's challenges of Christianity.

What Is Scientology?

Scientology is a 20th-century religion invented by a man as a variation of religious humanism that might rightly be called Hubbardism. Unlike other humanistic religions in this volume, Scientology tends to meld self-help psychology with Eastern religions and even borrows some Christian ideas.

From the Scientology website we read how they view the name scientology:

> Scientology: *Scio* (Latin) "knowing, in the fullest sense of the word," *logos* (Greek) "study of." Thus Scientology means "knowing how to know." Developed by L. Ron Hubbard, Scientology is a religion that offers a precise path leading to a complete and certain understanding of one's true spiritual nature and one's relationship to self, family, groups, Mankind, all life forms, the material universe, the spiritual universe and the Supreme Being.
>
> Scientology addresses the spirit — not the body or mind — and believes that Man is far more than a product of his environment, or his genes.
>
> Scientology comprises a body of knowledge which extends from certain fundamental truths. Prime among these are:
>
> • Man is an immortal spiritual being.
> • His experience extends well beyond a single lifetime.

---

5. L. Ron Hubbard, "Off the Time Track," lecture of June 1952, excerpted in *Journal of Scientology* issue 18-G, reprinted in *Technical Volumes of Dianetics & Scientology*, vol. 1, p. 418.
6. "The Creed of the Church of Scientology," February 18, 1954, http://www.scientology.org/what-is-scientology/the-scientology-creeds-and-codes/the-creed-of-the-church.html.

- His capabilities are unlimited, even if not presently realized.[7]

As with any religion, Scientology seeks to help humanity understand what is broken in the world and how to fix it. By understanding the Eight Dynamics (more on this in a moment) and how man relates to both the physical and spiritual realms, each individual can achieve a spiritual awareness that will lead to ultimate fulfillment and longevity. Focusing on improving relationships and communication, counselors offer "auditing" to help individuals recognize the things from their past that are blocking the expression of their potential.

Church of Scientology

The Church of Scientology International is the mother church under which individual Church of Scientology groups are organized. With its headquarters in Los Angeles, the 11,000 local churches or groups exist in over 160 nations.[8]

Scientology's Scriptures

It is important to understand that the Church of Scientology regards the teachings of Hubbard as authoritative. These materials are essentially the "Bible" for scientologists where Hubbard is seen as the only "prophet." In order to properly contrast the beliefs of scientology with those of Christianity, there must be an emphasis on the writings and teachings of Hubbard.

On the Church of Scientology's website under the question "Does Scientology have a Scripture?" we read:

> Yes. The written and recorded spoken words of L. Ron Hubbard on the subject of Scientology collectively constitute the scripture of the religion. He set forth the Scientology theology and technologies in tens of millions of words, including hundreds of books, scores of films and more than 3,000 recorded lectures.[9]

Although Scientology sees Hubbard's writing as authoritative, they claim to be tolerant of other religious views.

Scientology, like many of the dominant religions such as Islam, Buddhism, and Mormonism, has a single author as the revealer of truth. The

---

7. "What Is Scientology?" Scientology.org, accessed July 18, 2016, http://www.scientology.org/scientology.html.

8. "Scientology Religion Facts," Scientology.org, accessed July 18, 2016, http://www.scientologynews.org/quick-facts/scientology.html.

9. "Does Scientology have a Scripture?" Scientology.org, accessed July 18, 2016, http://www.scientology.org/faq/background-and-basic-principles/does-scientology-have-a-scripture.html.

authors of these religions have all attested to some sort of "private" interpretation or revelation, and they alone have the authority in its message.

The Bible is different to the scriptures revered by other religions. There is ultimately only one author for Scripture — God the Holy Spirit who moved through human authors to communicate His perfect and eternal message.

> Knowing this first, that no prophecy of Scripture is of any private interpretation, for prophecy never came by the will of man, but holy men of God spoke as they were moved by the Holy Spirit (2 Peter 1:20–21).

> All Scripture is given by inspiration of God, and is profitable for doctrine, for reproof, for correction, for instruction in righteousness, that the man of God may be complete, thoroughly equipped for every good work (2 Timothy 3:16–17).

Not only is the Holy Spirit the author of Scripture, He is also the one who opens our eyes to receive the truth that God gives to us.

> Revelation is God's making his truth known to humankind. Inspiration guarantees that what the Bible says is just what God would say if he were to speak directly. One other element is needed in this chain, however. For the Bible to function as if it is God speaking to us, the Bible reader needs to understand the meaning of Scriptures, and to be convinced of their divine origin and authorship. This is accomplished by an internal working of the Holy Spirit, illuminating the understanding of the hearer or reader of the Bible, bringing about comprehension of its meaning, and creating a certainty of its truth and divine origin.[10]

Wayne Grudem further illustrates this point.

> It is one thing to affirm that the Bible claims to be the words of God. It is another thing to be convinced that those claims are true. Our ultimate conviction that the words of the Bible are God's word comes only when the Holy Spirit speaks in and through the words of the Bible to our heart and gives us an inner assurance that these are the words of our Creator speaking to us. Apart from

---

10. Millard J. Erickson and L. Arnold Hustad, "The Power of God's Word: Authority," *Introducing Christian Doctrine*, 2nd ed. (Grand Rapids, MI: Baker Academic, 2001), p. 77.

the work of the Spirit of God, a person will not receive or accept the truth that the words of Scripture are in fact the words of God.[11]

There is also complete harmony in Scripture when compared to the disharmony of holy books of other world religions. Even though the Scriptures were written by men from different times, lands, professions, and ways of life, they all consistently attest to the glory of God and the revelation of the Messiah who would redeem people from their sin. Consider the argument from Living Waters:

> If just 10 people today were picked who were from the same place, born around the same time, spoke the same language, and made about the same amount of money, and were asked to write on just one controversial subject, they would have trouble agreeing with each other. But the Bible stands alone. It was written over a period of 1,600 years by more than 40 writers from all walks of life. Some were fishermen; some were politicians. Others were generals or kings, shepherds or historians. They were from three different continents, and wrote in three different languages. They wrote on hundreds of controversial subjects yet they wrote with agreement and harmony. They wrote in dungeons, in temples, on beaches, and on hillsides, during peacetime and during war. Yet their words sound like they came from the same source. So even though 10 people today couldn't write on one controversial subject and agree, God picked 40 different people to write the Bible — and it stands the test of time."[12]

View of God

The theology of Scientology will sound somewhat familiar to Christians, but the words have very different meanings. While they speak of a Supreme Being or God, it is not the Creator God of the Bible.

> In Scientology, the concept of God is expressed as the Eighth Dynamic — the urge toward existence as infinity. This is also identified as the Supreme Being. As the Eighth Dynamic, the

---

11. Wayne Grudem and Jeff Purswell, "The Authority and Inerrancy of the Bible." In *Bible Doctrine: Essential Teachings of the Christian Faith* (Grand Rapids, MI: Zondervan, 1999), p. 36.
12. "The Bible Stands Alone," Living Waters, accessed July 18, 2016, http://www.livingwaters.com/witnessingtool/Biblestandsalone.shtml.

Scientology concept of God rests at the very apex of universal survival. As L. Ron Hubbard wrote in *Science of Survival*:

> No culture in the history of the world, save the thoroughly depraved and expiring ones, has failed to affirm the existence of a Supreme Being. It is an empirical observation that men without a strong and lasting faith in a Supreme Being are less capable, less ethical and less valuable to themselves and society. . . . A man without an abiding faith is, by observation alone, more of a thing than a man.[13]

Based on his observation, Hubbard asserts that faith is an important element of humanity, but he does so in an arbitrary way. He points not to any real authority, but to personal experience. He also asserts that an atheist is of less benefit to society than a person who believes in a Supreme Being of some sort, but does not provide any justification for his claims. The explanation continues:

> Unlike religions with Judeo-Christian origins, the Church of Scientology has no set dogma concerning God that it imposes on its members. As with all its tenets, Scientology does not ask individuals to accept anything on faith alone. Rather, as one's level of spiritual awareness increases through participation in Scientology *auditing* and *training*, one attains his own certainty of every dynamic. Accordingly, only when the Seventh Dynamic (spiritual) is reached in its entirety will one discover and come to a full understanding of the Eighth Dynamic (infinity) and one's relationship to the Supreme Being.[14]

From the quote, it is worth noting that even though the Church of Scientology used the words "Supreme Being," it clearly rejects the teachings of the biblical God and absolutely rejects the Trinity. As will be discussed later on in this chapter, the Church of Scientology has been heavily influenced by Eastern thought, like Hinduism.

Their book (*A World Religion*) on world religions leaves little doubt that the Hindu Brahma is closely paralleled with Scientology's

---

13. "Does Scientology Have a Concept of God?" Scientology.org, accessed July 18, 2016, http://www.scientology.org/faq/scientology-beliefs/what-is-the-concept-of-god-in-scientology.html.
14. Ibid.

understanding of the Supreme Being. Here God is spoken in terms of Hinduism. Though Hubbard provides no strict definition of the Supreme Being, his descriptive characteristics are enough for the Christian reader to see its unbiblical nature. Hubbard rejects the Christian doctrine of the trinity. His *Phoenix Lectures* state "The Christian god is actually much better characterized in Hinduism than in any subsequent publication, including the Old Testament." Again, he said, "The god the Christians worshipped is certainly not the Hebrew god. He looks much more like the one talked about in the Veda (Hindu scripture). What he mistakenly assumed is that the Hindu "triad" is the basis for the Christian "Trinity."[15]

The Bible rejects the idea of multiple gods and affirms that there is one true God (Deuteronomy 4:39; Isaiah 43:10; 1 Timothy 2:5). The Bible always provides a clear distinction between God and man. Unlike other religions that mix the two and even attribute deity to human beings (not to be confused with being made in the image of God), the Bible clearly shows the difference between God and man, depicting God's incommunicable attributes as something beyond man's grasp (Numbers 23:19).

In scientology, this view of a Supreme Being is more like Eastern Mysticism's transcendental heavens, though it differs in that it holds that *infinity* is that Supreme Being. So the concept of a God like the God of the Bible is absent in scientology. This means it operates like an atheistic or dualistic religion. As a religion, it is essentially a cross between atheism and Eastern Mysticism (e.g., Taoism, Hinduism, Jainism, New Age, etc.) where each individual forms their own view of the god of the Eighth Dynamic.

View of Christ

It isn't a surprise that Hubbard has no reverence for Christ and sees him as just another moral teacher among many. In his Phoenix Lectures from 1968, Hubbard believes Jesus was "the Christ legend as an implant in preclears a

---

15. Walter Martin, "Jehovah's Witnesses and the Watchtower Bible and Tract Society," in *The Kingdom of the Cults*, 3. Rev. and Expanded ed. (Minneapolis, MN: Bethany House Publishers, 1985), p. 83. "Christianity does not believe that the Trinity was incarnate in Christ and that they were 'three-in-one' as such during Christ's ministry. Christ voluntarily limited himself in His earthly body, but heaven was always open to Him and He never ceased being God, Second Person of the Trinity. Even in the Incarnation itself (Luke 1:35) the Trinity appears (see also John 14:16 and 15:26). Of course it is not possible to fathom this great revelation completely, but this we do know: There is a unity of substance, not three gods, and that unity is One in every sense, which no reasonable person can doubt after surveying the evidence."

million years ago." In these lectures, he also casts doubts upon the authenticity of Jesus as Messiah. He states:

> Now the Hebrew definition of messiah is one who brings wisdom, a teacher, in other words. Messiah is from messenger. But he is somebody with information. And Moses was such a one. And then Christ became such a one. He was a bringer of information. He never announced his sources. . . . Now here we have a great teacher in Moses. We have other messiahs, and we then arrive with Christ. And the words of Christ were a lesson in compassion, and they set a very fine example to the western world, compared to what the western world was doing at that moment.[16]

Hubbard makes a mistake here in reference to the meaning of Christ. The name "Christ" means "anointed" and is a proper name or title of "the Anointed One" to translate the Hebrew word "Messiah."[17] This is further explained by the apologists at Got Questions, when they write:

> To the surprise of some, "Christ" is not Jesus' last name (surname). "Christ" comes from the Greek word *Christos*, meaning "anointed one" or "chosen one." This is the Greek equivalent of the Hebrew word *Mashiach*, or "Messiah." "Jesus" is the Lord's human name given to Mary by the angel Gabriel (Luke 1:31). "Christ" is His title, signifying Jesus was sent from God to be a King and Deliverer (see Daniel 9:25; Isaiah 32:1). "Jesus Christ" means "Jesus the Messiah" or "Jesus the Anointed One."
>
> When someone was given a position of authority in ancient Israel, oil was poured on his head to signify his being set apart for God's service (e.g., 1 Samuel 10:1). Kings, priests, and prophets were anointed in such fashion. Anointing was a symbolic act to indicate God's choosing (e.g., 1 Samuel 24:6). Although the literal meaning of *anointed* refers to the application of oil, it can also refer to one's consecration by God, even if literal oil is not used (Hebrews 1:9).[18]

---

16. L. Ron Hubbard, "General Background Part III," (lecture, Phoenix, Arizona, July 19, 1954), The Phoenix Lectures, p. 19, accessed at http://www.stss.nl/stss-materials/English%20Tapes/EN_BW_CR_Phoenix_Lectures.pdf.

17. A.T. Robertson, *Word Pictures in the New Testament: Matthew* (Grand Rapids, MI: Christian Classics Ethereal Library, 1985), p. 3.

18. http://www.gotquestions.org/what-does-Christ-mean.html#ixzz3U2Tn7BTR.

Not only is Jesus Christ the true Messiah promised in the Old Testament by the prophets, He is also fully God and fully man, a view that would be rejected by the Church of Scientology.

Among the many passages that attest to the deity of Christ,[19] three passages specifically stand out. The first is:

> In the beginning was the Word, and the Word was with God, and the Word was God. He was in the beginning with God. All things were made through Him, and without Him nothing was made that was made (John 1:1–3).

In verse one, John uses "was" to illustrate Jesus' pre-existence and eternal personhood as part of the Trinity. John further illustrates that Jesus was eternal by saying that the "Word was with God and the Word was God." Christ was in an intimate fellowship with God the Father before time existed. John's thoughts flow from Christ leaving the glories of heaven and putting on humanity.

In verse 14 of John 1, John says, "And the Word became flesh and dwelt among us, and we beheld His glory, the glory as of the only begotten of the Father, full of grace and truth." John MacArthur in his commentary on John states:

> While Christ as God was uncreated and eternal . . . the word "became" emphasizes Christ's taking on humanity (cf., Heb. 1:1–3, 2:14–18). This reality is surely the most profound ever because it indicated that the infinite became finite; the Eternal was conformed to time; the invisible became visible; the supernatural One reduced Himself to the natural. In the incarnation, however, the Word did not cease to be God but became God in human flesh, i.e., undiminished deity in human form as a man (1 Tim. 3:16).[20]

In referencing the word "begotten," skeptics suggest Jesus was a created being instead of eternal. Again, MacArthur speaks to this very issue.

> The term "only begotten" is a mistranslation of the Greek word. The word does not come from the term meaning "beget"

---

19. Bodie Hodge, "God Is Triune," Answers in Genesis, February 20, 2008, https://answers-ingenesis.org/who-is-god/the-trinity/god-is-triune.

20. John MacArthur, *The MacArthur Study Bible, NKJV,* John 1:14 (Nashville, TN: Word Publishing, 1997), p. 1574.

but instead has the idea of "the only beloved one." It, therefore, has the idea of singular uniqueness, of being beloved like no other. By this word, John emphasizes the exclusive character of the relationship between the Father and the Son in the Godhead (cf., 3:16, 18; 1 John 4:9). It does not connote origin but rather unique prominence.[21]

The Apostle John had no doubt that Jesus was the eternal Son of God with full deity in His nature.

A second passage which refutes the view of the Church of Scientology in regard to the person of Christ is:

> He has delivered us from the power of darkness and conveyed us into the kingdom of the Son of His love, in whom we have redemption through His blood, the forgiveness of sins. He is the image of the invisible God, the firstborn over all creation. For by Him all things were created that are in heaven and that are on earth, visible and invisible, whether thrones or dominions or principalities or powers. All things were created through Him and for Him. And He is before all things, and in Him all things consist (Colossians 1:13–17).

In this passage, Paul's letter to the church at Colossae highlights the fact that not only is Christ eternal but He is also Creator of all things. According to Greek scholar A.T. Robertson, "all things were created" has the idea of "stand created" or "remain created." Robertson adds, "The permanence of the universe rests, then, on Christ far more than on gravity. It is a Christ-centric universe."[22]

A third passage that clearly refutes Scientology's view of Jesus is found in the opening of Hebrews.

> God, who at various times and in various ways spoke in time past to the fathers by the prophets, has in these last days spoken to us by His Son, whom He has appointed heir of all things, through whom also He made the worlds; who being the brightness of His glory and the express image of His person, and

---

21. Ibid.
22. David Guzik Commentary, http://www.studylight.org/commentaries/guz/view.cgi?-book=col&chapter=001.

> upholding all things by the word of His power, when He had
> by Himself purged our sins, sat down at the right hand of the
> Majesty on high having become so much better than the angels,
> as He has by inheritance obtained a more excellent name than
> they (Hebrews 1:1–4).

God spoke through the prophets by means of parables, poetry, historical narrative, psalms, proverbs, and prophetic confrontation. God chose to pronounce His message through a time span of 1,600 years and 40 different authors reflecting different locations, times, cultures, and situations. What was the message? Even in the midst of the failure of Israel, God would redeem them through a perfect Savior.

From the very Fall of mankind, God had promised to send a Savior to restore the corruption that entered through sin. God would preserve the seed promised in Genesis 3:15: "And I will put enmity between you and the woman, and between your seed and her Seed; He shall bruise your head, and you shall bruise His heel." Throughout the narrative of the Old Testament, God promises once and for all through His Son's death and Resurrection to deliver His people from sin.

The Jews understood the "last days" to mean the time when the Messiah would come. Although it can be said that Jesus had a message from the Father, even truer is the statement that HE IS the message from the Father. The author of Hebrews also says Jesus has been "appointed heir of all things," showing that Jesus has been given the authority to save and to judge.

The author of Hebrews further states that Jesus Christ is the Creator of all things. He made the worlds. This statement is damaging to the view that Christ is not fully God since Scripture states He is "the brightness of His glory and express image of His person." The Greek denotes the radiance shining forth from a source of light. The idea of exact likeness as made by a stamp is reference to Christ being of the same substance as God. Both of these expressions point clearly to the deity of Christ.

When we read that Jesus is "upholding all things by the word of His power," we see that He is maintaining or actively sustaining the universe. We see this manifested in the ministry of Jesus Christ, as He is able to heal, forgive sins, cast out demons, and calm nature's fury.

Another comparison is that of Christ vs. all other religious leaders. All of them, including L. Ron Hubbard, Joseph Smith, Charles Taze Russell,

Muhammad, Buddha, and so forth, died. Jesus did too, but unlike these others, Jesus resurrected. Jesus, being God, had the power to lay down His life and take it up again.

> Therefore My Father loves Me, because I lay down My life that I may take it again. No one takes it from Me, but I lay it down of Myself. I have power to lay it down, and I have power to take it again. This command I have received from My Father (John 10:17–18).

Only Christ has power over death as proved by His Resurrection. Only He is in a position to inform us what happens after death.

For all of Hubbard's teachings that through one's self they can solve their problems, everyone still dies — even Scientologists. Those in scientology, even its founder, could not conquer death. Ron Hubbard finally died of a stroke. According to the Bible, death is a punishment for sin as far back as the first sin with Adam and Eve in Genesis 3 (see also Genesis 2:17 and Romans 5:12).

View of Man and Sin

Scientologists believe that "man is basically good."

> A fundamental tenet of Scientology is that Man is basically good; that he is seeking to survive; and that his survival depends upon himself and upon his fellows and his attainment of brotherhood with the universe. However, his experiences in the physical universe, through many lifetimes, have led him into evil, where he has committed harmful acts or sins, causing him to become *aberrated* (departing from rational thought or behavior). These harmful acts further reduce Man's awareness and innate goodness as a spiritual being.
>
> Through Scientology, one confronts these acts, erases the ignorance and aberration which surrounds them, and comes to know and experience truth again.
>
> All religions seek truth. Freedom of the spirit is only to be found on the road to truth. Sin is composed, according to Scientology, of lies and hidden actions and is therefore untruth.[23]

---

23. "Does Scientology Believe Man Is Sinful?" Scientology.org, accessed August 23, 2016, http://www.scientology.org/faq/scientology-beliefs/does-scientology-believe-man-is-sinful.html.

This raises the question of who defines "good." By what standard is something good or bad in this religion? Scientologists consider things that are constructive and enhance survival as good and things that are destructive as evil. The exact outworking of one's actions in light of the Eight Dynamics is determined by the individual, so there is no absolute view of right and wrong.

Scientology, like Eastern religions, also holds to a form of reincarnation, though it is slightly different. They have a varied understanding of the soul (which they call a *thetan*) that endured countless lifetimes. They also hold to a multitude of races of mankind.

Each person is seen as a spirit or thetan (what makes you, you) that has a mind (the expression of thoughts and emotions) and inhabits a body (a temporary physical expression of the self). Hubbard described the odd account of the origin of man in *Scientology: A History of Man*. The book has gone through several editions, but the history of the thetans and their origin on alien planets and subsequent evolution is described in detail. The engrams of trauma in these previous lives hinders survivability and must be removed through auditing. These ideas are solely the product of Hubbard's imagination and have no foundation in any facts. As such, his teaching has been ridiculed by many people.

Contrary to the teachings of the Church of Scientology, Scripture paints a completely different narrative regarding man's origin and nature and the nature of sin. Man was made by a perfect God in original perfection (Genesis 1:26–27, 31; Deuteronomy 32:4). We were made in the image of the God who created us. Man's original perfection was marred when Adam and Eve, the first two people and our direct ancestors, sinned (Genesis 3). Thus, we die and are in need of a Savior. Morally, mentally, and socially, man fell into sin and had to deal with a Curse upon the ground for man's sake (Genesis 3:17). This culminates in death (Romans 5:12), which results in the second death (e.g., Revelation 21:8) if we do not get saved from death and sin through Jesus Christ, who is the ultimate substitutionary atonement for our sin (1 Peter 2:24).

In Genesis 3, man goes from a having a perfect relationship with God and a perfect nature, to a relationship which is severed and a nature that is sinful. Genesis 3 describes this historical account of the Fall. Genesis 3:6–7 states:

> So when the woman saw that the tree was good for food,
> that it was pleasant to the eyes, and a tree desirable to make one

wise, she took of its fruit and ate. She also gave to her husband with her, and he ate. Then the eyes of both of them were opened, and they knew that they were naked; and they sewed fig leaves together and made themselves coverings.

In Romans chapter 5, Paul ties this account into his reasoning on the topic of justification by faith through grace, which is found in Christ.

> Therefore, just as through one man sin entered the world, and death through sin, and thus death spread to all men, because all sinned — (For until the law sin was in the world, but sin is not imputed when there is no law. Nevertheless death reigned from Adam to Moses, even over those who had not sinned according to the likeness of the transgression of Adam, who is a type of Him who was to come. But the free gift is not like the offense. For if by the one man's offense many died, much more the grace of God and the gift by the grace of the one Man, Jesus Christ, abounded to many. And the gift is not like that which came through the one who sinned. For the judgment which came from one offense resulted in condemnation, but the free gift which came from many offenses resulted in justification. For if by the one man's offense death reigned through the one, much more those who receive abundance of grace and of the gift of righteousness will reign in life through the One, Jesus Christ.) Therefore, as through one man's offense judgment came to all men, resulting in condemnation, even so through one Man's righteous act the free gift came to all men, resulting in justification of life. For as by one man's disobedience many were made sinners, so also by one Man's obedience many will be made righteous. Moreover the law entered that the offense might abound. But where sin abounded, grace abounded much more, so that as sin reigned in death, even so grace might reign through righteousness to eternal life through Jesus Christ our Lord (Romans 5:12–21).

In a moment, Adam's disposition changed from absolute worship of God to whatever his sinful heart desired. Throughout the Old and New Testament, the authors of Scripture paint a narrative not only of the sinful condition of man but his actions, which show that he has a fallen nature. In the Old

Testament, God implemented a sacrificial system to remind us of the need for a sacrifice and to point to the One who would redeem mankind from their sin. In the New Testament, we have the ultimate and final sacrifice in the crucifixion of Christ on a Cross to show the need for God's wrath to be satisfied. Christ, being God, was an acceptable sacrifice to endure the punishment from God the Father. Jesus said:

> Therefore My Father loves Me, because I lay down My life that I may take it again. No one takes it from Me, but I lay it down of Myself. I have power to lay it down, and I have power to take it again. This command I have received from My Father (John 10:17–18).

Upon death, God will judge man based on His Word. Those who die without receiving Christ, who covers all our sin with His death, burial, and Resurrection, will die an eternal death in hell (described as eternal fire). There will be no rest from this punishment.

God reveals to us, out of His infinite knowledge, that man's heart is deceitful and wicked (Genesis 8:21; Jeremiah 17:9). Since sin came into the world, our hearts and minds have been corrupted and can only be set free through the Lord Jesus Christ.

Yet the entirety of Scientology comes from the mind and actions of one man, L. Ron Hubbard. The authority of God has been replaced with authority in a man. Thus, in the simplest sense, it is merely a variant form of humanism. But man is not the authority. Even God writes of man:

> Stop regarding man in whose nostrils is breath, for of what account is he? (Isaiah 2:22; ESV).

View of Creation

As with any religion, Scientology has an explanation for the origin of the physical universe.

> In Scientology, this view flows from the theory of theta (the life force, or spirit) creating MEST (a coined word for the physical universe, Matter, Energy, Space and Time). In fact, it could be said that the creation of the universe is an inseparable part of that theory. The origins of theta and the creation of the

physical universe set forth in Scientology are described in *The Factors*, written by L. Ron Hubbard in 1953.[24]

Theta is expressed as an impersonal force or spirit manifested in individual thetans which created the physical universe. The thetan is the impersonal creator or god for Scientology (hence the name Thetanism is sometimes used).

Scientologists recognize that a god exists and this god is mentioned twice in the Creed of the Church of Scientology.[25] *The Thetan* (original) is claimed to be the creator, but this is not to be confused with the *Operating Thetan*, which is a level a person can supposedly achieve and then is able to study the advanced materials of Hubbard. Even so, it is tricky to understand as *one is a thetan* and doesn't *have a thetan*, somewhat equivalent to the soul or spirit of a man. Even so, when "God" is mentioned in scientology, it is referring to one moving "toward existence as infinity."[26]

The age of the earth is not addressed by the Church of Scientology specifically on their website. However, tidbits on their website reveal they believe in an older earth, as opposed to the biblical age of the earth. For example, they write, "Based upon the tradition of fifty thousand years of thinking men, Scientology beliefs are built upon the fundamental truths of life."[27]

Couple this with their view of nearly infinite past lives for individuals makes for a very old existence. So the concept of millions and billions of years is a common factor among scientologists. Hubbard dates some of the early events in his creation myth to a quadrillion years in the past. So naturally you can see the friction between Scientology's origins account and six-day creation as described in the Bible. Curiously, Hubbard once wrote, "Dianetics is a science; as such, it has no opinion about religion, for sciences are based on natural laws, not on opinions."[28]

---

24. "What Are Scientology Religious Beliefs about the Creation of the Universe?" Scientology.org, accessed July 18, 2016, http://www.scientology.org/faq/scientology-beliefs/what-are-scientology-religious-beliefs-about-creation-of-the-universe.html.

25. "The Creed of the Church of Scientology," Scientology.org, accessed July 18, 2016, http://www.scientology.org/what-is-scientology/the-scientology-creeds-and-codes/the-creed-of-the-church.html.

26. "Does Scientology Have a Concept of God?" Scientology.org, accessed July 18, 2016, http://www.scientology.org/faq/scientology-beliefs/what-is-the-concept-of-god-in-scientology.html.

27. "Scientology Beliefs," Scientology.org, accessed July 18, 2016, http://www.scientology.org/faq/scientology-beliefs.html.

28. L. Ron Hubbard, "Dianetic Auditor's Bulletin," October issue, 1950; see also https://sites.google.com/site/scientologyschafftunsab/scientology-is-not-a-religion.

In the Internet age, however, many details have come to light about Hubbard's origins account. It is clearly in conflict with the Bible's account of material creation.

Salvation

There are many erroneous beliefs built into the Church of Scientology regarding salvation. The first issue is the problem of reincarnation.

> The orthodox Hindu idea of reincarnation teaches that when you die, your soul does not go to heaven or hell. Instead, you soul goes into some other kind of body here on earth. This body can be an insect, fish, animal or human body. [29]

Scientologists prefer to use rebirth instead of reincarnation to describe their means for salvation even though reincarnation is included in many of their teachings. Hubbard believed that the way to salvation is to end the continuous cycle of birth and rebirth — a distinctive of Eastern religions. The key to the Scientologist view of salvation is the idea of "auditing."

> One of the fundamental principles of scientology is that a person can improve his condition only if he is allowed to find his own truth about himself. In Scientology, this is accomplished through auditing. Auditing is the process of asking specifically worded questions designed to help and find areas of distress. This is done with an auditor, meaning one who listens. An auditor does not offer solutions or advice. They are trained to listen and help you locate experiences that need to be addressed. But some experiences are so deeply buried in the mind, they are not easily recalled. The auditor helps you pinpoint these with an aid of an "e" meter. If you think of something that has upset or has stress connected to it, this shows up on the meter. Your attention can now be directed to that thought. Through auditing, one is able to look at their own existence and discover the past experiences that are holding them back against their will. [30]

---

29. Kirk Cameron and Ray Comfort, "Reincarnation," in *The School of Biblical Evangelism: 101 Lessons: How to Share Your Faith Simply, Effectively, Biblically — the Way Jesus Did*, 1st ed. Vol. 1 (Alachua, FL: Bridge-Logos Publishers, 2004), p. 511.

30. "What Is Auditing?" Scientology.org, accessed July 18, 2016, http://www.scientology.org/faq/scientology-and-dianetics-auditing/what-is-auditing.html.

Many cultists realized a system that teaches that people can be reincarnated into animal or insect would not appeal to Western thought, so they decided to change the concept.

> Using the Western concepts of evolution and progress, they taught that through reincarnation the soul always progressively evolves up the scale of being. Thus you cannot regress back into an insect or animal body once you have reached the human stage. You are either born into another human body or you are absorbed back into oneness depending on your karma.[31]

Karma is the teaching that your present condition in life is a result of your actions from a previous life. Scripture answers the question of reincarnation with two important passages found in the Gospel of John. In chapter 3 which is a familiar account among people who are saved and not saved, a Pharisee named Nicodemus wants to have a meeting with Jesus. He was an influential and educated leader within the Sanhedrin. He comes to Jesus by night and begins the conversation with a startling statement for a Pharisee. He says "Rabbi, we know that You are a teacher come from God; for no one can do these signs that You do unless God is with him" (John 3:2).

Multiple times throughout His ministry, Jesus's miracles were discredited by the Pharisees and even attributed as works of Satan. Following this confession, Jesus makes an even greater statement that confused Nicodemus. Jesus said, "Most assuredly, I say to you, unless one is born again, he cannot see the kingdom of God" (John 3:3).

Nicodemus's confusion is further illustrated when he asked Jesus in verse 4, "How can a man be born when he is old? Can he enter a second time into his mother's womb and be born?" Jesus was not referring to a physical rebirth or reincarnation. He was referring to a state of regeneration. The word translated "born again" literally means "to be born from above." Jesus was telling this man Nicodemus that the only way to achieve salvation was to have a change of heart through faith in God.

Another passage in Scripture which attacks the idea of reincarnation and karma is found in John chapter 9 where Jesus heals a blind man. As Jesus passes the blind man with his disciples, they ask, "Rabbi, who sinned, this man or his parents, that he was born blind?" (v. 1).

---

31. Cameron and Comfort, "Reincarnation," in *The School of Biblical Evangelism*, p. 511.

In our Western culture, we might think this to be an insensitive remark, however, it was a common belief among the Jews that physical illness resulted from sin. It isn't necessarily the same definition of karma, but the implications are the same. Jesus corrected His disciples and told them this was done for God's glory. The reason this man was blind was not due to a personal sin, his parent's sin, or any other circumstance. He was experiencing the results of the Fall, and Jesus was going to give the man a new nature beginning with the healing of his blindness.

The second problem in their view of salvation is the idea that there can be multiple lifetimes to correct past behavior. In the process of auditing, a person is mentored as they look into their "history" to discern the conditions that have put them in their current condition. This is done through the help of an E-meter that pinpoints areas that are causing stress in their lives. As an individual processes these events and frees themselves of the influence of implants or engrams experienced in previous lives or the present life, they advance toward a state of "clear." To be clear is to free one's "reactive mind" from any engrams that cause anxiety as well as toxins that impair the physical body.

Much like a pastor would guide a Christian in dealing with indwelling sin, an auditor assists in understanding the principles of affinity, reality, and communication (represented as an ARC triangle) to become clear. At this point, the secretive teachings of the Operative Thetan levels are studied to advance in understanding toward the Eighth Dynamic and spiritual freedom. There is no concept of a future state of heaven or hell, only spiritual freedom in a future that is built through right actions and thinking in the present.

The Bible paints a completely different narrative in regard to past lifetimes. There is only mention of the current life and the brevity of it. Hebrews 9:27 states, "And as it is appointed for men to die once, but after this the judgment." Another passage is found in Luke chapter 16 in the Parable of the Rich Man and Lazarus. While the rich man enjoyed the luxuries of life, Lazarus was confined to the gate where he would beg for the crumbs that fell from the rich man's table.

On the other side of eternity, the rich man makes a request of Abraham. The dialogue goes:

> "I beg you therefore, father, that you would send him to
> my father's house, for I have five brothers, that he may testify

to them, lest they also come to this place of torment." Abraham said to him, "They have Moses and the prophets; let them hear them." And he said, "No, father Abraham; but if one goes to them from the dead, they will repent." But he said to him, "If they do not hear Moses and the prophets, neither will they be persuaded though one rise from the dead" (Luke 16:27–31).

Both these passages affirm the teaching of the Bible that an individual only has their current life to trust through saving faith in Christ. Our existence today is the only one we have known and the only one we will ever live. After our time on earth has been completed, we will stand in judgment before God to give an account of our lives.

Conclusion

The Church of Scientology shares the same worldview as all the false religions of the world. They share in a rejection of the deity of Christ and His offer of salvation as being the only acceptable way of being right with God, the Bible as the only word of God, eternal judgment, and absolute authority. Scientologists have a pluralistic belief system that allows the individual to embrace whatever lifestyle they choose in order to make them happy.

> The goal of Scientology is making the individual capable of living a better life in his own estimation and with his fellows. Although such a statement may seem simple and modest, the ramifications are immense and embody the dream of every religion; the attainment of complete and total rehabilitation of man's native, but long obscured abilities — abilities that place him at knowing cause over matter, energy, space, time, form, thought and life. Yet even well before one reaches this state, the changes Scientology can bring are profound. Personal relationships can be repaired or revitalized. Personal goals can be realized and happiness restored. Where once there were doubts and inhibitions, there can be certainty and self-confidence. Where once there had been unhappiness and confusion, there can be joy and clarity.[32]

In contrast, the Bible tells us that "There is a way that seems right to a man, but its end is the way of death" (Proverbs 14:12), and it calls us to repentance

---

32. "The Bridge to a Better Life," In *What Is Scientology?: The Comprehensive Reference on the World's Fastest Growing Religion* (Los Angeles, CA: Bridge Publications, 1992). p. 173.

and faith in Christ, because we have sinned against a holy God. We are called to be reconciled to God (2 Corinthians 5:20–21) through Christ, and we would call all those in the Church of Scientology to do the same.

Summary of Scientology Beliefs[33]

Doctrine	Teachings of Scientology
God	Deny the existence of the biblical God, but believe in a supreme force (*theta*) and manifestations of that force (*thetan*). The Eighth Dynamic is the infinite expression of the Supreme Being. Reject Jesus as anything more than a good man.
Authority/ Revelation	The writings of L. Ron Hubbard, especially *Dianetics*.
Man	All men are basically good. The self is a *thetan* that has a mind and inhabits a body.
Sin	Sin is anything that leads to destruction or inhibits survivability, though each person must determine what constitutes wrong actions and truth for themselves.
Salvation	The *thetan* is impaired by engrams that must be removed through auditing so that the *thetan* can achieve spiritual freedom. There is no concept of heaven or hell.
Creation	MEST (matter, energy, space, and time) was created by *thetans* at some point beyond a quadrillion years ago. The creation of worlds and humans reads like a science fiction novel including alien life and other planets.

33. *One God, Many Gods: Bible Studies for Postmodern Times,* Student/Stdy Gd edition (St. Louis, MO: Concordia Publishing House, 1998), p. 72.

Chapter 7

Communism: The Failed Social Experiment

Dr. Nathan Merrill

"The control of the production of wealth is the control of human life itself." — Hilaire Belloc

As the summer heat faded in 1989, the Autumn Revolutions of Eastern Europe began to dismantle the most bellicose socialist economic system to ever govern human civilization. Citizens of the West sat transfixed to their television sets, watching as the Germans tore down the Berlin Wall, the Romanians executed their dictator, and the USSR dissolved into the Commonwealth of Independent States. Undoubtedly, communism had failed.

The Communist utopia — a society of equality and abundance for all — was never realized; there was only equal poverty for the greater populace and lavish abundance for the privileged few. The chief reason for this epic failure was communism's mistaken worldview. The errors are plentiful because the philosophical foundation of communism misunderstands the true nature of man and denies the supernatural. Thus, it is manifestly different than Christianity, which acknowledges the existence of the supernatural and correctly apprehends man's true nature. The philosophical incongruences are numerous, the chief of which will be highlighted in this chapter.

Communism, as many Enlightenment Age ideas are, is rooted in philosophical humanism. Humanism teaches that man alone can bring about an earthly utopia if only inequality and oppression are abolished. Karl Marx, the father of communism, springboards off this notion to formulate the Communist ideology. He postulated an economic system that would abolish the economic divide between the rich and poor. Society would be forced to distribute its wealth equally among all its people. Each person would receive a comparable wage (no matter the amount of time or effort labored), possess a similar size house, receive equal amounts of food, have equivalent amenities, etc. Thus, there would be no more rich or poor.

The above pictures, taken by this author in his hometown of Sibiu, Romania, depict the vast economic inequality between the greater populace (left picture) and the Communist leaders (right picture). The building on the left is where a normal citizen of the Communist state would reside. The state gave each family a small, unremarkable apartment within one of these buildings. All the apartments were basically the same size and layout. The large house on the right is where a Communist official in Sibiu, Romania, once lived. The Communist leaders generally lived in lavish residences in this most desirable part of the city.

Communism's Metaphysical Incongruencies with Christianity

Atheism Is Incongruent with Christianity

Though Marx posited an egalitarian society, he ended up creating an economic system of equal poverty for the greater populace and lavish abundance for the privileged few. This is because he presupposed the erroneous worldview of philosophical materialism. Materialism posits that matter is the elemental building block of reality; all processes and phenomenon, including feelings, thought, will, etc., are ultimately the result of material agencies.[1] There is no Supreme Being or supernatural realm. Man was created via natural processes without purpose or cause. He lives life merely to fulfill his animal instincts and to ensure the propagation of his species. Atheism and evolution are core doctrines of communism. Thus, communism is fundamentally contrary to Christianity. Christians believe man was created by a personal God for God's glory (Isaiah 43:7). Moreover, no Christian can deny God and the supernatural realm since these are the central tenets of its teaching.

Furthermore, the atheism of communism is not of the benign philosophical type (traditional atheism). It is a militant atheism which persecutes religious followers (new atheism). Communist regimes have razed thousands of religious buildings, banned religious gatherings, censored religious books, and imprisoned and murdered religious leaders. Vladimir Lenin, the father of Soviet communism, wrote:

> We must combat religion — that is the ABC of *all* materialism, and consequently of Marxism. But Marxism is not a materialism which has stopped at the ABC. Marxism goes further. It says: We must *know how* to combat religion, and in order to do so we must explain the source of faith and religion among the masses *in a materialist way*. The combating of religion cannot be confined to abstract ideological preaching, and it must not be reduced to such preaching. It must be linked up with the concrete practice of the class movement, which aims at eliminating the social roots of religion. . . . And so: "Down with religion and long live atheism; the dissemination of atheist views is our chief task!"[2]

Communism, being a totalitarian system, views religion as a threat (all religious views but its own, of course). It calls for undivided allegiance from its subjects. There can be no higher cause above the Communist state. Since religions teach a higher allegiance than the state, in the Communist mind

---

1. Merriam-Webster Online, s.v. "Materialism," accessed December 1, 2014, http://www.merriam-webster.com/dictionary/materialism.
2. Vladimir Ilyich Lenin, *The Attitude of the Workers' Party to Religion*, Marxist Internet Archive, accessed December 1, 2014, http://www.marxists.org/archive/lenin/works/1909/may/13.htm.

they usurp the authority of the state. Religion for the Communist is like an "opiate" by which the bourgeois control the masses in order to protect their interest.[3] Thus, religion is seen as an obstacle, since the Communist regime alone must wield the power to ensure a classless society. The regime must either utterly control a said religion or eradicate it.

Communism Denies the Depravity of Man

Communism, deeply entrenched in humanistic ideology, envisages a future earthly utopia. Unlike Christianity, however, this utopian dream is not brought about by a sovereign God. It is the result of a group of exceptionally benevolent, elite human planners who supposedly can foresee and understand all the contingencies involved in effectuating a human paradise.[4] This conception of an earthly utopia occasioned by munificent social organizers (the governing body of a Communist State) presupposes the essential goodness of the human nature. It is a direct contrast to Christianity, which teaches the depravity of mankind due to sin. For example, the prophet Micah states:

> The faithful man has perished from the earth, and there is no one upright among men. They all lie in wait for blood; every man hunts his brother with a net. That they may successfully do evil with both hands — the prince asks for gifts, the judge seeks a bribe, and the great man utters his evil desire; so they scheme together. The best of them is like a brier; the most upright is sharper than a thorn hedge; the day of your watchman and your punishment comes; now shall be their perplexity (Micah 7:2–4).[5]

Thus, men — as magnanimous as they may be — will only usher in pain and destruction; God alone can establish an earthly utopia as will be done with a new heavens and a new earth (Revelation 21:1) where the Curse has been removed (Genesis 3:14–17; Revelation 22:3).

Communism Denies the Dignity of Man

Though communism holds a few human beings to be exceptional (elite), in reality it denies the dignity of man. It believes man is nothing more than a

---

3. Karl Marx, *Deutsch-Französische Jahrbücher*, Marxist Internet Archive, accessed December 1, 2014, https://www.marxists.org/archive/marx/works/1843/critique-hpr/intro.htm.

4. Ronald H. Nash, *Poverty and Wealth: Why Socialism Doesn't Work* (Richardson, TX.: Probe Books, 1986), p. 68.

5. Consider also Genesis 8:21 and Jeremiah 17:9.

This highlights how *un-utopian* communism really is. The common citizens wait in long lines to get food for their families (left picture). Moreover, they are only rationed a certain amount of food per week (right picture: a ration card from communist-era Romania). Food outside the common staples, luxury items, and other non-essential commodities are scarce and hardly ever obtained by the common citizen. (Wikimedia; left photo: Scott Edelman)

cog in a machine to be shaped and discarded at will by the "all-wise" state.[6] Men have value only as part of the collective whole. They have no individual liberty, will, or self-worth. Once they cease to be useful for the collective cause they are no longer of any consequence. Thus, according to the arbitrary assertions of Communist theory, there is no room for individuality or personal liberty. Trofimov stated:

> In the Soviet Union under the guidance of the Ail-Union Communist Party (B.) a new type of man is being shaped — the man of Communist society. . . . He is not an individualist sealing himself up in a shell, and therefore he is not poor and empty spiritually. Soviet man has been fused with the whole people and the socialist fatherland.[7]

Hence, a man's value is merged with that of the Communist state. There is consequently marked ambivalence toward improving the individual's standard of living. For example, within Communist countries, housing is often

6. Mary E. Ali, *Through Three Miracles . . . Pulling the Sail in Together and Resetting "the Middle of the Political Spectrum"* (Pittsburgh, PA: Dorrance Publishing, 2013), p. 24.

7. P. Trofimov. "Edinstvo Eticheskikh i Estetichekikh Printzipov v Sovietskom Iskusstvo" ("Unity of Ethical and Aesthetical Principles in Soviet Art"), Bolshevik, No, 18 (1950): 34. as cited from Dr. Kazys Gečys, "Communist Ethics," accessed December 1, 2014, http://www.lituanus.org/1955/55_23_03Gecys.htm.

inadequate, personal possessions are few, and wages are meager. No solution is ever proposed to alleviate the long food lines. There is no such thing as workplace safety. Roads, houses, and other structures are ill designed. Services are poorly rendered and goods are shoddily manufactured. There is little time for entertainment or self-advancement because it is spent in advancing the goals of the Communist Party.[8]

This materialist view of man is utterly amiss. The Bible proclaims that human life is sacred. Individuals are not mere pawns of the state to be used and disposed of at will. They have individual freedom and self-worth. Their value is not determined by their role within the collective. Human dignity is innate; it is endowed by God because man is created in His image with special care and forethought (Genesis 1:26–27). The Psalmist writes:

> For You formed my inward parts; You covered me in my mother's womb. I will praise You, for I am fearfully and wonderfully made; marvelous are Your works, and that my soul knows very well. My frame was not hidden from You, when I was made in secret, and skillfully wrought in the lowest parts of the earth. Your eyes saw my substance, being yet unformed. And in Your book they all were written, the days fashioned for me, when as yet there were none of them (Psalm. 139:13–16).

Thus, humans, created in God's image, are to be served by the state, not exploited by it as a means to achieve the Communist utopia.

Communism Denies Private Property

In connection with denying the dignity of man, communism dictates the abolition of private property. Marx regarded private property as a great detriment to society. He believed it spawned the pernicious class struggle between the rich and poor; hence, the first mandate of his *Communist Manifesto* stipulated the "abolition of property in land and application of all rents of land to public purposes."[9] The second mandate appealed to the "abolition of all right of inheritance."[10] Acknowledgement of private property and

---

8. David A. Law, *Russian Civilization* (New York: MSS Information Corp., 1975), p. 138–39.
9. Karl Marx and Friedrich Engels, *Communist Manifesto*, Marxist Internet Archive, accessed December 2, 2014, https://www.marxists.org/archive/marx/works/1848/communist-manifesto/ch02.htm.
10. Ibid.

inheritance laws are fundamental to the biblical ethic. The confiscation of private property by state is a blatant violation of the biblical commands "you shall not steal" and "you shall not covet" (Exodus 20:15, 17). Moreover, these commandments become irrelevant without private ownership.

Christianity's influence on a society safeguards private ownership for institutions, families, and individuals. It reinforces inheritance practices (Numbers 27:6–11), exhorts individuals toward good stewardship, and makes laws against robbery and covetousness. By abolishing private property, communism disavows God's pre-ordained structure for society. Furthermore, the domination of all property rights in a sense equates the state with God himself; God is the sovereign owner of creation not the state. If God endows men with property and safeguards it via biblical mandates (Deuteronomy 27:17; Ezekiel 46:18), who is the state to alter this divine establishment?

Communism's Ethical Incongruencies with Christianity

In addition to being at variance with Christianity regarding the views of God and the nature of man, communism also differs ethically. It adheres to a form of ethical relativism which teaches right and wrong are determined by that which is most expedient for effecting a classless society. Lenin explained to a group of Communist youth:

> Communist morality is based on the struggle for the consolidation and completion of communism. . . . [It] is what serves to destroy the old exploiting society and to unite all the working people around the proletariat, which is building up a new, communist society.[11]

For the Communist, the end justifies the means. Hence, it is admissible in their ethical system to use any means necessary to achieve the Communist utopia. For example, Lenin declared one "must be ready to employ trickery, deceit, law-breaking, withholding and concealing truth. There are no morals in politics. There is only expedience.[12]

For the Communist there are no moral absolutes. Something is deemed moral by the party leaders if it promotes their agenda and immoral if it hinders it.

---

11. Vladimir Lenin, *On Culture and Cultural Revolution* (Rockville, MD: Wildside Press LLC, 2008), p. 137,139.
12. Oleg Kalugin, *Spymaster* (New York: Basic Books, 2009), p. 297.

Christianity, on the other hand, espouses moral absolutism. It argues that right and wrong are such because God's immutable nature makes them so. "All His precepts are sure. They stand fast forever and ever" (Psalm 111:7–8). Thus, Christianity posits an ethical system of moral absolutes. It does not propound that the end justifies the means as does communism. Something is moral or immoral because God makes it such (if it agrees or disagrees with His nature and subsequent law), not because it is expedient for a given cause.

The disparity between the ethical systems of communism and Christianity is clearly illustrated in how they operate practically within society. For example, communism promotes hatred, violence, coercion, and deceit to accomplish its objective, i.e., the classless society.[13] One must trample on the enemy to attain victory and retain power. Lenin explains, "The revolutionary dictatorship of the proletariat is rule won, and maintained, by the use of violence, by the proletariat, against the bourgeoisie, rule that is unrestricted by any laws."[14] Furthermore, "if you exploiters attempt to offer resistance to our proletarian revolution we shall ruthlessly suppress you; we shall deprive you of all rights; more than that, we shall not give you any bread, for in our proletarian republic the exploiters will have no rights, they will be deprived of fire and water, for we are socialists in real earnest, and not in the Scheidemann or Kautsky fashion."[15] So communism declares one must be hard and merciless when it comes to defeating the enemy.

Christianity, on the contrary, advocates love for one's enemies. Christ urges his followers to love their enemies and "do good to those who hate you" (Luke 6:27). Likewise, the Apostle Paul exhorts the Church to "be kind to one another, tenderhearted, forgiving one another, even as God in Christ forgave you (Ephesians 4:32). Thus, the ethical difference between communism and Christianity is clear. Communism adopts whatever means necessary — even hatred and ruthless violence — to achieve its ends. Christianity charges its followers to abide by peace and love no matter the cause.

Despite the obvious ethical differences between Christianity and communism, some still regard Christianity and communism to be morally

---

13. Nash, *Poverty and Wealth: Why Socialism Doesn't Work*, p. 64.
14. Vladimir Lenin, "How Kautsky Turned Marx Into a Common Liberal," in *The Proletarian Revolution and the Renegade Kautsky*, Marxist Internet Archive, accessed December 2, 2014, http://www.marxists.org/archive/lenin/works/1918/prrk/.
15. Ibid., "The Soviet Constitution."

compatible since they both share a concern for humanity. Communism claims to be the defender of the common man, but it has demonstrated otherwise. Indeed, there has been no other political system in human history that has caused so much human misery and bloodshed.[16] It has been variously estimated that communism killed between 85–100 million people in less than 70 years.[17] This unheard of level of violence and destruction is the result of an ethical system that maintains the end justifies the means — even the harshest means.

Some Christians have tried to draw support for communism by referencing the actions of early Christians in Jerusalem. Acts 2:44–45 states:

> Now all who believed were together, and had all things in common, and sold their possessions and goods, and divided them among all, as anyone had need.

However, this was a specific group in a specific area that knew what was going to happen to Jerusalem. It was foretold by Christ of the desolation that would come upon Jerusalem (e.g., Luke 21:20, 13:34–35). So it was wise to sell what you had there and not make life in that place. Better to sell and give to those in need. Plus, the words of the Apostle Peter to Ananias in Acts 5:4 make plain that this was not a mandatory giving up of goods and possessions, but was wholly voluntary by the individual. Soon after this, these Christians were scattered to various places anyway (Acts 8:1–4). So any use of this specified example in the Book of Acts to support a communistic mindset is not the best.

Conclusion

Communism is not merely an economic ideology — it is a religion in that it explains the cause, purpose, and nature of life. The economic aspects are merely an outworking of its inherent humanistic and atheistic religious system. Furthermore, it espouses an ethical code, gives hope for a better tomorrow, and seeks undivided devotion – all hallmarks of religion. Unlike Christianity, which values the individual and preaches love, communism is a somber religion. It devalues the individual and preaches envy, hatred, and violence to achieve its utopian polity. This earthly utopia, how-

---

16. Stéphane Courtois, *The Black Book of Communism: Crimes, Terror, Repression* (Cambridge, MA: Harvard University Press, 1999), p. ix–xx.

17. Ibid., p. 15.

ever, was never realized. In fact, most Communist regimes were toppled in fewer than 90 years after they began because they failed to offer the paradise they had promised. Instead, they brought about equal poverty for the greater populace and lavish abundance for a privileged few. These negative economic results stem from communism's erroneous worldview. Any economic system that begins with a mistaken worldview cannot work practically; it will have severe economic and social ramifications, as seen among Communist states.

Given that communism is a religious system that still affects a major portion of the world's population (China, Cuba, Laos, North Korea, and Vietnam), Christians should be very much interested in understanding it. Its negative implications for God's Kingdom are far-reaching since it denies God and endeavors to completely dominate or eradicate any semblance of organized religion. Christian believers must stand strong against such a system that promotes militant atheism, debases human value, and attempts to spread its materialistic message through hatred and violence.

Summary of Communist Beliefs

Doctrine	Teachings of Communism
God	Deny the existence of God. Man is viewed as the supreme being.
Authority/ Revelation	The writings of various authors are appealed to, though there is no notion of an authoritative revelation.
Man	Man is the measure of all things and basically good. Certain individuals are intended to lead others, but there is broad equality in humanity.
Sin	Sin is not a prominent concept. Right and wrong are relative to achieving the goals of the state.
Salvation	The goal of humanity is to achieve equality. There is no view to an afterlife.
Creation	Most would accept evolutionary views.

Chapter 8

Postmodernism

Dr. Carl J. Broggi

I was recently on an airplane where, as God sometimes allows to happen, the subject of conversation was turned to religion and Christianity. The individual sitting next to me was a pediatrician from Thailand. I asked her if she had ever considered the claims of Jesus Christ upon her life. She said, "There is no need to. All religions are the same." Then she added, "No one can claim that one religion is right and another is wrong. One can believe whatever they wish, as long as they believe it sincerely. All religions can be equally true."

This woman, who said she was a Buddhist, told me that this is what Buddhists have believed for centuries. Her statement reminded me of what God said through King Solomon, "There is nothing new under the sun" (Ecclesiastes 1:9). This perspective, that all religions are equally valid, and that no one can dogmatically say that one religion is more valid than another is known as postmodernism.

This notion, held by this Buddhist physician, is a perspective that many Americans are now embracing.

Postmodernism Defined

Defining postmodernism is a difficult process because the term can be used differently between disciplines. To understand the word, it might be helpful to break it down. Historically, when the word "modern" was used in a philosophical context, it referred to a worldview based on the principles of the Enlightenment. During the 17th and 18th centuries, the Enlightenment emphasized the autonomy of the individual, trust in the power of reason, conviction that human reason is objective, and that truth can be discovered by the rational human mind.[1] The "modern" mindset valued scientific investigation, absolute truth, logical and pragmatic organizations, and orderly surroundings.[2]

For this reason, long-established institutions that were deeply rooted in society, such as religion and the government, began to be questioned. There was a new and greater emphasis being placed on man's ability to reform the world by his own thought, by scientific investigation, and skepticism.[3]

Someone might think, "Well, what is wrong with that? What is wrong with using your mind and using science to determine what is true or false?" Please understand, the Bible is not necessarily against using our minds — it simply recognizes the limitations of human thought. God Himself says, " 'Come now, and let us reason together,' says the Lord" (Isaiah 1:18). Even the casual reader of Scripture is familiar with the Apostle Paul, who when evangelizing the lost people would "reason from the Scriptures" the truths concerning Jesus Christ (Acts 17:2, 18:4). God made us with minds, and in the commandment that the Lord referred to as the greatest of all the commandments He said, "You shall love the Lord your God with all your heart, with all your soul, and with all your mind" (Matthew 22:37).

But the Scriptures also recognize that man's mind is fallen. God tells us that the natural man, someone without a spiritual birth, "does not receive the things of the Spirit of God, for they are foolishness to him; nor can he know them, because they are spiritually discerned" (1 Corinthians 2:14). For the same reason, the Apostle Paul can declare, "For the wisdom of this world is foolishness with God" (1 Corinthians 3:19). This is why he warns us, "Beware lest anyone cheat you through philosophy and empty deceit, according to the tradition of men, according to the basic principles of the world, and not according to Christ" (Colossians 2:8). For this reason, once we receive Christ as our Savior and are given this second birth, making us

---

1. B.E. Benson, "Postmodernism" in *Evangelical Dictionary of Theology*, 2nd ed., ed. Walter A. Elwell (Grand Rapids, MI: Baker Academic, 2001), p. 939–945.
2. Gene Edward Veith Jr., *Postmodern Times: A Christian Guide to Contemporary Thought and Culture* (Wheaton, IL: Crossway Books, 1994), p. 42.
3. Skepticism is the process of applying reason and critical thinking to determine whether something is valid.

new persons inside (2 Corinthians 5:17), we are then commanded to let God renew our minds through the truth of the Scripture (Romans 12:2). The fact that the Bible tells us that our minds need to be renewed informs us that from God's perspective they have been damaged by the Fall.

Logically, most people can understand the principle that all human reasoning is not necessarily good. Hitler, with his reason, believed the Jewish people were an inferior race that needed to be exterminated. While the modernism of the Enlightenment period encouraged people to look to reason and science as a source of authority, if man's mind is fallen, if man's mind is by nature rebellious as the Bible reveals (Romans 3:10–12), then the conclusions one may make from science and reason alone will at times be faulty.

Scientific thought has been proven wrong on many occasions. There was a time when a minority of the scientific world was convinced that the world was flat. In hindsight, it did not matter how confidently they believed and taught it to be true — their position was still erroneous.[4] Modern secular science goes against a literal six-day creation despite the fact that God clearly reveals this truth.[5]

So when we speak of *modernism*, we are referring to a term that goes back to the time of the Enlightenment where man's autonomous reason was considered sovereign.[6] The problem with modernism is that it did not recognize that man's reason must be brought under the authority of the Bible (hence, "autonomous"). Therefore, it is not surprising that today in theological realms, *liberalism*, the rejection of the Bible as the absolute and final authority, was once called *modernism*.[7]

Bible-believing evangelicals recognize that "reason" is valuable in that God has called us to use our minds, but only to the degree that our reasoning process is tempered and corrected by Scripture. Those of us who

---

4. Had they only tempered their scientific discoveries with passages like Isaiah 40:21–22 or Proverbs 8:27 they would have discovered that their scientific conclusions were false.

5. For a good discussion on this subject, see "Could God Have Created Everything in Six Days?" in *The New Answers Book* by Ken Ham, ed., (Green Forest, AR: 2006), p. 88–112; available online at https://answersingenesis.org/days-of-creation/could-god-really-have-created-everything-in-six-days.

6. Essentially, man's ideas were elevated to a position of absolute authority by leaving the Bible out of it. It is a religion where man is basically seen as replacing God.

7. Today, when a person departs from theological orthodoxy, we say that he has embraced theological *liberalism*. Interestingly, during the late 19th century and during the first part of the 20th century, theologians who departed from orthodoxy were said to be guilty of *modernism*. Such people, who have departed from biblical Christianity, place their mind and reason above the authority of the Bible.

believe the Bible to be the inspired, inerrant, and infallible word of God tend to emphasize biblical thinking formed by logical analysis, propositional teaching, and a historical, grammatical interpretation of Bible passages. We embrace theological and moral absolutes as forming the foundation of our faith and typically are unafraid to challenge those who do not fully agree with this perspective.

But while we would say that we have "reasoned our way" to this position, we would also acknowledge that this "reasoning" was not done without the help of the Holy Spirit and apart from submitting any conclusions we have made to the litmus test of Scripture. In other words, we would say that our use of logic and reasoning are still predicated on the ultimate authority of God and His Word. Christ promised this helping ministry of the Spirit when He said, "when He, the Spirit of truth, has come, He will guide you into all truth" (John 16:13). The Holy Spirit's guidance never contradicts the Bible that He Himself inspired. For this reason, the Apostle Paul taught us that conclusions about life and God and the world around us that are contrary to what has been revealed in Scripture, are to be rejected.[8] So while the "modern" of the Enlightenment used his mind, he rejected the Bible as the final authority to guide it. In his thinking, if reason and science dictated the Bible was wrong, then it must be wrong.

So what do we mean by postmodernism and how can we best define the term? As previously stated, it can be difficult to define, and definitions tend to differ. Earl Creps posits that due to its absence of a central, unifying trait, trying to define postmodernism "is like nailing Jell-O to the wall."[9] Students of the social sciences generally agree that there was a shift that began to take place in the way some people began to think as early as the 1930s.[10] While some date postmodernism to the 1930s, most agree that it did not begin to take root in the West and in the United States until the 1960s and '70s, progressing ever since.[11]

Initially, the term "postmodernism" gained popularity as a term used to describe a period of architecture and art that began to emerge especially

---

8. Romans 16:17; 2 Thessalonians 3:14; 1 Timothy 6:3–4.

9. Earl G. Creps, "Moving Target: Reframing Discipleship for Postmoderns," *Enrichment Journal* (Winter 2008), p. 68.

10. For a discussion of this shift, see Stanley J. Grenz, *A Primer on Postmodernism* (Grand Rapids, MI: Eerdmans, 1996), p. 173; see also Heath White, *Postmodernism 101: A First Course for the Curious Christian* (Grand Rapids, MI: Brazos Press, 2006), p. 12–17.

11. Grenz, *A Primer on Postmodernism*, p. 17.

during the 1970s. Many found modern art and modern architecture to be confusing because it seemed to lack a sense of order, rhyme, and reason. By previous standards, this new expression of art and architecture seemed so bizarre, because it had abandoned traditional standards for new ideals. These new "postmodern" standards rejected a previous way of thinking about life based on objectivity and reason.

The Fruit of Modernism

Modernism began to deviate into a man-centered reality (as opposed to a God-centered reality) — postmodernism is like the fruit of this man-centered religion. It goes one more step toward relativism. Where modernism still retained certain aspects of Christianity (such as absolute conclusions) within its parameters, postmodernism tried doing away with any semblance of Christian influence (no absolutes).

Postmodern art and architecture had abandoned all previously held conventional standards in these fields. As a young man, when I would see this new kind of art and architecture, my first reaction was typically, "This is rather odd and confusing to me." The rejection of absolutes — the rejection of being able to rationally define something as acceptable or unacceptable — eventually made its way into the realm of theology.

Postmodernism is a philosophy that says absolute truth, solid concrete values, does not necessarily even exist. Since the postmodernist thinks there is no real valid way to measure truth from error, acceptable from unacceptable, or right from wrong, all beliefs and perspectives are determined to be equally valid. This way of thinking is determinatively different from the way Americans and Westerners have thought in the past.

A survey of research and literature indicates that Americans under the age of 35 have been raised in a postmodern culture, with many having distinctly different values and preferences from those in earlier generations.[12] At least with the person raised under the influence of the Enlightenment, through the process of reason, someone would come to a conclusion. Sometimes, a proper conclusion is made, consistent with the revelation of God in Scripture, and sometimes an improper conclusion. But in either case, a decision could be formulated, such that they would view an opposing decision as wrong.

---

12. Webber, *The Younger Evangelicals*, p. 41.

However, in postmodernism it is argued that each decision is equally valid and that two opposing decisions can be true at the same time.[13] Postmodernism embraces relativism to the highest degree. Relativism is the idea that truth and moral values are not absolute but are relative to the persons or groups holding them.

This means that what is right for one person, may not necessarily be right for another person. Therefore, truth is not really knowable. Truth is whatever you want it to be. This makes truth a moving target. What one believes, what one considers to be right or wrong, is really left up to the individual. I'm OK; you're OK — the famous saying brought to us by the psychology of the past — is an effective mantra for this viewpoint. What is true for you might not be true for me. In the thinking of the postmodernist, no one is really wrong except for those who hold to absolute truth.

But how can they know that those who hold to absolute truth are wrong? Are they absolutely sure? In their religion, there were no absolutes! By their own admission, they can't know the most basic tenant of their own religion! So they are inconsistent and self-refuting at their most basic level. More on this as we progress in the chapter.

The Postmodernist and Tolerance

Today, those who embrace postmodernism ridicule Christianity as intolerant, egotistical, and arrogant because of its exclusive claims about God and morality. To say that there is only one way to heaven through Christ[14] is viewed as intolerant by those who say there are many paths to heaven. To embrace a strict moral code that condemns sexual perversion like homosexuality[15] or sexual permissiveness like fornication or adultery[16] is to be restrictive, judgmental, and lacking sophistication. The battle cry of the postmodernist is a redefined understanding of "tolerance."

Because truth cannot absolutely be known in their religion, the highest virtue for the postmodern man is tolerance, but not as the word has traditionally been defined. In the past, when Americans used the term *tolerance*, it was understood to mean that everyone has a right to have their viewpoint respected. When brought over into the realm of religious belief, while you

---

13. For a discussion of this shift in thought, see Heath White, *Postmodernism 101: A First Course for the Curious Christian*, p. 12–17.
14. Clearly, this is what the Bible teaches in John 14:6 and Acts 4:12.
15. Leviticus 18:22; Romans 1:26–27; 1 Corinthians 6:9–11; 1 Timothy 1:8–10.
16. Exodus 20:14; Matthew 5:27–28; Galatians 5:19; Ephesians 5:3–5; Hebrews 13:4.

might reject someone else's religious system because you believed it was inferior or just wrong, you still allowed that person the right to embrace it. You might even try to convince someone that you believe his or her beliefs are wrong.

Nonetheless, because everyone is made in the image of God and are free moral agents, you recognize they are free to choose and tolerate their choice. However, in the postmodern worldview, no one has a right to say that his or her viewpoint is better or more correct than someone else's point of view (except, of course, the postmodernist who is imposing this belief system on others). "Tolerance" for the postmodernist is to be extended only to those who embrace a relativistic worldview. In practice, since postmodernism cannot possibly coexist with a worldview that embraces absolute truth, they are intolerant of those who do not agree, particularly Christians.

Postmodernism and Biblical Christianity

Some postmodernists argue that evangelical Christians are intolerant, not allowing other positions to exist or express their viewpoints. However, to paint this picture of Bible-believing Christians is utterly incorrect. It is true that in the history of the Church there have been some people who, in the name of Christianity, have not allowed other people to embrace or present their viewpoints. In this sense, such people were truly intolerant. However, what they did was contrary to Scripture, for the Lord Jesus said, "If anyone wills to do His will, he shall know concerning the doctrine, whether it is from God or whether I speak on My own authority" (John 7:17). This statement that Christ made to those who questioned His authority, implies the opportunity to decide for oneself.

Christianity is not intolerant in prohibiting people from considering certain options. But when postmodernists accuse Christians of intolerance, what they really mean is that because Bible-believers insist their point of view concerning moral absolutes and salvation in Jesus Christ is correct and other views are aberrant, they should be defined as intolerant.

Such a premise is a misunderstanding of tolerance. There is a difference between tolerating a belief and refuting it (showing it to be false). It is impossible for two viewpoints that contradict each other to be true.[17] They might

---

17. In formal logic this is known as the law of non-contradiction. Those who adopt a postmodern mindset seem to be comfortable with logical inconsistencies like this one in many situations.

both be false, but they cannot both be true at the same time. Therefore, just because Christ claimed to be the only way to God, and because Christianity maintains that there are moral absolutes, does not by definition make it intolerant. It would only be intolerant if it did not allow people the freedom to believe their viewpoints. The postmodern man will allow the conservative evangelical to have a place at the table for discussion, only if we quit being conservative evangelicals. We must leave Jesus' unique claims, the truth of the gospel, fiat creationism,[18] moral absolutes, and the offensive teaching about hell on the back shelf. In postmodern thought, exclusive claims about Jesus and His work violate the highest virtue of their understanding of tolerance, and so they want it silenced in the name of their religion.

Unfortunately, this kind of thinking has now permeated the university campuses of America. To spend any time in a meaningful discussion with the average college student, you soon discover that this way of thinking is widespread. Today, if you are a Christian on the secular university campus, you will be told that since all viewpoints are equally valid, what is right for one group is not necessarily right or true for someone else.

The most obvious example is sexual morality. For instance, Christianity teaches that marriage is defined as a union between a man and a woman because God created a man and woman. Therefore, by definition homosexual behavior and homosexual "marriage" are wrong.[19] Yet, more and more young Americans who have adopted a postmodern point of view would simply claim that such a position might pertain to some Christians but not to other Christians or to those who do not follow Christ at all. Following this line of thought to its logical conclusion, postmodernism argues that the Judeo-Christian ethic on which our legal system was built, is now antiquated.

18. Millard Erickson, in his systematic theology, defines succinctly the biblical revelation of fiat creationism: "This is the idea that God, by a direct act, brought into being virtually instantaneously everything that is. Note two features of this view. One is the brevity of time involved, and hence the relative recency of what occurred at creation. . . . Another tenet of this view is the idea of direct divine working. God produced the world and everything in it, not by the use of any indirect means or biological mechanisms, but by direct action and contact." Millard Erickson, *Christian Theology* (Grand Rapids, MI: Baker, 1988), p. 479–480).

19. Many who support same-sex "marriage" and the promotion of privileges for gays argue that, since Jesus never mentioned homosexuality, He did not consider it to be sinful. While it is technically true that Jesus did not specifically address homosexuality by name in the Gospel accounts, He did speak clearly about sexuality in general as well as in the rest of His Word (the Bible). In Matthew 19:4–6 Jesus clearly referred to Adam and Eve and affirmed God's intended design for marriage and sexuality.

So it is now maintained that while homosexual behavior was once considered against the law, such statutes should now be considered archaic. There was a time in the recent past when most Americans viewed homosexual behavior as objectionable. Prior to 1962, sodomy was a felony in every state, punished by a lengthy term of imprisonment and/or hard labor.[20]

There was a time in our nation's history when the average American would have had little or no problem with the Apostle Paul's instruction to Timothy, his young pastor protégé in the faith:

> But we know that the law is good if one uses it lawfully, knowing this: that the law is not made for a righteous person, but for the lawless and insubordinate, for the ungodly and for sinners, for the unholy and profane, for murderers of fathers and murderers of mothers, for manslayers, for fornicators, for sodomites, for kidnappers, for liars, for perjurers, and if there is any other thing that is contrary to sound doctrine (1 Timothy 1:8–10).

In this passage, God plainly tells us that laws are to be written not to condone this kind of behavior, but to curb it. However, if you believe that truth is different for each person, which is at the core of postmodernism, then you will favor laws endorsing any lifestyle the individual chooses. History demonstrates, and God's Word illustrates, that when the sin of homosexuality is left unchecked it will destroy a nation and invite the judgment of God.[21] Of course, to group the lifestyle of a homosexual with those that God refers to as *lawless, insubordinate,* and *ungodly* — not to mention *murderers of fathers and murderers of mothers* along with *kidnappers* and *perjurers* — informs us that this behavior is not some genetic predisposition. Just as murder and perjuring oneself and kidnapping are moral issues, so also is homosexuality.

Yet, while God's Word, the Bible, tells us that laws are to be written against this deviant lifestyle, our politicians, who have been influenced by

---

20. For a helpful discussion tracing the sodomy laws in American history and the changes that began to slowly take place after 1962, see Margot Canaday, "We Colonials: Sodomy Laws in America," *The Nation*, September 3, 2008.

21. If someone really wants to understand how God feels about the sin of sodomy, all they need to do is read Genesis chapter 19. In fact, in the New Testament, God uses the judgment that fell on Sodom and Gomorrah as an example of the wrath that is yet to come on all those who reject God's Son (Jude 7).

postmodern thought, have written laws in favor of this behavior. The same could be said concerning the use and legalization of marijuana. Postmodernism is turning our legal system upside-down because those things that were once consider wrong are now being embraced as right.

What Is Truth?

Hours before the Crucifixion, Jesus Christ stood before Pontius Pilate, and, as the Apostle John records:

> Pilate therefore said to Him, "Are You a king then?" Jesus answered, "You say rightly that I am a king. For this cause I was born, and for this cause I have come into the world, that I should bear witness to the truth. Everyone who is of the truth hears My voice." Pilate said to Him, "What is truth?" (John 18:37–38).

Pilate's question, "What is truth?" has reverberated down through history. It does not appear that Pilate was looking to find the answer, but rather was giving a cynical, indifferent, even irritated reply to Jesus' answer. However, if the postmodern man were to attempt to answer Pilate, he would say, "Truth cannot be known definitively — truth is whatever you want it to be." A profound response to that would be, "How do you know that is true?"

Of course, in our day Americans have differing definitions of what truth is, due to the influence of postmodernism. Some would say that truth is whatever works. The pragmatic outlook embraces that the end justifies the means. It is easy to see the fallacy in this line of thinking. For instance, one could lie and accomplish the objective they were trying to achieve, all the while doing it in a non-truthful way. Still, some would argue that truth is whatever makes you feel good. Many people build their morality on this proposition. However, if truth is what makes you feel good, what will the postmodernist do with bad news that one knows to be true but makes them feel miserable?

Others would say that truth is what the majority of people think is correct. Upon a recent visit to Yad Vashem, the World Center for Holocaust Research in Jerusalem, I was reminded again that during World War II, the Jewish people fled to nation after nation, including America, only to be turned away, with no place to go but back to Germany. While the majority of nations embraced the thought that the Jewish people should not be received into their countries, clearly the majority was wrong in light of the peril they faced in Germany.

Postmodernism has also influenced the popular position that truth is based on sincerity. It is reasoned that if you sincerely embrace something, then it is must be true. But if you pause and think about it, you will meet people who are sincere, but sincerely wrong. A person who is wrong but sincere is deceived, like so many in the various cults. Being sincere is not enough. The physician I sat next to in the airplane said, "It doesn't matter what you believe, just as long as you are sincere." Of course, people who say this typically only apply this fallacy to morality and religion, but never to other disciplines like mathematics or mechanics or medicine. They fragment their worldview and apply it selectively. I reminded her of some absolutes that she embraced as a practicing physician, for which she had no argument. I mean, who would want to have a heart surgeon operate on you who thought it did not matter what you believed concerning the function of the heart? Who would want a pediatrician to unnecessarily prescribe an antibiotic for a virus like the common cold because he believed it was best for your child? It doesn't matter how much one sincerely believes a wrong key will fit a door, if it is not the right key, the lock cannot be opened. Truth is unaffected by sincerity.

Someone who picks up a bottle of poison and sincerely believes it is lemonade will still suffer the unfortunate effects of the poison. My pediatrician friend from the airplane was quick to concur that believing two plus two equals five is foolish no matter how sincere you may be. Yet, what is sometimes so mind-boggling is that when it comes to spiritual truth, the one area of life that determines your spiritual destiny, people will tell you to believe whatever you want. Encounters like this serve as constant reminders that we are in a spiritual battle.[22] Indeed, the question Pilate asked, "What is truth?" is a very important question.

I find it interesting that in the Bible the Hebrew word for truth is *emeth* — which literally can be translated as "firmness," "constancy," or as "duration."[23] In other words, truth is something that is rock-solid and unchanging. In the original language of the New Testament, the Greek word for "truth" is *aletheia*, which literally means to "un-hide" or "to reveal."[24] It

---

22. 2 Corinthians 4:4; Ephesians 6:12.
23. See *Strong's Exhaustive Concordance*, #571.
24. For a good discussion on truth versus postmodernism, see B.E. Benson, "Postmodernism," in *Evangelical Dictionary of Theology*, 2nd ed., edited by Walter A. Elwell (Grand Rapids, MI: Baker Academic, 2001), p. 939–945.

conveys the thought that truth is always there, always open and available for all to see, with nothing being hidden or obscured. Unlike the postmodernist's perception of truth, God reveals that truth is knowable and available for those who desire to find it.[25] Truth is simply telling it like it is because truth reflects a sure and certain reality that exists and is unchanging. Truth comes from an unchanging God who is the truth.

Evangelizing the Postmodernist

Remember, the focus of this entire volume is to better equip those reading to become sharper tools in God's hand for breaking through the inaccuracies of our day. We are studying subjects like postmodernism not simply for our own edification, but rather to "always be ready to give a defense to everyone who asks you a reason for the hope that is in you, with meekness and fear" (1 Peter 3:15).

So precisely how do we reach so many who have embraced this faulty way of thinking? Please note, I did not say a *new* way of thinking because there really is nothing new under the sun. This premise of questioning truth, questioning what God has clearly revealed, is as old as the Garden of Eden.[26]

Critical to evangelizing those who are lost is to ask, "Why have they believed postmodernism to begin with?" Generally speaking, people embrace any error about God and morality for one of two reasons. Some are just deceived. In describing Satan, the Lord Jesus said to the Pharisees, "He was a murderer from the beginning, and does not stand in the truth, because there is no truth in him. When he speaks a lie, he speaks from his own resources, for he is a liar and the father of it" (John 8:44). Satan has a very simple strategy, and it is to sow error, that people might believe falsehood and be captured in his kingdom forever.[27] Some embrace postmodernism because the first to reach them deceived them. Unfortunately, many of God's people are not as faithful and fervent in sharing the truth as some of Satan's ambassadors are in sharing error.[28] It is essential that as Christians we are obedient to the Great Commission that Christ has entrusted to us. In many ways, postmodernism appears to be winning because so many of God's people are silent when it comes to sharing the gospel. So first, some

---

25. John 7:17.
26. Genesis 3:1–7.
27. Matthew 13:37–42.
28. 2 Corinthians 11:13–15.

embrace postmodernism simply because they are deceived. And the reason they are deceived is because they have not yet heard the truth, only error.

Still, others embrace postmodernism because they have heard the truth, but have chosen to reject the truth, driven by a love for sin.[29] Somebody once said that first God made us in His image, and ever since we have been returning the compliment. As rebellious sinners, we often like to make God in our image — as we would like Him to be.

The truth of Christianity is inevitably a threat to some because it immediately raises the question, "Who is going to be God in your life?" Some are not willing to admit that as created people, we have no right to tell the Creator what to do.[30] Some are not willing to admit that our hearts are desperately wicked and rebellious and that we need salvation from the coming wrath of God.[31] However, if one believes that they should be the center of their own universe, until their attitude changes, they are not going to consider the claims that Jesus Christ makes on their lives. Some people embrace postmodernism because while they may have understood something about God's truth, they have chosen to suppress that truth, and as a result have believed a lie.[32]

The Apostle Paul describes in the first chapter of Romans the downward progression into error that people take when they refuse to believe what they know in their hearts and minds to be true.[33] In their rebellion against God they "exchanged the truth of God for a lie" and as a result God gives them over, "to uncleanness" and, "to vile passions" and, ultimately, "to a debased mind."[34] The Greek word for "debased" is translated in many languages of the world as, "an upside-down mind."[35] In other words, a rejection of the truth results in a warping of values, where one calls right to be wrong and wrong to be right.[36] People who sin against God's revelation because of a love for sin can easily embrace falsehood.

For such people, postmodernism becomes a coping mechanism of sorts by which they can justify their guilty consciences and their sinful behavior.

---

29. John 3:19–20.
30. Romans 9:19–20.
31. Jeremiah 17:9; Luke 19:12–27.
32. John 12:35–41; 2 Thessalonians 2:8–12.
33. Romans 1:18–32.
34. Romans 1:24, 26, 28.
35. All of the Slavic languages of the world translate the Greek word in this fashion.
36. Our generation would do well to heed the warning of Isaiah 5:20.

The old adage is true, that a man's theology is often dictated by his morality. Nonetheless, people who are caught up in postmodernism are by no means unreachable for Christ. Even after the Apostle Paul gives a long list of sins describing depraved idolatrous behavior, he can still say of such people, "who, knowing the righteous judgment of God, that those who practice such things are deserving of death, not only do the same but also approve of those who practice them" (Romans 1:32).

When evangelizing the lost, we must never forget that even when a person is in the depths of sinful choices, they still do not totally lose the reality that they are sinning against clear absolute standards set by a holy God. We should be encouraged by the fact that even those who have been deceived into thinking that truth is not knowable and morality is relative still know better.

When describing those individuals who had never even read a Bible, God can say of them in Romans chapter 2, "For when Gentiles, who do not have the law, by nature do the things in the law, these, although not having the law, are a law to themselves, who show the work of the law written in their hearts, their conscience also bearing witness, and between themselves their thoughts accusing or else excusing them" (Romans 2:14–15). Gentiles who do not have the written Law or Scripture, nevertheless by nature, "do the things" required by "the Law."

You may be thinking, "How can we explain this paradox that although they do not have the Law, they appear to know it?" Paul's answer is that they "are a law to themselves." Not in the sense that they can frame or make up their own laws, as in postmodernism, such that truth can be whatever one wants it to be. But they, "are a law to themselves" in the sense that their own human person is their "law" because God created them as people with consciences.

Although the Gentiles being described in Romans chapter 2 do not have the Bible "in their hands," they do have some of the requirements of the Bible "in their hearts" because God wrote it there. This is the reason that people innately have a sense of what is right and wrong, what is just and unjust, what is fair and unfair. They understand principles of morality and justice because God wrote His moral dictates into our persons. It is important that we understand this as we attempt to evangelize the postmodern man. I asked the pediatrician on the airplane if she thought it was ok if I broke into her home, murdered her husband and children, and stole all her valuables. She saw my point. All truth is not relative. All truth is not whatever we want it to be. There are some absolutes.

Some Questions to Ask the Postmodernist

When I was in campus ministry working with many a skeptical college student, some who were trying to justify their immoral lifestyle, I was trained to ask three questions about statements students would make that clearly contradicted biblical truth.

First, "How do you know that is true?" Second, "Where do you get your information?" Third, "What if you are wrong?"

How Do You Know That Is True?

In asking this question, you want someone to examine the foundation of why they believe what they believe. For the postmodernist, you are asking them to explain why it is that they think their belief that "truth is not absolute" is correct. Of course, if they give the standard answer that truth cannot be definitively known, you can ask them, "Are you absolutely sure?" If they respond positively, they have revealed the absurdity of their position.

When the postmodernist states that there is no such thing as absolute truth, he is either stating that as an absolute or not. Obviously, if they are stating it as an absolute, then there is absolute truth. Whether his answer is in absolute terms or with a degree of uncertainty, we can still reason with him on the basis of the moral code written in his heart. In addition, we have the promise of the Holy Spirit's help working behind our witness.[37] If they are open to investigating the nature of truth, then you will have the opportunity to present the evidence for why you believe what you believe.[38] The Christian's faith is an issue of fact — God really did enter into human history, and there is either evidence for this or there is not. This is what contrasts Christianity with all the other religions in the world. Virtually all the other religions of the world are based upon an inner faith experience. They are not based on any objective, factual foundation. Knowing, as the Bible teaches, that God has written a sense of eternity into our hearts,[39] I find it helpful to remind people that eternity

---

37. John 16:8.
38. 1 Peter 3:15.
39. Ecclesiastes 3:11.

is for a long, long time. I am trying to help them see that it is at least worth their consideration to examine the objective evidence Christians claim to have.

Where Do You Get Your Information?

A second question I often ask the postmodernist is, "Where do you get your information?" Remember, everything you believe, and everything I believe, is based on something. You either made it up in your mind, someone told you, or possibly you read it in a book somewhere. There is always some basis, some source for an individual embracing the belief system he or she embraces. This becomes a good lead-in to remind them that everything the Christian believes is based on the Bible.

That opens the door for them to ask, "Why should I believe the Bible?" Of course, our argument is that the Bible is the only book on planet Earth that God ever inspired. Think about it, since God actually is the author behind the human authors of Scripture, and since the Bible is the only book God inspired, then it stands to reason that humanity has a reliable standard of absolute truth. Based on this premise, anyone can take any belief they have and look into the mirror of Scripture to see if it is true. If you need help in defending the unique authority of the Bible, you might find helpful the chapter that I authored in the book, *How Do We Know the Bible Is True*.[40]

What If You Are Wrong?

A third question I sometimes ask is, "What if you are wrong?" I finished my time with the physician on my long airplane ride with a challenge. I reminded her that her perspective on God and the afterlife was so broad that, according to her belief system, we could both believe what we believe and we would be just fine when we die. But then I reminded her that my viewpoint, really the Bible's viewpoint, is so narrow that both cannot be true. Jesus did not claim to be a good way to God, or even the best way to God, but the *only* way to God.[41] Unlike in postmodern thought, all roads do not lead to God. If one takes the position that all roads lead to God

---

40. "Why is the Bible Unique?" Dr. Carl J. Broggi, found in *How Do We Know the Bible Is True, Volume 2*, edited by Ken Ham & Bodie Hodge (Green Forest, AR: Master Books, 2012), p. 53.
41. John 14:6.

because all roads can be equally true, then that person is going against the clear teaching of the Bible.

Again, since the Bible is absolutely true, then they are embracing human opinion when they take a position that opposes the Bible. They are basing their eternal outcome on assertions others (mere people) have made, who have no authority to make them, because unlike Jesus Christ, they have not risen from the dead. It is much wiser to put one's faith in the objective evidence of the Resurrection, which demonstrated Christ's deity,[42] and proved His assertion that He is the only way to heaven. Facts are facts, and facts cannot be disputed. For some, their problem is that they are afraid to examine the evidence. However, a wise person will be willing to examine the objective evidence that the Christian faith is built on. Eternity is for a long time, and the Bible reminds us that, someday, "every tongue should confess that Jesus Christ is Lord."[43]

The issue is not whether one will do this, but when one is going to do this. People will either do it now, when it will bring them salvation, or they will do it when it is too late and they are eternally separated from God.[44] This is why the Apostle Peter boldly proclaimed, "Nor is there salvation in any other, for there is no other name under heaven given among men by which we must be saved" (Acts 4:12).

I reminded my physician friend that I was going back to my home in South Carolina and she was headed back to her home in Thailand. She could certainly continue to believe what she believed and never give it another thought. So I challenged her with the question, "What if you are wrong?" You see, if she is right and I am wrong, it really does not matter because, according to her postmodern position, we will both be just fine in the end. According to her belief system, my narrowness will someday be broadened to her perspective, but in either case we both would be just fine. If she is right and I am wrong, it really does not matter.

However, I reminded her, if I am right and she is wrong, then nothing else really matters. I gently reminded her that if the Bible is true, that means she is spiritually bankrupt and without salvation.[45] It is one thing to claim a belief, but it is quite another to stake your life and eternity on it.

---

42. Romans 1:4.
43. Philippians 2:11.
44. Matthew 7:23, 25:46.
45. 2 Thessalonians 1:8; Revelation 20:14–15.

Conclusion

As we think about evangelizing the postmodernist, as Christians we are to be involved in both apologetics and evangelism. Evangelism is the presentation of the gospel. The gospel is defined in 1 Corinthians 15 in the following words: "that Christ died for our sins according to the Scriptures, and that He was buried, and that He rose again the third day according to the Scriptures" (1 Corinthians 15:3–4). The death, burial, and Resurrection took place just as the Old Testament Scriptures prophesied centuries before would happen. Evangelism presents the essence of Christianity — that God came to earth in Christ and by His death and Resurrection provided a means by which we could be forgiven. We must never forget that evangelism is our primary responsibility and apologetics is our secondary responsibility.

Apologetics comes into play just as soon as people have objections. If a person raises an objection like Christ never lived, or the Bible is not true, or all truth is relative, then we should attempt to address these issues. As Christians, we need to be prepared to show the unbeliever that they cannot rationally justify unbelief. This means that as ambassadors for Christ we cannot remain intellectually lazy but must study to be able to respond to their objections. If someone remains a non-Christian, if someone embraces postmodernism, they will do so in the face of the evidence, but not because there is a case for unbelief.

In this day, many of God's people are distracted by the entertainments of the world, and so they have lost their edge in being used of God to win people to the Savior. Just before his death, the Apostle Paul reminds Timothy in his *last will and testament* to, "Be diligent to present yourself approved to God, a worker who does not need to be ashamed, rightly dividing the word of truth" (2 Timothy 2:15). This verse reminds us that not all Christians can be usable in God's hand, because not all are "approved."

Certainly, the Bible is clear that all who have been saved are equally loved and accepted by the Father.[46] But as Paul reminds Timothy, while all may be equally loved, not all are equally approved. Clearly, some are more usable than others because of their willingness to *study* the Scriptures and their readiness to *share* the Scriptures. If the instrument that the Holy Spirit uses to bring about conversion is the word of God,[47] then we would be wise

---

46. John 17:23; Romans 8:38–39; 2 Corinthians 5:21.
47. Romans 10:17; James 1:18; 1 Peter 1:23.

to study it and be ready to defend it. May God help us to be faithful to this high and holy call.

Summary of Postmodern Beliefs

Doctrine	Teachings of Postmodernism
God	Deny the exclusivity of the God of the Bible. Various positions exist, but all would deny the exclusivity of Jesus as Savior.
Authority/ Revelation	Holds a humanistic view of truth, looking to man as the source of truth.
Man	All men are able to determine truth on their own. Various positions exist on the nature of man, but most would view man as basically good.
Sin	Sin is a relative concept and generally denied. The Bible cannot be seen as the absolute authority on what is sinful.
Salvation	Most would hold the position that if there is an afterlife, there are many different paths to get there.
Creation	Most would hold to evolutionary views, though positions vary.

Chapter 9

Epicureanism and Evolutionary Religions

Bodie Hodge with Troy Lacey

What Is Evolution?

Evolution is a fundamental tenet in many religious philosophies. It is believed and held with fervor by its adherents as the religious origins model in most secular religions.

Most people in the Western world are familiar with evolution, since this religious view is openly taught in state-funded schools. It is inherent to many textbooks, secular media, secular museums, and even kids programming and books.

When most hear the word "evolution," they think of the "*general theory of evolution (GTE)*," or in laymen's terms "molecules-to-man," "electron-to-engineer," or "goo-to-you" evolution. But there are really four types of evolution that make up the broad view of evolution:

- *Cosmological/Astronomical Evolution:* The big bang (everything came from nothing) created the universe and gradually formed into elements, stars, galaxies, and planetary systems

- *Geological Evolution:* Millions of years of slow, gradual accumulations of rock layers, including fossils

Chemical Evolution: Life came from non-living matter, otherwise called abiogenesis

Biological Evolution: A single, simple life form gave rise to all other life forms down through the ages

These four aspects make up pure evolution, or an essentially evolutionary worldview. This is materialistic/naturalistic evolution, not to be confused with theistic evolution where God is mixed in with the evolutionary origins account and chemical evolution is optional (more on this in chapter 11 on syncretism in this volume).

There is a widespread belief that evolution originated with Charles Darwin, but this is not true. Darwin described a modern form of biological evolution, but even it has changed since Darwin's day. Darwin built his biological understanding of evolution on Charles Lyell's understating of geological evolution. What makes these modern forms of evolutionary religion so disruptive is how it has been devastating the Church. Many within the Church, particularly the youth, have been indoctrinated to believe this religious view . . . or at least aspects of it.

Many Christians have little training in the defense of the Bible and Christian doctrine. At the same time, many of these same people are being taught by the state school system and secular media. Many Christians then yield (knowingly or unknowingly) and mix these two religions. See the chapter on syncretism in this volume to see how modern Christians try to mix these very different religions and the problems therein.

Regardless, this causes a problem within the Church because some members have walked away from doctrine that was set forth in the Bible and moved from biblical positions to beliefs that incorporate evolution. Some Christians even criticize those biblical Christians who say that you should not mix these religions! This brings us to an interesting question. What would Paul say about this?

If Paul Were Around Today, Would He Argue against Evolutionists?

We don't have to wonder if Paul would have argued against evolutionists, because he did — the Epicureans!

If we go back to Paul in the Book of Acts and consider his missionary journeys, sermons, and epistles, he saw a great number of people and surely encountered a great number of beliefs. Taking a closer look at the Scriptures, consider:

> Then certain Epicurean and Stoic philosophers encountered him. And some said, "What does this babbler want to say?" Others said, "He seems to be a proclaimer of foreign gods," because he preached to them Jesus and the resurrection (Acts 17:18).

In the greater context, we find Paul forced into a debate with Epicureans and Stoics. Because they disagreed with Paul, they take him to Mars Hill (the Areopagus) to defend his views in front of the whole assembly of philosophers. Paul masterfully begins his defense with God as Creator, which has gone on to become the basis for creation evangelism.[1]

Epicureans

Most readers skim past the Epicureans with the basic understanding that this group of people was obviously not Christian and held to some other views. Though this is true, it is only the half of it. The Epicureans were the evolutionists of the day. They typically held a belief derived from Epicurus that there were no gods that intervened in the world. They did not believe in the typical Greek gods. The Epicureans viewed the alleged Greek gods as mere material that sat on shelves in the homes of many Greeks.

The Epicureans further believed that over long ages, atoms, the basic component of all matter, gave rise to life. Then that life gave rise to higher life such as mankind. But there was no God or gods involved.

Sound familiar? It should; because in its basic form the Epicurean beliefs mimic the evolutionary worldview of today. Of course, there are some differences from the modern views of evolution (Lamarckian, Traditional Darwinian, Neo-Darwinian — more on this in a moment), but this is likely the first time an evolutionary worldview held any prominence with a group of people (from around 300 B.C.).

The Famous Epicurean Mantra

The materialistic Epicureans were known for their argument against God (and alleged gods) using the problem of evil:

---

1. For more on the method of creation evangelism, see Ken Ham, *Why Won't They Listen?* (Green Forest, AR: Master Books, 2002).

God either wants to eliminate bad things and cannot, or can but does not want to, or neither wishes to nor can, or both wants to and can. If he wants to and cannot, then he is weak — and this does not apply to god. If he can but does not want to, then he is spiteful — which is equally foreign to god's nature. If he neither wants to nor can, he is both weak and spiteful, and so not a god. If he wants to and can, which is the only thing fitting for a god, where then do bad things come from? Or why does he not eliminate them?[2]

Even today, evolutionists try to use this claim without realizing that Christ Himself addressed it:

> Another parable He put forth to them, saying: "The kingdom of heaven is like a man who sowed good seed in his field; but while men slept, his enemy came and sowed tares among the wheat and went his way. But when the grain had sprouted and produced a crop, then the tares also appeared. So the servants of the owner came and said to him, 'Sir, did you not sow good seed in your field? How then does it have tares?' He said to them, 'An enemy has done this.' The servants said to him, 'Do you want us then to go and gather them up?' But he said, 'No, lest while you gather up the tares you also uproot the wheat with them. Let both grow together until the harvest, and at the time of harvest I will say to the reapers, "First gather together the tares and bind them in bundles to burn them, but gather the wheat into my barn" ' " (Matthew 13:24–30).

The existence of evil is no surprise to Christians, and God explains this in the Bible. In Genesis 3, God explains the origin of evil — and its final demise at the end of Revelation 20. God will destroy evil just as He has said in numerous places, but it will happen at the time appointed by God (harvest), not on the timing or desires of humanity — as the Epicureans tried to force upon God (i.e., if God doesn't do it *now*, then He can't exist).[3] God is not subject to man, but man to God.

---

2. As stated by Lactantius, an early Christian who responded to this claim; Lactantius, *De Ira Deorum*, 13.19.
3. Imagine if some used this argument for the existence of the president of the United States. They could say, "If the president doesn't take care of this economic problem *now*, then he doesn't exist." It would be a ludicrous argument!

In the same manner, God could have created everything in one second, but selected six days for the benefit and pattern of our workweek (Exodus 20:11). So God has an appointed time for the elimination of evil for the benefit of man.[4]

But consider how the Epicureans would answer the question, "On what basis, in your Epicurean worldview, does evil exist?" They must borrow from the biblical concept of evil to argue against the God of the Bible! So, they refute themselves by posing the very thing they believe refutes the existence of God!

Paul's Response to the Epicureans

You can see why the Epicureans opposed Paul! They didn't want God to exist, and they did not want Him to be the Creator (recall they view a god or gods as being material idols simply made from matter). Rather, they believed that people ultimately came from matter — a view where ultimately nothing *matters.*

Paul responded to these claims. In Acts 17:24, Paul defines God as the "God, who made the world and everything in it since He is Lord of heaven and earth." He refutes the Epicurean ideas that a relational, Creator God does not exist and that there is a spiritual realm, refuting their materialistic thinking.

Then Paul says that God "does not dwell in temples made with hands. Nor is He worshiped with men's hands, as though He needed anything" (v. 24–25). He refutes the belief that God is limited to materials (idols), and this is proper, since God is spirit (John 4:24). Greek culture often made images of their gods, and the Epicureans realized these idols were made of materials, which is why they argued against them. So, Paul is distancing the God of the Bible from what the Epicureans were used to arguing against.

Next, Paul says God "gives to all life, breath, and all things" (v. 25). Paul explains the true origin of life and refutes that atoms came together to form life of their own accord. But notice how Paul actually goes further in a presuppositional argument here. If the Epicureans start with matter, where did the matter come from? Paul reveals that God created it ("all things"). Paul, through the beginning of verse 29, continues to explain that all people come from one person ("one blood") and that person came about as a result

---

4. "For the earnest expectation of the creation eagerly waits for the revealing of the sons of God" (Romans 8:19). The harvest is taking place.

of God supernaturally creating him. This explanation refuted their views of evolution and established God as the special Creator of mankind.

In the rest of verse 29 and into 30, Paul reiterates his devastating critique of their materialistic understanding of God. Paul also points out that mankind is really acting as the ultimate authority by worshipping man-made gods when he says, "We ought not to think that the Divine Nature is like gold or silver or stone, something shaped by art and man's devising. Truly, these times of ignorance God overlooked." Then Paul gives the call to repent and presents the gospel.

Lastly, Paul mentioned that God confirmed this to all by the Resurrection of Jesus. It was at this point that Scripture says "some mocked" (Acts 17:32). This would have been the Epicureans, who did not believe in a bodily resurrection. They believed that once the body died, there was nothing else. In fact, a common Epicurean epitaph found on many Greek and Roman graves of the time was the phrase: "I was not; I was; I am not; I do not care."[5]

How Should Christians Deal with Evolutionism?

Paul did not compromise his stand on Genesis (alluding to Genesis 1–11), which he used as the foundation for understanding the gospel when he spoke at Mars Hill in front of the Epicureans, Stoics, and others. He did not encourage them to mix some of the evolutionary ideas the Epicureans were espousing with the Bible, but told them to repent and acknowledge God as Creator and Savior.

So, if Paul were around today, would he argue against the evolutionists? Well, he *did!*

Other Early Evolutionists

Epicurus was not the "inventor" of the belief in the materialistic origin of everything. It appears that the atomist school of thought went back almost a hundred years before to the Greek philosophers Leucippus (fifth century B.C.) and Democritus (c. 460–c. 370 B.C.). Little is known about Leucippus, but Democritus' beliefs have been preserved through the writings of Aristotle (384–322 B.C.) and Diogenes Laertius (early third century A.D). Democritus believed that all matter was made up of indivisible particles called atoms (the

---

5. Eric Gerlach, "Epicurus and Epicureanism," accessed August 2, 2016, https://ericgerlach. com/greekphilosophy14.

Greek meaning is "no parts," an indivisible particle). To Democritus, every atom was eternal and could neither be created nor destroyed.[6]

His idea of the universe was entirely materialistic, with no guiding order, intelligence, or purpose, and no god or gods who controlled the destiny of humanity.[7] Democritus even proposed that the human soul was nothing more than a collection of atoms. Since no intelligence produced atoms, nor organized them, then according to Democritus, atoms must be self-organizing. But knowing that organization takes time, Democritus postulated an infinite number of atoms and an eternal and infinite universe, moving in an infinite void; and even more so, he postulated infinite other universes.[8] In the view of Democritus, infinite possibilities exist in an infinite universe, and so inevitably lead to life.

It is against this backdrop that Epicurus refined the teachings of Democritus (he rejected the concept of an infinite number of atoms, for example[9]) and expanded the materialistic atomist philosophy into an argument for practical atheism. If nothing created atoms, and everything is made up of self-organized atoms, then any discussion of a god or gods becomes meaningless. In the view of Democritus, and later the Epicureans, the gods were merely a collection of atoms as well. Likewise, all matter and all life is merely a collection of self-organizing atoms. This abiogenesis hypothesis, as well as the concept of an unlimited past (later refined to finite, but deep time of billions of years) would be grasped as fundamental principles by later evolutionary proponents.

When discussing Epicureanism, it is difficult to ignore the lifestyle of many Epicureans — based on the religious aspect of hedonism. Epicurus, along with Cārvāka, Artippus, and the Cyrenaics are all counted as formulating early Hedonism in India and Greece (600–300 B.C.). Here is a quick evaluation of hedonism.

Hedonism

In simplicity, hedonism is a belief that individual pleasure is the ultimate goal in life. However, even Solomon, whose wisdom was unsurpassed in

---

6. Robert C. Solomon and Kathleen M. Higgins, *A Short History of Philosophy* (New York: Oxford University Press), 1996, p. 37.
7. Ibid., p. 38.
8. David Sedley, *Creationism and Its Critics in Antiquity* (Berkeley and Los Angeles: University of California Press), 2007, p. 136.
9. Ibid., p. 161.

judging the people of Israel (e.g., 1 Kings 3:7–12), tried to find pleasure in a great many things such as women, money, and labor (e.g., Ecclesiastes 2:10).

But in all of his endeavors he found pleasure to be ultimately meaningless apart from God (e.g., Ecclesiastes 2:1, 12:8). This is what the Book of Ecclesiastes is all about — realizing hedonism is not the chief goal, but rather to "fear God and keep His commandments, for this is man's all" (Ecclesiastes 12:13).

Even so, cultures around the world dive into hedonism, often failing to realize it. They pursue pleasure and personal happiness at the detriment of others, and this often comes without concern (James 5:4–6).

Pleasure is not of itself a bad thing — it is a gift from God. Pleasure is bad when people engage in the love of wicked pleasure (evil things) or place the pleasure above God instead of recognizing its rightful place (2 Timothy 3:2–7).

There are variations among modern hedonism such as Normative, Prudential, Utilitarianism Hedonic Calculus, and Motivational. Without getting lost in terminology, just understand that much of this is based on the focus of pleasure such as external/physical pleasure versus internal/mental pleasure regarding levels and types of pain; future happiness versus happiness now, and so on.

However, few who might currently be described as hedonists have contemplated their underlying philosophy for pursuing their own pleasures. As a big picture, major divisions in hedonism are simply qualitative versus quantitative hedonism. Qualitative is focusing on the quality of pleasurable things (e.g., demanding good wine rather than cheap beer) while quantitative focuses on the quantity of pleasurable things.

Consider it this way. Two hedonists are arguing. One is a qualitative hedonist and the other is quantitative. The qualitative hedonist says his goal is to get a Ferrari (a very nice and expensive car). The quantitative hedonist says that his goal is to have 11 cars that are all much cheaper — one for each aspect of his lifestyle.

There is a t-shirt that has been popular that says, "He who dies with the most toys wins." This is the battle cry of quantitative hedonism. What few understand is that he who dies with the most toys still dies — and will then face judgment. Hebrews 9:27 says:

And as it is appointed for men to die once, but after this the judgment.

Modern Evolutionary Religious Beliefs

Darwin didn't invent the idea of evolution; he just popularized a particular form of it to attempt to explain life without God. When variant forms of Epicureanism began to revive in the late 1700s and early 1800s with men such as Mr. Erasmus Darwin (Charles Darwin's grandfather) and Professor Jean-Baptiste Lamarck, evolutionists needed a way to explain how new features arise in organisms over time.

Evolutionists today basically adhere to this same religious mythology that Paul argued against in the first century in Acts 17. But it has changed in its mechanisms. Today, instead of a tiny particle as the Greeks proposed, secularists propose that a cosmic egg or an almost infinitely dense hot particle somehow popped into existence from nothing, to begin the universe in accordance with the big bang. Now we arrive at the various modern views of biological evolution.[10]

Lamarckian Evolution

When Epicureanism was rehashed in the late 1700s and early 1800s, the leading view was called Lamarckian evolution. The view was promoted and popularized by Professor Jean-Baptiste Lamarck in France[11] and Dr. Erasmus Darwin (Charles Darwin's grandfather) in England.[12]

This view is famous for its teaching that the giraffe's neck became longer because it kept reaching for leaves that were higher and higher. Then, supposedly, this feature of a longer, stretched neck was passed onto the next generation of giraffes.

Charles Darwin's grandfather Erasmus even wrote a book on Lamarckian evolution called *Zoonomia*.[13] Most people don't know that Charles Darwin used a form of Lamarck's ideas in his book, to give a supposed explanation

---

10. For an extensive discussion on these views, see Terry Mortenson and Roger Patterson, "Do Evolutionists Believe Darwin's Ideas about Evolution?" in Ken Ham, gen. ed., *The New Answers Book 3* (Green Forest, AR: Master Books, 2010), p. 271–282.
11. For his collective works, see: Jean-Baptiste Lamarck, http://www.lamarck.cnrs.fr/index.php?lang=en.
12. Erasmus Darwin, *Zoonomia; or, the Laws of Organic Life*, Volume I (London, England: J. Johnson Publishers, 1796).
13. Ibid.

for new characteristics appearing in new generations. Modern evolutionists would, of course, reject this idea today — even though they hold Darwin's book *On the Origin of Species* as the "Bible" of the evolution movement.

But anyone can test Lamarck's ideas of acquired inheritance. For instance, growing up as a farmer, I (Hodge) can tell you that if you cut the tail off of a sheep (docking) generation after generation, the baby lambs will still come out with a tail! So the evolutionists still needed a different mechanism to try to make evolution work.

Traditional Darwinism

A Christian named Ed Blyth published a number of papers on variations within the kinds of creatures that God created, discussing how the environment influences why such variations succeed or not. He did this about 25 years before Charles Darwin published his seminal work. Darwin, trained as a theologian, read these papers and thought *maybe this is the mechanism that will lead to evolution*. Darwin called this process "natural selection."

Creationists, by and large, believe in the observable process of natural selection (often referred to as "adaptation" or "variation"). Such a process only operates on the information already contained in the genome of a particular kind. No new information is generated — just different combinations of already existing information. This is why we have variations within the dog kind, for example.

Also, sometimes information is corrupted by mutations (cancer, deformations, or extra copies of something such as extra fingers or toes are examples of mutations). These things (selection and mutations) along with created genetic diversity help explain variations in animals (and the formation of different species within a kind — we have several species of the one dog kind like coyotes, wolves, dingoes, etc.). But Darwin thought this process would lead to evolution in the production of brand new characteristics that weren't previously present.

Of course, Darwin was emphatic about natural selection (and some Lamarckian process, too), being the mechanism for this in the first edition of *Origin of Species*. But by the sixth edition, Darwin had backed off of this significantly in his wording, knowing that it wasn't turning out to be the mechanism he desired.[14]

---

14. R. Hedtke, *Secrets of the Sixth Edition* (Green Forest, AR: Master Books, 2010).

But Darwin had now repopularized naturalistic evolution (one kind changing into a different kind — molecules-to-man evolution), and it had started to become a mainstream idea in the population — even though it still lacked a viable mechanism and had no directly observed evidence. Keep in mind that speciation is not evolution in the molecules-to-man sense.

So basically, traditional Darwinism said that natural selection (with aspects of the Lamarckian process of passing along these newly acquired traits, e.g., Darwin's proposed "gemmules"), plus long periods of time would somehow lead to evolution of new kinds of living things (amoeba-to-man).

Neo-Darwinism

Later evolutionists (called Neo-Darwinists), with an understanding of DNA as the molecule of heredity, postulated that *mutations* were supposedly the mechanism to increase complexity by generating new information in the genome. Neo-Darwinists differ from traditional Darwinists who appeal to natural selection alone as that mechanism. Neo-Darwinists do appeal to natural selection as part of the mechanism, but not the process for originating complexity from existing information. They see natural selection as a process for filtering out organisms to allow a more suited (or "better") one to take its place.

This sentiment is what shows like *X-men*, *Spiderman*, *Heroes*, and so on appeal to as well. So basically, Neo-Darwinism could be described this way:

> Natural selection, plus mutation, plus long periods of time leads to evolution.

Many learned evolutionists and creationists alike recognize what mutations really do — they are generally rather detrimental (though in some cases they are nearly neutral or do not affect function too much).[15] But they simply do not result in brand new complex information being generated and added into the genome — despite evolutionists' false claims to the contrary.[16] So,

---

15. See, for example, John Sanford, *Genetic Entropy and the Mystery of the Genome* (Waterloo, New York: FMS Publications, 2005); Lee Spetner, *Not by Chance* (Brooklyn, New York: Judaica Press, Inc., 1997).

16. The best example to date that I've seen evolutionists propose for new information is the nylon-degrading bacteria. However, this was only based on preprogrammed design changes in the plasmids, which are extrachromosomal segments that are autonomous to the bacterial DNA. So with a proper understanding, it doesn't support evolutionary changes at all. Please see Georgia Purdom and Kevin Anderson, "A Creationists Perspective of Beneficial Mutations in Bacteria," *Answers in Depth*, May 27, 2009, https://answersingenesis.org/genetics/mutations/a-creationist-perspective-of-beneficial-mutations-in-bacteria.

a new mechanism is still required for evolutionists to attempt an explanation for the complexities of life forms they believe diversified from a simple common ancestor.

The reason is that we do not observe mutations (the billions that we should be seeing if evolution were true) moving in a positive direction. Cancers, for example, are the result of mutations. Furthermore, after years of experiments on fruit flies, for instance, bombarding them with radiation to cause mutations, they never improve with brand new characteristics (generated by new information), not previously possible! Dr. Lee Spetner states:

> No mutations have ever been observed that have converted an animal to a markedly different species, say from a fly to a wasp.[17]

Punctuated Equilibrium

The problem of mutations gets worse since we do not find the gradual changing of creatures in the fossil record from one to another as evolutionary scientists, especially Darwin, have predicted. This was particularly troubling to evolutionist Dr. Stephen J. Gould from Harvard University, who became the popular advocate of the Punctuated Equilibrium idea, though not all evolutionists jumped on board his particular evolutionary view.

Essentially, Gould argued that things didn't change much over long periods of time, but rather the change happened in short spurts or bursts of evolution in isolated populations. This hypothesis was proposed to eliminate the problem of no undisputed transitional forms in the fossil record.

The idea was that changes happened so fast that you don't see the results of these in the fossil layers, much like you wouldn't see all of the action of a football game if you just looked at a few pictures taken throughout the game. So basically, the evolutionists were not finding evidence for molecules-to-man evolution in the fossil layers (it was nice Dr. Gould was honest about that). Then the evolutionists proposed that they didn't need any fossil evidence because they could explain this away using the concept of punctuated equilibrium.

So punctuated equilibrium suggests that mutations plus natural selection produce short bursts of evolution over long ages — we just don't have a record of it in the fossils. We've heard creationists explain it this way:

---

17. Spetner, *Not by Chance*, p. 177.

It used to be that the reason for no transitional forms in the fossil record and why we don't see molecules-to-man evolution happening, is because it happens slowly over a long time. Now it is proposed that the reason we don't see evolution happening or find transitional forms is because it happened so fast we missed it!

But in the end, the evolutionist still doesn't have an observable and repeatable process to change one kind of organism, like a relatively simple alga, into a totally different kind, such as a more complex dog. The only mechanisms they propose are natural selection and mutations. But both of these are actually working in the wrong direction for evolution.[18]

Modern Evolution's Shortcomings

What new complexity has mutated on a dog to make, say . . . feathers? We see misplaced copies of information, like extra toes or extra fingers (polydactyl, which are actually detrimental), but we don't see totally new characteristics arising like hair on a fish. We observe the result of genes that turn on and off, but that information was already there, and turning these on and off has nothing to do with molecules-to-man evolution (i.e., turning microbes eventually into turkeys).

If evolution is possible, considering the enormous (really incomprehensible) amount of information in living things, where is just one example of matter producing new information? Where do we observe matter generating the code for a brand new characteristic that was not previously present? The evolutionist accepts these things on blind faith.

Religious Nature of Evolution

Evolutionary religions are subsets of the greater secular humanistic religion. Many try to equate evolution as science, but that just gives science a bad name. Science, which simply means knowledge, is observable and repeatable, while molecules-to-man evolution is neither. It is merely a materialistic and naturalistic religion that many have been duped into believing is science. Consider the words of a famous Neo-Darwinist on his religious conviction to evolution:

---

18. We understand that there are variations within these models like neo-Lamarckianism or hopeful monster (an even faster model of punctuated equilibrium), but none offer a viable mechanism for evolution.

We take the side of science in spite of the patent absurdity of some of its constructs, in spite of its failure to fulfill many of its extravagant promises of health and life, in spite of the tolerance of the scientific community for unsubstantiated just-so stories, because we have a prior commitment, a commitment to materialism. It is not that the methods and institutions of science somehow compel us to accept a material explanation of the phenomenal world, but, on the contrary, that we are forced by our a priori adherence to material causes to create an apparatus of investigation and a set of concepts that produce material explanations, no matter how counter-intuitive, no matter how mystifying to the uninitiated. Moreover, that materialism is an absolute, for we cannot allow a Divine Foot in the door.[19]

Another leading evolutionist writes:

Christianity has fought, still fights, and will fight science to the desperate end over evolution, because evolution destroys utterly and finally the very reason Jesus' earthly life was supposedly made necessary. Destroy Adam and Eve and the original sin, and in the rubble you will find the sorry remains of the son of god. Take away the meaning of his death. If Jesus was not the redeemer that died for our sins, and this is what evolution means, then Christianity is nothing.[20]

Naturalistic evolutionists even recognize that evolution is an opposing religion to Christianity. It has competing religious claims. For example, you cannot have both special creation by God of an organism and naturalistic evolution of the same organism with no God at the same time. It is logically contradictory. These are two competing religious claims. Biblical Christians recognize this, and naturalistic evolutionists recognize this — the only ones who seem to fail to realize this are the compromised Christians who try to synchronize these very different religions in the oddest of ways.

---

19. Richard Lewontin, "Billions and Billions of Demons," *The New York Review*, January 9, 1997, p. 31.
20. G. Richard Bozarth, "The Meaning of Evolution," *American Atheist*, September 20, 1979, p. 30.

Refutations

Besides Paul's refutations, there are many more to choose from. For example, the Epicureans and other evolutionists are materialists, which means logic cannot exist in their worldview since logic is not material. Logic is an abstract, immaterial concept that has no grounding in a materialistic worldview, so it is inconsistent for a materialist to appeal to logic in an argument. So the materialistic evolutionists can't even make a logical argument against Christianity to favor evolution without leaving their religion behind them and borrowing from a biblical worldview!

The evolutionists cannot consistently argue that anything is "right" or "wrong" since absolute morality is not material either. The evolutionist cannot logically suggest that biblical creation is wrong without standing on a foundation that evolution (materialistic and naturalistic) is false.

Consider scientific inquiry. Repeatable and observable science is predicated on the concept of God upholding and sustaining the universe in a consistent fashion (e.g., Genesis 8:22; Hebrews 1:3). Christians describe the way God does this and call them the laws of nature. This is what makes repeatable science possible. God upholds laws of nature consistently so we get the same result when we do our experimentation. We have a grounding for our belief in the uniformity of nature that is consistent with our worldview.

Thus, as Bible believers, we know the future will be like the past because an all-knowing God who knows the future has revealed this to man in His Word. This explains why people who generally trusted the Bible developed most fields of science.

But how can the naturalist or materialist, thinking from a worldview without God, know the future? They can't. The consistent evolutionist must admit that the laws of nature could change tomorrow even though they believe in the uniformitarian view of natural processes. In the evolutionary story, at the beginning there were no laws of nature and then there were laws of nature. So if the laws changed in the past, why wouldn't they change in the future?

If the evolutionist argues that they know the laws of nature will remain the same in the future "because they were like that in the recent past," they commit the fallacy of begging the question (a form of a vicious circular argument). They still don't know the future, and knowing the past is irrelevant to knowing the future.

Allow me an illustration to get the point across. What if someone were to state, "Dr. Richard Dawkins, a famous evolutionist, will never die." You might ask, how do you know that this person knows the future — that Dr. Dawkins will never die. And they respond by saying, "The future is like the past and Dr. Dawkins has never died in the past, so therefore he will not die in the future." Do you see the fallacy? The same can be said for the uniformitarian view of history.

Conclusion

Evolution is a fundamental tenet of many religious philosophies. It is also a religious origins account borrowed by many humanistic religions (simply because evolution is one of the few religious models that tries to offer an explanation of origins apart from God or gods). Many have bought into evolutionary ideas so deeply that we might think of them as holding to the religion of evolutionism — looking to evolutionary ideas to account for the origin of the universe and the meaning of existence.

We must acknowledge that evolution fails both theologically and scientifically and cannot account for logic, morality, or uniformity in nature. It is a failed system and *false* religion.

Chapter 10

Dualism and the Types of Religions

Bodie Hodge

Stop regarding man in whose nostrils is breath, for of what account is he? (Isaiah 2:22; ESV).

For the ways of man are before the eyes of the LORD, And He ponders all his paths. His own iniquities entrap the wicked man, and he is caught in the cords of his sin. He shall die for lack of instruction, and in the greatness of his folly he shall go astray (Proverbs 5:21–23).

Preliminary Comments about Approaching Dualism

I think we could all agree there are a lot of strange beliefs in the world. So many that all cannot be dealt with in this book series on world religions, cults, and philosophical systems. To deal with dualism, it is appropriate to understand the three major forms of non-Christian religions from another angle.

So how do we deal with all these other religious systems? In the introductory comments of this book series we pointed out there were several ways to lump or group religions. We selected one method for the book series and continued with that scheme throughout the volumes.

But this chapter utilizes a different way of grouping religions that would typically be used to categorize philosophically religious systems. So it is a complementary look from a different angle. This will give us an overview of most religious models and categorize them in a way that we could take these belief systems and place them neatly into one of three categories (the remaining would fall under Christian religious appeals/openly Christian-based religious, four total).[1]

As you read this, there will likely be some new terminology that I will try to briefly define, but don't let this set you back. You should still be able to gather the main points without needing to memorize the technical lingo.

Categories of Religious Belief Systems

In this system, the three major categories are:

1. Spiritual Monism: all things are spiritual/nonmaterial; that is, all things really consist of nonmaterial aspects like a concept world or ultimate reality or ultimate being (e.g., Hinduism, Taoism, or New Age).
2. Materialistic Monism/Atomism: all things are material and there is no immaterial or spiritual realm (e.g., atheism, secular humanism, and materialism).
3. Philosophical/Non-religious/Secular Dualism: there are two (hence *dual*) opposing principles or substances that exist and cannot be broken down any further: *mind/conceptual* (non-material or *ideal* realm) and *matter* (e.g., modern dualism or Platonism).

In brief, these three non-Christian positions are (1) only non-material/spiritual exists, (2) only material exists, and (3) non-material/spiritual (secularistic or no god(s) involved) *and* material exists (in opposition to each other). When you understand the first two it will be much easier to understand secular dualism.

I'd like to add a caveat here. When discussing the dualistic viewpoint, we are not discussing the immaterial or spiritual realm as understood in a Christian sense. We are looking at a secular form of it, as dualism holds to a secular view that rejects any concept of a god. Although there are various forms of dualism, dualists typically still maintain that their immaterial

---

1. These are Bible-based religions or those that borrow heavily from the Bible but then deviate. Volume 1 of the *World Religions and Cults* dealt extensively with these counterfeits of Christianity, showing biblical Christianity as the only viable option.

conceptual realm is not the same as that of most religions, even though it is often denoted as "spiritual."

This is why religions that do entertain a true spiritual sense are dealt with extensively in their own chapters in this book series and not confined to this section. This would be that fourth section — *religious* (like what you see in the first volume of this book series on the Counterfeits of Christianity).

Another caveat also needs to be discussed. There is "religious dualism" which counterfeits Christianity, but this is a polytheistic religion with at least two equal and opposing "gods" where one is good and the other is evil. Not that secular dualism is itself unreligious — it is very religious — but it tries to do so in a *secular* sense without god(s). But the primary and leading form of dualism is Platonism (Idealism) developed by Plato, so that is what will be discussed here. So even though there are various forms of secular dualism, the king of dualism, Plato, will be our focus here.

1. Spiritual Monism

Spiritual Monism is united in proclaiming that "everything is one" or "all is one." In other words, the spiritual monist claims that all things are part of one spiritual entity, whether they appear to be physical or not. For example, *all of nature* or *all of the universe* and *all of the conceptual realm* or *realm of the mind* would be understood as merely being a part of one spiritual reality or one ultimate concept of being.

I know what you are thinking — "But we have physical, material things right in front of us!" But this view maintains that what we think and envision as the material world is actually a part of the spiritual realm. In other words, the material realm really doesn't exist in this view; people are merely mistaken to think it does — it is really an illusion (e.g., this concept is called *maya* in Hinduism). Most Eastern religions (Hinduism, Jainism, New Age, Taoism, etc.) are simply variations of this religion outlook.

The argument put forth by spiritual monists is that there is no distinction between the material and immaterial/spiritual realm. They would further argue that "everything is one" and there is really no distinction between anything since "all is one."

As the spiritual monist teaches, humanity's problem is that we misperceive reality by making distinctions when, in reality, there are no distinctions (we fail to properly understand). The goal of humanity is to work to understand how distinctions are not really there, bringing us closer to the "infinite sea of being" or a "state of nirvana" where we are again united with this ultimate state of spiritual reality or being.

Some popular forms of Spiritual Monism are Hinduism and its religious sisters, New Age, and Taoism, although others could be lumped under this religious system. Any philosophical system that is pantheistic (which in a general sense is: "all is God" or "everything together consists of God" or "all is part of God" or "the universe/cosmos is God") is spiritually monistic.

An Arbitrary Worldview?

To evaluate this worldview, we can ask a simple question — How do you know that all is one? The only way to know that all is one is to know all things! And yet, there is no authority within Spiritual Monism except the fallible and limited opinions of man, which are arbitrary. Arbitrariness, like an opinion, carries no weight in a debate. The entire religious set is predicated on the alleged human sages who developed the concept that all is one. And yet, one can't really know all is one outside of an arbitrary assertion!

Building a worldview on arbitrary claims is not a great foundation. If someone proclaimed 2+5=3 and you asked them how they know that 2+5=3, would you believe them if they just said they believed it was so? Not at all! Appealing to ideas of fallible man as an absolute truth shows that the argument has been refuted.

An Inconsistent Worldview?

Consider that the ultimate reality, ultimate spirituality, or ultimate nature is not personal (as taught in Taoism, New Age, Hinduism, etc.). It has never been personal, nor then is it capable of providing personal revelation to assert that truth. That is, if the ultimate spiritual being (all is one) was some form of absolute truth in the first place (after all, *truth* and *error* are one and the same in this view)! Being that it is not personal, how then could personal beings have any revealed knowledge of this ultimate reality or ultimate spiritual state? Such a contradiction provides a devastating argument against this worldview.

Furthermore, if there are no distinctions and our path is supposed to be understanding that there are no distinctions, then this introduces a grand inconsistency. That very claim is a distinction! In other words, it is contradictory at its very premise by saying, there are no distinctions in reality and then claiming we have failed to understand that distinction!

A Necessary Foundation for Logic and Truth?

If all is one, then absolute truth and absolute falsity are also one — therefore truth cannot really exist! If knowledge and lack of knowledge are one, then knowledge breaks down to be meaningless. Spiritual Monism (and the many religions that would be categorized under it) is utterly refuted as a coherent worldview by the fact that it has *no basis* for truth, knowledge, and the like.

Consider the actions of spiritual monists in light of their beliefs. If all is one and there is no distinction, then why do they buy a house for their possessions when there is no distinction between their house and possessions and someone else's house and possessions? Why would they kiss their children and wife (and not someone else's) as if they were special and unique? After all, there would be no distinction between their family and a pile of nuclear waste.

Why not have the monists give you their purse or wallet if there is no distinction between you and them? The religions grounded in Spiritual Monism break down into meaninglessness, arbitrariness, and inconsistency by their own perspective. They do not behave in the world in a way that is consistent with the fundamental beliefs of their worldview.

If one were to respond, "Well, that is the beauty of Spiritual Monism, we don't have to go use that Christian logic in our view, so you can't refute our view using logical arguments." Then we can respond by saying, "Yes, you do believe in logic because you just attempted to make a logical argument to prove me wrong. Thus, you have refuted your own position."

Since contradictions are allowed in their philosophical system, then simply contradict their view — what are they going to do? Are they going to appeal to the logic that they just gave up? The Spiritual Monistic view is easily refuted as an incoherent worldview.

2. Materialistic Monism

In exact opposition to Spiritual Monism, Materialistic Monism maintains that everything is material. In this view, there is no spiritual aspect of reality whatsoever. Everything is seen as material, and there is no spirit or non-material in existence. Everything in reality is an expression of matter and energy interacting. Hence, there is no God or gods whatsoever in this view.

Arbitrariness, Inconsistency, and Foundational Problems

Of course, holding to a strict materialistic concept causes problems because concepts cannot exist since concepts are not material (i.e., immaterial). Nor can logic, truth, knowledge, love, dignity, dreams, conclusions, mind, caring, and so on, because they are not material. These things have no mass and are abstract in their nature. So none of these really exist in the materialistic framework.

What does this mean for the materialistic worldview? It means they cannot even debate the subject without giving up their view and borrowing from a Christian worldview! In other words, to discuss the subject using abstract concepts and logic means that the atheistic position is wrong!

So many materialists, when they become aware of their own limitations, tend to be materialistic by profession but act like dualists to say reason, logic, and so on exist — but they just don't want God involved. But then they have to deal with the arbitrariness, inconsistencies, and other issues that we discussed in the Spiritual Monism section above. But strict materialism is self-refuting (inconsistent) since it cannot account for logic and reasoning in the first place.

3. Philosophical Dualism (Idealism)

As mentioned previously, this is not to be confused with *moral* or *religious dualism*, which is the view that there are two opposites (gods) that govern existence and oppose each other: good and evil. They merely share the same name (dualism).

Though the dualistic nature of religious dualism is related to Idealism, they are different subjects. In light of the pervasiveness of the religious dualistic view in our culture, there is the faulty idea floating around that God and Satan are equal and opposites, but this is not the case (i.e., two opposing eternal gods of good and evil, respectively).

However, Satan was created by God and has no power next to the infinite God of Scripture. The Bible teaches that Satan was once created perfect (Ezekiel 28:15; Deuteronomy 32:4; Colossians 1:16) and very good (Nehemiah 9:6; Genesis 1:31), but fell into sin. One day, God will cast Satan into hell (eternal punishment). Thus, there is no possibility of Satan being any form of co-equal, yet opposite, with God. Hence, Christianity doesn't fall under the *religious dualism* aspect, which is really polytheism (two opposing equal gods).

Returning to the subject at hand — Philosophical Dualism (Idealism) understands that everything is not material, but also recognizes that everything is not spiritual. Platonic dualism (the leading form that goes back to Plato) realized there are absolutes (e.g., logic, truth, concept forms) that do not change alongside our material universe that does change. So he held to a dualistic view of reality.

Plato believed that there is an ideal or immaterial realm of absolute forms or ideas, which he viewed as the first realm since it is unchanging. For example, logic doesn't change and absolute truths do not change, so they must be a part of the ideal realm. And then, there is our material world, which he viewed as a secondary realm because it undergoes constant change.

Plato held that things have *a form* in the first realm that does not change like a "class concept," whereas the world in which we live is subject to that first realm because things here do change but represent an unchanging ideal. What do I mean by class concepts? It means things like letters or numbers or things we can classify.

Consider this example. I can write a "B" on a piece of paper, and you would recognize it as a "B." If I were to erase this "B" and now there is no longer a material "B" on my paper, does that mean that "B-ness" no longer exists in the universe? Not at all. The *concept* of "B" is not dependent on *that material* "B" that I had written with pencil on the paper. There is a class concept of "B" that is not dependent on material — and yet we often use a material "B" to represent this immaterial concept. The same ideal can be represented in different materials as pixels on a digital screen, ink on this page, or carving it into the sand. The ideal form is constant, though its material expression can change.

As another example, I've seen big dogs, hairy dogs, black dogs, hairless dogs, plush-toy dogs, photographs of dogs, stick-figure dogs, shadows of dogs, and we can easily recognize that *concept* of dog. If a new image of some form of dog is found, we can easily classify it as a dog, even though we have not seen every single possible expression of a dog ideal. We recognize the concept of "dog" or "dogness." It was not dependent on the material of a single picture or drawing of a dog or a single living dog.

There is "dogness," "B-ness," truth, logic, absolute morality, and other *concepts* according to Plato that don't change. We see changes here in the material world (e.g., dogs die and return to dust as new dogs are born), yet the forms, ideas, class concepts, logic, and so on do not change. We don't have half logic or half "B-ness."

So Plato and other dualists postulate there is an unchanging, abstract realm of perfect ideas or forms (ideal realm) that they say exists that is not bound to the material universe. But they also assert that the material universe is subjected to this ideal realm so that "dogness," "B-ness," and the law of non-contradiction can exist in the material realm.

Today, we see many people following the basic tenets of Platonism, even if they don't realize they are dualists! Believe it or not, many professing atheists are actually dualists and don't realize it. They argue for materialism, but then agree that truth, love, conclusions, absolute morality, reason, concepts, theoretical mathematics, logic, and other abstract, immaterial concepts exist.

For example, I speak to a lot of atheists who say our existence is purely material, and then they go on to argue for absolute morality (e.g., murder is never acceptable). Or they agree that logic exists even though they say our reality is strictly material. These atheists are acting like dualists when they do this. Now I could go on, but this should explain that dualists hold there are both material and immaterial concepts in their view of the world that are separated in two realms — the realm we are in and an "ideal" realm of perfect ideas/concepts.

With all this in mind, remember that dualism has no God or gods involved — there is no being who governs or created both realms.

Arbitrariness and Inconsistency

Plato's brightest student, Aristotle, proposed a devastating argument that ultimately led to strife between the two. Aristotle basically posed to Plato, *"How do these two realms interact or inform each other?"*

You see, the universe in which we live is still subject to logic. The universe in which we live has "B-ness" in it and has recognizable "dogness" in it. So how does this first realm or ideal realm affect this world (secondary realm)? To which Plato, who was no doubt a brilliant mind, could not answer without telling a myth!

Plato knew he had no answer (see his book *Parmenides*) and realized that any answer he would give was a *mere opinion* (fallacious assertion).[2] It is arbitrary to assume in your own opinion that there is an abstract realm

---

2. Aristotle further elaborates this devastating case as the "Third Man argument" as a refutation.

that informs or interacts with our world. So all Plato could do was appeal to himself for this explanation, which is merely arbitrary and refuted. And even today, this devastating refutation still persists among professing dualists. So the dualistic viewpoint ultimately breaks down into arbitrariness.

Preconditions Problem

It would be inconsistent for dualists to use logic based on an arbitrary realm. The fact that Plato and other dualists use logic would be resting on arbitrariness as well. So why do they try to inconsistently use it to arrive at their positions?

Absolute and invariant logic does exist, after all. But not because it is confined to another realm as they arbitrarily proposed, but it exists as a tool because a logical God created all things and we are made in His image to use that tool! The universe obeys logic because God upholds the universe. The point is that logic exists because of God, and these dualists must borrow logic from God to make sense of anything.

In fact, nothing has meaning without God who gives meaning to things as His creations. Communication exists because we are made in the image of a communicating God. Absolute morality exists because God, an absolutely holy being, sets morality for all. Class concepts belong to God as they reflect His creations. Being made in His image, we can classify things too. So "B-ness" and "dogness" exist because of a God who gives rational meaning to things. And we as image bearers reflect this rational nature.

So immaterial things like logic, concepts, and morality exist not because of some proposed alternative realm, but because of the existence of the God of the Bible. The dualist has no God to connect absolutes to the material world and is left in the desolated rubble of arbitrariness and meaninglessness. When you delete the God of the Bible, things become meaningless.

> The fear of the LORD is the beginning of wisdom, and the knowledge of the Holy One is understanding (Proverbs 9:10).

Conclusion

These three forms — Spiritual Monism, Materialistic Monism, and Philosophical Dualism (Idealism) — all fall short logically and have inconsistencies within their own story. They are arbitrary and cannot make sense of the world in which we live.

The answer to truly understanding the world we live in lies in biblical Christianity, the king of the *religions*. It is not arbitrary, but stands on the authority of the absolute authority, who, by His very nature, is not arbitrary. Biblical Christianity is not inconsistent, as it rests on the consistent and logical all-knowing God who consistently upholds the universe just as He promised by His ultimate power. God is predicated for all knowledge and reasoning to exist.

The answer is clear.

> Where is the wise? Where is the scribe? Where is the disputer of this age? Has not God made foolish the wisdom of this world? (1 Corinthians 1:20).

Chapter 11

Christian Syncretism with Evolution and Other Belief Systems (Compromise)

Bodie Hodge

We live in strange times — I probably don't have to convince you of that.[1] Perhaps all one needs is to read the news over the course of about one week to get a small grip on the complexities of our era.

An example of a strange occurrence is found when we looked at Latin American Syncretism in Volume 2 of the World Religions and Cult series. We, in the Western world, can easily spot where Roman Catholicism had *blended* with paganism, and the adherents couldn't easily see it. We see compromise all around us where two opposing viewpoints are meshed into one strange concoction (brought "in sync" with each other, or when applied to religions, syncretized).

The Israelites were prone to do this from Moses' day (Numbers 25:1–9) through Solomon's day (1 Kings 11:1–4) and made complete in the day of our Lord (when the Israelites joined with Caesar over Christ as their ultimate authority — John 19:15).

One would think it a crazy notion to believe that solid churches that paved the road for Christianity in many parts of the world would have now become intertwined with false religions. But, with sadness, it is true.

---

1. There is nothing new under the sun (Ecclesiastes 1:9).

As citizens of once dominant Christian countries, we Christians in the USA, UK, Germany, etc. never expected such compromise to fill our own backyard. We expect to see this elsewhere, but not in our own pews . . . right? How wrong we are if we think such a thing. Does the Church in many parts of the Western world realize they have done the same thing as the pagans and other syncretists?

As an example, a Christian from Latin America can come to the USA or the UK and easily spot where Christians, leaders and laymen, have mixed our Christianity with the religion of evolution. So often, our compromised Christian brethren do not believe they have done the same thing that the Israelites did when they mixed their godly worship with Baal worship — they are just using the modern religion of the day, which is a secular view of evolution.

It is time to step back and have a look at our Christianity. Is it purely biblical or is it blended into a strange concoction with the evolutionary religion of our culture — or other religions like those in the East (New Age, Hinduism, Mysticism, etc.)?

The Four Aspects of Evolution

What is evolution? In its broadest sense, evolution is the naturalistic explanation of the origin and function of the universe, the *"general theory of evolution (GTE)"* or, in laymen's terms, "molecules-to-man," "electron-to-engineer," or "goo-to-you." But within this concept there are really four types of evolution, which are intrinsically connected to make up the whole naturalistic worldview explaining the universe without the need for a divine being. Evolution is a key tenet of the religion of Secular Humanism.

Cosmological/Astronomical Evolution: The big bang (everything came from nothing) created the universe and gradually formed into elements, stars, galaxies, and planetary systems.

Geological Evolution: Millions of years of slow, gradual accumulations of rock layers, including fossils.

Chemical Evolution: Life came from non-living matter, otherwise called abiogenesis.

Biological Evolution: A single, simple life form gave rise to all other life forms down through the ages.

Within the church, there are those who try to fit astronomical evolution, geological evolution, chemical evolution, or biological evolution into the Bible. Some Christians accept one, some, or all of these in their attempts to accommodate the secular beliefs with God's Word. This acceptance undermines the authority of the Word of God. This is ultimately undermining the gospel as it undercuts the Word of God from which the message of the gospel comes.

Let me explain this further, as it is quite important to grasp. The concept of millions of years (geological evolution) is a vital foundation for an evolutionary worldview. Without millions of years, there is no possibility of evolution — even evolutionists concede this (i.e., we don't have evolutionists arguing that all things evolved over the course of about 6,000 years from a single-celled organism). They *must* have millions of years.

Since God said He created all things in six days and rested on the seventh, how do syncretistic Christians deal with the millions of years? Virtually all Christians who have bought into an old earth (i.e., millions and billions of years or long ages) place the millions of years *prior* to Adam.

We have genealogical lists that connect Adam to Christ (e.g., Luke 3). For the compromising Christians, it would be blatantly absurd to try to insert millions and billions of years into these genealogies and say that Adam and Eve were made at the beginning of creation.[2]

Instead, old-earth creationists (as they are often denoted[3]) take these long ages and insert them somewhere prior to Adam; hence creation week has been a divisive point in Christianity ever since the idea of long ages became popular in the 1800s.

Biblically, How Old Is the Earth?

The primary sides are:

- Young-earth proponents (biblical age of the earth and universe of about 6,000 years)[4]
- Old-earth proponents (secular age of the earth of about 4.5 billion years and a universe about 14 billion years old)[5]

---

2. In Mark 10:6, Jesus says, "But from the beginning of the creation, God 'made them male and female.' "

3. In many other cases, those Christians who adhere to long ages are called "compromised Christians" since they are compromising by mixing these two religions' origins accounts (Secular Humanism and Christianity).

4. Not all young-earth creationists agree on this age, though the number is typically thousands, not millions.

5. Some of these old-earth proponents accept molecules-to-man biological evolution and so are called theistic evolutionists. Others reject neo-Darwinian evolution but accept the evolutionary timescale for astronomical and geological evolution, and hence agree with the evolutionary order of events in history.

The difference is immense! Let's give a little history of where the *biblical calculation* came from. We will discuss the old-earth development in the subsequent chapter on philosophical naturalism.

Where Did a Young-Earth Worldview Come From?

Simply put, it came from the Bible. Of course, the Bible doesn't say explicitly anywhere, "The earth is 6,000 years old." And it's a good thing it doesn't; otherwise it would be out of date the following year. But we wouldn't expect an all-knowing God to make that kind of a mistake.

God gave us something better. In essence, He gave us a "birth certificate." For example, using a personal birth certificate, a person can calculate how old he is at any point. It is similar with the earth. Genesis 1 says that the earth was created on the first day of creation (Genesis 1:1–5). From there, we can begin to calculate the age of the earth.

Let's do a rough calculation to show how this works. The age of the earth can be estimated by taking the first five days of creation (from earth's creation to Adam), then following the genealogies from Adam to Abraham in Genesis 5 and 11, then adding in the time from Abraham to today.

Adam was created on day 6, so there were five days before him. If we add up the dates from Adam to Abraham, we get about 2,000 years, using the Masoretic Hebrew text of Genesis 5 and 11.[6] Whether Christian or secular, most scholars would agree that Abraham lived about 2000 B.C. (4,000 years ago). So a simple calculation is:

> 5 days (creation to Adam)
> + ~2,000 years (Adam to Abraham)
> + ~4,000 years (Abraham to present)
> _____
>
> ~6,000 years

At this point, the first five days are negligible. Quite a few people have done this calculation using the Masoretic text (which is what most English translations are based on) and, with careful attention to the biblical details, have arrived at the same age of about 6,000 years, or about 4000 B.C. Two of the

---

6. Bodie Hodge, "Ancient Patriarchs in Genesis," Answers in Genesis, https://answersingenesis.org/bible-characters/ancient-patriarchs-in-genesis/.

Table 1: Jones and Ussher

Name	Age calculated	Reference and date
James Ussher	4004 B.C.	*The Annals of the World*, A.D. 1658
Floyd Nolen Jones	4004 B.C.	*The Chronology of the Old Testament*, A.D. 1993

most popular, and perhaps best, are a recent work by Floyd Jones[7] and a much earlier book by James Ussher[8] (1581–1656). See table 1.

The misconception exists that Ussher and Jones were the only ones to arrive at a date of 4000 B.C.; however, this is not the case at all. Jones[9] lists several chronologists who have undertaken the task of calculating the age of the earth based on the Bible, and their calculations range from 5501 to 3836 B.C. A few are listed in table 2 with a couple of newer ones and their reference.

As you will likely note from table 2, the dates are not all exact, even though the majority lie between 3950 and 4050 B.C. — hovering on each side of 4000 B.C. There are two primary reasons chronologists have different dates.[10]

Some used the Septuagint, or another early translation, instead of the Hebrew Masoretic text. The Septuagint is a Greek translation of the Hebrew Old Testament, completed around 250 B.C. by about 70 Jewish scholars (hence it is often cited as the LXX, 70 in roman numerals). It is good in most places, but appears to have a number of inaccuracies. For example, one relates to the Genesis chronologies where the LXX indicates that Methuselah would have lived past the Flood without being on the ark!

Several points in the biblical timeline are not straightforward to calculate. They require very careful study of more than one passage. These include exactly how long the Israelites were in Egypt and what Terah's age was when Abraham was born. (See Jones and Ussher for a detailed discussion of these difficulties.)

---

7. Floyd Nolen Jones, *Chronology of the Old Testament* (Green Forest, AR: Master Books, 2005).
8. James Ussher, *The Annals of the World* (Green Forest, AR: Master Books, 2003), translated by Larry and Marion Pierce.
9. Jones, *Chronology of the Old Testament*, p. 26.
10. Others would include gaps in the chronology based on the presences of an extra Cainan in Luke 3:36. But there are good reasons this variant is a transcription error and not part of the original text.

Table 2: Chronologists' Calculations

Age of the Earth (range B.C.)	Chronologist
3800–3850	A. Helwigius (c. 1630)
3850–3900	N/A
3900–3950	M. Beroaldus (c. 1675), J. Scaliger (d. 1609)
3950–4000	A. Salmeron (d. 1585), J. Haynlinus, P. Melanchthon (c. 1550), C. Longomontanus (c. 1600), J. Claverius, E. Reusnerus, W. Dolen (2003), Krentzeim, Becke, Frank Klassen (1975), D. Petavius (c. 1627)
4000–4050	James Ussher (c. 1656), Floyd Nolan Jones (1993), E. Faulstich (1986), E. Greswell (1830), J. Cappellus (c. 1600), E. Reinholt, W. Lange, Martin Anstey (1913),
4050–4100	H. Spondanus (1600), Jacob Salianus (c. 1600), J. Ricciolus, M. Michael Maestlinus (c. 1600),
4100–4150	Thomas Lydiat (c. 1600)
4150–4200	Jim Liles (2013),* L. Condomanus, Marianus Scotus (c. 1070)
4200–4950	N/A
4950–5550**	John Jackson, Julius Africanus, Dr. William Hales, George Syncellus, Eusebius, Dr. Benjamin Shaw***

    * Jim Liles, *Earth's Sacred Calendar* (Tarzana, CA: Bible Timeline, 2013).
   ** Utilizing the LXX (Septuagint).
 *** Benjamin Shaw, "The Genealogies of Genesis 5 and 11 and Their Significance for Chronology," BJU, December, 2004. Dr. Shaw states the date as "about 5000 B.C." in appendix I, but the specific date is derived from adding 1,656 years (the time from creation to the Flood) to his date of the Flood, which is stated as 3298 B.C. on p. 222.

The first four in table 2 (bolded) are calculated from the Septuagint (others give certain favoritism to the LXX too), which gives ages for the patriarchs' firstborn much higher than the Masoretic text or the Samaritan Pentateuch (a version of the Old Testament from the Jews in Samaria just before Christ). Because of this, the Septuagint adds in extra time. Though the Samaritan and Masoretic texts are much closer, they still have a few differences (see table 3).

Table 3: Septuagint, Masoretic, and Samaritan Early Patriarchal Ages at the Birth of the Following Son

Name of Father	Masoretic	Samaritan Pentateuch	Septuagint (LXX)
Adam	130	130	230
Seth	105	105	205
Enosh	90	90	190
Cainan	70	70	170
Mahalalel	65	65	165
Jared	162	62	162
Enoch	65	65	165
Methuselah	187	67	167
Lamech	182	53	188
Noah	500	500	500

Using data from table 2 (excluding the Septuagint calculations and including Jones and Ussher), the average date of the creation of the earth is 4045 B.C. This still yields an average of about 6,000 years for the age of the earth.

Extra-biblical Calculations for the Age of the Earth

Cultures throughout the world have kept track of history as well. From a biblical perspective, we would expect these dates given for creation of the earth to align much closer to the biblical date than billions of years.

This is expected, since everyone was descended from Noah and scattered from the Tower of Babel. Another expectation is that there should be some discrepancies about the age of the earth among people as they scattered throughout the world, taking their uninspired records or oral history to different parts of the globe.

Under the entry "creation," *Young's Analytical Concordance of the Bible*[11] lists William Hales' accumulation of dates of creation from many cultures. In most cases, Hales says which authority gave the date (see table 4).

---

11. Robert Young, *Young's Analytical Concordance to the Bible* (Peabody, MA: Hendrickson, 1996), referring to William Hales, *A New Analysis of Chronology and Geography, History and Prophecy*, Vol. 1 (1830), p. 210.

Table 4: Selected Dates for the Age of the Earth by Various Cultures

Culture	Age, B.C.	Authority listed by Hales
Spain by Alfonso X	6984	Muller
Spain by Alfonso X	6484	Strauchius
India	6204	Gentil
India	6174	Arab Records
Babylon	6158	Bailly
Chinese	6157	Bailly
Greece by Diogenes Laertius	6138	Playfair
Egypt	6081	Bailly
Persia	5507	Bailly
Israel/Judea by Josephus	5555	Playfair
Israel/Judea by Josephus	5481	Jackson
Israel/Judea by Josephus	5402	Hales
Israel/Judea by Josephus	4698	University History
India	5369	Megasthenes
Babylon (Talmud)	5344	Petrus Alliacens
Vatican (Catholic using the Septuagint)	5270	N/A
Samaria	4427	Scaliger
German, Holy Roman Empire by Johannes Kepler*	3993	Playfair
German, reformer by Martin Luther	3961	N/A
Israel/Judea by computation	3760	Strauchius
Israel/Judea by Rabbi Lipman	3616	University History

* Luther, Kepler, Lipman, and the Jewish computation likely used biblical texts to determine the date.

Historian Bill Cooper's research in *After the Flood* provides dates from several ancient cultures.[12] The first is that of the Anglo-Saxons, whose history has 5,200 years from creation to Christ, according to the Laud and Parker Chronicles. Cooper's research also indicated that Nennius' record of

12. Bill Cooper, *After the Flood* (UK: New Wine Press, 1995), p. 122–129.

the ancient British history has 5,228 years from creation to Christ. The Irish chronology has a date of about 4000 B.C. for creation, which is surprisingly close to Ussher and Jones! Even the Mayans had a date for the Flood of 3113 B.C. (the biblical date being 2349 B.C.).

The meticulous work of many historians should not be ignored. Their dates of only thousands of years are good support for the biblical date somewhere in the neighborhood of about 6,000 years, but not for millions or billions of years.

Origin of Geological Evolution

Prior to the late 1700s, precious few believed in an old earth. The approximate 6,000-year age for the earth was challenged only rather recently, beginning in the late 18th century. These opponents of the biblical chronology essentially left God out of the picture.

Old-earth advocates included Comte de Buffon, who thought the earth was at least 75,000 years old; Pièrre-Simon Laplace imagined an indefinite but very long history; and Jean-Baptiste Lamarck also proposed long ages.[13]

However, the idea of millions of years really took hold in geology when men like Abraham Werner, James Hutton, William Smith, Georges Cuvier, and Charles Lyell used their interpretations of geology as the standard, rather than the Bible. Werner estimated the age of the earth at about one million years. Smith and Cuvier believed untold ages were needed for the formation of rock layers. Hutton said he could see no geological evidence of a beginning of the earth; and building on Hutton's thinking, Lyell advocated "millions of years."

From these men and others came the secular consensus view that the geologic layers were laid down slowly over long periods of time based on the rates at which we see them accumulating today. This view is known as uniformitarianism since it proposes steady geologic processes over long periods of time. Hutton said:

> The past history of our globe must be explained by what can be seen to be happening now. . . . No powers are to be employed that are not natural to the globe, no action to be admitted except those of which we know the principle.[14]

13. Terry Mortenson, "The Origin of Old-earth Geology and Its Ramifications for Life in the 21st Century," TJ 18, no. 1 (2004): 22–26, online at www.answersingenesis.org/tj/v18/i1/oldearth.asp.
14. James Hutton, *Theory of the Earth* (trans. of Roy. Soc. of Edinburgh, 1785), quoted in A. Holmes, *Principles of Physical Geology* (UK: Thomas Nelson & Sons Ltd., 1965), p. 43–44.

Though some, such as Cuvier and Smith, believed in multiple catastrophes separated by long periods of time, the uniformitarian concept became the ruling dogma in geology.

Thinking biblically, we can see that the global Flood of Genesis 6–8 would wipe away the concept of millions of years, for this Flood would explain massive amounts of fossil layers. Most Christians fail to realize that a global Flood could rip up many of the previous rock layers and redeposit them elsewhere, destroying the previous fragile contents. This would destroy any evidence of alleged millions of years anyway. So the rock layers can theoretically represent the evidence of either millions of years or a global Flood, but not both. Sadly, by about 1840 even most of the church elite had accepted the dogmatic claims of the secular geologists and rejected the global Flood[15] and the biblical age of the earth.

After Lyell, in 1899 Lord Kelvin (William Thomson) calculated the age of the earth based on the cooling rate of a molten sphere instead of water (Genesis 1:2).[16] He calculated it to be a maximum of about 20–40 million years (this was revised from his earlier calculation of 100 million years in 1862).[17]

With the development of radiometric dating in the early 20th century, the age of the earth expanded radically. In 1913, Arthur Holmes' book, *The Age of the Earth,* gave an age of 1.6 billion years.[18] Since then, the supposed age of the earth has expanded to its present estimate of about 4.5 billion years (and about 14 billion years for the universe). But there is growing scientific evidence that radiometric dating methods are completely unreliable.[19]

---

15. Some still accepted a global Flood, but considered it geologically insignificant. This position is often called the Tranquil Flood theory. But when the devastating effects of even a local flood are observed, a tranquil global Flood becomes an absurdity.

16. The earth was without form, and void; and darkness was on the face of the deep. And the Spirit of God was hovering over the face of the waters.

17. Mark McCartney, "William Thompson: King of Victorian Physics," *Physics World*, December 2002, physicsworld.com/cws/article/print/16484.

18. Terry Mortenson, "The History of the Development of the Geological Column," in *The Geologic Column*, eds. Michael Oard and John Reed (Chino Valley, AZ: Creation Research Society, 2006).

19. For articles at the layman's level, see www.answersingenesis.org/home/area/faq/dating.asp. For a technical discussion, see Larry Vardiman, Andrew Snelling, and Eugene Chaffin, eds., *Radioisotopes and the Age of the Earth*, Vol. 1 and 2 (El Cajon, CA: Institute for Creation Research; Chino Valley, Arizona: Creation Research Society, 2000 and 2005). See also "Half-Life Heresy," *New Scientist*, October 21 2006, p. 36–39, abstract online at www.newscientist.com/channel/fundamentals/mg19225741.100-halflife-heresy-accelerating-radioactive-decay.html.

Table 5: Summary of the Old-Earth Proponents of Long Ages

Who?	Age of the earth	Date
Comte de Buffon	78 thousand years	1779
Abraham Werner	1 million years	1786
James Hutton	Perhaps eternal, long ages	1795
Pièrre LaPlace	Long ages	1796
Jean-Baptiste Lamarck	Long ages	1809
William Smith	Long ages	1835
Georges Cuvier	Long ages	1812
Charles Lyell	Millions of years	1830–1833
Lord Kelvin	20–100 million years	1862–1899
Arthur Holmes	1.6 billion years	1913
Clair Patterson	4.5 billion years	1956

Christians who have felt compelled to accept the millions of years as fact and try to fit them into the Bible need to become aware of this evidence. Today, secular geologists will allow some catastrophic events into their thinking as an explanation for what they see in the rocks. But uniformitarian thinking is still widespread, and secular geologists will seemingly never entertain the idea of the global catastrophic Flood of Noah's day.

The age of the earth debate ultimately comes down to this foundational question: Are we trusting man's imperfect and changing ideas and assumptions about the past, or are we trusting God's perfectly accurate eyewitness account of the past, including the creation of the world, Noah's global Flood, and the age of the earth?

When we start our thinking with God's Word, we see that the world is about 6,000 years old. Ancient cultures around the world give an age of the earth that confirms what the Bible teaches. The age of the earth ultimately comes down to a matter of trust — it's a religious issue. Will you trust what an all-knowing God says on the subject or will you trust imperfect man's assumptions and imaginations about the past that change regularly?

Sadly, many theologians in the 1800s began mixing geological evolution (millions of years) with the Bible — even before Darwin had published his work on biological evolution. This opened the door to accepting other forms of evolution as well. Let's take a look at these positions that theologians developed to accommodate evolutionary ideas.

Christian Syncretistic Positions

Here are some of the differing positions within the church — but all having one common factor — endeavoring to somehow fit geological evolution into the Bible.

Gap Theories

In general, these theories accommodate geological and astronomical evolution by placing vast ages in a "gap" in the first few verses of Genesis.

Pre-time Gap: This view adds long ages prior to God creating in Genesis 1:1.[20] The pre-time gap falls short for a number of reasons such as death before sin, allowance of man's ideas about millions of years to supersede God's Word, and the like. As another example, how can one have millions of years of time prior to the creation of time? It is quite illogical.

Ruin-reconstruction Gap: This is the most popular gap theory, which adds long ages between Genesis 1:1[21] and Genesis 1:2.[22] Scottish pastor Thomas Chalmers popularized it in the early 1800s. This idea is promoted in the Scofield and Dake Study Bibles and is often associated with a Luciferian fall and flood — but that would make Lucifer (Satan) in his sinful state very good and perfect since God said everything He made was "very good" after Adam had been created (Deuteronomy 32:4[23]; Genesis 1:31).[24]

Modified Gap/Precreation Chaos Gap: This view adds long ages between Genesis 1:2[25] and 1:3,[26] and it is primarily addressed in the International Conference on Creation article listed in this reference.[27]

---

20. In the beginning God created the heavens and the earth.
21. Ibid.
22. The earth was without form, and void; and darkness was on the face of the deep. And the Spirit of God was hovering over the face of the waters.
23. He is the Rock, His work is perfect; for all His ways are justice, a God of truth and without injustice; righteous and upright is He.
24. Ken Ham, "What About the Gap & Ruin-Reconstruction Theories?" in *The New Answers Book*, Ken Ham, Gen. Ed. (Green Forest, AR: Master Books, 2006); for a technical response see also, W. Fields, *Unformed and Unfilled*, (Burgener Enterprises, 1997).
25. The earth was without form, and void; and darkness was on the face of the deep. And the Spirit of God was hovering over the face of the waters.
26. Then God said, "Let there be light"; and there was light.
27. One refutation of this view is in the Proceedings of the Sixth International Conference on Creationism, 2008, by John Zoschke, *A Critique of the Precreation Chaos Gap Theory*, ed., Andrew Snelling.

Soft Gap: This also includes a gap between Genesis 1:2[28] and 1:3,[29] but unlike previous views, it has no catastrophic events or destruction of a previous state. Furthermore, it merely proposes that God created the world this way and left it for long periods of time in an effort to get starlight here. In essence, this view has a young earth and an old universe. The problem is that stars were created after the proposed gap (day 4), and it is unnecessary to make accommodations for long ages to solve the so-called starlight problem.

Late Gap: This view has a gap between chapters 2 and 3 of Genesis. In other words, some believe that Adam and Eve lived in the Garden for long ages before sin. This view has problems too. For example, Adam and Eve were told by God to be "fruitful and multiply" in Genesis 1:28,[30] and waiting long ages to do so would have been disobeying God's Word. This doesn't make sense. In addition, there is the problem of Adam only living 930 years as recorded in Genesis (Genesis 5:5[31]).[32]

When someone tries to put a large gap of time in the Scriptures when it is not warranted by the text, this should throw up a red flag to any Christian.

Day-Age Models

Each of these views adheres to some form of astronomical and geologic evolution, but most would reject chemical and biological evolution (or at least Darwinian evolution). The name comes from equating each of the days of Genesis 1 to a long period of time.

Day-Age: This idea was popularized by Hugh Miller in the early 1800s after walking away from Chalmers' idea of the gap theory. This model basically stretched the days of creation out to be millions of years long. Some would accept biological evolution (to varying degrees), but most would believe in the special creation of humans even if they allow for other living things to evolve. Of course, lengthening the days in Genesis to accommodate

---

28. The earth was without form, and void; and darkness was on the face of the deep. And the Spirit of God was hovering over the face of the waters.
29. Then God said, "Let there be light"; and there was light.
30. Then God blessed them, and God said to them, "Be fruitful and multiply; fill the earth and subdue it; have dominion over the fish of the sea, over the birds of the air, and over every living thing that moves on the earth."
31. So all the days that Adam lived were nine hundred and thirty years; and he died.
32. Bodie Hodge, *The Fall of Satan* (Green Forest, AR: Master Books, 2011), p. 23–26, https://answersingenesis.org/bible-characters/adam-and-eve/when-did-adam-and-eve-rebel/.

the secular evolutionist view of history simply doesn't match up with what is stated in Genesis 1.[33]

Progressive Creation: This is a modified form of the Day-Age idea (really in many ways it's similar to Theistic Evolution) led by Dr. Hugh Ross, head of an organization called Reasons to Believe. He appeals to nature (actually the secular interpretations of nature) as the supposed 67th book of the Bible, and then uses these interpretations to supersede what the Bible says, thus reinterpreting Genesis to force these ideas into Scripture. Dr. John Ankerberg is also a leading supporter of this viewpoint.[34] This view proposes that living creatures go extinct repeatedly over millions of years, but God, from time to time, makes new kinds and new species all fitting with a (geologically and cosmologically/astronomically) evolutionary timeframe of history.[35]

Theistic Evolutionary Models (each basically adhere to geological, astronomical, and biological evolution)

Theistic Evolution (Evolutionary Creation): Basically, the straightforward reading of Genesis 1–11 is thrown out or heavily reinterpreted to allow for evolutionary ideas to supersede the Scriptures. This view is heavily promoted by a group called BioLogos. They accept the prevailing evolutionist history, including the big bang, and then add God to it, giving Him credit for setting the laws of nature in place to bring about mankind. BioLogos writers have different ways of wildly reinterpreting Genesis to fit evolution into Scripture. Many would say that Genesis 1–11 has nothing to do with how God created, only to offer the Israelites a creation myth like the surrounding nations had.

Framework Hypothesis: Dr. Meredith Kline (1922–2007), who accepted some evolutionary ideas, popularized this view in America.[36] Today,

---

33. Terry Mortenson, "Evolution vs. Creation: The Order of Events Matters!" Answers in Genesis, April 4, 2006, https://answersingenesis.org/why-does-creation-matter/evolution-vs-creation-the-order-of-events-matters/.

34. J. Seegert, "Responding to the Compromise Views of John Ankerberg," Answers in Genesis, March 2, 2005, https://answersingenesis.org/reviews/tv/responding-to-the-compromise-views-of-john-ankerberg/.

35. Ken Ham and Terry Mortenson, "What's Wrong with Progressive Creation?" in Ken Ham, Gen. Ed., *The New Answers Book 2* (Green Forest, AR: Master Book, 2008), p. 123–134.

36. It was originally developed in 1924 by Professor Arnie Noordtzij in Europe, which was a couple of decades before Dr. Kline jumped on board with Framework Hypothesis.

Bruce Waltke holds it in esteem. It is very common in many seminaries today. Those who hold this view treat Genesis 1 as poetry or semi-poetic, with the first three days paralleling the last three days of creation. These days are not seen as 24-hour days, but are taken as metaphorical or allegorical to allow for ideas like evolution/millions of years to be entertained. Hence, Genesis 1 is treated as merely being a literary device to teach that God created everything.[37] However, Genesis 1 is not written as poetry, but as literal history.[38]

Cosmic Temple/Functionality View: Dr. John Walton agrees the language of Genesis 1 means ordinary days, but since he believes in evolution he had to do something to reconcile the biblical text to this belief. Walton proposes that Genesis 1 has nothing to do with material origins, but instead is referring to what he calls "God's Cosmic Temple." By disconnecting Genesis 1 from material origins of earth, he is free to believe in evolution and millions of years.

Other attempts to include evolutionary ideas into Genesis include Revelatory Day View by J.P. Wiseman, Analogical (Anthropomorphic) Day View by C. John Collins, and the Promised Land View (a modified gap theory) by John Sailhamer. In each case, the Bible's plain reading is demoted to allow for evolutionary ideas.

Problems with Evolutionary Syncretism

Global or Local Flood?

> The flood was indeed a river flood. . . . The language of Genesis allows for a regional flood. . . . The parts of modern Iraq which were occupied by the ancient Sumerians are extremely

---

37. Tim Chaffey and Robert McCabe, "What Is Wrong with the Framework Hypothesis?" Answers in Genesis, June 11, 2011, https://answersingenesis.org/creationism/old-earth/whats-wrong-with-the-framework-hypothesis/.

38. Hebrew expert Dr. Steven Boyd writes: "For Genesis 1:1–2:3, this probability is between 0.999942 and 0.999987 at a 99.5% confidence level. Thus, we conclude with statistical certainty that this text is narrative, not poetry. It is therefore statistically indefensible to argue that it is poetry. The hermeneutical implication of this finding is that this text should be read as other historical narratives. . . ." Dr. Steven Boyd, Associate Professor of Bible, The Master's College, *Radioisotopes and the Age of the Earth*, Volume II, Editors Larry Vardiman, Andrew Snelling, and Eugene Chaffin, ICR and CRS, 2005, p. 632. I would go one step further than Dr. Boyd, who left open the slim possibility of Genesis not being historical narrative, and say it is historical narrative and all doctrines of theology, directly or indirectly, are founded in the early pages of Genesis — though I appreciated Dr. Boyd's research.

flat. The floodplain, surrounding the Tigris and the Euphrates rivers, covers over 50,000 square miles which slope toward the gulf at less than one foot per mile. . . . Drainage is extremely poor and flooding is quite common, even without large rainstorms during the summer river-level peak (when Noah's flood happened).[39]

A Christian who believes that Noah's Flood was local and did not cover the entire globe penned these words. In fact, the idea of a small regional flood in Noah's day is often promoted by Christians who mix the Bible's clear teaching with "millions of years" of supposed naturalistic history!

As a reminder, you need to understand that the idea of millions of years comes from the belief that rock layers all over the world were laid down slowly over long ages without any major catastrophes. In other words, the idea of millions of years is predicated on the idea that there could NOT have been a global Flood. Otherwise, a global Flood would disrupt rock layers that exist and rearrange the sediment and lay down new rock layers!

What Does the Bible Say?

Did Noah experience a local flood, which left only a few sediment layers as floods do today? God's record is clear: the water covered the entire globe and killed all the land-dwelling animals on earth not aboard the ark. Such unique conditions are the only consistent way to explain worldwide fossil-bearing layers thousands of feet deep.

Scripture is clear about the historic reality of a global Flood in Noah's day. Genesis 7:17–23 specifically says:

> Now the flood was on the earth forty days. The waters increased and lifted up the ark, and it rose high above the earth. The waters prevailed and greatly increased on the earth, and the ark moved about on the surface of the waters. And the waters prevailed exceedingly on the earth, and all the high hills under the whole heaven were covered. The waters prevailed fifteen cubits upward, and the mountains were covered. And all flesh died that moved on the earth: birds and cattle and beasts and

---

39. Don Stoner, "The Historical Context for the Book of Genesis," Revision 2011-06-06, Part 3: Identifying Noah and the Great Flood, http://www.dstoner.net/Genesis_Context/Context.html#part3.

every creeping thing that creeps on the earth, and every man. All in whose nostrils was the breath of the spirit of life, all that was on the dry land, died. So He destroyed all living things which were on the face of the ground: both man and cattle, creeping thing and bird of the air. They were destroyed from the earth. Only Noah and those who were with him in the ark remained alive.

The Scripture is clear that "all the high hills under the whole heaven were covered" as "the waters prevailed fifteen cubits [that is about ~26 feet,[40] or ~8 m.] upward." All air-breathing land animals and people who were outside the ark who lived on the earth also died (Genesis 7:22–23).

Today, many people, including Christians, unfortunately do not accept the biblical account of a worldwide flood because they have been taught that most rocks and fossils were deposited over millions of years (and therefore not by a global Flood). Until the 1800s, most people from the Middle East to the Western world believed what the Bible records about creation and the global Flood. The secular idea of millions of years did not gain extensive popularity until the 1830s, under the influence of a man named Charles Lyell — who opposed a global Flood!

Based on how slowly some rock layers seem to form today (assuming no catastrophes), Lyell rejected the Bible's claims and declared that the earth's many rock layers must have been laid down slowly over millions of years. But he never witnessed the actual formation of the earlier rocks to see whether a unique, one-time global Flood unlike anything we observe today could lay the majority of the rock layers with fossils.

Lyell's claim was based on his own preconceptions and belief in the religion of naturalism, not his observations. Lyell's idea took hold in Western universities and spread throughout the Western world.

As a response, many Christians simply tried to add this idea of long ages to the Bible. What these Christians should have done was stand on the authority of the Bible and defend the global Flood, which can easily account for the bulk of fossil-bearing rock layers we find all over the world. Naturally, we have had some rock layers since the time of the Flood with local catastrophes such as volcanoes or local floods. But the bulk of the rock layers with fossils came from the Flood of Noah's day.

---

40. Using the long cubit of about 20.4 inches.

Some Christians have tried to put millions of years of rock formation before the global Flood to explain the bulk of the rock layers that contain fossils. But the problem is that the floodwaters would have ripped up a number of these old rock layers and laid down new ones! So this compromise not only fails to explain the rock layers, but also dishonors the clear claims of Scripture. The global Flood makes perfect sense, and it is foolish to stray from God's Word just because some men disagree that it happened.

Although there is tremendous physical evidence of a global flood, ultimately it is a matter of trust in a perfect God who created everything (Genesis 1:1),[41] knows everything (Colossians 2:3),[42] has always been there (Revelation 22:13),[43] and cannot lie (Titus 1:2).[44] The only alternative is to trust imperfect, fallible human beings who can only speculate on the past (see Romans 3:4).[45]

Local Flood Problems

Additionally, there are many problems with the claim that Noah's Flood was local. For instance:

- Why did God tell Noah to build an ark? If the Flood had been only local, Noah and his family could have just moved to higher ground or over a local mountain range or hills to avoid the floodwaters.
- The wicked people that the Flood was intended to destroy could have escaped God's judgment in the same manner. They could have used small boats or floating debris to swim to the edge of the flooded region and survive.
- Why would Noah have to put birds on the ark when they could have flown over the hills to safe ground?
- Why would animals be required to be on the ark to keep their kinds alive on the earth (Genesis 7:2–3)[46] if representatives

---

41. In the beginning God created the heavens and the earth.
42. In whom [Christ] are hidden all the treasures of wisdom and knowledge.
43. I am the Alpha and the Omega, the Beginning and the End, the First and the Last.
44. In hope of eternal life which God, who cannot lie, promised before time began.
45. Certainly not! Indeed, let God be true but every man a liar. As it is written: "That You may be justified in Your words, and may overcome when You are judged."
46. You shall take with you seven each of every clean animal, a male and his female; two each of animals that are unclean, a male and his female; also seven each of birds of the air, male and female, to keep the species alive on the face of all the earth.

of their kinds existed all over the earth outside of the alleged local Flood area?

- Did God fail at His stated task where He said that He would destroy all land animals on the earth since the Flood was *local* (Genesis 6:17)?[47]

- Why would a flood occur over the course of about a year if it were local?

- Why did Noah remain on the ark for about seven months after coming to rest after a little river flood? Does a local flood really have about five months of rising and five months of falling in a river valley? Such a flood would merely carve out a deep valley and wash Noah downstream to the ocean!

- How could the ark have landed in the mountains of Ararat far upstream (and up in the mountains above) from the alleged river valley when all flow is going to take the ark in the opposite direction toward the Persian Gulf?

- The Flood occurred about 1,656 years after creation. If all people outside the ark were judged and drowned in this little local river Flood (e.g., Genesis 7:23;[48] Matthew 24:39[49]) then they were all still living in this one little region on earth. Why didn't the Lord previously confuse their languages and scatter them for disobeying his command in Genesis 1 to be fruitful and multiply (Genesis 1:28)?[50] It only took about 100 years or so after the Flood for God to judge mankind for not scattering at Babel.[51]

The proposal of a local Flood for Genesis 6–8 simply doesn't make sense in the context.

---

47. And behold, I Myself am bringing floodwaters on the earth, to destroy from under heaven all flesh in which is the breath of life; everything that is on the earth shall die.

48. So He destroyed all living things which were on the face of the ground: both man and cattle, creeping thing and bird of the air. They were destroyed from the earth. Only Noah and those who were with him in the ark remained alive.

49. And did not know until the flood came and took them all away, so also will the coming of the Son of Man be.

50. Then God blessed them, and God said to them, "Be fruitful and multiply; fill the earth and subdue it; have dominion over the fish of the sea, over the birds of the air, and over every living thing that moves on the earth."

51. Bodie Hodge, *Tower of Babel* (Green Forest, AR: Master Books, 2013), p. 37–42.

Rainbow Promise

Another problem presents itself. If the Flood were local, then God would be a liar. God promised in Genesis 9:11[52] never to send a Flood like the one He just did to destroy the earth again. Yet the world has seen many local floods. Why the rainbow promise? The Bible says:

> Thus I establish My covenant with you: Never again shall all flesh be cut off by the waters of the flood; never again shall there be a flood to destroy the earth." And God said: "This is the sign of the covenant which I make between Me and you, and every living creature that is with you, for perpetual generations: I set My rainbow in the cloud, and it shall be for the sign of the covenant between Me and the earth. It shall be, when I bring a cloud over the earth, that the rainbow shall be seen in the cloud; and I will remember My covenant which is between Me and you and every living creature of all flesh; the waters shall never again become a flood to destroy all flesh. The rainbow shall be in the cloud, and I will look on it to remember the everlasting covenant between God and every living creature of all flesh that is on the earth." And God said to Noah, "This is the sign of the covenant which I have established between Me and all flesh that is on the earth" (Genesis 9:11–17).

This rules out the idea of a local flood. Some have commented that they think rainbows didn't exist until this point in Genesis 9. However, the Bible doesn't say this. Like bread and wine used in communion, so a rainbow now takes on the meaning as designated by God.

Each old-earth Christian worldview has no choice but to demote a global Flood to a local flood in order to accommodate the alleged millions of years (geological evolution) of rock layers (a global Flood would have destroyed these layers and laid down new ones).[53]

---

52. Thus I establish My covenant with you: Never again shall all flesh be cut off by the waters of the flood; never again shall there be a flood to destroy the earth.
53. Jason Lisle and Tim Chaffey, "Defense — A Local Flood?" in *Old Earth Creation on Trial* (Green Forest, AR: Master Books, 2008), p. 93–106, https://answersingenesis.org/the-flood/global/defensea-local-flood.

Big Bang

Also, the compromise views that accept the big-bang model of the origin of the universe have accepted a view that contradicts Scripture. They have adopted a model to explain the universe without God. So if God is added to the big bang idea, then really . . . God didn't do anything because the big-bang model dictates that the universe really created itself.[54]

Death before Sin

Each view also has an insurmountable problem in regard to the issue of death before sin that undermines both the authority of God's Word and the gospel.[55] The idea of millions of years came out of naturalism — the belief that the fossil-bearing rock layers were laid down slowly and gradually over millions of years before man.

This idea was meant to do away with the belief that Noah's Flood was responsible for most of the fossil-bearing sedimentary layers. Now in the fossil remains in these rock layers there is evidence of death, suffering, thorns, carnivory, cancer, and other diseases like arthritis.

So *all* old-earth worldviews have to then accept death, suffering, blood-shed, thorns, carnivory, and diseases like cancer before Adam's sin. Now, after God created Adam, He said everything He made was "very good" (Genesis 1:31).[56] This is confirmed as a *perfect* creation by the God of life in Deuteronomy 32:4[57] since every work of God is perfect.

But if one has accepted the millions-of-years idea to explain the fossil record, then millions of years of death, bloodshed, disease, thorns, suffering, and carnivory existed before man. But as the Bible makes clear, it was Adam's sin that caused death (Genesis 2:16–17,[58] 3:19[59]), suffering (e.g., Genesis

---

54. J. Lisle, "Does the Big Bang Fit with the Bible?" in K. Ham, Gen. Ed., *The New Answers Book 2* (Green Forest, AR: Master Books, 2008), p. 103–110, https://answersingenesis. org/big-bang/does-the-big-bang-fit-with-the-bible.

55. Hodge, *The Fall of Satan*, p. 68–76.

56. Then God saw everything that He had made, and indeed it was very good. So the evening and the morning were the sixth day.

57. He is the Rock, His work is perfect; For all His ways are justice, A God of truth and with-out injustice; Righteous and upright is He.

58. And the LORD God commanded the man, saying, "Of every tree of the garden you may freely eat; "but of the tree of the knowledge of good and evil you shall not eat, for in the day that you eat of it you shall surely die."

59. In the sweat of your face you shall eat bread till you return to the ground, for out of it you were taken; For dust you are, and to dust you shall return.

3:16–17),[60] thorns, (Genesis 3:18)[61] and the whole reason why we need a new heavens and a new earth (e.g., Isaiah 66:22;[62] 2 Peter 3:13;[63] Revelation 21:1[64]) — because what we have now is cursed and broken (Romans 8:22).[65]

Also, originally, the Bible makes it clear in Genesis 1:29–30[66] that man and animals were vegetarian — however, the fossil record has many evidences of animals eating animals. Genesis 1:30 is verified as a strictly vegetarian diet since man was not permitted to eat meat until after the Flood as recorded in Genesis 9:3.[67] This new provision only makes sense in contrast to the command in Genesis 1:29.[68]

To accept millions of years also means God called diseases like cancer (of which there is evidence in the fossil record) "very good." And because "without shedding of blood there is no remission" (Hebrews 9:22),[69] then allowing the shedding of blood millions of years before sin would *undermine* the atonement. Really, believing in millions of years blames God for death and disease instead of blaming our sin, from which Christ came to rescue us.

Some compromised Christians have objected, saying, *"But that just means the death of humans entered (Romans 5:12),*[70] *but animals could have*

---

60. To the woman He said: "I will *greatly multiply your sorrow* and your conception; *In pain* you shall bring forth children; your desire shall be for your husband, and he shall rule over you." Then to Adam He said, "Because you have heeded the voice of your wife, and have eaten from the tree of which I commanded you, saying, 'You shall not eat of it': "*Cursed is the ground* for your sake; *in toil* you shall eat of it all the days of your life" [emphasis added].

61. Both thorns and thistles it shall bring forth for you, and you shall eat the herb of the field.

62. "For just as the new heavens and the new earth which I make will endure before Me," declares the LORD, "so your offspring and your name will endure" (NASB).

63. Nevertheless, we, according to His promise, look for new heavens and a new earth, in which righteousness dwells.

64. Then I saw a new heaven and a new earth; for the first heaven and the first earth passed away. Also there was no more sea.

65. For we know that the whole creation groans and labors with birth pangs together until now.

66. And God said, "See, I have given you every herb that yields seed which is on the face of all the earth, and every tree whose fruit yields seed; to you it shall be for food. Also, to every beast of the earth, to every bird of the air, and to everything that creeps on the earth, in which there is life, I have given every green herb for food"; and it was so.

67. Every moving thing that lives shall be food for you. I have given you all things, even as the green herbs.

68. And God said, "See, I have given you every herb that yields seed which is on the face of all the earth, and every tree whose fruit yields seed; to you it shall be for food."

69. And according to the law almost all things are purified with blood, and without shedding of blood there is no remission.

70. Therefore, just as through one man sin entered the world, and death through sin, and thus death spread to all men, because all sinned.

died for billions of years." But this neglects that the first recorded death of animals (to replace fig leaf clothing with animal skins — the first blood sacrifice) in the Bible came as a direct result of human sin in the Garden of Eden (Genesis 3:21).[71]

One cannot deny biblically that there is a relationship between human sin and animal death. Just briefly look at the sacrifices of animals required for human sin throughout the Old Testament. This sacrifice began in the Garden of Eden (the first blood sacrifice as a covering for their sin, a picture of what was to come in the Lamb of God who takes away the sin of the world), that points to Jesus Christ, the ultimate and final sacrifice: . . . for this He did once for all when He offered up Himself (Hebrews 7:27).

Jesus Devastates an Old-Earth View

Allow me to relate this refutation with a discussion I had with a syncretistic Christian. I was attending a Christian conference and staffing an Answers in Genesis booth. As I walked around to look at the other booths at the beginning of this conference, a man quickly came up to me (from his booth), even though there was a crowd waiting to speak with him. He evidently felt the need to confront me (in front of the crowd at his booth) because he saw that I was wearing an Answers in Genesis conference badge.

In a hostile tone, the first thing out of his mouth was something akin to, "Is Answers in Genesis here at the conference? Well, I guess I am going to have to find your booth and set you straight about the age of the earth!" Clearly, I was dealing with a syncretistic (compromised) Christian.

Perhaps you are thinking, "I'm glad I wasn't in that situation." Well, I don't like those situations either! But for some reason, I tend to be in the middle of debates way too often. What ran through my head was, "How did I get myself into *this* situation? I was only walking through the conference halls!" But I realized there was a crowd of people staring as this man began his diatribe, so there I was, blindsided and thrust into a debate.

Needless to say, 2 Timothy 2:24–25 and 1 Peter 3:15 say to always be prepared to give an answer and be ready in season and out of season to rebuke and correct with gentleness and patience. I realized this "out of season" debate was going to occur, but I still needed to do it with gentleness, while being bold.

---

71. Also for Adam and his wife the LORD God made tunics of skin, and clothed them.

I asked this man, "In the context of the first marriage between Adam and Eve, do you think Jesus was wrong in Mark 10:6 when He said that God made them male and female at the *beginning of creation*? Or do you believe that the creation has been around for 13 billions years and marriage first came about near the *end of creation* a few thousand years ago with Adam and Eve?"[72]

Allow me to explain why I asked the question this way. If you start with the Bible, Adam and Eve were created on the sixth day of creation. So Adam and Eve were created about five days after the initial creation event on day 1. Then if you add up the genealogies from Adam to Jesus, you get a few thousand years (about 4,000 years) as discussed above. Most chronologists agree on this point.

But all Christians who have bought into an old earth have much more than 4,000 years between creation and Christ. They insert about 13–15 billion years, to be more precise, between the creation event that they call the big bang and marriage between the first human male and female. They further state that Adam and Eve only showed up a matter of thousands of years ago. So all old-earth scenarios have marriage (between human male and female, which first began with Adam and Eve) about 13–15 billion years after creation, which is the *end of creation*, nowhere near the *beginning of creation*.

Returning to the questioner, it was apparent that he was not ready for that question. What I did was contrast his stated position against what Christ clearly said. And this man knew it right off the bat. So did the crowd watching. They wanted to hear his answer, and so did I.

Realizing he was trapped in a "catch-22," this man immediately changed the subject to talk about what secular scientists believe about the age of the earth. Notice how he shifted from the authority of God's Word to the alleged authority of man regarding evolutionary ideas. I wasn't going to let him do that. He needed to address what Jesus said.

So I again kindly asked, "Was Jesus wrong in your view?" This man who had been so confident and aggressive began to squirm right where he stood. He responded, "I don't want to deal with that."

---

72. In *any* long-age scenario, mankind only showed up on the scene a matter of thousand years ago; so, in a long-age scenario, it would be impossible for marriage between a man and woman to be any earlier than the *very end* of creation about 13 billion years later. The Bible also affirms that we are at the end (Acts 2:17; Hebrews 1:2; 1 Peter 4:7).

At this point, I concluded our conversation by saying, "That is the crux of the issue: either you trust God's Word, or you don't." Hopefully, it was apparent to the crowd that this man was not standing on what Christ said in His Word, but was clinging to outside influences and did not want to address what Christ had said. Frankly, I was nervous, but I was being bold and seeking to be kind and gracious.

Why Is Mark 10:6 So Powerful?

Jesus said the following in the context of marriage and divorce:

> But from the beginning of the creation, God "made them male and female" (Mark 10:6).

> And He answered and said to them, "Have you not read that He who made them at the beginning 'made them male and female' " (Matthew 19:4).

If one believes Christ is Lord and is dedicated to following the words of Jesus, then accepting millions of years becomes an enormous problem. According to any old-earth or old-universe scenario, the creation began many billions of years ago, with man arriving on the scene a matter of thousands of years ago. How could any professing Christ-follower think that Jesus was in error and that marriage between that first man and a woman (whom Jesus clearly believed were Adam and Eve because in the context of Mark 10:6 he quotes from Genesis 1 and 2) only happened at the tail end of 13 or so billion years?

Jesus, the Creator, makes it clear that the first marriage between man and woman (Adam and Eve) came at the *beginning* of creation. From the chronological information given in Genesis 5 and 11 and in other biblical passages, Jesus was speaking about 4,000 years after this creation (an act He was responsible for).

Since the days in Genesis are regular 24-hour days and Jesus was speaking about 4,000 years later,[73] then the first marriage on day 6 was at the beginning of creation, speaking in non-technical language as Jesus was. If the earth is indeed billions of years old, then the first male and female came

73. Ken Ham, *The New Answers Book 1* (Green Forest, AR: Master Books 2006), p. 88–112, http://www.answersingenesis.org/articles/nab/could-god-have-created-in-six-days; Bodie Hodge, *The New Answers Book 2* (Green Forest, AR: Master Books, 2008), p. 41–52, http://www.answersingenesis.org/articles/2007/05/30/how-old-is-earth.

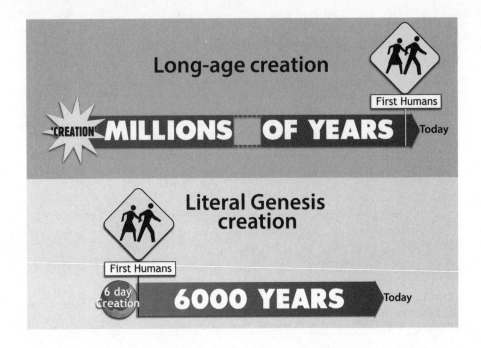

nowhere near the beginning of creation, but at the tail end of creation. This is a major theological problem because it calls into question the truthfulness of Christ in any old-earth/old-universe scenario.

Possible Responses to Mark 10:6

Those who religiously and unquestionably believe in the evolutionary time scale over God's Word (when they syncretize the two religions), yet profess Christ as Lord, have tried to respond. It is because they understand this is a devastating argument from Christ Himself against a "billions-of-years-ago" creation. Of course, the man at the conference did not want to give an answer, but others have tried. There are three common responses that need to be examined.

Some say biblical creationists have the same problem by appealing to Mark 10:6 because Adam and Eve were created on day 6, not day 1 of creation, which they claim *is* the "beginning of creation."

Some insert words into Mark 10:6 to change the meaning to "beginning of the creation *of marriage.*"

Some suggest that *beginning* is referring to an entire figurative "six-day" creation period or creation week, regardless of its length.

Looking at Response 1

This popular response by some theologians was dealt a fatal blow by Dr. Terry Mortenson.[74] But let's consider it briefly here. The argument incorrectly makes the assumption that the "beginning of creation" means the "first day of creation." The Bible doesn't say day 1 of creation; it says the "beginning of the creation" (or simply, "the beginning" in the parallel passage of Matthew 19:4).

If you were to watch a movie and then tell a friend about the beginning of the movie, would that consist of only the first word or frame of the movie? Absolutely not; it would be a range of time surrounding the beginning of the movie and the events that get the movie going.

There are other places in the New Testament that affirm "the beginning" was *near* the events of the beginning that range from the absolute beginning to the events that even occurred soon after creation week, such as the fall into sin. Let's look at some of these.

The absolute beginning: "In the beginning was the Word, and the Word was with God, and the Word was God. He was in the beginning with God" (John 1:1–2).

Upon the creation of Adam and Eve (the first marriage): "He said to them, 'Moses, because of the hardness of your hearts, permitted you to divorce your wives, but from the beginning it was not so'" (Matthew 19:8).

After the "very good" creation was completed (Genesis 1:31) but prior to Adam's sin: "He who sins is of the devil, for the devil has sinned from the beginning. For this purpose the Son of God was manifested, that He might destroy the works of the devil" (1 John 3:8).

After sin entered the world so that tribulation can be possible: "For in those days there will be tribulation, such as has not been since the beginning of the creation which God created until this time, nor ever shall be" (Mark 13:19).

If an old-earth proponent uses response 1, then he is conceding that Jesus was wrong. But can Jesus err? No. But for the sake of argument, if Jesus erred on this point, then perhaps Jesus erred in passages concerning salvation. If this were the case, then it would undermine the gospel, which

74. Terry Mortenson, "But from the Beginning of . . . the Institution of Marriage?" Answers in Genesis, November, 1, 2004, http://www.answersingenesis.org/articles/2004/11/01/from-the-beginning-of-marriage.

a professing Christian claims to believe. The point is that the entire Bible stands or falls on Christ's truthfulness.

Looking at Response 2

Who is fallible, sinful mankind that he should try to add to Scripture to change the meaning of that Scripture in order to "correct" God's Word to fit with man's fallible ideas about the past? Years ago, when I seriously contemplated the idea of millions of years and the big bang, this was the conclusion at which I finally arrived.

I realized that when I try to add millions of years into Genesis, that I would be required to reinterpret God to "correct" Him. Then it hit me. God is always right, and if we have to "reinterpret" God's Word over and over again to mean something other than what it plainly says, then we, as fallible people, are the ones in error (Exodus 20:11; Matthew 19:4–5; Mark 10:6; and so on)!

Allow me to give a glaring instance of something like this as a preface to responding to this second response on Mark 10:6. When I hear someone add to Scripture in order to make it align with views not clearly expressed in Scripture, I think of the treatment of John 1 by Jehovah's Witnesses.[75]

What Do the "Witnesses" Do?

Jehovah's Witnesses view Jesus as a created archangel named Michael. So John 1 becomes a major problem for Jehovah's Witnesses because Jesus, the Word, is the Creator of all things that has been created. They change the Scriptures in their New World Translation (NWT) to align more closely with their religion:

> In the beginning was the Word, and the Word was with God, and the Word was God (John 1:1).

> Jehovah's Witness change: In [the] beginning the Word was, and the Word was with God, and the Word was a god (John 1:1; NWT).

Notice the change to the Word was "a god" as opposed to "God." Sadly, this is done to change the Bible to conform to Jehovah's Witnesses' fallible,

---

75. See Bodie Hodge, Appendix 2, *World Religions and Cults*, Volume 1 (Green Forest, AR: Master Books, 2015), p 409–424.

unitarian theology, even though the NWT really argues for polytheism (more than one God) in this instance. But the point was to try to demote Christ from being God.[76]

This obvious example causes problems for Jehovah's Witnesses because a created Christ (in their view) really cannot endure and satisfy the infinite wrath of God for sin. The only person who could do that is Christ, *who is God*, as the infinite Son who could satisfy the wrath of an infinite God to truly pay the debt in full. The Jehovah's Witnesses have a false, created Christ who cannot save them, since that created Christ could never take the punishment we deserve any more than we could.

Should We Be Doing the Same Thing as the "Witnesses"?

In a familiar but different fashion, old-earth creationists (syncretists) that utilize response 2 do something quite similar. They essentially insert "of marriage," which changes the meaning. Unlike Jehovah's Witnesses, they do not add this to a new translation, nor does it affect the character of Christ, so I wouldn't dare call my old-earth brethren cultic, but I must admit that this tactic is identical to what many cultists do. I do not want my brothers in Christ to go down that path — as I once traveled down that path myself!

But in common, both Jehovah's Witnesses and old-earth creationists have taken outside ideas and imposed them on the Bible, making it mean something other than what *the text says*. It is essentially either mixing with Unitarian religious beliefs or, in this instance, mixing with secular humanistic religious beliefs (e.g., millions of years).

When people try to interpret Mark 10:6 in a way that makes it compatible with the idea of millions of years, then what is the difference between that and what cultists do with the text? Don't mistake what I'm saying here; old-earth proponents can still be saved as long as they trust in Jesus Christ, the Creator, alone for their salvation. They, unlike those who hold Unitarian views of a created Jesus, still believe in the Jesus of the Bible who is God. But their handling of Scripture, like that of cultists, undermines the truth and authority of the Bible.

Let's now turn our attention to why adding "of marriage" to Mark 10:6 is not a viable interpretation of the text. In refuting Drs. John Ankerberg and Norman Geisler, Dr. Terry Mortenson states the following:

---

76. Bodie Hodge, "Is Jesus the Creator God?" *Answers in Depth*, December 12, 2007, http://www.answersingenesis.org/articles/aid/v2/n1/jesus-the-creator.

They argue that *ktisis* (which is actually the noun "creation" not the verb "create," as [Ankerberg/Geisler] say) in Mark 10:6 should be translated as "institution" so that Jesus should be understood to be talking about the beginning of the institution of marriage, not the beginning of creation. They base this interpretation on the fact that in 1 Peter 2:13 *ktisis* is translated in the NIV as "to every authority instituted among men" or in the NASB as "to every human institution." But they have not paid careful attention to the presence of "among men" (NIV) and "human" (NASB) in this verse.

The Greek text is clear. The phrase under question is *pasē anthrōpinē ktisei,* where the whole phrase is in the dative case (so literally "to every human creation") and the adjective *anthrōpinē* ("human") modifies *ktisei* ("creation"). An institutional authority (such as kings, governors and slave masters, which Peter discusses in the context) is indeed a "human creation." But this is a very different contextual use of *ktisis* than we find in Mark 10:6, where no adjective is used to modify "creation." Furthermore, in Mark 10:6, Jesus could have easily said "from the first marriage" or "from the beginning of marriage" or "since God created man" or "since God created Adam," if that is what He meant.

Finally, if we give *ktisis* in Mark 10:6 the meaning "authority" or "institution," it makes no sense. What does from the beginning of authority or beginning of institution mean? To make it meaningful, Ankerberg and Geisler would have to add a word to the text, which would have no contextual justification.[77]

Furthermore, the Jews and pre-"millions-of-years" commentator Dr. John Gill also affirm this was the beginning of the creation, meaning the creation "of the world." Dr. Gill writes the following:

> Of the world, or of man . . . "from the beginning of the creation of the world," is a way of speaking often used by the Jews [Bereshit Rabba, sect. 3. fol. 2. 3. & sect. 4. fol. 4. 1].[78]

> This may be read in #Ge 1:27 and from thence this sense of things collected; that God, who in the beginning of time, or of the creation, as Mark expresses it, made all things, the heavens,

---

77. Mortenson, "But from the Beginning of. . . ."
78. J. Gill, Commentary notes on Mark 10:6.

and the earth, and all that is therein, and particularly "man," as the Vulgate Latin, and Munster's Hebrew Gospel supply it here, made the first parents of mankind, male and female.[79]

When it comes down to it, contrary to Christian syncretists' intentions, advocates of this second response are indirectly doing something that the cults also do — they are adding words to Scripture not to make it consistent with some other religious writings, but with the majority view in the scientific community rather than a cult.

Looking at Response 3

If one concludes that "from the beginning of creation" (and likewise "from the beginning" in Matthew 19:4) means "all of the creative period, regardless of its length," then this is saying that there are 13 billion years of time in the "creative period," which is the beginning, *middle,* and even encompasses the bulk of the *end* of the creation by the time Jesus made this statement (see also Acts 2:17; Hebrews 1:2; 1 Peter 4:7)!

It is strange that one would think that 13 billion years or so have passed and that all of it is the beginning of creation — and now suddenly we are at the end after a few measly thousand years. Going back to our movie illustration, this would be like telling someone that the end was the last second of a movie and that the other two hours of it were only the beginning.

So here, old-earth advocates are changing the definitions of the words *middle* and *end* to also mean "beginning." So they are changing the meanings of words to make them align with their old-earth/old-universe view. Such a redefinition of terms is unwarranted.

Conclusion of the Matter

Jesus' statement in Mark 10:6 is reasonable and accurate in the young-earth view, and *any* view of an old earth fails when trying to deal with marriage of man and woman being at the *beginning of creation.* In short, Jesus's words here devastate the concept of an old earth or old universe. Thus, from the perspective of a perfect Christ, there is no reason to mix millions of years and the evolutionary religion with Christianity.

So it makes sense why this man at the conference didn't want to address my question about Mark 10:6. In fact, in retrospect, his response was better

---

79. John Gill, Commentary notes on Matthew 19:4.

than most. At least he realized there was a problem and opted to remain silent and not reinterpret Christ's words. So for that, I commend him.

Sadly, many others are more than willing to try to reinterpret Christ's plain meaning in Mark 10 because of their absolute adherence to millions and billions of years. Mixing these religions undermines the authority of the Bible, and in many cases it directly undermines the gospel itself.

Conclusion

My hope is that Christians who have bought into belief in an old earth and syncretized the evolutionary beliefs with their Christianity will repent and return to the plain teachings in the Bible and stop mixing God's Word with secular beliefs that clearly contradict God's revelation and undermine the gospel by blaming God for death instead of our sin. I do not say this lightly; for once in my past I did very similar things.

Another point to make regarding syncretism is the issue of salvation. Some have asked, can a syncretist get saved? If they repent and believe in the Jesus Christ of Scripture, that He died, and resurrected on the third day, then of course they can be saved.

As a result, some have remarked that mixing these religions is not a big deal. But this is not true. It *is* a big deal. It is an issue of the authority of God vs. the authority of man. If someone compromises by opening the door to mix their Christianity with another religion, then their witness and testimony to others is that they can do that too!

Why would the next generation stop there and not open the door entirely and give up the whole Bible? Based on statistics, the next generation does push the door open and walks away from the Bible and Christianity.[80] So mixing the religions is not an acceptable avenue but needs to be warned against.

---

80. See the statistics in *Already Gone* and *Ready to Return* by Ken Ham et al. (Green Forest, AR: Master Books).

Chapter 12

The Religion of Naturalism

Dr. Terry Mortenson

Naturalism, or philosophical naturalism, is one of the most popular religions in the world today, although most people don't recognize it as such because it has no *obvious* worship centers, clergy, liturgy, or holy book. It has adherents in every country and dominates many countries, especially among the intellectual elites in the culture. It is therefore important to understand this major religion and how it became so popular. But sadly, it has also had a very significant and largely unrecognized influence on the worldview of many Christians, which is an even greater reason for Christians to understand it.

Naturalism is known by other names: atheism, scientific materialism, and secular humanism. Atheists, secular humanists, and other advocates of naturalism will protest that their view is a religion, but would say it is the opposite of religion. So we need to begin by defining "religion." According to the 11th edition of *Merriam-Webster's Collegiate Dictionary*, one definition of religion is "the service and worship of God or the supernatural." That obviously doesn't apply to atheism. But another given by that dictionary certainly does apply: "a cause, principle, or system of beliefs held to with ardor and faith." Many people who hold to naturalism are just as passionate about their belief as the most convinced Christians, Muslims, Hindus, or adherents of any other religion.[1]

---

1. For a good example of this firm belief, see Tim Chaffey, "Feedback: Is Atheism a Religion?" Answers in Genesis, accessed 9/19/2016, https://answersingenesis.org/world-religions/atheism/feedback-is-atheism-a-religion/.

Defining Naturalism

So what are the beliefs of naturalism? The most fundamental belief from which all others flow is that nature or matter is all that exists. It has always existed or it came into existence from nothing. There is nothing outside or before nature, i.e., the material universe that is studied by modern science. There is no God and no supernatural. Although nature has not always existed in its present form, what we see today is the result of time and chance and the laws of nature working on matter. Miracles are not possible, because they would be a violation of the laws of nature. Non-material things such as hopes, plans, behaviors, languages, logical inferences, etc., exist, but they are the result of and determined by material causes.

As Christian philosopher and theologian Ronald Nash summarizes:

> Nature is a self-explanatory system. Any and every thing that happens within the natural order must, at least in principle, be explainable in terms of other elements of the natural order. It is never necessary to seek the explanation for any event within nature in something beyond the natural order.[2]

With this belief in place, other beliefs follow. So, there is no purpose or meaning to life — we are simply the product of time and chance and the laws of nature; there are no moral absolutes that apply to all people in all times; moral values are simply personal beliefs or opinions, which themselves are the result of chemical and physical processes controlling matter. Likewise, there is no life after death, for the laws of nature still apply and our bodies simply decay over time and are mixed in with other non-living matter in the earth.

The late William Provine, atheist and evolutionary professor of history of biology at Cornell University, put his naturalistic view this way:

> Let me summarize my views on what modern evolutionary biology tells us loud and clear — and these are basically Darwin's views. There are no gods, no purposes, no goal-directed forces of any kind. There is no life after death. When I die, I am absolutely certain that I am going to be dead. That's the end for me.

2. Ronald H. Nash, *Worldviews in Conflict* (Grand Rapids, MI: Zondervan, 1992), p. 120.

There is no ultimate foundation for ethics, no ultimate meaning to life, and no free will for humans, either.[3]

The world's most famous atheist, Richard Dawkins, similarly said, "The universe we observe has precisely the properties we should expect if there is at bottom no design, no purpose, no evil and no good. Nothing but blind, pitiless indifference. DNA neither knows nor cares. DNA just is, and we dance to its music."[4] The first *Humanist Manifesto* was published in 1933. The first two articles of that document state, "FIRST, religious humanists regard the universe as self-existing and not created" and "SECOND, humanism believes that man is a part of nature and that he has emerged as a result of a continuous process." Flowing out of those two starting points, the fifth states, "FIFTH, humanism asserts that the nature of the universe depicted by modern science makes unacceptable any supernatural or cosmic guarantees of human values. . . . Religion must formulate its hopes and plans in the light of the scientific spirit and method."[5]

It will readily be clear to any thoughtful non-naturalist that this worldview is self-refuting. If nature is all that exists and everything is the result of time and chance and the laws of nature, then the naturalist or atheist can have no trust that his thoughts are telling him the truth for they are the result of chemical and physical processes operating in his brain. In fact, in his religion or worldview, objective absolute truth does not exist. Of course, if everything is the result of material causes, then the naturalist has no valid explanation for the origin or truth of the laws of nature that he relies on to understand the world. And if there is no absolute right and wrong, then the atheist cannot object to what Hitler did to the Jews or to what Muslim suicide bombers do to innocent civilians in a shopping mall. Nor could he object if someone entered his home, robbing him of all his valuables and murdering his family. Hitler, the suicide bomber, and the robber/murderer are just doing what they think is right, but their thoughts are dictated by their own DNA, which is produced by purposeless, directionless chemical and physical processes. Of course, neither Provine, nor Dawkins, nor anyone else can really live according to this religion of naturalism. In fact,

3. William Provine, "Darwinism: Science or Naturalistic Philosophy?" *Origins Research,* vol. 16:1/2 (1994): 9.
4. Richard Dawkins, *River Out of Eden* (New York, NY: Basic Books, 1995), p. 133.
5. "Humanist Manifesto I," American Humanist Association, accessed September 19, 2016, http://americanhumanist.org/humanism/humanist_manifesto_i.

to live, the naturalist must steal from the Christian worldview to argue that there is some truth (including the laws of nature) and some things that are absolutely right or wrong.

How Naturalism Became a Dominant Religion

Today, the religion of naturalism/atheism culturally dominates the Western world and the communist world and is widespread among the cultural elites in many other countries dominated by other religions. In addition, many people who profess to believe another religion are significantly influenced by naturalism in their thinking, and outside of their attendance at religious services at their house of worship they actually live like a naturalist/atheist. How did naturalism become such a widespread belief?

The roots of this modern dominance of the naturalistic religion or worldview can be found in the Enlightenment, an intellectual movement of the late 17th and 18th centuries in Europe that elevated human reason to the place of supreme authority for determining truth and understanding ultimate reality. As a result, such thinkers rejected the authority of the Christian church and the Bible. From this philosophical starting point, both deism and atheism became popular in those same centuries.

Deism is a halfway house on the way to atheism and holds that there is a God who created the universe and endowed it with the laws of nature and then left it to operate and develop according to those laws. So God is distant and has not been involved in the creation since the beginning. Apart from the deists' belief in a rather vaguely defined Creator God and a supernatural beginning to the creation, they were indistinguishable from atheists in their views of Scripture and physical reality.[6] In deism, as in atheism, the Bible is merely a human book, containing errors, and not the inspired Word of God, and the history and function of the creation can be totally explained by the properties of matter and the "inviolable laws of nature" in operation over a long period of time.

Deists and atheists often disguised their true views, especially in England and America where they were not culturally acceptable. Many of them gained influential positions in the scientific establishment of Europe and America, where they subtly and effectively promoted naturalistic thinking.

---

6. A good brief discussion of deism is found in James W. Sire, *The Universe Next Door* (Downers Grove, IL: InterVarsity Press, 2009, 5th ed.), p. 47–65.

Brooke, noted historian of science, comments on the subtle influence of deistic forms of naturalism when he writes:

> Without additional clarification, it is not always clear to the historian (and was not always clear to contemporaries) whether proponents of design were arguing a Christian or deistic thesis. The ambiguity itself could be useful. By cloaking potentially subversive discoveries in the language of natural theology, scientists could appear more orthodox than they were, but without the discomfort of duplicity if their inclinations were more in line with deism.[7]

But the effects of deistic and atheistic philosophy on biblical studies and Christian theology also became widespread on the European continent in the late 18th century and in Britain and America by the middle of the 19th century. As Reventlow concluded in his massive study:

> We cannot overestimate the influence exercised by Deistic thought, and by the principles of the Humanist world-view which the Deists made the criterion of their biblical criticism, on the historical-critical exegesis of the nineteenth century; the consequences extend right down to the present. At that time a series of almost unshakeable presuppositions were decisively shifted in a different direction.[8]

Historians of science agree that modern science was born in the womb of the Christian worldview. The Bible teaches that the Creator is a God of order who created an orderly world to reveal His glory (Psalm 19:1–6). Also, man was created in the image of God with a rational mind, and from the beginning man was commanded to rule over the creation (Genesis 1:27–28). Therefore, man could and should study the creation to discover that order and learn how to use the creation for the good of mankind and the glory of God.

So the biblical worldview, which had dominated the Western nations for centuries, was rapidly being replaced by a naturalistic worldview. Science

---

7. John H. Brooke, *Science and Religion* (Cambridge, UK: Cambridge University Press, 1991), p. 194.

8. Henning G. Reventlow, *The Authority of the Bible and the Rise of the Modern World,* John Bowden, transl. (London: SCM Press, 1984), p. 412.

became the main instrument for producing this transformation. Scientists became the priests of that religion, and through them many others were won to that faith. To understand how this happened, we need to distinguish between two broad categories of science. I like to call them operation science and origin science.

Operation science (also called experimental science or observational science) is what most people have in mind when they hear the word "science." I define it this way:

> The use of observable, repeatable experiments in a controlled environment (usually in a laboratory) to understand how things operate or function in the present physical universe to find cures for disease, produce new technology, put a man on the moon, etc.

Most of biology, chemistry, physics, medical research, and engineering research are in the realm of operation science. Scientists in these fields are studying how things in the natural world operate or function so they can manipulate, copy, utilize, or destroy (harmful) things for the improvement of human life or the environment. This kind of science works on the assumption that the laws of nature are constant and apply everywhere in the universe. Without this assumption scientists would not be able to discover cures for disease or develop new technologies. So this kind of science is essentially naturalistic in methodology: God and miracles are not considered or invoked as an explanation of how things operate.

Bible-believing creation scientists engage in operation science the same way other scientists do, for Scripture indicates that what we call today the laws of nature are simply descriptive of how God normally upholds His creation by His sovereign providence and care (e.g., Genesis 8:22; Jeremiah 31:35–36; Colossians 1:17; Hebrews 1:3). But the laws of nature are not absolute and unchangeable (so that not even God can "violate" them). He altered or suspended some of those laws at the Fall when He cursed His "very good" original creation (Genesis 1:31) because of man's sin (Genesis 3:14–19; Romans 8:19–23) and at the Flood (Genesis 8:21) and in other localized events when He performed miracles, such as the parting of the Red Sea (Exodus 14:19–31), the crossing of the Jordan River (Joshua 3:14–17), and in connection to the ministries of Old Testament prophets, New Testament

Apostles, and Jesus. Bible-believing scientists also cannot categorically rule out the possibility of God doing a miracle today (e.g., in a supernatural physical healing), although Scripture would lead them to believe that these would be on a personal level and extremely rare.

But while operation science is a source of new technology and cure for diseases, it cannot answer the question of how the Grand Canyon formed, for example. How did those horizontal layers of limestone, sandstone, and shale form? They are tens or hundreds of feet thick and cover thousands or tens of thousands of square miles. How were they deposited? In an ocean? In a desert? How long did it take for each layer to form and how much time passed between the layers and how long ago did it all happen? And how did the canyon form? It is 280 miles long (including Marble Canyon at the northeast end), 4–18 miles wide, and a mile deep. Was it carved by a little water eroding hard rock over a long period of time? The work of the Colorado River? Or was it caused by a lot of water eroding wet sediments or relatively soft rock in a short period of time?

Or how did stars and galaxies and the solar system come into existence? How did the first apple trees or rabbits or butterflies or people come into existence and how long ago? How did human language come about? These are historical questions. We can't create any of these things in the laboratory. We can't repeat these events and observe them occurring in the present. We want to know what happened in the unobserved past to produce what we observe in the present. Operation science can't answer these questions because it is studying observable, repeatable processes in the present. At best, we can observe, say, erosion and sedimentation events today and *by analogy* suggest the cause or causes in the past that produced the Grand Canyon and the layers we see exposed. But we can't re-create the Grand Canyon in the lab, and it dwarfs any canyons and sedimentary layers we see forming in recent times.

For historical questions we need what I like to call origin science (or historical science). I define it this way:

> The use of reliable, eyewitness testimony (if any is available) and presently observable evidence to determine the past, unobservable, unrepeatable event or events which produced the observable evidence we see in the present.

Origin or historical sciences include historical geology, paleontology, archeology, and cosmology. They study things in the present to attempt to reconstruct the past. As Martin Rudwick, the leading historian of geology, explains:

> Even at the opening of its "heroic age," geology was recognized as belonging to an altogether new kind of science, which posed problems of a kind that had never arisen before. It was the first science to be concerned with the reconstruction of the past development of the natural world, rather than the description and analysis of its present condition. The tools of the other sciences were therefore inadequate. The processes that shaped the world in the past were beyond either experiment or simple observation. Observation revealed only their end-products; experimental results could only be applied to them analogically. Somehow the past had to be interpreted in terms of the present. The main conceptual tool in that task was, and is, the principle of uniformity.[9]

The success of operation science in producing technology, curing diseases, and raising the general standard of living caused people to trust science as the path to truth about the world. This trust was passed on to the new science of geology and then further to other areas of origin or historical science. So today, many people consider scientists or the scientific consensus to be the authority for determining truth.

As seen in the statements above by Provine and Dawkins, Darwinian evolution is a naturalistic reconstruction of the past to try to explain the origin of living organisms: microbes, plants, animals, and people. However, naturalism's control of origin science did not begin with Darwin's theory of evolution, but over 50 years earlier with the idea of millions of years in geology. In the late 18th and early 19th centuries, deist and atheist scientists attempted to explain the origin of the world and unravel the history of the rocks and fossils. They did so by rejecting the truth of Genesis 1–11 and using the assumptions of naturalism, that nature is all there is and everything must be explained by time, chance, and the laws of nature.

---

9. Martin J.S. Rudwick, "The Principle of Uniformity," *History of Science*, Vol. I (Chicago, IL: University of Chicago Press, 1962), p. 82.

Three prominent French scientists were very influential in this regard. In his *Epochs of Nature* (1778), Georges-Louis Comte de Buffon (1708–88) postulated that the earth was the result of a collision between a comet and the sun and had gradually cooled from a molten lava state over at least 75,000 years (a figure based on his study of cooling metals), though his unpublished writings indicate that he actually believed that the sedimentary rocks probably took at least three million years to form.[10] Buffon was probably a deist or possibly a secret atheist.[11] Pierre Laplace (1749–1827), an open atheist, published his nebular hypothesis in *Exposition of the System of the Universe* (1796).[12] He imagined that the solar system had naturally and gradually condensed from a gas cloud during a very long period of time. In his *Philosophy of Zoology* (1809), Jean Lamarck (1744–1829), who straddled the fence between deism and atheism,[13] proposed a theory of biological evolution over long ages, with a mechanism known as the inheritance of acquired characteristics.

New theories in geology were also being advocated at the turn of the 19th century as geology began to develop into a disciplined field of scientific study. Abraham Werner (1749–1817) was a German mineralogist and a deist[14] or possibly an atheist.[15] Although he published very little, his impact on geology was enormous, because many of the 19th century's greatest geologists were his students. He theorized that the strata of the earth had been precipitated chemically and mechanically from a slowly receding universal ocean. According to Werner's unpublished writings, he believed the earth was at least one million years old.[16] His elegantly simple oceanic theory was quickly rejected (because it just did not fit the facts), but the idea of an old earth remained with his students.

James Hutton (1726–1797) in Scotland was trained in medicine but turned to farming for many years before eventually devoting his time to

---

10. Buffon's fear of contemporary reaction to this great date led him to put 75,000 years in the published book. See "Buffon, Georges-Louis LeClerc, Comte de," in Charles C. Gillispie, ed., *Dictionary of Scientific Biography* [hereafter DSB], 16 vol. (New York, NY: Scribner, 1970–1990), p. 579.
11. "Buffon, Georges-Louis LeClerc, Comte de," *DSB*, vol. 2, p. 577–78.
12. Pierre Laplace, *Exposition of the System of the Universe*, 2 vol. (Paris: Cercle Social, 1796).
13. Brooke, *Science and Religion*, p. 243.
14. Leroy E. Page, "Diluvialism and Its Critics in Great Britain in the Early Nineteenth Century," in Cecil J. Schneer, ed., *Toward a History of Geology* (Cambridge: MIT, 1969), p. 257.
15. A. Hallam, *Great Geological Controversies* (Oxford: Oxford University Press, 1992), p. 23.
16. Alexander Ospovat, "Werner, Abraham Gottlob," *DSB*, vol. 14, p. 260.

geology. In his *Theory of the Earth* (1795), he proposed that the continents were gradually and continually being eroded into the ocean basins. These sediments were then gradually hardened and raised by the internal heat of the earth to form new continents, which would be eroded into the ocean again. With this slow cyclical process in mind, Hutton could see no evidence of a beginning to the earth, a view that precipitated the charge of atheism by many of his contemporaries, though he was possibly a deist.[17]

Hutton is considered by many to be the father of modern geology. He laid down this rule for reconstructing the past history of the earth: "The past history of our globe must be explained by what can be seen to be happening now. . . . No powers are to be employed that are not natural to the globe, no action to be admitted except those of which we know the principle."[18] By insisting on this rule of geological reasoning, he rejected the biblical accounts of creation and the Flood before he ever looked at the geological evidence. Neither creation nor the Flood were happening when he wrote those words, and according to the Bible, creation week was a series of supernatural, divine acts, and the Flood was initiated and attended by supernatural acts of God.

Elsewhere Hutton wrote, "But, surely, general deluges [i.e., global floods] form no part of the theory of the earth; for, the purpose of this earth is evidently to maintain vegetable and animal life, and not to destroy them."[19] He rejected the global Flood because he insisted on a principle of absolute uniformity and was reasoning that the present is the key to the past. He assumed that the processes of nature have always operated in the past in the same way that we observe today. This was a fundamental error, for the totally trustworthy eyewitness testimony of the Creator in His Word is the key to the past and the present. But Hutton rejected that testimony because of his deistic or atheistic religious views.

Charles Lyell (1797–1875), an Oxford-trained lawyer who became a geologist, was probably a deist (or Unitarian, which is essentially the same).[20] Building on Hutton's uniformitarian ideas in his three-volume *Principles*

17. Dennis R. Dean, "James Hutton on Religion and Geology: The Unpublished Preface to his *Theory of the Earth* (1788)," *Annals of Science*, 32 (1975), pp. 187–93.
18. Quoted in A. Holmes, *Principles of Physical Geology*, 2nd ed. (Edinburgh, Scotland: Thomas Nelson and Sons Ltd., 1965), p. 43–44.
19. James Hutton, *Theory of the Earth* (Edinburgh, Scotland: William Creech, 1795), vol. 1, p. 273.
20. Colin A. Russell, *Cross-currents: Interactions Between Science & Faith* (Leicester, UK: Inter-Varsity Press, 1985), p. 136.

of Geology (1830–1833), Lyell insisted that the geological features of the earth can, and indeed must, be explained by slow, gradual processes of erosion, sedimentation, earthquakes, volcanism, etc., operating at essentially the same average rate, frequency, and power as we observe today. He also insisted,

> I have always been strongly impressed with the weight of an observation of an excellent writer and skillful geologist who said that "for the sake of revelation as well as of science — of truth in every form — the physical part of Geological inquiry ought to be conducted as if the Scriptures were not in existence."[21]

This feigned concern for the Bible was actually an attack on the Bible. It would not be a problem to do geology as if the Scriptures were not in existence, if the Bible said nothing about any globally significant geological events. But it describes two: the third day of creation when dry land appeared (presumably as God raised part of the earth's crust above sea level, which would have been a great erosion and sedimentation event), and Noah's Flood, which was intended to destroy the surface of the earth and would have caused an enormous amount of erosion and sedimentation and buried many plants and animals that would become fossils. To a fellow uniformitarian geologist, Lyell wrote in a private letter that he wanted to "free the science [of geology] from Moses."[22] In other words, he wanted to silence God's eyewitness testimony about the supernatural origin of a fully functioning universe of stars, planets, plants, animals, and people and His testimony about the global Flood of Noah that disrupted the normal course of nature as God initiated some processes and accelerated others to bring about His judgment of the world. Creation and the Flood were rejected for philosophical/religious reasons, not because of anything Lyell and Hutton saw in the rocks and fossils. By the 1840s, Lyell's view became the ruling paradigm in geology.

One more fact needs to be mentioned about geology at this time. The world's first scientific society devoted exclusively to geology was the London Geological Society (LGS), founded in 1807. From its inception, which was at

---

21. Charles Lyell, Lecture II at King's College London on May 4, 1832, quoted in Martin J.S. Rudwick, "Charles Lyell Speaks in the Lecture Theatre," *The British Journal for the History of Science*, vol. IX, pt. 2, no. 32 (July 1976): 150.
22. Charles Lyell, quoted in Katherine Lyell, *Life, Letters and Journals of Sir Charles Lyell, Bart* (London: John Murray, 1881), Vol. 1, p. 268.

a time when very little was known about the geological formations of the earth and the fossils in them, the LGS was controlled by the assumption that earth history is much older than and different from that presented in Genesis. Not only was very little known about the geological features of the earth, but at this time there were no university degrees in geology and no professional geologists. Neither was seen until the 1830s and 1840s, which was long after the naturalistic idea of an old earth was firmly entrenched in the minds of those who controlled the geological societies, journals, and university geology departments.

In *Origin of Species*, Charles Darwin reveals how important Lyell's thinking was for his own theory of evolution: "He who can read Sir Charles Lyell's grand work on the *Principles of Geology*, which the future historian will recognize as having produced a revolution in natural science, yet does not admit how incomprehensibly vast have been the past periods of time, may at once close this volume."[23] In private correspondence he added:

> I always feel as if my books came half out of Lyell's brains and that I never acknowledge this sufficiently, nor do I know how I can, without saying so in so many words — for I have always thought that the great merit of the *Principles* [*of Geology*], was that it altered the whole tone of one's mind & therefore that when seeing a thing never seen by Lyell, one yet saw it partially through his eyes.[24]

So naturalism took control of geology, then spread to biology through Darwin, and astronomers have applied the same assumptions in their hypotheses about the evolution of stars, galaxies, and the solar system. Science has been controlled by an anti-biblical naturalistic philosophical/religious worldview for over 150 years. In the widely seen 2014 documentary television series, "Cosmos: A Spacetime Odyssey," which has now been developed into a curriculum to teach public school children to believe in cosmological, geological, biological, and anthropological evolution,[25] the

---

23. Charles Darwin, *The Origin of Species* (London: Penguin Books, 1985, reprint of 1859 first edition), p. 293.
24. Charles Darwin, *The Correspondence of Charles Darwin*, Vol. 3 (Cambridge, UK: Cambridge Univ. Press, 1987), p. 55.
25. For a critique of each episode of this 8-part TV series promoting cosmological, geological, and biological evolution, see the series of web articles by Elizabeth Mitchell at https://answersingenesis.org/countering-the-culture/cosmos-a-spacetime-odyssey/. The articles have also been published as a study guide, *Questioning Cosmos*.

well-known atheist astrophysicist Neil deGrasse Tyson expresses this naturalistic religion memorably:

> Our ancestors worshipped the sun. They were far from foolish. It makes good sense to revere the sun and stars because we are their children. The silicon in the rocks, the oxygen in the air, the carbon in our DNA, the iron in our skyscrapers, the silver in our jewelry — were all made in stars billions of years ago. Our planet, our society, and we ourselves are stardust.[26]

Early 19th-Century Christian Compromise with Naturalism

During the early 19th century, many Christians made various attempts to harmonize these old-earth geological theories with the Bible, not realizing that they were compromising with naturalism. In 1804, the gap theory began to be propounded by the 24-year-old pastor Thomas Chalmers (1780–1847), who after his conversion to evangelicalism in 1811 became one of the leading Scottish evangelicals.[27] Chalmers began advocating this gap theory before the world's first geological society was formed (in London in 1807), and over two decades before Lyell's theory was promoted (beginning in 1830). In part because of Chalmers' powerful preaching and writing skills, the gap theory quickly became the most popular reinterpretation of Genesis among Christians for about the next half-century. However, the respected Anglican clergyman, George Stanley Faber (1773–1854), began advocating the day-age theory in 1823.[28] This was not widely accepted by Christians, especially geologists, because of the obvious discord between the order of events in Genesis 1 and the order according to old-earth theory. The day-age view began to be more popular after Hugh Miller (1802–56), the prominent Scottish geologist and evangelical friend of Chalmers, embraced and promoted it in the 1850s after abandoning the gap theory.[29]

---

26. Episode 8 ("Sisters of the Sun"). The show was a follow-up to the 1980 television series "Cosmos: A Personal Voyage," which was presented by the atheist Carl Sagan.

27. William Hanna, *Memoirs of the Life and Writings of Thomas Chalmers* (Edinburgh, 1849-52), Vol. 1, p. 80–81; Thomas Chalmers, "Remarks on Curvier's Theory of the Earth," *The Christian Instructor* (1814), reprinted in *The Works of Thomas Chalmers* (Glasgow, Scotland, 1836–42), Vol. 12, p. 347–72.

28. George S. Faber, *Treatise on the Genius and Object of the Patriarchal, the Levitical, and the Christian Dispensations* (London, 1823), Vol. 1, p. 111–166.

29. Hugh Miller, *The Two Records: Mosaic and the Geological* (London, 1854) and *Testimony of the Rocks* (Edinburgh: W.P. Nimmo, Hay & Mitchell, 1856), p. 107–74.

Also in the 1820s the evangelical Scottish zoologist, Rev. John Fleming (1785–1857), began arguing for a tranquil Noachian deluge[30] (a view which Lyell also advocated, under Fleming's influence). In the late 1830s the prominent Congregationalist theologian, John Pye Smith (1774–1851), advocated that Genesis 1–11 was describing a local creation and a local flood, both of which supposedly occurred in Mesopotamia.[31] Then, as German liberal theology was beginning to spread in Britain in the 1830s, the view that Genesis is a myth, which conveys only theological and moral truths, started to become popular.

Not all Christians went along with these old-earth ideas in geology in the early 19th century. A number of theologians and scientists, who collectively became known as the scriptural geologists and some of whom were very knowledgeable in geology, raised biblical, geological, and philosophical arguments against the old-earth geological theories and the various old-earth reinterpretations of Genesis. Their Christian opponents largely ignored their arguments. But many Christians still held to the literal view of Genesis because it was exegetically the soundest interpretation. In fact, up until about 1845, the majority of Bible commentaries on Genesis taught a recent six-day creation and a global catastrophic Flood.[32]

The Continuing Christian Compromise with Old-Earth Naturalism

Phillip Johnson was a long-time professor of law at University of California–Berkeley and the driving force behind the modern Intelligent Design movement. His first book on the subject of origins was *Darwin on Trial* (1991), in which he persuasively showed that the scientific evidence did not support the theory of evolution. He avoided discussion of Genesis and the age of the earth but made it clear that he was not a young-earth creationist. Elsewhere he wrote about the origins debate:

> To avoid endless confusion and distraction and to keep attention focused on the most important point, I have firmly put aside all questions of biblical interpretation and religious

---

30. John Fleming, "The Geological Deluge as Interpreted by Baron Cuvier and Buckland Inconsistent with Moses and Nature," *Edinburgh Philosophical Journal*, 14 (1826): 205–39.
31. John Pye Smith, *Relation Between the Holy Scriptures and Some Parts of Geological Science* (London: Jackson & Walford, 1839).
32. For more on these historical developments, see Terry Mortenson, *The Great Turning Point: the Church's Catastrophic Mistake on Geology — Before Darwin* (Green Forest, AR: Master Books, 2004).

authority, in order to concentrate my energies on one theme. My theme is that, in Fr. Seraphim's words, "evolution is not 'scientific fact' at all, but philosophy." The philosophy in question is naturalism.[33]

Johnson and the other old-earth advocates in the Intelligent Design movement (led by the Discovery Institute in Seattle) apparently have not gone back far enough in their historical studies. He appears to think that naturalism only took control of science after Darwin, or maybe even at the time of the 100th anniversary of Darwin's book. Speaking of the famous international celebration of about 2,000 scientists in Chicago in 1959, Johnson writes:

> What happened in that great triumphal celebration of 1959 is that science embraced a religious dogma called naturalism or materialism. Science declared that nature is all there is and that matter created everything that exists. The scientific community had a common interest in believing this creed because it affirmed that in principle there is nothing beyond the understanding and control of science. What went wrong in the wake of the Darwinian triumph was that the authority of science was captured by an ideology, and the evolutionary scientists thereafter believed what they wanted to believe rather than what the fossil data, the genetic data, the embryological data and the molecular data were showing them.[34]

Nancy Pearcey likewise seems historically shortsighted. In her excellent discussion of the victory of Darwin's theory, she speaks of the Christians who tried to make peace with Darwinian evolution. She states, "Those who reformulated Darwin to accommodate design were hoping to prevent the takeover of the idea of evolution by philosophical naturalism. They sought to extract the scientific theory from the philosophy in which it was imbedded."[35] But those Christians and many before them had for over 50 years

33. See Johnson's introduction to Fr. Seraphim Rose, *Genesis, Creation and Early Man* (Platina, CA: St. Herman of Alaska Brotherhood, 2000), p. 50.
34. Phillip Johnson, "Afterword: How to Sink a Battleship," in William Dembski, ed., *Mere Creation: Science, Faith and Intelligent Design* (Downers Grove, IL: InterVarsity Press, 1998), p. 448–49.
35. Nancy Pearcey, "You Guys Lost," in Dembski, ed., *Mere Creation*, p. 84.

allowed and even advocated (albeit unknowingly) the takeover of geology by naturalism and then advocated the day-age theory or gap theory and local Flood theory to save the old-earth theory. I attended the ID movement conference in 1996 where Pearcey originally presented her paper on this subject. When in the comment period after the presentation I remarked about philosophical naturalism taking control of science decades before Darwin through old-earth geology, and referred to my just-completed Ph.D. work on this matter, I got no response from anyone, either publicly or privately. It seemed that the old-earthers did not want to know about naturalism's involvement in the development of the idea of millions and billions of years of history.

William Dembski has been a prominent voice in the ID movement. He clearly sees naturalism's control of biology when he writes:

> Why does Darwinism, despite being so inadequately supported as a scientific theory, continue to garner full support of the academic establishment? . . . Why must science explain solely by recourse to undirected natural processes? We are dealing here with something more than a straightforward determination of scientific facts or confirmation of scientific theories. Rather we are dealing with competing worldviews and incompatible metaphysical systems. In the creation-evolution controversy we are dealing with a naturalistic metaphysic that shapes and controls what theories of biological origins are permitted on the playing field in advance of any discussion or weighing of evidence. This metaphysic is so pervasive and powerful that it not only rules alternative views out of court, but it cannot even permit itself to be criticized. The fallibleness and tentativeness that are supposed to be part of science find no place in the naturalistic metaphysic that undergirds Darwinism. It is this metaphysic that constitutes the main target of the design theorists' critique of Darwinism.[36]

But what Dembski should have said is:

> In the creation-evolution controversy *and the age-of-the-creation controversy* we are dealing with a naturalistic metaphysic

---

36. William A. Dembski, *Intelligent Design: The Bridge Between Science and Theology* (Downers Grove, IL: InterVarsity Press, 1999), p. 114.

that shapes and controls what theories of biological, *and geological and cosmological* origins are permitted on the playing field in advance of any discussion or weighing of evidence.

Naturalism controls all of science and all three aspects of evolution: biological, geological, and cosmological. But Dembski apparently doesn't see this control in geology and astrophysics, for elsewhere he has said:

> I myself would adopt [young-earth creation] in a heartbeat except that nature seems to present such strong evidence against it. . . . In our current mental environment, informed as it is by modern astrophysics and geology, the scientific community as a whole regards young-earth creationism as untenable.[37]

However, it is not *nature* that presents strong evidence against believing what Genesis 1–11 so clearly teaches. It is the *naturalistic interpretations* of the geological and astrophysical evidence that is against young-earth creation. And the scientific community as a whole regards as equally untenable Dembski's and others' rejection of biological evolution and advocacy of intelligent design. Rejecting biological evolution while at the same time accepting millions of years reveals a serious failure to recognize or admit the role of anti-biblical naturalistic assumptions controlling the interpretation of the scientific evidence.

Even a few young-earth creationists do not seem to see naturalism's control of all of science. Nelson and Reynolds state in their "debate" with old-earth proponents, "Our advice, therefore, is to leave the issues of biblical chronology and history to a saner period. Christians should unite in rooting out the tedious and unfruitful grip of naturalism, methodological and otherwise, on learning."[38] But there never will be a saner period, because the problem here is not intellectual, but spiritual. Sin will continue to darken the minds of people who do not want to submit to their Creator and His Word, causing them to suppress the truth (Romans 1:18–20 and Ephesians 4:17–18). Nelson and Reynolds are also mistaken when they say that "the key thing is to oppose any sort of attempt to accommodate theism

---

37. William A. Dembski, *The End of Christianity: Finding a Good God in an Evil World* (Nashville, TN: B&H Publishing, 2009), p. 55.
38. Paul Nelson and Mark John Reynolds, "Young-Earth Creationism: Conclusion," in J.P. Moreland and John Mark Reynolds, eds., *Three Views of Creation and Evolution* (Grand Rapids, MI: Zondervan, 1999), p. 100.

222 — World Religions and Cults • Volume 3

and naturalism."[39] No, the key is to oppose the accommodation of biblical revelation with naturalistic interpretations of the creation, which is what all old-earth reinterpretations of Genesis are attempting to do. The issue is not a vaguely defined *theism's* marriage with naturalism but rather the adulterous union of *biblical teaching* and naturalism.

Thus, fighting naturalism *only* in biology will not work. Ignoring the Bible, especially Genesis, and its testimony to the cosmic impact of sin and God's judgments at the Fall, the Flood, and the Tower of Babel, even while arguing for design in living things (and even *God's* designing activity), will not lead people to the true and living God, but rather away from Him and His holy Word. Nor will fighting naturalism only in biology, while tolerating or even promoting naturalism in geology and astronomy, break the stranglehold of naturalism on science.

In his book about his "wedge strategy," Johnson explains how Christians should proceed in what he thinks is the coming public dialogue between religion and science. He says, "The place to begin is with the Biblical passage that is most relevant to the evolution controversy. It is not in Genesis; rather, it is the opening of the Gospel of John."[40] He then quotes and discusses John 1:1–3 and then Rom 1:18–20. While those passages are certainly relevant, they do not directly address the creation-evolution and age-of-the-earth debates, as Genesis does. Furthermore, John and Paul clearly believed Genesis was literal history and based their teaching on Genesis, as Jesus did.[41] The following year, in an interview in 2001, Johnson also stated:

> I think that one of the secondary issues [in the creation-evolution debate] concerns the details of the chronology in Genesis. . . . So I say, in terms of biblical importance, that we should move from the Genesis chronology to the most important fact about creation, which is John 1:1. . . . It's important not to be side-tracked into questions of biblical detail, where you just wind up in a morass of shifting issues.[42]

---

39. Ibid.
40. Phillip Johnson, *The Wedge of Truth: Splitting the Foundations of Naturalism* (Downers Grove, IL: InterVarsity Press, 2000), p. 151.
41. See Terry Mortenson and Thane H. Ury, eds., *Coming to Grips with Genesis: Biblical Authority and the Age of the Earth* (Green Forest, AR: Master Books, 2008), chapters 12–13.
42. Peter Hastie, "Designer Genes: Phillip E. Johnson Talks to Peter Hastie," *Australian Presbyterian*, no. 531 (Oct. 2001) 4–8, http://members.iinet.net.au/~sejones/pjaustpr.html (web article pages 5–6), accessed Oct. 15, 2009.

On what basis does Johnson make the assertion that the most important fact about creation is John 1:1? He has never provided a theological or biblical argument to defend this assertion. It is difficult to see how Johnson's comments indicate anything but a very low view of and indifference to the inspired inerrant text of Genesis 1–11. I suggest that Johnson's failure to see (or to explain to his listeners, if he does see) that the idea of billions of years of geological and cosmic history is nothing but philosophical naturalism masquerading as scientific fact is the reason that he avoids the text of Genesis.

So the "wedge" of the ID movement does not appear to me to be a wedge at all. It is simply a nail, which will not split the foundations of naturalism, as Johnson hopes. It will not lead the scientific establishment to abandon the naturalistic worldview and embrace the biblical view of creation, nor will it lead most people to the true God, the Creator who has spoken in only one book, the Bible.

This failure to see the full extent of the influence of naturalism in science, even by a person warning about the danger of naturalism, is further illustrated in a paper by one of America's greatest evangelical philosophers, Norman Geisler. In 1998, Geisler was the president of the Evangelical Theological Society. As such he gave the presidential address at the November annual meeting of the ETS.[43] In it he warned of a number of dangerous philosophies that are assaulting the Church and having considerable influence. The first one he discussed is naturalism, which he said has been one of the most destructive philosophies. Therefore, he devoted more space to it than any of the other dangerous philosophies that he discussed. As far as his remarks went, it is a very helpful warning about the dangers of naturalism. He even said that, "James Hutton (1726–1797) applied [David] Hume's anti-supernaturalism to geology, inaugurating nearly two centuries of naturalism in science."[44]

What is terribly ironic and very disappointing is that Geisler has endorsed the writings of Hugh Ross, who promotes naturalistic assumptions and thinking in the Church by persuading Christians to accept millions of years and the "big bang" as scientific fact. Also, in Geisler's own *Encyclopedia of Christian Apologetics*, published in the year *after* his ETS presidential

43. Norman Geisler, "Beware of Philosophy: A Warning to Biblical Scholars," *JETS*, 42:1 (March 1999), p. 3–19.
44. Ibid., p. 5.

address, he tells his readers, "Most scientific evidence sets the age of the world at billions of years."[45] But it is not the *evidence* that sets the age at billions of years, it is rather the naturalistic *interpretation* of the evidence that leads to this conclusion. Because of this confusion of evidence and interpretation of evidence, Geisler rejects the literal-day interpretation of Genesis 1 and believes that the genealogies of Genesis 5 and 11 have gaps of thousands of years, even though he says that "*prima facie* evidence" in Genesis supports literal days and no genealogical gaps in Genesis.[46] After laying out the various old-earth reinterpretations of Genesis (all of which are based on naturalistic interpretations of the scientific evidence, have serious exegetical problems, and have been refuted by young-earth creationists) he mistakenly concludes, "There is no necessary conflict between Genesis and the belief that the universe is millions or even billions of years old."[47]

But Geisler is not the only evangelical philosopher who is highly trained to spot philosophical naturalism and yet has missed it in this issue of the age of the earth. I am not aware of any leading evangelical philosopher who is a convinced young-earth creationist. Paul Copan, who favors the day-age view and whose book *That's Just Your Interpretation* is enthusiastically endorsed by Ravi Zacharias and J.P. Moreland, says:

> Second, the ultimate issue here is not young-earth versus old-earth creationism or even creationism versus evolutionism (although I myself do not find biological evolution compelling). Rather, the crux is naturalism (all reality can be explained by and operates according to natural laws and processes) versus supernaturalism (a reality exists *beyond* and is not reducible to nature — God, miracles, and so on). What is most critical is *that* God created; *how* he created is a secondary matter. [48]

Herein we see the bewitching influence of naturalism imbedded in old-earth thinking that causes men to ignore or reject God's clear Word. The crux is naturalism versus biblical teaching. Genesis just as clearly teaches *when* and *how* God created as it teaches *that* He created.

---

45. Norman L. Geisler, *Encyclopedia of Christian Apologetics* (Grand Rapids, MI: Baker, 1999), p. 272.
46. Ibid., p. 270 (on the creation days) and 267 (on the genealogies).
47. Ibid., p. 272.
48. Paul Copan, *That's Just Your Interpretation* (Grand Rapids, MI: Baker, 2001), p. 146.

Conclusion

Naturalism is a religion, a worldview, and a philosophy. It dominates science and the thinking of most of the cultural elites in the world. This study shows the error of the statement of C. John Collins in his highly endorsed book on science and faith. Collins is an old-earth proponent and respected Old Testament scholar. He states at the end of his book's section on geology, "I conclude, then that I have no reason to disbelieve the standard theories of the geologists, including their estimate for the age of the earth. They may be wrong, for all I know; but if they are wrong, it's not because they have improperly smuggled philosophical assumptions into their work."[49] He could not be further from the truth on this subject. Without the uniformitarian assumptions of philosophical naturalism controlling geology, there is no evidence for millions of years.

So the age of the earth matters enormously, if we truly want to fight naturalism's control of science and if we want to be faithful to the inspired, inerrant Word of the Creator of heaven and earth, who was there at the beginning of creation and at the Flood and has faithfully and clearly told us what happened.

The evidence is abundant and clear. The enemy has invaded the holy citadel. Naturalistic (atheistic) ways of thinking have captured the minds of millions of people around the world and increasingly polluted the church over the last 200 years through millions-of-years, evolutionary "scientific" theories and through liberal theology. Will we take up the sword of the Spirit (Eph 6:17), especially Genesis 1–11, and help expel the enemy of naturalism? The only alternative is to ignore the invasion and pollution and further abet it by compromise with the evolutionary belief in millions of years.

---

49. C. John Collins, *Science and Faith: Friends or Foes?* (Wheaton, IL: Crossways, 2003), p. 250.

Chapter 13

Materialism

Dr. Tommy Mitchell

The term *materialism* conjures in the minds of most an image of people who pursue a life devoted to the acquisition of material possessions. Materialistic people value comfort and wealth more than spiritual pursuits. They often gauge their success based on having more wealth and possessions than others.

However, there is another type of materialism.

Materialism is a worldview based on the belief that physical matter is all that exists. In essence, to the materialist, matter is all that matters because nothing else is real. In the materialistic worldview, all that exists is material.

Those who adhere to this philosophical outlook maintain that the origin of the world and all the complex things it contains is explainable in material terms. That is, everything that exists is the result of matter and its interactions.

Matter and energy, we observe scientifically, act and react based on so-called "laws of matter" or "physical laws." These physical laws describe how the measureable things in nature — matter, energy, gravity, and time, for instance — behave and interact. The laws of motion, the laws of gases, the laws of thermodynamics, and, as we have learned in more recent decades, the laws of quantum mechanics — these scientific laws set the stage and provide the limits and boundaries for our understanding of matter and energy.

The laws of matter are observable, testable, and consistent. The materialistic philosophy goes beyond these observable laws of science, however, declaring that nothing immaterial even exists.

At one level this does seem to have at least some merit. After all, a bat hits a ball. A glass hits the floor. Fingers hit a keyboard. A plane flies through the air. A frog hops into a pond. Just matter interacting with matter, right? Well, up to a point, perhaps. But let's take a closer look at matter.

Matter

If a materialistic worldview contends that everything we see is the result of matter and its interactions, it would be helpful to know just what matter is.

Matter is the stuff around us. And it is the stuff we are made of. The stuff we can see, feel, touch, and hold. Even the air we breathe, though invisible, is matter. Matter is the physical stuff that exists in our universe. It takes up space and it has mass. You know, stuff.

The nature of matter has been considered and explored for centuries. The ancient Greeks were the first to postulate that there was a fundamental unit of matter. This unit was called an atom. Of course, in those days there was no way this could be scientifically tested or analyzed. Although this concept proved useful to philosophers of that day as they sought to understand the world around them, the idea of the atom was then more of a philosophical construct than a concept subject to scientific scrutiny. The idea that the atom was the fundamental unit of matter did, however, at least to a certain degree, turn out to be correct.

As the centuries passed, man's understanding of the physical world increased. The work of such scientists as Newton and Kepler aided in our knowledge of matter and motion and time. Apples fell from trees, and man's understanding of gravity grew. Planets moved through space, and keen observers discovered that their movements could be analyzed mathematically and accurately predicted. These ideas led many to view the universe as something that worked like a vast clock or some gigantic machine whose movements or outcomes could be precisely determined if all the initial condition were known. Ah, if only life were that simple. . . .

Scientific advances in our day have revolutionized our understanding of matter and motion and time and energy and gravity. While the atom is the basic building block of an element, we once incorrectly thought the atom was the smallest indivisible unit of matter. But now we know the atom consists of subatomic particles whose interactions determine how an atom behaves. We also now know that mass and energy are interchangeable and can be converted one to another. Time once seemed constant, but we now know that time changes with velocity and gravity.

Physics in the modern era is now not so much about atoms and particles, but more about energy and fields, quantum states and probability, space-time and gravity, dark matter and black holes. These are the things that now captivate us. And rightly so, for the more we understand about these things, the more we are awed by just how incredible the world around us really is.

Is That All There Is to It?

As science has advanced, we have learned much, much more about matter. What it is. What it isn't. How it behaves. How it changes. How it interacts with other matter.

But is that all that there is to reality? Actually, no. And does discovering how matter behaves reveal where it came from? Again, no.

We do indeed understand more about matter than ever before. This understanding comes from our observations and experimentation in the PRESENT. That is, we understand how matter acts NOW. We can see and test and evaluate now. We praise God for our ability to examine and evaluate our world in such minute detail.

But . . . does our understanding of matter allow us to conclude that everything that exists is merely the result of matter and its interactions? The materialist would reply that it does indeed provide us the means to conclude that, in fact, matter is all that matters. Many philosophers and scientists have for centuries argued just that, and many still do.

This materialist philosophy, or one of its variations, to one degree or another underlies many modern worldviews. Most prominently, evolution (in the molecules-to-man sense) is dependent on this materialist worldview. The foundation of evolution is the concept that over millions (and billions) of years, living things became gradually more complex. From the simplest one-celled creature until man arrived on the scene, matter interacting with matter caused it all.

Wanting something to be true does not make it true, however, no matter how earnestly the materialist wishes it to be so. The evolutionary materialist will wax endlessly philosophic about how matter rearranged itself to form living things. After all, the very existence of life is proof it MUST HAVE HAPPENED, because materialists can accept no creator other than matter itself.[1] Materialists argue this because they cannot (or will not) accept that there is a God who created.

> For the wrath of God is revealed from heaven against all ungodliness and unrighteousness of men, who suppress the truth in unrighteousness (Romans 1:18).

> . . . who exchanged the truth of God for the lie, and worshiped and served the creature rather than the Creator, who is blessed forever. Amen (Romans 1:25).

Materialism, like molecules-to-man evolution, is merely a way to try and explain how things got here without God. It fails in so many ways.

What's the Matter with Materialism? (See What I Did There?)

As stated, materialism and its variations have been the foundation of many worldviews and philosophies throughout the ages. This fact is staggering given that materialism fails on so many fronts. Here we will consider only a few.

First and foremost, if one holds to materialism as the foundation for understanding the world and how it works, it seems quite reasonable that the materialist should answer the question, "Where did matter come from?" Seems a simple starting place, right?

As it turns out, for the materialist this is not so simple and far from straightforward. The usual response to this question revolves around something called the big bang, which is the most widely accepted secular view of the origin of the universe. It is said by adherents to the big-bang account of history that thirteen and a half billion years ago (give or take a few hundred million years), the universe sprang into existence in a great fireball. From nothing, or so it was once taught.

More recently, many secular scientists have rejected the idea that the universe came from nothing. Their view of this "origin" event has evolved. Now many say that something WAS there in the beginning. Views differ about just what was there.

Big-bang supporters agree that all of space and energy was originally contained in a point called a "singularity" which then rapidly expanded.

---

1. This is the fallacy of begging the question — assuming materialism to prove materialism.

One school of thought argues that it is pointless to talk about how the singularity got there or what came before it because this singularity marks the beginning of time itself. There can be no "before the beginning." There is a certain logic to this, but it does not account for the existence of the singularity. The universe does have a beginning in time, and things that have a beginning require a cause. Yet, this view denies any sufficient cause to create the singularity or to cause it to expand. Indeed, there can be no cause for the singularity if nothing beyond physical material exists, since all material was supposedly contained in the singularity.

Another group of scientists postulates that in this "beginning" there existed some type of gravitational force and that gravity created matter. Although this position is self-defeating, as time (i.e., space-time) and gravity are connected to the material creation, so they really haven't answered the question.

Neither of these scenarios can be documented to have happened using the scientific method. Nevertheless, they are considered to be reasonable scientific explanations for how the universe began. Scientists know this sort of origin event happened, not because they have proven it scientifically but only because matter exists, and no non-materialistic explanation is acceptable to them.

But the same scientists who hold to the big-bang origins theory actually violate scientific laws by their belief. For instance, there is the first law of thermodynamics. A scientific law like this is known to be true because scientific observations never disobey it. The first law of thermodynamics tells us that matter and energy can neither be created nor destroyed. They can only be changed from one form to another, or transferred from one place to another.

Simply put, scientific observations always confirm that you can't get something from nothing. There are no exceptions. Except in the beginning, it seems!

You see, the materialist has to presume that an unobservable exception to the laws of thermodynamics happened in the beginning in order for this universe — a universe in which everything obeys the laws of thermodynamics — to come into being. Thus, the very foundation of the materialistic worldview is shaky at best, being in complete violation of the very laws it supposedly created through random natural processes. It is inconsistent for the universe to come into existence by means of neglecting the very laws that supposedly come from it.

So does physics rescue the materialist? Richard Vitzthum, an expert in philosophical materialism, writes that it has not:

> Yet there should be no confusion on one crucial point. Modern physics is not materialism, and materialism is not modern physics. Materialism makes metascientific assumptions about reality that are irrelevant to the aims of working physicists. In the first place, it assumes as axiomatic that the continuity and interconnectedness of things never ends. The universe did not pop out of nothing, either through supernatural fiat or through vacuum quantum fluctuation. If, as seems increasingly likely, some fifteen billion years ago our cosmos flashed into being in a fireball of inconceivable heat, energy, and violence, it did so from some kind of background state or dimensionality linked to it by processes as consistent and natural as those that link the earth to that first fireball. We don't yet understand the laws and processes that govern whatever kind of material reality lies outside the space-time-mass-energy manifold of our cosmos, hidden as they are beyond or within the so-called singularities, like black holes or the Big Bang, where the physical laws we can define no longer appear to hold. Maybe we never will.[2]

Taking this a step further, some big-bang supporters argue that our universe sprang from another — that the singularity was caused by a quantum fluctuation in another universe. In this view, our universe is just one of many, one part of a cosmic "multiverse." Aside from the fact that this speculation is entirely untestable, it merely pushes the problem back. If our universe came from another, then where did that other universe come from? Some might speculate that the multiverse is itself eternal, and therefore needs no first cause. But where is the evidence that such a multiverse even exists?

As philosopher Thomas Nagel explains, "Well, there is the hypothesis that this universe is not unique, but that all possible universes exist, and we find ourselves, not surprisingly, in one that contains life. But that is a cop-out, which dispenses with the attempt to explain anything."[3]

2. Richard C. Vitzthum, *Materialism* (New York: Prometheus Books, 1995), p. 179–180.
3. Thomas Nagel, *Mind and Cosmos* (New York: Oxford University Press, 2012), p. 95.

In other words, the idea of the "multiverse" takes an origins problem that physics cannot solve and multiplies it into an infinite number of origins problems that physics cannot solve. Materialism is a worldview that demands a materialistic beginning for the universe but fails to explain scientifically how that could happen.

The Origin of Life

Just as the materialist cannot easily deal with the problem of the origin of matter, the process by which inert matter combines to form living things is equally challenging. For life to arise spontaneously, the law of biogenesis must be violated.

Simply put, the law of biogenesis states that life comes from life. Period. Living things do not originate from nonliving matter. This is not a matter of speculation or assumption. It is a matter of pure observational science. Throughout history, based on things that have been observed, life has only arisen from life. Without exception. A law with a 100 percent track record is a very reliable law, right?

For the materialist, finding an exception to this law would be a fundamental step in supporting his worldview. No exception has ever been found. Not one. Frankly, materialism fails on this issue alone.

The Mind and Thought

Even if there were one single exception to the law of biogenesis and life did arise spontaneously long ago, there are still a vast number of things to account for. Let's just take one issue to make the case against materialism even stronger: the mind. How did the mind develop? How do our thoughts occur? What defines human consciousness?

Again, for the materialist, this is not an insignificant issue. How does matter give rise to consciousness and thought? Or even logic, reason, truth, knowledge, morality, conclusions, or any concept? These things are clearly immaterial. How can atoms and molecules, randomly interacting, give rise to something as amazing and complex as human thought?

Consider the artistry of Michelangelo, the genius of Albert Einstein, and the humor of Will Rogers. Are these things just the result of matter acting on matter, chemicals bumping around in their brains and in the brains of those who marvel at their genius? For the consistent materialist, the answer must be that creative and scientific genius are material. That is, people's choices, actions, consciousness, awareness — even their very identity — are merely the results of chemicals acting in the brain.

Even Charles Darwin considered this: " 'Even human thoughts,' Darwin provocatively wrote in his notebook, 'were little more than secretions from the brain, no more wonderful than inert matter being subject to gravitation. "Oh, you materialist!" he spluttered gleefully in conclusion.' "[4]

One might argue that in Darwin's time there was not as much understood about the brain. In our day and age, this is still a stumbling block for the materialist, as Thomas Nagel admits:

> Consciousness is the most conspicuous obstacle to a comprehensive naturalism that relies only on the resources of physical science. The existence of consciousness seems to imply that the physical description of the universe, in spite of its richness and explanatory power, is only part of the truth, and that the natural order is far less austere than it would be if physics and chemistry accounted for everything. If we take this problem seriously, and follow out its implications, it threatens to unravel the entire naturalistic world picture. Yet it is very difficult to imagine viable alternatives.[5]

Materialism comes up short once again.

Where Does All That Information Come From?

In a materialist worldview, at some time in the distant past, atoms randomly bumping together formed complex molecules, and these complex molecules randomly bumping together formed the first living cell. And so on. As we have seen, this scenario violates the law of biogenesis and therefore could not have ever happened. Even if it did (for the sake of argument), the materialist runs headlong into another problem. The problem is called information.

For a single-celled organism to evolve into a more complex creature, a vast amount of information must be added to the genetic material to code for this increase in complexity. Clearly, a horse is much more complex than an amoeba. So where does all this information to make hair and eyes and legs come from? An excellent question, it seems, as the materialist has no

---

4. Janet Browne, *Charles Darwin, Voyaging* (Princeton, NJ: Princeton University, 1995), p. 383.

5. Nagel, *Mind and Cosmos*, p. 35.

answer. You see, information is not material. It is not made of matter. It exists, but its origins elude the materialist.

What observational science reveals is that information does not arise spontaneously. Information never pops into existence from nowhere. As Werner Gitt, information technology expert and long-time professor at the prestigious German Federal Institute of Physics and Technology, explains:

> There is no known law of nature, no known process and no known sequence of events which can cause information to originate by itself in matter.[6]

Information always comes from a higher source of information. That source of information is merely a speculation for the materialist. For the Christian, this poses no difficulty whatsoever.

The Laws of Nature

In a materialist universe, how does one account for the fact that the universe itself operates consistently according to many so-called "laws"? From the earliest years in school, children are taught about how the universe works. We understand the motion of planets, the properties of gases, and the manner in which certain atoms interact. We can calculate the instant that a space probe will land on a distant planet or the precise point at which a hardened steel beam will break under pressure. These things are possible only because the universe functions consistently and logically according to physical laws that we have been discovering and describing in detail using science over the past few hundred years.

Just how did these "laws" come into existence? They are not material. Far from it. The laws of chemistry and physics apply to how matter functions and interacts, but they themselves are not material. Mathematics exists. Without it we could not hope to understand the material world, but mathematics itself is immaterial. The laws (or principles) of logic also exist, and neither are they material.

Some materialists have attempted to argue that these laws and principles are merely of human invention. This viewpoint is woefully insufficient, for it ignores the question entirely. It is true that the laws of the universe have been extensively studied and understood by man. Again, we praise

---

6. Werner Gitt, *In the Beginning Was Information* (Green Forest, AR: Master Books, 2006), p. 106.

God for giving us the ability to examine the manner in which the universe works and define the consistent patterns we find. But describing these things is not the same as inventing these things. Man uses logic. Man did not invent logic. The same can be said for the laws of physics or the principles of mathematics.

These laws and principles do not randomly change. There is uniformity in the operation of our world. If these laws did not operate in the past just as they operate in the present, then the materialist is bound to explain why.

For the Christian, understanding the origin of an orderly universe is simple. After all, the Christian serves the Creator God who by His nature is orderly, consistent, and logical. God put into operation an orderly universe that is bound by consistent laws and principles. It is not arbitrary or random. In Jeremiah 33:25 we read about "the ordinances of heaven and earth" which God put into place to govern the operation of the physical world.

How do you explain the immaterial in a materialist worldview? You cannot. Here, again, we see the problem.

Why Then . . .

If this worldview is so inconsistent, so unsupportable, then why do people believe it, support it, and promote it? As with so many worldviews, the materialist is trying to explain the nature of our world without acknowledging God as Creator.

If God is who He claims to be, and frankly all one needs to do is look at the world around us to understand that He is, then we are accountable to Him. You cannot explain or logically understand the universe without acknowledging God as the One who made all things (e.g., Proverbs 1:7, 9:10). The origin of matter, the origin of life, the consistency and orderliness of the universe — all these pose no problem whatsoever for the Christian.

But there are those who deny God. People who look to themselves as the authority. Those who yearn to be as gods, making their own rules and answering only to themselves. They must deny the One who created. To do that they must then be able to explain how everything got here without a Creator.

Every attempt to do so has failed. Materialism is but one example.

Still, man keeps trying, determined to talk around the possibility that God the Creator even exists. Harvard evolutionary biologist and geneticist Richard Lewontin admitted as much in a book review he wrote in 1997:

> Our willingness to accept scientific claims that are against common sense is the key to an understanding of the real struggle between science and the supernatural. We take the side of science in spite of the patent absurdity of some of its constructs, in spite of its failure to fulfill many of its extravagant promises of health and life, in spite of the tolerance of the scientific community for unsubstantiated just-so stories, because we have a prior commitment, a commitment to materialism.
>
> It is not that the methods and institutions of science somehow compel us to accept a material explanation of the phenomenal world, but, on the contrary, that we are forced by our a priori adherence to material causes to create an apparatus of investigation and a set of concepts that produce material explanations, no matter how mystifying to the uninitiated. Moreover, that materialism is absolute, for we cannot allow a Divine Foot in the door.[7]

It is fitting that we conclude this chapter on the highly intellectual subject of materialism by giving the eternal God — who created all that is material and all that is not — the final word on this subject:

> Professing to be wise, they became fools (Romans 1:22).

7. Richard Lewontin, "Billions and Billions of Demons," *The New York Review of Books,* Jan. 9, 1997, 31.

Chapter 14

Empiricism

Bryan Osborne

"Don't you believe in flying saucers?" they ask me. "Don't you believe in telepathy? — In ancient astronauts? — In the Bermuda triangle? — In life after death?"

"No," I reply. "No, no, no, no, and again no."

One person recently, goaded into desperation by the litany of unrelieved negation, burst out, "Don't you believe in anything?"

"Yes," I said. "I believe in evidence. I believe in observation, measurement, and reasoning, confirmed by independent observers. I'll believe anything, no matter how wild and ridiculous, if there is evidence for it. The wilder and more ridiculous something is, however, the firmer and more solid the evidence will have to be."[1]

There it is, empiricism in a nutshell. Colorfully illustrated by famed professor, science fiction author, and humanist Isaac Asimov. The general (less vibrant) definition for empiricism is as follows, "the doctrine that all knowledge is derived from sense experience."[2] Empiricism is a worldview that essentially believes all knowledge is gained from observations of what you can see, smell, taste, touch, and hear (even through the use of various

---

1. Isaac Asimov, *The Roving Mind* (Prometheus Books, 1983), p. 43.
2. Dictionary.com, s.v. "empiricism," http://dictionary.reference.com/browse/empiricism.

instruments). Actually, the disciple Thomas unintentionally gives a pretty good summary of empiricism in John 20:25:

> The other disciples therefore said to him, "We have seen the Lord." So he said to them, "Unless I see in His hands the print of the nails, and put my finger into the print of the nails, and put my hand into His side, I will not believe."

Although Thomas relegated himself to empiricism on this point at this time in his life, he was not an empiricist. But there appears to be a growing number of people who are empiricists in this day and age. This makes sense because we are seeing an increase in the religion of humanism in the Western world, and empiricism is a specific outworking of humanism.

According to a study published by Pew Research in 2012, roughly one in six people around the world (1.1 billion, or 16%) claim no "religious affiliation."[3] Ironically, this makes the "Religiously Unaffiliated" the third-largest religious group in the world. Of course, not everyone in this group is an empiricist, but it's probably safe to say that a decent percentage hold to some form of empiricism.

This should get our attention because, as we'll see in more detail later, empiricism is totally antithetical to the biblical worldview. With that in mind it should be noted that the majority of secular scientists and a large portion of higher education academics seemingly embrace some form of empiricism. And many of these same professors believe it is their job, even their "calling," to shape the worldview of their students into their own image. This should put us on alert because, as Adolf Hitler famously said, "He alone, who owns the youth, gains the future."[4]

Take Bill Savage for example, a self-identified political liberal, teacher of English, and college adviser at Northwestern University in Evanston, Illinois. Check his response to data that showed conservative "red" states are producing more children than liberal "blue" states and why he's not worried about it:

> The children of red states will seek a higher education, and that education will very often happen in blue states or blue islands in red states. For the foreseeable future, loyal dittoheads will continue to drop off their children at the dorms. After a

---

3. "The Global Religious Landscape," Dec. 18, 2012, http://www.pewforum.org/2012/12/18/global-religious-landscape-exec/.
4. http://www.brainyquote.com/quotes/quotes/a/adolfhitle378177.html.

Size of Major Religious Groups, 2010
Percentage of the global population

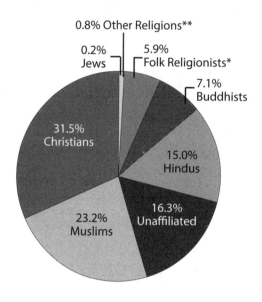

0.8% Other Religions**

0.2% Jews

5.9% Folk Religionists*

7.1% Buddhists

31.5% Christians

15.0% Hindus

16.3% Unaffiliated

23.2% Muslims

* Includes followers of African traditional religions, Chinese folk religions, Native American religions, and Australian aboriginal religions.

** Includes Baha'is, Jains, Sikhs, Shintoists, Taoists, followers of Tenrikyo, Wiccans, Zoroastrians, and many other faiths.

Percentages may not add to 100 due to rounding.

Pew Research Center's Forum on Religion & Public Life • Global Religious Landscape, December 2012

teary-eyed hug, Mom and Dad will drive their SUV off toward the nearest gas station, leaving their beloved progeny behind. *And then they are all mine* (emphasis added).[5]

That's right, Mom and Dad, you spend all your love, time, energy, and money raising your kids for 18 years and then in four years he'll transform their worldview into the "right" one — his. Children from Christian homes, for example, will be trained to be humanists and empiricists. And this even happens much earlier than college age — as early as middle school and high school![6]

History

The general premise of empiricism is surely as old as human history. The idea was initially articulated in philosophical terms around the third century B.C. in the Greek schools of Stoicism and Epicureanism. Different elements of empiricism flutter within various minds throughout history until Sir Francis Bacon, a creationist nonetheless, gathered them together to a more permanent philosophical home in the 16th century.

---

5. Bill Savage, "Lessons Learned," *The Stranger*, June 9–15, 2005.
6. Ken Ham, Britt Beemer, and Todd Hillard, *Already Gone* (Green Forest, Arkansas: Master Books, 2009).

For Bacon, the knowledge of primary importance to man was to be found empirically in the natural world. Truth required evidence from the real world and should be pursued through systematic observation, collection, and arrangement of data. As a result of these convictions he became the first to formulate the principles of the modern scientific method.

But it wasn't until the late 17th century that a British philosopher by the name of John Locke explicitly formulated the doctrine of Empiricism. Locke contended that the mind is a *tabula rasa* ("clean slate") on which experiences leave their imprint and shape an individual's thinking.[7] He concluded, for the most part, that humans do not have innate ideas, and knowledge is only possible through experience.

In the early 18th century, Bishop George Berkeley, an Irish philosopher, argued for a radical form of Empiricism eventually to be called Subjective Idealism.[8] In this variation, things only exist because an entity perceives them or by the action of being perceived. He essentially believed that existence was tied to experience, and things continue to exist as a result of the perception of God.

The final "founding father" of modern Empiricism was the Scottish philosopher and atheist David Hume. In many ways, his views on Empiricism were a fusion of the ideas of Locke and Berkeley and are probably best summarized by his quote "the science of man is the only solid foundation for the other sciences."[9] In other words, human experience is the closest thing we are going to get to truth, and the foundation for any logical argument is observation and experience. Hume was a rigid Empiricist who moved the philosophy to a new level of skepticism. His work proved extremely influential on subsequent Western philosophy by impacting many well-known names, including philosopher Immanuel Kant.

These four individuals laid the groundwork for the many variations of Empiricism that would arise over time. Some of these variants include:

- Phenomenalism
- Pragmatism
- Radical Empiricism
- Logical Positivism
- the list could go on

7. John Locke, *An Essay Concerning Human Understanding*, 1690.
8. Bishop George Berkeley, *Treatise Concerning the Principles of Human Knowledge*, 1710.
9. David Hume, *A Treatise of Human Nature*, 1738.

Each one brandishes its own specialized nuances, but all agree to the same core principles. The situation is summarized well in this quote.

> All empiricists hold that experience rather than reason is the source of knowledge. This very general thesis has received very different emphases and refinements, and as such lead to very different kinds of empiricism. Nevertheless, empiricists are united in the claim that knowledge ultimately depends on our senses, and what we discover by them.[10]

It is this "united claim" and general definition that we will consider. Time does not permit us to address each branch of this philosophical tree, so we will direct our attention to the trunk.

Authority

At first glance, it would appear the empiricist appeals to "science" and "nature" as their ultimate authority. For the most part, they see themselves as unbiased witnesses who astutely listen and record what these "forces" have to "say" through observation. Phrases like "The rocks and fossils tell us," "The evidence speaks for itself," "Science says the earth is billions of years old," or "Nature teaches us that evolution is true" are uttered without a second thought. The echoing sentiment in the shadow of these statements is, "These are the facts and they are not to be trifled with — deal with it."

Of course, the inherent problem here is nature, science, evidence, rocks, radioisotopes, etc. do not think or speak. This is the logical fallacy of reification, "attributing a concrete characteristic to something that is abstract,"[11] or personification, attributing a human characteristic to something non-human. These evidences are handled, observed, utilized, and ultimately interpreted by a person who does think and speak. Herein lies the key — every person comes to the evidence with a worldview, a set of basic assumptions presupposed to be true about reality, which is used to form their observations. Ultimately, it is a person's worldview that is used to interpret the evidence. And at the foundational level, there are only two worldviews to choose from — either you start with God's Word as the authority or you trust man's word. Either the revealed Word of God is the foundation on which we stand to

---

10. Norman Geisler and Paul Feinberg. *Introduction to Philosophy- A Christian Perspective.* 10th ed. (Grand Rapids MI: Baker, 1999), p. 113.
11. https://answersingenesis.org/logic/the-fallacy-of-reification/.

understand all of reality, past, present, and future, or it is false, and man, by default, becomes the measure of all things. Empiricism, by its very nature, rejects the idea of supernatural revelation and is thus left with man and his interpretations of reality as its sole authority.

Foundational Beliefs

Evolutionary, Atheistic, or Agnostic Empiricism

In regards to origins, the typical empiricist is going to fully embrace all that naturalistic evolutionary dogma has to offer. With God out of the way and man left as sole authority, evolutionary ideology becomes man's best attempt to explain life in the vacuum of God's absence. So the empiricist readily accepts the major cosmological, geological, and biological evolutionary components. Big bang, billions of years, and molecules-to-man evolution are all confidently asserted as factual history. These things must be true, because in the worldview of empiricism "the facts speak for themselves."

Now to be fair, empiricists do not have to be atheists, they can just as easily be staunchly agnostic. Whereas the atheist says definitively that there is no God, the agnostic says it is impossible to know if a god exists. To the agnostic, God is unknown and unknowable and this makes the idea of an agnostic Christian an oxymoron.

Deistic Empiricism

The God of the Bible has revealed Himself not only in His creation, but also more importantly in Christ and through His Word. At best, an agnostic empiricist can be a deist. A deist concedes that an unknown god started the universe and then let go. God wound the watch, so to speak, and then disappeared without a supernatural trace. All man can know about this god is through observation of the universe; there are no supernatural writings, incarnations, or revelations of any sort. Thus, you can see how the empiricist can feel right at home within this perspective.

With those cards on the table, let's do a quick, though far from exhaustive, comparison between the biblical God and empiricism's possible deistic god. The God of the Bible is omnipotent, omniscient, and omnipresent. He is the Alpha and Omega, Creator and sustainer of all things visible and invisible. His initial creation was perfect, and man has the distinct privilege of being made in His image. Upon man's choice to rebel and violate the

God-given command not to eat of a certain tree, perfect fellowship with God was broken, and death and the Curse entered this world.

From this point onward, the biblical narrative is focused on the Messiah who will come as the ultimate ransom for sin's debt, the Redeemer of mankind and restorer of all things. The Old Testament points to His coming, the New Testament records His coming, and Revelation anticipates His Second Coming, demonstrating His perfect will, sovereignty, and love for us! How do we know all this? Quite simply: the Bible tells us so as God has revealed Himself in Jesus Christ and through His Word, displaying His love and character for all to see.

The deistic god, on the other hand, is quite a different entity. Since he has declined to reveal himself, we can only infer things about him from what we observe (often referred to as natural law). But even then, that cannot really be known. It's fair to say that since he is not intimately involved with his creation he is a bit of an introvert. Does he love us? I guess we can't know for sure, but if he did, don't you think he would want to be with us? If he cared for us, don't you think he would want us to know it and would want to tell us how to live lives that have true meaning, purpose, and direction? It would hardly be groundbreaking to suggest that any child that has been abandoned by one or both parents could testify that is not love.

Also, look at the mess of his creation! Yes, there's beauty, but it's also full of death, suffering, pain, diseases, catastrophes, evil, violence, injustice, malice, etc. And he made it this way! Evidently this is how a deistic god wants things to be with no end in sight. If this is all that is to be known about the deistic god, I'm not sure he is somebody worth meeting.

Afterlife and Salvation in Empiricism?

What happens after death? Well, the biblical God has told us that we all spend eternity somewhere. The question is location, location, location!? In empiricism, whether of the atheist or deistic persuasion, the afterlife is unobservable and therefore unknown and unknowable.

As one might expect, empiricism's view of Jesus Christ is polar opposite of Christianity's. Christianity reveals that Jesus is Immanuel — God with us, God become flesh, 100 percent God and 100 percent man. This hypostatic union is critical to the gospel and Christian doctrine. Empiricism at its best would concede that Jesus was maybe a good teacher, but nothing more, and certainly not God — man is the ultimate authority in Empiricism.

246 — World Religions and Cults • Volume 3

And what about salvation? Biblical teaching says that salvation comes by grace through faith alone in Christ alone. In Empiricism, what do you need saving from? Either god does not exist or he hasn't revealed himself to man. Either way, no standard has been revealed and no instructions for salvation given. Thus, each person decides the parameters of their own salvation — but it has nothing to do with biblical salvation.

Arbitrariness, Inconsistencies, and Refutations

Arbitrariness

As mentioned earlier, empiricism suggests that truth is unveiled through man's senses, observations, and interpretations. Thus, in the empiricist worldview, man is the ultimate authority. But this view is inherently arbitrary. If man is the authority, then which man?

Whose senses, observations, and interpretations rise above all others to be standard-bearer? How can any person's observations and conclusions be trusted as "truth" when so many conclusions of the past have been shown to be egregiously mistaken?

Some might argue that a consensus of a majority can determine "truth," but one needs to look no further than Nazi Germany to realize that is fallacious. Using man as the ultimate authority for your worldview is like trying to nail gelatin to a wall. No matter how many times you try or different strategies you employ, it just won't stick!

Also, empiricism assumes from the start that either God doesn't exist or hasn't revealed Himself. Both of these ideas arbitrarily assume their conclusions. If one chooses to assume a god does not exist, can that person prove it scientifically? Think about it. To prove a god does not exist through empirical means, you would have to know everything. You would have to exist in all places at all times to make sure a god wasn't hiding somewhere. And you would have to be all-powerful to do those things. So in order to prove there is no god, you would have to be god; god would therefore exist, and it's a self-defeating argument.

In like manner, the agnostic empiricist also assumes what they cannot know. They assume that an unknown god does not reveal himself supernaturally. But how do they know that? Did they find this truth by empirical means? No. Did god supernaturally reveal to them that he does not reveal himself supernaturally? How can one simultaneously claim that god is not knowable but know how he chooses to operate? Again, it's a self-refuting argument.

What about the empiricist's view that Jesus was just a good man? Of course, this idea is not restricted to empiricism; it's safe to say the majority of worldviews outside of Christianity hold this view of Christ. But by what standard can they even measure good? What senses did they use to converse with Christ? Off the cuff, this idea may seem rational, but a quick look at the Word of God reveals the impossibility of such a view. Why? Because Jesus Himself plainly states numerous times that He is God. This sentiment reverberates throughout the Bible from cover to cover. Therefore, since Jesus claims to be God, it is impossible for Him to be "just a good man." To paraphrase what C.S. Lewis famously said in his book *Mere Christianity*, Jesus is either a liar, lunatic, or Lord. Either He is who He claims to be — the very Son of God — or He is a madman or the devil in disguise. These are the only options Jesus left us, and each person directly or indirectly chooses one of these three.[12]

Inconsistencies

As noted time and again throughout this book series, the ultimate confirmation of the biblical worldview is that it alone provides the preconditions necessary to make knowledge and life possible. Only the biblical worldview does this while remaining self-consistent.

Every other worldview, including Empiricism, is ultimately suicidal; it blows itself up by its own assumptions. This highlights Empiricism's most egregious inconsistency: it cannot be proved by its own standard! According to Empiricism, all knowledge is gained through observation.

Now it should be noted that it's perfectly consistent with Scripture to conclude that *some* knowledge can be gained by observation. This makes sense within the biblical worldview that tells us God made everything, He holds it together by the power of His Word, and He made our senses to be able to study the universe He created.

The problem with Empiricism is that it claims *all* knowledge is acquired by observation. Here's the key question; how does the empiricist know that all knowledge is attained by observation? Is this something he observed? Since knowledge itself cannot be "seen," obviously not. But if that's the case, how can Empiricism be verified if indeed all things are known by observation?

12. Later writers have added the option of "legend" to Lewis's trilemma.

If Empiricism is substantiated by something other than observation, it disproves itself. The conclusion is, if Empiricism were true, it would be impossible for the empiricist to actually know it or prove it. Empiricism refutes itself.

This problem is exponential when you realize that many people's observations are not trustworthy. Consider the observations of a person under the influence of drugs; to the empiricist, are their observations truth?

If things weren't already bad enough for the empiricist, their worldview also forces them to practice behavioral inconsistencies. This is the basic principle that "actions speak louder than words." Things like morality, justice, and love are not actually observable, but the empiricist unwittingly acknowledges their truth by his actions.

In essence, the empiricist proclaims one worldview but lives by another. Consider the empiricist who dogmatically claims evolution must be true — that life in all its splendor is merely a series of cosmic accidents such that origin and meaning are reduced to time plus chance and matter. But when he gets home from work he pets his dog with fondness and embraces his family with hugs and kisses, as if they are much more than chemical accidents. And how would he respond if a child of his was brutally murdered?

Would he say, "Oh well, it's a random chance universe and that event was just one chemical accident reacting with another chemical accident. You know, like when baking soda reacts with vinegar. No big deal." Of course not! He would be shocked, broken-hearted, outraged, and in desperate need of justice!

In both scenarios, the actions of the empiricist are quite contrary to his beliefs. He may profess empiricism, but he's actually living according to a different worldview. This shows that in his heart of hearts he knows that his worldview is insufficient to explain the realities of life. Things like freedom, morality, love, and justice are truths easily taken for granted, but only the biblical worldview can adequately account for them. It is only the biblical worldview that makes sense of the totality of reality, both physical and immaterial.

Refutations

So if empiricism, like every other non-biblical worldview, cannot account for the totality of reality, how does the empiricist function in the everyday world? He borrows from the biblical worldview, whether he realizes it or not. A few examples: the uniformity of nature, laws of logic, and absolute morality only make sense within a biblical worldview.

How does the empiricist account for these things within his own world-view? He boldly declares that all truth is discovered by one's senses, but you cannot see a law of logic, trip over a law of nature, or smell absolute morality. All of these things are unobservable and immaterial, yet absolutely true and necessary for life and knowledge.

Only the Bible reveals the omniscient, omnipotent, omnipresent God who created time, space, and matter and is not limited by them. The Creator God, who made all things both visible and invisible, holds them together by the power of His Word and has revealed Himself through His creation and the Scriptures. Outside of this, there is no accounting for the immaterial truths that flood our reality.

So what is the empiricist to do? He trespasses! He stands on biblical principles, probably unaware, and assumes all of these truths with no foundation for them in his proclaimed worldview. Ironically, the empiricist, like every other non-believer, is standing on the biblical worldview to try and argue against the biblical worldview.

The empiricist may contend that this is not the case; that he has morality and uses laws of logic just fine without believing in God. But you do not have to *confess* a belief in God to use the laws and principles He has put in place. The questions in play here are not "Are they true and do you use them?" but rather, "Where did they come from and why are they true?" Ultimately, the empiricist has no answer for these questions. Can he use these laws? Absolutely. Can he explain them within his own worldview? Absolutely not. Therefore, he lives in a fundamentally inconsistent way from his declared worldview.

Conclusion

So why accept a lacking and faulty worldview? In Romans 1:18 we are told that the unbeliever suppresses the truth in unrighteousness. Sinful man does not like the idea of being held accountable to a holy and just God, so he is willing to believe a lie as opposed to facing the truth. The truth is that "all have sinned and fall short of the glory of God" (Romans 3:23) and that "the wages of sin is death" (Romans 6:23). If you are reading this and are not sure that you have fallen short of God's glory, take a look at Exodus 20, the Ten Commandments, God's basic moral code for mankind.

Realize that since God is perfect and perfectly holy, He requires absolute perfection and flawless righteousness to be in His presence. Therefore, to attain entrance into heaven you must have kept His law perfectly, never breaking any of His standards, not even once.

> For whoever shall keep the whole law, and yet stumble in
> one point, he is guilty of all (James 2:10).

Not only that, God is omniscient (all knowing), knowing our thoughts, attitudes, and motives, which also must be completely pure and holy in His sight (see Matthew 5:21–30). One adulterous thought, vindictive motive, or malicious word makes a person a lawbreaker, guilty and fallen short of the glory of God.

You might be thinking to yourself that this kind of standard is impossible — no one can do this! You're right, and that's the point! We are all sinners by nature and by choice because we are all descendants of that first man Adam, who passed on his heritage of sin to all of us. We are incapable of saving ourselves and indeed this is the worst kind of news. But that is what makes the "Good News" so good — the good news that God became flesh, the Last Adam, Jesus Christ, lived a perfect life and died as a flawless sacrifice to pay a debt we never could!

> But God demonstrates His own love toward us, in that while
> we were still sinners, Christ died for us (Romans 5:8).

But that's not the end! Then He rose from the dead, defeating death, so that all who put their faith in Him have their sins forgiven, are clothed in the perfect righteousness of Christ, and have eternal life with Him!

That if you confess with your mouth the Lord Jesus and believe in your heart that God has raised Him from the dead, you will be saved (Romans 10:9).

Christianity provides the ultimate hope for the present and eternity, while Empiricism is an impotent religion of hopelessness that's unable to make sense of the senses or eternity.

That's a truth that resonates with all the senses.

Chapter 15

Afterlife: "What Must I Do to Be Saved?"

Eric Hovind

If you are like me, you skipped to the end of this book to read the conclusion. Seriously, no cheating. Go back and read what you skipped!

Whether this is the first chapter or the last chapter for you, you are still reading this book, which means either you are searching for answers for yourself, or seeking to educate yourself for a defense for what you already believe. Throughout these pages, we discovered that *all religions are not the same* and that tolerance of every religion is not the same as "accepting every religion as true." Even the claim by some that *all religions point to the same goal turns out to be a myth.*

You may describe yourself as an atheist, a skeptic, an agnostic, a seeker, a mystic, or a believer. Regardless of your title, are you certain about your eternal future? Are you unsure of which religion represents truth? Man, am I ever glad you asked that question!

I have some good news and some bad news to share. I'm the kind of guy that wants the bad news first, so that is where I am going to start.

Bad News First

The bad news? Statistics show that ten out of ten people die! I'm going to die one day. Of course I am going to make that the last thing I ever do, but it is going to happen. You too are going to die one day, and the question I have is "Why?"

Have you ever stopped to consider why people (and other things) die? Consider this, if you had a car that repaired itself every time it was damaged, it would last forever. Well, your body has the ability to heal itself and theoretically SHOULD be able to last forever. But it doesn't. Why? In an evolutionary worldview where life just came from matter and figured out how to repair itself, why didn't it figure out how to live forever? Or as a Hindu where nothing is ultimately real, why does death happen to everything? Or in Islam, why would it be the "will of Allah" to make life that simply . . . dies?

The truth is, death was not a part of God's original creation. He had created all of the animals and humans as vegetarians. There was no disease, no suffering, and no death. Death entered the world through the act of sin, which is any thought, word, or deed that breaks God's Law.

When the first man, Adam, and his wife, Eve, sinned, they were sentenced to death (Genesis 3:19). They had been warned, and it was true, death is the punishment for sin. In Adam, and individually, we have all sinned, so we are all sentenced to death. Remember that statistic? Ten out of ten people die. Sin really is the reason for death. When Adam sinned in the Garden of Eden, everything under his dominion fell into decay and death. This included the animals who were under Adam as his dominion (Genesis 1:26–28). When a spiritual being like Satan fell into sin, he was sentenced to death as well — not physical, but eternal hell, or the "lake of fire" (what is called the "second death" in Revelation 20:14).

Physical death is not the end of man, but God revealed that the man who sins will also endure the eternal punishment of the second death as well (Revelation 21:8). Why is it *eternal*? Because we have been made in the image of an *eternal* God. Our soul will continue after death for eternity. So the question of eternity in heaven or hell is arguably one of the most important questions of your life.

This is the reason you think about death and the afterlife. It is why you keep asking the question, "What happens after I die?"

I've heard people say that regardless of which religious organization you identify with, that basically when you die, good people go to heaven and bad people go hell.[1] The Bible teaches this. It says that the unrighteous, or

---

1. There is a misconception about hell in today's culture that Satan rules in hell. But this deception has gone on long enough. Even Satan is a captive there. The description of a fire is quite apt for hell, for all victims are being tormented forever without rest and none are "ruling," not even Satan.

"bad people," will not inherit the kingdom of God (1 Corinthians 6:9). All we need to know now is the definition of righteous and unrighteous. You probably have some of your own standards that you have developed as you have gone through life. Most of us have developed a personal standard of what is good and bad, and most of us feel that our good outweighs our bad. Based on this, many are satisfied that they have a pretty good chance of going to heaven (or a type of paradise in the afterlife) on the merit of their good works. *In fact, every world religion at which we have looked bases any hope of eternal bliss on our good works.*

Since individuals and religions have different ways of determining right and wrong, who is truly responsible for setting "the standard," for determining good and bad? The Bible says that God is the just judge of all of His creation. Do you think the God of the Bible considers you to be a good person? Let's find out.

How many lies have you told in your life? Too many to count, right! What do you call someone who tells a lie? A liar. Lying is not wrong simply because God says so. This standard of righteousness is because God is not a liar, and you have been made in the image of God.

How many times have you taken something that doesn't belong to you? Don't lie about this! What do we call someone who takes things that don't belong to them? A thief. Here again, we see the standard based on God's righteousness. It is wrong to steal because God does not steal.

God is perfectly faithful. His standard of righteousness says that we are to be perfectly faithful. That is why it is wrong to commit adultery. Then Jesus, who was God in human form, said that even looking with lust causes us to commit adultery in our hearts. Who can say that they have never looked with lust? Once again, we fall short of God's standard of righteousness.

Because God is perfect, He says that the use of His name is to be perfect. That's why He says, "Thou shalt not take the name of the Lord thy God in vain." Have you ever taken God's name and used it to swear? That is called blasphemy and it is a very serious sin.

The Bible sets the benchmark for "good" very high. *God's standard of a good person is "perfection!"* (Romans 5:8). Yet, nobody's perfect! Everyone has sinned! The word "sin" is an old archery term that means to "miss the mark." You and I have missed the mark of God's perfection, and not just by a little bit either!

Now, knowing God's standard, do you still consider yourself to be a good person? Do you think a just and holy God should let liars, thieves, adulterers, and blasphemers into heaven, a perfect place where people who miss the mark of God's perfection are not allowed to be?

The reason: If a perfect God allowed imperfect sinners into a His perfect heaven, it would no longer be perfect! Heaven would be no better than the sin-cursed and broken world we live in now. You wouldn't want that forever, and I wouldn't either.

Of course, God can't allow sinners into heaven. He tells us that all adulterers, the sexually immoral, liars, murderers, and so on will not inherit the kingdom of God (1 Corinthians 6:9; Revelation 22:15). He says that He will not hold them guiltless who take His name in vain (Exodus 20:7). Liars and thieves will have their part in the lake of fire (Revelation 21:8). Isaiah 59 says that your sins have cut you off from God. Romans 3:23 says "All have sinned and come short of the glory of God."

Working for Righteousness

Yes, the bad news is that you have missed the mark of perfection. Big revelation, I am sure, but it gets worse. *You can't do enough good works to outweigh the bad works.* In other words, Christianity, unlike every other religion in the world, focuses on trying to fix the problem of sin instead of ignoring it in hopes of good works outweighing the bad.

The Bible even says that all of our "good works" are as filthy rags to God (Isaiah 64:6). He is telling us that there is no way for us to get out of this situation on our own. We are trapped and doomed without someone to rescue us and save us from the destruction we deserve from our past sinful actions. We need someone to save us.

There is more bad news. When we break man's law, we pay man's penalty. When we break God's law, we pay God's penalty. Remember what the Bible says the penalty for sin is? "The wages of sin is death" (Romans 3:23). That is why ten out of ten people die and it has been like this since the first sinners (Adam and Eve).

We are born as sinners into a sin-cursed world (Psalm 51:5) and we all personally choose to sin (Ecclesiastes 7:20; 1 John 1:8), and that sin separates us from God and carries a death penalty that must be paid.

Many in our world fully embrace a sinful, humanistic lifestyle and justify our sinful actions. This humanistic worldview teaches "the end of all being is the happiness of man." In other words, this life is all about making yourself happy. But this statement could mean anything to anybody — one person's happiness could be another's misery. And, that worldview is a dead end! People have tried all kinds of things to obtain fulfillment and purpose, but money, power, and popularity never lead to true, lasting happiness.

That's the bad news. Now let me give you the good news!

Good News

Although we are sinners, God still loves us. God, Himself, even wrote out the plan for our redemption in the Bible so that we could be sure of the path to freedom, forgiveness, and hope. We were created for the purpose of enjoying a relationship with our Creator. We are made in His image after all. There is a path to discover true happiness. True joy is discovered when we realize that the end of all being is not the happiness of man, but the glory of God!

Did you notice something from the other religions addressed in this book? All the major religions of the world claim to POINT to truth. The Hindu scriptures, such as the Vedas, say truth is elusive and hard to find. At the end of his life, Buddha said, "I'm still searching for the truth." Muhammad wrote, "I point to the truth." Jesus Christ never claimed to point to truth. He said, "I am the way, the truth and the life. No one comes to the Father except through Me" (John 14:6).

I have talked to many that would assert the Christian belief that Christ is the only way to heaven is intolerant, dogmatic, and even uneducated in light of the many world religions. By now, if you really read the previous chapters like you were suppose to, you should be able to see through that assertion. We have seen that in reality, there are only two world religions: those that espouse God's Word as truth and those that do not.

Those that reject the Bible are actually the ones being intolerant — intolerant of the ultimate authority, choosing rather to determine truth for themselves. The path to redemption is made plain in Acts 4:12, "Nor is there salvation in any other, for there is no other name under heaven given among men by which we must be saved."

The good news about Jesus Christ being *the* way, *the* truth, *the* life is called the gospel. It is good news because God made a way for us to be saved, to be redeemed from the penalty of sin. God the Son, Jesus Christ, came and lived among men. He lived a perfect life. He never sinned one time. Then

He laid down His life and allowed Himself to be the sacrifice, the payment for our sin. We miss the mark of God's standard of perfection, but God the Son didn't (John 10:15).

Jesus Christ was crucified on a Cross, taking upon Himself the sins of the world — past, present, and future. Three days later, He literally rose from the dead, giving Him victory over death and sin. He paid the debt that we deserved to pay and proclaimed that anyone who believes, who accepts His payment, putting their faith and trust in what He did on the Cross, can be saved from paying that eternal death penalty themselves.

How much does this sin debt cost? In 1978, I was given physical life. It didn't cost me a thing, but it cost someone else a lot. In 2001, I was given spiritual life. My spiritual birth didn't cost me a thing, but it cost Christ everything. Romans 6:23 says, "the *gift* of God is eternal life through Jesus Christ our Lord." It's a gift! You can't earn it. You can't buy it. It is a gift received by faith alone (Ephesians 2:8–10; Titus 3:3–7).

Let us consider this debt further with regards to sin. One sin is worthy of . . . an *infinite* punishment. God is infinite (Psalm 147:5; Isaiah 40:28; Romans 1:20), so naturally the punishment for offending Him would also be infinite. The punishment from an infinite God upon sin, *our sin*, would also be infinite! There is no escape in and of yourself, because you cannot undo your offenses against a holy God.

In fact, the only one in a position to take that punishment for you is God Himself. Which is what He did in the person of Jesus Christ. The infinite Son of God took the punishment for sin upon Himself, and the infinite Father delivered that punishment, so the debt is paid in full.[2]

And God is so powerful that the person of Jesus Christ delivered the proof of everlasting life in the Resurrection (John 10:17). Not only did Christ die the punishment we deserve, but He also came back to life afterward! All that is required of you is faith — involving repentance of your sin and belief in the death, burial, and Resurrection of Jesus Christ alone.

What Is Faith?

Faith sometimes gets a bad rap, being described as something only needed by the weak-minded. The truth is, everyone practices faith! You have faith in

---

2. The Father and Son are not two different "gods," but are one God. The Father, the Son, and the Holy Spirit are the three persons of the one triune God. See the Appendix on the Triune God in volume one for further elaboration.

the food you eat and the air you breathe. You even put faith in drivers that you have never met, trusting that they will not cross those strips of yellow paint on the road as you fly past each other only a few feet apart. Faith is a part of our everyday lives. The most important faith questions we need to ask are, in what or in whom do we place our faith for our eternal destiny and how much faith do we need?

I could put lots and lots of faith in a rickety old chair to hold me; however, my faith won't determine whether the rickety old chair will hold me. I could put very little faith in a rock-solid chair to hold my weight, but my little faith won't change the fact that the sturdy chair has no problem holding me up. You see, it is not the amount of faith, it is the *object* of our faith that matters.

In what are you placing your faith? Good works? Religion? Science? A church? A pastor? A spouse? The Bible teaches us that there is only one thing in which we can put our trust to have salvation — the death, burial, and Resurrection of the Lord Jesus Christ. If you are putting your trust in anything other than Jesus Christ, then you need to repent. That word means "to change your mind." You need to change your mind about what you place your trust in for salvation. Your faith must be in *Christ alone*.

If you have never put your trust in Jesus Christ, forsaking your sin and turning to the one who died on the Cross and rose again to provide the way of salvation for you, then I invite you to do that today. My friends Matt and Sherry wrote a poem as a prayer for people who desire a relationship with God. While there are no magic words to communicate your heart to God that you are sorry for your sin and are seeking His forgiveness, you could make this poem your simple prayer for salvation.

Jesus, You died upon the Cross and rose again to save the lost.

Forgive me now of all my sin; come be my Savior, Lord, and friend.

Take my life and make it new, and help me, Lord, to live for you.

The Bible says in Romans 10:13 that "whoever calls on the name of the Lord shall be saved." That's a promise from the Creator of the universe. His promise is not based on our emotions or feelings, our good works or bad. Salvation is based on the object of our faith, the perfect, infinite, and eternal Jesus Christ.

The God of the universe loves you and desires to have a relationship with you. He wants to give your life true purpose and joy. The gospel really is simple.

Admit that you are a sinner who has come short of the glory of God, and because of your sin, you deserve to be punished.

Believe that Jesus Christ died, was buried, and rose triumphantly over death and sin, paying the punishment for you on the Cross.

Call upon the Lord Jesus. Repent of your sin and of trusting anything but Christ alone for salvation and you can be saved from eternal destruction and be assured of a home in heaven forever.

Our Authority Is the Bible — God's Word

No other world religion has a book of such miraculous power. No other book offers you a loving relationship with a God who loves you enough to let His only Son die for you. No other world religion has a resurrected Savior who came back from death to prove He alone knows what happens after death. Trust Jesus Christ and begin your God-quest journey with your Creator today!

Appendix A

The Bible versus Other Alleged Holy Books

Bodie Hodge

But how do you know the Bible is the right one to pick when there are so many holy books like the Upanishads, Confucius's writings, Book of Mormon, Vedas, Studies in the Scriptures (Charles Russell), and the Qur'an?

It sounds like a buffet where you pick what you want, doesn't it? Many mistakenly think that people just line the holy books up and make their best guess. In other words, you pick based on what *you* think is the truth. But this is not the case at all.

If YOU are the authority on the truthfulness of a religious book, then God (or a god or a set of gods) CANNOT be. Let me state this differently. If one argues that God is the absolute authority by appealing to their own opinions as the ultimate authority, then that person refutes himself or herself. It sounds complicated, but either man is the authority or God is.

So let's look at this issue in more detail.

What Is the Bible Really Up Against?

Some "Holy Books" Do Not Claim to Be the Word of God

This might surprise you, but many "holy books" aren't holy, and they admit it! In other words, they do not claim to be the Word of God. They are like any other writing.

For instance, take the writings by ancient Hindus. The Vedas, Upanishads, or even the Bhagavad Gita are not the revealed word of their god, Brahman (other gods in Hinduism are considered manifestations of Brahman). Brahman is not a personal god, so revelation (i.e., communication) from Brahman would not be a possibility since communication is a personal attribute.

These alleged holy writings are merely various opinions of their ancient sages on the subject. The alleged holy books of Hinduism are nothing more than errant books of man, nothing that should be confused as the inerrant (without error) Word of God, like the Bible. Any writing of an alleged *impersonal* god (e.g., New Age, Scientology, Taoism, etc.) is in the same camp.

Obviously, any book about religions that have no god (e.g., secular religions or many moralistic religions) cannot be a book that could be confused as the Word of God either. So there goes any Buddhist, Confucianist, Epicurean, Stoic, and atheistic writing. Believe it or not, this eliminates Satanism's writings, too (LaVey's *The Satanic Bible* and *The Devil's Notebook* for example). LaVey was actually an atheist arguing for atheism in the books!

Multi-god systems like Germanic or Greek mythologies, Shinto, and so forth are little more than ancestor worship where people were elevated to a god-like status. Oden and Thor are listed in ancient genealogies and were real people who later had god-like attributes attached to them.[1] Again, it would merely be the arbitrary and fallible opinions of man anyway you look at them.

Pagan religions like witchcraft, voodoo, and animism do not have a supreme god who reveals his or her will. This explains why there are such varied beliefs among pagans. It comes down to the mind of mankind anyway. There are no unified, absolute scriptures for paganism.

A deistic god generally remains distant from his creation, so there is no need for this alleged god to communicate with beings within his creation. So by the story of most deists, there should be no Word of God!

Other "Holy Books" Agree the Bible Is True!

Other alleged holy books or prophets often agree the Bible is true. More often than not, they want to add to the Bible.

---

1. Woden/Oden and Thor/Tror are even in my own genealogy that extends back to Noah and Adam.

Jehovah's Witnesses and Charles Taze Russell (their founder and supposed prophet) affirmed that the Bible is true. Russell just opted to *add* his works to it. The Watch Tower Bible and Tract Society (Jehovah's Witnesses) has continued in the same trend as Russell.

Alleged prophet Joseph Smith (founder of the Mormons) and subsequent Mormon leadership also agree that the Bible is true (insofar as it is accurately translated), although, Smith attempted to *add* the Book of Mormon, the Pearl of Great Price, and the Doctrines and Covenants as Scripture. Alleged prophetess Ellen White agreed the Bible is true though her writings were seen by many early Seventh Day Adventists (SDA) as inerrant — an *addition* to Scripture. Encouragingly, we see many SDA today who no longer hold Ellen White in such high esteem and now see the Bible as the *sole* source of doctrine.

Even Muhammad, the prophet of Islam, agreed the Bible is true, and this appears several times in the Qur'an (e.g., Surah 2:40–42, 126, 136, 285; 3:3, 71, 93; 4:47, 136; 5:47–51, 69, 71–72; 6:91; 10:37, 94; 21:7; 29:45–46; 35:31; 46:11–12). But the Qur'an was seen as the true revelation.

Within Roman Catholicism, they agree the Bible is true, but then try to *add* the Apocryphal books (and Papal/Ecumenical authority, which is a response called an "infallible pronouncement" on faith and moral issues if they are called into question). The Jews agreed on much of the Scripture (Old Testament) but then *add* the Talmud, Mishna, etc. (oral traditions put to writing beginning about A.D. 200) while rejecting the New Testament.

This list could continue, but the point is that many who have professed additional writings from God still agree that the Bible is true. So the issue with them is not the Bible. It is their alleged additions that need to be judged and tested by the Bible (previous Scripture). There is little dispute on the Bible.

There is no reason to be exhaustive here. The point is that the Bible has very little competition when you actually look at the issue. It is by no means a buffet line from which to pick and choose. The questions are, "Does the competition even come close?" and "Is the Bible true?" Let's begin with the latter question.

The Authority of Scripture

The God of the Bible is absolute by His very nature. He is the ultimate authority on all things — by extension, His Word is the ultimate authority on all things.

	Bible is true?	But wants to add . . .
Mormons	Yes	Book of Mormon, the Pearl of Great Price, and the Doctrines and Covenants
Jehovah's Witnesses	Yes	Studies in the Scripture, *Watchtower*, and *Awake*
Islam	Yes	Qur'an and Hadith
Seventh Day Adventist	Yes	Ellen White's writings
Roman Catholicism	Yes	Apocrypha and Papal authority
Judaism	Most (OT)	Talmud (Traditions)
Orthodoxy	Yes	Some Apocrypha and Patriarchal authority
Syncretism	Yes	Humanistic Origins (various degrees of evolution)
Bah'ai	Yes	Qur'an and Bahaullah's writings and his sons, modern prophets and the House of Justice
Biblical Christianity	Yes	**Nothing**

God, being the ultimate and final authority, can only reveal Himself by final and absolute authority. In other words, there is no other authority to "prove" God and His Word, as all other authorities are *lesser* than God.

This is why *I, a mere man*, am not in a position to prove God and His Word. If I appealed to my arbitrary opinions on God or His Word, I would be a lesser authority than God — being a fallible and imperfect man.

Can I use *logic* to try to prove God? Even logic is dependent upon God and His being as the ultimate authority. Logic and reasoning are tools that we use to "think God's thoughts after Him." But even logic is a lesser authority than God. All things (man, logic, angels, governments, etc.) are lesser than God, and thus lesser in authority than God and His Word. So only God is left in the position to prove Himself and His Word.[2] God alone is in

---

2. Some might object and appeal to logic that this is a circular argument, thus fallacious. However, circular arguments are *valid* logically. What makes a circular argument fallacious is when it is an *arbitrary* circle. God, being absolute and final, is non-arbitrary. Thus it is valid and sound, so one cannot appeal to this being a fallacious argument.

the spot to reveal to us His absolute existence and His absolute Word. And He did it with the first few words of Genesis.

In the beginning God . . . (Genesis 1:1).

This initial phrase is the foundation of the rest of Genesis 1:1. Genesis 1:1 is the foundation for the rest of Genesis 1. Genesis 1 is the foundation for the rest of the Book of Genesis, and Genesis is foundational to the rest of the Bible.

The Bible, from start to finish, is equal in authority and is our absolute starting point for all matters.[3] The Bible, the 66 books of Scripture, is the authority in all things — even the existence of God. Any objector would be a lesser authority and, therefore, not in a position to usurp the authority of God.

Man vs. God?

Secularists (humanists) like atheists, agnostics, Epicureans, Nazis, communists, and post-modernists merely appeal to their own authority. Mankind is seen as the absolute authority in their religious convictions. They have no God to which they can appeal. So whether people appeal to Darwin, Hitler, Stalin, or the like, it is always a person or group of people.

People do not have absolute authority. They are arbitrary and lesser authorities. Any argument they try to present to attack God and His Word is flawed from the onset because they are not a sufficient authority on the issue.

"But the Bible Was Written by Mere Men!"

Secularists and others who hold to a "no god" position want to demote God's Word to be like their arbitrary writings. They want to argue that God was not involved in the Bible (since they suppress His existence) and that it is merely a human document. They present a case that the Bible is no different from Darwin's book *The Descent of Man* or Plato's book *Critias*. They rebut, "The Bible was just written by men!"

When it comes to the authorship of the Bible, of course men were involved — Christians would be the first to point this out. Paul wrote letters to early churches and these became Scripture. David wrote many of

---

3. This is called the Transcendental Argument for the Existence of God (TAG). It is not an argument per se, but is the foundation that makes all argumentation possible.

the psalms, Moses wrote the Pentateuch (the first five books of the Bible), and so on. In fact, it is estimated that over 40 different human authors were involved.[4]

But this is not the real issue. The real issue is whether God had any involvement in the authorship of the Bible.

Let's think about this for a moment. When someone claims that the Bible was written by men, they really mean to say it was written by men *without God's involvement.*

This is an absolute statement that reveals something extraordinary. It reveals that the person saying this is claiming to be . . . transcendent. For a person to validate the claim that God did not inspire the human authors of the Bible means he must be omniscient, omnipresent, and omnipotent to know this is the case!

1. *Omniscient:* This person is claiming to be an all-knowing authority on the subject of God's inspiration in order to refute God's claim that Scripture was inspired by Him (2 Timothy 3:16).
2. *Omnipresent:* This person is claiming that he was present, both spiritually and physically, to observe that God had no part in aiding any of the biblical authors as they penned Scripture.
3. *Omnipotent:* This person is claiming that, had God tried to inspire the biblical authors, they had the power to stop such an action.

So the person making the claim that the Bible was merely written by men alone is claiming to be God since these three attributes belong to God alone. This is a religious issue of humanism versus Christianity. People who make such claims (perhaps unwittingly) are claiming that *they* are the ultimate authority over God and are trying to convince others that God is *subservient* to them.

When responding, I prefer to address this claim with a question that reveals the real issue — and there are several ways to do this. For example, referring to omnipresence, I can ask, "Do you really believe that you are omnipresent? The only way for you to make your point that God had no involvement would be if you were omnipresent." Then I can point out that

---

4. Josh McDowell, *A Ready Defense* (Nashville, TN: Thomas Nelson Publishers, 1993), p. 27.

this person is claiming to be God when he or she makes the statement that God had no involvement in the Bible.

Or, in regard to omnipotence, perhaps I can ask, "How is it that you are powerful enough to stop God from inspiring the authors?" Or I could direct the question to the rest of the listeners by simply asking, "Since the only way to refute the fact that God inspired the Bible is to use attributes of God such as omnipresence, omnipotence, and omniscience, do the rest of you think this person is God?" Naturally, I may have to explain it further from this point so the listeners will better understand.

I could also ask, "How do you know that God was not involved?" Other responses include undercutting the entire position by pointing out that any type of reasoning apart from the Bible is merely arbitrary. So the person trying to make a logical argument against the claims of the Bible (i.e., that God inspired the authors) is doing so only because he or she is assuming (though unintentionally) the Bible is true and that logic and truth exist! It is good to point out these types of presuppositions and inconsistencies.[5]

Someone may respond and say, "What if I claim that Shakespeare was inspired by God — then you would have to be omniscient, omnipresent, and omnipotent to refute it."

Actually, it is irrelevant *for me* to be omniscient, omnipresent, and omnipotent to refute such a claim. God, who is omniscient, omnipresent, and omnipotent, refutes this claim from what He has already stated in the Bible. Nowhere has God authenticated Shakespeare's writings as Scripture, unlike Christ the Creator God's (John 1; Colossians 1; Hebrews 1) approval of the Old Testament prophetic works and the New Testament apostolic works — the cap of the canon is already sealed.[6]

A Presuppositional Authority

God exists and His Word, the Bible, is the truth. This is the starting point.

God simply opens the Bible with a statement of His existence and says His Word is flawless (Genesis 1:1; Proverbs 30:5). The Bible bluntly claims to be the truth (Psalm 119:160), and Christ repeated this claim (John 17:17).

---

5. Jason Lisle, "Put the Bible Down," Answers in Genesis, December 5, 2008, www.answersingenesis.org/articles/2008/12/05/feedback-put-the-bible-down.
6. Bodie Hodge, "A Look at the Canon" Answers in Genesis, January 23, 2008, www.answersingenesis.org/articles/aid/v3/n1/look-at-the-canon.

In fact, if God had tried to prove that He existed or that His Word was flawless by any other means (i.e., a lesser means), then any evidence or proof would be greater than God and His Word — which would be contradictory to God's nature. However, all other things are lesser than God.

God knows that nothing is greater than He (e.g., Hebrews 6:13) and by extension, His Word, and therefore He doesn't stoop to our carnal desires for such proofs — instead God offers proof by the impossibility of the contrary (more on this in a moment).

The Bible also teaches us to have faith that God exists and that having faith pleases Him (Hebrews 11:6). Accordingly, we are on the right track if we start with God's Word. God's Word is presupposed as the truth and our starting point, and this is what makes all knowledge, all logic, all argumentation, all intellectual endeavors, etc. possible.

How Do We Know the Bible Is True?

Allow me to dive in a little deeper here by starting with God and His Word as the absolute authority. The Bible is true because any alternative would make knowledge, logic, and truth impossible. The Bible is the only book that has the preconditions for knowledge/logic/truth (i.e., intelligibility). Stated otherwise, the Bible must be predicated as true to make reasoning, truth, and intelligence a possibility.

All other worldviews must borrow from the Bible for the world to make sense. Science, morality, and logic all stem from the Bible being true. If the Bible were not true, then knowledge would be impossible. In other words, if the Bible were not true, nothing would make sense — good or bad . . . everything would be meaningless and pointless.

This doesn't mean someone has to *believe* the Bible to be true, but that the Bible is true regardless. Consider someone who says he doesn't believe air exists. He makes convincing verbal arguments and openly says he doesn't believe in air . . . all the while using air to breathe and speak his argument. It is like this with the critics of the Bible. They argue the Bible is not true and that they have knowledge to say so, all the while borrowing from the Bible, which accounts for truth and knowledge.

Think of it this way: Unless the Bible is true, which accounts for (1) knowledge and (2) truth existing and (3) that we are made in the image of an all-knowing, logical, God of truth (so we can seek to understand the answer), then no one and no worldview can even proceed to answer the question "How do we know the Bible is true?" unless they borrow these attributes from God's Word.

This is called the "impossibility of the contrary" that proves the Bible to be true by God's own Word. By starting with God and His Word as the absolute authority, no other possibility can exist to make knowledge possible.

Additional or Competitive "Holy Books"?

Scripture (God's Word) comes from God, and God cannot contradict Himself. If God were to contradict Himself, then nothing can be trustworthy or known. All knowledge would be arbitrary and nothing could ever really be known. Thus, when God reveals Himself, it will not be in contradiction.

Previous Scripture Is the Judge of Latter Scripture

Furthermore, when God revealed more about Himself in subsequent Scripture, it was consistent with the previous revelation. New revelation builds on previous Scripture as the *previous* judges the latter (newer Scripture). The Holy Spirit revealed this through Moses (e.g., Deuteronomy 13; Acts 1:16).

This is why the New Testament is built on a defense using the Old Testament to prove the New Testament (e.g., Acts 17:10–11). We saw Jesus, the Apostles, and others in the New Testament using the Old Testament witness as their proof of Jesus as the Messiah, for example. The Old Testament judged the New Testament. The New Testament was not contradictory to the Old Testament, but instead fulfilled what the Old Testament was looking toward and built upon its foundation.

A red flag should go up when you hear someone say that previous Scripture (e.g., the Old or New Testament) should be judged based on their alleged "new scripture." They have it backward. In fact, it would be too convenient if the new were to judge the old instead of the old judging the new because anyone could make that claim and put themself into a position of authority greater than God! And many have tried to do just that.

It is all too convenient when the new revelation is seen as authoritative and then the Bible is demoted. Yet this is a trademark for those who pay lip service to the Bible. For example, Mormons say the Book of Mormon and other Mormon writings are the authority and the Bible is secondary based on the interpretation and translation of the Bible according to Mormon teaching. They place the latter Mormon writings in a superior position to the previous (Bible).

The Jehovah's Witnesses do the same thing. The Bible is secondary to their writings and subject to the Watchtower Organization and Charles Russell's view of the Scripture. They have the latter in a superior position to the previous. Islam fairs the same with the Qur'an in a higher position than the Bible. Again, this is back to front.

The same worn-out case is found with Ellen White's writings. Her writings take the forefront and the Bible takes a secondary role, being interpreted based upon her view of the Bible. At the very least, if these alleged prophets viewed their works to be equal to the Bible, then they should have held to the position that their works were equal to but not greater than the previous! Instead, like clockwork, they elevate their own alleged revelations to supersede the Bible. That should be a red flag to anyone.

Sadly, this method of taking the new as authoritative and neglecting the old in light of it is nothing new. Did you realize Jesus had to deal with this? The Jews had been walking away from the Old Testament. They had held to the traditions of the elders (later written down and called the Talmud) as superior to Moses and the Old Testament prophets. They reinterpreted meanings in the Old Testament that destroyed the meanings of passages all for the traditions of man and made useless the commands of God.

The New Testament did not do that. The New Testament Apostles consistently argued their case, *based* upon the Old Testament and gave equal authority to their New Testament Scripture as a fulfillment to the Old Testament. The New Testament books were not seen as superior documents to the Old Testament that now need reinterpreting.

The same occurred throughout the Old Testament. When Old Testament prophets came forth with the Word of God, they did not say their books were superior and that Moses now needs to be seen as secondary or reinterpreted based on their new book. By no means. Their prophetic works were seen as building on the foundation of Moses.

Previous Scripture is to be used to judge latter Scripture. When an alleged new prophet claims the opposite, they stand in contradiction to the Bible and thus are false prophets.

God Will Not Contradict Himself

Another way to know that other religious writings are not from God has to do with contradictions. They contradict God's already stated Word, the Bible.

In the Bible we read that God cannot lie (Titus 1:2; Hebrews 6:18). This is significant because it means that God's Word will never contradict itself. Though skeptics have alleged that there are contradictions in the Bible, every such claim has been refuted.[7] This is what we would expect if God's Word were perfect.[8]

Yet the world is filled with other "religious writings" that claim divine origin or that have been treated as equal to or higher than the Bible on matters of truth or guidelines for living. In other words, these writings are treated as a final authority over the Bible.

Any religious writing that claims divine inspiration or authority equal to the Bible can't be from God if it has any contradictions: contradictions with the Bible, contradictions within itself, or contradictions with reality.

Examples of Contradictions in Religious Writings

A religious writing can be tested by comparing what it says to the Bible (1 Thessalonians 5:21). God will never disagree with Himself because God cannot lie (Hebrews 6:18). When the Bible was being written and Paul was preaching to the Bereans (Acts 17:11), he commended them for checking his words against the Scriptures that were already written. If someone claims that a book is of divine origin, then we need to be like the Bereans and test it to confirm whether it agrees with the 66 books of the Bible. Paul's writings, of course, were Scripture (2 Peter 3:16).

Religious books, such as Islam's Koran (Qur'an), Mormonism's Book of Mormon, and Hinduism's Vedas, contradict the Bible, so they cannot be Scripture. For example, the Koran in two chapters (Surah 4:171 and 23:91) says God had no son, but the Bible is clear that Jesus is the only begotten Son of God (Matthew 26:63–64).

The Book of Mormon says in Moroni 8:8 that children are not sinners, but the Bible teaches that children are sinful, even from birth (Psalm 51:5). The Book of Mormon, prior to the 1981 change, says that Native Americans will turn white when they convert to Mormonism (2 Nephi 30:6).

---

7. There are websites and books dedicated to this subject. To get started, I suggest *Demolishing Supposed Bible Contradictions*, Volume 1 and 2, (Green Forest, AR: Master Books, 2010 and 2012).

8. Keep in mind a crucial point here. *If* the Bible were not true and not from God, then contradictions are acceptable! It is from a biblical perspective that contradictions are a bad thing. If a secular worldview were correct (no God and no Word of God), why not contradict yourself?

Few would dispute that the Vedas and other writings in Hinduism are starkly different (thus contradictory) from the Bible as previously discussed.

Also, such religious writings contain contradictions within themselves that are unanswerable without gymnastics of logic. In the Koran, one passage says Jesus will be with God in paradise (Surah 3:45) and another states that He will be in hell for being worshiped by Christians (Surah 21:98).

None of the apocryphal books of Romanism or Orthodoxy claim inspiration from God. One apocryphal book, Maccabees (1 Maccabees 9:27, 4:46, and 14:41) points out that no prophets were in the land and hadn't been for some time. Since prophets were the mouthpieces of God, how can these books, written during this time that prophets weren't present in Israel, be the Word of God?

The Talmud, which is "the traditions of the elders, tradition of the fathers," "law of the fathers," or "tradition of men," was strictly opposed by Jesus and the New Testament (e.g. Matthew 15:2–6; Mark 7:3–13; Acts 22:3; Galatians 1:13–14; 1 Peter 1:17–19). They are obviously incompatible with the Bible.

If these writings were truly from God, such discrepancies couldn't exist.

False Prophecy

False prophecy is an obvious hallmark of false prophets. A prophet is one who claims to speak for God, often foretelling events. The Holy Spirit, speaking through Moses, writes,

> But the prophet who presumes to speak a word in My name, which I have not commanded him to speak, or who speaks in the name of other gods, that prophet shall die. And if you say in your heart, "How shall we know the word which the LORD has not spoken?" — when a prophet speaks in the name of the LORD, if the thing does not happen or come to pass, that is the thing which the LORD has not spoken; the prophet has spoken it presumptuously; you shall not be afraid of him (Deuteronomy 18:20–22).

Matthew 7:15–20 reiterates a warning against false prophets. How have the alleged prophets since the Bible fared?

Islam

In the Hadith tradition of Sunan Abu Dawud, Book 37 Number 4281–4283, Muhammad claimed that the Antichrist (*Dajjal*) was supposed to

Contradictions with Some Popular Alleged New Scriptures and the Bible

	Bible	New Scripture Claims
Koran (Qur'an)	Jesus is God who became a man as well (Colossians 2:9)	Jesus is not God (Surah 5:17, 5:75)
Koran (Qur'an)	Jesus was crucified (1 Peter 2:24)	Jesus was not crucified (Surah 4:157)
Koran Qur'an)	The Holy Spirit is God (Acts 5:3-4; 2 Corinthians 3:15-17)	The Holy Spirit is the created angel Gabriel (Surah 2:97, 16:102)
Book of Mormon	Salvation is by faith through grace apart from works (Ephesians 2:8–9)	Salvation is by grace and works (2 Nephi 25:23)
Book of Mormon	One God exists (Deuteronomy 6:4; 1 Chronicles 17:20; 1 Timothy 2:5)	Multiple gods exist (Doctrine and Covenants, Section 121:32, 132:18–20)
Jehovah's Witnesses	Jesus is the Creator God (John 1:1–3; Hebrews 1:1–9; Colossians 1:15–19, and distinguished from angels (Hebrews 1:4–8)	Jesus is the created angel, Michael*
Jehovah's Witnesses	Hell is a place of eternal torment for those who do not receive Christ (e.g., Daniel 12:2; John 5:28–29; Matthew 25:41–46; Mark 9:43–48; John 3:36; 2 Thessalonians 1:9; Revelation 14:9–11)	Hell is not a place of eternal torment**
Jehovah's Witnesses	God created in 6, 24-hour days as defined by an evening and a morning in Genesis 1 and rested on the seventh day (Genesis 1:1–2:3; Exodus 20:11; Exodus 31:15–17)	God created in 49,000 years with each day being 7,000 years in duration (Charles Russell, *Studies in the Scripture*, Volume 6, p. 19)

  * "Who Is Michael the Archangel," JW.org, accessed August 30, 2016, https://www.jw.org/en/publications/books/bible-teach/who-is-michael-the-archangel-jesus/.

  ** "What Is Hell? Is It a Place of Eternal Torment?" JW.org, accessed August 30, 2016, https://www.jw.org/en/bible-teachings/questions/what-is-hell/.

come forth six months after the conquest of Constantinople by the Muslims. At the same time, Medina (Yathrib) would be left in ruins.

The Muslim conquest was much later than Muhammad's day, finally occurring in May of A.D. 1453. But no Antichrist ascended in November of 1453 and Medina was not left in ruins.

Mormons (Church of Jesus Christ of Latter-day Saints)

The Mormons have not fared any better.

> Yea, the word of the Lord concerning his church, established in the last days for the restoration of his people, as he has spoken by the mouth of his prophets, and for the gathering of his saints to stand upon Mount Zion, in which shall be the city of New Jerusalem. Which city shall be built, beginning at the temple lot, which is appointed by the finger of the Lord, in the western boundaries of the State of Missouri, and dedicated by the hand of Joseph Smith, Jun., and others with whom the Lord was well pleased. Verily this is the word of the Lord, that the city New Jerusalem shall be built by the gathering of the saints, beginning at this place, even the place of the temple, which temple shall be reared in this generation. For verily this generation shall not all pass away until an house shall be built unto the Lord, and a cloud shall rest upon it, which cloud shall be even the glory of the Lord, which shall fill the house. (Doctrine and Covenants 84:2–5)

> Therefore, as I said concerning the sons of Moses for the sons of Moses and also the sons of Aaron shall offer an acceptable offering and sacrifice in the house of the Lord, which house shall be built unto the Lord in this generation, upon the consecrated spot as I have appointed. (Doctrine and Covenants 84:31)

The Mormon's New Jerusalem and temple was not built in Missouri and definitely not in that generation, which came and went many years ago.

The Mormons have an extensive seven-volume set of the *History of the Church* which was originally *History of Joseph Smith*. It includes Smith's writings and subsequent comments by Smith's secretaries and scribes (those close to him). Then it picks up with Mormon historians once Joseph Smith died. In volume 2, we read:

President Smith then stated that the meeting had been called, because God had commanded it; and it was made known to him by vision and by the Holy Spirit. He then gave a relation of some of the circumstances attending us while journeying to Zion — our trials, sufferings; and said God had not designed all this for nothing, but He had it in remembrance yet; and it was the will of God that those who went to Zion, with a determination to lay down their lives, if necessary, should be ordained to the ministry, and go forth to prune the vineyard for the last time, for the coming of the Lord, which was nigh — even fifty-six years should wind up the scene.[9]

So Smith marked the date of being no later than 56 years for the Second Coming of Christ Jesus. By the context it should be over well before that. This was stated in 1835, before his death in 1844, but 1891, 56 years later, came and went.

Jehovah's Witnesses

The Watchtower Society or Jehovah's Witnesses, who have claimed Charles Taze Russell as the continuous prophet, have had the most failed prophecies in modern times.

1889 True, it is expecting great things to claim, as we do, that within the coming twenty-six years, all present governments will be overthrown and dissolved.[10]

1889 Remember that the *forty years'* Jewish Harvest ended October, A.D. 69, and was followed by the complete overthrow of that nation; and that likewise the forty years of the Gospel age harvest will end October, 1914, and that likewise the overthrow of "Christendom," so-called, must be expected to immediately follow.[11]

For just one sample of the Watchtower Society's failed prophecies surrounding the year 1925, consider:

---

9. Joseph Smith, *History of the Church*, Vol. 2 (Salt Lake City, UT: Deseret News, 1902), p. 182.
10. Charles Russell, *Studies in the Scriptures*, Vol. 2 (Pittsburgh, PA: Watchtower Bible and Tract Society,1889), p. 98–99.
11. Ibid., p. 245.

- In 1918, they wrote, ". . . and since other Scriptures definitely fix the fact that there will be a resurrection of Abraham, Isaac, Jacob and other faithful ones of old, and that these will have the first favor, we may expect 1925 to witness the return of these faithful men of Israel from the condition of death, being resurrected and fully restored to perfect humanity and made the visible, legal representatives of the new order of things on earth. . . . Therefore we may confidently expect that 1925 will mark the return of Abraham, Isaac, Jacob and the faithful prophets of old, particularly those named by the Apostle in Hebrews chapter 11, to the condition of human perfection."[12]

- In 1923 they wrote, "Our thought is, that 1925 is definitely settled by the Scriptures."[13]

Jehovah's Witnesses have failed to predict the end of the world on many occasions including 1908, 1914, 1918, 1925, 1941, and 1975. Their prophecies continue to fail.

Other False Prophets

In the previous section we have focused on three major groups in our culture, but there are plenty of other false prophets. Some are specific and wrong.[14] Others, like Nostradamus, are so vague that they become meaningless. Here are just a few in our modern times (including some secular predictions):

- Harold Camping falsely prophesied that the end of the age would be in 1994 in his book *1994?* That didn't happen. Then Camping revised his date and said it would occur on May 21, 2011. The date came and went. He changed it to October of the same year. That came and went.

- Charles Darwin predicted the Caucasians would exterminate all other races within the not very distant future (measured by

---

12. J.F. Rutherford, *Millions Now Living Will Never Die* (Brooklyn, NY: International Bible Students Association, 1920), p. 88.
13. *Watchtower*, April 1, 1923, p. 106.
14. E.g., (1) Herbert Armstrong (too many to list), (2) Ellen White (claimed to have a vision of heaven in *Early Writings of Ellen G. White*, 1882 (Washington, DC: Review and Herald Publishing Association, 1945), p. 32, http://www.gilead.net/egw/books2/earlywritings/ewindex.html, where she saw the Temple in the Holy City, but the Bible says there is no Temple in heaven in Revelation 21:22), and (3) Jim Jones (who murdered his flock).

centuries at the most).[15] Now we know there is only one race — the human race. This is known from the Bible all along and now confirmed by DNA. This prediction by Darwin never happened and, based on his warped understanding of the human family, never will.

- Clarence Larkin believed the Second Coming would commence no later than A.D. 2000 with a rapture occurring (7 years before).[16]

- Edgar Whisenant's book *88 Reasons Why the Rapture Will Be in 1988* also failed.

- Pat Robertson falsely predicted that Mitt Romney would be elected the president of the United States in 2012, have two terms, and the economy would turn around under his presidency. He attributed this directly to the Lord. Instead, Romney, a Mormon, lost the election.

- William Miller (father of Millerites and Adventism), predicted that Christ would return on March 21, 1844, and then later said October 22, 1844. Clearly, this didn't transpire.

- Al Gore (evolutionist) predicted in January of 2006 that the global warming point of no return for a true planetary emergency would occur in just 10 years. It came and went.[17] This is a failed prophecy.

- Stephen Hawking, Richard Dawkins, Neil deGrasse Tyson, and others have predicted we will find aliens. I'll let you ponder these prophecies!

- Nigel Barber claimed the world would be won as atheism is predicted to defeat religion by the year 2038.[18] Of course,

15. Charles Darwin, *The Descent of Man* (New York: A.L. Burt, 1874, 2nd ed.), p. 178.
16. Clarence Larkin, *Dispensational Truth* (Philadelphia, PA: Rev. Clarence Larkin Est. Publisher, 1918), p. 16.
17. For more false prophecies regarding Al Gore see Larry Tomczak, "10 Ways Al Gore Was Wrong About Global Warming," *Charisma News*, February 16, 2016, http://www.charismanews.com/opinion/heres-the-deal/55185-10-ways-al-gore-was-wrong-about-global-warming.
18. Nigel Barber, "Atheism to Defeat Religion by 2038," *Huffington Post Science*, June 5, 2012, http://www.huffingtonpost.com/nigel-barber/atheism-to-defeat-religion-by-2038_b_1565108.html.

atheism *is* a religion so that would be impossible. But I hope readers will take note of this and test it when the time comes.

This is but a taste of the false prophets who have been. Even in the New Testament they dealt with false prophets (e.g., Bar-Jesus in Acts 13:6). We've seen false prophets; the early church had to deal with false prophets (e.g., Marcionism),[19] and it has continued right up to the current times.

The point of this exercise is that if you can't trust alleged prophet or prophecies from someone when they speak, why trust their other proclamations? Jesus wisely said to Nicodemus:

> If I have told you earthly things and you do not believe, how will you believe if I tell you heavenly things? (John 3:12).

Conclusion

Since such alleged holy books and prophets are not from the perfect God, who are they from? They are from deceived, imperfect mankind. They may also be based on deceiving spirits and demons as the Bible reveals:

> Now the Spirit expressly says that in latter times some will depart from the faith, giving heed to deceiving spirits and doctrines of demons, speaking lies in hypocrisy, having their own conscience seared with a hot iron, forbidding to marry,[20] and commanding to abstain from foods[21] which God created to be received with thanksgiving by those who believe and know the truth (1 Timothy 4:1–3).

Even the doctrines of demons come through the mind of man in their manifestations. Mankind's fallible reason is not the absolute authority. God and

---

19. A cult in the second century that taught the heretic Marcion of Sinope should be trusted. Essentially, Marcion wanted the Old Testament to be thrown out as Scripture. He also threw out most of the New Testament with the exception of ten of Paul's letters.
20. Many secularists today forbid and oppose marriage and attack this doctrine. We see these various forms as *perversional* or *adulterous humanism* pervades this culture since the "sexual revolution" that began blooming in the 1960s and is now in full flower.
21. This is the case with alleged prophetess Ellen White. We see this with others too (e.g., Messianic Judaism) which is Peterism. B. Hodge, "Peterism — a False Doctrine that Still Tries to Invade the Church," Biblical Authority Ministries, February 11, 2016, https://biblicalauthorityministries.wordpress.com/2016/02/11/peterism-a-false-doctrine-that-still-tries-to-invade-the-church.

His Word are. Other books may have value, such as historical insight; but they are not the infallible Word of God.

The Bible warns that false philosophies will be used to turn people from the Bible (Colossians 2:8). So people need to stand firm on the Bible and not be swayed (1 Corinthians 15:58; 2 Thessalonians 2:15).

There are two options: place our faith in the perfect, all-knowing God who has always been there, or trust in imperfect, fallible mankind and his philosophies. The Bible, God's Holy Word, is superior to all other alleged holy books. God will never be wrong or contradict Himself. So start with the Bible and build your faith on its teachings so that you please Him.

Is there a need for new revelation after the Bible? Consider the biblical Book of Jude which says:

> Beloved, while I was very diligent to write to you concerning our common salvation, I found it necessary to write to you exhorting you to contend earnestly for the faith *which was once for all delivered to the saints* (Jude 1:3, emphasis added).

Appendix B

What Makes a Christian Martyr Differ from Other Faiths' "Martyrs"?

Troy Lacey

He was a martyr for a good cause." A person is put to death (often quite brutally) because he refuses to recant his beliefs and teachings when he is demanded to do so by angry opponents. So we have Muslim martyrs, Jewish martyrs, communist martyrs, Christian martyrs, Buddhist martyrs, Hindu martyrs, etc. They are all the same, right? Not really.

What Is a Martyr?

The English word "martyr" is an almost direct transliteration from the New Testament Greek word *martus*, which originally meant a "witness." It was especially used in the early church to signify those who were witnesses of Jesus Christ's death, burial, and Resurrection (e.g., Acts 1:22). Consequently, many of those Apostles died giving testimony of their Lord. In current usage it usually means one who is killed for refusing to renounce their religious faith, practices, and beliefs.[1]

The unspoken assumption is that if the person would renounce his beliefs then he would not be put to death, avoiding martyrdom. History is replete with tales of martyrs, from Old Testament believers, to the Apostles, to the

---

11. *American Heritage Dictionary of the English Language*, s.v. "martyr" (Boston, MA: Houghton Mifflin Company, 1980).

early Church Fathers, and down to our time, especially in areas like Sudan, the Middle East, the Philippines, Indonesia, and parts of South America. For the most part, these have been either Jewish or Christian martyrs, and the logical question to ask would be "Why?" Why not Buddhists or Taoists or Hindu martyrs to the same extent? We will consider that question in due course.

A martyr is someone who believes so strongly in his religion that he is unwilling to compromise when faced with external pressures to convert to another religion. He would rather face death than dishonor himself and his god (either a false god or the true and Living God of the Bible). He does not deem it right (even in those situations where the threat of death is imminent) to even outwardly conform to a "religious conversion," even if he knows he would internally keep his original belief system. This would be construed as failing his god, lying to himself, and giving a poor testimony to the world about his god and religion. Shadrach, Meshach, and Abednego are perfect examples of this type of mindset, although they were divinely spared from becoming martyrs (Daniel 3).

Radical Muslims who blow themselves up in a suicide bombing to kill others are occasionally called martyrs by some, but this is a misnomer. The suicide bomber is not a martyr, but one who has chosen his (or her) own death and is actively pursuing it. He is not dying because he refuses to convert to Christianity (or Buddhism or Hinduism), but rather because of a choice to be an offensive weapon of terror.

For most polytheistic religions, martyrdom is usually not much of a concern, since another belief system can be incorporated into the pantheon of deities and beliefs already present. For example, this is why in India today we can see Jesus Christ being added by Hindu worshipers to the religious festivals and even the pantheon of deities. They will even venerate Jesus as a god without recognizing that He is actually *the Creator God* (John 1; Hebrews 1; Colossians 1).

This is not to say that Buddhist or Hindu adherents never become martyrs. The Tibetan Buddhists have, for many years, been persecuted and martyred by the Chinese government for their refusal to convert to atheistic communism. And Muslims have killed Hindus for their refusal to convert to their version of monotheism as well.

As in all cases of conflict, however, one must remember that religion may not be the only factor in persecution. In the case of the Hindu/Muslim conflict, much of the conflict lies in nationalistic animosity between Pakistanis and Indians. In the case of the Tibetan Buddhists vs. Communist Chinese government, it is as much a conflict about self-government and independence versus centralized government as it is about religion. Therefore, deaths on either side may be the result of skirmishing as opposed to actual cases of direct religious persecution leading to martyrdom.

Why Christian Martyrs Are Often Different

Nevertheless, we do know that such persecution and martyrdom does take place. So what makes the Buddhist or Hindu martyr different from the Christian martyr? How does a Christian missionary to Indonesia who is martyred differ from the Tibetan monk who is martyred?

It basically boils down to two things. First, what was the person who was martyred engaged in doing? What was his lifestyle and business that caused him to be a target? Second, what was the martyr killed for? In the above-mentioned cases of Hindu and Buddhist martyrs, some are engaged in violent or revolutionary activities against another government and so are not true martyrs because they are killed as "enemy combatants."

But many people in this situation are innocent bystanders living in areas viewed as hostile to the government in question. They may be killed inadvertently (or deliberately) because of nationalistic reasons. These deaths would actually be war casualties or genocide, not martyrdom in the religious sense. Others are killed mainly for religious reasons, but without a direct threat to convert or die. These killings are still mostly nationalistic in intent, not true martyrdom. The killing of non-Christians simply because of their religious beliefs and their subsequent refusal to convert to another religion is rare (although not unheard of).

The killing of Christians simply because of their belief and their refusal to deny Christ and convert to a different religion has been recorded countless times since the martyrdom of Stephen in Acts 7 (ca. A.D. 32–35) up to the present time. In fact, it has been said that more Christians are suffering martyrdom today than ever before — up to 100 thousand per year.[2]

There is often additional persecution to Christian populations that causes loss of property, forced displacement from their homeland, or even

---

2. Todd Johnson, "The Case for Higher Numbers of Christian Martyrs," Gordon-Conwell Theological Seminary, accessed January 15, 2016, http://www.gordonconwell.edu/ockenga/research/documents/csgc_Christian_martyrs.pdf.

ends in forced labor camps.[3] According to David Barrett, the "persecution of Christians is more common in our generation than ever in history. The oft-quoted statistic is that more people died for their Christian faith in the last century than in all the other centuries of recorded history combined."[4]

The Christian organization, *Voice of the Martyrs,* lists 52 countries that are currently persecuting Christians.[5] This persecution includes verbal assault, property confiscation, physical assault, unlawful imprisonment, threatenings, torture, psychological intimidation, kidnappings, and murder. In Sudan alone it is estimated that hundreds of thousands of Christians have been martyred and up to 2 million forced to flee their homes, simply for refusing to renounce their Christian faith.[6]

The Romans, Huns, Goths, Vikings, Muslims, Hindus, and other religious groups (including atheism and humanism) have perpetrated martyrdom of Christians since the time of the Apostles, mainly because of their Christian faith. The vast majority of these Christian martyrs were not revolutionaries or dissidents, but ordinary citizens trying to live peaceably among their neighbors. According to principles laid down in Scripture, they paid their taxes, honored the king and governors, loved their neighbors, and gave no cause for offense (Romans 13:1–8; 1 Peter 2:13–17).

Why Christians Are Targets

How then can we account for this vitriol directed at Christianity in excess of other inter-faith conflicts? The answer lies in the exclusivity of the Christian faith and the means of salvation. True Christianity does not teach a multiplicity of ways to "come to God." It does not teach that humans are basically good (Genesis 8:21; Jeremiah 17:9) and just need a divine nudge to get on the right track. It does not teach that man can earn merit with God (e.g., Galatians 2:16). True Christianity teaches what Jesus Christ taught, that He alone is "the Way, the Truth and the Life: no man comes to the Father except through Me" (John 14:6).

Christianity is intricately tied to the authority of the Bible, which details mankind's separation from God due to sin, the remedy that God provided

---

3. "Worldwide Persecution of Christians," Seeking Truth, accessed January 15, 2016, http://www.seekingtruth.co.uk/persecution.htm.
4. David Barrett, *International Bulletin of Missionary Research,* January 2007.
5. Voice of the Martyrs. *Foxe 33 A.D. to Today,* (China: Codra Enterprises, 2007), p. 341–473.
6. Ibid., p. 459–462.

through the death and Resurrection of Christ, how God wants to be worshiped, and how we are to conduct ourselves as ambassadors for Christ. Ephesians 2:1 says that we are all dead in sins until Christ makes us alive; and in verses 8–9 Paul tells us that we are saved (from God's judgment) by the grace of God through faith in Jesus Christ, not by our own good works or merit.

Romans 3:10–18 teaches that we are not righteous in our natural state and that we do not seek after God. Then we read in 1 John 4:10 that God demonstrated His love for us by sending His Son to be the propitiation (substitutionary sacrifice) for our sins. Just as by one man (Adam) judgment came upon all men to condemnation, so by the righteousness of one man (Jesus Christ), the free gift of salvation comes (Romans 5:15–18) through faith if they believe (Romans 3:22).

Therefore, Christians preach a gospel that teaches that all men are sinners, that we all need a Savior, and that Jesus Christ took our sins upon Himself on the Cross to pay for our transgressions. We are told to repent of our sins, believe on the Lord Jesus Christ, and make confession with our mouth (Acts 17:30–31; Romans 10:9–19). Christians understand that God has given us the insight to comprehend His Word. In our natural state we are at war with God and could never understand or please God (Romans 8:7–8). Consequently, we recognize that salvation is of the Lord (Psalm 3:8).

It is this teaching, that we cannot in and of ourselves please or earn merit with God, nor can we work toward our own salvation, that makes Christianity different from all other religions. It is not by works of righteousness, which *we* have done, but according to His mercy that He saves us (Titus 3:5). People do not like to hear that they are sinners, and that they can never please God by their own works or righteousness (Galatians 2:16). Nor do sinners like to hear that God will one day judge every man according to his works (Revelation 20:11–15) and that those works will be deemed at best "filthy rags" in the sight of God (Isaiah. 64:6).

It is for this gospel that Christians are persecuted, some to the point of martyrdom, even today. Jesus Himself told us to expect persecution because they persecuted Him. Therefore, others would persecute His followers (John 15:20). The Apostle Peter wrote that we are not to think it strange that we Christians should suffer persecution (1 Peter 4:12–13). And Paul told Timothy that "all who desire to live godly in Christ Jesus will suffer persecution" (2 Timothy 3:12). It is for this reason that the world hates us. As Jesus said in John 15:18–19, "If the world hates you, you know that it hated Me before it hated you. If you were of the world, the world would love its own. Yet because you are not of the world, but I chose you out of the world, therefore the world hates you."

The Apostle James wrote much about persecution, suffering, and endurance. He wrote that we are "to count it all joy when [we] fall into various trials, knowing that the testing of [our] faith produces patience. But let patience have its perfect work, that [we] may be perfect and complete, lacking nothing" (James 1:2–4). James understood that Christians would suffer persecution, but urged them to continue to spread the gospel, using the example of the Old Testament prophets' proclamation of the Word of the Lord even in times when that message was reviled.

> Therefore, be patient, brethren, until the coming of the Lord. See how the farmer waits for the precious fruit of the earth, waiting patiently for it until it receives the early and latter rain. You also be patient. Establish your hearts, for the coming of the Lord is at hand. Do not grumble against one another, brethren, lest you be condemned. Behold, the Judge is standing at the door! My brethren, take the prophets, who spoke in the name of the Lord, as an example of suffering and patience. Indeed we count them blessed who endure. You have heard of the perseverance of Job and seen the end intended by the Lord — that the Lord is very compassionate and merciful (James 5:7–11).

Christians in America and other Western nations have been blessed to live in lands that legislated religious freedom (a biblical principle, by the way, e.g., Joshua 24:15). Sadly, America is one of just a handful of countries that has such liberty. Most of our Christian brothers and sisters around the world suffer for their faith in one form or another — either at the hands of their government or at the hands of angry mobs bent on silencing their witness for Christ. We are enjoined by our Lord to "weep with those who weep" (Romans 12:15), for we know that we are all of one body in Christ (Romans 12:5). Therefore, we should pray for our brothers and sisters in Christ and also help provide for their needs (Romans 12:13).

Thankfully, we serve a God who providentially works all things in our lives for our good. Nothing ever catches Him by surprise. He will then use even the most trying circumstances to make us more like His Son, Jesus Christ.

> And we know that all things work together for good to those who love God, to those who are the called according to His purpose. For whom He foreknew, He also predestined to be conformed to the image of His Son, that He might be the firstborn among many brethren (Romans 8:28–29).

Some Martyrs and Concluding Remarks

Lastly, let's look at the reaction of some Christian martyrs as they faced their own death. First, we should remember the words of our Lord as He hung on the cross, "Father, forgive them, for they know not what they do" (Luke 23:34).

Next we have recorded in Scripture, the words of Stephen as he was being stoned to death, "Lord, do not charge them with this sin" (Acts 7:60). We read of eyewitness testimony of Polycarp, a disciple of John.

> While being burned to death on a pyre he remarked "I bless You that You have considered me worthy of this day and hour, to receive a part in the number of the martyrs in the cup of Your Christ."[7]

In each of these cases, and many more examples (e.g., *Foxe's Book of Martyrs*), the Christian martyr did not rail against his persecutors, nor curse them. Rather, either they prayed for their persecutors, or they thanked God for allowing the Christian to be a witness unto death for Him.

Many modern-day examples are happening right before our eyes, with Christians (as well as Muslims) being martyred by Boko Haram in Nigeria, Chad, Cameroon, and Niger,[8] and by ISIS/ISIL in Syria, Afghanistan, Iraq, Ethiopia, and other parts of the Middle East.[9] While some of these attacks

---

7. Ibid., p. 52.
8. "Nigeria: Abducted Women and Girls Forced to Join Boko Haram Attacks," Amnesty International, accessed August 23, 2016, https://www.amnesty.org/en/latest/news/2015/04/nigeria-abducted-women-and-girls-forced-to-join-boko-haram-attacks.
9. Greg Bothelo, "Faith Turns Christians into Terrorist Targets," CNN, accessed August 23, 2016, http://www.cnn.com/2015/04/24/world/terrorists-attacks-on-christianity.

are indiscriminate terrorist attacks that simply target areas with large concentrations of civilians, many are directly aimed at Christians, with the aim to make converts to Islam or kill those who will not convert.

As we look to God's revealed Word as our absolute authority and live lives that reflect its truths, we as Christians should be both salt and light. That light will stand out in a dark world (Matthew 5:14–16) exposing the darkness of sin (Ephesians 5:11). It will also mark Christians as different from the rest of the world and again make them targets for hatred, just as Christ was hated (John 15:18).

As Christians striving to live godly lives, we are to expect persecution (2 Timothy 3:12; Hebrews 12:1–4), whether it be in the form of mockery, being called foolish and scientifically illiterate, having our rights impinged on or denied, or, as we see in many countries around the world, physical persecution and even martyrdom. But we can be exhorted with the words of Christ on this matter: "And you will be hated by all for My name's sake. But he who endures to the end shall be saved" (Mark 13:13) and the promise that Jesus will never leave us nor forsake us (Hebrews 13:5).

Appendix C

Do Secularists Have a Foundation for Morality?

Ken Ham and Avery Foley

Secularists and atheists frequently accuse Christians of behaving "immorally" and religion of being "evil." But such objections to religion bring up an interesting question: how does the secular humanist or atheist define evil and morality and by what authority do they make such statements?

Nothing but Subjective Opinion

For the atheist or secular humanist, there is no foundation for morality besides his or her own subjective opinion.[1] These individuals often throw around words such as *evil, immoral, moral,* or *ethical,* often in the context of Christian religion or Christian individuals. They will say things such as "religion is evil"[2] or that teaching creation to children is "child abuse," but what do they mean by these phrases?

In their worldview, what makes anything immoral or wrong? Really it boils down to nothing more than their opinion.[3] They *believe* that something is wrong and therefore it *must* be. But who is to say that their opinion

---

1. Opinions are arbitrary, and thus fallacious.
2. Clearly, they mean Christianity. They do not argue that their religion of atheism or humanism is evil.
3. Opinions are pointless, as they are not a measure of truth in the least. Consider if someone was of the opinion that 2+2=-9. Such an opinion is worthless.

is the right one? After all, there are many different opinions on what is right and wrong. Who decides which one is right and which one is wrong?

The argument that atheism and secular humanism cannot provide a foundation for morality is a strong argument. Here are a few responses that you may hear if you bring up this objection.

Society Decides Morality

Some atheists will argue that morality is simply decided by the society. For example, here in America our society has decided that murdering an innocent human being is wrong, and therefore that action is morally wrong. But this kind of thinking simply does not hold up to scrutiny.

Society often changes its opinion. One clear example of this is in regard to gay "marriage." What was considered morally wrong by most of society is now legal, applauded, and celebrated by some groups. In this view, homosexual behavior went from being morally wrong to being morally acceptable. What if our society decides that murder is acceptable, as it did in the case of *Roe v. Wade* when America legalized the killing of unborn children? Does murder suddenly become morally acceptable too? What about adultery, stealing, lying, or any other manner of morally reprehensible actions? Would the atheist or humanist accept a society that decides that that society can kill all atheists and humanists? If society is the moral compass, then the compass never points north but rather jumps all over the place and changes with every generation.

Also, if society determines morality, how can one society tell another society what is right or wrong? Most people would agree that the abhorrent actions of the Nazi death camps were morally wrong. But why? Nazi Germany decided as a society that these actions were morally acceptable. What right does our society have to judge their society if morality is simply a societal preference?

Or what about certain Muslim groups? Few would agree that blowing up innocent civilians, slaughtering hundreds of people from other religious groups, kidnapping and enslaving young women, or using children as suicide bombers is morally acceptable. Yet if morality is simply a societal preference, what right does our society have to tell their society that their actions are wrong and must be stopped?

The consistent atheist or humanist can say nothing if that is the ethic a society has decided is right. In this view, the atheist, based on his arbitrary opinion, might not agree with their ethic, but they have no rationale to say anything or try to put a stop to it. If morality is simply decided by societal preference, it fails to make any sense and becomes arbitrary, subject to change by time and culture.

Human Reason

The problem only gets worse when you break it down to a personal level. Some secularists will argue that morality is an individual decision and no one has the right to tell another person what to do (this is called "autonomous human reason"). Of course, the irony of such a statement should be evident. By saying that no one should tell someone else what to do, they have just told someone else what to do!

If the secularists really believed this, then they couldn't say, "religion is evil" in the first place, since it is not their place to say.

If this view of morality is true, then our justice system cannot exist. After all, why should one judge, legislative assembly, or government body impose their view of morality on another individual? If stealing, killing, raping, or abusing is right for one individual, what gives another individual the right to say that view of morality is wrong?

Now this personal morality or human reasoning view stems from the idea that people are basically good and that, left on our own, humans tend to do right and not wrong (again, who defines right and wrong?). But humans aren't basically good! Human experience shows that throughout history humans have committed atrocities, even in our supposedly enlightened Western world. The Bible describes the fallen human heart this way:

> The heart is deceitful above all things, and desperately wicked; who can know it? (Jeremiah 17:9).

> And the LORD smelled a soothing aroma. Then the LORD said in His heart, "I will never again curse the ground for man's sake, although the imagination of man's heart is evil from his youth; nor will I again destroy every living thing as I have done" (Genesis 8:21).

> To the pure all things are pure, but to those who are defiled and unbelieving nothing is pure; but even their mind and conscience are defiled (Titus 1:15).

Autonomous human reason simply does not provide a sufficient foundation for morality.

Did Morality Evolve?

From human experience, we seem to naturally and intuitively know that actions such as murder, stealing, and child abandonment are wrong for all people everywhere. But where does this intuitive sense come from?

Evolutionists, by necessity, believe that morality (along with everything else) is simply the result of evolution. Somehow, after billions of years of death, struggle, atrocities, disease, and suffering, man realized that we should strive to do the opposite! Man should oppose survival of the fittest and try to be moral. In their worldview, we are nothing more than highly evolved animals, and our brains are nothing more than chemical reactions.[4] We are simply the product of our DNA.

This view raises the question of how the strictly naturalistic process of evolution leads to the development of an immaterial, absolute moral conscience that somehow applies to all people everywhere? And what happens if this conscience evolves? Does morality change again?

Furthermore, if we are simply animals, why are we held morally accountable? After all, we certainly don't hold animals accountable for their actions. No lion court exists to punish lions that maul gazelles to death and then eat them. No one jails a female cuckoo for abandoning her babies or forces male rabbits to pay child support. These are simply the things animals in this cursed world do, and no one faults them for doing it. If we are just animals, what makes humans so different?

The problem gets even worse if you argue that our brains are nothing more than random chemical reactions and that we are at the mercy of our DNA. If we are just programmed DNA, then how can we be held accountable for any of our decisions? There is no free will in a view such as this; therefore, there is no accountability for decisions or actions.

Morality simply cannot be the result of naturalistic processes over millions of years. This view does not hold up to close examination, and really is the opposite of what we know to be true from human experience and the Bible's teachings.

---

4. Recall that in the atheistic or humanistic worldview, all things are *natural* and *material*. Nothing immaterial really exists. So the mind cannot exist. But neither can logic, truth, knowledge, *morality*, and so on.

Moral Atheists?

When faced with their worldview's inability to provide a foundation for morality, many atheists respond by claiming that you don't have to be religious to be moral. It's true that plenty of atheists are moral citizens. But those who argue this way have missed the point.

Atheists certainly can be moral. Actually, starting with a biblical worldview, this is to be expected. God has put His law in all our hearts (Romans 2:15) so even atheists, who claim that they don't believe in the Creator God, can adhere to this law and be moral. But the point is that they have no foundation for this morality in their own worldview. They have no basis for saying something is right or wrong, moral or immoral.

The Bible Provides a Foundation for Morality

Secular humanism and atheism cannot account for the existence of morality in their worldview. But what about the biblical view?

According to God's Word, humans were specially created in the image of God (Genesis 1:27). We are not animals nor are our brains simply chemical reactions. As He has from the very beginning, our Creator holds us accountable for our actions (Genesis 2:17) and expects us to be able to choose and distinguish between right and wrong.

As Creator, only God has the authority to tell us what is right and what is wrong. And this standard is not arbitrary. It is based on the unchanging character of the righteous, holy, and perfect Judge of the universe. For example, all murder is wrong because God has created us in His own image and forbids the taking of a human life (e.g., Genesis 9:6; Exodus 20:13; Romans 13:9).

God, the Creator, has given us the Bible — His revealed Word,[5] which clearly lays out what is morally acceptable and what is not. It provides a firm foundation from the very Creator on which we can base our morality.

What is more, God has placed His law in all of our hearts (Romans 2:15). We know right from wrong because of the conscience that God has given all of humanity, and we are held accountable to Him for our actions and decisions (Romans 2:1–16) based on this knowledge of Him that we have.

It should be obvious to anyone who has lived in this world that no one fully obeys God's law. We all fall short of God's perfect standard, as Scripture

---

5. His Word is absolute and not arbitrary, like the opinions of man.

makes abundantly clear (Romans 3:23). We even fall far short of imperfect human standards! Why is this? Genesis gives us the answer.

The first two people, Adam and Eve, were created morally perfect, but they chose to rebel against their Creator (Genesis 3). No longer were they morally perfect; now they had a sin nature, which they passed on to each of their children (Romans 5:12–21). All of their descendants — every person on earth — is now a slave to sin (John 8:34) and in rebellion against God.

The Bible provides a firm foundation for morality and provides the answer for why all people have a moral conscience and why we cannot live up to this knowledge of morality. But there's more.

The Answer Is the Gospel

Not only does the Bible explain why there is a universal moral code, why everyone knows it, and why no one can consistently live up to it, but the Bible also provides the solution to our shortcoming. When Adam and Eve sinned, they received the penalty that their rebellion deserved — death (Genesis 2:17). We all sinned and continue to sin in Adam, so we all deserve the penalty of death (Romans 5:12). No matter how hard we try, we can never live up to God's perfect moral standard (Romans 3:23). We certainly are in a dire position, deserving nothing but condemnation and death.

But because of His great love for us and according to His mercy (Ephesians 2:4), the Creator came to earth as the God-man, a descendant of Adam just like us (1 Corinthians 15:45). But unlike us, He perfectly kept God's law (Romans 10:4). He then chose to *become* sin for us (2 Corinthians 5:21), taking the sins of the whole world upon Himself when He died on the Cross (1 John 2:2).

He took the penalty that we all deserve — death — for us (Romans 4:25, 5:8). But He didn't stay dead. He rose victoriously from the grave, defeating death (2 Timothy 1:10; Hebrews 2:14). He now offers forgiveness and eternal life to all who will repent (Acts 3:19), believe (John 3:18), and trust in Him (Romans 10:9).

Only the Bible provides a consistent foundation for morality that applies to all people everywhere. And only the Bible provides the hope that we need through the person of Jesus Christ, our Creator, Savior, and Lord.

Appendix D

Intelligent Design Movement

Dr. Georgia Purdom

The Intelligent Design Movement (IDM) entered the modern origins debate in 1991 with the publication of Phillip Johnson's book *Darwin on Trial*. Johnson was a lawyer who essentially "tried" Darwinism in a court of law. He found the evidence for Darwinism so lacking that he decided it could not "win" the case as a viable explanation for the origin of living things. Since that time, the IDM has gained increasing recognition and publicity for challenging Darwinism.

What Is Intelligent Design?

The Discovery Institute's Center for Science and Culture is the flagship organization of the IDM. On their website they state, "The theory of intelligent design holds that certain features of the universe and living things are best explained by an intelligent cause, not an undirected process such as natural selection."[1] The ID theory does not name the intelligent cause, and it does not claim that everything is designed. Many proponents of the theory still hold to certain aspects of evolution (e.g., common ancestry of apes and humans) and believe the earth and universe are billions of years old.

The modern IDM has its historical roots in the natural theology movement of the 18th and 19th centuries. Christian philosopher William Paley

---

1. "Frequently Asked Questions," Discovery Institute, accessed September 19, 2016, http://www.discovery.org/id/faqs/.

(1743–1805) reasoned that if one walked across a field and came upon a watch, the assumption would be that there had to be a watchmaker — the complexity and purpose of the watch points to the fact that it is not the result of undirected, unintelligent causes, but the product of a designer.

Natural theology sought to support the existence of God through nature (general revelation) apart from the Bible (special revelation), since the Bible was facing much criticism at that time. The scientific knowledge of the complexity of living things was grossly deficient, leading some to believe that natural causes were sufficient to bring everything into existence. Natural theology was an affront to that line of thinking, much like the ID theory is to Darwinism in modern times.

In the last 100 years or so, there has been an explosion of knowledge about the complexity of cells, DNA, and microorganisms. Thus, the need for a designer has become even greater. The current IDM has more than just philosophical arguments for a designer; it uses scientific evidence drawn from biology, chemistry, and physics.

Irreducible Complexity = Design

The Discovery Institute lists three areas in which they think the evidence for design is apparent.

1. Evidence for design in physics and cosmology — these evidences focus on the laws of the universe necessary for life on earth.
2. Evidence for design in the origin of life — these evidences focus on the "complex and specified information" (CSI) necessary for the origin of life.
3. Evidence for design in the development of biological complexity — these evidences focus on the CSI necessary for living things.[2]

I will focus on the evidence for design in biological complexity since this is the area for which the IDM is most well known.

The ID theory purports that the hallmark of designed living things is *irreducible complexity*. Dr. Michael Behe, ID proponent and author of *Darwin's Black Box*, defines irreducible complexity as:

---

2. "What Is the Science Behind Intelligent Design?" Discovery Institute, May 1, 2009, http://www.discovery.org/a/9761.

A single system composed of several well-matched, interacting parts that contribute to the basic function, wherein the
removal of any one of the parts causes the system to effectively
cease functioning.[3]

Some examples are the biochemistry of vision, the mammalian blood-clotting
pathway, and the bacterial flagellum. These biological pathways and structures consist of many factors, and *all* the factors and parts are necessary for
the pathway or structure to function properly.

Behe further explains that the gradual process of Darwinian evolution
cannot form these irreducibly complex systems:

An irreducibly complex system cannot be produced directly
(that is, by continuously improving the initial function, which
continues to work by the same mechanism) by slight, successive
modifications of a precursor system, because any precursor to an
irreducibly complex system that is missing a part is by definition
nonfunctional.[4]

Evolution works via the mechanism of small, gradual steps of random
chance mutation that "keeps" only that which is immediately helpful. The
changes must confer a survival advantage to an organism that allows it to
survive better than others of its kind. Better survival means the organism is
more likely to reproduce and pass on the changes to the next generation and
increase the number of organisms carrying the changes. The mechanism by
which evolution works actually prevents organisms from evolving complex
biological pathways and structures.

For example, if only three of the many proteins involved in vision were
formed in an organism (at one time by random chance), the organism could
not see. There would be no survival advantage and so that organism would
not necessarily survive better than others to pass on those changes to the
next generation. Evolutionary processes do not allow the organism with the
changes to preferentially survive and reproduce in the hopes that in a future
generation the rest of the vision proteins will form.

Evolution is goalless and purposeless; it does not have a mind and
cannot see or plan for the future. The information in the DNA for the vision

3. Michael Behe, *Darwin's Black Box* (New York, NY: Simon and Schuster, 1996), p. 39.
4. Ibid.

proteins is likely to be lost in future generations since it serves no immediate purpose that confers a survival advantage. Since evolution cannot accumulate the vision proteins in a step-wise fashion, it would have to start at square one again in each organism to develop the proteins (by random chance mutations) necessary for vision. It's improbable that all the necessary vision proteins would evolve by random chance in a single organism; thus, evolution does not have a mechanism to develop these complex biological pathways and structures.

How Is Irreducible Complexity Detected?

The question of whether a feature of a living organism displays design can be answered by using what is called an explanatory filter. The filter has three levels of explanation:

1. Necessity or Law — did it have to happen?
2. Chance — did it happen by accident?
3. Design — did an intelligent agent cause it to happen?[5]

This is a logical, common sense approach used by individuals every day to deduce cause and effect. For example, consider the scenario of a woman falling:

1. Did she have to fall? If the answer is no, then we have to ask the next two questions.
2. Was it an accident?
3. Or was she pushed?

Crime scene investigators use this explanatory filter every time they examine a crime scene. They need to decide if what happened was an accident or if a crime was committed by a "designer."

If we apply this explanatory filter to living organisms, a feature must be designed if the first two questions are answered no. Let's evaluate the vision pathway that results in sight with respect to these questions:

1. The vision pathway is compatible with, but not required by, the natural laws of biology and chemistry. It is not a necessity specified by natural phenomena.
2. It is complex because the vision pathway is composed of many proteins so it could not have happened by chance. Complex

---

5. William Dembski, "Signs of Intelligence," in: William Dembski and James Kushiner, eds., *Signs of Intelligence* (Grand Rapids, MI: Brazos Press, 2001), p. 171.

structures fall into two categories: ordered complexity and specified complexity. A snowflake is structurally complex, but does not contain information (specified complexity) so it represents a form of ordered complexity. It is the direct result of natural phenomena rather than a product of intelligent design.[6] DNA, on the other hand, does contain information and is an example of specified complexity that does require an intelligent designer.

3. The vision pathway has specified complexity because it has information that results in sight. All the proteins must be present and interact with each other in a specified manner in order for vision to occur. The vision pathway meets all the requirements for irreducible complexity so it must be the product of intelligent design.

Is the IDM a Religion, Science, or Neither?

ID proponent and theologian William Dembski states:

ID is three things:
a scientific research program that investigates the effects of intelligent causes [science];
an intellectual movement that challenges Darwinism and its naturalistic legacy;
and a way of understanding divine action [religion].[7]

The IDM focuses on what is designed rather than answering the questions of who, when, why, and how. Those within the movement believe this promotes scientific endeavor by looking for function and purpose in those things that are designed, whereas an evolutionary mindset presupposes waste and purposelessness and aborts further scientific thinking.

I would agree that the IDM challenges Darwinism; however, I would not say that it is science or religion, even though it has religious and scientific aspects. It's a worldview that acknowledges a "higher power" which will affect how those who hold it view the natural world and do science. In addition, many ID proponents hold a variety of religious views in regard to the "intelligent designer," making it difficult to define the IDM as a religion.

6. While snowflakes are not the direct result of intelligent design, it was God who designed and created the natural laws by which snowflakes form.
7. William Dembski, "Science and Design," *First Things* 86, October 1, 1998.

Evidential vs. Presuppositional Approaches

Proponents of IDM take an evidential approach when looking at the natural world. For example, the vision pathway (evidence) is irreducibly complex, so it must have been designed. But that is essentially where the ID argument ends. It does not answer who the designer is or when, why, or how the designer designed it.

The reason they do this is to have a "big tent" strategy in which they get as many people as possible (regardless of their religious beliefs about the who, what, where, when, and why of the designer) to oppose Darwinism. The hope is that the more people who oppose it, the more seriously their ideas will be taken and the more progress they can make in scientific and educational realms.

Christians in IDM look at it as a "first step" toward getting people to acknowledge a designer which they hope will result in further conversations that might lead them to know the designer is the God of the Bible.

Biblical creationists tend to take a presuppositional approach and use the framework of the inerrant Word of God when looking at the natural world. We would agree that the vision pathway is designed, but we know that because of the Bible. This also allows us to answer the other questions of who (God), when (approximately 6,000 years ago), why (His will), and how (by His Word). Everything in the natural world has been designed by God (Genesis 1) but corrupted by man's sin (Genesis 3) and impacted by a global Flood (Genesis 6–9). This context is very important because without this understanding the IDM runs into a major problem when it comes to the identity and characteristics of the intelligent designer (discussed later).

It is simply not sufficient to say what is designed without answering the questions that are sure to naturally follow — who, when, why, and how. The IDM is unable and unwilling to answer these questions because their "big tent" strategy means that people in the movement hold to a variety of answers to these questions. Many within the IDM would categorize their evidential approach to science as neutral since they only ask if things in the natural world are designed. However, no approach is neutral because every scientist has certain beliefs or presuppositions when they approach the evidence.

It is ironic that ID proponents refuse to see this about their own approach, considering that they claim the problem with Darwinism is the presupposition that nothing supernatural exists. ID proponents at the very least begin with the presupposition that allows for a supernatural intelligent designer.

The natural theology movement of the 1800s failed because it did not answer the next logical question: if it is designed, then who designed it? Most within this movement claimed that design pointed to the God of the Bible, but by divorcing general revelation (nature) from special revelation (the Bible) they opened the door to other conclusions. Deism (another movement of the same period) took the idea of excluding the Bible to the extreme and said God can only be known through nature and human reason, and that faith and revelation do not exist.

Since IDM proponents do not adhere to a particular theological framework, most have no problems with the universe and earth being billions of years old (i.e., the big bang and no global Flood) and still allow biological evolution (possibly being more guided) to play a role. For example, many in the IDM believe in common descent, (the evolutionary tree of life) including that humans and chimps share a common ancestor.

However, they fail to understand that a belief in long ages for the earth formed the foundation of Darwinism. Without billions of years, evolution doesn't have the time to accomplish the evolution of all living things from a single-celled common ancestor. The IDM thus fails to challenge and even accepts one of the core tenets of Darwinism, rendering it much less effective in providing a viable alternative to origins. The IDM is not opposed to evolution, only a purely naturalistic form of evolution.

IDM Is Not Silent about the Designer

Even with claims of neutrality and just answering the question of "what" is designed, the IDM by default is making certain claims about the intelligent designer. The design says something about its designer. For example, if someone designs a raincoat but it doesn't keep the person wearing it from getting wet, we would say the designer was incompetent. Without the biblical framework, what does the natural world "say" about the designer?

Michael Behe in his book, *The Edge of Evolution*, tries to answer this question in relation to the parasite that causes malaria:

> Malaria was intentionally designed. The molecular machinery with which the parasite invades red blood cells is an exquisitely purposeful arrangement of parts.

What sort of designer is that? What sort of "fine-tuning" leads to untold human misery? To countless mothers mourning countless children? Did a hateful, malign [sic] being make intelligent life in order to torture it? One who relishes cries of pain?!

Maybe. Maybe not. A torrent of pain indisputably swirls through the world — not only the world of humans but the world of sentient animal life as well. Yet, just as undeniably, much that is good graces nature. Many children die, yet many others thrive. . . . Does one outweigh the other? If so, which outweighs which? Or are pleasure and pain, good and evil incommensurable? Are viruses and parasites part of some brilliant, as-yet-unappreciated economy of nature, or do they reflect the bungling of an incompetent, fallible designer?

Maybe the designer *isn't* all that beneficent or omnipotent. Science can't answer questions like that.[8]

I agree that scientists can't answer those questions without a biblical worldview, which is why it's so important to have a biblical framework when doing science! The design says something about its designer and without the proper framework to understand it Behe describes a horrific designer. He believes the designer purposefully designed malaria to infect people, resulting in death for some. He suggests this might be some sort of "population control" by the designer and that maybe the designer is not all that nice and not all-powerful. Although Behe is Roman Catholic, this is certainly not a picture of the Creator God we know from the Bible.[9]

These beliefs of Behe shouldn't be all that surprising — as I have stated previously, many IDM proponents believe in various forms of evolution. If they also believe in the God of the Bible, then they believe He used millions of years of death, disease, and suffering as recorded in the fossil record to bring about mankind and every other living thing. Death is integral to evolution — it's all about survival of the fittest. Rather than death being a punishment for sin (Genesis 2:16–17 and 3:19), death existed for millions of years before mankind existed to sin. What does this say about God?!

Scripture is clear that death is the last enemy (1 Corinthians 15:26) and that death is the punishment for sin (Romans 6:23). Scripture is clear that

---

8. Michael J. Behe, *The Edge of Evolution* (New York, NY: Free Press, 2007), p. 237–238.
9. Many Roman Catholics would disagree with Behe on this point, as well.

originally everything was "very good" (Genesis 1:31), including the organism that in a fallen world causes malaria. Originally, its molecular machinery did something different that did not inflict pain or harm or cause disease. But as a result of sin, all creation is cursed (Romans 8:22) and organisms have changed as a result of mutations and other processes, allowing them to cause much human misery.

How could God use evolution, which is filled with millions of years of death, disease, and suffering, and then call it "very good"? God becomes the author of evil instead of evil being the result of man's actions (Genesis 3:6). Rather than God being loving, patient, kind, good, merciful, etc. as the Scripture describes Him, He is cruel, vicious, and unloving. If ID ideas without a biblical framework are to be a first step in leading someone to know more about God, why would anyone want to take the next step?

And if God is the author of evil, how can He be the solution to evil? Scripture makes it clear that because of the sin of the first Adam we need the death and Resurrection of the Last Adam, Jesus Christ (1 Corinthians 15:21–22, 45). The problem of sin begins in Genesis (Genesis 3), and the solution of sin is found in Jesus Christ (Romans 10:9). If instead, as many Christians within the IDM believe, God used death and suffering to bring about mankind and every other living thing, then death cannot be the punishment for sin. What then is the purpose of Jesus Christ dying a physical death on the Cross if the punishment for sin is not death? What did Christ die to redeem us from if the punishment for sin is not death?

The IDM does not necessarily acknowledge the God of the Bible as Creator or Redeemer, so the "designer" they postulate is not only responsible for the origin of evil but offers no final solution for the evil in this world. And by all appearances, evil will continue to reign supreme. A "god" like this is nothing more than any other false god in this world religions series.

However, when we trust the Bible, we read that evil was brought into this world by man's actions (Genesis 3), Jesus clearly conquered death by His Resurrection (Romans 6:3–10), and one day death will no longer reign (Revelation 21:4).

The Creator Cannot Be Separated from His Creation

Romans 1:20 states that all men know about God through His creation. However, just recognizing that there is a designer is only one part of it —

which is enough to leave a person without excuse. Colossians 1:15–20 and 2 Peter 3:3–6 point to the inexorable link between God's role as Creator *and* Redeemer.

In Colossians, Paul talks about God, in the person of Jesus, as Creator, and moves seamlessly to His role as Redeemer. Paul sees creation as a foundation for redemption. In 1 Peter, Peter states that people started disbelieving in the Second Coming of Christ because they started doubting God's role as Creator. Again, God's role as Creator is foundational to His role as Redeemer.

Recognizing a designer is not enough to be saved; submitting to the Redeemer is also necessary. While some might consider the IDM a noble attempt to counter the evolutionary indoctrination of our culture, it falls far short of a thoroughly biblical response and even embraces much evolutionary thinking.

We must not separate the creation from its Creator — knowledge of God must come through both general revelation (nature) and special revelation (the Bible). The theologian Louis Berkhof said, "Since the entrance of sin into the world, man can gather true knowledge about God from His general revelation only if he studies it in the light of Scripture."[10] It is only then that the *entire* truth about God and what is seen around us can be fully understood and used to help people understand the bad news in Genesis and the good news of Jesus Christ.

---

10. Louis Berkhof, *Introductory Volume to Systematic Theology* (Grand Rapids, MI: Eerdmans Publishing Co., 1938), p. 60.

Appendix E

Is Evolutionary Humanism the Most Blood-stained Religion Ever?

Bodie Hodge

Introduction: Man's Authority or God's Authority . . . Two Religions

If God and His Word are not the authority . . . then by default . . . who is? *Man* is. When people reject God and His Word as the ultimate authority, then man is attempting to elevate his or her thoughts (collectively or individually) to a position of authority *over* God and His Word.

People often claim that "Christians are religious, and the enlightened unbelievers who reject God are *not* religious." Don't be deceived by such a statement — for these nonbelievers are indeed religious . . . *very* religious, whether they realize it or not. For they have bought into the religion of humanism.

Humanism is the religion that elevates man to be greater than God. Humanism, in a broad sense, encompasses any thought or worldview that rejects God and the 66 books of His Word in part or in whole; hence, *all* non-biblical religions have humanistic roots. There are also those that *mix* aspects of humanism with the Bible. Many of these religions (e.g., Mormons, Islam, Judaism, etc.) openly borrow from the Bible, but they also have mixed *human* elements into their religion where they take some of man's ideas to supersede many parts of the Bible, perhaps in subtle ways.[1]

---

1. For example: in Islam, Muhammad's words in the Koran are taken as a higher authority than God's Word (the Bible); in Mormonism, they have changed nearly 4,000 verses of

There are many forms of humanism, but secular humanism has become one of the most popular today. Variant forms of secular humanism include atheism, agnosticism, non-theism, Darwinism, and the like. Each shares a belief in an evolutionary worldview, with man as the centered authority over God.

Humanism organizations can also receive a tax-exempt status (the same as a Christian church in the United States and the United Kingdom) and they even have religious documents like the *Humanist Manifesto*. Surprisingly, this religion has free rein in state schools, museums, and media under the guise of neutrality, seeking to fool people into thinking it is not a "religion."[2]

Humanism and "Good"

Christians are often confronted with the claim that a humanistic worldview will help society become "better."[3] Even the first *Humanist Manifesto*, of which belief in evolution is a subset, declared: "The goal of humanism is a free and universal society in which people voluntarily and intelligently co-operate for the common good."

But can such a statement be true? For starters, what do the authors mean by "good"? They have no legitimate foundation for such a concept, since one person's "good" can be another's "evil." To have some objective standard (not a relative standard), they must *borrow* from the absolute and true teachings of God in the Bible.

Beyond that, does evolutionary humanism really teach a future of prosperity and a common good? Since death is the "hero" in an evolutionary framework, then it makes one wonder. What has been the result of evolutionary thinking in the past century (20th century)? Perhaps this could be a test of what is to come.

Let's first look at the death estimates due to aggressive conflicts stemming from leaders with evolutionary worldviews, beginning in the 1900s, to see the hints of what this "next level" looks like. See Table 1.

---

the Bible to conform to Mormon teachings and add the words of Joseph Smith and later prophets as superior to God's Word; in Judaism, they accept a portion of God's Word (the Old Testament) but by human standards, they reject a large portion of God's Word (the New Testament) as well as the ultimate Passover lamb, Jesus Christ.

2. Although the U.S. Supreme Court says that religion is not to be taught in the classroom, this one seems to be allowed.

3. One can always ask the question, by what standard do they mean "better"? God is that standard, so they refute themselves when they speak of things being better or worse. In their own professed worldview it is merely arbitrary for something to be "better" or "worse."

Table 1 Estimated deaths as a result of an evolutionary worldview

Who/What?	Specific event and estimated dead	Total Estimates
Pre-Hitler Germany/ Hitler and the Nazis	WWI: 8,500,000[a] WWII: 70 million[b] [Holocaust: 17,000,000][c]	95,000,000
Leon Trotsky and Vladimir Lenin	Bolshevik revolution and Russian Civil War: 15,000,000[d]	15,000,000
Joseph Stalin	20,000,000[e]	20,000,000
Mao Zedong	14,000,000–20,000,000[f]	Median estimate: 17,000,000
Korean War	2,500,000?[g]	~2,500,000
Vietnam War (1959–1975)	4,000,000–5,000,000 Vietnamese, 1,500,000–2,000,000 Lao and Cambodians[h]	Medians of each and excludes French, Australia, and U.S. losses: 6,250,000
Pol Pot (Saloth Sar)	750,000–1,700,000[i]	Median estimate: 1,225,000
Abortion to children[j]	China estimates from 1971–2006: 300,000,000[k] USSR estimates from 1954–1991: 280,000,000[l] U.S. estimates 1928–2007: 26,000,000[m] France estimates 1936–2006: 5,749,731[n] United Kingdom estimates 1958–2006: 6,090,738[o] Germany estimates 1968–2007: 3,699,624[p] Etc.	621,500,000 and this excludes many other countries
Grand estimate		~778,000,000

a. *The World Book Encyclopedia*, Volume 21, Entry: World War II (Chicago, IL: World Book, Inc.), p. 467; such statistics may have some variance depending on source, as much of this is still in dispute.
b. Ranges from 60 to 80 million, so we are using 70 million.
c. Figures ranged from 7 to 26 million.
d. Russian Civil War, http://en.wikipedia.org/wiki/Russian_Civil_War, October 23, 2008.
e. Joseph Stalin, http://www.moreorless.au.com/killers/stalin.html, October 23, 2008.
f. Mao Tse-Tung, http://www.moreorless.au.com/killers/mao.html, October 23, 2008.
g. This one is tough to pin down and several sources have different estimates, so this is a middle-of-the-road estimate from the sources I found.
h. Vietnam War, http://www.vietnamwar.com/, October 23, 2008.
i. Pol Pot, http://en.wikipedia.org/wiki/Pol_Pot, October 23, 2008.
j. This table only lists estimates for abortion deaths in few countries; so, this total figure is

likely very conservative as well as brief stats of other atrocities.

k. Historical abortion statistics, PR China, compiled by Wm. Robert Johnston, last updated June 4, 2008, http://www.johnstonsarchive.net/policy/abortion/ab-prchina.html.

l. Historical abortion statistics, U.S.S.R., compiled by Wm. Robert Johnston, last updated June 4, 2008, http://www.johnstonsarchive.net/policy/abortion/ab-ussr.html.

m. Historical abortion statistics, United States, compiled by Wm. Robert Johnston, last updated June 4, 2008, http://www.johnstonsarchive.net/policy/abortion/ab-unitedstates.html.

n. Historical abortion statistics, France, compiled by Wm. Robert Johnston, last updated June 4, 2008, http://www.johnstonsarchive.net/policy/abortion/ab-france.html.

o. Historical abortion statistics, United Kingdom, compiled by Wm. Robert Johnston, last updated June 4, 2008, http://www.johnstonsarchive.net/policy/abortion/ab-unitedkingdom.html.

p. Historical abortion statistics, FR Germany, compiled by Wm. Robert Johnston, last updated June 4, 2008, http://www.johnstonsarchive.net/policy/abortion/ab-frgermany.html.

Charles Darwin's view of molecules-to-man evolution was catapulted into societies around the world in the mid-to-late 1800s. Evolutionary teachings influenced Karl Marx, Leon Trotsky, Adolf Hitler, Pol Pot, Mao Zedong, Joseph Stalin, Vladimir Lenin, and many others. Let's take a closer look at some of these people and events and examine the evolutionary influence and repercussions.

World War I and II, Hitler, Nazis, and the Holocaust

Most historians would point to the assassination of Archduke Francis Ferdinand on June 18, 1914, as the event that triggered World War I (WWI). But tensions were already high, considering the state of Europe at the time. Darwinian sentiment was brewing in Germany. Darwin once said:

> At some future period, not very distant as measured by centuries, the civilized races of man will almost certainly exterminate and replace the savage races throughout the world. At the same time the anthropomorphous apes . . . will no doubt be exterminated. The break between man and his nearest allies will then be wider, for it will intervene between man in a more civilized state, as we may hope, even than the Caucasian, and some ape as low as a baboon, instead of as now between the negro or Australian [Aborigine] and the gorilla.[4]

Darwin viewed the "Caucasian" (white-skinned Europeans) as the dominant "race" in his evolutionary worldview. To many evolutionists at the

---

4. Charles Darwin, *The Descent of Man* (New York: A.L. Burt, 1874, 2nd ed.), p. 178.

time, mankind had evolved from ape-like creatures that had more hair, dark skin, dark eyes, etc. Therefore, more "evolved" meant less body hair, blond hair, blue eyes, etc. Later, in Hitler's era, Nazi Germany practiced *Lebensborn*, which was a controversial program, the details of which have not been entirely brought to light. Many claim it was a breeding program that tried to evolve the "master race" further — more on this below.

But the German sentiment prior to WWI was very much bent on conquering for the purpose of expanding their territory and their "race." An encyclopedia entry from 1936 states:

> In discussions of the background of the war much has been said of Pan-Germanism, which was the spirit of national consciousness carried to the extreme limit. The Pan-Germans, who included not only militarists, but historians, scientists, educators and statesmen, conceived the German people, no matter where they located, as permanently retaining their nationality. The most ambitious of this group believed that it was their mission of Germans to extend their kultur (culture) over the world, and to accomplish this by conquest if necessary. In this connection the theory was advanced that the German was a superior being, destined to dominate other peoples, most of whom were thought of as decadent.[5]

Germany had been buying into Darwin's model of evolution and saw themselves as the superior "race," destined to dominate the world, and their actions were the consequence of their worldview. This view set the stage for Hitler and the Nazi party and paved the road to WWII.

Hitler and the Nazis

World War II dwarfed World War I in the total number of people who died. Racist evolutionary attitudes exploded in Germany against people groups such as Jews, Poles, and many others. Darwin's teaching on evolution and humanism heavily influenced Adolf Hitler and the Nazis.

Hitler even tried to force the Protestant church in Germany to change fundamental tenets because of his newfound faith.[6] In 1936, while Hitler was in power, an encyclopedia entry on Hitler stated:

5. *The American Educator Encyclopedia* (Chicago, IL: The United Educators, Inc., 1936), p. 3914 under entry "World War."
6. *The American Educator Encyclopedia* (Chicago, IL: The United Educators, Inc., 1936), p. 1702 under entry "Hitler."

. . . a Hitler attempt to modify the Protestant faith failed.[7]

His actions clearly show that he did not hold to the basic fundamentals taught in the 66 books of the Bible. Though some of his writings suggest he did believe in some form of God early on (due to his upbringing within Catholicism), his religious views moved toward atheistic humanism with his acceptance of evolution. Many atheists today try to disavow him, but actions speak louder than words.

The Alpha History site (dedicated to much of the history of Nazi Germany by providing documents, transcribed speeches, and so on) says:

> Contrary to popular opinion, Hitler himself was not an atheist. . . . Hitler drifted away from the church after leaving home, and his religious views in adulthood are in dispute.[8]

So this history site is not sure what his beliefs were, but they seem to be certain that he was not an atheist! If they are not sure what beliefs he held, how can they be certain he was not an atheist?[9] The fact is that many people who walk away from church become atheists (i.e., they were never believers in the first place as 1 John 2:19 indicates). Hitler's actions were diametrically opposed to Christianity . . . but not atheism, where there is no God who sets what is right and wrong.[10]

Regardless, this refutes notions that Hitler was a Christian, as some have falsely claimed. Hitler's disbelief started early. He said:

> The present system of teaching in schools permits the following absurdity: at 10 a.m. the pupils attend a lesson in the catechism, at which the creation of the world is presented to them in accordance with the teachings of the Bible; and at 11 a.m. they attend a lesson in natural science, at which they are taught the theory of evolution. Yet the two doctrines are in complete contradiction. As a child, I suffered from this contradiction, and

---

7. Ibid., p. 1494 under entry "Germany."
8. Religion in Nazi Germany, http://alphahistory.com/nazigermany/religion-in-nazi-germany/, April 3, 2013.
9. Romans 1 makes it clear that all people believe in God, they just suppress that knowledge, and this is also the case with any professed atheist.
10. For an extensive treatise on Hitler's (and the Nazis') religious viewpoints, see J. Bergman, *Hitler and the Nazi Darwinian Worldview* (Kitchener, Ontario, Canada: Joshua Press Inc., 2012).

ran my head against a wall. . . . Is there a single religion that can exist without a dogma? No, for in that case it would belong to the order of science. . . . But there have been human beings, in the baboon category, for at least three hundred thousand years. There is less distance between the man-ape and the ordinary modern man than there is between the ordinary modern man and a man like Schopenhauer. . . . It is impossible to suppose nowadays that organic life exists only on our planet.[11]

Consider this quote in his unpublished second book:

The types of creatures on the earth are countless, and on an individual level their self-preservation instinct as well as the longing for procreation is always unlimited; however, the space in which this entire life process plays itself out is limited. It is the surface area of a precisely measured sphere on which billions and billions of individual beings struggle for life and succession. In the limitation of this living space lies the compulsion for the struggle for survival, and the struggle for survival, in turn contains the precondition for evolution.[12]

Hitler continues:

The history of the world in the ages when humans did not yet exist was initially a representation of geological occurrences. The clash of natural forces with each other, the formation of a habitable surface on this planet, the separation of water and land, the formation of the mountains, plains, and the seas. That [was] is the history of the world during this time. Later, with the emergence of organic life, human interest focuses on the appearance and disappearance of its thousandfold forms. Man himself finally becomes visible very late, and from that point on he begins to understand the term "world history" as referring to the history of his own development — in other words, the representation of his own evolution. This development

11. Adolf Hitler, 1941, translated by Norman Cameron and R.H. Stevens, *Hitler's Secret Conversations*, 1941–1944 (The New American Library of World Literature, Inc., 1961).
12. Adolf Hitler, edited by Gerald L. Weinberg, translated by Krista Smith, *Hitler's Second Book* (U.K.: Enigma books, 2003), p. 8.

is characterized by the never-ending battle of humans against animals and also against humans themselves.[13]

Hitler fully believed Darwin as well as Darwin's precursors — such as Charles Lyell's geological ages and millions of years of history. In his statements here, there is no reference to God. Instead, he unreservedly flew the banner of naturalism and evolution and only mentioned God in a rare instance to win Christians to his side, just as agnostic Charles Darwin did in his book *On the Origin of Species*.[14]

One part of the Nazi party political platform's 25 points in 1920 says:

> We demand freedom of religion for all religious denomina-
> tions within the state so long as they do not endanger its exist-
> ence or oppose the moral senses of the Germanic race. The Party
> as such advocates the standpoint of a positive Christianity with-
> out binding itself confessionally to any one denomination.[15]

Clearly this "positive Christianity" was an appeal to some of Christianity's morality, but not the faith itself. Many atheists today still appeal to a "positive Christian" approach, wanting the morality of Christianity (in many respects), but not Christianity.

Christianity was under heavy attack by Hitler and the Nazis, as documented from original sources prior to the end of WWII by Bruce Walker in *The Swastika against the Cross*.[16] The book clearly reveals the anti-Christian sentiment by Hitler and the Nazis and their persecution of Christianity and their attempt to make Christianity change and be subject to the Nazi state and beliefs.

In 1939–1941, the Bible was rewritten for the German people at Hitler's command, eliminating all references to Jews and made Christ out to be pro-Aryan! The Ten Commandments were replaced with these twelve:[17]

13. Hitler, *Hitler's Second Book*, p. 9.
14. In the first edition of *Origin of Species*, God is not mentioned, in the sixth edition, "God" was added several times to draw Christians into this false religion. See Randall Hedtke, *Secrets of the Sixth Edition* (Green Forest, AR: Master Books, 2010).
15. "Nazi Party 25 Points (1920)," http://alphahistory.com/nazigermany/nazi-party-25-points-1920/.
16. B. Walker, *The Swastika against the Cross* (Denver, CO: Outskirts Press, Inc., 2008).
17. "Hitler Rewrote the Bible and Added Two Commandments," Pravda News Site, 8/10/2006, http://english.pravda.ru/world/europe/10-08-2006/83892-hitler-0/; Jewish References Erased in Newly Found Nazi Bible," Daily Mail Online, August 7, 2006, http://www.dailymail.co.uk/news/article-399470/Jewish-references-erased-newly-Nazi-Bible.html.

1. Honor your Fuhrer and master.
2. Keep the blood pure and your honor holy.
3. Honor God and believe in him wholeheartedly.
4. Seek out the peace of God.
5. Avoid all hypocrisy.
6. Holy is your health and life.
7. Holy is your well-being and honor.
8. Holy is your truth and fidelity.
9. Honor your father and mother — your children are your aid and your example.
10. Maintain and multiply the heritage of your forefathers.
11. Be ready to help and forgive.
12. Joyously serve the people with work and sacrifice.

Hitler had *replaced* Christ in Nazi thought; and children were even taught to pray to Hitler instead of God![18] Hitler and the Nazis were not Christian, but instead were humanistic in their outlook, and any semblance of Christianity was cultic. The Nazis determined that their philosophy was the best way to bring about the common good of all humanity.

Interestingly it was Christians alone in Germany who were unconquered by the Nazis and suffered heavily for it. Walker summarizes in his book:

> You would expect to find Christians and Nazis mortal ene-mies. This is, of course, exactly what happened historically. Christians, alone, proved unconquerable by the Nazis. It can be said that Christians did not succeed in stopping Hitler, but it cannot be said that they did not try, often at great loss and nearly always as true martyrs (people who could have chosen to live, but who chose to die for the sake of goodness.)[19]

Hitler and the Nazi's evolutionary views certainly helped lead Germany into WWII because they viewed the "Caucasian" as more evolved (and more spe-cifically the Aryan peoples of the Caucasians), which to them justified their adoption of the idea that lesser "races" should be murdered in the struggle for survival. Among the first to be targeted were Jews, then Poles, Slavs, and then many others — including Christians regardless of their heritage.

---

18. Walker, p. 20–22.
19. Walker, p. 88.

Trotsky and Lenin

Trotsky and Lenin were both notorious leaders of the USSR — and specifically the Russian revolution. Lenin, taking power in 1917, became a ruthless leader and selected Trotsky as his heir. Lenin and Trotsky held to Marxism, which was built, in part, on Darwinism and evolution applied to a social scheme.

Karl Marx regarded Darwin's book as an "epoch-making book." With regard to Darwin's research on natural origins, Marx claimed, "The latter method is the only materialistic and, therefore, the only scientific one."[20]

Few realize or admit that Marxism, the primary idea underlying communism, is built on Darwinism and materialism (i.e., no God). In 1883, Freidrich Engels, Marx's longtime friend and collaborator, stated at Marx's funeral service that "Just as Darwin discovered the law of evolution in organic nature, so Marx discovered the law of evolution in human history."[21] Both Darwin and Marx built their ideologies on naturalism and materialism (tenants of evolutionary humanism). Trotsky once said of Darwin:

> Darwin stood for me like a mighty doorkeeper at the entrance to the temple of the universe. I was intoxicated with his minute, precise, conscientious and at the same time powerful, thought. I was the more astonished when I read . . . that he had preserved his belief in God. I absolutely declined to understand how a theory of the origin of species by way of natural selection and sexual selection and a belief in God could find room in one and the same head.[22]

Trotsky's high regard for evolution and Darwin were the foundation of his belief system. Like many, Trotsky probably did not realize that the precious few instances of the name "God" did not appear in the first edition of *Origin of Species*. These references were added later, and many suspect that this was done to influence church members to adopt Darwinism. Regardless, Trotsky may not have read much of Darwin's second book, *Descent of Man,* in which Darwin claims that man invented God:

---

20. *Great Books of the Western World*, Volume 50, Capital, Karl Marx (Chicago, IL: William Benton Publishers, 1952), footnotes on p. 166 and p. 181.

21. Gertrude Himmelfarb, *Darwin and the Darwinian Revolution* (London: Chatto & Windus, 1959), p. 348.

22. Max Eastman, *Leon Trotsky: The Portrait of a Youth* (New York: Greenberg, 1925), p. 117–118.

> The same high mental faculties which first led man to believe in unseen spiritual agencies, then in fetishism, polytheism, and ultimately in monotheism, would infallibly lead him, as long as his reasoning powers remained poorly developed, to various strange superstitions and customs.[23]

Vladimir Lenin picked up on Darwinism and Marxism and ruled very harshly as an evolutionist. His variant of Marxism has become known as Leninism. Regardless, the evolutionist roots of Marx, Trotsky, and Lenin were the foundation that communism has stood on — and continues to stand on.

Stalin, Mao, and Pol Pot, to Name a Few

Perhaps the most ruthless communist leaders were Joseph Stalin, Mao Zedong, and Pol Pot. Each of these were social Darwinists, ruling three different countries — the Soviet Union, China, and Cambodia, respectively. Their reigns of terror demonstrated the end result of reducing the value of human life to that of mere animals, a Darwinistic teaching.[24] Though I could expand on each of these, you should be getting the point by now. So let's move to another key, but deadly, point in evolutionary thought.

Abortion — The War on Babies

The war on children has been one of the quietest, and yet bloodiest, in the past hundred years. In an evolutionary mindset, the unborn have been treated as though they are going through an "animal phase" and can simply be discarded.

Early evolutionist Ernst Haeckel first popularized the concept that babies in the womb are actually undergoing animal developmental stages, such as a fish stage and so on. This idea has come to be known as *ontogeny recapitulates phylogeny*. Haeckel even faked drawings of various animals' embryos and had them drawn next to human embryos looking virtually identical.[25]

---

23. Charles Darwin, *The Descent of Man and Selection in Relation to Sex,* chapter III ("Mental Powers of Man and the Lower Animals"), 1871, as printed in the *Great Books of the Western World*, Volume 49, Robert Hutchins, ed. (Chicago, IL: Wiliam Benton Publishers, 1952), p. 303.

24. R. Hall, "Darwin's Impact — The Bloodstained Legacy of Evolution," *Creation* Magazine 27(2):46-47, March 2005, http://www.answersingenesis.org/articles/cm/v27/n2/darwin.

25. Lithograph by J.G. Bach of Leipzig after drawings by Haeckel, from *Anthropogenie* published by Engelmann; public Domain, https://commons.wikimedia.org/w/index.php?curid=8007834.

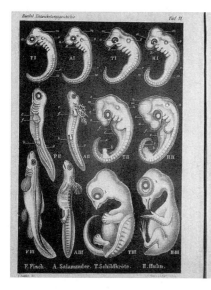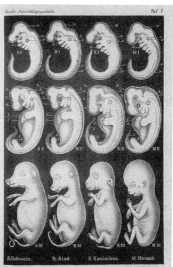

These drawings have been shown to be completely false.[26] Haeckel himself partially confessed as much.[27] However, this discredited idea has been used repeatedly for a hundred years! Textbooks today still use this concept (though not Haeckel's drawings), and museums around the world still teach it. Through this deception, many women have been convinced that the babies they are carrying in their wombs are simply going through an animal phase and can be aborted. Author and general editor of this volume, Ken Ham, states:

> In fact, some abortion clinics in America have taken women aside to explain to them that what is being aborted is just an embryo in the fish stage of evolution, and that the embryo must not be thought of as human. These women are being fed outright lies.[28]

26. Michael Richardson et al., *Anatomy and Embryology*, 196(2):91–106, 1997.
27. Haeckel said, "A small portion of my embryo-pictures (possibly 6 or 8 in a hundred) are really (in Dr Brass's [one of his critics] sense of the word) 'falsified' — all those, namely, in which the disclosed material for inspection is so incomplete or insufficient that one is compelled in a restoration of a connected development series to fill up the gaps through hypotheses, and to reconstruct the missing members through comparative syntheses. What difficulties this task encounters, and how easily the draughts — man may blunder in it, the embryologist alone can judge." The Truth about Haeckel's Confession, *The Bible Investigator and Inquirer*, M.L. Hutchinson, Melbourne, March 11, 1911, p. 22–24.
28. Ken Ham, *The Lie: Evolution*, chapter 8, "The Evils of Evolution" (Green Forest, AR: Master Books, 1987), p. 105.

Evolutionary views have decreased the value of human life. Throughout the world the casualties of the war on children is staggering. Though deaths of children and the unborn did exist prior to the "evolution revolution," they have increased exponentially after the promotion of Darwinian teachings.

Conclusion

Is evolution the cause of wars and deaths? Absolutely not — both existed long before Darwin was born. Sin is the ultimate cause.[29] But an evolutionary worldview has done nothing but add fuel to the fire.

In spite of the wars and atrocities caused by those who subscribed to an evolutionary worldview in recent times, there is still hope. We can end the seemingly endless atrocities against the unborn and those deemed less worthy of living, including the old and impaired.

In Egypt, Israelite boys were slaughtered by being thrown into the Nile at the command of Pharaoh (Exodus 1:20). And yet, by the providence of God, Moses survived and led the Israelites to safety, and the Lord later judged the Egyptians.

In Judea, under the Roman Empire, subordinate King Herod the Great commanded the slaughter of all the boys under the age of two in and around Bethlehem. And yet, by the providence of God, Jesus, the Son of God, survived and later laid down His life to bring salvation to mankind as the Prince of Peace. Herod's name, however, went down in history as an evil tyrant and murderer.

In this day and age, governments readily promote and fund the killing of children, both boys and girls, and sometimes command it, through abortion. By providence, however . . . you survived. While we can't change the past, we can learn from it. If we are to stop this continuing bloodshed, we must get back to the Bible and realize the bankrupt religion of evolutionary humanism has led only to death — by the millions. We need to point those who think humanity is the answer, to the Savior who took the sins of humanity on Himself to offer them salvation.

---

29. *The New Answers Book 1*, gen. ed. Ken Ham, chapter 26, "Why Does God's Creation Include Death and Suffering?" (Green Forest, AR: Master Books, 2006), p.325–338, http://www.answersingenesis.org/articles/nab/why-does-creation-include-suffering.

Appendix F

Responding to Atheist Propaganda

Ken Ham

Christians need to understand that many secularists have put together a very effective propaganda machine as a part of their effort to impose their atheistic religion on the Western culture. They intimidate Christians and influence the government to limit freedom of religion (particularly in regard to Christianity).

To help counteract this aggressive effort, Christians — wherever they are in the West — need to be aware of the terms being used in the secularist campaign and what Christians need to be doing to help counter this campaign.

Secularists know the adage that if you "throw enough mud at the wall, some of it will stick." If enough false information and misleading accusations are spread, people will begin to believe them. This is nothing new, as Nazis did this very thing leading up to WWII. In our day and age, this has happened in a number of places.

1. The use of the word *science*

Here is how I discussed the word *science* during my debate with Bill Nye "The Science Guy":

> Public school textbooks are using the same word *science* for observational and historical science. They arbitrarily define *science* as naturalism and outlaw the supernatural. They present

molecules-to-man evolution as fact. They are imposing the religion of naturalism/atheism on generations of students.[1]

I also stated the following during the debate:

> The word *science* has been hijacked by secularists in teaching evolution to force the religion of naturalism on generations of kids. . . . The creation/evolution debate is really a conflict between two philosophical worldviews based on two different accounts of origins or historical science beliefs. The word *science* is defined as "the state of knowing: knowledge as distinguished from ignorance or misunderstanding."[2]

Scientific pursuit needs to be broken into two parts: experimental (observable or operational) science and origins (historical) science. Both creation and evolution involve historical science (belief about the past) and observational science (such as the study of genetics, mixing chemicals in test tubes, or building computers).

Experimental science that builds our modern technology is accomplished through the scientific method. Origins or historical science is the non-repeatable, non-observable science dealing with the past — which enters the realm of beliefs (really, religion).

In almost all of today's government-run educational systems, the religion of secular humanism — with its foundation of naturalistic evolution based on man's word/beliefs about the past (molecules-to-man evolution) — is guised in textbooks, lectures, and secular museums as so-called "science." But the same word, *science*, is used for the experimental science that helps build technology.

Because students aren't taught the difference between historical and observational science, they are brainwashed into thinking that molecules-to-man evolution is the same science as what has built technology — which it is not. It is what we call a "bait-and-switch fallacy" (a fallacy in logic). It's really a conflict between two philosophical worldviews that are based on two different accounts of origins or historical science beliefs.

---

1. Ken Ham and Bodie Hodge, *Inside the Nye-Ham Debate* (Green Forest, AR: Master Books, 2014), p. 33.
2. Merriam-Webster Online Dictionary, s.v. "science," http://www.merriam-webster.com/dictionary/science.

Because of this misuse of wording by the secularists, Christians need to be using the terms *observational science* and *historical science* over and over again! The secularists hate these terms, for they don't want people to know they actually have a religion (a worldview) they are trying to impose on the masses. Their propaganda campaign, which confuses the meaning of the word science and attempts to indoctrinate people in evolutionary ideas, has been very successful.

To help counter their efforts, we need to keep delineating between "observational" and "historical" science as much as we can — much to the consternation of the secularists!

2. The use of the word *religion*

The word *religion* has a variety of definitions, but one of the main definitions (as given by the *Merriam-Webster Dictionary*) is "an interest, a belief, or an activity that is very important to a person or group."[3]

Atheists have effectively propagandized the culture to indoctrinate people to think that if you believe in God as Christians do, then that is religion — however, if you don't believe in God and believe the universe and all life arose by natural processes, then supposedly that is not a religion! But as we constantly point out, atheism and humanism are religions — beliefs meant to explain life by natural processes, without the supernatural involved.

Atheists go ballistic when I say in many articles that they are trying to impose their religion of naturalism on the culture. But the point is, they are!

Just because atheists refuse to acknowledge it does not mean they are not doing it. In fact, due to the atheist propaganda effort, it's one of the reasons we are losing Christian symbols (crosses, Nativity scenes, and so on) across the nation.

Furthermore, in the United States and other Western countries, the government is imposing a religion on millions of children when they insist that schools only teach evolution in science classes and not biblical creation. Officials insist that evolution is deemed to be "science" and creation is "religion." Evolutionists have been indoctrinating people with a false view of the words *science* and *religion*.

I am encouraging Christians, as much as they can, to use the word *religion* to describe secularism. When a secular group like the Freedom from

---

3. Merriam-Webster Online Dictionary, s.v. "religion," http://www.merriam-webster.com/dictionary/religion.

Religion Foundation or Americans United for the Separation of Church and State lodge a lawsuit to get a cross removed from a public place or a statue with someone praying, and so on, then we need to make sure to be vocal about the fact that secularists have imposed their religion of atheism.

Furthermore, why are these same organizations refusing to sue for the removal of symbols of atheism, evolution, and naturalism? It is a double standard.

Some secularists want to deny that humanism and atheism should be considered religions, but even various U.S. courts have ruled and described in their decisions that humanism should be viewed as a religion. In Oregon, an inmate sued, with the assistance of the American Humanist Association, to have a humanist study group recognized as a religious study group along with Bible studies in the prison.

Arguing based on the Establishment Clause of the First Amendment, the inmate won the right as the district judge ordered secular humanism to be viewed as a religion. Even so, humanism had previously been viewed as a non-theistic religion in the rationale for the Supreme Court case of *Torcaso v. Watkins*. This is the first ruling that clearly establishes atheistic secular humanism as a religion whose practice should be protected under the First Amendment.[4]

Additionally, the U.S. military has commissioned humanist chaplains to serve those soldiers who deny God's existence.

3. The word *intolerance*

Intolerance/intolerant is defined in the *Merriam-Webster Dictionary* this way:

> Unwilling to grant equal freedom of expression especially in religious matters; unwilling to grant or share social, political, or professional rights.[5]

Intolerantly, secularists often accuse Christians who, for example, take a stand on marriage being one man for one woman based on the Bible, as being intolerant. But in fact, Christians are the ones who are tolerant of

---

4. The U.S. Supreme Court in *Torcaso v. Watkins*, 81 S.Ct. 1681 (1961), stated the following: "Among religions in this country which do not teach what would generally be considered a belief in the existence of God, are Buddhism, Taoism, Ethical Culture, Secular Humanism, and others."

5. Merriam-Webster Online Dictionary, s.v. "intolerant," http://www.merriam-webster.com/dictionary/intolerant.

others. You see, Christians who stand on God's Word will authoritatively speak against gay marriage, but they should not be intolerant of the people who disagree with them.

I find that those who call Christians "intolerant" are really the ones who are intolerant! So when a fire chief in Atlanta, Georgia, is fired by a city council because his personal beliefs concerning marriage are based on the Bible, Christians need to be vocal about the city council's being intolerant and imposing their humanistic religion on people under their jurisdiction!

4. The word *proselytize*

The *Merriam-Webster Dictionary* has this definition of *proselytize*:

> To try to persuade people to join a religion, cause, or group.[6]

Actually, America's courts have not been able to give an accepted definition of this word. Some people claim that just telling someone about the gospel of Jesus Christ is supposedly trying to force one's belief on someone (their definition of proselytizing). Christians will certainly share their beliefs and the hope of forgiveness of sins with others, but they recognize that they cannot force someone to become a Christian. Only God can change people's hearts.

In reality, it's the secularists who are trying to force their religion on others as they intimidate people to accept the basic tenets of their religion, such as evolutionary naturalism. Many atheists don't necessarily use the word *proselytize*, but they claim that a Christian working in a government institution or a government-funded place cannot bring their Christianity into the workplace.

Yet many professors at government-subsidized universities will openly proclaim their atheism (and even attack the Bible and the Christian faith) in their classes, but if a professor were to admit he was a Christian and make statements about his religious beliefs to the students, he would likely be disciplined or fired.[7]

More and more we see intolerant secularists trying to limit the Christian influence by attempting to intimidate Christians not to bring their

---

6. Merriam-Webster Online Dictionary, s.v. "proselytize," http://www.merriam-webster.com/dictionary/proselytize.

7. For some examples, see Jerry Bergman, *Slaughter of the Dissidents* (Southworth, WA: Leafcutter Press, 2012), https://answersingenesis.org/store/product/slaughter-dissidents/?sku=10-2-345.

Christianity into their workplace — all the while they want the freedom to impose theirs. They ultimately want Christianity eliminated altogether from the public arena. Meanwhile, secularists are free to exercise their religion wherever they want to.

Conclusion

As secularists are successful in getting the governments to teach evolution as fact to millions of students in Western nations and will not allow biblical creation to be taught in science classes, we should be pointing out their deceptive use of terms. Indeed, the secularists continually misuse the word *science* as they indoctrinate people into a false worldview of naturalism so they can impose that religion on young people. At the same time, they exhibit their intolerance of Christianity and Christians in the culture.

The secularists want to express their beliefs throughout society and want Christians to keep their beliefs inside their churches. In reality, governments are sanctioning the religion of naturalism and that it be imposed on millions of children and teens. At the same time, Western nations have supported a growing intolerance of anything Christian and are limiting free speech and the freedom of religion in trying to squelch the free exercise of Christianity.

I challenge Christians, especially Christian leaders, to be more vocal in this battle, boldly proclaiming the gospel to unbelievers and calling Christians back to the authority of the Bible. As we stand firmly and boldly on the truths of Jesus Christ as the Creator and Savior in our apologetic arguments, we must also use correct terms like *historical science, observational science, religion,* and *intolerance* when engaging the secularists in the ongoing war against Christianity in Western nations.

That is why you will find Answers in Genesis using these terms in our articles, billboards, and other outreaches, as we do our best to help undo the work of the atheists' propaganda campaigns and point people to the hope that we have in Jesus Christ, as we give a defense of the Christian faith.

Appendix G

Responding to Skeptics

Roger Patterson

The humanistic thinking that underlies the philosophy of a majority of those in the West has colored every aspect of life. And that makes perfect sense — culture is a reflection of the religious views (cultus) of the people who make up the society. As go the people, so go the schools, the government, entertainment, etc. One of the key areas where this influence is seen is in the government-run schools.

In America and other Western countries, there is a naturalistic bias that permeates the science classrooms and a progressive bias that colors the social studies classes. Science is limited to only anti-God, naturalistic ideas, especially those promoting evolutionary ideas (cosmological, geological, and biological). While there is some latitude in social studies classrooms to discuss various religious ideas, Christianity is certainly demonized in many settings. However, is it really the public school's job to offer religious instruction? Well, if our religious views color everything we do, then there is no separating the sacred from the secular activities of our days.

So how would you respond to someone in a discussion of what should be taught in the public schools? That response is going to depend on a lot of factors, but the following exchange shows how to expose the false beliefs and arbitrary claims of a skeptic while directing them to the truth found in the

Bible and ultimately declare the glorious gospel of Jesus Christ.[1] The original letter appears as block quotes with the responses inserted between.

Can Public Schools Be "Neutral"?

> Insofar as the Humanist Manifesto declares there is no God, public schools must not be humanist. But neither may they endorse any particular creed they must be deity neuter. Public schools, since they are supported by mandatory taxation, must not teach any religious viewpoint (including atheism). Would you like it if your children were taught to reverence Vishnu?
>
> You say you want Creationism taught along with Evolution? Fine, but whose Creation mythos — Aztec, Greek, Norse, Hindu, etc?
>
> Yes, science means knowledge but knowledge is achieved only through observation and reasoning never revelation. Revelation is not repeatable (on demand) and hence not subject to the scientific method. Even Scripture acknowledges that God is unknowable. The basis of scientific study is the presumed constancy of physical laws but since God is an entity and therefore capable of mercy, no analysis can predict His actions.
>
> — L.W., U.S.

I agree that humanism should not be promoted in the public school systems, but the fact remains that it *is* the dominant worldview presented to children. If science in the public schools is restricted to teaching only naturalistic explanations for the origin and history of life on earth, then this is biased against any deistic religion, and therefore is promoting the humanist religion above any other religion that does not hold this philosophy (more on this in a moment).

Humanist groups are accepted as "religious" institutions on college campuses and are granted tax-exempt status by the government in the same way that churches and traditional religious denominations are. If schools must be "deity neutral," then the public school system fails to meet this standard. Man is the measure of all things and becomes the de facto deity in the religion of

1. This feedback originally appeared on the Answers in Genesis website in response to an email received concerning an article written by Ken Ham. Roger Patterson, "Can Public Schools Be 'Neutral'?" Answers in Genesis, accessed October 7, 2016, https://answersingenesis.org/public-school/can-public-schools-be-neutral.

humanism. So, if humanism is promoted in the classrooms, then the classrooms are not deity neutral.

There are other religious worldviews that do not believe in a distinct deity — Buddhism and Taoism are two examples — but the U.S. Supreme Court has recognized that these worldviews should be considered religions as is evident in the following statement:

> Among religions in this country which do not teach what would generally be considered a belief in the existence of God, are *Buddhism, Taoism*, Ethical Culture, *Secular Humanism* (emphasis added), and others. (*Torcaso vs Watkins*, 81 S.Ct. 1681 (1961))

If we look at the Humanist Manifesto III, we see that three of the major tenets of the religion of humanism are:

1. Knowledge of the world is derived by observation, experimentation, and rational analysis. Humanists find that science is the best method for determining this knowledge as well as for solving problems and developing beneficial technologies. We also recognize the value of new departures in thought, the arts, and inner experience — each subject to analysis by critical intelligence.

2. Humans are an integral part of nature, the result of unguided evolutionary change. Humanists recognize nature as self-existing. We accept our life as all and enough, distinguishing things as they are from things as we might wish or imagine them to be. We welcome the challenges of the future, and are drawn to and undaunted by the yet to be known.

3. Ethical values are derived from human need and interest as tested by experience. Humanists ground values in human welfare shaped by human circumstances, interests, and concerns and extended to the global ecosystem and beyond. We are committed to treating each person as having inherent worth and dignity, and to making informed choices in a context of freedom consonant with responsibility.[2]

2. "Humanism and Its Aspirations, Humanist Manifesto III," American Humanist Association, http://americanhumanist.org/Humanism/Humanist_Manifesto_III.

If science in the public schools is based on the idea that "[k]nowledge is derived by observation, experimentation, and rational [read: "without supernaturalism"] analysis," then, again, it is promoting the humanist religion above any other religion that does not hold this philosophy.

If science teachers in the public schools are only allowed to teach that "humans are an integral part of nature, the result of unguided evolutionary change," then it is promoting the humanist religion above any other religion that does not hold this philosophy.

If the public school system is teaching that "ethical values are derived from human need and interest as tested by experience" (as is evident in the teaching of situational ethics and the absence of any absolute truth), then it is promoting the humanist religion above any other religion that does not hold this philosophy (see a pattern?).

Since all of the above conditions can be shown to be true, then the public school systems are promoting the religion of secular humanism, an atheistic religion, above all other views, cleverly and deceptively worded as "science," while other religions are relegated to "humanities" or "religious studies."

The problem that we face is related to the myth of neutrality — every system of thought must begin with a set of assumptions and is, therefore, not neutral. The public school systems cannot be neutral on the issue of the origin and history of life on earth. They are choosing to teach one view at the exclusion of others, which is not exactly neutral.

> Public schools, since they are supported by mandatory taxation, must not teach any religious viewpoint (including atheism)

But the fact is that they *do* promote atheistic, humanistic philosophies, as I have detailed above!

The irony is that the most outspoken proponents of removing religion from the public schools are those who place their faith in the humanist religion. They claim that they are trying to achieve the "separation of church and state" (a phrase and concept absent from the U.S. Constitution or its amendments), while they are instilling their religious values in the students attending public schools.

> Would you like it if your children were taught to reverence Vishnu?

No, I would not like it if my children were taught that Vishnu, Brahman, autonomous human reasoning, Zeus, or any other false god should be reverenced. There is only one true God who has revealed Himself to mankind in the Bible. To teach my children to reverence any other false god would be to violate the first and second of the Ten Commandments. But if my children were in public schools, they would be taught to reverence autonomous man and human reasoning above God, and that is no different. Children in public schools are still being taught to worship "a god made in man's image" — an idol in the eyes of the one, true living God.

Biblically, I am required to teach my children that some other people worship false gods, and that act of worship goes against the clear teaching of the Bible (Proverbs 22:6; Exodus 20:3–4; Psalm 40:4, 34:11). That is why I homeschool my children and why Ken Ham was encouraging Christian parents to think carefully and biblically about placing their children in a "temple of humanism."

You say you want Creationism taught along with Evolution?

I am not sure where you got this idea, but Answers in Genesis does not promote the mandatory teaching of biblical creation in public schools. However, we do not agree that naturalistic evolution, a tenet of Secular Humanism, should be the only idea taught to explain the history of life on earth, particularly if even naturalistic inconsistencies with this position are also censored.

It would be unwise for a Christian to expect a teacher trained by the humanistic, evolutionary university system to present creation in a respectable fashion anyway. As I was being trained to be a science teacher in two different state universities, I was taught everything from an antibiblical psychological, humanistic, and evolutionary perspective. At that time, I was an atheist myself, and I embraced the philosophies. I believed that human reasoning was the absolute source of truth — and I was trained to teach my students that view. Now that I am a Christian, I rely on the Bible for authority in every area of my life (to the best of my ability), and as I look back, I realize that in an atheistic view, there was no such thing as absolute truth anyway.

The relatively new, purely naturalistic view is not the only view of the history of life on earth. As mentioned in the article you are responding to, there is no valid reason that science should be arbitrarily limited to only naturalistic explanations. If science is to be based solely on those things that can be observed, tested, and verified by repeating the event, then neither the evolutionary origin of life from non-living matter nor any supernatural creation account should be taught in the science classroom. If public school systems are not going to allow views that are not observable and repeatable, then why accept the unscientific humanistic view that has the same problem? The only answer is that there is a bias toward the humanist religion in the "neutral" public school systems.

> Fine, but whose Creation mythos — Aztec, Greek, Norse, Hindu, etc ?

As I recall from my public school days, the mythology and religious views of the Babylonians, Greeks, Romans, and Egyptians were taught in great detail. In fact, one of the most memorable social studies units of my youth was a detailed description of the Egyptian culture and religious views. Why can public schools teach these religious ideas openly but may face the threat of lawsuits if the name of Christ is even mentioned with respect to a major religious holiday? But the question still remains: Why does the humanistic evolutionary myth get free reign in the classroom, particularly in the sciences? Religion *is* taught in schools — just not the Christian religion!

> Yes, science means knowledge but knowledge is achieved only through observation and reasoning never revelation.

How can you be so emphatic? To say that a transcendent God cannot communicate with man (revelation) means you are claiming powers of transcendence (an attribute of God). To make this claim you are claiming to know every single thought and conversation, whether in thoughts, dreams, or aloud, of every single person who has ever lived to say God never communicated with them, which is omnipresence and omnipotence (attributes of God). This sort of statement reveals a humanistic reasoning: that people are seen as the final authority — "as gods" themselves.

Furthermore, you may make this claim, as was made in the *Humanist Manifesto III* mentioned above, but on what grounds do you make it? This is an arbitrary definition and is based on the religious beliefs of humanism at this point in history. What does it mean to reason, if your brain is the product of random, unguided interactions of matter and energy? How can you trust such reasoning? If the universe exists as the result of random, unguided processes, then why should we expect to find order in it? Why should natural laws be consistent if they are the result of random processes?

As I view the world from a biblical perspective, I have a reason to believe in reasoning. The God of the Bible is a God of order, and He has created the universe in a logical way. Even the great scientists of the past based their work on this belief. Kepler said that science was an act of "thinking God's thoughts after Him." He obviously believed in a Creator that used logic and order in His creation. It is because God has made the world to operate in an orderly way that we can study the world and expect the natural laws to behave in a consistent way. Science is possible because of God, not in the absence of God.

On what basis do you make the claim that revelation never provides knowledge? With the Bible as my authority, I make the claim that the fear of the Lord is the beginning of wisdom and that we could understand nothing if we had not been created in His image (Job 28:28; Psalm 111:10; Proverbs 1:7, 29, 2:5, 9:10, 15:33, etc.).

> Revelation is not repeatable (on demand) and hence not subject to the scientific method.

Neither is the origin of life from unguided, evolutionary processes, nor rational thought, nor an emotion, nor the existence of logic, nor the origin of information, nor the formation of the first stars, nor Abraham Lincoln's life, nor even your birth!

In order to be consistent in your thinking, you must also claim that none of the items mentioned above are scientific. I think you fail to recognize the difference between operational science and historical science.

> Even Scripture acknowledges that God is unknowable.

Where does the Bible say this? It says in Isaiah 55:8–9 that His *ways* are higher than our ways, but not that God is unknowable. In fact, Jesus, who is the Creator God says:

> "I am the good shepherd; I know my sheep and my sheep know me" (John 10:14; NIV).

> "If you really know me, you will know my Father as well. From now on, you do know Him and have seen Him" (John 14:7; NIV).

Romans 1:18–23 also makes it clear that some attributes of the Creator can be known from His creation, so all are without excuse. Science can help us understand how the world works, but only when we look at the world from a biblical perspective. If you want to properly understand a 3-D picture, you have to look at it through the proper, colored lenses. If you want to understand the universe that was created by God, you have to look at it through the lens of Scripture.

> The basis of scientific study is the presumed constancy of physical laws but since God is an entity and therefore capable of mercy, no analysis can predict His actions.

Once again I must ask how naturalistic science can explain the constancy of the laws of nature without using a circular argument. There are many reasons to assume consistency with the God of the Bible. We start with the Bible as our authority, so we have a basis for making our claim.

I am not sure how you conclude that because God is an entity that He must be capable of mercy. There is no logical reason that conclusion is necessary. I do agree with your conclusion, as it is consistent with the Bible, but you may not realize that you are borrowing from the Bible to make such a claim. God is described as a God of mercy, but He is also described as a God of wrath because He is a just God. How could we know mercy if we did not know wrath?

We can predict one future action of God because He has revealed it to us in the Bible. We can be certain that He will one day act as the just judge of everyone. This is because we are all guilty of sinning against our Creator by breaking His commandments — and because God is a just judge, He must punish sin. I know that I am guilty of sinning against a perfectly holy and eternal God and that I deserve to spend an eternity paying that fine. I recognize God's wrath, but I also recognize His mercy — both described in the Bible.

In God's mercy He has made a way that we can have our penalty for sin placed on the account of His Son Jesus Christ. Jesus came to the earth and lived a perfect, sinless life, died on the Cross, was buried, and rose again on the third day. If anyone will receive Jesus Christ as Lord and Savior through repentance and faith, God's wrath will be turned away from them, and they can receive His mercy. If they do not, then God's justice demands their punishment. So, the biggest question is not whether we should teach creation in public schools or if nature follows certain patterns, but where we will spend eternity.

How about you? If God judges you, as the Bible tells us He will, will you have the innocence that only Christ can give you or your own guilt? I would ask that you seriously consider that question above all of the other things mentioned. We can debate the merits of social systems and scientific understanding, but where we will spend eternity is much more important than any of those things.

Appendix H

Evolution (Not Creation) Is a "God of the Gaps"

Prof. Stuart Burgess

When a false god is called upon to solve gaps in knowledge, this is sometimes referred to as "god of the gaps."[1] For example, if someone did not know that ice is formed when water freezes and proposed that there was an "ice god" that occasionally causes ice to spontaneously appear, then they would be guilty of using a "god of the gaps" explanation. Mythologies are known for their various "gods of the gaps."

Biblical Creation Is Not a "God of the Gaps"

Atheists have often accused Christians of invoking God to fill in a gap in scientific knowledge. Even the great scientist Isaac Newton has been accused by atheists of using a "god of the gaps" explanation when he said that the universe reveals evidence of design.[2] But creationists like Newton do not believe in a god of gaps, but a God of absolute necessity. Newton recognized that the universe could not exist without the supernatural creative power of an Almighty Creator.

Newton and most of the other founding fathers of science could see that the universe can only be fully explained with a combination of natural and

---

1. When doing this, it is a form of arbitrariness.
2. Marcelo Gleiser, "What the 'God of the Gaps' Teaches Us About Science," *WPSU*, April 8, 2015, http://radio.wpsu.org/post/what-god-gaps-teaches-us-about-science.

supernatural explanations. Creationists invoke God in origins, based on the revelation of this supreme God, and supernatural action is necessary as it steps beyond the laws of science. For example, according to the conservation of matter and energy (the first law of thermodynamics), it is impossible for a universe to come into existence without the supernatural intervention of an all-powerful being.

The Bible is scientifically correct when it states that divine supernatural power is required to create the universe (Genesis 1:1) and life (Genesis 2:7) and different kinds of creatures (Genesis 1:24). The Bible is also scientifically accurate that divine supernatural power is required to uphold all things (Colossians 1:17) — which include the laws of science. Rather than being accused of superstition, the Bible should be commended for correctly identifying the areas of origins where a supernatural Creator is necessary.[3]

Biblical Creation Is Not Anti-Science

Creationists are sometimes accused of ignoring scientific evidence and being anti-science. But belief in God in no way diminishes zeal for how life works and how the universe operates. The great pioneer scientists of the 17th to 20th centuries were inspired by their belief in God. Likewise, modern-day scientists who are biblical creationists find their belief in a purposeful universe to be helpful in their work.

Biblical creationists are always eager to learn from real scientific discoveries in every area of science. I personally have designed rockets and spacecraft for the European Space Agency and NASA using the latest scientific knowledge in physics and engineering. I have a patent on a special gearbox that was used on the world's largest civilian spacecraft and have been awarded three national prizes for the development of technology for spacecraft.

The only "science" that creationists do not use is the speculative "science" of evolution that has nothing to do with useful operational science (observable and repeatable science). Evolutionary ideas like "apelike creature-to-man charts" that supposedly chart human evolution are based on pure speculation and not useful to science and technology in any way.

---

3. These instances are not arbitrary appeals, but based on the absoluteness of who God is in how He works to create and uphold creation.

Evolution Is Guilty of "God of the Gaps" Explanations

Ironically, it is actually evolutionary believers that are guilty of "god of the gaps" explanations. When secular biology books attempt to explain why creatures or plants have a certain design, the answer is almost always "evolution did it" or "natural selection did it" without any explanation as to how the design feature could evolve by chance.[4]

This is what leading atheist and evolutionist Dr. Richard Dawkins has written about the origin of life:

> We have no evidence about what the first step in making life was, but we do know the *kind* of step it must have been. It must have been whatever it took to get natural selection started . . . by some process as yet unknown.[5]

The above quote is a classic example of evolution being a "god of the gaps" explanation. There is a total gap in what evolution can explain about the origin of life, and Dawkins invokes the god of evolution to fill in the gap and asserts that natural selection "must" have gotten started somehow. But natural selection by itself cannot create anything; it can only "select" or filter things already created.[6]

When my daughters did a two-year advanced biology course at high school in the United Kingdom, the teachers kept saying that "evolution did this" and "natural selection did that" for the origin of features like fins and wings and hearts and lungs. Near the end of the course, one of my daughters challenged the teacher and said, "Miss, you keep saying 'evolution did it,' but you never actually explain how evolution did it." The teacher had to confess that my daughter made a valid criticism, and the rest of the class agreed.

Since evolution has no credible evidence, biology books use examples of adaptation as supposed examples of evolution. Darwin's finches and resistant bacteria are held up as classic examples of evolution even though they are not evolution at all. These adaptations involve no new information, but simply a

---

4. These are reification fallacies.
5. Richard Dawkins, *The Greatest Show on Earth: The Evidence for Evolution* (New York: Free Press, 2009), p. 419 (emphasis Dawkins').
6. This observable process called *natural selection* was described in detail long before Charles Darwin, by a creationist named Ed Blyth.

shuffling of existing genes, which is what is expected with natural selection. Natural selection and adaptation are actually in opposition to onward-and-upward evolution.

Evolution Is Guilty of Being Anti-Science

Ironically, it is evolutionists, not creationists, who are guilty of ignoring scientific evidence.[7] Over the last 70 years there have been many thousands of experiments with sophisticated equipment trying to create life in the laboratory (called "abiogenesis") from dead matter and energy.[8]

However, all of these experiments have clearly demonstrated that life cannot come about by chance. Evolutionists have a choice. Either they accept the laboratory experiments or ignore them and put faith in the god of evolution. They have chosen to ignore the evidence and exercise blind faith in chance.

Evolutionary philosophy holds back scientific progress by seeking false evolutionary explanations of origins. If you refuse to believe that a jumbo jet was designed, it will affect the way you investigate the complexity of the aircraft. If you believe that the aircraft evolved by chance, you will not have your mind open to possibilities of coordinated design.

When the human genome was discovered to have far more information than expected, evolutionists immediately jumped to the conclusion that it was "junk" DNA because evolution predicts bad design not sophisticated design. However, subsequent work showed that the junk DNA was not junk at all, but highly coordinated information with important functions. That example shows how evolutionary assumptions hold back science.

A few years ago, I spoke to a senior professor of microbiology at my university (who is an agnostic) and asked what he thought of the theory of abiogenesis — the theory that life can evolve from dead matter. He said the concept was a type of "superstitious black magic." The biology professor had no Christian bias and had been taught the dogma of evolution for decades, but he could still see that abiogenesis was not real science but so speculative that it could be called black magic.

---

7. Elizabeth Mitchell, "Evolutionary Call to Arms," Answers in Genesis, June 1, 2012, https://answersingenesis.org/creation-vs-evolution/evolutionary-call-to-arms/.
8. Ken Ham, "Challenging Atheists at the Kentucky State Fair," *Around the World with Ken Ham* (blog), September 2, 2014, http://blogs.answersingenesis.org/blogs/ken-ham/2014/09/02/challenging-atheists-at-the-kentucky-state-fair/.

The Missing Link: Yet Another Gap in Evolution's Knowledge

When Darwin published his *Origin of Species* more than 150 years ago, one of the problems with his model was that there was a missing link between man and apes. That missing link is still missing today despite extensive searches for fossil evidence of evolution all over the world.

Based on fossil evidence, humans have always been strikingly different from apes. Humans walk on two legs, whereas apes walk on all four limbs. Humans have an arched foot, whereas apes have a flexible foot like a hand. Fossil evidence shows that no ape-like creature has ever had an arched foot for walking upright. As with every other aspect of the evolutionary religion, the evolutionist ignores the gaps and encourages everyone to put their faith in the god of evolution.

Evolution Is Like a Magic Wand

I recently talked with another senior professor of microbiology at my university (another agnostic), and he made a surprisingly frank admission about evolution being a "god of the gaps." He is not a creationist but like many biologists can see the serious weaknesses in evolution (although he keeps his views discreet for fear of losing his job).

This microbiologist told me that evolution could be described as a "magic wand." He said that he has noticed how even the experts say "evolution did this" and "natural selection did that" without any actual explanation being given and no demonstration in the laboratory. He said that the evolutionist could explain any aspect of origins by simply waving a magic wand and saying "evolution did it."

Paying Homage to the God of Evolution

Evolution makes no useful contribution to scientific and technological advances. However, there is an unwritten rule in the modern secular biology community that after completing a scientific study (on a topic not linked to evolution), evolution is mentioned in the write-up as being the explanation for the origin of features of design.

In the same way that a religious essay is finished by paying homage to a particular god, so in modern secular biology, essays are finished by paying homage to evolution. I have personally worked on biology-related projects where this is exactly what has happened. The end result is that the community blindly believes that the god of evolution must be true.

A Battle of Worldviews

Biblical creation versus evolution is not "faith versus science," but a worldview that includes God versus a worldview that has excluded God. Evolution is not a scientific theory because it has an unjustified assumption that God was not involved in origins. It is wrong for Christians to be accused of having a hidden religious agenda, because biblical creation openly declares its worldview.

Ironically, it is actually evolution that hides its atheistic agenda by pretending to be just science. If Isaac Newton and the other great scientists were here today, they would be astonished and saddened at the atheistic bias in modern secular science.

Giving Credit to the Creator

In modern society, a scientist is not allowed to say, "God did it" for any aspect of creation, whether it is ultimate origins or the origin of any detailed design feature. The phrase "God did it" is seen as anti-scientific. But if God is the author of creation, then He deserves acknowledgment and credit for His work. And if God is the author of creation, then scientific investigation can only be helped by recognizing God as Creator.

If you refused to believe that a jumbo jet had been designed, then that would be dishonoring to the designers. How much more dishonoring it is when secular science and the secular media refuse to acknowledge that creation has a Designer. Thankfully, there are many scientists today who are prepared to acknowledge the Creator despite the risk to their jobs and careers.

Such scientists can have the satisfaction of knowing they stand shoulder to shoulder with the greatest scientists that ever lived such as Newton, Kepler, Pascal, Faraday, Maxwell, Kelvin, and Flemming. And by the way, the last three great scientists in this list knew of Darwin's theory and rejected it — a fact that secular science has never publicized.